WITH *Amusement* FOR ALL

WITH *Amusement* FOR ALL

A HISTORY OF AMERICAN POPULAR CULTURE SINCE 1830

LeROY ASHBY

THE UNIVERSITY PRESS OF KENTUCKY

Scholarly publisher for the Commonwealth,
serving Bellarmine University, Berea College, Centre
College of Kentucky, Eastern Kentucky University,
The Filson Historical Society, Georgetown College,
Kentucky Historical Society, Kentucky State University,
Morehead State University, Murray State University,
Northern Kentucky University, Transylvania University,
University of Kentucky, University of Louisville,
and Western Kentucky University.

Editorial and Sales Offices: The University Press of Kentucky
663 South Limestone Street, Lexington, Kentucky 40508-4008
www.kentuckypress.com

12 13 14 15 16   5 4 3 2 1

The Library of Congress has cataloged the hardcover edition as follows:

Ashby, LeRoy.
With amusement for all : a history of American popular culture
since 1830 / LeRoy Ashby.
p.   cm.
Includes bibliographical references and index.
ISBN-13: 978-0-8131-2397-4 (hardcover : alk. paper)
ISBN-10: 0-8131-2397-6 (hardcover : alk. paper)
1. Popular culture—United States—History. 2. Amusements—United
States—History. 3. United States—Civilization. 4. United States—Social
conditions. I. Title.
E169.1.A8525 2006
306.4'80973—dc22
                           2006002558
ISBN 978-0-8131-4107-7 (pbk. : alk. paper)

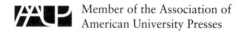 Member of the Association of
American University Presses

To Mary, my best friend and the love of my life,
for all the right reasons

CONTENTS

INTRODUCTION TO THE
PAPERBACK EDITION

In the brief seven years since I finished writing this book in 2005, popular culture has continued to change at a dizzying pace, vastly expanding the number and variety of options as well as ways to access them. Familiar patterns remain, certainly. Corporate behemoths keep jockeying for position and profits. New technology relentlessly brushes aside old systems and devices. Interactions between mainstream amusements (in the tradition of the circus's fabled big tent) and riskier, marginalized sideshows continue to reshape boundaries of respectability, acceptability, and controversy. Themes of centralization and homogenization persist. But, more than ever, fragmenting, disintegrating forces are apparent. These fracturing, splintering tendencies pose urgent new questions about the role of entertainment in a nation beset by disturbing expressions of disunity, acrimony, and resentment.

"If you don't know where you are going, you might wind up someplace else," said Yogi Berra, the former New York Yankees catcher turned street sage. By the twenty-first century's second decade, America's sprawling amusement culture seems adrift—as confused and disparate as the nation itself. Entertainments have never been uniform or synchronized, of course, but the rapidly proliferating sideshows make the big tent harder to find. "We have become a nation of niches," asserts media commentator Neil Gabler.[1] This trend has gathered momentum against a backdrop of jarring events: the nation's longest war, the worst economic crisis since the Great Depression, a technological upheaval of revolutionary proportions, and a bitterly divided political environment.

Responding to what President George W. Bush labeled the "war on terror," popular culture created a take-charge, laconic hero in the John Wayne tradition: Jack Bauer, a fictional counterterrorism expert who time and again saved the country, even if he sometimes had to use torture. He was so popular that leading officials such as Supreme Court Justice Antonin Scalia praised him, prompting one journalist to wonder "if they were aware that Jack Bauer is a character on a TV show, *24.*" By 2012, after ten seasons on Fox (2001–2010), Bauer was gone from TV, and the seemingly endless war was at last winding down. On May 2, 2011, U.S. Navy Seals killed Osama bin Laden, and in December, the last American combat troops left Iraq. Soldiers in Afghanistan are supposed to be home by the end of 2014. The wars produced grim statistics: by 2012, their costs had soared to over $2.5 trillion. American deaths alone surpassed 4,600. Tens of thousands of veterans returned home with severe physical and emotional injuries. Yet 63 percent of young adults could not locate Iraq on a map. Such numbers help explain why the entertainment industry has had difficulty finding wartime narratives with wide appeal.[2]

Identifying and courting audiences became even more complicated as the Great Recession struck the United States with unexpected fury in mid-2007. Over the next frightening months, as Americans lost homes, jobs, and businesses, the amusement industry took a pummeling. The challenge was not simply that of "competing for people's entertainment dollars," according to one chief executive: "We're going up against milk and orange juice." By 2009, 25 percent of the wealth of average American households had disappeared. Consumer confidence was shattered. Income and wealth inequities worsened. "The banker grows fat / Working man grows thin," lamented Bruce Springsteen on his 2012 album *Wrecking Ball.* The "epic breakdown" began to stabilize only after federal actions bailed out the banking system, rescued the auto industry, and injected almost $800 billion into an economic stimulus program.[3]

By then, however, the combined effects of the economic catastrophe, the controversial rescue programs, and the slow recovery had stoked public rage. While the 2008 election of the nation's first African American president raised hopes that the United States had turned a racial corner, it also injected an additional dose of bitter partisanship into American politics. On talk radio, Rush Limbaugh communicated the rising level of vitriol when he asserted that Barack Obama's election would encourage black kids to assault whites on school buses.[4]

The ravaged economy was critical to Obama's election, but popular culture also played a role. In 2010, when Oprah Winfrey was sitting next to Obama at the Kennedy Center, comedian Chris Rock joked about "the most powerful person in the world. And right next to her, Barack Obama! Hey, he didn't get her a job—she got him a job." The joke had more than an element of truth. By then, Winfrey had forged such an extensive "pop-culture empire" that, according to one commentator, "future generations may remember TV as 'the thing Oprah was on.'" According to another observer, hers had "been the hand that rocks the cradle across America."[5]

Over several decades, the rise of entertainment icons such as Winfrey (who appeared on the cover of *People Magazine* a record fifteen times between 1987 and 1998), Bill Cosby, Michael Jackson, and Michael Jordan had been pivotal in reordering America's racial attitudes. One interpretation of Obama's election pointed to the "Huxtable effect"—a reference to the pathbreaking role of the lovable black family on the *Cosby Show* (1984–1991). In the words of one columnist, an entire generation came "home after school to Oprah on television, with Bill Cosby selling them Jell-O during the commercial breaks." Meanwhile, Jackson had broken down what the *Washington Post* described as "the cultural apartheid of MTV and pop radio." In sports, Jordan's popularity attested to a world in which blacks dominated professional football and basketball, while black and Hispanic athletes filled major league baseball rosters. In turnarounds that would have been unthinkable only several decades earlier, movies and TV series featured competent and commanding black presidents, such as Morgan Freeman in the film *Deep Impact* (1998) and Dennis Haysbert in *24*. In that context, arguments that popular culture helped prepare the ground for Obama's election made sense. As writer Darryl Pinckney said, "Obama had a 'color-coded' popular culture of television, film, and radio that offered him 'an arcade of images' to choose from."[6]

While Obama benefited from popular culture, the 2008 Republican vice presidential candidate, Sarah Palin, used politics to transform herself into a pop culture celebrity. Virtually unknown previously, she leveraged political attention from the 2008 campaign to obtain lucrative book deals, get her own reality TV show, become a television commentator, and make news as she toured the nation in her own bus. Her boosters described her as a "babe" and a "smoking-hot chick." When comparing her to Obama, Louisiana senator David Vitter said, "I'll take a TV personality over a community organizer any day."[7]

Equally telling, however, were comedian Tina Fey's brilliant impersonations of Palin—so perfect in tone and appearance that Fey humorously defined Palin for many Americans. During the 2008 campaign, Fey appeared on *Saturday Night Live*, wonderfully parodying Palin's views on subjects such as foreign policy—for example, saying that she could see Russia from Alaska. Two weeks before the election, when Palin herself was a guest on the program and appeared onstage with her look-alike, politician and comedian seemed interchangeable. Comedy's influence on politics was moving far beyond where humorists such as Mark Twain, Will Rogers, or Johnny Carson had taken it. Indeed, as historian Peter Robinson has argued: "In the early twenty-first century the political comedians would be invested with the sort of comprehensive sovereignty that presidents and candidates only dream of: political influence, economic power, and cultural celebrity."[8]

There are no better examples of humor's influence on politics than the Comedy Channel's Jon Stewart and Stephen Colbert, "masters of truth through fakery." For several million viewers, most of them young, *The Daily Show* and the *Colbert Report* are their main sources of news. "You simply can't understand American politics in the new millennium without *The Daily Show*," asserts one prominent commentator about Stewart's exceptionally popular weekday program. Meanwhile, Colbert satirizes politics by posing as a political reactionary. Coining the term *truthiness*, he humorously extols perceptions of reality that come "from the gut" rather than from critical thought and factual evidence. "I'm not a fan of facts," he says. "Facts can change all the time, but my opinion will never change."[9]

Truthiness describes all too well the content of much political discussion, especially in the media. In April 2011, Senator Jon Kyl (R-AZ) shrugged off an outlandishly inaccurate characterization of one organization by saying his information "was not intended to be a factual statement." Similarly, Bill Sammon, vice president and Washington managing editor of television's Fox News, admitted that his network's attacks on President Obama were "rather farfetched" and, indeed, were "mischievous speculation." Although Fox News touts its programming as "fair and balanced," it ingeniously blurs opinion and journalism into what one of its former news directors calls a "propaganda machine." When network head Roger Ailes hired Glenn Beck—a purveyor of innuendo, misstatement, and hyperbole—Ailes informed Beck that the primary objective was to block Obama's administration: "I see this as the Alamo."[10]

Ironically, following the economy's near collapse in 2007–2008 and the onset of the Great Recession, a spirited defense of unregulated capitalism gained traction. One sign was the popularity of novelist Ayn Rand's works, especially *Atlas Shrugged* (1957). Rand's writings had long influenced libertarians, including her best-selling *The Fountainhead* (1943), which in 1948 inspired a popular movie starring Gary Cooper. By 2010, Rand's growing audiences were helping to shape Republican policies and fuel conservative opposition to Obama. There had been, of course, earlier examples of popular fiction's impact on American politics—most notably, Harriet Beecher Stowe's *Uncle Tom's Cabin* (1852), which helped spread antislavery sentiments, and Upton Sinclair's *The Jungle* (1902), which sparked passage of the Pure Food and Drug Act in 1906. The expanding popularity of *Atlas Shrugged*, fifty years after its publication, was nevertheless a puzzle: the book champions an unregulated market even though several decades of corporate greed, financial chicanery, and corruption have resulted in a terrible economic bust.[11]

Rand (1905–1982), who fled Soviet Russia for the United States in 1926, celebrates strong, creative individuals who defy larger public currents in the name of unrestricted individualism. *Atlas Shrugged* is her magnum opus, a ringing defense of brilliant, inventive entrepreneurs pitted against villainous government bureaucrats and unimaginative conformists who threaten capitalism, which Rand calls "the noblest, cleanest, and most idealistic system of all." A question surfaces throughout the novel: "Who is John Galt?" He is an inventor and the most mythical of Rand's heroes, the driving force behind a hidden capitalist utopia in Colorado's mountains. Rand devotes no fewer than sixty pages of her thousand-plus-page novel to Galt's radio address to the nation, a cry for glorious individualism and unsullied capitalism. (When her editor insisted that she reduce the speech, she stood firm, reportedly asking, "Would you cut the Bible?")[12]

Atlas Shrugged gained a wide audience. When a 1998 Modern Library poll asked readers to name the 100 greatest books of the twentieth century, *Atlas Shrugged* ranked first, and *The Fountainhead* was second. In 1993, *Atlas Shrugged* trailed only the Bible when the Library of Congress and the Book of the Month Club asked readers to identify the book that had most influenced their lives. Up to the end of the twentieth century, sales of *Atlas Shrugged* and *The Fountainhead* remained brisk, exceeding 300,000 copies a year. Curiously, in 2007–2008, as the economic crisis seared America, sales of *Atlas Shrugged* nearly tripled. Rand had become "a more active presence in American culture," according to one biographer, "than she was during her own lifetime." In 2011, the first installment of a projected movie trilogy based on *Atlas Shrugged* reached theaters.[13]

By then, the impact of *Atlas Shrugged* on American politics was indisputable. The novel had become a virtual handbook for leading Republican conservatives who were intent on shrinking government, "liberating" business from regulations, and rewarding entrepreneurial initiative with increased wealth. "Going Galt" became a rallying cry to reduce government. Calling for "a strike of small businesses against the movement for global socialism" and on behalf of "free market capitalism," an activist in the Republican "Tea Party" wing quoted from the conclusion of the 2011 movie *Atlas Shrugged—Part I:* "I'm on strike!" Other champions of *Atlas Shrugged* included conservative talk-show hosts Rush Limbaugh and Glenn Beck. Wisconsin Representative Paul Ryan, who in 2010 became chair of the powerful House Budget Committee, required all his staffers to read *Atlas Shrugged* and praised Rand in YouTube videos. Ryan, like many conservatives who saw themselves as rescuing America from a collectivist government, echoed John Galt's words: "We have . . . no terms to bargain about, no compromise to reach. You have nothing to offer us. We do not need you."[14]

Although *Atlas Shrugged* grew in popularity a half century after its publication, many people were now reading it and other books on electronic devices that jeopardized the centuries-old printed format. The book business was in such upheaval that some people speculated about its obsolescence. Indeed, in 2011, Amazon.com sold more electronic books than it did printed ones, and the long-established book chain Borders closed. Over the previous decade, 20 percent of independent bookstores had disappeared. Effects of the rapidly emerging digital age stretched to magazines, newspapers, and beyond the print world to movies and television.[15]

For generations, technology had reshaped the entertainment world, but never with such stunning rapidity or breadth as at the turn of the twenty-first century. Almost overnight, a staggering assortment of inventions and developments transformed the media landscape, producing a revolution that reporter Ken Auletta compared to Gutenberg's invention of the printing press in the 1400s. As Auletta notes, in 1990 "there was no World Wide Web, no DVDs, no satellite TV, no mobile phones or PDAs, no TiVos or DVRs, no digital cameras, no iPods, no PlayStation or Wii games." The changes came so quickly and from so many directions that Microsoft founder and CEO Bill Gates half-seriously joked: "I fear someone in a garage who is devising something completely new."[16]

The technological breakthroughs surprised even some of the most established media entrepreneurs. In 1994, Viacom's Sumner Redstone asserted: "I will believe in the 500-channel world only when I see it." He also dismissed the World Wide Web as little more than "a road to fantasyland." Time Warner dismissed the Internet as "just for nerds."[17]

Around 2002, however, that situation changed with lightning speed. The general public had viewed the first Internet generation as reclusive, "Ivy League–educated geeks." Then, virtually overnight, the Internet transformed from something distant and irrelevant to an essential part of everyday life. New computer technologies such as high-speed connections and WiFi-enabled laptops facilitated the change. So did the hunger for social connections. Much as the telephone had done decades earlier, the Internet's rapidly expanding social-networking sites allowed people to connect and interact in breathtaking ways. By 2009, 230 million Americans had Internet access. A vibrant Internet culture was being born in public schools and libraries as well as in individual homes, bringing with it enormous implications for the production and distribution of entertainment. The old media world of print, music, movies, and television was on the defensive, courtesy of Internet companies and devices with names such as Google, Amazon, iTunes, YouTube, MySpace, and Facebook.[18]

Google, founded in 1998, was especially important. Its search engine soon provided individuals with unprecedented access to an astounding amount of Internet information. In 2006, for a staggering $1.65 billion, Google purchased YouTube, a year-old, user-generated Web site that allowed rank-and-file computer users to post and view videos online. Visitors could upload all sorts of things, from grainy, homemade clips to on-the-scene coverage of news events. The results often resembled the clutter of a college dorm room or "user-generated anarchy." More and more clips, however, came from television shows, movies, and music videos—although, according to YouTube, the clips were not supposed to exceed fifteen minutes. By March 2009, YouTube's 90 million visitors constituted two-thirds of all Web video traffic. Fifteen months later, YouTube's traffic was reportedly "nearly double the prime-time audience of all three major US television networks combined."[19]

Aware that "you can't compete with free," media giants such as Viacom sued Google and YouTube for copyright infringement. Under fire for Internet theft, YouTube fought back, claiming that it provided only a platform; user-generated uploads supplied the content. YouTube was willing to take down videos, but only after the content owners demanded their removal.[20]

Defenders of the Internet assumed that it implicitly "favored its users, 'the people,' over centralized authorities," as writer Steve Coll observed. But what if the Internet retraced radio's trajectory? Radio's once-open airwaves had initially belonged to amateurs and offered a freewheeling medium. Then corporations such as RCA took command. There was no guarantee that the Internet would be any less vulnerable to monopolization. In that sense, according to one commentator, the fight between Internet powers and the corporate giants of the old media resembled that "between Godzilla and King Kong." A healthy skepticism about both sides of the debate over intellectual property was essential.[21]

The ongoing battles resembled earlier ones over the player piano, jukebox, VCR, and other devices that encouraged easier and cheaper methods of copying and distributing content. DVDs and TiVo, for example, jeopardized television broadcasters' profits by letting viewers skip the ads. In 2007, when Netflix enlarged its DVD-by-mail business to include video streaming, it allowed subscribers to watch and change movies at will, bringing "channel-surfing to movies," as Netflix's Robert Kyncl said. Kyncl wanted to develop "the skill set" that would "bridge Silicon Valley and Hollywood—an information culture and an entertainment culture." The challenge was how to merge the massive amounts of free information flooding the Internet with the entertainment business's need to control and restrict content in order to protect profits.[22]

Technology was touching off fierce—and familiar—debates with high stakes. At risk was nothing less than the entertainment industry's power structure. A 2008 study, for example, showed that Americans between the ages of eighteen and twenty-seven spent more time on the Internet each week (on average, two and a half hours more) than they did watching television. That reality forced collaborative efforts between the new "participatory media" and the professional programming of traditional media companies. Thus, to promote its programs, CBS uploaded hundreds of short clips on YouTube. It also allowed YouTube to use pirated video from the network if it agreed to split revenues from advertising.[23]

The legendary Steve Jobs was largely responsible for advancing the computer's role as a "digital hub" for music, videos, texting, and photos. A college dropout who started the Apple Computer business in his parents' garage in 1976, he shrewdly focused on making computer products more user-friendly and attractive. Despite his reputation as a modern Henry Ford, he was less an inventor than a marketing genius—more "P. T. Barnum than Thomas Edison," as one person said. With great flair, he enlarged the Internet's place in daily lives with such mass-marketing successes as the iPod, the iTunes Store, the iPhone, the iPad, the iBookstore, and the App Store. While companies such as Dell made hardware for computers, and while Microsoft wrote software programming, Apple did both—facilitating what Jobs proudly described as a "digital lifestyle."[24]

In October 2001, Jobs introduced a key component of that lifestyle: the iPod. "This amazing little device," he said as he held it up, "holds a thousand songs, and it goes right in my pocket." Owners of Apple computers could download the music free from Apple's iTunes playlist, courtesy of an agreement Jobs struck with several nervous recording companies that hoped advertising profits would be a sufficient trade-off. Jobs went further. In order to offer new music and manage the issue of copyright infringement, he made a deal with several top music companies. His new iTunes Store, which opened in April 2003, would sell digital songs for ninety-nine cents; the recording companies received seventy cents. Customers could now own downloaded songs rather than simply renting them through subscription services. Additionally, customers could create a kind of "digital jukebox" by purchasing individual songs rather than entire albums. Within six days, the iTunes Store sold a million songs—"a turning point in the music industry," as Jobs dubbed it. Jobs next made deals with top recording artists. U2, one of the world's most popular bands, agreed to make a free TV commercial for Apple in return for "royalties from the sale of a special U2 edition of the iPod," as Jobs's biographer explained. "The album sold 840,000 copies in its first week and debuted at number one on the *Billboard* chart."[25]

The Internet upheaval was profoundly democratizing. It gave tremendous creative power to "average everyday folks" who could challenge the mainstream amusement industry. The ability to upload amateur videos on Web sites such as YouTube meant that "anyone with a camera" might become a star. Individuals could circumvent traditional media gatekeepers. By using "blogs, social networking tools, video sharing, and digital downloading," they could, in the words of one sociologist, "act as their own record company, publicist, or publishing company."[26]

"The days of walking into a record label and giving them your demo" were over, as rapper Wade pointed out. "Now it's like, 'Get your own buzz. Get your own thing rockin,' maybe do some YouTubes. Prove yourself like that.'" In that regard, Wade believed Southern rapper Soulja Boy "kind of revolutionized" the hip-hop business. As a young teenager, Soulja Boy had used basic digital software to record songs that he posted on sites like MySpace. When he attracted half a billion views on YouTube, he became "the first megastar rapper of the Internet age," according to one account. YouTube also propelled thirteen-year-old Justin Bieber, a Canadian, to stardom. Bieber's working-class mother started posting his performances on YouTube, and in 2008 a U.S. marketing executive accidentally clicked on one of the videos. He signed Bieber to a recording contract, and within months, the youngster was one of entertainment's biggest names, performing at the White House. Jackie Evancho was even younger when she rocketed to stardom after receiving the most fan votes on the YouTube competition sponsored by the *America's Got Talent* TV show and subsequently placed second on the show itself.[27]

In 2011, YouTube dramatically expanded the Internet's role as an agent of popular culture. By inaugurating YouTube Original Channels, it moved television closer to a radically new era. Working with Netflix's Robert Kyncl, it commissioned more than a hundred channels for which professionals from the traditional media would provide content. Among those signing on were Madonna, Amy Poehler, Shaquille O'Neal, the *Wall Street Journal,* and even Disney. The new channels would revolve around a host of programming choices for a wide range of interests, including rapper Jay-Z, skateboarding, fashion, and shows for Latin American young adults. Many questions surrounded YouTube's move to include professionally scripted and produced content. One was whether it might alienate its original constituency of everyday people. Another was whether it could ever generate real television hits. But one thing was sure: the trend of entertainment expansion and audience fragmentation would accelerate. Evidence of the rise of small audiences—connected by demographics, tastes, and ideologies—is overwhelming. In 2011, television's most popular show, *American Idol,* claimed only 9 percent of all U.S. TV viewers. As writer John Seabrook predicts, with YouTube's Original Channels, "niches will get nichier."[28]

The Internet has accelerated that trend in areas such as advertising. By purchasing search keywords on Google, advertisers can target potential buyers more precisely than ever. Rather than blanketing various outlets in the hope of finding potential customers, advertisers can simply track the items individuals search for on the Internet. Thus, people looking for a certain book might find an accompanying "Sponsored Link" from Amazon. By 2009, according to one source, "paid search" constituted "more than 40 percent of the online advertising market" and was becoming "the ultimate holy grail for advertisers."[29]

Hollywood—facing Internet technologies, economic pressures, and fractured audiences—necessarily made adjustments of its own. In May 2006, even before the Great Recession hit, *Entertainment Weekly* issued a disconcerting report on the movie industry: "After decades of seemingly unlimited star paydays, studios are fretting over declining audiences and rising production costs, and taking a hard new look at those eye-popping price tags." Over the previous six years, the cost of making an average movie had spiraled from $54.8 million to $65.8 million; the price of prints and ads jumped from $27.3 million to $34.5 million. Meanwhile, between 2002 and 2005, domestic box-office receipts had dropped from $9.52 billion to $8.99 billion, despite escalating ticket prices. The corporate acquisitions and consolidations of the 1990s had left the studios even more reliant on outside financing, mainly from six global entertainment behemoths: Warner Brothers (Time Warner), Disney, Sony, Universal (GE), Fox (News Corp.), and Paramount (Viacom). Wall Street hedge fund investors covered half the production costs for Warner Brothers' mid-2008 release of Christopher Nolan's *The Dark Knight*, a blockbuster hit. Former venture capitalist Thomas Tull, working with partners who were mostly new to movie investments, played a key role—along with JP Morgan—in working out the deal with Warner Brothers. The onset of the Great Recession, however, caused hedge fund investors and banks to pull back. Even the home video market shrank. Faced with tightening finances, the studios resorted to budget cuts and layoffs.[30]

As they struggled with budget problems, competition from other amusements, and the expectations of outside investors, the studios developed several strategies. They relied less on stars, who had become both increasingly expensive and less important to audiences—almost 40 percent of filmgoers were in the twelve to twenty-four age bracket. They produced fewer original films and more franchise movies, often built around concepts and characters from comic books. They increasingly shifted from 35mm film, which had long dominated the medium, to digital technology; by 2011 (a "tipping point" in the replacement of celluloid film), more than half of U.S. projection booths were reportedly digital. The studios also tapped a renewed interest in 3-D movies. They increasingly used product placement. (So many products appeared in the James Bond movie *Die Another Day* [Lee Tamahori, 2002] that some comedians renamed it "Buy Another Day." For the twenty-third Bond film, *Skyfall* [Sam Mendes,

2012], Heineken paid millions of dollars to have 007 order its beer in place of his trademark vodka martini, "shaken, not stirred.") More than ever, the studios looked to the international market. (Three-fourths of the theatrical gross for *Pirates of the Caribbean: On Stranger Tides* [Rob Marshall, 2011] came from abroad.) The studios also shifted to a multiplatform distribution that included electronic media and Internet delivery. Hollywood had moved a long way from 1982, when industry head Jack Valente warned that the "VCR is to the American film producer and the American public as the Boston strangler is to the woman home alone." Within twenty-five years, DVD rentals and sales had become a crucial income source for Hollywood, exceeding theatrical gross box-office revenues. Worrisome in that regard was the fact that, in 2008, revenues from the top ten DVDs fell by 15 percent.[31]

Another reality that influenced Hollywood was the continuing dominance of young audiences. In response, the studios produced more PG-rated movies (doubling from 15 percent in 2003 to 30 percent in 2007) and fewer R-rated films (down from 20 percent in 2003 to 15 percent in 2007). By 2012, one person was asking: "You know what's a drag about being a grown-up? Nobody makes movies for me anymore." Longtime movie critic Roger Ebert reported that "some studio divisions have been forthright about their decision to stop making grown-up movies at all."[32]

The decline in movies for older audiences reemphasized Hollywood's basic caution and unwillingness to produce "message" movies." For example, few films dealt with the wars in Iraq and Afghanistan; those that did performed poorly at the box office. Although a 2007 Gallup poll suggested that 60 percent of Americans viewed the war as a mistake, audiences showed little interest in that year's small cluster of movies questioning it. Despite strong casts, movies such as *Rendition, In the Valley of Elah, Grace Is Gone, Lions for Lambs,* and *Stop-Loss* lacked appeal. According to Brad Thor, a rising author of terror best sellers, "In Middle America people want to see their values triumph."[33]

Spurning pessimism, mainstream movies stuck with "big tent" franchises—often sequels—that were bursting with explosions, car chases, superheroes, and winners. Of the top ten domestic box-office draws, three featured comic-book heroes (Batman and Spider-Man), two were animated features (*Shrek 2* and *Finding Nemo*), two were from *The Lord of the Rings* trilogy, and the others were episodes from *Pirates of the Caribbean* and *Star Wars.* Other top moneymakers included *The Matrix Reloaded, The Chronicles of Narnia: The Lion, the Witch, and the Wardrobe,* and two Harry Potter films. Losers were virtually absent from the big screen, except for several small-budget "independent" films—movies the major studios typically "outsourced" to "specialty satellites" such as Fox Searchlight. "Whenever I see a movie that impresses me, I always wonder how it occurred," said the cocreator of television's superb series *The Wire*. "Like how did they thread *that* one through the needle."[34]

Television also pursued the lowest common denominator, especially with its proliferating "reality" shows. Such shows are 50 to 75 percent cheaper to make than scripted programs, and they are also very popular. Forty million viewers turned the first-season finale of *Joe Millionaire* (in which Joe chose the woman of his affections) into the decade's third most-watched TV episode. *Joe Millionaire*, *The Bachelor*, and myriad look-alikes that are supposedly "unscripted" portray "real people" dealing with "real emotions." But as TV celebrity Pamela Anderson said of her lettuce bikini: "It's partially real and partially not real—just like me."[35]

Reality shows are in fact carefully crafted, tapping familiar narratives about love and romance. Great attention goes into securing the "right" kind of participants and reactions, even to the point of revising reality. A producer of *The Bachelor* admitted: "We have even gone so far as to 'fran-kenbite,' where you take somebody saying, 'of course I'd like to say I love him' and cutting the bite together to say 'of course I love him.'" On another show, a woman said she loved one man, but editors inserted someone else's name. Editors compare themselves to "puppeteers" who manipulate footage "cleverly and often." The popularity of reality shows partly reflects how well they reaffirm the American dream of success. "I can't believe I'm saying this," said *Joe Millionaire*'s winning participant, "but I do believe in fairytales." Beneath the fantasy and romance, however, are darker themes of humiliation, class anxieties, consumerism, and stereotyped gender roles. Female participants, in the words of *The Bachelor*'s executive producer, "have to look good in the hot tub." According to media critic Jennifer Pozner, reality TV typically portrays women as bitches, morons, skanks, and gold diggers. Reality television, she argues, "was built on a foundation of garden-variety misogyny" and constitutes "our most vivid example of a pop cultural backlash against women's rights and social progress."[36]

Questions nevertheless remain about audience preferences. *Joe Millionaire*'s popularity quickly faded, for instance. After its big first-season finale, it lost 80 percent of its audience and survived only one more season. Ultimately, viewers have much to say about the fate of programs. In that regard, as gender studies scholar Kathy Davis argues: "Women are not merely the victims of the terrors visited upon them by the beauty system. On the contrary, they partake in its delights as well."[37]

Reality TV in fact has some redeeming features. *America's Got Talent* can be downright silly, but it also provides breakthrough opportunities for gifted entertainers. *American Idol* and *The Voice* do the same thing. "No major label would've signed a gay, 27-year-old white theater dude without *Idol*," said Adam Lambert after almost winning on the show's eighth season.

So You Think You Can Dance has introduced a wide range of dance styles and talented young performers to larger audiences. Programs such as *The Amazing Race* provide views of various parts of the world and many different cultures. Most offerings on channels such as Home and Garden TV are informative. An outpouring of reality shows about "manly men doing manly things" has boosted cable networks such as History, Discovery, A&E, and the National Geographic Channel. One commentator believes that programs about everyday people engaged in blue-collar activities (e.g., *Pawn Stars, Swamp People, The Greatest Catch, Ice Road Truckers, Ax Men, Dirty Jobs*) offer "male viewers a sense of wish fulfillment in a struggling economy." "Testosterone TV" also draws substantial female audiences.[38]

Although reality shows have continued to spread, often seeming to clone one another, an important segment of television has entered new territory with thoughtful, unpredictable offerings—so good that, according to *Newsweek,* "Television is running circles around the movies." Media scholar Heather Hendershot agrees: "The best of contemporary television is simply more compelling than most contemporary American cinema." This development was possible, Hendershot explains, because TV's "multi-channel, niche-audience environment allows for long-term character development, genre innovation and aesthetic risk-taking." Producer-writer Paul Schrader and others now favor "long-form television" because of the diminishing prospects for "grown-up films and creative projects."[39]

Television owes most of its innovation to digitalized cable systems, whose subscribers tripled to 30 million between 2000 and 2005. "It's not TV. It's HBO," proclaims Home Box Office, which has aired a number of pathbreaking programs. *The Sopranos* (1999–2007), for example, was a pioneering series about the mob that the *New York Times* judged to be "the greatest work of American popular culture of the last quarter century." The series' creator, David Chase, had come to "loathe and despise almost every second of" network television, which he considered "propaganda for the corporate state," full of mawkish lessons "that 'life is nothing but great.'" Chase stunningly brought to television the gangster themes that marked classic crime movies such as *The Godfather,* and in doing so, he explored a variety of subjects—aging, masculinity, ethnicity, and women's roles. The result was a kind of television "palace coup." When the series came to an indeterminate end in 2007, Chase left viewers with few illusions and no sense of redemption.[40]

In tone, mood, and creativity, *The Sopranos* helped open the door for other landmark series. The sixty episodes of HBO's *The Wire* (2002–2008), set in Baltimore, brilliantly dissected urban America—its underclass, politicians, police, educators, and journalists. One viewer watched it "with a kind of mesmerized dread," noting that "almost everyone who tries to buck the system and do right is punished." Other notable HBO serial dramas include *Deadwood* (2004–2006), which reworked Old West themes; *In Treatment* (2008–), which sensitively conveys the dynamics and emotions of psychotherapy; *Game of Thrones* (2011–), which inverts the fantasy genre, replacing friendly hobbits and good guys with a treacherous world where compromised heroes do not always survive; and *Boardwalk Empire* (2009–), about unprincipled people at every level during the Prohibition era. Showtime has had some noteworthy series of its own: two lavishly produced period pieces full of corruption and unscrupulous power seekers—*The Tudors* (2007–2010) and *The Borgias* (2011–)—plus *True Blood* (2008–), a much-remodeled and very erotic vampire story. In 2011, Showtime won an Emmy Award for its first season of *Homeland,* in which a returned prisoner of war from Afghanistan is in fact a domestic terrorist. Meanwhile, Starz Channel's *The Boss* (2011–) depicts urban politics at its slimiest.[41]

Nonpremium cable channels have added to the list of exceptional serial dramas. AMC's *Breaking Bad* (2008–) focuses on a dying high-school chemistry teacher who, to provide for his pregnant wife and their physically disabled son, starts a meth lab with a former student. But even after his cancer goes into remission and he has built a comfortable nest egg, the teacher is so obsessed with his drug cooking that he increasingly reveals his own murderous side. "Mr. Chips" becomes "Scarface," as the show's creator said. From one critic's perspective, *Breaking Bad* is "one of the grimmest sagas of our time, an ambitious bid to explore an American dream gone horribly wrong." AMC's *Mad Men* (2007–) is another much-praised, highly popular series. It provides a searing look at a fictional advertising agency in the 1960s, examining sexism, racism, greed, envy, and the sleazy world of image making.[42]

FX has weighed in with adult series such as *Rescue Me* (2004–2011), in which post-9/11 New York City firefighters struggle with bad memories, personal demons, and booze; *Sons of Anarchy* (2008–), about a deadly motorcycle gang for which things go badly; and *Justified* (2010–), in which a flawed federal agent deals with a nightmarish setting of former friends and neighbors in Kentucky's backwoods. Some viewers drew eerie comparisons between the Sci Fi Channel's *Battlestar Gallactica* (2004–2009)—which asked, "Is our way of life even worth saving?"—and the post-9/11 world. Like film noir following World War II, these television serial dramas convey a sense of claustrophobia, systemic corruption, failed dreams, the taint of money, and life's randomness.[43]

Although movies generally spurned such dark perspectives, a distinguished few conveyed a *Breaking Bad*–type sense of unease. *There Will Be Blood* (Paul Thomas Anderson, 2007) focuses on the greed and ambition of both a turn-of-the-century oil man and a revivalist preacher. *No Country for Old Men* (Joel and Ethan Coen, 2007) relentlessly portrays the crumbling of an aging Texas lawman's world. *The Road* (John Hillcoat, 2009) follows the desperate journey of a father and his young son through a postapocalyptic America. In *The Hurt Locker* (Kathryn Bigelow, 2008), a soldier defines himself through the violence and thrill of war. Many of these films drew on critically acclaimed novels. Together, the novels, movies, and cable dramas have built "a cavalcade of bleakness."[44]

A strongly disquieting mood has also surfaced in an unexpected place: novels for young adults. Dystopian fiction for young people is not new, of course. By 2010, however, a boom in that genre was under way, with several dozen titles under contract. Suzanne Collins's sensational *The Hunger Games Trilogy* (2008–2010) led the way, quickly moving into film. "The brutality of war. An elite class exploiting the masses. Children hungry and hopeless"—such are the themes that mark Collins's best-selling series, which *Parade* magazine described as "one of the biggest hits in young adult literature—ever." Not surprisingly, *The Hunger Games* and other novels with deteriorating, oppressive surroundings also include teen heroines and romantic interests. Still, their menacing settings of moral bankruptcy, war, injustices, inequities, authoritarian threats, and a largely ruined world are of sterner stuff than that found in most young-adult fiction. One writer's guess is that "the grim dystopia boom" means "that teens in our mismanaged times are demanding to read 'something that isn't a lie.'" Social criticism may not have been the main purpose of the novels, but they nevertheless reflect, in the words of one critic, "the course of adolescent disaffection."[45]

Even comic-book superheroes are caught in a deeply troubled society. In 2003, conservative pundit Michael Medved objected to the "betrayal of Captain America" and accused left-wing ideologues of subverting the comics. Medved certainly would not have approved three years later when Marvel Comics reacted to the Iraq war and the Patriot Act by running a short series about America's new "civil war"—one that pitted superheroes against one another. The story line has the federal government, in the name of fighting terrorism, requiring people with superpowers to register with, and fall under the purview of, the government. Those who refuse are designated "unlawful combatants" and disappear without trial into secret prisons. Captain America leads some superheroes (including an initially conflicted Spider-Man) in an underground resistance movement against the government crackdown; others, with Iron Man at the head, defend the government's position. In the shocking conclusion, as authorities take the handcuffed Captain America into the courthouse, he is assassinated. Two years later, changing circumstances demanded his return. According to Marvel's executive editor, the Great Recession helped account for the five-part series *Captain America Reborn*: "It feels like there's a desire for hopefulness, a desire for heroes and for somebody to show us that we can be our better selves and to help pull us all up by our bootstraps and get out of the situations that we find ourselves in."[46]

This had long been the mission of comic-book superheroes. But the results did not necessarily amount to a mindless patriotism or triumphalism, as Captain America's assassination in 2007 attested. The longtime trajectory of the superhero narrative—from Superman in 1938 onward—was bent toward securing American ideals of social justice, freedom, fairness, and democracy. Increasingly, too, the comics celebrated diversity and tolerance regarding religion, race, ethnicity, and, more recently, sexual preference. In the 1980s, Marvel's position was "No Gays in the Marvel Universe," but in 2002, its revived *Rawhide Kid* became "the first openly gay comic book character to star in his own magazine." In response to complaints that the character would corrupt children, Marvel posted an "Adults Only" label on its cover.[47]

In 2011, despite objections that political correctness had "run amok," Marvel introduced a black and Latino Spider-Man. DC Comics decided to publish revised versions of fifty-two superhero titles, giving its characters, including Superman, new outfits and more complex personalities. The *New 52* relaunch included, with her own title, a lesbian Batwoman, whom DC had introduced in 2006 but then relegated to minor roles following a wave of criticism; a bisexual African American woman named Voodoo; and an openly gay Latino superhero, Bunker. DC also brought Midnighter into its main offerings; in DC's earlier 2002 Wildstorm imprint, he had married his boyfriend, Apollo, and subsequently adopted a daughter. In 2010, despite the outcry of the American Family Association, even Archie Comics introduced a gay character; he was so popular that he had his own series within two years. The comic-book industry was unquestionably responding to dropping sales—by 7 percent in 2010 alone—and trying to rebuild its audience. Over several decades, that audience had declined as comic books lost their once unique hold on "youth sensibilities" to a host of competing entertainments. Nevertheless, the comic industry's evolving choice of narrative themes and twists says much about changing American attitudes.[48]

Despite the multicultural turn of comic-book heroes and the grown-up themes of significant cable television dramas, audiences for these entertainment outlets have been comparatively small and almost secluded. TV shows such as *Mad Men* (with fewer than 3 million viewers per episode in its Emmy Award–winning fourth season) attest more to "class-based niche viewing" than to broad popular appeal. Television is "no longer the one-size-fits-all broadcast monolith of the [baby] boomers' childhood," writes media critic Tom Carson, who compares it to "something more closely resembling the landscape of Los Angeles itself: nugget-like conclaves without even a freeway exit in common." Historically, of course, media representations of togetherness and national consensus were selective and incomplete, ignoring groups, ideas, and events that did not fit. Still, by the twenty-first century's second decade, there are worrisome signs that Americans' sense of collective identity is shrinking. Indeed, there are now so many channels and programs that finding someone with similar tastes has become uncommon. "I'm always blown away when this happens," said one TV viewer. The expansion of social media has facilitated individuals' abilities to find—and isolate themselves within—like-minded but narrow communities. When coworkers gather to discuss a TV show, the odds are getting better that most of their associates will not have seen it. One journalist even wonders whether such a discussion could be divisive: "Could it fuel an US and THEM vibe?"[49]

Certainly network television's growing reliance on political advertisements exacerbates political polarization. Whereas political advertising in 1990 accounted for only about 3 percent of commercial stations' revenues, by 2010, that figure had jumped to 20 percent ($2.8 billion). Estimates placed spending for political ads at $5 billion in 2012. TV's new "cash cow" resulted from the Supreme Court's 2010 ruling *Citizens United v. Federal Election Commission,* which allowed corporations to pour unprecedented amounts of money into political campaigns. Multimillionaires and billionaires used "super-PACs" to flood television with misleading and often ugly advertisements. "The money and media election complex" is redefining American politics, making it less democratic and more noxious.[50]

By 2011, strident partisanship had brought government to a virtual halt. Journalist George Packer wrote that finding "a common cultural narrative" is almost impossible. Long gone was the romanticized world of the 1960s *Andy Griffith Show:* "The America that the show idealized—a society in which every man had a job, inequalities of wealth were muted, and people were bound together in a tight community—no longer existed." Instead, political divisions were hardening into "mutually hostile and unintelligible universes." The sense of unity and purpose immediately following the 9/11 attacks was over. Packer feared the nation was "coming apart."[51]

For people seeking magical "water-cooler" moments that evoke feelings of communal solidarity, sports still has much to offer. The 2012 Super Bowl, for example, attracted an audience of 111.4 million—the most people that have ever watched a TV show. "In a fragmented cultural landscape," *Sports Illustrated* announced, "the TV-perfect NFL unites all." The fact that twenty-three of the previous year's top twenty-five television shows featured NFL games strengthened that argument. So did "the sheer breadth of the NFL's cultural penetration," which extends to advertising, gambling, fantasy football games, and the social network. After the New York Giants rallied in Super Bowl XLVI to defeat the Boston Patriots 21–17, the 12,233 Internet tweets per second set a record; no other English-language event matched those numbers.[52]

Skeptics take little comfort in such statistics, however. The obsession with athletics constitutes "the Achilles heel of our culture," laments sports columnist Norman Chad. "We spend more money on stadiums than schools. At our institutions of higher learning, we care more about basketball than biology." The details of football games receive closer scrutiny than the war in Afghanistan. "Let's put the games on pause and pick up our lives," Chad pleaded.[53]

There is unquestionably reason to complain about the relentless commercialization of sports. Television dollars still drive the process. Professional football has become America's most popular sport largely because of TV coverage. A 2011 deal strengthened this longtime partnership even more. Within three years, NBC, CBS, and Fox would pay the NFL more than $1 billion annually; ESPN would pay $1.9 billion a year for *Monday Night Football* and other content rights. Those arrangements amounted to an incredible 60 percent increase above what TV had been paying, and they would last into the 2020s. There was speculation that the NFL's television revenues could reach $8 billion by 2014.[54]

Proliferating sports channels and coverage have encouraged a "culture of more" in college athletics as well. As universities jump conferences in pursuit of money and publicity, "a me-first anarchy of realignment" occurs. Pittsburgh and Syracuse departed the Big East for the Atlantic Coast Conference (ACC). Nebraska, Colorado, Missouri, and Texas A&M abandoned the Big 12 for three other conferences; Texas agreed to stay, but only after securing its own lucrative television arrangement. Texas Christian University and West Virginia bolted their leagues to join the Big 12. The ACC commissioner had "never seen this level of uncertainty and potential fluidity in schools and conferences." One writer quipped that the difference between prostitution and college football is that "hookers don't have as much trouble deciding which street corner to work."[55]

Soaring coaches' salaries and the obsession with winning facilitate corruption. At Ohio State, legendary football coach Woody Hayes made $40,000 a year; less than four decades later, Urban Meyer signed a guaranteed six-year contract for $24 million. After the University of Alabama won the 2011 national football championship, coach Nick Saban signed a new contract worth $5.3 million for the next season and ranging up to $6 million by 2020, making him the highest-paid college coach. Defenders emphasize that such salaries come from athletic, not academic, budgets and that Alabama's athletic department generated $31 million in 2011. Still, as the percentage of state dollars for academics shrinks across the country, dramatically forcing up tuition and eliminating programs, university priorities understandably come under fire.[56]

Meanwhile, sports scandals are constantly in the news. Particularly unpleasant revelations involved pro football's New Orleans Saints, which had come to symbolize the tenacity of a city recovering from the disaster of Hurricane Katrina. News broke in 2012 that several dozen players had participated for three years in a "bounty" system whereby they received payments for injuring their opponents. In college football, Ohio State coach Jim Tressel resigned after the 2010 season amid allegations that his program had violated rules for years. In 2011, yet another booster-financed scandal prompted *Sports Illustrated* to run its second cover story in sixteen years titled "Why the University of Miami Should Drop Football." A few weeks later, the magazine's cover story shifted to "The Failure and Shame of Penn State," when a child-abuse scandal involving a former assistant coach resulted in the firing of celebrated coach Joe Paterno, the university's president, and the athletic director. Illegal benefits cost the University of Southern California its 2004 national title. UCLA's storied basketball program struggled in 2012 with reports of "guys drinking, guys doing drugs, guys not taking practice seriously, guys fighting." College sports has developed into a "monster," *Newsweek* asserted.[57]

There were also issues surrounding the public financing and approval of sports arenas. Plans to use a $300 million bond issue to fund a new professional football stadium in Los Angeles moved ahead despite the city's huge financial shortfall and slashed budgets for the police, firefighters, libraries, and parks. In early 2012, the Sacramento city council approved the use of public funds to cover two-thirds of the cost of a new NBA arena. Not only was Sacramento "on the verge of insolvency," as one enraged city council dissenter pointed out, but the real beneficiaries of the public bailout would be the millionaire owners. Meanwhile, most people could not even afford tickets.[58]

There had been a time when working-class fans could afford football, basketball, and baseball tickets, but soaring prices have increasingly limited that pastime to a privileged few. At an average price of $27, tickets to professional baseball games are still relatively inexpensive. Pro basketball tickets, in contrast, average $59; pro football, $113. Tickets for NFL games in the 110,000-seat Dallas Cowboys Stadium, which includes a massive 160- by 72-foot jumbotron screen, range up to $500,000 for luxury boxes. A family of four pays, on average, almost $760 to attend a Cowboys game. As NBA commissioner David Stern said: "We went from a league playing in beat-up buildings to this model of video boards and sound systems and restaurants and suites and clubs and, oh yes, there's a basketball game in here somewhere." Or, as one person joked about the patrons of sprawling new sports facilities: "They're buying tickets to a mall that happens to be a baseball stadium."[59]

Much in sports does seem to be out of whack, yet athletic competitions continue to have enormous appeal. "Sports, not religion, is the opiate of the people," explains one journalist. Economics partly accounts for sports' popularity. Many jobs (ranging from concession workers to janitors and security guards) were at stake in 2011 when a dispute between NFL owners and players—billionaires and millionaires—threatened the upcoming season. In all the NFL cities combined, around 110,000 jobs and $5 billion in income at hotels, restaurants, and bars were on the line.[60]

As always, however, sports' hold on the public imagination goes far beyond pocketbooks. "To most of us," writes one fan, "they're still about the stories we tell one another, the transcendent moments that lift us—the very way we define ourselves." It's about "dreams and escape," revered announcer Vin Scully said of baseball, "now more than ever." Close contests, surprising upsets, old loyalties, and unexpected new stars feed an ongoing public hunger. In early 2012, little-known Taiwanese American Jeremy Lin became an overnight NBA sensation after coming off the bench to energize the drooping New York Knicks with stunning performances. "We Are Linsane" and "The Sky's the Lin It" read some signs, while others touted a "Linderella Story." Elsewhere, the news was about "Detroit Rising," as successful seasons for the Detroit Lions, Tigers, and Red Wings meshed with a rebounding auto industry to instill a beleaguered American city with hope and a sense of community.[61]

While sports can strengthen feelings of kinship on a variety of levels, they also feed the insatiable appetite for celebrities. For decades, commentators have discussed the public's need to identify with people who are famous for being famous—"intimate strangers." But with the Internet, the speed with which celebrities are created has quickened. Moreover, the Great Recession, combined with accelerating social changes, may have strengthened the obsession with pop idols, who implicitly confirm the American dream of opportunity and triumph. They show that fame and fortune rest with individuals rather than with class, race, gender, or institutions. Less comforting, of course, is how short-lived celebrity success can be. Just a few weeks after Jeremy Lin's scintillating debut with the New York Knicks, and even before an injured knee ended his remarkable season, "Linsanity" merchandise was available for half price. "There seems to be a new shot clock on our celebrity culture," said a bemused reporter; "even the best stories get old fast."[62]

The fascination with celebrities can easily obscure social realities and divert attention from entertainment woes. In 2007, *Rolling Stone* magazine reported that "the record business has plunged into historic decline." After Warner Music Group's stock prices fell by 42 percent in twelve months, it laid off 400 employees. Between 2003 and 2007, 2,700 music stores (around 38 percent of the total) closed, leaving the bulk of sales to box stores like Wal-Mart. According to a well-established industry source, "Here we have a business that's dying. There won't be any major labels pretty soon." The rapid slide in CD sales (dropping 52 percent between 2000 and 2009) convinced one executive that the CD era was almost over. The Great Recession further pounded the music business. In 2010, concert attendance plunged by 25 percent, even though ticket prices dropped from the previous year's average of $65 to $61; gross sales fell by 26 percent. The next year was reportedly the worst ever. As revenues shrank, so did the number of major recording labels. Going into the decade, there had been six; after Universal purchased EMI in 2011, there were only three (including Warner and Sony, which had merged with BMG Entertainment).[63]

Despite the recording industry's turmoil, music is "everywhere," as the president of *American Idol*'s production company insists. The Internet has been a culprit in the "industry's slow fade," but it also prompted the move toward the file-sharing services that turned Apple's iTunes Music Store into the world's largest music retailer. Meanwhile, streaming services such as the Danish-based Spotify were having a huge impact, reflecting the music labels' growing willingness to license their content. In mid-2011, after two years of negotiating, Spotify finally gained access to the U.S. market; within six months, it had 10 million users. With a subscription service that included 15 million songs by 2012, Spotify offers a "freemium" package whereby users pay nothing to hear a limited number of songs interspersed with ads. For $4.99 a month, subscribers can omit the ads and stream as much music as they want. They can also use the "Rolling Stone Recommends" app to hear many of the songs reviewed by the magazine. "We think Spotify is like the ultimate jukebox," says *Rolling Stone* editor Jann Wenner. Spotify formed a partnership with Facebook as well. According to critic Steve Knopper, Spotify and other newly launched "cloud-based music services"—Apple's iTune Match, Google Music, and Amazon Cloud—made 2011 the year in which "the digital-music revolution took its biggest step since iTunes launched in 2003."[64]

While the Internet refashioned the music business, a rising group of new stars such as Taylor Swift and Lady Gaga enlivened it. Dubbed the "poet laureate of puberty" by the *Washington Post,* Swift released her first album in 2006, when she was sixteen. Within five years, her annual income was $45 million and she had won virtually every country music award. She had sold a record-setting 20 million albums and—more than any other country singer—25 million digital tracks. She wrote her own material. And she carefully cultivated a clean image. "Taylor Swift is the greatest thing that's ever happened to country music," extolled the legendary Dolly Parton. According to one commentator, Swift "tapped into an audience that hadn't previously been recognized: teen-age girls who listen to country music." And the story she offers them is basically "an underdog saga" about the triumph of niceness over meanness.[65]

Lady Gaga likewise treats her fans with great care, sensitivity, and even affection. The former Stefani Joanne Angelina Germanotta is considerably more daring and provocative, however. Serious and tireless, she writes her own songs and choreographs her performances. She even recorded most of her smash album *Born This Way* (which sold 1.1 million albums in its first week) on a studio-equipped bus, "surging down the highway, wind in my hair." Describing herself as a "free bitch," she wears outrageous, suggestive costumes, makeup, and hairdos. But it is her persona as a champion of misfits and outcasts that especially energizes her young followers: she is the "Mother Monster" of all the "Little Monsters." Recalling how students bullied her in an all-girl Catholic school in New York City, she pleads with her teenage followers to shed their insecurities and be proud of who they are. In the words of one expert, she "reshaped pop in her own image, telling kids it's cool to be gay or freaky or unpopular." She also evokes controversy. The Catholic League condemned her single "Judas," in which the twelve apostles are a motorcycle gang and she is Mary Magdalene. Within three years after her career first took off in 2008, talent and controversy had combined to make her an entertainment phenomenon with reported earnings of $100 million.[66]

Hip-hop has much to celebrate as well. By 2010, after five slumping years, it was rebounding. Eminem's *Recovery* album was one reason, but so was the popularity of rappers such as Lil Wayne, who by 2007 had become a dominant solo act. In 2008, his *Tha Carter II* outsold all other albums in every genre. Significantly, Lil Wayne's emergence helped to mark rap's Southern turn. Gritty neighborhoods in Miami, Atlanta, and Houston had incubated "a largely grassroots movement" that, according to writer Ben Westhoff, "succeeded in spite of, not because of the big record labels." New York in the 1980s and the West Coast in the 1990s had framed the rap phenomenon. But in 2009, Southern artists accounted for 75 percent of *Billboard*'s Top 40 rap songs. The songs have a distinctive sound with lots of "hyper-regional slang" as well as "chants, grunts, and shouts." Some critics worried that Southern rap's "nursery rhyme jingles," along with its "shucking-and-jiving ditties," might place it uncomfortably in the "minstrel show" tradition. Westhoff and others have found much to like, however. It is music to "sing along with," as one producer says. Westhoff lauds it as "the true populist music of its time," in the tradition of the Mississippi blues—sympathetic to poor people and humble origins, and opposed to corporate manipulation. As "party music," it is good for dancing, less "lyrically focused" and cerebral than New York rap. And it is indisputably popular. "Why they hittin' on me?" raps Soulja Boy. "I didn't do nothin' to them, but count this money."[67]

More than money is involved, however. In less than four decades, hip-hop's cultural impact has been phenomenal. It has fostered what Steve Stoute, an inductee into the Advertising Hall of Achievement, dubbed "the tanning of America." He refers to hip-hop's role as a "catalytic force" among young people. It blurs differences "by allowing for a cultural exchange between all comers, groups of kids who were black, white, Hispanic, Asian, you name it." Hip-hop has shaped "a generationally shared mental complexion." In the words of rapper DJ Kool Herc, "It wasn't a black thing. It was a 'we' thing."[68]

The "tanning" phenomenon has raised both hopes and fears. A reassuring perspective is that popular culture—by "normalizing, individualizing and humanizing"—facilitates adjustments to new, unsettling developments. "The 'Will and Grace' theory" thus suggests that the highly rated NBC television comedy's treatment of gay characters from 1998 to 2006 influenced a dramatic shift in public opinion. In the early 2000s, polls showed that two-thirds of Americans opposed gay marriage; a decade later, more than half supported it. One study found that TV characters had influenced about one-third of individuals who ultimately viewed gays and lesbians more favorably.[69]

Such shifts in opinion have also spawned an angry and anxious backlash among Americans who are worried that they are losing the country they once knew. Immigration, cultural diversity, an African American president, same-sex marriage, sexuality, and even birth control are hot-button issues with fierce political implications. In that charged political setting, 2012 Republican presidential aspirant Rick Santorum asserted that Satan had captured popular culture. As had happened before, the question of "whose America is this?" tore at the national fabric.[70]

Like the United States generally, entertainment includes a widening range of diffuse and segmented parts. As popular culture splinters into a mind-boggling number of options and audiences, it follows the trajectory of an increasingly varied society without a unifying center. In many respects, American amusements and their many assorted participants—like the nation itself—seem to be forming into virtually separate worlds, with insular identities and orbits.

Despite the exponential growth of the Internet, specialized audiences, and programs, there is reason to believe that popular culture's images, narratives, and experiences will continue to be consolidating forces. It was, after all, pop culture agencies such as Wild West shows, vaudeville, Tin Pan Alley, movies, radio, sports, and television that helped forge nineteenth-century villages into a nation. That process was anything but seamless or free of controversy. Many times, it was disruptive. Still, as writer John Powers has argued, "The love of entertainment is central to our national character." Over time, popular culture has unified more than divided. Indeed, "in these extreme times," writes Powers, "our shallow, trivial, ephemeral popular culture may be what's keeping America from falling apart."[71]

Centrifugal technological and social trends pose massive challenges nonetheless. So does a battered, unpredictable economy and a toxic political environment. One can only hope that American amusements—long the "art of democracy" and often the nation's most inclusionary force—are up to the increasingly severe test.

NOTES

1. Neil Gabler, "Celebrity: The Greatest Show on Earth," *Newsweek*, December 21, 2009, 65.

2. Leonard Pitts Jr., "Torture Turned up Only Shame," *Spokane (WA) Spokesman-Review*, November 13, 2009, B8 (Jack Bauer); Linda J. Bilmes and Joseph E. Stiglitz, "America's Costly War Machine," *Los Angeles Times*, September 18, 2011; Ron Powers, "The Cost of War," http://usmilitary.about.com/od/terrorism/a/iraqdeath1000.html?p=1 (accessed March 14, 2012); John Powers, "Same as It Ever Was," *American Prospect*, September 2011, 35 (Iraq on map).

3. Matthew Futterman, "Fans, Sponsors, No Slam Dunk," *Spokane (WA) Spokesman-Review*, October 19, 2008, E1 ("orange juice"); James Suroweiki, "The De-Leveraging Myth," *New Yorker*, November 14, 2011, 30 (25 percent); Thomas Frank, *Pity the Billionaire: The Hard-Times Swindle and the Unlikely Resurgence of the American Right* (New York: Metropolitan Books, 2011), 3 ("epic breakdown"), 13–14, 32; John Cassidy, "The Economy: Why They Failed," *New York Review of Books*, December 9, 2010, 27–29.

4. David Frum, "Rush to the Bottom," *Newsweek*, March 19, 2012, 29.

5. Rob Sheffield, "The United States of Oprah," *Rolling Stone*, May 26, 2011, 38; Leon Wynter, *American Skin: Pop Culture, Big Business and the End of White America* (New York: Crown Publishers, 2002), 181 ("rocks the cradle").

6. Wynter, *American Skin*, 118 (*People Magazine*); Lynn Elber, "Did '80s Show Help in '08 Election?" *Spokane (WA) Spokesman-Review*, November 13, 2008, D7 ("Huxtable effect"); Gil Troy, "Michael Jackson: The King of Pop Made His Mark," http://hnn.us/blogs/68.html (accessed July 2, 2009); Darryl Pinckney, "Dreams from Obama," *New York Review of Books*, March 6, 2008, 42. See also Steve Stoute, *The Tanning of America: How Hip-Hop Created a Culture that Rewrote the Rules of the New Economy* (New York: Gotham Books, 2011), 240, 244–47.

7. "Palin: What's Her Political Legacy," *Week*, October 21, 2011, 17; Joann Wypijewski, "Rawhide," *Nation*, October 10, 2011, 6; David Sirota, "In Celebrities We Trust," *In These Times*, April 2011, 35 (Vitter).

8. Peter M. Robinson, *The Dance of the Comedians: The People, the President, and the Performance of Political Standup Comedy in America* (Amherst: University of Massachusetts Press, 2010), 222 (Fey's impersonation of Palin), 214 ("political comedians").

9. Henrik Hertzberg, "The Debate Debate," *New Yorker*, February 13 and 20, 2012, 32 ("fakery"); Robinson, *Dance of the Comedians*, 220 ("simply," "the gut"); Maureen Dowd, "America's Anchors," *Rolling Stone*, November 16, 2006, 54 ("not a fan").

10. Leonard Pitts Jr., "Casual Lying a Real Threat," *Spokane (WA) Spokesman-Review*, April 18, 2011, A9 (Kyl); Eric Alterman, "The Liar's Network," *Nation*, April 25, 2011, 10 (Sammon); Tim Dickinson, "The Fox News Fear Factory," *Rolling Stone*, June 9, 2011, 57 ("propaganda machine"), 82 (Ailes).

11. Explanations of the Great Recession are substantial, but see, e.g., Paul Krugman and Robin Wells, "The Busts Keep Getting Bigger: Why?" *New York Review of Books*, July 14, 2011, 28–29.

12. Jennifer Burns, *Goddess of the Market: Ayn Rand and the American Right* (New York: Oxford University Press, 2011), 63 ("noblest"); Anne C. Heller, *Ayn Rand and the World She Made* (New York: Anchor Books, 2009), 279 ("cut the Bible").

13. Heller, *Ayn Rand*, xii, 287 (polls); Burns, *Goddess of the Market*, 2 ("own lifetime"), 283–84.

14. Burns, *Goddess of the Market*, 284 ("Going Galt"); Adam Kirsch, "Ayn Rand's Revenge," *New York Times*, November 1, 2009; William Rivers Pitt, "A Moment of Pure Astonishment, Again" (proposed strike), http://www.truth-out.org/moment-pure-astonishment-again/1319390406 (accessed October 16, 2011); Thomas Frank, "More Government, Please!" *Harper's Magazine*, December 2011, 8; John Nichols, "Representative Paul Ryan," *Nation*, December 6, 2010, 11. Other discussions of Rand's influence on recent politics include E. J. Dionne's comments on the July 20, 2011, *Rachel Maddow Show* (CSNBC); Jane Mayer, "State for Sale," *New Yorker*, October 10, 2011, 94, 96; and Dave Johnson, "Concern over Republican Embrace of the Ayn Rand Poison," http://ourfuture.org/print/67834 (accessed September 24, 2011).

15. Michael Guilfoil, "Shelf-Life Support," *Spokane (WA) Spokesman-Review*, March 4, 2012, D1, D7.

16. Ken Auletta, *Googled: The End of the World as We Know It* (London: Penguin Books, 2009, 2010), 305 (Gutenberg), 14 ("no Web"), 28 (Gates).

17. Ibid., 12 (Redstone); Sarah Lacy, *The Facebook Story* (Surrey, England: Crimson Publishing, 2009), 138–39 ("nerds").

18. Lacy, *Facebook Story*, 59–60, 105–8; Auletta, *Googled*, 14 (Internet access).

19. John Seabrook, "Streaming Dreams," *New Yorker*, January 16, 2012, 24–25 (dorm, "anarchy"); Lacy, *Facebook Story*, 1–2; Auletta, *Googled*, xi (2009 statistic), 152; Glenn Chapman, "YouTube Serving up Two Billion Videos Daily," May 16, 2010 ("nearly double"), http://www.google.com/hostednews/afp/article/ALeqM5jK4sI9GfUTCKAkVGhDz pJ1ACZm9Q (accessed May 24, 2012).

20. Rob Fischer, "A Ninja in Our Sites," *American Prospect*, January/February 2012, 30–31 ("free"); Seabrook, "Streaming Dreams," 25.

21. Steve Coll, "The Internet: For Better or for Worse," *New York Review of Books*, April 7, 2011, 22, 24; Danny Goldberg, "Kill the Internet—and Other Anti-SOPA Myths," January 24, 2012, http://www.thenation.com/print/article/165837/kill-internet-and-other-anti-sopa-myths (accessed January 25, 2012).

22. Auletta, *Googled*, 152, 169–71, 238, 263; Seabrook, "Streaming Dreams," 27 (Kyncl).

23. Auletta, *Googled*, 146 (2008 study), 240 (CBS); Fischer, "Ninja in Our Sites," 28–30.

24. Sue Halpern, "Who Was Steve Jobs?" *New York Review of Books*, January 12, 2012, 24–26; "Steve Jobs: Does He Deserve All the Adulation," *Week*, October 21, 2011, 16 ("Barnum"); Walter Isaacson, *Steve Jobs* (New York: Simon and Schuster, 2011), 373, 378–425 (379, "lifestyle").

25. Isaacson, *Steve Jobs*, 392 ("pocket"), 403 ("turning point"), 421–23 (U2); Auletta, *Googled*, 230 ("digital jukebox").

26. Auletta, *Googled*, 14; Lacy, *Facebook Story*, 112 ("everyday folks"); Karen Sternheimer, *Celebrity Culture and the American Dream* (New York: Routledge, 2011), 223 ("camera"), 214 ("their own"). Lacy, *Facebook Story*, 109–18, is very helpful regarding the roles of open-source software and peer-to-peer networks in this transition.

27. Ben Westhoff, *Dirty South: Outkast, Lil Wayne, Soulja Boy, and the Southern Rappers Who Reinvented Hip Hop* (Chicago: Chicago Review Press, 2011), 237–38 (Wade), 232–33 ("megastar"); "Justin Bieber," Billboard.com, http://www.billboard.com/artist /justin-bieber/1099520#/artist/justin-bieber/bio/1099520 (accessed May 24, 2012); "Jackie Evancho Biography," http://www.jackie evancho.com/us/bio (accessed May 24, 2012).

28. Seabrook, "Streaming Dreams," 24, 26, 28–30.

29. Lacy, *Facebook Story*, 98–99, 164–65.

30. Alex Ben Block and Lucy Autrey Wilson, eds., *George Lucas's Blockbusting* (New York: it Books, HarperCollins, 2010), 723, 811–17 (813, "fretting"), 898–900.

31. Ibid., 811–21, 835, 838, 839, 898–901; Tom Doherty, "The Last Bow for 35mm Film," February 20, 2012, http://hnn.us/articles/law-bow-35mm-film (accessed February 20, 2012); *NBC Nightly News*, April 8, 2011 (James Bond); David Denby, "Crash Landing," *New Yorker*, March 26, 2011, 109 (*Pirates*); Fischer, "Ninja in Our Sites," 30 (Valente, DVDs).

32. Rafer Guzman, "Focus on Young Viewers Aside, Grown-ups Had Worthy Options," *Spokane (WA) Spokesman-Review*, December 12, 2011, C3; Roger Ebert, "Sequel Madness," *Newsweek*, May 23 and 30, 2011, 76.

33. Stephen Prince, *Firestorm: American Film in the Age of Terrorism* (New York: Columbia University Press, 2009), 296–305; Thor quoted in Jacob Bernstein, "The Right's Thriller King," *Newsweek*, July 29, 2011, 70. *Stop-Loss*, scheduled for release in 2007, was postponed until 2008.

34. Ebert, "Sequel Madness," 74–76; Block and Wilson, *George Lucas's Blockbusting*, 810, 817 (box office); Heather Hendershot, "Losers Take All," *Nation*, May 30, 2011, 40; Devin Gordon, "Why TV Is Better than the Movies," *Newsweek*, February 26, 2007, 54 ("outsourced," "needle").

35. Jennifer L. Pozner, *Reality Bites Back: The Troubling Truth about Guilty Pleasure TV* (Berkeley, CA: Seal Press, 2010), 8, 12, 14 (costs); *Us*, July 7–14, 2003, 48 (Anderson).

36. Pozner, *Reality Bites Back*, 26, 28, 33, 71, 19, 17.

37. Davis quoted in Kelefa Sanneh, "The Reality Principle," *New Yorker*, May 9, 2011, 74–75.

38. Matt Diehl, "Adam Lambert Storms the Dance Floor on New LP," *Rolling Stone*, December 8, 2011, 20; Michael Schneider, "You've Got Male," *TV Guide*, March 19–April 1, 2012, 24–25.

39. Gordon, "Why TV Is Better," 53; Hendershot, "Losers Take All," 40–41; Ebert, "Sequel Madness," 76 (Schrader).

40. Marc Peyser, "'The Sopranos': Making a Mob Hit," *Newsweek*, January 17, 2000, 71 (quoting *New York Times*); Geoffrey O'Brien, "A Northern New Jersey of the Mind," *New York Review of Books*, August 16, 2007, 18 (Chase, "coup"). David Simon, *Tony Soprano's America: The Criminal Side of the American Dream* (Boulder, CO: Westview Press, 2002), conveys a sense of the series' richness.

41. Lorrie Moore, "In the Life of 'The Wire,'" *New York Review of Books*, October 14, 2010, 24. On *Game of Thrones*, see Adam Serwer, "A Liberal's Guide to Middle Earth," *American Prospect*, April 4, 2011, 33–35, and Rob Sheffield, "No Country for Old Hobbits," *Rolling Stone*, May 12, 2011, 28.

42. On *Breaking Bad*, see Andrew Romano, "The Most Dangerous Show on Television," *Newsweek*, July 4 and 11, 2011, 59–62 (60, "Mr. Chips"); Andrew Leonard, "The Downward Spiral," *Rolling Stone*, June 23, 2011, 45–46 ("grimmest"); and Rob Sheffield, "Men at Work," ibid., August 18, 2011, 30. On *Mad Men*, see Eric Konigsberg, "A Fine Madness," *Rolling Stone*, September 16, 2010, 43–49; and Stephanie Coontz, "'Mad Men': A Postseason Retrospective," November 1, 2010, http://www.hnn.us/articles/133064.html (accessed November 1, 2010).

43. Joshua Alston, "Battlestar Gallactica," *Newsweek*, December 22, 2008, 52–53.

44. Powers, "Same as It Ever Was," 36 ("bleakness"), 37.

45. Emily Listfield, "Game On!" *Parade*, March 18, 2012, 11; Abby McGanney Nolan, "Hell's Belles," *American Prospect*, March 2012, 58 ("boom"), 59; Laura Miller, "Fresh Hell," *New Yorker*, June 14 and 21, 2010, 132–35 ("disaffection").

46. Julian Sanchez, "The Revolt of the Comic Books," *American Prospect*, November 2007, 43–47; *Captain America 5*, no. 25 (March 2007); Katherine G. Aiken, "Superhero History: Using Comic Books to Teach U.S. History," *Organization of American Historians Magazine of History*, April 2010, 43 (*Reborn*).

47. "LGBT Themes in American Mainstream Comics," http://en.wikipedia.org/wiki/LGBT_themes_in_American_mainstream_comics (accessed February 10, 2012).

48. Leonard Pitts Jr., "A Superhero for a New Age," *Spokane (WA) Spokesman-Review*,

August 15, 2011, A7; "Gay Caped Crusaders," *Rolling Stone,* November 10, 2011, 70; Gene Demby, "Masked Identity Politics," *American Prospect,* June 2011, 29–31; "The Man of Steel Gets a Makeover," *Parade,* September 25, 2011, 4 (sales); *CBS's Sunday Morning,* September 25, 2011; "Comics Alliance," http://www.comicsalliance.com/2010/0211 /captain-america-tea-party-controversy/ (copy in author's possession); "LGBT Themes in American Mainstream Comics"; "The New 52," http://en.wikipedia.org/wiki/The_New_52/ (accessed February 10, 2012); Bill Berkowitz, "Archie Comics Defies Religious Extremists and Celebrates Gay Marriage," http://blog.buzzflash.com/print/13387 (accessed March 21, 2012); Bradford W. Wright, *Comic-Book Nation: The Transformation of Culture in America* (Baltimore: Johns Hopkins University Press, 2001), 282–83 ("sensibilities").

49. Tom Carson, "Old Frontier," *American Prospect,* September 2011, 56; Dave Itzkoff, "The Top Man at 'Mad Men' Isn't Mad Anymore," *New York Times,* March 11, 2012, A&L, 14 (*Mad Men* viewers); Paul Turner, "Watching What We Say," *Spokane (WA) Spokesman-Review,* March 11, 2012, D7 ("blown away," "vibe"); Gregory Rodriquez, "Why Social Media Isn't," *Los Angeles Times,* June 20, 2011.

50. John Nichols and Robert W. McChesney, "The Money & Media Election Complex," *Nation,* November 19, 2010, 11–17 (12, ad revenues); Nichols and McChesney, "The Assault of the Super PACs," ibid., February 6, 2012, 11–18.

51. George Packer, "Coming Apart, " *New Yorker,* September 12, 2011, 67, 65, 69.

52. Tim Layden, "The Power of the Game," *Sports Illustrated,* February 13, 2012, 15–16; Stephen Battaglio, "NBC Scores Big with the Super Bowl," ibid., February 20–March 4, 2012, 12; Paul Turner, "A Charlie Brown Super Bowl," *Spokane (WA) Spokesman-Review,* February 5, 2012, D6.

53. Norman Chad, "Slouch Says Sports Fixation Has Our Priorities Skewed," *Spokane (WA) Spokesman-Review,* January 3, 2012, B5.

54. "Broadcast Networks Reach New Contracts with League," *Spokane (WA) Spokesman-Review,* December 5, 2011, B2; Peter King, "Game Time," *Sports Illustrated,* August 1, 2011, 37. On the NFL's marketing campaigns, see Michael Oriard, *Brand NFL: Making and Selling America's Favorite Sport* (Chapel Hill: University of North Carolina Press, 2007).

55. John Blanchette, "Reason Wins the Day for PAC-12, Washington State," *Spokane (WA) Spokesman-Review,* September 21, 2011, B1, B7 ("culture of more," "anarchy," "hookers"); Joedy McCreary, "ACC Adds Pitt, 'Cuse," ibid., September 19, 2011, B3 ("uncertainty"); Austin Murphy, "What Just Happened to College Football," *Sports Illustrated,* June 21, 2010, 16–17.

56. Dave Zirin, "The Year I Learned to Hate College Football," Nation.com (posted December 31, 2011; accessed January 2, 2012); Adam Kramer, "Nick Saban's Contract: An Ugly Style Translates to Wins, Dollars, Dominance," bleacherreport.com/ . . . /1122501-a -beautiful-ugly-nic-saban-style-tr . . . , March 28, 2012 (accessed April 4, 2012).

57. Peter King, "Way Out of Bounds," *Sports Illustrated,* March 12, 2012, 34–41 (Saints); George Dohrmann with David Epstein, "The Fall of Jim Tressel," ibid., June 6, 2011, 40–46; Alexander Wolff, "16 Years Later, It's Time to Get Real," ibid., August 29, 2011, 33–35 (Miami); L. Jon Werthem and David Epstein, "This Is Penn State," ibid., November 21, 2011, 40–53; "Not the UCLA Bruins Way," ibid., March 5, 2012, 60 ("guys"); Buzz Bissinger, "Open Secrets," *Newsweek,* November 21, 2011, 4.

58. Connie Bruck, "The Man Who Owns L.A.," *New Yorker,* January 16, 2012, 44–56; Norman Chad, "Once Again Sports Public a Victim of 'Stadium Abuse,'" *Spokane (WA) Spokesman-Review,* March 13, 2012, B1, B5 ("insolvency").

59. On prices, see Michael Kazin, "Why Baseball Is the Best—and Least Exploitative—American Sport," *New Republic,* March 31, 2012; Sally Jenkins, "Does Football Cost Too Much?" *Parade,* November 29, 2009, 14–15; Bruck, "Man Who Owns L.A.," 48 (Stern); Michael Kimmelman, "At the Bad New Ballparks," *New York Review of Books,* November 19, 2009, 23 ("mall").

60. Robyn Norwood, "Too Big to Fail?" *USA Today,* June 10–12, 2011, 2A; David Remnick, "Speaking of Sports," *New Yorker,* November 28, 2011, 75 ("opiate"); Ellen Gibson and Paul Wiseman, "Gridiron Gold," *Spokane (WA) Spokesman-Review,* October 10, 2011, A8.

61. Terry McDonnell, "In My Tribe," *Sports Illustrated*, November 28, 2011, 68–69 ("define ourselves"); Joe Posnanski, "Loving Baseball," ibid., July 25, 2011, 56 (Scully); Pablo S. Torre, "From Couch to Clutch," ibid., February 20, 2012, 48 (Lin puns); Pablo S. Torre, "A Run Like No Other," ibid., February 27, 2012, 30–35; Marisol Bellow and Steve Gardner, "Detroit Rising," *USA Today*, October 10, 2011, 1–2A. See also Lee Jenkins, "Best. Night. Ever." *Sports Illustrated*, December 12, 2011, 101–10, on the 2011 baseball season.

62. Richard Shickel, *Intimate Strangers: The Culture of Celebrity in America* (1985; reprint, Chicago: Ivan Dee, 2000); Sternheimer, *Celebrity Culture and the American Dream*, 1–24, 214–40; Richard Hoffer, "Over in a New York Minute," *Sports Illustrated*, March 26, 2012, 21–22 ("new shot clock").

63. Brian Hiatt and Evan Serpick, "The Record Industry's Slow Fade," *Rolling Stone*, June 28, 2007, 13–14 ("decline," "dying"); Stoute, *Tanning of America*, 256 (CD sales); Steve Knopper, "Is the CD Era Finally Over?" *Rolling Stone*, March 1, 2012, 13–14; Knopper, "Concert Biz Collapses as Fans Flee," ibid., January 20, 2011, 19; Knopper, "Touring, Downloads Stall in Worst Year on Record," ibid., February 3, 2011, 17; Knopper, "Universal Buys EMI for $1.9 Billion," ibid., December 2, 2012, 15.

64. Steve Knopper, "Music Rules Prime-Time TV," *Rolling Stone*, June 23, 2011, 17 ("everywhere"), 20; Hiatt and Serpick, "Record Industry's Slow Fade," 14; Knopper, "Is the CD Era Finally Over?" 14; Simon Vozick-Levinson, "Spotify Finally Hits America," *Rolling Stone*, August 4, 2011, 17–18; "Rolling Stone and Stopify Team Up," ibid., December 22, 2011–January 5, 2012, 10 (Wenner); Knopper, "Digital Music's Cloud Revolution," ibid., 16.

65. Lizzie Widdicombe, "You Belong to Me," *New Yorker*, October 10, 2011, 104 ("poet laureate"), 106 (Parton), 110 ("tapped," "saga").

66. "Lady Gaga Sells 1.1 Million Albums in a Week," *Rolling Stone*, June 23, 2011, 22; Neil Strauss, "The Broken Heart and Violent Fantasies of Lady Gaga," ibid., July 8–22, 2010, 68 ("bitch"); Brian Hiatt, "Monster Goddess," ibid., June 9, 2011, 42 ("freaky"), 46 (Catholic League); "The Hits," ibid., February 3, 2011, 18 (income); Ramin Setoodeh, "Gaga's Oprah Moment," *Newsweek*, June 6, 2011, 50.

67. Westhoff, *Dirty South*, 18 ("succeeded"), 3–4 ("jingles"), 9 ("sing along," "party music"), 268 ("populist"), 237 ("count this money"); see ibid., 243–53, on Lil Wayne.

68. Stoute, *Tanning of America*, xvi–xvii, 231 (Herc).

69. Leonard Pitts Jr., "Another Opportunity Lost," *Spokane (WA) Spokesman-Review*, March 12, 2012, A7 ("normalizing"); Dahlia Lithwick, "Extreme Makeover," *New Yorker*, March 12, 2012, 77 ("Will and Grace"); Ramin Setoodeh, "Kings of Queens," *Newsweek*, November 23, 2009, 56.

70. Hendrick Hertzberg, "Satanic Reverses," *New Yorker*, March 5, 2012, 24 (Santorum).

71. Powers, "Same as It Ever Was," 38.

PREFACE

"WE SELL FUN," SAID MARK CUBAN, THE owner of the Dallas Mavericks basketball team, in 2002. "We sell the answer to 'What do you want to do tonight?'" Cuban's comment neatly sums up the history of popular culture in the United States.[1]

This book is an interpretive synthesis of almost two hundred years of American entertainment: the sale, and purchase, of fun. Popular culture must enjoy at least fairly broad support from ordinary people and be accessible to them. But what separates it from noncommercial neighborhood and family games, for instance, is that its creators and/or disseminators seek to profit from it; they are in the business of merchandising entertainment. Over the years, new technologies, shifting values and moods, economic conditions, political pressures, consumer expectations, and demographics have dramatically formed and transformed the nature of that business and its products.[2]

In that regard, popular culture both reflects and shapes the larger society. How it does so is anything but simple. It can refract as well as mirror, breaking the larger society into a wide range of images and meanings. It can follow well-worn paths and set new directions. American entertainment has never comprised a neatly homogenized set of diversions. Instead, it is full of contradictions and speaks in many voices, some louder and more influential than others. Its messages can be liberating and confining, reassuring and unsettling. Conflicts, sometimes violent, have frequently accompanied efforts to establish what kinds of amusements are acceptable and on whose terms. Shifting historical contexts have been crucial in determining what is popular, how it emerges, and what forms it takes. In that regard, popular culture has mirrored social, economic, and political changes. But it has also been an agency of change, influencing attitudes, breaking down barriers, facilitating upward mobility, and causing social collisions.

It has both provided important cultural ties in times of crisis and triggered conflict.[3]

The processes by which assorted amusements have become mainstream entertainment have resembled the dynamics between a circus's big tent and the outlying sideshows. The owners of the big tent typically move cautiously, courting relatively well-to-do and respectable middle-class audiences. In order not to offend people with money and status or create problems with local authorities, the big tent's offerings must be decent, reputable, and not overly controversial. Yet acts that are too bland or uninteresting may fail to attract customers. In that regard, the sideshow exhibits have played crucial roles. Sideshows aim to shock. They appeal to society's allegedly baser instincts. For a small fee, customers can peek briefly into forbidden or unsettling worlds—the worlds of freaks, nudity, the risqué, the exotic, and the erotic. In their quest for new, exciting fare, operators of the big tent have historically reached, however tentatively, into the sideshows for material. Despite ongoing resistance from authorities and moral guardians, the sideshows have eventually influenced what happens in the big tent. But it is only as tamer, cleaner versions that sideshow acts have eased into the spotlight. The acts must qualify as "respectable" fare, fit for general audiences. As a result, it is only in sanitized form that many once-boisterous, daring, lower-class entertainments have eased into more prosperous, bourgeois venues. But, even as the big tent incorporates and tames the sideshows' more risqué and edgier elements, it is invigorated and energized by them.[4]

The history of popular culture has consisted of ongoing exchanges and sometimes brutal struggles between society's outsiders and insiders. Sometimes outsider status has been primarily a state of mind, a result of perceived snubs and slights. In most instances, however, American entertainers have truly come from society's margins—from the difficult worlds of new immigrants, racial minorities, the working class, and women who chafed under the restrictions of a patriarchal environment. Lacking power and influence, and often struggling against discrimination, prejudice, and poverty, they have looked to entertainment as a "way out." The amusement business, although harsh and demanding, has been alluring as a place in which to demonstrate talent, achieve individual attention, and perhaps—as a few have done—become rich and famous. Too often, talented and innovative people who helped clear the way for their more celebrated successors have labored in obscurity. In a number of instances, the environments in which they have worked have been hostile. Still, in significant ways, popular culture has provided a ladder of opportunity for some gifted individuals who have lacked financial resources, education, social connections, and status. As products of society's peripheries, and while laboring against considerable odds, they have helped forge and disseminate a variety of amusements that in notable instances influenced society.

Such influence has not come smoothly or without opposition. Elite groups have typically feared or denounced much of popular culture because of its lower-class origins—its vulgarity, its lack of taste, its crudeness, its threats to traditional sources of authority. It has seemed especially pernicious to privileged groups precisely because of its appeal to people within their own ranks, especially the young. The story of popular culture in the United States has, thus, been as much about efforts to contain and control it as about its intrinsic character and content.

New entertainments have, nevertheless, proved marvelously adaptive, and, over time, many diversions that once existed only in society's nethermost regions have become part of mainstream fare. Indeed, popular culture as a whole has moved from the nation's economic and social fringes to a central place in American life. By the end of the twentieth century, it not only constituted a vital component of the national economy but also was America's leading export. New technologies have played a pivotal role in the diffusion of an entertainment culture. Over several generations, audio recordings, movies, radio, television, and other inventions helped create a set of national images, sounds, and narratives. While such technology has had a centralizing effect that often overwhelms local distinctions, it has, ultimately, also encouraged fragmentation. The creation of hundreds of cable television channels by the end of the twentieth century, for instance, segmented the very audiences that the several networks had earlier pulled together.

Ironically, as the pop culture market has splintered into a multitude of niche audiences, corporations in the amusement business have merged and consolidated at a quickening rate. Government facilitated the mergers by championing policies that favored large corporations. A few critics judged this concentration of power in the mass media as nothing short of obscene. But the dominant controversies revolved—as they had time and again—around entertainment's spreading impact on American morals.

The hybrid nature of American popular culture has been striking. Entertainments have grown via mixing or "crossing over," whether from the margins to the center or across the boundaries of race, class, and gender. Whites, for example, have continually incorporated—or stolen, as some critics charge—materials from African Americans in their own music and other entertainment. But blacks have borrowed and adapted as well. These cultural "skin grafts," as the writer Leon Wynter has termed them, have helped transform America's race relations. Long before the Supreme Court's 1954 *Brown v. Board of Education* court decision outlawed racial segregation in public schools, African Americans were gradually making significant inroads into an increasingly integrated entertainment world. In turn, by the end of the twentieth century, a fundamental truth had solidified: "*American* does not mean 'white,'" as Wynter has argued. "The preferences, presence, and perspectives of people of color" have increasingly altered long-standing assumptions about the American identity. Popular culture has facilitated new ways of defining what an American is. Phrases like "as American as Ray Charles" or ". . . Oprah Winfrey" do not shock mainstream sensibilities within which the norm was once emphatically white.[5]

From this perspective, popular culture has been America's most democratic art form. Granted, much racism, discrimination, and injustice have marked it. But the perception that the United States is an open society arguably has no more forceful basis than in the evolving messages and images of popular culture.

The world of entertainment has bridged not only racial lines but also those of class and gender. Examples have been legion. They include the immigrant founders of Hollywood's studio system, the white "cracker" kid Elvis Presley, and female performers such as Mae West and Carol Burnett.

But, even as popular culture has helped shape a more open, diversified society, its commercial matrix has functioned like a sponge, absorbing contrary, dissenting views so efficiently that even radical ideas become mere consumer items. In mid-1969, for example, Paul Goodman's highly critical examination of American society, *Like a Conquered Province*, appeared in a *New York Times Magazine* advertisement. The book was a vigorous critique of the United States as an "empty society" in which, among other things, middle-class citizens wandered aimlessly across the barren terrain of a consumer culture. In the ad, however, the book's message was completely absent. The ad was not even about the book. Instead, it endorsed a particular brand of women's beach wear. Goodman's book was only a prop in the hands of a leggy model displaying a new-style swimsuit. Around the same time, the box for a board game "for kids from 8 to 80"—Class Struggle—featured pictures of Karl Marx, whose nineteenth-century writings called for a proletarian revolution, and Nelson Rockefeller, a scion of one of the nation's wealthiest families and a powerful Republican politician. The box portrayed the two men engaged in an arm-wrestling contest. In such ways, popular culture could strip protest of political meaning. Its capacity to do so has frustrated people fighting for change as well as traditionalists who celebrate the market economy even as its pursuit of novelty and profit demolish the "good ol' days."

This study draws mainly from the gathering flood of scholarly publications on popular culture over the past several decades. I am deeply indebted to the many people who have done pioneering work in a field that scholars not long ago dismissed as frivolous. The subject is, in fact, full of intellectual surprises, revealing, in the words of one of its leading students, "terrains of conflict and struggle in the most unexpected places and allies in the most improbable individuals."[6]

Although I am well aware of the important place of theoretical material in much recent literature, I have chosen not to discuss theory but to write what I hope is an accessible historical narrative of U.S. popular culture. I hold no illusions that my treatment of this vast topic is comprehensive. Invariably, some people will wonder why I have overlooked particular entertainers or events or given them briefer treatment than they deserve. I had to make choices. Given the limits of time and space, I have tried to cast a large net that covers a wide range of amusements and places them in historical context.

For over a decade, I have benefited from the resources that the late Claudius O. and Mary Johnson have provided with their endowed professorship at Washington State University. Those resources have allowed me to collect many of the materials that were vital to this project. I appreciate the support that I have received from Roger Schlesinger, the History Department's chair, for the past twelve years, and from Pat Thorsten, the department's administrative manager. Pat's assistance was indispensable, especially regarding the photographs and managing the Johnson professorship's budget. The readers who produced critiques of my manuscript for the University Press of Kentucky deserve my deepest gratitude. Their suggestions were careful and extremely useful.

I owe special thanks as well to Bob Zieger at the University of Florida, John Donnelly, Sara Donnelly, and Ann Roberts for reading most of the manuscript and offering perceptive insights and encouragement. My wife, Mary, has been a wonder, reading the manuscript many times, giving helpful suggestions, and reminding me—during the sometimes dark days of writing—that I really could finish this project. Of course, I owe her for so much more. The enthusiasm of our son, Steve, for popular culture has also been a big help. As a musician and the owner of a music store, he has taught me much. Our daughter-in-law, Kris, has also followed the evolution of this project with good humor and encouragement.

I must also thank two of my graduate assistants who recently helped me develop ideas for my courses on American popular culture, John Hausdoerffer and Robin Payne. Nate Gilbert aided me in locating images, and I am grateful for his help. At the University Press of Kentucky, Steve Wrinn has been a terrific editor, enthusiastic, thoughtful, and accommodating. His staff is excellent. The copyeditor, Joseph Brown, was exceptionally thorough and knowledgeable. I would be remiss if I failed to thank, too, the many students who over the years have made the classroom such a rewarding place in which to spend time.

PROLOGUE

Popular Culture on the Brink

In November 1829, some twelve thousand people, many of whom had paid for a good view, watched the famous falls jumper Sam Patch leap off a scaffolding and plunge 125 feet into the roiling waters at the foot of Genesee Falls in upstate New York. It was his last jump. Drunk before he leaped, he did not survive. He could hardly have guessed that his jump from that platform marked a symbolic moment in the history of American popular culture. When Patch bounded into the void, American entertainment was in the process of stepping into a turbulent new era.[1]

That new era was the product of several developments that owed much to the American Revolution. Initially a colonial war for independence, the Revolution hastened many changes. "A fundamental mistake of the Americans has been that they considered the revolution as completed when it was just begun," observed Noah Webster, a young member of the revolutionary generation, in 1787. One of the rebellion's ongoing consequences was a spreading political environment that celebrated personal autonomy, social mobility, and popular sovereignty. Another was an emerging market economy that prized the individual's freedom to profit from producing and selling goods. Much irony existed in the fact that such changes came at the considerable expense of the republican ideals that shaped much of the Revolution's ideology. But the paradoxes and unintended consequences so central to that story also helped give rise to the kinds of entertainment that leading revolutionaries feared. It would have been of little comfort to those revolutionaries to realize that such entertainment derived in significant ways from their own ambivalence about accommodating the expectations and tastes of society's increasingly assertive lower ranks.[2]

Although the developing commercial amusements differed substantially from the folk games, festivals, and celebrations that had marked societies around the globe for centuries, they nevertheless tapped similar desires for fun and pleasure just as they stirred familiar apprehensions about those desires. The England from which most of the colonists had come to the New World in the seventeenth and eighteenth centuries included many traditions of play and entertainment that were woven into time-honored religious commemorations of saints and martyrs, seasonal holidays, and county fairs. There were sporting events that foreshadowed modern baseball and football. There were horse races and a variety of blood sports such as cockfighting and animal baiting. Fairs included puppet shows and displays of human "freaks." But such amusements also provoked concern and opposition. Sometimes authorities banned events that had become too violent. In 1762, for example, England's Southwark fair was so disruptive that officials abolished it. Among the critics of such popular diversions was the poet William Wordsworth, who cringed at a fair: "What a shock / For eyes and ears! What anarchy and din, / . . . Albinos, painted Indians, Dwarfs, / The Horse of knowledge, the learned Pig, / . . . the man that swallows fire, / . . . All out-o'-the-way, far-fetched, perverted things, / . . . A Parliament of Monsters. . . ."[3]

When individuals such as Wordsworth lamented this "vast mill vomiting," they expressed elite worries about upheavals from society's lower classes, but another significant source of tension flowed from religious concerns. A dilemma in this regard was that the line between sacred and secular often blurred. It was to aid the Protestant revolt against the Catholic Church, for example, that England's King James I in 1618 issued his *Book of Sports*: "Our good people," he proclaimed, should not be "discouraged from any lawful recreation, Such as dancing . . . Recreation . . . and the setting up of Maypoles and other sports." The king reasoned that banning such activities would only make Catholicism more appealing. In that regard, the sacred and the secular were entwined in an uneasy relation that resembled "a dance," as one historian has written, "sometimes graceful, sometimes awkward."[4]

Even the fiercely devout Puritans in New England's Massachusetts Bay colony recognized the importance of having fun. They accepted "worldly delights" as long as such pleasures did not interfere with godly pursuits, occur on the Sabbath, smack of Catholicism, or otherwise threaten the colony's religious mission. "It spoils the *bow* to keep it always straight," asserted the minister Benjamin Colman. "I am far from inveighing against sober mirth," he wrote in 1707; "on the contrary, I justify, applaud, and recommend it. Let it be pure and grave . . . yet free and cheerful." In sum, there was nothing wrong with mirth as long as it was tempered or, in Colman's words, free of the "carnal and vicious." Colman opposed anything that "stops devotion, cramps industry and is big with idleness." Even gambling was permissible when it was part of a lottery to raise funds for worthy causes. Play, as the historian Bruce Daniels has written, "had to be interwoven with Scripture, workplace, village, meetinghouse, home, family." Leisure and labor were interconnected, not polarized. The Puritans approved recreations that they deemed moral. Play "must tend also to glorify God," wrote one minister. Productive activities such as archery and athletic contests that boosted the participants' health and served the public welfare were acceptable. Unproductive diversions were unsuitable. The theater was among proscribed activities because critics believed that its setting encouraged illicit behavior and the actors engaged in deception. "Plays," according to one minister, "were sucked out of the Devil's teats to nourish us in idolatrie, heathenrie, and sinne." This aversion to stage plays was so widely shared that almost every colonial legislature banned them.[5]

"Have fun, but not too much"—this implicit guideline, as Daniels has pointed out, attested to the New Englanders' ambivalence about leisure. The difficulty was in defining what constituted too much fun and who said so. Over time, as the Puritans' hold on New England weakened, "sober mirth" made room for "fancy frolics." Throughout the eighteenth century, dancing spread despite the minister Increase Mather's condemnation of it in 1684 as "a regular madness." The role and place of music also changed. From 1620 to the 1720s, although the Puritans had incorporated music in their church services, they spurned instruments, direction, and musical scores, which they associated with Catholicism. One result was that the singing of psalms was sometimes so awful that, according to one satirist, "a certain gentlewoman miscarried at the ungrateful and yelling noise of a deacon." By the 1720s, however, congregations were singing by note; within another half century, music in New England was becoming a source of entertainment in a number of sites. By then, leisure and play increasingly offered a variety of diversions outside the tightly knit community of saints that the Puritans had initially envisioned. The Puritan dream of a strictly homogenized society could not keep pace with events or an expanding population, which in Boston had grown to eight thousand by 1708.[6]

By then, the serious business of religion sometimes threatened to slip into entertainment. In their efforts to stoke the fires of religious passion, Puritan leaders used a tactic that was hardly unique: describing sin's terrible consequences in sensational ways. Published execution sermons, for instance, increasingly depicted horrible crimes in lurid detail. A goal of these sermons was to warn that such lesser sins as drunkenness and Sabbath breaking could lead to worse misdeeds, including murder. By shocking readers and listeners, preachers hoped to drive home the importance of salvation and the necessities of clean living. But the hellfire images of later sermons, which included graphic descriptions of torture and other bloody actions, could easily slip into titillation, or even pornography. Over time, the lines between moral instruction and escapist fantasy were sometimes thin.[7]

Still, before the 1680s, escapism of any kind from duties and onerous work was for the most part limited for most people in the English colonies. In the Chesapeake and Southern regions, the widely dispersed population discouraged the replication of Old World amusements. Play overlapped labor, and displays of prowess typically were rooted in arduous yet often irregular work tasks. In the Chesapeake Bay area, for instance, the brutal conditions of the emerging tobacco economy allowed little time for recreation. "So soon as it is day," said an indentured servant in a ballad, "to work I must away."[8]

By the end of the seventeenth century, however, popular diversions began to take a more regular shape, one that bore the imprint of distinct social classes. For an emerging group of "gentlemen"—propertied men with status—activities such as billiards, lawn bowling, and horse racing were popular. Thoroughbred horse racing also served to remind propertyless observers of the aristocrats' wealth and status. In 1674, a county court in Virginia emphasized that horse racing was "a sport for gentlemen only." The races allowed the gentry to display their authority and valuable possessions, including slaves, who sometimes rode as jockeys for their masters in high-stakes races. Moreover, according to the historian Nancy Struna: "This generation of provincial gentlemen had begun to construct a specific notion of leisure as a distinctive time and set of experiences." From the participants' perspective, such experiences were separate from labor but not in opposition to it; horse racing, for instance, had a number of practical purposes, including separating out the best horses for breeding.[9]

While horse racing probably added to the amount of social deference that the gentry enjoyed, the lower classes found alternative spheres of recreation in fields, streets, and taverns. In many respects, as Struna has written, "taverns offered the 'only game in town.'" Proprietors often sponsored "inn games" or various entertainments, including cards, dice, bowling, shooting contests, and cockfighting. The popular cockfights had a leveling tendency because both poor and rich could enter their fighting birds in the contests. By the 1730s, elites increasingly complained that taverns were becoming the haunts of "loose, idle, and disorderly" individuals of "the poorer sort"—"the very dregs of people," according to a Virginia minister. Georgia's ruling council fretted that "the common people" were using taverns to "debauch themselves." Lower-class rowdiness was also evident in fist fighting and cock shailing, whereby observers hurled rocks and sticks at a chicken that a man led down the street, sometimes hitting passersby and damaging property as well. Elites complained about such behavior but had, in fact, done much to identify recreation as enjoyable on its own terms, quite separate from work, churchgoing, or community service.[10]

Among the diversions that the wealthy enjoyed in some cities by the 1750s was the professional theater, which had begun to gain some legitimacy, particularly outside New England. To win the support of leading citizens, traveling actors often invited them to benefit performances. One actor's announcement humbly requested that "the Gentlemen and Ladies will be so kind as to favor him with their company." Theaters at that point were aristocratic institutions that were generally too expensive for workers to attend.[11]

As revolutionary fervor grew in behalf of American independence, however, the elite's hold on aristocratic rituals and establishments was increasingly tenuous. Threats came from several directions. One was in the form of what the historian Gordon Wood has described as an "assault on aristocracy." Another, which encouraged that assault, was a developing colonial economy that increasingly provided common folks with access to a variety of consumer goods as well as recreation and entertainment.[12]

The ideology of republicanism, so critical in fueling the independence movement and antiaristocratic sentiments, was not simply political, aimed at government's proper function and structure. It was also cultural. Revolutionaries used the concept of virtue as a way to contrast the colonists and their imperial rulers. According to republican thought, luxury and artificial privilege had corrupted England, turning it into a decaying society from which the colonists had to free themselves.

Against that backdrop, the theater again became a target, with critics assailing it now on political as well as moral grounds, associating it with British decadence. "The money thrown away in one night at a play would purchase wood, provisions and other necessities, sufficient for a number of poor," railed one New York newspaper in 1768. The situation had already turned ugly. Two years earlier, rioting members of the Sons of Liberty had attacked the Chapel Street Theater, driving out the audience, dismantling the building, and building a bonfire from the wood. In 1772, at Philadelphia's Southwark Theater, lower-class protesters—"Ruffians," according to one account—left the theater intact but disrupted the performance. Issues of social class and independence merged in these incidents, which reflected anger at colonial aristocrats as well as the British.[13]

The presence of "Ruffians" in the audience attested to a dramatic transformation in the colonial economy. That transformation was a by-product of what historians have described as a "consumer revolution" in eighteenth-century England. Many goods that had once been available only to privileged people now seemed within reach of the larger population. In the mid-eighteenth century, a growing flood of British imports into the colonies whetted appetites of ordinary but more prosperous colonists for an array of consumer goods ranging from dishes to assorted textiles, shoe buckles, and even silk shirts and handkerchiefs. Although a rising standard of living in the colonies particularly benefited the rich and made the distribution of wealth even more unequal, ordinary citizens were also better off. More than ever, commoners were able to tap into what the historian T. H. Breen has dubbed "an empire of goods."[14]

The variety of goods and the consumer choices that accompanied them were disquieting on several levels. Wealthy colonists worried about the fate of traditional social hierarchies. "We run into . . . Extremes as to Dress," fretted the *Boston Gazette* in 1765; "there is scarce any Distinction between Persons of great Fortune, and People of ordinary Rank." Another writer complained that "the lowest rank of men would pass for a middle sort; and every one lives above his condition." For the evangelical minister William Tennent, this trend was especially ominous because "our common and Country People seem to vie with the first Classes of Mankind in Vices."[15]

Tennent's comment underlined another level of concern: the ways in which those goods threatened republican virtue in the colonies. During the revolutionary era, the colonial governments responded by trying to seal off the menace of luxury, decadence, and corruption that they associated with the British monarchy and ruling class. Revolutionaries from Sam Adams to Thomas Paine emphasized that civic virtue was essential to sustain a republic; citizens needed to repudiate selfish individualism for the common welfare. Social rank in the American republic was supposed to rest on virtue, merit, and natural ability—not birth, artificial privilege, or riches. "I was not sent into this world to spend my days in sports, diversion, and pleasures," insisted John Adams, a leading republican theorist.[16]

In 1773, Connecticut's Act for the Suppressing of Mountebanks thus banned "any games, tricks, plays, juggling or feats of uncommon dexterity and agility of body" that drew "great numbers of people, to the corruption of manners, promoting of idleness, and the detriment of good order and religion." A year later, the Continental Congress in Philadelphia set forth a moral program that prohibited racing horses, fighting cocks, playing cards, rolling dice, attending the theater, and indulging in other expensive entertainments. The recreations that the congress identified were especially associated with England. Banning them would supposedly demonstrate the moral superiority of the revolutionary colonists in contrast with the depravity of the British. Enforcement rested with local communities and typically relied on public humiliation, including tarring and feathering and drumming offenders out of town. Usually, however, communities tolerated considerable deviation, unless the offenders were English sympathizers. The moral strictures were, in that sense, largely symbolic, aimed at unifying colonists during a time of revolutionary crisis. Once America had established its independence, the activities that the Continental Congress had targeted as vices quickly regained legitimacy. By the 1790s horse racing and cockfighting were thriving again in many places, and theaters gained popularity in cities along the Atlantic seaboard. Still, as late as 1819, New York State declared it illegal to "exhibit or perform for gain and profit any puppet show, wire dance, or any other idle shows, acts or feats."[17]

Citizens of the new nation thus wavered between the moral strictures of earlier eras and the results of democratizing and market trends that encouraged individual choice and the pursuit of economic success. The dramatist William Dunlap provided an especially poignant example of the postrevolutionary struggles between past and future. A firm believer in the Revolution's ideals, he saw the theater as an agency to promote republicanism and demonstrate America's cultural strengths. Moreover, attitudes concerning theaters mellowed somewhat after the American Revolution, particularly in light of arguments that governments could not repress individual freedoms. One Philadelphia resident warned: "The same authority which proscribes our amusements, may, with equal justice dictate the shape and texture of our dress or the modes and ceremonies of our worship." With opposition weakening, theaters grew in number and popularity. Dunlap, who had experienced the Revolutionary War as a boy, hoped to use the stage to exhibit the new nation's greatness. In that regard, he said, "the wise and the good" should "set proper exhibitions before a free and well-ordered people." In 1789, his play *The Father; or, American Shandyism*—"homespun fare," as he described it—opened successfully in New York. In several subsequent plays, he showed his ability to please audiences and reflect on republican virtue. In 1796, convinced that he had a "duty to take the direction of so powerful an engine as the stage," he became a co-owner of the American Company, which quickly constructed the two-thousand-seat Park Theater in New York City.[18]

But disappointment quickly followed. Audience numbers were low, and revenues sagged. To his despair, Dunlap was forced to resort to staging novelty acts such as jugglers and acrobats during intermissions. "To support the treasury," he wrote woefully, "the stage was degraded by the exhibitions of a man who could whirl around on his head with crackers and other fireworkers attached to his heels." In 1802, the company featured *Bunker's Hill*—"vile trash," in Dunlap's words—but its revenues were high. An even bigger moneymaker was *The Glory of Columbia,* which Dunlap described as "amusements for holiday fools." To his chagrin, patrons seemed less interested in virtue than in jingoistic patriotism and "shameful exhibitions of monsters, and beasts, and other vulgar shows." Despite his expectations, aesthetic standards seemed to clash with popular sovereignty—a crucial element of republicanism. In 1805, a bankrupt Dunlap lost his property, and his theater closed. Disillusioned, he blamed the masses and the marketplace. "The uneducated, the idle, and the profligate" demanded foolish entertainment, turning the stage into "a breeding ground for ignorance and depravity." Aiding them were commercial forces that displayed the "vilest and most hateful qualities." In his opinion, obsession with profits was "incompatible with virtue." To save theaters from market greed, he now advocated government patronage. As the historian Joseph Ellis has written: "Dunlap was warning against the commercialization of art and the creation of mass culture at precisely the moment they were becoming dominant."[19]

When Dunlap's theater fell victim in 1805 to a rising democracy and market pressures, commercialized entertainment was still in its early form. Dramatic changes nevertheless hastened its development. A rapidly expanding population, increased per capita wealth, and the growth of cities were major factors. So too were spectacular developments in transportation and communication. After 1815, steamboats began to revolutionize travel. The construction of canals further opened water transportation. Particularly stunning was the completion in the 1820s of the Erie Canal, connecting the Hudson River and the Great Lakes. By the 1830s, railroads were starting to form what over the next several decades would become a giant web of tracks tying cities and towns together, facilitating as never before the transport of goods and people. Improvements in printing and literacy rates were spawning a host of new publications, a number of which by the 1830s enticed ordinary readers with cheap prices and attention to popular amusements.

In important ways, these developments helped provide their own kind of scaffolding for Sam Patch's famed jumps. The completion of the Erie Canal allowed curious onlookers an easier opportunity to witness his feats. Increased wealth encouraged the growth of leisure and tourism that brought many visitors to Niagara or Genesee Falls, sites at which Patch performed. And many of those visitors were city people responding to advertisements and publications hailing the wonders of rustic settings, beautiful scenery, wild nature—and Sam Patch plunging down a waterfall.

Patch's short career illustrated notable trends in the emerging popular culture. For one thing, it showed how amusements bubbled up from society's lower ranks. At the age of seven or eight, Patch had started working in Samuel Slater's textile mill in Pawtucket, Rhode Island. As one of America's first generation of factory employees, he labored for Slater before moving to another cotton mill in Paterson, New Jersey. By then he was an accomplished boss spinner, using his skills to operate one of the biggest machines in the unfolding industrial revolution. He had also honed his jumping prowess by leaping time and again, as many of the mill boys and young men did, into the river below Pawtucket Falls, a drop of over fifty feet. Leaps from the top of one of Slater's mill buildings covered eighty feet.[20]

In September 1827, Patch jumped seventy feet down the Passaic River Falls outside Paterson, disrupting the commemorative opening of a bridge, and illuminating another trend in popular culture's evolution: the conflict over recreational space and time. In this instance, the Paterson mill owner Timothy Crane was turning what had been public grounds into a private area—Forest Garden, "a place of rational amusement" for "decent people" and "ladies and gentlemen" who conducted themselves in an orderly manner. Access to the garden was over Crane's newly constructed toll bridge. But the day Crane had set aside to celebrate his technological and entrepreneurial achievement turned instead into Patch's moment. Patch conquered the waterfall by jumping into it, not by building a bridge over it. "Crane has done a great thing," Patch said before he leaped, indicating that he intended "to do another." The next year, again on July 4, while Paterson's elite was enjoying an Independence Day banquet, Patch jumped down Passaic Falls once more. Most of the city's plain people—perhaps as many as five thousand—watched him. "Some things can be done as well as others," was now Patch's motto, contrasting the accomplishments of laborers such as himself with those of industrial entrepreneurs like Crane.[21]

A few weeks later, Patch jumped from a ship's mast into the Hudson River at Hoboken, New Jersey, a distance of ninety feet. The publicity marked a turning point for him. Patch, in his late twenties, left the textile mills and entered the budding world of entertainment. In 1829, he made several jumps at Niagara Falls, which was by then becoming an attraction for affluent tourists. To sustain the area's businesses during weaker periods, hotel keepers had started staging events. In September 1827, for example, perhaps as many as fifty thousand spectators had watched an old schooner go over the falls with human effigies and a number of animals on board, while several brass bands performed and nearby sideshows flourished, including one with a caged African lion. The emerging press gave Patch considerable publicity. Some writers placed him in the ranks of President Andrew Jackson's unwashed democracy—"*universal suffrage folks,*" as the wealthy New York editor William Leete Stone wrote disdainfully. Patch not only made several breathtaking jumps—one from a height of 120 feet into the Niagara River—for which local proprietors paid him, but he also exhibited himself at Jonathan McCleary's recently opened museum in Buffalo. He further cultivated a showman's style by walking around town with a pet black bear on a chain. Usually he was drunk, just as he was when he made his fatal jump at the Genesee Falls. By then, and for years after, his name surfaced in newspapers, books, shows, and even a cigar brand. "What the Sam Patch?" became a popular expression. President Jackson named his horse after the falls jumper.[22]

Elites cringed. A genteel speaker at Dartmouth College sniffed that "Sam Patch, leaping over Genesee Falls, could gather a greater crowd than Daniel Webster," the famous lawyer and U.S. senator. A new kind of fame was taking shape, one built around entertainment. Patch, an undistinguished common worker, had ascended "from low beginnings to make a name known throughout the republic—simply by leaping waterfalls," as the historian Paul Johnson has written. He had demonstrated "that anyone could be famous. Democracy, commerce, and new kinds of popular imagination were rising all at once." The decade after Patch's death would provide ample evidence of the rapidly expanding influence of popular culture.[23]

I

BLACKFACE, BARNUM, AND
NEWSPAPER BALLYHOO

IN 1832, THOMAS DARTMOUTH RICE, A YOUNG FORMER carpenter's apprentice wearing blackface, electrified his boisterous working-class audience by spinning around on a Bowery stage with a curious, jerky motion and singing: "Weel about and turn about, / And do jis so; / Eb'ry time I weel about, I jump Jim Crow." A year later, the newspaper publisher Benjamin Day, age twenty-three, launched a newspaper that was about one-third the size of other papers, sold at the incredibly cheap price of one cent, and highlighted sensational murders, tragedies, and gossip. And, in mid-1835, Phineas Taylor Barnum, a twenty-five-year-old refugee from the dry goods business, exhibited a decrepit, partially paralyzed, blind slave woman who supposedly was 161 years old and had nursed and cared for "dear little George" Washington, the nation's first president.[1]

Here, in the early 1830s, within a few brief years and within a few blocks in New York City, the scaffolding for modern popular culture in the United States took shape. The pillars of this rapidly emerging world of cheap, accessible, and rambunctious entertainments included blackface minstrelsy, which "Daddy" Rice's "Jim Crow" performance elevated to new levels of popularity; the penny press, which heralded a revolution in America's print industry; and "the show business," as Barnum dubbed it and which he, as much as anyone, helped define and fit with the era's democratic sensibilities. Each benefited from ongoing changes in communications and transportation. Each initially catered to enthusiastic working-class audiences, much to the chagrin of nervous social elites and an upstart middle class whose members worried that raucous amusements threatened civility and good character. Each in one way or another ultimately helped blur boundaries separating races, genders, and classes. Each attested to the force of the rising democratic politics that Andrew Jackson symbolized as well as the upheaval of the emerging market economy. And each helped put in motion trends and patterns that continued to play out generations later.[2]

In the late 1820s, even before T. D. Rice took his little song and dance to what he described as "unsophisticated" Bowery audiences, a friend of the fledgling songwriter Stephen Foster observed that "Jim Crow was on everybody's tongue." Its popularity had spread after Rice first introduced his Jim Crow steps and little tune in Louisville, when he was acting in a play, *The Rifle*. He reportedly did so after observing a slave, who was cleaning a stable, do the odd, jerky movements, hunching his shoulders, shuffling, spinning around on his heel, and singing. In fact, however, according to one minstrel scholar: "No single stable hand made up or taught the song. Instead there was a widespread African-American folk dance impersonating—delineating—crows, based in agricultural ritual and, some say, 'magical in character.'" Whether or not Rice realized that he was adapting a regional folklore character, he soon added, between acts of *The Rifle*, other "Negro" performances. Singing "Me and My Shadow," for example, he danced while a child actor in blackface mimicked his steps. By the time Rice took his talents to New York City, he enjoyed a popular stage reputation as "*the negro*, par excellence."[3]

Although "jumping Jim Crow" elevated Rice from obscurity and made him one of the best-known actors of his era, blackface performances were far from new. Indeed, they were deeply rooted in the carnivals and festivals of early modern Europe. A carnival served as "an anti-holiday (literally an unholy feast)," and the line between celebration and criminality or violence was thin. Rowdy celebrants, often hiding their identities behind costumes and masks, defied propriety and traditional roles and assumed the identities of other people. Centuries later, during Mardi Gras in New Orleans, participants continued to carry that tradition into the streets, momentarily celebrating disorder and reversing roles. Similarly, in Finland, citizens staged an annual revelry—Vappu—by donning masks, parading through the streets with drinks in their hands, ringing doorbells, and urinating in public. During these "inversion rituals," as scholars would later describe them, boisterous, sometimes riotous participants momentarily turned the existing social order upside down, switching roles, repudiating decorum, and threatening traditional authority figures.[4]

Sometimes during such carnivals, a commoner would become "King for a Day," or a "Lord of Misrule," briefly playing out a charade in which the subjects took charge while the obliging ruling classes allowed their "inferiors" to unleash grievances and blow off steam. One such European ritual was mumming, when costumed young men, singing, drinking, and making all kinds of noise, demanded food and beverages from owners of wealthy homes and businesses. During some of these inversion rituals, white workers blackened their faces with chimney soot, changing their identities and, for the moment, becoming someone they were not: the Other. By the 1820s and 1830s, young workers in American cities such as Philadelphia and New York celebrated the new year by dressing outlandishly, making "night hideous" with street bands that created noise with anything from horns to pots and pans, and disguising their faces with grease and soot. When T. D. Rice jumped Jim Crow in New York City's Bowery, he thus drew on complex but familiar social rituals that were loaded with cultural meaning.[5]

The rise in the 1830s of blackface minstrel acts as mass entertainment in the United States very much reflected the influence of economic change, social class, and the growth of mixed-race amusements on the margins of the burgeoning commercial society. The dockside area where minstrelsy first thrived in New York City was heavily working class and included a considerable mixing of blacks and whites. Similarly, in Western frontier river towns such as Louisville, Cincinnati, and Pittsburgh, black and white laborers mingled and observed each other on and off the job.

When "Daddy" Rice brought to New York City's Bowery area the little dance that he had watched the black stable hand performing in Louisville, he provided an "instance in American commercial culture of an outland form exported to the northeastern city," as the historian Eric Lott has written.[6] Generations later, minstrel critics would attack the racist caricatures and messages of minstrelsy, but blackface performances initially contained more complex and ambiguous meanings as well. As racial hybrids, the spreading minstrel acts attested, however unconsciously, to black influences on whites and, at the same time, provided a way for lower-class groups to mock social elites.

Such was certainly the case in the rough-and-tumble, impoverished southeastern section of lower Manhattan, which fronted New York City's East River. Around areas such as the Catherine Street Market—where T. D. Rice was born and raised—laborers battled economic hardship, harsh working conditions, and disease. By the early nineteenth century, a large proportion of New York City's nine thousand blacks (constituting around 8 percent of the city's population) lived and worked there, mixing with poor whites, and forming what a historian has described as an "urban shadowland" or "subversive landscape" where prostitution, drinking, and gambling flourished. Here, quite literally, was a marginal world, occupying the edges of the nation's fastest-growing commercial city.[7]

While some of the racial intermingling was intimate, much of it was informal, casual, part of a daily give-and-take that accompanied residing, working, and playing in close proximity. An 1840 raid on a New York City gambling house found some twenty people "of all sizes and colors"; the apparent "master of ceremonies" was "an out-and-out darkey," while off to one side "a little black rascal of twelve years, assisted by two little white ones of eleven or under were roaring a love song." Elsewhere in the room, whites and blacks applauded a black man "who was jumping Jim Crow."[8]

Black dancers, whether jumping Jim Crow or dancing for eels in street competition, constituted a common sight in and around the Catherine Street Market. A number of them came from Long Island (where slavery continued to exist until 1827) "to engage in a jig or breakdown," recalled a white butcher, Thomas De Voe. According to De Voe: "Each had his particular 'shingle' brought with him as part of his stock in trade." While a companion beat time with a heel or by striking a hand against a leg, the dancer performed on the board for monetary or other rewards, such as fish and eels. Another observer could well have been Micah Hawkins, a white man who owned a grocery store nearby and, in 1815, wrote an early black-face song. Sometimes, black fiddle players provided the backdrop for electrifying breakdown contests featuring the popular Bobolink Bob or the legendary "Juba"—William Henry Lane, who reportedly had no equal. Lane, from lower Manhattan, dazzled Charles Dickens when the famed English novelist watched him perform in a seedy underground dance hall.[9]

For African Americans, the dancing, the music, and the laughter not only elicited small rewards from white spectators but also provided momentary release from hard times. Whether dancing for eels in the streets or entering the noisy, multiracial world of taverns, oyster houses, and gambling dens, they found brief alternatives to the rigors of work and hardscrabble existence.

Not all blacks approved of such frivolity, of course. Some African Americans objected on religious grounds. Some warned that poor individuals were wasting their meager resources on liquor and vices. Others were concerned that such loose living only confirmed white perceptions of blacks as shiftless, immoral, and lewd. But, to many African Americans, the urban shadowland of streets and taverns was a welcome place where, in the words of one historian, they "shucked off the problems of a workaday existence, reclaimed their bodies as instruments of pleasure not toil, and showed that the night time was the right time." Some, such as William Johnson, a free black resident of Natchez, Mississippi, even enjoyed the sight of whites in blackface doing their own versions of jigs and jumping Jim Crow. In the mid-1830s, Johnson watched "Daddy" Rice perform.[10]

In turn, as Rice and other white minstrel performers looked for material to use onstage, they observed and studied black workers, dancers, and singers.[11] One white minstrel, Ben Cotton, recalled spending time with blacks along the Mississippi, "twanging" the banjo with them: "They did not quite understand me. I was the first white man they had seen who sang as they did; but we were brothers for the time being and were perfectly happy." Such "crossing over" into the black world could also be a source of escape and satisfaction. In that regard, performers such as Cotton and Rice made career choices that took them, not into the emerging environment of middle-class respectability, but into the suspect arena of the theater and entertainment. "Marginalized by temperament, by habit (often alcoholism), by ethnicity, even by sexual orientation," as Lott has written, "these artists immersed themselves in 'blackness' to indulge their felt sense of difference." Thus, the *New York Tribune* reported that "a white negro" sang a minstrel song. If blackface minstrels qualified as "white Negroes," whites in the audience could also sense the thrill of crossing over. In the 1830s, the young Lew Wallace (who later wrote the best-selling novel *Ben Hur* [1880]) excitedly watched an actor who was passing through a small Indiana town perform "plantation songs and jigs, executed in costume—burned cork, shovel shoes, and all." Among the songs was "Jump, Jim Crow." "As I walked home through the night," Wallace remembered, "I felt that the world was full of fun and life worth living, if only for fun."[12]

While blackface minstrels drew heavily on their impressions of African Americans, they tapped other cultural veins that social elites also typically judged as disreputable—circus clowning and the "ring-tale roaring" of Southwestern humorists. Clowns, like blackface minstrels, engaged in the "doubleness" of masking and disguise, and a goodly number of minstrel men started out in the circus.[13]

The celebrated clown Daniel McClaren III, who sometimes engaged in "nigero singing and dancing," as he put it, changed his last name to Rice to capitalize on the popularity of T. D. "Daddy" Rice, whom young Dan may have seen in New York City. George Washington Dixon, the son of a barber and a washerwoman, also started out in the circus before turning, in 1829, a minstrel song, "Coal Black Rose," into what may have been the first blackface farce. Traveling circuses incorporated horseback riding, menageries, and various acts such as ropewalkers, but blackface was so common that owners usually indicated if they did not include "negro pantomime." Performers moved back and forth from theaters to minstrel shows and circuses. White and blackface clowns competed for laughs in adult-oriented programs that were racy and raucous. Sometimes local rowdies got downright threatening, and performers had to protect themselves with their fists. "Respectable" people stayed away from this tawdry and even dangerous setting of animal smells, loud noises, rowdy spectators, and acts that sometimes included partial nudity. But the circuses were extremely popular among working-class audiences, who joined in the performances by shouting back at the clowns.[14]

The "roaring" or "whooping" exploits of Southwestern humorists such as Davy Crockett and Mike Fink provided blackface performers with another useful source on which to pattern their acts. According to Lott: "The most common characters of antebellum minstrelsy . . . were often little more than blackfaced versions of heroes from southwestern humor." Crockett, the famed Tennessee frontiersman, trumpeted his own exploits in the immensely successful *Crockett Almanacs*. He touted his ability to out-drink and outfight anyone. As a child, he supposedly consumed a pint of whiskey with his breakfast and a quart with his lunch. In one fight, he re-portedly bit his opponent's big toe off. After another, he "picked up three heads and half a dozen legs an [*sic*] arms, and carried 'em home to Mrs. Crockett to kindle fire with." Once, just as he prepared to pop an adver-sary's eye out ("like taking up a gooseberry in a spoon"), the fight ended. Similarly, river boatmen such as Mike Fink boasted reputations as "half horse, half alligator."[15]

Like Crockett and Fink, who humbled and thumbed their noses at snobbish aristocrats, the Jim Crow stage character quickly evolved into a brawling, boisterous tough guy, proclaiming, as Rice did: "When I got out I hit a man, / His name I now forget, / But dere was nothing left / 'Sept a little grease spot." Rice could supposedly "wip my weight in wildcats" or "eat an Alligator." He was part "snapping turtle, / Nine-tenths of a bull dog. I've turned the Mississippy, / All for a pint of grog."[16]

The blackface acts of the 1830s helped express a developing working-class consciousness and often contained messages of contempt for privi-leged groups. It was not by accident that minstrel shows found exuberant audiences in places such as the Bowery section of lower Manhattan. Nor was it coincidental that minstrelsy became a popular rage among laborers when it did. By the 1830s, the U.S. economy was clearly in the throes of a dramatic transformation. The opening in 1825 of the Erie Canal, an engi-neering triumph, provided a powerful symbolic marker of the changes un-der way. The 364-mile channel connected Lake Erie with the Hudson River, allowing goods and people to move, as never before, to and from the north-ern frontier areas and New York City. Virtually overnight, the small up-state town of Rochester became a bustling commercial city and a microcosm of the economic adjustments that marked an emerging industrial system in the Northeast. In cities such as Rochester, a social wall increasingly sepa-rated laborers and their employers, who had once worked in small shops alongside each other, talking and drinking together, and sometimes even sharing living quarters. As businesses became more lucrative, the owners tended to relocate to residential sites outside the industrial districts, leaving behind a kind of working-class ghetto, a low-rent area with a floating pop-ulation and a reputation for vice and crime—and a target for a growing body of moral reformers from the swelling ranks of an identifiable bour-geoisie. An economy of self-sufficient artisans increasingly gave way to one of wage earners in the employ of industrial and merchant entrepreneurs. New forms of work discipline accompanied the shifts to more mechanized production. As laborers experienced the shocks of the budding free-labor economy, the unsettledness of economic fluctuations, the sense of diminished power, and the formation of distinct areas of working-class sociability in taverns and boardinghouses, they also enlarged their sphere of entertainments and amusements. In New York City's Bowery, for example, the urban underworld of cheap dance halls, prostitution, and arenas for blood sports such as cockfighting quickly expanded.[17]

It was to the Bowery Theater in 1832 that T. D. Rice brought his act, exciting his audience so much that he had to repeat his Jim Crow song twenty times, ultimately with so many viewers coming onstage for a closer look that he could barely dance. In a few brief years, the Bowery Theater had moved from featuring "respectable" programs to a sideshow atmosphere that included animal acts, blackface minstrels, and red-flannel-shirted audience members who stood, according to one newspaper, "with their chins resting on the lamp board, chanking peanuts and squirting tobacco juice upon the stage." Here was a world far removed from bourgeois fare and institutions. Indeed, as the poet Walt Whitman observed, applause in the Bowery was "no dainty kid-glove business, but electric force and muscle from perhaps 2000 full-sinew'd men."[18]

In that context, the minstrel shows of the 1830s served their white, male, working-class audiences as a kind of "antitheater" or "underground theater." The blackface mask facilitated the ridicule of respectable society. Behind a camouflage of burned cork, minstrels could take a roundhouse swing at the "legitimate," pretentious society that did not respect them, fleeced them, and tried to control them. "An [sic] I caution all white dandies," Rice sang in 1832, "Not to come in my way, / For if dey insult me, / dey'll in de gutter lay." Granted, minstrelsy's indirect resistance hardly disturbed the economic arrangements against which its allies protested, but it nevertheless provided a notable instance of popular culture as an oppositional voice. "The blackface character boots the behind of authority every chance he finds," according to a leading student of minstrelsy. "Jim Crow, Gumbo Chaff, Ginger Blue, and Bone Squash—they all outwit and supersede their white employers."[19]

Common citizens lacked economic and social power, but they could at least lay claim to their own entertainment, one that bubbled up from the streets. And through it they could challenge the high culture of their social betters. The critics might dismiss their low-class entertainment as trash, but its supporters could reply that they willingly chose it, making it at least *their* trash. As a popular culture scholar would later write: "Mass entertainment may have begun as the democrats' revenge against the elites they despised." But the revenge of the commoners could be inherently and ironically flawed, as minstrel shows demonstrated. Minstrelsy's blackface weapon wounded others on society's margins: women, for example, who were largely absent from the audiences and whom cross-dressing males typically portrayed as "wenches" or other unflattering types.[20]

Undeniably, the stage persona of blacked-up whites all too often belittled and demeaned African Americans. On this level, black caricatures provided a means by which whites grappled with the anxieties and insecurities that the shifting economy provoked. The new industrial work discipline emphasized punctuality, regularity, sobriety, sexual abstinence, and orderly habits as the means to success. In contrast, the old preindustrial routines that allowed for such things as drinking, gambling, and extensive holidays were turning into prescriptions for failure. Many workers resisted the altered economic guidelines even as they internalized them. The process was difficult and stirred considerable tension and unease. Blackface may, from this perspective, have allowed whites to displace their conflicted emotions onto African Americans, identifying them with permissive, lackadaisical preindustrial habits that could evoke both nostalgia and scorn. By "acting black," whites could momentarily step outside the new work discipline and into the freewheeling, "natural" disposition that African Americans supposedly enjoyed. They could invent, as the historian David Roediger has said, "a new sense of whiteness by creating a new sense of blackness." And they could remove the cork when they wanted, asking humorously, "Why is we niggas like a slave ship on de Coast of Africa?" and replying, "Because we both make money by taking off the negroes." Ironically, minstrel shows grew in popularity at the same time that state and local governments in the Northeast took steps to curtail black celebrations such as Negro Election Day, a festive holiday that lasted almost a week. As one white reformer objected in Lynn, Massachusetts: "Excesses of the negroes gave rise to the vile manner in which [Negro Election] was observed by some of the lower class of our own complexion." Behavior that was unacceptable for whites in the streets could, however, find an outlet onstage.[21]

Moreover, when blackface performers appropriated elements from African American culture, they were engaged in a kind of theft. Any semblance of racial collaboration was, after all, hardly equal. When blacks danced for eels at the Catherine Street Market, they were not performing as minstrels; many of them were simply, as one student later observed, "slaves dancing for eels."[22]

The cultural dynamics of minstrelsy were, nevertheless, considerably more complex and nuanced than simple racism would allow. In notable ways, whites onstage and in the audiences identified with the African Americans who, like them, lived and worked in the integrated areas of lower Manhattan. A minstrel parody of Shakespeare thus bore the title "Black and White Niggers," and Rice sang: "Aldough I'm a black man, De white is call'd my broder."[23] Whites could share with blacks a sense of being victims and exploited. Young, white, working-class males could, according to one interpretation, "see themselves in the hounded image of the free/escaped black continually on the lam." For them, blackface disguise and the weapon of laughter provided an indirect means to strike back at more powerful and privileged groups.[24]

In this regard, minstrelsy's theatrical attack included two main characters: "Jim Crow" and "Zip Coon." In 1834, George Washington Dixon, whose song "Coal Black Rose" had already turned him into a blackface star, introduced Zip Coon—"Zip" serving as the abbreviated version of "Scipio," then a common African American name. Whereas the shuffling, ragamuffin Jim Crow was the caricature of a slave, Zip Coon personified a Northern urban dandy, a swaggering parody of fashion and pretense. Together, in their own ways, the two popular blackface characters took on the attributes of roistering Davy Crocketts and Mike Finks. Like them, the blackface creations provided the socially weak with symbolic power. In the style of a Crockett or a Fink, Jim Crow and Zip Coon poked fun at foppish urban gentlemen and celebrated common folks' wisdom over the formal education of the elites, echoing lines that evoked lusty cheers from Bowery-style audiences: "An [sic] den I show my science—prenez gardez vous / Bung he eye, break the shin, split de nose in two." Or as the song "Zip Coon" joked: "O ole Zip Coon he is a larned skoler . . . / Sings possum up a gum tree an [sic] coony in a holler."[25]

At first glance, the humor of the "Zip Coon" lyrics, with references to "coons" and "possums," seemed to target African Americans. But the bulk of the song reflected Dixon's working-class leanings by positing a political alliance between Davy Crockett and Zip Coon: "De bery nex President, will be Zip Coon . . . / Zip shall be President, Crockett shall be vice / And den dey two togedder, will habe de tings nice." Even if the song's intention was to ridicule the unlikelihood of a black president, democratic sympathies linked Zip and Crockett.[26]

The music implicitly contained a class message. Songs such as "Jim Crow" and "Zip Coon" countered the respectable parlor music and classical orchestrations of the middle and upper classes with what was in effect "antimusic"—even "noise." Such "rough music" was in the tradition of carnival misrule, in which exuberant gangs paraded through the streets, banging on pots and pans, hollering, ringing bells, blowing horns, and creating what one New York newspaper dismissed as sounds "rarely heard by ears of mortals." Similarly, the early blackface shows of the 1830s offered a clashing counterpoint to the polished, harmonic music of more socially privileged circles.[27]

On minstrel stages, the instruments of choice were fiddles and banjos, both of which were common to African American culture. A striking number of newspaper notices described escaped slaves as fiddle players, and black folklore was full of tales of "demon fiddlers." In 1838, one reporter sniffed at the fiddle's dire effect: "The poor can but share / A Crack'd fiddle in the air, / Which offends all sound morality." The banjo, in turn, was a West African instrument that entered America via the slave trade. As late as the 1820s, blacks were virtually the only Americans who played the gourd-shaped, handmade instrument. In proper circles, the banjo was thoroughly disreputable—a "terror to all Pianos, Harps, and Organs," according to an 1840 handbill. One aristocrat was so appalled by the musical deficiencies at the Bowery Theater that he and his associates "in an agony of tears . . . rushed from the house." Walt Whitman, with his plebeian sympathies, took a different view; a genuine "American opera," if he had his way, would "put three banjos (or more?) in the orchestra."[28]

Blackface performances, where banjos and fiddles were center stage, served additional notice that American culture was splintering—moving in New York City quite literally along different streets. The broad avenue of the Bowery, the workers' domain, served as "the plebeian counterpart of elegant Broadway to the west," a few blocks away. Minstrel songs celebrated the Bowery, which was quickly becoming a symbolic center of working-class culture. According to one minstrel tune, workers could find in a Bowery theater "entertainments of de best." The plush Astor Place in a wealthier section of Manhattan was another story: "If *you* go thar, jest wash your face! / Put on your 'kids,' an fix up neat, / For dis am de spot of de eliteet!"[29]

Early minstrelsy thus contained a strain of social criticism that reflected the fears and anxieties of the emerging working class. Blackface performers joked fondly about the preindustrial work ethic. One song contended that the creation of the world was supposed to take eleven days but stopped on the seventh because "de carpenters got drunk, and de masons couldn't work, / So de cheapest way to do it was to fill it with dirt." Other songs poked fun at moral reformers bent on curbing sexuality: "When de whites dey go to bed, / The devil is working in de nigger's head." These words cut several ways, implying envy over African American eroticism, and also reinforcing images of lustful blacks.[30]

Although Rice supported President Andrew Jackson, he otherwise expressed disdain for politicians: "For de duties ob de Semblyman / I tink is very funny, / For dey only hab to eat dinners, / And spend de people's money." Financial institutions were no better. "How is it banks suspend and break / and cause such awful times?" minstrels asked. The answer was simple: bank officials were thieves, "pocket[ing] all the dimes."[31]

Initially, at least in the 1830s, minstrel shows—ever evolving and for the most part still single song-and-dance acts, not yet formal blackface quartets or full-evening shows—thus offered a kind of working-class commentary. Granted, performers hid their social criticism behind blackface masks, typically airing working-class grievances only indirectly and by substituting parodies of the upper- and middle-class moral reformers for messages about economic injustices and conflicts. Blackface racism further muted minstrelsy's critiques of the new industrial discipline by imputing to supposedly inferior blacks looser, and increasingly suspect, preindustrial work habits—"It's them, not us," a white viewer could conclude.[32]

Still, particularly in its opening burst of antebellum popularity, minstrelsy undeniably contained significant political themes that reflected and articulated, however obliquely, the wishes and needs of the emerging working class. Within a few years, by the 1840s, that situation changed. As minstrel shows turned into entire evenings that focused on what advertisements hailed as the "oddities, peculiarities, eccentricities, and comicalities of that Sable Genus of Humanity," they blunted class critiques, rendering them more acceptable to wider audiences.[33]

In the 1830s, however, minstrelsy exhibited a notable element of social class by celebrating rank-and-file people (even though the focus was admittedly on white males), jabbing at more privileged "respectable" groups, and helping transform the urban shadowland into a growing source of mass entertainment. It emerged from social and cultural margins—from the urban underbelly; from performers such as Rice and Dixon, who wound their way through struggling circuses and seedy venues in search of new material that would provide their main chance in show business; and from the Bowery-type settings that constituted theater's fringes. Unlike the "respectable" culture of social elites, it reveled in the excitement, variety, temptations, and dangers of city life,[34] even as it lodged an implicit protest against the threats and travails of the changing market economy.

As minstrelsy helped construct the budding new world of popular amusements, it found a significant ally in the "penny press," a centerpiece of what was becoming the first information explosion. Between 1790 and 1835, the number of newspapers in the United States surged from 106 to 1,258. The federal government's postal system played an instrumental role in this development. A symbol of republican ideals, the postal system reflected the revolutionary leader Benjamin Rush's argument in 1787 favoring the circulation of "knowledge of every kind" to citizens throughout the country. With the Postage Act of 1792, Congress in effect subsidized newspapers with special discount rates and privileges. By the 1830s, the postal service was shipping far more newspapers than letters; indeed, newspapers constituted 95 percent of the weight of the service's mail while providing only 15 percent of its revenue.[35]

In this supportive environment, a growing flood of inexpensive magazines, paperbacks, and news sheets rolled off revamped presses, undermining "the once well-ordered and controlled world of print," in the words of the historian Isabelle Lehuu, and creating a virtual "carnival on the page" that was cheap, playful, and sensational. This print transformation owed much to changing technology, popular demand, the instincts of creative newspaper pioneers such as Benjamin Day and James Gordon Bennett, and an economic moment that allowed artisan printers with working-class sympathies to enter the mass circulation field. Quickly, it began to turn upside down the traditional print business, challenging what had, in effect, been a product of and for the nation's elite. And it marked a major journalistic turn toward entertainment.[36]

Going into the 1830s, newspapers typically depended financially on political parties or government contracts and sold for six cents, a price that substantially limited the readership. Because of their size—sometimes two by three feet per page—they were known as "blanket sheets." Copies were seldom available on the streets and were the province of wealthy subscribers, particularly commercial and professional men. For rank-and-file citizens, newspapers were, thus, for the most part inaccessible and, in any case, addressed primarily the concerns and interests of people who enjoyed money, power, and influence.[37]

On September 3, 1833, Benjamin Day, a shrewd former printing press operator who had already aligned himself with a failed effort to publish a mass circulation paper that would convey "the distress which pervades the producing classes of this community," broke dramatically from the genteel newspaper business by starting a new and quite different daily paper, the *New York Sun*. The *Sun* sold for only one cent, was small in size (nine by twelve inches), received no financial support from political parties or government, and depended entirely on street sales and advertising. Within three months, a circulation of five thousand copies made the *Sun* the most popular paper in New York City. Two years later, circulation figures approached twenty thousand. The relatively low costs of entering the business facilitated Day's ventures and, soon, those of other penny pioneers—such as Arunah Shepherdson Abell and William Swain, who both worked for the *Sun* before starting the *Philadelphia Public Ledger,* and James Gordon Bennett, who with only $500 launched the *New York Herald*. "Capital! Bless you," Day recalled, "I hadn't any capital." What he had were his contacts with printers and a willingness to try out developing technologies. Day initially relied on a hand-cranked flatbed printer that produced only two hundred copies an hour. Within a short time, he had accelerated the output to two thousand copies an hour by using a rotating cylinder to move the paper across the form. In 1835, he implemented a steam-driven process with two cylinders, more than doubling the number of sheets per hour from two to five thousand. By 1840, that figure had jumped to an astounding forty thousand. Day actively courted a wide reading public by filling those sheets with offbeat, entertaining stories—rowdy, gossip filled, often lurid, and in defiance of genteel tastes.[38]

Day's success caught the attention of the volatile Bennett, a former clerk, teacher, and proofreader from Scotland, who, in 1835, founded the *New York Herald.* Bennett quite literally produced a "rag," using paper that he manufactured from bleached rags, a new process that was far cheaper than using wood pulp. As competition between the *Sun,* the *New York Transcript* (which three men with strong working-class ties started in 1834), and the *Herald* galvanized a burgeoning readership, the penny press became more than a journalistic sideshow. Soon, it inspired imitators in Philadelphia, Baltimore, Boston, and smaller cities.[39]

It did so by bringing carnival techniques to the print world. Like sideshow barkers, newsboys (often with reputations as "street rats") wandered the city, shouting out reasons why customers should buy a paper and, especially on slow news days, embellishing considerably what was actually in the papers. Although newspapers, including even most of the new penny dailies, continued to be visually drab compilations of words, Bennett experimented with images in the *Herald* in the 1830s and 1840s, paying for woodcuts illustrating current events. And, because the *Herald,* the *Sun,* and their counterparts relished gossip, they opened private lives and events to public scrutiny.[40]

With profits dependent entirely on advertising and sales, the penny press quite deliberately targeted a previously untapped market, particularly commoners and members of the working class who were hungry for inexpensive literature that addressed their needs and interests, sympathized with them, and helped them make sense of the swirl of city life. Significantly, eight of the ten publishers of the first wave of penny press dailies had artisan roots: seven were printers and one a cabinetmaker. Bennett, although not an artisan, had been a wage earner who at one point had been unemployed. Benjamin Day, who took pride in reaching beyond "the rich aristocrat who lolls in his carriage to the humble laborer who wields a broom in the streets," delighted in saying that the *Sun*'s readers were as smart as the social elite. "The public," he said, "have as good an opportunity of forming as correct an opinion" as did people of wealth and authority. The *Sun* would enable workers to "understand their own interest." Bennett weighed in with equal fervor. "Formerly no man could read unless he had $10 to spare for a paper," he wrote. "Now with a cent in his left pocket, and a quid of tobacco in his cheek, he can purchase more intelligence, truth, and wit, than is contained in such papers as the dull . . . or the stupid" expensive papers over three months. The *Philadelphia Public Ledger* distinguished itself from "those dull papers who have the arrogance to call themselves 'respectable,'" while the *Baltimore Sun* sought "the ear of the before neglected mass," who represented hard work rather than the "indolence, luxurious ease," and questionable morals of the elite few.[41]

Deliberately courting working-class readers, the penny press published lengthy, often gory accounts from police court reports that revealed hypocrisy and scandal in the ranks of the middle and upper classes. In this context, news that seemed apolitical in fact contained a sharp political edge. Stories of sex, crime, and manners could expose the misplaced pretensions of privileged groups who presumed to lecture their inferiors about proper conduct.[42]

As penny papers attracted a growing and more diverse readership, they were agents of democratization, blurring lines of deference and newsworthiness. Without doubt, from the perspective of the old print world and its upper-class clientele, the penny dailies were a disruptive force. Although members of America's social elite reportedly dismissed as a sad joke comments such as, "I read it in a newspaper, and it must be true," they sensed nervously the truth in the writer Edgar Allan Poe's statement: "Words— printed ones especially—are murderous things."[43]

Significantly, the new mass circulation press published news about common people and local events that the blanket sheets had not deemed worthy of attention, except perhaps as low comedy. Newly hired reporters began to cover local news and lively human interest stories. Here was democracy in print: all stories, even those that did not deal with "important" people or events, were worthy of scrutiny. As part of unfolding stories, even ordinary individuals (e.g., witnesses or victims) could momentarily become public figures. "The news of a day—of a week—is supposed by the superficial blockheads who conduct newspapers and govern nations—or cheat the public—or shave in Wall Street, to be of trifling moment," the *Herald* said caustically. "And so it is to them. To the philosopher who dips into things, it is different." Even the pennies' advertisements had a democratic tilt, moving beyond the traditional legalistic notices about shipping or public sales to products such as patent medicines that addressed bodily needs. "One man has as good a right as another to have his wares, his goods, his panaceas, his profession, published to the world in a newspaper," announced the newly founded *Boston Daily Times* in 1837, "provided he pays for it." And, unlike the traditional six-centers, whose advertisements remained the same year after year (like the brass plates that identified businesses and professional offices), the penny dailies frequently changed ads, adding to a sense of change and movement. The diminished size of the penny paper also had democratic implications. Whereas the blanket dailies spread out over store counters or desks, the penny publications were easy to fold and fit in pockets. Readers could examine them while standing in line—or even sitting in an outhouse. In 1836, according to the new *Philadelphia Ledger*: "These papers are to be found in every street, lane, and alley; in every hotel, tavern, counting-house, shop, etc. Almost every porter and drayman, while not engaged in his occupation, may be seen with a paper in his hands."[44]

A sensational ax murder in 1836 provided exactly the kind of material on which the cheap press fed. The murder victim was a twenty-three-year-old prostitute, Helen Jewett, who died in Rosina Townsend's Palace of the Passions in New York City. Her killer had struck her head with an ax and then set fire to the bed in hopes of destroying the evidence. Within a short time, authorities arrested a dry goods clerk, Richard Robinson, age nineteen, whose trial became a celebrated event. Each day, spectators lined up outside the courtroom, hoping at least to see Robinson, an apparently respectable young man whose father had served eight terms in the Connecticut legislature. Some youthful clerks became his fans, wearing Robinson-style caps, and cheering for him in the courtroom. Ultimately, after five days of testimony, the jury acquitted him because of a lack of evidence. The crime went unsolved. Fascination with the Jewett case spread far beyond New York City. For at least two months, the public seemed unable to get enough information about the lurid case, and the penny press rushed to cover the story. Prior to the shocking murder and trial, the one-cent papers had limited their crime reports to short accounts, leaving more detailed coverage to the publishers of increasingly popular sixteen- and twenty-four-page octavo pamphlets, inexpensive publications that provided graphic descriptions and crude, titillating illustrations. With Jewett's murder, however, the penny press began focusing on crime stories with a vengeance. No trial had previously received such attention from the American press. From Mississippi to Maine, newspapers carried lengthy reports. Coverage of Jewett's murder and the search for her killer was full of sex, blood, and recrimination—which was probably why elite sixpenny publications deigned to give the matter only limited attention, and then with apologies for the "disgusting" tale. In contrast, the *New York Herald* churned out endless print columns, boosting its circulation from five to fifteen thousand, as the penny dailies scrambled to report the goriest details, construct crime scenarios, and impute guilt or innocence.[45]

As papers such as the *Herald* and the *New York Sun* competed fiercely in their coverage of remarkable events such as the Jewett case, rank-and-file readers looked to them as welcome sources of hidden information. Common, working-class people had long been outside the elite communications network of sixpenny papers and other expensive publications. But the cheap press, with its juicy revelations of fraud and misconduct, could transform them into insiders, privy to even the most concealed truths.[46]

But those truths could be significantly different, depending on whether the *Herald* or the *Sun* or some other paper was the source. In that regard, the penny press editors provided conflicting explanations that different communities of readers embraced. At stake were varying popular myths with which individuals shaped their understandings of the world. The Jewett murder case served as a prime example. Benjamin Day and James Gordon Bennett each claimed to have the facts on his side and warned readers not to trust the rival editor. According to Day, Bennett's "only chance of dying an upright man will be that of hanging perpendicularly upon a rope." In turn, the volatile and fiery Bennett was quick to bring lawsuits or engage in fisticuffs; three times, he lost badly in fights to another editor, James Watson Webb.[47]

In their coverage of the Jewett case, Day and Bennett summoned up contrasting mythologies about fallen women—that of "the Poor Unfortunate," a "victim, a trusting innocent from the country" (in the media scholar Andie Tucher's words), versus that of "the Siren," the predatory Eve with her apple of sin. As Tucher has observed: "The real 'news' about Jewett's death [had] more to do with these traditions than with facts." At stake were opposing perspectives about what was happening in the United States generally. When Day (as well as the *Transcript*) portrayed Jewett as the exploited victim of privileged middle- or upper-class men, he advanced an argument with which many working-class readers could identify. Bennett, on the other hand, did not wish to offend respectable middle-class readers who might expand his base of customers. He thus placed Jewett in the "Siren" category and blamed New York City's deviant groups for her fate. Meanwhile, publishers of small country weeklies confirmed suspicions among rural readers that New York City, like all metropolises, was a sinful place. In such ways, the spreading print revolution reflected as well as shaped public thinking.[48]

Although different print mythologies resonated among different groups, the penny press nevertheless touched a powerful grassroots desire to make sense of the rapidly changing urban environment. Swelling city populations created a setting of increasing anonymity in which it was difficult to identify whether strangers were friends or foes. Against that nervous backdrop, the penny press performed a number of functions that boosted its popularity. It helped mark boundaries between "us" and "them," thereby building feelings of belonging to a shared community. In the words of one historian, "daily papers reinforced emerging modes of anonymous, market-oriented, urban sociability" whereby strangers coalesced within a world of print. News stories that illuminated previously private lives (such as Jewett's or Robinson's) could, thus, serve as substitutes for human contact, allowing a sense of familiarity through human-interest tales. On this level, the penny press fulfilled the traditional cohesive role of village gossip, supplying a sense of order, control, and democratic empowerment. And, just as significantly, the penny dailies moved the expanding urban discourse from elite business houses and salons to the streets. This was precisely what minstrel shows were doing, as was Phineas Taylor Barnum.[49]

Probably no individual in the antebellum era took advantage of the appeal of the penny press as effectively as did the incomparable P. T. Barnum, a brilliant promoter of himself and his exhibits. In the summer of 1835, before he displayed Joice Heth, who supposedly was 161 years old and had nursed the infant George Washington, Barnum shrewdly set up a private interview between her and key New York City newspaper editors, including Benjamin Day. With well-rehearsed lines, she told them of her time as an African princess, her sale into slavery, and her conversion to Christianity—and also, of course, about caring for little George. Barnum, moreover, enthusiastically publicized the Heth exhibit by placing hundreds of bold advertisements in the newspapers: "JOICE HETH, the NURSE OF WASHINGTON . . . 'SHE RAISED HIM!'" The ads described her as perhaps "the oldest specimen of mortality," a tiny, forty-six-pound woman who "converses freely, sings numerous hymns, relates many interesting anecdotes of the *boy* Washington, *the red coats,* &c." As the new penny press editors competed for sensational stories, Barnum happily provided them with spectacular material, helping sell newspapers, boosting his own recent entry into show business, and, during his display of Joice Heth, pocketing as much as $1,500 per week.[50]

Phineas Taylor Barnum, ultimately America's leading pioneer of popular entertainment, started out inconspicuously enough. Born in 1810, he lived an uneventful childhood in Bethel, Connecticut, where his grandfather was one of the town's wealthiest individuals. Barnum's later celebrations of himself as "a tailor's son" and "a poor inexperienced boy" who soon had to "shift for myself" revealed mainly his fondness for hyperbole. Still, even though his life did not quite match the rags-to-riches saga that he liked to tell, he knew what it was like to be on the social and cultural margins. When he was growing up, the Congregational Church still controlled the state, which imposed harsh blue laws, kept theatrical and other commercial amusements at a minimum, and taxed citizens on behalf of religion. At age sixteen, following his father's death, Barnum briefly took a job as a clerk in Brooklyn and then in New York City, where he much enjoyed attending the theater and took an early fling at the entertainment business himself. For a short time, he worked with a traveling comedian, apparently exhibiting an "educated goat." The act did not last long but perhaps taught Barnum something about how controversy can enliven a performance. The controversy developed when an old woman claimed that Barnum was guilty of a hoax. There was no learned goat, she asserted, only "a show-actor dressed in goatskin." The woman was so certain she was correct that she picked up some of the goat's droppings, dismissed them as "nothing but dried cherries," ate them, and then promptly became ill and fled the building.[51]

After a year away from Bethel, Barnum returned, eventually operating a country store, dabbling in real estate, and, at age twenty-one, launching a small newspaper, the *Herald of Freedom*. His short-lived journalistic experiment mainly allowed him to vent his anger against the "*purse-proud overbearing lordlings,*" aristocrats, and overzealous Congregationalists who ran the state. Such attacks, besides revealing his plebeian sympathies, opened him to criticism and lawsuits. After he mysteriously accused a church deacon of "taking *usury* from an orphan boy," he served a sixty-day jail sentence. His supporters, however, celebrated his departure from jail by staging a parade, shooting off cannons, and undoubtedly thrilling Barnum with the excitement of being the center of attention.[52]

But New York City continued to lure Barnum, who, in 1833, got a job clerking in a lower Manhattan dry goods store. As a financially strapped denizen of the low-life Bowery area, he identified with the working class, frequented taverns and gambling dens, and cultivated his distaste for what he described as the "codfish aristocracy"—the privileged elites with their "many fine ladies" or the prudish middle class with its zeal for moral uplift. He apparently felt a kind of instinctive tie to the Bowery toughs, even as he looked for his main chance, his own formula for fame, fortune, and respectability.[53]

In 1835, two years after Barnum returned to Manhattan, he took a bold step, quitting his job, borrowing money, and joining the itinerant "hawkers and walkers" who trudged the countryside with acts and exhibits ranging from animals to peep shows and freaks. Barnum, however, had a particularly audacious exhibit: Joice Heth, whom he touted as "The Greatest Natural and National Curiosity in the World"—natural because of her alleged age of 161 years and national because of her ability to tap patriotic emotions regarding the great American hero, George Washington. She was, as Barnum advertised her, "the first person *who put clothes on the unconscious* infant who was destined . . . to lead our heroic fathers to glory, to victory, and to freedom." When Barnum first learned about the aged slave whom two men, including R. W. Lindsay, were showing in Philadelphia with only modest success, he examined her carefully and, as he later wrote, "was favorably struck with the appearance of the old woman." The decrepit, wizened slave "might almost as well have been called a thousand years old as any other age." She could barely move, and her left arm and both legs seemed paralyzed. "She was totally blind, and her eyes were so deeply sunken in their sockets that the eyeballs seemed to have disappeared altogether. She had no teeth, but possessed a head of thick bushy gray hair." Despite her infirmity, she seemed "in good health and spirits" and, much to Barnum's delight, sang and spun tales of "her protégé, 'dear little George,' as she termed the great father of our country." Heth's proud claim, "I raised him," was something that she told one audience after another. A supporting document, which her owners showed Barnum, indicated that George Washington's father had owned her. Barnum, sensing profits in Heth's aging body, joined Lindsay. For $1,000, half of which was a loan, Barnum became her co-owner, or at least (the arrangements were ambiguous) purchased the right to exhibit her.[54]

Via one of the new railways that facilitated the movement of various kinds of entertainment, Barnum transported Heth to New York City, where, in mid-1835, he displayed her for two and a half weeks at Niblo's Garden. Niblo's, which had been open for only seven years, was located on the corner of Broadway and Ann Street, some distance from lower Manhattan. It was one of the city's developing "pleasure gardens," featuring elaborate flower beds and a promenade, barring prostitutes, and catering, as one patron said, to "the aristocratic or at least the toffish Broadway set." Barnum observed wryly that these "shining lights of righteousness" strictly avoided theaters, whose customers were supposedly "on the high road to damnation." Over the next several months, he exhibited Heth in front of large crowds throughout a number of cities and towns in New England as well as in Albany, New York, and again in Manhattan. In doing so, he tapped audiences' fascination with Heth's accounts of raising the beloved Washington (thereby linking a new generation with the storied, but fading, exploits of the revolutionary era), her age, and her race. "Whereas a focus on her body degraded her," the Barnum scholar Benjamin Reiss has written, "the connection to Washington exalted her. . . . She elicited an unsettling mixture of disgust and envy." On the one hand, she was a shriveled, ancient-looking African American woman (a "living mummy") whose deformities and blackness unsettled and even repulsed many white viewers. Yet, on the other hand, she offered the reassuring presence of a happy slave, one who had engaged in the exalted domestic drama of child rearing and faithfully served the family of the nation's first president.[55]

Barnum, displaying an absolute genius for marketing, devised several strategies to publicize the Heth exhibit and fend off critics. Working with Levi Lyman, whom he hired as an advance man, he scheduled special opportunities for ministers to meet Heth, showing them baptismal documents that he and Lyman had forged. In order to reassure abolitionists, he planted a newspaper story that the exhibit was actually an antislavery benefit. He published a short biography, "The Life of Joice Heth, the Nurse of George Washington," further heightening the tensions over her identity. Audiences could view her as a pious, moral, patriotic woman or as an aged, black freak—as, in Reiss's words, a "spiritual vessel" or a "human grotesque," both of which lured spectators and lined Barnum's pockets. Or

spectators could even conclude that she was not human at all. In this respect, Barnum cleverly seized on charges that Heth was, in fact, a fraud. He
planted newspaper stories and staged incidents suggesting that she was actually made of whalebone and India rubber (itself one of the era's wonders)
and that the contraption's voice came from a ventriloquist. As Barnum
snickered: "Many who had seen her were equally desirous of a second
look, in order to determine whether or not they had been deceived."
Whether they paid once or twice, Barnum reaped the dividends. In his efforts to extend his clientele beyond upper-class patrons, he also sought to
lure female workers in factory towns such as Lowell, Massachusetts, and
added to the exhibition a "Signor Vivalla," who specialized in balancing
and spinning such items as plates as he danced around, sometimes on stilts.
Barnum changed Vivalla's name from Antonio (which to Barnum did not
sound foreign enough), paid him a fairly hefty salary, and required that he
bathe more frequently. Ultimately, Barnum ventured beyond the posh settings of the early tour and brought Heth and Vivalla to the quite unfashion-
able Bowery, where working-class audiences reportedly turned out to see
them in large numbers. Walking a kind of cultural tightrope, Barnum was
attempting to craft an audience that bridged the elegant Niblo's and Bowery
dives. For the next two decades, he would do so with uncanny success.[56]

Joice Heth, for her part, served the cause exceedingly well. On an important level, certainly, she had little choice; she was Barnum's commodity
to display. Still, as she became an early media celebrity, she may have relished the attention as well as the opportunity to step beyond traditionally
restrictive roles for slaves and most women. In a real sense, she created her
own persona, even as Barnum, Lyman, and the audiences shaped her in the
images they wanted. And she did so by demonstrating considerable theatrical talents. Perhaps, too, she appreciated the relatively decent care that
Barnum provided, including a black female attendant to help her, a soft
bed, tobacco, and whiskey. Perhaps, even more important, she found em-
powering the chance to enact her own version of a familiar slave strategy
of "puttin' on ol' massa," embellishing to her great advantage the hoax
that she was Washington's nurse. She may even have come to believe many
of her own stories about herself.[57]

In any case, Heth was a superb performer. For eight to fourteen gruel-
ing hours per day, six days a week—except when she was traveling, an or-
deal in itself—she was on display, resting, singing hymns, smoking a pipe,
spinning tales about the baby Washington, shaking hands, letting people
take her pulse, eating her food, joking, and answering questions playfully
and imaginatively. How long had she smoked? One hundred twenty years,
she replied. When she quipped that she hoped soon to buy a wedding dress,
a man asked whom she expected to marry. "Yourself sir," she replied, "if I
can find *no one else*." She added that there "are a great many others *too*

old for me." She also poked fun at fashion, stating her dislike for one person's cologne: "Clear out with your *muskrat,* don't bring such stuff about me." And, to much laughter, she spurned broiled mutton, saying: "I'd tank you to understand dat I am *Lady Washington,* and want as good victuals as any body." But, finally, on February 18, 1836, after Barnum had exhibited her for eight months, the old woman died.[58]

Even after Heth was dead, however, Barnum brought her out for one last performance. In Manhattan's City Saloon on Broadway, he made another $700 by charging admission to a public autopsy to determine her real age. Some fifteen hundred individuals paid to watch a leading surgeon, Dr. David L. Rogers, dissect her body. When Rogers concluded that she could not have been older than eighty years of age, Barnum claimed that he, too, had been the victim of a hoax. He also helped fuel another hoax: a rumor that Heth was actually alive and living in Hebron, Connecticut, and that the dissected corpse was that of a black woman from Harlem.[59]

By 1841, when Barnum entered the museum business to great fanfare, he was, thus, no stranger to the world of commercial amusements. He had toured with hardscrabble circuses and variety acts, including an "educated goat," the crockery-spinning Signor Vivalla, and an African American whom he blacked up. He had also performed in blackface himself—to much applause, as he recalled with some surprise. Although, by 1838, he was "thoroughly disgusted with the life of an itinerant showman," the Heth exhibits had unquestionably whetted his showbiz appetite. The challenge now was to find a profitable venue and build an audience—but to do so by building a "respectable, permanent business," as he put it.[60]

In that respect, his choice in 1841 hardly seemed promising. For several decades, the once-proud museum business had been descending rapidly toward the disreputable. The early museums in the United States had been the pet projects of influential philanthropists such as Thomas Jefferson's friend Charles Willson Peale, who viewed their institutions as vehicles for uplift and information, enlightened training grounds for educated, responsible, civic-minded citizens of the new republic. "Whoso would learn Wisdom, let him enter here!" was the motto of Peale's famous Philadelphia collection of paintings, artifacts, stuffed animals, and other exhibits. In Cincinnati, a physician who shared Peale's scientific perspective opened the Western Museum. But even he and Peale learned that the best educational intentions had to reckon with the pull of entertainment. When people donated a host of private curiosities to Peale, for example, he typically felt an obligation to display even the most bizarre items, including a four-legged chicken and a murderer's finger. In the early nineteenth century, in order to keep the museum interesting, Peale grudgingly bowed to his son's recommendation to include live entertainers. When the son subsequently took over the museum, he boosted revenues by featuring a growing list of popular attractions. A second museum that the son opened, this one in New York City, displayed such eccentricities as a "learned dog" and a calf that had, among other things, two heads and six legs. Meanwhile, the appeal of Cincinnati's dusty Western Museum declined so much that the stockholders, unable even to sell the collections, gave the institution to a curator who promptly lured audiences by exhibiting moving skeletons and the head and heart of a local murderer. "Dime museums" grew in popularity, setting their admission at ten cents, although adults more commonly paid twenty-five cents. Although some museums still paid lip service to the goal of education, their increasingly sensational and weird exhibits were turning them primarily into amusement centers—ones that reflected the raucous spirit of New York's Bowery, "the capital of dissipation" and "the main street of the lower classes," according to one of the city's chroniclers.[61]

As a former Bowery inhabitant, Barnum certainly had no quarrel with that spirit, which was evident in his earlier use of foreign jugglers, blackface, and Joice Heth. If anything, Barnum hoped to capitalize even more on the appeal of the excessive and the bizarre. Bowery patrons were surely welcome when he opened the doors of his own museum a few blocks away—on Broadway, no less, the commercial heart of a city with nearly 300,000 residents (third largest in the world). Although Broadway was assuredly not free of dirt or lowlife, it had been the first street in the city to have a brick sidewalk, numbered houses, and gas lighting.[62]

The museum in downtown Manhattan that Barnum purchased in 1841 became, under his inventive leadership, nationally known and, for a while, New York City's most popular attraction. The five-story building had formerly been John Scudder's American Museum but had fallen on hard times. Barnum bought it with no more than his own "brass," as he put it, although he used some Connecticut real estate for collateral on the $15,000 purchase. The museum was strategically located at the city's emerging commercial center, the corner of Ann and Broadway, bridging upscale shopping establishments and the crowded Bowery tenements.[63]

With formidable show business savvy, Barnum skillfully implemented vigorous advertising, stunning decorations, and, of course, controversy to publicize a breathtaking range of exhibits and experiences. He later delighted in relating how, in 1842, he had manipulated the city's Independence Day celebration to his advantage. One of his plans was "to run out a string of American flags across the street on that day, for I knew there would be thousands of people passing the Museum with leisure and pocket money"; the flags "would arrest their patriotic attention, and bring many of them within my walls." Vestrymen from St. Paul's Church threatened to scuttle his plan, however, when they objected to his attaching any rope to their churchyard tree. Early on July 4, Barnum defied them, hanging flags from a rope with one end tied to that very tree. By 9:30 A.M., when the vestrymen discovered what he had done, festive crowds were already thronging the street between the church and the museum. Barnum seemed accommodating enough when the vestrymen came to his office in angry protest. But, after persuading them to join him outside, he said loudly: "Really, gentlemen, these flags look very beautiful; they do not injure your tree." Rolling up his sleeves, he then dared the vestrymen to take down the flags and threatened to "show you a thousand pairs of Yankee hands in two minutes" if they tried "to take down the stars and stripes on this great birthday of American freedom!" By now, Barnum had successfully captured the attention of the crowd, including some loud patriots who were determined to protect the flags at all costs. The vestrymen quickly relented. Barnum's gambit had worked so well that by 1 P.M. his museum was so crowded that additional customers could not get in. To avoid repeating that situation, Barnum devised a gimmick for future use. Several months later, when the museum was again full, he fooled some of the customers into leaving prematurely by hanging up a sign that said "To the Egress." Curious spectators, anxious to see whatever this egress was, found themselves exiting into the back alley, thereby allowing Barnum to sell more tickets up front.[64]

Within three years, Barnum's exceptionally popular American Museum featured perhaps as many as thirty thousand exhibits, including waxworks, displays of armor and weapons, and live animals. The huge menagerie eventually included exotic creatures ranging from tigers to giraffes, crocodiles, sloths, and a hippopotamus. By 1857, new aquariums featured even whales. A satirist compared the collection to "a Connecticut chowder," mixing "bears, reptiles, reprobates, bugs, bulls, bells, bats, birds, petrifactions, putrefactions."[65]

On the upstairs floors, patrons could gawk at some of the most popular and controversial exhibits: "human curiosities," or "freaks," such as bearded ladies, legless individuals, albinos, giants, and midgets. From later perspectives, the exhibiting of such individuals for profit was reprehensible and exploitative. Barnum, however, took great pride in his collection of human curiosities. He believed not only that he treated them well (even though he once threatened to have a family of albinos—the Lucasies—arrested because they were being "disagreeable") but also that he provided useful employment, opportunities to live in a shared community, and even a chance to become celebrities. Moreover, he was drawing on an entertainment phenomenon that had a long history, evident, for example, in sixteenth-century English fairs. By helping turn such human curiosities into featured museum exhibits, Barnum was, nevertheless, instrumental in forging what became a subculture of freaks within the nascent popular amusement industry.[66]

"Freak shows" both thrilled and reassured audiences, who viewed human oddities with combinations of fear, inquisitiveness, and feelings of superiority. Spectators who were trying to make sense of the often terrifying and confusing whirl of a rapidly industrializing, urbanizing society could measure and define themselves against those strange Others whose presence helped distinguish the normal from the deviant. In that regard, of course, the nature of the exhibits revealed much about contemporary anxieties concerning sexuality, race, and power.[67]

Barnum thus toyed with issues of sexuality when he exhibited Josephine Clofullia, his Swiss bearded lady. Ever mindful of the benefits of controversy, he encouraged rumors that she was, in fact, a man. After paying a customer to accuse her of being a fraud, Barnum brought the phony case to court, where doctors, as well as Clofullia's husband, testified that she was truly a female. The big winner, of course, was Barnum, who used the case's notoriety to boost his museum. Similarly, he profited from public speculation over the sex lives of Chang and Eng, the famed Siamese twins who performed all kinds of astonishing physical feats before enthusiastic audiences. Joined at the chest, they had escaped desperate poverty in Siam (later Thailand) by touring as a circus act. Never before had joined twins been exhibited in the United States. By the time they joined up with Barnum, Chang and Eng were fairly wealthy U.S. citizens. In 1843, they married sisters and, soon thereafter, began having children—ultimately, twenty-two of them. Museum customers were curious about how Chang, Eng, and their wives engaged in sexual intercourse. What, too, museum visitors wondered, about the sex lives of the fat woman and the thin man? Here was a mysterious world full of ambiguity, one that, as a dime museum scholar has written, "challenge[d] the conventional boundaries between male, female, sex, self, and other."[68]

Race as a subject was never more evident than in Barnum's "What Is It?" exhibit. In this instance, Barnum pressed beyond some of the racial issues that had surrounded his Joice Heth tour. In 1860, he undoubtedly took advantage of intensified public speculation, following the recent publication (in 1859) of Charles Darwin's *On the Origin of Species,* about connections between humans and monkeys. Barnum had devised earlier exhibits to suggest such connections, but never before had he used a black man as, according to advertisements, the "CONNECTING LINK BETWEEN MAN AND MONKEY." The man was William Henry Johnson, under five feet tall, with a small, pointed head, a large nose that seemed to start at the hairline, and diminished intellectual capacity. "Zip" was his stage name, perhaps echoing that of the "Zip Coon" minstrel character. Although Johnson was more than likely born in New Jersey, Barnum claimed that a group of explorers in Africa, looking for gorillas, had found him and an entire race just like him, living nude in the trees. Johnson had supposedly been the only survivor among the several of his species whom the explorers brought to the United States. He reportedly walked initially on all fours and ate raw meat as well as fruit and nuts. One of Barnum's advertisements claimed that Johnson "has been examined by some of the most scientific men we have, and pronounced by them to be a CONNECTING LINK BETWEEN THE WILD AFRICAN AND BRUTE CREATION." Other museum ads suggested that "it seems to be a sort of cross between an ape species and a Negro" or "between the WILD NATIVE AFRICAN AND THE ORANG OUTANG." As white museum customers watched Johnson, they could wrestle with questions of race, secure at least in the knowledge that the "missing link" was apparently black.[69]

At least one skeptical reporter suspected that the act was fraudulent. He observed that, when the keeper was delivering his "What Is It?" lecture to the audience, the "It" made "many sly manoeuvers that lets in the light on the humbug terribly." Illuminating "the humbug"—here, perhaps, was a significant key to the astounding popularity of Barnum's museum. "Vive la humbug!" Barnum had himself chortled earlier, after he had convinced members of the clergy to endorse his Joice Heth exhibit. "Emancipation and blarney carried all before them, and I pocketed the rhino," he wrote.[70]

Barnum's clever gambits fit superbly in the antebellum era, when American culture, as one historian has described it, "was a jamboree of exaggeration, chicanery, flimflam, and bunkum." Against a backdrop of wrenching change, citizens understandably worried about making sense of what was happening all around them. Rapid technological developments, ranging from railroads and steamboats to the telegraph and new methods of printing newspapers, were revolutionizing communication and transportation. Industrialization and the emerging free-labor market made social positions and personal finances more tenuous and fluid. Rapidly growing cities filled the streets with anonymous strangers. The era's voracious land speculation hinged on the credibility of promoters, just as the flood of paper money rested on creditors' faith. What could individuals believe? How could they understand the workings of the new technology? Whom could they trust? How could one distinguish the truth from outright lies? Finding answers to such questions was even more difficult because of the expanding numbers of people who engaged in trickery, wearing disguises to fool innocent citizens and mastering the art of the swindle. A fast-talking New Yorker named William Thompson inspired the label *confidence man* by convincing strangers to loan him their watches, which he promptly stole. In 1857, with Thompson in mind, Herman Melville published his novel *The Confidence Man*. The penny press reported regularly about con artists and "painted ladies" who adopted poses in order to fleece unsuspecting individuals. Benjamin Day's *New York Sun* practiced its own deceits with stories about the recent discovery of winged men on the moon. The era's famed writer Edgar Allan Poe, who himself spun whoppers about an alleged three-day balloon crossing of the Atlantic, believed that confidence games were central to the nation's culture: "A crow thieves; a fox cheats; a man diddles. To diddle is his destiny."[71]

Within this "burgeoning marketplace of playful frauds," Barnum competed for customers. Indeed, the era's fascination with human oddities was so large that some individuals—"Horatio Algers of the underworld who cannily faked their uncanniness," as one historian has characterized them— tried to cash in on the phenomenon by posing as freaks. One such imposter donned a wig and passed himself off as a "dog-faced boy." No fewer than forty men posed as the Lost Dauphin (Louis XVII). Barnum, who himself played fast and loose with the truth, had to guard against individuals who might, in turn, take advantage of him. "I really believe she is honest," he insisted, after the penny press exposed one of his acts, "Miss Darling," as a prostitute who had spent some time in an insane asylum. Then, of course, there was the matter of Joice Heth. In his 1855 autobiography, Barnum claimed to know nothing about her as an imposter, even though he had allegedly boasted about the ruse to the journalist Albert Smith. At the least, despite his subsequent claims of innocence, he had chosen not to inquire too closely into her background.[72]

Overall, Barnum more than held his own when it came to inventive deceptions, some of which he termed his "side shows." He once advertised for free viewing of a wild buffalo hunt. Fifteen of the animals, which he had purchased for $700 from the Western frontier, were on a farm in Hoboken, New Jersey, across the Hudson River from Manhattan. On one day, twenty-four thousand passengers jammed on ferryboats to see these fearsome animals. To their chagrin, they discovered not magnificent beasts but ones that were mangy, emaciated, "so weak and tame that it was doubtful whether they would run at all," as Barnum later admitted, and so terrified that they fled into a nearby swamp. Still, because, except for the cost of transportation, the buffalo exhibit was free, viewers masked their disappointment with humor. When one of them on a departing boat shouted to passengers who were just arriving at the New Jersey wharf that the exhibit "was the biggest humbug you ever heard of!" the incoming audience cheered. Barnum, meanwhile, happily pocketed his share of the transportation fees, courtesy of a deal he had struck with the ferryboat owners, and made a profit of $3,500.[73]

Intuitively, Barnum seemed to recognize that the phenomenon of "diddling" not only stirred public anxieties but was also a rich source of entertainment. While the confidence man loomed as a frightening specter of social disorder, he could just as easily be a beloved rogue, a trickster in the mold of a Davy Crockett or a Yankee peddler, like the fictional character Simon Suggs, who joked, "IT IS GOOD TO BE SHIFTY IN A NEW COUNTRY." Deception perhaps played an important role in many of the new amusements because it continually tested the viewers' abilities to distinguish fact from fiction, the authentic from the artificial, and what was legitimate from what was pretense.[74]

In that regard, one of the era's most popular exhibits—and one from which Barnum drew much inspiration—was a mechanized chess player. Viewers could wonder whether it was truly a thinking machine or a glorious hoax. It came from Europe, where, in the late eighteenth century, a Hungarian official had used it to astonish royalty and aristocrats. The automaton, wearing a Turkish robe and turban, sat with a chessboard behind a cabinet with two front doors. The Hungarian would open each door to prove that they concealed only levers and wheels and had no additional room. Then, while the machine's owner called out the moves as they occurred, the mannequin would play chess with human challengers who sat on the audience side. Time and again, the automaton won, once besting the visiting Benjamin Franklin. In 1826, Johann Maelzel, a German student who had purchased the machine, began to exhibit it in the United States. Among those trying to solve its mystery was Edgar Allan Poe, who suspected that the machine was a hoax and not really "a *pure machine,* unconnected with human agency in its movements." By late 1835, when Barnum met Maelzel in Boston, the automaton chess player was no longer attracting huge crowds because the novelty was wearing off and the prevailing assumption was that the act was, indeed, a fake. Two years later, a Philadelphia newspaper exposed the trick. A human hid behind false panels inside the cabinet, shifting from one side to the other as the owner opened each door for examination. When the chess game started, the concealed person was able to manipulate the automaton's arm and fingers in response to the moves that the owner described. Barnum was particularly impressed with how Maelzel, following exposure of the ruse, in effect reinvented himself as a creator of elaborate hoaxes rather than thinking machines. Deception, even once the secret was out, could still be a source of profit. Controversy and doubt—not conclusive demonstrations of truth—were magnets for audiences.[75]

With that lesson in mind, Barnum cultivated his growing reputation as the "prince of humbug," a term that he proudly applied to himself. "Now and then," he recalled, "some one would cry out 'humbug' and 'charlatan,' but so much the better for me. It helped to advertise me." Humbugging was, from his view, different from swindling or even lying. It depended on the participation of the "victim"; typically, the object of the deception enjoyed the ruse or was at least so gullible that others could laugh. "When people expect to get 'something for nothing' they are sure to be cheated, and generally deserve to be," Barnum wrote. Humbug was like an inside joke, and it was an expected part of merchandising. Barnum recalled that, when he was clerking in general stores as a youngster, "the customers cheated us in their fabrics: we cheated the customers with our goods. Each party expected to be cheated. . . ." Barnum implicitly nudged viewers in the rib and gave a wink; participants agreed to join the game, just as they had done when they were purchasing goods from the general stores at which he had worked: "Our cottons were sold for wool, our wool and cotton for silk and linen; in fact nearly everything was different from what it was represented." Thus, later in his museum, the ballyhooed "Man-Eating Chicken" turned out to be a "man eating chicken," and "THE GREAT MODEL OF NI-AGARA FALLS, WITH REAL WATER!" (an exhibit that city officials initially feared would demand a huge amount of water) was, in fact, only eighteen inches high and used a barrel of water per month.[76]

Such artful deception meshed well with the antebellum era's celebration of democracy—evident, for instance, in the leveling rhetoric of President Andrew Jackson, whom Barnum warmly endorsed. John Quincy Adams could write, but Jackson could fight, as one poet observed in 1828. Similarly, the art of deception was open to common scrutiny, regardless of wealth, privilege, or education. Any individual could try to figure out the puzzle, solve the mystery, discover the hoax. In that spirit, at a time when science and technology were opening vast areas for inquiry, Barnum was urging rank-and-file citizens to join the debate. A prime example was his infamous "Feejee Mermaid," a manufactured curiosity with a monkey's head attached to a fish's body whose exhibition virtually tripled the museum's receipts in just four weeks. Barnum publicized it as the discovery of London's Dr. J. Griffin (actually Levi Lyman, Barnum's advance man during the Heth exhibit). Spectators could reach their own conclusions about the mermaid's authenticity. The opinions of common citizens in effect counted as heavily as did those of famous scientists, who, according to Barnum, were themselves deeply divided over whether the exhibit was a fake. To entice people to view his "critter," he contemplated an advertisement that asked: "Who is to decide when the doctors disagree?" Barnum's museum thus encouraged a kind of cultural democracy; truth rested with the majority.[77]

Even low-life Bowery residents were welcome at the museum and could join the debates over whether exhibits were phony or genuine. Upper-class patrons could take offense, "but I worked for the million," wrote Barnum, which was also "the only way to make a million." He admittedly greeted Bowery types in part because he recognized that their dimes and quarters matched in value those of everyone else. Moreover, he liked to tweak the respectable folks who sneered at him and his amusements, complaining, as one did, about "crowds rushing, ready to break their necks, to witness a vile imposter, a gross humbug" who exhibited "stunted children, pasteboard mermaids, wooly horses, and other 'wonderful inventions.'"[78]

But Barnum apparently also felt a kind of kinship with working-class toughs such as the "Bowery b'hoys" and their counterparts in other cities.

They were generally young, single males for whom the emerging factory economy seemed to hold diminishing opportunities for self-employment. Many belonged to, or associated with, volunteer fire departments, which were rowdy centers of boisterous, highly competitive urban gangs who sometimes fought over the right to extinguish fires. Sporting the title *b'hoys* (reflecting the Irish and street pronunciation of *boys*), they strutted and bragged about their talents as lovers and brawlers, typically defining themselves in opposition to middle-class decorum and respectability. Their own sense of class came less from participation in the era's organized labor movement than from identifying with a cultural style built around their dress, mannerisms, use of leisure time, and popular culture. Taking advantage of a dramatic drop in the prices of theater tickets in the 1820s and early 1830s, they turned places such as the Bowery Theater into popular gathering spots in which raucous b'hoys demanded their kind of entertainment. "When their mouths were not filled with tobacco and peanuts," recalled one minstrel performer about their conduct, "they were shouting to each other at the top of their voices." "Their chief pastime between the acts, when not fighting, was to catch up a stranger or countryman, and toss him from hand to hand over their heads until forced from fatigue to desist."[79]

In 1848, when the play *A Glance at New York* opened in the Bowery's Olympic Theater, the b'hoys enthusiastically greeted a character made in their image: "Mose." When he took the stage, Mose evoked an outcry of recognition. According to one account: "He stood there in his red shirt, with his fire coat thrown over his arm, the stovepipe hat . . . drawn down over one eye, his trousers tucked into his boots, a stump of a cigar pointing up from his lips to his eye, the soap locks plastered flat on his temples." He was spoiling for a fight yet quick to rescue women and children. "The fireboys may be a little rough outside, but they're all right here," he said, touching his chest. "Lize," a Bowery g'hal, was his besmitten female friend. Her character suggested that the b'hoys were willing to share some social and cultural room with females who, although still supposedly subservient, deserved at least some courtesy and respect. Moreover, she attested to the growing numbers of young workingwomen who took advantage of the cities' new resources and opportunities and who, like Lize, made their own class statement with colorful dresses, outgoing manners, and the repudiation of ladyhood. "Her very walk has a swing of mischief and defiance in it," wrote George Foster, a leading observer of the city's nightlife.[80]

Youthful, urban male workers found the same defiance in Mose, who quickly became a hero as far away as Nashville, Tennessee, but was part of the "civic scum" that infuriated the likes of the wealthy George Templeton Strong. One gentleman complained that the Olympic Theater's "boxes no longer shone with the elite of the city; the character of the audiences was entirely changed, and Mose, instead of appearing on stage, was in the pit, the boxes, and the gallery. It was all Mose, and the respectability of the house mosed too."[81]

Although Barnum gladly opened his doors to Boweryites and regularly featured Irish performances and songfests in order to attract the swelling ranks of working-class immigrants from the Emerald Isle, he did not want his museum "mosed." His quest for profits as well as respectability turned his attention elsewhere, to the emerging middle class. While he gave the impression that he welcomed the scorn of fashionable people, he probably resented descriptions of his kind of museum as nothing more than "a place for some stuffed birds and animals, for the exhibition of monsters, and for vulgar dramatic performances," as the educated and aristocratic Henry Tappan described it—"a mere place of popular amusement." Although Barnum liked to say that he would "rather be kicked than not noticed at all," he privately regretted that he had "(foolishly) stuck my worst side outside." As he tried to bridge the expanding cultural gap between the Bowery and Broadway, he leaned increasingly toward the prosperous and the respectable. And, in that regard, he mirrored trends in other amusements, including the minstrel shows and the press.[82]

2

TAMING ROUGH AMUSEMENTS
1840s-1860s

A PIVOTAL ANTEBELLUM DEVELOPMENT WAS THE emergence of a middle class with an expansive set of values and beliefs. That development profoundly influenced popular culture. For the burgeoning amusement sector, this middle class was both an obstacle, swelling the ranks of social and cultural reformers who targeted "immoral" diversions, and a boon, enlarging the pool of potential, and relatively more affluent, customers. Popular culture proved remarkably adaptive, accommodating dramatic social changes, yet never completely losing its oppositional and resistant features. While important amusement pockets (including such blood sports as boxing) continued to provide refuges from the spreading dictates of middle-class morality, rising entertainment entrepreneurs such as P. T. Barnum shrewdly adjusted their offerings. By the 1840s, Barnum's museum, blackface minstrel shows, the penny press, holiday celebrations (especially Christmas), and the publication of increasingly popular sentimental fiction and etiquette books evolved via a tentative, often conflicted association with the expanding middle class.

By the middle of the nineteenth century, according to the historian E. J. Hobsbawm, "the era of the triumphant bourgeois" had arrived. This rising middle class was a creation of the proliferating market economy. As household production gave way to the budding world of small industries, a modern system of capitalist production emerged. For manual laborers, a system of wages and piece rates increasingly shouldered aside long-established apprentice arrangements, whereby employees learned a trade and moved toward economic independence. That same "urban-industrial revolution," in the words of the historian Stuart Blumin, allowed people in the formative middle class to "redefine themselves, and elevate themselves, in ways that were not possible in the craft economies and the little urban worlds of the eighteenth century." More and more, it was possible to distinguish between what a writer in 1847 described as "head-work and hand-work." By 1860, perhaps 40 percent of the workforce in American cities was engaged in nonmanual labor, or what was, in effect, a growing number of white-collar positions. Whereas in the eighteenth century proprietors had typically performed manual tasks, in the nineteenth the ascendant kinds of work involved not making things but, in Blumin's words, "buying, selling, shipping, and the managing of other people's production." Here was the economic base of a nascent middle class—one whose lifestyles and manners ultimately fit the *Victorian* label of its counterpart in Queen Victoria's nineteenth-century England.[1]

The members of that nascent middle class ranged from merchants, professionals, retailers, and wholesalers to sales managers, supervisors, book-keepers, and clerks of various kinds. Their workplaces tended to be in stores and offices, typically separate from the uncomfortable, dirty, noisy environs where people who engaged in "hand-work" actually built things. Their income was significantly higher than that of manual laborers, and even low-paid clerks anticipated eventually making more than skilled workers. Their dwellings were usually larger and more prosperous. They were particularly susceptible to the religious fervor of what has come to be known as the Second Great Awakening, an evangelical revival that swept across huge chunks of the country in the early nineteenth century. And they typically defined themselves in ways that emphasized their material and moral superiority to those who engaged in other than "head-work." One writer in 1843 referred condescendingly to manual workers' "low station, their wants, and their drudgeries," which encouraged sordid, coarse, and rude behavior and temperaments.[2]

While members of this growing middle class measured their existence in terms of wealth, occupation, and moral discipline, they also formed distinctive views of the family, public life, and gender. As traditional family responsibilities increasingly became the province of new public institutions such as hospitals, schools, and poorhouses, middle-class homes were inclined to retreat to a "family circle" that was private and protected.[3] While public life—that of business, politics, and careers—belonged to men, the domestic setting turned rapidly into a sphere particularly for women, whose primary responsibilities were to raise children, provide emotional support for their spouses, and serve as society's moral anchors. As the productive capacity of children in such homes declined, the "value" of offspring depended more and more on their affectionate ties with parents.

These trends helped forge a romanticized ideology in which children were vulnerable innocents and mothers had special responsibility for protecting them from worldly corruption. Architecture and fashion reflected this ideology. The middle-class house took on the look of what a sociologist has described as "a virtual feminine theme park," with a neat parlor set off from the rear of the house, providing a barrier against the dirt and filth of the outside world. To demonstrate their dependence, physical weakness, passivity, and moral purity, middle-class women were supposed to seek beauty through cleanliness, proper diet, and simple hairstyles. And, to distinguish themselves further from the lower classes, they needed to wear dresses that reflected bourgeois sincerity and character—dresses that, by the late 1830s, limited movement by billowing outward from narrow waists over padded hips to the floor and featured snug bodices worn over tightly laced corsets.[4]

Accompanying these changing fashions was an outpouring of advice literature containing elaborate instructions on bourgeois standards of respectability, decorum, and self-control. In the three decades after 1830, around seventy etiquette manuals appeared. "Remember," advised the *Handbook for the Use of the Lady in Polite Society* (1860), "that every part of your person and dress should be in perfect order . . . and avoid all such tricks as smoothing your hair with your hand, arranging your curls, pulling the waist of your dress down." The 1855 *Treatise on the Art of Politeness, Good Breeding, and Manners* described as "truly indecent" the act of running fingers through hair; people who engaged in such conduct "might as well bring in their whole paraphanalia [*sic*] of the toilet and exhibit before their friends the interesting performance." Publications included instructions ranging from "How Not to Cough" to "How to Dress Well and Tastefully, with Rules for Courtship, Marriage, Etc.," "How to Write a Good Hand," and "The Art of Making Home Happy, with Rules for Games, Recreations, Home Amusements, Tableaux, etc., etc."[5]

Particularly for young males, a small flood of advice manuals warned against sinful sexual thoughts and practices. Self-control was never more essential than when it applied to sexuality. Masturbation—the "solitary sin" or the "secret vice"—was especially dangerous. According to the moral crusader Sylvester Graham, "the wretched transgressor" who failed to control the sex drive "finally becomes a confirmed and degraded idiot" with "deeply sunken and vacant, glossy eye, and livid shrivelled countenance, and ulcerous, toothless gums, and fetid breath, and feeble, broken voice, and emaciated and dwarfish and crooked body . . . and a ruined soul!"[6]

Increasingly, antebellum reformers set out to police the nation's morals, providing messages of uplift, attacking drunkenness and rowdiness, and censuring bad conduct. As one magazine declared in 1851: "Let our readers, one and all, remember that we were sent into the world, not for sport and amusement, but for labor; not to enjoy and please ourselves, but to serve and glorify God."[7] The rising world of popular amusements would have to reckon with such moralists.

P. T. Barnum's eagerness to court the rapidly evolving middle class and his willingness to square his entertainments with bourgeois expectations flowed easily from his interest in profits and respectability. Barnum was always quick to admit that his primary motive in the amusement business was to make money. "My disposition is, and ever was, of a speculative character," he wrote, "and I am never content to engage in any business unless it is of such a nature that my profits may be greatly enhanced."[8] Moreover, despite his often flippant comments about high society and manners, he also sought approval. After exhibiting Joice Heth, he wanted to find "a respectable, permanent business," one in which he could "settle down into a respectable calling."[9] Even though his entertainment offerings included, as he said, "a little 'clap-trap' occasionally," he claimed, no doubt with considerable hyperbole, that he personally "relished a higher grade of amusement, and . . . was a frequent attendant at the opera, first-class concerts, lectures, and the like." While he liked to joke that the "old 'fogies'" who criticized his exhibits of "'stuffed monkey skins'" ultimately "paid their quarters to see them," he undoubtedly wished that such "fogies" would take him more seriously.[10] It was, thus, not coincidental that, at a time when the theater summoned up images of raunchiness and vice, Barnum would advertise his museum as "the special place of FAMILY AMUSEMENT IN THE UNITED STATES." Some observers might see his museum "as an annex of the Bowery," but he increasingly took pains to endorse themes of temperance and domesticity: Bowery toughs, although welcome in his museum, needed to leave their rowdiness at the door.[11]

To burnish his middle-class credentials, Barnum needed to make some personal adjustments of his own. Much about his background contradicted bourgeois values. In 1841, during a stint selling Bibles, he leased under a friend's name the Vauxhall Gardens saloon and featured variety acts. "I thought it would be compromising my dignity as a 'Bible man' to be known as the lessee of a theater," he joked later.[12] Moreover, he could offer only weak claims as a family man, and his lifestyle was morally flawed. Although he had, in 1837, momentarily abandoned his itinerant showmanship because he favored "home sweet home" and his "dear family," in the early 1840s he spent much of his time on the road, despite the death of his two-year-old daughter and the illness of his wife, Charity. He complained that Charity, whom he had married in 1829, seemed to fit a little too well the moral standards of the middle class. "Her ideas of morality and propriety," Barnum wrote, "savored too much of the old blue law school of Connecticut" and also made her suitable company for New York City's "old maids." His own defiance of that "old blue law school" included a great deal of carousing. He enjoyed card playing, cigar smoking, and particularly drinking. He admitted that his "appetite for liquor" was increasing "month to month." Charity had reason to worry that he was heading down "a drunkard's path"; by 1847, he was downing at least a bottle of champagne each evening and was sometimes unable to work by the afternoon. A year later, however, convinced that he was, indeed, "pursuing a path of wrong-doing," he destroyed the sixty or more bottles of champagne in his basement, signed "the teetotaler pledge," and joined the temperance movement.[13]

He soon noted proudly that he had banned intoxicating liquors from his museum: "I would not even allow my visitors to 'go out to drink' and return again without paying a second time, and this reconciled them to the 'ice-water' which was always profuse and free on each floor." Moreover, he had hired "half a score of detectives dressed in plain clothes, who . . . turned into the street every person of either sex whose actions indicated loose habits." In that context, he distinguished his "lecture room" from a theater so that he could, in his words, "catch the quiet country people . . . who have the old puritanical horror of the ordinary theatrical performance." By the 1850s, the expanded room held more than three thousand people and featured "moral drama" and lectures. In mid-1850, with hopes of "minister[ing] to a refined and elevated popular taste," Barnum opened performances of *The Drunkard; or, The Fallen Saved,* an antiliquor play, and provided copies of the teetotal pledge for individuals to sign. In 1865, he claimed that "no vulgar word or gesture and not a profane expression was *ever* allowed on my stage."[14]

Barnum was, in effect, trying to reshape the American theater, reclaiming it "from both puritanism and vice," as a trio of Barnum scholars has written, and transforming it into "a reputable, middle-class institution."[15] To forge a place of family entertainment was a formidable challenge, however. Not only did theaters labor under tawdry, dissipated reputations, but they had increasingly become arenas of class warfare.

Over several decades, class fissures had been growing within and between theaters. For a while, some theaters provided common ground for laborers and elites, who gathered under the same roofs but sat in different places. The pit was directly beneath the stage. Typically, it seated a "mixed multitude," as one Bostonian wrote in 1820, including artisans and mechanics. Sometimes it resembled, in the words of the writer George Foster, a "wild and sullen tumult, like a red flannel sea agitated by some lurid storm," with "the roaring crush and clamor of tobacco chewing." The second tier contained boxes, with individual seats for fashionable, society people, eager to show off their clothes and themselves: "gentlewomen," according to one observer, "famous for their delicacy" as well as "the dandies, and people of fine respectability and fashion." The cheapest section, at the back of the auditorium, was the third-tier gallery, from which tum-

bled, as Foster said, "the yells and screams, the shuddering oaths and obscene songs" of the Bowery b'hoys and their compatriots. Prostitutes often
conducted business in the gallery. Within theaters, these class distinctions
increasingly became sources of tension. Prosperous elites complained about
the "gallery gods," as the writer Washington Irving dubbed them, who hollered, whistled, coughed, sneezed, and, when they disliked the performance,
threw objects at the stage, sometimes also hitting people in the pit. Even the
pit was not free of the boorishness that offended visitors such as England's
Frances Trollope. "One man in the pit was seized with a fit of vomiting,
which appeared not the least to annoy or surprise his neighbors," she complained. "The spitting was incessant." Irving described what happened
when the gallery spectators objected to the music: "They stamped, hissed,
roared, whistled and groaned in cadence until the musicians" played something "more suited to their tastes."[16]

As audiences "called the tune," they claimed their authority and importance in a nation awash with the democratic rhetoric of a Davy Crockett
or an Andrew Jackson. "We (the sovereigns) determine to have the worth
of our money when we go to the theater," remarked one individual. Theater
lighting, which still lacked the technology to focus on the stage and illuminated the entire house, added to the impression that all audience members
had equal parts in the show.[17]

More and more, however, the socially heterogeneous audiences that sat
under single theater roofs began to fragment. Unhappy that the "shirt-
sleeve crowd"—Frances Trollope's term for people in the pit and gallery—
was taking over, members of polite society tried to take control. One
strategy was to separate respectable venues and moral entertainment from
the kinds of vulgar contamination that "Boweryisms" represented.[18]

In 1832, for example, a group of evangelists purchased the Bowery's
Chatham Theater and briefly turned it into a chapel. A powerful evangelical movement—the Second Great Awakening—was by then sweeping much
of the Northeast and fueling a host of reform movements ranging from sabbatarianism to abolition. Among its ranks were some of the new-style entrepreneurs who helped mold the emerging middle-class world and led a
series of moral-uplift crusades. The Tappan brothers, Arthur and Lewis,
whose piecing-out system of production included close scrutiny of their
employees' private lives, founded Oberlin College on the Ohio frontier,
helped establish an Asylum for Indigent Boys, and became tenacious abolitionists. Arthur helped launch the American Tract Society, which distributed to poor people small booklets with scriptural messages. William E.
Dodge, who moved from a small Connecticut town to New York City,
where he became wealthy in the metals business, was a founder of the
American Bible Society, taught Sunday school classes, and backed the
Young Men's Christian Association. Such evangelicals turned their atten-

tion to the Chatham Theater, where Frances Trollope had found "a general level of contempt for the decencies of life." By mid-1832, just a few months after the evangelists took control of the Chatham, the famed preacher Charles G. Finney was saving souls where blackface minstrels had performed shortly before. Although the short-lived experiment ended in 1839, when the theater returned to popular management and minstrel shows, the evangelicals had demonstrated their commitment to social uplift.[19]

An additional strategy to undercut perceived threats from the great unwashed was to increase managerial control over audiences and to orient theater fare toward more polite preferences. "If the public has rights, so has the manager," asserted an advocate of change.[20] In a related development, "the ermined ranks of fashion," as one magazine described the patrons of the Astor Place Opera House, turned increasingly to the opera as their preserve. For years, opera, although often in bowdlerized versions, had attracted both grassroots and elite audiences. But by raising ticket prices substantially and insisting that performers sing in the original tongue—not English—social elites asserted their authority.[21] Commoners objected to such effete snobbery and putting on of "airs." "If he could once break through the shell of the library and mingle with the world," wrote one satirist of a Boston gentleman who disdained popular music but attended a high-class performance of *Don Giovanni*, "he would become a glorious fellow . . . not so *precious* as now. So we will even let him vegetate."[22]

Among the kinds of theatrical entertainment that appealed particularly to middle-class audiences was melodrama, ultimately one of popular culture's most familiar and compelling elements. As part of the effort to bring some restraint and virtue into the theater, melodrama celebrated bourgeois values of respectability, status, and self-discipline while emphasizing that moral certitudes would prevail. Melodrama portrayed a world in which clear-cut morals, innocence, heroism, and virtue invariably triumphed. It invited teary-eyed spectators to empathize with beleaguered but worthy victims, who succeed through hard work, honesty, and a capacity to suffer. Onstage, there was no room for moral ambiguities as good defeated evil.[23] Stock characters included the hero, an honorable and patriotic man with a pure heart; the heroine, who embodied the "true woman," sincere, unsullied, vulnerable; and the villain, a thoroughly reprehensible individual. The plots typically centered on romantic love—chaste and restrained—and predictably brought the hero and heroine together, despite terrible odds. Home and hearth provided innocent spaces. Melodrama made an idealized world seem real. Moreover, by around 1845, it had shifted from heroic scenarios that males favored to what a historian has described as "moral reform melodramas," catering to "an audience of respectable Protestant families, most of whose female and youthful auditors were new to theatergoing."[24]

Against the efforts to make the theater more genteel, patrons of a variety of competing venues fought off respectability. Concert saloons, for example, were deliberate refutations of the "proper" theater. Springing up along low-life streets, they featured variety acts, lots of liquor, and blood sports such as rat baiting and boxing. In one Bowery saloon around 1830, a trained fox terrier, in an eight-foot-long pit, raced the clock as boisterous spectators placed their bets on how many of one hundred rats he could kill. Kit Burns's Sportsman's Hall was a particularly notorious tavern, including a famous "pit" in which dogs killed rats, or starving rats fought other rats, or men engaged in bare-knuckle fights. Burns's son-in-law, Jack the Rat, would himself bite off a mouse's head for a dime or a rat's for a quarter.[25]

In 1849, the struggles over who controlled America's theater erupted in the Astor Place Riot, a bloody symbol of how class was dividing American culture. A growing rivalry between the popular American actor Edwin Forrest and the renowned British performer William Charles Macready touched off the violence, but class antagonisms were the root cause. To working-class theater patrons, the Astor Place Opera House epitomized luxury and wealth. Built in 1847 with money from 150 affluent New Yorkers, it required "freshly shaven faces, evening dress, fresh waistcoats and kid gloves for gentlemen." Macready, who had criticized the taste of working-class Americans, seemed to represent aristocratic privilege. Forrest's muscular, athletic style, on the other hand, as well as his typical role as a common man fighting for freedom and honor, received criticism from the elite *Knickerbocker* magazine as representing "the affected, ranting school" while winning applause from the Bowery b'hoys. When visiting England in 1845, Forrest had exercised the kind of audience sovereignty that was common in the United States by hissing during a Macready performance. In the spring of 1849, Macready received even worse treatment when he performed in places such as Cincinnati. Furious at the behavior of theater "ruffians," he retreated to New York's Astor Place. But, when he walked on its stage, he encountered yet another cascade of rotten eggs, vegetables, and even chairs from the gallery, which was packed with Forrest's fans. By the third act, Macready had experienced enough. He left the theater, declaring that he was returning to England. At that point, a group of influential New Yorkers convinced him that a civil, appreciative audience would welcome his return in a few days to the Astor Place stage. Posters appeared around the city threatening a showdown: "WORKINGMEN, SHALL AMERICANS OR ENGLISH RULE THIS CITY?" There were references to "the English Aristocratic Opera House" and cries for workers to "stand by your lawful rights!" With over three hundred police inside and outside the theater, and with militia troops nearby, Macready initially received a fifteen-minute ovation from his supporters. The opposition rallied shortly, however, as the police made arrests in the pit and the gallery. Outside the theater, thousands of demonstrators started heaving rocks through the windows and at authorities. A full-scale riot erupted. By the time the violence ended, the militia had killed at least twenty-two people.[26]

Against this tense and volatile backdrop, Barnum's effort to refashion theater audiences along middle-class lines was bold, shrewd, and quite successful. His lecture room was "so judiciously purged of every semblance of immorality," according to the upscale journal *Gleason's Pictorial Drawing-Room Companion* in 1853, "that the most fastidious may listen with satisfaction, and the most sensitive witness without fear." But Barnum was not engaged in a lonely venture. In some respects, he followed the lead of Boston's Moses Kimball in domesticating the theater setting, which working-class males had increasingly claimed as their turf. In the early 1840s, Kimball had opened a "museum theater" and used his resident company to stage such performances as *The Drunkard*. By offering family entertainment, and by scheduling matinees for women, Kimball, Barnum, and other theater owners helped enlarge and alter popular culture's domain.[27]

The pursuit of respectable female audiences was a major trend in the theater business. By the 1850s, a number of entrepreneurs offered weekly matinees. "As no public establishment can succeed unless patronized by ladies, and as ladies cannot possibly countenance a place of public entertainment where the other sex are disorderly," announced an Alabama theater owner as early as 1841, "it is the intention of the Manager to make every effort in his power to maintain that decorum in the theater which is observed in the drawing room." Even some theater pits included more women. "Respectability," argued the *Spirit of the Times,* "wants room—wants to take its wife and daughter to the play—and Shilling Democracy must give way." American drama was swinging on a hinge of gender. As more and more middle-class women constituted the audience, men began to seek their own amusements elsewhere; to fill their seats, theater owners had to recruit female patrons even more energetically, trying to lure them to evening performances, not just afternoon shows. Moreover, unlike the rowdy, working-class males who had loudly demanded their money's worth a few years earlier, these audiences were far more reserved, polite, and passive.[28]

Swaggering male stage characters in the mold of rip-roaring Mike Fink or the Bowery b'hoys' Mose increasingly made room for the likes of Joe Morgan, the reformed alcoholic in *Ten Nights in a Barroom,* a dramatization of Timothy Shaw Arthur's 1854 novel. Few plays resonated more with bourgeois reform sentiments. At the beginning of the play, Joe Morgan has a wholesome family, steady employment, and a bright future. But, once he discovers liquor, his life falls apart. He loses his job, mistreats his wife, and watches drunkenly while his family slides into poverty. In an emotional scene, his angelic older daughter, Mary, pleads with him to leave the saloon and return home, where little Benny is terribly ill: "Father, Dear Father, Come Home with Me Now," she wails. Soon it is too late. Benny—whose last words were, "I want to kiss Papa goodnight"—is dead. As Mary, back again, tells her father the crushing news and urges him to come home, the drunken tavern owner throws a glass, which kills her. Joe, suffering from an onslaught of delirium tremens, remembers his pledge to the martyred Mary that he will stop drinking. By the end of the play, he is a reformed alcoholic, leading the prohibition movement and urging audience members to join him in halting "the accursed liquor traffic." *Ten Nights in a Barroom* stirred audiences across the country, including those in Barnum's lecture room. As Barnum said: "My plan is to introduce into the lecture room highly moral and instructive domestic dramas, written expressly for my establishment and so constructed as to please and edify while they possess a powerful *reformatory* tendency."[29]

Two reassuring symbols that Barnum used to great advantage in his bid for respectability were the midget Charles S. Stratton and the "Swedish Nightingale," Jenny Lind. Stratton, who was born in Bridgeport, Connecticut, had virtually stopped growing at seven months of age. He was five years old and barely two feet tall when, in 1842, Barnum learned about him, immediately rented him from his family (initially for $3 weekly), and displayed him as "General Tom Thumb," supposedly age eleven. As Barnum explained: "Had I announced him as only five years of age, it would have been impossible to excite the interest or the curiosity of the public."[30] Stratton cooperated in this deception by growing only slightly.

Under Barnum's careful tutelage, Tom became an extremely popular exhibit, singing songs, dancing, and imitating a range of characters from Cupid and Hercules to Napoléon. Stratton, a natural performer, thrived. Onstage, when Barnum asked for volunteers to come up and contrast their size to Tom Thumb's, the diminutive "general" piped up, to the audience's approval, "I'd rather have a little miss." Dwarfs as entertainers were not new, of course; for centuries, kings and others had shown them as exotics. But, because Stratton was normally proportioned and cute, audiences could view him without feelings of repulsion or discomfort. He was forever small, a kind of man-child, or, as Barnum described him, a "man in miniature." Tom Thumb summoned up images of childlike innocence at a time when, in middle-class families, the productive capacity of children declined and the "value" of offspring was tied increasingly to their affectionate ties with parents. In 1863, Barnum happily paid for a much-publicized wedding in his museum in which Stratton, now twenty-four, married another normally proportioned and pretty midget whom Barnum had discovered, Lavinia Warren Bump. She was thirty-two inches tall and twenty years old. President Abraham Lincoln welcomed the newlyweds as guests at the White House. By then, Barnum had found a Tom Thumb equivalent, George Washington Morrison Nutt, twenty-nine inches tall and "an attractive little man," as Barnum described him. Nutt, whom Barnum dubbed the "Commodore" and the "Prince of the Lilliputs," was another childlike figure who meshed nicely with the increasingly romanticized bourgeois family.[31]

The place of children within that family was something Barnum extolled. Not only did his museum guidebooks show couples with youngsters, but he promised parents that they need not worry about encountering "anything calculated to corrupt the mind or taint the juvenile imagination." He proudly claimed in 1850 that "fully one third" of the museum's patrons were children. In 1855, he began hosting baby shows, giving cash prizes in such categories as the "finest twin," the "finest triplet," and the "finest baby." The shows were overwhelming successes, once attracting more than sixty thousand patrons over four days and inspiring a song sheet, "Barnum's Baby Show Polka."[32]

While Tom Thumb, Commodore Nutt, and baby shows touched a middle-class chord, Barnum's use of Jenny Lind in the early 1850s fit superbly with the ideology of "sentimental womanhood." As part of his effort to link his entertainments with bourgeois respectability, Barnum hired the Swedish singer for a staggering $1,000 per night for as many as 150 nights. Before he made the offer in 1849, Barnum had never heard her perform, and, at the time, few Americans knew about her. But, from the start of her unprecedented tour in September 1850, he touted her as the very embodiment of middle-class domesticity and true womanhood—a model for American females. Small, demure, and plain, she dressed in simple white gowns, wearing "her virginity on her sleeve." Epitomizing sentimentalism, "she wept when she saw the American flag," according to one newspaper, "she wept when they serenaded her—she wept nearly all the time, if some of the paper[s] be true, and doubtless fell asleep crying." The rugged poet Walt Whitman scoffed that her facial expression was "a sort of moral milk and honey," but that was all the better for Barnum's purposes.[33]

Lind symbolized purity, not seduction. Indeed, according to Barnum's broadsides, her lovely soprano voice might even bring "an erring man" back to his family by reminding him of "his childhood's home, his mother's love, his sister's kiss, and the sinless pleasure of his early days." Moreover, to appreciate her musical talents, listeners need not read books or defer to aristocrats or formal learning; they could rely instead on that great source of democratic knowledge: feeling. And, in celebrating the Nightingale, her American audiences could implicitly give the lie to Europeans who dismissed them as gauche, shallow, and grasping. By celebrating Jenny Lind, as Barnum made clear, Americans were celebrating themselves.[34]

With Barnum astutely churning out publicity, Lind's tour indeed shook the country. As a student of the era later wrote: "The entire country was whipped into a pop frenzy, 'Lindomania.'" Merchandisers offered Jenny Lind hats, gloves, furniture, pianos, and even chewing tobacco. Chambermaids sold hairs from her hairbrush, and the finder of one of her gloves charged people who wanted to kiss it. One eighteen-year-old youth walked for three days, covering sixty miles, in order to hear her sing in Wheeling, West Virginia. He repaired clocks en route so that he could buy an admission ticket. Huge crowds greeted her wherever she appeared. Among the thirty thousand who jammed Canal Street in New York City were many working-class people, some of whom had participated in the Astor Place Riot not long before. Volunteer fire companies in cities from New York and Philadelphia to New Orleans championed her, and lower-class women were as eager as anyone to buy Jenny Lind merchandise.[35]

Lindomania attested to Barnum's ability to build a cross-class following but also revealed the difficulties of holding such a coalition together. In many respects, the tour separated Barnum even more from the lower classes, who usually could not afford the ticket prices. While large numbers of working-class people gathered outside concert halls to see Lind or perhaps even hear her voice through open windows, middle- and upper-class audiences enjoyed the performances inside. Several times, disgruntled crowds outside grew violent. In one city, the police fended off some five hundred rough-looking individuals who tried to force their way into the hall. In Boston, people in the streets threw dirt through the open windows. In Cincinnati, authorities eventually fired warning shots to drive off a crowd that tried to see Lind through the windows. The Lind phenomenon thus cut across classes but ultimately demonstrated the difficulties of building a mass entertainment "big tent." Ultimately, Jenny Lind's tour attested mainly to the middle class's growing box-office strength and cultural muscle.[36]

By the 1840s, minstrel shows increasingly displayed a similar trend, still incorporating some of their original working-class appeal while drifting steadily toward middle-class commercialism. In the process, the format and content of minstrelsy also began to change. Increasingly, minstrel shows moved from being mere parts of larger programs to being a full evening's entertainment. In the process, minstrelsy muted its critiques of the emerging factory order and privileged elites. Class commentary faded, and the music became more melodious, less "noisy."[37]

Indeed, the music, which often constituted two-thirds of a show, in effect turned minstrelsy into musical theater. One result was that minstrel shows became more popular than ever, especially among the middle class. The music, according to one magazine in 1855, "is sung in the parlor, hummed in the kitchen, and whistled in the stable."[38] The nation's economic depression of the late 1830s helped literally to set the stage for these shifts. By 1842, with the United States still hanging on the edge of financial crisis, the theater business had touched bottom. In a New York City hotel, four blackface performers, now unemployed, anxiously discussed their futures. One of them, perhaps Dan Emmett (although Billy Whitlock insisted that he deserved credit), suggested that they form a blackface troupe that would present a whole show on minstrelsy. In 1843, describing themselves as a "surpassingly melodious ethiopian band, entitled the VIRGINIA MINSTRELS," they opened a show that created an immediate sensation. The advertisement they took out in James Gordon Bennett's *New York Herald* was telling. The act was "an *exclusively musical entertainment* . . . entirely exempt from the vulgarities and other objectionable features, which have hitherto characterized negro extravaganzas." Theirs was "A NEGRO CONCERT," toned down and less raucous than its predecessors. It fit the trend that was already tipping theaters from working-class to more upscale audiences. "Chaste, Pleasing and Elegant!" read one satisfied editorial, noting that the troupe was "liberally patronized by the elite" of New York City: "This species of amusement . . . cannot fail of making it acceptable to the most refined and sensitive audience."[39]

Although the Virginia Minstrels stayed together less than six months, they pointed the direction in which minstrelsy would go. Their success directly inspired Edwin P. Christy—a ballad singer, traveling shoe seller, and circus performer from Philadelphia—to establish the Christy Minstrels. Christy, always more manager than performer, was determined to go beyond the Virginia Minstrels in having a clean show, one at which women and children would not take offense. Around 1845, one of his playbills announced that his group's "CHASTE AND INIMITABLE CONCERTS . . . have been received with every mark and favor by the Elite and Fashion." He was, apparently, correct. According to one contemporary, the Christy Minstrels attracted "'good families' and 'nice people,' who were glad to go for a hearty laugh and an hour's enjoyment of the pretty music."[40]

Over the next few years, minstrel shows, without losing altogether their characteristic irreverence toward white authority figures,[41] increasingly shed class messages in favor of more overtly racist themes. The caricatures of African Americans became uglier, emphasizing violence, drunkenness, and a lack of sexual control. Minstrel shows also countered the antislavery movement with benign views of slavery. "There is some folks called abolition," went one verse from "Old Dan Tucker," "Want to mend de nigger condition, / If dey would let the niggers alone, / The niggers will always have a home."[42]

By the 1850s, as minstrelsy's racist tone became more prominent, blackface entertainment's larger, more professional shows also increasingly offered a new format. In act 1, the entire company typically paraded and sang in blackface before forming a semicircle with an interlocutor, or straight man, who had the superior airs of the upper class or humanitarian reformers. While he pompously lectured the audience, the end men, misusing language and mispronouncing words, made him look the fool. At one end sat "Tambo" (because he played the tambourine); at the other was

"Brudder Bones," who played castanets, often made from horse ribs. Act 2 usually included a variety segment, known as the "olio." "Feller-fellers and oder fellers," a blackface comedian might say, "when Joan of Ark and his broder Noah's Ark crossed the Rubicund in search of Decamora's horn, and meeting dat solitary horseman by de way, de anapulated in de clarion tones of de clamuour rooster, de insignification of de—de—de hop-toad." Other comedians, jugglers, and singers would also perform. Act 3 evolved from plantation skits, with Sambo and Mammy figures, to including also burlesques of serious dramas and familiar plays. Throughout, blackface dialect provided a key source of humor, and blacks were comic figures.[43]

In notable respects, the changing minstrel shows resembled Barnum's efforts to juggle entertainments so that they attracted a broad spectrum of patrons. Like Barnum, minstrelsy cast a wide net, including both "respectable" audiences as well as "the b'hoys and their seamstress sweethearts" that the *Literary World* identified in 1849. And, again, like Barnum, blackface entertainment cultivated a respectable reputation. Supposedly, minstrel performances even lured men away from saloons and into a more mixed, family setting. One playbill, similar to many others, promised a show that was "chaste, moral and free from vulgarity. . . . No improper person (male or female) admitted. . . . FRONT SEATS RESERVED FOR LADIES." Gentlemen were not even supposed to tap their toes to the music.[44]

Although blackface buffoonery was hardly high-toned or respectful of fashion, it nevertheless increasingly pursued a middle-class, family audience. The acts were cleaner. And the friendlier family fare included much sentimental music, appropriate to the bourgeois parlor. Minstrelsy's door was opening to Stephen Foster, a true pioneer of American popular music. Foster's life, like much of the popular culture that he helped invent, was full of contradictions. His songs celebrated the rural South, but he resided mainly in Pittsburgh, where he was born in 1826, and Cincinnati, where he worked for a while. Both cities were important cogs in the nation's industrial revolution; Pittsburgh's coal industry fueled much of the factory economy, while Cincinnati's business revolved around Ohio River steamboat trade, manufacturing whiskey, and slaughtering hogs—some 375,000 per year. Nostalgia for home suffused Foster's music, but he knew little of rootedness, bouncing from place to place and living with various relatives in Pittsburgh and Ohio communities such as Youngstown. His songs idealized family life, yet his father was a financial failure, his mother had a nervous breakdown when he was five, and his own marriage failed. But one thing was constant: his interest in entertainment. By age nine, he was onstage with a group of neighbor boys, belting out comic songs in blackface dialect.[45]

At that time, American popular music was still very much in gestation. Its delivery came through a budding sheet music industry that was another product of the antebellum era's legal, economic, and technological upheavals. Just as new laws increasingly defined and protected such emerging corporate entities as railroads, so, in 1831, revamped copyright laws boosted the sale of sheet music. Until 1831, U.S. copyright law left out musical compositions, which meant that American publishers had little incentive to pay songwriters for original material. The revised copyright protections bolstered that incentive, while, simultaneously, the manufacture of sheet music benefited from the breakthroughs in print technology that launched the penny press, including such things as a high-speed rotary steam press and new processes to make paper from rags. The canals, steamboats, railroads, and telegraph that spread the print revolution also helped distribute newly published music.[46]

Ultimately, Stephen Foster provided yet another prime example of the cultural fusions, mixings, and tensions that suffused and defined popular entertainment. Like the nascent music industry, he felt the pull of competing cultural poles, one centered in the middle-class home and the other in minstrelsy's less respectable street traditions. Parlor music—appropriate for pianos in bourgeois residences—dominated sheet music sales because the industry depended primarily on a female audience. Full of sentimentality, parlor music dealt with the triumphs and tragedies of domestic life. Many songs evoked tears by telling of homeless orphans, the fragility of family ties, and the sorrows of death. Parlor music was proper, designed not to "offend the most fastidious ear," as *The Parlour Companion, or Polite Song Book* pledged in 1836. An 1832 songbook pledged that it would not "mantle the cheek of beauty with the faintest blush." Nostalgia was another characteristic of parlor music. One early songwriter, Henry Russell, who traveled around the country playing the piano, singing, and selling sheet music, was responsible for such songs as "The Old Arm Chair," "The Old Night Lamp," "The Old Farm Gate," "The Old School House," and "The Old Water Mill." Another thoroughly genteel source of parlor music was Henry Klebert, who owned a Pittsburgh music store, gave local concerts, and taught music lessons. Stephen Foster studied with Klebert and subsequently wrote a large number of haunting parlor ballads, including "Jeanie with the Light Brown Hair," "Beautiful Dreamer," "Gentle Annie" (about a child's death), and "Nelly Was a Lady" (about a deceased spouse). But, as Foster grew up in the 1830s, he was well aware of a competing kind of music—the raucous, antiparlor sound that was spilling out of the blackface phenomenon. He was drawn to this rough music, which he knew well.[47]

By the late 1840s, these contrasting musical styles tugged at Foster as, still in his early twenties, he made a risky move toward full-time songwriting—a new vocation. Lacking financial resources, he was reliant on commercial realities and what people wanted to buy. Although parlor music initially held the advantage, its street-inspired minstrel competition grew rapidly in popularity and, by the early 1850s, paid ten times more per song (about $310). There was also the matter of Foster's reputation: parlor ballads enjoyed bourgeois respectability, which was important to the young songwriter, while blackface songs were still shaking off the stigma of the alley. "Should he hearken to the genteel muse or heed the siren call of blackface?" Such, in his biographer's words, was Foster's dilemma. "At the outset Foster zigzagged."[48]

Minstrelsy inspired some of Foster's most memorable creations, especially "Oh! Susannah" and "De Camptown Races." "Oh! Susannah," which he published in 1848 at age twenty-two, became hugely popular within the next several years. Its lyrics were in blackface dialect: "I come from Alabama / With my banjo on my knee / I's gwine to Lou'siana / My true lub for to see." Its series of comic non sequiturs echoed blackface performances: "It rained all night the day I left, / The weather it was dry, / The sun so hot I frose to death; / Susanna dont you cry." And it also soared into a kind of American anthem by celebrating the technology (trains, steamboats, and telegraph) that was transforming the nation and then expressing the anxieties that such inventions produced. "I really thought I'd die," Foster wrote regarding the explosion of a steamboat boiler; "I shut my eyes to hold my bref / Susanna dont you cry." According to his biographer, Ken Emerson, Foster had constructed, "in the foothills of popular culture," a classic work that was "at once jaunty and forlorn," lamenting a lost "past even as it hurtles into the future." In 1850, as "Oh! Susanna" swept the nation like wildfire, Foster published sixteen more original works, including "De Camptown Races." That the tune's "Camptown ladies" were, presumably, prostitutes immediately set the song apart from genteel offerings. Moreover, the repeated lines and chorus resembled the call-and-response technique that had marked slave songs.[49]

To increase his still-meager profits, Foster in 1851 sold "Old Folks at Home" to the Christy Minstrels but withheld his name from the credit. As he told E. P. Christy a year later: "I had the intention of omitting my name on my Ethiopian songs, owing to the prejudice against them by some, which might injure my reputation as a writer of another style of music." Those words pointed up Foster's dilemma. His blackface songs were extremely popular but blocked the respectability that he sought. One article praised his music but warned that its association with "negro idioms" precluded its acceptance among the parlor set. The article urged him to "devote himself principally hereafter to the production of 'White men's music.'"[50]

Foster vacillated. In 1852, he decided that he should get credit for "Old Folks at Home." He pleaded unsuccessfully with Christy to add his name to the sheet music cover: "I find that by my efforts I have done a great deal to build up a taste for Ethiopian songs among refined people. . . . Therefore I have concluded to establish my name as the best Ethiopian song writer."

He spoke with some bravado, however, because he subsequently omitted blackface dialect from "My Old Kentucky Home" and, throughout most of the 1850s, avoided "darky songs." On the eve of the Civil War, he again reversed himself, writing several blackface songs. "Old Black Joe," one of the more memorable efforts, echoed African American spirituals but also sentimentalized slavery. By the 1860s, a discouraged and impoverished Foster was living in the Bowery, drinking himself to death. In January 1864, at age thirty-seven, he died, just as popular music was on the verge of becoming a big business. The press had by then identified him as "the author of most of the popular Ethiopian melodies now afloat." As his biographer later wrote, Stephen Foster occupied "the heart of the tangled, tortuous interchange between whites and blacks that both dishonors America yet distinguishes its culture."[51]

Ironically, the choice between commercial appeal and social respectability that plagued Foster proved far from insurmountable in the evolving music business. As Foster himself suspected in early 1852, his "Ethiopian songs" were finding a refined audience. And, as troupes such as the Christy Minstrels adopted his blends of blackface and parlor ballads (e.g., "Old Folks at Home" and "My Old Kentucky Home"), they helped move minstrelsy from the streets to a more reputable status. By 1868, the *New York Clipper* could describe minstrelsy as good family entertainment: "clean, bright amusement."[52]

While cleaned-up minstrel shows became safer havens for the middle class, a coalition of elite New Yorkers, new industrialists, and antebellum reformers transformed the annual celebration of Christmas into a veritable bourgeois preserve. In the process, Christmas changed from a rowdy folk celebration into a family-centered, increasingly commercialized holiday, although new middle-class rituals often masked its business side. The change did not come easily. And, like the struggles over museums, the theater, and music, the battle for Christmas revolved around the question of cultural authority in the United States.

Considering the centuries-old traditions that had surrounded the Christmas season, the rapid reordering of the holiday celebrations was a remarkable achievement. For centuries, those celebrations had drawn on carnivalesque traditions of misrule. The time of year was partly responsible for the disorderly festivities. In the fourth century, the church had identified December 25 as Christ's birth date and started holding the Feast of the Nativity. That date had nothing to do with religion because no one knew for sure exactly when Christ had been born. The church had settled on late December simply because that time of the year marked the coming of the winter solstice, an event that had, in northern agricultural societies, long provided several weeks of carnival between the end of the fall harvest and the onset of winter. For centuries, the church, trying to contain the challenge of pagan cults, tolerated festivities that had traditionally accompanied this shift in seasons—rowdy, sometimes violent festivities that included masking, role reversals, and revelry, typically through Christmas and the advent of the new year. Peasants mocked gentlemen. Wandering bands of poor young males demanded food and drink from wealthy families. An early form of wassailing—or caroling—included the threat: "We've come here to claim our right . . . / And if you don't open up your door, / We will lay you flat upon the floor." But with the Protestant Reformation came religious resistance to such Christmas celebrations, which had no scriptural basis and smacked of Catholic rituals. In 1644, the English parliament attacked Christmas for "giving liberty to carnall and sensual delights." And, in the English colonies, the Pilgrims in Plymouth dismissed the Christmas revelry as evil and went about the business of clearing land, while Puritans at Massachusetts Bay outlawed Christmas celebrations by imposing fines on individuals who did not work on December 25 (unless it happened to fall on a Sunday). Such efforts proved inadequate, however, and bouts of feasting, carousing, and partying continued to surface. By the mid-eighteenth century, even in the Puritans' New World heartland of Boston, some of the poorest residents engaged in Christmas misrule.[53]

By the early nineteenth century, respectable citizens in cities such as Boston and Philadelphia cringed at the approaching Christmas season. They battened down for another round of carnivalesque disorder as mobs from working-class neighborhoods poured forth, engaging in various acts of debauchery and "making night hideous." Celebrants had a different perspective, of course. From their viewpoint, the festivities supplied a momentary buffer against the harsh times of winter, which often brought unemployment and special hardships for poor people. The revelry, with its undertone of desperation and distress, was a last opportunity to make merry for a while—a chance to bid farewell to the old year and "fire in" the new with noise, disguises, and demands for free food and drink. To the despair of social elites, young men in costumes caroused through city streets, looking for treats or fights, and frightening exponents of law and order.[54]

All this was about to change—and with surprising speed. A combination of economic trends and influential individuals would move the Christmas celebration from the streets to homes, turning it into a family- and child-centered religious holiday. The transformation attested to the growing power of the new economic discipline and the accompanying bourgeois cult of domesticity.[55]

A distinct New York social group played a crucial role. The Knickerbockers, as they were known, represented a significant element of the city's wealthy old aristocracy. They were of British descent and politically reactionary. With fear and trepidation, they watched the era's swelling democratic currents. Democracy was, from their privileged vantage point, nothing less than mob rule. By the early nineteenth century, the mob posed a growing threat to New York City, where poverty, homelessness, and crime marked the rapidly growing population. The Christmas season was particularly susceptible to violence and misrule. "The beastly vice of drunkenness among the lower laboring classes is growing to frightful excess," complained the propertied John Pintard. At one point, Pintard had helped establish a group to halt public begging and reduce the spiraling costs of poor relief, but, by 1828, he confessed that the problems of poverty and violence "baffled all our skill." Pintard thought that new social rituals might help reestablish a sense of decorum and order. In that regard, he found an important ally in another prominent New Yorker, the writer Washington Irving, author of such famed short stories as "Rip Van Winkle" and "The Legend of Sleepy Hollow." Irving had once been among the unlucky targets of "a discharge of apples, nuts & gingerbread" when he was attending the theater: "I can't say but I was a little irritated at being saluted aside of my head with a rotten pippin, and was going to shake my cane at them," he wrote. He refrained from protesting after another patron said that "they are only *amusing themselves* a little at our expence." In 1819, Irving, who clearly could have done without such amusement, published a series of tales, set during Christmas, in which he waxed nostalgic about how all classes celebrated together under a paternalist umbrella. The fact that Irving had not, in fact, observed such customs seemed not to bother him. But it was the thoroughly aristocratic Clement Clark Moore who penned the defining Christmas script, "A Visit from St. Nicholas."[56]

Moore had earlier written political tracts attacking the radicalism of Thomas Jefferson and his followers. He was an extremely conservative country gentleman who owned five slaves. In 1822, when he wrote "A Visit from St. Nicholas," he was much worried about a conspiracy of workers that threatened New York City. In his famous poem, Moore replaced radical workers with a friendly plebeian, Santa Claus. On Christmas Eve, Santa, a carnivalesque figure, came to visit—but with gifts and good cheer, not with wassailing, drunkenness, and demands. Gone in Moore's and Irving's tales were rowdy street celebrations. In their versions, the "real" Christmas was quiet, nonthreatening, and orderly. Its central elements included, as the historian Stephen Nissenbaum has written, "*keeping the poor away from the house*" and keeping "one's own children *inside.*"[57]

Here were ingredients with which the emerging middle class could easily identify. And the battle lines were familiar: "the parlor or the street," in Nissenbaum's words. As Christmas moved inside, its domestication mirrored the evolving concept of domesticity itself. The tranquil family home, so central to the bourgeois ideal, readily welcomed the quickly developing range of holiday rituals, including decorated Christmas trees, dinners, and presents for the children. By 1860, *Godey's Lady's Book,* which had become the leading fashion magazine since its creation thirty years earlier, described what was now a familiar Christmas scene, with an evergreen tree "reaching almost to the ceiling" and containing room on the parlor floor beneath it "for *all* the family presents."[58]

The appearance in 1842 of Charles Dickens's vastly popular novella *A Christmas Carol* illuminated connections between the new holiday rituals, the attractions of middle-class domesticity, and the unfolding economic order. Dickens, the famed English author, had visited the United States shortly before publishing his novella and had a considerable American audience. On one level, *A Christmas Carol* celebrated domesticity in the form of Bob Cratchit's family—poor but polite, civil, and happily together at home for the holiday dinner. On another level, Bob Cratchit embodied the best habits of the new industrial discipline. Granted, he was an office clerk, not a factory worker. Still, his values and conduct reflected the kind of discipline that business owners increasingly wanted in their salaried employees. He was punctual and respectful and spent his wages carefully, without going on drunken binges or carousing in the streets. His model behavior on the job carried over into his responsibilities for his child-centered family.[59]

Not surprisingly, a growing number of merchants endorsed these revised Christmas celebrations. Such festivities reinforced important family values and work habits while clearing the streets of riotous behavior. And, when it came to Christmas charity, Dickens's fictional employer, Ebenezer Scrooge, pointed the way: he was willing to provide a turkey for Bob Cratchit's deserving family, but he avoided the kind of indiscriminate giving that, from the view of people such as John Pintard, only encouraged public begging. While the new-style holiday celebrations did not favor the advice of the old English phrase, "please put a penny in the old man's hat," they did something else. In a historian's words, they "helped intensify and legitimize a commercial kind of consumerism." This consumerism represented a break from the republican ideology of the American Revolution, which had warned that luxury, excess, and unnecessary goods would undermine citizens' virtue. In contrast, Christmas giving seemed innocuous, even as it facilitated a new commercialism. It symbolized domestic intimacy and altruism rather than moneygrubbing selfishness. In that context, Santa was an especially critical figure. He was not concerned with profits. Moreover, he reinforced the myth that presents came from him, not from commercial stores, and that he made them himself. And, reassuringly, his "workshop" harked back to the days of household production. By the 1840s, merchants eagerly used Santa Claus as a device to bring children into their stores. Not coincidentally, in 1843 advertisements for Christmas tree decorations began appearing in New York City newspapers.[60]

In three short decades, from the 1820s through the 1840s, the shapers of the newly designed Christmas celebration had "invented a tradition"[61] that wedded domesticity and commercialism, the sacred and the secular. These cultural reformers had effectively moved Christmas celebrations from the street to the middle-class, child-centered home. In the process, they had also provided, however inadvertently, the emerging commercial culture with one of its most important footholds. The problem in that regard was that Christmas wavered between market and hearth. Piety mixed with profits, the sacred with the profane. By 1870, when Congress declared Christmas a national holiday, the domesticated, commercialized celebration was well in place, and so were often-repeated warnings that the date was losing its religious meaning.[62]

In place, too, was St. Valentine's Day, which, during the antebellum era, took on new meanings that also reflected bourgeois sentimentality and the pull of the market. The reinvention of Valentine's Day moved parallel with that of Christmas. St. Valentine was originally a Christian saint. In the late fourteenth century and the early fifteenth, writers like Chaucer had helped link him to patterns of courtship, inspiring a folk holiday when young people chose lots to see who should get their valentine greetings. Not until the 1840s, however, did Valentine's Day gain much notice in the United States. It did so as a commercial product. Printers began to produce cards and poems for sale, marketing expressions of affection and romance. "VALENTINES! VALENTINES!" trumpeted a New York bookseller: "Come ye Lovers, one and all, / Be ye great or be ye small, / Into [this store] make a dash, / There's the place to spend your cash. / Every Lover there will find / Valentines to suit his mind." Such greetings promised to facilitate courtship. "COQUETRY cured in 10 minutes," read one advertisement. "PROUD MAIDENS rendered soft and tender on reasonable terms. . . . OLD BACHE-LORS entrapped." References to "Cupid's Grand Carnival" directed people not into the streets for carnivalesque celebrations but into stores that featured a variety of Valentine's cards. In an increasingly complex society, such cards became, as a historian has described them, "ambassadors between people," distributing packaged feelings between friends, family members, and lovers. The whole process fit well with the new domesticity and the bourgeois emphasis on restraint, civility, and order.[63]

Valentine greetings, along with the increasingly familiar icons of Christmas (from decorated evergreen trees to family dinners and Santa Claus), were important parts of popular culture's spreading big tent. That big tent included a curious mixture of impulses, motives, and trends. Regarding Christmas, for example, there was, as the historian Leigh Eric

Schmidt has argued, "no sweeping march of secularization, but instead a dance of the sacred and the secular, sometimes graceful, sometimes awkward."[64] Similar kinds of dances—graceful yet awkward—invariably characterized popular culture's comings, goings, and transformations.

Among the champions of embourgeoisement that so powerfully influenced antebellum popular culture were writers such as Harriet Beecher Stowe and Susan Warner, who enlisted the print revolution in the cause of home, family, and sentimentalism. Although the male author Nathaniel Hawthorne dismissed them as "damned female scribblers," they developed a large audience, mainly female.[65]

In best-selling tales of pious domesticity, Stowe, Warner, and others created selfless female protagonists trying to live up to an ideal of Christian virtue. They served God by helping others and, in the agonizingly emotional process, endured considerable psychological suffering. Plots typically orbited around home, family, the power of love, and spiritual redemption. Before Stowe published her famously influential *Uncle Tom's Cabin* (1852), no American novel had sold a million copies. Her achievement, according to one scholar, was in weaving with stunning effect "a conventional sentimental story of youthful female suffering" with a critique of slavery.[66]

Godey's Lady's Book, a monthly fashion magazine that Louis Antoine Godey launched in 1830 in Philadelphia, provided another major outlet for sentimental literature. Within two decades, it grew from forty-eight to over ninety pages. While it represented an arresting challenge to the predominantly male print culture, and while it was notable for its use of striking images (including watercolor plates), its message was reassuringly domestic and genteel. In *Godey's,* true women, although typically looking frail and dependent, nevertheless reigned in their separate sphere, the home, as gentle, loving mothers and wives.[67]

By the 1840s, as Stowe and other "female scribblers" infused the print world with sentimental messages, the penny press was taking on a more bourgeois aura. A major reason was financial. On one level, the wrenching depression from 1837 to 1842, which had closed 90 percent of American factories during its first six weeks alone, wiped out many of the dailies, including the *New York Transcript.* On another level, by introducing the increasingly expensive new technology, the penny pioneers ironically priced themselves out of the market, basically shutting down opportunities for the kinds of worker-oriented artisan printers (like Benjamin Day) who had transformed the newspaper business. Whereas in 1835 James Gordon Bennett had reportedly founded the *New York Herald* with only $500, sixteen years later a group of investors supplied Henry Raymond with $100,000 to start the *New York Times.* A college graduate, Raymond came from a class background resembling that of the old sixpenny press editors.

Although Horace Greeley had been a journeyman printer, he enjoyed substantial financial backing when in 1841 he launched the *New York Tribune* and aligned himself with the business-oriented Whig political party. As bourgeois capital entered the penny field, the class lines between owner-publishers and working printers, which had narrowed briefly in the early 1830s, widened once again. One result was the blunting of the penny press's initial working-class bent.[68]

As the mass circulation press increasingly mirrored the middle-class revolution, Bennett's *New York Herald* became both an "immoral" target of the old sixpenny press and an ally of bourgeois values. In 1840, the six-cent papers opened a "Moral War" against the *Herald*, trying to run it out of business. Although the news coverage in the expensive journals increasingly resembled that of the penny press, the sixpenny publications claimed that no self-respecting man or woman would read the *Herald*—that "dirty sheet." Such a claim, of course, suggested an important development: the *Herald* was attracting a well-to-do clientele. With more and more success, the fiery Bennett, who was determined to expand his readership beyond the working class to more genteel readers, shrewdly moved his paper to the middle ground. From the *Herald*'s beginnings in 1835, he had stated how it "differs from the other small daily papers" in its diffusion across "all classes—but principally among the business and commercial, private families, and men of leisure." While he attacked the dull and expensive "Wall Street press" as a mouthpiece for "the banks and corrupt *cliques* of men," he crowed in 1840 about the *Herald*'s accomplishment: "No newspaper establishment, in this or any other country, has ever attained so extensive a circulation, or is read by so many of the business, educated, and intelligent classes." Other penny papers, he charged, lacked intelligence, knowledge of the business world, and an appreciation of society. The *Sun,* he contended, was useful mainly "for wrapping up tea and enveloping hog's lard"; it was "a dirty, sneaking, drivelling contemporary nigger paper." Although he still published boxing news, despite the sport's rapidly sinking reputation, he started printing disclaimers next to the fight stories. He also took a tough law-and-order stance, defending the right of respectable folks to defend themselves against the robbers, poor people, free blacks, and foreigners who threatened the social order. Bennett positioned the *Herald* as a defender of the rising middle class against society's margins.[69]

Significantly, the news story that Bennett seized to ward off his critics during the "Moral Wars" was the unsolved, brutal murder in mid-1841 of a young tobacco girl and boardinghouse keeper, Mary Rogers. Bennett cannily mixed salacious details regarding Rogers's battered body and the imagined scenario of her death with descriptions of the threats that the city's marginal groups posed to law-abiding citizens. According to the *Herald:* "A young and beautiful girl has been seduced from her home."

Bennett portrayed Rogers as both a virtuous maiden and "the Beautiful Cigar Girl" who symbolized the threat of unrestrained female sexuality. And he took a tough law-and-order stance in concocting a theory that Rogers was a victim of New York City's violent underside—either a "gang of negroes" or one of the "fire rowdies, butcher boys, soap-locks, and all sorts of riotous miscreants." Bennett was seeking to have it both ways: to print sensational accounts and to place the *Herald* on the solid moral ground of the middle class.[70]

This turn of popular culture toward the middle class did not go uncontested. Old-style celebrators of the Christmas holiday season continued to "make night hideous," although they focused their street-oriented revelry more on New Year's. On January 1, for decades to come, thousands of costumed individuals strutted, drank, and made loud noises in mummers' parades. Similarly, even the sweetly commercialized St. Valentine's Day was not free of the older carnivalesque traditions. Competing with the often-gushy sentimental greetings were mock valentines that poked fun at all groups, manners, and customs. Full of grotesque stereotypes and phallic symbolism (e.g., showing Mose, as a volunteer fireman, with a giant hose nozzle sticking up between his legs), they lampooned romantic courtesies, youthful wooing, and domesticity. Around 1850, amid the growing antebellum struggle for women, one mock valentine derided the victim of a nagging wife: "You old henpicked wretch, you are quite a disgrace, / Let your wife mind the baby and keep her place, / Be more of a man, don't allow her to roam, / make her leave off the breeches and keep her at home." Other popular targets included female flirts and, especially, old maids: "You ugly, cross and wrinkled shrew, / You advocate of woman's rights, / No man on earth would live with you. / For fear of endless fights."[71]

Additional challenges to sentimentality and polite amusements appeared in concert saloons, where men gathered to drink and enjoy a variety of blood sports such as cockfights and boxing matches. Bare-knuckle fighting was an especially popular plebeian sport. Workers were, of course, far from a monolithic group, and some embraced the bourgeois world, seeking prosperity through hard work, discipline, and self-control. But many working-class males resented the changing economic order in which bosses tried to exert more authority over them on and off the job. They proudly joined the volunteer fire brigades with its "Mose" heroes, rejected the middle class's moral arrogance by enjoying the camaraderie and refreshments of the tavern, and viewed the brutality of the boxing ring as a way to thumb their noses at respectable society. Workers in the skilled trades, particularly butchering, appreciated boxing as a craft and cheered what, to them, was a manly art. At the same time, the boxing ring became a place in which ethnic rivalries found an outlet. And, insofar as embittered native workers blamed foreigners for problems of lost jobs and diminished autonomy in the changing economy, those rivalries became more violent.[72]

Although bare-knuckle boxing was less brutal than the no-holds-barred, rough-and-tumble kind of fighting that flourished in the frontier backcountry, it was still a bloody and dangerous affair. After 1838, boxing matches typically occurred under the new rules of the London prize ring, which abolished rough-and-tumble practices such as gouging out eyes, biting, and ripping off fingers. "We found the combatants . . . fast clinched by the hair," wrote one horrified traveler in Georgia regarding a no-holds-barred match, "their thumbs endeavoring to force a passage into each others eyes; while several of the bystanders were betting upon the first eye to be turned out of its socket." Place-names along the frontier such as Gouge Eye thus had a very real meaning, as did phrases such as *saving face*.[73] But, even under the London rules, bare-knuckle boxing could be deadly. In 1842, Christopher Lilly and Thomas McCoy continued a rivalry that grew out of a quarrel and an exhibition match in a New York City saloon. In the so-called Battle of Hasting, twenty-five miles outside the city, they fought for almost three hours. Granted, under the 1838 rules, a round ended each time one of the fighters was knocked down—and McCoy was floored eighty times. Still, in the 119th round, McCoy died, choking on his own blood. The fatality touched off another outcry to outlaw boxing, but such crusades only forced boxing further underground and did not prevent it from becoming, by the end of the 1840s, the nation's most popular spectator sport.[74]

For some competitors, boxing could also be quite profitable. In 1849, Tom Hyer and Yankee Sullivan faced off in rural Maryland, with a light blanket of snow around them, for a $10,000 purse. The match bristled with ethnic animosities. Hyer, a butcher and a native-born American, wore an outfit with stars and stripes on it. Sullivan, an Irish immigrant who had sold licenses to Irish butchers, wore the Emerald Isle's green. In only seventeen minutes, Hyer beat Sullivan, but the fight provided a major news story as papers obtained results via new telegraph lines. Within a month, Massachusetts joined states that had banned prizefighting. The sport flourished nevertheless as steamboats took spectators to distant sites and as newspapers carried boxing news.[75]

While bare-knuckled prizefighting flaunted middle-class manners and decorum, there were other expressions of unease regarding the new bourgeois order, especially its expectations about family and gender. A veritable explosion of interest in murder literature aired this unease, however indirectly. In the 1830s, the penny press had tapped the public fascination with urban crime. By the 1840s, many readers were drawn to the "mysteries of the city" fiction, with its descriptions of a sleazy urban underworld. But it was the growing prevalence of detailed, lurid stories about domestic homicide that particularly revealed concerns that all was not well in America's domestic Eden, the last place where evil was supposed to lurk. These bloody accounts of "families run amok" were, as the historian Karen Haltunnen has argued, "nightmares of the companionate marriage gone bad." From one angle, certainly, tales of husbands such as Michael McGarvey, who whipped his wife to death, were shocking indictments of unchecked male power and summoned up support for the growing women's rights movement. Yet, from another angle, the stories contained disturbing subtexts of resistance to that movement and questioned whether romantic love should be the basis for marriage. "It was a damned bad country that would not allow a man to beat his wife," McGarvey reportedly complained, explaining that he had whipped his wife so that she would learn to keep her place. "She had it coming"—the abusive husband's typical defense—undoubtedly resonated among readers who resented women who did not know their proper roles. Hence, printed accounts described a situation in which one husband "slapped her chops, and stopped her tongue." A spouse who had buried an ax in his wife's skull blamed the feminist advocate Frances Wright for what had happened: Wright, allegedly a destroyer of marriages, was the truly guilty party.[76]

"There was a woman in the case"—these words in 1829 from an attorney defending a wife killer touched a popular chord. A kind of sexual murder narrative took shape, featuring a variety of female characters. Some were victims of seduction. Others were sexually depraved. All raised questions about female sexuality, a subject that haunted a wave of sensational stories, some real and many fictional, about "female fiends." Two small Northeastern publishers cranked out dozens of such stories, often in relatively cheap pamphlet form. Apparently, many middle-class readers—including women—purchased them. Often in these stories, a married woman was the murderer. While some of these women were defending themselves and their children against violent abusers, the message often was that they would have killed anyhow because, deep down, they refused to accept their wifely obligations. Hence, Lucretia Cannon became a serial killer, eventually slaughtering at least eleven adults and throwing one baby into a fire. Such stories seemed implicitly to find the seeds of terror in the romantic and marital ideals that ultimately created these fictional female victims/fiends. The popularity of such tales suggested that considerable nervousness accompanied the growth of the bourgeois family.[77]

Female impersonators on the minstrel stage voiced a similar nervousness. Although some women played female roles on the minstrel stage, cross-dressed male performers were more typical. And their images of women were usually negative, either as sexual prey, silly devotees of fashion, or disobedient wives. "Oh! Buffalo gals, will ye come out tonight," went one popular song about prostitutes or women that men desired. Poking fun at fashion, men appeared in the elaborate dress of "ladies," some with huge shoes visible beneath their skirts. Songs endorsed the male right to have sexual liaisons: "Pray turkey buzzard, / Now lend me your wing, / 'Til I fly o'er de river, / To see Miss Sally King." In some cases, the husband threatens to punish his nagging spouse: "If she makes a scolding wife, / As sure as she was born, / I'll tote her down to Georgia, / And trade her off for corn." He delivers another warning: "And if Lucy doesn't mind me, / This fellow will cut and run." Marriage in these blackface songs is typically a remorseless prison in which unhappy men deal with shrewish wives: "When I was a single feller, / I lived in peace and pleasure, / But now I am a married man, / I'm troubled out of measure." Wives scold and bully their beleaguered mates. Hence, as one husband sings: "De pain ob death came on her, / Some did cry, but I did laugh, / to see de breff go from her." Granted, by the 1850s, as minstrel shows shifted to family entertainment, playbills dropped songs such as "Buffalo Gals" in favor of less vulgar and more sentimental messages. Still, for a while, men in blackface registered their disapproval of middle-class domesticity and all that went with it.[78]

A notable group of female actresses who performed in breeches also felt the sting of that domesticity and resisted it. For several centuries, women in tight-fitting knee-length pants had played male characters onstage. In the antebellum United States, as the bourgeois concepts of separate gender spheres and true womanhood gathered momentum, a number of actresses used the "male mask" of breeches to ward off the newly constructed gender boundaries and the cult of the home. By playing male and female roles, a leading actress such as Charlotte Cushman (who appeared, e.g., as Shakespeare's Romeo) not only transcended gender lines but implicitly questioned their artificiality. During the 1830s, in tandem with the appearance of more women in factories, religious revivals, and voluntary associations as well as a budding women's rights movement, breeches performances enjoyed growing popularity. They simultaneously fell victim to growing fears about women who, outside the theater, might "wear the breeches"—"mannish women, like hens that crow," as the *New York Herald* fretted when ridiculing "hen-pecked husbands" who "ought to wear petticoats." Against that cultural backlash, female breeches performers were unquestionably making political statements. Indeed, offstage, Cushman and others assumed a number of male responsibilities by managing theaters and serving as their families' primary breadwinners. To the despair of such women, breeches roles diminished in the antebellum era. Women in breeches were increasingly limited to parts as young boys, innocent, immature, weak, irrational, and in need of protection from adult male heroes—in sum, more stereotypically childish and feminine. Although in the 1840s and 1850s an international star such as Cushman still "passed" as a man onstage (and off), defying and subverting gender categories, by the mid-1850s breeches performances were in sharp decline, increasingly identified with the "low theater" of the Bowery.[79]

As lines of resistance to the trend of embourgeoisement wavered, even bare-knuckle fights gave ground. In the battle for cultural supremacy, few amusements were more central than boxing. Young, urban males, resentful of a changing economy that victimized them, resisted middle-class standards and won symbolic victories in the ring against the drift of modern society. Yet even these symbolic victories typically contained impulses that accommodated the emerging industrial and bourgeois order. Boxing, for example, in its own ways represented a significant search for order and control. Granted, it undoubtedly reflected the arbitrariness, bloodiness, and uncertainty of a world full of underemployment, poverty, and often early death. Yet the ring also provided rules and structure, removing some of the randomness of life.[80]

Similarly, adjustments to the new order marked even the habits of the rowdy Bowery theater audiences. Ironically, the taming influences came in part from stage stars such as the b'hoys' heroes Edwin Forrest and Frank Chanfrau, who first played Mose. While theater managers, including P. T. Barnum, moved to take control of their venues, Forrest and other popular actors shrewdly adopted techniques that allowed them more command over their performances. Forrest and Chanfrau turned their huge popularity to their advantage, using the respect that audiences awarded them to shift power from the patrons to the actors. These early stars cannily involved audiences in a process that was stage-managed, giving the patrons the impression that they were still "calling the tune" when, in fact, they were responding to the promptings of the skillful Forrests and Chanfraus. Through such subtle processes, b'hoy-style opposition slipped more and more toward incorporation, a trend that increasingly characterized the growth of the nascent entertainment industry.[81]

Paradoxically, however, as middle-class currents reshaped that industry, the revamped amusements in turn included elements that threatened crucial bases of the bourgeois world. There was, in that regard, the problem of humbuggery. From one angle, a P. T. Barnum offered an implicitly reassuring message: the older, revered powers of reason could still allow people to distinguish between the authentic and the fraudulent, the real and the fake, the true and the false. But, from another angle, a nagging set of worries plagued the middle class as it tried to learn, via the proliferating etiquette manuals and urban guidebooks, what was respectable and how to act and dress. Was the middle class itself, through its obsession with impressions and images, built on a kind of tricksterism? And what would prevent any huckster from using those same advice books or watching those moral plays such as *Ten Nights in a Barroom* in order to set up some new confidence game? At the heart of these questions was a radical, and frightening, possibility: things are not necessarily what they seem. And, if that were the case, how could respectable middle-class people discern who among them was a deceiver?[82]

A related, and equally chilling, issue haunted the emerging commercial economy and the extent to which deception ruled it. As people grew more dependent on products that strangers made and advertised, the growing challenge was to distinguish legitimate from fraudulent goods. Again, Barnum's experience was instructive. His playful humbugs not only fed on anxieties about con artists but also suggested that deceptions such as the Feejee Mermaid were, in fact, reflective of the market economy itself. "In what business is there not humbug?" Barnum asked. In that regard, he could but wonder why his museum customers tended to suspect that all his museum exhibits—even authentic ones—were fakes. Here was a problem with which the emerging world of commercial entertainment would have to reckon. The "Prince of Humbugs" was helping forge, probably far more than he realized, a brave new world of tricksterism. Increasingly, entertainment entrepreneurs would have to deal with the expanding cynicism of audiences "raised on a steady diet of Barnumesque hoaxing."[83]

While Barnum tried to negotiate that cultural tightrope, his attempt to turn his museum into an amusement venue for all classes ultimately failed. Granted, in 1865 a devastating fire hardly helped his cause. At noon on July 13, a fire broke out; within an hour, the entire building was in flames. Although no human was killed, virtually all the animals (including two beluga whales) were destroyed, along with all the inanimate exhibits. A few months later, Barnum opened a new museum farther up Broadway, but, by then, the museum business as a whole was in tatters. The reputation of museums would sink rapidly over the next several decades. As seedy representatives of cheap entertainment that lacked all traces of middle-class respectability, they would line streets such as New York's Bowery. Despite Barnum's herculean efforts, the museum business fell victim to a trend that events such as the Astor Place Riot had signaled: the segmentation of audiences and entertainment.[84]

Additional evidence of such segmentation was apparent in the growth of downtown shopping districts, which at the same time showed ways in which subversive elements infiltrated middle-class entertainments. The new shopping districts benefited from women's matinee attendance at theaters, a critical factor in domesticating the stage. Shopping and going to the theater coincided nicely, both enjoying the support of female customers. But the implicit messages of these emerging commercial spaces contained a new siren song of consumption that elevated self-indulgence over the prized bourgeois value of self-control. The rising middle class was surely altering America's mass amusements, but not without itself undergoing change.[85]

Sentimental fiction provided additional evidence of cultural counter-currents. Although on one level such fiction affirmed middle-class attitudes regarding gender, on another level it constituted an implicit protest against the lack of female economic and political power. Harriet Beecher Stowe's triumph in *Uncle Tom's Cabin* was, according to one interpretation, in transferring "the center of power in American life, placing it not in the government, nor in the courts of law, nor in the factories, nor in the marketplace, but in the kitchen"—under the command of women, not men. The message was radical.[86]

In sentimental celebrations of home and heart, moreover, sensationalism (a dreaded adversary of bourgeois decorum and reason) increasingly surfaced with a vengeance. As problems such as liquor, poverty, and vice battered the optimism of antebellum reformers, the outpouring of moralistic tracts, pamphlets, and novels steadily awarded more attention to sin's consequences than to virtue's rewards. Trying to shock the wayward into improving their behavior was hardly a new strategy, of course; many preachers had long tried to convert sinners with graphic descriptions of hell and the penalties of immorality. But, by the 1840s, the apparent intractability of society's problems eroded the optimism of many reformers, who more desperately turned to chilling accounts of ruined lives, moral collapse, and the gap between righteous and evil conduct. "I have been called 'humbug,' a 'theatrical performer,' a 'mountebank,' a 'clown,' a 'buffoon,'" said a leading temperance lecturer, John Bartholomew Gough, in defense of his lurid stories about the effects of liquor. But Gough insisted that he needed to make clear the ravages of liquor. The era's didactic literature turned similarly to more shocking descriptions of vice in order to discourage illicit behavior. In the process, the line between titillation and moral uplift blurred. Some critics of *Uncle Tom's Cabin* believed that Stowe had moved from respectable fiction into pure sensationalism with her bloody accounts of brutality and her dark musings about theological questions: "Who knows anything about anything?" wails a character after little Eva dies. "Is there no more Eva,—no heaven,—no Christ,—nothing?" One of Stowe's readers objected strenuously to such subversive doubts about God and moral certainty: "Are scenes of license and impurity, and ideas of loathsome depravity and habitual prostitution to be made the cherished topics of the female pen, and the familiar staple of domestic consideration of promiscuous conversation?"[87]

By the 1850s, such scenes of license, impurity, and skepticism dominated the popular mysteries of the city novels that probed the hidden horrors of urban America. A prime example was George Lippard's *The Quaker City; or, The Monks of Monk Hall* (1845), which sold over 210,000 copies in six years. Before *Uncle Tom's Cabin*, no American author had written a book that sold more copies. Lippard liked to observe that, despite attacks on it as "the most immoral work of the age," his novel had become "more read, and more attacked, than any work of American fiction ever published." In 1848, none other than *Godey's Lady's Book* announced, although unhappily, that he was "the most popular writer of the day."[88]

Even *Godey's*, however, just like many of the era's domestic novels, contained ambiguous messages about the bourgeois home and family. In 1851, for example, a story entitled "The Constant" described a woman reflecting sadly about how she has neglected her husband and experiencing a moral revelation about her need to be a good wife. Yet the accompanying pictorial plate, which shows her studying her husband's picture, contains scenes around its border of other men admiring her as she looks at them appreciatively, even flirtatiously. The outside and inside images cut two ways, sending competing messages.[89]

Despite—or, perhaps, because of—such contradictory currents, popular amusements continued to grow in power. Moving into the last decades of the nineteenth century, their appeal was undeniable. During the antebellum era, popular culture had proved that it had a distinct edge in the struggles between individuals who warned against the dangers of leisure—and who preached the virtues of thrift, sobriety, and discipline—and those who experienced the lure of growing entertainment opportunities. The famed minister Henry Ward Beecher learned this fact firsthand. From the 1840s into the 1870s, he sold sixty thousand copies of his moralistic *Lectures to Young Men* (1844), an attack on virtually all forms of popular amusement. Such sales constituted an impressive figure, but one that failed to match even the number of individuals who in just two years visited the developing resort city of Saratoga Springs, New York. Beecher himself, while maintaining his opposition to amusements, ended up taking two-month summer vacations.[90] Moreover, between 1841 and 1865, when the U.S. population grew to 35 million, Barnum sold 38 million admission tickets to his American Museum.[91] Broadway had come to resemble a more upscale version of the Bowery. As the actor Leon Beauvallet observed in wonder, New York City was like "a gigantic billboard for a traveling circus," and Broadway fairly swarmed with "showmen"—"quack doctors, tooth-pullers, exhibitors of bearded negresses, wild animal trainers. . . . It is as if one were walking through an immense village fair."[92]

As the nineteenth century wound down, popular culture was clearly gaining an expansive audience, and if any group could claim to have constructed a big entertainment tent, it was the middle class. But that claim had to be tentative because, even though the middle class had substantially influenced a number of amusement venues, a host of vibrant alternative entertainments existed on the still-disreputable social margins. Over the next several decades, a number of those alternatives would continue to push toward the respectable and profitable center, altering it in the process. Relatedly, and just as importantly, popular culture was becoming a big business.

3

BUILDING AN ENTERTAINMENT INDUSTRY

In the early 1880s, audiences from New England to the Midwest and the Great Plains took turns packing themselves into a massive traveling canvas tent to watch "the Greatest Show on Earth"—the circus extravaganza of P. T. Barnum and his new partner, James A. Bailey. In town after town, excitement would build for weeks about the show's impending arrival: "circus day," when performers, trainers, and animals, in sixty or more special cars, rolled into the local railroad station. Communities came to a standstill for the unloading of the cars, parades down main streets, and the performances themselves, which featured acrobats, clowns, sideshow exhibitions, and a vast menagerie that included Jumbo, reputedly the largest elephant in captivity. Several decades later, circuses continued to be the most-awaited entertainment event in towns across the nation. As the writer Hamlin Garland remembered about growing up in rural Iowa, the circus "brought to our ears the latest band pieces and taught us the most popular songs. It furnished us with jokes. It relieved our dullness. It gave us something to talk about."[1]

Popular amusements such as the circus indeed provided much to talk about in the late nineteenth century. As the Greatest Show on Earth traversed the nation, a U.S. entertainment industry emerged. This development reflected trends in the larger economy, where sprawling corporations such as John D. Rockefeller's Standard Oil fought to bring order, predictability, and control to entire business sectors. Just as burgeoning companies like Standard Oil tried to rationalize their businesses through cutthroat practices and tighter organization, popular culture forms—the circus, Wild West shows, enlarged minstrel shows, and sports, for example—offered instructive, although smaller, models of organization. Barnum's circus represented, according to advertisements, "Centralization of All That Is Great in the Amusement Realm." And, like the sprawling industrial combinations, the circus and its amusement counterparts utilized superbly the ongoing revolution in transportation and communications, involving especially electricity, railroads, and print. Similarly, in an era that celebrated the likes of Rockefeller and the steel magnate Andrew Carnegie as "self-made men," the entertainment world featured its own "captains of industry"—Barnum, for instance, by then in the last stages of his phenomenal career, or his circus partner James A. Bailey, or Wild West star Buffalo Bill Cody, or professional baseball organizer Albert Spalding.[2]

The prizefighter John L. Sullivan provided another variation of the self-made success story. Although Sullivan was never adept at business, he symbolized a new kind of hero in American life: the celebrity, someone who was famous not for winning elections or battles or leading reform causes, but for holding a prominent place in the spreading domain of mass amusements. Sullivan's fame, like that of a Cody or a Barnum, revealed an important and continuing paradox: even as the emerging popular culture industry reflected the move toward efficiency, organization, incorporation, discipline, and punctuality in the larger society, at the same time it persistently went against the cultural grain, pitting excess and escapism against discipline, fun against work, titillation against traditional morality, muscular individualism against organization, playful informality against restrictive etiquette, pleasureful abandon against restraint, and unfamiliar, alternative worlds against the traditional and the respectable.[3]

The circus pointed the way, with none other than the remarkable Barnum playing a pivotal role. In 1868, after his American Museum burned down for the second time in less than four years, he had briefly retired. But, in 1870, Dan Castello and William Coup, who, in frontier regions such as California and Missouri, had operated small sideshows and wagon circuses—"mud" shows because of the roads they often had to maneuver—convinced Barnum to join them, bringing with him his famous name, his genius for marketing, and his money. Circuses were far from new, certainly. But Barnum, in his inimitable way, would alter their organization, their scale, and their reputation, helping launch their golden age from roughly 1870 to 1914.[4]

Organizationally, Barnum's circus epitomized the new industrial rhythms and system of the rising corporate America. After 1872, when Barnum put his circus on rails, he tied the circus more tightly than ever to schedules and organization. It was a prisoner of the calendar, following strict timetables from place to place; the performances themselves moved like clockwork, with a ringmaster and musical scripts coordinating the procession of acts—an even more impressive accomplishment when the Greatest Show on Earth spread from two to three rings. Here, indeed, was the world of the clock that increasingly influenced American lives. In 1876, the popular song described how "Grandfather's Clock" marked the entire life of one man: "Ninety years without slumbering, tick, tick, tick, tick," until "the old man died." Even as that fabled clock stopped ticking, businessmen increasingly relied on fob watches, railroads on newly defined time zones, towns on the railway timetables, factories on time clocks, and sports more and more on timed events (such as boxing's move to three-minute rounds). While the circus adhered rigorously to time schedules, it was also a marvel of superbly coordinated activities, from the loading and unloading of the railroad cars to the raising and lowering of the big top. For the job of driving in tent stakes, a "sledging gang" of as many as twelve men stood in a circle, taking rapid-fire turns at hitting the stakes with machine-like precision. By the 1890s, the U.S. War Department was studying circuses for information about how to move large numbers of personnel and animals. "Routing a big circus is like maneuvering an army in time of war," claimed one of Barnum's press agents, while another appreciative onlooker believed that moving "a city that folds itself up like an umbrella . . . would have staggered Napoleon himself."[5]

In 1880, when Barnum merged his big show with Bailey's, the circus took on gargantuan proportions, becoming what was, in effect, a traveling company town. The storied elephant Jumbo symbolized Barnum's tendency toward excess. Utilizing his brilliant skills as a promoter, Barnum turned Jumbo into a phenomenally popular exhibit. The exhibit's attraction attested to the growing American interest in animals that resulted partly from urbanization and partly from controversies over Charles Darwin's 1859 *On the Origin of Species* and that found expression in municipal zoos, animal protection societies, and a flood of books and stories attributing human qualities to pets and other animals. In 1882, Barnum paid the London Zoological Gardens $10,000 for the huge elephant, which was more than twelve feet tall and weighed six and a half tons. When Jumbo, seeming to protest his departure from England, lay down at the gate of the London zoo, Barnum rejoiced: "Let him lie there as long as he wants to. The publicity is worth it." By spring, the animal was in the United States traveling in "Jumbo's Palace Car," a brightly colored private railroad car that Barnum had prepared for him. For over three years, the elephant was the centerpiece of the Greatest Show on Earth. After a locomotive accidentally struck and killed Jumbo in September 1885, Barnum contrived a melodramatic version of the animal's death. He claimed that Jumbo had died in the process of saving a dwarf elephant named Tom Thumb and that Jumbo's "widow," a cow elephant that the circus had also acquired from the London zoo, was in mourning. Barnum displayed the "widow" with Jumbo's preserved carcass and developed an act in which the other circus elephants, in memory of Jumbo, wiped their eyes with large handkerchiefs.[6]

Barnum's other lasting influence was in elevating the reputation of circuses. Antebellum mud or "dog and pony" shows, which moral organizations such as the American Sunday-School Union condemned, had catered to adults, not children. In 1858, a Kenosha, Wisconsin, newspaper editor denounced circus audiences as "a nuisance and a pest"—sorry "dregs of American population" that had "the most vulgar passions." The troupers were equally reprehensible, in his opinion, and should hang "by their rascally necks till they were dead." Unruly circus patrons responded vociferously to racy jokes and anticipated seeing a bit of nudity, or at the least female legs in tights. Sometimes the noisy, often drunken, crowds moved beyond laughing and shouting at the clowns and other performers and started throwing punches. "Hey, Rube!" became a chilling cry by which circus people, under attack, signaled their compatriots for help. River, mining, and college towns could be especially violent. The great clown Dan Rice noted, for example, that he and his colleagues had to administer "unnumerable thumpings" to Yale men in order to earn some respect.[7]

Still, especially in rural America, these traveling circuses exerted a growing appeal. In 1839, the population of a community such as Cooperstown, New York, increased from twelve hundred to four thousand when the circus was around. Even a local attorney who complained about the "disagreeable" and "vulgar" audiences took his children and then later went to the show yet again with several women. As early as the 1830s, certainly, there had been efforts to broaden circuses' appeal via such attractions as free street parades, featuring local bands. In 1846 in New York City, an elegantly ornamented bandwagon joined fifty carriages and 150 horses in what a newspaper described as "one of the most splendid pageants ever got up in this country." In 1858, the steam calliope appeared. By then, the circus owner and performer Dan Rice was downplaying his roguish reputation. In 1855, claiming that he offered "higher" entertainment, he renamed his company Dan Rice's Great Show and dropped the word *circus* from advertisements. Describing himself now as a *humorist* rather than a *clown,* he shed his clown outfit for the suit and tie of a middle-class gentleman and featured uplifting songs, sermons, and patriotic speeches. He insisted that his performers were religious as well as refined; at least once, he marched them into the services of a small church. In 1857, one magazine claimed that Rice had driven "the groveling babbler in spotted dress, and the low buffoon . . . from the ring."[8]

More than anyone, however, Barnum transformed the circus from an unsavory source of cheap adult entertainment into a purified setting for children, young and old. In 1851, when he was still in the museum business, he had taken a traveling show on the road but carefully dubbed it his Asiatic Caravan, Museum, and Menagerie—not a circus. And, in 1872, when he joined up with Coup and Castello, he again avoided the word *circus,* calling his entertainment P. T. Barnum's Great Traveling Museum,

Menagerie, and World's Fair. For two years, starting in 1874, he and Coup ran a second traveling road show, P. T. Barnum's Great Roman Hippodrome, which was alcohol free. "NOTHING CONNECTED WITH THIS ESTABLISHMENT RESEMBLES A CIRCUS," his advertisements claimed grandly and misleadingly. Barnum emphasized that his "elevating and unobjectionable" amusements were ones "to which a refined Christian mother can take her children with satisfaction." Newspapers agreed, referring to "the Great Moral Show." The *New York Times* believed that Barnum's "establishment has already become the resort of ladies and little ones, who seem especially delighted with what they see," and a religious publication, praising the "decency and good morals of the show," tendered Barnum "the heartiest thanks of all good Christian people." Cultivating the same reputation that he developed at his American Museum, Barnum declared that he was "the Children's Friend" and that "children of all ages" would enjoy his show. In this context, Mark Twain had his fictional character Huck Finn exclaim: "It was a bully circus. It was the splendidest sight that ever was." By the 1890s, the Greatest Show on Earth and many other circuses enjoyed reputations as places for youngsters; orphanages made a point of sending their young residents, sometimes courtesy of local businesses, who also occasionally provided tickets for sick and other needy children. Not coincidentally, in 1902, the National Biscuit Company created Barnum's Animals crackers.[9]

Barnum's efforts to elevate the circus's reputation benefited also from his partner, James Bailey, as well as from rival organizations such as that of the Ringling Brothers. The stern "Mr. Bailey," as even Barnum called him, managed their partnership with steely rigor, tolerating no difficulties with employees. Born in 1847, orphaned at age eight, and subjected to regular beatings at the hands of his oldest sister, Bailey had fled to a circus when he was eleven. Later, even as the Greatest Show on Earth flourished, he longed someday to run a more "tasteful" and exclusive entertainment, one that catered to fashionable elites. Barnum, of course, sought respectability, but not at the expense of excluding the masses. The night before Barnum died, on April 7, 1891, his last request was reportedly to know what the day's circus receipts were. As the *Times* of London wrote on his death: "He knew that 'the people' means crowds, paying crowds." And, unquestionably, by the late nineteenth century, large, paying crowds were turning circuses into mainstream amusements with huge and varied followings. In the 1870s and 1880s, a number of circuses had formed, taking advantage of the rapidly spreading railroad system. Between 1884 and 1889, the number of traveling shows jumped from fourteen to twenty-two, with the Ringling Brothers troupe prominent among them. Sons of August Rüngeling, a German immigrant harness maker in Wisconsin, the brothers may have cut legal corners (a smaller competitor accused them of a price-fixing arrangement with the railroads), but, by the mid-1890s, their banning of liquor and gambling had earned their circus a *Sunday school* label from the press. Still, it was Barnum who, according to the popular *Literary Digest* on his death, had done more than anyone "to preserve the circus from vulgarity." By then, the old man had essentially retired, allowing Bailey to take control of the business (which, in 1888, became officially the Barnum and Bailey Greatest Show on Earth). Barnum had, nevertheless, occasionally toured with the show in his last years, once jumping through flaming hoops to prove that his performing horses were safe. On another occasion, he rode in a carriage around a London arena, calling out: "I suppose you all come to see Barnum. Wa-al, I'm Barnum."[10]

Despite the elevated image of circuses by the end of the nineteenth century, they in fact had a more titillating, subversive side—offering what a former clown described as "G-strings with a G-rating." As early as 1874, even as Barnum emphasized the moral nature of his circus, he collaborated with several entrepreneurs in setting up "Barnumville," a number of sideshows. One that he personally owned featured scantily clad women. Sideshows, most of which were owned independently or operated as concessions, became a regular part of circuses. By the 1880s, large circuses typically included a dozen or so small tents. "Ten-in-one shows" offered ten acts for one price. "Pit shows" usually displayed one human oddity, or "freak," per ticket. Customers flocked to the freak shows and other side exhibitions as they negotiated the "midway" path to the big top and main performance.[11]

Hence, while circuses cultivated an image as family entertainment, they continually transgressed the lines of "normality," predictability, and socially defined distinctions. Human acrobats could soar like birds, while "learned pigs" and other animals took on human accoutrements. Clowns used vulgar language and then, as the size of shows grew, employed slapstick to mock authority and acceptable behavior; often acting like children, they were disruptive pranksters who functioned outside conventional rules and relished a simpler, preindustrial world. When the circus came to town, it indeed brought a diverse collection of social outsiders who constituted a "nomadic community of oddballs."[12]

On gender issues, these bizarre communities walked their own social tightrope, trying simultaneously to titillate yet reassure. Shows in the late nineteenth century included more female performers, challenging on a number of levels the dictates and expectations of Victorian womanhood. On the one hand, athletic, daring, often partially disrobed and sexually attractive women defied respectable middle-class norms by appearing as animal tamers, acrobats riding horses and elephants, "ballet girls" performing exotic dances, and trapeze artists swinging through the air. Indeed, some turn-of-the-century acts, such as Barnum and Bailey's "Statue Girls," featured virtually nude women who, by posing in greasepaint as examples of ancient sculpture, supposedly represented culturally acceptable art. Even aerial performers who wore full dresses, as did those in the Adam Forepaugh and Sells Brothers Circus in 1896, exposed parts of their legs as they swung above the audience. More typically, female acrobats wore tights, displaying their bodies in various positions as they soared through the air. As the historian Alison Kibler has argued, these trapeze artists offered a kind of metaphor for the much-publicized New Woman, who was displaying more independence outside the home. A growing number of females were attending college, working in the public sphere, engaging in physical exercises such as bicycling, pushing for the right to vote, seeking information about birth control, and having fewer children. Such developments suggested that Victorian prescriptions for proper and true womanhood were wavering. Female snake charmers in the circus also poked fun at such prescriptions. "To see her lithesome figure, her strong muscular arms and shapely limbs bravely caressing the huge squirming boa constrictors, never fails to produce a great impression," wrote one press agent of one snake charmer. Another, who worked with Barnum and Bailey in the 1880s, channeled her maternal instincts in a curious way: "I give [my snakes] as much attention as a mother does a child. Regularly every Saturday night they are washed in lukewarm water and wrapped in blankets." Startled audiences sometimes discovered that the "women" were, in fact, men in drag, further confounding gender lines and suggesting the illusion of appearances. Similarly, grease-painted male clowns, wearing women's clothes and gargantuan rubber breasts, toyed with gender norms.[13]

Although circuses always struggled with a "low" entertainment image because of their association with sawdust, dirt, animal smells, and the bizarre, they grew in popularity and largely avoided the kinds of state regulation with which moral reformers targeted many public amusements. This relative immunity from "the prowling prudes," as *Billboard* magazine called such reformers, may have reflected the circus's transient nature, but it flowed too from marketing strategies that emphasized propriety and education. By cultivating what one scholar has described as a "paradoxical image of domesticated eroticism," circus entrepreneurs quite successfully contained moral criticism. Programs thus referred to the animal trainer Mabel Stark as "the Lady Dainty" and claimed that female performers were respectable "ladies . . . of good breeding." "The domestic instinct is very strong among circus women," argued Barnum and Bailey show programs. Indeed, one writer asserted that their domestic urges were so strong that "the thoughts of many of them as they go flying through hoops or whirling through the air on a trapeze, are in some faraway home with their children." An Iowa newspaper reassured citizens that perceptions of circus women as "Cigarette Smoking Chatter Boxes, Paint-Bedaubed, Etc.," were wrong: the performers were, in fact, "Just Like All Human Beings."[14]

But circuses were, perhaps, able to circumvent much moral criticism because they offered upbeat, optimistic spectaculars that audiences ultimately found reassuring. For P. T. Barnum, such reassurances came naturally. At peace with the late nineteenth century, the aging entertainer was able to provide the kind of happy, encouraging diversions that many people welcomed in a topsy-turvy world.[15]

Cities were growing at an accelerating rate, putting enormous strains on municipal resources, bogging down in corruption as political machines scrambled for urban spoils, and undergoing a massive demographic upheaval as people migrated from rural America while millions of immigrants entered the United States, particularly from Southern and Eastern Europe. Chicago, for example, after experiencing a devastating fire in 1871, reached a population of 500,000 by the 1880s and then doubled its numbers to become the second-largest city in the Western Hemisphere by the 1890s. By 1900, moreover, four-fifths of Chicago's residents were either new immigrants or first-generation Americans, a fact that stirred nativistic impulses among the many old-stock citizens who watched with alarm the changing ethnic and religious composition of urban America. In the late nineteenth century, labor violence shook Chicago and other cities that were still experiencing the birth pangs of the industrial system. The nation's economy resembled a roller coaster, sliding into and out of devastating depressions in the mid-1870s, mid-1880s, and mid-1890s. Against that backdrop, citizens anxiously debated the dangers of business monopolies, financially strapped agrarians forged angry protest organizations, and urban violence mounted. In contrast, the Greatest Show on Earth and other circuses provided social scripts that were less disturbing—ones that ignored grim industrial realities while implicitly endorsing a surging predilection for wonder and the grandiose.

Wild West shows, which had much in common with circuses, similarly offered both ostentatious entertainment and suggestions that American expansionism came without consequences. Since the 1860s, cowboys had engaged in roping, steer-riding, and bronco-busting contests, but it was William F. "Buffalo Bill" Cody who seized the moment. In 1883, Cody launched a greatest show of his own that ultimately "Out-Barnumed Barnum," as one journalist enthusiastically reported, bringing an exciting and romanticized adaptation of the American West to eager audiences who often knew little about the region. Cody's extravaganza quickly became a national—and then an international—phenomenon, combining rodeo-style competition with dramatic theatrical productions that celebrated the "winning" of the West and turned the cowboy into a hero. There were authentic

Native Americans, albeit now in unthreatening roles—curiosities to ponder rather than rampaging savages to fear. There were also demonstrations of cowboy skills, reenactments of frontier battles, and exhibits of buffalo, wild horses, and even mountain lions. The ultimate result was a sympathetic rendering of America's Western history that provided onlookers with a sanitized past, minus the bloody destruction of territorial expansion. Here was a staged history lesson that was fun, uplifting, and comforting—American history as a form of immaculate conception. "Foes in '76—Friends in '85" read one program that showed Cody shaking hands with Sitting Bull, the Hunkpapa Sioux chief who toured briefly with the show, often attracting hisses and boos from the crowd.[16]

Cody's triumphs owed much to his own credentials, talents, and timing. For one thing, he was an authentic frontier product who cut a handsome figure—tall and with flowing hair, a moustache, and a goatee. Born in Iowa in 1846, he had as a boy in Kansas Territory once watched perhaps a thousand covered wagons heading west, met Native Americans, and warily eyed some rugged-looking whites with "huge pistols and knives in their belts." By his early thirties, he claimed to have tracked Indians for the U.S. Army, participated in fourteen military campaigns against Indians, killed buffalo for the Kansas Pacific Railroad, herded oxen, ridden with the Pony Express, commanded a wagon train, and stolen horses for the Union Army during the Civil War. He had been only twenty-three when he encountered Edward Zane Carroll Judson, a shady character who had helped instigate the bloody 1849 Astor Place Riot, spent time in jail, shot a man, survived an attempted lynching, and—under the pseudonym Ned Buntline—started cranking out cheap fiction for the Beadle and Adams publishing firm. In 1869, after meeting Cody a few months earlier, Buntline published a serial novel, *Buffalo Bill, the King of the Border Men*.[17]

Initially, Cody thus inhabited the far regions of the entertainment business. As a ripsnorting character in sensationalized dime novels, he was far removed from genteel fiction. Yet, as the subject of perhaps ultimately 550 of these cheap books by many authors, he became a notable figure, indeed, an early action hero, in the developing popular mythology of the West. In early 1872, wearing buckskins, he took a bow in New York City's Bowery Theater during a dramatized version of Buntline's *King of the Border Men*. That December, he performed as himself when the play *The Scouts of the Prairie* opened in Chicago. At one point, he forgot his lines and shouted, to the audience's laughter: "Hello Mamma! . . . Oh, but I'm a bad actor." For the next decade, he rotated summer scouting assignments in the West with an acting career during the winter months, typically playing himself in trite, wildly plotted melodramas that nevertheless drew loudly approving crowds, including "fully seven hundred boys and men paying for admission to the gallery alone." He claimed also to have written some dime novels himself.

"I am sorry to have to lie so outrageously in this yarn," he reportedly apologized to his publisher. "My hero has killed more Indians on one war-trail than I have killed in all my life. But I understand this is what is expected in border tales." Still, he chafed at his position on the entertainment world's fringes and sought to build a broader and more reputable following. At age thirty-three, he thus published his autobiography, advancing his credentials as a respectable gentleman as well as a tough, heroic Westerner. He described how he had avenged General George Custer's death at the Battle of the Little Bighorn by killing "Yellow Hand a Cheyenne Chief in a single-handed fight." (Later, onstage and in his Wild West show, he thrilled audiences by holding up Yellow Hand's scalp and shouting: "*The first scalp for Custer.*") In 1883, after the stage manager Nate Salsbury urged him to move beyond "dime novel thrillers," Cody opened his career as a Wild West entrepreneur.[18]

As P. T. Barnum had done earlier with his museum and circus, Cody revealed a special knack for advertising and pitched his show as respectable entertainment. Implementing advertising strategies that would have made Barnum proud, Cody put up posters that were 9 feet high and almost 150 feet long. Parades, with Cody on horseback at the front, sometimes lasted well over two hours. "Our entertainment don't want to smack of a show or circus," he said. "Must be on a high toned basis." He wanted to attract a "better class of public" than did less reputable amusements. To that end, he astutely included domestic imagery that would please middle-class audiences. For twenty-three years, starting in 1884, he consistently featured a reenactment of an "Attack on the Settlers' Cabin," which typically came as the show's grand finale. As whooping Indians circled a burning frontier home, a white family huddled inside until, at the last moment, Buffalo Bill and his cowboy friends rode to the rescue. The scene of men defending the home, saving the woman and children inside, meshed neatly with the idealized roles and domestic setting that helped define the middle class. By the 1890s, pictures in the show's program made much of Cody's own journey from "lassoing wild horses on the Platte in old days" to his modern home and ranch. A poem extolled Cody's treatment of his baby daughter; with his "rifle and knife laid by, / He coos and tosses the baby, / Darling 'apple of his eye.'" Representing his Wild West extravaganza as "genuinely American" and tailored for women and children, Cody charged a relatively expensive amount for tickets—fifty cents for adults, twenty-five cents for children. Despite the pricy admission charge, crowds packed the arena, hungry for entertainment that, from their perspective, combined education and amusement, historical authenticity and action-packed fun.[19]

Cody's timing could hardly have been better. On one level, he rode the swelling wave of mass amusements. On another level, he tapped a growing interest in the American West. By the late nineteenth century, there were expressions of anxiety in print and artistic sources that the nation's storied frontier was disappearing. Indeed, according to the 1890 census report, it was already closed. The frontier now survived mainly as memory, in still-popular dime novels that glorified such Western heroes as Daniel Boone and Buffalo Bill—or in Wild West shows. Cody's success owed much to a public mood that was both jittery about the future and nostalgic for the past.[20]

On yet another level, Wild West shows—like circuses generally—appealed to audiences at the very moment when imperial ambitions were again stirring the nation. As expansionists embraced "the white man's burden"—civilization, Christianity, and commerce—the United States enlarged its influence in the Caribbean and added island territories in the Pacific. In 1898, for example, the United States annexed Hawaii and drove Spain out of the Philippines and Cuba; a subsequent, longer and bloodier war against insurgent Filipinos solidified control of the Philippines. Capturing the mood that fueled such expansion, Buffalo Bill Cody offered a glorious saga of Manifest Destiny. "The bullet is the pioneer of civilization," claimed his 1885 program, "for it has gone hand in hand with the axe that cleared the forest, and with the family bible and school book." By 1899, Cody's Wild West show—by then known as Buffalo Bill's Wild West and Congress of Rough Riders of the World—invited spectators to see "Strange People from Our New Possessions." The show also included a reenactment of the Battle of San Juan Hill, which celebrated the victorious charge of Theodore Roosevelt and his Rough Riders against Spanish troops in Cuba. According to the program's notes, Roosevelt's troops were courageous, "virile," and "manly," while the Spanish were "wine-soaked" cowards. In 1901, Cody included another spectacle, "The Rescue at Pekin," showing the rescue of Americans during China's Boxer Rebellion; Native Americans played the parts of the Chinese Boxers.[21]

"As moral cheerleaders of expansionism," Wild West shows and circuses helped audiences adjust to the enlarged international role played by the United States, cloaking it in adventurous and innocent terms. Territorial expansion fused neatly with entertainment. Indeed, in 1901, one reporter believed that the war against Filipino rebels resembled a Wild West show: "The theory of the Administration is that the trouble in the Philippines is like the Wild West show. It isn't war, but it looks a good deal like it." Several years earlier, when word of the U.S. victory over Spain arrived at a circus in Beloit, Kansas, the audience broke into cheers, and the band played the national anthem. Circuses and Wild West shows provided not only patriotic displays but also opportunities for patrons to view "Genuine Natives of India and Ceylon," "Australian Bushmen, the Lowest in the Human Scale of All the Peoples of the Earth," "South Pacific Savages," or "every shade, color and kind of savage people from mountain, valley, forest, jungle or cave." These exhibits underlined the racial inferiority of non-whites, reaffirmed stereotypes concerning the sexual promiscuity and laziness of "savage" peoples, and highlighted the march of civilization. According to an 1895 Buffalo Bill Wild West program, for example, Native Americans were "doomed . . . to . . . extinction, like the buffalo they once hunted."[22]

These "visions of empire" were apparent also in the era's several international expositions, which attracted millions of spectators and wove their images into the larger culture. A prospectus for Omaha's 1899 Greater America Exposition illustrated the prevailing message with a drawing of Uncle Sam reaching around the world and pointing to the Philippines and Cuba; stretching beneath his arms was a ribbon reading: "The White Man's Burden." Expositions ranging from Chicago's in 1893 (at which Buffalo Bill's Wild West played just outside the entrance) to others in Omaha, Buffalo, St. Louis, and elsewhere featured ethnological villages on the fairgrounds and midway shows alike. Visitors could, thus, see exhibits arranged according to what one journalist described as a "sliding scale of humanity" at the Chicago Midway (including African pygmies and Egyptians), a bare-breasted Samoan woman at San Francisco's 1894 fair, a Chinese Village concession in Nashville's 1897 fair, or, at St. Louis's 1904 Louisiana Purchase Exposition, some half-nude Igorots among the twelve hundred residents of the Philippines Reservation. Through all these exhibits ran Darwinian themes of racial progress and celebrations of U.S. power. In 1898, the circus proprietor Peter Sells summed up the dominant theme: "We have taken our place at the very head in the front rank of nations."[23]

Cody's use of Native Americans unquestionably reinforced that message. Although Indians had appeared in many previous exhibits and road shows, Cody elevated the concept of show Indians. In several respects, he treated them better than did competing shows such as that of W. H. Barten, who made the Indians purchase their costumes from him and refused to pay them regularly lest they waste their money on liquor. And Cody, whose own hair grew to his shoulders, hardly sympathized with reformers who sought to assimilate Native Americans into white society via such strategies as requiring short hair. Still, the Wild West's format encouraged evolutionary views that placed Indians among "vanishing races." "The departing Red Man," according to one of Cody's programs, "has kept an always backward pace. . . . His day on earth is apparently short." Undoubtedly, too, the Wild West show perpetuated unflattering stereotypes and even stirred animosities when, for example, crowds jeered Sitting Bull. Even more favorable characterizations of the show Indians served white needs. When Wild West publicity hailed them as "nature's *noblemen* in physique, fearless audacity, consummate skill," it both complimented the hardy pioneers who had "conquered the wilderness" and chastised their descendants "for crowding into cities and living as do worms." In either case, whites—not Native

Americans—were the protagonists of the frontier tale. Show Indians them-selves, however, often found different meanings in their performances. Working for Cody, they had opportunities to travel, to earn a modest in-come, to reaffirm at least parts of their native culture, and to act out old battles. As Black Elk, an Oglala Sioux, recalled: "I liked the part of the show we made but *not* the part the Wasichu [whites] made." What the Indians read into the mock battles was not necessarily the same as what whites saw. As Joe Rockboy, an Ihanktonwan-Sicangu Sioux, remembered, performing "gave me a chance to get back on a horse and act it out again."[24]

On several levels, the evolution of the Wild West shows of the late nineteenth century and the early twentieth corresponded with that of black-face minstrelsy during the same period. Indeed, Cody and Nate Salsbury considered producing minstrel-like entertainments. Cody's Wild West oc-casionally included black entertainers as musicians or clownlike figures. In 1895, Salsbury created a colossal "Black America" show that included some 620 African American performers but lasted only a few months.[25]

Like the Wild West shows, the still-popular minstrel shows became more organized, extravagant, and racially demeaning. Black performers, who appeared with growing frequency, faced many of the same dilemmas as did show Indians. By blacking up, African American minstrels—like the show Indians—often helped strengthen and perpetuate ugly racial stereo-types. Yet, again like the show Indians, they demonstrated the tangled com-plexities of the racial thicket that constituted so much of the unfolding mass culture.

Following the Civil War, competition in the amusement industry forced minstrel troupes to make important adjustments. These alterations reflect-ed the era's drive toward consolidation, expanded the sizes of troupes (in some cases to eighty members), and offered musical extravaganzas as wholesome family entertainment. In notable instances, minstrel troupes al-tered their formats so much that they became almost indistinguishable from other amusements by featuring such Barnum-style freaks as an eight-foot, two-inch Chinese giant and an "African dwarf," a strongman, a champion wrestler, people who posed as "Roman statuary," and extrava-gant costume skits about, for example, a "Turkish Barbaric Palace in Silver and Gold." In some cases, they even dropped blackface itself. As the min-strel star George Thatcher remembered: "We were looking for novelty and for a change tried white minstrelsy, singing and dancing in 'Shakespearean costumes' and 'Louis XI court dress.'" The occasional departure from blackface grated on the white minstrel comedian Lew Dockstader. "They have refined all of the fun out of it," he complained. "Minstrelsy in silk stockings, set in square cuts and bag wigs, is about as palatable as an amusement as a salad of pine shavings and sawdust with a little salmon, lobster, or chicken."[26]

The more expensive productions devastated smaller troupes, particularly as the nation's unsettled economy lurched up and down. As a result, in the ten-year period before 1877, the number of companies reportedly plummeted from sixty to twelve. In the move toward consolidation, the biggest winner was J. H. Haverly, minstrelsy's P. T. Barnum. Echoing Barnum, Haverly stated that his only goal was "to find out what the people want and then give them that thing. . . . There's no use trying to force the public into a theater." In the 1870s, viewing minstrelsy from the perspective of a promoter and manager, he decided to form a troupe "that for extraordinary excellence, merit, and magnitude will astonish and satisfy the most exacting amusement seeker in the world." He promptly absorbed four companies into "HAVERLY'S UNITED MASTODON MINSTRELS," which featured forty performers: "FORTY—40—COUNT 'EM—40—FORTY." His advertisements claimed: "Forty is a magical and historical number. In the time of Noah it rained forty days and nights. The Children of Israel wandered forty days in the wilderness. Haverly's famous forty are just as important." By the early 1880s, Haverly had parlayed his investment to include theaters in Brooklyn, Chicago, San Francisco, and New York City (where he owned three), four touring theater groups, three minstrel troupes, and several mining and milling businesses. One of his minstrel programs parodied Barnum's circus: "PEA-TEA-BAR-NONE'S KOLLOSAL CIRKUSS, MUSEUM, MENAGERIE AND KAYNE'S KICKDROME KAVALCADE," which included acrobats, stunt riders, and clowns.[27]

As minstrelsy cut a broader entertainment swath, it even included several all-female casts. In 1870, M. B. Leavitt put together Madame Rentz's Female Minstrels, who performed in tights. The main focus in these shows was "shape," as one woman admitted. "We give a tough show, draw tough houses, and have a tough time." Here, however, was a rougher kind of show that still claimed to fit with minstrelsy's overall image of family entertainment. "Nothing to offend," promised one show. "FUN WITHOUT VULGARITY. Heads of families can bring WIVES AND DAUGHTERS" and not worry about "COARSE AND VULGAR WITTICISMS."[28] Minstrelsy's continued popularity undoubtedly reflected its ability to accommodate other forms of entertainment, but more was involved. Like mass amusements generally, minstrelsy appealed to audiences' desires to deal with the changing world around them. Although the sharp class commentary that had first marked blackface performances had long since faded, minstrel shows nevertheless did not ignore the flux of an increasingly urban and immigrant nation. Hence, acts jabbed at crime, high taxes, unclean streets, expensive rents, and dangerous transportation. "Whoever you meet, look for their little game" was one warning. A favorite joke was about how not a single bug existed in the house because they were all married and with children. Critiques often had a racial and imperial edge resembling that in Wild West shows and circuses. Thus, in 1872 and 1873, several troupes performed a skit, "Life on the Indian Frontier; or, The Comanches," that concluded with the "downfall of the Savages," after the army saved innocent villagers from drunken, murderous Native Americans. "WARPATH, SCALPING, KNIVES, TOMAHAWKS" were part of another skit. In the mid-1860s, several troupes portrayed the "jap-oh-knees"; twenty years later, a number of burlesques of the popular musical *Mikado* were featured, with a cast that included a Japanese "no-account" and "a smart Coon." Such references to "coons" attested to minstrelsy's enduring roots in blackface.[29]

Those roots, along with the minstrel show's quest for novelty, opened the postbellum minstrel stage to "real coons," or "genuine sons of Africa," as advertisements and observers described them. African Americans were not altogether new to minstrelsy, of course. In 1845, the great black dancer William Henry "Juba" Lane had appeared with white minstrels, and, a decade later, several small troupes of what one newspaper described as "real 'culled pussons'" had emerged. At the end of the Civil War, Brooker and Clayton's Georgia Minstrels—"the Only Simon Pure Negro Troupe in the World"—did well on a Northeastern tour. In 1878, none other than J. H. Haverly, by then the king of minstrelsy, purchased the Georgia Minstrels and put them on the road as the Haverly Colored Minstrels, eventually a company with one hundred members. Advertising for these shows emphasized the performers' supposed authenticity. According to one newspaper in 1880, Haverly's black troupe conveyed a sense of plantation life "with greater fidelity than any 'poor white trash' with corked faces can ever do.'"[30]

Minstrelsy's fascination with "natural" representatives from the slave era tapped the ongoing nostalgia for an idealized rural America. As urbanization and industrialization steadily gripped the nation, many citizens longed for a mythical America of quiet, innocent villages. This nostalgia encouraged fantasies of happy plantation days, fantasies captured in a host of popular songs such as the 1871 "The Little Old Cabin in the Lane," the 1877 "Dem Good Ole Times," James Bland's 1878 version of "Carry Me Back to Old Virginny," and the 1884 "My Home in Alabama," about an elderly black couple now living sadly in a city tenement. Here was a world that contrasted sharply with the turbulent setting of the late nineteenth century. "In de evening by de moonlight / when dis darkies work was over, / We would gather round de fire, / 'till de hoecake it was done," an 1880 song remembered.[31] One minstrel performer, who described himself as a genuinely "black Efiopian," promised that his show would stir fond memories of the "good old plantation." "De darky will be hisself once more and forget that he ever had any trouble," while white observers would end up wishing that they were "brack as dese brack fellers up dere dat am making all dis music" and having such a great time.[32]

Such affectionate portraits of an imaginary past came more and more at the expense of African Americans. By the late nineteenth century, minstrel shows had solidly replaced their earlier class resentments against wealth and power with ever uglier representations of blacks, who increasingly appeared as reprehensible, violent brutes. Minstrel songs reflected a fear of African Americans that gripped many cities in the wake of emancipation and growing black neighborhoods. An 1883 song, "New Coon in Town," warned about a fancy-dressed, bejeweled black gambler who cheated. Two years later, singers feared "De Coon Dat Had de Razor": "I went to a ball de other night, / At Susie Simkins hut, / Where dem coons all carry razors; / And how dem niggers cut." By the end of the century, "coon songs" became a kind of fad. The fact that the 1896 hit "All Coons Look Alike to Me" came from Ernest Hogan, a free black man who had performed on the minstrel stage, revealed much about the challenges, tragedies, and paradoxes that haunted the African American entry onto the minstrel stage.[33]

Despite the dangers and racial debasement that confronted black minstrel performers, the African American composer W. C. Handy insisted that, at that time, minstrelsy was "one of the greatest outlets for talented [Negro] musicians and artists. All the best [black] talent of that generation came down the same drain. The composers, the singers, the musicians, the speakers, the stage performers—the minstrel show got them all." Black minstrelsy unquestionably provided a crucial vehicle for the nation's first professional black performing artists.[34] It also raised a dilemma. Black minstrel performers faced a risky challenge that haunted not only them but their comedic descendants as well. The challenge, as Mel Watkins, a leading authority on African American humor, has observed, was how to handle "the conflict between satirizing social images of blacks and contributing to whites' negative stereotypes of blacks in general."[35]

One strategy—familiar to all groups on the margins of power and authority—was to take at least some control of those stereotypes, however covertly and indirectly. As the novelist Ralph Ellison later advised: "Change the joke and slip the yoke." Creative performers could, thus, work to turn the stereotype inside out, adding nuances and meaning. In blackface masks, they could disarm audiences, resisting and even mocking dominant attitudes—"exaggerating the exaggerations of our enemies," as the former slave Frederick Douglass said of one black troupe.[36] Slaves had used this tactic when they developed the cakewalk, a rendition of dances that whites performed. When the slaves subsequently high-stepped and strutted through the cakewalk, amused white audiences saw only failed sophistication, thereby overlooking the joke: the slaves were, in fact, making fun of the master class's pretensions. "They did a take-off on the high manners of the white folks in the 'big house,'" recalled a ninety-year-old ex-slave, "but their masters who gathered around to watch the fun missed the point." On the minstrel stage, black performers could, thus, twist the familiar Old Darky character, a happy slave as whites interpreted him, into a tragic figure who longed for his wife and children on another plantation.[37]

But efforts to reshape blackface images could be tricky and even dangerous. Indeed, for African Americans, the minstrel circuit itself often posed considerable risk, especially in the South. The black performer Tom Fletcher remembered Southern towns that displayed signs that said: "NIGGER, READ AND RUN." Sometimes, Fletcher said, "there would be added 'and if you can't read, run anyway.'" When a show was over, black minstrels moved as a group to the railroad car. "If there were no trains leaving that night," according to Fletcher, "we would hire an engine and get right out of town without delay." In one Texas town, white rowdies threw rocks at W. C. Handy's group when it was parading to the theater. Handy himself once had to hide from a lynch mob. Louis Wright died at the hands of such a mob in Missouri. After Wright cursed whites who threw snowballs at him, local authorities arrested the entire troupe, beating up several members in an unsuccessful effort to make them identify him. Ultimately, the sheriff turned Wright over to the mob, which lynched him and removed his tongue.[38]

Still, for many aspiring black performers, minstrelsy offered opportunity as well as risk. It gave them, in Handy's words, "a glimpse of another world" in which they could travel, be onstage, dress smartly, and make more money than most black laborers. By 1882, the great Billy Kersands was the highest-paid black minstrel, making $80 a week, which was comparable to the earnings of most white minstrel stars. Kersands, whose act reinforced the caricatured image of an ignorant black man, dazzled audiences by dancing slowly to Stephen Foster's song "Swanee River" while holding a cup and saucer and stuffing several billiard balls in his mouth. But most black performers made far less. According to the 1890 census, there were around fifteen hundred black entertainers, but, almost certainly, others labored in small troupes around the country. For a few of these entertainers—W. C. Handy, for example—minstrelsy provided a springboard into the wider world of show business.[39]

Handy noted perceptively that a "large section of upper-crust Negroes" wanted nothing to do with black minstrels such as himself. More common African Americans, however, were great fans of black minstrels. On one level, they enjoyed watching other blacks perform. Many identified with these resourceful artists who, as Handy remembered, "bought smart outfits" and flirted with young women. On another level, black audiences could laugh uproariously at the shows themselves, albeit for different reasons than white patrons did. Whereas most whites were inclined to take the caricatures of blacks at face value, blacks recognized that the humor rested on exaggeration and the trickster's legendary guile. The tragedy, of course, was that, as the black intellectual James Weldon Johnson observed, "minstrelsy . . . fixed the tradition of the Negro as only an irresponsible, happy-go-lucky, wide-grinning, loud-laughing, banjo-playing, singing, dancing sort of being."[40]

Although, by the late nineteenth century, minstrel shows were giving way to other entertainment forms such as vaudeville, minstrelsy continued to extend its legacy. It was while watching a blackface act in Missouri in 1889—a performer in drag acting the role of a cook and singing "Old Aunt Jemima," a song that Billy Kersands had earlier adapted from an old slave work tune and popularized—that a white entrepreneur, Chris Rutt, settled on the image of a slave mammy—Aunt Jemima—to promote his new self-rising, ready-mix pancake flour. By then, urbanization, transportation, and innovations in food packaging (such as paper boxes) were inspiring a range of national brands of crackers, breakfast cereals, and other products. Rutt may have acted on a whim when he chose his product's trademark. But, as a familiar figure on the minstrel stage, Aunt Jemima was waiting to be discovered. And, by the time Rutt did so, heavyset mammy cooks were a staple in popular culture, joining such stereotypical black male servants as Sambo and Uncle Tom on trading cards, posters, cartoons, and advertisements. In 1890, when Rutt's company faltered because of weak marketing, the new owner, R. T. Davis, adopted a promotional strategy whereby a real black woman assumed the role of Aunt Jemima, promoting the pancake flour across the country with the catchphrase "I'se in town, honey." Davis thus fused "the mammy and the mass market," removing Aunt Jemima from the minstrel stage, and presenting her as "a 'real' slave woman." Even as minstrel shows faded as mass entertainment, they thus provided the inspiration for one of the most familiar, and ultimately controversial, of trademarks: the "slave in a box" who appeared on containers of pancake flour and countless advertisements. For decades, Aunt Jemima, wearing a brightly colored bandanna over her hair, smiling, and eager to serve, would continue to summon up nostalgic images of the mythical Old South. As a contented, nurturing mammy, she attested to minstrelsy's effectiveness in reaffirming the myths regarding idealized plantations and dutiful slaves.[41]

In contrast, by the late nineteenth century, the banjo—one of minstrelsy's defining musical instruments—had assumed new social meanings that distanced it from its slave and minstrel roots. An 1893 advertisement in *Stewart's Banjo and Guitar Journal* for a banjo concert at Philadelphia's Academy of Music thus asserted that "the banjo of to-day is altogether another instrument" from that which "was once monopolized by Negro minstrel performers." By then, one genteel banjo teacher proudly claimed that he had "a good class of pupils of the best society people." This transformation occurred largely through the efforts of a white entrepreneur, Samuel Swain Stewart, the scion of a moderately wealthy Philadelphia family in the patent medicine business. Although his parents had hoped that he would become a serious musician, Stewart settled on the banjo after attending a New York City minstrel show. By the time he died in 1898, he had established a kind of banjo empire through the mass production and marketing of the instrument, its parts, instruction books on how to play it, and sheet music. His story, as two banjo scholars have written, was about "how an instrument once marginalized because of its associations with lower classes became iconic of American culture at all levels, and in particular of middle-class pretensions to gentility." Indeed, by 1900, some people claimed that the banjo was the "National Musical Instrument."[42]

"Banjo culture" emerged quickly. In the early 1840s, even in New York City, it was virtually impossible to find a place that sold banjos. But, by 1866, according to one writer, there were "over 10,000 instruments" in New York, and one could hear their "rich melody" stretching "from the marble fronts of Fifth Avenue down to the slums of Baxter Street." Such expanding popularity owed much to several entrepreneurs, none more important than S. S. Stewart, who dedicated himself to elevating the instrument's reputation.[43]

A master of advertising, Stewart not only broadened the business of banjo production but deliberately set out to uplift it, enhancing its respectability and denying its African American roots. He argued that the banjo was "not of negro origin," criticized people who used the banjo in "vulgar" ways, claimed that "the Banjoist who cannot read music today is like the man who is unable to read a sign-post or a newspaper," and urged musicians to frequent the "parlor or drawing room . . . among gentlemen and ladies" rather than "go around among variety halls or drinking saloons to hear some negro or mountebank attempt to play the instrument." Still, although he chastened the boorish musician with "a cigar stump in the corner of his mouth . . . and Banjo in a bag under his arm," he was not opposed to selling his own instruments to such a person. At least once he even advised a student to "Black Up" and form a minstrel troupe. Although his banjos ranged in price from $10 to $100, Stewart increasingly identified them with, in his words, "the parlor, the drawing room, and the select musical entertainment." To buy a Stewart banjo would signify the consumer's edified status. Stewart's national promotional campaigns far surpassed those of others in the banjo business and helped spread the instrument's appeal into fashionable circles, including college campuses.[44]

The banjo's elevated position was, however, less securely anchored in the respectable genteel order than Stewart and others hoped. Ironically, for instance, some college students favored the banjo because they associated it with a lack of respectability. "How in the name of common sense," asked a Massachusetts newspaper in 1888, could "people who are supposed to be cultured" embrace an instrument "which was never intended for anything more than a barbaric sort of accompaniment, for the weird and wild songs and dances of the uncultivated Negro race"? But it was precisely because the banjo offered a counterpoint to the prevailing emphasis on order and discipline that many students embraced it. As the writer Mark Twain had laughingly insisted: "When you want *genuine music*—music that will come right home to you like a bad quarter, suffuse your system like strychnine whisky, . . . and break out on your hide like the pin-feather pimples on a pickled goose—when you want all this, just smash your piano, and invoke the glory-beaming banjo." An 1891 publication thus claimed that the banjo's "half barbaric twang" was a welcome contrast to the piano's "conventional" sound or the violin's "thin and tame" music: "The banjo sends out its lusty note in a charmingly stimulating way." It was this hint of decadence, rule breaking, and boundary crossing that attracted even upper-class, privileged white females to the instrument. Paradoxically, by 1900, the banjo had gained respectability by becoming something other than "the Negro instrument," but its spreading popularity also owed much to its less proper cultural baggage. "Give me the banjo," Mark Twain wrote, comparing it to "a hot whisky punch."[45]

That desire for the likes of "a hot whisky punch"—a defiant rejoinder to staid Victorian ideals—also helped explain the popularity of the celebrated boxer John L. Sullivan. A roughhouse brawler from Boston's Irish Catholic neighborhoods, Sullivan rose to fame in what had been an outlaw sport. By the mid-1880s, the Boston "Strong Boy" had become the recognized heavyweight champion of the world and arguably the century's most celebrated athlete.

Sullivan's popularity was crucial to boxing's rise in the 1880s from the depths to a modicum of respectability even among genteel groups. Over the several previous decades, the reputation of boxing—always suspect because of its blood-sport origins—had slipped even more because of its association with underworld crime and corruption, fixed fights, mob violence, and shaky organization. During the 1880s, the gradual adoption of the more "civilized" Marquis of Queensbury rules, the bringing of more order and stability to the sport, and creative journalistic coverage were vital in preparing the ring for the "Great John L."[46]

In that transition, no one was more important than the publisher Richard Kyle Fox and his *National Police Gazette*. The weekly paper, which had emerged in the 1840s by emphasizing social sins, crime, and sports, was sinking financially until Fox assumed control in 1876. He had arrived from Ireland only two years earlier, taking a job at the slumping

Gazette. Promptly, he resuscitated the failing journal, printing it on pink pages laced with themes of sex and violence. Despite the efforts of censors such as Anthony Comstock's Society for the Suppression of Vice to block its publication, the *Gazette* became a truly national publication—a staple in cheap hotels and male preserves such as saloons and barbershops, where it was known as the "barbershop bible." The *Gazette* "offered a particular kind of vulgarity," as one historian has written: "at the edge of acceptability but not quite beyond the pale," opening a small window on society's underside and peppering its contents with gossip, scandal, pictures of partially clad women, and stories about such individuals as Colorado's champion opium smoker (Beefsteak Mike). Crime stories typically focused on love crimes, providing lurid coverage of sexual misdeeds and illustrations of female victims with their skirts "in abandoned disarray," as a reader recalled: "It was the ankles and legs that really got me." By the 1880s, Fox was also including pictures of semiclothed female performers and featuring stories about alluring women—"gold diggers"—who victimized wealthy gentlemen. "Write! Write a lot!" he allegedly instructed his stable of hack writers when he locked them—and a supply of whiskey—in a room from Saturday afternoon until Monday morning. "Write the stuff the dailies don't dare use. Be as truthful as possible, but a story's a story." In 1883, the dapper-looking Fox opened a newly constructed seven-story building that highlighted New York City's skyline. By then, he was not only providing graphic accounts of blood sports such as cockfights and boxing but also asserting himself as a grand organizer of prizefighting, which was illegal in many states. It was Fox, always seeking news to boost his paper's circulation, who set out to clean up the sport, sponsoring bouts, classifying boxers by weight (light, middle, and heavy), guaranteeing the stakes, and widening boxing's audience.[47]

Although Sullivan and Fox reportedly disliked each other from their first meeting in 1881, their relationship proved symbiotic. Fox viewed Sullivan as an "unreliable boaster" but recognized the fighter's appeal, particularly after March 1881, when Sullivan knocked out an opponent known as "the Bull Head Terror" on a barge in the Hudson River. For Sullivan, born in 1858 to struggling Irish Catholic immigrant parents, Fox's promotion of boxing helped provide a shaky ladder of opportunity from Boston's mean and impoverished streets. Unlike his father, a common laborer whose jobs included digging trenches for sewers, John L. would seek esteem and social mobility in the world of sport. In 1878, after handily winning his first "exhibition" match, he began to attract attention. Three years later, he launched an audacious national tour, offering fifty dollars to anyone whom he could not knock out in four three-minute rounds. "I can lick any son-ofabitch in the house," he reportedly claimed. Never before had a single athlete set out on such a project. The tour made Sullivan a nationally recognizable figure and netted him over $6,000—"triple what a skilled laborer could make in a year," according to his biographer. He then set his sights on the "American champion," Patrick "Paddy" Ryan, "the Trojan Giant" from Troy, New York. Ryan, with Richard Kyle Fox speaking for him, agreed to a "championship of the world" match—apparently the first usage of that description. Fox subsequently publicized the contest grandly, touting Ryan as the "world's champion." On February 7, 1882, the bare-knuckle fight—illegal under Louisiana and Mississippi laws—occurred just across the Mississippi state line, allowing the boxers to cross quickly back into Louisiana at the end of the bout. Sullivan won in less than eleven minutes. Barely twenty-three, he was now the heavyweight champion of the world.[48]

Over the next several years, Sullivan became an entertainment wonder. In 1884, he conducted his most spectacular tour, which lasted eight months. Crisscrossing the country by train, and fighting in cities and small towns alike, he now offered $250 to anyone who could last four rounds with him. As his biographer has written, he "was literally challenging all of America to fight"—with the notable exception of African Americans, whom he refused to box because he saw himself as the champion of white America. Significantly, too, Sullivan fought under the Queensbury rules, spurning bare-knuckle boxing for gloves in order to protect his hands. The rules' three-minute rounds and ten-second limit on how long a fighter could stay down also worked to his advantage. Under the old London Prize Ring regulations, a knockdown ended a round, and the fallen opponent had thirty seconds to recover before resuming the fight, gaining valuable time against Sullivan, who worried little about conditioning and hoped to score a quick knockout. The tour earned him $80,000, more than the salary of the president of the United States. He soon learned that fans would pay just to see him even outside the ring, whether he was in skits onstage or showing up at exhibition baseball games (for which he once pocketed half the gate, almost $1,600). In the mid-1880s, he traveled with a minstrel show, earning $500 per week for twenty weeks, posing as "model statuary"—a gladiator, for example. The burgeoning sheet music industry produced songs about him, such as "Our Champion." His picture hung in taverns across the nation. Moreover, as the very proper E. L. Godkin observed in the genteel *Nation* magazine, Sullivan's popularity was no longer limited to the "coarse and uneducated and vicious class"; the fighter also enjoyed support "from higher sources."[49]

The Great John L. was, nevertheless, a curious object of such "higher" attention, not only because of his association with a much-disparaged gutter profession, but also because he did nothing to hide his own unsavory, loutish behavior. An alcoholic, he went on inebriated binges, scrapping in saloons, beating up on bystanders, and pummeling his wife, with whom he lived for a while out of wedlock. After a short-lived marriage, she took their son and left Sullivan. Still, the Boston Strongboy became one of the most famous Americans of his time. And he did so not as a heralded inventor, politician, entrepreneur, or general, but as a professional athlete—a previously improbable calling for a public hero. Ironically, his much-publicized character flaws only added to his aura. He wasted money rather than saving or investing it. He was a bully. He was a drunk. He spurned physical training to keep in shape, sometimes ballooning to over three hundred pounds.[50]

Still, his legend grew. For one thing, his success story resonated in a culture that extolled self-improvement, individual effort, and personal triumph. For another, in an increasingly mechanized era that celebrated power—both individual and national—he resembled a "magnificent machine of flesh and blood" and a "wonderful engine of destruction," as people described him. And, of particular importance, his raw, undisciplined character contradicted the "civilizing" trends of system, order, and regimentation. As his biographer has observed: "In an age that sought to discipline itself in the school, the factory, and the office, he seemed a wild throwback to a more ungoverned time." Yet, while he pushed against modernizing trends, he aided others—for instance, boxing's development as a commercial sport and the athlete-as-celebrity phenomenon. His fame rested on two worlds, old and new. Sullivan's 1889 defense of his title against Jake Kilrain in the last championship fight under the old London rules—a brutal affair that lasted seventy-five rounds and more than two hours under a sweltering Mississippi sun—and even his defeat in 1892 at the hands of "Gentleman Jim" Corbett, when Sullivan absorbed a withering punishment before finally falling, only added to his mystique. After he stopped boxing, he remained an entertainment legend. By the time he died in 1918, males young and old liked to brag about how they had shaken the hand of someone who had shaken the hand of the great John L. Sullivan.[51]

Although Sullivan achieved fame as a prizefighter, he had always wanted to play baseball—a sport that by the 1870s also drew on roistering athletes and audiences and offered a possible springboard to public recognition and even wealth. Ultimately, however, like much of popular entertainment, it combined nostalgia with modernizing trends. Baseball, like boxing, merged older values with the centralization, standardized rules, and marketing strategies that characterized America's spreading industrialization. Over several decades in the mid-nineteenth century, the game emerged as a truly national sport with standardized rules and a tightening business structure. Going into the 1850s, the nature of the game had varied from place to place. No firm understandings had existed regarding such questions as how many players composed a team, how many outs would retire a side, whether hitting base runners with a thrown ball could constitute an out, and even what shape the field should be. By the Civil War, however, the "New York game" (which included a diamond-shaped field, foul lines, nine players per team, three outs per inning, and nine innings per game) was dominant. It took hold in part because of the technology that helped distribute other forms of popular culture across the nation—the railroad, the telegraph, and the growing national press—but also because corporate-minded individuals consciously fashioned the game to fit their own tastes, substituting, in the words of the historian Jules Tygiel, "the chaos of townball . . . with a more ordered, rational variation."[52]

At first glance, much about baseball seemed alien to the new industrialized world and resembled a throwback to an earlier, pastoral era. After all, baseball, unlike the emerging economy, was outside the domain of the clock. Games moved according to their own momentum, working through outs and innings, not the number of minutes left to play. "Take your time, kid," teammates could call to their pitcher, "all the time in the world." The playing area itself, especially the expansive outfield, summoned up images of rural America, uncrowded and leisurely. Yet, in major ways, baseball meshed well with the emerging corporate culture. Like the urban, corporate world, it had rules, regularized procedures, and standardized areas. Play, it turned out, contained important lessons for work. Baseball players, like factory workers, learned the skills of particular assignments and played specialized positions. They also learned the importance of practice and discipline. Teamwork was crucial; indeed, the word *sacrifice* in baseball summed up a moment when the batter deliberately abandoned individual success in order to advance a teammate around the bases. And the much-quoted consolation, "That's the way the ball bounces," was ideal for an industrial world that blamed misfortunes and disastrous times on bad luck, not on the system itself.[53]

It was, however, the emphasis on statistics that especially aligned baseball with the industrial mind-set. "Almost from the beginning," according to one baseball expert, "the new sport of baseball was a mathematical wonder." Baseball's statistical dimension was the creation of an English immigrant, Henry Chadwick, who, in 1860, devised the first "box score," a capsule summary that charted the hits, runs, and outs of each player in a game. Soon Chadwick was computing the batting averages and "earned runs" that allowed factual comparisons of players' records. This appeal of statistics resonated perfectly in an era that found truth in quantification. In the post–Civil War period, insurance companies devised actuarial tables, the federal census bureau started cross-tabulating data, and emerging social science disciplines such as sociology relied on statistical studies. Through numbers, according to one reformer, it was possible to "measure a nation's moral and religious improvement; its health, wealth, strength, and safety." Certainly, Chadwick shared this faith in the power of statistics to effect beneficial social change: baseball's numbers and uniform standards could inspire "a moral recreation" to counteract urban evils. From Chadwick's perspective, box scores were, thus, nothing less than "mini-morality plays," as Jules Tygiel has written, serving "accountability," efficiency, and the proper distribution of rewards. Before his death in 1908, Chadwick played a pivotal role in transforming baseball from an amateur game into a truly national sport that was big business and featured professional athletes.[54]

Baseball's evolution in the latter half of the nineteenth century met a number of shifting needs. Prior to the 1860s, social need gave rise to a "base ball fraternity." In Eastern cities, dozens of fraternal organizations emerged, drawing primarily from a middle-class base of clerks and small proprietors, but also including many skilled workers and even members of volunteer fire companies. These clubs included bylaws, officers, membership dues, dances, dinners, and other events that spanned cultural lines. "The game appealed simultaneously to the culture of the urban streets," according to one interpreter, "and to the respectable and newly vigorous culture of middle-class Victorian men." In 1858, these amateur baseball clubs established the National Association of Base Ball Players, aimed at protecting the game's fraternal elements. By the late 1860s, some 350 clubs across the nation were part of the association.[55]

In the wake of the Civil War, baseball also met a patriotic need. Some observers hoped that the game, whose popularity had spread among the soldiers, would have a unifying influence. Baseball might, as one newspaper asserted, "close the National Wounds opened by the late war," substituting friendly competitive fields for those "lately crimsoned by their brothers' blood in mortal combat." In that context, a series of myths grew around baseball, tying it to national ideals and values. It was supposed to provide, for example, a ladder of social mobility by which poor boys could find success. In reality, the belief that baseball furnished such opportunity was much exaggerated, certainly in the professional ranks. Although a few of the new immigrants from Southern and Eastern Europe prospered in the professional leagues, almost all players were native-born Americans from lower-middle- and middle-class backgrounds. In the impoverished, crowded urban neighborhoods of the new immigrants, there was seldom the space or the time for or any interest in a game where established players tended to resent and mistreat new arrivals with Jewish, Italian, and Slavic roots. Moreover, although several dozen African Americans had played organized baseball in the 1870s and 1880s, by the century's end professional club owners agreed informally to keep blacks out of the game. Still, the powerful myth that baseball allowed lower-class youths to pull themselves up the social and economic ladder was significant: however untrue, it verified beliefs that the United States was, indeed, a democratic nation that rewarded hard work and individual striving. Baseball's democratic impulses supposedly influenced even onlookers. "The spectator at a ball game is no longer a statesman, a lawyer, broker, doctor, merchant, or artisan," insisted one individual, "but just plain every-day man, with a heart full of fraternity and good will to all his fellow men." "Baseball," agreed the player and sports entrepreneur Albert Spalding, "is a democratic game."[56]

While baseball helped confirm democratic values, it also met the emotional needs of a growing number of young males, who, by the 1880s, supplied the bulk of the game's players and spectators. On this level, according to one scholar, baseball reflected "a youth movement, fomented in the face of disapproving authority" that was both "a counterpart to 19th-century revivalism and temperance," and "a precursor to 20th-century movies and rock and roll." It supplied a powerful feeling of camaraderie at a time when immigration and dramatic population shifts made cities especially disorienting places. A team, like a gang or a club, provided "instantaneous community." "We were a band of brothers," recalled one fellow about his team. Moreover, the game's structure encouraged individual recognition, whether the focus was on the batter, the pitcher, or the fielder. Even the box scores ratified the importance of individual members of teams. The sport likewise supplied a welcome sense of order with its fixed boundaries, positions, and responsibilities; in a disorderly, risky world, the baseball field supplied a kind of sanctuary. Distracted and busy parents might chastise their adolescent sons for playing ball instead of doing chores, but the young men found security and fun in what the historian Ronald Story has described as the baseball diamond's "country of the young."[57]

Baseball fulfilled a variety of social and cultural needs, but it also grew as an economic institution. And its economic trajectory, like that of industrialization generally, was toward consolidation, monopolistic control, and labor conflict. The professional game developed quickly following the organization in 1869 of the Cincinnati Red Stockings, the first all-salaried team. Paying its players an attractive salary averaging around $1,000 per year at a time when common laborers earned around $350, the team traveled as far as California on the newly completed transcontinental railroad, drawing substantial crowds. The Red Stockings also showed other cities that a baseball team could boost its home base. "Glory, they've advertised the city," commented a happy Cincinnati entrepreneur, "advertised us, sir, and helped our business."[58]

In 1871, the lure of profits encouraged owners of other teams to start a new league, the National Association of Professional Base Ball Players, in nine cities in the Northeast and Midwest. Instability haunted these early efforts, however, as teams came and went. Rowdy, drunken fans sometimes interrupted the games. After the league fell apart in 1875, William Hulbert, a wealthy wholesale grocer and coal dealer, took the lead in forging the National League of Professional Baseball Clubs. Determined to elevate the game, Hulbert, the president of the Chicago White Stockings, banned the sale of liquor at games, boosted ticket prices to fifty cents at a time when laborers' wages averaged from $1 to $3 daily, and scheduled afternoon games during the week when few working-class people could attend. In 1882, to entice workers back to the ballparks, six rival owners, four of whom owned breweries, launched the American Association of Baseball Clubs. They halved the price of tickets and sold beer. They also infuriated the National League by luring away players with higher salaries. But this cutthroat competition did not last long. Demonstrating the growing power of management, the leagues quickly signed an agreement establishing a $2,500 salary cap and embracing a "reserve" clause, which blocked players from changing teams during the season. In 1885, angry players formed a labor union, the National Brotherhood of Baseball; four years later, some of them started their own league, the Brotherhood of Professional Baseball Players, which banned the reserve clause and endorsed profit sharing. The established leagues fought back, labeling the players as revolutionaries bent on establishing, in Henry Chadwick's words, "a system of terrorism." Starved for resources, the players' organization crumbled.[59]

While baseball's formative history included the cutthroat economic competition and labor conflicts that marked the late nineteenth century, it also provided its own versions of upstart entrepreneurs with riches and monopolistic control on their minds. A prime example was the talented player Albert Spalding, who ultimately joined management and aspired to be the John D. Rockefeller of baseball. Just as Rockefeller integrated the oil business, controlling it from drilling to sales, Spalding established a highly lucrative sporting-goods business in which his plants manufactured baseball gloves, balls, and bats and moved the products through more than twenty thousand retail accounts.[60]

On one level, baseball's soaring popularity thus attested to the power of the emerging industrial, bureaucratic order to assimilate Americans to a new regimen. But, on another level, the story—like that of popular culture as a whole—demonstrated common Americans' ingenious ways of adapting to that new order, of shrewdly and creatively adjusting to the rising force of a corporate world while still having fun. "*Play* ball!" in that regard was a summons to enjoy oneself, not a subscription to the machine age. Baseball provided temporary escape from daily routines. In an industrial world of rapid flux and unfamiliar circumstances, baseball was intelligible. Like the detective novel, which made its debut at roughly the same time, baseball featured clear-cut endings as well as examples of individual excellence and heroism. For good reason, the sport struck a popular chord. Grassroots enthusiasm, from youngsters' proliferating sandlot games to town teams, accompanied and boosted the game's professional development. In the several decades after the Civil War, Midwestern villages fielded amateur teams and held tournaments. A passerby in Croswell, Michigan, asked what a crowd was all about. "Ball, you d—d fool," shouted some small boys. Baseball had become so important that newspaper editors sometimes felt compelled to offer excuses when local teams lost. Although the team sport of baseball in many ways fit with the emerging industrial script, the game caught on because of its association with daily experiences, conversations, memories, and community loyalties.[61]

Amid economic conflicts and modernizing trends, baseball offered a symbol of stability and rootedness. In that sense, perhaps nothing was more important than the concept of the "home team," whose support provided a counterpoint to the dizzying mobility that accompanied immigration and urban growth. In order to score runs, players had to cross "home plate." A familiar refrain in a song that ultimately became the sport's anthem, "Take Me Out to the Ball Game," pledged the fan to "root, root, root for the home team." And the game's official—the umpire—assumed villainous characteristics when he seemed to jeopardize the hometown team's chances. Team owners discovered that umpire baiting could be profitable. Albert Spalding thus claimed that fans who criticized umpires were simply participating in democracy's wondrous rituals of opposing tyrants. "Mother, may I slug the umpire, / May I slug him right away," asked one poet in 1886. "Let me climb his frame, dear mother, / While the happy people shout; / I'll not kill him, dearest mother, / I will only knock him out."[62]

Baseball's soaring popularity—like that of John L. Sullivan or the emerging sport of college football—reflected the growth by the late nineteenth century of a sporting ideology replete with masculine anxieties. A kind of masculinity crisis was building, particularly among middle-class and privileged males who feared that a host of social and economic changes jeopardized their manhood. Economically, the growing corporate world seemed to threaten the ideals of autonomy and independence, turning increasing numbers of men into cogs for a "banker's world," as the writer Henry Adams described it. Additionally, as the frontier closed, many observers fretted that rapidly expanding cities were producing a male "milksop" who lived "an unambitious namby-pamby life," in the words of one magazine. The expanding number of women in the workforce was another source of worry. The fact that women now constituted a substantial majority of elementary school teachers stirred concerns that females were educating a bunch of "sissies"—effeminate boys, "flabby, feeble, mawkish . . . chicken-hearted, cold and fearful," according to *Cosmopolitan* magazine. Even the large number of female Sunday school teachers bothered some men. "The boy is a hero-worshipper," one male insisted, "and his hero cannot be found in a Sunday school which is manned by women." Meanwhile, in the rising professions of law, medicine, engineering, and industrial management, there was less contact with the time-honored virtues of physical labor. Success manuals increasingly recommended combining "brain power" with "muscular vigor" and "manly sport."[63]

By the 1880s, popular mass sports, which the middle class had once rejected as debilitating wastes of time, were booming. Sports, according to the emerging ideology, would improve health, advance a moral social order, build character, discourage effeminacy, and divert sexual energies from the bedroom to the more innocent setting of the playing field. Even the mere watching of an athletic contest could reportedly be a transforming experience. "It is far better for the young boys and the old boys to be out in the light and the open air, watching a clean and thrilling struggle that is played where all may see," argued one writer, "than to sit with legs crossed under a taproom table, dealing out grimy cards or grimier stories."[64]

For many wealthy and upper-middle-class sons of America's elite, football held a special appeal. "The game is a mimic battle-field," wrote Caspar Whitney, the future editor of an outdoor magazine. A player, he continued, must "be trustworthy, observant, vigilant, have courage, pluck, fortitude, daring, and a spirit of self sacrifice to duty. . . . [He must] have a well-balanced manhood, a healthy mind in a sound body." That perspective turned football into what two sports historians have described as "the consuming collegiate passion of the late nineteenth century."[65]

While boxing and baseball initially tapped the support of marginal economic and social groups, college football depended on a strikingly different clientele: privileged young men who attended the nation's premier academic institutions. It was from the campuses of private Eastern schools such as Harvard, Yale, and Princeton that football emerged. Students at first took the initiative, playing informal games with as many as twenty-five players per team, no uniforms, and no coaches. The games at that point resembled soccer matches; players could neither run with nor throw the ball, and each side tried to kick or bat the round ball through goal posts. Harvard, however, favored rules that tilted the contests more toward rugby, with ball carriers and the use of physical force to stop them. In 1875, when Yale first played Harvard, rugby-style football took hold. By the 1880s, the game was extremely violent, with rules that permitted players to hit each other with closed fists. Several of the elite colleges began playing Thanksgiving Day games, which became major events, attracting the nation's social elite. Before the 1893 Thanksgiving clash between Yale and Princeton, for example, a parade up New York City's Fifth Avenue took four hours, while multimillionaires such as Cornelius Vanderbilt watched.[66]

Football's violence and changing rules reflected a merger of masculine and corporate ideologies. The desire among middle-class and privileged males to build "virile, manly qualities," in Theodore Roosevelt's words, was pivotal. Roosevelt believed that football's brutality provided an important training field in manly efficiency. The sport's violence, which caused broken limbs, smashed faces, and even several deaths, seemed essential to offset the dangers of "softness" and overcivilization. Yale's Frederick Remington, before heading West to paint scenes that glorified a mythical frontier of rugged males, spread slaughterhouse blood on his football uniform in order to create the proper effect. Princeton president Francis Patton was convinced that "some of the very best elements of manhood may emerge" on the football field. Another university official admired players with "a broken collar bone occasionally" and scorned young men "dedicated to croquet." Harvard president Charles Eliot concurred that "effeminacy and luxury are worse evils than brutality." A University of Pennsylvania medical doctor wrote excitedly after Penn won a game in a "quagmire of cold mud" that "those eleven frozen, purple, shivering, chattering players" deserved praise from "every one who loves manliness and courage." It was, thus, not coincidental that Theodore Roosevelt selected a football metaphor when he urged Americans to "hit the line hard: don't foul and don't shirk, but hit the line hard."[67]

But, if manliness was a vital goal, so was corporate efficiency. In that regard, as the historian David Wallace Adams has observed, football was both antimodern and modern, blending raw violence with tight organization, "creating the new American man—half Boone, half Rockefeller." Unlike baseball, football was very much a game of the clock; appropriately, the man who more than anyone "invented" the modern version of the game was Walter Camp, an employee of the New Haven Clock Company. A weak and sickly child, he had dutifully cultivated athletic skills before playing football at Yale, where he remained as an unpaid coach for years. Still working at the nearby clock company, he was determined to bring corporate order, systematization, and rigor to football. He coached his Yale team as if it were a hierarchically ordered business; players were supposed to learn the benefits of discipline, efficiency, and teamwork. Under Camp, the coach's role resembled that of another symbol of the industrial world: the engineer. And, like an engineer, Camp redesigned football. He helped distinguish football from rugby by allowing tackling below the waist. And, as Yale's representative at the annual rules conventions in the late nineteenth century, he devised two major rules changes. One established a line of scrimmage that gave the ball to one team at a time (requiring someone to snap the ball to a quarterback); the other required a series of downs during which the offensive team had to advance the ball a required yardage (initially, five yards) or relinquish it to the opposition. Under Camp's tutelage, Yale turned into a football powerhouse.[68]

While the ideologies of masculinity and corporate efficiency molded college football, it was largely the practical needs of the evolving newspaper business that popularized the sport beyond the Ivy League campuses of the Northeast. Not since the days of the penny press had there been such a revolution in the print industry. By the end of the nineteenth century, improvements in transportation, communication, and technology had inspired a flourishing book trade, a host of new or expanded magazines, and the astounding success of fledgling newspaper publishers such as Joseph Pulitzer and William Randolph Hearst. In 1883, Pulitzer bought a floundering daily, the *New York World,* boosting its circulation within a decade from 15,000 to 2 million. He did so through sensationalistic stories, illustrations, Sunday supplements, women's features, comics, and sports coverage. After Hearst purchased the *New York Journal* in 1895, he used Pulitzer's strategies to his own spectacular advantage. College football was a major beneficiary as well. Courtesy of newspapers such as the *World* and the *Journal,* a sport whose following was initially limited to elite universities in the Northeast found a national audience.[69]

The marriage between newspapers and college football was, in many respects, coincidental. By November, with the baseball and horse-racing seasons at an end, newspapers were looking for sports stories. Thanksgiving football games helped fill the void. So did the fact that football contests occurred on Saturdays, typically slow news days because the courts and city offices were closed. For the expanded Sunday editions, football provided a convenient and welcome source of news.[70]

The press did more, however, than broaden football's audience; it also linked the sport to dominant—but also conflicting—cultural beliefs, myths, and narratives about work, play, success, college life, morality, heroism, manliness, gender, and race. "Football reporting of the 1880s and 1890s was highly formulaic," as the historian Michael Oriard has shown, and reporters filled their columns with hyperbolic accounts of heroic struggle, rugged exploits, and community spirit. "It was a royal battle of gladiators, such as were fought in the days of Hector and Ajax," the *New York World* exulted about the 1891 Harvard-Yale game. A year later, when Yale played Princeton, the *World* cheered the glories of manly personal encounter: "For two hours it had been muscle against muscle, and bone against bone, and every body among them had met a foe-man worthy of his steel. Then again, every athlete among them was a freeborn college boy and a fighter from way back." Illustrations typically added a powerful visual narrative to such purple prose about the "meanings" of football, which circulated across the country via the wire services and newspaper syndicates.[71]

These written and illustrated narratives were loaded also with telling descriptions of comely women who cheered on their brave warriors. One illustration showed two attractive young women comforting a battered player, who had bandages on his head and arm. At the 1892 Harvard-Yale game, the *New York Herald* located "the American 'best girl,' no longer demure and retiring but roused to a high state of tension" as she rooted "for the lads whose ribbons she wore." Elsewhere in the crowd, "pretty girls who never behaved so surprisingly before threw themselves into their escorts' arms." From this perspective, the era's emerging New Woman (whom the popular press identified as a college-educated, independent-minded, and professional female outside the traditional women's sphere) remained manageable, still rooting for her man. As the *New York Times* reported about one game: "The college girl was there and numerous. . . . When her particular Ivanhoe lay down on his back in a puddle, . . . she simply clapped her hands. The tighter he hugged the ball the more she loved him."[72]

While football's narratives turned women into cheerleaders, they also provided commentaries on race—particularly when the Carlisle Indian School played the Eastern powerhouses. Richard Henry Pratt, who founded the coeducational school in Pennsylvania in 1879, was among an important group of humanitarian reformers hoping that forced acculturation would separate young Native Americans from their tribal heritage, imbue them with the ways of white civilization, and thereby save their race from extinction. In 1893, after several dozen Carlisle students begged Pratt to let them play football, he relented. Several years earlier, after a player broke his leg, Pratt had halted the school's program. But now he saw an opportunity to counter the images of treacherous and savage Indians that prevailed in the Wild West shows. "Buffalo Bill travels all over the land parading what he intends the people to believe to be the particular qualities of the Indian," he stated angrily. "No man ever put a greater lie before the public than Buffalo Bill." Pratt instructed his young charges that, in order "to make a record for your race," they must never hit a rival player and must play the best teams in the country. Soon Carlisle, which lacked a stadium of its own, became a legendary road team, competing with the nation's top football programs and sometimes beating them. But, while Pratt waxed enthusiastic about how Carlisle's players would improve whites' perceptions of Native Americans, Carlisle's games in fact evoked images of frontier warfare. Thus, when Carlisle lost to Columbia in 1900, the *New York Journal* observed that "brawn, muscle and speed scrapping over a slippery football" had replaced historical battles involving "tomahawks and rifles with lives at stake. Of course, the redskins were beaten. They always were." After Brown beat Carlisle in 1897, the *New York Herald* noted that the "victorious paleface" had "lured the wily redskin into the open, and there scalped him with his own tomahawk." A year earlier, the *New York World* had described the Brown players as "representing the highest type of New England culture," while Carlisle drew "from the uncivilized sections of the far West. . . . Brains won in the contest, as they always do in the long run."

When Carlisle played Yale, according to the *Journal*, the result was "a new and modernized phase of the Indian question."[73]

That complicated "Indian question" could, nevertheless, stir mixed emotions, as white rooters for Carlisle made clear. One sympathetic cartoonist portrayed Sitting Bull commenting on a football game: "In old days pale faces whip old Injuns heap. Now young Injuns lick palefaces." Some whites who cheered for Carlisle may, like Pratt, have been looking for evidence that Native Americans were adapting to non-Indian culture. "The Indians have invaded the East, and the people have not been scalped, burned alive or tomahawked," wrote one reporter. At least a few whites no doubt believed that their nation had treated Native Americans badly and wanted Carlisle's players to win at least symbolic victories on the gridiron. But perhaps "many white spectators cheered for the Indians, not because they were civilized, nor because they had been wronged, but merely because they were Indians," the historian David Wallace Adams has speculated. "Without Indians there would have been no Frontier Myth. . . . To imagine the American story without the Indian was, in effect, to imagine an America not worth imagining. In this sense, the villain in the American drama was as vital to the play as the hero." Against the larger historical backdrop, whites did not lose even if Carlisle won. "Here was the beauty of it all," according to Adams. "It was all just a game. However fans might play out their imaginations on the mythic space of the gridiron, real space—that is to say, the frontier—was safely in white hands. Clearly, it was a win-win situation." Still, the Carlisle Indians could claim some symbolic victories of their own. They had played in entertainment venues that belonged to the nation's elite. In doing so, they had, as the star player Bemus Pierce said, demonstrated that they could "do most anything." The legendary Jim Thorpe thus would never forget the moment when he stood in the center of Harvard's field, with "the biggest crowd I had ever seen watching us," and kicked the winning goal. The larger society hardly provided an equal competitive setting. But, on the stage of popular culture, the social script was sometimes more fluid and flexible.[74]

When whites cheered for Carlisle, perhaps engaging in what Adams has described as "a kind of border-crossing, a diluted form of . . . 'playing [Indian],'" they also aligned football with a significant impulse in the developing entertainment industry. Border crossing was much of what popular culture was about. That theme was evident in the circuses, the Wild West shows, J. H. Haverly's minstrels, and a variety of sports where the public could peek across at the other side—a side that contrasted with the tightening hold of the job, or the restrictions of traditional morality, or the organized efficiency of the modern, corporate age. Yet audiences could enjoy a sense of security as they paid their admission because they were, after all, only momentarily peeking at different worlds—and, ironically, worlds with rules and tendencies that in themselves fit, and even helped shape, the emerging industrial society.[75]

4

"THE BILLION-DOLLAR SMILE"

From Burlesque to Vaudeville and Amusement Parks

During the late nineteenth century and the early twentieth, the entertainment industry expanded at a furious rate. Joining circuses, enlarged minstrel shows, and sports were burlesque and vaudeville. Like their amusement counterparts, burlesque and vaudeville reflected the industrial trend of consolidation. Yet they followed contrasting audience trajectories: burlesque moved from several lavishly staged spectacles in respectable theaters to "leg shows"; its initially clever satires, which drew large, mixed crowds, increasingly featured seminude females who danced for largely male audiences in seedy surroundings. Vaudeville, on the other hand, worked steadily to shed its questionable reputation, courted family audiences, and gave voice to immigrant America. Meanwhile, many of those urban, immigrant patrons turned to yet another creation: amusement parks, of which Coney Island alone eventually featured several dazzling venues. Burlesque, vaudeville, and the amusement parks, all in their own ways, both threatened and accommodated still-powerful Victorian values. They also underlined ways in which marginal and controversial entertainments moved from the peripheries, helping forge an amusement economy—"the billion-dollar smile," as one publicity agent described it, stretching "from Seattle to New York, from Bangor to the Gulf," mirroring and advancing the developing consumer culture of display and spectacle.[1]

That "billion-dollar smile" hardly delighted the nation's more privileged groups, however. In the late nineteenth century, the spreading web of inexpensive amusements sent cultural elites scurrying for more protected sanctuaries, where they attempted to turn high art into something almost sacred, free from vulgar tastes and transmutations. This "sacralization of culture" represented an elite effort to reclaim music, drama, and the arts from the unwashed masses. As the orchestra leader Theodore Thomas said condescendingly: "Those old giants [the great classical composers] said their prayers when they wished to write an immortal work. The modern man takes a drink." Self-styled cultural arbiters such as Thomas sought to preserve art for the "better class, the most refined and intelligent of our citizens," the "high-minded, the pure and the virtuous" people who appreciated true quality and beauty. A leading symbol of cultural sacralization was the Boston Symphony Orchestra, which the stockbroker Henry Lee Higginson founded in 1881. As one editor said: "The Boston Symphony Orchestra is Mr. Henry L. Higginson's yacht, his racing-stable, his library, and his art gallery, or it takes the place of what these things are to the other men of wealth with other tastes." To Higginson and his wealthy compatriots, great artistic and musical works should be inviolate, separate from what elites saw as popular drivel. The purpose of high culture was to uplift. Respectful, quiet, and passive audiences should absorb the civilizing messages and cultural truths of classical music and literature—courtesy of a select few definers of taste. Frivolous entertainment and the untutored, poorer classes had no place in the hallowed halls of the emerging artistic institutions of America's privileged groups. Hence, in 1876, the report to the Smithsonian Institution in Washington, DC, of its secretary, Joseph Henry, asserted "that the Institution is not a popular establishment and that it . . . is in a considerable degree incompatible with continued interruption from large numbers of visitors." Similarly, one writer joked in 1884 that New York City's Lenox Library really wanted to keep people away: "*But why?* To keep the pretty books from being spoiled. *Why! Who would spoil the pretty books?* The public. *How?* By reading them." The writer Mark Twain mocked the new rules of an art museum, which required that he leave his cane in the cloakroom. "Leave my cane! Leave my cane!" he responded wryly. "Then how do you expect me to poke holes through the oil paintings?"[2]

As "high" art and "low" entertainment separated in the late nineteenth century, the popular theater verged on becoming a male-only province. Especially appealing to male audiences were a variety of performances that were more and more sexual in nature. Some drew on a form that had emerged in the 1840s—"model statuary," in which semiclad performers posed as "living reproductions" from biblical stories or ancient sculpture and paintings. While some of these "living pictures" tried not to offend middle-class audiences, many were mere excuses for sexual display. One newspaper speculated that audiences attended "because of depraved taste rather than pure love of art." Enthusiastic male patrons stomped, cheered, and whistled in their eagerness to see the women. Theater managers typically hired anonymous women at low wages to titillate the audiences. Concert saloons combined alcohol with female waitresses and performers, turning into places of "avowed Bacchus and Phallus worship," according to a New York City newspaper in 1862.[3]

In the decade before the Civil War, the English immigrant Laura Keene momentarily resisted such risqué entertainment by attempting to provide respectable theater that appealed particularly to women. Her efforts to succeed in the world of male theater managers were fraught with difficulty and controversy, however, and, ultimately, she herself became a reluctant popularizer of leg shows. Keene came to New York City in 1851, after a failed marriage to a vagrant husband. With two daughters to support, she jumped from acting to the tough, competitive world of theater management. In 1856, she opened Laura Keene's Theater on Broadway, promising a clean environment with no cheap gallery section or liquor. She courted a middle-class female audience with "problem plays," dealing sympathetically with women as victims of seduction and prostitution, and critiquing the male sexual double standard. Keene faced huge challenges. For one thing, a growing backlash against the rising women's rights movement, which the 1848 Seneca Falls conference had done much to publicize, encouraged male critics to dismiss Keene's efforts as another attempt at "petticoat government." Also, her failed marriage helped stigmatize her as a "woman with a past." This questionable reputation hardly benefited from the fact that funding for her theater venture came largely from a married man who had left his wife. One male theater critic, although conceding that Keene was an effective manager, complained that she was "also a woman and an actress; in other words, she is mentally unstable and professionally vain." Her plays nevertheless often drew substantial numbers of women, and she produced the hit of the 1858–59 season, *Our American Cousin.* Although she paid $1,000 for the script, two Philadelphia managers hired a secretary to sit in the audience and copy the dialogue, which they then used to restage the drama in their own theater, to considerable profit. When Keene sued, a judge ruled that the play was a public performance and anyone could use it.[4]

In 1860, desperately seeking new formulas that would keep her theater alive, Keene devised a play, *The Seven Sisters,* featuring women in what the *New York Clipper* described as "shockingly low-necked dresses" and "tight-fitting clothes." Keene was aware that the legitimate theaters were quickly disappearing, unable to compete with the booming concert saloons. And she recognized that the market favored male audiences. The financial power of such patrons was evident when *The Seven Sisters* ran uninterrupted for a record eight and a half months. Male reviewers hailed the "short-petticoated ladies," their "hundred miscellaneous legs in flesh-colored tights," and their plunging necklines: "a bevy of beauties, dressed in good, tight-fitting clothes," as one man happily described them. Keene, who had set out to please female audiences, had ended up providing visual delights for men.

Suffering from ill health, she soon left the theater, leaving behind an ironic legacy: a leg show, built around displays of the female body.[5]

In mid-1861, a year after Keene's *The Seven Sisters* opened, a phenomenon known famously as "the Menken" further enlivened such female spectacle. Performing at the Green Street Theater in Albany, New York, as the male protagonist in *Mazeppa*, Adah Isaacs Menken catapulted to fame by wearing skin-colored tights that made her appear naked. The play, which had become a theater staple, included a scene in which enemies tied the noble Mazeppa to the back of a wild horse to die of exposure. Traditionally, because actors were reluctant to undertake the stunt, the scene had included a cloth dummy. But Menken accomplished the feat herself. Spread-eagled, and tied faceup, she stayed atop the horse as it cantered up a wood-and-canvas mountain that towered forty feet off the back of the stage. Over the next five years, she drew huge audiences as she toured from the Northeast to San Francisco, then to Europe, and finally to New York City's prestigious Broadway Theater. Menken was a sensation, not simply because she played the male role and performed the dangerous stunt, but because she revealed so much of her body. When publicity about the play suggested that she was truly naked, she deliberately refused to deny that possibility. One advertisement revealingly displayed a woman, partially unclothed, tied provocatively to a rearing horse's back. Menken's largely male audiences turned her into perhaps the world's highest-paid actress, while photographs and imitations of her, as well as songs such as the "Mazeppa Waltz" and the "Mazeppa Gallop," became a minor industry.[6]

Intelligent and free-spirited as well as alluring, Menken took pride in her independence, learning six languages and aspiring to be a serious poet. Critics believed that she needed "taming down," but she delighted in subverting the Victorian roles of true womanhood and the frail woman. She smoked in public, wore crimson lipstick, and reveled in the scandalous gossip about her stormy marriage to and divorce from the prizefighter John Heenan as well as her much-publicized affairs with the French novelist Alexandre Dumas père and the English poet Algernon Charles Swinburne. (She rejected Swinburne after he told her: "My darling, a woman with such beautiful legs need not bother about poetry.") She was married and divorced at least four times. Marriage, she wrote, reduced women to "nonentities": "Good wives are rarely clever and clever women are rarely good." Like P. T. Barnum, she recognized the importance of controversy in advancing a performer's career and, thus, carefully kept reshaping who she seemed to be. "She claimed fathers from the margins of society," according to her biographer, "from groups most Americans considered not quite white; they were usually Jewish, Irish, or Spanish." Such ambiguities added to the mysteries and suggestion of danger that surrounded her.[7]

Menken's appeal also owed much to the destabilizing effects of the

Civil War and changes within the middle class itself. Her Albany appearance as Mazeppa came barely two months after the war began. The bloody conflict initially devastated theater attendances, forcing many theaters to close. Large crowds nevertheless turned out to see Menken throughout the rest of the year. By then, the war was boosting the economies of Northern commercial cities, providing spending money that more people could use for entertainment. Menken undoubtedly offered a provocative diversion from wartime anxieties. But how she did so was significant. Among the Civil War's disruptive aspects was its challenge to identity—that of the nation itself, certainly, but also that of gender. As women participated in the war effort, working in hospitals, planting fields, and running family businesses, traditional gender lines blurred. Against that backdrop, Menken's cross-dressing acts were particularly meaningful. As a woman in the part of a man, she raised questions about her identity anyhow, but her rumored nudity pushed her beyond such noted breeches performers as Charlotte Cushman, who spurned erotic exhibitionism and the reputation of a "shape actress." Male audiences might see the alluring Menken as sexually available, but women could envy her freedom from corsets and billowing skirts. One San Francisco writer rebuked her for "bewitching" young, innocent females. The danger that Menken posed from this angle was in her implicit message that gender was, indeed, only a role, a performance.[8]

In that regard, Menken's acts resonated with many in the middle class who were engaged in their own "performances." The gathering flood of manuals and magazines on proper dress and behavior had, in effect, created a theater of "bourgeois etiquette." While printed guides had helped the antebellum middle class define itself, by the 1860s a new generation was engaged in considerable redefining. The evolving, broadening middle class was becoming more worldly, chafing under strict genteel codes, and loosening former restrictions of self-display concerning such things as cosmetics and fine dress. According to the historian Karen Haltunnen: "The American middle classes after 1850 were beginning to accept the necessity and legitimacy of social forms they had once condemned as social hypocrisy and to accept a new view of character as a theatrical part to be played by respectable men and women." As one etiquette author wrote in 1855: "Hypocrisy is the homage that vice pays to virtue." This changing middle-class perspective facilitated Menken's rise to stardom, allowing her to rise from working-class theaters such as New York City's Old Bowery to upscale venues by the 1860s, bringing a dose of low-class concert halls to respectable stages.[9]

In the process, Menken also accelerated the developing fascination with celebrity. Within the increasingly fluid setting of cities and commerce, many people hungered for personal reference points. The media helped to fill that need not only by publicizing various individuals but also by focusing on their private lives. Menken thus became a phenomenon—"the Menken" in the press. She basked in the public limelight, constructing a persona that was seductive and scandalous, yet seemingly accessible. After she died of a mysterious illness in 1868 at age thirty-three, papers were full of stories about her—but, ironically, given all the intimate details the public had learned about her, there was little agreement on when or where she was born, who her parents were, where she died, or the cause of her death, let alone what kind of person she really was.[10]

Although many critics saw Menken as a threatening figure—a female who crossed the boundaries of gender and Victorian etiquette—the press generally contained that threat by focusing on her sexuality. Onstage, as Mazeppa, she implicitly made a point common to cross-dressing female performers: gender was an act, a role. But the popular press largely undercut that subversive message by focusing on her as an object of male titillation—a source of erotic entertainment for men. In that regard, although Menken died at a young age, she widened the entryway for the emerging "girlie" shows.[11]

In 1866, *The Black Crook,* arguably the first Broadway musical, moved through that entryway with a flourish. The production of a French ballet company, it opened at the fashionable Niblo's Garden after New York City's Academy of Music burned down. Ballet had, of course, enjoyed considerable legitimacy in the United States since the 1830s. Although the scanty costumes had stirred some criticism, ballet's association with high European culture had eased concerns. Moreover, the dancers' moves seemed not deliberately sensuous. *The Black Crook,* on the other hand, so tested the limits of acceptable ballet that an outraged James Gordon Bennett of the *New York Herald* attacked it as "one of the grossest immoral productions that was ever put on the stage." Such criticism aside, the play indeed provided a spectacular evening of entertainment, with elaborate sets and a program that initially lasted over five hours, combining a huge cast, music, melodrama, speciality acts, and—whenever the action dragged—dancing women. It was, however, the "beautiful bare-legged girls" that caught the attention of people such as the writer Mark Twain: "Nothing but a wilderness of girls—stacked up, pile on pile, away aloft to the dome of the theater." The "large number of female legs" was particularly striking in "The Demon Dance," which the women performed in pantaloon costumes that lacked skirts and sleeves—"no clothes to speak of," according to the *New York Times.* The *New York Clipper* joked: "It used to be that Menken's undress uniform 'took the rag off,' but these demons at Niblo's have scarcely a rag left upon them to take off." Men increasingly flocked to the show, and the elite Union League Club reserved a theater box for a month. On opening night, women reportedly constituted over half the audience, but, as moral critics targeted the play, they tended to stay away, although some attended anonymously with veils covering their faces. For a record-setting 474 performances, lasting over sixteen months, *The Black Crook* was a huge box-office success, grossing a million dollars. Some male customers showed up regularly just to see "The Demon Dance." Indeed, the manager conveniently printed a timetable of the various acts so that a man "may drop in, take a peek at his favorite scene, or dance, or leg or something and enjoying the sight, return to the bosom of his family."[12]

By the time Lydia Thompson's English troupe, the British Blondes, launched its landmark American tour in 1868, the girlie or leg show stood at a crossroads in the evolving tradition of burlesque. One path pointed toward straightforward display of females as sex objects with little or no purpose beyond performers' exposing as much of their body as they could get away with. The other path, which Thompson's group initially followed, used scantily clad women and racy scenes to make social comments, satirizing conventional attitudes, Victorian fashion, and gender roles. Burlesque, in Thompson's hands (or "licentious legs," as one critic described them), retained elements of the disturbing, mocking, subversive, transgressive amusements that had marked street festivals, masquerades, parades, and early Christmas celebrations, momentarily inverting cultural hierarchies and power relationships. Thompson-style burlesque, according to one historian, "took wicked fun in reversing roles, shattering polite expectations, brazenly challenging notions of the approved ways women might display their bodies and speak in public."[13]

By September 1868, when the thirty-two-year-old, British-born Thompson opened her play *Ixion* in George Wood's newly renovated and quite respectable museum and theater in uptown New York, perhaps no one suspected how much she would shake up theatrical entertainment. She had, after all, achieved a considerable stage reputation in Europe. Moreover, in 1862, the New York state legislature had cracked down on concert saloons, closing many of them; and, by then, the notorious third tiers, where prostitution had thrived several decades earlier, had virtually disappeared. Audiences no longer disrupted performances. Theater managers enforced rules of behavior. Individual, padded seats had replaced the wooden benches in the gallery. And, in small-town theaters across the country, melodrama continued to reward true womanhood and family in plays such as *East Lynne,* which began a series of long runs in 1861, and *The Old Homestead,* which opened in 1876. From 1865 to 1904, audiences thrilled to Joseph Jefferson III's portrayal of Rip Van Winkle and his lines: "Well, here's [to] your good health, and your families' good health, and may they all live long and prosper!" Against that backdrop, Laura Keene's *The Seven Sisters,* Adah Menken's "Naked Lady," and *The Black Crook* stood out by placing women onstage in controversial roles. Yet, as the burlesque scholar Robert Allen has argued, even "*The Black Crook* was not a burlesque. There was no impertinent, inversive burlesque humor in the piece; it was played straight, not for laughs."[14]

At Wood's Museum and Theater, at Niblo's Garden a few months later, and then during a cross-country tour, Lydia Thompson and her British Blondes offered a genuinely transgressive burlesque that, in Robert Allen's words, "combined visual elements of feminine spectacle with the impertinence . . . of the burlesque form." The result, according to Allen, was "the most thoroughly feminized form of theatrical entertainment in the history of the American stage to that time. Indeed, no form of American commercial theatrical entertainment before or since has given the stage to women to a greater degree." Like the girlie shows, the British Blondes displayed the female body in tantalizing ways. They wore, for example, breeches and tights that revealed their lower thighs. On one level, they could justify their costumes because they were playing the parts of men; on another level, in line with the leg show, the goal was not to look masculine but to emphasize feminine charm and shape. Thompson's Blondes went further, however, mocking fashionable dress and gender ideals. In one skit, Thompson wore a silly hat with a stuffed squirrel on top and smoked a cigarette. Moreover, in contrast with the sentimentalized female, who was frail and weak, the Blondes were voluptuous, emphasizing their ample breasts and hips and encouraging what one reporter referred to as "these rebellious days." To the dismay of a number of bourgeois males, some middle-class women, in the spirit of independence and experimentation, took cues from Thompson and her troupe, dying their hair blond and wearing heavy cosmetics. In that regard, the Blondes implicitly reflected and encouraged larger changes concerning women's roles in the developing urban, commercial setting. Onstage, the Blondes swaggered, talked, and acted in unladylike ways, exhibiting a kind of male cockiness. Thompsonian burlesque was irreverent and insubordinate—and it played in a major theater like Niblo's Garden, no less.[15]

In the early 1870s, the popularity of the British Blondes inspired a veritable "culture of leg-work," according to the New York Tribune. A range of burlesque troupes, like Thompson's show, turned the bourgeois world upside down, providing images of female power and using cross-dressed women to satirize men ("an idiotic parody of masculinity," complained the New York Times). The color posters that advertised the traveling burlesque troupes were in themselves remarkably suggestive regarding female sexual power and dominance. Some showed women in traditional men's roles. In the poster for "Bend Her," a burlesque of the popular story of Ben Hur, two well-endowed women whipped their horses during the chariot race. Another poster portrayed women dressed as soldiers, but with tight-fitting leggings and prominent busts—"Imperials Always to the Front," according to the caption. Other advertisements showed attractive, shapely females manipulating wealthy men, like puppets "on the string." In the poster "Dining a

High Roller Girl after the Show," a portly, balding rich man has passed out while the woman, who has rifled his wallet, lights up a cigarette.[16]

In these posters, however, and increasingly in the burlesque shows generally, more was at stake than gender; as with the early minstrel shows, class issues were strongly evident. Indeed, class was a key reason why burlesque ultimately moved from upscale venues such as Niblo's Garden to much seedier and disreputable settings. Attacks from the mainstream press diminished the number of fashionable women who initially attended the British Blondes' performances. During the 1870–71 tour of Thompson's troupe, "respectable" people relinquished their seats to tougher, rowdier patrons, who, according to one condescending observer, simply wanted "to see legs and busts, and listen to double entendres and all that kind of thing." In turn, the growing working-class male audiences who laughed and cheered for powerful, dominant females did so because the women's hapless victims were wealthy men from the starched-shirt set who lacked the right stuff. In that regard, a telling publicity poster showed that a chorus girl could control rich, effete males but was no match for those at the bottom of the economic order, who strung her up by her feet and dipped her in a tub of beer. In sum, working-class audiences could enjoy the physical attributes of a woman with Amazonian proportions and yet feel secure in their own power. An ultimate casualty of the evolving burlesque show by the late nineteenth century was the woman whose authority on stage went beyond her looks. By the 1890s, Lydia Thompson noted regretfully that audiences had "retired" her kind of entertainment—full of female rebelliousness and empowerment—in favor of the unqualified sexual display of women. The burlesque road was leading to belly dances, strip shows, and, in 1917, the "runway" on which voiceless women paraded and danced provocatively in front of male audiences.[17]

Another, more respectable kind of female sexual exhibitionism nevertheless found expression in the late nineteenth century, largely through the budding efforts of Florenz Ziegfeld Jr. A Chicago native, Ziegfeld had a Barnum-style bent for hokum as well as a keen eye for spectacle and show, key elements in the growing commercial world of department stores and consumer goods. "I invented the showgirl," he later boasted, referring grandiosely to the uneasy combination of respectable gentility and sensuality with which he carefully packaged sexual images for middle-class audiences. Born into a cultured household in 1868, he early on championed popular amusements rather than the classical music that his parents hoped he would embrace. (His father, a German immigrant, founded the Chicago Musical College, which became a reputable institution within the city's higher cultural circles.) Junior claimed to have joined Buffalo Bill's Wild West show when he was seventeen, a story that may have been apocryphal but illustrated his fascination with entertainment. At age twenty-two, he unveiled in a Chicago park "the Dancing Ducks of Denmark." For fifteen cents, amazed customers could watch the quacking ducks jump on a small table as Ziegfeld played music. In fact, however, the ducks were from a nearby farm, not Europe, and lighted gas jets under the table forced them to "dance." Authorities ultimately closed down the act and, subsequently, another in which people who paid to see "the Invisible Brazilian Fish" found nothing but a tank full of water. P. T. Barnum would undoubtedly have been proud, but Ziegfeld clearly needed another gimmick if he was to have a show business future. In the 1890s, young Florenz began to strike pay dirt, not with ducks or invisible fish, but with magnificently shaped humans: first the strongman Eugen Sandow and then the voluptuous Anna Held, around whom he first began to develop his reputation as "the man who invented women."[18]

Ziegfeld first saw Sandow in 1893 when the German-born muscleman was performing in a New York City variety show, claiming to be the strongest man in the world. The audience was small, but Ziegfeld noticed how the few women in attendance responded to the impressively built Sandow. Ziegfeld quickly contracted him to perform in Chicago's new Trocadero theater, not far from the grounds of the world's fair. Under Ziegfeld's skillful direction, and with the help of his ingenious publicity, "the Great Sandow" emerged as a national celebrity. Ziegfeld blanketed Chicago with posters touting Sandow as "the strongest man on earth!"—"the modern Hercules"—and offered substantial rewards to any man who could duplicate his performances, which included lifting over his head two full-grown gentlemen in baskets attached to a barbell, or a piano with the musician seated on top, or a board holding nineteen people (including Ziegfeld) and a dog. In a brilliant publicity stroke, Ziegfeld said that women who paid $300 to charity could feel the strongman's muscles backstage, an offer that some of the city's most fashionable ladies, including the wives of millionaire entrepreneurs Potter Palmer and George Pullman, hastily accepted. In a situation that would otherwise have been vulgar or sexually dangerous, the women could run their hands across Sandow's rippling body in a safe, regulated setting. Once, according to the *National Police Gazette,* when a bashful young woman hesitated to touch Sandow, he urged her on: "These muscles, madam, are hard as iron itself, I want you to convince yourself of that fact." He then guided her gloved hand across his body. "It's unbelievable!" she said as she swooned.[19]

For the next three years, Ziegfeld promoted and toured with the world's "perfect man." Increasingly, Sandow revealed more of his body, replacing traditional tights with only a handkerchief-sized strip of silk and even an artificial fig leaf. Sandow's rising celebrity helped redefine masculinity in the United States—at a time when the crisis of American manhood seemed to demand the appearance of "real men," whether on the football field or on the public stage in the form of Theodore Roosevelt–style leaders. As a physical specimen, Sandow presented a new image of the ideal white male. Indeed, he ultimately posed for a sculpture of the "perfect type of European man." With his hard, sculpted body, whipcord muscles, forty-six-inch chest, twenty-nine-inch waist, and tremendous strength, he exuded control, character, and confidence—and always with a gentlemanly demeanor. The fact that he had once been a sickly boy held out the possibility of self-transformation in an era that extolled fitness and exercise. This "theme of metamorphosis lies at the heart of bodybuilding," as the historian John Kasson has argued. "A longing for male metamorphosis lay deep in the culture of the United States . . . at the advent of the modern age." Moreover, according to Kasson, Sandow "adapted older traditions of manly physical challenge to promote a new mass culture of entertainment," combining the appeal of heroic, primitive warriors—free of civilization's emasculating features—with modern "scientific" training, methods, and nutritional advice. He used his body not for physical labor but as a showpiece.[20]

Florenz Ziegfeld had been instrumental in launching Sandow's long, famous career, but his own future rested far more with exhibiting beautiful women, starting with his masterful promotion of Anna Held. His triumph was in negotiating the fine line between the risqué and the respectable, using female sexuality to tantalize without offending upscale audiences. In 1896, shortly after his collaboration with Sandow ended, Ziegfeld discovered Held performing in a Paris music hall. By then, the popularity on Broadway of French-imported revues like the famed Moulin Rouge, with its lines of dancing girls, offered him an opportunity to exploit. Always adept at advertising, he trumpeted in U.S. publications that he had just hired a star from the Folies-Bergère at a staggering $1,500 per week salary. His marketing of her arrival rivaled that which P. T. Barnum had used years earlier with Jenny Lind. By the time the twenty-three-year-old Held debarked in New York City by climbing on a yacht with a thirty-piece band, Ziegfeld had already turned her into a much-awaited celebrity. Reporters gathered in her lavish hotel suite, where, following Ziegfeld's script, she answered questions in a semitransparent negligee. Ziegfeld not only set up the interviews but also capitalized on a rumor that he had planted, namely, that she took daily baths in fresh milk. To enhance the drama, Ziegfeld ingeniously staged an event, arranging for milk to arrive at the same time the reporters did. Ziegfeld then protested that the four hundred gallons of milk were not fresh and sued the milkman, who was in on the hoax. News that the incident was fake simply spawned more news. "The fake story became more than part of our job," recalled a publicist who worked for Ziegfeld; "it was a matching of wits with city editors and the filling of a demand for news far in excess of the supply"—an assignment for "professional liars." A year after Held's arrival, the *New York World* announced that her name was as familiar to Americans as was that of their president. By the early twentieth century, what the press described as "the Anna Held craze" had spawned a host of consumer products carrying her name, including corsets and face powders.[21]

Ziegfeld astutely recognized that Anna Held's background was part of her mystique. Although he marketed her as a fashionable singer from Paris, rumors about her Eastern European and Jewish origins enhanced the mystery and exoticism surrounding her. Held had, in fact, been born in Warsaw, Poland; her father was French and Jewish, while her mother was Polish and Catholic. Her show business origins were in London's Yiddish theater. She thus combined the elegance of the Old World with its darker mysteries. In the United States, as the number of women in public places grew and the need for a managed sexuality seemed increasingly important to many nervous citizens, Held offered a tantalizing combination of "the fashionable and the filthy," of high fashion and saucy earthiness. On the one hand, she dispensed high-society beauty advice from Europe; on the other hand, she sang suggestive songs such as "Won't You Come and Play Wiz Me," "I Just Can't Make My Eyes Behave," and "Would You Like to See a Little More of Me" with a sexy French accent while offering advice on "how to flirt with a parasol." She discussed "the art of the corset," offering her own curvaceous hourglass shape (without, in fact, exposing her body onstage) as an example of that garment's usefulness. Her ruminations on the corset came at a time when, according to one male: "If you want a girl to grow up gentle and womanly in her ways and feelings, lace her tight." In this context, the sensuous Held endorsed traditional and confined roles for women by recommending marriage (even though she and Ziegfeld maintained only a common-law arrangement) and expressing doubts about whether women should vote. "I don't care at all who is president if the lace on my bodice is right," she said coyly. According to one scholar: "Ziegfeld's genius was his uncanny ability to package titillation and naughtiness with the label of middle-class respectability, to blend idealism and voyeurism."[22]

Ziegfeld's marketing talents also intuitively reflected the emphasis on spectacle that heralded the growth of the emerging bourgeois consumer culture. Like Ziegfeld, the new urban department stores, with their expansive windows and display cases, aimed to "show things off." New-style merchandisers such as Philadelphia's John Wanamaker turned their stores into gigantic exhibits. In 1876, Wanamaker converted an abandoned railroad depot into what was perhaps the nation's first department store. Within a short time, Macy's in New York City, Marshall Field's in Chicago, and Filene's in Boston were also in business, despite the opposition of small retailers and organized labor, which Marshall Field, for example, banned forcefully. Some of these entrepreneurs were themselves uneasy about the consumer society they were helping create. The very devout Wanamaker denied that he was a "capitalist" and regretted that society was "worshipping the most helpless god of all that is in or out of heathen temples—MONEY." Yet he, as much as anyone, shaped an economy in which acquisition reportedly held the key to happiness. As another merchant said, the best advice was: "Amuse thyself, take care of yourself." Day and night, the huge windows of the developing department stores enticed consumers with goods. The stores helped "democratize desire" by suggesting access to those goods; at the same time, they put up barriers—the windows—with the implicit message that people should look, not touch. Store products, like Anna Held on the stage, were close yet far, things to see, to dream and fantasize about. Like Held, the goods offered theatrical entertainment, a connection that was evident in the increasingly realistic store mannequins. Police in one city had to break up a crowd that pressed against a store's windows to see the revealing gowns and lingerie on some of the full-bodied mannequins. In this emerging culture of display, Ziegfeld's "showing" of Anna Held thus fit neatly: "the Ziegfeld stage–as–department store."[23]

Ziegfeld, Sandow, and Held all moved ultimately into one of the era's most important entertainment forms: vaudeville. The word *vaudeville* apparently originated in the Vive River valley in France, an area known for its drinking songs, where it eventually came to refer, broadly, to street voices or, more specifically, to light plays with musical interludes. In the United States, however, *vaudeville* came to mean a series of short variety acts, together lasting as long as two hours—"something for everybody." That agenda, as well as the backgrounds of the performers and small-time entrepreneurs who provided it, demonstrated powerfully the various ways in which American popular culture was a democratic art. Variety entertainment was certainly not new, but vaudeville drew like a sponge from many antecedents: from minstrelsy's specialty acts or "olios"; from the circus's traveling acrobats and trained animals; from the backcountry's wandering singers and magicians; from the theater's musical, dancing, and comedy acts; and from the risqué offerings of burlesque and concert saloons. It emerged not according to any design but through the efforts of small-time entertainers seeking amusement formulas that drew crowds, made money, and benefited from middle-class respectability. And, as much as any popular culture form, it moved, unevenly and crab-like, from the margins of the amusement industry to the center of mass entertainment, providing a potpourri of inexpensive diversions in towns and cities across the country. By the turn of the century, vaudeville had become the most popular entertainment form in the United States. Its trajectory was familiar to the general history of American amusements, a history that moved toward economic consolidation, catered to the expanding middle class, and negotiated the treacherous but intriguing path between traditional decorum and "sinful" distractions.[24]

Significantly, vaudeville cobbled diverse forms of amusement into a national amusement network with schedules, rules, and thousands of traveling entertainers. Ultimately, as one performer said, vaudeville circuits "strung America together just as surely as did the railroad tracks." Starting in the 1870s at the local level, theater people such as Tony Pastor had experimented with variety acts that bridged the lines between vulgar and upscale material and audiences. Born in New York City in the 1830s, the colorful Pastor had performed in minstrel shows, Barnum's museum, and circuses before taking his own variety show on the road. In 1875, he replaced his Bowery-style acts and clientele with higher-class offerings and audiences in an upscale Broadway venue. He reportedly once disguised prostitutes as fashionably dressed patrons in order to attract proper audiences, including refined females.[25]

Pastor's success in combining racy and proper acts and in attracting respectable patrons captured the attention of, in particular, Benjamin Franklin Keith and Edward Franklin Albee, who jointly turned vaudeville into an entertainment empire that stretched coast-to-coast. Like Pastor, both men had worked the tawdry fringes of the amusement world, touring with circuses. Albee, born in Maine, had been an "outside ticket" man, trying to entice audiences to see such things as "the wild man, eating bumbergriff. . . . Get your tickets here. . . ." Keith, a product of New Hampshire, opened a Barnum-style museum in Boston in 1885 and was a kind of con artist, selling such novelties as "blood testers," which, he said, "the famous Professor Spivins spent 42 years perfecting." But, in the mid-1880s, Albee and Keith joined forces to offer cleaned-up variety offerings suitable for the entire family. Although they claimed that their goal was to offer moral entertainment, they were interested primarily in selling tickets to prosperous middle-class audiences. Within a few years, they established what some people mocked as "the Sunday School Circuit." They prohibited their performers from using suggestive language, by which they meant, among other things, all "words unfit for the ears of ladies and children," as one warning sign said. According to a notice that Albee himself tacked up: "Remember this theater caters to ladies and gentlemen and children. Vulgarity will not be tolerated." Among the forbidden words were *liar, son-of-a-gun, devil, sucker, damn, hell, spit,* and *cockroach.* Also barred were references to questionable locales such as taverns. Albee boasted: "The old variety houses used to be filthy places, but we changed all that. We believed in soap and water, and in a strict censorship on the stage."[26]

By the early twentieth century, what critics called the Keith-Albee "octopus" exerted enormous power over the vaudeville business. Taking a cue from six entrepreneurs who in 1896 formed a booking syndicate that established a virtual monopoly over road shows for legitimate theater performances, Keith and Albee became the primary booking agents for vaudeville. They hired and controlled acts, moving them along prearranged routes and collecting 5 percent of each performer's salary. A number of actors resisted, forming a kind of labor union known as the White Rats, but these unionization efforts largely failed. By 1907, the Keith circuit dominated big-time vaudeville on the East Coast; three years later, Keith joined with the Orpheum circuit, the big-time operation along the West Coast. The circuits sometimes blacklisted acts that rejected salary offers, virtually assuring that such performers would never succeed except on the entertainment margins. Vaudeville, like most of the industrial economy, moved to the beat of bureaucratic organization, centralization, and consolidation. By the twentieth century, vaudeville's industrial format, with its unified booking system and continuous performances, employed perhaps fifteen thousand performers.[27]

While Keith and Albee controlled much of big-time vaudeville and also operated several of their own fashionable theaters, Marcus Loew formed what one person has described as "vaudeville's version of baseball's minor leagues." Developing a reputation as "the Henry Ford of show biz," Loew expanded his small-time theater business in New York City until, by 1918, he operated over a hundred theaters aimed at working-class audiences and providing what one magazine said was "the poor man's hour of fun." Theaters such as Loew's were anything but posh, and the audiences were frequently rowdy. "Amateur nights" were particularly raucous. Eddie Cantor, who went on to become a big-name star, recalled working one night in a Bowery theater with the crowd shouting: "Go to work, you bum!" Sometimes unpopular performers got "the hook," jerking them off the stage before their acts were finished.[28]

For entertainers on the road, life was harsh and demanding, especially in vaudeville's small-time hinterlands, which bore such nicknames as "the Death Trail" and "the Aching Heart." Traveling from town to town, performers might stage thirty shows in a week. The Marx Brothers found the Midwestern circuit especially painful. "We played in towns I would refuse to be buried in today," recalled Groucho. "Looking back," remembered his brother Harpo, "I simply don't know how we survived it. Those early days on the road were sheer, unmitigated hell." To Harpo, the cheap hotels were "bug sanctuaries." Another famous vaudeville product, Fred Allen, marveled especially at ways in which female performers continued to care for their families: "The female of the species foaled on trains, in dressing rooms, in tank towns, and in big cities. The show must go on. . . . The smalltime vaudeville mother had the endurance of a door-knob. She did three or four shows a day as part of the act. She cared for her baby. . . . She did the family washing. . . . The kids were packed like sardines into upper berths." Charlie Chaplin found the cheap vaudeville circuits "bleak and depressing." Sophie Tucker, who eventually became a star, described some of the theaters in which she played as "drafty old firetraps, no toilets, filthy dirty cracked walls that let in the wind and the rain. . . . Never enough heat." Life on the circuit was often lonely and hostile. While Groucho Marx never forgot the "suspicion and contempt" with which townspeople regarded him, Harpo recalled how difficult audiences could be: "We were pelted with sticks, bricks, spitballs, cigar butts, peach pits and chewed-out stalks of sugar cane."[29]

Vaudevillians endured such treatment and isolation because they viewed the stage as a ladder of economic and social mobility. They came overwhelmingly from poor backgrounds; many were recent immigrants or the sons and daughters of newly arrived families. Sophie Tucker, whose Jewish parents ran a delicatessen downstairs and rented rooms upstairs in their Connecticut home, said: "We all sprang from the same source, the same origin. We were all swept to the shores of this country on the same tidal wave of immigration, in the same flight from prejudice and persecution. Our life stories are pretty much the same." As products of underprivileged circumstances, they found the lure of national stardom and possible salaries of $1,500 per week enthralling, even though only a few reached the big time. "Where else can people who don't know anything make so much money?" asked Minnie Marx. The rags-to-riches stories were legendary. Eddie Cantor was orphaned at age two and raised in the tough streets of New York's Lower East Side. After changing his name from Isidore Iskowitz, he had climbed the entertainment ladder from amateur contests to blackface shows, saloons, and burlesque reviews to become one of the nation's famed entertainers. George Burns performed as a child on street corners. As a teenager, he danced on roller skates in a bar. "We were the only act," he reminisced. "The guys would get full of beer and fall asleep. The minute they'd fall asleep, we had to go on, and the noise of the skates woke them up. So that's the job we had—waking up drunks. Big future there." Elsewhere, working-class women, for whom independent careers were virtually nonexistent, could find inspiration in the vaudeville stardom of Maggie Cline (the daughter of a shoe factory foreman), Fanny Brice (who started performing in amateur shows in Brooklyn as a teenager), and Sophie Tucker.[30]

While most vaudeville performers came from impoverished backgrounds, they were typically also social outsiders and representatives of marginalized groups. "Theatrically, we were at the bottom of the social ladder," recalled Groucho Marx. "Five performances a day in a ten-cent vaudeville theater was about as low as you could get. The only things below us were the carnival shows, one-ring circuses, and the crooked medicine hustlers." The Marx Brothers felt "like unwanted gypsies," according to

Harpo. "One: we were stage folks, in a class with gypsies and other vagrants. Two: we were Jewish. Three: we had New York accents."[31]

Those New York—or at least urban—accents profoundly shaped not just vaudeville but popular culture generally. Vaudeville humor very much reflected the nation's accelerating transition from a rural base to cities. Fast-paced jokes, suggestive of the frenzied action of city streets as well as the clock-oriented tempo of factories, department stores, and offices, replaced the slower, rambling talk of the village storyteller. Through vaudeville, small towns encountered big-city manners and pace. And, in the crowded cities themselves, vaudeville's wordplay, full of malapropisms and verbal misunderstandings, resonated with immigrants who were trying to learn a new language. "Vatever I don't know, I teach you," said one of the characters in the famous poolroom sketch of Joe Weber and Lew Fields, Jews from New York's Lower East Side who played roles as Germans.[32]

Rapid verbal exchanges could also poke fun at ethnic differences and help people adjust to the varied rhythms of city life. Hence, Fred Allen, a vaudeville star who subsequently became one of radio's funniest comedians, enjoyed turning family relationships upside down: "He's a good boy—everything he steals he brings right home to his mother." Or, regarding authority figures, Allen would say: "I could tell he was a policeman—he had his hat off and the woodpeckers were starting to congregate." Here was humor that was constant chatter and motion, full of gags, one-line jabs, and short bits. In one of the many anarchic Weber and Fields exchanges, the doctor asks the uninsured patient, "If you die, what will your wife bury you with?" "With pleasure," responds the patient. Subsequently, the doctor demands $10 for his advice, to which the patient replies, "Ten dollars for your advice? Well, doctor. Here's $2. Take it, that's *my* advice." The Marx Brothers similarly delighted in creating verbal bedlam, making wild leaps from one zany reference to another, refusing to stay within language's restraints. Typically, vaudeville comedy was also rough physically, featuring pratfalls, eye jabbing, and other forms of slapstick. Audiences could laugh when the "nut act" of Duffy and Sweeney took turns slapping each other because no one was actually injured. As the comedian George M. Cohan pointed out: "The most successful tricks or jokes are all based on the *idea* of pain or embarrassment."[33]

Performers, of course, always had to gauge their audiences' tastes and wishes if they hoped to keep their jobs and certainly if they hoped to play in the big-time houses. Once they had designed an act that worked, they could typically recycle it again and again. But they also had to protect their material. Comedians in particular often stole each other's jokes. Indeed, as George Burns recalled, theft was so common that a manager in one North Dakota theater posted a sign "listing about 100 jokes and warning, THESE JOKES HAVE ALREADY BEEN USED IN THIS THEATER—DO NOT USE THEM."

Burns noted that "nobody used them there, but everybody wrote them down and put them in their act for the next booking." Or, as the comedian Milton Berle joked about stealing lines from another comic, "He was so funny I almost dropped my pad and pencil."[34]

In their efforts to cultivate favorable audience responses, vaudevillians necessarily worked from material that observers recognized, including well-established stereotypes. In 1911, a team known as Morris and Allen appeared as "two Jews singing Irish songs with a little talk and some bag pipe playing," according to the manager R. E. Irwin. This kind of "synthetic ethnicity" fused a host of stock traits of various groups such as rural hicks and country bumpkins, the drunken Irish "mick," or the Jewish cheapskate. Such stereotypes and caricatures served as "identifying markers," reference points for audiences amid a society in tremendous flux. Through laughter, audiences could try to control an often strange and disconcerting world. Stage stereotypes could, indeed, reflect outright bigotry, insensitivity, and ignorance of diverse ethnic and racial groups. The use of such demeaning portraits allowed at least some native-born Americans to reaffirm their feelings of superiority over new immigrants by laughing at the caricatures onstage of "kikes," "wops," and "dirty little Greeks." In turn, many performers with recent origins in Eastern Europe performed in blackface. Eddie Cantor and Al Jolson were prime examples of Jewish vaudevillians who became famous partly because of the roles they played in burned cork. Blacked-up white female performers appeared in "pickaninny acts" and sang "coon songs." By 1906, Sophie Tucker was a "World Renowned Coon Shouter." May Irwin sang about "Crappy Dan de Spo'tin' Man," who liked to gamble and "allus got his gun." African Americans, who were often limited to the black theatrical circuit, typically had to work within the confines of racist stereotypes as black dandies and buffoons, wearing funny clothes and speaking in dialect. Touring, for example, with the white-owned Theatre Owners Booking Association (TOBA—which some entertainers read as "Tough on Black Asses"), black performers also had to fend off the resentment of elites within their own communities. Ethel Waters recalled that she was "considered not much better than cattle by respectable Negroes." Whites, on the other hand, would tolerate what she did on the stage but view her with utter disdain outside the theater. "So," she said, "we found ourselves applauded by the ofays in the theater and insulted by them in the streets."[35]

But the popularity of racial and ethnic stereotypes on the vaudeville stage was more complicated than simple prejudice suggested. Among vaudevillians, for example, bigotry could be less prominent than it was in the larger society. The white performer Al Fanton insisted that, for the most part, "there wasn't any prejudice backstage. . . . We were travelers, like in space. There were Arab tumblers, there were Hungarian teeterboard performers, Spanish dancers, there were Negro dancers, there were Jew comics. . . . And you had to get along." A number of whites reluctantly applied burned cork because blackface allowed them additional freedom onstage. As one audience member asserted, blackface performers "were loose in their emotions; it was a free thing, they had voices, they could deliver the song." Ned Wayburn, who had been a coon singer and later choreographed dances for Florenz Ziegfeld's Follies, thus had seventeen white chorus girls apply blackface in front of the audience so that, in their burned-cork roles, they could become wild women. For some white performers, blackface offered opportunities that may not otherwise have existed. Sophie Tucker, for example, was a large woman about whom one stage manager had an emphatic recommendation: "This one's so big and ugly the crowd out front will razz her. Better get some cork and black her up." Tucker resented her blackface persona, however, and jettisoned it once she got established. White women with reputations for being too large and unattractive to perform as sexy chorus girls sometimes found that blackface opened their stage careers. May Irwin, whom one critic dismissed as so ample that "at her entrance [she] looks like a sister team," thus initially turned a blackface "mammy" role to her advantage and sang "coon songs." Even though the immensely popular singer and dancer Eva Tanguay reportedly had an affair with the African American performer George Walker, she used black racial stereotypes onstage.[36]

Stereotypes could be ugly and demeaning, but they also provided opportunities for satire. The comedian Ed Wynn could come onstage as a top-hatted "gentleman" with a college cheer, "Rah, rah, rah. Who pays my bills. Pa and Ma." Pat Rooney's 1880 song "Is That Mr. Riley?" envisioned a time when the Irish had power: "I'd set Ireland free; / On the railway you'd never pay a fare. / I'd have the United States under my thumb, / And sleep in the president's chair. / I'd have nothing but Irishmen on the police. / Patrick's Day would be Fourth of July." Moreover, performers could play off the stereotypes, trying to reshape them. "This is what others think of us," said the black actor Ronald Stephens years later, "but let's take it and make it our own." The contrasting ways in which different ethnic groups interpreted the material were also significant. When Pat Rooney had his working-class Irish character say that his favorite stone was a brick, non-Irish audiences might laugh at his lack of taste, while patrons with Irish roots could applaud the nonpretentious, hardworking laborer. Or there was an expression of fierce pride in the response of Mike, a typical Irish character, to the news that an explosion has killed forty "Eyetalians" and one Irishman: "The poor man."[37]

Jewish comedians were not alone in finding humor in their own experiences and trying to use their outsider status as a source of commentary on broader aspects of American life. Jack Benny, who grew up as Benjamin

Kubelski in Waukegan, Illinois, before entering vaudeville, softened the stereotype of tightfisted Jews by developing a character whose stinginess was
laughably endearing; for example, he promised his date that he would bring
her seeds rather than flowers. Jewish comics like Benny often wrestled with
themes that related not just to their ethnic identity but to larger issues of
assimilation and adaptation. As the number of Jews in New York City
alone jumped from 80,000 in 1880 to 1.25 million in 1910, the new immigrants encountered considerable prejudice. Comedy provided an acceptable avenue out of the ghetto. "Audiences were used to laughing at ethnic
stereotypes, including Jewish stereotypes," as one scholar has observed.
"The door may have been open for the wrong reasons, but many Jews recognized that at least the door was open, and they walked right in"—forging some of the best-known examples of American humor and becoming
some of the nation's most familiar entertainers. According to Jack Benny,
ethnic humor had redeeming qualities: "I think it was a way that America
heated up the national groups and the ethnic groups in a melting pot and
made one people of us—or tried to do so." Although vaudeville's ethnic
humor could be insulting and confining, it was also somewhat elastic. "If
you're playing Bushwick," noted one vaudevillian, "you make fun of
Flatbush, if you're playing Flatbush, you make fun of Bushwick. That's an
old game."[38]

Still, especially for African Americans, vaudeville's stereotypes exacted
a costly economic, psychological, and creative toll. Bert Williams, who performed with George Walker as "Two Real Coons," observed wryly that it
was inconvenient being black in America. The shuffling character that he
played onstage was, he insisted, "not me." Williams had graduated from
high school at a time when most Americans did not do so, and he enjoyed
reading Mark Twain and Nietzsche. To observers who believed that blacks
onstage represented "a free thing," Williams replied: "If I were free to *do
as I like,* I would give both sides of the shiftless darky—the pathos as well
as the fun. . . . But the public knows me for certain things. If I attempt anything outside those things I am not Bert Williams." The genius of actors
such as Williams and Walker was evident in the ways in which they stretched
otherwise confining roles. Williams's famous song "Nobody" revealed a
genuine humanity in his character, for whom nothing seems to work. "I am
the 'Jonah Man,'" explained Williams, "the man who, even if it rained soup,
would be found with a fork in his hand and no spoon in sight, the man
whose fighting relatives come to visit and whose head is always dented by
the furniture they throw at each other." Williams also tried to bring depth
to his character: "Show this artless darky [onstage] a book and he won't
know what it is all about. He can't read. He cannot write. But ask him a
question and he'll answer it with a philosophy that's got something."[39]

Black vaudevillians like Williams and Walker could enjoy the attention they received onstage, but outside the theater they encountered constant reminders of their inferior status. A white mob in one small Southern community stripped them, gave them burlap sacks to wear, and ran them out of town. When, after one performance, Williams headed for the back elevator that blacks were supposed to use, Eddie Cantor observed real sadness on his face. "It wouldn't be so bad, Eddie," Williams remarked, "if I didn't still hear the applause ringing in my ears." W. C. Fields, who started his vaudeville career as a juggler, said that Bert Williams was "the funniest man I ever saw and the saddest man I ever knew." The African American leader Booker T. Washington believed that, despite the high personal price, Williams "has done more for the race than I have. He has smiled his way into people's hearts."[40]

That smile was haunted, however, just as vaudeville's ethnic humor generally was. Not surprisingly, as various immigrant groups tried to enhance their positions in American society, they took issue with the unflattering stereotypes. A number of ethnic organizations protested against insulting portraits of their people. The Russell Brothers learned an unhappy lesson in this regard. Once popular for their skits about two Irish servant girls, they were bewildered when the Ancient Order of Hibernians eventually took them to task and audiences started booing them. Theater managers became more cautious lest they offend groups. An act with "Hebrew" comedy thus bothered one manager, who warned: "Someday the Hebrews are going to make as big a kick as the Irish did against this kind of burlesque of the nationality." In order to enhance vaudeville's reputation and appeal, the Keith-Albee chain sought to downplay low, ethnic comedy.[41]

Such efforts to discipline low comedy presented a host of challenges, however, revealing the managers' limited power as well as the audiences' conflicting desires. Managers nervously tried to control their shows even as they recognized that patrons typically preferred acts that were reputable yet edgy. On this level, according to one interpretation, popular culture involved far more than "a process of homogenization and embourgeoisement." As "a work in progress," mass culture at the turn of the century did two things at once: "It uplifted low culture and unraveled high culture." Despite the considerable claims of vaudeville impresarios such as Keith and Albee that they provided uplifting fare, their exuberant and often irreverent stage offerings weakened the Victorian ideals of gentility, social hierarchy, postponed gratification, and morality.[42]

Women's place in vaudeville provided a telling example of popular culture's mixed relation with mainstream values and expectations. Attempts to make entertainment safer and more wholesome for women certainly fit with Victorian concerns about domesticity. At the same time, amusements such as vaudeville had the practical effect of bringing women into public spaces. The acts themselves were also full of contrary messages and images. "Our bright soubrette," as a trade journal noted, was "just as saucy as she's sweet"; yet, although "over all the world she'll roam," she remained true to her one love "at home." Determined to sell tickets, managers often wavered over acceptable sexuality. One of them conceded that the dancer Dora Ronca's movements were quite sensual and that she might not even be that talented; nevertheless, "Miss Ronca . . . catches the boys." Theater owners pledged their homage to traditional feminine standards while noting that the fig-leaf-wearing strongman, Eugen Sandow, was, as a Detroit manager described him, "a hit with the women folk." Controversial women also tended to draw well at the box office. A number of them who were involved in sex scandals or well-publicized trials went on vaudeville tours. After two women shot a lover, they performed at Hammerstein's Victorian Theater in New York as "the Shooting Stars." The chorus girl Evelyn Nesbit became famously popular after her millionaire husband murdered a man with whom she had lived previously, the celebrated architect Stanford White. Another performer, after a jury acquitted her of a murder charge, lost her contract "unless," as an owner cynically advised her, "you shoot another man."[43]

Unless women performers were sexy and shapely like Anna Held, they typically struggled under limiting circumstances. In comedy, even conventionally attractive females had difficult times. Male audiences were especially uncomfortable with pretty women who were aggressively humorous or told questionable jokes. Such women typically had to make themselves less threatening sexually by wearing silly disguises or playing "Dumb Dora" roles in which they appeared witless. Humor in which women were the object of the jests was usually more acceptable.[44]

Despite and because of such limitations, female performers used a variety of strategies to forge their careers—strategies that pecked away at proper Victorian expectations regarding domesticity, true womanhood, and respectability. Joking that "nobody laughs at a skinny woman," Trixie Friganza made much of her large size, even padding her body. Sometimes she would appear onstage wearing many costumes simultaneously, discarding them one by one. Discussing "the troubles of a fat girl," she kidded audiences. Laughingly, she suggested that managers should have to pay female comics "by the pound." Marie Dressler likewise made much of her substantial body, developing a theme song, "A Great Big Girl Like Me," and doing a Spanish fandango in which her hips pounded the performers around her as if they were, according to one account, "rubber balls batted with a sledgehammer." Both Friganza and Dressler took advantage of the stereotype that "fat people" have unrestrained sexual appetites. "Won't Someone Kindly Stake Me to a Man," Friganza sang provocatively. Using a kind of stealth humor, such female comics often hinted at gender wars. Friganza wrote that the female comedian should establish a particular rapport with women, that "her attitude must be 'My dear, I know just what a time you have with your husband,'" and "oh it's fierce to be a woman, but we're all women together—leagued against a common enemy." Lillian Shaw was more demure but apparently received sympathetic responses from female patrons by poking fun at marriage. When she asked whether marriage was a good idea, a woman she had planted in the audience shouted: "No." According to one reviewer: "Her exposition of the woes of married life made every bachelor maid in the house congratulate herself." Women in particular enjoyed her song "If I Was Single Once Again."[45]

By far the most unruly and the most popular of the female vaudevillians, however, was the irrepressible Eva Tanguay, who combined sexual innuendo with such childlike energy and willful abandon that she disarmed moral critics and ultimately earned $3,500 weekly—which may have made her the highest-paid actress in America. Born in Canada in 1878 and raised in rural poverty near Holyoke, Massachusetts, she entered show business as a child, worked her way through low-class theaters and burlesque, and finally burst to stardom in her mid-twenties. The formula for her success was unique. With a voice that reviewers compared to a buzz saw and "a hairshirt to the nerves," she was hardly a great singer. Her dancing resembled "a mad dog fleeing a mob of small boys." Physically, Tanguay struck many observers as somewhat chunky. Yet, onstage, her ebullient personality, raw emotional intensity, constant motion, and suggestive material made her a sensation. One dazzled reviewer believed that "she gave an exhibition of abandon I never have seen equaled"; her prancing, hopping, and endurance seemed nothing less than "abnormal." Another reviewer compared her to "a tornado, a whirlwind, a bouncing bundle of perpetual motion. She shouts, she twists and turns, she is a mad woman, a whirling dervish of grotesquerie. She is unlike any other woman on stage." Earning such nicknames as "the Little Cyclone on Legs," "the Queen of Perpetual Motion," and "the Evangelist of Joy," Tanguay struck one observer as comparable to "a bunch of firecrackers in an overheated stove." Her constant movement, her revealing yet ridiculous costumes (e.g., pennies glued to skimpy dresses), her wildly frizzy hair, and her aura of craziness allowed her to exhibit a provocative sexuality in respectable venues to appreciative males and females.[46]

In her inimitable style, Tanguay chipped away gleefully at Victorian concerns about proper appearances and femininity. Onstage, she presented a continuing challenge to the host of nineteenth-century advice books on public decorum, manners, dress, and cultured taste. She spoofed the famous ballerina Anna Pavlova by cavorting ungracefully around the stage in a tutu, singing "When Pavlova Sees Me Put It Over." She delighted in being who she was, unconventional, eccentric, and independent, with songs such as "There Goes Crazy Eva," "I Want Someone to Go Wild with Me," "I'm

Crazy about That Kind of Love," "It's All Been Done but Not the Way I Do It," and, especially, her theme song, which she introduced in 1902, "I Don't Care": "They say I'm crazy, got no sense, / But I don't care / . . . I don't care! I don't care! / What they think of me, / I'm happy go lucky / Men say I am plucky, / So jolly and care free / . . . My voice may be funny, / But it's giving me money, / So I don't care." Carefully, on- and offstage, Tanguay cultivated a risqué image. She was supposedly writing an autobiography, *A Hundred Loves,* including incidents that "some people will recognize." She rode in hot-air balloons, hunted big game, posed for photographs with tigers, and laughingly denied that she was "naughty" because "I never drink" and "I never smoke." She mocked marriage with songs like "That Wouldn't Make a Hit with Me": "When you marry some old guy / Who hasn't the decency to die, / Or you marry some old pill / Who you can neither cure nor kill, / That wouldn't make a hit with me." At one point she sang a "drinking song" while soaking her unruly, almost electrified hair with a bottle of champagne and shaking her breasts and hips. "Tanguay drew in a public eager to flirt with her brand of outrageous abandon," according to the historian Marybeth Hamilton. "They could toy with it without committing themselves to it, without being forced to live with its consequences." She had, as one theater manager said, "that Vaudeville something that makes her worth every dollar," disarming her critics so effectively that even the Keith-Albee "Sunday School Circuit" featured her.[47]

Female vaudevillians such as Tanguay thus demonstrated time and again, as the historian Alison Kibler has observed, that it was not the ladies of social rank who held all the power; "for brief moments, at least, the rank ladies ruled," shredding Victorian ideals of social class and respectability. According to Caroline Caffin, who in 1914 wrote a pioneering study of vaudeville, these "personal and unashamed" vaudeville women stared audiences "straight in the face" with a defiant message: "Look at ME! I am going to astonish you!" Kate and May Elinore provided additional examples. During their fifteen popular years in vaudeville, from 1894 to 1909, they developed a series of Irish American characters who mocked gentility and propriety. In one skit, "Dangerous Mrs. Delaney," Kate played a working-class Irish immigrant who becomes rich from a lawsuit following her husband's death in a city sewer. Her daughter, played by May, keeps trying to make Kate a proper Victorian woman. Competing with May's cultivated messages—a nod to genteel respectability—was the humor of Kate's behavior as she spits in public places and hurls punches as well as insults. At one point, she brags that she hit a "little weasel of a man . . . so hard that I had to go to the hospital to have me fist cut out of his ribs." In another skit, a high-society woman mistakes Kate, playing an unemployed maid, for her rich aunt; the audience cheers for the working-class Kate, who seems genuine, as opposed to the woman of status, who fawns and grovels for attention and money.[48]

Some of the most daring challenges to Victorian boundaries came, however, from a surprising source—the highly respectable and extremely popular black vaudeville team the Whitman Sisters. The four sisters grew up in a very proper middle-class family in Lawrence, Kansas. Their father was a preacher for the African Methodist Episcopal Church. The dates of their births are not precisely known, but Mabel was born around 1880, Essie two years later, Alberta around 1888, and Alice in approximately 1900. The three oldest sisters started performing in church, singing and dancing while their father preached. When they were in their teens, they sang jubilee songs (joyful spirituals full of jubilation about individual blessings and a better future) in a rented hall. Increasingly, they added tunes like "Adam Never Had No Mammy" and "Black Like Me" to their repertoire. By the turn of the century, they had become one of the few black groups to tour with white vaudeville troupes. Their mother chaperoned them and served as their manager. In the early twentieth century, they formed their own troupe, whose program featured jubilee songs and coon shouts; dancing, comedy, and specialty acts, including the young Ethel Waters; a "befoh da wah" plantation skit that was reminiscent of minstrel shows; and even a jazz band with Bill Basie, later famous as Count Basie. The sisters skillfully courted the support of elite African Americans as well as church groups, and their reputation as a "class act" made them not just acceptable to white audiences but, ultimately, influential enough that they could sometimes refuse to perform before segregated audiences.[49]

Despite their irreproachable images, the Whitman Sisters continually disrupted expectations regarding race, gender, and power. They explored volatile themes and issues obliquely, implicitly raising a number of disturbing questions: "How do we know a black woman when we see one?" "What happens when the signs we have learned to read no longer signify the expected?" "Who has the power: the watcher or the watched?" "What is beautiful?" The answer to how people could identify a black woman seemed simple enough, but the sisters complicated it by performing in black-haired wigs and blackface, then returning to the stage with blonde wigs and without burned cork. Because they were light skinned, the audience could wonder: "Who are those white women?" Subtly, the Whitman Sisters simultaneously suggested that reality was what the performers intended, not simply what the spectators saw. In the troupe's chorus line, the sisters deliberately mixed fair-skinned and dark-skinned women, blurring assumptions about what chorus girls should look like. They also toyed with gender lines. Essie did a drunk act, and Alice tap-danced at a time when men typically provided such entertainment. Alberta was an accomplished male impersonator, and, wearing any of a number of men's costumes, she would dance with the very feminine Alice. Time and again, the Whitman Sisters revised traditional representations and images. They also bridged low and high culture. The chorus lines and Alice in particular hinted at burlesque and flirted with the risqué; Alice's singing could sound sultry and inviting. Yet the sisters countered coon shouts, suggestive acts, and the fact that they were running an entertainment business with constant reminders of their religious background and beliefs. Offstage, they dressed fashionably, visited elite women's clubs, contributed to church budgets, and hailed the "family" ambience of their whole troupe, which included a number of children whom the sisters reportedly treated as their own. In careers that spanned four decades, they turned, as their biographer has shown, "the vaudeville stage into a site of resistance." [50]

In many ways, of course, all vaudeville constituted such a site. Verbal jabs, slapstick comedy, inversions of true womanhood, Tanguay-style eccentricity, disruptions of social hierarchies, skimpy attire, and ribald humor all pushed against the boundaries of respectability, disrupting what was supposed to be an orderly, well-mannered world. By the 1920s, for example, a comic could joke: "A few words mumbled by a minister constitute a marriage. A few words mumbled by a sleeping husband constitute a divorce." Or: "Marriage is an institution. So is a lunatic asylum." While Benjamin Keith and Edward Albee claimed that they featured only "clean" entertainment, they knew intuitively that it could not be too clean or refined lest it lose its appeal. "They were well aware," as the historian David Nasaw has quipped, "that Sunday Schools did not attract many paying customers." Although one critic of inexpensive amusements predicted that the high-culture "genius of Sophocles, of Shakespeare, or Moliere" would soon render vaudeville a mere sideshow, the future was not on his side. The entire culture was being "vaudevillized." [51]

Technology hastened this transformation. Railroads moved vaudeville troupes around the country, along with circuses, Wild West shows, baseball teams, and the British Blondes. The coming of the age of electrical power was also crucial. Thomas Edison's incandescent bulbs illuminated vaudeville theaters as well as department store windows and sporting arenas, while breakthrough discoveries in the use of alternating currents electrified the great White City of Chicago's 1893 world's fair and, next to it, the wonders of the Midway. Meanwhile, the Midway's colossal Ferris wheel helped introduce an exciting new dimension of entertainment's "billion-dollar smile": the amusement park. [52]

Early amusement parks—such as Bigelow's Gardens in Worcester, Massachusetts—revealed some of the cultural strains that accompanied the budding world of commercial entertainment. Horace Bigelow was a self-made man who started making shoes in a small shop, became a wealthy shoe manufacturer, invested in real estate, and developed lakeside property. In 1881, he converted a skating rink that had catered to Worcester's better sort into a downtown amusement emporium for a larger and more broadly based clientele. Local moralists objected when he operated his gardens on Sundays. To many working-class families, however, Sundays provided rare opportunities to enjoy commercial amusements. Bigelow faced a decision. He himself courted the elite classes, building summer homes and an "elegant" boat club for them; moreover, he was a teetotaler who had descended from New England Puritans fiercely protective of the Sabbath. Yet he ultimately sided with the "Liberty Loving" workers, defending their right to ride his swings and carousel and to attend his band concerts on Sundays. "It was," he argued, "no worse for a poor man to ride a wooden horse on Sunday that it was for a rich man to ride behind a living animal." Bigelow, of course, gained from selling tickets on the Sabbath. But he also resented the local elite, which had long made him feel like a social outsider. In that regard, he took his revenge, helping move Sunday recreation—which one critic attacked as "a modern Sodom of license and riot"—closer to the mainstream culture. Over the next few years, Bigelow developed a reputation as the "Great Amusement Caterer," in 1905 opening a full-scale amusement park with rides and sideshows. By then, such parks existed around the nation, most famously at Coney Island, "the people's playground."[53]

Perched on a spit of land less than ten miles east of Manhattan, on the southern edge of Brooklyn, Coney Island had, before the Civil War, been a seashore retreat for such celebrated visitors as P. T. Barnum, Jenny Lind, senators Daniel Webster and Henry Clay, the penny press entrepreneur James Gordon Bennett, and the writer Washington Irving. Even then, Bennett's *New York Herald* complained of the "hordes of outside barbarians" who took advantage of the unrestricted beach. By the mid-1880s, improved roads, several railroad lines, and steamboats that ferried people from New York City had transformed the area. It featured exotic hotels, cafés, boardwalks, carousels, bathing pavilions, racetracks, an aquarium, a huge roller coaster, musical entertainment, and reassembled structures from the 1876 Philadelphia Exposition, including an amusement tower that, at three hundred feet, was taller than any existing building in the United States and provided a breathtaking twenty-mile view. One hotel was in the shape of a giant elephant and featured a shopping mall along with its thirty-four guest rooms. At a refreshment kiosk, dairymaids drew iced milk from the mechanical udders of a large metal cow. Sunday crowds on the island reportedly reached 100,000, resembling "New York moved down to the sea," as one journalist wrote. Among them, in the words of the *New York Herald*, were many "working men and their families, young clerks and saleswomen—the toiling dwellers in the crowded tenements."[54]

The coming of this working-class "multitude"—"a motley throng," as *Harper's Weekly* described them—attested to a remarkable transition in the history of America labor. During the several bloody decades after the Civil War, clashes between industry's forces and striking workers resulted time and again in deadly violence. Battles for workers' rights nevertheless persisted. In late 1889, hundreds of trade unionists thus paraded through Worcester, Massachusetts, bearing a banner that read: "Eight Hours for Work, Eight Hours for Rest, Eight Hours for What We Will." Workers wanted not only improved working conditions and higher pay but also more leisure time. "A workingman wants something besides food and clothes in this country," one laborer told a Senate committee in 1883. "He wants recreation. Why should not a workingman have it as well as other people?" The demand for more free time had already produced a series of struggles that spilled out of the workshop into recreational spaces, as the debates surrounding Bigelow's Gardens demonstrated. Those struggles, moreover, made a difference, slowly encouraging shorter workdays and more leisure time. Factory employees faced a more disciplined work regimen, but they eked out more time for socializing off the job. During each of the nineteenth century's last five decades, the nonagricultural workweek declined by around 3 percent, ultimately providing an average of fifteen more hours for leisure each week. "A *full quarter of the year* is now practically made unproductive time," complained one disgruntled employer. Between 1900 and 1910, the trend nevertheless intensified, reducing the average workweek another 10 percent to slightly over fifty hours. In contrast to the regimentation and subordination that typically marked those long hours on the job, the recreational and commercial entertainments in places such as Coney Island offered up hard-won freedom—the opportunity to do "what we will" and with a sense of equality. After all, Coney's surf treated rich and poor alike: "Old Ocean is a grand old Democrat," the *New York Times* asserted.[55]

By the end of the nineteenth century, wealthier citizens continued their search for more exclusive beach settings, helping seal Coney Island's reputation as, according to one guidebook, the "great democratic resort—the ocean bathtub of the great unwashed." The privileged and resentful George Templeton Strong scoffed that "civic scum" had taken over the island—"the fast-man, whore, and Bowery girl" and the "vermin that hot weather roasts out of its homes in town." But it was precisely this clientele that several rising amusement entrepreneurs shrewdly tapped.[56]

Preeminent in this group of entertainment impresarios was the brilliantly innovative Frederick Thompson, whom the *New York Sun* described in 1905 as "capitalist, amusement inventor and perennial small boy." His personality and temperament meshed superbly with the developing world of fun and play, whose cause he so happily advanced. Born in 1873, Thompson grew up in a series of Midwestern steel cities, where his father was a skilled iron-worker in a volatile, conflict-ridden economy. Young Fred apparently concluded that work in the mills was not for him. Except for his interest in mechanics and machinery, he seemed unfocused, mainly getting in trouble at home and at school. Such youthful insubordination and rebelliousness were common, but Thompson sustained into adulthood his reluctance to "grow up" or to acquire "manly" attributes of self-restraint and responsibility. Likewise, he found little that was appealing in evangelical religion, noting wryly his preference for churches that closed for picnics. Machines fascinated him, but primarily as sources of pleasure; he liked the manufacturing process, while hating the confinements of work. Ultimately, he looked for ways to hang onto childhood pleasures and make money from them. Indeed, his crucial insight was in seeing, as his biographer has observed, "the market value of play"—in sum, how "concepts of play and childhood" could be financially lucrative. A "boy's wish for fun," excitement, and personal gratification seemed more important than prescribed duties. Thompson himself stated that "the trouble with this present age" was easy to explain: "too much work and too little play." He set out to remedy that problem. In his opinion, a child's resistance to sitting still, taking orders, following rules, and emphasizing responsibilities was entirely defensible, and he applauded youngsters' love of excitement, pleasure, and good times. Here was a formula for the emerging consumer culture whose building blocks were desire, adventure, novelty, and illusion—a culture that such new institutions as department stores and advertising agencies were already molding.[57]

After studying drawing and design in his uncle's distinguished architectural firm, Thompson settled on becoming, in his words, "an inventor and constructor of shows." At age twenty-six, he captured attention as the key designer for the midway at the 1901 Pan-American Exposition in Buffalo, New York. To the chagrin of the promoters, people spurned the exposition's uplifting instruction in favor of the midway's delights. Especially popular was Thompson's staging of a Trip to the Moon, by which customers participated in an illusory voyage, replete with a sense of motion, views of the receding earth, and chances to see a replica of the moon up close, full of green cheese, brilliant fountains, and dancing maids. With attendance at the exposition still flagging after three months, Thompson successfully staged a "Midway Day," elevating the midway shows above the fair itself. "An exposition is not, nor should it be, a serious thing," he explained. "Amusement should predominate. It should be billed like a circus." Over 105,000 people attended Midway Day, a record crowd at that point for the fair. Although a spirit of unrestrained carnival marked the festivities, Thompson carefully orchestrated all the events. The Buffalo newspaper was ecstatic: "For once the Pan-American Exposition lost its identity and became the Midway, all Midway and nothing but the Midway." Several of the fair's managers reluctantly concurred that the exposition should offer more fun. Thompson urged them to turn it into the equivalent of Mardi Gras: "Get down to the level of the masses. Provide what they want and provide it liberally." His argument failed, but he articulated his own entertainment philosophy—a philosophy that he implemented at Coney Island in 1903 when he opened the spectacular Luna Park.[58]

Two amusement parks preceded Luna at Coney Island, but all three represented an ongoing battle to counter the island's growing reputation as "Sodom by the Sea." Although diminishing numbers of wealthier people still basked in the expensive hotels on the eastern end of the five-mile-long island, the western side attracted rougher elements and had a tenderloin section known as the Gut, a cradle of prostitution and gambling. Before Thompson's arrival, several entrepreneurs had already set out to improve the surroundings.

In 1895, Captain Paul Boynton opened the nation's first enclosed amusement park, just behind the Elephant Hotel. He was a legendary swimmer who, in a watertight rubber suit, negotiated a host of waterways (including the English Channel, the Strait of Gibralter, and 450 miles of the Rhine River). At Coney Island, his Sea Lion Park featured a roller coaster that maneuvered a circular loop and, most famously, a Shoot the Chutes water amusement ride. In 1897, George Tilyou, whose father had developed a number of the island's attractions, opened the second enclosed park: Steeplechase, which guaranteed "ten hours' fun for ten cents." It was a five-acre showcase with at least fifty amusements lining its midway, including a Ferris wheel, a roller coaster, water rides, and, most of all, the celebrated Gravity Steeplechase Race Course. Customers rode mechanical horses around the park's borders to enjoy, as the ride promised, "half a mile in half a minute, and fun all the time." Tilyou's park was located in an area known as "the Bowery at Coney Island." There, Tilyou sought to balance the island's tougher and more elegant extremes while catering to a working- and lower-middle-class clientele. The fact that Sea Lion and Steeplechase parks were both enclosed made a powerful statement: management intended to screen out undesirables yet profit from entry fees that were cheap enough to attract working-class families. Seeking more spectacular amusements, Tilyou in 1902 persuaded Fred Thompson to reconstruct his Trip to the Moon ride at Steeplechase as an independent concession. A year later, Thompson, with his partner Elmer "Skip" Dundy and the silent backing of the wealthy industrialist John W. "Bet-a-Million" Gates, leased Boynton's flagging Sea Lion Park and launched a more ambitious enterprise, Luna, the most popular of Coney's amusement venues.[59]

On May 16, 1903, the throng of perhaps sixty thousand customers on hand for Luna's grand opening encountered a wondrous environment, the epitome of amusement parks. Designed architecturally as an "Oriental dream"—a "Baghdad by the Sea"—Luna was also the first theme park. Its architectural design reflected "the spirit of carnival," as Thompson described it. For an admission price of ten cents, customers could wander the grounds for hours, enjoying the colors, lights, ornamental structures, towers, spires, minarets, canals with gondoliers, Japanese gardens, elephant and camel rides down the "Streets of Delhi," circus acts, thrilling mechanical rides, and the dream-like atmosphere that was like "a world removed—shut away from the sordid clatter and turmoil of the streets," as a reporter depicted it. Thompson himself guessed that the patrons "do not want to encounter seriousness. They have enough seriousness in their everyday lives. . . . Everything must be different from ordinary experience." Or, as he said on another occasion, Luna's customers were "big children who have come to fairyland and want the fairies to make them laugh and show them strange things." On the park's first Fourth of July, 142,000 customers showed up. For most of them—individuals with few resources—the park's ostentatious setting suggested that they could depart, however briefly, from plain, everyday lives and bask in the majestic grandeur of wealth and privilege. While rich industrial families such as the Vanderbilts enjoyed the stunning opulence of Newport, Rhode Island, Luna Park provided what one historian has described as "a Newport for the masses."[60]

Thompson assuredly delighted in bringing fun to the masses, but he sought an audience a few notches above what one observer depicted as the island's "spectacle of poverty in spangles." The clientele that Thompson favored came from America's rising group of employees: white-collar clerks and salaried managers. He hoped also to draw on the expanding domestic tourist industry. In his opinion, he was helping Coney Island shed its trashy image. He claimed that, before he had started Luna Park, Coney "was a byword for all that was vulgar, vicious and deplorable." Luna brought respectability. It was, according to advertisements, "the Place for Your Mother, Your Wife, Your Daughter and Your Sister." In 1908, Thompson bragged in a respectable women's magazine that he was "Amusing the Million" in a wholesome way. Indeed, he claimed personally to have "soundly thrashed" one "rowdy" who tried to enter the park, apparently forgetting that "his mother and sister" might be there. Like so many of the amusement entrepreneurs, from P. T. Barnum to William F. Cody and the vaudeville magnates B. F. Keith and Edward Albee, Thompson recognized the importance of middle-class respectability. At one point, he candidly admitted that he dreamed of a day when midway entrepreneurs would no longer have to believe that they occupied "some long street in a back yard"—some "sideshow to be more or less ashamed of."[61]

Luna Park might be a place for the "pure and good," as Thompson described it, but he recognized that the business of "amusing the million" necessarily required—as he himself had advised the Buffalo exposition board—"get[ting] down to the level of the masses." And, in that regard, he had clearly found a winning formula; within just the first three months, he and Dundy got back virtually all their investment. Most of the money came from ticket sales, but the owners added to their profits by leasing out most of the concessions to independent operators, who typically also paid percentages on earnings.[62]

In 1904, largely because of Luna's resounding success, a business consortium opened yet another amusement park on Coney Island: Dreamland. In many respects, from its 370-foot tower to its longer rides and menagerie of wild beasts, Dreamland was even grander than Luna Park. It also sought to be more educational and "morally instructive." Thompson fought back, expanding Luna by sixteen more acres, a project that included a miniature Himalayan mountain. For the next several years, even though Dreamland never quite matched Luna's appeal, the two parks were in heated competition, each trying to outdo the other with more exciting rides and spectacles. Meanwhile, George Tilyou continued to develop Steeplechase Park, enlarging it and, after a fire in 1908, renewing it under the label of "An Effulgence of Amusement." Like Thompson, Tilyou favored "clean fun," banning intoxicating beverages and vulgar performances from the grounds. "People are just boys and girls grown tall," he said, sounding a lot like Thompson. The offerings of the giant amusement parks meant that, according to the *New York Times,* "Coney is regenerated, and almost every trace of Old Coney has been wiped out." Although a good deal of "Old Coney" still lingered in the many independent amusement venues that lined the long boardwalk outside the amusement parks, by 1910 Coney Island was, indeed, a towering symbol of the nation's evolving mass culture.[63]

Thompson's Luna Park exerted particular influence. Within five short years, according to one writer, it "set the pace for every other modern amusement park in the world." By then, at least four hundred amusement parks existed in the United States, with almost forty in Illinois and more than seventy in Ohio. If one counted fairgrounds and other resorts, there were perhaps two thousand such parks by 1910. Attendance around the country was reportedly high, from the 3 million in 1903 at Willow Grove Park in Philadelphia to the 600,000 at Olentangy Park in Columbus, Ohio. In 1905, Chicago's White City Amusement Park drew 2.25 million. Two parks near Los Angeles attracted 3 million. Moreover, parks usually touted their clean, safe environments. "No Objectionable Persons Permitted on Grounds," warned Cleveland's Euclid Beach Park. "If you come here," assured a brochure from Newark's Olympic Park, "you have no fear of contamination with the undesirable element. . . . Representatives of the rowdy element will not be tolerated." Even at Philadelphia's Washington Park, where the clientele came from "the less orderly class," according to a 1904

Rand McNally guidebook, the park's patrols kept out "the really 'tough' element." Liquor was rarely available in any amusement park.[64]

Like so much of the emerging popular culture, amusement parks were both disturbing and reassuring, offering safe thrills, balancing the risqué with the respectable, and providing modes of adjusting to a society in rapid flux. When the Russian critic Maxim Gorky sadly dismissed Coney Island for imposing "a slimy marsh of boredom" and "dismal ugliness" on working people, crushing their spirit and taking their hard-earned money, he scarcely spoke for workers who found the parks liberating and fun. Gorky's visit to Coney in 1906 convinced him that manufactured amusements were "the new opiate of the people," distracting them from an oppressive social and economic system. But the millions of lower-middle- and working-class patrons of Coney, many of whom were new immigrants from Eastern European nations, hardly shared such a bleak assessment. Where Gorky lamented their rushing "into the cages like black flies," they justifiably saw themselves as enjoying the fruits of recently won freedom and opportunity, using their prized leisure time as a welcome diversion.[65]

On one level, in fact, the amusement parks were all about breaking from cages—the cages of workaday roles, convention, respectability, responsibility, self-control, rigidity, and the scrutiny of prying neighbors and other cultural watchdogs, even within one's own family. "Coney Island in effect declared a moral holiday for all who entered its gates," as Kasson has written. "Against the values of thrift, sobriety, industry, and ambition, it encouraged extravagance, gaiety, abandon, revelry." Like preindustrial carnivals with their inversions of roles, expectations, and hierarchies, Coney Island provided a touch of the carnivalesque—in this case, "a Feast of Fools for an urban-industrial society."[66]

There were, for example, booths with imitation china dishes at which customers could throw objects. "If you can't break up your own home, break up ours!" urged the sign. In the Barrel of Fun, strangers bumped against and sometimes briefly held on to each other. Couples entered the Cannon Coaster with a sense of possibility; "WILL SHE THROW HER ARMS AROUND YOUR NECK AND YELL?" asked the advertisement. "WELL, I GUESS, YES!" According to another sign, the revolving Barrel of Love beat "love in a cottage" by "a mile." Or, in the words of one fun house operator: "The men like it because it gives them a chance to hug the girls, the girls like it because it gives them a chance to be hugged." Hints of sexuality were everywhere. As customers filed into Steeplechase, compressed-air jets blew women's skirts upward. After passing through this Blowhole area, former victims could sit in the Laughing Gallery and enjoy the embarrassment of subsequent visitors. "Greetings from Coney Island," proclaimed a postcard that showed a couple embracing on the beach. Another postcard carried the message, "I AM HAVING A H . . . OF A GOOD TIME AT CONEY ISLAND."[67]

More rambunctious fun lined Surf Avenue, which ran through the amusement district and where one observer encountered the "most bewildering, noisy approach to bedlam that we know of in America." Packed into a short stretch were vaudeville and burlesque theaters, cabarets, sidewalk vendors, roulette games, taverns, dance halls, calliopes, roller coaster rides, public swimming beaches, and, as one person wrote in 1908, "a streaming river of people arched over by electric signs."[68]

Granted, the merriment sometimes came at the expense of other individuals and groups, echoing the prejudices that shaped the outside society. Just as vaudeville shows included demeaning stereotypes, amusement parks manifested prevailing views on such subjects as beauty, normality, and race. Dreamland, for instance, had its collection of "human oddities," including a woman "So Fat That It Takes Seven Men to Hug Her," a collection of "aborigines," and, by 1912, William Henry Johnson, the "What Is It?" from P. T. Barnum's museum a half century earlier. One concession at Coney Island asked customers to "Hit the Nigger—Three Balls for Five [Cents]," the goal being to knock the black man off his perch with a rubber ball, dumping him in a tank of water. Variations on these Kill the Coon and African Dodger ball-throwing games included foreign targets such as Turks. Elsewhere, Chicago's Riverview Park had its African Dip and three Kansas City parks had Coontown Plunges. At Coney, African Americans encountered unofficial color lines requiring them to use separate bathhouses and swim in separate areas. As late as 1928, two-thirds of Northern amusement parks practiced some form of racial segregation.[69]

But, while amusement parks reinforced some social divisions, they helped dissolve others, forging new communities in which strangers mingled, however briefly, in the pursuit of common pleasure. The parks allowed people to venture into cultural borderlands, experiencing environments with brash possibilities—sideshow frontiers where, for example, women moved beyond their traditionally prescribed separate sphere into more open mixed-gender settings; where public forms of play overshadowed the revered privacy and quiet of the home; where etiquette norms wavered; where one could find the different, the unexpected, the exotic; where economic and class status blurred among the crowd; and where clothing worn in public, especially at the beach, could be looser, informal, and (especially for women) somewhat more revealing. An observer in 1892 believed that the less modest clothing affected behavior, reporting that "the haughty dowager, the exquisite maid, the formal-minded matron" took on "a devil-may-care disregard for the conventions of fashion."[70]

Even the efforts of proprietors such as Fred Thompson to emphasize their parks' decency and respectability (an advertising strategy that Thompson claimed had "increased the value of the property about five times in as many years") were misleading. As the writer O. Henry quipped, the morally uplifting process consisted mainly of raising prices "and hirin' a blonde named Maudie to sell tickets instead of Mickey, the Bowery Bite." On a variety of levels, the parks—like mass culture generally—deliberately bent the lines of respectability. In these public venues, it was possible to test roles that were otherwise unacceptable or at least questionable. Here, one could take "the brakes off," as Tilyou's son Edward observed: "People out for a good time forget all about the dress parade of business and social life. They cut loose from repressions and restrictions." Moreover, in an increasingly anonymous world, places like Coney Island allowed strangers to find common ground. While they waited in lines or laughed and screamed during exhilarating mechanical rides, they could momentarily discover a flickering sense of community where fear and suspicion gave way to feelings of camaraderie and shared adventure.[71]

But ironies and contradictions suffused this often daring, engaging, and thrilling domain of amusement and entertainment. Coney's "Sodom by the Sea" image competed with the claims that parks such as Luna were for moms, wives, daughters, and sisters. Even Fred Thompson admitted that Luna had its "frisky" side, albeit within well-policed limits. Morever, although Thompson insisted that "everything must be different from ordinary experience," most of the wondrous mechanical rides reflected, like a fun house mirror, the larger world of machines and technology. The difference was that, as Kasson has observed, "instruments of production and efficiency were transformed into objects of amusement." After all, the mechanics by which thrill seekers raced down Steeplechase's Gravity Ride were much like those that lowered miners into coal shafts, although, admittedly, roller coasters moved with more speed and within a holiday atmosphere. Indeed, the inventor of Coney's Switchback Railroad got his idea from watching customers pay to ride gravity-powered coal cars into abandoned mines. Similarly, except for its breathtaking vertical loop, Sea Lion Park's Flip-Flap Railway resembled elevated city trains. And even the uniqueness and audacity of the amusement parks' mechanical rides became more predictable and mundane, especially as entertainment venues proliferated. Significantly, too, despite their magical, carnivalesque qualities, amusement parks were, at bottom, managed environments, fenced in and providing illusions of disorder and risk. "The Greatest Sensation of the age," promised the Loop the Loop ride: "No danger whatever." Strangers might strike up a momentary friendship as they shared the thrills of that ride, but it was the purchase of a ticket that bound them briefly together in an increasingly commodified environment. It was, in sum, easy to exaggerate the extent to which amusement parks resisted and challenged the world outside their gates. In remarkable ways, the worlds on both sides of the fence moved in tandem, however uneasily and controversially. In both areas, privatized and commercialized spaces were the rule.[72]

Such implicit meanings were, nevertheless, of little consequence to the millions and millions of people from working- and lower-middle-class backgrounds who anticipated and relished their visits to places such as Luna Park. In those settings, participants could revel in the opportunities to shed inhibitions, take risks without real danger, enjoy a carnival atmosphere, and have a good time. The growing popularity of places like amusement parks was also, however, a rising concern to reformers who viewed the expanding mass culture as exploitative and often immoral. By the early twentieth century, a major struggle was under way over what critics dismissed as "Coney Island stuff."[73]

5

THE "LEISURE PROBLEM" AT THE TURN OF THE CENTURY

"'LOOPING THE LOOP' AMID SHRIEKS OF STIMULATED TER-
ror or dancing in disorderly saloon halls are perhaps the natural reactions
to a day spent in noisy factories and in trolley cars whirling through the
distracting streets," wrote Jane Addams in 1909, "but the city which per-
mits them to be the acme of pleasure and recreation to its young people,
commits a grievous mistake." Addams was no reactionary. She was an advocate for women's suffrage, an early member of the National Association
for the Advancement of Colored People, a defender of immigrant America
and beleaguered workers, and a founder of the helping profession of social
work. Yet she expressed alarm at ways in which commercial interests were
shaping mass entertainment, from amusement parks to budding movie
theaters and popular music. She had no quarrel with having fun or finding
joy in life. Like other turn-of-the-century reformers known as "progressives," Addams worried, nevertheless, about a leisure problem that reflected a broader set of social, economic, and political threats to America—threats
such as the monopolistic concentration of wealth, the exploitation of the
working class, political graft and corruption, and eroding moral values. To
rescue the victims of industrialization and urbanization, to reinvigorate the
nation's traditional democratic ideals, and to restore America's moral center, progressives such as Addams forged one of the most important reform
eras in U.S. history, lasting from the 1890s through World War I. Although
they accomplished much that was significant and substantial, they built on
shifting sands, including those of popular culture, where social and economic outsiders continued to produce and revel in the "Coney Island
stuff."[1]

A sense of crisis in the late nineteenth century and the early twentieth galvanized progressive reformers. The United States seemed at a turn-

ing point as dangers proliferated from many sources. Industrialization was one source, creating huge disparities in wealth, triggering class conflict, producing a monied elite with a "public-be-damned" mentality, and fostering powerful economic combinations. To challenge these massive corporations, whether to regulate them or to protect the ideal of economic competition, coalitions of reformers rallied to a "new politics" dedicated to protecting the "general welfare" and the "public interest." A related danger was apparent in the burgeoning cities, where urban bosses ran corrupt machines via graft and favoritism and a flood of new immigrants crowded into impoverished neighborhoods and overwhelmed urban services. During the forty years after 1880, approximately 23 million immigrants came to the United States; by the end of that time, foreign-born individuals constituted, for example, 40 percent of New York City's population. In Chicago, by 1890, roughly four of five residents had at least one immigrant parent. Reformers dealt with these issues on a variety of fronts and with varying strategies. Some who hoped to broaden the democratic process backed such political changes as direct primary laws, direct election of senators, voter recall of officials, and women's suffrage. Others with a more elitist bent favored "management" in place of "politics" and emphasized the need for credentials, expertise, and social efficiency. Some, such as Jane Addams, sought to aid disadvantaged groups by battling inequities and injustices; others worried more about controlling the "dangerous classes." But most agreed that the spread of mass entertainment presented a host of moral dilemmas that demanded attention.

Progressives tended to define issues in moral terms. The journalist William Allen White recalled the "profoundly spiritual" aspects of progressivism, which he described as "an evangelical uprising." Another reformer, Frederic Howe, remembered that "early assumptions as to virtue and vice, goodness and evil remained in my mind long after I tried to discard them." This progressive-style evangelism attested to the heavy influence on many reformers of mainline Protestantism, particularly its Social Gospel messages urging believers to respond, like the Bible's Good Samaritan, to the needs of workers, new immigrants, and the poor.[2]

Although the label *progressive* connoted a forward-looking perspective (which, indeed, characterized the reformers' views on, say, government's activist role), progressives tended to be cultural traditionalists, always more at home in the Victorian moral world from which they came. "Designate me an old fogey," wrote the California senator Hiram Johnson to his sons after reading that several thousand women had attended a boxing match in 1919, "but really, I prefer the womanhood of old to the non-child-bearing, smoking, drinking, and neurotic creature sitting at the ring side." Johnson, who, in 1912, was Theodore Roosevelt's vice presidential running mate on the Progressive Party ticket, remembered watching many "exciting" fights as a youth; yet he resented reports that many women attended the recent bout and that the fighters reportedly received $300,000 and $200,000, "what decent men cannot acquire in a lifetime of earnest, active and honest endeavor." In such developments Johnson saw not progress but regression.[3]

To Johnson and most other progressives—"ministers of reform," as one historian has described them—leisure and entertainment should always serve a wholesome, uplifting moral purpose. President Theodore Roosevelt thus described one of the Russian novelist Leo Tolstoy's works as "unhealthy," "vicious in its teaching to the young," and the product of "a sexual and moral pervert." The three-time presidential candidate William Jennings Bryan warned young readers against "the yellow back novel" and "literary trash" such as "'blood and thunder' Indian and detective stories." He urged boys to read books that educated, stimulated "worthy ambitions," emphasized morality, and taught "wholesome lessons without being namby-pamby." In 1909, Addams attacked the "trashy love stories" that were the fare of many cheap theaters, full of "flippant street music" and extolling "the vulgar experiences of a city man wandering from amusement park to bathing beach in search of flirtations."[4]

Charles Sheldon's phenomenal best seller *In His Steps* (1897) was a quintessential progressive novel demonstrating that moral works could find huge audiences at the turn of the century. In the mid-1890s, after studying for the ministry in New England, Sheldon brought a strong Social Gospel message to the pulpit in Topeka, Kansas. There, he sympathized with the downtrodden working class, whom decent, middle-class Christians should, he believed, assist. At the beginning of *In His Steps,* an unemployed tramp unsuccessfully appeals for help from a local preacher. Still desperate, the tramp subsequently shows up at the Sunday church service and tells the congregation that he has no job, his wife is dead, and he is having trouble caring for his small daughter. After imploring the good churchgoing people to look out for the less fortunate, he faints from hunger and exhaustion. The incident so shocks the minister that the next Sunday he asks the church members to go about their daily business for one month by asking what Jesus would do in the situations they confront. That request has a transforming effect. One by one, citizens in the community alter their conduct by attempting to follow in Christ's steps, putting Christianity into action. By the novel's end, the town is in the midst of an inspiring reform upheaval, in which middle-class individuals work to "do good" by battling corporate corruption, defending the disadvantaged, and uplifting the working class. Moreover, the town's conduct proves infectious, catching the attention of ministers in cities such as Chicago, where the reform spirit begins to stir.[5]

The upstanding middle-class leaders in Sheldon's fictional town had their counterparts in the Merriwell brothers, the heroes of almost 250 children's books, whose total sales of 500 million copies surpassed those of the

Bible between 1896 and 1918. "I always take the side of the underdog," proclaimed Frank Merriwell after stopping a bully from beating up a "little popcorn vendor." Unlike the main characters of many earlier dime novels for young readers, such as Horatio Alger's Ragged Dick, the Merriwells exuded genteel values as top students at prep school and Yale. Their creator was Gilbert M. Patten, a longtime dime novelist whom the Street and Smith publishing firm contracted in 1895 to write a series about a prep school youngster. Over the next twenty years, writing under the name Burt L. Standish, Patten ground out one story after another. Most of the plots focused on the athletic field, where the Merriwells were unbeatable. Mainly, however, the brothers were paragons of virtue. Although they were somewhat privileged youngsters, they battled to uphold the "old democratic spirit" of Yale and help the little fellow, directly and through their own example. "I don't know w'y it is," said one tough boy, "but jes' bein' wid you makes me want ter do de square t'ing." The Merriwells always played fair. They neither smoked nor drank. They also had courage and stood up for what is right. "I'll give you the licking you deserve!" Frank told one bully.[6]

The mischievous Penrod Schofield, the amazingly popular hero of Booth Tarkington's juvenile novels *Penrod* (1914) and *Penrod and Sam* (1916), lacked the crusading instincts of the Merriwells but manifested the sweet innocence of childhood that moralists prized. Despite his reputation as "the Worst Boy in Town," Penrod's harmless misbehavior resulted mainly in embarrassment. In his knickerbockers, and with "his wistful dog," Penrod provided a nostalgic portrait of a youth growing up in a Midwestern town, dreaming and creating most of his entertainment in his own backyard. L. Frank Baum's 1899 classic *The Wizard of Oz* was another influential children's book full of moral lessons.[7]

The best-seller list at the turn of the century suggested that many adults, as well as young people, relished books of good cheer—"Glad-books," or books that were packed with uplifting themes and subjects. In 1901, Alice Hegan Rice's *Mrs. Wiggs of the Cabbage Patch* was so popular that it inspired at least seven stage productions. "Looks like ever'thing in the world comes out right, if we jes' wait long enough," says Mrs. Wiggs, who endures a succession of troubles and woes. In 1913, Eleanor H. Porter created a character who came to symbolize blind optimism: Pollyanna, "the Glad Girl." The message of Harold Bell Wright, a minister whose many novels—especially *The Shepherd of the Hills* (1907)—were exceedingly popular, offered similar advice: keep the faith, and problems will go away. Gene Stratton-Porter, a druggist's wife in Indiana, wrote sentimental books such as *Freckles* (1904), about an orphan, and *Laddie* (1913), about a dog. One critic dismissed her books as "molasses fiction," but the thousands of letters she received from satisfied readers steeled her resolve: "I shall keep straight on writing of the love of joy and of life I have found in the world, and when I have used the last drop of molasses, I shall stop writing." Ultimately, her Indiana home became a tourist shrine.[8]

Several optimistic poets also developed huge followings. James Whitcomb Riley, who wrote verses from 1877 until his death in 1917, was so popular that his stage tours across the country were national events. In poems such as "The Old Swimming Hole," "When the Frost Is on the Punkin," and "The Raggedy Man," he celebrated old-fashioned values and the joys of childhood, marriage, and productive work, especially in small-town, rural America. Eugene Field and Edgar Allen Guest became famous as "newspaper poets," writing syndicated verses that appeared in papers across the nation. Field died suddenly in 1895, at age forty-five, but audiences continued to enjoy such favorites as "Wynken, Blynken, and Nod" and "Little Boy Blue," which recounted bittersweet memories about a dead child. Starting in 1899, Guest wrote thousands of poems that, he said, celebrated home, work, and God. "Somebody said that it couldn't be done," one poem recounted, "But he with a chuckle replied, / That maybe it couldn't but he'd be the one / Who wouldn't say so till he tried." The last words of the verse were: "*It couldn't be done, but he did it!*"[9]

Such optimism was ready-made for a generation of progressive reformers who believed that they were standing up against evil—a theme that suffused some of the era's most popular novels about the West. Owen Wister dedicated *The Virginian* (1902), probably the seminal adult western, to his friend Theodore Roosevelt. Although Wister's sympathies rested too much with big business to qualify him as a genuine progressive, his novel featured a classic shoot-out pitting a good and decent man against a well-defined villain. The forces of virtue also triumphed in the westerns of Zane Grey, an Ohio dentist who, during the 1910s and into the 1920s, wrote one best seller after another, including *Riders of the Purple Sage* (1912) and *Lone Star Ranger* (1915). "Never lay down your pen," urged one appreciative fan. "You are distinctively and genuinely American. . . . The good you are doing is incalculable."[10]

Despite considerable evidence that the Victorian cultural world was intact, progressives nevertheless had much to be nervous about. Moreover, they themselves helped open doors through which "Coney Island stuff" would move. There was, for one thing, the matter of technology, which seemed to provide the physical means by which to solve many problems. For reformers, breathtaking technological breakthroughs involving X-rays, automobiles, airplanes, audio recordings, and moving pictures heralded all kinds of promise for such areas as medicine, transportation, and education. Yet these innovations also produced unintended consequences. By shifting sources of information and agencies of change away from traditional institutions such as schools, churches, and families, they helped create a crisis in cultural authority.

For another thing, there was the role that much of the reform literature inadvertently played in advancing the cult of celebrity, which all too easily defined people in terms of visibility and notoriety, not character. In order to expose urban and corporate corruption and irresponsibility, "muckraking" journalists such as Lincoln Steffens and Ida Tarbell wrote powerful, colorful indictments of city bosses and industrialists like John D. Rockefeller. By exposing "the shame of the cities," Steffens and others hoped to alert the public to the need for political and economic reforms. In order to provide the "inside dope" on individuals, making them appear more real and less abstract, the muckrakers typically emphasized the personalities and memorable quirks of, say, Cincinnati's "Boss" Cox. But, by humanizing the "bad" as well as "good" guys (such as Theodore Roosevelt), and often by placing themselves in their stories, muckrakers pushed along a celebrity journalism that emphasized scandals, gossip, and private lives as the keys to understanding real people—sensational material that easily tipped toward entertainment.[11]

Progressives recognized, moreover, the importance that amusements could bring into drab and stunted lives. After all, even the fictional Penrod typically got into mischief because of boredom. The "craving to be amused," as the economist Simon Patten advised, offered an opportunity that reformers should seize. Efforts to repress entertainments were foolish and counterproductive because people, especially those in the crowded slums, needed recreational outlets. The problem was not with play but with the way in which commercial hucksters perverted it, fostering illicit thoughts and actions. In responsible hands, however, amusements could provide "attractive social control," as Patten put it.[12]

The challenge, in other words, was to provide uplifting kinds of entertainment, taking it out of the hands of what the settlement house worker Belle Moskowitz described as "those ungoverned, unlicensed, unregulated amusement resorts" that hoped only to make profits without regard to the types of fun they provided. One progressive strategy was to use licensing laws and the imposition of curfews to remove vice from entertainment. A second strategy enlisted cities to sponsor clean forms of fun, substituting "attractive virtues for attractive vices," as the journalist Walter Lippmann wrote. Municipal dance halls and athletic leagues needed to exist because, as Addams argued, "when commercialized recreation is left to its own devices, social neglect and lax enforcement of the law go hand in hand." Or, in the words of another reformer: "If the Christian worker is to win the boy of the street, he, too, must put in his bid for him."[13]

To provide uplifting amusements, in contrast to those that sacrificed

youngsters for profit, influential reformers launched a playground movement in the early twentieth century. Their goal was to encourage well-
ordered and carefully supervised play that would teach proper values
regarding the importance of cooperation, friendly competition, and law-
abiding conduct. "The playground is something more than a mere means
of pleasant diversion," wrote the newspaper editor Edward Booth. "It is,
in fact, a school, where instruction of no less value than that of the school
proper is given." Some of these playgrounds resembled military camps.
According to one observer in New York City, a pianist struck a chord at
1:00 P.M., "and all the children assembled fall in line for the grand march.
At a signal, the flag is saluted; then two or three patriotic songs are
heartily sung, after which the order is given to 'break ranks.'" In such
an environment, children reputedly learned values that would make
them dependable employees: "As a child plays," reported Booth, "so will
he later work."[14]

The playground movement was instrumental in moving basketball to
the city streets. James Naismith, who had trained for the ministry but became a physical educator, invented the game in 1891 in New England to
help occupy boys during the winter. His game was supposed to channel
their energies, improve their health, and enhance good sportsmanship. In
rural areas such as Indiana, where harsh winter conditions drove people
inside, basketball enjoyed wide support. But it was also popular on cold
outdoor playgrounds in the immigrant neighborhoods of cities such as
New York because it did not require large athletic fields or special equipment. "Everywhere you looked," recalled the Brooklyn-born Red Auerbach,
"all you saw was concrete, so there was no football, no baseball, and hardly any track there. Basketball was our game." Play reformers and settlement house workers were quick to use basketball as an urban recreation
program, introducing the sport into working-class communities, where it
developed strong ethnic followings. Indeed, New York City was soon "the
basketball capital of the world."[15]

Although basketball became a popular city game, youngsters' responses to the supervised playground movement indicated some of the obstacles
that reformers faced when they tried to compete with commercial amusements. As one eleven-year-old complained: "I can't go to the playgrounds
now. They get on me nerves with so many men and women around telling
you what to do." Or, as a fourteen-year-old observed: "I can't see any fun
playing as school ma'ams say we must play." Progressives discovered that,
if they hoped to attract slum children to the playgrounds, they had to be
more flexible and bow somewhat to the youthful desire for spontaneity and
roughness.[16]

Progressives such as Theodore Roosevelt certainly had no quarrel with
roughness. "We do not admire the man of timid peace," asserted Roosevelt.

"We admire the man who embodies victorious effort; the man who never wrongs his neighbor, who is prompt to help a friend, but who has those virile qualities necessary to win in the stern strife of actual life." Anxious about the decline in masculinity that seemed to afflict so many middle-class males at the turn of the century, Roosevelt and other reformers found much to admire in organized sports. The challenge was to encourage expressions of clean, muscular Christianity that avoided violent excesses and corruption.[17]

It was, thus, not coincidental that Roosevelt threw his support behind efforts to soften the brutality of college football. Although he had no sympathy with "baby act" talk about abolishing the sport, he was concerned about the excessive violence and unsportsmanlike conduct that harmed the game. In 1905, following a rash of deaths on the gridiron, he hosted a meeting at the White House with representatives from Yale, Harvard, and Princeton to discuss the need "to play football honestly." When Yale's Walter Camp helped draft a statement banning "unnecessary roughness, holding, and foul play" from the game, Roosevelt agreed. The White House meeting laid the groundwork for the formation of a voluntary organization to oversee college athletics, a good example of progressive strategies to boost fairness and civility in American life. The transition was, nevertheless, sometimes bumpy. At the University of Wisconsin in 1906, students, some armed with guns, responded to rumors that the administration might abolish football by marching on faculty homes and shouting: "Death to the faculty." "Put him in the lake," they shouted at one professor, and, before disbanding, they burned effigies of three faculty members.[18]

Like college football, professional baseball was a sport that benefited from a cleaned-up image during the Progressive Era. By the 1890s, the game was in serious trouble. The agonizing economic depression of the decade assuredly hurt, but fans stayed away also because of unruly, often inebriated crowds. One writer objected to an atmosphere that "reeked with obscenity and profanity." In 1893, owners of several Midwestern teams hired a thirty-year-old sports editor, Byron Bancroft "Ban" Johnson, to rescue their Western League. The three-hundred-pound Johnson implemented a number of strategies: clean up the game's image by squelching rowdy behavior and gambling, and challenge baseball's kingpins in the National League by, for instance, raiding their rosters. He changed the name of the Western League to the American League, increased the number of teams, and enhanced the game's respectability. In 1902, the American League enticed 220,000 more fans to its games than did the older, but embattled, National League. Over the next few months, the two leagues arrived at a "peace" settlement, agreeing to coexist and not take each other's players. In 1903, the champions of each league played in what became a "World Series," fueling more interest in a sport that was regaining its hold on the American imagination.[19]

Important in reinforcing baseball's mythical status were four legendary people who helped found the American League—Charles Comiskey, Connie Mack, Clark Griffith, and John McGraw. The careers of all four men resonated with the nation's love for rags-to-riches stories. Products of recent immigrant backgrounds or of poor Southern farms, they accumulated wealth and fame. Although they had very different personalities, they provided evidence that the American dream was achievable. Starting out with neither status nor privilege, they used baseball as a ladder of mobility. As players who became owners, they differed from the "magnates" of the National League, who had made fortunes in other businesses before buying teams. Moreover, Mack and McGraw especially tried to enhance the sport's respectability by, for example, requiring the players to dress in business suits on road trips. "I will not tolerate profanity, obscene language or personal insults from my bench," declared Mack. "I will always insist . . . that my boys be gentlemen." The presence in the major leagues of players with college backgrounds added to the game's status; although less than 5 percent of the college-age population of males had received any higher education in 1910, almost 26 percent of players had. Ten college-trained players were on Mack's 1906 team. The New York Giants, which McGraw managed after abandoning the American League, included the college-educated pitcher Christy Mathewson, whom the press hailed as a model Christian gentleman, living clean and playing fair. According to one magazine, Mathewson's influence on youths "quite overshadow[ed] George Washington and his cherry tree."[20]

By the early twentieth century, baseball—with a refurbished image, colorful individuals who symbolized the American dream, and more orderly fans—was, thus, on the rebound; between 1903 and 1909, game attendance doubled. By 1910, one magazine observed: "It has . . . [become] almost impossible to pick up a magazine that [does] not contain some kind of an article on baseball." The sport's strong middle-class influence was apparent everywhere, from the stands to the progressive ideology that hailed the game as a source of community, stability, traditional values, democracy, and (despite the absence of African American players) opportunity for anyone to succeed through merit and hard work. As fans gathered at the ballparks, Jane Addams wondered optimistically whether this was not evidence "of the undoubted power of public recreation to bring together all classes of a community in the modern city unhappily so full of devices for keeping men apart?"[21]

Boxing, which was still illegal in most states, posed a severer test for reformers. The sport had assuredly moved a considerable distance from its outlaw origins. Yet even Theodore Roosevelt, once an amateur boxer at Harvard who as president liked to put on gloves and spar at the White House, fretted that "a prize-fight is simply brutal and degrading. The people who attend it and make a hero of the prize fighter, are . . . to a very great extent, men who hover on the borderlines of criminality." Race was a complicating issue, especially after the African American fighter Jack Johnson won the heavyweight title in 1908. With a few notable exceptions, most progressives believed firmly in Anglo-Saxon superiority. Johnson's ascendancy challenged such beliefs. Granted, between 1890 and 1908 there were five black champions, but Johnson stood out because he fought as a heavyweight, the classification that John L. Sullivan had made preeminent, and because of his relationships with white women, his jaunty confidence, and his showy clothing. In 1910, when he defeated the "Great White Hope," the former champion John Jeffries, he taunted his opponent. "Package being delivered Mister Jeff," he said before he hit him; and he mocked the ex-champion Jim Corbett, who was at ringside. Many whites invested much hope in Jeffries, who, according to one sportswriter, "had Runnymede and Agincourt behind him, while Johnson had nothing but the jungle." Following the match, white mobs rioted in many places throughout the country. Elite African Americans disliked Johnson because he stirred white anger and made blacks more vulnerable, but he was a hero to the black masses. As one street song put it: "The Yankees hold the play / The white man pulls the trigger; / But it makes no difference what the white man say / The world champion's still a nigger." Johnson's defeat of Jeffries helped publicize boxing but also further endangered its reputation as a national sport. Thanks to the efforts of certain reformers, the Johnson-Jeffries fight film was banned in a number of states, as were prizefight films generally in some others. In 1913, the federal government indicted Johnson on morals charges. After he fled the United States, he reportedly agreed in 1915 to lose a title fight in Havana in exchange for the government's dropping the charges against him. Thereafter, into the 1920s, boxing resumed its search for a wider audience, with growing success.[22]

While coercive-minded antivice crusaders favored shutting down morally questionable kinds of entertainment such as prizefighting and dance halls, progressives such as Jane Addams followed different strategies. Addams and her allies sought to remove conditions by which illicit activities attracted working-class and poor people, to protect especially children from commercial exploiters, and to render amusements uplifting and educational. In tandem with advocates of the playground movement, progressives who saw music as a means of cultural elevation thus sponsored public concerts and free music instruction for children from, in the words of one reformer, "the alleys," not "the avenues."[23]

Two new technologies—the phonograph and motion pictures—seemed especially promising as agencies for uplift. Initially, however, the famous inventor Thomas Edison viewed his creations more as toys than as instruments of mass instruction. In 1877, after Edison designed a machine that recorded and played back his own voice, his Edison Speaking Phonograph Company staged practical demonstrations that mainly aroused curiosity about how the technology worked. With tinfoil wrapped around a cylinder and a stylus that indented the foil, the hand-cranked instrument reproduced speeches and other sounds. During exhibitions, notable people in a crowd (e.g., the mayor) would come onstage, say a few words into a mouthpiece, and then listen in amazement, along with the audience, to the words coming back through a funnel. But interest in the exhibitions faded after about a year, and Edison began developing his incandescent light. Only after Alexander Graham Bell and others in the early 1880s developed their own recording machine—the graphophone—did Edison return to his phonograph, "my baby," as he described it: "I expect it to grow up and be a big feller and support me in my old age." Even then, however, he was interested primarily in how businesses might adapt it for stenographic purposes; it was, his company claimed, better at taking dictation than was a woman, who all too often got sick, thought about men, or wanted a raise. Other entrepreneurs nevertheless turned to the phonograph as a source of entertainment. Some, such as Lyman Howe, charged ten-cent admissions to "concerts" where they used "horns" to project the sounds of recordings to audiences composed largely, if the catalog advertisements were correct, of refined, well-to-do listeners. In 1889 in San Francisco, a company set up two slot machines through which, for a nickel, a customer could listen to recorded sounds. The successful venture soon attracted other businesses to the field, including the Columbia Phonograph Company, which began to record popular music. By the 1890s, "phonograph parlors," containing coin-operated phonographs, were joining the spreading ranks of commercial entertainments.[24]

Even after Edison grudgingly opened his own phonograph parlor in New York City, his company and others that quickly dominated the recording industry (Columbia and the Victor Talking Machine Company) wanted to make their machines high-class instruments that middle- and upper-middle-class customers would buy and that would remove any stigma of low culture. They thus launched major publicity campaigns on behalf of respectable music that reflected cultivated tastes and preferences. At Victor, Eldridge Johnson designed a new record player, the Victrola, to produce music "for the classes, not the masses," as one trade publication contended. Unlike Edison's machine, which used a wax cylinder, the Victrola operated with flat disks. According to a 1910 advertisement: "It represents all the Victor repertoire of high class music in an attractive setting. . . . It appeals to the best class of people." An ad two years later applauded the opportunity to listen to great music at "your summer home, your yacht, and out on your lawn." Such advertisements typically portrayed expensively clothed, genteel people listening in their parlors to phonographs that fit nicely next to pianos and other symbols of Victorian domesticity.[25]

Victor took pride in offering opera music along with traditional parlor songs, such as Stephen Foster's "My Old Kentucky Home," or music that evoked sentimental images of home and family. In 1904, on its newly established Red Seal line of celebrity records, it signed the opera singer Enrico Caruso to an exclusive contract. A Red Seal record, which was supposed to be a sign of cultural polish, typically cost $2, about $1.25 more than the average recording. Indeed, in 1908, Victor sold one opera record, featuring Caruso and several other singers, for $7. "Not all of your customers can afford to purchase a $7.00 record," the company told its dealers, "but the mere announcement of it will bring them to your store as a magnet attracts steel." The stirring, patriotic music of military-style marching bands—particularly that of John Philip Sousa—was also available. Such marching music would, according to industry publicity, make "you wish you were going to war or doing something daring and heroic." The music was reassuring and safe.[26]

For progressives such as Jane Addams, who favored music outreach programs as ways to build community spirit and civic engagement, the persistent challenge was, nevertheless, to find music that bridged middle-class parlors and immigrant, working-class neighborhoods. To that end, Addams and her associates at Hull House, Chicago's famous social settlement, were remarkably innovative and open-minded. In order to appeal to larger audiences, they did not limit themselves, as some reformers did, to bringing serious, canonical classical European music to the masses. Addams believed instead that it was necessary to include "very 'popular' music" in the Hull House–sponsored concerts "in order to hold the attention of the hearers, as a whole." The concerts thus mixed children's songs, folk songs, and traditional ballads with light-classical fare. Such a musical blend could, in Addams's opinion, help people "forget their differences." Similarly, Hull House's musical instructors gave free lessons in an atmosphere that encouraged artistic freedom. In the Hull House Boys Band, for example, was a young clarinetist, Benny Goodman, who developed the talents that later made him a famed jazz musician. Still, invariably, Addams and her progressive cohorts hoped to contain the rebellious elements and settings of the rising commercial amusement culture. Addams thus objected to the "vulgar type of music," such as ragtime, that prevailed in dance halls. She hoped that Hull House–style entertainment would allow immigrants to come "in contact with a better type of American," even as it allowed them "to preserve and keep whatever of value their past life contained." As the head of the Hull House Music School observed, Addams (like Mary Rozet Smith, who funded the school) "believed in the civilizing and ennobling influence of good music."[27]

It was against that ideological backdrop that Addams and other re-formers saw the phonograph as a means to elevate the lives of working-class people, counteracting the more sensual offerings of dance halls and the streets. From this reform perspective, the phonograph allowed poorer citizens to discover the high culture of classical European music and enjoy soothing reminders of peaceful domesticity. As the head of the Victor Talking Machine Company's education department warned, youngsters particularly needed to hear music that was "not flimsy trash"; indeed, "worthless so called 'melodies,' with their accompanying verses of vulgar slang and coarse innuendo[,] . . . set a standard of musical taste to your children that is as morally dangerous as it is musically misleading."[28]

While the phonograph stirred a combination of hopes and fears among reformers, motion pictures also raised expectations and anxieties. By the turn of the century, movies, like the phonograph, were emerging as a pow-erful new medium. And, like the phonograph business, motion pictures moved from novelty status to mass entertainment despite the intentions of Thomas Edison when he first experimented with cameras and projectors. The idea of projecting moving images long preceded the work at Edison's laboratories, of course. Almost five centuries earlier in Italy, Giovanni da Fontana had used a lantern to cast shadows on a wall. In 1645, the Jesuit scholar Athanasius Kircher used a mirror and lens to reflect light on a screen. For years thereafter, lanternists told stories by pulling pictures through lanterns to create movements of images on a wall. In the mid-nineteenth century, the growth of photography facilitated making multi-ple copies of images. By the 1880s, "illustrated lectures," often dealing with travel, were popular among cultural elites and church-based groups. With such devices as long panoramic slides or turning glass wheels, pro-jectors could move a series of images across a screen. Individual pictures, if moved quickly enough, could give an illusion of continuous motion.[29]

By the 1890s, Edison's laboratory had devised a machine to show a short series of moving pictures that wealthy families would, he believed, find useful, if only as a hobby. Soon, however, he adapted visual images to his nickel-in-the-slot phonograph idea. Whereas patrons had previously lis-tened for a few seconds through earphones to a phonograph, they could now view short motion pictures through peepholes. In 1893, at a private showing at the Brooklyn Institute of Arts and Sciences, a select group of guests briefly watched tiny pictures moving along a perforated, celluloid film of Edison's assistants acting as blacksmiths. A visiting businessman ar-ranged to exhibit this Edison "kinetoscope" at the Chicago world's fair. A year later, several brothers contracted with Edison to open a kinetoscope parlor in New York City, showing fifteen- to twenty-second films that Edison made in a small studio with a roof that opened to let in sunlight and pivoted on circular rails to allow for the best illumination. The subjects ranged from the strongman Eugen Sandow flexing his muscles to Buffalo Bill, performers from Barnum and Bailey's circus, and a man getting a shave. As the popular kinetoscope parlors spread to other urban areas, competitors tried out different technologies for peephole shows, including the use of a drum with photographs mounted on it that customers rotated with a mechanical crank. Some of the films catered to men by focusing on exotic dancers or subjects such as *How Girls Go to Bed* or *How Girls Undress*. By then, however, the peephole business was losing its novelty and slipping into disrepute.[30]

Meanwhile, exhibitors pressed for technology that would project images on a screen. With a projector, they could increase revenues by using only one machine to show pictures to many individuals at the same time. Customers, moreover, would appreciate the larger images. Edison was, nevertheless, reluctant to develop such technology because he did not want to hurt sales for his kinetoscope. "Let's not kill the goose that lays the golden egg," he reportedly said. But, in 1895, when C. Francis Jenkins, an impoverished inventor and government clerk, along with the real estate entrepreneur Thomas Armat, asked him to market their newly developed projector under his famous name, he agreed. A year later, "Edison's Vitascope" made its debut to considerable publicity. "The Latest Marvel: The 'Vitascope' a new machine . . . is probably the most remarkable and startling in its results of any that the world has ever seen," one notice proclaimed. Soon, however, several other companies were also in the market, most especially the French-based Lumière firm and the Biograph company in the United States. Each was a complete motion-picture organization, making its own equipment and controlling the production and exhibition of its films. The pressing challenge was to make enough films to keep audiences coming back. To help in that regard, in 1896 the Edison Company had a photographer move around New York City with a portable camera, taking pictures of subjects that ranged from elevated trains to children playing in the streets. "It did not much matter *what* was filmed," as one media scholar has observed, "just that it *moved*." Edison also filmed the first kiss, featuring two actors from the stage show *The Widow Jones*. Although "the May Irwin Kiss" lasted only a few seconds, it stirred considerable controversy; one New York newspaper devoted almost a full page of commentary and illustrations to it.[31]

These short films began to appear in slide presentations, vaudeville programs, and, by the early twentieth century, traveling movie shows that periodically brought motion pictures to small towns. In 1897, Alva Roebuck of the rapidly expanding Sears, Roebuck mail-order business introduced a Department of Public Entertainment Outfits and Supplies that sold such items as movie projectors, films, and phonographs to people who dreamed of owning their own businesses. At a time when self-employment seemed increasingly remote for many individuals, advertisements declared that the movie business offered a chance for someone to make a profit and be "independent, . . . not subject to any individual company, corporation or community. You have no boss or bosses, you conduct the business to suit yourself." Albert (Bert) Cook and his wife, Fannie Shaw Cook, aspiring musicians and actors, thus purchased a projector and launched a "High Class Moving Picture Company." Working out of Wilkes-Barre, Pennsylvania, they circulated with their two-hour program from one small town to another. She sold tickets while he ran the projector for a lineup of twenty to twenty-five brief movies; the couple also sang melodies, sometimes matching the songs with the film images.[32]

To keep the novelty of movies from wearing off, exhibitors devised new strategies. Some colored the film by hand. Some implemented various kinds of sound effects, using pianists, narrators, phonograph recordings, and loud bangs. And some courted specific audiences, ranging from church groups to boxing fans (who could see the exhibition of fight films even if their states forbade prizefighting). Producers discovered the popularity of films that told stories, especially after the phenomenal success in 1903 of Edison's *The Great Train Robbery,* which the influential Edwin Porter produced and photographed. Although *The Great Train Robbery* was filmed in New Jersey, it provided the key ingredients of what became one of the most enduring of film genres, the western. Only about ten minutes in length, it was about a train robbery and the posse's chase to track down the outlaws.[33]

Movies became less dependent on other entertainment venues in mid-1905 when the Pittsburgh vaudeville magnate Harry Davis and his brother, John P. Harris, opened a remodeled storefront in nearby McKeesport for the single purpose of showing films. They showed fifteen minutes of film continuously from 8:00 A.M. until midnight and charged a five-cent admission. The venture was so popular that Davis, who was also a real estate speculator, opened fourteen more movie theaters in Pittsburgh. The "Pittsburgh idea" quickly spread to other cities; Davis himself owned theaters in Rochester, Toledo, Buffalo, and Cleveland. In order to elevate the five-cent theaters' status, owners dubbed them *nickelodeons,* adapting the Greek word for theater: *odeon.* By 1910, as many as ten thousand of what critics called "nickel dumps" had reportedly opened across the country. One magazine claimed that they were "multiplying faster than guinea pigs." *Billboard,* a trade journal for the amusement business, dubbed them the "jack-rabbits of public entertainment." Many of these nickel theaters were one-person operations, with the owner collecting admission, cranking the projector by hand, and sometimes providing narration and even singing. As economically shaky as these nickelodeons often were, they nevertheless allowed the movie business to establish more firmly its own entertainment niche.[34]

Although nickelodeons in small towns, as well as those in more upscale urban settings, attracted a middle-class clientele, their predominant location in working-class, immigrant neighborhoods established their "nickel-dump" reputation. In 1911, a Russell Sage Foundation study of New York City nickelodeons discovered that 72 percent of the audiences came from the working class. "The movies," as the famed entertainer Milton Berle recalled, "were something for the lower classes and immigrants." For a cheap admission price, individuals could sit anywhere they wanted, at any time of day, and watch escapist films that did not require an understanding of the English language. "It doesn't matter whether a man is from Kamchatka or Stamboul, whether he can speak English or not," explained one movie manager. "He can understand pictures and he doesn't need to have anyone explain that to him." In that regard, one commentator observed in 1909 that the medium's "very voicelessness makes it eloquent for Letts, Finns, Italians, Syrians, Greeks, and pigtailed Celestials." Moreover, clerks from stores near the nickelodeons—many of whom were young women—could watch films during their lunch hours, and factory workers could drop by on their way to and from the job. A 1907 article in *Harper's Weekly* described audiences of "workingmen[,] . . . tired drudging mothers of bawling infants [and] the little children of the streets, newsboys, bootblacks, and smudgy urchins." One person recalled: "They were called silent pictures. Maybe the pictures were silent, but the audience certainly wasn't."[35]

While the noisy settings added to the nickelodeons' disreputable image, so did rumors of thieves and pickpockets, although "there isn't an ounce of plunder in sight," joked *Harper's*. The odor of people jammed into stale rooms with little air circulation was another problem. "There were five hundred smells combined in one," sniffed one suburban visitor; "people with sensitive noses should not go slumming." Given this kind of environment, refined people reportedly stayed away or checked nervously to ensure that no one noticed them if their curiosity enticed them through the doors. The association of nickelodeons with the "canned beans" crowd and questionable entertainment piqued reformers' concerns that movies were "recruiting stations of vice."[36]

A growing sense of alarm gripped many progressives as they tried to understand this rising new medium. They fretted that "promoters of pleasure" were ruining a promising "educational medium." Traditional elites, who saw themselves as the distributors of proper culture, feared that motion pictures were contributing to lower-class disorder. "Undeveloped people, people in transitional stages," as the reform-minded *Outlook* magazine referred to immigrants and lower-class individuals, were particularly susceptible to the tawdry nickelodeon environment. "When a large percentage of the patrons of such theaters is made up of minors, or adults without education," in the words of another reformer, the situation was ominous.

According to a 1909 Chicago study, children constituted one-third of the audiences. Moreover, they were "mostly children of the poor," fretted the *Chicago Tribune,* which observed one boy leaving a nickelodeon "with his eyes popping and his mouth open in wonderment"; he seemed "ready to kill." Interviews with five hundred newsboys in St. Louis indicated that 87 percent regularly attended. Additionally disturbing was the finding that at least 40 percent of movies that the Ohio Humane Society examined in 1910 were "unfit for children's eyes." Darkened theaters only heightened the dangers.[37]

In 1907, to combat what *Harper's Weekly* dubbed "nickel madness," Jane Addams and her associates launched a three-month experiment, opening a three-hundred-seat "uplift theater," as one magazine described it, at the Hull House settlement. The environment was sanitary and offered such wholesome educational fare as travelogues, film adaptations of literary classics (including *Uncle Tom's Cabin*), and nature films like *Otters at Play.* But the brief experiment was a failure. On one occasion, only thirty-seven children attended. "It ain't lively enough," one boy explained. "People like to see fights 'n' fellows getting hurt, 'n' love makin', 'n' robbers and all that stuff. This show ain't even funny, unless those big lizards from Java was funny." The Hull House reformers soon closed their theater, whose offerings of *Sleigh Riding in Central Park* could not compete with *The Pirates* and *Car Man's Danger* down the block.[38]

More strident antivice reformers tried to shut down nickelodeons on Sundays or establish licensing laws. In New York State, there was talk about limiting motion-picture theater licenses to U.S. citizens. Such legislation, according to one magazine, was "aimed . . . at the horde of foreigners who operate the moving picture shows." Although the law apparently never passed, it revealed the ethnic undertones that influenced much criticism of the movie business. By 1913, a number of states and cities had passed legislation requiring more lighting in theaters as well as adult supervision of young children, although such regulations proved hard to enforce. There was also mounting discussion of the need to censor movie contents.[39]

Reformers were no match, however, for rapidly proliferating amusements that included the phonograph and motion pictures. In a variety of ways, American society as a whole was experiencing a formidable sea change of urban modernity—a transition that entertainments accelerated. The flood of technological, demographic, and environmental changes in cities at the turn of the century rudely and relentlessly shocked the senses. Time and space seemed disturbingly more fluid in the face of urban subway and elevated train systems, electric illumination, automobiles, billboards, advertisements, department store windows, a mass press with illustrations and comics, widespread tourism, and new social practices such as shopping and unchaperoned female mobility as well as the noisy, unruly environment of jostling crowds and congested traffic. In a rapidly urbanizing America, the frenzied pace, the constant visual and aural bombardment, and the continual warnings about dangerous streetcars and other machinery had a disorienting effect that forced new ways of seeing and understanding—an "aesthetics of astonishment."[40]

Movies—like amusement parks or the rapid-fire format of vaudeville—reflected this emerging aesthetics with special force. For one thing, motion pictures were all about movement. Comedies, in particular, unfolded with racetrack speed. Time and again in Mack Sennett's popular Keystone Kops movies, for instance, the ineffectual police frantically chased hapless culprits. The breathtaking action serials of the 1910s were similarly full of pursuits, explosions, escapes, and rescues—"Fisticuffs, kisses, falls, chases!" as one observer wrote.[41]

Smaller communities were hardly immune to the jolting transformations that rocked urban America. The new entertainment spilled over into scattered towns at a time when they were wrestling with escalating controversies involving unfaithful spouses, consensual sex, and female sexuality. In courtrooms around the country, juries found such issues increasingly muddled and ambiguous; innocence and respectable behavior were not always easy to measure. Conduct that was once unacceptable could now more commonly appear relatively harmless. Rhetoric about moral transgressions was one thing; applying that rhetoric in specific cases was another matter. These local dilemmas played out against a backdrop of messages from popular culture. As the historian Sharon Ullman has written: "A vast array of sexual images permeated turn-of-the-century American culture at the very moment that shifts in sexual attitudes, both subtle and striking, found voice in local communities." Granted, movies typically had little to do with reality. More often, they offered escape from and even contradicted it. Films like the Edison Company's *Why Mr. Nation Wants a Divorce* (1901) and Biograph's *The Threshing Scene* (1905) focused humorously, for instance, on henpecked husbands who were victims of asexual, nagging wives and desperately wanted out of their unhappy marriages. In fact, however, by then women were the primary instigators of divorce suits, and their complaints about unhappy sexual relationships were far from unusual. Although movies—like popular culture in general—were full of distortions and exaggerations, they tapped the public's growing anxiety and ambivalence regarding, as well as its fascination with, variant behavior. Films and other entertainments engaged audiences in discussions of changing conduct in ways that moral reformers did not. A number of screen images thus hinted at female sexuality and dealt playfully with it. Many Americans, trying to negotiate the shifting and increasingly complex terrain of modern sexuality, could identify more with popular culture's "scandalous" and sensational messages than with those of crusading moralists, whose Victorian guidelines seemed further and further removed from daily experience.[42]

Sensationalism had, of course, defined popular culture since the days of P. T. Barnum's Joice Heth exhibit and the penny press, but new technologies disseminated it at a quickening rate. It still owed much to the lower-class ambience of the urban streets, but now a kind of "low-rent amusement network" extended ever more widely from working-class, immigrant neighborhoods into cheap theater, burlesque, vaudeville, Coney Island, nickelodeons, and pulp magazines. The overwhelming objective of this network was to entertain, not elevate. Cheap theater, for example, provided rowdy and lurid melodramas. As one of its products, Mae West, recalled: "There were sassy things with music in which any excuse to get the girl into tights and drawers was all right, if they showed their lacy derrieres. Murder, rape, wrecks . . . also served us."[43]

The pulps, like most cheap entertainment, offered a counterpoint to respectable amusements. In contrast to the new mass circulation magazines like the *Ladies Home Journal* and *Cosmopolitan,* which depended on the middle and upper classes, the pulps—with about 120 untrimmed pages in a seven-by-ten-inch format—were anything but slick. Printed on rough, inexpensive wood-pulp paper, they soon specialized in fictional genres ranging from westerns to adventure, detective, and romance stories. Frank Munsey was the publisher who in effect started the "magazine revolution" that included the pulps. A farmer's son from Maine who entered the publishing business in the 1880s, Munsey in 1893 cut the price of *Munsey's Magazine* from a quarter to a dime, looking for a wider audience than periodicals had traditionally courted. Indeed, before Munsey, magazines had been the province of wealthy, educated readers whose elite monthlies, such as *Century* and *Harper's,* focused on high culture and travel. By lowering prices from the twenty-five- to thirty-five-cent cost of the genteel magazines, and by seeking a mass audience, Munsey inspired a new breed of publishers. In 1896, he took another important step, saving his floundering *Argosy* magazine by dropping photographs and printing only fiction on low-cost paper. The revamped magazine, full of adventure stories, soared to a circulation of over 700,000. Other publishers soon moved into the pulp business, including Street and Smith, which had previously printed boys' magazines. In 1912, Munsey launched other titles such as *Cavalier,* the first weekly pulp. By then, the dozens of competing pulps, all wholly dependent on newsstand sales, vied for customers with color covers that were increasingly suggestive and sensational. Moral uplift, education, and spiritual truths seldom intruded on the pulps' world, where low-paid writers in "fiction factories" churned out formulaic stories.[44]

While the pulps provided escapist literature for the masses, the music business discovered a huge audience for ready-made songs. Demands for sheet music and songbooks had grown since the 1850s, especially in middle-class homes, where residents more typically owned pianos and could read music. But music publishing had been unorganized, chaotic, and leisurely. Like owners of old country stores, sheet music publishers offered only a limited selection and seemed oblivious to marketing techniques. Most songwriters wrote for a few dollars and were virtually anonymous. Charles K. Harris, a self-taught banjo player from Wisconsin, changed this situation dramatically and helped introduce the modern music business. In the 1880s, he hung a sign up outside his shop: "SONGS WRITTEN TO ORDER." Although he could not write music himself, he dictated songs to someone who could, thereby producing music by request for special occasions. In 1892, he broke into the big time. His waltz "After the Ball," which he had placed with a variety show, unexpectedly became a colossal hit. Within a few months, he sold 400,000 copies of the sheet music. By the year's end, he was making $25,000 per week. Harris astutely relied on the emerging system of national marketing, especially advertising, to push sales into the millions.[45]

After Harris demonstrated that popular music could generate substantial profits, an aspiring group of entrepreneurs—often Jewish immigrants—entered the business. Most of the firms were grouped together in lower Manhattan, on Twenty-eighth Street, with at least twenty-one of them existing during a short time on one block at the turn of the century. This concentration of music-publishing firms—the location of which shifted several times over the years ("usually in close proximity to the source of the next dollar," according to one joke)—was known as Tin Pan Alley. When people walked down the street during the summer, they could hear hundreds of musicians banging out new compositions on pianos, generating sounds that resembled, according to one person, "a tin pan to a passerby with a sensitive ear for music." By 1910, through aggressive marketing that included mail-order houses and department stores, these new businesses were selling 30 million copies of sheet music annually.[46]

Many of the writers came from the millions of immigrants who streamed into the United States at the turn of the century, largely from Eastern and Southern Europe. Often untrained in music, they typically worked in teams, churning out songs in assembly-line fashion. "Most of my songs were written in less than 15 minutes," recalled one of them; the popular hit "Tea of Two" "was written in less than four minutes." Intuitively, they produced music that resonated with the immigrant working class.[47]

Theirs was music that bubbled up from the streets. Like a vaudeville show, it was rambunctious and full of rough edges. "A good song embodies the feelings of the mob and a songwriter is not much more than a mirror which reflects those feelings," said Irving Berlin, one of Tin Pan Alley's most famous composers. "The mob is always right," he added respectfully. "I write a song to please the public—and if the public doesn't like it in New Haven, I change it." His advice to other songwriters was to mingle with audiences and "watch what they're humming": songs should be "easy to sing, easy to say, easy to remember and applicable to everyday events." Berlin signaled not only a musical revolution but also, as the historian Ann Douglas has written, "a broad-based linguistic revolution" that popularized slang and common talk—an eclectic, democratic idiom.[48]

Like many of the Tin Pan Alley creators, Berlin was Jewish. In 1893, at age five, he had fled Russia's horrific pogroms with his parents and five siblings, traveling steerage to the United States with a few pieces of luggage. Originally named Israel Baline, he lived in the grim sweatshop poverty of New York City's Lower East Side. He learned English but dropped out of school after five years. By age thirteen, he was scraping out a living in the Bowery, sleeping in flophouses and hallways as he waited tables in seedy dives, played the piano in saloons, and sang for nickels and dimes. He could sound like an Italian, an Irishman, a German, or a member of a number of other ethnic groups. Although he never learned to read or write music, he began composing as many as seven songs a week, tunes that mixed ethnic parodies, sugary ballads, and novelties. For the rights to his first song, he received thirty-seven cents.[49]

Berlin's music, like that of Tin Pan Alley overall, provided the sounds of "a new nation being born," as the writer Jody Rosen has argued: "melting pot music, the sound of a polyglot America emerging from its Victorian past and striding jauntily into the century it would claim as its own." The music was fun, full of possibilities and suggestions of breaking loose—"My Wife's Gone to the Country (Hurrah! Hurrah! Hurrah!)." It was sexually suggestive. In the 1904 hit song "Meet Me in St. Louis," a man finds a note from his wife: "It ran, 'Louis dear, / It's too slow for me here, / So I think I will go for a ride.'" If her husband will follow her to the St. Louis fair, however, she promises to be his "tootsie-wootsie." A 1909 hit described a man wondering: "Who's kissing her now, / Wonder who's teaching her how . . . / I wonder who's buying the wine / For lips that I used to call mine, / Wonder if she ever tells him of me, / I wonder who's kissing her now." Other songs had titles such as "There's Yes in Your Eyes" and "If You Talk in Your Sleep Don't Mention My Name." Some music was nostalgic about the "good old days": "Down by the Old Mill Stream" and "I Want a Girl (Just Like the Girl That Married Dear Old Dad)." Some dealt with new machinery and technology: "The Elevator Man Going Up, Going Up, Going Up" and "Come Away with Me Lucille in My Merry Oldsmobile." Some focused on geographic settings, such as the Swanee River that Stephen Foster had made famous. The writers of "Swanee, How I Love Ya," Irving Caesar and George Gershwin, had not seen the river. "We'd never been south of the Battery in New York," admitted Caesar. "When we finally did see the river, however, on a trip to Florida, it was a good thing we had written the song first because the Swanee turned out to be just a nice muddy stream."[50]

The accessibility and openness of this melting-pot music was evident in Irving Berlin's 1911 instant hit "Alexander's Ragtime Band," which quickly sold 1.5 million copies. It joyfully welcomed listeners to "Come on and hear! Come on and hear!" Here was music from the nation's social margins. It opened up traditions, as the music historian Gary Giddins has written, spreading "underclass musical styles" and welcoming people to join "cross-cultural assimilations." Although the melting-pot ideal fell far short of reality in the larger society, Tin Pan Alley was remarkably receptive to ethnic and racial influences, including music from the black lower classes.[51]

African American elites typically despised such low-class music—an "epidemic" of "vicious trash," according to the *Negro Music Journal* in 1902. Members of the black upper social stratum usually patterned their social events after those of whites in the genteel South, sponsoring formal balls and charitable events. Detroit's Summer Club, which formed in 1890, specifically banned working-class kinds of entertainment, including popular dancing. In sharp contrast, the rural jook joint had a notable lack of social polish. It was, as the writer Zora Neale Hurston recalled, "a Negro pleasure house. It may mean a bawdy house. It may mean the house set apart . . . where men and women dance, drink, and gamble." Often little more than dirty shacks, the jooks catered to the postslavery Southern black workforce. "Musically speaking," wrote Hurston, "the Jook is the most important place in America. For in its smelly shoddy confines has been born the secular music known as the blues." The jooks formed the basis of what became the storied "chitlin circuit" for many underpaid black performers. Meanwhile, the honky-tonk—the urban equivalent of the jook—generally catered to black wage earners outside agriculture. African American elites, who saw themselves as cultural arbiters and models for their race, watched contemptuously as black working-class amusements spread. Especially disturbing were the popular musical sounds from dives and brothels: the blues and ragtime.[52]

The blues were a home-brewed American musical form with a variety of roots, including West African rhythms, the slave experience, spirituals, field hollers, Saturday night parties, and prison work songs. Among poor blacks, for whom the end of slavery held out the promise of new opportunity yet typically resulted in disappointment and discrimination, the music was particularly poignant. It reflected pain, a keen awareness of life's anguish and hardships, and a stoic determination to survive at least through the night. "Singing the blues is like being black twice," observed the fabled bluesman B. B. King. According to the writer Ralph Ellison: "The blues is an impulse to keep the painful details and episodes of a brutal experience alive in one's aching consciousness, to finger its jagged grain, and to transcend it." A sense of loss as well as an awareness of evil—outside and inside oneself—suffused the music. "You can't hide from yourself," as Teddy Pendergrass would sing later, "Everywhere you go, there you are." Or, in the words of the blues singer Robert Johnson: "Early this morning, you knocked upon my door. And I said hello Satan, I believe it's time to go." In such phrases, the black writer Langston Hughes discovered "the kind of humor that laughs to keep from crying." Blues singers often characterized their music as "a feeling"—for example, "a feeling that a sound would put you into," as Leonard "Baby Doo" Caston once described it. W. C. Handy, who became a musician despite the advice of his father (a minister who warned that he was selling his soul to the devil), claimed that he first heard the blues in 1903, when he was traveling on a train with a minstrel troupe through Mississippi. In his legendary account of musical discovery, Handy described how "a lean, loose-jointed Negro had commenced plunking a guitar beside me while I slept." "As he played, he pressed a knife on the strings of a guitar," giving it a wailing sound. "The effect was unforgettable."[53]

Given the blues' social origins and subject matter, which often included sexual themes, it was not surprising that many whites as well as respectable black churchgoers shunned the music. The blues certainly had no elite musical pedigree. "What I mean is you can't put down the music in the blues on no paper," as the singer Big Bill Broonzy later said. No wonder that W. C. Handy was not sure initially "if anybody besides small town rounders and their running mates would go for such music." He changed his mind, however, when he discovered "the beauty of primitive music" while watching "a local colored band" in Cleveland, Mississippi. To his surprise, this music from the "cane rows and levee camps" elicited an enthusiastic audience response, and "a rain of silver dollars began to fall around the outlandish, stamping feet" of the band. "My idea of what constitutes music," he recalled wryly, "was changed by the sight of that silver money cascading around the splay feet of a Mississippi string band." Ultimately, Handy became one of the music's prime disseminators, laying his claims as "Father of the Blues" by publishing in 1912 his popular "Memphis Blues" (for which he received only $100) and, two years later, his spectacular hit "St. Louis Blues," whose polished sounds had a Tin Pan Alley quality. Although the song was "a pretty tune" with a "kind of bluesy tone," according to the singer T-Bone Walker, it did not truly qualify as "the blues. You can't dress up the blues." Still, however dressed up, "St. Louis Blues" was a musical landmark that found a huge audience.[54]

Handy's songs contained elements of ragtime, already part of a national music craze following the release in 1899 of Scott Joplin's sensationally popular "Maple Leaf Rag." "The term 'ragtime,'" according to Ann Douglas, "probably derived from 'ragged [or broken] time' and meant 'tearing time apart'; the phrase 'to rag' meant to tease. . . . Playing ragtime on the piano, the right hand was literally teasing the left." Ragtime combined the classical European music style with the popular expressions of the new immigrants and African Americans: "It was a tease and a put on." Through the process of "syncopation," the musician played "against the beat" by emphasizing the weak melodic offbeats.[55]

There were other ragtime composers, but Joplin justifiably attracted the most attention. His shortened, tragedy-filled life started in 1868, when he was born on the Texas-Arkansas border. He taught himself to play the piano, so impressing a German music professor that the man gave him free instruction in classical European music. As a youth, Joplin hit the road, reportedly working in taverns and bawdy houses. In Sedalia, Missouri, he studied at a small college for African Americans, composed music, and worked at the short-lived Maple Leaf Club. John Stark, a white man who had sold ice cream before entering the music-publishing business, liked what Joplin was playing and, in 1899, agreed to pay a one-cent-per-copy royalty to publish "Maple Leaf Rag." The rather unusual royalty agreement ultimately benefited Joplin because, at the time, most publishers still paid a flat fee of $25 or $50 for a piece of music. Within a decade or so, customers bought almost half a million copies. Living with his new bride on the edge of St. Louis's red-light district, Joplin continued to write music, but his life was unraveling. His wife left him after their baby daughter died, and his second wife died of pneumonia within a few months of their marriage. Joplin battled terrible bouts of depression, ending up in a state hospital, where he died in 1917 at age forty-nine. "A homeless itinerant, he left his mark on American music," wrote John Stark in a brief but insightful eulogy.[56]

For a moment, "ragging" became a way to protest subtly against genteel music. Even ragtime's energetic, percussive-like use of the piano countered the staid and stiff parlor tradition of the respectable middle class. Within reserved Victorian homes, the piano had become a symbol of femininity and moral uplift. In the 1920s, President Calvin Coolidge said grandly: "We cannot imagine a model . . . home without the family Bible on the table and the family piano in the corner." Ragtime—like much of the music that was coming out of Tin Pan Alley—was partly a reaction to that Victorian ethos and its cloying, moralizing domesticity, a fact that did not escape traditionalists, who attacked "nigger whorehouse music" that was "artistically and morally depressing." The National Federation of Women's Clubs expressed its determination to recapture music from "the hands of the infidel foreigner" and poor blacks. And, in 1914, the *Musical Observer* stated that morally pure Christian homes should oppose ragtime.[57]

"You know," Irving Berlin later claimed, "I never did find out what ragtime was." Yet he helped popularize it and, by doing so, manifested one of popular culture's most creative dynamics: a process by which Jews drew on black culture and helped introduce it to the mainstream. In the big-city streets of the North, a host of Jewish youths honed their entertainment skills by watching and listening to African Americans. "A colored fellow used to move and dance on our street," recalled the comedian Joe Sulzer, who grew up in the 1890s on New York City's Lower East Side. "He had sand and threw it on the sidewalk and danced. The sound of the sand and the shuffle of his feet fascinated me and I would try to dance like him." According to Sulzer: "We'd pick up routines from the street." As a young-ster, George Gershwin, who ultimately became one of Tin Pan Alley's prime talents, listened to ragtime in Harlem and Coney Island. Blackface acts were common to many Jewish performers, especially early in their careers. Eddie Cantor blacked up with Bert Williams in a "Follies Pickaninnies" act in which they sang Berlin's "I Want to See a Minstrel Show." Burned cork became such "an inseparable part of my stage presence," Cantor said, that "I feared the day might come when I could never take it off." Al Jolson, born in Russia as Asa Yoelson, and so nervous as an actor that he often vomited between scenes, recalled another performer who advised him early on: "You'd be much funnier, boss, if you blacked your face like mine. People always laugh at the black man."[58]

Such burned-cork performances reportedly provided a vehicle by which Jewish immigrants assimilated themselves into the larger culture. But there were larger meanings. Significantly, the implicit message from amusement sources like Tin Pan Alley was that American culture was inclusive.[59]

Granted, these cross-cultural exchanges were complicated and ambigu-ous. A musical hybrid such as "Alexander's Ragtime Band," for example, was open to various interpretations. On one level, it unquestionably per-petuated minstrel stereotypes. In coon songs and minstrel shows, the name Alexander typically identified a highfalutin black man with comical preten-sions. Still, on another level, Irving Berlin's song added to the ragtime craze and may even have encouraged cultural mixing. From the perspective of the Jewish magazine *Forward* at the time, Jews in blackface represented "a sign of intense cultural bonding" across racial lines. Invariably, of course, the question was who gained and at whose expense. As Ann Douglas has observed: "American entertainment, whatever the state of American soci-ety, has always been integrated, if only by theft and parody." In this sense, Tin Pan Alley's cultural collaboration was skewed. Although Berlin hardly personified ragtime, many people thought he did. The English hailed him in 1913 as "the King of Ragtime." Within two years, Berlin himself assert-ed that he had "started the ragtime mania," and, by 1920, he was claiming that America's popular music came from people of "Russian birth and an-cestry"—individuals of "pure white blood." The African American writer James Weldon Johnson found all this perplexing. He recognized that popular culture grew from a "plurality of voices" and believed that it could be a weapon against prejudice and for the integrated world that he favored. By the mid-1920s, he nevertheless worried about white appropriation of black creativity—about white cultural imperialists who colonized black music. "The first of the so-called Ragtime songs to be published," he wrote, "were actually Negro Secular folk songs" to which whites had "affixed their own names as the composers." Although popular culture was, thus, more responsive to outsiders than the nation was as a whole, it mirrored the larger society in which some people were more equal than others.[60]

Still, as Tin Pan Alley demonstrated, popular entertainment time and again represented a cultural upheaval from the nation's margins. Not coincidentally, criticism of the emerging music business contained strong nativistic warnings about the "suggestive" lyrics and racial rhythms of "Hebrew Broadway jazz" or ragtime ("symbolic of the primitive morality and perceptible moral limitations of the Negro type," according to the *Musical Courier*). Similarly, a genteel citizen such as Henry Seidel Canby, the proud product of an elite culture "in which one quickly knew one's place," apprehensively viewed working-class people who "let themselves go": "These indeed were our barbarians."[61]

But it was precisely those barbarians whom one encountered on phonograph records and in movies—courtesy of an entertainment business that did not wish to limit sales. Hence, the Edison Company told its dealers that, while "Grand Opera lovers are saving up money to buy more records, the good old 'ragtime-coon songs . . . sentimental ballads' crowd will still be on the job buying . . . until there's frost on the sun." And, despite the Victor Talking Machine Company's expensive Red Seal recordings and its commitment to music "for the best class of people," it nevertheless made cheaper "Black Label" records for a larger audience. One of Victor's most popular singers was Ada Jones, the daughter of an English saloon keeper who had moved to Philadelphia. By age six, Jones was performing onstage as "Little Ada Jones"; when she was twenty, she reportedly became the first woman to make a commercial solo recording. "I believe," she said, "that the world is enriched by the melodies and sentiments that come from the masses." Many of her songs were, thus, about single working-class females who were having fun. In "Coming Home from Coney Isle," she reveled in their enjoyment of good times. She also poked fun at middle-class propriety and the sentimentalized family. In one song, she joked about a young woman whose boyfriend marries her mother: "And Now I Have to Call Him Faaather."[62]

Even people who detested Tin Pan Alley music complained that it imprisoned them. "God sent us the Victrola, and you can't get away from it," lamented one person about the power of the phonograph. "It's everywhere, this Victrola: in the tenements, the restaurants, the ice-cream parlors, the candy stores. You lock your door at night and are safe from burglars, but not from the Victrola."[63]

Movies could be equally unsettling. While the rapidly flickering images reflected the sheer momentum of social and economic changes, the films often battered Victorian standards of decorum, manners, and authority. Even though Thomas Edison declared that "nothing is of greater importance to the success of the motion picture interests than films of good moral tone," he was quite willing to make exceptions. His 1899 *Tenderloin at Night* had the ingredients of an urban morality tale, but, two years later, *What Happened on 23rd St., NYC* simply showed a strong wind lifting women's skirts. Once, when he was screening films of female dancers, he reportedly clapped his hands and said: "That is good enough to warrant our establishing a bald-head row, and we will do it too." The bald-head row probably liked the Edison Company's *What Demoralized the Barbershop* (1897), which showed how the sight of two women's legs could disrupt a cellar barbershop. As the legs pass into view at the top of the movie frame, men scramble to get a better look up the women's skirts, and the distracted barber accidentally puts shaving cream in the mouth of his unsuspecting customer. Biograph's *The Pajama Girl* (1903) showed a partially unclothed young woman taking a bath.[64]

Companies such as Biograph also cranked out risqué films, including Biograph's *Peeping Tom* (1897) and *One Girl Swinging* (1897), in which the woman reveals her undergarments as she swings toward the camera. In another movie, the audience gets a close view of a woman's lower leg when she is trying on shoes. As the nearby chaperone reads the paper, the male clerk touches the young woman's calf. When the chaperone discovers the clerk and woman kissing, she clobbers him with her umbrella. In Biograph's *The Story the Biograph Told* (1903), an office boy uses a camera to take movies of his boss passionately kissing his young female secretary. That night, the boss and his wife are at the theater when suddenly the pictures on the screen are those the boy took of him and his secretary. At the film's end, the angry wife hires a male secretary for her husband.[65]

A number of movies, particularly those of David Wark Griffith at Biograph, were strongly sympathetic to the working class. Griffith had worked on a lumber schooner and in an iron mill, picked hops, jumped rides on freight trains, and lived in flophouses. Between 1908 and 1913, he made some five hundred films for Biograph; each lasted about ten minutes, and many portrayed decadent monopolists exploiting workers and bankrupting innocent people. Although he cared little about the fate of African Americans, he used his camera to champion white laborers.[66]

Griffith's injection of social commentary into early films was not unusual. Workers and political radicals made movies that dealt with strikes and the evils of monopoly. They sometimes found allies among progressive reformers, who hoped that movies might inform the public about such ills as child labor and prostitution. In turn, large businesses and organizations like the National Association of Manufacturers sought to enhance their public images with industrial films celebrating the wonders of the new technology or arguing that corporations were improving safety on the assembly lines despite careless workers. The Ford Motor Company had a Department of Motion Pictures, and the Heinz ketchup company provided theaters for its employees. Some employers' associations convinced conservative film producers to provide antiunion messages yet not alienate working-class audiences. A common strategy was to praise workers while portraying labor organizers as radical agitators. In 1917, Edison's *Courage of the Commonplace* thus depicted nonunion laborers drinking lemonade while shabby foreigners in saloons plotted vile union deeds. Women's issues also received attention, particularly in Lois Weber's movies. Weber had started out as a street-corner missionary before turning to the stage. By 1917, after writing, starring in, and directing several one-reel movies, she was producing her own films, focusing on issues of fairness to women, hypocrisy, birth control, poverty, child abuse, and capital punishment. "I can preach to my heart's content," she said happily about her movies, although censorship groups criticized her for dealing with taboo subjects. In sum, battles over film contents and ideology buffeted the emerging movie industry.[67]

The rise of independent moviemakers—many of whom were recent Jewish immigrants from Eastern Europe—exacerbated these battles. Edison and the other film pioneers were overwhelmingly Anglo-Saxon Protestant Americans. Their views of the new immigrants were made clear in the Biograph film *The Fights of Nations* (1907), which portrayed Jews as money-loving con artists and showed inferior ethnic groups deferring to a very genteel and white Uncle Sam. But, by around 1910, some of those very immigrants were making movies of their own. A number of these upstarts were newcomers to the United States who had struggled initially on the economic fringes in rough, emerging businesses such as ready-made clothing. Sensing the magical effects of motion pictures on audiences, some had opened storefront nickelodeons in poorer neighborhoods. Soon they spotted opportunities in distributing and making—not simply showing—movies, particularly because the several thousand working-class theaters typically needed twenty or so new films every week in order to keep patrons coming back. Edison tried to freeze out this growing competition. In late 1908, he persuaded eight of the established producing companies (including Biograph and Vitagraph) to join the Motion Picture Patents Company: "the Trust." Members agreed to use only Eastman Kodak raw film stock; in return, Eastman would sell only to them. Although theaters were supposed to pay for licenses to show Patents Company films, at least two thousand refused to do so. The Trust's formation ignited a series of lawsuits to break up the monopoly and intensified competition from the independents, who scrambled to find film stock and equipment that the Trust had not licensed and also to serve the unlicensed theaters. When, in desperation, the independents started pirating licensed machines, the Trust struck back, sometimes violently. It was partly to distance themselves from the Trust that many independents moved to the southern California coast, where, moreover, the weather was conducive to year-round filming.[68]

Through pluck, ingenuity, and a knowledge of storefront nickel theaters and inexpensive entertainments, the independents were soon ascendant. Largely the products of the impoverished, foreign-born working class, they had found in the movies an alternative ladder of economic success, one on the margins, with a questionable reputation but still very much developing. "A Jew could make a lot of money at this," Adolph Zukor remembered thinking. Born in Hungary, and orphaned by age eight, Zukor had come to the United States after reading about it in dime novels. He arrived at age sixteen with $40 from a Hungarian orphanage board. "A newborn person," as he described himself, he attended night school, apprenticed in a furrier's shop, established Zukor's Novelty Fur Company, and then turned to amusements, operating a penny arcade and, by 1908, a small string of nickelodeons. His interest in making movies was not simply mercenary. Like many of his immigrant compatriots, he sought to channel his considerable energies in fresh directions. From his perspective, Edison's Trust "belonged entirely to technicians." Zukor had a grander vision: "What I was talking about—that was show business." In late 1912, after Zukor had produced several movies, the *New York Evening Journal* declared that he was "the most notable figure in the moving picture field today." The middle-class Protestant movers and shakers of the pre-1907 movie business were quickly giving way to people who would soon dominate the industry: future Hollywood studio "moguls" such as Zukor, William Fox, Carl Laemmle, the Warner brothers, Samuel Goldwyn, and Louis B. Mayer.[69]

For genteel Protestants such as Henry Seidel Canby, who worried that "barbarians" threatened refinement, the movies provided disconcerting proof. In film after film, the official representatives of respectable society looked absurd and foolish. In Mack Sennett's Keystone Kops movies, for example, the police were befuddled and incompetent. "Authority had been ridiculed!" Sennett explained gleefully. "That was exactly the artistic effect I was after." The son of a blacksmith and a former plumber's assistant, Sennett saw himself on the side of the "little guy." In his opinion: "Nearly everyone of us lives in the secret hope that someday before he dies he will be able to swat a policeman's hat down around his ears." Sennett's working-class experiences, like those of many silent-movie comedians, influenced his cynical view of authority. His films, like slapstick comedy in general, featured simple heroes who suffered ritualistic indignities, injustices, and defeats but ultimately survived. "They whaled the daylights out of pretension," Sennett said of his common protagonists. "They made fun of themselves and the human race. They reduced convention, dogma, stuffed shirts, and Authority to nonsense, and then blossomed into pandemonium." The writer and film critic James Agee remembered that "'nice' people . . . condemned the Sennett comedies as vulgar and naive" while "the laughter of unrespectable people" showed that they were "having a hell of a fine time."[70]

It was hardly surprising that such "unrespectable people" found Charlie Chaplin's "Little Tramp" character so appealing. Chaplin was a product of the London slums and had grown up in the Hanwell School for Orphans and Destitute Children. He identified instinctively with the working class and did nothing to discourage speculation, although untrue, that he was Jewish. "Born in the poorest class in England," he said, "with no past, nor castles, nor ancestors to defend, I was not a man to encumber myself with prejudice. If they wanted me Jewish, they would have me Jewish." Onscreen, his liberating antics continually subverted social order and pomposity. With his trademark baggy trousers, bowler hat, narrow moustache, and splay-footed walk, the Little Tramp dreamed of love and modest success even as disappointment and hard times besieged him. In the 1915 film *The Bank,* Chaplin plays a janitor who thinks he is kissing the lovely secretary that he secretly loves only to realize that he has been dreaming and is, in fact, embracing a wet floor mop. In *The Immigrant,* made two years later, he lacks the money to pay his restaurant bill and ineptly spills beans into his coffee as he looks longingly at the woman across from him. Time and again, Chaplin played a lonely, poverty-stricken outsider, desperately seeking acceptance and love in a cruel world. Events and modern technology continually plague him, but he survives with dignity and grace. And he does so by distinguishing himself from the hypocrisy and phoniness of wealthy, pretentious, and privileged people. In *The Floorwalker,* a 1916 film, the shabby-looking but honest Tramp draws the wrath of a suspicious department store manager, who harangues him while two rich people, unnoticed, shoplift at will. Chaplin's lovable character stood out as a model of strength and innocent virtue, offering a poignant example to working-class audiences, whose lives were also full of hard knocks.[71]

Movies thus often offered a view from the bottom up. And they typically did so in cheap nickel theaters full of the great unwashed. Perhaps invariably, reactions to films during their first twenty or so years cut across class lines. It was, for example, fear of lower-class disorder that stirred the progressive reformers' largely failed efforts to use films as agencies of moral uplift. To immigrant workers, class was an important issue, too. For many of them, movies offered inexpensive moments of fun, relaxation, and escape and typically did so by lampooning high society, elite snobbery, and institutions. For at least some plebeian viewers, the nascent film business also meant something else—a chance to break loose and explore new opportunities.[72]

Young, working-class women, for example, discovered thrilling new worlds by watching motion-picture serials about daring and adventuresome female heroines. In mid-1912, the Edison Company collaborated with a lowbrow "mail order journal," the *Ladies' World,* to make twelve monthly film installments for theaters of *What Happened to Mary.* Each segment lasted about twenty minutes. In the series, Mary, who is orphaned at the end of the first installment, encounters a host of exciting adventures and close calls that eventually bring her social recognition. The popularity of *What Happened to Mary* inspired other female adventure series and, after only five episodes, boosted sales of the *Ladies' World* by 100,000. The magazine, and others like it, had gotten revenues not from subscriptions but from printing mail-order advertisements. Readers came from the working and lower middle classes, an audience that the Edison Company clearly wanted to tap. At the end of each *What Happened to Mary* episode, words on the screen urged viewers to check the *Ladies' World* for pictures and information about the series and offered a $100 reward for the best essay on "What Happened to Mary Next?" In 1913, another movie company struck a deal with the *Chicago Tribune* to coordinate newspaper stories and bi-weekly film installments of *The Adventures of Kathlyn.* A year later, the William Randolph Hearst publishing chain contracted with Pathé Studios for a serial, *The Perils of Pauline.* Shortly, with the production of competing installments, including the *Hazards of Helen* (with 119 episodes) and *Lucille Love, Girl of Mystery,* "serialitis" was reportedly seizing female fans.[73]

Series such as *What Happened to Mary* demonstrated the film industry's growing courtship of working women. Between 1880 and 1910, the number of females in the paid labor force doubled to 20 percent and in some cities tripled. By 1910, perhaps as many as 60 percent of young single women in urban America were working before they married; across the country as a whole, that percentage had climbed to 40 percent. Work aside, more women were visible in public. Increasingly, they enjoyed the kind of freedom that had traditionally been a male privilege as they shopped, rode electric trolleys and bicycles, visited amusement parks, and attended movies. By 1910, females constituted 40 percent of the working-class film audience.[74]

Against that backdrop, it was not surprising that the serial-queen melodramas on film emphasized female power and portrayed young females in roles ranging from detectives to reporters. The protagonist of the *Hazards of Helen* series, which began in 1914, was a female telegraph operator who engaged in such breathtaking feats as leaping from one train car to another as she escaped crooks. Significantly, mothers were virtually nonexistent in these serials, and the heroines spent little time in domestic settings. Although the films focused on heroic female workers, they nevertheless carefully avoided topics that involved political action or strikes. And, paradoxically, the "perils" and "hazards" that faced fictional stars such as Helen provided lingering reminders of female victimization and, sometimes, the need for male rescuers. Viewers could have it both ways. "It may be that I shall consent to marry Harry some day," Pauline says, "but you know my adventurous spirit and my desire to live and realize the greatest thrills"; yet, after many escapades, she declares: "I have once and forever finished with this life of adventure. I am quite prepared to marry you, Harry, and we shall be happy at last." Although the serials included double-edged messages, they recognized the growing importance of a female audience and sparked imaginations about the world "out there." The opening lines of *What Happened to Mary* offered some tantalizing possibilities: "Mary's eyes were smoldering that day with the fire of strange yearnings. She moved about her work as one walking in a dream—burning with a life that was not the life around her."[75]

While fictional working-class characters such as Mary, Helen, and Pauline broke from traditional social restraints, they had a real-life counterpart in Harry Houdini, a Jewish immigrant who built a career around sensational staged escapes. After toiling for a number of years on the entertainment margins, he became an inspiring model of self-liberation, using much-publicized stunts to free himself from numerous fetters, including handcuffs, straitjackets, and chained boxes. Houdini, a master illusionist, dazzled audiences with implicit evidence that the unadorned individual can prevail over the institutions and technology of the modern world.[76]

Born in Budapest, Hungary, in 1874 as Erik Weisz (later Ehrich Weiss), Houdini had immigrated at age two with his family to Appleton, Wisconsin, where his father became a rabbi in a small German Jewish congregation. Times were harsh, and, at one point, the family relied on a local relief society to get through the winter. With creditors in pursuit, the Weiszes moved to New York City, where both Erik and his father worked in a necktie factory. Not long after his father's death in 1892, Erik became an entertainer. After several years of performing in dime museums, variety theaters, circuses, and burlesque shows, he was ready to quit show business. Yet he soon established himself as a breathtakingly popular illusionist. Although he changed his stage name to Harry Houdini, some gossiping detractors doubted that "this low-minded Jew has any claim on the word American." No one, however, could dispute his talents as an escape artist. "MANACLES DO NOT HOLD HIM," announced the *Kansas City Times* after he proved that he could get loose from restraints that professional police officers placed on him. In 1906, he freed himself from the "escape-proof" tombs in a Boston prison. Dangling high in the air from downtown buildings, he also electrified throngs of viewers in numerous cities by shaking loose from straitjackets. Bound with handcuffs, he jumped off bridges into deep water and emerged with his hands free. Onstage, he had authorities lock him in a milk can full of water, from which he escaped before drowning. Similarly, he extracted himself from the "Chinese Water Torture Cell." When he died in 1926, it was from a ruptured appendix, not because he had failed to shed any restraints.[77]

Again and again, the Great Houdini symbolized the victory of common human beings over social and technological restrictions. He represented, in the words of the historian John Kasson, "a modern David pitted against institutional Goliaths." Institutions could not imprison him, nor could representatives of the impersonal corporate economy. At one point, he let a manufacturer of automobile tire chains handcuff his wrists, shackle his ankles, padlock six chains around his body, and chain him to an automobile wheel and tire. Yet he escaped. According to Kasson: "In an age of often bewildering obstacles and intimidating authorities, he dramatized the ability of a lone figure to triumph over the most formidable restraints and the most implacable foes and against the most impossible odds."[78]

Undoubtedly, the theme of breaking loose characterized mass amusements on many levels, from Coney Island to movies and Tin Pan Alley. Popular culture, growing from urban sensationalism and lower-class entertainments, was itself moving outward and upward. And, significantly, its liberating messages increasingly resonated with the sons and daughters of middle-class America.

6

POPULAR CULTURE AND MIDDLE-CLASS RESPECTABILITY IN THE EARLY TWENTIETH CENTURY

EDGAR RICE BURROUGHS WAS BORED. AS THE SON OF A SUC-cessful entrepreneur whose company made storage batteries, he had grown up during the late nineteenth century in a middle-class Chicago family. "Nothing interesting ever happened to me in my life," he recalled. "I never went to a fire but that it was out before I arrived. . . . The results were always blah." Uninterested in academics, he dropped out of prep school, suffered through the rigid discipline of a military academy, and sought excitement in brief stints as a cowboy, gold miner, railroad police officer, and member of the U.S. Cavalry. When he settled down with a wife and children, he was a bookkeeper, sold pencil sharpeners, and worked, he said, "as a very minor cog in the machinery" of the Sears, Roebuck mail-order company. His restlessness grew as he toiled in the business world, where the emphasis was on organization, efficiency, and system—a world that Burroughs viewed as an iron cage. To challenge the restrictions of the modern technological society, he decided to write stories about heroic individuals who were strong, free, and fiercely independent. He had no illusions about his limited writing talents, but his perusal of a few pulp fiction magazines convinced him that he need not worry. "If other people got money for writing such stuff," he said later, "I might, too, for I was sure I could write stories as rotten as theirs." Ultimately, he became a best-selling author of some one hundred books, including many about one of the most successful fictional heroes ever: "Tarzan, Lord of the Apes," whom the thirty-seven-year-old Burroughs introduced in 1912 in the pulp magazine *All-Story*.[1]

Burroughs's venture into the low-culture world of the pulps mirrored the longing of many young people from reputable middle-class backgrounds who helped bring popular culture into the commercial mainstream. "We wish to escape . . . the restrictions of man made laws, and the inhibitions that society has placed upon us," Burroughs said tellingly. "We would each like to be Tarzan. At least I would; I admit it."[2]

In the early twentieth century, that emotional urge to break loose from daily routines boosted the amusement sector, making it more central to American society. And, as popular culture strengthened its influence on American life, it repeated the familiar theme of adapting sideshow material to mass entertainment's ever-growing big tent. Ironies aplenty marked that process. Burroughs, for example, created a Tarzan character who represented an appealing and romantic counterpoint to modern constraints and regimen, yet Burroughs ended up as a virtual slave to his writing, complaining that "the work is so hard." Averse to "system," he nevertheless kept a strict accounting of his word output, cranking out 413,000 words in 1913 alone. Starting in 1914, he wrote a new Tarzan book (along with other stories about warrior heroes) almost every year until 1939, when heart troubles slowed him down.[3]

While Burroughs adjusted his own life to the impersonal modern order that he opposed, similar paradoxes abounded elsewhere. Sports, which were increasingly organized and commercialized, produced individualistic heroes whose motivations supposedly came purely from a love of the game. Immigrant newcomers to the United States ironically created movies that strengthened and shaped deeply rooted American myths regarding opportunity, democracy, and freedom. Budding entertainment entrepreneurs, lagging behind their competitors, became major innovators. Corporate elites, by hailing the pleasures of consumerism, not only enticed citizens to purchase new products but also inadvertently subjected traditional values to "the seductive power of the new popular culture," which included risqué stage shows, entertainment celebrities with enhanced power over taste and conduct, and "undignified" kinds of music such as jazz and "hillbilly." Moreover, individuals with reputations for "cleaning up" such diversions as music and dances helped popularize what had been previously suspect.[4]

Insofar as Americans "wanted to be like Tarzan," sports offered a number of larger-than-life models. By the end of the 1920s, several figures had assumed legendary status, particularly football's Harold "Red" Grange, boxing's Jack Dempsey, and baseball's George Herman "Babe" Ruth. They were, in effect, "compensatory heroes" who helped their fans make up for feelings of lost individual power in a changing world of tightening rules and systems, bureaucracies, and schedules. These athletes seemingly shrugged off the restraints of modern society, asserting themselves as flamboyant individuals while reaffirming traditional dreams of personal success over tremendous odds.[5]

Timing played a predictably crucial role in the emergence of these sports heroes. Ruth, for example, helped rescue baseball from the dispiriting "Black Sox" scandals of 1919–20. But, as much as any factor, America's 1917 entry into the Great War, which for almost three years had already taken a horrific toll across the Atlantic, set the stage for sport's huge burst in popularity.

U.S. participation in the war initially encouraged athletics by echoing the turn-of-the-century exhortations about strenuous lifestyles and muscular Christianity. The reform-oriented psychologist G. Stanley Hall believed: "War is, in a sense, the acme of what some now call the manly protest. In peace women have invaded nearly all the occupations of man, but in war male virtues come to the fore, for women cannot go 'over the top.'" A man in the U.S. Army, according to Hall, grew "hair on the chest not only of his body but of his very soul." In order to win what President Woodrow Wilson described as "a war to end war" and what prominent ministers saw as "America's holy war" or a "twentieth-century crusade," Americans needed to be physically fit. In that context, the armed forces were aghast to learn that about 30 percent of military-age males were unfit for military service. The military thus organized a number of recreational programs, assuming that competitive sports created better soldiers. "Never before in the history of this country have so large a number of men engaged in athletics," observed one newspaper. Relatedly, the war placed women in more physically active roles, including industrial jobs. Criticism of "ungirlish" militarism receded as membership in organizations such as the Girl Scouts took on patriotic meanings.[6]

Meanwhile, to prepare American soldiers and boost their morale, the military established football teams at each of the training camps and hired people such as the Yale coach Walter Camp to help. Camp contended that learning to throw a football was good training for lobbing hand grenades, a viewpoint that the *American Boy* magazine ratified in an article entitled "Athletics' Aid to War." Physical education teachers for the Young Men's Christian Association (YMCA) compared boxing to bayonet practice. Basketball's inventor James Naismith directed the YMCA's wartime Bureau of Hygiene. And professional baseball teams conducted close-order drills with bats over their shoulders.[7]

The postwar mood also boosted the popularity of sports and athletic heroes. Although the war ended in November 1918 with the United States on the winning side, tensions and disillusionment were quickly apparent. The bloody conflict had highlighted technological weaponry and organizational efficiency far more than individual heroism and courage. Moreover, it was soon apparent that the war to end wars and to make the world safe for democracy had not realized those idealistic goals. The Bolshevik Revolution in Russia in 1917, coupled with the wartime search for traitors, ignited a "Red Scare." A dramatic economic slump right after the war touched off a wave of strikes that exacerbated fears of Communist subversion. And divisions worsened between Americans with loyalties to traditional village values and the largely urban residents who represented a more cosmopolitan, diverse world. By the early 1920s, these strains and anxieties were fueling ugly political battles over immigration restriction, a revived Ku Klux Klan, enforcement of Prohibition, and censorship. Mass entertainments negotiated these treacherous cultural crosscurrents by incorporating changes while reinforcing familiar, valued traditions. In sports, this process helped produce a kind of golden age.

College football benefited particularly from a series of postwar trends that stimulated excitement about sports. State-supported universities boomed, ultimately tilting the balance on the gridiron away from the elite Eastern schools that had dominated the game. Important also in collegiate football's shifting power were a number of private schools with large Catholic followings, especially Notre Dame. Under the storied leadership of Knute Rockne, Notre Dame became a dominant gridiron force during the 1920s. Rockne became such a coaching celebrity that Wilson Sporting Goods paid him to put his name on its footballs and helmets; by the end of the 1920s, he was giving pep talks to Studebaker's salespeople for $75,000 a year, more than the company's president received. His Notre Dame teams were a multiethnic collection—"Rockne's Irish, Swedes, and Poles," as an Atlanta newspaper described the 1927 version. "GEORGIA TECH BEATS MICKS" read a headline in Dallas a year later. In 1931, during what was becoming an intense intersectional rivalry, the University of Southern California defeated Notre Dame, according to one sportswriter, because of the superiority of the former's "native American stock."[8]

The surge in football's popularity was evident elsewhere, including the construction of new stadiums. During the early 1920s, no fewer than twenty colleges and several cities built stadiums with more than twenty thousand seats. These structures were often memorials to the Great War's dead soldiers—Chicago's Soldier Field and Los Angeles's Memorial Stadium, for example. The rise of the automobile culture facilitated trips to these sporting arenas. Closed autos made even winter drives to games more feasible. In 1919, only about 10 percent of the nation's cars were enclosed; by 1927, that figure had leaped to 85 percent. According to a 1923 University of Illinois publication, soon "five million people will be within five hours drive of the Stadium," which "is to be one great agency in putting the University before the state of Illinois." Meanwhile, the ongoing communications revolution continued to popularize sports such as football. New techniques of transmitting photographs by wire meant that pictures of athletic competitions were available to newspapers across the country within several hours. Movie newsreels, which began in 1911, increasingly included sports footage. And, by the late 1920s, the new medium of radio was providing instant coverage of athletic events.[9]

Crucial to the postwar sports craze, however, was the public hunger for heroes. Such heroes supplied evidence that, in a rapidly modernizing world, traditional values and virtues still counted. Red Grange was a dazzling example. For believers in small-town, rural America, he seemed to show that the modern world of cities and technology had met its match. Hailed as a poor boy from rural America, he symbolized the continuing resilience of the countryside. In many respects, that image was much exaggerated. Although Grange had, indeed, been born in a rural area in Pennsylvania, his family moved to Wheaton, Illinois—thirty miles from Chicago—when he was five. If he was no country bumpkin, neither was he poor. His father was the town police officer, earning a salary exceeding that of most industrial laborers. Despite the discrepancies between reality and perceptions that surrounded Grange, he was a superb football player who electrified the nation on October 18, 1924, scoring four touchdowns in the first twelve minutes of the University of Illinois's homecoming game against a formidable University of Michigan team that had won twenty consecutive contests over two years. Before the game was over, Grange scored another touchdown, passed for another, and rushed for a total of 402 yards—a scintillating performance that became the stuff of legend. Moreover, he accomplished these feats before a record football crowd in the Midwest—sixty-seven thousand—and did so on the day that the university dedicated its new stadium to honor Illinois's war dead. Within a few days, movie audiences across the nation could see flickering black-and-white images of Illinois's "Galloping Ghost" weaving across the screen. Shortly thereafter, the national magazine *Literary Digest* published an article on Grange, "The First All-American Iceman," extolling his work ethic and humility. Suddenly, Grange's summer job delivering ice became part of his mythology, additional evidence of his solid rural virtues.[10]

The press descended on the university campus, staying outside Grange's fraternity house for several days, hungrily gathering bits and pieces of news about the redheaded football star. "I had no privacy," Grange recalled about his newfound celebrity status. "This man Grange of Illinois is three or four men and a horse rolled into one for football purposes," wrote the sportswriter Damon Runyon. "He is Jack Dempsey, Babe Ruth, Al Jolson, Paavo Nurmi [Finland's great distance runner] and Man o' War. Put them all together, they spell Grange." All this attention piqued the interest of a colorful con artist, Charles C. Pyle, who quickly helped develop the concept of a sports agent. Pyle had embarked on many moneymaking schemes over the years, including a traveling theater company in which he played the tuba and had a drunk act. By the 1920s, he owned three movie theaters in Illinois. Pyle convinced Grange to sign a contract with Chicago's professional football team, which he would join the next fall even though he had not yet finished his college career. In 1925, Grange turned professional, despite a storm of university protests about the intrusion of pro football—"a dirty little business run by rogues and bargain-basement entrepreneurs," as one sportswriter said. Over the next several years, in fact, Grange helped popularize the professional game, which had lacked status, fielded teams in a variety of Midwestern "tank towns," and attracted fans whom one writer associated with the roller derby. Grange's pro debut attracted a standing-room-only crowd of thirty-six thousand to watch the Chicago Bears play. The Bears' owner, George Halas, was ecstatic: "There had never been such evidence of public interest since our professional league began in 1920. I knew then and there that pro football was destined to be a big-time sport." Over the next few years, Grange continued to elevate the professional game while also appearing as the top bill, "C'mon Red," for a vaudeville tour and starring in several movies, including a twelve-part serial, *The Galloping Ghost,* that did well at the box office. He had contracts as well to endorse "Red Grange chocolates," a soft drink, and various kinds of clothing.[11]

For a public searching for heroes who personified self-made success and familiar values, Grange provided an answer. From one angle, certainly, the fact that he loved driving automobiles at high speeds and appeared in movies placed him in the modern age. From another angle, however, his popularity perhaps reflected his ability to accommodate different eras and different values.[12]

The heavyweight boxing champion Jack Dempsey played a similar cultural role. He, too, was in notable ways a media creation for anxious times. Despite his reputation as "Jack the Giant Killer," his ring record was far from sensational. After he won the heavyweight title from Jess Willard in 1919, he defended his title only six times in seven years—and often against questionable competition. But, whatever his actual accomplishments, he captured the public imagination and helped immensely in boxing's push for respectability.

The war had already assisted boxing in that regard. No less an authority than General John J. "Black Jack" Pershing, the supreme commander of the U.S. troops, had declared that boxing "is what makes the American Army the greatest in the world." In the military camps, boxing was extremely popular, and the prizefighter Mike Gibbons showed soldiers how boxing techniques could fend off bayonets. Moreover, the terrifying realities of a war that included mustard gas and machine guns made the brutality of the boxing ring appear quite civilized.[13]

Canny promoters such as George L. "Tex" Rickard cultivated that image in their successful drives to legalize boxing, as New York did in 1920, and turn the sport into a truly big business. Such legalization constituted a shrewd compromise: state regulation, the middle ground between prohibiting the sport and allowing unchecked corruption. Rickard, the "King of Ballyhoo" and a promotional artist, used a number of strategies to add "re-

fined" people to boxing's constituency. In 1921, for example, he established a special "Jenny Wren" section for female spectators at a championship
bout. "Women," he said, "have given us insurance for the future of boxing." He also searched for a fighter who could draw crowds, something that
Jess Willard had not done. Indeed, after Willard defeated Jack Johnson in
1915, he did not defend his title for three years, choosing instead to tour
with a Wild West show.[14]

Rickard found his fighter in William Harrison "Jack" Dempsey. Born
in tiny Manassa, Colorado, Dempsey was the ninth of thirteen children of
a poor Irish American family that sometimes received charity assistance
from a local church. He learned to box in taverns, hobo jungles, and mining camps. "I can't sing and I can't dance," he would announce in cheap
bars, "but I'll lick anyone in the house." If he won the ensuing fight, he
passed the hat for donations. Otherwise, he nursed his wounds and headed
off to the next place. He was virtually unknown when Rickard discovered
him and paired him as the underdog against Willard in a mid-1919 heavyweight championship fight. In Toledo, Ohio, with the heat soaring to 106
degrees, the 180-pound Dempsey faced off against the massive Willard,
who was six feet five and almost 300 pounds and had already killed one
fighter. Fans gasped in surprise when Dempsey knocked the champion to
the mat seven times during the first round, sending Willard to his corner
with a broken jaw and missing teeth. In the fourth round, Willard sat dazed
on his stool while his assistants tossed a bloody towel into the ring. Dempsey
had catapulted to fame. Rickard made sure that he stayed there. In 1921,
he matched Dempsey against France's Georges Carpentier, the light heavyweight champion of Europe. Carpentier weighed only 170 pounds, but
Rickard blew the fight out of proportion, touting it as a battle between a
"foreign foe" and an American, and spreading rumors that the Frenchman
was working on a mysterious punch. Over eighty thousand fans brought in
boxing's first million-dollar gate and watched Dempsey knock out
Carpentier in the fourth round. ("He can't fight," Rickard had told Dempsey
before the fight. "I could lick him myself. So I want you to be careful and
not kill him.") In September 1923, Dempsey fought an Argentinean, Luis
Firpo, whom Rickard touted as the "Wild Bull of the Pampas." During the
electrifying first round, Firpo knocked Dempsey out of the ring. Still, the
champion needed only five minutes to win the bout, flooring his opponent
nine times. By then, Dempsey had established himself as the "Manassa
Mauler," a celebrity who could earn $500,000 annually in vaudeville
shows, movies, and other appearances outside the ring.[15]

Dempsey became boxing's first millionaire champion, the poor kid who
ultimately made it to the big time, eating at fancy restaurants, mixing with
famous people, and receiving an invitation to the White House. He also
blended many of the era's paradoxes. On one level, he fit with the emerging

modern world of show business, marketing, public relations, and advertising. He was impulsive, enjoyed fast cars, and relished the glitter of the movie industry. On another level, he was quiet and modest outside the ring, emphasized the importance of his parents, gave talks on clean living, made movies with moral lessons, and saw himself as unremarkable: "I was just a big kid that God blessed with a good punch." But, to average citizens who had their own personal difficulties to overcome, Dempsey was a larger-than-life champion. This son of a frontier family had become an "everyman, fighting our battles," as the sportswriter Paul Gallico wrote: Dempsey "crystallized something that all of us at one time or another long for—to be able to [stand] 'up' to someone, a giant, a bully, a tough guy, without qualm or tremor, and let him have it." In that spirit, young kids scuffling in the streets would say: "Aw, who do you think you are—Jack Dempsey?" A poem portrayed Dempsey as a defender of common citizens: "Knock down the big boss, / O, my little Dempsey, / my beautiful Dempsey / with that Godinheaven smile / and the quick, god's body leaping, / not afraid, leaping, rising— / hit him again, he cut my pay check, Dempsey."[16]

"Dempseymania" revealed a split in the newspaper business over the growing power of sports departments, which some editors believed were "going hog wild." Since the early twentieth century, sports coverage had increased by half, with "no end in sight." The growing complaints from more senior press members echoed their larger concerns about the "Typhoid Marys of journalism" who turned news into entertainment with an exaggerated tabloid style. The sorry objective, lamented one reporter, "is to buy white paper at three cents a pound and sell it at ten cents a pound." In turn, advocates of more sports coverage feared that the trend toward newspaper consolidation was standardizing the nation's 1,250 newspapers. The sportswriter Heywood Broun favored putting "the power of imagination" into writing and resisting "the standardization of the copy desk." Moreover, journalists such as Broun could point to studies showing that one in four readers looked mainly to the sports section, which tapped into the proliferating amusement economy. Indicative of entertainment's hold on the public, Americans sang the phenomenal hit of the mid-1920s, "Yes, We Have No Bananas," according to one observer, more times than they did "'The Star Spangled Banner' and all of the hymns in all of the hymnals put together." In that context, although a writer like Ring Lardner might dismiss "Dempsey worship" as a "national disease," it reflected an expanding public demand.[17]

Even in defeat, Dempsey's mystique grew. He lost twice to Gene Tunney, an ex-marine. The first time was in 1926, in front of over 120,000 spectators; the second time was in September 1927, in the famous "long count" fight with over 104,000 fans watching. Debates continued for years over whether Dempsey would have won the second fight had he gone immediately to a neutral corner after knocking Tunney down. "I couldn't move," Dempsey later explained. "I just couldn't. I wanted him to get up. I wanted to kill the son of a bitch." Because the referee did not start counting until Dempsey finally retreated to the proper corner, Tunney gained an additional few seconds to compose himself and go on to win the match. Tunney never won over the fans, however. His "scientific" style of boxing was efficient but not exciting, and his drab personality summoned up comparisons to "a no account clerk" or "a man in an arrow collar." Dempsey, on the other hand, exuded a kind of outlaw spirit in the ring, the kind of rebellious demeanor that suggested he could smash through modern constraints, compensating for the powerlessness that most people felt.[18]

Babe Ruth brought that same spirit to baseball. He did so, moreover, at a moment when the sport was trying to shed a shocking scandal that jeopardized its image as the nation's favorite pastime. In September 1920, at the conclusion of baseball's most successful season ever, the public learned that eight Chicago White Sox players had taken bribes to lose the 1919 World Series. Despite the players' confessions and a grand jury indictment, the trial ended up in acquittals. Spectators at the trial erupted with cheers and applause when the verdict came in. One writer was convinced that a guilty verdict would have been as crushing a blow as learning that "Daniel Boone had been bought by the Indians to lose his fights in Kentucky." But baseball's owners realized that they had to remedy a bad situation. They dissolved the governing commission that had existed since the 1903 truce between the American and National leagues and brought in the federal judge Kenesaw Mountain Landis—a formidable name, one that matched his appearance and reputation—as baseball's single high commissioner. Landis quickly used his quasi-dictatorial powers to ban the Chicago players, even though a jury had acquitted them, and crack down on any hint of gambling, rigged games, and even off-the-field legal scrapes. His high-handed actions nevertheless won general approval. According to the *New York Evening World*: "The supreme court of baseball is not governed by the same restrictions as a court of law. It is concerned primarily in protecting the game and not the technical rights of the players." But Landis had done more than protect the game. Just as important, he had protected the game's image, buttressing a myth that the notorious "Black Sox scandal" constituted baseball's solitary moment of sin.[19]

While the white-haired, firm-jawed Landis had reportedly given baseball "a character bath," as the *Chicago Tribune* described it, Babe Ruth rejuvenated the sport with a new style of play. Between 1919 and 1921, he radically altered the game's offense. Before Ruth, players such as Ty Cobb had focused on low-scoring, disciplined, "scientific" hitting: "hit-and-run, the steal and double steal, the bunt, . . . the squeeze, . . . the ball punched through openings in the defense for a single," as Cobb later wrote. Ruth, on the other hand, swung with power, coming up and under the ball, trying to knock it out of the park. In 1919, he hit a record-setting twenty-nine home runs; the next year, he hit an incredible fifty-four, more than accumulated by any other team combined except his own; and, in 1921, he hit fifty-nine. Other players quickly began to swing for the fences as well. But it was Ruth who became the "Sultan of Swat," packing fans into stadiums. "Baseball, year by year, had grown more scientific, more a thing of accepted rules, of set routine" explained the *Baseball Magazine* writer F. C. Lane in 1921 regarding "the home run epidemic": "But every so often some superman appears who follows no set rule, who flouts accepted theories, who throws science itself to the winds. . . . Such a man is Babe Ruth."[20]

Ruth symbolized triumphant individualism. His famous home runs, like Dempsey's heralded knockout punches or Grange's breakaway runs, set him apart. "Now and then," as F. C. Lane observed, "a superman arises in the domain of politics or finance or science and plays havoc with kingdoms or fortunes or established theories." Ruth—like Grange and Dempsey—qualified for "superman" status. And, like them, he became a media star beyond his sport, appearing in vaudeville and movies, and attaching his name to an array of products such as Babe Ruth Home Run Shoes, Babe Ruth Gum, and Bambino Smoking Tobacco. He was, according to the *New York Times,* "an appealing, swashbuckling, roistering, boisterous figure that is as natural a showman as the late Phineas T. Barnum." As early as October 1920, *Current Magazine* concluded that he was "the most talked of American." According to the *Literary Digest* in 1922, "Everybody knows him." In fact, more people recognized Ruth than recognized President Warren G. Harding. Stories of Ruth's herculean feats on and off the field dominated the news. Yet he remained an accessible, unpretentious man. He was the "babe," with a child's love of fun. He was the Baltimore slum kid who had grown up in an institution for orphans and delinquents and gone on to become baseball's highest-paid player. And he believed deeply in the American dream: "The greatest thing about this country is the wonderful fact that it doesn't matter which side of the tracks you were born on, or whether you're homeless or homely or friendless. The chance is still there. I know." By the end of the 1920s, he was making more money than the president of the United States, but he clearly played baseball out of a love for the game, not for the money. He appealed to his fans in part because he was a throwback to earlier, simpler times. Yet he would never have reached his heroic proportions without the new technologies and media forms that publicized him, from tabloid newspapers (such as the *New York Daily News,* which hired a year-round Babe Ruth correspondent) to magazines, advertisements (which quadrupled on billboards and in newspapers and magazines between 1917 and 1929), radio, Tin Pan Alley—and, of course, movies, including the news films that four companies were showing in theaters by 1919, when Ruth started the "Home Run Epidemic."[21]

Far beyond the work they did publicizing figures such as Ruth, motion pictures were particularly important in illuminating popular culture's paradoxes and strengthening the place of mass amusements in American life. By 1920, the United States dominated world filmmaking. Several factors had given American film production a substantial edge: immigrant audiences and filmmakers who stimulated the industry; the cheap real estate and favorable weather in southern California (where most of the business had relocated); and the devastating impact of the Great War from 1914 to 1918 on Europe and foreign film competition. Within the United States itself, silent movies had overtaken the vaudeville stage as a chief source of entertainment. Between 1912 and the early 1920s, weekly film attendance leaped from 16 million to 40 million. Although films had become fairly common on vaudeville programs, movies had increasingly emerged as distinct entertainments with their own theaters. Yet, even as vaudeville lost ground as a favored entertainment, it continued to exert a powerful influence on the movie business. On one level, it provided a major doorway through which performers and their employers moved. On another level, vaudeville's pace and separate variety acts unquestionably shaped early film comedy, which typically worked around a series of gags that could stand alone. But movies also drew from vaudeville's energy, creativity, and ability to respond to audience needs and expectations.[22]

In reacting to audiences' wishes, movies displayed a remarkable ability to plumb deeply resonant myths in American culture regarding democracy, virtuous commoners, mobility, and starting anew. Heroic figures, who were at once self-reliant individuals and decent democratic citizens, triumphed. Abstractions such as liberty and equality seemed real. "Movies breathe the spirit in which the country was founded, freedom and equality," contended William Fox's *Exhibitor's Bulletin* in June 1914. That same spirit was evident in the motion-picture theaters themselves, where, according to Fox, "there are no separations of classes. Everyone enters the same way. . . . In the movies the rich rub elbows with the poor and that's the way it should be. The motion picture is a distinctly American institution." Fox's claim was generally true. The one-price admission fee to sit anywhere (excluding blacks, whom many theaters barred or segregated) in fact differed from the ticket prices of most earlier forms of theatrical entertainment, which were scaled according to seat location. Movie sites also encouraged sexual egalitarianism by urging women to attend and by keeping prices low enough to attract working-class females. Children, too, enjoyed exceptional access to movies.[23]

And, because they were built around visual display, films suggested ways in which viewers could re-create themselves and enjoy second chances. "The task I'm trying to achieve," said the influential filmmaker D. W. Griffith, "is above all to make you see." And part of what viewers saw involved implicit instruction regarding how to conduct themselves, dress, and look. Fan magazines seized on the growing fascination with movie actors by including advertisements and articles such as "The Fifth of a Series on How to Use the Motion Picture to Suggest Furnishings for Your Home." New immigrants and others could, thus, learn from the movies how to construct themselves as Americans. In that regard, according to a film historian, "the country found a voice by keeping silent," and motion pictures helped define the nation. In 1915, the poet Vachel Lindsay wrote excitedly that "our soil has no Roman coin or buried altar or Buddhist tope"; but it did have film, which provided, Lindsay believed, a "new hieroglyphics" for a democratic people.[24]

Those hieroglyphics came primarily from a small group of Jewish filmmakers who "invented Hollywood." Most were recent immigrants or their children and had roots in Central and Eastern Europe. Invariably, they felt the sting of being social and economic outsiders, and their personal stories were often quests for acceptance, respect, and cultural legitimacy. Harry Warner once bet that his brother Jack did not know the Lord's Prayer. Jack took the bet and then began nervously: "Now I lay me down to sleep." At that point, Harry interrupted him and gave him the money, adding: "I didn't think you knew it." Carl Laemmle, an immigrant from Germany in the mid-1880s, drifted from one failed job to another until he ended up in Chicago one rainy night to investigate the prospects of opening a small clothing store. He happened to attend "one of those hole-in-the-wall five-cent motion pictures" and decided, instead, to enter the movie business, subsequently leading the successful legal battles against the Edison Trust for its monopolistic practices, and eventually creating Universal Pictures. When a newspaper called him a "film magnate," he was elated: "See, I told you I'd make them recognize me."[25]

These "movie Jews" earned the label *moguls*, pioneering a system whereby several large production studios dominated the motion-picture industry for decades, churning out and distributing feature films, often through their own theater chains, and wielding almost absolute power over thousands of contract personnel. After Adolph Zukor took command of Paramount Studios in 1916, he moved from producing and distributing films to acquiring and building theaters. By 1921, his three hundred–plus theaters were part of Paramount's budding film empire, which included, as did William Fox's, production, distribution, and exhibition.[26]

Critics saw the Hollywood Jews as unlettered gate-crashers—"alien ex-buttonhole makers and pressers"—who built what the *New Yorker* magazine in 1925 dubbed a "mongrel industry." As social and cultural outsiders, they desperately sought acceptance and respectability. "I yearned to trespass on Quality Street," said Jesse Lasky. After working with his sister in a vaudeville act, he established his own booking agency for performers and then teamed up with Adolph Zukor at Paramount.[27]

Trying to discard their outsider status, the Hollywood moguls carefully, even obsessively, pursued esteem for themselves and their product. Personally, they often tried to obliterate their pasts, typically changing their names and embracing passionately the dominant American culture. "People are gonna find out you're a Jew sooner or later," Jack Warner advised one young actor, "but better later." Louis B. Mayer, whose family fled Russia when he was around three, changed his birth date to July 4. He then honored Independence Day by closing his Metro-Goldwyn-Mayer (MGM) studio and hosting picnics, parades, and his own flag-waving orations. Columbia Pictures' founder Harry Cohn, whose parents had immigrated from Europe (his father from Germany and his mother from Russia), once asked a screenwriter about his ethnic origins. When the man answered, "I'm an American and a Jew," Cohn replied, "I like that. American first." Cohn rejected a Jewish relief fund's request for a contribution with a shout: "Relief *for* the Jews! How about relief *from* the Jews!"[28]

To enhance the reputation of movies, the Hollywood Jews pursued two central strategies: improve the theaters and make bigger and better films. Both strategies were supposed to attract what Zukor described as "a higher class trade." In the mid-1910s, to lift motion pictures from their nickelodeon status, a number of theater entrepreneurs built huge new theaters whose luxurious comforts made audiences feel special and privileged. "The motion picture has risen from the peep show novelty," announced Samuel "Roxy" Rothapfel, who, by 1916, owned ten of these "luxury" houses, most notable among which was the Strand, which opened in 1914 with four thousand seats. The Strand's debut left the *New York Times* drama critic Victor Watson breathless. Earlier, if anyone had told him "that the time would come when the finest looking people in town would be going to the biggest and newest theater on Broadway for the purpose of seeing motion pictures," he would have promptly referred them to "the doctor who runs the city's bughouse." Rothapfel's motto set the tone for the majestic new theaters: "Don't 'give the people what they want'—give 'em something better." In 1926, Rothapfel opened the Roxy ("the cathedral of motion pictures"), which had more than sixty-two hundred seats. "Picture palaces" such as Rothapfel's included lobbies, gardens, large orchestra pits, organs, statues, rugs, uniformed ushers, elegant staircases, and cushioned seats. "Mama—does God live here?" asked a child in a *New Yorker* cartoon. According to Rothapfel: "I want to make the truck driver and his wife feel like a king." In the theater, differences in social class would dissolve: "The man who comes to the theater on foot rubs elbows with the man who arrives in a limousine, and no favoritism is shown one way or the other." Rich and poor might, indeed, bump into each other, but "the Paramount plan," as Zukor explained it, "meant better times for theater patrons in providing them high-class amusement." According to the director of a theater managers training school: "People come to the motion picture theater to live an hour or two, in the land of romance. . . . For a small charge they can be picked up on a magic carpet and set down in a dream city amidst palatial surroundings where worry and care can never enter."[29]

Even in much less opulent small-town theaters, which still accounted for a majority of the nation's movie-theater seats, the emphasis was on middle-class respectability. "A nice place to spend a half-hour: With the children! With your wife! With your girl!" promised the Star Theater in Lexington, Kentucky, which had three hundred seats and offered a "special school children's matinee." Theater owners such as the Star's developed close ties with their local communities, working with downtown retailers to host "Merchant's gift night," special parties for merchants' employees, and benefits for charities. Such events also underlined the extent to which outside commercial entertainments such as movies were weaving into the daily lives of citizens across the country.[30]

While theaters tilted more and more toward middle-class audiences (Rothapfel "gave the 'movie' a college education," according to one writer), the film industry followed Zukor's lead in producing longer, more lavish, "feature" films. As early as 1911, Zukor began to make five-reel, one-hour films, disproving the Edison Trust's contention that the "time is not ripe for feature pictures, if it ever will be." As Zukor predicted, the movies' future rested with dramatic narratives.[31]

D. W. Griffith's colossal 1915 production *The Birth of a Nation* was a milestone in that regard. Lasting two and a half hours, and costing at least $2 per ticket, the twelve-reel movie focused on a white Southern family in the Civil War era. Griffith used a variety of techniques, including shifting the camera's point of view and intermixing stunning panoramas with iris shots that highlighted faces. He also employed a large cast and staged spectacular battle scenes. The landmark film evoked a storm of controversy, however, by treating African Americans disparagingly and portraying the Ku Klux Klan as a heroic movement that saved the white South from the ravages of black rule. Despite protests from organizations such as the National Association for the Advancement of Colored People, President Woodrow Wilson endorsed the film as "like writing history with lightning." Louis B. Mayer perhaps earned $500,000 as a chief distributor of the film.[32]

The shift to multireel films such as *Birth of a Nation* helped end the nickelodeon era, which had depended on short shows and quick turnover. Longer feature movies often required more than one projector and larger theaters. But, as Zukor had guessed, the feature films appealed to a growing middle-class audience and maintained working-class support.[33]

The nature of those movies also attested to the ingenuity of filmmakers struggling for respect. Shrewdly, the moguls constructed a powerful film version of what the United States represented. Because most were newcomers to the United States, they worked intuitively to understand American culture and—like vaudeville performers in front of diverse audiences—they honed a sense of what customers wanted. They understood firsthand, of course, the dreams and hopes of other Americans with immigrant and working-class backgrounds. And, from their experiences in the fashion, retail, and entertainment businesses, they learned to gauge public taste. "They *were* the audience," as another movie producer said. Desperate to win recognition as red-blooded Americans, they made much of their own patriotism. Onscreen, they created a mythical America that expressed their own vision of the country's history, ideals, and values. This idealized movie nation was so compelling that Americans from wide-ranging backgrounds identified with it; in effect, the mythical America that the Hollywood studios created became the real America in many citizens' minds. "By making a 'shadow' America," as the entertainment scholar Neal Gabler has written, "the Hollywood Jews created a powerful cluster of images and ideas—so powerful that, in a sense, they colonized the American imagination. No one could think about this country without thinking about the movies."[34]

The U.S. entry into World War I in 1917 gave the moguls an opportunity to confirm their—and movies'—100 percent American credentials. As Zukor said, the industry was anxious "to show its patriotism [and] to prove beyond all question its worth to the Government as well as to the people of the United States." Films, which critics had attacked as immoral, could now exude a positive civic image and stave off government regulation. "KEEP YOUR HANDS OFF WAR PICTURES," industry publicity warned censors: "THESE PICTURES ARE A PART OF THE FIGHTING FORCES OF THE UNITED STATES. . . . SUPPRESS ANY PART OR ANY ONE OF THESE PICTURE MESSAGES AND—WHETHER YOU ADMIT IT OR NOT—YOU ARE PLAYING THE GAME OF GERMANY." Such assertions of "reel patriotism" were also evident in a number of movies that applauded American soldiers: "I promised Dad I'd get six!" says one soldier as he bayonets Germans. Movies like *Miss Jackie of the Army* (Lloyd Ingraham, 1917), *Her Country First* (James Young, 1918), *Battling Jane* (Elmer Clifton, 1918), and *Every Mother's Son* (R. A. Walsh, 1918) focused on how Americans at home, particularly women, could help the cause. Others, including *The Claws of the Hun* (Victor L. Schertzinger, 1918) and *The Kaiser, the Beast of Berlin* (Rupert Julian, 1918), vilified the enemy and even urged audiences to "hiss the kaiser" whenever his picture appeared. According to the *Motion Picture News*, the movie *The Kaiser* "dramatizes patriotism. . . . Its appeal to red blooded Americans is boundless."[35]

After the war, as the "Red Terror" gripped the United States, filmmakers continued to establish their patriotic credentials by targeting radicalism. In 1919, the federal government successfully implored the movie industry to help "carry on a nation-wide campaign to combat Bolshevism and radicalism" that would "crush the Red movement in America." Anti-Bolshevik films would reaffirm movie patriotism, make profits, and protect the industry from censors. A small wave of antiradical movies included *The New Moon* (Chester Withey, 1919), which portrayed sweet young females as hapless victims of evil Bolsheviks.[36]

The strong tilt toward antiradical politics spun easily out of the industry's accelerating pursuit of middle-class support. Although working-class families initially provided the backbone of movie audiences, the filmmakers—many of them refugees from the slums—were anxious to find broader support. To do so meant increasingly avoiding working-class themes and topics. "If you want to send a message," Samuel Goldwyn said, "send it Western Union."[37]

In fact, of course, the films were full of cultural messages, many of which mirrored and accelerated the shift from genteel Victorian values to ones more cosmopolitan and novel. By the 1920s, the United States was in the grip of an intensifying cultural struggle. Traditionalists feared that the morals and lifestyles they favored were losing ground to an emerging polyglot culture rooted in immigrant, urban America. Social barriers indeed appeared to be slipping as a growing number of people seemed determined to take chances, act spontaneously and informally, live on the edge, and experience new things at the expense of deeply rooted customs. Irving Berlin's popular 1911 song "Everybody's Doin' It Now" summed up the developing mood. As Neal Gabler has written: "The social history of America in the 1920s was the story of the combat between these two Americas—one new and ascendant, the other old and declining." The battle lines included Prohibition, sabbatarianism, censorship, and immigration restriction. Against that backdrop, the movie industry stirred controversies and concerns. "No American born actors or directors have a prominent part," reported the *St. Louis Post Dispatch* in 1927, noting also that the "majority of American movie picture producers are of foreign birth."[38]

The famed automaker Henry Ford expressed the anxieties of many Anglo-Saxon Protestants when he attacked the Jews as primary threats to 100 percent Americanism. "The motion picture influence of the United States . . . is exclusively under the control, moral and financial, of the Jewish manipulators of the public mind," read a 1921 article in Ford's publication the *Dearborn Independent*. The article classed Jews with "an

Oriental ideal—'if you can't go as far as you like, go as far as you can.' It [that ideal] gravitates naturally to the flesh and its exposure, its natural psychic habitat is among the more sensual emotions. The Oriental view is essentially different from the Anglo-Saxon, the American view." Even people who did not necessarily share Ford's blatant anti-Semitism worried about the "movie problem," worries that were evident in the censorship laws that at least thirty-seven state legislatures debated. Celebrations of Charlie Chaplin as a "national hero, whose funny hat, walk, cane, and mustache are now better known than the prayer book," according to the *National Labor Tribune* in 1915, hardly reassured deeply religious citizens.[39]

By then, however, Chaplin himself was beginning to adjust his screen persona so that it would be less "vulgar." As he told one interviewer in 1916: "I am now trying to steer clear from this sort of humor and adapt myself to a . . . finer shade of acting." Chaplin indicated that, although he had little formal education, he read Shakespeare and other great authors. By the 1920s, his films allowed for romantic relationships, a shift that broadened his following—among men, who typically experienced courtship rituals in which they lacked wealth and money and, like Chaplin's character, all too often failed at love; among women, who appreciated the more tender Chaplin; and among moralists, who valued his undaunted determination to improve himself. Chaplin now preferred that people call him Charles, not Charlie.[40]

Like Chaplin, the movie industry as a whole dealt with its opponents by turning to self-censorship and making films that bridged the cultural divide. In 1922, to stave off the censors, studio executives formed the Motion Picture Producers and Distributors of America (MPPDA) and hired Will Hays as its overseer. Some movie people chafed at the choice. "We are against any kind of censorship, and particularly against Presbyterian censorship," Charlie Chaplin said at a private party, after which he attached a "Welcome WILL HAYS" sign to the door to the men's toilet at the studio. Ultimately, however, Hays turned out to be a shrewd selection. For one thing, he was an elder in the Presbyterian Church; for another, he had impressive political credentials and connections. A conservative from Indiana, he chaired the Republican National Committee and served as President Warren G. Harding's postmaster general. The Hays office took a number of steps to reassure citizens that the motion-picture industry was in good hands—for example, establishing voluntary production codes that imposed time limits on movie kisses and including morality clauses in employees' contracts. Although evangelicals such as the Reverend Bob Shuler saw Hays as nothing more than "the hired man of a bunch of rich Jews," the MPPDA provided the industry with a moral cloak. In 1929, Hays declared that the film industry constituted "the quintessence of what we mean by 'America.'" Privately, he indicated that he had no intention of eliminating sex from the movies. Its treatment simply had to be "passionate but pure," he told Carl Laemmle, "giving the public all the sex it wants with compensating values for all those church and women's groups."[41]

By then, Hollywood's filmmakers were cannily making movies that synthesized traditional and modern values as well as the expectations of working- and middle-class audiences. Movies celebrated sex and money while, at the same time, providing reassurances that America was still deeply moral. Biblical spectacles provided a useful channel for such mixed messages. In 1923, for example, Cecil B. DeMille's *The Ten Commandments* adroitly mixed bacchanalian scenes with moralistic messages. Nine years earlier, DeMille had entered the movie business with his close friend Jesse Lasky and Lasky's brother-in-law, Samuel Goldfish. When making their first film, *The Squaw Man* (1914), the trio at first punched the sprocket holes on the film negative incorrectly, adding to movie lore about how inexperienced amateurs had fumbled their way into the business. But DeMille had since become Adolph Zukor's leading director, with a special talent for titillating without offending audiences. As early as 1917, DeMille had received a memorandum advising him that "what the public needs today is modern stuff with plenty of clothes, rich sets, and action." He soon began to meet those expectations, although he occasionally removed some of the clothes; in *Male and Female* (1919), for instance, Gloria Swanson briefly revealed her breasts. DeMille's brother William laughingly described how Cecil's celebrated bathroom scenes had turned the bath into "a mystic shrine," bathing into "a lovely ceremony rather than a merely sanitary duty," and undressing into "a progressive revelation of entrancing beauty," "a study in diminishing draperies." But Cecil DeMille's real accomplishment, according to one historian, was in his ability "to free the subject of marriage from the overstuffed parlors of Victorian melodrama, to infuse it with wit, style, vicarious pleasures, and above all, practical hints on contemporary ways to behave."[42]

DeMille excelled in making fantasy stories about the power of love in crossing class lines and solving all problems—a favorite theme of many movies going into the 1920s. In his *Orchids and Ermine* (1927), for example, a telephone operator falls in love with Jack, a valet to a Tulsa millionaire. When she consents to marry Jack, she learns that he is the millionaire, who had disguised his identity in order to fend off money-hungry women. Such films ignored social problems and showed the triumph of personal fulfillment through romance and consumerism.[43]

In several dozen comedies, DeMille touted not only consumption but a freer sex life as well, and he did so by suggesting that such values could, in fact, save marriages. By bringing passion "into the bonds that the Bible has lain down," as he explained in 1920, sex between husbands and wives could reinforce and energize marital bonds: "The breaking of the law comes from adultery, not sex." In films with suggestive titles such as *Old Wives for New* (1918), *Don't Change Your Husband* (1919), and *Why Change Your Wife?* (1920), DeMille showed bored spouses who seek excitement beyond their restricted social roles and routines. A husband, for instance, turns to a new "jazz baby" and leaves his wife, who is morally rigid and wants nothing to do with his "Oriental ideas" and "physical music." In frustration, he breaks loose from the stuffy Victorian constraints. "I want a sweetheart, not a governess," he says. But his new freedom brings disenchantments of its own. In one film, for example, the man discovers that his chorus girl lover is unfaithful. "If this is the gay life," he concludes, "I'm going back to my wife." Meanwhile, the abandoned spouse has also moved to new experiences. One ex-wife decides: "I've been foolish enough to think a man wants a wife decent and honest." She buys a revealing dress, one that will allow her to "go the limit. . . . Thank God I'm still young." In a common plot device, the former mates rediscover each other, initially without recognizing who the other is, and they fall in love again. But, in the meantime, each has become more adventuresome, more daring. Their newly found sexual freedom invigorates their relationship and strengthens their home. "Ladies," warns a final caption, "if you want to be your husband's sweetheart, you must simply forget when you are his wife." Such films thus critiqued traditional values, but with reassuring outcomes.[44]

While movies touted the virtues of playful marriages and—through lavish sets and costumes—consumerism, they also provided glimpses of other lifestyles. In *Prodigal Daughters* (Sam Wood, 1923), according to the caption, the father "catches his daughters in the act of returning from a ball *after midnight*." The collisions between old and new cultures sometimes played out in plots whereby accidents or kidnappers temporarily remove a young woman from her proper Victorian household and plunge her into a world of gypsies, robbers, or foreigners. After learning to dance to ragtime or the tango or to dress more exotically, she ends up back in her original environment, albeit with more venturesome ideas.[45]

Remarkably, by the 1920s, people from working-class, new-immigrant backgrounds were teaching moviegoers from all groups about matters of etiquette, fashion, and behavior. In that regard, films were short-circuiting the traditional sources of instruction—families, schools, and churches. And, despite the cultural counterrevolution that found expression in anti-Semitic and anti-Catholic sentiments, immigration restriction, and Prohibition, mass amusements such as motion pictures were forging a shared culture. That culture was, of course, notably different from what the older, genteel America had pursued.[46]

Among the new tastemakers, few were more influential than celebrities, who owed much to fans, advertising, and a modern consumer mentality built around style and personality. The concept of personality reflected growing concerns about how people could express, present, and distinguish themselves in a mass society. Such concerns had unquestionably existed for decades, as the antebellum fascination with humbuggery and the arts of deception made clear; but, by the early twentieth century, they had intensified. Technological changes, urban congestion, and the movements of large numbers of rural residents to cities and of new immigrants to the United States had exacerbated feelings of anonymity and unfamiliarity. In an environment with more and more strangers, how could an individual stand out and excel? By the early twentieth century, in articles such as "The Secret of Making People Like You," popular psychologists and writers generally agreed that success rested with a "striking personality." Not surprisingly, that 1919 essay appeared in *Film Fun* magazine.[47]

By then, movie stars were rising cultural authorities. They owed their existence to the passionately engaged movie audiences who, by around 1908, flooded film studios with questions about actors. Anything but passive viewers, these fans actively identified with their screen idols and wanted to know more about them, asking, for example, who was "the girl with the curls"? At first, some film studios responded by publicizing performers' names and even offering pictures of them on trading cards. But it was the producer Carl Laemmle who responded most ingeniously. His Biograph company had received so many queries about "the Biograph girl" that he devised an inventive publicity stunt. In March 1910, he planted a phony news story that she—Florence Lawrence—had died in a streetcar accident. He followed that account with charges that a studio competitor had circulated the "cowardly" lie about her death. When he sent Lawrence to St. Louis as evidence that she was very much alive, ecstatic fans nearly crushed her. An actress had become a star. Letters poured in to "Dear Miss Flo." One fan apologized for writing "without ever having met you," but "I feel that I almost know you." Other film studios quickly boosted their own stars. The president of Vitagraph, J. Stuart Blackton, even commissioned a waltz, "The Vitagraph Girl," from a Tin Pan Alley firm for one of them.[48]

From the outset, the creation of movie stars was intertwined with the film industry's quest for respectability. In 1911, Vitagraph's Blackton published the inaugural issue of what became the first movie fan journal, *Motion Picture Story Magazine*. Initially, Blackton gave little attention to actors. He was interested primarily in attracting middle-class readers as evidence that movies' appeal extended beyond illiterate immigrants. The magazine at first published Vitagraph movie plot summaries and advertised male as well as female products. Over the next few years, however, the magazine's focus evolved significantly. In response to readers' pressing interests, it included more information about movie stars and tried to entice young females with stories of romance and beauty. The magazine's restyled fan became a young, independent woman around eighteen who loved mass culture. "The man I marry must be twice the movie fan I am," was a typical line.[49]

At this point, however, the efforts to enhance the respectability of movies via the time-honored uplift strategy of attracting female audiences took a problematic turn. Movies that appealed to young women often contradicted refined, moralistic messages. Popular serials such as *What Happened to Mary?* subverted traditional feminine roles with stories of liberated females who engaged in swashbuckling adventure. Moreover, the females who cheered for the likes of the imperiled Pauline were anything but sedate, reserved, and "ladylike." Their rowdy behavior encouraged caricatures of "movie-struck girls" who suffered from what *McClure's* in 1916 labeled "Filmitis . . . the most modern of diseases." The good news for the film industry, as Universal's general manager Joe Brandt observed, was, nevertheless, that, "because of the millions of movie-struck girls in America, the moving picture theaters flourish." Indeed, during the 1920s, females reportedly constituted from 60 to an astounding 83 percent of film audiences. The bad news was the perception that "Little Miss Movie-Struck," in the words of the *Woman's Home Companion,* might be a kind of social rebel; according to the magazine, she needed to learn that "the best moving picture in which she can play a leading role is one entitled 'Home.'"[50]

To counter the disreputable stereotype of movie fans as hysterical teenage females, the editor of *Photoplay* set out to convince advertisers that movie fans were, in fact, middle-class consumers whom businesses should court. *Photoplay* had made its debut in 1912, but, in 1917, a well-established figure in the print business, James Quirk, became the editor. One of Quirk's goals was to publicize the link between movie stars and consumerism. Initially, the film industry and other businesses were reluctant to link movie stars and products. When, in 1916, for example, the rising star Mary Pickford signed a $500 advertising contract to endorse Pompeian skin cream, Samuel Goldwyn and her attorney believed that she was making a mistake. Such a contract would be "undignified and risky," according to her attorney. "Your name should stand for motion pictures and not as an advertisement for evening gowns, cosmetics," and such products. Pickford went ahead with the advertising deal anyhow, appearing regularly in the cold-cream ads for five years, and helping connect film stars with products other than movies. Mary Fuller, of *What Happened to Mary?* fame, endorsed Coca-Cola and a perfume bearing her name. Meanwhile, at *Photoplay,* Quirk labored energetically to break the stereotype of film audiences as poor working-class immigrants who lacked purchasing power. Movie fans, he argued, were, in fact, "perfect consumers." "Here's Your Audience!" *Photoplay* informed advertisers: well-to-do young females (and sometimes males) from the middle class. "Today," Quirk argued, "the enlightened eyes of college professors and car conductors and bank presidents and scrub women follow Charlie [Chaplin]" and other stars. These people would buy products that they associated with their favorite movies. They left theaters with "new desires for the better things of life—desires that are yours to capitalize on when you use the advertising pages of *Photoplay*." The fact that they were young was an added bonus because, unlike their frugal and stuffy elders, they were interested in "the joy of living and having."[51]

In this mixture of consumerism and fandom, film stars emerged as models of conduct and personality. They provided important building blocks for a nascent culture of teenage girls, who used stars' pictures to decorate rooms and construct scrapbooks. In 1915, the *Ladies Home Journal* identified Mary Pickford as the "best known girl in America." She had risen from an impoverished childhood (in which she was onstage at the age of five) to the title of "America's Sweetheart," earning $1 million a year by 1920. One fan gushed: "I don't suppose a day has ever passed . . . that I haven't thought of her at least once. She has never been a movie star to me—but a person, a friend, an ideal." That ideal exuded youthful innocence. Pickford regularly dispensed instruction on diet, dress, cosmetics, health, happiness, and how to be true to oneself. On- and offscreen, she skillfully negotiated the constraints of gender, combining Victorian purity and femininity with youthful independence and fun, merging old and new. The ghostwritten "Mary Pickford's Daily Talks" appeared in 150 newspapers across the country. Pickford's advice about such things as "rice powder and olive oil on the skin" reinforced emerging beliefs that people could re-create themselves through consuming goods.[52]

New advertising strategies cultivated those beliefs by focusing less on products themselves than on what the products could do for the users by enhancing their looks, self-confidence, and success—indeed, by making them more like movie stars. A magazine study in the early 1920s found a "revolutionary change" in middle-class buying patterns: consumers sought vicarious links to media celebrities. Statistics bore out that impression; between 1914 and 1924, middle-class spending on items such as cosmetics and beauty aids increased by eight times. As a poem in the fan magazine *Movie Weekly* in 1921 put it: "My life is ruled by standards of the moving picture screen / The moods my missus cultivates depict a movie queen / She wears her hair like Pickford and she has a [Theda] Bara stare." According to a variety of other sources, she would also have been more and more concerned with "S.A."—sex appeal.[53]

While movie stars and advertising promoted consumer products and set standards for beauty, personality, and sexuality, the famed Ziegfeld Follies made additional contributions. In his first Follies in 1907, Florenz

Ziegfeld had turned a $13,000 stage investment into a handsome $100,000 profit with a snappy mixture of comedy, dancing, and glamorous women in flimsy costumes. The idea had come from his wife, Anna Held, who guessed correctly that a Parisian-style review would be popular. The previous year, Ziegfeld's lavish production *The Parisian Model* had starred Held, who appeared in a corset and flesh-colored stockings with a number of bare-legged chorus girls. It ran thirty-three weeks on Broadway, to which it returned after a lengthy tour. Each year from 1907 through the 1920s, long after he had separated from Held, Ziegfeld produced a new Follies. Although the spectacular shows included great vaudeville performers such as Eddie Cantor, Al Jolson, Fanny Brice, and Bert Williams, the Ziegfeld Girls most identified the productions. Ultimately, the women were like brand-name products. According to one newspaper headline: "ZIEGFELD TRADE-MARK ASSET TO CHORUS GIRL: MEANS BEAUTY, YOUTH, ANIMATION, STAGE SPARKLE, AND KNACK OF WEARING CLOTHES CHIC-LY." As a historian has written: "The Ziegfeld Girl, like Heinz pickles, gained national product identity by measuring up to an advertised standard."[54]

Ziegfeld defined that standard, casting himself as the sole architect of feminine beauty. He bragged that, from some five thousand applicants, he personally selected the "thirty girls" who "are the most beautiful women in the world." In his estimation, he could turn even a "shop girl" into "a stunning beauty."[55]

Ziegfeld girls had several notable traits. They were disciplined and nonthreatening. And they were also white—"*the American type*," in Ziegfeld's words. "Not only are they native-born, but their parents and grandparents and remoter ancestors were also natives of this country." At a time when Victorian ideals about a woman's proper domestic role were slipping and new immigrants were streaming into the country, Ziegfeld's standards of female beauty were loaded with political meaning.[56]

Showing that they knew their proper roles, Ziegfeld girls danced in strictly choreographed routines. Ziegfeld's dancing director, Ned Wayburn, was reportedly "an efficiency expert in girls." He claimed that he did not want dancers who were "too intelligent" because it might be difficult to teach them. As Ziegfeld put it: "Beauty and brains are not often found together." Onstage, the dancers demonstrated the precision of a machine, moving in unison. In one revue, the chorus girls performed as part of "The Rotisserie," in which they resembled chickens that men were cooking. "Take a little broiler home with you," went the accompanying song, "Take a little broiler do. / . . . Ev'ry one will fill you with delight / Tickle up your appetite. . . . / So try a little tender thing / How about a leg or wing / We've every kind of chick for you." Although the dancers wore little clothing and were alluring, Ziegfeld did not want them to seem sexually threatening. "Most people do not like the 'vampire' type of beauty," he explained. His girls looked dependent and vulnerable. And certainly, according to one song, not one of them was "That Ragtime Suffragette" who, "while her husband is waiting home to dine. / . . . is ragging up and down the line." The goal of Ziegfeld girls was to "attract men," Ziegfeld insisted, and to offer "a promise of romance and excitement—the things a man dreams about when he thinks of the word *girl* . . . that haunting quality."[57]

Unlike Anna Held, Ziegfeld's first star, who exhibited an exotic and foreign mystique, the Follies women increasingly represented a taller, whiter, and more Anglicized image. Blond, long-legged Lillian Lorraine was a prime example. Distinguishing his "showgirls" from chorus girls, Ziegfeld emphasized their wholesome sexuality, their combination of "sensuality and niceness." When he said, "Bring on the girls," he—like the movie industry and advertisements—offered up idealized images of what females should be. Moreover, the Follies' popularity suggested that Ziegfeld had found a winning formula. By striking a balance between naughtiness and niceness, Ziegfeld—like celebrities such as Mary Pickford—constructed a world that consumers could enter safely, yet with excitement.[58]

By the 1920s, however, some entertainments threatened that delicate balance, suggesting that wilder currents were moving through popular culture and within the middle class itself. There were striking examples. Burlesque shows increasingly centered on female strippers. Performers, such as the "bad girl" Mae West, toyed with sexual and racial boundaries. The darkly mysterious movie star Rudolph Valentino tapped a smoldering sexual energy in mature women and reworked traditional masculine images. New York City's Harlem bubbled with a raw energy that attracted white "slummers."

Burlesque's exposure of female flesh was an ironic beneficiary of the progressive reformers' victory over the liquor industry. The Eighteenth Amendment, which, in 1919, made the sale and transport of "intoxicating liquors" unconstitutional, inadvertently helped encourage more titillating stage performances. Because theater owners could no longer sell alcohol, they featured more nudity onstage in order to attract audiences. In illegal speakeasies as well, female entertainers sometimes removed their clothes. Paradoxically, the antivice reformers' success in securing Prohibition thus further jeopardized old moral codes. Traditional Victorian rules were already under assault as Tin Pan Alley songs proclaimed that "everybody is doing it now," public dancing became both more common and more exuberant, hemlines lifted, cosmetic sales grew, and the so-called New Woman attracted attention.[59]

Various displays of the female body had, of course, been challenging those rules for several decades. At Chicago's 1893 Columbian Exposition, the performer known as Little Egypt had dazzled and infuriated visitors to the Midway sideshows with her notorious "cooch" (belly or "muscle") dance. Despite protests against what the moralist Anthony Comstock described as "one of the most outrageous assaults on the sacred dignity of womanhood," the cooch spread quickly to amusement parks, carnivals, silent movies, state and county fairs, parts of vaudeville, and burlesque stages. Some dancers began removing parts of their costumes, although they typically did so behind backlit screens or when wearing flesh-colored tights. On the several burlesque circuits, and especially within the cheaper and more salacious "stock" burlesque companies, acts became more daring. Between 1915 and 1922, the American Burlesque Association highlighted its cooch dancers. "We're not producing Sunday school shows," conceded one of the association's founders, Isidore Herk, as he jabbed at reformers. But, in April 1925, it was the four Minsky brothers (Billy, Abe, Herb, and Mort) who achieved legendary status courtesy of a famous police raid on one of their theaters after "Mademoiselle Fifi" (Mary Dawson) bared her breasts at the end of her act.[60]

The Minskys were the sons of a Jewish immigrant who had come to New York City in 1883 and worked his way up from peddling to real estate. The brothers turned to show business. Starting out with a building on the Lower East Side and presenting shows mainly to immigrant audiences, they ran a low-budget show patterned after the Ziegfeld Follies. The show hinted at elegance but included a red warning light backstage to alert performers if police were in the audience. The Minskys claimed to have invented the burlesque striptease act. Supposedly, one night in 1917, as Mae Dix exited the stage after performing a high-spirited version of an old Anna Held number, she started removing her detachable cuffs and collar so that they would not get dirty. A customer, thinking she was still doing her act, applauded. Energized, Dix returned to the stage and started unbuttoning her top, at which point the house manager doused the lights. Around that time, the Minskys reportedly came up with another innovation: the runway. After Abe visited the Folies-Bergère in Paris, he excitedly told his brothers about how the women had paraded on a runway that extended from the stage. The Minskys promptly built their own runway. Mort recalled that, as six women performed, the mostly male audience "could look right up their legs." The dancers were "so close to the audience" that customers "could actually smell their perfume and hear their heavy breathing. It was sensational!"[61]

Other burlesque houses soon included their own runways, on which bare-legged females strutted, discarding garments and teasing the onlookers. Cleveland's Empire Theater advertised the dancer Carrie Finnell as "the girl with the $100,000 legs." By 1926, Finnell had her own troupe, Carrie Finnell and Her Red-Headed Blondes, and was using her "educated bosom" to twirl tassels that were stuck to her nipples. In Mort Minsky's words: "Burlesque was on its way to becoming nothing more than a legal way of selling the illusion of sex to the public."[62]

Not everyone agreed with critics who attacked striptease as nothing more than the exploitation of women. Years later, in the 1950s, the writer Francine du Plessix Gray, fresh out of college, watched a New Jersey strip show in wonder, finding in the dancers examples "of defiance that I was searching for in my own life." "Are these girls ever in charge!" she remembered thinking. "They seemed to be saying, 'I'll do whatever I like with my body, because it's no one's but my own.'" The stripper Seph Weene attested to the sense of empowerment that she received during her performances. Once she recognized that "[her] sexuality was a product," she was liberated: "I knew the mind of my enemy." She argued that performers onstage sought control. "The thrill I got from stripping was power. . . . I felt powerful." Whether one agreed that strippers were "gender warriors," as another former stripper, Lily Burana, believed, there was no doubt that striptease pitted repression against transgression, a dialectic that characterized much entertainment.[63]

Mary Jane "Mae" West, an early-twentieth-century burlesque performer, relished such transgression and delighted in undercutting Victorian values. A child of the working class, she was born in 1893 and grew up in Brooklyn. Her father was a muscular, temperamental man of Irish extraction who was a boilermaker, night watchman, bouncer, and boxer. Her mother was a German immigrant who dreamed of a theatrical career and helped push her daughter into show business. By age eight, Mae had left school and was performing on the stage. "I was a hard-boiled, wise-cracking kid, doing anything to get a laugh," she said. Her stage career took her into stock theater, vaudeville, and burlesque, where she exhibited "a raunchy streetwise style," defying boundaries and displaying an uninhibited, disreputable persona. A vigorous sexuality marked her life. On the burlesque stage, she performed fan and cooch dances. In vaudeville, her act included a muscle dance, in which she sat in a chair, wriggling suggestively to a ragtime beat; when the strap on her gown "accidentally" broke, she nonchalantly straightened it over her partially exposed breast. Viewing herself as a social outsider, she early on used her acts as critical commentaries on sexual hypocrisy and male privilege. "I thought white men had it their own way too long, and should stop exploiting women and blacks and gays," she said later. Two of her stage models were Eva Tanguay, who enjoyed shredding Victorian sentimentality, and especially Bert Williams, whom West met as a little girl. "I knew black people from the beginning," she said later. "So I realized they weren't stereotypes, they were people like me, but darker." Like Tanguay and Williams, West continually played with various constructions of identity.[64]

In the mid-1920s, West collided with moralists and the law. In April

1926, her play *Sex,* about a prostitute and class conflict, opened on Broadway with financial backing from two businessmen. She wrote and starred in the "comedy-drama," which ran for almost a year. The production drew the wrath of New York City's moral reformers. "We were shown not sex but lust—stark naked lust," protested one critic. "Street sweepings," complained the *New Yorker.* "MONSTROSITY PLUCKED FROM GARBAGE CAN, DESTINED TO SEWER," claimed the *Daily Mirror.*[65]

By then, however, the New York stage was experiencing strong countercurrents. Theatrical modernists such as Eugene O'Neill were intent on rejecting dramas of Victorian uplift and exploring psychological and sexual issues in realistic ways. At the same time, emerging Broadway impresarios such as Earl Carroll and the Shubert brothers were eager to bring sexuality into their productions. In 1923, Carroll launched his Vanities revue, which featured as many as one hundred women in poses more revealing than those found in Ziegfeld's Follies. "Let Flo spend money dressing them," Carroll said of female revue performers. "I plan to undress them." The Shuberts countered with their own revue that featured Broadway's first topless women. After watching the Shubert show, one critic estimated: "In the last ten years, the American male has seen so many female legs that the sight of it excites him as much as the sight of a carrot on a vegetable stand." The critic's reaction hardly accounted for the enthusiastic and changing theater audience that buoyed up New York City's seventy-one theaters. The fact was that many middle-class young people were as eager as the O'Neills and the Carrolls to challenge the older generation's reticence about sex. These new patrons reveled in a tabloid style that stressed the sensational and voyeuristic.[66]

Against that backdrop, as one journalist remembered, "some of the so-called highbrows" approached Mae West's theater as if they were going "on a slumming tour." In January 1927, while moralists were excoriating *Sex,* West wrote and directed *The Drag,* advertised as a "homosexual comedy-drama." The New York rehearsals in January 1927 drew large groups of spectators. "That production," objected one Broadway producer, "strikes at the decency of manhood." *The Drag* was full of mixed messages about homosexuality. While it contained offensive stereotypes, it also provided a novel moment in which gay men not only played gay men but also ad-libbed their lines while West modified her script. "West's purpose was radical," according to a biographer; "she intended to bring her depiction of male homosexuality and drag queens into New York City's great theater culture."[67]

Whatever West's motives, officials quashed *The Drag*'s opening, and, while a thousand spectators cheered in her behalf, the police closed down *Sex* and arrested her for indecency and corrupting morals. On April 5, 1927, after she was led from the courtroom following the jury's guilty verdict, West cheerfully told reporters: "I expect it will be the making of me." During her eight days in jail, she received considerable publicity. To much fanfare, the press covered her departure from prison, at which she donated $1,000 to improve the prison library and said that her only complaint concerned prison underwear. West was achieving stardom by opposing the conventional and reputable. "Censorship *made* me," she said later.[68]

Issues of sexuality whirled around Rudolph Valentino no less than around West. In late 1913, the eighteen-year-old Rodolfo Guglielmi, as he was then called, arrived in New York City from Italy. By then, Italian immigration to the United States was peaking at 300,000 annually. Almost immediately, he became a dancer for hire in the city's flourishing cabarets, or nightclubs, where unescorted women received dancing lessons from partners, or gigolos. Worried moralists viewed these "taxi dancers" as lower-class males who hoped to take advantage of rich women. Despite the seamy nature of his job, Valentino used his considerable dancing talent as a stepping-stone to the entertainment world that beckoned him. Within a few months of his arrival in New York, he got bit parts in movies and then a job touring on the Keith vaudeville circuit. In 1917, he traveled to Los Angeles, where he played the villain in several films. At a time when the most popular leading men were clean-cut, all-American types, his chances for stardom seemed remote. "He's too foreign looking," said D. W. Griffith. "The girls would never like him." Griffith overlooked, however, a major shift by the 1920s in the preferences of the overwhelmingly female audiences. In 1921, that shift became shockingly apparent in the emotional reactions to Valentino's appearance in Rex Ingram's epic film *The Four Horsemen of the Apocalypse.* "Rudolph Valentino played [the Argentinian character] Julio," reported *Photoplay,* "and immediately the film world knew it had the continental hero, the polished foreigner, the modern Don Juan in its unsuspecting midst."[69]

In *The Four Horsemen of the Apocalypse,* Valentino dazzled audiences with a steamy tango dance in which he looked like a gaucho, with a flat-brimmed hat, serape, billowing pants, and boots with spurs. The next year, in George Melford's *The Sheik,* he played an Arab, albeit one whose parents were from Europe. And, in *Blood and Sand* (Fred Niblo, 1922), he was a matador who died in the bullring. Within a short time, Valentino's dark complexion, "foreign" look, intimations of sexual menace, piercing eyes, and sultry grace as a dancer had catapulted him to stardom. Ironically, he became a box-office idol at the same time that fears of foreigners generated support for the 1924 Immigration Restriction Act (reducing, e.g., the number of Italian immigrants to fewer than two thousand a year) and the Ku Klux Klan reemerged as a significant national force. One fan magazine guessed that Valentino's popularity derived from the very fact that he was different: "He does not look like your husband. He is not in the least like your brother. He does not resemble the man your mother thinks you ought to marry." Nor was he even "like the nice boy who takes you to all the high-school dances." The screenwriter Frances Marion jokingly referred to his spell over female audiences as "*The Shreik,* for if you tuned in . . . the female voices borne by the wind . . . the sound they made carried his name in a sort of passionate paean." That paean, moreover, reportedly issued from females of all ages, not simply young women.[70]

The substantial female obsession with Valentino sparked a male backlash. "He made mainstream husbands and boyfriends feel mundane and unromantic," wrote a psychologist in *Motion Picture Magazine;* he was "the Phantom Rival in every domestic establishment." Although some young males tried to imitate his looks, other men dismissed him as a "pink powder puff," not a real man. Calling him "Vaselino," they joked about his slicked-down hair. His endorsement of cosmetics also drew fire. In 1923, Mineralava products subsidized a national tour in which he danced and promoted the company's beauty clay. In ads, Valentino, wearing a gaucho hat, appeared above the caption: "Every man and woman should use Mineralava, I would not be without it." His role as a prettified French nobleman in *Monsieur Beaucaire* (Sidney Olcott, 1924) prompted one critic to anticipate that men would not much like this "dolled up" fellow "in his white wig, silks, lace and satin knickers." A *Chicago Tribune* editorial in mid-1926 protested "this degeneration into effeminacy" that Valentino symbolized. "Better a rule by masculine women than by effeminate men," the writer said.[71]

By the time Valentino died suddenly in August 1926 at age thirty-one (of postsurgical peritonitis), he had revealed much about new definitions of masculinity and women's sexual longing as well as about the growing influence of popular culture. Whereas the death of the former Harvard president Charles W. Eliot merited one obituary column, news of Valentino's death and funeral filled entire pages for weeks. "What a power is this fragile strip of celluloid in which he played!" extolled *Moving Picture World* when using Valentino as an example of film's "all-conquering" might. Onscreen, according to another movie fan magazine, Valentino had supposedly also symbolized something else—namely, that "dark people are always more alert, intense, energetic. They have more concentrated power and nervous force."[72]

It was this image of the exotic Other that made Harlem, located in the northwestern part of Manhattan, a magnet for white partygoers. Over several decades, but particularly during the African American demographic shift north in the late 1910s, Harlem had switched from a white to a black neighborhood. By the 1920s, a remarkable infusion of black talent had launched a much-heralded artistic upheaval. There was, indeed, considerable hope among participants in this Harlem Renaissance that art might help solve the nation's race problems. By demonstrating their artistic achievements, African Americans might win the respect of the white community. While the amount of respect generated was questionable, large numbers of whites indeed pursued excitement and fun in Harlem's nightspots. Beyond famous places such as the Cotton Club, however, Harlem had a more hidden side—an impoverished, hand-to-mouth environment that was turning into a slum. Some residents, in order to come up with lodging money, staged rent parties where dozens of people crowded into flats to hear local musicians such as the great pianist Willie "the Lion" Smith. Although the Harlem Renaissance provided the artistic climate for musical experimentation, its high-culture advocates generally kept their distance from "the low-life world" of the other Harlem. As one jazz musician recalled: "We in music knew there was much going on in literature, for example, but our worlds were far apart. We sensed that the black cultural as well as moral leaders looked down on our music as undignified."[73]

That music was largely jazz. According to the historian Ann Douglas: "The term 'jazz' was used very loosely to include everything from ragtime to blues, from Louis Armstrong to sheer Tin Pan Alley pop. But what 'jazz' always meant was a loosened beat and Negro sources." It also represented, as a music critic said, "the blending together of cultural elements that had existed separately." The musical roots of jazz were in New Orleans, partly because in 1817 that city had legalized slave dances, unlike other locations in the South that banned slaves' use of drums, horns, and other loud instruments. By the late nineteenth century, New Orleans was on a grim economic downslide, but its music flourished at festivals, funerals, street parades, and honky-tonks such as the original Funky Butt. In the late 1910s, when around a half million Southern blacks moved north, jazz was part of their cultural baggage, moving upriver to Chicago and elsewhere, including New York City. One of its chief messengers was the incomparable Louis Armstrong, an illegitimate child who spent his early years in a ramshackle, violent neighborhood known as "the Battlefield" before entering the Colored Waif's Home, where he learned to play the cornet. Although he had been born on August 4, 1901, he elected to celebrate his birthday on July 4, Independence Day. Bashful, humble, and gripped with a sense of worthlessness, he looked to his audiences for approval. "Anyone can steal anything but my applause," he once told a friend. He played for a while with the King Oliver Creole Band in Chicago and then moved to New York.[74]

The new mass market technologies of dissemination, including mechanical pianos and phonographs, were vital in spreading African American music to larger audiences, including many white youths. In 1918, the fifteen-year-old Bix Beiderbecke first heard jazz recordings in his Davenport, Iowa, home after his brother returned from wartime service with a phonograph and some records. To his parents' despair, he purchased a cornet and started learning how to play jazz. A few years later, a group of white students listened to some jazz recordings on a windup Victrola in a local soda parlor outside Chicago. "Were we excited by it!" recalled one of them. "We were used to hearing commercial dance bands, but this sound was something else." According to another member of the group: "Right then and there we decided we would get a band and try to play like those guys."[75]

Jazz fascinated such white youths in part because it contained strong hints of rebellion. Its vitality and spontaneity presented a refreshing counterpoint to the stolid, genteel music that represented respectability and (high) culture. Whereas culture smacked of the traditional and exclusive and required formal training, jazz was new and discordant and invited audiences to join in, clapping, cheering, and dancing. Against genteel culture's order and stability, jazz offered a chance to escape. Hoagy Carmichael, who later wrote such classics as "Lazy River" and "Stardust," remembered a "hot Negro band" from Louisville playing at a high school dance in Bloomington, Indiana, in 1919. He had never heard such music. "I'm a Congo medicine man!" he suddenly shouted. An "insane dancing madness" swept over him and his partner as they moved to the "disjointed, unorganized music, full of screaming blue notes and a solid beat. . . . Jazz maniacs were being born and I was one of them." "The music poured into us like daylight running down a dark hole," remembered Eddie Condon. Another distinguished white jazz player, Mezz Mezzrow, put it well: "We were teenage refugees from the sunny suburbs." Their refugee status took on a courageous luster in the face of mainstream criticism. "Does jazz put the sin in syncopation?" asked the president of the National Federation of Women's Clubs in the *Ladies Home Journal*. John Philip Sousa, the composer of marching music, contended that jazz "does not truly represent America to the world." An Episcopal preacher in New York City believed that jazz "is retrogression. It is going to the African jungle for our music," and the *New York Times* equated jazz "to the humming, hand-clapping, or tomtom beating of savages."[76]

Whites such as Beiderbecke, Condon, and Mezzrow not only resisted the hold of culture but also helped confirm the kinds of mixing and crossovers that characterized so much American music. Jazz history, according to the music historian Richard Sudhalter, constituted a "picaresque tale of cooperation, mutual admiration, cross-fertilization, comings-together and driftings apart—all *despite* . . . the segregation of the larger society." Racial barriers blurred. Young white jazz musicians looked to blacks as mentors. But the respect went both ways. When Louis Armstrong heard Beiderbecke in Chicago in the mid-1920s, he was most appreciative: "I'm tellin' you, those pretty notes went right through me." And Armstrong, when playing with the white musician Jack Teagarden, reportedly said: "You an ofay, I'm a spade. Let's blow!"[77]

Jazz was a musical hybrid, but its origins were African American, and the continuing African American influence was profound. As the young William Dixon observed in his Harlem neighborhood: "It did seem, to a little boy, that . . . white people *really* owned everything. But that wasn't entirely true. They didn't own the music that I played."[78]

In one way, of course, Dixon was correct, but, in another way, he was not. As the popularity of jazz increased, the music industry grew more interested in capitalizing on and controlling it. Initially, businesses such as the Victor Talking Machine Company refused to record black artists; the assumption was that black performers would sully Victor's prestige and that white customers would shun them. In 1917, when Victor made the first jazz record ever, it featured the all-white Original Dixieland Jazz Band. When, a few months later, the band performed in England, the *London Daily News* emphasized that the musicians were "all white—as white as they can be." The bandleader, Nick LaRocca, went on to insist that whites had created jazz. "Our music is strictly white man's music," he maintained. "My contention is that the Negroes learned to play this rhythm and music from the whites. . . . The Negro did not play any kind of music equal to white men at the time."[79]

By the 1920s, the so-called King of Jazz was a white bandleader from Denver's middle class, Paul Whiteman, who also insisted that jazz had nothing to do with African Americans. Whiteman was a classical musician who admitted that he initially found it difficult to "jazz it up" because he felt "too tight inside," unable "to sway and pat and enjoy myself." He first used jazz in 1914 as a lark. While performing in New York City, his band set out to poke fun at a jazz hit, "Livery Stable Blues." To his surprise, the audience responded enthusiastically. "They hadn't realized the attempt at burlesque," he recalled. "They were ignorantly applauding the thing on its merits." Thereafter, he increasingly added his arrangements of black rhythms to his band's playlist, but he was determined to tame the music with refined symphonic sounds—to make "a lady of jazz." The members of Whiteman's Ambassador Orchestra could all read music, unlike a number of black musicians (or Tin Pan Alley composers such as Irving Berlin), who, through lack of opportunity, had received no formal training. "I didn't need the schooling," Louis Armstrong insisted. "I had the horn." According to Armstrong, the singer Bessie Smith "always just had her blues in her head; sometimes made them right up in the studio." Whiteman, however, did not hire black musicians no matter how talented, remarking once to the brilliant African American pianist Earl Hines: "If you were only white." Racism certainly influenced Whiteman's hiring decisions, but so did his desire to elevate the music's status and make it less culturally threatening. One result was that his 1926 autobiography, *Jazz,* incredibly ignored the contributions of blacks. Although he considered himself a "jazz mission-ary," he admitted that the music "puzzled" him. He compared "its un-couthness" to that of "an uneducated man struggling ungrammatically to express a true and original idea." The kind of "sweet," smooth music that he popularized as jazz discouraged improvisation: "Every member knows exactly what he is to play every minute of the time," he said. The music also contained little hint of the blues. But it served well the Victor recording company's needs. Playing it safe, Victor released many watered-down dance records featuring white orchestras. Whiteman's—"a jazz band with strings," playing from scores—produced dozens of hit records and sold millions of copies. The black activist and writer Amiri Baraka later referred to money-making bands such as Whiteman's when he wrote that the jazz age "had rushed into the mainstream without so much as one black face."[80]

But, in the 1920s, jazz was among the powerful magnets that drew large numbers of white slummers to Harlem's nightclubs. In those clubs, whites could, as the music historians Larry Starr and Christopher Waterman have written, "experience black culture without proximity to black peo-ple." Or, at least, they could experience their own versions of black culture, which seemed full of risk and temptation. Mae West dubbed Harlem "the Paris of the Western Hemisphere—a museum of occult sex, a sensual oasis in the sterile desert of white civilization, where conventional people can in-dulge in unconventional excesses." "Harlem!" read one advertisement: "The City that Never Sleeps! . . . A Strange, Exotic Island in the Heart of New York! . . . Rent Parties! . . . Number Runners! . . . Chippies! . . . Jazz Love! . . . Primitive Passion!" Here, supposedly, in contrast to an inhibited, repressed white culture, one could find an expressive, spontaneous lifestyle full of excitement and fun. When a white drama critic decided that the per-formers in one black dance review were too "dressed up and dignified," he complained that he wanted them to be "different [and] distinct" from whites. He preferred "picks [pickaninnies], Zulus, cannibals and cotton-pickers." From such a perspective, as the historian Nathan Huggins later argued, Harlem offered white slummers a "convenient" adventure: "It was merely a taxi trip to the exotic for most white New Yorkers. . . . No safari! . . . no tropic jungle. . . . thrill without danger."[81]

If these cultural excursions encouraged a sense of daring without risk, so did the kind of social dancing that Vernon and Irene Castle so famously popularized. Like Paul Whiteman, who believed that he "made an honest woman of jazz," the Castles saw themselves as cleansing forces for some of the era's new dance fads—"naughty diversions," as one newspaper in 1912 described them. Largely in response to ragtime's popularity, a succession of dance crazes began to sweep the nation. "The town is dance mad," one ob-server said of New York City. Working-class youths in particular engaged in a style of "tough dancing" that included "shaking the shimmy," dipping, and twirling. The New York socialite Elizabeth Marbury worried that respectable families needed "a place where their children could go to learn the dance without being exposed to the discredited elements." Marbury looked to the Castles, who could, she thought, bring "an uplifting influence" to the dance fads, and persuaded several of her wealthy friends to help establish Castle House, where young people could learn new steps in a polite setting.[82]

During the 1910s, the Castles became some of the media's biggest celebrities, giving dancing lessons, writing the best-selling instruction manual *Modern Dancing* (1914), appearing in silent films, and marketing their names on clothing and other consumer goods. Their backgrounds hardly matched their fashion-setting reputations. Vernon Castle was an Englishman who came to the United States with an engineering degree but ended up performing in musical comedies and burlesques. In 1910, he married Irene Foote. Born into a respectable middle-class family in New Rochelle, New York, Irene had initially seemed too "awkward" for the stage. But she and her new husband headed to France, where, after failing in a musical, they attracted success as a dance team in a Paris café. They returned to the United States in 1913, starring in a Broadway musical comedy, *The Sunshine Girl*, in which they performed the tango. That dance had developed in Buenos Aires, but the Castles turned it into a major American fad. Although the tango was originally quite sensual, the Castles' version was much more restrained. "If Vernon would have ever looked into my eyes with smoldering passion during the tango," Irene wrote later, "we would have both burst out laughing." Portraying themselves as aristocrats, the Castles became models of elegance, carefully putting distance between their dance styles and those of the lower classes. "We get our dances from the Barbary Coast," Irene explained. "Of course, they reach New York in a very primitive condition, and have to be considerably toned down before they can be used in the drawing room." She indicated that "a nigger dance" had recently arrived but that she and her husband "may try and make something of it." *Theatre Magazine* applauded them because they "spiritualized the dances thought to be hopelessly fleshly." "Do not wiggle the shoulders," the Castles advised. "Do not shake the hips. Do not twist the body." Dancing, Vernon emphasized, should be stately, graceful, and smooth. "It should not be done in a romping spirit."[83]

Despite the elements of control and restraint that they brought to dance and music, the Castles and Paul Whiteman played significant roles in popularizing new styles and challenging Victorian limits. Their respectable images disarmed critics and provided somewhat more room for experimentation, bringing popular dances and sounds into the ballroom. "We were clean-cut," explained Irene Castle; "we were married and when we danced there was nothing suggestive about it." She became an influential fashion-setter, bobbing her hair, urging women to shed their corsets, and presenting an appearance of innocent fun. Like Cecil B. DeMille's movies, the Castles demonstrated that "new freedoms could revitalize marriage without destroying it." As the historian Lewis Erenberg has written: "They uplifted the low-life sensuality of the city and made it eligible for the home." Similarly, Whiteman helped legitimize jazz, despite its muted form. By dismissing jazz's moral critics as "jazz-klanners," by hiring talented white musicians such as Bix Beiderbecke, and by taking his sweetened form of jazz around the country, Whiteman helped, however inadvertently, to widen the boundaries of popular music. For African Americans, of course, his "whitened" jazz was all too familiar at a time when the heavyweight champion Jack Dempsey refused to fight blacks, baseball's major leagues were segregated, and football included only a handful of black players.[84]

By the 1920s, popular culture was, nevertheless, steadily eroding much that was old and traditional. "When a good orchestra plays a 'rag,'" observed Vernon Castle, "one has simply *got* to move." Or, as the wife said in the 1915 *McClure's* story "Dance-Mad Billie": "I want—I want—I want to en-*joy* myself too." Her husband responded enthusiastically: "Let's go out to-night and have a lark!"[85]

An increasingly significant aspect of the broad social and cultural transformations that mass entertainment encouraged was a revolutionary "turn to listening." The phonograph had set the course, and recorded sounds ultimately dominated the music industry. In 1919, for the first time, a recorded song became a hit before it appeared as sheet music; "Mary," a dance tune from the Victor company, sold 300,000 copies in only three months. Within a half dozen years, phonograph records were outselling sheet music and coming off factory lines at the rate of almost 100 million per year. Because of microphones, the recordings were better than ever. First used in 1925, microphones meant that engineers had more control over particular sounds and that performers no longer had to project into large megaphones.[86]

The burgeoning record industry scrambled to find talent and cultivate audiences. Victor, for example, despite its high-toned image, hoped to take advantage of dance crazes such as the tango. In 1913, it thus urged dealers to push the company's new list of dance records: "Take advantage of the current desire for this type of dance to reap a profitable harvest." And, although Victor's concerns about jazz's suspect reputation discouraged the company from pressing many jazz records until the mid-1920s, it was Victor that introduced the Original Dixieland Jazz Band in 1917. Still, because the dominant music companies such as Victor and Columbia were so cautious and grudging about recording many forms of popular music, they opened opportunities for fledgling operations such as Okeh Records.[87]

Okeh was established in 1918, the creation of Otto Heinemann, a German immigrant who three years earlier had incorporated the General Phonograph Company in New York City. Heinemann's goal was to produce "the most popular of popular records." In 1920, Okeh released the first popular recordings by an African American female, Mamie Smith. When her "Crazy Blues" sold seventy-five thousand copies in one month, mainly in black communities, it was clear that Okeh had discovered a music audience outside the commercial mainstream. Polk Brockman, who ran Okeh's Atlanta dealership, helped with that discovery. While running his family furniture store, Brockman noted that people without much money would buy phonograph record players because the windup motors did not require electricity. Moreover, blacks in the Atlanta area bought substantial numbers of jazz and blues recordings, while poor whites looked for "country" music. His litmus test was overwhelmingly financial. "My interest in hillbilly music and black music is strictly financial," he candidly admitted. In his opinion: "The customer is always right." Sensing the existence of a largely overlooked market, Brockman started driving white and black performers long distances to recording studios. Soon Okeh took the lead in sending talent scouts—particularly the influential Ralph Peer—through the South in search of new sounds and singers. Because it was cheaper to record in regional centers than to bring the artists to New York City, Okeh started using portable recording equipment. Other small independents, such as the Wisconsin Chair Company's Paramount Records, quickly rushed into this budding market. The bigger companies followed.[88]

As companies began to record "race music" such as the blues, jazz, and gospel singing, Okeh in 1923 released the first commercially successful hillbilly record. The event was virtually an accident. Ralph Peer was in Atlanta to record a singer from a local church. But, when the individual could not attend because of a family illness, Polk Brockman brought in Fiddlin' John Carson. Carson was by then around fifty years old and lived in Cabbagetown, a working-class factory town outside Atlanta. He had long participated in fiddling championships and identified with the rebellious political tradition of impoverished whites from the hill country. Although Peer cringed at what he thought was Carson's "pluperfect awful" music, the recording sold well in the Georgia area. "I decided to stop makin' liquor and go to makin' phonograph records," joked Carson. "So," Peer later said, "the beginning of the hillbilly [recording industry] was just this effort to take up some time. . . . I can't claim there was any genius connected with it—not on my part, not on his part."[89]

In 1927, Peer made even bigger discoveries—ones that constituted country music's "big bang." By then, he had moved to the dominant Victor Company, where, he said, the label alone guaranteed sales of at least forty thousand copies of each record. His contract with Victor was strategically brilliant: his income would come from copyright royalties on agreements that he worked out with the artists; the company would earn money from the sales and would not need to pay him a salary. Victor, which did not see much future in country music, thought that it had a favorable deal. In August 1927, Peer held recording sessions in Bristol, Tennessee, where he signed on the Carter Family: A. P. ("Doc"), his wife, Sara, and his sister-in-law, Maybelle. Over the next fifteen years, the Carters made over three hundred recordings, including the classic "Wabash Cannonball" and "Will the Circle Be Unbroken."[90]

Peer's other Bristol discovery was Jimmie Rodgers, a product of rural Mississippi who by the age of twelve was performing with carnivals and minstrel shows. Later, on the road with a small band, he at least once found no one in the audience. "If I can't get 'em in town," he resolutely told his wife, "we'll go to the woods." By the time he reached Bristol, his band had broken up, but he auditioned anyhow, commencing a storied but short singing career. Like many of the performers from society's margins, he could not read music. Still, until he died of tuberculosis in 1933, he melded blues, jazz, and country sounds into a unique and influential sound. Rodgers and the Carters staked out the two major dimensions of country music: while the Carters hauntingly evoked images of church, family, and roots, Rodgers celebrated the open road and movin' on. Although hillbilly records sold in far fewer numbers than did mainstream popular records, sales of Rodgers's first nine releases reportedly approached 4 million.[91]

Despite country music's popularity, the "hillbilly stuff" embarrassed the music producers, who recorded it reluctantly. Considering themselves sophisticated urbanites, they generally viewed country singers and audiences with contempt. As a result, starting in the 1920s, they patched together images of the hillbilly constituency as rural rustics, thereby reinforcing perceptions that country music was for bumpkins—geezers, hicks, plain women in polka-dot dresses, or, in the words of the entertainment industry's trade journal *Variety*, people "of 'poor white trash' genera" who were "illiterate and ignorant, with the intelligence of morons."[92]

Ralph Peer nevertheless had much to cheer about. Although he had long envied the commercial mainstream of the music industry, he learned that a specialized minority market—an entertainment niche—bore its own fruit. During one quarter in 1928, he reportedly earned $250,000.[93]

Ironically, economic difficulties in the recording industry had provided the opportunity for Peer to develop that specialized music niche. Although record sales boomed from 1919 to 1921 with companies annually pressing almost 100 million disks, Columbia's pretax profits during those years dropped from $7 million to $4.3 million, a harbinger of what was to come; in 1923, the bankrupt company, although still making records, tumbled into receivership. Meanwhile, between 1921 and 1925, Victor's sales plunged by

half, from $51 to $25 million. Technology, which had buoyed up the record industry, was now undermining it. Just as phonograph recordings displaced sheet music, radio was suddenly the ascendant technological force.
Rapidly declining record sales raised an important question: Why would
people buy records when they could listen to the songs for free over the radio? That question helped explain the recording industry's sudden interest
in exploring new markets and attested to radio's rapidly emerging music
format.[94]

Going into the 1920s, radio had been the preserve of scientific researchers and amateurs. After 1896, when the Italian Guglielmo Marconi trans-
mitted the first "wireless" coded message through the air, the American
scientist Lee De Forest developed an oscillating vacuum tube that allowed
for transmitting human voices. Three years later, in 1909, Charles D.
Herrold played music for his students on his College of Engineering's
fifteen-watt station in San Jose. In mid-1920, an electrical engineer from
Westinghouse, Frank Conrad, started transmitting two-hour "programs"
on a regular basis from his garage in a Pittsburgh suburb, where he played
phonograph records and chatted with friends and guests. A local music
store provided the records in exchange for Conrad saying where he had
gotten them. On November 2, 1920, a small radio station in East Pittsburgh,
Pennsylvania, broadcast the results of the presidential election to several
hundred listeners. Meanwhile, amateurs built wireless sets and shortwave
transmitters to talk with each other, giving rise to legends about "boy heroes" who helped rescue ships at sea. During the early 1920s, broadcasting
touched off a national fad. By the end of 1922, 1.5 million radio sets and
more than 550 stations speckled the country. Seventy-four colleges and
universities had established their own radio stations. A mining engineer in
a remote area conveyed a sense of the wonders of this new medium. He described his "three bosom friends . . . here in the shack with me—my ax, my
dog, and my wireless receiving set," which provided music, stories, and information about the larger world. "I may be at 'the back of the beyond,'
but the whole world has marched right up to the edge of the little copper
switch at my elbow."[95]

Predictably, cultural battle lines soon formed around radio. What was
its main purpose? What kinds of sounds would issue from it? Who would
control it? As had been the case with the phonograph and movies, some
reformers and intellectuals looked to radio as a source of cultural unity and
uplift. They believed that it would bring together diverse groups by providing instruction, shared values, and high culture.

Early on, however, radio became the domain of the commercial and the
popular. In 1922, the federal government acted to ensure that unsupervised
amateurs did not reduce the airwaves to chaos and threaten middle-class
homes with unacceptable kinds of material. Despite arguments that, in a

democracy, the airwaves should be open to all, the Department of Commerce (using its licensing powers under the 1912 Radio Law) distinguished between *amateurs* and *broadcasters*. Amateur radio licenses forbade broadcasting "entertainment" or reports such as the weather or news. As the radio historian Michele Hilmes has written: "Early radio regulation exhibited a tendency to *exclude* more than include—to set up barriers to popular expression." For people curious about who would pay for broadcasting, an answer appeared on August 8, 1922: a real estate company bought ten minutes of New York station WEAF's time to advertise an apartment. The giant American Telephone and Telegraph Company (AT&T) owned WEAF, exemplifying the eagerness of numerous major corporations, department stores, and newspapers to establish radio stations. Among the company-sponsored programs on WEAF was the *Eveready Hour*. It first aired in late 1923 to promote the National Carbon Company's Eveready batteries. But it also revealed radio's receptivity to popular tastes. A number of companies attempted to associate their products with high culture by sponsoring orchestras (e.g., the Lucky Strike Orchestra) that played classical music— or "potted palm music," as one critic described it. But, in January 1924, Eveready bowed to "vaudeville culture" by hiring Wendell Hall as one of its stars. A novelty singer, Hall had appeared briefly on a Westinghouse Company station. Eveready, however, worked through a national advertising company, N. W. Ayer, to sign him up after his 1923 song, "It Ain't Gonna Rain No Mo'," swept the country. Sponsored entertainment quickly became the backbone of radio programming. By the end of 1924, AT&T had used its telephone lines to hook up twenty-six stations, coast-to-coast, that paid a toll for broadcast time.[96]

The growing importance of sponsors led in 1926 to the formation of the first national radio network—the National Broadcasting Company (NBC). Initially, the network had two parts—NBC-Red, with twenty-two stations, and NBC-Blue, with six. Within fifteen years, NBC-Red numbered seventy-four stations and NBC-Blue ninety-two. The fact that NBC's owner was the Radio Corporation of America (RCA), which AT&T had helped form in 1919, manifested corporate America's early dominance of radio. In 1927, Columbia Records, hoping to promote its artists and their songs, launched the Columbia Broadcasting System (CBS) with sixteen stations. After a few months, however, the recording company jettisoned its financially strapped radio network, selling it to the Paley family, owners of the Philadelphia-based Congress Cigar Company. The NBC and CBS networks allowed affiliated stations (which they did not own) to air network programs and share production costs. Ultimately, the networks' widely scattered distributors helped disseminate an increasingly national popular culture.[97]

That culture's emphasis on consumerism became even firmer via radio's reliance on advertising. To the disappointment of some elites and intellectuals, it was the market—not high culture—that decided what aired over the radio. Because broadcasting developed commercially, without direct government subsidy or state involvement, negotiations between advertisers, sponsors, networks, and stations determined radio's contents. The mediated results most certainly privileged some voices at the expense of others. Still, because advertisers and broadcasters sought large audiences, they were less constrained by traditional class, religious, ethnic, and regional boundaries. A significant result was that myriad sounds and messages—and, thus, myriad points of view—flooded the airwaves.[98]

Even the few pockets of noncommercial radio were caught in cultural crosscurrents. At the University of Wisconsin, for example, professors hoped that agricultural programming at the state-operated WHA station would educate and uplift. In the opinion of the station's broadcast chief, who had shed the farm clothes of his youth to teach physics at the university, "old time fiddler" music and "other worthless material" were "beneath the dignity of the University to add to it." Rural listeners bridled at such talk, which seemed yet another example of snobbish, urban, intellectual thinking. "Give us something with melody," pleaded one individual, although some listeners, particularly women, appreciated the university's high-toned programming as an enriching and welcome alternative to rural isolation. Radio countered such isolation in other ways as well. WHA's coverage of the university's football games, for example, reached across the state, tying together communities of loyal fans. And, if rural audiences sometimes found radio too full of urban sounds, at least a few believed that it protected rural America. Whereas automobiles "have tended to take farmers away from home," explained one person, "the radio . . . tends to keep these same folks at home."[99]

Radio ultimately cast a wide and rapidly expanding audio net, capturing listeners through a variety of sounds, some local, some national; some familiar, some disturbing; some genteel, some vulgar. Even local programming had many nuances. In Butte, Montana, for example, listeners called in requests for particular tunes. "Request hour, hell," one person alerted the announcer. "You're advertising every whore in Butte." When "Gladys at 2 Upper Terrace" or "Dorothy at 8 Lower Terrace" called in, they were simply taking advantage of local broadcasting's commercial benefits.[100]

And, while the act of listening to the radio at home could put up barriers, isolating individuals from rough crowds and discouraging them from going out, it also broke down barriers, admitting the Other into the home via the airwaves. As a student of radio has written, it "allowed 'race' music to invade the home, vaudeville to compete with opera in the living room, risqué city humor to raise rural eyebrows, salesmen and entertainers to find a place in the family circle." Whites who chafed at the restraints of "Main

Street, USA," for example, could, in the words of one media historian, "play hooky in the safety of their own homes, far away from the ghettos, brothels, and gin joints that produced such music, such truancy." In that regard, radio was an "auditory turnstile between cultures," between the world "out there" and everyday life. One person recalled fondly how his neighbors in West Virginia's hill country gathered on the highest point on Saturday nights to listen to a country music show that the National Life and Accident Insurance Company's Nashville station inaugurated in 1927: *The Grand Ole Opry*. People arrived from miles around to listen to Uncle Salter's radio, which ran off the car battery: "All of us would sit up there under the stars and listen to it until it went off the air at night. It was fine."[101]

Not until 1927 did the sound revolution reach the movies, however. Motion pictures had, of course, never been completely silent. Not only were the audiences often noisy, but theater managers had also used pianos, orchestras, narrators, phonograph records, and various in-house sound effects as audio backdrops to the moving images. But it was Alan Crosland's landmark film *The Jazz Singer,* which premiered in New York City on October 6, 1927, that first synchronized words with the pictures.

As has frequently happened in popular culture, the innovative forces came from the industry's margins. The established studios were reluctant to experiment much with sound lest it require expensive changes in producing and showing movies. When making silent pictures, filmmakers could place sets in close proximity, making several movies at once, and shouting instructions to the actors. "Sound is a passing fancy," MGM producer Irving Thalberg told his wife of efforts to synchronize it with motion pictures. "It won't last."[102]

Newcomers such as the Warner brothers, determined to gain a foothold in the industry, developed a conscious strategy to use sound to challenge the big studios' dominance. "Every worthwhile contribution to the advancement of motion pictures has been made over a howl of protest from the standpatters, whose favorite refrain has been, 'You can't do that,'" Jack Warner asserted. "And when we hear that chorus now, we know we must be on the right track." The brothers saw themselves as unappreciated underdogs. Their parents had immigrated to the United States from Poland in 1876, reportedly picking up the Warner name at Ellis Island when an official substituted it for a word he could not figure out. Twelve children were born into the economically strapped family. Eventually, four of the brothers (Sam, Harry, Albert, and Jack) established a small chain of nickelodeons in Ohio and Pennsylvania towns. At one point, according to Harry, they had to borrow chairs from the undertaker's place next door. With profits from their nickelodeons and a loan, they rented a small movie studio in Hollywood, turning out cheap films that glamorized small-town life and played outside the major theater chains. Fascinated by the sound revolution, they opened a radio station in Los Angeles—the third station to exist in the area and the only one owned by a Hollywood movie company. Seeking ways to finance a synchronized sound system for film, they secured a loan from the Western Electric Company (a branch of AT&T), which hoped to manufacture and sell sound equipment for theaters and had developed a sound-on-disk process known as Vitaphone. The Warners, running the only family-owned and family-operated Hollywood studio, were determined to catch up with such majors as MGM, Universal, and Paramount.[103]

They were, however, in a race with William Fox, a more established moviemaker who was bent on surpassing the bigger studios. A Hungarian, Fox had immigrated to the United States at the age of nine months and grown up as one of thirteen children on New York City's Lower East Side. When he was twenty-five, he and two partners started a nickelodeon in Brooklyn. Soon he owned an expanding chain of theaters that, by the end of the 1920s, numbered over five hundred houses. By then, however, he had concluded that the real money rested in producing movies, not simply showing them. Beginning in 1914, he started making melodramas and action films that starred the sultry Theda Bara and the cowboy hero Tom Mix. As he began to develop impressive picture palaces, he decided also to produce more prestigious films. A workaholic, he refused to carry a watch because he did not care about the time and reportedly dreamed of a day when he would control the entire movie industry. Sound seemed to offer opportunities to elevate his company into the top ranks.[104]

In this race between two studios hungry for big-time success, the Warner brothers came out ahead. Although Fox produced a fully orchestrated symphonic sound track for the film *Seventh Heaven* (Frank Borzage, 1927) and synchronized some street sounds in *Sunrise* (F. W. Murnau, 1927), the Warners were the first to mesh spoken words with the moving pictures. *The Jazz Singer* in fact combined silence and sound, using written words on the screen except for songs and several extemporized comments, particularly Al Jolson's "Wait a minute! Wait a minute! You ain't seen nothin' yet." When Jolson, a well-known theatrical and recording star, burst into song, the experience was electrifying. "Jolson, Jolson, Jolson!" screamed the audience at the end of the New York City premiere showing. According to one observer, the spectators resembled "a milling, battling mob." The Warners' investment reaped dividends. Costs of equipping the two theaters that showed the movie reached $500,000, but the studio's assets soared from $5 million in 1925 to $230 million in 1930. Quickly, the other major filmmakers were trying to catch up with the Warner brothers, whom MGM and the other big studios had viewed contemptuously as "low-rent upstarts."[105]

The Warners had turned the movie industry upside down. According to a Western Electric sound engineer: "Producers now realized it was a case of sink or swim." Within three years, in 1930, the major studios stopped silent-film production. Ironically, the new instructions, "All quiet on the set," signaled the full-scale arrival of the sound revolution in film. The costs of accomplishing that momentous transition, however, made the industry even more vulnerable to the Great Depression, which shattered the American economy and jeopardized all popular culture.[106]

7

BATTLING THE GREAT DEPRESSION

THE CATACLYSMIC EVENTS OF THE GREAT DEPRESSION CONSTI-
tuted a major turning point in U.S. history, but they also tested and, eventually, strengthened popular culture's place in the nation's life. Virtually all
areas of mass entertainment reeled during the early 1930s as the economic
crisis deepened. Ultimately, however, commercial amusements flourished,
producing what one writer later characterized as "the first great period of
American popular culture." The entertainment business rebounded as citizens sought to escape dispiriting realities by attending athletic events and
movies, listening to the phonograph and the radio, reading magazines and
comic books. Such amusements enlarged the shared experiences of common citizens, eroding provincial boundaries and increasing fascination
with the world "out there." In a variety of ways, popular culture also reflected and reaffirmed the activities and spirit of President Franklin Roosevelt's New Deal programs for economic recovery.[1]

Yet, while popular culture was a powerful unifying force, it also conveyed different meanings and competing images. The staggering unemployment figures gave a disturbing twist to old worries about the "problem of
leisure." During the Depression, a host of moralists and social scientists renewed the call for "guidance in the right use of leisure" that had earlier
motivated progressives to launch such reforms as the playground movement. A sociologist argued that "leisure and how we spend it becomes of
paramount importance to us educationally and morally, individually, and
as a nation." Such concerns invigorated censorship campaigns against commercial amusements, which elites still judged as low-class diversions.
Citizens "have been fed on jazz," warned a 1935 publication of the
Methodist Episcopal Church: "They may not know good music when they
hear it. . . . They have been accustomed to getting their amusements in
'canned form.'" Meanwhile, even entertainment with a reputation for up-

lift sent conflicting messages. In 1937, for example, Walt Disney's first feature-length cartoon movie, *Snow White and the Seven Dwarfs*, elicited praise for affirming traditional moral values. But one woman who worked with slum children believed that they missed "the beauty of this extraordinary film" and its lessons. Instead of viewing *Snow White* as one of life's "finer cultural experiences," as the woman hoped they would, they seemed interested mainly in such details as the scary trees and the violence.[2]

During the 1920s, the unprecedented heights and level of influence to which popular culture had risen hardly prepared it for the devastating economic collapse that became the Great Depression. Granted, in the 1920s, just as some groups—particularly farmers—had experienced severe economic setbacks, pockets of the entertainment industry suffered financial woes. Between 1921 and 1925, for example, sales in the recording industry fell from a high of $106 million to about half that amount. Still, via improved technology, enhanced advertising, new talent, and a recognition of diverse audience interests, the record business had rebounded, momentarily holding off the growing threat of radio, which, by 1926, was in only half the number of homes that owned phonographs.[3]

In the early 1930s, however, the challenge of dealing with competition in the amusement sector paled beside the problem of finding consumers as thousands of banks and businesses closed and unemployment soared to staggering levels. A sense of desperation gripped the nation as a great army of unemployed citizens took to the road or the rails, waited in soup lines, took refuge in proliferating shantytowns, or hunkered down nervously with beleaguered families. Between 1929 and 1932, total national income and industrial production fell by half; income from wages dropped by around 60 percent. By 1932, layoffs in the automobile industry had idled a quarter of a million workers in Detroit alone. The ranks of the unemployed swelled to 624,000 in Chicago and 800,000 in New York. Shockingly, perhaps as much as 28 percent of the population had no income at all. Even among those who held jobs, possibly one-third worked only part-time. National income plunged from $81 billion in 1929 to $41 billion in 1932. "The real problem in America," observed one person, "is not to feed ourselves for one more winter, it is to find what we are going to do with ten or twelve million people who are permanently displaced." Public and private relief agencies could not meet escalating demands. As one newspaper editor commented: "We can no longer depend on passing the hat, and rattling the tin cup. We have gone to the bottom of the barrel."[4]

Not surprisingly, the fortunes of the entertainment industry plummeted. At the end of 1931, the trade journal *Variety* summed up the grim situation: "Show business, as the current year closes out, is in the most chaotic condition it has ever known." From the record business to theaters, athletic arenas, and amusement parks, the Depression relentlessly pounded away. "People seemed to be hiding," recalled one individual. "They simply did not have the money to waste on baseball games or amusements." Even the Ziegfeld Follies, for years an entertainment jewel, could not survive in its old form. In mid-1931, Florenz Ziegfeld fought off bankruptcy to open his last Follies, but it lasted only 165 performances. On July 22, 1932, he died, virtually broke. That drama season, two-thirds of New York City's theaters were closed, and 80 percent of the stage productions failed.[5]

Although huge crowds continued to take advantage of the low subway and trolley fares from New York City to Coney Island, the amusement parks struggled through disastrous times. Coney, which the *New York Times* had described in 1922 as a "paradise of the proletariat," still drew massive crowds, but the island's concessionaires complained that people no longer spent money. Instead, poor families brought their own food, ignored the sideshows, and slept on the beach by the thousands, sometimes all night. "Nowadays you have to half kill 'em to get a dime," lamented one performer. "Thirty-five years ago I could do more business with 60,000 visitors than I can do with 500,000 now," moaned another individual. Charles Feltman, a German immigrant who had invented the hot dog and for years had operated the largest pavilion on the island, slashed prices and released two-thirds of his twelve hundred employees in an effort to stay afloat. Still, one by one, Coney's rides, galleries, and traditional landmarks closed down. By the end of the 1930s, perhaps half the island's attractions had disappeared. The epithet "the Poor Man's Riviera" took on shabbier meanings, as Coney declined from its once-storied position as an entertainment highlight to what its historian has described as "the resort of last resort for those who could afford little more than the nickel it took to get there on the subway."[6]

Circuses fared no better, enduring their worst decade since the Civil War. Early on in the Depression, a number of smaller shows folded their tents for the last time. In September, the D. C. Robbins Brothers Circus literally threw off the train protesting workers whom the owner had given $1 each and then fired; several were injured badly, and one died. Even the Greatest Show on Earth—Ringling Brothers and Barnum and Bailey (which had netted $1 million in 1929)—ended up in receivership. John Ringling had made the costly mistake of purchasing the American Circus Corporation and its five medium-sized shows just before the 1929 stock market crash buried circus stocks. In 1928, he had been one of America's ten richest people; when he died six years later at age seventy, he had a mere $311 in the bank, although his estate was still substantial. In 1937, his nephew John Ringling North obtained sufficient money to regain family ownership of the Greatest Show on Earth and helped revitalize it, partly with a much-ballyhooed gorilla named Gargantua the Great—"the most terrifying creature the world has ever seen," as North described it. Meanwhile, in the mid-1930s, Tom Mix briefly parlayed his fame as a popular cowboy from Wild West shows and movies into his own circus, but his show closed in 1938.[7]

One of the few circus success stories during the Depression was that of Clyde Beatty, a wild animal trainer, who seemed to meet a national hunger for symbols of courage, resilience, and overcoming the odds. Holding a chair to fend off the dangerous animals and cracking a whip, he would enter a cage with as many as forty lions and tigers. He performed for the Greatest Show on Earth in New York's Madison Square Garden and in Boston and then hit the road with a smaller circus. During a practice session in January 1932, a lion mauled him badly. For weeks, an anxious public followed extensive radio and newspaper coverage of his struggle to live. Three months after the attack, he was back in the cage, facing off the animals. "In this Depression year of 1932," a circus historian has written, "Beatty seemed to express the national longing for recovery, and the belief that an American boy could overcome the 'Law of the Jungle.'" Beatty starred in several movies and, in 1937, appeared on *Time* magazine's cover. Overall, however, the Depression brought only bad times to the circus business. By the 1940s, Ringling Brothers and Barnum and Bailey was the only large circus still operating, while a few small-scale operations performed at county fairs and in places such as community ballparks.[8]

For several painful years, the movie industry also floundered badly. Because of Hollywood's expensive transition to "talkies," the Depression could hardly have hit at a worse time. Studios had invested heavily in new cameras, film, and soundstages, while theaters—70 percent of which were equipped with sound systems by 1930—had gone heavily into debt. The Depression subsequently drove theater admissions from 80 million in 1930 to 55 million in 1932. By mid-1932, as ticket sales sagged, sixty-five hundred of twenty thousand theaters closed their doors. Groucho Marx quipped that the only problem with the movies was that people no longer attended. "God knows where they go," he said. "They certainly don't go to bed and, judging from business conditions, they don't go to work." The toll on the studios was heavy. By early 1933, for example, RKO and Paramount were bankrupt, Universal was in receivership, and Fox, Warner Brothers, Columbia, and United Artists were barely afloat. Scrambling to offset this unprecedented crisis, the movie industry begged Congress, itself desperate for revenues, not to impose a proposed tax on theater tickets. The studios argued that they provided a crucial public service in a time of great need, distracting citizens momentarily from the Depression's misery and thereby boosting morale. "Every darkened theater is a victory for the forces of discontent and disorder in the United States," a Hollywood attorney warned a congressional committee.[9]

The question, of course, was what kind of escapist fare would lure people off the streets. "The function of movies is to ENTERTAIN," proclaimed Will Hays, who, since 1922, had presided as a kind of cultural watchdog over the Motion Picture Producers and Distributors of America (MPPDA). Such entertainment, according to the Production Code that the MPPDA adopted in March 1930, was supposed to be "wholesome" and "directly responsible for spiritual or moral progress." The Code, exuding reformist faith in the power of moral leadership and uplift, insisted that "no picture shall be produced which will lower the moral standards of those who see it." Predicated on the assumption that "art can be morally evil in its effects," the Code warned against movies that, among other things, sympathized with "crime, wrongdoing, evil, or sin"; dishonored the institution of marriage; included obscenities, profanity, "*sex perversion*," or "excessive and lustful kissing"; featured "*indecent or undue exposure*"; or ridiculed the law or showed disrespect for the flag. But the studios, awash in red ink, were increasingly less concerned with the Code's dictates and the $25,000 fine for films that lacked the Production Code Administration's seal of approval than with filling seats.[10]

Against that backdrop, Hollywood briefly took more chances than it would otherwise have been inclined to do. It made a number of films with implicit political messages, explored real problems besetting the nation, and sometimes even questioned hallowed American myths. A few movies exhibited the sense of despair that gripped many citizens. Although the Hays office struggled to ensure that Hollywood produced respectable entertainment, the studios for a while took a riskier approach to violence, unsettling characters, and sexuality.

One result was "sin-ema," or what the Hays office rebuked as "sex films." Despite the Production Code, a number of these movies included partial and, occasionally, full nudity. In Paramount's 1932 *Time of the Cross,* Cecil B. DeMille embellished his old technique of combining risqué scenes with a biblical story. In one scene, for example, a pagan lesbian tempted a virtuous Christian slave woman. "Rome burns again!" said the studio publicist excitedly. "The sets are marvelous and the costumes spell sex. There's Claudette Colbert in a milk bath. And Frederic March using the sensuous Joyzelle [a dancing lesbian] to break down the resistance of [the Christian slave woman]—mentally, and how!" In Paramount's *Girl without a Room* (Ralph Murphy, 1933), Joyzelle Joyner danced in nothing but body paint. A totally nude model posed in MGM's *Another Language* (Edward H. Griffith, 1933).[11]

"Sin-ema" dripped with sexual references, innuendo, and double entendres. "As long as they have sidewalks, you'll have a job," one woman jabbed at another in *Footlight Parade* (Lloyd Bacon, 1933). In *42nd Street* (Lloyd Bacon, 1933), the song "Any Time Annie" included the line: "She only said 'no' once, and then she didn't hear the question." In *Finishing School* (George Nichols Jr. and Wanda Tuchock, 1934), a female insisted that trying to put a brassiere on her small-bosomed sorority sister would be "like putting a saddle on a Pekinese." Elsewhere, in *Employees' Entrance* (Roy Del Ruth, 1933), a male boss told the blonde who entered his office: "Oh, it's you—I didn't recognize you with your clothes on." Or, in *No More Women* (Albert S. Rogell, 1934), when a man said to a woman, "You know, I always like to take an experienced girl home," she replied innocently, "I ain't 'experienced.'" He responded: "Well, you ain't home yet."[12]

This was the setting in which Mae West rocketed to film stardom. Going into the 1930s, she may have been "fat, fair and I don't know how near forty," as the columnist Louella Parsons criticized her, but she almost single-handedly rescued the Paramount studio from bankruptcy. Initially, Hollywood had spurned her because of her reputation for scandal. But, in 1932, reeling through a record annual loss of $21 million and headed toward receivership, Paramount turned to her precisely because of her notoriety. Playing a bit part in Archie Mayo's *Night after Night,* she "stole everything but the cameras," according to the movie's star, George Raft. When, in the film, the checkroom girl commented, "Goodness, what beautiful diamonds," West—in lines that she had rewritten—scoffed memorably: "Goodness had nothing to do with it, dearie." Paramount decided to turn her play *Diamond Lil*—a 1928 Broadway hit that the Hays office had placed on its "banned list" of theater and literary works as unsuitable for screen adaptation—into a movie, *She Done Him Wrong* (Lowell Sherman, 1933). Indeed, the financially desperate studio even offered West total script control. At Warner Brothers, when Harry Warner learned that "Paramount has arranged to make *Diamond Lil* with Mae West," he immediately wired Hays: "Recollect that it was absolutely definite that *Diamond Lil* . . . was not to be produced." Warner had no personal objection to making such a film, but he wanted to know what restrictions still applied to his own studio. After Hays called an emergency meeting to deal with the matter, Paramount indicated its willingness to obey the Code by portraying the women in the movie as dancers and singers rather than as prostitutes, avoiding offensive subject matter, and making no connection to *Diamond Lil* in any advertising. West masterfully finessed the situation, combining humor and innuendo with exaggerated sexuality. She swayed suggestively across the screen, issued salty pronouncements such as "When women go wrong, men go *right after them*," and sang "I Like a Guy What Takes His Time." The movie was a box-office hit across the country. According to one female reviewer, it was "the most flagrant and utterly abandoned morsel of sin ever attempted on the screen, and I must confess that I enjoyed it enormously." Paramount continued to give West freedom over her scripts and performances. Her second film, *I'm No Angel* (Wesley

Ruggles, 1933), earned twelve times what it cost. *It Ain't No Sin* was the original title of her third movie—before the censors objected and it became *Belle of the Nineties* (Leo McCarey, 1934). Oozing sexuality, West was by 1934 reportedly the highest-paid woman in the country, appearing not simply on screen but in advertisements and on Lux soapboxes. Moreover, she had sufficient power at Paramount to get the studio to drop its opposition to putting black musicians onscreen and allow Duke Ellington and his band to appear in *Belle of the Nineties*.[13]

There was certainly nothing new in using titillation to build audiences. But, in the early 1930s, in the context of a growing public cynicism, filmmakers often reversed the traditional moral formula in which fallen women paid dearly for their transgressions. Now, lusty women slept their way to success, mostly enjoying luxury and good times. "He's a man, ain't he," Jean Harlow said in *Red-Headed Woman* (Jack Conway, 1932), attesting to her manipulative powers over wealthy males. Playing a prostitute that same year in Victor Fleming's *Red Dust,* Harlow laughingly tempted Clark Gable as she bathed in a rain barrel. In *Iron Man* (Tod Browning, 1931), the nipples of the two-timing Harlow's breasts were clearly visible through a filmy negligee. Moreover, the message in such films suggested that poor people sometimes had to use illicit measures in order to survive. Hence, audiences could sympathize with Loretta Young's need, in *Employees' Entrance* (Roy Del Ruth, 1933), to surrender to the department store manager's sexual demands.[14]

While the Hays office struggled to bank the fires of film sexuality, it faced additional worries in a spate of early 1930s horror and crime movies. Not only was Tod Browning's vampire film *Dracula* Universal's top revenue producer in 1931, but it also inspired several dozen other horror films over the next five years, including especially *Frankenstein* (James Whale, 1931), *Dr. Jekyll and Mr. Hyde* (Rouben Mamoulian, 1931), and *King Kong* (Merian C. Cooper and Ernest B. Schoedsack, 1933). One of the worst years of the Great Depression, 1931 "would be the best year ever for monsters," in the words of the film scholar David Skal. "With a yearlong flourish, the monsters were loose," providing screen metaphors for what millions of Americans sensed—"that they were no longer completely in control of their lives" and that "faceless, frightening forces" were at work.[15]

In a terrifying time, audiences could discover a variety of meanings in horror films. They may even have found—however subconsciously—messages of class conflict. The aristocratic Dracula, after all, resembled "a sanguinary capitalist," as Skal has argued, someone who has moved "from Transylvania after draining the local peasants." In contrast, the more proletarian Frankenstein's creature fit with "an army of abject and abandoned laborers, down to his work clothes and asphalt-spreader's boots." Certainly, the actor Boris Karloff wanted the creature to appear both "innocent" and "pathetic," a victim—like most humans—of events. Karloff later said that he could never forget "the fantastic numbers of ordinary people that got this general air of sympathy. I found all my letters heavy with it. . . . It was one of the most moving experiences of my life." At the least, despite the horror genre's eerie music, unsettling atmosphere, and scary situations, the movies could be reassuring. After all, the monsters were well defined, and the villagers prevailed at the end. Implicitly, too, the monster films offered a cautionary lesson for a nation in turmoil: embrace the familiar, and do not seek dramatic change—unlike the mad doctors and scientists who try to create life or unearth mummies. "I meddled in things that man must leave alone," warned the protagonist in *The Invisible Man* (James Whale, 1933).[16]

Nevertheless, by the end of 1931, the Code enforcer Jason S. Joy wrote nervously to Will Hays about the horror phenomenon: "Is this the beginning of a cycle that ought to be retarded or killed?" Other studios, according to Joy, had noted that *Frankenstein* was "taking in big money at theatres which were about on the rocks." At Paramount, for example, an executive observed enthusiastically: "If we had a picture like that we'd clean up." Shortly thereafter, Mamoulian's *Dr. Jekyll and Mr. Hyde* was a box-office hit for the studio. When Joy contemplated the distressing possibility that his "children might see FRANKENSTEIN, JEKYLL, or the others," he wondered whether such movies had crossed a moral line.[17]

Gangster films were potentially greater threats to the Code, which warned against motion pictures where "the *sympathy* of the audience is thrown on the side of crime" or "criminals seem heroic and justified." In 1931, Mervyn LeRoy's *Little Caesar* and William A. Wellman's *The Public Enemy* stood out in a flurry of popular crime movies. The studios were aware that the films were vulnerable to censorship and argued, with some validity, that such movies in fact proved that crime did not pay. After all, the gangsters died at the end. "Mother of Mercy, is this the end of Rico?" asked the mortally wounded Little Caesar as he died from police bullets. Or, in *Scarface* (Howard Hawks and Richard Rosson, 1932), a revolving sign above the body of the dead gangster flashed mockingly: "THE WORLD IS YOURS." "I ain't so tough," gasped the gangster in *The Public Enemy* as he died in a gutter. The Warner Brothers production head Darryl F. Zanuck tried to reassure Jason Joy that *The Public Enemy* (made in three weeks for only $150,000) had "a very strong moral theme," proving that breaking the law "ultimately ends in disaster to the participants." Will Hays, who obviously had doubts about such claims, guessed incorrectly that the American public would "vote thumbs down" on crime films. At the opening of *Little Caesar* in New York City, some three thousand people showed up, eventually breaking the theater's glass doors; *The Public Enemy* proved even more profitable. Quickly, over two dozen gangster movies were in production.[18]

Despite Hays's optimistic prediction, crime movies tapped a growing vein of public anger and disillusionment that was evident elsewhere. Gangsters were a powerful presence in other areas of popular culture, such as the pulp magazines, whose titles included *Gangland Stories, Complete Gang, Gang World, Gangster Stories, Gun Molls, Underworld, Greater Gangster Stories,* and *Prison Stories.* In the early 1930s, in fact, the popularity of criminals such as John Dillinger, "Baby Face" Nelson, Bonnie Parker, and Clyde Barrow greatly disturbed law enforcement officials, particularly the fiercely outspoken director of the Federal Bureau of Investigation, J. Edgar Hoover. As the Depression deepened, crime proved to be not only "the last profession in America . . . that still attracted crowds of applicants," as the notorious mobster Alvin Karpis wisecracked, but also a source of idealized folk heroes. By 1933, when bank robberies averaged two per day in the United States, stories circulated of "beloved badmen" or "social bandits" who—like Robin Hood—stole from the rich and gave to the poor. Legends of social banditry involving such earlier outlaws as Jesse James unquestionably went deep into oral tradition, but the mass media of the 1930s were crucial in spreading the lore surrounding Dillinger and his counterparts. Newsreels, radio, magazines, and newspapers built modern myths of social outcasts who used fast cars to elude the authorities. "If you are still in need / *Of something else to read* / Here's the story of Bonnie and Clyde," wrote Bonnie Parker in a poem to a newspaper. As the media churned out information about such outlaws, a variety of citizens were eager to jump on the publicity wagon or air their grievances against a failed system. A man who knew Dillinger "heard a lot of people say that he'd give money away so people could have something to eat and a roof over their head. He never killed anybody either, like a lot of people have said." When the citizens of Dillinger's hometown of Mooresville, Indiana, petitioned the governor on behalf of their most infamous citizen, they claimed "that most of the financial institutions of the state have just as criminally robbed our citizens."[19]

Strong social currents were, thus, at work, allowing audiences to identify with romanticized "celebrity bandits" like "Pretty Boy" Floyd or screen gangsters such as the charismatic Tom Powers, whom the actor James Cagney portrayed so compellingly in *The Public Enemy.* Tom, unlike his hardworking brother, whom he chastised for "learning how to be poor," fought back against an unfair system. Although Tom died at the end, his brother—perhaps like many in theater audiences—may have questioned an unjust, deeply flawed system.[20]

Additionally, whatever the studio heads intended, some of the people who made the movies had no doubt that they were looking realistically at hard social truths. The cowriters of the movies *Little Caesar* (John Bright) and *The Public Enemy* (Francis Faragoh) had left-wing sympathies, and W. R. Burnett, who wrote the novel *Little Caesar* (1929) and scripted the movie, believed: "If you have this type of society, you will get this type of man." Burnett consciously rejected the old formula by which "the criminal was just some son-of-a-bitch who'd killed somebody and then they got 'em. I treated them as human beings. Well, what else are they?" And Edward G. Robinson, who played Little Caesar, viewed the movie as "the drama of the humblest, the most despised, seeking to break his way out of the anonymity of ignorance. . . . While Rico's goals were immoral and anti-social, we had this in common . . . somehow we would be different, above, higher." Certainly, too, despite his assurances to Jason Joy, Darryl Zanuck at Warner Brothers wanted to purge *The Public Enemy* of any moral sentimentality. "Everyone in this movie is tough, tough, tough," he reportedly kept reminding the director. "People are going to say the characters are immoral, but they're not because they don't have any morals. They steal, they kill, they lie, they hump each other because that's the way they're made." The technology of sound enhanced the realistic effects of the crime movies. Audiences could hear gunfire, screeching tires, and rough, vernacular talk.[21]

On several levels, then, the gangster phenomenon made authorities uneasy. Reports that "children applaud the gang leader as a hero" were especially disconcerting. *Little Caesar* infuriated the head of New York State's Motion Picture Division, Dr. James Wingate. "Children," he fretted, "see a gangster riding around in a Rolls-Royce and living in luxury, and even though some gangster gets it in the end, the child unconsciously forms the idea that he will be smarter and will get away with it." Wingate was convinced that "there is a general break-down in respect for all laws."[22]

This general disrespect was also evident in the films of "guerrilla comedians"—Mae West, W. C. Fields, and especially the Marx Brothers, who gleefully subverted authority, logic, and virtually every cultural and social norm they approached. In 1929, Paramount contracted the Marx Brothers, who had battled through vaudeville's lower reaches to the big time, to make a series of movies. The brothers' entry into film coincided with the arrival of the Depression, which unquestionably facilitated their attacks on everything official and respectable, ranging from universities to high society and government. "Most people at some time want to throw things around recklessly," said Harpo. "They don't—but we do." In movies such as Norman Z. McLeod's *Monkey Business* (1931) and *Horse Feathers* (1932), the brothers tweaked social mores and lampooned etiquette and language. As irreverent tricksters, they struck back at a society that had too often made them feel like outsiders. Once, reportedly, when Groucho took his son to a club that banned Jews, he had rebuked the management for its restrictions, arguing that the child should be able to enter the swimming pool at least up to his knees because he was only half Jewish. Likewise, when a Long Island hotel confirmed Harpo's reservations on the premise that he was a gentile, Harpo—dressed up to look Irish—showed up at the establishment and registered as "Harpo MacMarx." He then asked directions "to the near-r-rest Jewish temple."[23]

For those many theater audience members from immigrant, working-class backgrounds who had themselves felt the sting of cultural prejudice and economic hard times, the Marx Brothers provided a welcome revenge against the wealthy, the powerful, and failed institutions. In *Animal Crackers* (Victor Heerman, 1930), Groucho twits a conservative who complains that "the nickel is not what it used to be." What this country needs, Groucho responds, is "a seven-cent nickel. . . . If that works out, next year we could have an eight-cent nickel. Think what that would mean. You could go to a newsstand, buy a three-cent paper, and get the same nickel back again. One nickel carefully used would last a family a lifetime!" In *A Night at the Opera* (Sam Wood, 1935), Chico ultimately sums up the Marx Brothers' perspective on the world with the line: "There ain't no sanity clause."[24]

In 1932, several soberer, harsher films grappled with life's uncertainties and unfairness. *Freaks* and *I Am a Fugitive from a Chain Gang* exuded a despair that was uncommonly dark, even for this bleak period. Todd Browning, the director of *Dracula,* made *Freaks* for MGM. In this case, the traditional sideshow freaks—the "human curiosities" that had been the staple of P. T. Barnum's museums and endless numbers of carnivals and circuses—are, in fact, not the monsters; instead, the trapeze woman and the circus strongman, supposedly among the "beautiful" people, are the true grotesques, abusing the "freaks" and even trying to kill one of them. But it is the strongman who ends up missing, while the acrobat has herself become a sideshow freak—the "chicken lady"—with the body of a chicken and a misshapen human head. Browning took what was supposedly normal and turned it upside down. Nothing was what it seemed. People who looked monstrous according to traditional standards were, in fact, decent and loving, whereas supposedly normal individuals with exemplary looks performed evil deeds. Although Browning later defended *Freaks* as a compassionate study of people whom society has historically exploited, the film proved too graphic and controversial. MGM executives, particularly the studio president, Louis B. Mayer, were reportedly irate, and, when the film lost money, they wanted nothing more to do with Browning, whose Hollywood career virtually ended.[25]

I Am a Fugitive from a Chain Gang, directed by Mervyn LeRoy, offered another dismal rendering of social injustice. The story was about a decorated World War I veteran, James Allen, who, during the immediate postwar economic slump, ends up in a Southern chain gang for a crime he did not commit. The movie portrays chain gang life with vivid brutality. Allen escapes and flees to Chicago, where he restarts his life, becoming economically and socially successful. But his past catches up with him, and he has to return to the chain gang for a symbolic ninety days. When the authorities violate their end of the bargain, Allen must again escape—but this time into the midst of the Great Depression. On the run in an economically devastated society, he has no way out. The movie ends with Allen, staring wide-eyed into the camera as he fades into the night, explaining how he will live: "I steal." At the Warner Brothers studio, Jack Warner conceded that the movie "will make us some enemies."[26]

More than the other studios, Warner Brothers made films about social problems and drew stories from the news—"headlines" pictures, in the words of Darryl Zanuck. But Hollywood as a whole was far more concerned with profits than with social justice. Temperamentally, most major studio heads probably did not relish interpretations in which film gangsters like Little Caesar became stand-ins for greedy American entrepreneurs in a capitalistic system run amok. The movie industry's innate political conservatism was abundantly clear during California's 1934 gubernatorial election, when the major studios engaged in a mean-spirited, nasty campaign to defeat Upton Sinclair, a socialist who surprisingly had won the Democratic primary election. MGM, for example, filmed phony newsreels showing radical-looking individuals with foreign accents endorsing Sinclair.[27]

By then, however, Hollywood was caught in powerful crosscurrents. One involved the swirling tensions between the search for profits, the political conservatism of the more established studios, and an increasingly active coalition of censors that included the Hays office, religious groups such as the Catholic-based Legion of Decency, and numerous politicians. Cries for censorship resulted in what the trade press called "the storm of '34." Increasingly fearful of outside interference, the movie industry reiterated its traditional commitment to self-regulation and, in mid-1934, created a Production Code Administration (PCA) that would more rigorously enforce the 1930 rules. This agreement attested in part to how Hollywood's financial exigencies early in the Great Depression had tilted control of the movie industry toward New York financiers. Now, according to the president of the Bank of America, financing would go only to films with PCA approval. Under the leadership of Joseph I. Breen, a former newspaper reporter whom Hays selected to enforce the Production Code, the Hays office flexed its muscles. Mae West in particular battled to hold off the censors, scripting decoy scenes that would distract them. "I wrote scenes for them to cut!" she explained later. "These scenes were so rough that I'd never have used them"—"scenes about a man's fly and all that." Paramount, trying to demonstrate its willingness to adhere to the Code, attempted to reform West's image. In turn, MGM cut from *Tarzan and His Mate* (Cedric

Gibbons, 1934) a prolonged underwater scene with full frontal female nudity. "The woman was stark naked," Breen protested. MGM more than likely suspected that it could not include such a scene and willingly sacrificed it to placate the censors.[28]

Another of the crosscurrents pulling and tugging at the movie industry involved a notable shift in cultural authority that favored popular over high culture and endorsed a commoner's vision of American ideals. As has so often been the case in mass entertainment, this transformation owed much to the influence of people and groups on society's edges. At the turn of the decade, companies such as Warner Brothers, Disney, and Columbia achieved major status. Indeed, Walt Disney built his company by isolating himself even within the movie culture. Specializing in animation, he avoided associating with stars, agents, and the movie moguls, whom he, a Midwestern Protestant, described as "those Jews."[29]

Independent studios nearly doubled in number from around fifty in the 1920s to ninety-two in 1934. Although most of them lasted only a few years, their film production—between a third and half of movies in the 1930s—rivaled that of the established major studios, such as MGM and Paramount. And, because the independents typically operated with little-known performers, beneath the attention of the censors, and served smaller theaters, they staked out a bit more maneuvering room. In notable ways, the Depression nudged the aspiring William Fox back into this group. In the 1920s, Fox had, indeed, sought to identify his movies with wealth and status. But, when the Depression bankrupted his company, he reembraced his earlier commitments, which had included membership in the Socialist Party and a desire to provide entertainment for the working class. Fox wanted, in his words, to put "entertainment and relaxation within the reach of all." Blaming his company's bankruptcy on financiers and his own momentary aloofness to audience taste, he—along with a host of other small producers—now embraced reform themes. Those themes typically championed the little folk and emphasized the evils of big business. By one count, the percentage of rich characters who were "morally evil or a social danger" increased twelvefold, from 5 to over 60 percent. Accompanying these portraits was a conscious effort on the part of a number of writers to replace what one dubbed as the "bloody revolting English of the Broadway stage" with "dialogue for ordinary people"—or the "Woolworth touch," as another writer described it. In that spirit, when W. R. Burnett scripted *Little Caesar,* he deliberately shunned "literary English. . . . I dumped all that out. I just threw it away. It was a revolt in the name of a language based on the way the American people spoke."[30]

By the mid-1930s, this cultural realignment was evident across much of popular culture and resonated with the mood and aspirations of

Franklin Roosevelt's New Deal. When Roosevelt entered the White House in March 1933, his immediate goal was to seek relief from the Depression via an energetic federal government. With a mind that resembled "a spacious, cluttered warehouse, a teeming curiosity shop," as the historian David Kennedy has written, Roosevelt "was open to all number and manner of impressions, facts, theories, nostrums, and personalities." He wanted to use that activist government, not simply to fight the Depression, but, over the long run, to advance the collective public interest over selfish ends, advance the principles of a political democracy over an economic plutocracy, bring more equity to American life, and make ordinary Americans more secure. Because the Great Depression hit so many people so hard over such a long time, he had a rare opportunity to act on his principles. "The Depression and the New Deal," according to Kennedy, "were Siamese twins, enduring together in a painful but symbiotic relationship that stretched to the end of the decade." During the Roosevelt administration's first months, the so-called Hundred Days Congress rapidly passed legislation that called for unprecedented federal action to deal with the banking and agricultural crises, establish the largest public relief program in U.S. history to that point, and encourage industrial recovery. Granted, these programs followed no single pattern or strategy, and they hardly fazed the enduring Depression, but they characterized Roosevelt's willingness to experiment with even contradictory programs and set a tone.[31]

That tone had profound cultural implications. Just as Roosevelt forged a political coalition that was more inclusive—more open to previously marginal groups—so did he symbolize the gathering cultural shift toward the common citizenry. Within the New Deal, that shift was evident in such things as the decision in 1933 of the relief administrator Harry Hopkins to send the journalist Lorena Hickok around the country to document the Depression's impact at the grassroots level and get a sense of what was happening to the "ordinary citizen." It was evident as well in the New Deal's work-relief agency, the Works Progress Administration, which, among other things, sought to get culture to the masses by, for example, sponsoring free art and music lessons and sending groups of previously unemployed actors, artists, and musicians to communities around the country to stage concerts and theater productions.[32]

A genuine appreciation for the lives of common people surfaced also in "bottom dog literature," a small flood of short stories and novels that focused on immigrant neighborhoods, the working class, and the impoverished. A string of authors on the political Left, ranging from Robert Cantwell to Jack Conroy, James T. Farrell, Erskine Caldwell, Daniel Fuchs, and Richard Wright, drew from their own experiences to write fiction that some people labeled *proletarian.* John Steinbeck, in novels such as *In Dubious Battle* (1936) and, especially, *The Grapes of Wrath* (1939), wrote about "plain people" struggling to survive. "Rich fellas come up an' they die, an' their kids ain't no good, an' they die out," says the Oklahoma farm migrant Ma Joad in famous lines from *The Grapes of Wrath* that reappeared in John Ford's 1940 movie version: "But we keep a-coming. We're the people that live. Can't nobody wipe us out. Can't nobody lick us. We'll go on forever, Pa, 'cause we're the people." The folksinger Woody Guthrie also helped memorialize the experience of the "Okie" migrants, who fled to California from the dust storms of the Great Plains. "A folk song," he wrote, "is what's wrong and how to fix it, or it could be whose [sic] hungry and where their mouth is, or whose [sic] out of work and where the job is." Guthrie's stated goal was "to sing songs that will prove to you that this is your land," songs "that will make you take pride in yourself and your work."[33]

Perhaps the comedian Will Rogers best conveyed a sense of the cultural dimensions of the New Deal, however, even though he died in a plane crash in mid-1935. He had become a much-beloved entertainment celebrity in a variety of forums—the Wild West show, vaudeville, the Ziegfeld Follies, a nationally syndicated newspaper column, radio, and dozens of silent and sound movies. In the early 1930s, his radio commentaries and newspaper columns reached an estimated 40 million people, and he was the top box-office attraction in film. Dressed like a cowboy, he liked to remind audiences: "You know, I'm an Indian, my parents are Cherokee." He championed an America that was open to all groups, saying: "I have a different slant on things . . . for my ancestors did not come over on the Mayflower. They met the boat." And he used humor to articulate a street-level view of American society and politics. "All I know is what I read in the newspapers," he joked, as he proceeded to give the perspective of what he called "my kind of people . . . the underdog." Scratching his head, and smiling shyly, he jabbed at economic and social privilege: "Why is it alright for these Wall Street boys to bet millions and make that bet affect the fellow plowing a field in Claremore, Oklahoma?" The state in the Soviet Union, he said, "owns everything . . . a little like bankers here." He poked fun at Mother's Day, which supposedly honored mothers but hardly increased their purchasing power. His movies between 1931 and 1935 dealt with community alliances that bonded people across racial and gender lines, and his radio commentaries earned him the sobriquet "Number One New Dealer." Gentle, caring, and generous with his time and money, he was what one drama critic described as "what Americans think other Americans are like."[34]

The pluralistic nation that Rogers favored and that found expression in Roosevelt's expanding political coalition was also apparent in American music, especially the swing jazz phenomenon that began sweeping the country in the mid-1930s. Initially in the Depression, the music industry almost failed. In 1927, 100 million records had been sold; by 1932, that figure had dropped to 6 million. Phonograph production was down 96 percent. Thomas A. Edison, Incorporated, folded altogether. Columbia, which had been around since the 1890s, sold for a mere $70,000 to the American Record Company, which specialized in selling bargain disks with unknown singers to Woolworth's and other chain stores. The once-proud Victor company remained afloat only through the backing of the Radio Corporation of America (RCA).[35]

Into this shambles stepped Jack Kapp, whose Decca company virtually resurrected the recording business. Kapp had considerable grounding in the music industry. Four years after his birth in Chicago in 1901, his Russian immigrant father had started distributing Columbia records and then opened a small shop that sold phonographs and sheet music. When Jack turned twenty-one, he and his younger brother started their own record store on the city's West Side, where many of their customers came from the nearby African American neighborhood. In 1926, Jack became a talent scout and producer for Brunswick Records, a subsidiary of an Iowa-based company that made such things as bowling balls. Although he could neither read nor play music, he worked around a simple question, "Where's the melody?" trying to anticipate what customers who lacked an interest in high culture might want. Building a reputation as a "man of no taste, so corny he's good," he recruited superbly talented people to Brunswick, especially the gifted Bing Crosby, a rising star of radio and film. In 1934, Kapp agreed to start an American branch of the struggling English company Decca. Despite a terrible first year, he turned Decca into a musical powerhouse that featured such talents as Crosby, Louis Armstrong, Ethel Waters, the Mills Brothers, and Guy Lombardo.[36]

Kapp took risks. He cut the price of Decca's records by half, selling them for thirty-five cents, or three for a dollar, at a time when the prevailing price was seventy-five cents. "What's the use?" wondered the shocked trade journal *Variety*, if Decca could not get the traditional price for something like a Crosby recording. To Kapp, the answer was simple: the sheer volume of sales would boost profits. Advertising heavily, Kapp emphasized that Decca was not selling budget renditions of songs: "*Not* obsolete records, cut in price to meet a market, but the latest, newest smash hits." And he seized on a new outlet for recordings that the repeal of the Eighteenth Amendment in 1933 had encouraged. With Prohibition's end, taverns suddenly flourished again, perhaps quadrupling the number of drinking establishments that had existed earlier in the form of illegal speakeasies. Many of those taverns, as well as restaurants, could not afford to provide live music and, thus, turned to coin-operated "automatic phonographs," or jukeboxes, which jumped in number from 25,000 in 1933 to 225,000 by 1939. By the mid-1930s, perhaps 40 percent of the records in the United States were playing in jukeboxes; in 1939, that figure was 60 percent. And two-thirds of all those records came from Decca. Companies that earned concessions off the jukeboxes understandably wanted to keep stocking their machines with popular records, a demand that Kapp willingly met by supplying twenty-one-cent Decca records and churning out "hits." "I know how to keep my pulse on the multitude," Kapp would say later about his success at Decca. By doing so, he created what the music historian Gary Giddins has described as "the people's record company": "Parents handed their children a dollar bill and told them to bring back three new Deccas."[37]

To attract consumers, Kapp shrewdly developed a distinctive kind of music that was gentle and soothing. The "Kapp sound" countered Depression woes, helping people through harsh times. A prime example of this warm, dreamy music was perhaps most evident in a style of singing known as "crooning." There was no more famous "crooner" than Bing Crosby. With an intimate style and a richly mellow baritone voice, he conveyed the sadness of homeless citizens with his mournful tune "Brother, Can You Spare a Dime?" just as effectively as he summoned up the hope of young lovers with "Just One More Chance" and expressed nostalgia for familiar times. Significantly, few songs at Decca or elsewhere focused on the Depression. "Brother, Can You Spare a Dime?" was a rare exception; more typical were Crosby's "I've Got the World on a String" and "Wrap Your Troubles in Dreams." For the most part, Tin Pan Alley's popular tunes of the 1930s urged people to "Get Happy," to look for better times "On the Sunny Side of the Street," to discover that "Life Is Just a Bowl of Cherries," to believe that "We're in the Money," and to "Smile, Darn Ya, Smile." For Tin Pan Alley, sticking with previously successful formulas seemed the best way to cope with uncertainty.[38]

It was, nevertheless, what *Variety* in 1935 called a "freak tune" that catapulted Decca into the black. After Kapp learned about a song, "The Music Goes 'Round and Around," that a band was playing at a club near his office, he got the musicians to provide lyrics. Within a few months after Decca released the recording, it swept the country. "At least everyone can sing Whoa-ho-ho-ho," Kapp explained, "and that is what made the song a hit." Here was a peppy, catchy tune whose popularity suggested that a good many listeners preferred exuberant music to soft ballads. In a few months, consumers purchased 100,000 records, while copies of the sheet music were reportedly selling at "a-copy-a-minute" rate, and the song filled the airwaves. As one writer observed: "It was like an echo that followed you around through the night and into the quiet and deserted streets of New Year's Day, 1936."[39]

Although "The Music Goes 'Round and Around" was essentially a silly novelty piece, *Time* magazine said that it was "fundamentally a 'swing' tune." However misplaced *Time*'s characterization might have been, the magazine's mention of "swing" was significant because it referred to a building music revolution in the mid-1930s—one that combined popular songs and jazz. Swing music became "the paradigm for popular music in America," the jazz historian Ted Gioia has said. "Never again would popular music be so jazzy, or jazz music so popular." This development reversed jazz's fortunes, which had declined sharply during the early 1930s. That decline came partly because some people equated jazz with the excesses of the 1920s. For others, the mood of the Depression favored "sweet bands," not groups that played "hot" jazz with its rowdier sounds and improvised style. By the mid-1930s, a jazz lover in Chicago lamented that jazz musicians were now "looked on very poorly—even by their wives."[40]

Against that backdrop, few events were perhaps more surprising than the one on August 21, 1935, that, by most accounts, marked the birth of the Swing Era. On that evening, in Los Angeles's Palomar Ballroom, the Benny Goodman band unexpectedly ignited a jubilant response from the patrons. Probably no one could have predicted that famous moment. A few weeks earlier, New York City's Hotel Roosevelt had fired Goodman's orchestra because it was too loud. "Just by way of *contrast*," one customer had complained, "why not play something sweet and low?" The musicians had subsequently started a discouraging cross-country tour, limping across the United States, encountering one humiliation after another. In a Michigan ballroom, barely thirty people attended; in Denver, dancers who wanted softer music turned hostile and demanded their money back; in Grand Junction, Colorado, unhappy customers pelted the band with whiskey bottles; in Pismo Beach, California, the band played in a fish barn. By the time Goodman's orchestra reached Los Angeles, it was running out of geographic and emotional space. The lethargic Palomar audience was not responding even to the melodic kinds of music that Goodman had reluctantly concluded that patrons wanted. "Let's cut the shit," trumpeter Bunny Berigan finally shouted, prompting Goodman to move the band to a livelier beat. As the crowd responded wildly, Goodman sensed that he was at a turning point: "After traveling three thousand miles, we finally found people who were up on what we were trying to do, prepared to take our music the way we wanted to play it." By the time the band got back to New York a year later, following a hugely successful stint in Chicago, the Swing Era was in full force, Goodman was the "King of Swing," and his band was, according to *Billboard* magazine, "one of the top drawing cards in show business."[41]

Goodman was uneasy with the King of Swing title and insisted that *swing* simply meant "jazz": "'hot' jazz and 'improvised' jazz, as distinguished from the 'sweet' jazz and the 'symphonic' jazz so popular some years ago." Although swing was, indeed, rooted in the musical margins that had earlier inspired jazz, it became in the mid-1930s "the defining music for a whole generation of Americans." And, in the process, it boosted spirits during a grim period and encouraged the blurring of long-standing racial boundaries.[42]

The generational support for swing attested to the emergence of a mass youth culture. During the 1930s, the lack of jobs and economic opportunities encouraged more youths to stay in high school. Before the Depression, only about half of individuals in the fourteen- to eighteen-year-old age bracket remained in school; by 1940, around 75 percent were doing so. This youth cohort developed more of a sense of its own identity, which included such distinguishing markers as musical preferences. In that regard, youths refashioned popular entertainment to meet their own expectations. While the music industry—as well as Hollywood—continued to court general audiences and generally ignored high school students as special consumers, young people were creating an identifiable teenage culture. Records, like movies, were not simply commodities on the market. They also formed the basis of daily lives in conversations, socializing, dating, daydreaming, sorting through emotions, and forging memories about growing up. The capacity of young teenagers to inject meaning into music was apparent at swing concerts when they would, as the *Los Angeles Times* observed, "jump out of their seats and actually hold a Carnival in the aisles." The song "Taint What You Do (But the Way That Ya Do It)" expressed a sense of newfound freedom. The timing of swing's popularity attested as well to the modest success of New Deal programs that boosted the economy somewhat, providing a bit more money for entertainment and encouraging more hope for the future.[43]

Swing and the New Deal meshed on a cultural level, too. "Swing," according to the historian David Stowe, "was the preeminent musical expression of the New Deal: a cultural form of 'the people,' accessible, inclusive, distinctively democratic . . . ever more egalitarian and progressive." In that regard, it mirrored the political tendencies of the Roosevelt coalition, whose motley collection of formerly marginalized groups blurred racial, ethnic, and geographic distinctions. The links between swing and New Deal politics were especially evident in the lives of a number of musicians whose work implicitly championed the fabled American melting pot. Although Benny Goodman was no civil rights crusader, his appreciation of musical talent moved him to challenge racial barriers. His own background facilitated his efforts. Like many of the shapers of popular culture, he came from new-immigrant, urban roots. Growing up in an impoverished Jewish family in Chicago, he knew what it was like to be a cultural and ethnic outsider. In the 1930s, as he enjoyed his King of Swing reputation, he became a leading symbol of racial integration in the music business. The "difference of race, creed or color has never been of the slightest importance in the best bands," he argued. Although his big band remained all white until 1939, he appeared earlier in integrated performances and formed several small-combo units, including the Benny Goodman Quartet with the African Americans Lionel Hampton and Teddy Wilson. Hampton remembered that "Bennie would not back down. He once bopped a guy in the head with his clarinet when the guy told him that he should 'get those niggers off his show.'" Goodman liked to say: "I am selling music, not prejudice." Other whites who knew and worked with Goodman—Artie Shaw and Gene Krupa, for example—took the same position.[44]

On January 16, 1938, swing's pluralistic tendencies were dramatically visible. That night, Goodman's orchestra introduced swing to a packed Carnegie Hall, that staid bastion of high culture. "Sure, I'm nervous," admitted the trumpet soloist Harry James. "You know—Carnegie Hall—after all." Indeed, as the concert started, James observed that he felt "like a whore in church." When someone asked Goodman how long the intermission should be, he replied: "I dunno, how much does [Arturo] Toscanini have?" Goodman's own racially integrated trio and quartet also performed, and Goodman played with black musicians such as Count Basie. After the performance, which had people dancing in the aisles, Goodman and several other musicians left Carnegie Hall and headed uptown to Harlem's Savoy Club to watch the fabled black bands of Count Basie and Chick Webb compete. It was an electric evening. Swing, within a few hours, had bridged the concert hall, African American culture, and popular entertainment.[45]

In many respects, of course, swing—no more than the New Deal—was hardly free from traditional inequities. The fact that Goodman was white allowed him to enjoy far more opportunities than did black bandleaders. Black bands usually toiled with little pay and in poor conditions, sometimes traveling several hundred miles between one-night stands, and typically dealing with segregated accommodations, even in Northern cities such as Moline, Illinois. And sometimes the musicians faced violence, as did the badly beaten Don Albert. Discrimination also plagued the careers of female singers, who learned daily how much of the music world belonged to men. Still, swing betokened change and possibility, prompting critics to worry about the "jitterbug ecstasy" of some 100,000 joyous fans who celebrated a Swing Jamboree on August 24, 1938, at Chicago's Soldier's Field—"the world's largest crowd . . . for a musical event," according to one newspaper.[46]

In sports, the melting pot was not boiling over, as the *Chicago Tribune* reported that it did at Swing Jamboree, but there were signs of lowered social barriers and a more open society. College football was one example. Like entertainment generally, the sport reeled during the early years of the Depression, with attendance falling 25 percent between 1929 and 1933 and athletic budgets tumbling into debt. By the mid-1930s, however, football was rebounding. In the South especially, football victories became a way of measuring state pride and accomplishments. As Louisiana's governor in the early 1930s, Huey Long had pointed the way in this regard, sometimes attending Louisiana State University's practices, delivering locker-room speeches, sitting on the team bench during games, and even proposing to give state jobs to men whose sons the team was recruiting. In 1935, teams in the Southeastern Conference started giving scholarships purely for football (although, certainly, conferences such as the Big Ten were already providing do-nothing jobs or other subsidies for players). To many beleaguered Southerners, intersectional victories over Northern teams were a symbolic way of reversing the outcome of the Civil War. Meanwhile, a number of cities across the South tried to raise revenues by establishing their own versions of the Rose Bowl in Pasadena, California. The Orange, Cotton, and Sugar bowls were among the most prestigious, but a host of smaller bowl games carried names such as Celery, Grape, and Salad.[47]

Although football remained strictly segregated in the South and only a few Northern schools included African American players, the game took on more pluralistic features. The shift in football dominance from the exclusive, private Northeastern schools to private institutions such as Notre Dame and to state universities continued. Moreover, the athletes came increasingly from new-immigrant, blue-collar backgrounds. As products of steel and mining communities, for example, they helped open the doors of higher education in America. Among them were such all-American players as the University of Minnesota's Bronco Nagurski, a Ukrainian, and Fordham's Alex Wojchiechowicz. "I feel at home with this squad because they're big and I can't pronounce their names," joked the Fordham coach. Such developments helped confirm *Sports Story* magazine's 1930 claim: "Football has ceased to be a game of the classes and has become a game of all the people. . . . It has become a truly democratic sport, open to boys who come from all social levels." According to the magazine, football was equalizing the playing field between "rich man's son and poor man's son."[48]

Baseball, like football, rallied from a severe economic downturn and became somewhat more inclusive. Although 1930 was such a good year for the sport that *Baseball Magazine* thought the game might be Depression proof, ticket sales promptly dropped. In 1933, attendance at major-league games fell to around 6 million, down from the 1930 figures by 40–45 percent. Indebted teams reduced rosters and slashed salaries. Even Babe Ruth felt the pinch. When his salary dropped from $80,000 to $35,000 between 1930 and 1934, *Baseball Magazine* said: "Babe now knows what millions of others have found out, how it seems to take a fifty per cent cut." By 1934, however, the sport began to revive economically. That recovery so closely matched the overall economy's stirrings under the Roosevelt administration's policies that it deserved the epithet "New Deal Baseball." The Depression still held the nation in a terrible grip, but New Deal relief programs had provided some spending money. American League attendance alone in 1934 jumped by 1 million. In 1936, overall major-league attendance was up to around 8 million, and nine of sixteen franchises were out of the red. Ticket sales reached 9.5 million the next year. Moreover, by 1939, the names of players suggested that the major leagues were drawing from an increasingly diverse ethnic base. *Sporting News* pointed to players with names such as Krakauskas, Bordagarary, Lodigiani, "Lou Novikoff . . . the mad Russian," and Alex Kampouris, "the only Greek in the big show," as evidence that baseball was "the nation's greatest force of democracy . . . the melting pot of sons of all languages, the caldron of equal big opportunity."[49]

In contrast, African American baseball players—whom the major-league teams had informally barred since the late nineteenth century—had little to celebrate in the 1930s. Their situation, like that of blacks generally during the Great Depression, was abysmal. By 1932, when 75 percent of blacks in Detroit and 69 percent in Pittsburgh were unemployed, black baseball was in pitiful shape. The several professional leagues that had done rather well in the 1920s had folded. Several black entrepreneurs nevertheless improved the situation somewhat by reviving the Negro National League (NNL) in 1933 and forming the Negro American League (NAL) in 1937. William A. "Gus" Greenlee, who had profited from illegal speakeasies and the numbers racket in Pittsburgh, took a lead role. He was the driving force behind the rejuvenated NNL, made the Pittsburgh Crawfords into a talented team, built (for $100,000) the first black-owned baseball park (with seating for six thousand), and put into motion strategies to forge a "race baseball" that was free of white financing and more attractive to black fans. Given the depressed economy, Greenlee's efforts were daring. The results were mixed, however, and would remain so after the formation of the rival NAL. To a number of black critics, the erratic scheduling, shifting teams, high player turnover, and sorry conditions for the players were farcical. Still, as one player noted: "There was always sun shining someplace." He referred to opportunities to play baseball year-round, from the United States to countries such as Mexico, Venezuela, and Cuba. Moreover, "in Mexico they treat you royally," observed one player. "No segregation." But, even in the United States, many off-season barnstorming tours pitted black professionals against white. While those contests hardly fazed the all-white major leagues' opposition to signing blacks and sometimes even reinforced prejudices, they also hinted at change. "Sure," said the white player Leo Durocher, "I've seen plenty of colored boys who could make it in the majors. Hell, I've seen a million." Pie Traynor, the manager of the Pittsburgh Pirates, could make no sense of "why the ban against Negro players exists at all." Even though the ban continued, it could not stop black communities from rooting for the likes of such baseball legends as Josh Gibson and Leroy "Satchel" Paige. Black fans could undoubtedly take pride also in a white journalist's grudging praise that black "baseball is to white baseball as the Harlem stomp is to the sedate ballroom waltz."[50]

In professional football as well, African Americans had to settle for marginal roles. At a February 1933 meeting in Pittsburgh, nine white owners informally agreed to ban black players, thereby reversing integration practices that had marked the National Football League (NFL) since its founding thirteen years earlier. Economic calculations influenced the decision. Three NFL teams had just gone broke, and the Boston Braves were struggling with red ink. "Gentlemen," said the Braves' owner George Preston Marshall, "it's time we recognized we're not only in the football business but in the entertainment business as well." It was, thus, imperative to infuse the games with more excitement and hoopla—but also not to alienate white patrons who might resent the hiring of blacks during hard times. Although the owners subsequently denied that they practiced segregation, they found excuses not to sign black players. In 1935, hoping to break down the NFL's unofficial color line, several former African American stars in the league—particularly Fritz Pollard—put together a Harlem-based team, the New York Brown Bombers. For the next three years, the Bombers built a winning record against leading white semiprofessional and independent teams. But NFL teams refused to play Pollard's squad, which folded after the 1937 season. Segregation prevailed in the NFL, although some minor leagues—such as the American Professional Football Association in the New York metropolitan area and the Pacific Coast Football League—included black players.[51]

Outside the major leagues, baseball likewise provided examples of racial integration. In 1935, Satchel Paige pitched for a Bismarck, North Dakota, team that included five white and six black players and won the first national semiprofessional baseball championship. That tournament, which occurred in Wichita, Kansas, featured thirty-two teams from twenty-five states. Although Wichita's restaurants and hotels remained segregated, thousands of black and white fans watched the unfolding of an interracial event that included, according to the local newspaper, players from "four different races." One team included a Native American, several were all-black, and some—such as Bismarck's—were mixed. This was not the first time that local people had witnessed interracial competition. In 1930, for example, they had watched baseball's first night game when the all-black Kansas City Monarchs came to town; in 1932, two Mexican American teams had played in the city league. The extent to which baseball weakened racial barriers in the 1930s was, of course, problematic. The triumph of the integrated North Dakota team in 1935 nevertheless had symbolic importance. "I'd cracked another little clink in Jim Crow," was how Satchel Paige interpreted the moment.[52]

In the mid-1930s, there were other symbols that marked the beginnings of baseball's better times. Among them was the 1934 World Series. For one thing, the opposing teams that year came from middle-American cities that the Depression had struck with special force: Detroit, which had suffered excruciating layoffs in the automobile industry, and St. Louis, a victim of slumping agriculture and Mississippi River traffic. For another thing, the Detroit Tigers' first baseman was Henry Greenberg, the leading Jewish player to that point. "I don't think anybody can imagine the terrific importance of Hank Greenberg to the Jewish community," recalled a Detroit resident. "He was a God, a true folk hero"—and at a time when anti-Semitism was still an ugly presence in a city all too familiar with anti-Jewish sentiments, ranging from those of Henry Ford and a revived Ku Klux Klan to Father Charles Coughlin's diatribes against an international Jewish banking conspiracy. "Being Jewish did carry with it a special responsibility," Greenberg admitted. He wearied of having "some son of a bitch call you a Jew bastard and a kike and a sheenie and get on your ass. . . . If the ballplayers weren't doing it, the fans were. Sometimes I wanted to go up in the stand and beat the shit out of them." But, in 1934, Greenberg's sterling season lifted his Tigers from obscurity to the Series and the highest attendance figure in the majors, triple what Detroit had drawn the previous year. The St. Louis Cardinals, in turn, were so underpaid that some observers called them "coolies." Yet they had a collection of colorful misfits that included especially Jerome "Dizzy" Dean, the son of an Arkansas sharecropper. In the fourth game of the Series, a thrown ball hit Dean on the head, knocking him unconscious. Recovering in the locker room, he pledged to pitch again the next day, saying: "You can't hurt no Dean by hittin' him on the head." Although Dean lost the next game, his brother Paul (nicknamed "Daffy") ultimately pitched the Series-winning contest for St. Louis.[53]

The Dean brothers, adept at attracting headlines, participated in another significant event in 1934: they became part of a three-person "team" that included Mildred "Babe" Didrikson. In one of her many efforts to show that she could compete athletically with men, Didrikson had gotten the Deans to join her in one-on-one pitching contests against big leaguers. The brothers probably signed on as a joke, but Didrikson was quite serious about challenging traditional male barriers in sports. A high school dropout from a South Texas working-class family, she had in 1932 won the national Amateur Athletic Union (AAU) track-and-field championships as a one-woman team, setting four world records and forcing into second place a team that had twenty-two athletes. That year in Los Angeles she won two Olympic gold medals. After her victories, a Dodge automobile advertisement in February 1933 featured her hurdling a car. Immediately, the AAU banned her from amateur competition, even though she claimed that Dodge had not paid her for the ad. To earn money, she made several stage appearances and started devising stunts, including the one-on-one pitching contests, to demonstrate her physical abilities. A 1933 sports movie showed her in twelve sports, including a staged event in which she played football with the Southern Methodist University team. Working-class females such as Didrikson had certainly participated in a variety of outdoor activities for years, from ice-skating on ponds to roller-skating on urban streets; and middle- and upper-class females had increasingly participated in the properly "beautiful" sports such as swimming and tennis. But Didrikson was another story, especially when she claimed openly that she could beat any man in any sport.[54]

Didrikson increasingly concentrated on the male bastion of golf, predictably evoking scorn and derision. The famed sportswriter Paul Gallico, whom she defeated in golf, set the tone of hostility. He dubbed her "the Texas Babe" and a "Muscle Moll." "Golf was never meant for women," he scoffed. "A girl can't do those things and still be a lady." Didrikson's open defiance of "ladylike" etiquette opened her to criticism for being unmarried, stepping outside proper gender roles, and earning money during the Depression when women were supposed to leave jobs open for men. When someone asked her about a diamond she was wearing, she snapped back: "Bought it myself. It was a diamond I wanted, not a man." She also shrugged off marriage, saying: "A girl can't get ahead that way." There were rumors that she was, in fact, a man. Once, when a female spectator hollered at her, "Where are your whiskers," Didrikson responded: "I'm sitting on 'em sister, just like you are!" True, as the 1930s wore down and she established her reputation as a golfer, Didrikson tried to appear more feminine. But there was no doubt that she was pioneering the gender boundaries of sport.[55]

While Didrikson challenged gender lines, Joe Louis undermined racial barriers in boxing. Born in 1914 in a sharecropper's shack in Alabama, Louis had moved at age twelve to Detroit. After dropping out of school by the sixth grade and working for a short time in an automobile plant, he had built a superb reputation as an amateur boxer. When he turned professional, however, he was entering a white man's sport. One of his African American managers, John Roxborough, recognized how crucial it was for Louis to distinguish himself from Jack Johnson. To that end, Roxborough established rules for Louis: he was never, for example, to have his picture taken with a white woman, and he needed to live and fight cleanly. Using his fists to speak for him, Louis won an incredible twenty-two bouts between July 1934 and June 1935, most by knockout. Several factors explained Louis's rising popularity. The Great Depression unquestionably raised the public's need to find heroes who overcame ferocious odds, and boxing fans were looking for new attractions that could energize the sport. White Southerners, who typically would have worried about Louis's race, were more inclined to accept him because he was from the South and did not pose the racial threat of a Jack Johnson. The Southern press thus referred to Louis as an "ex-pickaninny," a "southern colored boy," and a "good nigger." Northerners were more inclined to place Louis's exploits against an international backdrop that featured the menacing rise of fascism in Benito Mussolini's Italy and Adolf Hitler's Germany. On March 28, 1935, the twenty-one-year-old Louis, barely a heavyweight, pummeled the 260-pound former heavyweight champion Primo Carnera, allegedly Mussolini's "emissary." That September, before eighty-eight thousand spectators, Louis knocked out the ex-champ Max Baer in four rounds; the fight produced the largest gate since the second bout between Jack Dempsey and Gene Tunney. Afterward, an awed Baer said: "I could have struggled up once more, but when I get executed, people are going to have to pay more than twenty-five dollars a seat to watch it." The stage was set for a June 22, 1936, fight between Louis and Germany's Max Schmeling. But, in a shocking defeat, Louis lost in twelve rounds. When Hitler and his supporters used the fight as a propaganda piece for Nazi Germany, many Americans viewed Louis as a representative of their nation's hopes and pride and wanted a rematch. In the meantime, a number of whites fretted about a black champion, especially after Louis won the heavyweight crown from James Braddock on June 22, 1937. "I thought half my head was blowed off," said Braddock after the fight, when he also compared Louis's right-hand punches to blows from a crowbar.[56]

In mid-1938, when Louis again fought Schmeling, few Americans favored war with Germany, but many longed for an emblematic demonstration of democracy's strengths over fascism's. Louis reinforced such images by saying that he was "backing up America against Germany." Franklin Roosevelt concurred. He invited Louis to the White House and asked the champion to "lean over, Joe, so I can feel your muscles." Beaming, the president said: "Joe, we need muscles like yours to beat Germany." Louis subsequently pounded Schmeling to the canvas a little over two minutes into the first round. Afterward, even a syndicated columnist who still believed that whites were more intelligent than blacks concluded that "black boys" like Louis were, nevertheless, Americans: "For all their misfortunes and shortcomings they are our people—Negroes, yes, but our Negroes." African Americans across the United States embraced Louis as a conquering hero. "Champion of the world," remembered the novelist Maya Angelou. "A Black boy. Some Black mother's son. He was the strongest man in the world." Looking back, Malcolm X would recall how "every Negro boy old enough to walk wanted to be the next Brown Bomber." But Louis's importance stretched into white America as well. Right after Louis defeated Schmeling, the noted sportswriter Heywood Broun asserted that "the decline of Nazi prestige began with a left hook delivered by a former unskilled automotive worker" who "exploded the Nordic myth with a bombing glove." And, years later, the humorist Art Buchwald remembered several certainties that young Americans held at the time: "Franklin Roosevelt was going to save the economy"; "Joe Louis was going to save us from the Germans."[57]

When virtually two-thirds of American radio sets were tuned in to the second Louis-Schmeling fight, they demonstrated radio's staggering growth as a source of information and entertainment. During the Depression, radio was the largest disseminator of popular culture. It was also a potent inclusive force, although, ironically, that inclusiveness came through a process of separation. Except in rural areas, where "cracker-barrel" gatherings around a set remained popular, radio listening typically occurred in the privacy of homes. The sounds that listeners heard came increasingly from network programming.[58]

Network broadcasting indeed encouraged a kind of cultural homogenization, but there were so many different kinds of programs that were open to so many varying interpretations that radio was a constant reminder of exciting possibilities. "The boundaries of my world suddenly dilated beyond the sagebrush hills of Idaho," recalled one individual about radio's magic, "and through the hissing swish of static, like a bell pealing in a snowstorm, came the sweet, wavering voices of KHJ, Los Angeles, KDKA, Pittsburgh, and, one enchanted evening, Havana, Cuba." In 1933, to boost sales, RCA picked up on this theme, advertising opportunities to tour the nation via radio: "What will it be tonight—Hollywood, Wolf Point, Tupelo or New York?" Radio, in sum, could be both reassuringly familiar and breathtakingly new. And, because listeners could tune in for nothing, it offered a particularly welcome respite from hard times. Because it was "cheap, accessible, and generous in its provision of popular taste," as the cultural observer Gilbert Seldes noted, it served as "the poor man's library . . . his club." In the words of a woman defending her favorite soap opera, it offered "great pleasure that the poor man's wife as well as the rich man's wife may enjoy."[59]

Although, in the early 1930s, the radio business was arguably healthier than most other forms of entertainment, it did not completely escape the Depression's onset. In 1933, only about a quarter of 347 broadcasters showed a profit after taxes; in just two years, NBC's income toppled from $2.6 million to $600,000, and RCA also lost money. Radio stores declined in number by almost half. Even the 66 percent jump in radio sales in 1933 reaped disappointing dividends because, as businesses scrambled to attract consumers, they reduced the average price of radios from $133 in 1929 to

$48 in 1932. Yet the fact that the percentage of homes with sets virtually doubled between 1929 and 1932, from 31.2 to 60.6, was ultimately encouraging; by 1940, four-fifths of American families owned radios.[60]

The cultural implications of such statistics were profound. When speaking about the radio, people referred, as the essayist E. B. White observed in 1933, "to a pervading and somewhat godlike presence which has come into their lives and homes." During the Depression, the radio became a powerful means by which people could pass idle time and find welcome distraction from economic and social distress. "I feel your music and songs are what pulled me through this winter," said an unemployed listener in 1935. "Half the time we were blue and broke. One year during the Depression and no work. Kept from going on relief but lost everything we possessed doing so. So thanks for the songs, for they make life seem more like living." In rural America, which had long battled the problems of isolation and loneliness, the radio was especially welcome. By 1938, when over 40 percent of Americans still lived in rural areas, around two-thirds of farm families owned radios. "Of course we're shut in still," read one poem about the winter months. "But we've a radio with which to fill / The ice-bound chunks of silence with song."[61]

Such references to music were telling. By 1938, recordings of popular music constituted over half of all broadcast programs. Moreover, radio popularized musical forms that previously had small audiences. This assuredly was the case with country music. In 1930, for example, the station manager Glen Rice turned to it in a desperate effort to help his struggling KMPC in Beverly Hills, California. He did so with a ruse. After "disappearing" for several weeks and stirring speculation that something awful had happened to him, he appeared with a story about how he had gotten lost and stumbled by accident into an unknown "hillbilly" community that refugees from the Arkansas Ozarks had established in the California mountains a century earlier. He claimed that some of the residents were musicians and that he had invited them to perform at KMPC. For several weeks, he milked the story for all it was worth, saying that the hillbillies should arrive soon. On April 6, he excitedly informed the radio audience that they were, indeed, on their way: "Yes, yes, I see them getting off their mules, and there they are. Ladies and gentlemen, may I present the hill billies!" The musicians were, in fact, professionals from around the country with considerable experience playing jazz and other kinds of music. Performing now as the Beverly Hill Billies, they became a nightly hit at KMPC, drawing large and curious crowds. Soon, the musicians had various stage personalities. One who was allegedly a horse doctor started receiving questions about how to deal with sick animals. When another one, "Jad," said that his cabin had burned, kindhearted listeners delivered lumber, furniture, and food to the station parking lot. The group, with a changing membership, played at KMPC for two years, until moving to another Los Angeles station. In the meantime, Rice had reinforced country music's rustic, hillbilly image.[62]

That fabricated image had emerged in the mid-1920s courtesy of people such as George Hay, a newspaper journalist from Indiana who turned to broadcasting. Hay "didn't know music," according to one individual. "He wouldn't know the difference between 'Turkey in the Straw' and 'Steamboat Bill.'" Nevertheless, he became one of country music's most influential forces, first in Chicago as an announcer for the *Barn Dance* program at the new Sears station, WLS, where he was station manager, and then in Nashville, as radio director at WSM, one of the premier stations in the country. In 1925, the National Life and Accident Insurance Company had launched WSM, which soon became an NBC affiliate. Although Hay was only thirty, he had already developed a radio personality as "the solemn old judge." In December 1925, when WSM started its Saturday night *Barn Dance* program, Hay was probably simply acknowledging the popularity of old-time tunes. Still, those tunes squared with his own advice about music: "Keep it down to earth." In late 1927, as the NBC network show *Music Appreciation Hour* left the air and the locally produced *Barn Dance* commenced, Judge Hay said: "For the past hour we have been listening to music taken largely from the Grand Opera, but from now on we will present the Grand Ole Opry." That name quickly came to define one of the most popular radio shows, which WSM carried to at least half the nation. Soon, live audiences watched *The Grand Ole Opry*, and, as the crowds grew, the *Opry* shifted to different settings with more seats. Hay shrewdly exploited the hillbilly stereotypes that others were already associating with old-time music. He referred to "'talent' . . . from the back country" or to "Tennessee mountaineers." With the development of live performances, he also altered the cast's apparel and names. Members of Dr. Humphrey Bate's band, for example, exchanged their business suits for overalls and posed in cornfields as Dr. Bate and His Possum Hunters. Hay reportedly chose names for bands from a "colorful" list that he kept in his desk. By this process, the Binkley Brothers became the Binkley Brothers Dixie Clodhoppers; other bands had names such as the Fruit Jar Drinkers and the Gully Jumpers.[63]

These invented images that accompanied the rise of country music cut in several directions. Ralph Peer had admittedly used them as a way to distinguish white country sounds from the "race" music of blacks. "I invented the hillbilly and the nigger stuff," he said proudly. On another level, the label *hillbilly* tapped the kinds of antiurban, antimodern sentiments that still gripped many Americans. In contrast to the phony and artificial, the mythical hill country supposedly represented what was homemade, authentic, traditional, unpretentious, and rooted. When Hay and others contrived to make performers fit that image, they were "preserving" artificially constructed set pieces reminiscent of vaudeville's stock characters. Hence, George Hay required the daughter of Dr. Bate, a Vanderbilt graduate and medical doctor, to appear with her father in rustic attire, as if she had just come in from the farm. Unfortunately, the hillbilly images simply reinforced critics' perceptions that country music came from bumpkins and unsophisticated yokels.[64]

Nashville itself was hardly free of such perceptions. The city suffered a split identity. As the "Athens of the South," with two universities, a number of solid businesses, and privileged neighborhoods such as Belle Meade, it embodied high culture and society. But, as the "Buckle of the Bible Belt," it also summoned up images of "a cesspool of Baptists . . . and syphilitic evangelists," the description that the journalist H. L. Mencken had pinned on Dayton, Tennessee, during the infamous Scopes "Monkey Trial" in 1925. One Belle Meade product, Sarah Ophelia Colley, experienced firsthand the rebuke of Nashville's "better" class when she abandoned her wealthy finishing-school background for a traveling theater group and, in 1940, joined *The Grand Ole Opry*. Developing a character named Minnie Pearl, she became a legendary *Opry* performer. Minnie Pearl was precisely the rube that respectable Nashville despised. Wearing gingham dresses and a cheap straw hat with a $1.98 price tag hanging from it, Pearl concocted tales about her hillbilly family in Grinder's Switch and her failed efforts to get male attention. Once, supposedly, after a robber frisked her and asked, "Are you sure you ain't got any money," she had replied: "Nossir, but if you'll do that again, I'll write you a check." She became so well-known that fans' letters bearing no address except drawings of her trademark hat arrived at the *Opry*. "When I first came to Nashville," she remembered, "country music was not welcome in this town." In response to elites who "started talking down on us, we developed a saying: 'Nobody likes us but the people.'" And, by the end of the Depression, those people belonged to a growing constituency that had discovered country music via the radio and the *Opry*. By then, too, movie "horse operas" with stars such as Gene Autry, Roy Rogers, and Tex Ritter were replacing the hillbilly image with that of the singing cowboy armed with a guitar as well as a six-gun. As the country performer and historian Douglas Green observed: "No youngster in the thirties and forties ever wanted to grow up to be a hillbilly, but thousands upon thousands wanted to be cowboys."[65]

While *The Grand Ole Opry* and other barn dance radio shows that emerged in the 1930s promoted country music, programs such as *Your Hit Parade* aired the pop hits of Tin Pan Alley. Starting in 1935, Lucky Strike cigarettes sponsored the weekly show that played the nation's Top 10 hits. "Your Hit Parade!" the show announced as it came on the air. "We don't pick 'em, we just play 'em. . . . We check the songs you dance to . . . the sales of the records you buy . . . and the sheet music you play. And then, knowing your preferences, we bring you the top hits of the week!" The host then started the countdown from the number ten hit to "the top song in the country, Number One on Your Lucky Strike Hit Parade." The accuracy of the rankings was questionable, but the program drew young listeners from across the country.[66]

Behind all this entertainment, of course, were powerful commercializing forces. A rising entertainment bureaucracy marked the amusement industries, from movies to music and radio. Companies such as the Music Corporation of America (MCA) increasingly guided the careers of professional bands and musicians. MCA's founder was Julius Caesar Stein, the son of Lithuanian Jewish immigrants and an ophthalmologist who, in the 1920s, started booking bands in Chicago while he was practicing medicine. In May 1924, with his booking service earning ten times more than his medical practice, he incorporated MCA, signing up emerging dance bands such as Guy Lombardo's. He then clawed his way up in a cutthroat business, an unregulated world populated by shady clients and thugs. By the mid-1930s, perhaps 90 percent of dance bands and many other entertainers were under exclusive contract at MCA. Some performers viewed the corporation as a "Star Spangled Octopus" that controlled them just as plantation bosses did slaves. "I'm on the road for MCA," the trombonist Jack Teagarden once quipped. In 1936, Stein added motion-picture people to his list of clients, moving MCA's headquarters to Beverly Hills, California. His company strengthened links between musicians, radio networks, the movie industry, and advertisers. MCA likewise facilitated a revolution in Tin Pan Alley whereby movie studios increasingly co-opted major music publishing houses, transforming them into studio branches or contracting directly with musicians.[67]

Organizations also emerged in the music industry to deal with continuing problems over fair compensation. In 1914, the American Society of Composers, Authors, and Publishers (ASCAP) had formed to extend the protections of the 1909 copyright law, which required record companies to pay writers and publishers of songs. Although the law imposed fees on the purchase or "mechanical reproduction" of published compositions, ASCAP subsequently won court rulings in favor of additional payments for using its members' work in live settings, in movies, and on the radio. Tin Pan Alley benefited greatly from ASCAP, which, by 1939, licensed about 90 percent of its songs. But ASCAP generally ignored race and hillbilly music. Not until 1940 would blues and country musicians begin to break the ASCAP monopoly. They did so when radio broadcasters—angry at ASCAP's continuing pressure for higher fees—formed a rival licensing agency: Broadcast Music, Incorporated (BMI). Searching for tunes that ASCAP did not control, BMI helped increase copyright protection and airtime for African American and country music. Over the next few years, BMI grew stronger, eventually even loosening ASCAP's hold on Tin Pan Alley.[68]

Meanwhile, the commercial networks, which had feuded with ASCAP, consolidated their position atop the radio industry. In the late 1920s, the networks' dominance had been anything but certain during what was, in effect, a battle for the airwaves. Initially, several hundred nonprofit broadcasters, most of them on university campuses, were radio's pioneers, while private broadcasters struggled financially. Indeed, most of the private stations existed primarily to draw attention to the newspapers, stores, and companies that owned them. In 1927, the newly formed national networks of NBC, with twenty-eight affiliates, and CBS, with sixteen, accounted for only 6.4 percent of the nation's broadcast stations. Within a mere four years, however, NBC and CBS affiliates constituted 30 percent of the stations and provided 70 percent of U.S. broadcasting. By 1934, nonprofit airtime had plummeted to 2 percent. This dramatic turnaround resulted from fierce resistance to government support for noncommercial stations and a huge jump in advertising for the commercial networks. With the 1934 Communications Act, Congress delivered control of the airwaves to the Federal Communications Commission, which essentially agreed with NBC's David Sarnoff that "our American system of broadcasting . . . is privately owned because private ownership is one of our national doctrines. It is privately supported, through commercial sponsorship of its program hours, and at no cost to the listener, because ours is a free economic system." CBS's William Paley asserted: "He who attacks the fundamentals of the American system [of broadcasting] attacks democracy itself." The Depression unquestionably bolstered the networks' position. Sarnoff's point that listeners received programming "at no cost" was especially welcome during the harsh economic times. In turn, advertisers found that radio was an effective way to court consumers.[69]

Prior to the Depression, according to *Fortune* magazine in 1932: "Radio was polite. Radio was genteel. Radio was a guest in the home, not the salesman on the doorstep. . . . But some 18 months of further Depression have changed all that." The evidence was staggering. Between 1928 and 1934, the networks more than tripled their revenues from advertising.[70]

During the 1930s, NBC, CBS, and the Mutual Broadcasting System collectively tied together several hundred broadcasting affiliates; by 1938, Mutual, which started in 1934, included 110 stations. NBC—the product of arrangements with the corporate giants RCA, General Electric, and Westinghouse—had two networks, NBC-Red and NBC-Blue, which paid affiliates to broadcast nationally sponsored shows and, in turn, billed affiliates for locally sponsored programs. To determine listener preferences as well as the sizes and demographics of audiences, networks as well as stations and sponsors turned to market researchers, who conducted surveys, some via the telephone. Gauging popular taste was crucial because successful programs attracted sponsors, and, by 1938, commercials controlled one-third of broadcast hours, pushing radio revenue from advertising above that of magazines for the first time.[71]

By then, a crucial ingredient in radio's relentless search for advertisers was the daytime soap opera. In 1940, perhaps 60 percent of daytime network programming consisted of these serials aimed at women. The serial format had long preceded the soap operas, of course. In the nineteenth century, the famed English writer Charles Dickens had published a number of his novels in installments. In the United States, comic strips and movie serials such as *The Perils of Pauline* had continued the form. And, in radio, the spectacularly popular *Amos 'n' Andy* show featured a regular cast of characters and evolved through a daily narrative. The decisions to apply the serial format to women's shows grew directly, however, from advertising studies showing that women purchased 85 percent of household items and overwhelmingly constituted radio's daytime audience. On October 20, 1930, *Painted Dreams,* an early daytime serial aimed specifically at women, began on Chicago's WGN. Although the station manager, Henry Selinger, had pushed the idea of designing a serial to sell products to women, it was Irna Phillips who wrote and acted in *Painted Dreams.* Phillips, along with Anne and Frank Hummert of a Chicago advertising agency, became the driving figures behind the soap opera phenomenon, which soon included a host of programs such as *Ma Perkins, Just Plain Bill, The Romance of Helen Trent, Pepper Young's Family,* and *The Guiding Light.* By the end of the decade, the number of serials being broadcast had grown from three to sixty-one, ruling the weekday airwaves from 9:00 A.M. until 5:00 P.M. Half of American women reportedly listened to at least one serial on a regular basis. Because the Proctor and Gamble Company was the dominant sponsor, such programs earned the name *soap operas.* Social and cultural elites scoffed at these "washboard weepers," this "serialized drool." In 1939, one woman's club launched an "I'm Not Listening" boycott, which spread to clubs in thirty-nine states. An NBC executive characterized the typical listener as "the shop girl type"; indeed, he believed, she was probably a "neurotic who sits entranced before the radio, clutching a copy of 'True Confessions' and (possibly) guzzling gin and ginger ale." But, for both networks and sponsors, the soap operas were a gold mine; one survey indicated that 61 percent of female listeners bought the items that their favorite serials advertised. Hence, while the network executives extolled the cultural value of their nighttime offerings, they expanded, albeit with some embarrassment, their daytime menus. Such a strategy encouraged the "ghettoization" of programming for women, which *Variety* dismissed as a "malnutritious diet of pap."[72]

The growth of soap operas nevertheless demonstrated the greatly expanded influence of advertising agencies on the radio industry. In 1930, for example, the ad agency for the Saks and Company department store had to persuade the CBS head, William Paley, to air a fifteen-minute celebrity gossip show featuring the fast-talking columnist Walter Winchell. "I introduce myself to you as New York's most notorious gossip," said Winchell, as he launched his long and controversial radio career, "in case you have never read my drivel." But soon the advertising agencies, especially the J. Walter Thompson Company (JWT), themselves began to produce shows for sponsors and shop them around the networks, seeking favorable time slots and other advantages. As early as 1927, JWT had established a radio department to court radio clients. But, when Thompson concluded that NBC had produced an unacceptable half hour for one client, he concluded: "Hell, if that's the best you can do, we can do better, with our own writers and directors." Working in Hollywood, JWT produced at least five of the top shows in 1935, building programs around stars such as Bing Crosby, who was with *The Kraft Music Hall*. Worried that the ad agencies and the sponsors were taking over the radio business, the networks tried to regain control over such things as scripts. "Just another case of NBC B damned," complained an executive after one disagreement. Another programming head observed: "The agencies and clients have not reached the point where they agree with us on what is acceptable in the average American home." Significantly, of the eighty top shows between 1935 and 1942, JWT produced thirty-five.[73]

Angry at advertising's growing domination of radio, Lee De Forest, who with his vacuum tube had helped invent the medium, complained that "uncouth 'sandwich-men'" had taken control, churning out "a cold mess of ginger-ale and cigarettes." Another person concluded that radio had produced "a new and noisy method of letting peddlers into your home." Yet many listeners welcomed such intrusions. Indeed, sponsored programs may have helped big business regain some of the respect that it had lost with the coming of the Depression. Grateful listeners appreciated the corporations that provided radio's entertainment and sometimes even apologized to companies for not buying enough of their products. Radio thus strengthened the bonds between consumerism and pleasure, a key element of commercial entertainment.[74]

As consumers, listeners could even gain a sense of empowerment. They could take advertising as evidence of their strength and influence. "If Mary goes back to that worthless Joe," threatened one woman regarding a soap opera, "I will never use Kleenex again." Listeners could fairly conclude that a program sponsor cared what they thought because, after all, they bought the product. "Yes, we use Ivory Soap and Ivory Flakes," wrote one couple to Proctor and Gamble, the biggest sponsor of daytime programming, about the fate of a soap opera. Such words implicitly reminded the company that it should honor listeners' wishes. Radio thus played a major role in shaping consumer consciousness, but such consciousness was anything but passive. Sponsors recognized this fact and hired experts to assess what kinds of ads motivated and engaged listeners. Programmers and sponsors wanted, ultimately, to please.[75]

Radio's pleasures—like those of vaudeville, from which radio drew so much of its talent and format—often worried moralists, however. The networks were, thus, nervous as well. They did not want to alienate sponsors, agencies, and listeners, nor did they want to bring down the wrath of government censors. Like Hollywood, the networks thus relied on self-regulation. Starting in 1933, a song censor at NBC examined the lyrics of tunes that might be aired. A year later (at the same time that Hollywood put teeth in its Production Code), NBC established a Continuity Acceptance Department to review scripts and products. In 1937, that department opened an office in Los Angeles in order to keep closer track of radio productions there. An NBC booklet in 1938 maintained that "good taste and good radio are forged indelibly together. . . . The American people are *not* interested in radio programs dealing with sex or sex perversion." Efforts to ensure that programs met network standards, however, ultimately pointed up the challenges of interpretation. These challenges were abundantly clear when they involved spoken words. Listeners, operating in a "Theater of the Mind," as one announcer described it, were not passive; their imaginations turned sounds into images. Or, as Janet MacRorie, the head of NBC's Continuity Acceptance Department in New York, recognized: "It is not always possible to foresee in reading the script the exact shade of meaning that the actor will give the line when it is read."[76]

Such certainly was the case on December 12, 1937, when Mae West gave her own seductive rendering of a script that NBC's censorship board had approved for the popular variety show *The Chase and Sanborn Hour*. In a sketch about the Garden of Eden, West played a bored and sexually aggressive Eve who urges Adam to "take me outta this dismal dump and give me the chance to develop my personality." She even seduces the serpent, who urges her not to "be so rough. To me, love is peace and quiet." West responds suggestively: "That ain't love—that's sleep." One indignant listener wrote to Chase and Sanborn that West's "lewd" interpretation "makes one think she should wear a veil over the lower part of her face to hide her nudity." Caught off guard when many listeners objected, NBC, the J. Walter Thompson agency, and the sponsor scrambled, arguing that the problem was not with the script but with West's delivery of it. NBC not only declared West an "unfit radio personality" but barred its affiliates and performers from even mentioning her name. Criticism, in turn, of the network's response highlighted the difficulties of gauging public opinion. The

Chicago Daily News scoffed at the hypocrisy of NBC and the sponsors, who knew when they hired West that she was no Mary Pickford. And a random telephone survey for the *Radio Guide* showed that 59 percent of those listeners were on West's side.[77]

The Mae West episode illustrated the multiple levels on which a radio program stirred imaginations. Somewhere in that mix were reasons for the popularity of the 1930s' great radio shows, whose messages were, typically, contradictory. Whether the format was soap opera or comedy, the programs reinforced and questioned social norms, broaching controversial subjects and then softening them.[78]

Soap operas were, from one perspective, all about hope, romance, and traditional values. "I want you to put God on every page," Anne Hummert instructed her writers. (When one writer asked, "Who's going to play the part?" Hummert fired her.) For women in these shows, marriage, home, and family were defining ingredients. "Of course you want to get married," a mother assured her daughter. "Every girl wants to get married." At a time when economic troubles savaged many families, it was reassuring to hear a character discuss "the magic ring of happiness and home" and to listen to beleaguered people overcoming adversity. It was not coincidental that soap operas took hold during the Depression. From another perspective, then, the serials met felt needs by providing escapist relief from housework's drudgery and addressing genuine concerns, many of which the Depression exacerbated. Moreover, the messages were sometimes ambivalent. While there were assuredly "Cinderella" plotlines, there were also reminders of life's uncertainties: "All we can be sure of is that nothing is sure," said one character. The soaps even hedged sometimes on conventional gender roles. At the end of a 1932 episode of *Today's Children*, for example, Frances indeed decided that she would not enter a career back East but would stay and marry Bob: "I guess—yes, I guess my place is here—with Bob." But her "I guess" suggested lingering doubts about her decision. Earlier in the program, she wondered: "Must a woman's only reason for living be the raising of a family? Is it fair—is it right?" And she asserted that all men are "selfish, egotistical, vain—either woman must lose herself completely in the personality of the man, in her marriage, or the game is off." Although soap operas ultimately reinforced the domestic ideal, they raised other possibilities. And sometimes they simply provided examples of how to handle real-life situations. Hence, one woman drew a connection between a jealous male on one program and her own boyfriend. "Listening to stories like that," she said, "makes me know how . . . to tell my boyfriend where he can get off at."[79]

Radio comedy also had layered meanings. There was no better example than *Amos 'n' Andy,* the spectacularly popular and highly influential program that drew on the minstrel tradition. With two white men, Charles

Correll and Freeman Gosden, as black characters, the show drew an astounding 40 million listeners nightly in the early 1930s. Lasting for fifteen minutes six evenings a week throughout the 1930s, the program forced businesses to accommodate it. Store owners played it over loudspeakers so that customers could listen as they shopped, and movie theaters held intermissions in order to broadcast the program. Like minstrelsy, *Amos 'n' Andy* used stereotypes and caricatures of African Americans. The characters spoke with a thick dialect full of grammatical errors and malapropisms, and they bumbled through one problem after another surrounding the "Fresh Air Taxicab Company" in Chicago. Despite its racism, however, the program had an appeal that crossed racial lines, and its serialized story dealt with concerns common to much of society. It was, in effect, as a leading student of black humor has described it, "a comic, black-voice soap opera that, like minstrelsy, allowed America obliquely to scrutinize and laugh at its own problems"—including those of the Depression, or "repression," as Amos and Andy called it. Correll later explained: "We chose black characters because blackface could tell funnier stories than whiteface comics." Many white listeners seemed genuinely to identify with the slow-talking Amos's honesty, work ethic, and love for his wife, Ruby. When, during an October 1931 sequence, Amos was falsely accused of murder and on trial, listeners got so angry that the program's sponsor cautioned Gosden and Correll: "The country's mad! The Parent-Teacher Association is going to boycott the program if Amos is convicted." Even though the program hardly challenged the nation's racial status quo and, in some respects, may even have implicitly encouraged such practices as segregation, it was full of ambiguities. When white audiences seemed genuinely to care about black characters who were not stereotypical "mammies" and "uncles," they implicitly nudged deep-seated racist beliefs.[80]

The "linguistic slapstick" in *Amos 'n' Andy* was crucial to what made radio comedy as a whole so popular during the Depression. In this regard, comedy did far more than lift people's spirits during hard times. "Radio comedy was enacting much larger dramas about competition, authority, fairness, and hope during the greatest crisis of American capitalism," as the media scholar Susan Douglas has written. At a time when the nation's future seemed particularly uncertain, the radio comedians conducted a "linguistic rebellion" against the traditional and the proper. "Decorum and insubordination took turns," according to Douglas, "and they worked hand in hand." Time and again, radio comedy questioned the established social order, even as it left that order intact. The result was "an ongoing contest between the infantile and the rational, in which the rational wins out—we 'get' the joke—but up until then nonsense has a field day." Hence, a radio joke could describe a man walking by a "lunatic asylum" and hearing chants: "Thirteen, thirteen, thirteen." Curious, he looks through the door's peephole. A stick jabs him in the eye. From inside, he hears: "Fourteen, fourteen, fourteen."[81]

George Burns and Gracie Allen excelled in the nonsensical and, in the process, conveyed dual gender messages. The couple had met as vaudeville performers and married in 1926. In 1929, they moved their successful act to radio; within three years, they had their own show on NBC. The addled Gracie never seemed to understand the real world. When George wondered why she put straw in the water when she boiled eggs, she said sweetly: "So they'll feel at home." Yet she differed "from all the other dumb Doras," Burns later explained, because "Gracie played her as if she were totally sane, as if her answers actually made sense. We called it illogic-logic." At the end of each program, when George instructed her to "Say good night, Gracie," she responded: "Good night, Gracie." Her comments often did not make sense; yet, at the same time, in weird ways, they made complete sense. When George asked her if the nurse dropped her on her head when she was a baby, she replied: "Oh no, we couldn't afford a nurse. My mother had to do it." Significantly, Gracie's "illogic-logic" often undermined George's male authority. George, frustrated and confused, rasped: "Gracie, all I have to do is hear you talk and the blood rushes to my head." She told him: "That's because it's empty."[82]

Traditional images of male self-assurance and dominance also took a pounding in the comedy of Jack Benny. Like Burns and Allen, Benny too was a well-known vaudeville performer in the 1920s. In early 1932, however, he decided to learn more about radio. "I'm going to study this thing backward and forward," he said. He subsequently helped prove his point that "the big future in our business is the radio" by launching, in May 1932, one of the most successful of all programs. By 1937, he was making almost $400,000 annually from it. Shrewdly, he made his radio persona the main target of the show's humor. The character was inept, pretentious, wealthy but stingy, pompous yet insecure, thus displaying "all the faults and frailties of mankind," as Benny explained. "Every family has that kind of person." Playing a stooge and fall guy, Benny allowed Depression-era audiences to use him as a humorous scapegoat. His character was the opposite of a manly man. "The minute I come on," Benny said, "even the most henpecked guy in the audience feels good." Indeed, Benny's prissiness, as well as his vanity about age and looks, and his shrieking response to taunts—"Now cut that out!"—hinted strongly of a "feminine" side. His traits of helplessness and dependency, as well as his failure to develop romantic relationships, could evoke sympathy among listeners who had a sense of powerlessness; but those traits also played off cultural anxieties about gender and alternative sexuality. In 1935, NBC's Programming Department expressed concern about "a definite tendency toward effeminate characterizations" among comedians such as Benny and urged banning "anything of the lavendar [*sic*] nature." *The Jack Benny Show* perhaps softened its oblique sexual references by allowing listeners to relate to Benny in different ways and by taking a teasing approach to homosexuality. During one episode, for instance, Benny described an effeminate male as "a weird fella. I'm nervous." Ultimately in radio comedy, as one media scholar has noted: "Homosexuality . . . was represented as a comic quirk, valuable for its odd perspective but not as a basis for identity." Differences might exist, but society could contain them—a message that was both liberating and reassuring in an anxious time.[83]

While Depression-era anxieties fed the need for comedic relief, they did not stir much public interest in radio news, except regarding such sensational events as the 1932 kidnapping of the Lindbergh baby. A number of individuals nevertheless used the airwaves for political purposes. Father Charles Coughlin became a national personality with his Sunday broadcasts from Detroit, blaming the economic crisis on rich bankers in tones that were increasingly anti-Semitic. Louisiana senator Huey Long, before his assassination in 1935, purchased radio time on several occasions to champion his "Share the Wealth" ideas. In Kansas, John Brinkley, a medical doctor who specialized in goat-gland transplants to invigorate male sexuality, launched his nearly successful gubernatorial campaigns in 1930 and 1932 from his KFKB station. And, in 1938, the radio announcer Wilbert Lee "Pappy, Pass the Biscuits" O'Daniel's popularity on his Hillbilly Flour Company's weekly program was sufficient to make him the governor of Texas. But it was Franklin Roosevelt who most effectively demonstrated radio's political power with a series of "fireside chats" in which he informally addressed the nation from the White House. His first talk, on March 12, 1933, focused on the banking crisis so skillfully that Will Rogers quipped: "He made everybody understand it, even the bankers." In one poll, Roosevelt emerged as radio's most popular personality. Although the fit between radio and politics was clear, 1930s programming mainly reflected an advertising agency head's advice that, in the words of historian Tom Lewis, "America should laugh and dance its way out of the depression."[84]

By the mid-1930s, popular culture as a whole was supplying plenty of opportunities for dance and laughter as well as assurances that the system would prevail. The gangster hero of the Depression's early years gave way to a contrasting image of democratic authority: the government agent, or G-man. "Uncle Sam won't stand for it," said a character in *Special Agent* (William Keighley, 1935) regarding crime. With the active encouragement of the FBI director, J. Edgar Hoover, and perhaps reflecting a growing public faith in the federal government, Hollywood declared war on criminals. *"G" Men* (William Keighley, 1935) featured Jimmy Cagney, who had starred as the gangster Tom Powers in *Public Enemy* but was now on the side of the law. "Hollywood's Most Famous Bad Man Joins the G-Men and Halts the March of Crime," proclaimed Warner Brothers. The next year, in William Keighley's *Bullets or Ballots,* Edward G. Robinson switched from his *Little Caesar* persona to that of law enforcer. *Show Them No Mercy* (George Marshall, 1935) pitted the FBI against kidnappers; *Public Hero #1* (J. Walter Ruben, 1935) also had an FBI agent as its hero. Pulp magazines joined the swing to the side of law and order with publications such as *The Feds, G-Men Detective, Ace G-Man Stories, Crime Busters,* and a bunch of detective heroes. On radio, in 1935, the popular *Gang Busters* made its debut with machine-gun fire, sirens, and a rallying cry: "*Calling the police! Calling the G-men! Calling all Americans to war on the underworld.*" Four years later, Boston's WNAC started a series, *G-Men in Action.*[85]

Popular culture in various forms also reverberated with the rhetoric of democracy, the importance of the little folk, and the greatness of the American way of life. Movies were increasingly "pictures for the entire family," as Jack Warner described his studio's production schedule. Adolph Zukor agreed: "Paramount does not and will not make dirty pictures." Walt Disney similarly focused on family fare that emphasized hope and self-confidence. Cartoon characters such as Mickey Mouse championed average citizens' wisdom, dignity, and ability to survive. The characters also reflected Disney's daring assumption that children constituted entertainment's main audience. He put that assumption to the test in 1937 with *Snow White and the Seven Dwarfs,* the first feature-length animated film. Despite jokes in the movie studios about "Disney's Folly," not only was *Snow White* a box-office hit, but, like Mickey Mouse, it showed that the licensing of intellectual properties as dolls and other consumer items could yield huge profits. Although Disney marched to his own creative drum, his narratives about goodness triumphing over hardship and evil were anything but unique. Frank Capra directed movies about Mr. Deeds, Mr. Smith, and John Doe, all heroic, small-town commoners who help others and redeem the nation. "There you are, Norton—the people. Try and lick that," a reporter told the villain in Capra's *Meet John Doe* (1941). And, in 1939, a stunning screen presentation by Victor Fleming of Margaret Mitchell's best-selling novel *Gone With the Wind* concluded with Scarlett O'Hara's optimistic words: "After all, tomorrow is another day." That same year, another lavish Victor Fleming movie spectacle, *The Wizard of Oz,* also provided a nostalgic reminder of the importance of family and roots.[86]

Ambiguities abounded, however, despite the shared themes that linked most movies and other forms of Depression entertainment. In Hollywood, for example, "screwball" comedies and "women's films" treated matters of sexuality and gender roles quite differently. Screwball comedy emerged in the mid-1930s, largely as a strategy by which the studios could handle sexual themes without defying the Production Code. The plots staged seduction and courtship within a framework of humorous romantic battles and, in the process, toyed with gender roles. The comedies featured strong, independent-minded females who sparred verbally and physically with suave, good-looking males trying to protect their masculine authority. "Liberated" women asserted their rights and their sense of equality while the men struggled to contain such efforts. The films seemingly gave women permission to step outside their traditional domestic roles and typically suggested that male dominance was tenuous at best. Despite the somewhat open-ended possibilities of screwball comedies, movies as a whole strongly asserted the primacy of men while celebrating conventional female domesticity. So-called women's films—which critics dismissed as cinematic soap operas or "weepies"—provided females with opportunities to play main characters. But the predictably happy endings occurred because the women made the right choices; they suffered stoically, sacrificed for someone else, married, and raised children.[87]

Depression-era movies also widened and narrowed masculinity. The refined leading men of the 1920s generally gave way to tough, streetwise "city boys," such as James Cagney, John Garfield, and Humphrey Bogart. Resilient and inherently rebellious, they projected an urban, working-class style of manhood onto the screen. A competing masculine style appeared in the cowboy movies of especially John Wayne, whose characters harkened back to frontier days and exuded a quiet but commanding authority. Neither the city boys nor the cowboy figures challenged the traditional narratives of masculinity in America, which had long emphasized the male's need for independence and solitude as well as his obligations and responsibilities to others. Yet the city boy tended to be adaptive and malleable, trying to adjust to a changing world, while the Wayne-style cowboy was trapped in the past. The cowboy's manhood was locked in time, leaving the character fighting heroically to protect society but unwilling to live in it. That historically confined masculine role was also apparent in the extremely popular *The Lone Ranger,* which returned listeners *"to those thrilling days of yesteryear."* The radio show expanded from a three-station radio hookup in January 1933 to a nationwide program, a daily comic strip, juvenile novels, and movie serials. "Who *was* that masked man, anyway?" someone asks as the Lone Ranger and his faithful sidekick, Tonto, ride off from the town after saving it. The cowboy and city boy heroes, however different, were both instructive about constructing manhood at a time when the Depression sorely jeopardized the traditional roles of male breadwinners and protectors.[88]

Although the city boy and the cowboy models had different emphases, they were, nevertheless, in one way quite similar: they were white. African Americans and other ethnic minorities were left with supporting roles that typically recycled demeaning stereotypes. Even the sensual Latin lover that Rudolph Valentino had made famous in the 1920s faded in the 1930s.

Overwhelmingly visible among popular culture's images and themes by the latter half of the 1930s, however, were signs of a returning confidence in American ideals, citizens, and processes. Joining movies, radio, sports, and music were other striking examples: the board game Monopoly; Dale Carnegie's nonfiction best seller *How to Win Friends and Influence People* (1936); *Life* magazine; and one of the comic-book industry's most famous characters, Superman. Monopoly, which the Parker Brothers Company released in 1935, was all about the importance of money and property. Players could buy property on the board, build miniature houses and hotels, and even play the role of banker. A player's situation might look bleak, but a favorable turn of the dice could bring prosperity. While economic hard times tested the spirit of capitalism, Monopoly confirmed it. Carnegie's extremely influential self-help guide likewise maintained that the American dream was still achievable and that there was nothing wrong with the existing order as long as people adjusted themselves to it. The key to success lay in an individual's winning personality.[89]

Life, an exceptionally popular weekly picture magazine that the publisher Henry R. Luce first published on November 23, 1936, presented equally optimistic portraits of America's character and purpose. Luce wanted to use photographs—a "common denominator with low-brows," in his words—to offer a vision of the world that ultimately attested to the nation's greatness. As one photographer recalled, the idea was that "here, set down for all time, you may look at the average 1937 American as he really is" and "take stock of some of the abiding things which are magnificently *right* about America." In Luce's opinion, certain values were "infinitely precious and especially American—a love of freedom, a feeling for the equality of opportunity, a tradition of self-reliance and independence." These were values, Luce believed, that the United States should "spread throughout the world." *Life* quickly struck a public chord. By 1939, its circulation exceeded 2 million, but surveys suggested that between fourteen and eighteen people read each issue.[90]

While *Life* became one of the decade's icons, so did Superman. The cartoon character also transformed the comic-book business, which grew from publishing's seedier regions. Working in those regions was Harry Donenfeld, a Romanian immigrant whose inspirations included "girlie pulps" such as *Juicy Tales* and *Spicy Detective Stories.* Renewed crackdowns in New York City on obscenity in 1937 had sent Donenfeld scurrying for safer material in the still-small comic business, where he took over a failed company and renamed it Detective Comics, Incorporated (DC). At the time, comic publishing resembled "a kind of artistic ghetto," according to one cartoonist, and "had to suffer the disdain of the mainstream." The Depression hardly helped, because magazine distributors and vendors were reluctant to gamble on unproved comic books that sold for ten cents. On the other hand, the ailing economy allowed several small companies, drawing on limited capital, to find illustrators who badly needed work. In June 1938, DC introduced Superman in one of its publications, *Action Comics*. Donenfeld was soon getting reports from local dealers that kids kept asking for "the comic with Superman in it." The character was so instantly popular that, the next year, DC started publishing a comic book named after him. In 1940, *Superman*'s circulation grossed almost a million dollars. By then, Superman was also appearing in a nationally syndicated comic strip, a radio program, and toys and was headed for the movies. Harry Donenfeld was now rich, and the comic-book business had risen from a "junk culture industry" into a moneymaker and a centerpiece of American childhood. According to one survey, 90 percent of fourth and fifth graders said they regularly read comic books. Superman had touched off a comic-book fad. As one of the people at DC Comics observed: "Superman literally created this industry."[91]

Superman was the idea in 1934 of Jerry Siegel and Joe Shuster, high school students in Cleveland who felt very much like outsiders. The sons of Jewish immigrants with little money, they had found in popular culture an outlet for their dreams. Drawing on a host of images from the movies, comic strips, animated cartoons, and the pulps, they ingeniously crafted a character who mixed humor, danger, and fantasy. In Superman, they provided a character with whom many youngsters could identify. Although he comes from a distant planet, his earthly persona is Clark Kent, a bespectacled, mild-mannered man who gets little respect. But, once Kent dons his Superman costume, he becomes an invincible defender of the oppressed and needy. For "the young, alienated, and dispossessed 'Clark Kents' of society," according to the historian Bradford Wright, Superman met a deep need. Moreover, the early *Superman* issues echoed New Deal themes, championing the public welfare over corporate greed and injustice. "Superman's America was something of a paradox," Wright has argued. It was "a land where the virtue of the poor and the weak towered over that of the wealthy and the powerful. Yet the common man could not expect to prevail on his own in this America." Superman was an essential ally. Following his example, other "superheroes for the common man" rapidly emerged, including especially Batman, Captain Marvel, and Wonder Woman.[92]

Those superheroes—along with other representatives from popular culture—would shortly become worthy allies in another building crisis:

war. During the Depression, mass entertainment had rebounded from the financial depths, providing escape, reflecting anxieties and hopes, and leaving an indelible imprint on U.S. society. Although popular culture was still controversial in many respects, it had become a prominent definer of the American way of life—a role that World War II and the early Cold War would fortify.

8

BUILDING A WARTIME CONSENSUS
IN THE 1940s AND 1950s

In early December 1941, the Japanese attack on Pearl Harbor prompted *Time* magazine to displace its originally scheduled cover story regarding Walt Disney's new cartoon movie creation, Dumbo. After the December 7 attack on the Hawaiian Islands and Germany's declaration of war on the United States a few days later, Americans immediately focused on the spreading horror of World War II. The fate of the big-eared circus elephant in Disney's feature-length cartoon suddenly seemed trivial.[1]

Quickly, however, popular culture's place in the nation's life became stronger than ever. Indeed, over the next twenty years or so, during World War II and the early Cold War, the entertainment industry helped forge a national consensus celebrating the American way of life. Amusements and patriotism had often been intertwined, certainly during the crises of the 1930s, but that linkage tightened as Americans rallied to their nation's defense against the Axis powers and, subsequently, the Soviet Union and communism. The entertainment industry bolstered a victory mystique, provided opportunities for temporary amusement in an all-too-grim world, and profoundly influenced Americans' perceptions of themselves and their country.

In late 1941, when the United States plunged fully into World War II, the fate and role of popular culture were initially much in question. The spreading conflict's insatiable need for matériel and personnel threatened to drain the entertainment industry of crucial resources. Government-instituted rationing programs for products such as gasoline could strangle amusements such as circuses, music groups, and athletic teams that depended on travel. Wartime shortages of other matériel such as shellac and celluloid jeopardized the record and movie businesses. "Dim-out" and "blackout" regulations made Coney Island at night resemble a ghost town; at Steeplechase Park, a mere two thousand shaded bulbs replaced the sixty thousand bright lights that previously illuminated the area. Government insistence after 1943 on the reduction of paper usage by 15–20 percent created problems for newspaper, magazine, and comic-book publishers. And a number of prominent entertainers, ranging from Jimmy Stewart and Clark Gable in films to Joe DiMaggio and Ted Williams in baseball, joined the armed forces.[2]

But, as Dumbo's fortunes in December 1941 ultimately demonstrated, Americans hastily embraced popular culture. Although *Time* magazine exchanged Disney's character for war news on its cover right after the Pearl Harbor attack, the magazine did not completely ignore the cartoon elephant. Indeed, the December 29 issue included a story characterizing him as "the most appealing new character of this year of war." In the movie, the little elephant's ridiculously huge ears, which initially make him the target of jokes, ultimately lift him to heroic status as he saves the circus and becomes its star. "Among all the grim and forbidding images of A.D. 1941," *Time* conjectured, Dumbo's "guileless homely face is the face of the true man of good will." In fact, "*Dumbo* could only have happened here." Certainly, the story of the defenseless but courageous underdog who triumphed over injustice and hardship provided a ready-made script for a nation at war with aggressor forces.[3]

For good reason, then, President Franklin D. Roosevelt's administration recognized popular culture's importance for the war effort. The government's position was that the show must go on, although entertainment producers were supposed to ask of their products: "Will this help win the war?" The Office of Defense Transportation thus allowed circus trains to operate because circuses were crucial to "morale on the home front." For the same reason, Roosevelt ensured that Hollywood could continue producing commercial movies. "The American motion picture is one of the most effective mediums in informing and entertaining our citizens," he said. And, when he established a liaison between the government and Hollywood, he emphasized that he "want[ed] no censorship of the movies." Roosevelt turned also to the music industry: "The inspiration of great music can help to instill a fervor for the spiritual values of our way of life; and thus to strengthen democracy against [its enemies]." Even without such urging, the makers of popular culture—from movies to Tin Pan Alley, radio, sports, and comic books—eagerly raised the flag, seeking in the process to enhance their public image and worth.[4]

Comic-book publishers were an important example. For parents who fretted about comics' bad influence on youngsters, the war provided the comic business with an opportunity to demonstrate its patriotism. Virtually every comic-book hero (including the leading characters in newspapers' daily comic strips, such as *Joe Palooka* and *Terry and the Pirates*) battled the enemy abroad and at home. Superman, Captain Marvel, Wonder Woman, and Batman and Robin led the cause.[5]

But it was Captain America, a character that Marvel Comics created a few months before the attack on Pearl Harbor, who perhaps best symbolized the role of comic books in the war. One of the character's creators was Jacob Kurtzberg, the son of Jewish immigrants from Austria. Kurtzberg changed his name to Jack Kirby because he "very much wanted to be an American." In his opinion, comics represented a "strictly American" art form, one that reflected the nation's democratic strengths. In March 1941, eight months before the United States entered the war, he teamed up with Joe Simon to introduce Captain America, a muscular hero wearing a red, white, and blue costume and bearing a shield embellished with stars and stripes. The cover of the first issue showed Captain America slugging Adolf Hitler. Steve Rogers, the superhero's real name, starts out as a weakling unfit for military service before a leading American scientist transforms him into the nation's "super-soldier." Dedicated to protecting "a peace-loving America" against "ruthless war mongers," Rogers quickly captured the imagination of readers. Each month during the war, newsstands sold around a million copies of *Captain America* comics. Nor were youngsters the only readers. Significantly, comic books constituted 25 percent of all magazines that U.S. troops received overseas.[6]

While fictional heroes such as Steve Rogers enlisted in the war effort, a large number of real-life entertainment celebrities also donned uniforms. "He wants to have a hand in beating the living daylights out of the Nazis and the Japs and all the rest of the gang who because Uncle Sam is at heart a peace-loving old gent have had the effrontery to go to war against him," *Photoplay* magazine reported in November 1942 when the film star Robert Cummings joined the air force. "He is a typical American, Bob is, easy going, careless of his privileges until he finds them threatened; tolerant of the other fellows' vices until he is hit below the belt. And when he is mad, he knows how to fight."[7]

That same image of peace-loving, reluctant warriors defined the screen characters in war-related movies, which constituted roughly one-fourth of Hollywood's output from 1942 to 1944. John Wayne epitomized such characters, although time and again the most common of soldiers stood tall. "I'm no hero," says "Taxi" Potts, the jovial cabdriver from Brooklyn in *Guadalcanal Diary* (Lewis Seiler, 1943) as he awaits an enemy attack. "I'm just a guy. I came out here because somebody had to come, [but] I don't want no medals. I just want to go back home."[8]

While Hollywood films showed soldiers abroad and citizens at home sacrificing for their country, thousands of performers voluntarily raised money for war bonds or entertained the troops. Celebrity guests appeared on army posts and naval stations or at the famed Hollywood Canteen, which hosted many of the hundreds of thousands of soldiers moving through Los Angeles to the Pacific battle arena. More than three hundred movie stars participated in the government's first war bond drive in September 1942, selling over $838 million in bonds. Over the course of the war, the popular actress Dorothy Lamour reportedly sold $350 million in bonds. Sexy Hedy Lamarr kissed men who bought bonds worth $25,000. Meanwhile, many movie theaters functioned as "war-oriented community centers," sponsoring bond drives, showing government-made films, providing collection centers for critical war matériel such as blood plasma, using parking lots to gather scrap metal, and, especially in areas near defense plants, expanding schedules to accommodate swing-shift workers. In many respects, World War II marked Hollywood's finest moment.[9]

Although movies and other forms of wartime amusement advanced a victory narrative that extolled America's democratic virtues and strengths, popular culture generally settled on strategies that were less overtly propagandistic and more escapist. This trend was clear in music, where initially a call went out for "the great American war song." "What America needs today is a good five cent war song," said an enthusiastic member of Congress a few weeks after the United States entered the conflict. "The nation is literally crying for a good, peppy marching song, something with plenty of zip, ginger, fire"—like George M. Cohan's World War I anthem "Over There." Seeking to make music a "psychological fighting force," the government's wartime propaganda office, the Office of War Information (OWI), urged the music industry to produce "freedom songs" with lots of flag-waving. And, indeed, immediately after Pearl Harbor, according to the trade journal *Variety,* "writers kept rushing into publishers' offices with songs inspired by the event." With a few exceptions, however, the results were less than memorable. Songs like "Goodbye Momma, I'm Off to Yokohama," "They're Going to Be Playing Taps on the Japs," "Oh, You Little Son of an Oriental," "Slap the Jap Right off the Map," "To Be Specific, It's Our Pacific," "We're Gonna Find a Fella Who Is Yeller and Beat Him Red, White, and Blue," "When Those Little Yellow Bellies Meet the Cohens and the Kelleys," "Let's Put the Axe to the Axis," and "Let's Knock the Hit out of Hitler" for the most part stirred little passion. As early as October 1942, the head of the OWI's Music Committee complained that Tin Pan Alley was not doing as well as it should. "We want to give Hitler a more audible razzing than we've been doing," he urged, but Tin Pan Alley was settling for "just love songs . . . 'boy meets girl stuff.'"[10]

In fact, however, Americans in and out of uniform overwhelmingly preferred sentimental tunes about home, families, and girl- and boyfriends— not rip-roaring marching music. According to *Billboard* magazine, soldiers "don't want war songs . . . [in a] foxhole or training course—they like the same tunes" that they enjoyed before the war. On the home front as well, crooners such as Bing Crosby were particularly popular. By 1943, "loneliness songs" were increasingly in demand. Soft ballads such as "Don't Get around Much Anymore," "Saturday Night Is the Loneliest Night of the Week," "I Don't Want to Walk without You," and "I'll Walk Alone (Because to Tell You the Truth I Am Lonely)" expressed a growing sense of frustration with wartime sacrifice and separation. Significantly, the renowned "White Christmas" did not mention the war at all. Irving Berlin wrote the song, which Bing Crosby recorded in 1942 for Decca. Crosby's melancholy rendering of Christmases "just like the ones I used to know" tapped soldiers' homesickness as well as domestic longings for a mythical past. "White Christmas" became not only a kind of World War II anthem but arguably the most popular song ever in the United States. Crosby's 1942 version alone would sell over 31 million copies, reaching the hit parade nineteen times over the next twenty years.[11]

Ultimately, popular culture did less to evoke a martial spirit among citizens than it did to provide a much-needed diversion from wartime suffering and fear. Within two months of the Pearl Harbor attack, *Variety* observed that "an amusement rash" afflicted a public that desperately sought to escape grim realities. Hence, when an OWI official fretted in 1945 that Hollywood focused too much on entertainment when its main responsibility was to educate the public about the war, the industry replied that empty theater seats were of little use to anyone. "Film with a purpose must pass the same test that the escapist film easily passes," wrote the head of the Motion Picture Academy, Walter Wanger. "Theater-goers must want to see the picture." Similarly, radio advertisers were reluctant to stress martial themes. As the popular composer Frank Loesser observed, women listening to the radio soap operas did not want constant reminders of the war. "If you want to sell a housewife Jell-O," he advised, you don't tell her: "Madam, it is highly probable that your son is coming home a basket case, or at least totally blind, but cheer up, tonight choose one of the six delicious flavors and be happy with America's finest dessert."[12]

Popular culture entrepreneurs had to strike a delicate balance between wartime messages and entertainment. *Life* magazine achieved that balance so well that its circulation soared from 2.86 million in 1940 to 5.45 million in 1948. With twenty-one photographers in various combat zones, *Life* documented the war with special effect. But alongside its treatment of the war were stories about show business and everyday occurrences that illustrated those things that the magazine's publisher Henry Luce believed were particularly American, among them the spirit of cooperation and the desire to be free, independent, and self-reliant. During the war, *Life* moved closer to what Luce envisioned as its special role in unifying and defining the United States. "Although we did not plan *Life* as a war magazine," he said later, "that's the way it turned out to be." A weary postal worker in

Baltimore looked on *Life* as "the great backbreaker. . . . Every Baltimorean with a mailbox seemed to subscribe."[13]

World War II may have been *"made* for *Life,"* as one writer asserted, but even amusements that seemed to have little apparent connection to the conflict supposedly had an important role to play. In a May 1942 radio statement, the coach of the Chicago Cardinals professional football team lambasted "the bleeding hearts" who had criticized the game "because it involves body contact and it teaches violence." With the advent of the war, critics would, he believed, finally appreciate what the sport did to toughen up young men physically and mentally. "Football is the No. 1 medium for attuning a man to body contact and physical shock. It teaches that after all there isn't anything so terrifying about a punch in the puss." Whether or not fans believed that football was boosting America's defense by teaching toughness, in 1943 they turned out in sufficient numbers to give the National Football League its second-best financial season ever; attendance that year averaged over twenty-five thousand per game, up by around forty-five hundred over 1942. Finding players who were not in the armed forces was a problem, but the league prevailed by luring former athletes, such as Bronco Nagurski, out of retirement. "We held tryouts and signed up anybody who could run around the field twice," joked one coach. In 1943, the Philadelphia Eagles and the Pittsburgh Steelers combined temporarily into the "Pittsadelphia Steagles"; the next year, the Steelers merged with the Chicago Cardinals as the Card-Pitts ("Carpets").[14]

Baseball, however, persisted as the nation's most popular sport, in no small way because it especially seemed to reaffirm American values. According to the *Sporting News,* major-league baseball helped distinguish Americans from the treacherous Japanese. "Japan never was converted to baseball," proclaimed the magazine. "No nation . . . could have committed the vicious, infamous deed of . . . December 7, 1941, if the spirit of the game ever had penetrated their yellow hides." A Japanese battle cry, "Fuck Babe Ruth," only confirmed that wisdom.[15]

In early 1942, when the worried baseball commissioner, Judge Landis, asked Franklin Roosevelt whether baseball should disband during the war, the president demurred. "I honestly feel," Roosevelt replied, "that it would be best for the country to keep baseball going." Wartime employees, who would be working long hours, "ought to have a chance for recreation and for taking their minds off their work more than before." Granted, the quality of major-league baseball dropped. With more than two-thirds of the fifty-seven hundred major- and minor-league players—including stars such as Hank Greenberg and Joe DiMaggio—in the military, baseball was now in the hands of "the remnants, the retreads, the too young and too old," as one writer said. Players ranged in age from sixteen to forty-five and included even a one-armed outfielder.[16]

Because of the loss of players, in 1943 the Chicago Cubs owner, Phillip K. Wrigley, launched the All-American Girls Professional Baseball League (AAGPBL). Starting out with four teams (such as the Rockford, Illinois, Peaches), the league soon included eight, all in the Midwest, and all regularly drawing several thousand spectators. Initially more like fast-pitch softball, with underhand pitching, the all-girl version of the game increasingly resembled regular baseball. According to one player, the league "wanted the girls to conduct themselves as ladies at all times, but to play like men." The willingness to let them "play like men" reflected a wartime setting in which millions of women took jobs on factory lines to assemble weapons and other military equipment. Patriotism also marked the AAGPBL, the players lining up in a "V for victory" formation before each game for the national anthem. During the war, the AAGPBL—like baseball generally—thus provided chances to wave the flag and also find temporary respite from embattled times.[17]

Radio perhaps offered the best example of popular culture's blending of wartime service and entertainment. With radio sets in 90 percent of American homes, and with listeners tuning in daily for an average of three to four hours, radio affected more everyday lives than did any other medium. Indeed, a *Fortune* survey in 1939 revealed that only 14 percent of respondents believed that they could live without radios, as compared to 80 percent who were willing to give up movies; by 1945, the percentages were 11 and 84, respectively. Although far more Americans got their news from the radio than from other sources, the medium's main fare included soap operas, comedy shows, and music. Government arguments for more noncommercial, public affairs kinds of programs ultimately proved futile.[18]

"Radio is primarily an entertainment medium," insisted Douglas Meservey, a former executive at CBS and NBC who was now with the government. According to Meservey, the challenge was "to make the best possible use of radio for the war effort while still maintaining the tremendous audience which [made] the medium so valuable." To meet that challenge, in early 1942 government officials, network executives, and advertisers created the Network Allocation Plan. The plan included guidelines regarding how sponsored shows might best help the war effort. In the early months of the war, government "idealists" with strong New Deal sympathies sought to elevate radio's educational role. But, by 1943, the dominant decisionmakers were from private industry. These individuals, including people such as the former Coca-Cola vice president Price Gilbert, preferred commercialized, privatized strategies that favored program sponsors. The disappointed New Dealers resented this "Madison Avenue" strategy of tying patriotism to products. A poem summed up their frustrations: "Try this delicious health-building War! / Buy *all* you need—then buy some more! / *Never mind what we're fighting for! / Customers, customers, come and buy! / A short girdle does not bind the thigh. / We're the Salesmen of the OWI.*"[19]

This mixture of patriotism and profits nevertheless suffused entertainment. On the one hand, popular culture helped the war effort by boosting morale and providing outlets for public anxieties and nationalism. On the other hand, it ultimately prospered in the booming war economy, which finally ended the Great Depression. In early 1940, around 8 million Americans were still unemployed. Over the next few years, the war created some 17 million new jobs. With large numbers of men in the military and defense plants in desperate need of employees, the government urged women to take nontraditional jobs such as welding and construction. By mid-1943, women, many of them married, constituted almost one-third of the workforce. Incomes were growing, but many consumer items were either unavailable or rationed because of military needs. A good deal of spending money was, therefore, available for amusement. "Everybody had money and everybody was looking around for entertainment," as the baseball pitcher Satchel Paige recalled.[20]

Popular culture as a whole thus posted "stratospheric earnings," as *Variety* observed at the end of 1944. Radio's advertising income almost doubled. Major-league baseball, despite an early slump, rebounded; by 1944, attendance was growing and reached a record 10.8 million in 1945. Comic-book publishers distributed 125 titles monthly with total sales climbing from around 15 million in early 1942 to 25 million by the end of 1943. Coney Island thrived once again. In 1943, a record 46 million visitors crowded its amusement parks, which included Hit-the-Axis games and sold war bonds. For military personnel on leave, the legendary Coney was as essential to see as were the Statue of Liberty and the Empire State Building. Circuses also did well. Ringling Brothers combined "Let Freedom Ring" spectacles with elephant ballets, while others—such as the Clyde Beatty–Wallace Brothers Circus—expanded or opened. And, after experiencing the Depression's doldrums and a terrible first year of the war (when at least fifty-four plays failed), New York City's playhouses rebounded significantly, with Broadway's 1944–45 season becoming its most prosperous to date.[21]

The music industry flourished, too. Although fewer dance bands toured the country, booking demands and increased fees meant that business was very good overall. Record sales were high, despite cutbacks because of limited shellac supplies until mid-1944, rescuing several large companies that the Depression had almost bankrupted. By 1945, record sales climbed to $109 million, far above the $5.5 million during the Depression's low point. Before the war, a song that sold over 200,000 copies was a hit; during the war, songs that sold a million copies were not unusual. "A year of years" was how *Variety* described the music industry's rising fortunes in 1945. By then, the RCA, Victor, and Decca companies were each churning out 100 million records annually.[22]

Hollywood too had much to applaud. Profits for the largest eight studios (which controlled about 95 percent of the market) soared from some $20 million in 1940 to $60 million annually from 1943 through 1945. Gross box-office receipts rose steadily throughout the war via higher ticket prices and increased admissions. Because of surging attendance, studios routinely needed only twelve weeks in a film's first run to cover production costs.[23]

World War II did more for popular culture than increase profits, however. By uprooting millions of citizens for military service or defense jobs, and by merging classes, genders, and races in new ways, the long, bloody conflict opened up areas of entertainment. As geographic boundaries blurred, sights and sounds from society's margins eased into the mainstream. White migrants from the rural South, for example, exposed diverse groups in the North and West to country music. By 1944, according to *Billboard* magazine, perhaps as many as 40 million Americans listened to some six hundred regular country radio shows.[24]

Similarly, urban nightlife broadened. Although nightclubs had bounced back following Prohibition's repeal in 1933, the war enhanced their social role. At places such as New York City's Stage Door Canteen, tens of thousands of military personnel from all over the country experienced—free of charge—nightclub festivities in exciting new ways. Entertainment celebrities such as Marlene Dietrich often served as hosts, providing music, dancing with soldiers, and appearing in skits.[25]

But, as a provider of nightlife amusements, Las Vegas particularly benefited from wartime developments. Entering the 1930s, Las Vegas had been only the fourth-largest community in Nevada, a state with fewer than 100,000 residents. In 1931, as the Depression settled in across the nation, Nevada legislators had sought to attract outside money by reducing the waiting period for divorces to six weeks and legalizing gambling, which Progressive Era reformers had outlawed. Additional profits came during the mid-1930s when construction workers at Boulder Dam, some twenty-five miles away, poured into the bars and casinos along Las Vegas's two-block downtown area. With the dam's completion, however, the town slipped into little more than "a gritty, wind-whipped crossroads of faded whorehouses and honky-tonks with stuttering neon," as two students of the city later wrote.[26]

World War II revitalized Las Vegas. For one thing, thousands of military people, either in transit or located at various army installations in the area, flooded the town in search of good times. For another thing, the war provided the mobster Meyer Lansky with opportunities to turn Las Vegas into a gambler's paradise. Born in Poland in 1902 as Maier Suchowljansky, Lansky had grown up in poverty on New York City's tough Lower East Side before enriching himself through strategies that combined racketeering with legal businesses. By the 1940s, he saw huge potential in Las Vegas, despite its distance from population centers. "Vegas was a horrible place," he remembered, but even its remoteness could be a bonanza: "Once you got tourists there, after they had eaten and drunk all they could, there was only one thing left—to go gambling." Over the next few years, he established himself as the city's dominant force by typically working behind the scenes. "He's got a piece of every joint in Vegas," complained one gangster. World War II helped Lansky work out an accommodation with law enforcement authorities. In order to help quell disorder on New York City's docks and ease difficult situations abroad, the federal government found an ally in organized crime. The Office of Strategic Service's top secret "Operation Underworld" relied on Lansky and other mobsters to control unions and protect the Manhattan waterfront. The government also used its U.S. mob contacts to secure Mafia aid in Sicily for the 1943 invasion. By assisting the government, Lansky acquired virtual immunity from agencies such as the Federal Bureau of Investigation and began to build Las Vegas into a gambling and mob center. There were no lucky gamblers in his opinion, only "winners and losers": "The winners are those who control the game . . . all the rest are suckers."[27]

By the end of World War II, Lansky's build-it-and-they-will-come scheme started turning Las Vegas into an amusement empire. Its murky underworld arrangements were in place. "We don't run for office," said Lansky's partner, Benjamin "Bugsy" Siegel. "We own politicians." The city also tapped the public desire for risky but harmless fun, combining hints of danger with dreams of instant wealth—the "pathology of hope," as one writer has described it.[28]

That pathology of hope fed on the larger wartime glorification of the United States as a place of opportunity, fresh starts, freedom, and democracy. Popular culture endlessly reaffirmed those themes by portraying the nation as a melting pot that honored its common citizens. Before the war, for instance, the media had typically referred to the baseball star Hank Greenberg as the "Jewish first-baseman." But, after Greenberg volunteered for combat in the air force, he became "Captain Henry," an embodiment of "the American way of life."[29]

Other notable portraits of a pluralistic America where dedicated, God-fearing people earned respect and honor were evident in *The Fighting Sullivans* (Lloyd Bacon, 1944), a film salute to five Irish American brothers who died together when their ship went down fighting the Japanese, and

"The House I Live In," an award-winning song from the sensational young singer Frank Sinatra. The real-life Sullivans had grown up in a devout Catholic family in Waterloo, Iowa. The film treatment of their lives was tearfully sentimental. It emphasized that the brothers, proud of their familial and American roots, always stuck together. One of the movie's plot devices showed the youngest brother on several occasions running to catch up with his bigger siblings, even when they were headed for a fight with other neighborhood kids. "Hey," he would holler, "wait for me." As children, the Sullivans liked to climb the railroad station's water tower so that they could wave to their father, a train conductor. At the end of the movie, after the parents have learned that all their sons have died on the same ship, the father sadly and nostalgically remembers how his boys used to wave at him when his train pulled out of town. As the song "Anchors Away" swelled from the movie's sound track, the camera shifted upward, showing four of the uniformed brothers marching through the clouds. They look backward—and then, as always, wait for their youngest sibling to catch up with them.

Sinatra's "The House I Live In" similarly hailed a country that welcomed people from all races and religions, people who, in turn, were willing to sacrifice themselves for their country. As Sinatra said of his own father, an Italian immigrant: "He wasn't born here, rest his soul, but he made damn sure that I was." In the early months of World War II, Benny Goodman could still ask: "Who the hell is Frank Sinatra?" He was, in fact, a skinny young man from the working-class neighborhoods of Hoboken, New Jersey (a "sewer," as he later described the environment). After attending high school for only forty-seven days, he dropped out. Although he could not read music, he decided, after watching Bing Crosby, that he would be a singer, too. Fiercely ambitious, with a sexy, emotion-filled voice that conveyed a heartfelt passion, Sinatra became a musical force during the war. By late 1943, when he performed in a New York theater, it took 450 police to manage thirty thousand screaming teenagers, most of them female. "Whatever he stirred beneath our barely budding breasts, it wasn't motherly," recalled one such fan. The media called him "Swoonatra." His popularity, they said, constituted "Sinatrauma." Although his songs often expressed an aching loneliness, "The House I Live In" eloquently depicted a nation that was tolerant and inclusive. Moreover, he believed passionately in those ideals. When race riots broke out in New York City's Harlem in 1943, he spoke in two high schools, exhorting the youngsters to be colorblind. When white students in Gary, Indiana, refused to attend classes with African Americans, Sinatra addressed them in the school auditorium and sang "The House I Live In." In early 1945, Hollywood's short film *The House I Live In* won a special Academy Award. The movie showed Sinatra taking a recording break in the alley, where he stopped a gang of kids from beating up on a Jewish boy. After telling the youngsters that racial and religious differences "make no difference except to a Nazi or somebody who's stupid," he crooned the title song, extolling a nation of common citizens—the grocer, the butcher, or the person at "the little corner newsstand"—who get along with each other.[30]

A number of comic books echoed such pleas for social justice. In a 1944 example, the superhero Green Lantern replied angrily to a woman who objected to some children singing Christmas songs because "they ain't all real white 100% Americans! Their color is wrong and their religion is wrong and most of them is foreigners anyway!" After Green Lantern lectured the woman that, "when you hate a man for his race, creed, or color, you're just a sucker for those who hate America!" the woman apologized for being "a fool." Similarly, the Justice Society, another group of heroes who fight for truth and right, emphasized: "The United States is a great melting pot into which other races are poured—a pot which converts all of us into one big nation!" America's many ethnic groups, together, would win the war: "You can't beat that combination Adolf," one character warns Hitler. "It's too strong!"[31]

The heavyweight boxing champion Joe Louis also symbolized a racially diverse nation full of opportunity, and the government used him to ease growing racial tensions and conflict. As a private in the U.S. Army, he entertained the troops with almost one hundred exhibition matches. "Ain't fighting for nothing," he said, regarding his diminished salary as a member of the armed forces. "I'm fighting for my country." Privately, he opposed segregation. He emphasized that his boxing tour was "not for any one race group" and quietly intervened to help desegregate service athletic teams on army bases. But, in 1942, it was Private Joe Louis, a fighting African American patriot who opposed external enemies, who loomed from a famous government poster. In uniform, and with a bayoneted rifle pointing outward, he guaranteed that the United States would win the war because "we're on God's side."[32]

This vision of the United States as a special country of common, unified citizens—"Americans all"—suffused popular culture. *The Fighting Sullivans* lauded not only the assimilation of Catholics into society but also a way of life that rested on ordinary working-class families. In World War II movies, working-class characters were typically model citizens—like the Sullivans or Joe Louis, who appeared in the 1943 Warner Brothers/Michael Curtiz version of the War Department's extremely popular Broadway musical revue *This Is the Army*. The radio announcer Norman Corwin described the idealized American, particularly the everyday soldier, as well as anyone: "Take a bow GI. Take a bow little guy. The superman of tomorrow lies at the feet of you common men this afternoon." Or, as another show emphasized: "Hitler ain't fightin' kings and queens, no more. We're the only ones who can win it . . . the little people, all dressed up in our ha-loes and gas masks."[33]

Such egalitarian, liberating messages reinforced working-class perspec-tives that had long been central to popular culture. Even in trying circum-stances, plain folk felt the pull of deeply rooted ideals, ideals that wartime propaganda infused with new energy. Chester Himes, an African American novelist from Ohio, encountered ugly racism when he worked in California's defense plants. "Los Angeles hurt me racially as much as any city I have ever known," he recalled. Yet Himes could not ignore the idealism of the war-time messages. One of his later fictional characters summed up the point well: "I'd learned the same jive the white folks had learned. All that stuff about liberty and justice and equality. . . . That was the hell of it; the white folks had drummed more into me than they'd been able to scare out."[34]

As with Himes, the wartime experiences of many future entertainers ensured that much of popular culture would not soon lose touch with working-class fears, dreams, and values. The country singer Hank Williams was only one of many examples. A high school dropout who grew up in the crushing poverty of rural Alabama, Williams failed a medical exam when he tried to enlist in the military. During the war, he honed his working-class sympathies while working as a shopfitter's helper and welder in Mobile's shipyards and singing in seedy taverns. After the war, his songs continued to articulate the dreams and frustrations of struggling people. "This guy is hurting," thought the bluesman B. B. King, when he heard Williams singing over the radio. "He's hurting from inside." Even as his career soared, Williams remained suspicious of rich individuals. He once rejected a Montgomery banker's dinner invitation because, as he put it: "When I was starving in this town, the son of a bitch wouldn't buy me a hamburger. Now there's nothing too good for me. What's the matter, ain't I the same guy?"[35]

Although such populist leanings radiated throughout popular cul-ture, World War II entertainment also included contrasting messages and trends. Mass magazines, advertisements, and films lauded common citi-zens, but the words and images favored particular kinds of Americans— white, rural, Protestant, and male. Portraits of soldiers in popular journals such as the *Saturday Evening Post* and *Life,* and in books such as the war correspondent Bill Mauldin's *Up Front* (1944), typically depicted village settings and products. A soldier who died "chasing a bunch of Japs" in the Pacific "was a Wisconsin boy," reported one magazine. "He loved the blue lakes of Wisconsin, the cool winds, the bright farmlands." There was also the soldier who "was reared on the old Slagle farm, where generations of Slagles, country boys and proud of it, had been reared." The *Saturday Evening Post* described an officer who once "had a paper route" and "would stop and chat with old ladies and run to the store for them." When another soldier was growing up, he "had some fun on the side . . . swimming, hunting, fishing, tennis and golf." General Dwight Eisenhower as a youth in rural Kansas "had an orchard, a large garden, a cow and a horse, and always a dog." The *Saturday Evening Post* described America's soldiers as "kids who were in filling stations and stores, at soda fountains and on farms, kids from high school and maybe college, who went off to war in the flush of youth." During a time of enormous wartime stress and crisis, the dominant culture turned to images that were reassuring and familiar: "Truth became selective."[36]

As a result, recalled the cultural commentator Peter Schrag, the idealized American who emerged from the war was "part Leather-stocking, part Teddy Roosevelt, part John Wayne, with a little Ben Franklin thrown in for good measure." He was "red white and blue, free white and twenty-one, . . . didn't fire until he saw the whites of their eyes, damned the torpedoes, met the enemy (and it wasn't us), couldn't tell a lie, and regretted that he had but one life to give for his country." That perception of the 100 percent American exerted enormous force. "Our man. His country," according to Schrag. "We all wanted to learn the style, the proper accent." A "controlled assimilation"—rather than genuine pluralism—was the implicit goal. In movies, the multicultural platoon typically included representatives from various groups—Anglo-Protestants, Irish Catholics, and Jewish and Italian new immigrants. Few blacks or Asians were included. But, whatever the minority group, the assumption was that its members should look to Anglo-Saxon heroes as models. If ethnic actors such as William Bendix, Richard Conte, and Anthony Quinn died onscreen, they did so for a good cause. "If that boy was too Italian," Schrag remembered, "he might be a little suspect; but a good leg wound would Americanize him."[37]

Such potent cultural impulses helped circumscribe expressions of ethnicity, race, and gender. In that context, the Depression-era swing music of a Benny Goodman gave way to Glenn Miller's softened, whitened version of jazz. Unlike most jazz greats, Miller was a product of small-town settings in Iowa and Colorado and attended college for two years. His mother was a devout prohibitionist who headed a chapter of the Women's Christian Temperance Union. In the 1930s, Miller moved to New York City and formed a successful swing orchestra. His main goal, he told the critic John Hammond, was to make money. In 1942, Miller enlisted in the military, turning his Army Air Force Band into a national favorite. "The majority of people like to hear pretty tunes," he said. Because "none of the big bands played pretty tunes," he was determined to tone down the freewheeling, Goodman-style music, making it more melodic, harmonious, gentle, and romantic. The lyrics to his popular "Juke Box Saturday Night" neatly summed up his musical formula: "Mixin' hot licks with vanilla." His tight arrangements left no room for improvisation; indeed, even his musicians' dress had to be "just right." His resistance to hiring African Americans meshed with the military's opposition to integrated service bands. Miller was also reluctant to employ Italians and Jews, whom he considered "troublemakers."[38]

Miller's music squared with the growing public interest in home and sentimentality that increasingly characterized the ballads of a Crosby, a Sinatra, or the Andrews Sisters. When some critics accused Miller of playing bland and unadventurous music, one soldier responded that, while "it doesn't sound like . . . the Apollo midnight show" in Harlem, "the average G.I." disliked "weird harmonies" and preferred cheerful music laced with memories of home and "days when we were all happy." Images of harmonious, white village neighborhoods suffused Miller's tunes. The famed bandleader's disappearance in a plane over the English Channel in late 1944 added to his mystique. Certainly, his popularity suggested that the hard-charging, biracial swing music of the 1930s was losing favor. "Perhaps," according to the historian Burton Peretti, "the white majority once again craved dreamy, nostalgic evocations of an allegedly safer and simpler time, and saw music and dance no longer as an expression of urban culture but as a vehicle for escapism."[39]

Similarly, as women streamed into defense jobs, the extremely popular "pinup girls" signaled that traditional beauty standards and gender roles were safe. Unlike in World War I, when the military disparaged "naughty postcards" from France, the government promoted the pinup. Official military magazines such as *Yank* contained photographs of swimsuited entertainment stars in order to assure soldiers that they were fighting for real people who personified an American way of life.[40]

But, significantly, the most popular pinups exuded as much innocence as eroticism. And they overwhelmingly associated whiteness with beauty, as Rita Hayworth's visual transformation showed. Born as Margaret Cansino, Hayworth came from a Spanish family and, in her first movies, typically played Latin American or darkly sexy characters. Her emergence as a pinup reflected some notable makeovers: she changed her name to the rural-sounding Hayworth, died her hair strawberry blonde, underwent plastic surgery to make her nose thinner, and shed any trace of a Spanish accent. In one pinup photograph, her red, white, and blue swimsuit attested further to her "American" look. The actress June Allyson—supposedly "America's sweetheart" and the "girl the soldiers most want to marry"— was another example of the ideal woman; blond, "girlish," fun, and "compulsively clean," according to various descriptions, she reportedly wanted only to marry and have children.[41]

Betty Grable, named by Armed Forces Radio "America's ideal girl," was the most popular pinup. No other celebrity received more soldiers' fan mail. And no woman drew a higher salary. Less sultry than Hayworth, Grable reportedly became a kind of representative woman, an acceptable fantasy surrogate for wives and sweethearts. As one soldier told her, he and others in combat would "be exhausted, frightened, confused" until "suddenly someone would pull your picture out of his wallet. Or we'd see a decal of you on a plane and then we'd *know* what we were fighting for." Grable's "straight-arrow" appearance, "her peach-cheeked, pearl blond good looks," and her demeanor gave her appeal a kind of safeness. Even her famous legs, according to *Life* magazine, were "great American average legs." Grable concurred, claiming that "girls see me in a picture and feel I could be one of them." Moreover, her advice to women was that they should try to please men: "Remember to follow their lead, from dancing to conversation. Talk about *them*." Grable was, thus, a nonthreatening female—"an icon of good femininity," as one scholar has written.[42]

Nor did female athletes in the AAGPBL jeopardize good femininity. Playing for teams with nicknames such as "Slapsie Maxie's Curvaceous Cuties," they were clearly not impinging on male turf. *Newsweek* referred to them as "Babette Ruths." According to a league handbook: "*The more feminine the appearance of the performer, the more dramatic the performance.*" Their uniforms included short skirts, and their equipment contained beauty kits. In 1943 and 1944, the league mandated charm-school lessons so that the women would learn how to look, dress, and act as traditionally feminine as possible. Off the field, accompanied by chaperones, they posed awkwardly in high heels and dresses for newsreels and photographs.[43]

Such reassuring, rather than threatening, images and messages characterized wartime entertainment as a whole. In the process of reaffirming the American way of life, movies and other amusements said little about social inequality or needs. Instead, the emphasis was on minimizing differences while championing unity, loyalty, and teamwork. The messages of wartime films thus began to shift from those of the Great Depression. Movies in the 1930s had often reflected what the historian Lary May has described as a kind of "working-class Americanism"—a perspective that sympathized with common citizens who stood up against large institutions, especially corporations. Certainly, those Depression-era films had stressed traditional values and the nation's bedrock strengths. But, during the war, in May's words, "the basis of authority was realigned from the grassroots to the official institutions and patriotic causes." A significant result was that wartime movie narratives played down class differences and were friendlier to big business, which was now an essential part of the "arsenal of democracy." Films muted class and ethnic identities as well as a need for reforms. In *Keeper of the Flame* (George Cukor, 1942), for instance, the protagonist learned that his populist hero, who attacked big business, was nothing less than a Nazi agent. Whereas, during the Depression, film protagonists were inclined to shift their sympathies from the rich to the lower class or other outsiders, during World War II a reversal was under way: 30 percent of "conversion movies," according to May, "dramatized characters shedding their earlier oppositional class identity in favor of loyalty to official institutions" and moving "cultural authority from the bottom to the top of society."[44]

The increasingly favorable tilt toward big business and away from New Deal–era reform themes marked radio and advertising as well. Corporate sponsors and advertisers used commercial radio to enhance their images, tout products, and promote a privatized ideology of consumerism—in sum, "to sell free enterprise." Business had been "in the doghouse for a decade or more," as the president of the American Association of Advertising Agencies lamented in 1944. "Always on the defensive, we have been afraid of every tin horn bureaucrat in Washington." But the war offered an opportunity to fight back, humanizing the reputation of corporate America. According to an executive at the giant J. Walter Thompson advertising agency, it was now possible "to regain for business the leadership of our economy." Advertisers thus went to great lengths to tie their products to wartime needs and sacrifices. The federal government helped. Under the revised tax code of May 1942, businesses could deduct as much as 80 percent of advertising costs as long as the ads boosted defense needs. General Motors thus claimed: "Victory Is Our Business." Pennsylvania Oil supposedly would "Care for Your Car for Your Country." "Don't be a public enemy!" warned Kleenex tissues. "Be patriotic and smother sneezes with Kleenex to help keep colds from spreading to war workers."[45]

Radio especially reflected these advertising pitches. Smith Brothers cough drops sponsored news bulletins. Jack Benny's comedy show audiences heard his familiar greeting, "Jell-O" (in reference to the sponsor), and then learned that he had contributed his beloved 1924 Maxwell automobile to the War Salvage Drive. The Bob Hope show advised workers to "gargle with Pepsodent Antiseptic regularly" so that they would not fall ill and lose crucial time on the job. A poll indicated, moreover, that almost two-thirds of listeners either liked or did not object to radio advertising. "I might fuss about ads on the radio," said one woman, "but truthfully I would be lost without them."[46]

By the time World War II ended in August 1945, a political consensus was firmly in place, and mass entertainment had done much to construct it. Over the next few years, that consensus strengthened as yet another international conflict emerged, this one involving the threat of Soviet Russia and the terror of possible nuclear war. Against that frightening backdrop, increasingly homogenized and centralized aspects of popular culture constructed the equivalent of a master narrative in which a closely knit, classless, village-oriented, white America grappled with dramatic challenges at home and abroad.[47]

Popular culture responded to and influenced several developments that accelerated during and right after World War II: the migration of African Americans to cities outside the South; the corresponding "white flight" to the emerging suburbs; and the "baby boom." The movement north and west of Southern blacks already constituted one of the nation's most significant demographic shifts, but, during the 1940s and 1950s, it intensified. One result was a "blackening" inner core of many cities and a corresponding growth of "vanilla suburbs." Federal agencies facilitated this trend via discriminatory policies concerning such things as racially sensitive housing loans and property evaluations. During the 1950s, Chicago's black population jumped by 65 percent, while its white population fell by 13 percent. Brooklyn lost 476,094 white residents while gaining 93,091 who were nonwhite. Cities such as Detroit soon claimed black majorities. Many whites relocated to the burgeoning suburbs, taking advantage of newly constructed freeways and shopping malls. The nation's almost all-white suburban population rocketed in the 1950s at ten times the central cities' rate. Between 1950 and 1970, it mushroomed from 35.1 to 75.6 million. Southern California's Orange County suburbs exploded from 216,224 in 1950 to 703,925 in 1960; by 1970, the number of residents approached 1.5 million.[48]

Children accounted significantly for those numbers. In the two decades following World War II, the baby boom resulted in 80 million births, almost 40 percent of the U.S. population. In contrast, the previous generation consisted of only 30 million births. Birth rates started rising in 1942 but soared to a record rate in 1946, jumping 20 percent in one year. As families reunited after the war, and as new couples opted to build their households quickly, the number of children grew rapidly. In 1957, the peak of the boom, one baby was born every seven seconds on average. Some suburban housing developments boasted that producing children was their "greatest industry." Postwar prosperity encouraged the spiraling birth rate and also provided unprecedented amounts of money for a child-centered market that, by 1959, included over 50 million youngsters under age fourteen.[49]

These notable demographic transformations had a seismic effect on American society, including popular culture. Toy manufacturers and other amusement businesses scrambled eagerly to cash in on the surging baby-boomer market. Advertisements, movies, and the new medium of television reinforced images of disorderly, dangerous central cities as opposed to tranquil, family-oriented suburbs. And transplanted as well as new entertainment venues attested to the uneasiness of many whites regarding the changing racial composition of cities. In 1975, the singer George Clinton's hit "Chocolate City" observed: "There's a lot of chocolate cities around. We've got Newark, we've got Gary." But, to many whites in postwar America, Clinton's message symbolized a racial threat, not a reaching out or a proud statement about African Americans' "piece of the rock": "Movin' in and on ya, gainin' on ya! Can't you feel my breath, heh . . . All up around your neck, heh heh." Race was, thus, a factor in the construction of suburban shopping malls and new amusement parks in postwar America.[50]

The transformation of cities also helped explain why—for the first time in half a century—several major-league baseball teams relocated. Granted, the attraction of more lucrative markets was central to the moves. Moreover, the teams left cities that had other major-league franchises. In the 1950s, the Boston Braves moved to Milwaukee, the St. Louis Browns to Baltimore, the Philadelphia Athletics to Kansas City, the New York Giants to San Francisco, and the Brooklyn Dodgers to Los Angeles. When in 1953 the Braves drew as many fans in their first nine games in Milwaukee as in the entire previous season in Boston, they demonstrated the benefits of a new location. Moreover, as Los Angeles's Downtown Businessmen's Association was quick to observe of Milwaukee's success: "Overnight, big league baseball transformed a dull Midwestern city into blazing, dancing, fairy tale headlines." The association and other boosters believed that the same thing could happen in Los Angeles. The city's Merchants and Manufacturers Association predicted that tourists would flock to Los Angeles to see the Dodgers, leaving "a great deal of cash behind in the restaurants, night clubs, bars, hotels, gas stations, stores and in many other places." While team owners felt the tug of new opportunities, they were also anxious to flee declining neighborhoods. In Brooklyn, for example, a sportswriter complained about the "rough, tough bunch" that attended games at the aging Ebbets Field. As one white fan recalled: "When Blacks started coming to the game a lot of Whites stopped coming." He guessed that the Dodgers' owner, Walter O'Malley, had switched the team to Los Angeles for that reason: "Once [blacks] started to live in the neighborhood . . . it was time to move out." Meanwhile, in Los Angeles, local elites avidly courted O'Malley, reversing a 1951 plan to build public housing in the "blighted" Chavez Ravine area in favor of privatized, commercial development, which included Dodger Stadium. When someone wondered why people who objected to government subsidies for public housing could accept them regarding the stadium, O'Malley scoffed: "Son, look what the government did for the railroads to help develop the country." O'Malley and city officials subsequently marketed the safe, respectable, "wholesome" family nature of the Dodgers' games.[51]

The battle over the fate of Chavez Ravine also pointed to another development that severely affected American life after 1945: the onset of the Cold War. When Los Angeles's new mayor, Norris Poulson, attacked the city's Housing Authority for having endorsed low-rent "slum clearance" buildings for the Chavez Ravine area, he promised to oust the "communists" from that agency. His pledge tapped escalating fears that marked yet another Red scare in American history. The emerging Cold War would be instrumental in spreading a culture of conformity across society, from politics to entertainment.[52]

The emphasis on conformity paradoxically reflected a kind of "triumphalist despair." A sense of triumph grew from recent events that seemed to confirm the national success story. The nation's democratic and economic systems had weathered the Great Depression, and the United States had just won a righteous war against the Axis aggressors. The novelist John Updike summed up the exultant mood: "Where America is, there is freedom, and wherever America is not, madness rules with chains, darkness strangles millions. Beneath [America's] patient bombers, paradise is possible." In that spirit, *Fortune* magazine declared in September 1945 that the United States "has become the guardian and standard-bearer of western civilization." The publisher Henry Luce believed that "the American century" was at hand. Unlike vast sections of the world, the United States emerged from the war with its infrastructure intact and a booming economy. By the mid-1950s, a nation with only 6 percent of the world's population was producing more than half of the world's manufactured goods. Moreover, citizens viewed the United States as a model nation, notable for its workable government, its ideals of democracy and freedom, and its lack of ideological fanaticism. Most Americans saw no reason to "rock the boat" or dissent.[53]

But feelings of triumph did not necessarily preclude despair. Anxiety, as much as jubilation, helped mold the postwar consensus. Reality seemed to mock the script of Mervyn LeRoy's 1944 movie *Thirty Seconds over Tokyo,* in which an aviator told his buddies: "When [the war's] all over . . . just think . . . being able to settle down . . . and never be in doubt about anything." Despite the prevailing public desire to return to a mythical past— safe, known, and secure—the world was in frightening turmoil. Worldwide crises aside, Americans faced a variety of issues within their own nation, including race, sexuality, delinquency, and an expansive entertainment culture that raised old concerns about outside influences and alien lifestyles.[54]

These domestic issues posed serious challenges in themselves, but the developing Cold War made them seem even more frightening. The Second World War had barely ended when the nation's leaders identified the Soviet Union and communism as constituting a new threat: "Red fascism." Although the Soviets had been U.S. allies during the war, they now seemed to be the ideological equivalents of Nazis, constituting yet another totalitarian system with ambitions to control the world. In August 1949, when the Soviets exploded their own atomic bomb, the specter of nuclear war suddenly became all too real. To many worried Americans, Communists were also to blame for many unsettling changes at home. The young revivalist Billy Graham and the Federal Bureau of Investigation director, J. Edgar

Hoover, were among alarmists who warned that communism had targeted the American family. A grassroots anticommunism emerged to defend local morals, values, and lifestyles against amorphous yet pervasive threats.

One way in which to combat these dangers was to affirm traditional understandings of America's greatness and galvanize national pride. In the late 1940s and early 1950s, the nation staged myriad patriotic rallies, loyalty parades and pageants, Know Your America weeks, and I Am An American days. The emerging Cold War consensus heralded the United States as a counterpoint to the fanaticism that had fueled the Nazis and, now, the Communists. Unlike extreme ideologues, who tried to impose their will on others, Americans reputedly belonged to a free, classless, family-centered society whose politics sought agreement and compromise, not conflict. As the historian Daniel Boorstin wrote in his 1953 study *The Genius of American Politics*: "It is not surprising that we have no enthusiasm for plans to make society over. . . . Why should *we* make a five-year plan for ourselves when God seems to have had a thousand-year plan ready made for us?" Popular magazines such as *Life* hailed America's bounties and system of "people's capitalism," whereby everyone was an entrepreneur. "Our houses are all on one level, like our class structure," *House Beautiful* declared in 1953. By buying products, consumers not only prevented another depression but also demonstrated the economic vitality and appeal of the United States. "If America ever crashes, it will be in a two-tone convertible," quipped the banker Bernard Baruch. As a strategy for defeating communism, the president of Montgomery Ward thought that millions of mail-order catalogs would convert the Russians to capitalism. The sociologist David Riesman offered a variation of that plan: dropping nylon stockings by parachute into the Soviet Union.[55]

The contrasting moods of hope and fear that informed the postwar political consensus tapped roots that went deep in American history. Some hopeful Americans embraced the tradition of inclusion. Historically, such inclusion had been voluntary, tolerant, and visible in the nation's fabled melting pot of many ethnic and religious groups. But a contrasting, exclusive tradition also existed. Exclusion's strategies had included censorship, deportation, surveillance, and restricting rights to protect the nation against alien influences.[56]

Popular culture had long mirrored the tensions between these inclusionary and exclusionary tendencies, but Cold War fears regarding the threat of Soviet expansion and nuclear war raised the stakes. As had often been the case during national crises, much of the entertainment world responded by energizing the familiar narrative of American success. Optimistic examples abounded in movies and elsewhere of a nation with the inherent will and moral strength to survive the Communist threat. These positive images of the United States were so strong that taking issue with them was like trying, in the novelist Marge Piercy's words, "to stand up in a stadium during a football game and . . . read aloud a poem."[57]

The football analogy was apt in another sense as well: sports, in so many ways, had come to symbolize the American way of life. "Sports World," as the journalist Robert Lipsyte described it, was a special domain: "a sweaty Oz you'll never find in a geography book, . . . a place to hide that glows with that time of innocence when we believed that rules and boundaries were honored, that good triumphed over evil." Earl Warren, who became chief justice of the U.S. Supreme Court in 1953, claimed always to read the sports pages first when he opened the morning newspaper. "They record people's accomplishments," he said, not the failures that made up most of the rest of the news. Not surprisingly, against the backdrop of the emerging Cold War, the patriotic ambience of organized athletics was crucial in shaping the cultural consensus. "I never saw a ballplayer who was a communist," claimed the Idaho senator Herman Welker. From this perspective, athletics became a Cold War weapon. "I think Joe Stalin thinks he is going to show up our soft capitalistic Americans," laughed Bing Crosby in a 1952 Olympic telethon to raise money for U.S. athletes. "We've got to cut him down to size." In this context, the interweaving of athletics and America became even tighter, and sports' popularity reached new heights.[58]

"Men," the University of Oklahoma president George Cross told the school's board of regents in January 1946, "there is only one way to get this state back on track, and that's football, football, football." Quite deliberately, the university decided to build its football program in an effort to overcome the curse of the Great Depression. That curse took the form of a powerful set of lingering Depression-era perceptions that the state was little more than a dust bowl. During the 1930s, over a million down-and-out "Okies" had fled Oklahoma's droughts, dust storms, and broken dreams. "These god-damned Okies are thieves," said the unsympathetic observers in John Steinbeck's best-selling novel *The Grapes of Wrath* (1939). "They bring disease, they're filthy. . . . How would you like to have your sister go out with one of them?" Cross hoped to counter those prejudices. "The war is over and our state's upside down," he told the regents. "We must make sure that this does not translate into a downward spiral for this university." Football—so important in American life—would supposedly restore state pride, elevate the university's reputation, and show the rest of the nation that Oklahoma was synonymous with winning. Cross's strategy soon produced dividends. A series of successful seasons for the university football team culminated in a phenomenal forty-seven-game winning streak from 1953 until late 1957 that gained much national attention.[59]

By then, across the nation, college football's long-evolving spectacle and rituals had come to represent a wholesome, homegrown "autumn pastoral." "Football is everything America is," *Life* claimed in 1955: "fast, young, colorful, complex, efficient, aggressive." During the early Cold War, popular magazines touted football as embodying the best of American life. The sport provided a sense of cohesion and togetherness. It had carefully designated roles. Female cheerleaders, for instance, enlivened a gridiron script of football heroes and star-struck, "beautiful girls," as one song put it. "As outsiders," according to the football scholar Michael Oriard, "women played a key role in defining the center. The cheerleaders, majorettes, and adoring female fans . . . enhanced the masculinity of football players by contrast."[60]

By bolstering masculinity, football helped ease a vital set of Cold War concerns. Strident Cold Warriors fretted that some Americans were "soft" on communism, not tough enough to help a nation under siege. In the conservative *New York Daily News*, spineless males took the form of "Harvard lace cuff liberals" and "lace panty diplomats." Liberals also called for muscular leadership. In that setting, the press glamorized football coaches as makers of rugged, disciplined men. At the University of Kentucky, according to writers at the *Saturday Evening Post* and *Collier's,* Paul "Bear" Bryant's "tough-guy approach" had reportedly dispersed the team's pampered "horsey set." The *Post* applauded Georgia's Wallace Butts as an "exacting drillmaster" whose rigorous training camp drove half the players from the team.[61]

But it was professional football's image of violence and toughness that especially meshed with Cold War needs. In contrast to college football—whose undergraduates, alumni, marching bands, and Frank Merriwell–type heroes seemed oriented toward middle-class life—the postwar professional game allowed for "savagery on Sunday," as *Life* reported in 1955. Professionals could be hard-drinking roughnecks, "get[ting] in their licks with knees and elbows down under the pile." Here, said *Time,* was "a man's game." It was also a game with working-class allegiances. Unlike college football, with its bucolic campus settings, pro football was situated in Northern industrial cities. "This version of the game emerged on the soggy, snowbound fields of America's heavy-industrial belt, in gritty contests," according to one description. "Pro football players were . . . 'mud-rain-frost-and-wind boys,' playing out a gruntlike drama on a muddy swath of land under the frosted skies of smokestack America." Immediately after World War II, however, professional football's larger popularity was still in question. A low point occurred in 1952, when a Thanksgiving Day game attracted a mere three thousand fans, one-fifth the number who had attended a high school game that morning. But more prosperous times were on the way. Whereas the average attendance at a National Football

League game in 1950 was 25,000, by 1959 it was 43,600. Television coverage, along with that of popular magazines, certainly helped spread professional football's fan support, but the Cold War's emphasis on toughness was indispensable. Some players drew a literal connection. "In football, the Commies are on one side of this ball and we're on the other," the Green Bay Packers' Jim Ringo instructed Dave Meggyesy. "That's what this game is all about."[62]

The fact that football players—as well as athletes in sports such as baseball and basketball—came from a variety of ethnic backgrounds also fit well with Cold War celebrations of the United States as a land of opportunity, freedom, and democracy. By the postwar era, non-Anglo names dominated these sports, from Vic Janowicz, an all-American football player at Ohio State who was the son of poor Polish immigrants, to the baseball stars Joe and Dominick DiMaggio, sons of Sicilian immigrants. Rosters of city basketball players offered a miniature narrative of the melting pot in action. By 1950, City College of New York (CCNY)—with "sons of immigrants and grandsons of slaves," as the writer Stanley Cohen described them—epitomized basketball's ability to stir loyalty and pride in ethnically diverse neighborhoods. That year, when the top-ranked University of Kentucky's all-white team played CCNY in Madison Square Garden, the changing face of basketball was apparent. The legendary Kentucky coach Adolph Rupp had said that an African American would never play on his team. As the CCNY alumnus Marvin Kalb recalled, the heralded Kentucky players, tall and blond, "looked so all-American," and the coach was "Adolph Rupp—*Adolph* Rupp—shortly after World War II." When the Kentucky players refused to shake the hand of a black CCNY player at the beginning of the game, the New York school's Jewish coach, Nat Holman, seized the moment to motivate his team to a stunning victory.[63]

While the racial incident during the CCNY-Kentucky game pointed up critical fissures in the benign image that Americans hoped to project in the Cold War, the era nevertheless brought numerous signs of change. In 1946, when the Los Angeles Rams signed Kenny Washington and Woody Strode, the National Football League ended an informal twelve-year understanding among the owners that they would not hire black athletes. In Cleveland, future stars such as Bill Willis and Marion Motley helped integrate the sport. Opposing players, as Motley recalled, "found out that while they were calling us names, I was running by 'em and Willis was knocking the shit out of them. So they stopped calling us names and started trying to catch up with us." College football meanwhile experienced a number of years of embarrassing racial turmoil when Southern white schools refused, at least on their home fields, to play teams that had black players. Again, there were signs of change. In 1956, for example, the Georgia governor, Marvin Griffin, tried to block Georgia Tech from playing in the Sugar Bowl because the opposing Pittsburgh team included an African American. "The South stands at Armageddon," proclaimed Griffin. Many of the two thousand students who subsequently rioted, and many of the newspapers that objected to Griffin's rigidity, perhaps cared more about playing a football game than striking a blow for racial justice. Still, Georgia Tech ultimately played Pittsburgh, and the Atlanta press concluded optimistically: "In sports at least there is no place for racial discrimination or prejudice."[64]

During the postwar era, racial barriers were, indeed, slipping in sport.[65] In the early 1950s, professional basketball signed its first black players. In tennis, which had been the domain of country-club whites, Althea Gibson broke the color barrier, participating in 1950 in the previously all-white U.S. Lawn Tennis Association (USLTA). A Harlem product who had spent time in a home for troubled girls, Gibson became the decade's celebrated female athlete. In 1957, after she won her first Wimbledon title, New York City honored her with a ticker-tape parade, and the mayor awarded her the key to the city. But, as was so often the case in the early Cold War, these racial breakthroughs took on special ideological meaning. Not surprisingly, in 1955, the State Department sent Gibson on an extended international tour. And, in 1950, when a white former USLTA champion, Alice Marble, argued that the selection committee should allow Gibson to play in the national tournament at Forest Hills, she struck a patriotic note: "At this moment tennis is privileged to take its place among the pioneers for a true democracy."[66]

This same awareness of how sport reflected national ideals and values was most famously apparent in Jackie Robinson's debut in 1947 with the Brooklyn Dodgers, bringing down the decades-long segregation of major-league baseball. Robinson encountered numerous expressions of racism and hostility. Some Brooklyn whites resented him along with the black fans who came to Ebbets Field in growing numbers. "In the '40s the crowds had been all white," remembered one white person, "but by the mid-50s, after Jackie Robinson had been there a while, you go to a Sunday doubleheader, and the dominant smell in the ballpark was bagged fried chicken." Nevertheless, at the end of his first sensational year in the big leagues, polls showed him behind only Bing Crosby as the nation's most admired man. His story, as the writer John Gregory Dunne later said, helped validate "the comforting illusion that the nation is color-blind." *The Jackie Robinson Story*, Alfred E. Green's 1950 movie, made exactly that point. At the film's beginning, Robinson, perhaps age twelve, asks if he can field a few ground balls during a practice that includes only white youths. The two white coaches not only let him do so but are so appreciative of the youngster's ability that they give him an old baseball mitt as a gesture of encouragement. Respect—not racism—marks the coaches' and players' reaction to the black youth.[67]

Perhaps because of baseball's reputation in the sporting hierarchy, Robinson's integration of baseball dwarfed the Boston Celtics' signing in 1950 of the National Basketball Association's first African American player. By then, too, the press tended to portray integration in athletics as almost a natural process. From this angle, sport followed the logic of a color-blind meritocracy and market economy in which the search for the best product necessarily favored equal opportunity. Such a perspective facilitated optimistic conclusions that race problems were automatically disappearing and should neither require much analysis nor cause any real concern.[68]

Many other examples from popular culture boosted the Cold War consensus that the American system worked. Portrayals of U.S. citizens as hopeful, religious, and charitable abounded. "To hell with romanticizing gangsters, villains, whores, and pimps!" said the film director Frank Capra of his *It's a Wonderful Life* (1947), a heartwarming story about the importance of family and community ties. "To hell with psychosis, neurosis and halitosis. I'm going to make a picture about good people. People who eat, work, hope, dream and make love in the normal way." Ten years later, another movie, Sidney Lumet's *Twelve Angry Men* (1957), also focused on ordinary citizens. In this instance, they were jurors in a murder trial. Despite their early disagreements, they learned the importance of mutual understanding and open discussion. Justice triumphed because they ultimately set blind emotion aside, sorted out the facts, and discovered the truth.[69]

With a rash of postwar combat films, westerns, biblical epics, and musicals, Hollywood shaped the culture of "Cold War Americanism." Several John Wayne movies that ostensibly had nothing to do with the Cold War were, in fact, loaded with messages about it. In *Sands of Iwo Jima* (Allan Dwan, 1949) and three John Ford "Seventh Cavalry" films released around the same time, Wayne became the top box-office draw in the country, serving as a role model for anxious times. By playing lonely authority figures who bore huge responsibilities, he demonstrated "the power and resolution of America," in the words of the biographer Garry Wills. The cavalry films—*Fort Apache* (1948), *She Wore a Yellow Ribbon* (1949), and *Rio Grande* (1950)—all emphasized, in Wills's words, "the need for *regimentation* as necessary to survival under threat." The movies also romanticized Manifest Destiny and America's global responsibilities, themes that dominated a number of popular postwar history books. Westerns, with their emphasis on taking a stand and using violence to further righteous causes, meshed with a postwar U.S. foreign policy that increasingly used force to contain communism.[70]

Early Cold War biblical spectacles dramatized the era's strong religious underpinnings. Leading the decade's nonfiction best sellers was *The Power of Positive Thinking* (1952), by the Protestant minister Norman Vincent Peale. It remained on the best-seller list for 112 consecutive weeks; in 1954, only the Bible sold more copies. Peale attached faith to practical advice: readers should believe in themselves and avoid negative thoughts. Other nonfiction best sellers were *Life Is Worth Living* (the fifth-ranked best seller of 1953) by the Catholic bishop Fulton J. Sheen, Catherine Marshall's *A Man Called Peter* (1951), the evangelist Billy Graham's *Peace with God* (1953) and *The Secret of Happiness* (1955), and Jim Bishop's *The Day Christ Died* (1957). Even topics such as *The Power of Prayer on Plants* found large reading audiences. Fictional best sellers included Lloyd C. Douglas's *The Big Fisherman* (1948) and Thomas Bertram Costain's *The Silver Chalice* (1952). Among the top songs of the 1950s were a number about faith—"I Believe," "He," "Somebody Up There Likes Me," "A Wonderful Time Up There," "He's Got the Whole World in His Hands," "It's No Secret What God Can Do," "The Man Upstairs," and "The Big Fellow in the Sky." Spiritual programming such as *Billy Graham's Hour of Decision* and Bishop Sheen's *Life Is Worth Living*—both packed with anti-Communist messages—constituted a good deal of television's Sunday offerings. On *The Mickey Mouse Club*, Walt Disney's influential TV program, a sign reading "GOD BLESS THE MICKEY MOUSE CLUB" hung over the clubhouse door. In that setting, Hollywood's big productions—*Samson and Delilah* (Cecil B. DeMille, 1949), *Quo Vadis* (Mervyn LeRoy, 1951), *David and Bathsheba* (Henry King, 1951), *The Robe* (Henry Koster, 1953), and especially *The Ten Commandments* (Cecil B. DeMille, 1956) and *Ben-Hur* (William Wyler, 1959)—fit neatly.[71]

The religion that emerged from these examples was unquestionably Christian, but of a nondenominational variety. As President Dwight Eisenhower said: "Our government makes no sense unless it is founded in a deeply felt religious faith—and I don't care what it is." That faith represented what the theologian Reinhold Niebuhr described as "a rather frantic effort of the naturally optimistic American soul to preserve its optimism in an age of anxiety." Although 95 percent of Americans said that they were religious, only 53 percent could identify even one of the Gospels in the Bible. Here was a kind of secularized faith, concerned less with sectarian doctrine than with the religion of America itself. It provided a sense of belonging and reassurance. And, as the flood of popular culture examples demonstrated, it placed few demands on believers. The Hollywood star Jane Russell described God as "a living doll." Meanwhile, audiences who packed into *The Ten Commandments* seemed not to mind that Cecil B. DeMille's film was "serving up flesh in pots," as the critic Murray Kempton observed. The film drew parallels between the Cold War and early Christians' struggles against pagan tyranny. As DeMille stated at the movie's beginning, it was "a story of the birth of freedom." Yet it mixed urgency with a relaxed optimism. "Moses, Moses," said the Anne Baxter character, "you splendid, stubborn, adorable fool."[72]

Hollywood's postwar musicals were equally reassuring and owed much to the "Rodgers and Hammerstein revolution" that rejuvenated Broadway in the 1940s and 1950s. Between 1943 and 1959, Richard Rodgers and Oscar Hammerstein dominated the musical stage, producing six hit shows and several others. *Oklahoma!* inaugurated this revolution in 1943, creating what the theater scholar John Jones described as "the totally integrated musical," in which no song is superfluous or irrelevant to the plots and characters. Moreover, Rodgers and Hammerstein effectively combined escapist entertainment with social messages about "the need for eradicating racial, ethnic, and cultural prejudices, promoting tolerance and acceptance of differences, and bringing reconciliation, if possible." The music of *Oklahoma!* substituted Dust Bowl memories with pastoral scenes in which the corn grew as high as an elephant's eye and the wind whistled through the plains. Yet against that bucolic backdrop and the boy-meets-girl plot were lessons about the necessities of living together peacefully. In disputes over how to use the land, according to one song, farmers push plows, and cattlemen chase cows, but the two groups should still be friends. *Carousel,* which opened on Broadway in 1945, dealt with accepting ethnic and class dissimilarities. *South Pacific,* which ran for over 1,900 performances after opening in 1949, and *The King and I,* which started in 1951 and played 1,246 times, both focused on overcoming racial conflict and cultural differences. The 1958 production *Flower Drum Song* focused on the Chinese American community and the solving of intergenerational misunderstandings. In one song, America's melting pot resembled chop suey: "Everything is in it—all mixed up." At one point, the Chinese immigrants joined a square dance. The last Rodgers and Hammerstein collaboration was *The Sound of Music,* which appeared in late 1959, shortly before Hammerstein died of cancer. The play was about the Von Trapp family, which fled Austria to escape the spreading bigotry and tyranny of Hitler's Third Reich.[73]

In the 1950s, Hollywood jumped on the theater bandwagon by bringing Broadway hits to the screen. Fred Zinneman's *Oklahoma!* (1955), Henry King's *Carousel* (1956), and Walter Lang's *The King and I* (1956) were three of the most popular. And following close behind them in 1958 was Joshua Logan's *South Pacific.* Moreover, the flourishing postwar musical theater inspired a number of other popular 1950s films that meshed with the reassuring Cold War consensus: *Annie Get Your Gun* (George Sidney, 1950), *Kiss Me Kate* (George Sidney, 1953), *Guys and Dolls* (Joseph L. Mankiewicz, 1955), *The Pajama Game* (George Abbott and Stanley Donen, 1957), and *Damn Yankees!* (George Abbott and Stanley Donen, 1958). These movies, just like the musical theater that spawned them, attracted substantial audiences and portrayed a vibrant nation with much to celebrate.[74]

It was, however, Walt Disney who most effectively provided the narratives for the postwar American way—sentimental, wholesome, innocent. Through films, television, and the Disneyland amusement park that he opened in 1955, Disney promoted the basic values of individualism and freedom. Traditional village America was triumphant courtesy of technological ingenuity, material abundance, and decent citizens. According to the biographer Steven Watts, Disney "helped cement the Cold War American consensus by mediating a host of jarring impulses: individualism and conformity, corporate institutions and small-town values, science and fantasy, consumerism and producerism."[75]

To make his point, Disney often turned to history. In a host of movies and television programs, he reinvented the American past, showing how ordinary citizens had created a nation. Starting in the late 1940s, his films and cartoons applauded American folk heroes such as Johnny Appleseed, John Henry, Pecos Bill, and Paul Bunyan. Here, extolled one enthusiastic reviewer, was "history told with head high, chest up, heart bursting with pride." In the mid-1950s, Disney's rendering of history touched off a kind of popular culture earthquake: the "Davy Crockett craze." Following Disney's three-part television series about the legendary frontier hero, Crockett was virtually everywhere: in two Disney movies, a number one hit song ("The Ballad of Davy Crockett"), books, toys, puzzles, school lunch boxes, and coonskin caps. "Davy Crockett is bigger even than Mickey Mouse," asserted *Time* magazine. Fess Parker, the actor who played Crockett in the Disney TV and film productions, was even an honorary guest at dinners and luncheons in the nation's capital, where he sat—in buckskins and coonskin cap—with prominent politicians. His Crockett character symbolized a "plain-folks" hero who had battled for his beliefs in a seemingly less complicated age. "Americans are in trouble," Crockett said in the TV series as he headed off to the Alamo, where "freedom was fightin' another foe." Several members of Congress believed that Crockett's pronouncement, "Be sure you're right, then go ahead," would serve Cold War America well.[76]

Even Disney's innovative 1950s nature films implicitly endorsed the United States. Audiences could marvel at the sheer beauty of the American landscape as well as the technology that captured it on film; they could also watch at a safe distance the struggle for survival that marked the natural world. "Nature, in Disney's hands," as Steven Watts has written, "became another denomination in an American federation of religious institutions."[77]

Disney's America was full of happy families and open to all groups. Disney quite deliberately marketed his products as family entertainment—

products that, as he said, strengthened "the sanctity of the home . . . [and] all that is good for the family and for our country." During the 1950s, his movies and TV shows were, according to Watts, "assimilationist and inclusionary," showing how minorities had found their way "into the ranks of the virtuous American people." While Disney was no civil rights crusader, such Disney movies as *Tonka* (1958) and television shows as *Swamp Fox* (1959–61) and *Zorro* (1957–59) treated Native Americans, African Americans, and Hispanics sympathetically. Stereotypes nevertheless surfaced time and again. A Disneyland publicity sheet, for example, described the Frontierland section of Disneyland as "a land of hostile Indians and straight shooting pioneers." In Frontierland, visitors could also "relive the days of the Old South" by eating at a re-created Southern plantation kitchen, where a black woman dressed as Aunt Jemima dispensed "her famed pancakes everyday" while she sang.[78]

Especially at his amusement park, which opened in 1955 about eleven miles from downtown Los Angeles, Disney consciously aligned himself with suburban America and against disorderly city influences. "There's an American theme behind the whole park," he told the Hollywood reporter Hedda Hopper. "I believe in emphasizing the story of what made America great and what will keep it great." As Disneyland showed, that greatness came from small-town America. The park's "Main Street, USA," according to publicity statements, was "everybody's hometown" and "the heartline of America." It was implicitly the antithesis of New York City, which Disney disliked and whose residents, he suspected, did not share his values. Disneyland as a whole contrasted as well with Coney Island, which Disney criticized for its "tawdry rides and hostile employees." At Disneyland, in contrast, employees could not wear "heavy perfume or jewelry" or exhibit "raffishness." Workers were supposed to be "clean and natural without extremes." Visitors could, thus, enjoy a clean, predictable, orderly environment. Paradoxically, Disneyland celebrated village traditions with technology and corporate imprints. The prevailing assumption was, in the historian Eric Avila's words, "that social order could be marketed, not legislated." The corporate support that Disney received for his park was evident in the names of large companies, including Bank of America and General Electric, that accompanied many exhibits, concession stands, and other attractions. "The Disneyland premise," according to Avila, was "that corporations could make the world not only more exciting, uplifting, and convenient, but also better-tasting and sweeter-smelling."[79]

Probably, however, the millions of children and their parents, as well as many other adults, who visited Disneyland did not go away discussing its orderliness or sanitized setting. More than likely, they viewed their experience there as magical, thrilling, fun. Most would, presumably, have echoed the words used in later advertisements following major sporting events such as football's Super Bowl, when the game's most valuable player would answer the question about what he wanted to do next by shouting joyously: "Go to Disneyland!"

Despite such positive, upbeat perspectives, the postwar consensus nevertheless had a darker side. Anti-Communist fears combined with political opportunism to fuel a Red scare, reminiscent of that which followed World War I. Both major political parties engaged in Red-baiting opponents, but Republicans especially sought power by searching for Communist subversives in the United States. The Wisconsin senator Joe McCarthy became a national figure by accusing the Democrats of "twenty years of treason." And several congressional committees investigated possible dangers within entertainments, especially movies, television, and comics.

In 1947, the House Committee on Un-American Activities (HUAC) opened a series of highly publicized hearings regarding the Communist influence on Hollywood. The HUAC investigations reflected the bigotry of committee members such as Mississippi's John Rankin, a notorious racist and anti-Semite, who proclaimed: "Communism is Yiddish. I understand that every member of the Politburo around Stalin is either Yiddish or married to one, and that includes Stalin himself." In Rankin's opinion, Communists had headquarters in Hollywood, "the greatest hotbed of subversive activities in the United States." But the investigations also played off the nation's love/hate relationship with Hollywood and much of popular culture in general. For many Americans, the entertainment world had too often loomed as a powerful subversive force, more potent than traditional family, community, and religious institutions. "Communists are more rampant in Los Angeles than any other city in America," contended the revivalist preacher Billy Graham. It was a "city of wickedness."[80]

When the HUAC hearings on the film industry opened in October 1947, notable Hollywood entertainers such as Humphrey Bogart, Lauren Bacall, and Katharine Hepburn objected by forming a Committee for the First Amendment. "Once they get the movies throttled, how long will it be before we're told what we can say and cannot say into a radio microphone?" asked Frank Sinatra. "If you make a pitch on a nationwide network for a square deal for the underdog, will they call you a Commie? . . . Are they going to scare us into silence?"[81]

A number of prominent Hollywood people nevertheless believed passionately that the movie industry should show no quarter in the fight against communism. The director Sam Wood demonstrated his strong feelings on the subject by stipulating in his will that no relatives other than his wife could claim their inheritances without declaring that they "are not now, nor have they ever been, Communists." In 1944, Wood had joined Walt Disney and around fifteen hundred other members of the film community to set up the Motion Picture Alliance for the Preservation of American Ideals, which urged HUAC to resume earlier probes into possible un-American influences in Hollywood. The alliance published *A Screen Guide for Americans.* "Don't Smear the Free Enterprise System" and "Don't Show That Poverty Is a Virtue and Failure Is Noble" were some of the guide's instructions.[82]

Once HUAC launched its investigation in 1947, the studios seized the moment to deal with the industry's building internal problems. Turbulence had begun to unsettle Hollywood even as it enjoyed the wartime economic boom and, in 1946, record profits. A paralyzing and sometimes violent strike erupted in 1945, involving some seven thousand workers. Meanwhile, the Justice Department stepped up an antitrust campaign begun in 1938 against the major studios, particularly regarding studio ownership of theaters. Even more alarming, starting in 1947, movie attendance slumped disastrously. From 1946 to 1949, according to *Variety,* Hollywood's revenues plummeted by 21 percent.[83]

Several factors contributed to the decline in movie attendance. The postwar baby boom kept many families home. Although the drive-in theater phenomenon countered this tendency somewhat, the outdoor screens were a mixed blessing for the film industry because they diverted patrons from once-popular deluxe theaters. Another factor was the expanded number of entertainment options, including television. Jack Warner so despised the new medium that he banned the showing of TV sets in Warner Brothers movies. But numerous other amusement choices enjoyed newfound popularity. Bowling, once a marginal sport limited to sleazy venues, became a major draw. *Life* magazine described it as the nation's "most popular participant sport"—indeed, "a way of life." With automatic pinsetters and new, air-conditioned buildings, operators successfully marketed the sport as a family activity. By the mid-1950s, over 20 million regular bowlers helped turn bowling alleys into "the country clubs of America's blue-collar class." The critical fact was that Hollywood was losing the race for consumer dollars. During the war, it had gotten 25 percent of America's recreation expenditures; by 1950, that figure had slid by over half, to 12.3 percent.[84]

Battling slumping fortunes, the studios willingly joined the anti-Communist crusade by blacklisting suspected Communists, voluntarily cooperating with various government agencies, and making anti-Communist films. The studios wanted to protect the image they had long cultivated as thoroughly American institutions but also recognized opportunities to deal with unions and troublesome employees. Moreover, their anti-Communist bent reflected ongoing ideological shifts in the movie industry. Like the Motion Picture Alliance, the Motion Picture Producers and Distributors of America (MPPDA), the largest of the studio trade organizations, wanted to counter "the growing impression that this industry is made up of, and dominated by Communists, radicals, and crackpots." The MPPDA hoped to make films that diminished themes of "un-American" class conflict and were friendlier toward big business. Eric Johnston, who succeeded Will Hays as the organization's president in September 1945, epitomized this viewpoint. "We'll have no more *Grapes of Wrath,*" he instructed the Screen Writers Guild, "no more films that deal with the seamy side of life. We'll have no more films that treat the banker as villain." On November 15, 1947, shortly after the first round of HUAC hearings, Johnston said that Hollywood would not "be swayed by hysteria or intimidation" and then promptly added that the studios had agreed to keep out Communists and deal with "disloyal elements." The blacklisting process had begun.[85]

Some performers, such as Frank Sinatra, barely saved their careers. "SINATRA FACES PROBE ON RED TIES," blared a headline in 1947. By 1953, his name had surfaced a dozen times during HUAC hearings, and FBI files identified him as a Communist. Between 1947 and 1952, he lost his radio show and his film contract, his theatrical agency released him, and Columbia Records dropped him. Had it not been for a fortunate turn of events by which he got a role in the movie *From Here to Eternity* (Fred Zinneman, 1953) and received an Academy Award for best supporting actor, he might have been finished as a big-time performer.[86]

Numerous other Hollywood actors, screenwriters, and directors were less fortunate. Some virtually disappeared for years. The actor Zero Mostel turned to painting, describing himself as "a man of a thousand faces, all of them blacklisted." Writers sometimes hid behind pseudonyms in order to sell their scripts. In 1957, "Robert Rich" was not present to receive the Academy Award for his screenplay for Irving Rapper's *The Brave One;* he was, in fact, Dalton Trumbo, a blacklisted writer who had served a year in jail for refusing to answer HUAC questions ten years earlier.[87]

While the studios carefully avoided overt relationships with anyone whose associations might encourage anti-Communist groups to boycott films, they also established liaisons with government offices such as the Central Intelligence Agency. Paramount's contact with the CIA, for instance, was Luigi Luraschi. At one point, Luraschi objected to the script for *Arrowhead* (Charles Marquis Warren, 1953), a western starring Charlton Heston, on the grounds that its sympathetic treatment of Native Americans was "a story which the Commies could use to their advantage in Asia." The studio reworked the movie to show that personality conflicts—not injustices—underlay the feud between the Apaches and whites. Luraschi nevertheless fretted: "Commies will probably make the most of it."[88]

Hollywood also released dozens of explicitly anti-Communist movies. This flurry of activity was partly a reaction to a question that Richard Nixon asked Jack Warner in 1947: "How many anti-communist movies have you made?" Nixon, a newly elected California Republican who had just joined HUAC, was quickly establishing his anti-Red credentials. Over the next few years, the studios cranked out dozens of anti-Communist movies. Some, such as *The Red Menace* (R. G. Springsteen, 1949) and *I Was a Communist for the FBI* (Gordon Douglas, 1951), were little more than heavy-handed propaganda. John Wayne's *Big Jim McLain* (Edward Ludwig, 1952) stated its gratitude to HUAC. A number of other movies, some quite distinguished, addressed the Communist issue more obliquely. The Academy Award winner in 1954 for best film, *On the Waterfront*, implicitly applauded informants at a time when a number of people in the movie industry (including the film's director, Elia Kazan) were naming suspected Communists.[89]

Of all the entertainment sectors, however, television was the chief Cold War medium. This was hardly surprising given the timing of TV's emergence as a popular force. Although television technology had been developing for several decades and had constituted a dazzling exhibit at the 1939 New York World's Fair, TV did not start building a viewing public until the late 1940s. In 1946, there may have been no more than 7,000 sets in the entire country. The small-screen images on large sets were fuzzy and flickering, programming was extremely limited, and reception depended on antennae. In 1948, few American homes had a television. By then, however, sets were selling at a rate of 200,000 per month; in 1956, consumers were purchasing 20,000 sets daily. By 1959, almost 50 million homes—nine of ten—included television. Revenues of the networks and their affiliates soared from $1.9 million in 1947 to $943.2 million ten years later. Within roughly a decade, a veritable television revolution had occurred.[90]

And that revolution took place during the early intensification of the Cold War, when Americans worried about nuclear war with the Soviet Union, fought in the Korean War, and listened to hysterical warnings from Joe McCarthy and others about Communist subversion within the United States. In 1951, *Variety* declared that HUAC members strongly believed "that since television is such a powerful medium of propaganda and since it comes directly into the home, TV should get the most thorough going-over." Emerging in tandem, "the Cold War and the cool medium negotiated a cultural pact that demanded adjustments on both sides of the dial," as the historian Thomas Doherty has written. In October 1947, TV cameras were notably present at HUAC's inquiry into the movie industry, and they subsequently played a significant role in McCarthy's rapid ascent to political prominence. Moreover, because its programming depended on sponsors, TV was particularly susceptible to the pressures of freelance anti-Communist groups such as the American Business Consultants, which, in 1950, published the hugely influential *Red Channels: The Report of Communist Influence in Radio and Television*.[91]

Cover of an 1870 children's book on Sam Patch. (Courtesy of Paul Johnson, Department of History, University of South Carolina, Columbia.)

(Above) T. D. Rice as Jim Crow.
(Courtesy of the Harvard Theater
Collection, Houghton Library.)

(Right) P. T. Barnum caricatured as a
humbug, emblematic of the antebellum
era's fascination with exaggeration and
bunkum. (Courtesy of the Harvard
Theater Collection, Houghton Library.)

Mose, stage hero of the Bowery b'hoys, with his g'hal, Lize. (Courtesy of the Library of Congress.)

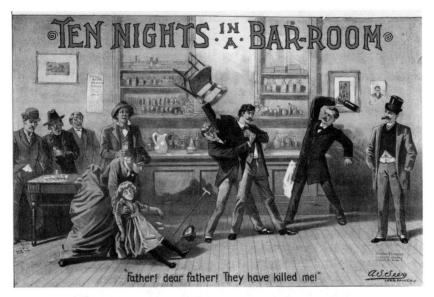

(Above) *Ten Nights in a Barroom* (1855), a prime example of the moral reform melodramas that illustrated the emerging middle class's fears of demon rum's ruination of families. (Courtesy of the Harvard Theater Collection, Houghton Library.)

(Below) With groups like the Virginia Minstrels, minstrelsy became more formalized and respectable, but more racist as well. (Courtesy of the Harvard Theater Collection, Houghton Library.)

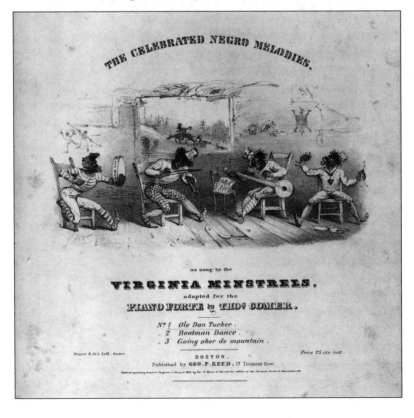

The family as the centerpiece of the newly "invented tradition" of Christmas, according to bourgeois publications such as *Godey's Lady's Book* with its December 1850 frontispiece "The Christmas Tree." (Courtesy of the Winterthur Library, Printed Book and Periodical Collection.)

Lurid antebellum stories of domestic violence suggested anxieties about families and female roles. (Courtesy of the American Antiquarian Society.)

(Above) Barnum and Bailey poster from 1915. Circuses courted family audiences but included a variety of subversive messages, challenging, for example, Victorian ideals of womanhood. (Permission from RINGLING BROS. AND BARNUM & BAILEY THE GREATEST SHOW ON EARTH. Courtesy of Circus World Museum, Baraboo, WI.)

(Right) William "Buffalo Bill" Cody, a spectacular figure in developing the popular mythology of the West. (Courtesy of the Print Collection, Miriam and Ira D. Wallach Division of Arts, Prints and Photographs, the New York Public Library, Astor, Lenox and Tilden Foundations.)

A tobacco card in 1869 of the first all-salaried baseball team, the Cincinnati Red Stockings. (Courtesy of the Library of Congress.)

(Left) A publicity poster of "the Menken"—Adah Isaacs Menken—as Mazeppa. (Courtesy of the Harvard Theater Collection, Houghton Library.)

(Below) Although they soon led to belly dances and strip shows, early burlesque troupes did more than display women's bodies in titillating ways; they also exhibited female rebelliousness, sexual power, and dominance. (Courtesy of the Library of Congress.)

(Above) The Great Sandow supporting the Trocadero Vaudevilles, with Florenz Ziegfeld at the center of the platform. (Courtesy of the Wisconsin Center for Film and Theater Research.)

(Left) Vaudevillian Eva Tanguay, combining sexual innuendo with childlike innocence and energy, was perhaps America's highest-paid actress. (Courtesy of the Harvard Theater Collection, Houghton Library.)

(Above) Under the guidance of a friendly adult supervisor, youths in 1911 play basketball on a New York City playground. Demonstrating reformers' desire to use entertainment as an agency of uplift and social control, the era's playground movement helped popularize basketball on city streets. (Below) Movie still from *Bird in a Gilded Cage* (1909) shows the kinds of action and danger that thrilled nickelodeon audiences and worried moralists. (Photos courtesy of the Library of Congress.)

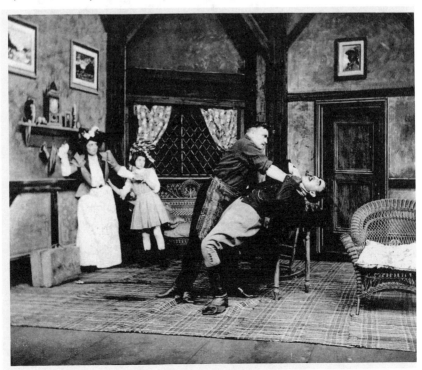

The Great Houdini, illusionist and escape artist, symbolized natural man breaking loose from the chains of modern institutions, restrictions, and technology. (Courtesy of the Library of Congress.)

(Left) Edgar Rice Burroughs's "Tarzan of the Apes" made its debut in 1912, in the pulp magazine *All-Story*. Clinton Pettee drew this first picture of Tarzan. The book version, *Tarzan of the Apes,* was published two years later. (Courtesy of the Edgar Rice Burroughs Collection, Ekstrom Library, University of Louisville.)

(Right) Harold "Red" Grange, the University of Illinois's "Galloping Ghost" in 1923, was later a key player in developing professional football. (Courtesy of the University of Illinois.)

(Right) Irene and Vernon Castle, authors of the best-selling instruction manual *Modern Dancing* (1914) and popularizers of sanitized versions of dances such as the tango, in 1913. (Courtesy of the Library of Congress.)

(Below) The Beverly Hill Billies (pictured here in 1930) illustrated the impact of radio as well as country music's widening popularity and the rustic hillbilly image that promoters initially attached to it. (Courtesy of the Folklife Collection, University of North Carolina, Chapel Hill.)

During the Great Depression, radio dominated entertainment with a wide variety of advertiser-sponsored programming, including music, comedy, and soap operas. Radio's messages both reinforced and questioned social norms. (Courtesy of Bettman/CORBIS.)

(Left) Superman, who made his debut in the June 1938 *Action Comics,* was a cartoon hero for depressed times, and he transformed the comic industry. ("Action Comics" #1, © 1938 DC Comics. All rights reserved. Used with permission.)

(Below) This World War II poster, featuring the heavyweight boxing champion Joe Louis, reflected the government propaganda that emphasized America's racial diversity and freedom. (Courtesy of the National Archives [Image #44 PA-87].)

John Wayne, World War II and Cold War icon, in *Fort Apache* (John Ford, 1948). (Courtesy of the Lilly Library, Indiana University, Bloomington.)

A family in mid-1957 watches TV, by then the leading Cold War medium. (Courtesy of the Library of Congress, Prints and Photographs Division, U.S. News and World Report Magazine Collection, LC-U9-927.)

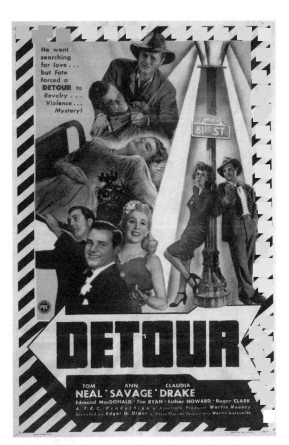

(Right) With a tiny budget, six-day shooting schedule, and dark themes, *Detour* (Edgar G. Ulmer, 1945) was an early example of film noir. (Courtesy of the Library of Congress.)

(Left) Horror comics in the early 1950s, by providing critiques of hypocrisies and injustices, parodied official truths but also provoked a congressional investigation and, in 1954, a stricter comics code. (*Crime SuspenStories* 22 [EC Comics, May 1954]. Art by Johnny Craig. Courtesy of William M. Gaines, Agent, Inc.)

Elvis Presley, whose sensational rise reflected crucial themes in rock and roll music—race, youth, sex, and the role of outsiders in transforming the cultural mainstream. (Courtesy of the Library of Congress.)

Bob Dylan, one of the most influential figures in American music.
(Courtesy of Bettman/CORBIS.)

(Right) In an increasingly divided nation, Muhammad Ali became one of the biggest and most controversial figures in sport, a symbol of principled integrity to his fans and of the disloyal American to his critics. (Courtesy of Bettman/CORBIS.)

(Below) Francis Ford Coppola's immensely successful *The Godfather* (1972) epitomized the New Hollywood, in which directors challenged studio power and a host of socially conscious movies signified a brief moment of doubt in a medium that was typically full of optimism and good cheer. (Courtesy of Bettman/CORBIS.)

(Above) *The Mary Tyler Moore Show*, a breakthrough program from the newly formed MTM Enterprises, in 1970 helped lead the way for some of TV comedy's greatest shows, including *All in the Family* and *M*A*S*H*. (Courtesy of Bettman/CORBIS.)

(Left) Richard Pryor was emblematic of the spectacular emergence by the 1970s of black comedians into entertainment's mainstream, using edgy street humor to become a huge racial crossover star. (Courtesy of AP/Wide World Photos.)

Tim LaHaye and Jerry B. Jenkins, the authors of the best-selling Left Behind novels, and prominent examples of fundamentalist Christians' growing influence on entertainment. (© Newsweek, Inc. All rights reserved. Printed by permission. Photo by Michael Kelley.)

American Business Consultants had already flexed considerable muscle. The creation of three former Federal Bureau of Investigation agents, it had, in 1947, started publishing a controversial weekly newsletter, *Counterattack: The Newsletter of Facts to Combat Communism,* which soon focused on the broadcasting industry. With freewheeling references to "commies," "pinks," and "dupes," *Counterattack* relied on distortion, rumor, and innuendo. Ed Sullivan, a columnist for the *New York Daily News* who, in 1948, launched a long-lasting television talent show, lauded *Counterattack* for doing "a magnificent American job." Sullivan admitted checking with the editors regarding the political backgrounds of his program's guests. In June 1950, all subscribers received a copy of the 213-page, paperbound *Red Channels.* The book, which also went on sale in stores for $1, argued a stunning thesis: the Soviet Union was increasingly dominating American radio and television. Indeed, Communists "now rely more on radio and TV than on the press and motion pictures as 'belts' to transmit pro-Sovietism to the American public." The eye-catching cover showed a red fist grasping a microphone. Inside the publication was a shocking list of 151 writers, directors, and performers who were aiding this fifth-column offensive. Among them were such well-known entertainers and authors as John Garfield, Judy Holliday, Lena Horne, Arthur Miller, Edward G. Robinson, Artie Shaw, Orson Welles, and Jean Muir.[92]

A few weeks after *Red Channels* appeared, Jean Muir lost her role as the mother in a scheduled TV version of the popular radio show *The Aldrich Family.* The program's sponsor, General Foods, said that it did not want to associate its product—Jell-O—with a "controversial" actor. Several other of the individuals whom *Red Channels* had named, including Ireene Wicker and Philip Loeb, soon also lost starring roles on TV programs because of sponsors' edicts. Meanwhile, the supermarket owner Laurence A. Johnson threatened sponsors of presumed subversive programs by saying that he would post signs on store shelves to identify companies whose shows employed "Stalin's little creatures." Johnson asked a toothpaste manufacturer "DO YOU WANT ANY PART OF YOUR PURCHASE PRICE TO BE USED TO HIRE COMMUNIST FRONTERS?"[93]

Network owners and program sponsors were soon on the run. In 1951, a CBS vice president asked whether a proposed composer for a program was "in the book." When the puzzled program director reached for the phone directory, the vice president plopped down *Red Channels* and remarked: "This is the book we live by." The *New York Herald Tribune*'s TV critic contended: "Everyone—ad agencies and networks—seems to have a little list. Heaven knows how anyone's name gets on these little lists." But lists indeed existed, and careers hung in the balance.[94]

Although ideology undoubtedly motivated some network executives and sponsors who were determined to drive suspected Communists out of entertainment, the main concern was to avoid controversy that might drive away consumers. Courting the largest possible audience, people in the TV business did not wish to offend or anger. One executive described this strategy as the "LOP" theory—"least objectionable programming."[95]

Such caution also dominated the outlook of large advertising firms. Going into the 1950s, uniformity and predictability were watchwords of the big Madison Avenue ad agencies. Using polling and psychological studies, the agencies sought to build a consensus that favored their products. From this perspective, consensus rested not on surprises but on repetition, continuity, and plain, simple messages. "The consumer tends to remember just one thing from an advertisement," said Rosser Reeves, head of the influential Ted Bates Agency. To build consumers' confidence, ads should tie products to scientific studies or expert advice; Colgate toothpaste's "Gardow," for example, supposedly cleaned teeth in three distinct ways, and Wonder Bread built "strong bodies twelve ways." Advertisements were not supposed to be complicated, confusing, or even liked. People detested a Reeves ad for Anacin because its images of a hammer pounding inside a human head were repetitive and unpleasant, but product sales zoomed from $18 million to $54 million within eighteen months of its debut. "How do you spell relief? R-O-L-A-I-D-S," went another of the era's most familiar ads. Images in ads were supposed to be reassuring and full of reminders of American prosperity and progress. Ads needed also to suggest ways in which a consumer could fit in, be secure, and belong. They should, thus, not "rock the boat," but reaffirm the familiar. "Mrs. Middle Majority," as one sociologist described her, was a key to marketing. Ads should urge conformity, not dissent. In that spirit, the Clairol company's 1955 ad took advantage of the perception that only 7 percent of women colored their hair: "Does she . . . or doesn't she?" The woman in the ad had "hair color so natural only her hairdresser knows for sure!" Over the next six years, Clairol sales of hair coloring jumped over 400 percent. According to the advertiser David Ogilvy, customers did not simply buy products; they purchased images.[96]

And, with television, images became more important than ever. "We discovered," said Rosser Reeves, "that this was no tame kitten; we had a ferocious man-eating tiger." That tiger paid staggering dividends, too. Between 1949 and 1951, Madison Avenue's television billings leaped from $12.3 million to $128 million. As an NBC vice president for marketing later observed, networks were "in the business of selling audiences to advertisers."[97]

In this increasingly high-stakes marriage of television and advertising, the last thing that either partner wanted was controversy. Hence, in 1952, the networks adopted a Television Code, which resembled the MPPDA Production Code. Stressing that TV was a "family medium" and a provider of "wholesome entertainment," the networks banned obscenities, vulgarities, and sexual and violent excess. Against that backdrop, the medium also screened out alleged radicals via blacklisting and loyalty oaths to "the American way of life." Starting in December 1950, all CBS employees had to answer several questions, including: "Are you now, or have you ever been, a member of the Communist Party, U.S.A., or any Communist organization?"[98]

In fact, however, actual political associations were less important than perceived connections. Sanka Coffee, a product of General Foods, thus demanded that the CBS program *It's News to Me* cut actress Anna Lee because her name had appeared on a blacklist. The show's producer, Mark Goodson, was flabbergasted. "This one is crazy," he told other network executives. "Anna Lee is about as leftist as Herbert Hoover." To Goodson's surprise, the executives conceded that she was the victim of a mistake; someone had confused her with a woman who wrote for a Communist newspaper. "We are going to drop Anna Lee anyway," said one of Goodson's bosses. "We're already starting to get mail, and we can't let the sponsor be involved with protests." After Goodson had stormed out of the meeting, he learned that his objections had sparked a question about his own loyalties: "Is he a pinko?" Anna Lee ultimately remained with the show, but even knowledge that she had been misidentified was almost insufficient to save her career. In retrospect, Goodson regretted the "conspiracy of silence" that had facilitated the blacklisting of innocent people.[99]

The Cold War pervaded early television in other ways as well. Initially, TV stations depended greatly on programs that government and private industry supplied. In 1950, the National Association of Manufacturers provided a series of minidocumentaries celebrating American business, and, within four years, some 234 stations had aired it. The U.S. Army produced another series, *The Big Picture,* which opened by saying: "All over the world the US Army is on the alert to defend our country—you, the American people—against aggression." One scene showed a mass of soldiers' graves with the comment: "You are looking at the face of Communism. Never forget it."[100]

Cold War messages were also interwoven through a myriad of entertainment programs that affirmed the American way of life. TV schedules included endless examples of the-system-works programs. Starting in 1956, the top daytime show was *Queen for a Day,* in which audiences chose which of several contenders—whose families all suffered from one kind of hardship or another—would get her wish (e.g., a vaporizer for an asthmatic child). But the winner also received a veritable cornucopia of goods, ranging from washers and dryers to various foods. During the 1950s, TV also included many police shows, such as *Dragnet,* and spy dramas, including *I Led Three Lives* and at least eighteen others. Westerns such as

Gunsmoke and *Maverick*—and there was a veritable flood of them in the 1950s—were exceptionally popular. Together, such shows provided constant reminders of the wonders of life in America, where little people fulfilled their dreams within a benign institutional framework. The surging popularity of quiz shows at the decade's end echoed themes of equality, opportunity, and success. "We're trying to show the country that the little people are really very intelligent," said the sponsor of *The $64,000 Question*.[101]

Hopeful, reassuring themes suffused family situation comedies, which idealized household life, middle-class lifestyles, suburban living, and traditional gender roles. In a 1958 episode of *Father Knows Best*, the older daughter, Betty, announced that she wanted to be an engineer and get a summer job with a surveying crew. "I hardly know what kind of towels to hang in her bathroom—His or Hers," the mother fretted. On the job, Betty had to deal with a handsome supervisor who reminded her that women always "cook their husbands' breakfast." That night the supervisor dropped by her house with a box of chocolates for her, and she heard him tell her parents that she might become "a darned good" engineer, but then some future husband would not have anyone "to come home to." At the end of the program, Betty decided not to return to the surveying crew. Instead, she accepted the box of chocolates and an offer for a Saturday night date. Similarly, in *The Donna Reed Show*, wife Donna told her husband and two teenage children that she was going to run for a city council office. Three days into her campaign, however, her household was in chaos. "I'm tired of losing my buttons, I'm sick of eating leathery eggs and carbon toast," moaned her husband. "We need you more than the country does." Wilting emotionally, Donna responded: "Say that again—that you need me." When she decided to quit the campaign, another woman told her: "If I had a family like yours, I'd give up all the dashing around [too]." The television family was like an anchor in a sea of change.[102]

This powerful consensus culture of the early Cold War was, nevertheless, full of fissures. Paradoxically, objects of praise—such as America's affluence—contained fault lines. Increasingly, Loyalty Day and other civic celebrations simply became occasions to seek a range of amusements. A day at an amusement park or the beach or a chance to go shopping overshadowed patriotic testimonies to national sacrifice, virtue, and traditional values. Ironically, America's vaunted consumerism and leisure weakened the anti-Communist fervor and fears that helped forge the Cold War culture. Soon the national loyalty director of the Veterans of Foreign Wars would lament: "The main problem today is that too many fine Americans, leading the 'good life,' are not inclined to become involved [in patriotic festivities]." Recreation and amusements indeed had their own siren call.[103]

Moreover, postwar society had set in motion or intensified a number of developments that challenged central assumptions within the postwar consensus. The continuing upheaval in sexuality, a building civil rights movement, and the demands of the emerging baby-boom generation constituted many of those challenges. And so did popular culture. Even as it reinforced themes of conformity, unanimity, and consensus, it contradicted them, as film noir, rock and roll, and other modes of entertainment soon showed.

9

COUNTERPOINTS TO CONSENSUS

"THE STREETS WERE DARK WITH SOMETHING MORE THAN NIGHT," the mystery novelist Raymond Chandler wrote in 1944. While mass entertainment during the 1940s and 1950s was packed with the reassuring images and rhetoric of the postwar consensus, Chandler's comment attested to another perspective, one full of danger, unpredictability, and striking reminders of popular culture's power to disturb and unsettle. Amid the triumphal mood of World War II and the early Cold War, a kind of guerrilla culture flourished on the social margins in areas such as radio thriller dramas, film noir, pulp fiction, comic books, comedy, and music. "Things are not what they seem" was a countervailing message, often cynical and bleak. Another message, more hopeful and energetic, was implicitly about "breaking loose" from a consensus world that critics found contrived and confining. Even supposedly "safe" and predictable amusements, such as television's family comedies, included contrary examples and encouraged parody. Although strategies of coercion and "taming" generally protected the cultural consensus through the 1950s, it was increasingly on the defensive. New departures vied with powerful continuities.[1]

By the end of World War II and into the early Cold War years, a victory narrative was virtually a cultural imperative. It undoubtedly reflected the fact that Americans had much to celebrate: the defeat of the Axis powers and the end of the Great Depression. "With 7 percent of the world's population in the late 1940s, America possessed 42 percent of the world's income and accounted for half of the world's manufacturing output," according to one account. "American workers produced 57 percent of the world's steel, 43 percent of electricity, 62 percent of oil, 80 percent of automobiles." Never before had the world seen such prosperity.[2]

But, paradoxically, fears and apprehensions haunted this amazing success story. The existence of nuclear weapons amid threats of continued international conflict stirred anxieties. Even the rising economy brought uneasiness as citizens wondered whether the terrifying jobless days might return. As Americans struggled to restore and build families, they worried about divorce rates and juvenile delinquency. Complicating these efforts was a nettlesome fact: the values that Americans most prized cut in several directions. The myth of the rugged individual collided with that of the close-knit community of helpful neighbors. Celebrations of change and progress competed with nostalgia for the "good old days." Relaxation and fun jeopardized traditional values regarding work and self-discipline. The growing stream of consumer products after World War II contrasted favorably with the perceived starkness of Communist societies, yet some critics worried that goods in fact jeopardized American goodness. Thus, while a 1951 *Time* magazine advertisement applauded the abundance of telephones in America, a 1952 Conrad Hilton ad in the *Saturday Evening Post* showed Uncle Sam on his knees asking God to save the United States from the evils of mammon. Moreover, while the phone company and Conrad Hilton both attested to America's entrepreneurial success, they also symbolized the growing power and control of large organizations. It was precisely such tensions and anxieties that the wartime political and cultural consensus tried to soothe. In the words of one historian: "It fell to popular culture to exorcise these demons and provide compensating, vicarious adventures in potency and dominion."[3]

But popular culture also provided outlets for feelings of uncertainty, doubt, and diminished personal power. "It doesn't take much to see that the problems of three little people don't amount to a hill of beans in this crazy world," said Rick Blaine, the Humphrey Bogart character in *Casablanca* (Michael Curtiz, 1942). The movie unquestionably reaffirmed the wartime emphasis on noble sacrifice, as the protagonists set aside personal needs on behalf of patriotism and the greater good; yet, on another level, it conveyed an abiding sense of sadness and loss. Events and large institutions were in control, defeating personal hopes and dreams. The film's melancholy song "As Time Goes By" exuded feelings of helplessness.[4]

These feelings of a world turned upside down, full of menace, dominated a veritable "noir mediascape" in popular culture that challenged the triumphalist consensus script. "Whichever way you turn," said the protagonist of the movie *Detour* (Edgar G. Ulmer, 1945), "fate sticks out a foot to trip you." This bleak mediascape relied on small budgets and existed on the entertainment industry's margins. It constituted a kind of underground culture—one with "private runways to the truth," as the film critic Manny Farber wrote in 1957.[5]

The brooding, pessimistic stories that constituted a "turn toward horror" in a small but significant number of radio programs and movies in the 1940s and 1950s owed much to the pulp magazines' hard-boiled crime fiction of earlier decades as well as the paperback publishing revolution that started in 1939. Writing in pulp journals such as *Black Mask* and *Dime Detective Magazine,* Dashiell Hammett and Raymond Chandler were among the most famous creators of pulp fiction in which institutional corruption was pervasive, betrayal lurked around every corner, violence and greed were rampant, individuals were trapped in a humdrum environment, and the lines between good and evil blurred. Weary, disillusioned private detectives such as Sam Spade pursued illusive truths more from a sense of personal loyalty and obligation than from confidence that justice would result.[6]

This somber viewpoint infiltrated radio during World War II in the form of programs such as *Inner Sanctum* in 1941 and especially *Suspense,* which made its debut in June 1942. These shows were so popular that, by mid-1945, they had inspired over forty other thriller dramas. Importantly, at a time when much of popular culture celebrated home and family, *Suspense* portrayed a grim world of troubles. A familiar theme involved the imperiled woman who has much to fear—including her husband. The wartime demographics of radio listening encouraged this plotline. During the war, radio responded to a decrease in male audiences by drawing ideas from the daytime soap operas, setting many of the thriller episodes within the home and using female leads or voice narrators. Throughout the 1940s, *Suspense* dealt often with domestic tensions and female perspectives. Female listeners could well have identified with characters who were at the mercy of circumstances and restrictive environments. One of *Suspense*'s most acclaimed and popular episodes was "Sorry, Wrong Number." It first aired on May 25, 1943, starring the esteemed actress Agnes Moorehead. The plot involved Moorehead as an invalid who discovers that her husband has hired someone to kill her. Desperately, she seeks help via the telephone, but no one will believe her. Her final call to the police is too late. The killer stabs her to death and hangs up the phone, saying: "Sorry, wrong number." The show was so popular that it aired eight more times over the next few years.[7]

Male characters were also vulnerable. One of them murdered a promoted coworker; another killed his abusive boss. In a 1949 show, James Stewart played a paralyzed, angry veteran: "Once in a while they dump me in a wheelchair and wheel me up and down the walk like I was a baby. Only babies can cry." Radio thrillers typically dramatized a haunted landscape of doubt, alienation, and horror.[8]

They had their movie counterparts. As the United States emerged from

World War II, a tough, weary realism found its way onto many screens. Because of their shadowy settings, grim mood, and dark subjects, these movies earned the label *film noir* from French critics. In contrast to upbeat movies regarding the American dream of success, opportunity, and shared values, noir films probed the nation's somber underside, revealing problems, alienation, failure, and depravity. Here, the American dream has gone bad, and, typically in this nightmare world, there is no way out. To the question, "Why me?" that haunted many of these movies, the answer was, according to the beleaguered protagonist in *Detour,* "For no good reason at all."[9]

Such pessimism was largely a response to "rips and tears in the social fabric," as the film writer and director Paul Schrader observed. The shocks and displacements of World War II made reacclimation difficult for returning veterans and their families. The reality of nuclear weapons haunted not just photographs and newsreels of Hiroshima and Nagasaki but visions of the future. In 1950, *Life* predicted "the growing likelihood of World War III" in the essay "How U.S. Cities Can Prepare for Atomic War." *Collier's* described a hypothetical atomic attack on New York City in "Hiroshima U.S.A.: Can Anything Be Done about It?" Postwar trauma and nuclear anxieties boosted the popularity of psychoanalysis, which—like film noir—probed the subconscious and sexuality. In dealing with themes of dislocation, readjustment, and vulnerability, noir films were, in the words of the critic James Greenberg, "movies about adults, made for adults who had just been through a war."[10]

By 1947, Hollywood's economic troubles gave the makers of noir an opening to make movies that undermined the consensus model. During the Great Depression, film distributors had typically offered double features—the back-to-back showing of two films—in order to attract audiences. Rental charges for the big-budget "A" releases were based on a percentage of the income from ticket sales. In contrast, there was a flat rental fee for each showing of the "B," or low-budget, films. Audience size, in other words, was irrelevant to distributors' B-movie rental costs. All the major studios had specialized B-movie units, but, as the demand for double-bill pictures grew, dozens of small, independent production companies flourished. Indeed, a veritable independent revolution had occurred, according to the vice president of United Artists, who, in 1958, claimed that the output of the "indies" had grown from 1 percent of Hollywood films in 1951 to almost half. Most noir films were B (or second-feature) movies and ran for only fifty-five to seventy-five minutes. Because they had small casts and depended on character studies, not action, they cost under $100,000 to make. As the actor Robert Mitchum later quipped: "Hell, we didn't know what film noir was in those days. We were just making movies. Cary Grant and all the big stars at RKO got all the lights. We lit our sets with cigarette butts." Along Hollywood's "Poverty Row," struggling studios such as Republic and Monogram cranked out the cheap productions. A forlorn, struggling studio, Producers Releasing Corporation (which detractors shrugged off as standing for Poverty Row Crap) took only six days to make *Detour,* a notable early example of American film noir.[11]

Because the B films were inexpensive and did not depend on large audiences, the directors who made them were subject to less financial pressure and enjoyed some creative license. Later, the director Martin Scorsese characterized them as "film smugglers." Luigi Luraschi, Paramount's liaison with the Central Intelligence Agency, complained that pictures "made outside of the major companies" were "difficult to keep track of." He found it hard to work with unorthodox directors such as Billy Wilder, one of whose movies Luraschi dubbed a "wonderful piece of propaganda for the commies." Wilder and John Huston were mavericks who clashed with other members of the Directors Guild, voting against a Cecil B. DeMille motion favoring loyalty oaths. One guild vice president guessed that "DeMille didn't give a damn about anybody's politics" and was simply determined to keep Congress at bay, but the meeting turned ugly when DeMille questioned the motives of those who opposed the oaths. "There were two of us against one hundred and there were whispers in the room," recalled Huston. "We were communists. That was the last Directors Guild meeting I ever attended. The sad part of the story is that the accusers . . . dirtied the soul of America." Huston and Wilder directed some of the best examples of film noir, partly by avoiding the large-studio executives—"cannibals," as Huston called them—and by making movies on location, beyond the constraints of studio lots. From this perspective, according to one writer, noir films were "distress flares launched onto movie screens by artists working the night shift at the Dream Factory."[12]

The noir style was spare, stark, and deadly. Shadows and darkness set a mood of entrapment. "I feel all dead inside," said a character in *The Dark Corner* (Henry Hathaway, 1946). "I'm backed up in a dark corner and I don't know who's hitting me." Film titles suggested claustrophobia, alienation, and paranoia—*Framed, Abandoned, Cornered, Desperate, Fear, Blackmail, The Hunted, Raw Deal, Trapped, Quicksand, Where Danger Lives, No Escape, Stolen Identity, The Night Holds Terror.* The characters were typically burnout cases, with few redeeming virtues. "We really didn't need the money, did we?" conceded a dying police officer who had turned crooked in *Pushover* (Richard Quine, 1954). "You're no good and neither am I," Jane Greer told Robert Mitchum in *Out of the Past* (Jacques Tourneur, 1947). The raised level of violence in these movies was also clear in titles: *The Killer That Stalked, Murder without Tears, Paid to Kill,* and *Witness to Murder.*[13]

Film noir and paperback books developed together and shared the same hard-boiled, grimly realistic themes of danger, violence, and obsession. Together, they subverted the consensus narrative by exposing, as one author has said, "the ignoble corners of life beyond the glow of . . . *Father Knows Best,* and the healthy, smiling faces in magazines advertising milk or frozen dinners or trips to California." They sharply countered the upbeat messages of the era's patriotic bombast and oratory with portraits of a hidden America, corrupt and mean. And each thrived on the culture's peripheries. Like most of the independents who produced film noir, the paperback entrepreneurs initially worked on the economic fringes.[14]

"OUT TODAY, THE NEW POCKET BOOKS THAT MAY REVOLUTIONIZE AMERICA'S READING HABITS," an advertisement announced on June 19, 1939, when a new publishing company launched a bold experiment. Starting out with ten paperback titles for twenty-five cents each, Pocket Books soon transformed the publishing business. Although cheap reprints and books bound in paper had existed for decades, Pocket Books, as the writer Geoffrey O'Brien observed, pushed "the nascent advertising/packaging/marketing revolution in one particular area—the retailing of literature." Advertisements hailed the new books as "kind to your pocket and your pocketbook." The first ten titles were all reprints of earlier best sellers (such as James Hilton's 1935 *Lost Horizon*) or of prestigious works of literature (*Five Great Tragedies* by Shakespeare). In 1941, with a growing list of titles, Pocket Books sold 12 million copies. The small, portable volumes were ideal for soldiers to carry during World War II. By mid-1942, GIs were consuming 250,000 each month. Over the next three years, Popular Library, Dell, and Bantam also got into the paperback business.[15]

But, in 1946, with 353 paperback titles in print, the market suddenly sagged. Veterans, in the process of rebuilding their lives, seemed less interested in the books. Quickly, the publishers tried to rebuild interest. For one thing, they embraced more actively the hard-boiled, realistic style of the once-popular pulp magazines. Indeed, many paperbacks were recycled versions of *Black Mask* and *Detective Fiction Weekly,* and the publishers had typically started out in the pulp magazine business. Usually, paperbacks and pulp magazines appeared in newsstands and bus depots, not standard bookstores, and shared the same groups of readers. Critics dismissed paperbacks as literary trash, but the publishers were willing to sacrifice respectability for sales.[16]

To that end, the publishers adopted pulp-style covers that accented sex. "The word went out," remembered one illustrator, "get sex into [that cover] somehow." Whereas a 1944 edition of Dashiell Hammett's *The Maltese Falcon* simply showed three hands reaching for a statuette, a 1947 edition was more tantalizing: while a woman undressed on the other side of a sheer curtain, a man sat with her panties on his leg and her high-heeled shoe in his hand. In 1948, Popular Library reissued the 1925 best seller *The Private Life of Helen of Troy* with a "nipple cover." Helen's nipples were clearly visible through her toga. Lurid covers with curvaceous women in various states of undress and erotic poses now characterized paperback covers. "I got all my sex education from books like this," recalled one man regarding those suggestive pictures. "Sex, sadism, and the smoking gun" constituted "the 3 S's" of cover art, which unquestionably attracted readers. By 1951, the business was booming, with 866 paperback titles in print. New companies were emerging. In 1950, Fawcett started an all-original paperback line, paying most authors $2,000 per book for publishing runs of 200,000 copies and giving authors such as Louis L'Amour and John D. MacDonald opportunities to get in print.[17]

It was mainly paperbacks that accounted for the mystery writer Mickey Spillane's phenomenal popularity. When E. P. Dutton published a hardbound edition of his first novel, *I, the Jury,* in 1947, the editor noted: "It isn't in the best of taste but it will sell." Initially, however, it did poorly. After the sale of only four thousand copies, Dutton passed the paperback rights to Signet, an imprint of New American Library. In January 1948, Signet released the novel with a tantalizing cover showing an alluring woman opening her blouse. Over the next two years, the twenty-five-cent paperback sold over 2 million copies, suddenly making Signet a big-time publisher. By 1953, Spillane had written six additional books, each with huge paperback sales, including the record-setting 2.5 million first printing of *The Big Kill* (1951). Incredibly, the decade's top ten fictional best sellers included those six books. The books were full of explicit descriptions of sex and violence. "I loved to shoot killers," Spillane's fictional tough-guy private detective, Mike Hammer, said. "I couldn't think of anything I'd rather do than shoot a killer and watch his blood trace a slimy path across the floor." The prevalence of urban sin, corruption, pluralism, and scarlet women often made the novels read like the last gasp of an older America caught in the suffocating grasp of a modern, cosmopolitan world. Hammer, operating like a vigilante redeemer, continually worked outside the law. For readers weary of bureaucratic rules and regulations, he symbolized someone who took action. "That Hammer!" said a character in John D. MacDonald's *The Neon Jungle* (1953). "There was a guy who knew how to live. They didn't mess with him. Not twice, anyway. He had what it took with women. He wasn't stuck in any two-bit grocery business."[18]

Many of the hard-boiled paperback characters were stuck, however. "I don't know what the game was," said a character in Cornell Woolrich's *I Married a Dead Man* (1948). "I only know its name: they call it life. I'm not sure how it should be played. No one ever told me. No one ever tells anybody." In the novels of Jim Thompson, there was "no familiar thing to cling to." Everything was topsy-turvy. As Thompson himself explained:

"There is only one plot—things are not as they seem." Hence, in one story, a small-town deputy sheriff was in fact a schizophrenic killer. "We're living in a funny world," the officer commented. "The police are playing crooks in it, and the crooks are doing police duty. . . . It's a screwed-up, bitched-up world, and I'm afraid it's going to stay that way." In the words of another writer, Thompson's works reduced to sawdust every "single plank in the platform of traditional heartland optimism" that underlay consensus America.[19]

In that regard, the lessons of hard-boiled paperbacks and noir films coiled tightly together. There was no room here for American innocence. Darkness and disorder prevailed. Paperback novels represented a depressing underside of 1950s America.[20]

It was, thus, hardly surprising that Congress, already scrutinizing Hollywood for suspected subversion, investigated the paperback publishers. In May 1952, the House of Representatives established a Select Committee on Current Pornographic Materials to examine "offensive matter," including undue emphasis on crime, violence, and corruption. The Kansas Democrat E. C. Gathing, the resolution's sponsor, was the committee chair. When the hearings opened on December 1, the committee stated that paperback publishers were spreading "sensuality, immorality, filth, perversion and degeneracy." Particularly offensive were the "lurid and daring illustrations of voluptuous young women on the covers of the books." The committee listened mainly to testimony from individuals who found the paperbacks objectionable. A written statement from the Newark, New Jersey, director of public safety placed the hearings in a Cold War context: "If the Communists are not behind this drive to flood the nation with obscenity, to weaken the moral fibre of our youth and debauch our adults, then it is only because the greedy business men are carrying the ball for them." After five days of testimony, six of the nine committee members signed a report attacking "the so-called pocket-size books" for such things as disseminating immorality and extolling "sexual aberrations." Although no legislation resulted from the hearings, local authorities and moral watchdogs cracked down on newsstands and books in the paperback racks. In Texas, imprisonment and fines awaited the designers of book covers and advertisements that were allegedly obscene; authors faced similar penalties.[21]

"Presumably," a writer joked later, the drive to purge the United States of immorality would leave nothing behind "but Gideon Bibles and civil-defense pamphlets." By the mid-1950s, such pressure was having an effect. Paperback cover art "became steadily more restrained. . . . The world had temporarily been made safe for the *Saturday Evening Post*."[22]

Changes in the paperback industry also played a role. By the mid-1950s, efforts were under way to make the business more predictable and orderly. In 1953, paperback inventories had soared to 175 million copies, and, each month, around ninety new titles appeared. "We're like Coca-Cola," lamented an executive. "We keep growing but our share of the market is falling." Increased competition and an oversupply of books were hurting profits. "The business had outgrown the seat-of-the-pants flying that characterized earlier days when a publisher could play fast and loose, experiment a little, and eat a mistake because the risks were lower," according to one historian. "No more. An increasingly sophisticated organization demanded more controls and efficiencies." By 1953, Robert Graff, the freewheeling founder of Pocket Books, held a largely ceremonial position in the company. In 1954, Bantam Books, one of the paperback industry's Big Four but now losing money, named a new president, Oscar Dystel. Although Dystel was a stranger to the paperback business, he had been an innovative marketer and editor for a number of trade journals and mass market magazines such as *Coronet* and *Collier's*. After graduating from New York University, he attended Harvard Business School. At Bantam, he tightened up distribution: "We were sending out a thousand soldiers to take over an objective and getting nine hundred killed," he said, regarding the number of books flooding the market. With new leaders such as Dystel, the streamlined paperback industry eased away from its "pioneering days." Undoubtedly, the pressure that paperback publishers were receiving from Congress and censorship campaigns influenced that transition.[23]

Comic books also fell under the scrutiny of Congress and numerous citizen watchdog groups. Costumed superheroes such as Superman and Captain America had helped elevate the comic industry's patriotic standing, but many readers now looked for edgier, more realistic fare. In the year after the war, superheroes' sales fell by about one-third, and, by the end of 1948, many of the characters had slipped off the pages in favor of the heroes of westerns and the heroes and antiheroes of the newly popular romance and crime genres. In 1947, DC Comics started publishing *Young Romance,* which sold millions and inspired dozens of competitors. *Crime Does Not Pay* also suddenly revealed a promising new market. When *Crime Does Not Pay* started in 1941, it was the only crime comic; in 1948, it led a pack of forty. In the immediate postwar period, a number of these comics—like paperbacks and movies—exhibited a noir sensibility.[24]

Despite the superheroes' decline, the comic industry grew dramatically into the early 1950s, when monthly sales reached 60 million copies. Statistics showed a wide audience across age and gender brackets. Among children aged six to eleven, 95 percent of boys and 91 percent of girls read comics. The figures among twelve- to seventeen-year-olds were 87 and 81 percent, respectively. The number of readers between the ages of eighteen and thirty was smaller but still significant: 41 percent of males and 28 percent of females. Even 16 percent of men and 12 percent of women over age thirty were readers. A growing number of publishers carved out specialties such as westerns and romance (by 1949, the top-selling genre, with almost one hundred titles each month). Moreover, comics, like the paperbacks, increasingly used sex, trying to entice male readers with scantily clad jungle queens or other females with bare legs and breasts so large that they inspired the nickname "headlight comics."[25]

Still, comics generally mirrored the triumphalist consensus of the early Cold War. American institutions and values reigned supreme. A 1950 issue of *Captain Marvel Adventures* focused on "Captain Marvel and the American Century," claiming that, "during the first half of this century, America has led all civilization in enormous strides forward toward the ideals of freedom, democracy, and peace. . . . The next half of the American Century from 1950–2000 is yours!" A November 1952 issue of *Atom-Age Combat* portrayed Americans winning the war against "Red Asians" under their evil commander, Boris "the Butcher" Kasilov. Elsewhere, heroes in comics such as *Spy Fighters, T-Man,* and *Kent Blake of the Secret Service* fought the "Red menace," and Captain America reappeared briefly as "Commie Smasher."[26]

But, as with paperbacks and film noir, an emerging group of highly popular comic books turned the American dream inside out, printing images and stories that tested consensus certainties. As more and more readers lost interest in costumed superheroes, they turned eagerly to crime comic books, which, by 1947, were proliferating. Despite titles such as *Crime Does Not Pay,* the stories mainly included graphic depictions of violence and brutality—stabbings, torture, dismemberment. In 40 percent of the panels in a 1948 issue of *Crime Must Pay the Penalty,* someone was shot. According to the historian Bradford Wright: "The crime comic books put forth a remarkably perverse and horrifying image of the affluent society turned upside down." And they found an eager and growing young audience. Not surprisingly, especially as postwar concerns about juvenile delinquency gained headlines, many adults talked of ways to regulate the comic-book industry.[27]

Against that backdrop, in 1950, a new company named EC Comics introduced *Tales from the Crypt* and, shortly thereafter, other horror titles such as *The Vault of Horror.* EC initially stood for Education Comics, a business that Max Gaines opened in 1946 after leaving DC Comics. Gaines published stories from the Bible and American history. When he died in a boat crash in 1947, his twenty-five-year-old son, William, took over a struggling company. Within three years, William reconstructed it entirely. EC now stood for Entertaining Comics. Gone was the educational series, and in its place were terrifying looks into worlds of horror and the grotesque. Gaines drew heavily from childhood memories of the pulps and radio shows such as *Suspense* and *Inner Sanctum.* "Into a self-satisfied culture of abundance and moral certitudes," as Bradford Wright has written, "EC injected a dose of sober revisionism and liberating anarchy." In place of Cold War celebrations of American values and institutions, EC offered satire, sharp criticism, and doubts. Brutal criminals looked "normal"; middle-class suburban families provided dysfunctional studies in psychosis; husbands dealt with independent wives by frying or boiling them; police officers murdered their own wives and raped teenage girls; teams played baseball with decapitated heads and other body parts; children killed their abusive parents; and cruel teachers and fathers met terrible fates in things like meat grinders. Bloody meat cleavers, axes, mallets, and ice picks were prevalent. Explicit drawings matched the grisly prose: "The flesh . . . rotted and stinking . . . fell from his bones." A worried Federal Bureau of Investigation decided to start a file on EC.[28]

While Gaines and his staff poked fun at society, they also hoped to make it better. Behind the gruesome pictures and stories was a social agenda to expose America's hypocrisies, injustices, and shortcomings. EC took direct aim at racial segregation, bigotry, history that ignored ugly realities, and phony patriotism. *Shock SuspenStories* included a story in which a black man is lynched for killing a white woman; after the hanging, someone else confesses to the crime. Another tale, "The Patriots," described how a mob beats a man to death after he keeps on his hat when the American flag passes by. Later, the townspeople discover that the "lousy Red" was a blind American veteran.[29]

In the early 1950s, the comic-book industry rode the horror phenomenon to record sales. Although EC was a quite small company, it set the pace. "When we found EC's horror books were doing well," recalled the editor of Marvel Comics, "we published a lot of horror books." Around one hundred titles from twenty-eight publishers were soon on store racks. And, of course, the popular crime comics also contained substantial gore.[30]

For an industry that was already under public scrutiny, however, the horror boom was very much a mixed blessing. The publication in 1954 of Frederic Wertham's *Seduction of the Innocent* proved that point all too well. Wertham was a respected New York psychiatrist who opposed racial segregation, advocated programs to help the poor and disadvantaged, and wanted to pare back censorship laws regarding adult literature. But he was convinced that comics encouraged antisocial behavior and violence among children. "To publish crime comics has nothing to do with civil liberties," he insisted. "It is a perversion of the idea of civil liberties." He wanted laws that blocked selling crime and horror comics to children under age fifteen. His best-selling four-hundred-page attack on comic books rang an authoritative alarm bell at a time when fear of juvenile delinquency was reaching epidemic proportions. *Seduction of the Innocent* reiterated an argument that Wertham had started advancing in the late 1940s, namely, that comic books were "a correspondence course in crime" and sexually deviant behavior. Although Wertham's evidence for that claim was thin at best, worried parents and authorities believed that they had the expert opinion they needed. Many were inclined to agree with Wertham's characterization of comic-book publishers as "racketeers of the spirit" who continued to corrupt children. And, however unintentionally, his warning that "as long as the crime comic-book industry exists in its present forms there are no secure homes" resonated with Cold War paranoia. "Would it not be simple for the Kremlin conspirators to put the comics to work for 'the cause' by infiltrating the ranks of the writers and artists?" asked one individual.[31]

Within a short time, over fifty cities limited comic sales, and more than half of state legislatures were discussing similar restrictions. In Binghamton, New York, volunteers canvassed neighborhoods, asking: "Are there any comics in this house?" The volunteers subsequently set fire to many comics, an incident that *Time* magazine photographed and that encouraged similar burnings elsewhere.[32]

Not surprisingly, the storm gathering around comic books prompted a Senate investigation at which Wertham was a star witness. On April 21, 1954, the Senate Judiciary Subcommittee to Investigate Juvenile Delinquency commenced its hearings in New York City on the comic-book industry with a slide show of bloody covers and panels from horror comics. "That committee was there to hang the comic publishers," said William Gaines, who tried to organize the other publishers to take a stand by testifying before the subcommittee. They preferred to keep low profiles, however, so only Gaines ultimately spoke for the industry. "I felt that I was really going to fix those bastards," he said later. But, after he read an eloquent defense of the intelligence of young readers, saying that "nobody was ever ruined by a comic," the relentless grilling wore him down, and he left the hearing in a daze. Although the subcommittee announced that its report would not be ready until 1955, its position was clear early on. "Not even the Communist conspiracy could devise a more effective way to demoralize, disrupt, confuse and destroy our future citizens," asserted Senator Robert Hendrickson (R-NJ), who chaired the subcommittee.[33]

Scurrying to avoid outside censorship, the comic industry did what the movie and TV industries had done under pressure: adopt a self-regulating code. The comic publishers had already established a code six years earlier, but, in October 1954, the newly formed Comic Magazine Association of America (CMAA) strengthened it, going so far as to ban the words *horror* and *terror* from comic-book covers. Under the revised rules, comics were to show respect for parents, marriage, and the family. These measures nevertheless failed to stop thirteen states from passing laws over the next few months to prevent sales of crime and horror comics. The industry's peak years were quickly receding. Within two years, the number of published titles fell by more than half, and eighteen companies quit. EC, which on principle had refused to join the CMAA, stopped publishing all its comics save one—*Mad,* which Gaines reshaped into a large format and called a magazine. Bristling with satire, *Mad* proudly defined itself as "trash" from "the usual gang of idiots." Its moving force was EC's gifted cartoonist Harvey Kurtzman, whose comics *Two-Fisted Tales* and *Frontline Combat* had already angered the U.S. Army. "These publications," according to the military, were "subversive because they tend to discredit the army and undermine troop morale." *Mad* soon showed that it would spare neither the military nor anything else from relentless spoofing. Moreover, when the fourth issue, which included a mocking satire of *Superman,* sold over a million copies, *Mad* signaled that many readers were eager to laugh at national icons. Granted, by the mid-1950s, comic books were back safely within the Cold War consensus. But, for some eight years, EC had taken a prominent role in staking out alternative imaginary worlds, questioning, mocking, and parodying the consensus culture's official truths. *Mad* continued that legacy.[34]

Elsewhere on the cultural fringes, established truths encountered additional challenges. In small, dingy urban dives and basement rooms, for instance, aspiring new-style comedians discussed politics and social issues such as race. And, in out-of-the-way taverns and dance halls known as honky-tonks, country musicians explored themes of loneliness, failed romance, and infidelity.

Technology was vital to disseminating this diverse material to larger audiences. Honky-tonk music spread via coin-operated record players called jukeboxes, whereas stand-up comedy benefited from the 33 1/3 rpm long-playing albums that first appeared in 1948. Despite their different venues and technologies, these and other entertainment forms provided their own critiques of American life.

If the "rebel comedians" marked their breaking-out debut at any particular point, it was probably December 25, 1953, when the little-known Mort Sahl took the stage at the "hungry i," a seedy dive with only eighty-three seats carved out of a San Francisco wine cellar. His humor was path-breaking but indebted to a host of Jewish comedians who had honed their comedy in the "Borscht Belt," a collection of small resorts that had developed along a narrow strip of the Catskill Mountains, about one hundred miles north of New York City. The resorts (in many cases, collections of small bungalow houses) had emerged from the 1920s into the 1940s to meet the needs of Jews who could not stay at exclusionary gentile resorts. As members of an "'outgroup' subculture," the tourists often depended on a figure with roots deep in Jewish culture: the "tummler," who resembled a comic jester at various celebrations. In the Catskills, the tummler served as a social director and trickster whose job was to make sure the guests enjoyed themselves. A large number of tummlers went on to develop well-known stage careers, among them Sid Caesar, Red Buttons, Lenny Bruce, Jerry Lewis, Shecky Greene, Judy Holliday, and Danny Kaye. For American comedy after World War II, the Catskills were the equivalent of baseball's minor leagues.[35]

What distinguished Mort Sahl from the older-style comics, however, was his eagerness to satirize American politics and social issues. Whereas they sought to amuse, not to change, society, he openly criticized the injustices and hypocrisies around him. His technique was that of "the hipster," not of a Bob Hope kind of "toastmaster." By the 1950s, Hope had become an establishment entertainer, one of the biggest stars of radio, film, and television. His famous one-liners were topical and funny but at the same time safe, innocuous, and patriotic. As someone later commented, his humor "rubbed but did not scratch." In contrast, Sahl's scratched, often brutally so. "Is there any group I haven't offended?" he liked to ask.[36]

Sahl had been born in Canada but grew up in Los Angeles and then moved to the San Francisco area. In 1953, in an audition for the hungry i, his joke about how Joe McCarthy's jacket resembled Eisenhower's, "only it's got an extra zipper that fits over the mouth," convinced the club owner, Enrico Banducci, to hire him. Banducci figured, "He can't hurt the place," and signed him on as a comedian for $75 a week. Dressed casually in slacks and a cardigan sweater, Sahl typically sauntered onstage with a newspaper. His "audacious position was that, basically, the fix was in," according to one media observer. In other words: "Life in the 1950s, and politics in particular, was a joke and . . . he was simply reporting what went on in Washington."[37]

Over the next few years, Sahl pioneered what the *San Francisco Chronicle*'s jazz expert Ralph Gleason described as "the new comedy of dissent." Using a free-form style like that of jazz, he shredded Cold War certitudes. "Joe McCarthy doesn't question what you say so much as your right to say it," he joked. He maintained that, if McCarthy questioned him about his activities, he would reply: "I didn't mean to be a subversive, but I was new in this community and I wanted to meet the girls." When he discussed the House Committee on Un-American Activities (HUAC), he said: "Every time the Russians throw an American in jail, the HUAC retaliates— by throwing an American in jail." He claimed that Vice President Richard Nixon had "been on the cover of every magazine except *True*." And he said that he was less interested in politics than "in overthrowing the government." When someone asked him to say something funny, he answered simply: "John Foster Dulles," Eisenhower's secretary of state. He also spoke out on issues of nuclear war, sex, and race. "Eisenhower says he's for integration but gradually; [the Illinois governor and Democratic presidential candidate Adlai] Stevenson says he's for integration but moderately," Sahl quipped. "It should be possible to compromise between those extremes." Of capital punishment, he announced firmly: "You've got to execute people. How else are they gonna learn?" Nevertheless, he liked to remind religious groups who favored the death penalty that they had "once made a Very Big Mistake." He was, according to *Time* magazine, "a sort of Will Rogers with fangs."[38]

Sahl and the hungry i galvanized the comedy world. In cities around the United States, small, cheap clubs with maverick performers spread like an underground movement outside the traditional posh showrooms, such as New York's famed Copacabana. Vibrant, socially aware satire began to burst loose, unleashing waves of antiestablishment humor. Long-playing recordings of comedy performances also broke new ground, attracting even more audiences from around the country. In 1951, the humorist Stan Freberg's "comedy albums" had led the way, but Sahl's first album in 1955 was reputedly the first recording of a live comedy performance. Soon rebel comedians such as Shelley Berman, Bob Newhart, Tom Lehrer, Elaine May, and Mike Nichols were producing successful recordings. Sahl's influence was profound. "He totally restructured comedy," contended Woody Allen, whose own comedic career owed much to him. "Sahl made it less difficult for all of us who came after him. He was like the tip of the iceberg. Underneath were all the other people who came along: Lenny Bruce, Nichols & May, all the Second City players." Sahl and the comedians whom he influenced did more than advance antiestablishment humor. They also elevated stand-up comedy, previously "a show-business subdivision" inhabited by "theatrical lowlife."[39]

The *Playboy* publisher Hugh Hefner played an important role in that process. Hefner was the product of a relatively prosperous and devout Chicago family that spurned swearing, drinking, and smoking. In late 1953, after serving in the army, graduating from college, starting a family, and working as a circulation manager for *Children's Activities,* the twenty-seven-year-old Hefner decided—with little money and no publishing connections—to start a new kind of men's magazine, *Playboy.* At that time, the standard publications came primarily in two types. One was the "sweaty-armpits" journal, such as *True, Stag,* or *Men,* which included lots of action, some sports, an essay on sex such as "Anything Goes in Fresno," and several pages of cheesecake photos or seminude drawings. The other kind was the "girlie magazine," with titles such as *Wink* and *Flirt.* Some of the publications included sexually explicit photographs and were available under-the-counter, but most were displayed openly in newsstands and drugstores. New publications such as *Male* raised the number of men's adventure magazines from five in 1950 to eleven in 1952. Increasingly, most featured pulp-style cover paintings in which rugged men fought off myriad dangers or revealingly clad women were victims of bondage and torture. The magazines combined contradictory messages. As one analysis has noted, the journals "spread the gospel of sexual repression—sex is dirty and dangerous—all the while providing sexual titillation for voyeuristic readers, without ever describing any real . . . well, sex."[40]

Convinced that blue-collar workers with high school diplomas read the traditional men's magazines, Hefner pitched his publication at a different audience: young urban males who had gone to college and hoped to succeed in business or a profession. *Playboy,* he said, would be "a pleasure primer styled for the masculine taste"—"a romantic men's magazine." It would provide guidelines for success for the upwardly mobile young man, with much emphasis on status, dressing stylishly, driving the right car, and owning a good stereo recording system. Other men's magazines liked to show men "thrashing through thorny thickets or splashing about in fast flowing streams," Hefner wrote, but not *Playboy.* "We plan spending most of our time inside." The dominant message was: "Enjoy yourself." To that end, *Playboy* took a recreational view of sex. This kind of sex, as Hefner argued, was "innocent," not sleazy or associated with quick-stop motel rooms. The women in *Playboy*'s famous centerfolds were supposed to seem wholesome, fun loving, warm, and unpretentious. The first of those women was none other than Marilyn Monroe, who, by 1953, was well on her way to becoming a sensationally popular movie star. For $500, Hefner was able to buy the rights to a nude photograph that she had let a calendar company take four years earlier, when she desperately needed money. Monroe's nude picture unquestionably helped turn the launching of *Playboy* into one of publishing's most striking success stories. Although Hefner was so skeptical about his magazine's future that he kept the date off the first issue, he need not have worried. Within a few years, he was well on his way to building a *Playboy* empire, including nightclubs.[41]

Hefner threw his growing influence behind the new rebel comics, featuring them in his magazine, putting them in his nightclubs, and boosting their national credentials. In 1956, for example, he published a *Playboy* interview with Sahl. (Sahl liked to joke that *Playboy*'s three-page foldout of nude women had created an entire generation of males who thought that women were folded several times and had staples in their navels.) Hefner also boosted the career of Lenny Bruce. After watching Bruce perform in a small San Francisco club, Hefner secured his booking at Chicago's upscale Cloister for $850 a week.[42]

In important ways, of course, *Playboy* and the new stand-up comics, like noir films, themselves fit the consensus culture, particularly on gender issues. The magazine and the clubs were basically men's worlds. "All woman wants is security," claimed an early feature article. "And she's perfectly willing to crush men's adventurous, freedom-loving spirit to get it." The cultural observer Peter Schrag believed that Hefner and Walt Disney had much in common, that "Disneyland and Playboyland" were both about indulging fantasies: "Where Disneyland offers a mermaid without nipples, Hefner serves up his playmates without warts, birthmarks or pimples." Granted, Hefner was less prudish than Disney and saw sex as "no longer dirty but healthy," wrote Schrag. In both instances, sex was, nevertheless, "as uncomplicated as ever."[43]

Mort Sahl seemed also to share that dream of an uncomplicated, idealized world. Like Hefner, he took many of his beliefs from Depression-era movies, particularly Frank Capra's. "My eyes get moist when I watch *Mr. Smith Goes to Washington*," he said. In any case, his views of women were often condescending and defensive. For a while, Sahl was married to a *Playboy* centerfold who said that "being a Bunny is my main career." The singer Julie London liked much about Sahl but claimed that "he likes the girly-girly type" and that "[his] male side is attracted to Vargas girls"—the cheesecake pinups of Alberto Vargas that appeared in *Esquire* magazine, calendars, and elsewhere. "He says men get a raw deal." That impression was not London's alone. "Chicks holler for equal rights," Sahl said. "What they really mean is they want men's rights and they're willing to give up theirs, which is a dumb bargain." He told *Playboy* that women dating him looked for "Hilarity. Alcohol. Adventure. Escape. Danger. Reflected prestige." He also said, "I don't expect them to be intellectuals," and quipped, "A woman's place is in the stove."[44]

Similarly, in film noir, independent women were often malevolent creatures who preyed on men. Movie titles included *Sinful Woman, Bad Blonde, Wicked Woman, Blonde Sinner, Man Bait,* and *A Dame Called Murder.* The ubiquitous femme fatale was the sexy human equivalent of a black widow spider with a victim caught in her web. "I want action," says Laurie, the short-skirted carnival woman in *Gun Crazy* (Joseph H. Lewis, 1949), to the gullible drifter, Bart, before they embark on a bloody crime spree. "You're a little man with a briefcase," the sensual Lizabeth Scott character goads an insurance agent in *Pitfall* (André De Toth, 1948). In Billy Wilder's *Ace in the Hole* (1951), the tough, scheming Jan Sterling refuses to pray for her dying husband: "I don't pray. Kneeling bags my nylons." According to one film scholar: "Noir's misogyny functioned as a kind of containment: beware, this is what happens when iron-willed women seize power over men."[45]

Still, although film noir, *Playboy,* the rebel comedians, and other contrary entertainment forms were clearly products of the mainstream society that they battled, they unquestionably pushed against many of that society's barriers. They were cultural troublemakers. In fundamental ways, they used a fun house mirror to examine many Cold War values and assumptions. *Time* magazine thus labeled the stand-up comics as "Sickniks" who displayed a "highly disturbing hostility towards the world." A sociologist lamented their impact on the nation: "It's like the last days of Rome." Nor could film noir's disillusioning treatments of marriage and family reassure traditionalists. "Home is where you come when you run out of places," said Barbara Stanwyck's Mae Doyle character in *Clash by Night* (Fritz Lang, 1952).[46]

The religion that stand-up comedian Lenny Bruce discussed, for example, was a far cry from that in Hollywood's reverential biblical spectaculars, Billy Graham's best sellers, or songs about "The Man Upstairs." From Bruce's perspective, modern con artists and greedy hustlers had turned organized religion into a racket. Christ, after all, was a bearded prophet who had driven the money changers from the temple and advocated peace—actions that would have made him a subversive in the America of Joe McCarthy and HUAC.[47]

Within pockets of popular culture, nothing seemed safe, including such consensus centerpieces as religion, marriage, family, and sweet girl-meets-boy romance. According to the idealized scenario, Americans were enjoying a new lifestyle, "togetherness," as the editors of the women's magazine *McCall's* described it in 1954: "Men, women and children are achieving it together . . . not as women alone, or men alone, isolated from one another, but as a family, sharing a common experience." *Playboy*, however, downplayed marriage commitments. According to one social commentator: "*Playboy* loved women—large-breasted, long-legged young women, anyway—and hated wives." The popular cartoonist Charles Addams often paired marriage and murder. "For heaven's sake, can't you do anything right?" a wife in one cartoon asked her husband after he tried to hang himself. Elsewhere, Addams showed a husband sneaking up behind his wife with a hatchet. Unaware of her impending doom, she said: "Now, don't come back asking me to forgive you." In film noir, seductive, deadly females were at the same time appealingly strong, complex, intelligent, and independent. They contrasted sharply with "the girl back home, or the faithful, long-suffering wife," who, in the words of the writer Nicholas Christopher, "was antiseptic, static, sexually repressed, socially rather dull." Males understandably looked outside the home for fun and excitement. Indeed, the family was seldom visible in film noir, and, when it was, it resembled a prison. "In sexual and social matters," according to Christopher, noir was "a subversive form, galaxies removed from the usual cinematic concerns of marriage, conventional romance, love as elixir."[48]

Country music also probed the darker side of marriage, courtship, and romance. Significantly, it was as a kind of minority report on domestic life that country music in the 1940s and early 1950s moved from entertainment's regional margins to the national mainstream. In the process, it shed much of its hillbilly reputation, found an urban audience, turned itself into a big business, and even helped the recording industry through a brief downturn.

Going into the 1940s, the hillbilly image continued to haunt country music, tainting it as a rube sideshow. In 1943, for instance, Tennessee governor Prentice Cooper refused to attend a party celebrating *The Grand Ole Opry*'s coast-to-coast radio hookup. The event was nothing but a "circus," he argued. He also accused *Opry* star Roy Acuff of turning Nashville into a laughable "hillbilly capital." Such rebukes were powerful reminders, as Acuff said, that "we had a ways to go before our type of music was to become respectable." In the meantime, some musicians struggled fiercely to find respectability. "That 'hillbilly' [label]," recalled Clayton McMichen, "we fought it, teeth and toenails, . . . [because] we wanted to make [country music] popular." The rising country singer Ernest Tubb threw down a gauntlet: "Smile when you call me a hillbilly."[49]

World War II was crucial in setting the stage for country's widening popularity and prosperity. By dispersing many rural Southerners to urban defense industries and into the military, the war helped widen country music's prospective audience. The popularity of jukeboxes and the American Federation of Musicians (AFM) strike, which started in August 1942, also made the music more accessible. The AFM contended that the 400,000 jukeboxes throughout the nation, along with radio's increasing reliance on phonograph records, were hurting songwriters and performers. When the major recording companies refused to establish a fund for unemployed musicians, the AFM went on strike. The federation's yearlong ban on recordings opened opportunities for small, independent record companies to take advantage of the demand for new music. Among these companies was the Nashville-based Acuff-Rose Publications, which Roy Acuff and Fred Rose founded in 1942 exclusively for country music, and the Capitol label, which the songwriter Johnny Mercer started that same year in Los Angeles. Capitol became the main source of West Coast country music recordings, particularly those of the cowboy movie star Tex Ritter. Ultimately, the AFM received more compensation for its members, but, in the meantime, many radio stations and jukebox operators discovered country alternatives to popular music. A growing number of listeners appreciated country music's treatment of experiences that the war exacerbated—suffering, loneliness, and death.[50]

Of the several varieties of country music that came out of the war, none proved more influential than that which was associated with the honky-tonks—small, roadside clubs scattered outside towns and along highways, especially in the Southwest. Honky-tonk songs were made for dancing, but they also articulated the difficulties that working-class rural transplants faced in urban America. The music probed as well the difficulties of overcoming the wartime separation of spouses and lovers and dealing with threats to traditional gender roles as large numbers of women entered the manufacturing workforce. "Should I Come Back Home to You?" asked Ernest Tubb in a 1945 song about a soldier who realized that his wife might have been unfaithful while he was away. The next year, Tubb's "Rainbow at Midnight" focused on a returning soldier's dream of reuniting with a woman he had left behind, settling down, and having "a baby or two." But postwar realities quickly took the measure of many such dreams as well as the happy, abundant future that advertisements and other wartime propaganda had set forth. As weariness, worry, and guilt competed with anxious optimism, honky-tonk music touched an emotional chord, dealing forthrightly with broken relationships and addressing themes such as infidelity. Right after the war, almost half the honky-tonk songs dealt with lost love and breaking up.[51]

Al Dexter's 1943 hit "Pistol Packin' Mama" set the tone of many "cheating" songs. It described a woman entering a bar with intentions of killing her husband's girlfriend. As Dexter later explained, Columbia Records' country recording director "Art Satherley . . . told me to write honky-tonk songs. When I told him I like pretty songs, he said . . . 'My lad, do you want to sing pretty songs or do you want to make money.'" "Pistol Packin' Mama" made lots of money, selling a million records within six months and becoming one of the war era's biggest hits.[52]

Although major record companies and radio stations initially rebuffed explicit treatments of unfaithful and failed relationships, a small flood of such songs emerged over the next few years. Among the most popular were Floyd Tillman's "Drivin' Nails in My Coffin," about a man who turns to drink to compensate for lost love; Tubb's "Walkin' the Floor over You," about a man awaiting the return of a woman who has left him; Hank Thompson's "The Wild Side of Life," about a husband's efforts to keep his wife from partying with other men; and Merle Travis's "Divorce Me, C.O.D." By the late 1940s, jukeboxes were popularizing songs about infidelity despite the uneasiness of mainstream recording companies and radio stations. Two of the most popular songs were "One Has My Name, the Other Has My Heart," about people trapped in unhappy marriages, and "Slipping A-round," about married people having an affair. In 1949, the Ernest Tubb version of "Slipping Around" became the top country hit, selling a million copies. Opposition to lyrics about sexual dallying was easing.[53]

Nevertheless, as late as 1952, *The Grand Ole Opry* and NBC banned Kitty Wells's extremely popular "It Wasn't God Who Made Honky Tonk Angels," which contended that there was "a man to blame" for every fallen woman—a direct response to Thompson's "Wild Side of Life." Despite such resistance, Wells's song soared to the top of the country charts. Although honky-tonk music for the most part expressed male frustrations and discontent in the postwar era, Wells's hit indicated that women were clearly anxious to express their own grievances. Certainly, the folk tradition in country music was full of songs that expressed a fierce female independence. But Wells recorded "the first massively popular woman's song of self-assertion in country music." Despite her image as a wholesome, old-time country sweetheart, the thirty-three-year-old mother in gingham dresses had provided a ringing answer to the male cheating songs. Country record companies remained skeptical about promoting female performers, however, because, as the country star Chet Atkins said, "they just didn't think they could make any money off them." That did not stop other women—including Jean Shepard, Charline Arthur, and Texas Ruby (Ruby Agnes Owens)—from singing about unfaithful spouses and unhappy relationships.[54]

The postwar rash of expressive, personal songs about sexual transgressions and domestic troubles reflected changes in the American family. Polls showed that around 75 percent of women regretted having to give up their wartime jobs. Additional studies in the 1950s indicated that only about one-third of working-class couples described themselves as happily married. The consensus portrait of blissful American families in which women delighted in performing traditional household duties did not match the actual experience of huge numbers of people. In 1946, the divorce rate leaped upward; during the 1950s, between one-third and one-fourth of new marriages failed. A number of "country jeremiads" such as "Dust on the Bible" fretted about the perceived collapse of traditional morals. The immensely popular Eddie Arnold, in his "Mother Please Stay Home with Me," told of a child who died while his mother was partying. But, while such "mother songs" celebrated women's familiar household roles, the cheating songs suggested that families were faltering. "Married by the Bible (Divorced by the Law)" summed up disturbing trends.[55]

By the early 1950s, the leading troubadour of heartbreak was Hank Williams. Williams's emotional intensity was legendary. Within a few years, before his death on New Year's Day 1953 at age twenty-nine, he recorded some of country music's most memorable songs. Many of them exuded sadness, alienation, and fractured relationships—"(You Don't Love Me) Half as Much (As I Love You)," "Your Cheatin' Heart," "My Son Calls Another Man Daddy," "I'm So Lonesome I Could Cry," "Why Don't You Love Me Like You Used to Do," "Cold, Cold Heart," "Lovesick Blues," "Lonesome Whistle," "May You Never Be Alone Like Me," "Take These Chains from My Heart," and "I'll Never Get out of This World Alive." Here were cries of anguish from a world of illicit sex, liquor, regrets, and lost love. "Hank Williams was a poet of limits, fear, and failure," the cultural analyst Greil Marcus wrote. "He went as deeply into one dimension of the country world as anyone could, gave it beauty, gave it dignity." With Williams, the fabled American road became "a lost highway." At one point when he was singing the religious standard "I Saw the Light," he stopped, turned to Minnie Pearl, and said, "Minnie, I don't see no light. There ain't no light." Even Williams's growing stardom weighed heavily on him. He feared that he was becoming just another commodity on the market. "They're slicing me up and selling me like baloney," he protested.[56]

The music industry, on the other hand, was delighted with country's growing profits and popularity. Indeed, when the record industry lost about 25 percent of its business between 1947 and 1949, honky-tonk helped ease the situation. While Tin Pan Alley songwriters avoided lyrics that reflected rising divorce rates, family instability, and a spreading sense that things were not quite right, the candor of honky-tonk musicians found a growing audience. As the country music writer and performer Ted Daffan observed, whereas "pop music was very flowery and sentimental," "country writers, me included, would tell it in straight, simple language, like it was": "It sounded much more real."[57]

As country music grew into a $70 million business by 1954, commercial considerations became even more important. The Nashville companies not only had solidified their hold on country's future but now hoped to expand from their working-class base to more cosmopolitan, middle-class patrons. As a result, going into the 1950s, major efforts were under way to soften and clean up the honky-tonk messages, turning them into "country pop." The success of "The Tennessee Waltz" was a milepost in that respect. In 1950, two years after Pee Wee King and his Golden West Cowboys first recorded the song, the pop singer Patti Page's version became a music sensation. In less than six months, record sales of Page's "Tennessee Waltz" approached 5 million. Although the song echoed the theme of broken romance so familiar to honky-tonk, Page's recording soared to the top of the pop charts. "It had the effect of breaking down barriers," according to the music publisher Wesley Rose. More than ever, country music producers and entertainers saw opportunities to "cross over" onto the lucrative pop lists. Established country stars such as Jimmy Wakely, Red Foley, and especially Eddie Arnold demonstrated the cross-chart marketability of country. Wakely began recording with full orchestras because, as he said: "It's always been my contention that country music should be sold to the, call it the upper echelon, or what have you." Arnold's soft, smooth, optimistic style elevated him into one of the era's most popular singers on both the country and the pop charts. "I never wanted to desert the country side," he explained. "I just wanted to broaden my thing." Nashville—"Tin Pan Valley," as *Time* dubbed it in 1951—also promoted new stars like Carl Smith and Faron Young, who downplayed subjects such as infidelity in favor of more upbeat, affirmative renderings of fulfilled love. Country music was clearly in transition.[58]

But, for a while in the late 1940s and early 1950s, honky-tonk—like the blues—revealed the underside of postwar prosperity and contentment.

Charlie Parker, the great jazz musician, listened to country for a simple reason: "The stories, man. Listen to the stories." Granted, those stories hardly attacked the nation's larger political, social, and economic institutions. "Private sins and worries" dominated. But, on that level alone, honky-tonk stories contradicted the good-news reports from the cultural mainstream.[59]

Powerful crosscurrents in fact surged all through that mainstream. Some were inadvertent creations of the government's own Cold War strategies. For example, in the mid-1950s, the State Department started sending well-known jazz musicians around the world as part of a "people-to-people" program aimed at contrasting U.S. freedom with the Soviet Union's closed society. Supposedly, "jam-bassadors" such as Louis Armstrong would also belie charges that the United States was a racist nation, despite the reality of segregation. Although these goodwill ambassadors quite successfully represented the image of a democratic America abroad, they in turn seized the opportunity to advance their own agendas concerning civil rights and the liberation of people from colonial powers. "Invited onto the margins of diplomacy," as one historian has written, "they refused to stay on the fringes as sidemen." At a time when the emerging civil rights movement in the United States elicited an increasingly violent response, the Cold War jazz tours emphasized black contributions to American culture. "After all," said Armstrong when he was in Ghana, "my ancestors came from here and I still have African blood in me." Between 1945 and 1960, forty countries in Africa and Asia won independence from imperial systems. When the jam-bassadors toured, there was little doubt that they identified with revolutionary change. Within the United States, Armstrong was an outspoken opponent of segregation. "The way they are treating my people in the South," he asserted angrily in 1957, "the Government can go to hell." It was this oppositional aspect of the performers' tours that resonated among many foreigners. In Greece, for example, anti-American students who objected to U.S. support for their country's right-wing dictatorship nevertheless carried jazz great Dizzy Gillespie on their shoulders. "Students Drop Rocks and Roll with Dizzy," reported one local newspaper. In 1962, following their goodwill tours, Armstrong and Dave and Iola Brubeck collaborated on a jazz musical review at the Monterey Jazz Festival in California. They poked fun at elements within the State Department efforts and also condemned racial segregation. "Look here," said Armstrong at one point, "what *we* need is a goodwill tour of Mississippi. . . . Forget Moscow—when do we play in New Orleans!" Although the State Department used the musicians as weapons in the Cold War, the musicians fired some volleys of their own.[60]

While the Cold War cultural exchanges meant different things to different people, popular culture sometimes evoked unexpected responses. Surprisingly, for example, one of America's most powerful Catholics, Francis Cardinal Spellman, recommended that his priests read Mickey Spillane's *One Lonely Night* (1951). The staunchly anti-Communist Spellman hardly approved of the novel's sexual material, but he liked the way in which the fictional hero, Mike Hammer, dealt with the Reds. As Hammer says: "Don't arrest them, don't treat them with the dignity of the democratic process of the courts of law . . . do the same thing they'd to do you! Treat 'em to the inglorious taste of sudden death."[61]

Popular culture's mixed messages were legion. Consensus and dissenting messages often appeared in the same places. A movie such as *The Wild One* (Lázló Benedek, 1953), about a motorcycle gang that tore apart a town, drew criticism for encouraging teenage rebellion and even giving propagandistic ammunition to the Communists. "What are you rebelling against?" asks a young woman of Johnny (Marlon Brando), the leather-coated gang leader. "Well, what ya got?" he replies, in one of the movie's famous lines. Meanwhile, Kathy, the waitress to whom he is attracted, dreams of finding a man who will help her escape from the small, boring town. Brando himself wanted the film to sympathize with rebellious outsiders and to criticize the middle-class world of "drones and Babbitts responding to the leather-jacketed bikers with a hysteria that had driven the group to violence in the first place." Ultimately, however, he was disappointed with compromises in the plot: "Somewhere along the way we went off track. The result was that instead of finding why young people tend to bunch into groups that seek expression in violence, all that we did was show the violence." At the film's end, Brando still seemed to be the alienated rebel. He climbs on his motorcycle and rides out of the town without Kathy. Yet audiences leaving the theater could hardly forget his voice-over commentary in the movie's opening scenes. "A girl got to me," he says, as he rolls down the road. "I changed." Audiences leaving the theaters could wonder how much he had changed and whether love had eventually prevailed, soon to bring him back to Kathy. Perhaps the wild one was no longer quite so wild—a reassuring message for mainstream America.[62]

Hollywood's ability to package rebellion with consensus was also apparent in *Rebel without a Cause* (Nicholas Ray, 1955). James Dean played an alienated high school student, Jim Stark. Advertisements and posters for the movie offered Dean as a symbol of teen disenchantment and revolt. He looked defiantly "cool," standing with a sullen expression, dressed in blue jeans, T-shirt, and red windbreaker, and holding a cigarette. Yet the movie's message was anything but radical. Ultimately, the film endorsed tight-knit families built on love and traditional gender roles—not permissiveness. Jim chafed at the outset in a permissive environment in which his father, who sometimes wore an apron, refused to exert authority. "When did I ever stop you from doing anything?" asked the father at one point. An important character in the movie was Ray, a kindly juvenile officer who tried to help troubled youngsters. On this level, the movie implicitly endorsed caring, therapeutic strategies as ways by which professionals could reduce social differences and discontent. These strategies mirrored the widespread interest in psychology in the postwar years. "Where's Your Personality?" asked the *Reader's Digest* in a typical article. "Stop! I'm a doctor. I can cure you," shouted a character in the movie *Panic in the Streets* (Elia Kazan, 1950). Norman Vincent Peale's best-selling nonfiction books also offered a cure: "positive thinking," which would allow an individual to "become . . . more popular, esteemed, and well-liked." Such therapeutic remedies suggested that problems rested with individuals, not institutions or larger social forces. In *Rebel without a Cause,* Jim primarily wanted acceptance and stability. By the film's end, he no longer had a reason to protest. Hollywood could tout the rebel images of Brando and Dean and still make the characters safe enough for the mainstream.[63]

Within that mainstream, rebel images nevertheless proved highly marketable. In the 1950s, Walt Disney films and television programs thus included *The Story of Robin and His Merrie Men* (Ken Annakin, 1952), *Rob Roy, the Highland Rogue* (Harold French, 1954), and, of course, *Davy Crockett, King of the Wild Frontier* (Norman Foster, 1955). Crockett epitomized the feisty American with a healthy antiauthoritarian attitude. "Crockett," warns one character, "if you go in there and speak against President Jackson's bill, you're through with politics." After punching him, Crockett responds: "Here's what I think of *your* kind of politics."[64]

Some film genres—especially the western—were particularly useful vehicles in addressing contradictory themes. Precisely because the western was "a safe vessel, its red-blooded Americanism beyond question," as a film historian observed, it "functioned as both a contained indictment and a reaffirmation of America, past and present." A number of postwar westerns at least indirectly explored current social problems and conflicts over values, rather than simply reaffirming old certainties. *The Gunfighter* (Henry King, 1950), for instance, thus had much to say about how power can create vulnerability and limit options. Gregory Peck played Jimmy Ringo, a gunfighter with a fabled reputation who simply wants to settle down with his family. He is tired of living with "fame," which has isolated him and made him the target of up-and-coming young gunslingers. Tragedy, not triumph, haunted the film. At the end, a young man shoots Ringo in the back. The dying Ringo claims falsely that the shooter outdrew him. Now the man who killed the famous Jimmy Ringo must also lead a life of doom. Here, wrote the historian Richard Slotkin, was a Western "parody of the Cold War." Ringo was "at once the most powerful and the most vulnerable man in the world."[65]

Cold War meanings may have been even clearer in Fred Zinneman's

1952 box-office hit *High Noon,* but viewers disagreed on how to interpret them. The movie was about a newly married marshal, Will Kane (a role for which Gary Cooper won an Academy Award), who must deal with a man whom he put in prison, Frank Miller. Now out of jail, Miller and his three brothers are returning to the community of Hadleyville to kill Kane. The marshal is unable to recruit any help from the cowardly townspeople. Finally, he takes to the street alone in a shoot-out with the Miller gang. At a crucial moment, he finds an ally in his Quaker wife, even though she opposes violence and had pleaded with him simply to flee the town. With the Millers dead in the street, the townspeople rush to congratulate Kane. But he disgustedly throws his badge on the ground and rides out of town with his wife. It was possible to view the movie as both a critique and a defense of McCarthyism. The scriptwriter, Carl Foreman, specifically intended the film to be a criticism of HUAC and of Hollywood for knuckling under to it. He wrote the screenplay at a time when HUAC had subpoenaed him to testify. "There must be times these days," asserted *The Nation* magazine, "when Mr. Foreman feels that he too [like Marshal Kane in *High Noon*] has been deserted by those who should have helped him stand off the bullies and the tough guys whose aggressions have so largely destroyed the moral fiber of the Western town that goes by the name of Hollywood." However, another publication regretted that the portrait of Hadleyville as weak provided grist for the Communist propaganda mill. John Wayne furiously dismissed the movie as "the most un-American thing I've ever seen in my whole life." How else, Wayne wondered, could one interpret "ole Coop putting the U.S. marshal's badge under his foot and stomping on it"? In contrast, other critics saw parallels between Kane's willingness to stand up for principles and America's resolute courage in opposing communism.[66]

Like westerns, established entertainment genres such as science fiction, war, and horror offered opportunities to comment at least obliquely on social issues. The creator in 1959 of television's *Twilight Zone,* Rod Serling had turned to science fiction out of frustration with networks and sponsors who shunned any kind of controversy. Serling, who had felt the sting of anti-Semitism, found that he could deal with such topics as prejudice, discrimination, and nuclear war with allegory. "Things which couldn't be said by a Republican or a Democrat could be said by a Martian," he noted of this "strange ritual of track-covering."[67]

In the 1950s, science fiction movies often mixed such "track-covering" with strong twists of the macabre that attracted substantial audiences. "Thank God for the horror pictures," rejoiced a drive-in theater owner. "They've saved us. . . . The girls yell and hang on to the boys and sometimes you've really got to keep an eye on those cars." Granted, on one level, the films were harmless entertainments that provided cheap thrills. They also often used familiar formulas of endangered women and echoed Cold

War fears about attacks on the United States. But, on another level, they supplied numerous reminders of public anxieties over atomic weapons and nuclear fallout. The producer of *Them!* (Gordon Douglas, 1954), Ted Sherdeman, hated nuclear weapons. "I just went over to the curb and started to throw up," he recalled, on learning of the Hiroshima bombing. *Them!* was about monstrous, irradiated ants who terrorize earth. "Everyone had seen ants and no one trusted the atom bomb, so I had Warner [Brothers] buy the story," he said. Apocalyptic themes suffused such productions. In *The Day the Earth Stood Still* (Robert Wise, 1951), an alien spoke of peace and refused to take sides regarding Cold War disputes. "My mission here," he said, "is not to solve your petty squabbles. It concerns the existence of every last creature on your Earth." *The Incredible Shrinking Man* (Jack Arnold, 1957) focused on the terrible fate of a man who was accidentally exposed to radiation. *On the Beach* (Stanley Kramer, 1959), based on a best-selling novel, dealt poignantly with the end of the world following a nuclear war and was the fifth-biggest box-office draw of 1960.[68]

An implicit target of many 1950s films was the modern organizational world that rested on rules, order, knowledge, and predictability. In *The Thing from Another World* (Christian Nyby, 1951), a scientist claimed: "Knowledge is more important than life. . . . We've split the atom." A listener interrupted him: "Yes, and that sure made the world happy, didn't it?" A number of 1950s war films applauded the heroism of ordinary soldiers but looked skeptically at the institutions, hierarchies, and bureaucracies that commanded them. *From Here to Eternity* (Fred Zinneman, 1953), *Attack* (Robert Aldrich, 1956), and *Pork Chop Hill* (Lewis Milestone, 1959) were notable examples. *Paths of Glory* (Stanley Kubrick, 1957) offered an even more directly powerful antiwar statement, but it did so by focusing on a French unit during World War I.[69]

Probably no one in the entertainment business looked more skeptically at the supposed orderliness of human affairs than did the movie and TV producer Alfred Hitchcock. Time and again, Hitchcock showed how evil and irrationality stalk innocent people. The so-called normal world masks the horror that lurks beneath. In *Rear Window* (1954), the James Stewart character, hobbled with a broken leg, watches his neighbors through binoculars. He is merely killing time, enjoying vicarious thrills; to his horror, he discovers that other kinds of killing are taking place, and he himself almost becomes a victim. In *The Man Who Knew Too Much* (1955), an unsuspecting family on vacation suddenly plunges into a deadly world of intrigue and murder. In *The Wrong Man* (1956), the protagonist endures his wrongful arrest and trial only to find that his wife has completely broken under the strain and no longer even recognizes him. In *Vertigo* (1958), things are never quite as they seem, and, when the protagonist finally solves the mystery, the result is the death of the woman he loves. *Psycho* (1960) demonstrated that normal activities such as taking a shower can be deadly.[70]

Even seemingly benign comic strips could include sharp social commentary, poking fun at dominant assumptions and portraying sweetly innocent protagonists as trapped in circumstances beyond their control. Starting in 1949, Walt Kelly's *Pogo* went into syndication, soon appearing in hundreds of newspapers. Pogo, a little opossum living in the swamp, was, in Kelly's words, "the reasonably patient, soft-hearted, naive, friendly little person we think we all are." But, as the writer Brad Leithauser later pointed out: "Pogo remained someone things happened around or to." It was "his instinct for tempered, proud, quiet retreat" that allowed him to survive in a world populated with the likes of Simple J. Malarkey, a wildcat stand-in for Senator Joe McCarthy, and P. T. Bridgeport, a capitalistic con artist à la Barnum.[71]

When Charles Schulz's immensely successful cartoon strip *Peanuts* debuted in October 1950, it included another representative of the beleaguered little guy: Charlie Brown. "Well! Here comes ol' Charlie Brown," said two children in the first strip. "Good ol' Charlie Brown. . . . Yes, sir! Good ol' Charlie Brown. . . . How I hate him." He is a hapless victim who perseveres despite life's constant battering. He lives with rejection, failure, anonymity, and feelings of insignificance. "I didn't even know you weren't here," retorted a party host after Charlie apologized for arriving late. Schulz's "strip vibrated with '50s alienation," said another cartoonist, Garry Trudeau. "Knowingly or not," according to the writer Henry Allen, "Schulz was an existential rebel against the good news being preached in America. . . . He created a world of irresolvable paradox in a country that invented the slogan 'can do.'" Readers could only laugh at the "cosmic absurdity" that Charlie Brown and his cohort of friends confronted day in and day out.[72]

Although early television reflected the consensus culture's quest for uniformity and wholesomeness, it too had an edgier side. In 1951, for example, *Variety* noted growing concerns about "below the belt humor" in the variety comedy shows of especially Milton Berle and Sid Caesar. Because these shows derived their format from vaudeville, people often referred to them as *vaudeo*. Like vaudeville, they included raucous, physical, slapstick humor with touches of the risqué.[73]

In the late 1940s and early 1950s, Berle was arguably television's biggest star. Born in Harlem in 1908 as Mendel Berlinger, he had gotten into show business at age five as a model for Buster Brown shoes. He moved to silent movies, appearing in more than fifty by the time he was eight years old, and at age sixteen had a solo vaudeville act. By the time he started hosting NBC's *Texaco Star Theater* in January 1948, he was able to draw on over thirty years of performing experience. Dubbing himself "Uncle Miltie," he became an overnight sensation, and his program enjoyed spectacular ratings, attracting a staggering 75 percent of the television audience. Millions of Americans bought their first TV set in order to see him—"Mr. Television." The first season, he worked live performances without writers, drawing entirely on his own gags and rambunctious displays of spontaneity. "You never knew what was going to happen," Berle remembered. According to *Time* magazine, he was "a six-foot-long banana with deadpan ears, Bugs Bunny teeth, a rubbery leer that threatened to meet the back of his neck, and the energy of a wildebeest stampede." He was fast-paced and frantic, changing costumes and characters many times during the show. "Anything for a laugh" was his motto. Sometimes he appeared in drag, once dressing up like the entertainer Carmen Miranda and kissing singer Tony Martin. Sexual innuendo was common: "I went to see the doctor. He wasn't in. I took a turn for the nurse." Soon a host of other network shows were copying Berle. "Vaudeville is back," said a *Variety* advertisement.[74]

But the Berle-style vaudeo was too spontaneous, bawdy, urban, and ethnic to last more than a few years. When Berle made his stunning debut, the networks offered only prime-time shows over a half million sets. NBC's seven affiliates were all on the East Coast. In 1950, TV sets were in only 9 percent of American homes. After 1951, the completion of a transcontinental coaxial cable expanded live TV to 90 percent of U.S. stations, stretching west to Los Angeles, where NBC and CBS set up studios that increasingly challenged New York as a production center. By 1954, there were 354 stations across the country, and advertisers were rushing to tap the swelling national audience. This expansion of television did not help Berle, however. While working- and lower-class New Yorkers loved him, his humor did not appeal to rural America. According to a 1954 survey, for instance, his rating in Charlotte, North Carolina, was a paltry 1.9 percent. Executives worried that their networks seemed too Jewish for general audiences. Concerned about offending viewers and program sponsors, the executives nervously watched freewheeling performers such as Berle and Sid Caesar. As early as 1951, the networks and TV stations, under growing pressure to rein in "offensive" humor, were reportedly telling comedians to "watch their step." The networks soon embraced scripted family situation comedies, which were easily controlled and, as one writer said, played well to "the front porches of Dubuque." Armed with the 1952 Television Code pledging a commitment to "wholesome entertainment," the networks began to move Berle, Caesar, and other vaudeo pioneers to the margins.[75]

Although Lucille Ball popularized the new domestic situation comedy and hastened Berle's downfall, she had troubles of her own, almost falling victim to the era's Red Scare. Ball ultimately prevailed because her top-rated show, *I Love Lucy*, was virtually untouchable. Earlier in her career, few could have guessed that she would become a colossal television celebrity. She had appeared in over fifty movies but never reached stardom. In fact, she had courted trouble by opposing HUAC's Hollywood investigations. Nevertheless, *I Love Lucy* became the number one program within only four months of its October 15, 1951, debut. Over the next six years, it led the ratings four times. In March 1953, O. Parker McComas, the president of the Philip Morris company, which sponsored the show, claimed that "three times more people see every Monday night's *I Love Lucy* show than watched all the major league baseball games last year. . . . As you can see, 'We Love Lucy.'" That September, however, headlines carried a shocking announcement: "Lucille Ball Named Red." Suddenly, Ball's career was in jeopardy. One hostile TV critic chortled that her retirement "may be a lot sooner than Lucy plans." A few days later, on September 9, with the show's future in doubt, her husband, Desi Arnaz, told a live TV audience that "Lucille Ball is no Communist. Lucy has never been a Communist, not now and never will be. . . . Lucille is 100 percent American. . . . Please, ladies and gentlemen, don't believe every piece of bunk you read in today's papers." Arnaz then introduced her as "my favorite redhead . . . in fact, that's the only thing red about her, and even *that's* not legitimate." As she came onstage, she received a standing ovation. Philip Morris stuck with her. The fact that her program had 50 million viewers a week spoke loudly. The company had financial reasons to love Lucy.[76]

Although *I Love Lucy* was a family situation comedy and Ball made much of the fact that she was "just a typical housewife at heart," the show's implicit challenge to traditional gender roles was quite bold. It offered a sharp contrast to the other domestic situation shows, such as *Father Knows Best* and *The Donna Reed Show*, where family members knew their socially assigned places. Lucy served as a surrogate for many American women who found housework boring and wanted more from life. In the words of one writer: "She is what happens when a woman is allowed to go to college, tantalized with career possibilities, asked to give her all to war-work, and then told to retreat to the kitchen because that's what good girls are supposed to do." *I Love Lucy* episodes often revealed Lucy's desire to step outside the home and into the public sphere, preferably into show business, where she could make money and be famous. To that end, she used all kinds of trickery. True, she invariably paid a price for resisting social conventions, but the show revolved around those very acts of defiance. She attempted to breach gender walls. Although Lucy's message was strikingly different from that of Margaret Anderson on *Father Knows Best*, magazines like *Cosmopolitan* continued to insist reassuringly: "At heart, she's a housewife." Importantly, at each program's conclusion, her forgiving husband took her back, and, for the moment, she appeared to have learned her lesson.[77]

Still, as *I Love Lucy* suggested, television did more than reflect caution and Cold War certainties. If TV helped make Joe McCarthy a powerful political figure, it also played a role in his political fall. The newscaster Edward R. Murrow was able to criticize the senator precisely because television had enhanced Murrow's public visibility and influence. And, for six weeks in 1954, ABC, an aspiring network in search of cheap daytime programming opportunities, televised Senate hearings that culminated in McCarthy's censure for conduct unbecoming a senator.[78]

Television sometimes took chances on touchy racial issues as well. In November 1956, NBC launched *The Nat King Cole Show* without sponsors. Only eight months earlier, five white men, hollering "Let's go get that coon," had beaten the singer onstage in Birmingham, Alabama. "I can't understand it," Cole said of the attack. "I have not taken part in any protests. Nor have I joined an organization fighting segregation." From the networks' point of view, of course, Cole's lack of involvement in controversial political issues made him a good choice as the first African American to host his own television show. Cole approached television with a purpose, convinced that he could best advance the cause of civil rights by entertaining large white audiences. "It could be a turning point," he said of his show. CBS had signed him earlier in 1956 but then lost interest. NBC aired the show, assuming that sponsors would sign on. Fearing boycotts of their products, however, sponsors stayed away. NBC refused to give up, enlarging the program from fifteen to thirty minutes. Big-time performers such as Tony Bennett, Harry Belafonte, and Peggy Lee appeared as guests, working for minimum wage. Finally, NBC dropped the show. Cole praised the network but criticized the advertising business for not being more helpful. "Madison Avenue," he said, "is afraid of the dark."[79]

Television's record on social and political issues was, thus, in the words of the historian Thomas Doherty, "schizophrenic: as an institution, more easily scared; as a medium, less easily silenced." As Doherty has argued: "Ultimately, the insatiable demand for material—more thought, more talk, more tales, more personalities—would override the timidity of the medium." The simple fact that "television needed to fill air time" helped open it up to more than one set of messages, sounds, and images.[80]

Wladziu Valentino Liberace provided ample proof, pushing against the familiar boundaries of sexual identity, and becoming a media star. "Prior to t.v.," he said, "I was what you might consider a successful unknown." By the 1950s, he had toured much of the country for over a decade, combining classical and popular music on the piano and showing that he was a consummate entertainer. "If you can produce this kind of show on television you'll be holding lightning in a bottle," the Los Angeles TV manager Don Fedderson told him. Fedderson took him on a drive in the Los Angeles area, pointing out that TV antennae were most prominent in the working-

and middle-class neighborhoods. The idea clicked with Liberace that TV viewers were not the so-called sophisticated people who dismissed popular entertainment. The people who watched television were, he concluded, "the solid backbone people of America. The ones who did the work, kept things going and were ready to be friendly to anyone who was friendly to them." On February 3, 1952, Liberace took that insight with him onto the air when *The Liberace Show* premiered on Fedderson's KLAC station. In about a week, he had signed a contract to make 177 half-hour programs with KLAC-TV and an independent filmmaker and syndicator, Guild Films. Significantly, the networks were not interested in Liberace, whose act and persona seemed too unconventional. Just as significantly, syndicated programs were emerging to meet the growing need of local stations to find enough shows. By the mid-1950s, some two hundred stations were airing *The Liberace Show*, and Liberace was one of the country's most celebrated entertainers. *TV Guide* declared that he was "America's first real television genuine matinee idol."[81]

Amazingly, Liberace soared to stardom amid rumors that he was homosexual, at a time when homosexuality was under attack in a variety of forums. In 1950, for example, a Senate subcommittee published the *Report on Employment of Homosexuals and Other Sex Perverts in Government.* Because Liberace emphasized his "sissy" eccentricities in the ways he talked, dressed, and acted, he became the target of scandal sheets such as *Hollywood Confidential,* which, by the end of 1955, sold more copies at newsstands than did any other magazine—over 4 million. Articles raised doubts about his sexual identity: "Don't call him mister." "Liberace and old lace." "Is he, or is he ain't?" One publication argued that "the American public expects . . . a little less lavender-water from their heroes."[82]

Liberace was, in fact, gay, and, according to the biographer Darden Pyron, his genius as an entertainer grew from his ability to play "his eccentricities . . . against the most conservative and traditional patterns." He negotiated "borders and margins against the center," maintaining himself as "the outsider in the middle of things." With affected mannerisms and speech, clothing that ranged from tuxedos to outlandish costumes, props such as a candelabra on his piano, and playful winks, he was, as a historian has said, "a harlequin poised at the outer edges of sexual acceptability." Yet his friendly, nonthreatening style, his constant emphasis on the importance of family, and his "just-folks" personality—combined with images of wealth and style—built him a large fan base among traditional, middle-of-the-road Americans. "I talked to the viewers as if they were my friends, my next door neighbors," Liberace explained. "We had a kind of over the back-fence relationship." Most viewers were women, often married, and ranging in age from twenty to sixty. Some saw him as the ideal son. Others viewed him as kindly and sensitive. According to one observer: "Liberace fills a void in the lives of millions of American housewives whose dull, un-romantic husbands can't tell the difference between a rose and a dandelion." But rumors of his homosexuality eventually took a toll. After 1955, his popularity began to slump. Cultivating a more conservative image, he returned to his origins in the hinterland's community concert venues, eventually regenerating himself so that, by the early 1960s, he was again a national celebrity, popular in Las Vegas and New York and on TV.[83]

TV's power to popularize uniqueness—and then tame it—was also evident in rock and roll music. Few entertainment examples were initially more unsettling or controversial to the mainstream culture than was rock and roll. It was a disturbing force within the music industry, between generations, and as an agent of major changes concerning race and sexuality.

Into the late 1940s and the 1950s, the big popular music recording companies such as Decca, RCA, and Columbia featured smooth sounds that echoed nicely the soothing messages of the postwar consensus. Bing Crosby remained popular, and his relaxed style inspired a number of imitators, particularly Perry Como. "I used to go to Perry's to borrow a cup of sleep," joked Dean Martin, another emerging crooner with a silky voice. The mainstream sounds from the established center of the recording industry honed a "perfected mellowness."[84]

Plenty of what critics deemed mere "noise" was, nevertheless, building on the industry's fringes, where literally hundreds of small, independent companies pushed the boundaries of the musical spectrum. The unwillingness of the major labels to record the blues and other marginal forms of music created opportunities for the indies, of which around a thousand opened shop between 1948 and 1954. "I looked for an area neglected by the majors and in essence took the crumbs off the table of the record industry," said Art Rupe, who, in 1945, started his Specialty company in Los Angeles. With only around $1,000, it was possible to rent a recording studio, book musicians, prepare a tape, and press five hundred singles. Little companies sprouted all over. The curmudgeonly Syd Nathan, for example, used an abandoned ice factory in Cincinnati when he founded King Records in 1943. He focused on what he called the "music of the little people"—race and country sounds that the big labels largely ignored. He also recorded "smutty" songs such as "I Want a Bowlegged Woman," which the established companies spurned. Herman Lubinsky, who started the Savoy label, claimed that his records were "for the man with the dinner pail and the lady over the washtub." The indies were far from equal, however. Most of them were fly-by-night, short-lived operations with meager budgets and sales, but a few were bigger operations. The owners were typically tight-fisted and difficult. Still, the independent companies energized the music business and provided the breeding ground for rock and roll.[85]

Radio played a crucial role, too. Seemingly destined for the scrap heap because of television, radio made major adjustments. As local stations competed fiercely for audiences and local advertisers, they turned to "narrowcasting": targeting special, segmented markets. One of the cheapest kinds of programming involved playing records. By the 1950s, the nature of the records being played was changing. A short time earlier, as Ahmet Ertegun (the cofounder of Atlantic Records) recalled: "You couldn't find a black performer on network radio. And when it came to disc jockeys on the big wattage stations, they wouldn't play a black record. We had a real tough time getting our records played—even Ruth Brown, who didn't sound particularly black." But in the early 1950s a number of disc jockeys moved in a new direction. Because music was so important to radio programming, the deejays—most of whom were white—enjoyed a growing autonomy. They developed colorful on-air personalities, targeted young listeners, and played music associated with African Americans. In mid-1951, Alan Freed pointed the way when he began playing rhythm and blues on Cleveland's independent station WJW. With his—and radio's—future seemingly in doubt, he accepted an offer from a local record store owner who was willing to provide R & B records and pay Freed for playing them on the radio. Dubbing himself the "King of the Moondoggers," ringing a cowbell, and engaging in energetic patter, Freed expanded his audience beyond black listeners and began getting requests from white teenagers. As deejays like Freed courted teenage audiences, they dropped the kind of official "announcer speak" that had traditionally marked radio, talked in hip terms, and even practiced sounding "black." By circulating music from the many new indie record companies, deejays on typically small, independent radio stations encouraged what a media scholar has described as "breakout listening"—"a conscious turn away from mainstream, adult, white culture."[86]

That turn had gained momentum during World War II with the development of a notable teenage subculture. Key ingredients in molding that subculture were demographics, dollars, and greater awareness of a special youthful identity. Wartime demands on families had meant that many youths were under less parental scrutiny. Many communities had established neighborhood recreation centers—"teen canteens"—where kids could gather to listen to jukeboxes, dance, play ping-pong, and relax over soft drinks. Although the music still met "clean" middle-class standards, it increasingly recognized the preferences of the youths themselves, especially the adolescent girls. For the first time, newspaper radio logs began to include a "youth listening" category. "Meet Soozie Cue . . . she knows who's who!" read a weekly half-page advertisement from Columbia Records that featured a teenage girl near a jukebox. In September 1944, the magazine *Seventeen* emerged, full of advice for teenagers. Americans were unquestionably becoming more "youth conscious," as a government report observed.[87]

When the war ended, *Seventeen* took the lead in touting the benefits of the teen market. The *Seventeen* editor Helen Valentine argued that postwar prosperity was putting money into young people's pockets and thus providing all kinds of business opportunities. By the end of 1945, the magazine's monthly circulation was over a million, enhancing *Seventeen*'s influence on advertisers. Valentine and her staff urged clothing manufacturers, for example, to produce fashions that spoke to "the way of life, the style of life, the time of life that teenagers represented." For Valentine, in her early fifties, however, adults needed to play a crucial role. She exhorted the older generation to guide young people toward responsible adulthood, family life, and the rituals of consumption. The postwar baby boom heightened that mission. Between 1946 and 1964, birth rates soared.[88]

But, even while the fabled baby boomers were toddlers and in elementary school, many entrepreneurs began to recognize the market power of an early wave of adolescent consumers. The number of teenagers in high school more than doubled between 1946 and 1960, from 5.6 to 11.8 million, and these youths had money to spend. "Our salient discovery," reported the founder of the newly established Youth Marketing Company right after the war, "is that within the past decade teenagers have become a separate and distinct group in our society," and their purchasing power was increasing. Many businesses took note. Publishers printed teenage advice books, such as Edith Heal's *The Teen-Age Manual: A Guide to Popularity and Success* (1948). In the early 1950s, Sam Katzman was cranking out some seventeen films and three serials a year, including B-movie matinee shows such as *Captain Video* for the preteen "cap pistol set" and a Jungle Jim series for older youths. "Lord knows, I'll never make an Academy Award movie," he said in 1953, "but then I'm just as happy to get my achievement plaque from the bank every year."[89]

Despite the hopes of people such as Helen Valentine, the rising generation paid little attention to adult suggestions. "It's the kids telling us, instead of us telling them," conceded the editor of *Profile of Youth* (1951), a series of *Ladies Home Journal* interviews with high school students. Clearly, a significant number of youngsters were looking outside middle-class models of behavior. Many, for example, paid little attention to the music that *Seventeen* reviewed. Instead, they turned to the race music on independent record labels. This was music with a difference, as one company claimed: "It Jumps . . . It Rocks, It Rolls." Moreover, it was precisely the music that many local deejays—constituting "a radio empire of the night"—played on programs such as *Hoot 'n' Holler* and *The Heebee Jeebee Show*. These deejays initially drew their listeners from "a growing underworld of working-class teenage 'cats' who had no intention of following adolescent rules," according to one interpretation. "By the mid-1950s," however, "teenage cats and high school rebels, not carefree bobby soxers, would symbolize teenage culture." And the bellwethers of change were "Elvis Presley and rock 'n' roll, not *Seventeen* and character builders."[90]

Young people had rallied earlier to the swing music of Benny Goodman, of course, but they had been part of a larger, intergenerational audience. Rock and roll was different. It helped define the emerging postwar generation. Songs focused on being young and dealing with the anxieties of growing up. Much of the music revolved around romance and the pull of sex. "We got a new generation," the movie producer Sam Katzman shrewdly observed in 1952, "but they got the same old glands." In that regard, the early rock tunes echoed the sexual innuendos of rhythm and blues. Indeed, *rock* typically referred to the sex act. "Work with me, Annie," sang Hank Ballard in a 1953 song that some towns banned: "Annie, please don't cheat, / Gimme all my meat." In another song, "Sexy Ways," Ballard's message was equally clear: "Any old way, just pound, pound, pound." "Shake it, baby, shake it," sang Jerry Lee Lewis in his 1957 hit. "Goodness, gracious, great balls of fire."[91]

While suggestive "leerics" angered rock's critics, so did its racial roots, connotations, and collaborations. *Billboard* magazine saw it as "mongrel music." In that regard, it fit with the history of American popular music as a whole, drawing from many sources, but especially from blacks. As the white singer Carl Perkins put it, rock and roll was "a country man's song with a black man's rhythm." To many young whites, such as the songwriters Jerry Leiber and Mike Stoller, that racial connection represented freedom. "Actually, I think we wanted to be black," recalled Leiber. "Black people had a better time. As far as we were concerned, the worlds we came from were drab by comparison. . . . I was alienated from my own culture and searching for something else." When sixteen-year-old Sam Phillips first visited the black section of Memphis and drove "down Beale Street in the middle of the night," he was flabbergasted: "It was *rockin'!* It was so active—musically, socially, God, I loved it!" In the mid-1950s, the African American singer Chuck Berry performed in Brooklyn before a largely white audience—a "multicult audience," as he described it—and was initially unnerved. The enthusiastic reaction jolted him. He could not believe that he was "finally being welcomed by an entirely unbiased and friendly audience, applauding without apparent regard for racial difference." Rock and roll was, in many respects, the music of integration. Like jazz, it involved blacks and whites drawing on each other's music. Chuck Berry viewed his hit "Maybellene" as a hillbilly song. Ray Charles, who played at one point with an all-white country band, "loved" listening to *The Grand Ole Opry*. Marvin Gaye said: "My dream was to become Frank Sinatra. . . . I also dug Dean Martin and especially Perry Como."[92]

Certainly, as a historian has argued, "not everyone who tuned in to the rock 'n' roll revolution embraced or even contemplated the revised racial order. Enough did, however, to make a difference." And, for that reason, white racists attacked rock as "nigger" and "jungle" music.[93]

Rock in its formative years was largely the creation of racial and working-class outsiders. Like earlier manifestations of popular music, it came mainly from untrained amateurs.[94] "What else can a poor boy do?" the Rolling Stones would sing years later in the 1968 "Street Fighting Man," "but sing for a rock and roll band?" Hence, in the mid-1950s, young black "doo-wop" singers harmonized with their own "homemade songs" on gritty street corners in places such as Harlem. One of them, Frankie Lymon, was by age ten pimping for prostitutes, getting a commission for each customer he found. Billy Lee Riley, a white singer who grew up in rural Arkansas near the town dump, remembered only two social classes: "The ones that had everything and those that didn't have anything." Another white singer, Carl Perkins, son of sharecroppers, was living with his wife in a government project in Jackson, Tennessee, when he wrote his hit song "Blue Suede Shoes." "You gotta be real poor to care about new shoes like I did," he said. He penciled the song's lyrics "on a potato sack—we didn't have reason to have writing paper around." Rock music's early performers came from society's edges. But so did the "teenage cats" who embraced their music. And these youths included "the high school students who never played the lead in teenage novels," as the historian Grace Palladino has written. "They were kids like Elvis Presley, the son of a ne'er-do-well truck driver and a part-time waitress in Memphis, Tennessee, who did not fit into the 'right' high school crowd and did not try to."[95]

But Presley was soon the one who attracted the crowds. Many singers, largely unheralded African Americans, had blazed the musical trail for him, but he became rock and roll's biggest-selling recording artist. The country singer Conway Twitty (the Mississippi-born Harold Jenkins, who, for a while in the mid-1950s, had his own rock and roll band) had no doubt about whom to credit for rock's breakthrough: "It was Elvis and no one else. He was the one. Nothing like it, period. He bowled people over. He changed the whole damn world." Within two years of his first recording for Sun Records in mid-1954, Presley rocketed to stardom, accounting for an astounding 10 percent of the music industry's total sales in 1956. That year, five of his songs were in the top nine, selling at a rate of seventy-five thousand per day, and his huge hit "Don't Be Cruel" was number one for eleven weeks.[96]

Presley epitomized many of the patterns that coalesced in rock and roll. Like most of the musicians from R & B, country, and rock, he was young, Southern, and poor. Born in 1935—the middle of the Great Depression—in Tupelo, Mississippi, he had grown up as a member of what more privileged groups condescendingly viewed as "white trash." "Poor we were," his father protested many years later. "I'll never deny that. But trash we weren't.

. . . We never had any prejudice. We never put anybody down." Elvis was almost three years old when he saw his father hauled off to prison for altering, and then cashing, a four-dollar check for the family hog. When Elvis was thirteen, his family moved to a government-assisted housing project in Memphis. "We were broke, man, broke," Elvis remembered. "We just headed for Memphis. Things had to be better." Presley never forgot his working-class roots. Later, after he became famous and wealthy, when someone asked him whether he had thought about attending college, he simply stared. Then he said: "You can't go beyond your limitations. I stay with my own people." The class element of rock and roll was evident when a Massachusetts representative, Robert MacDonald, attacked Presley "and all the other hundreds of musical illiterates, whose noises presently clutter up our jukeboxes and our airways."[97]

Independent recording companies provided rock's infrastructure, and, appropriately, Presley got his start at Sun Records, Sam Phillips's shoe-string operation in Memphis. Phillips, a high school dropout from rural Alabama, contended that he always looked for musicians who "had absolutely no formal training in music, didn't know one note from another." As the singer Sonny Burgess recalled: "None of us knew anything. Some of us Sun guys never got through high school." Carl Perkins remembered how Phillips would urge him on: "I'd say, 'Mr. Phillips, that's terrible.' He said, 'That's original.' I said, 'But it's just a big original mistake.' And he said, *'That's what Sun Records is.* That's what we are.'" Phillips welcomed aspiring singers, black and white, but viewed them as "my damn babies": "I knew how to paddle their butt when they needed it, I knew how to clean it when they needed it." It was with Phillips that Presley made his first recording, a recycled version of the black singer Arthur Crudup's "That's All Right."[98]

Celebrity disc jockeys had been crucial promoters of rock music, and so, again appropriately, it was one of the pioneer deejays—Dewey Phillips (a friend of Sam's but not related), at Memphis station WHBQ—who first played Presley's "That's All Right" and dubbed it a hit. Stories differed, but Phillips may have played the song seven times in a row. After dozens of people called, he summoned Presley to the station for an interview. "I asked him where he went to high school," Phillips remembered. "I wanted to get that out because a lot of people listening had thought he was colored."[99]

Given the strong theme of racial crossover in rock music, it was hardly surprising that race played a major role in Presley's career. Sam Phillips had once reportedly said: "If I could find a white man who had the Negro sound and the Negro feel, I could make a billion dollars." But Phillips knew he had to be patient. He did not want angry whites to ask: "Why should we give this nigger-loving sonafabitch a break?" Presley, he believed, was the solution. Moreover, he sensed that "*intuitively*" Presley recognized the importance of crashing racial barriers. "The lack of prejudice on the part of Elvis Presley had to be one of the biggest things that ever happened to us," Phillips later emphasized. Certainly, Presley never hesitated to acknowledge his debt to black musicians. "I dug the real low-down Mississippi singers, mostly Big Bill Broonzy and Big Boy Crudup," he said. "'Sinful music,' the townsfolk in Memphis said it was. Which never bothered me, I guess." He told a reporter in 1956: "The colored folks have been singing it and playing it just like I'm doin' now, man, for more years than I know and nobody paid it no mind till I goosed it up. I got it from them." He remembered his reaction to questions after he recorded "That's All Right": "When the record came out a lot of people liked it and you could hear folks around town saying, 'Is he, is he?' and I'm going, 'Am I, am I?'" In retrospect, Sam Phillips was convinced that he and Presley had "knocked the shit out of the color line." Their approach, as he described it, "was almost subversive, sneaking around through the music."[100]

Presley's spectacular rise to prominence also reflected another of rock's patterns: the role of young people in making the music a culture-shaking phenomenon. "Teenagers are my life and triumph," he told reporters in 1956. "I'd be nowhere without them."[101]

In the early part of his career, Presley was very much a work in progress, but he was willing to take chances. In high school, despite his shy, polite demeanor, he had rejected the look of the "clean-cut" middle-class students and displayed a rebellious approach to fashion and appearance. He wore lengthy sideburns, modeling himself after cross-country truck drivers—"wild-looking guys," as he described them. He also let his hair grow long, pomaded it in a wave, and swept the sides back in the "duck-tail" style popular among the allegedly tougher "low-class" element. When he refused to cut his hair, the football coach kicked him off the team. "Had pretty long hair for that time and I tell you it got pretty weird," he remembered. "They used to see me comin' down the street and they'd say, 'Hot dang, let's get him, he's a squirrel, he's a squirrel, get him, he just come down outta the trees.'" He liked to wear bright clothing from a store that blacks patronized on Beale Street. Quietly, he asserted his independence, demonstrating a mixture of resentment and burning ambition. After his eighth-grade teacher told him that he did not know how to sing, he brought his guitar to class and tried to prove her wrong, finally wresting at least an admission from her that she probably just did not appreciate his kind of music. And that music drew increasingly from a mélange of sounds—popular, country, blues, and gospel—that he heard over the radio and on records.[102]

As an outsider who was "hellbent for the mainstream," Presley was astutely sensitive to the reactions of his audiences. His success was hard earned, derived from playing many nights on the road in small Southern towns as he struggled to find his way. "He was," recalled his guitarist Scotty Moore, "very conscious of what got a reaction. He'd do something one time and then he would expand on it real quick."[103]

That responsiveness increasingly took him onto risky sexual grounds. On fundamental levels, Presley toyed with gender conventions. Although most males kept their hair short, he wore his long and also dyed it. Bill Black, a member of Presley's band, recalled that "all these guys with crew cuts and muscles resented a pretty boy," especially when girls seemed interested in him. Then there were his clothes—pink and chartreuse jackets, white pants, striped black pants, two-tone shoes. He chose the color pink quite deliberately, noting that the public associated it with girls. Because he liked the way the movie star Tony Curtis used mascara, he experimented with eye shadow, sometimes wearing a royal blue shade. In 1954, when he played at *The Grand Ole Opry,* the country great Chet Atkins was astounded: "I couldn't get over that eye shadow he was wearing. It was like seeing a couple of guys kissin' in Key West." Presley was helping create an androgynous side of rock music that would influence later performers such as Mick Jagger of the Rolling Stones. The guitarist Scotty Moore believed that Presley was "damn near too pretty to be a man." Moore recalled that, when he saw him, "I thought my wife was going out the back door." Elvis's hunching and humping moves onstage reminded some observers of a burlesque queen or stripper. That analogy was not far off the mark, as Presley's drummer D. J. Fontana admitted. Fontana had played in burlesque shows, hitting the drum to "catch their leg movements, their tassel movements, their rear end movements." Similarly, when Presley was performing, Fontana "played an accent wherever his legs were or wherever his rear end was, and I just learned to catch all that by watching these girls strip."[104]

Sexuality suffused Presley's performances. It stirred feelings among many white teenage girls, including those from "proper" families, who responded to Presley in ways they had not acted publicly before. They were experiencing the allure of the country's building sexual revolution. Although most probably shared the standard dreams of marrying, raising children, and living in the middle-class suburbs, they considered the prospects of sexual freedom. Sandra Scarbrough, who grew up in the white section of a small Mississippi town, remembered going with her older brother to a black juke joint and anxiously wanting to learn to dance like *that.* "Sex was everywhere [in high school]," she said, "and it's a wonder none of us got pregnant." As a member of the local Baptist Church, she attended Sunday services, but with thoughts on her mind about the previous night. "You'd go out on Saturday night . . . and then you'd come and rededicate your life on Sunday morning." Young teenagers like Scarbrough lived in competing worlds that included sexual restraint and sexual freedom. Presley's nervous energy onstage, the twitching of his legs and the movement of his hips, allowed them to respond in special ways. "Let's face it," remembered one of them, "Elvis gave us a heightened sense of our own sexuality," helping unleash pent-up emotions. "He isn't afraid to express himself," said a thirteen-year-old. "When he does that . . . I get down on the floor and scream."[105]

"I came offstage," recalled Presley, when he at first thought the audience was making fun of him with its wild reaction. "[But] my manager told me that they was hollering because I was wiggling my legs. I went back out for an encore, and I did a little more, and the more I did, the wilder they got."[106]

When Presley was onstage, the enthusiastic audiences transformed him. "It's like a surge of electricity going through you," he explained. "It's almost like making love. . . . Hell, I don't calm down till two or three hours after I leave the stage. Sometimes I think my heart is going to explode." Onstage, a fierce energy replaced his usual casual politeness. According to one writer, "vehement emotion" marked Presley's performances. Elvis offered up "the face of Dionysus, full of febrile sexuality and senselessness": "It flushed the skin of new housewives and made pink teenage boys reinvent themselves as flaming creatures." The aspiring rock singer Roy Orbison was taken aback when he first watched Elvis in early 1955. "I can't overemphasize how shocking he looked and seemed to me that night," Orbison recalled. Elvis had the same impact on him as David Lynch's 1986 film *Blue Velvet* did years later: "I just didn't know what to make of it. There was just no reference point in the culture to compare to it."[107]

In notable ways, however, Presley was less the creator of the moment than were those teenage girls who screamed so wildly, inflaming a public that was already in panic over the escalating rate of teenage pregnancy. Responding to their own awakening female sexuality, those girls made Elvis what they wanted him to be and publicly acted out their fantasies in defiance of society's traditional expectations. They cried in ecstasy when Presley, oozing eroticism, told them: "If you're looking for trouble, you've come to the right place." He explained his and James Dean's popularity: "I know why girls, at least the young 'uns, go for us. We're sullen, we're brooding, we're something of a menace."[108]

Here, indeed, was cultural dynamite. Predictably, protests erupted from the social mainstream about Presley and rock and roll. Printed sources referred to his performances as "an aborigine's mating dance," "suggestive and vulgar," a "kind of animalism." New York congressman Emanuel Celler believed that rock music "has its place . . . among the colored people." He found Presley's "gyrations . . . most distasteful." *Look* magazine dismissed Presley as "mostly nightmare." Radio stations smashed his records over the air. Some towns banned his performances. The Federal Bureau of Investigation started building a file on him. Even before Presley's emergence, the best-selling book *U.S.A. Confidential* (1952) compared rock music to "a heathen religion, . . . all tied up with tom-toms and hot jive and ritualistic orgies of erotic dancing, weed-smoking and mass mania, with African jungle background." An Alabama Klan member and head of the state's White Councils traced rock and roll back to "the heart of Africa, where it was used to incite warriors to such frenzy that by nightfall neighbors were cooked in carnage pots!" A Connecticut psychiatrist believed that the music was "a communicable disease" that drove "teenagers to do outlandish things."[109]

Some of the strongest resistance to rock and roll came from within the music industry itself. The major recording companies suddenly found their positions slipping. Of the 162 million-selling records between 1946 and 1952, the majors had been responsible for all but five; yet, in 1957, independents produced 76 percent of the hit singles. On radio, also, rock was shouldering aside Tin Pan Alley–style sounds; by the end of 1956, 68 percent of the records that deejays spun were rock and roll, up two-thirds from a year earlier. Some defenders of traditional musical styles resented the growing place of the electric guitar in rock music. After Leo Fender turned out the first mass-produced, solid-body electric guitar in 1950 (and four years later his popular Stratocaster), sales soared. "The boy with his guitar" was on his way to becoming a familiar sight. Chuck Berry, as much as anyone, with hits such as "Maybellene" and "Johnny B. Goode," helped introduce the electric guitar to rock music. "Powerful, flashy, unspeakably loud, . . . the electric guitar became the archetypal weapon in rock's attack on the decorum and orderliness of previous forms of fine music," according to the rock scholar Jim Miller. It assaulted the mainstream "empire of well-tempered tones and refined artistry."[110]

Not surprisingly, some people entrenched in the music industry's mainstream objected. One of Irving Berlin's longtime collaborators, Edgar Leslie, asked: "What are they trying to tell us, that all this talent that produced this wonderful [Tin Pan Alley] music has disappeared overnight?" An unhappy Berlin tried to prevent the playing of Elvis Presley's version of "White Christmas" on the radio. Frank Sinatra, no longer the teenagers' idol, believed that rock music "smells phony and false." It was "the most brutal, ugly, desperate, vicious form of expression it has been my misfortune to hear." In his opinion, rock and roll singers were "cretinous goons" responsible for "the martial music of every sideburned delinquent on the face of the earth." Dean Martin said that rock was the product of "unnatural forces." Sammy Davis Jr., a crooner who was a close friend of Sinatra's and Martin's, claimed: "If rock 'n' roll is here to stay I might commit suicide."[111]

As the evidence mounted that rock was no passing fad and carried the promise of substantial profits, however, the entertainment mainstream moved quickly to co-opt the music. In 1955, in Richard Brooks's *Blackboard Jungle,* Hollywood for the first time used a rock and roll sound track in a movie. "We don't like rock 'n' roll," admitted an executive at a big recording company. "But we discovered that's what teenagers want, and that's what we're going to give them." The majors now rushed to capitalize on record sales that, between 1954 and 1959, tripled to $613 million.[112]

Boosting those sales were two technological developments: the invention of the transistor in 1947 and the 45 rpm record that RCA developed in 1950. The Bell lab's tiny transistor meant that radios could be much smaller than those using electron tubes. The appearance of portable, transistorized sets on the market in 1954 facilitated "out-of-home" listening in automobiles and elsewhere. Young people now had more opportunities to hear what they wanted over the radio, away from supervising adults. The cheaper seven-inch 45s were perfect for rock and roll single recordings and also ideal for youths to carry around.[113]

The industry establishment nevertheless moved cautiously, much aware that it needed to improve rock and roll's image in the larger society. It was essential to "clean up" the music and the performers, disassociating them from delinquency and tying them to an innocent world of milk shakes and ponytails. The "great homogenizing" had begun.[114]

Again, Presley's career illustrated the dominant pattern. In late 1955, RCA Victor bought his contract from cash-starved Sun Records. A few months later, Presley broke the barriers in the entertainment medium that had been least receptive to rock and roll: television. Although his four appearances on CBS's low-rated *Stage Show* received little attention, his June 5, 1956, appearance on *The Milton Berle Show,* where he sang his hit "Hound Dog" and seemed at one point to be humping the microphone, stirred an angry reaction. NBC was determined to avoid such problems when Presley performed shortly thereafter on Steve Allen's show. "We won't stand for any bad taste under any circumstances," said one network executive. The result was a decidedly "purified" Elvis. Meanwhile, Ed Sullivan, whose CBS variety show was immensely popular, had pledged that there was no way he would feature Presley. Sullivan, whose stage demeanor was so restrained that he was "the only man who brightens a room by leaving it," according to the comedian Jack Leonard, wanted no part of Presley: Sullivan considered Elvis "not my cup of tea" and, indeed, "unfit for a family audience." Presley's soaring popularity nevertheless finally convinced Sullivan to sign him up for three appearances, in September and October 1956 and January 1957. But, by the third show, the camera would show Elvis only from the waist up. When the TV audience surpassed a whopping

80 percent during the first show, Sullivan hardly regretted his decision. At the end of the third performance, Sullivan bestowed the establishment's blessings on Presley, describing him as "a real decent, fine boy."[115]

A key to taming Elvis was to distance him from live audiences, particularly those swooning females. Television did that, as did movies. In 1956, in Robert D. Webb's *Love Me Tender*, he also launched his screen career, which, over the next decade, included more than two dozen films. Guiding his career by then was a genuine con artist with important show business connections, "Colonel" Tom Parker. On August 15, 1955, Parker signed on as "special adviser to Elvis Presley," negotiating the RCA contract. The following March, he became Elvis's sole manager. Parker was, in fact, an illegal alien whose real name was Andreas van Kukjk and who had sneaked into the United States, working at first as a sideshow barker and carnival concessionaire. He never liked Presley's music, but he saw in Elvis a commodity that virtually printed money. Parker managed Presley with minute care. "We do it this way, we make money," he told Elvis. "We do it your way, we don't make money." Under Parker's tutelage, an "Elvis song" had to be simple and have a happy ending. An "Elvis movie" also had to fit a wholesome image. The films would "never win any Academy Awards," Parker conceded. "All they're good for is to make money." Presley perhaps relied on Parker because the Colonel was, in the words of the Elvis biographer Bobbie Ann Mason, "a con man who could challenge the big dudes" in the entertainment industry; and, from the perspective of the Presley family, which never trusted bankers and company executives, those "big dudes" would ruin you if they could.[116]

Reshaping Elvis's image also involved promoting him as a 100 percent American in the Cold War. Thus, in 1956, he appeared in a TV show on board a battleship with an audience largely of young males (minus those troublesome teenage females). And, in 1958, Presley entered the U.S. Army. With his military uniform, he became a kind of a Cold War poster boy. Incredibly, in 1959, the Mississippi legislature resolved that Elvis was a "legend and inspiration to tens of millions of Americans."[117]

Presley's transformation into the "great Elvis Presley industry," as a top retail-sales promoter described it, symbolized what was happening to rock and roll generally in the latter half of the 1950s. Like Presley, who spawned a multimillion-dollar merchandising operation, rock became a giant business, increasingly centralized and predictable, and identified less and less with scattered, unpredictable local sources. Recording companies promoted a succession of new, clean-cut singers. Pat Boone, for example, attended Columbia University and posed in front of it for his first album cover. "Cleanliness is next to godliness," proclaimed his press guide. He sang a number of sanitized cover versions of blues songs. In concerts, he introduced Fats Domino's "Ain't It a Shame" as "Isn't It a Shame." Meanwhile, the family-friendly TV show *The Adventures of Ozzie and Harriet* brought forth another rock star, Ricky Nelson, who, despite his offscreen rebelliousness, which included smoking marijuana, was packaged as a wholesome, subdued teenager. "I had gone straight from singing in the bathroom to the recording studio," he recalled. Then, in August 1957, television introduced Dick Clark's *American Bandstand*. Clark knew nothing about any kind of music, let alone rock and roll. As a colleague joked, he could not distinguish Chuck Berry from a huckleberry. But, as Clark said revealingly: "I don't make culture, I sell it." He became the perfect master of ceremonies for a teenage dance show that associated rock and roll with respectability and helped the ABC network, which was fending off bill collectors, bolster its daytime offerings. He invited "housewives" to "roll up the ironing board and join us when you can." On radio, in the meantime, the emergence of a Top 40 format restricted the number of songs on the air and increasingly tied deejays to a playlist and more homogenized programming.[118]

These trends benefited the major recording studios. By 1959, almost 75 percent of total record sales went to four industry heavyweights—RCA Victor, Columbia, Decca, and Capitol. (In 1956, Presley accounted for 50 percent of RCA's pop music sales.)[119]

Granted, the Motown music empire that the black entrepreneur Berry Gordy started in 1958, with an $800 loan and a rented Detroit house, would soon make its mark, mass producing and selling music by black artists as no company had previously done; but Gordy was no less interested in gaining mainstream respect. During the 1960s, Motown's "sound of young America" reaped huge dividends. "After a while it was like Dial-A-Hit," according to a Motown songwriter. "Just like dialing the fire department." Gordy had reason to rejoice. "From $800 to $61 million," he would say later. "I had done it. I had won the poker hand." His achievement at a time when the civil rights movement and the quest for black empowerment were gaining momentum was assuredly full of political and racial implications. Certainly, Motown's scintillating collection of black talent—including Marvin Gaye, William "Smokey" Robinson, Diana Ross, and Stevie Wonder—attested to Gordy's ability to advance black cultural expression. Importantly, however, Gordy primarily wanted his "hit factory" to please mainstream America and capitalize on the white market. It would do exactly that. By 1967, white youths were purchasing 70 percent of Motown's records. "'Pop' means popular and if it ain't that, I don't know what it is," Gordy said. "I never gave a damn what else it was called." He described Motown as "a general-market company. Whether you were black, white, green or blue, you could relate to our music." He hired a finishing and modeling school to instruct his performers on matters of etiquette and elocution in order to facilitate what the choreographer Cholly Atkins described as the "transition from the chitlin' circuit to Vegas." Gordy thus avoided controversies that might restrict the size of his white audience. According to the Motown producer Mickey Stevenson, for example: "We would reject anything that had a strong blues sound to it."[120]

As the 1950s wound down, dissent and resistance seemed to be ebbing. In 1959, the University of California's new president, Clark Kerr, optimistically predicted that the incoming students "are going to be easy to handle." Trends in society and in popular culture seemed to justify such a conclusion.[121]

But the evidence was hardly unanimous. The new sensibilities that challenged the wartime consensus had not disappeared. Although high school students named *Life* as their favorite magazine, their second choice was the irreverently satirical *Mad*, whose circulation was 1 million. Almost 60 percent of college students read *Mad*. Cultural conflicts were brewing for the turbulent years ahead.[122]

10

POPULAR CULTURE AND 1960s FERMENT

During the 1960s, the United States entered a fiercely tumultuous era of social and cultural unrest. The civil rights movement became a powerful force, breaking down racial barriers and galvanizing both a larger "rights revolution" and fierce resistance. The United States and the Soviet Union faced off for thirteen terrifying days in October 1962 over missiles in Cuba, bringing the world to what President John Kennedy later described as a fifty-fifty chance of nuclear war. Assassins killed Kennedy, his brother Robert, and a number of people in the civil rights movement, including Martin Luther King Jr. Bloody urban riots launched a series of violent summers in dozens of cities. The U.S. military intervention in Vietnam deepened, fueling protests that, in turn, drew fire as un-American and unpatriotic. Representatives of a budding counterculture faced attack as "long-haired hippie freaks." Dramatic changes created both a yeasty sense of possibilities and fears that the nation was frighteningly off track. Racial conflict, campus unrest, more assassinations, and bitter social divisions over a host of issues pounded Americans. "It seems like it's been the sixties forever," moaned two writers in 1966. "We have had enough! Enough! . . . Let six years be a decade." But some of the worst violence was yet to come. One person recalled going into the 1960s with a firm belief in "sports, mom and dad, apple pie. I came out of it seeing American society as rotten to the core." Another believed that the upheavals had virtually destroyed the United States: "The inmates started running the asylum."[1]

Caught in this social, political, and cultural maelstrom, American entertainments spun with dizzying speed. Popular culture burst with renewed creativity. At the same time, it reflected the strong pull of tradition and a desire for order. Powerful continuities competed with startling changes.

For some embittered Americans, then and later, the 1960s gave birth to a regrettable wave of irresponsibility and permissiveness—nothing less than cultural treason. "In the nation's politics," as the cultural analyst Thomas Frank later wrote, "sixties- and hippie-bashing remains a trump card only slightly less effective than red-baiting was in earlier times." Critics of the 1960s tended to blame groups of "unpatriotic" Americans for assaulting the nation's treasured heritage and values. Such scapegoating typically overlooked the role of one of the most hallowed of American touchstones—the market—in disrupting tradition, promoting rebellion, and encouraging the pursuit of pleasure, however forbidden. "Consumer capitalism did not demand conformity or homogeneity," according to Frank; "rather, it thrived on the doctrine of liberation and continual transgression." Nothing less than one of the market's most potent mechanisms—the all-American institution of advertising—neatly helped prepare the way for the rule-breaking, countercultural ferment of the 1960s.[2]

During the 1950s, a small group of creative rebels on the margins of the advertising industry had begun to challenge the established views that promoted consensus-style conformity. "For creative people rules can be prisons," asserted Bill Bernbach, who hoped to turn the public's growing cynicism about advertising into a marketing ploy in itself. His relatively small company spurned quantitative research and broke the rules that an advertising giant such as Rosser Reeves had spelled out when he advised: "Tell 'em what ya gonna tell 'em, tell 'em, tell 'em what ya told 'em, and then do it again."[3]

In some brilliantly innovative ads at the end of the 1950s, for example, Bernbach conceded that Volkswagen cars were small and ugly. Here was a shocking departure from familiar advertisements that emphasized American automobiles' powerful engines, large size, and chrome-covered appeal. Bernbach's VW ads urged people to "think small" and buy a car they could drive cheaply—a kind of "anticar" or cute "love bug." In the 1960s, Bernbach continued his inventive techniques, replacing authority figures in ads with playful individuals who, for example, tried to eat their Campbell's pork and beans as they took a convertible through a car wash: "You can still taste the sauce." Starting in 1962, Bernbach's ads for the Avis rental car company did the unthinkable: admit that a company ranked second to its competitor. But, precisely because Avis needed clients to catch up, its motto was: "We try harder." Avis was initially skeptical about running the advertisements, but Bernbach prevailed, increasing the company's share of the rental car market by 28 percent within two years.[4]

Other rising companies, such as those of Leo Burnett and George Lois, also pushed new styles of advertising into the mainstream. Burnett, for example, used cartoon characters such as the Pillsbury Doughboy and Charlie the Tuna (a beatnik fish with sunglasses) to push products. Lois sought out eccentrics for his firm. "If you're not a bad boy, if you're not a big pain in the ass," he said, "then what you are is some mush, in this business." When a prospective employee shouted, "I don't need this horseshit," during an interview, Lois hired him. Lois believed that disorder encouraged creativity. In these budding firms, novelty trumped predictability, nonconformity was prized, and rebellion became a watchword. A disbelieving Rosser Reeves was convinced that crazy people were now running the ad business. The madness was, nevertheless, quite shrewd. Americans were wearying of old-style advertising. As early as the mid-1950s, the reporter Marya Mannes had observed, "The rebellion against commercials is rising daily." Even a General Electric district commissioner complained, "Television commercials have reached the point where I don't believe a doggone thing I hear on the air." The new strategy for calling attention to a product and making it attractive to cynical consumers was to do the opposite of what people expected. One scheme was, thus, to show what was wrong with the product. Hence, ads in 1966 for Benson and Hedges admitted humorously that the novel and larger cigarette could be difficult to smoke. Pictures showed a cigarette caught in an elevator door, not fitting in a cigarette case, and mashed against a telephone.[5]

A notable shift was under way. Before World War II, and in the post-war consensus culture, ads had advised people on how to dress and how to fit into the larger, modern society. They had shown idealized families in respectable settings doing respectable things. In this serious set of endeavors, there was little room for humor. The advertising heavyweight David Ogilvy adhered to a rigid set of rules, which included the omission of humor from ads. *Television Magazine* agreed: "A too-funny commercial runs the risk of obliterating the sell with its hilarity." But, by the 1960s, ads—in print and on TV—were reflecting the satirical influences of stand-up comedians such as Mort Sahl, Lenny Bruce, Elaine May, and Mike Nichols. Stan Freberg, who, in 1951, had made one of the first "comedy albums," turned to making funny commercials. In a 1961 TV spot for Chun King chow mein, he defied the advertising convention of never speaking negatively about one's product: "Ninety-five percent of the people in the U.S.A. are *not* buying Chun King chow mein." A 1962 Bernbach ad for Frito-Lay's Laura Scudders potato chips showed an old woman in a pose resembling that of Whistler's mother in the famous painting; after hearing that a chip was "extraordinarily crunchy," she bites into it. By then, TV commercials were pouring forth from more than 450 production companies. Some of the ads used rock and roll music—something that Coca-Cola had rejected as being "dirty and low-class."[6]

Many of these new ads emphasized themes of escape, individualism, freedom, diversity, authenticity, and not being ordinary. "Protest against the Rising Tide of Conformity," urged a Booth's gin ad in 1965. "Join the Dodge Rebellion," said another ad that same year. "Rise up. Break away from the everyday." Get a Dodge, and join "the charge on Dullsville." By the mid-1960s, the older, established ad agencies were rushing to join the industry's creative revolution. In 1965, the amount of "hip" advertising in magazines such as *Life* and the *Ladies Home Journal* jumped dramatically, typically characterizing half or more of the ads for such things as detergents, appliances, automobiles, and cigarettes. A "new hip consumerism" swelled throughout the rest of the 1960s. Breaking away from the crowd, being true to oneself, defying rules, rebelling, and spurning respectable status became advertising's dominant messages. "Men of the world, arise!" said a men's clothing store ad in 1968. "The revolution has begun and fashion is at the barricades." Such symbolic 1950s rebels as James Dean, Marlon Brando, and Elvis Presley had once seemed threatening; now they became mainstream icons. And crucial to this transformation were advertising, fashion, and business—all trying to divine market imperatives.[7]

The countercultural impulses of the 1960s thus coincided with the emerging antiestablishment messages of advertising and business. In 1968, 7-Up raced to catch up with soft-drink leaders Coca-Cola and Pepsi-Cola. To change their product's image, the people at 7-Up turned to the J. Walter Thompson agency. The agency, long a giant in the advertising world, was coincidentally undergoing a changing of the guard. As Thompson's John Furr recalled: "Here was a client who was trying to reinvent its brand . . . coming to an agency that was very much doing the same thing, in terms of its own . . . creative persona." The result of that matchup was the launching of the unorthodox but successful "Uncola" ad campaign. By portraying 7-Up as a daring outsider drink, the ads resonated with "this whole antiestablishment everything," according to Furr. "The timing was brilliant." So was the ad campaign several years later that portrayed Pepsi as hip and youthful as opposed to Coca-Cola, the leading soft drink. "Free to choose a new way," said the Pepsi jingle, "free to stand up and say, you be you, and I'll be me."[8]

Such ads unquestionably served to co-opt the messages of avowed social critics, threatening to render them politically meaningless. By the end of the 1960s, for example, while the growing feminist movement sharply critiqued gender roles and relationships, ads for Virginia Slims cigarettes featured their own version of women's liberation. "It used to be, lady, you had no rights. No right to vote, no right to property, no right to the wage you earned," said one of Leo Burnett's ads. The ad noted that times were changing from "back when you were laced in, hemmed in, and left with not a whole lot to do. That was back when you had to sneak up to the attic if you wanted a cigarette." From this perspective, the women's rights movement had triumphed with the right to smoke in public. Although such ads could trivialize important issues and movements, at the same time they offered "a grandiose cultural manifesto in an age of grandiose cultural manifestoes," as Thomas Frank has argued, "a vision of countercultural carnival." In the process, they helped popularize and legitimize the rhetoric that accompanied the era's rights rebellion.[9]

These changes in advertising betokened and facilitated the social and cultural ferment that continued to shake up the Cold War consensus. The Cold War mentality still gripped U.S. politics and foreign policy. But elements of dissent began to move more forcefully into the mainstream.

Bob Newhart's stand-up comedy was a prime early example—superficially mild-mannered and unassuming, yet with a knife's edge. Years later, when Newhart received the Mark Twain Prize for humor, the citation said that he had "found the befuddling lunacy that lurks beneath the surface of deceptive calm." And he had unearthed that lunacy at the dawn of the 1960s with his signature style—calm, quiet, deadpan. Unlike Mort Sahl, he rejected political material. And he avoided Lenny Bruce's run-ins with the law over the use of obscene words and raw humor. Indeed, Newhart's image was that of "Mr. Clean." Despite his reputation as a stand-up comedian, Newhart had never worked in a nightclub before cutting his first album. Born in 1929 to a middle-class Chicago family, he had gotten a B.S. degree in business at Loyola University of Chicago and attended law school for eighteen months before flunking out. As he held jobs selling shoes, writing copy, and keeping books, he judged himself "a dismal failure." But, in April 1960, his luck changed. After hearing only several of his audiotape comedy sketches, Warner Brothers Records, almost bankrupt, released *The Button-Down Mind of Bob Newhart*. It did so despite the reservations of Warner executive Herman Starr, who judged the effort "a mistake" because "comedy records don't sell." The album nevertheless quickly roared to the top of the charts for fourteen weeks, winning the Grammy Award for album of the year, launching Newhart's career, and rescuing Warner Brothers Records. "We couldn't press the records fast enough," recalled a jubilant James Conkling, the president of Warner's record company. Local radio personalities played cuts from the album, which was especially popular on college campuses. Before the year was over, Newhart's second hit album, *The Button-Down Mind Strikes Back*, was out. Almost overnight, Newhart had become a hot property, appearing in clubs and on TV talk shows, and, in 1961, briefly getting his own variety show on NBC.[10]

"All my humor is based on the fact that I'm the only sane person in a world gone completely mad," Newhart said later. Although his bland persona epitomized consensus conformity, that "button-down mind was fairly hot under the collar," as one individual observed. Newhart, in retrospect, preferred the word *outrage*. In a series of comedic set pieces, he expressed the trapped anguish of the little guy who is, as he later said, lost in "the impersonal corporate bigness in modern life." "I resent large corporations," he explained. "They flatten personalities. When I worked for a huge accounting firm, that's what happened to me. So I quit." In Newhart's opinion, the corporate system was so "outrageous that you *had* to make fun of it. It was the only weapon I had, or any of the other people. . . . Humor was the only way I could retain my sanity." His low-key, stammering style seemed innocuous, but his sketches mocked the modern systems of public relations, merchandising, and business. In various skits, Abraham Lincoln's political handler tries to talk the president out of revising his Gettysburg address ("Abe, will ya just give the speech the way Charlie wrote it?"); Sir Walter Raleigh strives to sell tobacco to a skeptical buyer ("Walt, . . . you're gonna have a tough time getting people to stick burning leaves in their mouth"); and the Wright brothers encounter an unenthusiastic reaction to their idea about starting airplane transportation ("You only went a hundred and five feet, huh?"). Newhart also turned a suspicious eye on the Cold War. In one routine, the Soviet leader Nikita Khrushchev supposedly participates in a television "walk-through" rehearsal at the Washington, DC, airport just before he formally commenced his September 1959 visit to the United States. The TV people prepare to spray Khrushchev's and President Dwight Eisenhower's bald heads to remove the shine from them; Khrushchev opens the airplane door too quickly, hitting the little flower girl; someone has to remove the golf putter from Eisenhower's hands. For those listening to Newhart's albums, particularly college students, the Cold War had become a joke.[11]

Although Newhart avoided social issues, African American comedians such as Dick Gregory were pushing onto that more perilous ground. They began moving black street humor from the Southern chitlin circuit into white venues in the North. Here was a style of humor that drew on daily routines and traditions of storytelling and verbal jesting. Popular culture in the early 1960s started opening to it, but the emerging black performers who helped introduce it to white audiences were bold gamblers. "There they stood, mike in hand, a ton of history on their backs, free to strangle it or uphold it or reinterpret it," as the writer Will Haygood later described them. "History written by jokesters. Just trying to get a laugh," working off of stereotypes and the pain of discrimination.[12]

Gregory came from the slums of St. Louis. In January 1961, at age twenty-eight, he made a breakthrough appearance at Chicago's Playboy Club, winning over an initially difficult group of whites who were in town for a business convention. His formula was "to make jokes about myself, before I can make jokes about them and their society." Suddenly, he was slipping in jokes regarding civil rights. "Wouldn't it be a hell of a thing," he asked, "if all this was burnt cork and you people were being tolerant for nothing?" Within two years, *Newsweek* announced that "from the moment [Gregory] was booked in the Playboy Club . . . Jim Crow was dead in the joke world." Although Gregory toned down the raunchier street humor, he jettisoned the clownish demeanor and speech that had long imprisoned black comedians. And, as the civil rights movement grew, his humor became more barbed: "If it hadn't been for Abe [Lincoln], I'd still be on the market." "I wouldn't mind paying taxes—if I knew they were going to a friendly country." "I sat at a lunch counter nine months. When they finally integrated, they didn't have what I wanted."[13]

The popularity of Newhart and Gregory among college students underlined the shifting tastes of many baby boomers, tastes that fueled a socially conscious folk music revival. According to a 1960 *Mademoiselle* magazine article, students were "desperately hungry for a small, safe taste of an unslick, underground world." A number of them found it in folk music, which represented "a tentative step in the direction of the open road."[14]

Folk music's long pedigree included sources ranging from the Appalachian mountains to hoboes and union organizers and mixing sounds from the blues, hillbilly, and various other regional styles. Untrained musicians using acoustic instruments had forged a "folk aesthetic" that betokened regional authenticity, progressive politics, and struggling underdogs. "[Folk music] hadn't been made to stand up and salute," said the songwriter and singer John Sebastian. For that reason, it had largely fallen victim to Cold War Red-baiting and blacklisting. But its unpackaged sounds remained alive in small coffeehouses scattered throughout major cities and college towns. As the singer Oscar Brand quipped: "You could walk from New York to California by just stepping from one coffeehouse to another without touching ground." In 1958, folk music suddenly found a national audience when the Kingston Trio, a "neatened up and depoliticized" group with college backgrounds, recorded "Tom Dooley," which rocketed to number one on the pop charts with sales of almost 4 million. The song was based on an old ballad about a man who killed his girlfriend and was hanged for his crime. Historically, folk music had been largely noncommercial, but it suddenly became big business after the Kingston Trio's emergence. Between 1958 and 1963, the group produced fifteen Top 10 albums; five reached number one.[15]

The trio—"bright, smiling, well-scrubbed young white men in collegiate sweaters," according to one description—had little interest in politics or social causes. Nor did *Hootenanny,* the ABC television show that premiered in April 1963 and rode the wave of folk music's burgeoning popularity. Shunning political controversy, the program banned traditional folksingers with left-wing credentials, such as Pete Seeger. While around 11 million viewers tuned in each week, *Hootenanny* staged concerts on various college campuses. To Seeger, *Hootenanny* missed folk music's defining spirit. It "was a bunch of white college kids all clapping inanely, no matter what song was sung, big smiles all over, and never a hint of controversy or protest. . . . I was pleased when they moved on to make money out of something else."[16]

By then, however, more and more young folksingers were injecting political meanings into their songs, addressing topics such as civil rights, nuclear weapons, and pacifism. In April 1961, a New York City park commissioner was so concerned that he banned folk singing in Washington Square. Presaging the violence that would soon mark the decade, police forcefully removed a defiant crowd as its members sang "We Shall Not Be Moved," an anthem of the labor and civil rights movements.[17]

Crucial to injecting political content into the revived folk music were such singers as Peter, Paul, and Mary, Joan Baez, Judy Collins, Phil Ochs, and especially Bob Dylan. Although Dylan's ambition was modest—"trying to be a singer without a dictionary, and a poet not bound with shelves of books"—he ultimately became one of the most creative forces in American music. In the early 1960s, Dylan emerged as an acoustic singer-songwriter whose works other singers often popularized. In 1963, for example, Peter, Paul, and Mary moved two of his singles—"Blowin' in the Wind" and "Don't Think Twice, It's All Right"—into the pop charts' Top 10. A product of northern Minnesota, Dylan had dropped out of the University of Minnesota after a year and headed for New York City's coffeehouses, where Columbia Records' John Hammond heard him and contracted his first album. Dylan quickly began building a legendary reputation with hauntingly poetic songs about racial injustice, generational differences, authority, and peace. He steered away from the showbiz side of the music business: "Fat guys chewing cigars, carrying around gold records, selling songs, selling talent, selling an image. I never hung out there." Instead he went to the racial battlefields in places such as Mississippi, playing his guitar and singing civil rights songs. In 1963, at the March on Washington for Jobs and Freedom, he sang "Only a Pawn in the Game," a ballad about the slaying of civil rights leader Medgar Evers. The music of Dylan, Baez, and other folksingers helped spread the ideals and social commitments of the civil rights movement to a growing number of young white Americans.[18]

Although, with the exception of folk, American music at the dawn of the 1960s generally avoided expressions of social conscience, some of it responded to issues such as the accelerating sexual revolution. In December 1960, for example, "Will You Love Me Tomorrow" became the number one pop hit. The song was not a typical sugary expression of teenage love but instead wondered openly about engaging in sexual intercourse. Should the girl believe all the warnings that she would lose respect if she did have sex? Or should she believe the boy's reassurances to the contrary? The song, as the media scholar Susan Douglas argued, captured teenage girls' confusion about the mixed and ambivalent sexual messages they received, but it also "was about having a choice": "For these girls, the decision to have sex was now a choice, and *this* was new." So too was the fact that "pop music became the one area of popular culture in which adolescent female voices could be clearly heard." Significantly, as well, a group of four black females, The Shirelles, performed "Will You Love Me Tomorrow?" Never before had such a group made a number one hit. Over the next several years, however, African Americans typically constituted the successful female groups. "And with the rise of the civil rights movement," according to Douglas, their "black voices conveyed both a moral authority and a spirited hope for the future." By rejecting messages of "sexual repression, of social complacency, or of homogenized commercialism," they anticipated the budding women's movement so important to the era's rights revolution.[19]

Elsewhere in the entertainment world, there were additional signs of cultural and social thawing. The comic-book business, for instance, began to shake off the lethargy that had set in following the mid-1950s attacks from Frederic Wertham, Congress, and local censors. By the 1960s, Marvel Comics had been around for several decades but was experiencing serious financial troubles. As a solution, Marvel's publisher asked his new editor, Stan Lee, to challenge the popularity of DC Comics' superheroes. Lee had started working for Marvel in 1940, when he was only seventeen, but had always thought that comics' superheroes badly needed a makeover. With his artists Jack Kirby and Steve Ditko, he set out to create characters who were more complex and believable—"a team such as comicdom had never known," Lee recalled. "They'd be flesh and blood, they'd have faults and foibles, they be fallible and feisty, and—most important of all—inside their colorful costumed booties they'd still have feet of clay." The result was a lineup of unusual, accidental, reluctant heroes who wrestled with mixed emotions about pursuing their own lives yet shouldering communal responsibilities. Some were fresh creations, such as the Thing and Daredevil; others—such as the Human Torch, the Sub-Mariner, and Captain America— had been around for a while but were now flawed and conflicted. All combined superpowers with human weaknesses.[20]

In 1962, Lee and his crew created the Incredible Hulk, a character whose very existence rebuked modern weapons and Cold War assumptions. The protagonist is a scientist, Dr. Bruce Banner, who warns a cigar-chomping general about the dangers of the army developing a new gamma bomb. The general shrugs off the warning: "A bomb is a bomb. The trouble with you is you're a milksop! You've got no guts!" Later, Banner exposes himself to gamma radiation by rescuing an imperiled boy. As a result, he develops another side that, when angered, turns into a powerful green monster—the Hulk. Although he wants only to survive and protect his privacy, he invariably has to fight to save humanity. Sometimes he battles another ugly superhero: the Thing, orange, covered with bumps, and—like the Hulk—totally antisocial. Stan Lee viewed himself as an outsider and cast his cartoon creations in a similar mold. At the beginning of one Hulk installment, Lee asked: "Can a man with green skin and a petulant personality find happiness in today's status-seeking society?"[21]

Marvel Comics' most ingenious creation, however, was Spider-Man, arguably the most significant comic-book superhero since Superman. Introduced in 1962, Spider-Man is, in fact, Peter Parker, a lonely high school student whom a spider bite has given miraculous powers. "He's the character with the Achilles Heel," said Joe Quesada, one of Marvel's editors, "the everyday schlub wondering how to get by." As Lee later explained: "I didn't want Peter Parker to look like a superhero. I wanted him to look like an average school boy." Moreover, unlike the adult superheroes such as Superman and Batman, Spider-Man suffered from the same adolescent confusions as did his readers, over grades, finances, dates, love, misunderstandings, and defining who he was. And it was he who most influenced the superhero genre as comic books entered this new phase.[22]

Stan Lee's "Marvel Universe" jolted the sluggish comic industry. Comic books never recaptured their popularity from the early 1950s, but they were on the rebound. On college campuses, Marvel Comics became popular fare. Indeed, an *Esquire* magazine college poll revealed that radicalized students liked Spider-Man as much as they did Bob Dylan and the South American revolutionary Che Guevara. By the mid-1960s, Marvel broke additional new ground by integrating African Americans into its cast of characters. The first black superhero, Black Panther, emerged in 1966. Within five years of the introduction of Spider-Man and the Hulk in 1962, Marvel's sales doubled and challenged the reigning industry giant, an initially befuddled DC. According to people who worked for DC, the larger company viewed Marvel with disdain and assumed that antiheroes would hurt "the house image." But, as the 1960s closed, DC's characters joined Marvel's in questioning authority and dealing with social issues. Comic books were becoming what one cultural critic described as "the scriptures of the cultural revolution."[23]

Television, in its own halting way, also wrestled with the era's convulsions. In the early 1960s, the networks even experimented with socially relevant programs. They did so, however, less for reasons of social conscience than because of a sudden need to clean up TV's image.

In 1959, a major scandal jolted the networks when word got out that immensely popular quiz shows were rigged. Shortly thereafter, in mid-1961, new Federal Communications Commission (FCC) head Newton

Minow described television as "a vast wasteland" and warned implicitly that government scrutiny of programming and licensing might increase. The networks reacted in several ways. On one front, they hastened steps to recapture their medium from the sponsors, solidifying a trend that had been under way for several years. For some time, advertisers had chafed at rising costs, which were making single sponsorship of programs an increasingly unrealistic notion. Participation (or shared) sponsorships now seemed more attractive. Under the emerging "magazine concept of telecasting," as one public relations firm said, "stations and networks would select and produce all programs"; advertisers and agencies would focus on commercials. The quiz show scandals certainly heightened the networks' awareness of the need to enhance their control of TV programming. Ironically, the networks' own search for cheap programs had encouraged the very game shows that had been so easy to fix. On another front, the scandals forced the networks to polish their reputations by including more public affairs segments as well as dramatic entertainment that replaced "fluff" with social awareness.[24]

As the 1960s opened, a small flood of TV series featured idealistic characters promoting social justice and helping people in need. There were teachers in *Mr. Novak* and *Channing,* a public-spirited state legislator in *Slattery's People,* sensitive doctors in *Dr. Kildare* and *Ben Casey,* and a psychiatrist in *The Eleventh Hour.* In *The Defenders,* high-minded attorneys handled cases involving blacklisting, capital punishment, civil liberties, civil rights, and abortion. In September 1963, CBS introduced *East Side/West Side,* a gritty drama about a crusading social worker who fought for urban renewal and the care of the mentally disabled and against discrimination. The show's producer, David Suskind, claimed that twenty-six Southern affiliates boycotted the program. Many of these series dealt with race and included African Americans in guest roles. A *Dr. Kildare* episode focused on sickle-cell anemia, a disease that afflicts mainly blacks. "In a sense I integrated Blair Hospital," laughed the scriptwriter Sy Salkowitz, as he reflected on the roles of guest stars Ruby Dee and Ossie Davis. *East Side/West Side* regularly featured a black social worker (played by Cicely Tyson), a professional, not the stereotypical mammy character. Even shows such as *Route 66,* about two young men on the road searching for adventure and meaning, often dealt with social issues. One episode was about how Tod and Buz reunited an old jazz band. It featured some of the era's great black jazz players, such as Coleman Hawkins, and suggested how important jazz was to American culture.[25]

Moral lessons, some regarding race, were also interwoven in *The Dick Van Dyke Show,* a genre-bending situation comedy that CBS introduced in October 1961 and that won more than a dozen Emmys over its five-year run. In terms of style alone, the comedy deserved attention for reshaping the family sitcom. Its focus on an aspiring, white, suburban family (Rob and Laura Petrie and their son, Ritchie) and its use of physical comedy such as pratfalls were familiar. So, too, was Laura's comment: "I don't want to be a dancer, I want to be your wife." The network's caution was probably also apparent in the casting of Missouri-born Van Dyke as Rob (from Illinois in the sitcom) in order to get around the "too-Jewish" rumors that had plagued Milton Berle and Sid Caesar. As the comedy writer Gerard Jones later wrote, the program switched from "matzoh to mayonnaise." Despite the show's familiar qualities, it still broke new ground, especially in giving special attention to Rob's workplace and the people there, who formed a kind of extended family. The show's creator, Carl Reiner, said that he wanted to make "the first situation comedy where you saw where the man worked before he walked in and said, 'Hi, honey, I'm home!'" What also distinguished the show from other family sitcoms was the focus on adults and their problems more than on issues of child rearing. The dialogue was notably quick, clever, and urbane. Politically, the program had a progressive orientation. Laura was committed to being a good wife, but she clearly had an independent streak. And she and Rob exuded an open-minded innocence, enthusiasm, and goodness in their response to the multiethnic world they encountered.[26]

Never before had a family sitcom included lessons about race relations. In one episode, when the Petries attend a fund-raiser for a civil rights organization, they wear white gloves to cover their hands, which they have accidentally died black. They bluff no one, of course, and learn that honesty is the best way to solve misunderstandings. In another episode, Rob believes that the hospital has mistakenly mixed up baby Ritchie with the child of a couple—the Peters—in the room next door. When the Peters show up in response to his frantic call, he discovers that they are African American. The live audience erupted in laughter—"the longest laugh in the whole five-year history of *The Dick Van Dyke Show*," recalled the producer Sheldon Leonard, "so long that it had to be trimmed to fit the episode into its allotted air time."[27]

Rarely, however, did the didactic lessons of *The Dick Van Dyke Show* or the socially relevant dramas cut very deeply. In that regard, the TV networks carefully avoided any suggestion that injustice, racism, and social conflict were endemic to the larger society. Instead, the episodes—dovetailing with consensus attitudes—reached optimistic and harmonious conclusions. A similar trend was evident in the popular western dramas of the 1960s, such as *Bonanza, The Virginian, Big Valley,* and *High Chaparral.* The shows occasionally struck blows for justice and morality and against unfairness and bigotry. Indeed, some Southern stations refused to air a *Bonanza* episode that dealt with race. On another level, however, these westerns were anything but radical. All of them were about large landowners who were courageous, honorable, and well-intentioned. On *Bonanza,* for instance, Ben Cartwright and his four sons lived on the sprawling Ponderosa ranch. Implicitly, these TV westerns reflected a worldview that fit neatly with bigness—whether in the form of corporations or nations—and suggested that giants can help little people in need. "Look at the setup of the show," said one of the stars of *Bonanza,* Pernell Roberts. "The Ponderosa is a little kingdom of very rich people, with Ben Cartwright as absolute monarch."[28]

While TV programs typically lauded America's economic and political systems, they also buttressed the role of professionals. The American Medical Association, for example, provided consultants for *Ben Casey* and *Dr. Kildare* and viewed the programs as "the best public relations the AMA ever had." A psychiatrist who worked with *The Eleventh Hour* explained why he did so. When he and other psychiatrists lectured to the public, few people attended. But, when publicity advertised the speaker as a consultant to the TV show: "We can fill the house." *The Eleventh Hour,* in sum, was a way of getting out the word: "There's a doctor here to help you." The National Education Association offered advice to *Mr. Novak,* particularly concerning any behavior that might reflect unfavorably on teachers.[29]

Even within ideological constraints, these TV series may, nevertheless, have altered perceptions and broken down social barriers. The African Americans on the shows were dignified, articulate, and "worthy of integration." TV, moreover, had a greater capacity than any other medium to breach the segregated spaces of private homes, bringing new images and lessons about tolerance. In 1956, state legislators in Louisiana had objected that television used "the communist technique of brainwashing for racial integration." Television programming in the early 1960s would have worried them even more. Although most of these socially relevant series were short-lived, television had briefly pressed the limits of its "least objectionable programming" formula.[30]

And, despite TV's retreat to safer ground with situation comedies such as *My Favorite Martian* and *Mr. Ed,* about a talking horse, nightly news broadcasts confronted audiences with searing images of a nation in turmoil. In September 1963, the networks enlarged their evening news programs from fifteen to thirty minutes. Via television, from which most U.S. citizens now got their news, came burning images of John Kennedy's assassination and the national mourning that followed, violent reactions against the civil rights movement, the expanding Vietnam War, urban riots, antiwar and campus protests, and an emerging counterculture.

While it was possible by the late 1960s to conclude with the singer Gil Scott Heron that "The Revolution Will Not Be Televised," at least on prime-time shows, TV could no more avoid the impact of the nation's upheavals than could any other aspect of popular culture. In various ways, it accommodated, however tentatively and obliquely, the turbulence surrounding issues of sexuality, race, gender, war, and protest. By doing so, it both promoted and contained powerful changes.[31]

In the mid-1960s, a host of examples illustrated the medium's schizophrenic qualities. Although racial issues virtually disappeared from prime-time TV after the early demise of the socially relevant programs, Bill Cosby in September 1965 became the first African American to have a starring role in a dramatic series. NBC's *I Spy* (1965–68) was about two spies—a white man who posed as a tennis professional and a black man who was supposedly his trainer but was, in fact, his social equal, knew seven languages, and was a Rhodes scholar. "This is the first time they called [an African American] up to play a spy instead of a problem," Cosby quipped.[32]

NBC worried about how white Southerners would react to an integrated pair traveling and rooming together. Four Deep South stations would not air *I Spy*. Cosby himself did not want the show to deal with racial issues, any more than he had been doing as a rising stand-up comedian over the previous several years. His comic strategy was to avoid political topics and, instead, spin funny stories about growing up with the likes of Fat Albert, Dumb Donald, and Ol' Weird Harold. Like Charles Schulz, the creator of *Peanuts,* Cosby tapped into the charming innocence of childhood in a color-blind world. His own childhood lacked that innocence. He had grown up in a rough housing project in Philadelphia. His working-class father drank a lot and abused Bill's mother, who cleaned houses. The family ended up on welfare. When someone later asked Cosby if his own childhood had been happy, he answered simply: "It will be, on stage." Some critics believed that his stand-up routines provided white audiences with "a showbiz backrub"—and did so as many young African Americans rejected Martin Luther King Jr.'s style of nonviolence for a more militant, separatist agenda. Cosby did not waver, however. He defined his contribution to the civil rights movement as showing "white people that Negroes are human beings with the same aspirations and abilities that whites have." On *I Spy,* he carefully avoided actions that might make him look submissive. "I don't sing, tap dance, juggle, or say 'Sir.' I am not a Rochester," he insisted. The role for which he won an Emmy as outstanding actor in a drama series was a constant challenge. He observed that he had to walk a "dozen thin lines" in order to make his "character acceptable not just to white America but to me and to Blacks everywhere": "It was a box I was in." Nevertheless, he believed that, in his own way, he had confronted the race issue in American entertainment and "moved us down the road a piece." The *Saturday Evening Post* dubbed him "the Jackie Robinson of television"— an apt analogy. Like Robinson, he hid his anger, won over whites with his nonthreatening demeanor, and helped open opportunities for successors.[33]

Television fenced with gender as well as racial issues. On all these issues, of course, the medium's own dynamics were at work. Some innovation, even within formalized genres, was usually necessary in order to attract viewers to a network. Ratings could also influence the willingness to experiment. A network in last place sometimes had to be inventive in order to stay competitive. And, certainly, outside trends and events exerted pressure. All these factors were evident by the mid-1960s in television's ambiguous handling of a swelling feminist movement that constituted an essential part of the era's rights revolution.[34]

Some programming suggested that prime-time television hardly took the women's movement seriously. The exceptionally popular *Beverly Hillbillies* (1962–71)—about a family of country rubes who become millionaires after accidentally discovering oil—occasionally poked fun at "women's lib." When the character Jethro saw a magazine entitled *Free Women,* he happily announced: "I'm gonna git me one of them." Elsewhere, family sitcoms such as *Bewitched* (1964–72) and *I Dream of Jeannie* (1965–70) perhaps worked off male sexual fantasies about attractive, magical women who seem eager to please. "Darling," says Samantha, the Elizabeth Montgomery character in *Bewitched,* "I'll be the best wife a man ever had." She sticks to that pledge even when her husband instructs her that she will "have to learn to cook and clean and keep house and go to my mother's house every Friday night." Females could, nevertheless, find other meanings in this quite conventional arrangement. Samantha was smarter and more capable than her incompetent husband, whom she constantly had to bail out of problems. Jeannie, a genie serving her master, was sillier than Samantha, but she too was clearly the person in control. As Susan Douglas argued: "Both shows anticipated feminism and hailed the prefeminist viewer." However much TV executives may have wanted to contain the building women's movement, they were unintentionally helping let a movement genie out of the bottle.[35]

A similar pattern was at work in *Honey West,* which was as pathbreaking for females as Cosby's *I Spy* role was for African Americans. Never before had TV featured a female protagonist outside sitcoms. As a no-nonsense private detective, Honey West resembled "Mickey Spillane in a skirt." Originally, she was a character in G. G. Fickling's novels about a "blonde bombshell" with measurements of "38-22-36." ABC gambled on a series about her as part of its effort to catch up with its bigger competitors at NBC and CBS. Rejecting the traditional television strategy of courting general audiences, ABC decided to target young, "swinging" adults who chafed at the confinements of both small-town America and suburban married life. In September 1965, the statuesque Anne Francis made her debut as the sexy, tough, independent private eye. ABC tried to ride the wave of the culture's expanding sexuality by dressing Francis in revealing outfits. It also recognized the growing feminist movement. In one scene, when a man says,

"A woman's place is in the home," Honey West uses quick karate moves to flip him. At the same time, the network moved cautiously, tailoring West so that she would not be too controversial in the prime-time schedule. As a result, a male friend often protects her, she shares an apartment with her aunt, and she goes out on conventional dates. But ABC's effort to negotiate its way through the sexual and gender upheavals of the era collided with CBS's smash hit *Gomer Pyle,* about a slow-witted soldier. After one year and thirty episodes, ABC canceled *Honey West.*[36]

Two years later, however, a different kind of gender breakthrough occurred with the opening of *The Carol Burnett Show* (1967–79)—the first comedy-variety hour hosted by a woman. Moreover, Burnett's comedy sketches typically challenged and parodied the traditional images of what constituted proper womanhood. She screeched, bullied, and manipulated. As the media scholar Molly Haskell wrote: "She's every aggressive, uncivil harpy who ever tried to elbow her way in front of you at the checkout counter." Her savage bits on the fictional blue-collar family of Eunice Higgins and her husband, Ed, skewered the 1950s TV family image. Burnett's Eunice was a trapped, exasperated woman, dealing with a worthless husband and an overbearing mother. Fighting—not goodwill or harmony—defined the Higgins home. The rawness of such humor grew from Burnett's own sad experiences as an emotionally abused child, coping with unloving, alcoholic parents and a grandmother, with whom she often lived, who constantly threatened suicide and had numerous affairs. Pessimism laced Burnett's humor. "Unattached women in the Burnett show don't make themselves over, Cosmo-girl style," according to Haskell; "they just sink further into misery." But audiences applauded Burnett's spunk and her bitingly funny renditions of characters such as *Gone with the Wind*'s Scarlett O'Hara. Burnett also neatly benefited from the talents of the regular group of performers around her—Harvey Korman, Tim Conway, and Vicki Lawrence.[37]

In 1967, the same year that CBS first aired Burnett's show, the network nervously courted young adults with another comedy-variety offering: *The Smothers Brothers Comedy Hour.* The humor worked partly off the clean-cut image that Tom and Dick Smothers brought with them from their earlier days as folksingers in the San Francisco area. They had first appeared on TV in 1963 on ABC's *Hootenanny.* According to Tom Smothers: "We prided ourselves on *not* taking any political stands." In contrast, their late 1960s show was full of barbed sketches about the Vietnam War, big business, religion, and a presidential "campaign" that the series regular Pat Paulsen staged. Events had radicalized the brothers, turning them into what the press described as "hippies with haircuts." Guests on the program included protest singers such as Joan Baez and Pete Seeger, who had been notably absent from *Hootenanny* and television generally. CBS was, nevertheless, so jittery about Seeger's appearance with the Smother Brothers that it cut his videotaped antiwar song, "Waist Deep in the Big Muddy," about the actual deaths of several soldiers after a military officer ordered them into a raging river. Five months later, however, the network bowed to viewers' protests by letting Seeger perform the song during his second appearance on the show.[38]

The episode illustrated the network's ongoing struggles to rein in the increasingly outspoken brothers. CBS censors objected to the song "Draft Dodger Rag" on grounds that the "introduction . . . seemed complimentary to draft dodgers." On another occasion, the head of CBS's Program Practices, W. H. Tankersley, tried to reassure an advertiser: "The Smothers Brothers like to poke fun at 'the establishment,' and we have the daily task of deciding just where they may be abusing the privilege." A problem, he noted, was the difficulty of finding "contemporary popular songs which do not contain some comment directly or indirectly on issues of public importance: war, peace, civil rights, patriotism, conformity, and the like." Although, in its first year, the show ranked eighteenth in the ratings and attracted the sixteen- to twenty-four-year-old age group, CBS bumped it in September 1969 for a country comedy series, *Hee Haw*. The Smothers Brothers' humor had become more politically charged and confrontational—more oriented specifically to an insurgent, countercultural audience. Some network affiliates objected to the "sick" show. *TV Guide* printed a special editorial endorsing CBS's decision. The magazine asked rhetorically: "Shall a network be required to provide time for a Joan Baez to pay tribute to her draft-evading husband while hundreds of thousands of viewers in the households of men fighting and dying in Vietnam look on in shocked resentment?"[39]

The comedian Goldie Hahn had a humorous answer: "I love Joan Baez; I've even got a set of her fingerprints." The comment came on *Rowan and Martin's Laugh-In* (1968–73), a summer replacement series that NBC gambled on in 1968, as CBS wrestled with the Smothers Brothers, and that surprisingly leaped to the top of the ratings. The more stylistically avant-garde *Laugh-In* was a self-styled "comedy happening" loaded with topical content and a striking countercultural ambience. With quick cuts and one-liners, comedians jabbed at the Vietnam War, conformity, and established institutions. "My church welcomes all denominations," said Henry Gibson in clerical collar, "but especially the five-dollar bill." As the crusty telephone operator Ernestine, Lily Tomlin satirized one of the nation's most powerful corporations. "This is the Telephone Company," she said in her nastiest nasal tone. "We are omnipotent. We handle 84 billion calls a year from everyone, including presidents and the pope. We don't need the business of scum like you, who owe us $18.34 for your last month's bill." Regarding the war in Southeast Asia, Dan Martin quipped: "You know, we only went into Vietnam as advisers. Last week we dropped over 400,000 tons of advice." On environmental issues, Henry Gibson stood, flower in hand, reading a poem: "I used to like fresh air / When it was there. / And water, I enjoyed it / Till we destroyed it. / Each day, the land's diminished. / I think I'm finished." One-liners tumbled from the "Joke Wall": "The KKK is full of sheet." "This is your slum. Keep it clean." "Miners get the shaft." There were also drug references. When one person said "Hi!" another replied, "You, too?"[40]

The producer of *Laugh-In*, George Schlatter, continually battled NBC's network's censors. "He literally once threw a chair across a studio because of something," recalled one of the show's writers, Allan Manings. "I said, 'Jesus Christ, George, let them have it.' But he was protecting something else that he felt he wanted." The bickering between the people on the show and the censors "became a game," said Manings. "They would see how much they could force us to give up. We would see how far we could push." The fact that *Laugh-In* topped the ratings during two of its five seasons undoubtedly gave Schlatter and his crew extra leverage.[41]

Despite network censorship, television programming encouraged wide-ranging changes across much of society, and perhaps nowhere more than in sports. Since its beginnings, TV had taken a strong interest in athletics. In the late 1940s and early 1950s, the search for cheap, uncomplicated programming had resulted in coverage of boxing and professional wrestling. Both those sports boomed momentarily, until the mid-1950s, when the networks turned especially to professional football, which, within a decade, became by far TV's most popular team sport.

In the early 1960s, third-place ABC added more sports programming to enhance summer weekend offerings and boost ratings. "We had no hit shows, no stars, and nothing in prospect but struggle," the network's president had said a few years earlier. Roone P. Arledge helped turn that situation around with a simple strategy: "We are going to add show business to sports." In 1960, when Arledge joined ABC to handle football coverage, he shrewdly recognized that the overall entertainment appeal of sporting events was more important than the contests themselves. The goal, he said, was "to take the viewer to the game!"—by providing a sense of excitement and color. Even if viewers "didn't give a damn about the game, they still might enjoy the program." To that end, the announcers and the crowds themselves would play critical roles. In 1961, Arledge began producing *The Wide World of Sports*, which took ABC's cameras to virtually any kind of athletic competition, including wrist wrestling, log-rolling championships, demolition derbies, and even rattlesnake hunting. As the sportscaster Vin Scully observed: "Legitimate sports, for the most part, have limited audiences. But when you give it another dimension—entertainment—you capture a new breed of viewer." Arledge saw opportunities for attracting female viewers. "We must gain and hold the interest of women who are not fanatic followers of the sport," he wrote. "Incidentally, very few men have ever switched channels when a nicely proportioned girl was leaping into the air," providing "honey shots," as he described such images. The entertainment strategy paid off throughout the 1960s as ABC's sports coverage lifted the network's fortunes.[42]

In the process, television reshaped the sporting world. For one thing, it accelerated the nationalization of sports. Earlier, the press, radio, and movies had made national figures of the Babe Ruths, Jack Dempseys, and Red Granges. But TV allowed fans from distant points to watch athletic events live, thereby blurring even more the boundaries between teams' traditional local constituencies and broader audiences. Starting in the 1960s, the newly enfranchised Dallas Cowboys football team advertised itself quite successfully as "America's team." The Dallas cheerleaders, whose sexy costumes and sideline routines received much television attention, were also known nationally. And, as TV developed more gimmicks to cover athletic contests—replays, slow motion, and different viewing angles—the fan base grew, and a dramatic trend emerged: increasing numbers of people said that they would rather watch TV coverage than actually attend events. Moreover, during the 1960s, television boosted professional football into the position of Americans' favorite sport.[43]

Television money attracted new sporting entrepreneurs such as the founders of the American Football League (AFL). After failing in the late 1950s to get National Football League (NFL) franchises, in 1960 the Texas millionaires Lamar Hunt and K. S. "Bud" Adams formed a rival league with eight teams. Previously, individual teams had negotiated their own TV contracts, but the new league as a unit worked out an agreement with ABC to cover its games. For the AFL, increased TV visibility proved far more valuable than the modest amount of money it received from the network. The NFL quickly took steps of its own, agreeing the next year to give CBS exclusive rights to cover its games. After a federal judge ruled that such contracts violated federal antitrust law, team owners prevailed on Congress to pass the Sports Broadcasting Act of 1961. According to the act, leagues could negotiate broadcasting agreements for all their teams. For teams far removed from large markets, the results were extremely important. Because franchises shared the revenues equally, weaker teams could stay afloat financially and also help keep the league intact. A geographically isolated team such as the Green Bay Packers still had a future. "We're 28 Republicans who vote socialist," joked the Cleveland Browns owner Art Modell of the NFL's television agreement.[44]

When, in 1964, NBC again lost the NFL television contract to CBS (which almost tripled its 1962 terms), the network turned to the new league, beating out ABC with a far more lucrative offer. With NBC's $42 million contract for five years, the AFL had even more money to lure top college players. In 1965, the Alabama star Joe Namath signed with the fledgling New York Jets for a record professional deal of $420,000 for three years. With TV money and more headline players, the AFL climbed to respectability. Moreover, the geographic distribution of pro football sites was spreading.[45]

Television and the new football league also influenced race relations. More than anywhere, on TV, sports provided visibility and income for African Americans. And that visibility increased as teams signed more black players. In its quest for fresh talent, the AFL was especially willing to cross the color line and recruit from small black colleges. At the end of the 1960s, the Kansas City Chiefs became the first pro football team to have a roster that was more than half black. As African Americans moved into the AFL, a number of them demonstrated the impact of the civil rights movement. Historically, most athletes shunned political activism. Jackie Robinson did not speak out on civil rights issues until after his retirement from baseball in 1956, and, even then, he was atypical in doing so. In the words of one sports historian: "Most African American athletes were symbols of social change rather than activists." By the 1960s, however, the civil rights movement was affecting a growing number of black athletes. In 1964, black players boycotted the AFL's all-star game in New Orleans because of that city's racial restrictions. The San Diego Chargers' Earl Faison remembered thinking: "As a black man I cannot go through that indignity and play a game here." (Two years earlier, black members of the Boston Celtics professional basketball team had refused to play an exhibition game in Lexington, Kentucky, for the same reason.) After the AFL moved its game to Houston, business and political leaders in Louisiana took steps to break down segregation and make their state more attractive to pro football franchises.[46]

Black players, especially in the AFL, also began to bring a style of play to the game that broke from staid tradition. Through such acts as dancing in the end zone and spiking the ball, they found innovative ways to make individual statements of pride and worth. As the sports educator and civil rights activist Harry Edwards explained, the players were creating "a vehicle to express that joy for which there is no mainstream language."[47]

A new professional basketball league, just as in football, encouraged creative stylistic expression and opened more racial opportunities. In 1967, several millionaires—including the singer Pat Boone—established the American Basketball Association (ABA). By then, the National Basketball Association (NBA) had existed for two decades and featured a conventional playing style. To challenge the old league, the ABA introduced such devices as a red, white, and blue ball, a three-point shot, and a slam-dunk competition for special occasions. Like the AFL, the ABA signed up young black players for what were then high salaries. Athletes such as Julius Erving—"Dr. J"—rejected the "buttoned-down game" of the NBA and brought a street style to the basketball court. One broadcaster compared Erving to Thomas Edison: "He was inventing something new every night." Erving and many of the other black players wore Afro hairstyles. Artis Gilmore's hair swept up six inches. The players also made striking fashion statements off the court, wearing such things as platform shoes and floor-length mink coats.[48]

Such styles of play and personal expression in athletic arenas mirrored a shift in the civil rights movement. By the mid-1960s, events were having a radicalizing effect. To Martin Luther King Jr.'s despair, black neighborhoods began erupting into violence; in mid-1965, some three dozen people died during bloody riots in the Watts section of Los Angeles. There were also more militant cries for black pride and black power. In sport, no one exemplified this shift more than Muhammad Ali.

In 1960, when the eighteen-year-old, cherub-faced Ali (then Cassius Marcellus Clay Jr.) won an Olympic gold medal in boxing in Rome, he seemed anything but radical. Indeed, for two days, the young man from Louisville's slums refused to take off his medal. At the Olympics, he told a Russian reporter that the "U.S.A. is the best country in the world, including yours." On the issue of America's racial inequality, he was reassuring: "Tell your readers we got qualified people working on that, and I'm not worried about the outcome." When people compared him to Joe Louis, he replied: "You know I'll be a credit to my race." But, shortly after his return from Rome, ugly examples of bigotry radicalized him. The owner of a segregated Louisville restaurant refused to serve him, and a motorcycle gang of white supremacists chased him. Thoroughly disillusioned, he threw his Olympic medal into the river. "I don't have to be what you want me to be," he began telling white America; "I'm free to be who I want." Unlike the soft-spoken Joe Louis, who had let his "fists do the talking," Ali brashly touted his abilities, often in rhyme. In mid-1963: he even made a phonograph record: *I Am the Greatest*. And, unlike Louis, he responded to American racism with growing anger and militancy. In 1964, after defeating the heavily favored Sonny Liston and winning the heavyweight boxing crown, he announced that he had joined the Nation of Islam and was changing his name to Muhammad Ali. His decision was so controversial that it prompted comments even on the floor of the U.S. Senate.[49]

Much of the press and some leading African American athletes, including Joe Louis, criticized Ali. The former heavyweight titleholder Floyd Patterson declared: "The image of a Black Muslim as the world heavyweight champion disgraces the sport and the nation." Ali's agonizing decision in 1966 to refuse induction into the military made him even more of a pariah to his critics. Young blacks and antiwar resisters, however, cheered him as a symbol of black resistance and pride. "Out of the womb of oppression he was our phoenix," extolled the singer-actor Harry Belafonte. Ali's spiritual adviser, the fiery Black Muslim preacher Malcolm X, predicted that Ali would be more of a hero to African Americans than Jackie Robinson had been. "Robinson is the white man's hero," Malcolm argued. When Ali rejected military service on religious grounds in February 1966, he recited a poem: "Keep asking me, no matter how long / On the war in Viet Nam, I sing this song. / I ain't got no quarrel with the Viet Cong." "Why," he asked angrily, "should they ask me and other so-called Negroes to put on a uniform and go 10,000 miles from home and drop bombs on brown people in Vietnam while so-called Negro people in Louisville are treated like dogs and denied simple human rights?" Boxing authorities promptly stripped him of his heavyweight title and withdrew his boxing license. In mid-1967, a Texas jury found him guilty of draft evasion. Facing five years in prison, Ali appealed his case through the courts, finally winning in 1971, when the Supreme Court overturned his conviction on a technicality. By then, Ali had become one of the biggest and most controversial symbols in sports. In 1968, black protesters boycotting the New York Athletic Club for refusing to admit blacks shouted: "Muhammad Ali is our champ!"[50]

The growing turmoil and conflict of the 1960s increasingly politicized athletics. While ABC's *Wide World of Sports* focused on "the thrill of victory and the agony of defeat," athletes and fans of varying political persuasions invested sport with a host of contrasting meanings. The 1966 college basketball championship game, for example, became a surrogate racial battleground. The number one–ranked, all-white University of Kentucky team (still coached by Adolph Rupp, who refused to recruit African Americans) suffered a stunning 72-65 defeat at the hands of an unheralded group from El Paso's Texas Western College, whose top seven players were black. Here, it seemed, was a spectacular blow against discrimination. Yet, at El Paso and elsewhere, a growing number of African American athletes complained that they were "hired guns" for the white establishment, which simply used them. Between 1967 and 1971, athletes protested at more than three dozen universities. White coaches at some of those schools dumped African Americans who objected to discriminatory racial policies. In one notable instance, the players were vindicated. When the Syracuse football coach Ben Schwartzwalder dismissed them for boycotting practice until he made changes (including the hiring of a black assistant coach), Schwartzwalder was himself fired.[51]

Evidence of the nation's spreading rights revolution was also evident in protests against coaches' authoritarian practices. Only a few years earlier, hard-nosed college coaches had enjoyed revered places in sports' character-building mythology. But, by the late 1960s, a growing number of players resisted abusive and demeaning methods. During the "Great Football Rebellion" at the University of Maryland in 1969, for example, 113 players petitioned successfully for the firing of their coach because of his fear tactics and physical mistreatment. Not long after, Vice President Spiro Agnew sympathized with beleaguered coaches. "In the New Left weekly rating of the people's enemies," he said, "the institution known as Football Coach ranks high in the top ten—not far behind the Joint Chiefs of Staff, General Motors, the CIA, the FBI, John Wayne, and yours truly."[52]

Agnew joined a number of fans, coaches, and players in objecting to what they saw as a countercultural invasion of sports' sacred grounds. To the Notre Dame football coach Ara Parseghian, hippies were simply "scum." At the University of South Carolina, Coach Paul Dietzel would not tolerate long hair on his football team. "You cannot wear these girl haircuts," he ordered, "because I like to make sure we are coaching boys." For a variety of reasons, then, Joe Namath, the gifted New York Jets star quarterback, sparked controversies. "Broadway Joe" let his hair grow long, wore a Fu Manchu mustache, played in distinctive white (rather than the usual black) shoes, and even posed for a TV ad in Beautymist pantyhose. Although he did not address political or social issues, his demeanor betokened a rebel image that contrasted sharply with the looks of another of the era's great quarterbacks, Johnny Unitas, whom *Sports Illustrated* applauded as "crew cut and quiet."[53]

Major-league baseball also reflected the era's fissures and strains. By the mid-1960s, players were pushing hard to enhance their salaries, pensions, and bargaining power with management. In 1969, the St. Louis Cardinals outfielder Curt Flood took aim at one of management's strongest weapons: the reserve clause, by which teams could trade players at will. When the Cardinals traded Flood to the Philadelphia Phillies, he went to court, seeking status as a free agent and claiming that the reserve clause violated antitrust law. "There ain't no way I'm going to pack up and move twelve years of my life away from here," Flood said pithily. "I do not feel that I am a piece of property to be bought and sold irrespective of my wishes," he informed the baseball commissioner. In 1972, the Supreme Court ruled against him, but the push for player empowerment continued to challenge baseball's traditional hierarchy.[54]

Racial issues continued to simmer in baseball's ranks as well. "I face more pressure every day just being a Negro," replied the Cardinals' great pitcher, Bob Gibson, when answering a question about the pressures he felt when he faced batters. Latin players also expressed a growing anger. Like African Americans, they had faced segregation and discrimination. "There is a lot of stuff I will never forget," recalled Cuba's Luis Tiant about his arrival in the United States in the early 1960s. "I remember when I first broke in, driving forty hours on the bus from Mexico City to Tulsa, and I couldn't even get in a restaurant." The number of Latins in the major leagues had grown from one regular player in 1948 to forty-eight in 1965, but they felt like a "minority within a minority," as the Puerto Rican–born Robert Clemente said. Clemente, who won four batting titles in the 1960s while playing with the Pittsburgh Pirates, was especially outspoken about the lack of respect that Latin players received, particularly from reporters, who stereotyped them as, for example, "hot-tempered." According to Clemente: "The Latin player doesn't get the recognition he deserves." Moreover, Clemente bridled at ways in which some reporters made him seem unintelligent. "They say 'Hey, he talks funny!' But they go to Puerto Rico and they don't talk like us. I don't have a master's degree, but I'm not a dumb-head and I don't want no bullshit from anyone." Oblivious to such feelings, in 1964 the San Francisco Giants coach, Alvin Dark, ordered his players to speak only in English. Orlando Cepeda objected vehemently: "Listen, I'm Puerto Rican and I'm proud of my language. I would feel foolish if I talked to [José] Pagan in English." Dark exacerbated the situation by telling a reporter: "We have trouble . . . because we have so many Spanish-speaking and Negro players on the team. They are just not able to perform up to the white ball player when it comes to mental alertness." Cepeda had heard about America's race problem, but, as he said later: "I never knew it was going to be that bad."[55]

Such discontent could only worry those Americans who believed, as Vice President Agnew did, that "sports—all sports—is one of the few bits of glue that hold society together." In mid-1968, Homer D. Babbidge, the president of the University of Connecticut, regretted that, "if the current undergraduate mood persists, intercollegiate athletics are going to be a target of criticism, disruption, and protest . . . a prime target." In Babbidge's opinion: "Our teams and our players, by and large, are the guys in the white hats—they keep their hair cut short, they're clean, they're orderly, aware of the importance of law and order and discipline." The California educator Max Rafferty agreed, describing football players as "the custodians of the concepts of democracy." Their critics were, in Rafferty's opinion, "kooks, crumbums and commies . . . hairy, loud mouth, beatniks."[56]

People who embraced athletics as a conservative, stabilizing force were, of course, able to find their own heroes. The football star O. J. Simpson ridiculed long-haired hippies and said that, to him, the concept of black power meant opportunities to make money. The Green Bay Packer coach Vince Lombardi attacked the era's permissiveness as well as "a society which seems to have sympathy only for the misfits, only for the maladjusted, only for the criminal, only for the loser."[57]

Yet Lombardi also spoke for racial and sexual tolerance, demonstrating the perils of typing people ideologically. As an Italian American who had endured such insults as *dago* and *wop,* he opposed discrimination. "If

I ever hear nigger or dago or kike or anything like that around here, regardless of who you are," he informed his team, "you're through with me. You can't play for me if you have any kind of prejudice." He declared that any Green Bay establishment refusing to serve his black players would lose the entire team's patronage. He also defended homosexuals. Once, when referring to a Packer who was homosexual, Lombardi warned: "If I hear one of you people make reference to his manhood you'll be out of here before your ass hits the ground."[58]

Sometimes, too, a team could unify a badly divided community. One year after Detroit's bloody race riots in 1967, the Tigers won the American League pennant. Their opponent in the 1968 World Series was St. Louis—reminiscent of that moment in the 1930s when the teams of Hank Greenberg and Dizzy Dean had faced off during previously troubled times. The Cardinals were defending world champions and three-to-one favorites. But, after the Tigers rallied to win the last three games and the Series, the city of Detroit erupted in jubilation. Confetti flew, and people danced in the streets. "What really struck me," recalled one of the team's stars, Gates Brown, "was how the blacks and whites were celebrating . . . hugging each other." The Detroit resident and black activist Herb Boyd remembered believing that "if we could come back after the devastation of 1967 and win a pennant and a World Series then there is possibility all over the place." In fundamental ways, of course, Detroit had not changed, but, as the sportswriter George Cantor said: "For those few months that surrounded the pennant race and that World Series, this was a wonderful place to live again."[59]

By the end of the 1960s, the sports world was, nevertheless, becoming more politicized. "As the '70s begin," observed the sportswriter Paul Hoch, "every U.S. sports event seems to be turning into a pro-war rally, complete with speeches from the Secretary of Defense at the baseball opener, Air Force jets flying overhead at football games, moments of silence for 'our boys in Vietnam.'" Continued efforts to link sports and patriotism only strengthened, of course, the symbolism of athletic contests.[60]

Like sports, music reflected and influenced the era's social ferment in numerous ways. Groups such as the Beatles and the Rolling Stones reinvigorated rock and roll, taking it in new directions. Bob Dylan upset the folk world by using an electric guitar. Lawrence Welk defended the "squares" against the counterculture. And country singers warred over exactly what defined their music.

The Beatles (John Lennon, Paul McCartney, George Harrison, and Ringo Starr) arguably influenced American music more than any other group had ever done. By the early 1960s, rock and roll seemed thoroughly tamed. Some relieved observers concluded that the popular mainstream was back in safe, orderly hands. But, with the Beatles in the vanguard, rock again emerged as a disruptive force—powerful enough, some believed, to alter the world.[61]

As poor kids growing up after World War II in the dilapidated, economically depressed port city of Liverpool, the Beatles had used bomb sites as playgrounds. And, as working-class outsiders in England's class-conscious society, they felt the sting of snubs. "People had a sense of humor," Lennon said, "because they're in so much pain." In the late 1950s, before Starr became the drummer, the group underwent several name changes and searched for an identity. Often wearing leather jackets and resembling local toughs, the musicians wound their way through shabby clubs in Liverpool and Hamburg's raunchy Reeperbahn district. But, by 1962, with Starr then in the band, the Beatles were building an English audience. The slipcover for their 1963 album *Introducing the Beatles* described them as "England's No. 1 Vocal Group." A few months later, their record sales jolted the music world. In January 1964, "I Want to Hold Your Hand" not only roared to the top of the pop charts but sold at the staggering rate of ten thousand copies an hour in New York City alone. The next month, the Beatles made their sensational live television debut on *The Ed Sullivan Show,* drawing a record TV audience of some 73 million viewers. By April, they had set another precedent, capturing the top five places on the *Billboard* chart. "Beatlemania" had arrived in the United States. "This isn't show business," sensed John Lennon. "It's something else. This is different from anything that anybody imagines."[62]

Timing was important in the Beatles' explosive impact in the United States. By the mid-1960s, the postwar baby-boom generation was coming of age and looking for something fresh. As one young fan declared: "My mother hates them, my father hates them, my teacher hates them. Can you think of three better reasons why I love them?" Another fan liked the group's 1964 movie *A Hard Day's Night* because "all the dreary old adults are mocked and brushed aside." Moreover, in the wake of John Kennedy's assassination on November 22, 1963, the freewheeling Beatles offered a welcome exuberance and optimism. It helped, too, that their new manager, Brian Epstein, had gotten the American media to turn the Beatles' U.S. arrival into a major event. *Time, Newsweek,* and *Life* all ran big stories. "Here come the Beatles," proclaimed *Life* on January 31, 1964. By then, Capitol Records had distributed 5 million "The Beatles Are Coming" stickers in every state. And radio stations played so many Beatles songs that a rival company objected, claiming that its records were little more than "spot commercials between Beatles tunes."[63]

Hype and timing helped account for Beatlemania, but the "Fab Four" indeed represented something different. For one thing, their personalities and style had an energizing effect. Although the Edwardian suits and ties that they had recently started wearing made them seem totally respectable, their hair—"great pudding bowls of hair," in *Newsweek*'s words—was longer than that of most males in 1964 and gave them a somewhat androgynous look. Indeed, according to Susan Douglas, the Beatles "challenged traditional gender lines" by showing "that all kinds of barriers could be finessed," that "you could mock conventions while obeying them." When they performed onstage and in their movies, as another cultural commentator observed, they were all "about having fun, beating the system, reinventing one-self and liberating us all from grimly earnest 'maturity.'" They brought a festive spirit with them, whimsically fielding banal questions from the press. When asked, "Do you hope to get haircuts?" they replied: "We had one yesterday." What did they think of Beethoven? "I love him," answered Starr. "Especially his poems." And, unlike anyone since Elvis Presley, they evoked expressions of female desire that accompanied the accelerating sexual revolution. "I think you are sexy and I don't even know what it means," wrote a self-described "little fan" to McCartney in 1964. A year later, in Seattle, police struggled to hold back hysterical girls who typically pleaded: "I have to talk to them! You don't understand!"[64]

The Beatles were different also because, unlike most popular singers, who recorded what others had written, they wanted to create their own music. "It's a different thing we're going for," Paul McCartney insisted, "it's something new." They thus resisted the traditional etiquette of the recording industry. "We weren't even allowed into the control room [at first]," McCartney recalled. "It was Us and Them." "Grown-ups" operated the controls—"guys in full-length lab-coats, maintenance men and engineers." On the other side of the glass, "there was us, the tradesmen." But the Beatles changed that equation: "We gradually became the workmen who took over the factory."[65]

Moreover, the Beatles tried to prevent showbiz conventions from defining them. In that regard, they were quite remarkable, agonizing over and resisting the confinements of stardom and celebrity. At the outset, Brian Epstein had gotten them to alter their appearance. "They were a scruffy crowd in leather," he thought when he first saw them in Liverpool, "not very tidy and not very clean." He reworked their image, getting them into suits. But the Beatles were uneasy about these changes. Lennon admitted: "[We] felt embarrassed in our new suits and being very clean. We were worried that our friends might think we'd sold out—which we had, in a way." They recognized that the entertainment business marketed performers as commodities, like soap or cereal. The once-innovative Elvis Presley had, thus, become predictable, a prisoner of designated roles and images. The Beatles desperately wanted to avoid that oppressive fate. They resented efforts to turn them into objects. "It's as though we were force grown, like rhubarb," complained George Harrison.[66]

"No official functions, ever," became the Beatles' position after the

British Embassy hosted an event in Washington, DC, to commemorate their first visit to the United States in 1964. In a setting that reeked of class snobbishness and condescension, the Beatles felt like curiosities on display. When the British ambassador, Sir David Ormsby-Gore, could not keep their names straight, they toyed with him. Lennon claimed that he was Fred and said that Harrison was John. When the ambassador addressed Harrison as John, Harrison laughed, "I'm Charlie," and introduced Ringo as John. Before the Beatles left, they took another playful jab at aristocratic pomposities by asking Ormsby-Gore: "And what do you do?" But humor was insufficient protection against the elite posturing around them. As wealthy, drunken guests groped at them, cutting a lock of Ringo's hair, a cursing Lennon fled the building.[67]

Fans' growing demands also bothered the Beatles, who were beginning to feel as if they were living in a fishbowl. "It's like we're four freaks being wheeled out to be seen, shake our hair about, and get back in our cage afterwards," Lennon remarked. "I reckon we could send out four waxwork dummies of ourselves." Some of the adulation was downright terrifying. Lennon recalled that, during the group's last tour of the United States in August 1965, "people kept bringing blind, crippled, deformed children into our dressing room. This boy's mother would say, 'Go on, kiss him, maybe you'll bring back his sight.' We're not cruel. But when a mother shrieks, 'Just touch him and maybe he'll walk again,' we want to run, cry and empty our pockets." George Harrison was so discouraged at the end of the tour that he threatened to quit.[68]

Against that backdrop, the Beatles' movies—*A Hard Day's Night* (Richard Lester, 1964) and *Help!* (Richard Lester, 1965)—served as metaphors of their troubled relationships with demanding fans. From one angle, the movies were inventive comedies about the joys of freedom and spontaneity. But, from another angle, they were unsettling. However unintentionally, the movies commented darkly on how fans developed fantastical expectations of entertainers. In *A Hard Day's Night*, the Beatles as themselves are constantly running from overzealous fans. A female character dismisses the real John Lennon because "you don't look like him at all." And, when another female fan sees the real Ringo Starr in working-class clothes, she says: "Get out of it, shorty." *Help!* similarly was about being on the run, trying with songs and laughter to hold off the surrounding chaos.[69]

Meanwhile, the 1965 U.S. tour took a heavy emotional toll. "There was no satisfaction in it," Harrison said. "We got worse as musicians, playing the same old junk every day." So the Beatles returned to England to explore new kinds of music. As McCartney put it: "The cute period had ended."[70]

As the Beatles began to transform themselves, they reflected the influence of Bob Dylan. They met him in 1964, in a New York City hotel, following their performance before sixteen thousand frenzied fans at a nearby facility. He introduced them to marijuana, showing them how to roll joints and inhale. Afterward, their music became more introspective—"a medium fit for communicating autobiographical intimacies, political discontents, spiritual elation, inviting an audience not to dance, but to *listen*—quietly, attentively, thoughtfully," in the rock historian James Miller's words. But Dylan also provided the Beatles with a role model as an independent artist with integrity. He was willing to take chances, reinventing himself and his music, and not tying himself to what audiences wanted or expected.[71]

In turn, Dylan admired the Beatles' creativity, which may have influenced his turn away from purely acoustic music. "I knew they were pointing the direction where music had to go," he said. On July 25, 1965, he took one of his biggest gambles at Rhode Island's annual Newport Folk Festival. Wearing a green polka-dot shirt and sunglasses in lieu of the customary folk musician's blue jeans and work shirt, and playing an electric guitar, he launched loudly into "Maggie's Farm," "Like a Rolling Stone," and a third song. Folk performers had always used acoustic guitars, leaving amplified instruments to commercial singers. Dylan was breaking that hallowed tradition. He had recently recorded an electrified version of "Like a Rolling Stone," a breakthrough record open to interpretation but memorably conveying a sense of a world in flux. Lasting six minutes, the longest 45 rpm pop single to that date, it would rise to number two on the charts. And now here was Dylan at Newport, where, according to the guitarist Michael Bloomfield, who accompanied him, rock and roll summoned up images of "greasers, heads, dancers, people who got drunk and boogied." When Dylan took the stage with his electric guitar, as his band member Barry Goldberg recalled: "The feeling was that the barbarians were at the gate." People shouted that Dylan was a "sellout" who should play authentic folk music. Someone from the audience hollered: "Go back to the Sullivan show!" "It's terrible," shouted Pete Seeger when he heard the electric guitar. "If I had an ax I'd cut the cable right now." According to Peter Yarrow of the folk group Peter, Paul, and Mary: "People were just horrified. . . . It was as if it was a capitulation to the enemy—as if all of a sudden you saw Martin Luther King, Jr., doing a cigarette ad." In Bloomfield's opinion: "Dylan should have just given them the finger."[72]

With Dylan's radical departures as a model, the Beatles were ready to move in new directions. By then, rock music was enjoying a magical moment. Dylan had gone electric and was injecting a potent social consciousness into rock. At Detroit's Motown recording studio, a marvelous lineup of African American singers—including Smokey Robinson, the Supremes, and Marvin Gaye—was turning out memorable hits. The Beatles were infusing the pop world with fresh innocence. And accompanying them on their 1965 tour was a group from the East Los Angeles barrio, Cannibal and the Headhunters, whose version of "Land of a Thousand Dances" reached number thirty on the pop charts—the highest ranking that any Latino band had achieved. The song became a kind of "anthem for East L.A." and demonstrated the immense variety of American culture. As had been the case in the mid-1950s, the energy across racial and ethnic lines was powerful. Rock's dominant mood expressed a "longing for community," as a rock historian later observed, "or at least tolerant pluralism." Its young followers felt a sense of empowerment, an opportunity to effect genuine change.[73]

In that spirit, the Beatles released in 1967 what *Rolling Stone* later judged "the most important rock and roll album ever made, an unsurpassed adventure in concept, sound, songwriting, cover art and studio technology . . . rock's greatest declaration of change": *Sgt. Pepper's Lonely Hearts Club Band*. The album took seven hundred hours to make, from late 1966 to April 1967. It was a concept album, not a collection of single songs. There had been other such albums, but this was the first not to release the songs individually. Technologically, the use of multitracking elevated studio recording to new levels. The album cover was itself a landmark. The Beatles in colorful band uniforms stand among a host of historical figures with countercultural associations, including Karl Marx, Lenny Bruce, Marilyn Monroe, Marlon Brando, James Dean, Bob Dylan, and Mae West. West laughingly granted permission to include her picture but asked playfully: "What would I be doing in a lonely hearts club?" The songs were full of drug references, such as the line: "I get high with a little help from my friends." Later, McCartney explained the origins of the album "in one word, drugs. Pot." Posing as an imaginary band playing an imaginary concert, the Beatles addressed their listeners at the beginning: "We hope you will enjoy the show." Throughout the album were sounds of laughter and random conversation. As Ringo Starr said: "*Sgt. Pepper* was our grandest endeavor." For over three years, it was on *Billboard*'s album charts. Incredibly, four young men with no formal musical training had made it.[74]

Meanwhile, another "bunch of bloody amateurs, ignorant as hell," were shaking the rock world. The description came from Mick Jagger, lead singer for that "bunch"—the Rolling Stones. Formed in mid-1963, the English group drew heavily from American blues singers such as Muddy Waters. Their manager, Andrew Logg Oldham, decided that the Stones needed to project an image that contrasted starkly with that of the "clean-cut choirboy" Beatles. "I wanted to establish that the Stones were threatening, uncouth and animalistic. . . . The opposite of those nice little chaps." During their second American tour in the fall of 1964, the Stones were a big hit, flaunting their rebellious reputation. "Would You Let Your Daughter Go with a Rolling Stone" was exactly the kind of headline they relished. "The Beatles may want to hold your hand," remarked the writer Tom Wolfe. "The Stones want to burn your town." Another writer compared them to "five unfolding switchblades." According to Jagger: "We never set out to make cultural changes. . . . Initially, I think the driving force was just to be famous, get lots of girls, and earn a lot of money." But their defiant attitude became a statement in itself. And, by 1968, songs such as "Street Fighting Man" had a definite political edge. "Hey," sang Jagger. "Said my name is called Disturbance." Although the song "Sympathy for the Devil" was basically a commentary on the personal evil that haunts every individual, the Stones were willing to let people interpret it as they wished.[75]

By the latter half of the 1960s, a wave of new rock performers was raising cultural and political consciousness. Their sounds, messages, and dress gave rock an even more radical edge. The Beatles shed their "lovable mop-tops" appearance for longer hair, drooping mustaches, and brightly colored clothes. Several members of a group known simply as The Band had beards. The Who, from England, sported a clean-cut "mod look" but represented "a single force which threatens a lot of crap which is around at the moment in the middle class and in the middle-aged politics or philosophy," according to the guitarist Pete Townshend. "My Generation" was The Who's rallying cry for youths against their elders. "Hope I die before I get old" was a line in the song.[76]

A number of rock groups and singers embraced the hippie counterculture. Substantial numbers of these bands included middle-class youths pushing against their respectable, restrictive backgrounds. Jim Morrison, whose father was an admiral, enrolled for a while at the University of California, Los Angeles, but opted, he said, for "anything about revolt, disorder, chaos." His songs provided him with a chance to "break on through to the other side." Janis Joplin described herself as "a weirdo among fools" in conservative Port Arthur, Texas. She rejected her family's middle-class values, the local racism, and a cheerleader-style femininity. At the University of Texas, students cruelly nominated her "Ugliest Man on Campus." She dropped out of college and carved a niche for herself in the heavily male world of rock and roll. When a fan asked, "D' you like what you're doing?" she replied: "I wrote the part." A lover of blues music, she assumed responsibility for much of the cost to place a tombstone on the great blues singer Bessie Smith's previously unmarked grave.[77]

Groups such as the Grateful Dead and the Jefferson Airplane sometimes staged free concerts as counterpoints to America's corporate, commercial culture. Joplin sang at the nonprofit 1967 Monterey Pop Festival, where Townshend shattered his guitar and Jimi Hendrix set his on fire. Jerry Garcia of the Grateful Dead objected to "being just another face in a corporate personality. There isn't even a Warner 'brother' to talk to. The music business and the Grateful Dead are in two different orbits, two different universes."[78]

Radio's "FM revolution" helped disseminate rock and roll's increasingly radical messages. The acronym *FM* stands for *frequency modulation,* or the modulation of the frequency of the carrier or radio waves. As early as the 1920s, the RCA company's technological wizard Howard Armstrong had varied the dimensions of radio waves in order to reduce static. He found that widening signal bands up to twenty times beyond the accepted AM model produced a much clearer sound. But RCA, especially during the 1930s, was reluctant to adopt FM lest the company's NBC network lose listeners who could not afford to buy new radios. FM thus remained on radio's fringes. By the late 1940s, there were a few FM stations, but AM stations in the same market owned 80 percent of them. Those FM stations basically recycled AM material. In 1964, however, an FCC ruling liberated a huge chunk of FM programming. The ruling, which would go into effect in 1967, stated that AM stations in cities of over 100,000 residents could not duplicate more than half their programming on FM. Coincidentally, the crowded AM frequencies made FM attractive to new stations. For those emerging stations, the question was what material to put on the air.[79]

The answer came from new-style disc jockeys such as San Francisco's Tom "Big Daddy" Donahue. A refugee from AM, Donahue identified with the growing counterculture. "Top 40 radio, as we . . . have known it for the last ten years, is dead, and its rotting corpse is stinking up the airwaves," he contended. "How many goddamn times can you play Herman's Hermits and still feel good about what you do?" He could not believe that a Grateful Dead concert could draw thousands of people in San Francisco but that no local radio station would broadcast that kind of music. On April 7, 1967, after convincing KMPX to let him play some of his own albums, he took to the air, saying: "This is Tom Donahue. I'm here to clean up your face and mess up your mind."[80]

The result was a kind of free-form programming that quickly proliferated via "underground" or "progressive rock" stations. Hip deejays like Donahue rejected the AM format, which rotated pop singles (never lasting more than three minutes) with commercials. The FM disc jockeys played longer songs and album tracks. They used commercials erratically, sometimes bunching them up after ignoring them for half an hour. And they typically disdained scripts, deciding on the spur of the moment what song to play next. "That's working without a net," said one deejay; "that's an artist." Also, their radio style was different from that of Top 40 announcers. As Cousin Brucie explained: "Where the most successful jocks on AM sounded like they'd love a piece of your bubble gum, the rising stars of FM sounded like they knew where you kept your stash of pot." When one exasperated station manager tried to impose a dress code, the response was incredulous: "A dress code. Was he kidding? Half of these people didn't ever wear shoes." On one occasion, the Los Angeles deejay Jim Ladd put on a twenty-four-minute track from a Grateful Dead album, snuck onto the fire escape to smoke marijuana, and discovered he had locked himself out of the studio. Such free-spirited, antiformula broadcasting was short-lived, but the so-called hippie stations dispensed rock and roll that was otherwise unavailable over the airwaves.[81]

By the late 1960s, however, rock was reaching a crossroads. In 1965, President Lyndon Johnson had started sending U.S. ground troops to Vietnam. As draft levels and the number of American deaths went up, and as violence increasingly shook the United States, the rock community's sense of empowerment and hope began giving way to fear. And, as rock and roll's messages became more radical—more strident as well as more introspective—the music started to fragment and encountered growing resistance.[82]

All along, of course, Middle America had clung to safe, familiar music and entertainment. For many traditionalists, there was no more reliable source than Lawrence Welk, whose weekly television show had a huge following. Welk was "one of us—the farm boy who made good," the *Saturday Evening Post* later reported. "He seems to personify all that is best in the American character, a man who made good by being good" and who intuited "the musical tastes of the average American." Welk was a German-Russian product from Strasburg, North Dakota. On local radio during the 1920s, he had popularized a musical variety format. Subsequently, his dance bands became so popular that, in 1955, ABC hired him to host a Saturday night TV show, *The Dodge Dancing Party*. His audience that year more than quadrupled, jumping from 7.1 to 32.5 million; the next year it approached 50 million. At that point, *Life* dubbed him "the most popular musician in U.S. history." Unlike Ed Sullivan, Welk ignored the hottest new acts and had his orchestra stick with polkas and old-style dance music—"champagne music" and "mom and dad music," as he described it. As one of his singers said: "He wanted to give people music he thought they could understand, and he didn't think they could understand Beatles songs."[83]

Through the 1960s, Welk's show remained a television staple with high ratings. His no-frills, unchanging format featured him with baton in hand, speaking in his "Wunnerful, wunnerful" style, and prompting his orchestra with "ah-one-and-ah-two-and-ah" commands. For viewers, his orchestra resembled an extended family, formally dressed but with casual, neighborly manners. The musicians and singers appeared on camera as folksy and friendly. They included "da luffly Lennon Sisters," young girls who exuded down-home innocence, and the accordionist Myron Floren, who beamed, nodded, and winked when the camera zeroed in on him. In Welk's words, they resembled "a little 'America' . . . democracy all its own." Welk imposed a dress code on all members of his cast. Critics joked that he was "the Geritol set's Elvis," but he refused to make adjustments. He recognized, as a TV commentator argued, "that a wide schism had developed between the urban coastal cultures and the more-populous 'other America.'" As Welk explained his popularity: "There seems to be a lot of midwesterners everywhere."[84]

Welk was, in many respects, an antidote to the unstable 1960s. His ordinary, amateurish demeanor struck a welcome chord. According to one reporter, his "shy, clodhopper charm" epitomized a "one-hundred percent Midwest American, red, white, and blue." Viewers could embrace the illusion, as another reporter wrote, "that life really is free and easy and we can merely dance our troubles away." One of the Lennon sisters explained that Welk was "a constant in the constantly changing world." To the critics who called him a "square," he responded simply: "When I was growing up, 'square' was a compliment. You gave a man a square deal, looked him square in the eye, stood four square on your principles. . . . I grew up in a community of squares." Squares were citizens who "enjoy clean fun, understandable music, pretty and wholesome girls." They were, he argued, people who "pay their bills . . . keep their children clothed and fed, send them to Sunday school, raise them to believe in God and this country." Such thinking assuredly resonated among people who longed for an older, more stable America.[85]

That America was evident also in television's immensely popular rural situation comedies, especially *The Andy Griffith Show, Petticoat Junction, Green Acres,* and *The Beverly Hillbillies.* Although critics scoffed at "hayseed TV," no TV genre had a larger following in the 1960s. *The Andy Griffith Show* premiered on CBS in 1960 and was a top ten show during all its eight seasons. At a time when the civil rights movement was shaking society, African Americans were strikingly absent from the fictional North Carolina village of Mayberry. So were other signs of social turbulence, as the town's "just plain folks" dealt with daily life humorously and in a neighborly fashion. In 1967–68, as violence and protests rocked the nation, the show achieved a number one rating. During the decade's building turmoil, it and the other rural sitcoms—like Lawrence Welk—supplied a kind of "cultural anaesthetic."[86]

Another rearguard action was evident in the men's adventure magazines such as *Male, Man's Story, All Man, Real Men, Man's Action, Men Today, For Men Only,* and *Man's World.* These offshoots of the pulp industry had started appearing in significant numbers during the early 1950s but boomed into the 1970s. Monthly sales per issue among even "the lower-tier magazines" ranged from 100,000 to 250,000. Most copies were available at train and bus stations, but the readership was an ill-defined group. "We never did find out with any precision exactly who 'our guys' were," recalled one editor, Bruce Jay Friedman. "We were reasonably sure our readers drank beer." They were also interested in World War II. Certainly, combat stories were central to the magazines. The "true" accounts were typically fabricated. Friedman once noticed that three stories in one issue that was ready for press dealt with Americans who had survived rat cages in Japan. Hurriedly, the printer reset the type to move one rat cage to Germany and another to Argentina. The writer Mario Puzo remembered getting letters from readers correcting mistakes in stories—"which was very funny, 'cause the whole piece was usually made up." Wherever the setting, and whatever the subject, the world of these magazines lacked ambiguity, presenting good and evil in stark terms. Rugged warriors battled monstrous villains amid warnings that sinful cities, sissified men, and independent women threatened American masculinity. Looking back, Friedman admitted that themes of racism, imperialism, and misogyny pervaded the publications. "That was the way things were," he said. "We didn't think twice about it."[87]

The magazines' cover illustrations were crucial, both in attracting readers and in setting a tone. That tone, according to the editor Adam Parfrey, was all about fear: "Fear of enemies, fear of animals, fear of women, fear of any loaded attack on the buyer's manliness." Sex received prominent attention, but, as the son of one illustrator recalled, the magazines "adhered to a strict censorship on nipples, bottoms and crotches, so the public could openly buy these magazines from displays at most newsstands and drug stores." Significantly, in the 1960s, many of the men's adventure magazines featured more and more cover stories about the brutalization of women or about cruel women, such as "the Bitch of Buchenwald," "Madame Torture," or the "Nazi She-Devil." The illustrations invariably portrayed female victims and torturers as large breasted and scantily dressed. Usually, female and male sadists appeared as Nazis or Communists. The cover of *Man's Exploits* in March 1963, for example, showed Chinese Communists flogging Anglo-looking women in "The City of Lust of Red China's Butcher General." Parfrey guessed that the adventure magazines disclosed "a suppressed side of the American male, percolating with hate and vengeance" at a time when feminism was a growing force.[88]

Such magazines promised "deliverance from women," in the words of one sociologist. By the 1970s, a revitalized *True* magazine hailed itself as "MACHO" and pledged to "bring the American man and American values back from the shadow . . . back from behind the frivolous skirts of libbers." A "masculine mystique" was finding more strident expression as issues of gender became more prominent.[89]

The tug-of-war between the more traditional America and the tumult of the 1960s also left a mark on country music. For years, pop and rock music had both repulsed and attracted the country industry. And, certainly, country music's "purity" was mythical given the genre's history of invented traditions—from the fabricated rusticity of the early *Grand Ole Opry* to the singing cowboys and the "beer-drinking music" of the honky-tonk in the 1930s. In the 1950s, rock and roll had battered the country industry by raiding young audiences and dominating radio. In an effort to adapt, country's recording studios developed the "Nashville sound." "We took the twang out of it," recalled one of that sound's innovators, the brilliant guitarist Chet Atkins, who had become RCA's main country producer. The goal, Atkins said, was simply "to make hit records" by capturing both pop and country markets—taking country "more uptown."[90]

Before Patsy Cline died in a plane crash in early 1963, she set a standard as a female artist who produced crossover hits. In 1961, her "I Fall to Pieces" and "Crazy" ranked one and two on the country charts, twelve and nine on the pop charts. She abandoned western clothes for evening wear, sequins, cashmere, knee-length dresses, and fur shawls. And, although she described herself as an "ol' hillbilly" who at one point had worked in a poultry plant cutting off chicken heads, she adopted a stylized sophistication. Even as she found a national market for the Nashville sound, however, she was uncomfortable. "It ain't country," she said of "Walkin' after Midnight," another of her big hits on both charts. "Doing something I don't believe in makes me feel like a whore." As Cline implied, the Nashville recording industry had to wonder how many adjustments it could make and still have "country." Jimmy Webb, the young writer of Glen Campbell's late 1960s crossover hits "Wichita Lineman" and "Galveston," asked laughingly of Nashville: "Which country is that?"[91]

Efforts to align country and pop nevertheless reaped dividends. In 1961, only 81 radio stations played country music; by 1969, that number was 606. Over the 1960s, country music's profits jumped by around 500 percent, to $200 million annually. Chet Atkins summed up the point as effectively as anyone. Jingling the change in his pants pocket, he said: "That is the Nashville sound." Yet he wondered what he had wrought. "People ask me whether I'm sorry I moved the Nashville sound so far uptown. Well, yes, in a way I am."[92]

That uptown transition angered some mainstays in the country industry, which could not escape the cultural fault lines that divided the rest of the nation in the 1960s. "The rock 'n' roll kids, the folk-rock, they're taking care of all the protest stuff," insisted 1930s cowboy movie star Tex Ritter, one of the first members of the Country Music Hall of Fame. "I don't want country music to fall into all of *that*. I don't mind to sing about mother and home and flag all of the time." Some country songs answered the wishes of Ritter and other Americans who resented "the protest stuff" and longed for more tranquil times. The best-selling country single of 1969 was Merle Haggard's "Okie from Muskogee," which became a kind of anthem to defenders of traditional values. Haggard had been riding through Oklahoma when his tour bus passed a road marker: "Muskogee—19 miles." A band member laughed: "Hell, I'll bet they don't smoke marijuana in Muskogee." The comment inspired Haggard, who took only twenty minutes to write the hit song about small-town America, where citizens were patriotic and spurned countercultural lifestyles.[93]

In 1969, the tensions within country music were evident in *The Johnny Cash Show* (1969–71). That year ABC had signed Cash, already a country icon, to a Saturday night show at Nashville's Ryman Auditorium, the site of *The Grand Ole Opry*. Cash chose Bob Dylan as his first guest, a choice that unquestionably raised eyebrows among some country fans. Three years earlier, when Dylan, well into his search for creative discovery, visited Nashville to make his album *Blonde on Blonde,* he was virtually a stranger. "All we knew was that Dylan looked very strange to us," said a member of the backup band. "We were still what you'd call rednecks." But Cash had admired Dylan for some time, defending him after the 1965 Newport Folk Festival incident, and recording some of his songs. Not everyone in Nashville shared Cash's admiration. When Dylan's friends Joni Mitchell and Graham Nash came to town to watch the TV show, they encountered considerable hostility. According to their manager: "People yelled, called them shaggy-hairs and hippies. They felt unsafe." Shortly thereafter, Cash again courted controversy—with country fans as well as the ABC network. The issue involved a song that Kris Kristofferson had written, "Sunday Morning Coming Down." "Now we got our own pet hippie," some critics scoffed at Kristofferson, who wore a beard and long hair. ABC wanted Cash to change a drug reference in the song: the word *stoned*. While Kristofferson watched nervously from the balcony, Cash defied the network by leaving the song intact. The struggle for country music's soul was heating up.[94]

Changes were also buffeting the movie industry, which was still trying to find its way in the television age. Grand epics such as *Spartacus* (Stanley Kubrick, 1960) and *Doctor Zhivago* (David Lean, 1965) continued to have box-office appeal, but some, like *Cleopatra* (Joseph L. Mankiewicz, 1963), *The Greatest Story Ever Told* (George Stevens, 1965), and *The Bible* (John Huston, 1966), were busts. Family movies such as *Mary Poppins* (Robert Stevenson, 1964) and *The Sound of Music* (Robert Wise, 1965) reaped substantial dividends, but *Doctor Doolittle* (Richard Fleischer, 1967) flopped.[95]

As the studios searched for winning formulas and audiences, they were somewhat more willing to deal with issues involving the Cold War, race, and the sexual revolution. By 1960, Hollywood was starting to back away from the ugly blacklisting era. That year Kirk Douglas not only hired the blacklisted Dalton Trumbo to write the script for *Spartacus* but also included Trumbo's name in the film credits. "The one thing in my career I'm most proud of," Douglas said later, "is the breaking of the blacklist." When, despite anti-Communist pickets outside some theaters, the film became the year's top moneymaker, Hollywood began to drop its ban on blacklisted writers, performers, and directors. The studios welcomed the change because, for some time, they had chafed as television reran old movies that owed much to the talents of people whom Hollywood had banned.[96]

In the early 1960s, Hollywood drew on best-selling novels to raise questions about the fear of communism and the threat of nuclear war: *Advise and Consent* (Otto Preminger, 1962), which obliquely addressed Red-baiting in government; *The Manchurian Candidate* (John Frankenheimer, 1962), which reversed the anti-Communist film images of the 1950s, portraying 100 percent Americans in the mode of Joe McCarthy as Communist stooges; *Seven Days in May* (John Frankenheimer, 1964), about a threatened right-wing military coup; *Fail-Safe* (Sidney Lumet, 1964), about efforts to deal with a mistaken U.S. nuclear attack on the Soviet Union. *Dr. Strangelove; or, How I Learned to Stop Worrying and Love the Bomb* (Stanley Kubrick, 1964), a pathbreaking film, used humor to satirize the perils of Cold War ideology and nuclear war. And, in 1965, Martin Ritt's *The Spy Who Came in from the Cold* was a successful film adaptation of John le Carré's disturbing best seller. The novel, which le Carré first published in England in 1963, became the top-selling book in the United States a year later. The movie accurately reflected le Carré's pessimistic view that the Cold War was about not victory and virtue but, in his words, "a condition of political misery" in which "distinctions between good and evil remain stubbornly elusive, and individual humanity stood dwarfed by vast ideological and bureaucratic systems." The story's protagonist, a burned-out British spy named Alec Lemas (played by Richard Burton in the movie), learns that the anti-Communist ally he is protecting is, in fact, a despicable ex-Nazi. At the end, after the woman he loves dies at the Berlin Wall, Lemas finds his own death preferable to living with the cynical duplicity of the government he serves.[97]

Westerns continued to provide a medium by which to critique social trends and problems. Granted, the lavish, star-filled *How the West Was Won* (John Ford et al., 1962) recycled in grand style the march-of-civilization theme, and John Wayne made several westerns that celebrated triumphant individualism. But a striking number of fine films—*The Misfits* (John Huston, 1961), *Lonely Are the Brave* (David Miller, 1962), *The Man Who*

Shot Liberty Valance (John Ford, 1962), *Ride the High Country* (Sam Peckinpah, 1962), and *Hud* (Martin Ritt, 1963)—raised doubts about modernizing, depersonalizing forces. At the beginning of *Ride the High Country,* old Judd (Joel McCrea), a retired law officer, rides his horse into town. He smiles and waves at the people lining the street because he thinks they are honoring him for his past heroic deeds. Instead, a policeman hustles him out of the way to allow for the real celebration: a camel race and an approaching carnival. At the end, when Judd dies in a shoot-out to protect a young woman, the audience could sense that an era was closing as well. In *The Man Who Shot Liberty Valance,* the James Stewart character builds a political career on the mistaken assumption that he rescued a town by killing a sadistic bully. Ultimately, he tells several journalists that someone else shot the detestable Liberty Valance, but they decide not to print the truth. As one of them says: "When the legend becomes fact, print the legend." From this perspective, of course, romantic illusions trumped harsh realities.[98]

Those realities concerning the American frontier had probably never looked harsher on movie screens than in three Sergio Leone films that lifted Clint Eastwood to stardom—*A Fistful of Dollars* (1964), *For a Few Dollars More* (1965), and *The Good, the Bad, and the Ugly* (1967). Opening in the United States in 1967, these so-called spaghetti westerns (Leone was Italian) presented an unlovely portrait of the Old West. Eastwood is the ultimate loner—"the man with no name." An amoral protagonist, he tries simply to survive. As he rides across a desolate landscape, he encounters only treachery, violence, and corruption.[99]

Hollywood similarly showed a willingness to face the nation's race problems somewhat more openly, albeit often in ways that fit within the Cold War consensus. John Sturges's popular 1960 *The Magnificent Seven,* for example, tied together American's fight for racial justice at home and for defenseless people abroad. In the opening scenes, two of the protagonists, the gunfighters Chris and Vin (Yul Brynner and Steve McQueen), defy local bigots who try to block the burial of a Native American in "Boot Hill." Then, with five comrades, they ride into Mexico to liberate a village from bandits. Although the men are professional gunfighters, just doing a job the villagers have hired them to do, they are also idealists who want to do the right thing: free the peasants from cruel aggressors. Pride, honor, professionalism, and a sense of justice motivate them. They have no desire to seek glory or rule others. At the movie's end, two of the surviving gunfighters ride off, presumably to save another beleaguered town. The image reinforced the perception that the United States had a similar role to play in international affairs, where it supposedly came as a liberator—not as an imperialist bent on plunder or subjugation.[100]

To Kill a Mockingbird (Robert Mulligan, 1962) dealt with Southern segregation and injustice, but its 1930s setting kept the volatile subject at a somewhat safe historical distance. Based on Harper Lee's best-selling 1960 novel, the story is about a young Alabama white girl's education in tolerance. The girl's father, Atticus Finch, is a kindly attorney who courageously defends a black man wrongly accused of rape. Although the black man dies trying to escape from jail, the story is, ultimately, reassuring. The girl learns the importance of a social conscience. And Atticus, a model of common sense and understanding, exemplifies a color-blind, fair-minded America.[101]

The admirable Atticus Finch character was white, but, in 1960s movies, African Americans began to play more sympathetic roles than had typically been available to them. As the actor Sidney Poitier wrote: "The image of the black man just scratching his head is changing." Poitier's own career was a notable example. Since 1950, he had emerged as one of a very few black film stars, and, in 1964, he became the first African American to win an Academy Award as best actor. Moreover, the part for which he received the Oscar was about the growth of racial understanding. Even then, however, the movie (*Lilies of the Field* [Ralph Nelson, 1963]) cautiously featured him as a black handyman working for a group of nuns—white women whose religious vows precluded any kind of sexual longing. Seven years earlier, in *Island in the Sun* (Robert Rossen, 1957), Hollywood had circumspectly approached interracial sexual attraction, allowing a white man to embrace a black woman (Dorothy Dandridge) for the first time in a major Hollywood production. Although the very talented Dandridge invariably played stereotyped roles as a seductive temptress, the movie industry was demonstrating more willingness to handle racial issues.[102]

Poitier continued to appear in roles that—in the context of the civil rights movement—were racially daring but left some black critics unhappy with his contrived screen image as an "ebony saint." In *Guess Who's Coming to Dinner* (Stanley Kramer, 1967), his role involved an interracial romance. He played a young doctor who meets his future white in-laws for the first time. They are shocked that their daughter plans to marry a black man, but they struggle toward acceptance. *In the Heat of the Night* (Norman Jewison, 1967) was a murder mystery in which Poitier, as the Northern police officer Virgil Tibbs, teams up with a white Southern sheriff (Rod Steiger) to solve the crime. The Academy Award–winning film dealt candidly with a reality that Hollywood had ducked for many years: the racism of the Southern legal system. "My God, what kind of people are you?" Tibbs asks incredulously of the Mississippi whites. "What kind of place is this?" Confronting bigoted white authorities, he instructs them: "Call me *Mister* Tibbs." In another scene, when a member of the white elite slaps him, Tibbs slaps him back. As Steiger later pointed out: "It was the first film I can think of in which the black man hit the white man." Significantly, Poitier himself changed the script to allow his character to retaliate.[103]

Ultimately, however, *In the Heat of the Night* hedged its social realism, thereby illustrating the movie industry's continued worries about offending white audiences. The writer James Baldwin rightly placed the blame on Hollywood, not Poitier. "The industry is compelled," he wrote, "to present to the American people a self-perpetuating fantasy of American life." A really truthful treatment of the nation's racism would demolish that fantasy. Baldwin forcefully defended Poitier. After all, the actor needed the work, and many people wanted to see him on the screen. Poitier's challenge as a black performer was to "smuggle in a reality that he knows is not in the script." The producer Walter Mirisch insisted that the movie as a whole had smuggled in some of that reality by saying "a lot of things we thought should be said." In the end, the film nevertheless displaced racism onto a white, working-class redneck and basically exonerated the white power structure. "The rise of the hillbilly from hell" would influence a number of movies in the near future—ranging from *Easy Rider* (Dennis Hopper, 1969) to *Deliverance* (John Boorman, 1972)—and also facilitated the "redemption of the southern lawman." *In the Heat of the Night* showed Steiger's sheriff shedding his bigoted persona and joining Poitier's Virgil Tibbs as a hero. "Literally overnight," according to one interpretation, "the enforcer of illegitimate law—states' rights and Jim Crow—metamorphosed into the protector and defender of legitimate law." The movie pulled as many racial punches as it landed. One unfortunate outcome was that Poitier's reputation suffered among some African Americans. Although his Tibbs character did and said things that would have been unthinkable on the screen only a short time before, some critics viewed Poitier "as a Stepin Fetchit in a gray flannel suit." The black playwright Clifford Mason, for instance, criticized him as "a showcase nigger" for white America, and others called him "a million-dollar shoeshine boy."[104]

Despite Hollywood's caution and the unfair attacks on Poitier's accommodationist roles, the movie industry was clearly opening its doors to African Americans. It showed fewer signs of change with other minorities, however. A rare exception concerning Latinos came early in the decade with *West Side Story* (Jerome Robbins and Robert Wise, 1961). The film won the Academy Award for best picture in 1962, and Rita Moreno received the Oscar for best supporting actress. Based on Leonard Bernstein's hit play, which opened in 1957 on Broadway and ran for 732 performances, the musical dealt seriously with urban ethnic conflict. It wove a love affair along the lines of that of Romeo and Juliet into a story of conflict between two juvenile gangs: the "American" Jets and the Puerto Rican Sharks. Significantly, according to the drama historian John Jones: "*West*

Side Story was the first Broadway musical to seriously question the universality of the American Dream." Neither the "Americans" nor the Puerto Ricans have much chance of realizing that dream. "I say this turf is small," says the Jets' leader, "*but it's all we got.*" In the play and the subsequent movie, as Jones pointed out, America's "streets are paved with—well, pavement." Ultimately, blood also covers those streets as the story ends in tragedy.[105]

By the 1960s, movies responded more fully to the sexual revolution. Signs of that revolution in the larger society were legion. Although *Playboy* confronted numerous legal challenges, its 5 million readers by 1958 had made it a publishing success. A year later, the Barbie doll had made her debut. Traditionally, dolls resembled babies, and girls who played with them supposedly rehearsed nurturing roles. In contrast, Barbie was no infant. She had a female adult body—albeit one with exaggerated breasts. She also suggested independence. And, with her emphasis on expensive clothes and possessions, she epitomized consumerism. Parents might fret that Barbie's sensuous look threatened childhood innocence, but many relented in the face of their children's demands, purchasing the doll as well as her costly wardrobe and accessories.[106]

In 1960, the sexual revolution entered a new phase with the marketing of "the Pill," an oral contraceptive for women. Two years later, Helen Gurley Brown's *Sex and the Single Girl* (1962) became a smash best seller, translated into ten languages. Although Brown believed that women should please men, hardly a feminist position, her book offered at least a partial call for women's sexual liberation. She urged women to enjoy their single status. They should get jobs and postpone marriage (a limited world of child rearing and "the jammed clothes drier"). Mainly, they should enjoy sex. "Theoretically," Brown wrote, "a 'nice' single woman has no sex life. What nonsense! She has a better sex life than most of her friends. . . . Her choice of partners is endless and they seek *her.*" Brown attracted so much attention that, in 1965, the Hearst Corporation hired her as the editor of *Cosmopolitan,* the well-established women's magazine, which she was supposed to make more risqué.[107]

Meanwhile, Hollywood's Production Code was crumbling. As the director Stanley Kubrick quipped in 1959: "The Code has become the loose suspenders that hold up the baggy pants of the circus clown. It allows the pants to slip dangerously, but never to fall." One reason was that, in 1954, Geoffrey Shurlock had replaced Joseph Breen at the Code office. Shurlock had a greater appreciation for movies with adult subject matter. Another reason was that the industry was at an organizational crossroads. The old moguls were stepping down or dying. Louis Mayer died in 1957 and Harry Cohn the next year. Some studios relied heavily on independent director-producers such as Alfred Hitchcock. In fact, film distribution—rather than production—was becoming the major studios' main focus. A telling statistic in that regard was that, "during the first six months of 1960, the major studios *made* only fourteen of the ninety-eight pictures they produced," according to two film experts. "The corporations sacrificed corporate identities for cash infusions." It was largely pressure from the independent producers that helped liberalize the Code somewhat in 1956. Except for nudity, sexual perversion, and venereal disease, other subjects were permissible "within the careful limits of good taste." Over the next few years, filmmakers continually tested those limits.[108]

One strategy was to approach sexual issues by capitalizing on the controversies surrounding best sellers. In 1957, for example, Mark Robson's somewhat tamer version of Grace Metalious's sensational novel *Peyton Place* (1956) appeared in theaters. The hardbound edition of the novel had reached number two on the best-seller lists, but Dell's 1957 paperback reprint was a publishing phenomenon, selling 3 million copies that year. Advertised as the book that "lifts the lid off a small New England town," *Peyton Place* in fact contained few explicit sexual passages. But it argued that women had sexual needs and desires, and it contradicted the old advice that "good girls don't." Metalious's fictional women enjoyed sex, and the anything-but-respectable village was a place of dark secrets dealing with abuse, infidelity, teen abortion, and hypocritical gossip. Hollywood snapped up the rights to the novel for $250,000, a high price at the time. Jerry Wald produced the film. Although he lauded the Code for protecting viewers from "an orgy of sin, smut, and sensationalism," he conceded that he had infused *Peyton Place* and several other films with "every bit of sexual relationship you can think of." Not surprisingly, Helen Gurley Brown's *Sex and the Single Girl* inspired a 1964 Richard Quine movie, two years after the best seller's publication. And, in 1967, Hollywood and Mark Robson leveraged Jacqueline Suzanne's sexy best seller *Valley of the Dolls* (1966) into a titillating box-office draw.[109]

The popular James Bond novels provided Hollywood with even better opportunities to incorporate sex into mainstream movies. Based on Ian Fleming's highly successful spy series, the Bond films (the first six of which appeared between 1962 and 1971) turned into a box-office and merchandising bonanza. On many levels, the films reflected the Cold War consensus, attesting to the triumph of Western technology, capitalism, competitive individualism, and consumerism. And even though the Bond character was a *Playboy*-style male—cool and a magnet for women—the alluring females he met were anything but domesticated. They were strong, athletic, independent, free, and very sexual. The Bond films moved carefully within the Production Code's lingering confines, but *Dr. No* (Terence Young, 1962), *From Russia with Love* (Terence Young, 1963), *Goldfinger* (Guy Hamilton, 1964), and *Thunderball* (Terence Young, 1965) pushed the boundaries. Even the name of the woman in *Goldfinger* was suggestive: Pussy Galore. In sum, the movie industry was increasingly testing the Code's sexual limits.[110]

Demographics and additional industry changes placed more pressure on the Production Code. As the movie audience moved toward an age distribution in which almost half were between sixteen and twenty-four, Hollywood had to take note. Trends in a range of amusements, from comics to music, made clear that the maturing baby-boom generation sought more serious fare than the mainstream had typically offered. In 1967, Mike Nichol's *The Graduate* drove home the importance of that youth market. The movie, which was about young adults trying to break loose from the phony, hypocritical world of their parents, grossed more than any film to that point except *The Sound of Music* and *Gone with the Wind*.[111]

Meanwhile, outside investors were dramatically altering the industry's longtime corporate structure and bringing in new leadership. Hollywood appealed to investors because the studio lots constituted valuable real estate, film libraries were rich resources for media such as television, and slumping studio stocks were cheap to buy. In 1959, Universal Studios, which Decca Records had purchased in 1952, merged with the Music Corporation of America (MCA). In 1966, Gulf and Western Industries, with holdings ranging from zinc mines to automobile parts, took over Paramount. In 1967, the giant financial services company Transamerica purchased United Artists. And, in 1969, Kinney National Services took over Warner Brothers and moved toward forming a leisure-time unit, Warner Communications, which included Atlantic Records. In the meantime, MGM was disappearing into the holdings of Kirk Kerkorian, whose other investments included Western Airlines and various Las Vegas hotels and gambling casinos. These diversified conglomerates expanded the concept of the entertainment marketplace, momentarily providing more maneuvering room for filmmakers. The movie industry was on the brink of a creative explosion.[112]

By the end of the 1960s, as Hollywood moved into one of its most formative eras, several inventive Broadway musicals also responded to the nation's social turbulence. Overall, certainly, most shows continued to serve as pleasant diversions. Mid-1960s productions such as *Hello Dolly, Funny Girl, Mame*, and *You're a Good Man, Charlie Brown* were several of the biggest hits. But the 1960s also inspired several "issue-driven musicals" whose plots contained social and political agendas.[113]

Cabaret, which opened in late 1966, used Germany in the early 1930s as a setting in which to explore current American racial issues. "To us," said director Hal Prince, "it was a play about civil rights, the problem of blacks in America, about how it [a Nazi system] can happen here." Opening in early 1969, *1776* also used history to comment on the present. Although audiences may have felt good about the achievements of the writers of the Declaration of Independence, the librettist Peter Stone sought a deeper meaning: "What of the similarities between those times and these (states rights *versus* federal rights; property rights *versus* human rights; privileged rights *versus* civil rights) and the differences (if any)?" But it was *Hair* (1968), billed as "the American Tribal Love-Rock Musical," that best captured the era's countercultural politics. The prefatory material to the play's published text made explicit the goal: "Gain greater understanding, support, and tolerance, and thus perhaps expand the horizons of active participation toward a better, saner, peace-full, love-full world." Not only did it defend the counterculture, but it also addressed issues of pollution, poverty, civil rights, and the Vietnam War. It also included full frontal nudity and obscene language. Offstage, it set major legal precedents. Challenges to road productions in several states ultimately resulted in Supreme Court rulings protecting nudity onstage and halting prior censorship of a theatrical production. *Hair, 1776,* and *Cabaret* were undoubtedly popular because—politics aside—they were entertaining. But they showed that Broadway musicals were not completely immune to the era's social upheavals.[114]

Ironically, even people who loathed political dissent sought their own kind of counterculture when they headed off to America's entertainment mecca, Las Vegas. Despite its connections to organized crime (the Chicago boss Sam Giancana claimed that his "personal take" exceeded $300,000 monthly), Las Vegas largely escaped association with the underworld. Residents happily touted "our city of churches and schools." During the 1950s, "a river of wealth" had built fabulous clubs such as the Sahara, the Showboat, the Riviera, the Dunes, the Tropicana, and the world's largest hotel—the Stardust. In the mid-1950s, over 8 million visitors passed through town annually to gamble and watch big-name performers for every taste, including Elvis Presley, Frank Sinatra, Bing Crosby, Milton Berle, Liberace, and the stripper Lili St. Cyr. Even dozens of nearby atmospheric nuclear tests drew tourists to the city. Casinos served "atomic cocktails" and advertised rooms with views of the blasts, while pinups sported the "atomic hairdo" and wore pieces of cloth shaped like mushroom clouds over their breasts. The dazzling image of what *Life* described as a "showgirl Shangri-La" conveniently obscured the city's darker underside: segregated casinos and hotels and a sexist world in which women, as some of them remembered, were displayed "like meat hanging on a hook."[115]

Las Vegas appealed in striking ways to people who otherwise had conservative political and cultural tastes. For a few days, older citizens on vacation from the nation's heartland could break from their otherwise staid lifestyles. They could watch the risqué "Lido de Paris" revue at the Stardust. Or they could enjoy the singing of Eddie Fisher, who had churned out Top

10 records in the 1950s, or the still-young Wayne Newton, belting out "Danke Schoen." They could stare at bare-legged waitresses wearing high heels, or play the slot machines, or marvel at the round-the-clock electronic stimulation of the flashing signs and the constant noise. In the late 1950s and early 1960s, they might also see Frank Sinatra's famed "Rat Pack," a small group that epitomized male "coolness." With drinks and cigarettes in hand, and surrounded by women, members of the Pack—Sinatra, Dean Martin, Joey Bishop, Peter Lawford, and Sammy Davis Jr.—partied and performed in the nightclubs. The Pack epitomized male bonding. According to one reporter, its members "were men behaving badly and being loved for it. They broke society's rules in a way that most men fantasized about breaking rules." In sum, Las Vegas was "the American Monte Carlo," wrote the journalist Tom Wolfe, "without any of the inevitable upper-class baggage of the Riviera casinos." Here, too, Wolfe said, was "a resort for old people . . . seeking liberation," briefly turning their backs on "the entire cupboard of Protestant taboos against drinking, lusting, gambling, staying out late, getting up late, loafing, idling, lollygagging around the streets and wearing Capri pants."[116]

All this resonated, of course, with advertising's hip celebration of outlaws and pleasure. The era's traumatic events and social tumult were shaking the nation in fundamental ways. As Americans tried to negotiate their way through deeply troubled years, popular culture provided a major vehicle. It promoted and facilitated dramatic changes, yet typically did so within familiar arenas and forms. Just as it had done since the days of P. T. Barnum, it combined a volatile mixture of transformation and stability, newness and nostalgia, the unexpected and the predictable. As the turbulence of the 1960s spun into the next decade, events would continue to test pop culture's responses to the demands of a divided nation.

II

UP FOR GRABS

Leaving the 1960s

As the United States entered the 1970s, popular culture provided wildly different signals about where the nation was headed. In 1970, a ninety-three-page novel with a bland title, *Jonathan Livingston Seagull*, came out of nowhere to become what *Time* described as "the decade's pop publishing miracle." According to the author, Richard Bach, the story was about "one little sea gull's search for freedom and his striving to attain perfection." The seagull separated himself from the mundane routines of the other birds, becoming their inspiration, simply because he "loved to fly." Several publishers had rejected the book, and Macmillan released it with almost no fanfare. The fable may have been "a mite too icky poo" for *Publishers Weekly,* but readers swept it up. The subsequent $1 million paperback rights set a record. While *Jonathan Livingston Seagull* topped the best-seller list, however, Hollywood was making dozens of movies in which the bird's fate would have resembled that of a canary in a polluted mine shaft. On one side, such movies spun grim, often depressing narratives; on the other side, the seagull presented a saga of triumphant escape.[1]

In such ways, entertainment served as a barometer of—and a refuge from—change. The pace of change and the turmoil accompanying it seemed relentless. The Vietnam War finally ended for U.S. combat troops in 1973, two years before a conclusive Communist victory. Scandals ripped the White House, driving both Vice President Spiro Agnew and President Richard Nixon from office. The movement culture of the 1960s had resulted in major breakthroughs for minorities and women, but debates still raged over questions of racial and sexual identity and justice. The economy, so central to America's post–World War II prominence, turned sluggish, revealing serious vulnerabilities and stirring considerable uneasiness about the future.

Such disquietude caused many Americans to embrace spiritual certainties and pursue personal fulfillment, a trend that was evident in the spectacular appeal of *Jonathan Livingston Seagull* and other best sellers. Hal Lindsey's *The Late Great Planet Earth* (1970)—an apocalyptic novel based on biblical prophecy—ultimately became the decade's top seller, reflecting a notable turn to religious answers. Among the leading nonfiction books, almost 15 percent were positive-thinking self-help guides along the lines of *I'm OK, You're OK* (1969).[2]

"America Now Up for Grabs," reported the *Berkeley Barb*. The unsettling prediction followed the Rolling Stones' December 6, 1969, concert at an old racetrack in Altamont, California, during which four people died and hundreds were injured. As the *Barb* interpreted the situation, the idealism of the 1960s rights revolution and counterculture was over: "Stones Concert Ends It." That ominous forecast was both misplaced and accurate. As the United States moved into the 1970s, the previous decade's ferment continued to spill over. Popular culture in many areas continued to jump with new perspectives, sights, and sounds. At the same time, various aspects of entertainment fragmented, reflecting exhaustion and disillusionment. By the mid-1970s, a retreat to older certainties was under way across much of the amusement world, providing a bridge to the upbeat rhetoric and imagery of Ronald Reagan's presidency in the next decade. But, even then, popular culture summoned up numerous minority reports on the health of the nation.[3]

In the movie industry, changes in the late 1960s briefly opened the door on a "cinematic golden age," in the minds of many critics. "Directors of that era, unshackled after 30 years of censorship and working before accountants and demographic analysts took over the industry, operated in an atmosphere of relative freedom," according to one of those critics, Mick LaSalle. "The freedom sometimes resulted in excess and self-indulgence, but often in experimentation and triumph."[4]

Hollywood had, of course, produced earlier examples of socially conscious movies. But what set the so-called New Hollywood apart was the sheer number of such films and their popularity. Right after World War II, noir films had, typically, been B productions. By the early 1970s, however, movies with similar themes of doubt and cynicism were box-office and critical successes.

This remarkable moment in movie history was a product of economic and demographic forces, a highly charged political context, and new talent. Economically, Hollywood had been struggling for around two decades to recapture its earlier cultural authority from other amusements, particularly television. By the 1970s, five studios were operating in the red as weekly ticket sales collapsed to around 10 percent of the "potential audience"; in

1946, that figure had approximated 75 percent. Sagging fortunes forced the film industry to make adjustments that redefined the contents of many movies.[5]

The baby boom influenced those adjustments. In the 1950s, certainly, Hollywood had targeted young audiences with "teenpics," typically sensational kinds of juvenile entertainment. But, even then, some canny individuals had tried to use such sensationalism to cloak serious messages—"termite art," as the film critic Manny Farber described the strategy. Roger Corman, basically a one-person studio, was a prime example. He cranked out films such as *Attack of the Crab Monsters* (1957). *A Bucket of Blood* (1959) took five days to film and *The Little Shop of Horrors* (1960) only two. "When I made movies with Roger Corman," laughed one actor, "the only way you did a second take was if the camera fell over." None of Corman's forty-nine features lost money. But Corman also had an artistic influence on a number of the people who soon became part of the New Hollywood, including Peter Fonda. "I prefer," Corman said, "the audience to go to see a commercially oriented film, and find to their surprise—and hopefully their delight—that there is more there." *Little Shop of Horrors* was, for instance, a parable about capitalist greed.[6]

By the late 1960s, a maturing baby-boom generation facilitated dealing with such topics more openly. Half of filmgoers were between the ages of sixteen and twenty-four, and they were less willing to settle for Hollywood's old feel-good formulas. Assassinations, the rights revolution and the violent backlash to it, the deepening Vietnam War, and the rise of the counterculture were hammering out new sensibilities. The actor Paul Newman spoke for many in that new generation when he said: "The old heroes used to protect society from its enemies. Now it's society itself that's the enemy."[7]

Cool Hand Luke (Stuart Rosenberg, 1967), Newman's movie about men in a prison chain gang, made that point dramatically. "What we've got here is a failure to communicate," says the brutal warden as he hits Luke, Newman's likeable character. Luke is less menacing and dangerous than the prison authorities are. Basically a harmless loner, he chafes at society's rules and regulations and wants people to leave him alone. But society cannot tolerate rule breakers, no matter how nonthreatening they may be. At the movie's end, the warden gives the order to shoot Luke. "Is this what you mean by failure to communicate," Luke shouts wryly just before a bullet rips into him.

At least two other movies in 1967 reflected the same antiestablishment ideology and were harbingers of things to come. The final scene of *The Graduate*, a film that the former stand-up comedian Mike Nichols directed, struck a blow for youth against the hypocritical older generation. As the young couple flees in search of happiness, Ben, played by Dustin Hoffman, holds up a cross to fend off his female friend's parents, just as he would need to do to ward off vampires.

Bonnie and Clyde directed an even more powerful blow against both old-style Hollywood filmmaking and the larger society. In order to put distance between themselves and the watchful Warner Brothers studio, the director, Arthur Penn, and the star, Warren Beatty, successfully fought to shoot the film in Texas. They were determined to make the film's violence as realistic as possible. "Let's not repeat what the studios have done for so long," said Penn. "It has to be in-your-face." Moreover, the movie romanticized the real-life 1930s bank robbers and killers Bonnie Parker and Clyde Barrow. When the elderly Jack Warner previewed the film, he was reluctant to release it. "Who wants to see the rise and fall of a couple of rats?" he asked. Beyond that, he had to take three bathroom breaks during the screening and had already warned Penn: "If I have to go pee, the picture stinks." But, a few weeks later, Warner sold his holdings in the studio for $32 million. His successors were more sympathetic to directors exercising artistic control. When the movie received ten Academy Award nominations and quickly became one of the top twenty–grossing pictures to that point, it sent a clear message to the industry. "The walls came tumbling down after *Bonnie and Clyde*," Penn believed.[8]

Among the biggest of walls to come down was the Production Code from the 1930s. Despite continuing efforts to make it more flexible, the Code had become a troublesome dinosaur. A growing number of movies in the 1960s, such as *The Cincinnati Kid* (Norman Jewison, 1965), initially included nude scenes that producers reluctantly cut in order to garner the Code seal of approval. But it was a contentious showdown over the "blue language" in *Who's Afraid of Virginia Woolf?* (Mike Nichols, 1966), a searing portrait of a troubled marriage, that marked a major turning point. The battle over the script ripped at the movie industry for three years, producing silly squabbles over whether phrases such as "Hump the Hostess" should be "Hop the Hostess." By then, the pressure had grown steadily to allow for a separate classification of movies for mature adults. Some in Hollywood, such as the producer Hal Wallis, resisted mightily, arguing that Hollywood should make moral—not "adult"—pictures. In mid-1966, the Motion Picture Association of America finally sanctioned the ribald dialogue in *Virginia Woolf*. The result in 1966 was a loosening of the Code that allowed for the labeling of some pictures as "suggested for mature audiences."[9]

The 1930s Code soon collapsed altogether. On November 1, 1968, a new ratings system buried it. Like its predecessor, the new system indicated that the movie industry was going to police itself voluntarily. Unlike the earlier arrangement, however, the new system, Hollywood officially declared, would "encourage artistic freedom by expanding creative freedom."

The exercise of such freedom was, of course, supposed to be "responsible and sensitive to the standards of the larger society." To alert audiences regarding film contents, the ratings now had four categories: "G," for all viewers; "M," for adults and mature viewers; "R," which required adults to accompany anyone under sixteen; and "X," which was closed to anyone under sixteen. Over the next few years, as the industry continued to refine categories—by adding, for example, a "PG" label for parental guidance—movies more commonly included nudity and blue language. Whereas only 25 R-rated films appeared in 1968, in 1973 there were 276. In 1973, three "hard-core" XXX-rated films with explicit sex scenes—*Deep Throat* (Gerard Damiano, 1972), *The Devil in Miss Jones* (Gerard Damiano, 1972), and *Behind the Green Door* (Jim and Artie Mitchell, 1973)—were among the fifteen biggest moneymakers. Indeed, *Deep Throat* cost only $25,000 to make but ultimately grossed a reported $600 million, record profits for any movie.[10]

A growing X-rated culture threatened to swamp even *Playboy*. Several developments facilitated pornography's diffusion into the mainstream. In mid-1970, the Commission on Obscenity and Pornography, which President Lyndon Johnson had appointed three years earlier, released a preliminary report finding "no evidence that exposure to pornography operates as a cause of misconduct in either youths or adults" and defending an "adults-only" principle on grounds that it was "wholly inappropriate to adjust the level of adult communication to that considered suitable for children." In 1973, the U.S. Supreme Court ruled that local—not national—standards should determine what was considered obscene. Shortly thereafter, the New York State Supreme Court decided that measuring community standards was impossible. By then, among other things, viewers in adult bookstores and sex shops were watching new-style peep shows: "loops," or short Super 8 porn films, "essentially a nickelodeon for the horny," in one historian's words. On New York City's Forty-second Street, which Mayor Abe Beame derided as "the porn capital of America," a veritable sex emporium featured viewing rooms and an in-the-round stage, where various combinations of couples engaged in live sex. Here, according to one author, was "the first supermarket of porn."[11]

Playboy, once riding the crest of the sexual revolution, now verged on becoming one of its victims. In the first six months of 1973, its circulation plunged by 300,000. Within a short time, circulation fell from 7.2 million to 6.4 million. Between the end of fiscal year 1973 and the end of fiscal year 1975, the magazine's pretax earnings plunged from $21.9 to $8.4 million. The Playboy Corporation's hotels, new film division, and records also revealed losses.[12]

One reason for this state of affairs was the start of the "pubic wars," courtesy of competitors such as *Penthouse, Gallery,* and *Hustler. Penthouse* had been an English publication until Bob Guccione imported it in 1969 and began to include full frontal nudity. "We give our readers the pictures without the lectures, the pinups without the hangups," Guccione declared. One advertising agent believed that *"Playboy* has lost a lot of pizzazz," whereas *"Penthouse* takes readers a step beyond titillation." In 1974, the strip-club owner Larry Flynt launched his even raunchier *Hustler* with the battle cry "Think Pink," in reference to photographs showing female genitals. Hefner resisted publishing "a cheap girlie magazine," but, by the mid-1970s, *Playboy* featured more explicit picture spreads. Some advertisers were furious, and Hefner himself was torn between his desire for respectability and the need to ward off his competitors. "What have they done to the girl next door?" asked *Esquire* magazine on its November 1976 cover, showing Hefner scowling at a copy of *Hustler.*[13]

After the collapse of the old Production Code, Hollywood also struggled with the issue of nudity: how much was acceptable and to what end? In 1969, three pivotal movies—Dennis Hopper's *Easy Rider,* Sam Peckinpah's *The Wild Bunch,* and John Schlesinger's *Midnight Cowboy*—demonstrated powerfully that Hollywood was navigating a watershed of sexuality as well as one of violence and unhappy endings. At first glance, *Easy Rider* hardly seemed the stuff of great moment. With a paltry budget, amateurish direction, a constantly changing script, and a filming time of only seven weeks, it resembled an old B movie. The plot was about two hippies, played by Dennis Hopper and Peter Fonda, who complete a drug deal in California and then head east on their motorcycles to see America. At one point, they pick up a failed, alcoholic attorney (played by Jack Nicholson), who puts on an old football helmet and rides on the back of one of the motorcycles. The protagonists encounter an America that is full of bigotry and suspicious of freedom. "This used to be a hell of a good country," Nicholson observes, shortly before a mob beats him to death. At the end of the film, two rednecks gun down both Fonda and Hopper on the highway. To perhaps everyone's surprise, the movie won a 1969 Cannes Film Festival award. It also indicated that new forces were at work in Hollywood. *Easy Rider* "opened up a path," according to the writer-actor Buck Henry. "Now the children of Dylan were in control." One film historian described Hopper and Fonda as "Hollywood-bashers, the Vietcong of Beverly Hills." Hopper liked to threaten the established industry leaders by saying: "Heads are going to roll, the old order is going to fall, all you dinosaurs are going to die."[14]

Easy Rider's stunning financial success spoke emphatically to the movie industry. With overall costs under $600,000, the film grossed a staggering $60 million. Moreover, a new group of movie producers accounted for much of that success and provided a model of what was to come. BBS Productions[15] had convinced Columbia Studios to distribute the movie. Columbia had little interest in anything that smacked of the counterculture, but—like the other studios—was economically struggling and needed an infusion of income. The subsequent success of *Easy Rider* awakened Columbia to the box-office potential of young filmmakers. BBS was able to negotiate an unprecedented agreement with the aging studio: Columbia would finance and distribute six BBS films and would not interfere with the movies as long as they cost less than $1 million each. BBS and Columbia agreed to split the profits. A small, artistically ambitious company, BBS provided an oasis for Hollywood outsiders. As one director recalled: "The possibility opened up that you could really do serious and interesting work, and survive commercially. We wanted to have film reflect our lives . . . the cultural changes that we were all part of."[16]

Other studios made adjustments of their own. Universal, for example, had slipped into the doldrums and was making more and more material for television. "These were aging gentleman who did not remotely understand where their audience had gone," remembered one studio employee. "They looked at a movie like *Easy Rider,* and they said, 'What in the hell is this?' It's against everything they thought was a value in this country." In an effort to discover what was happening in the industry, Universal in 1969 established a "youth division" and hired a young man from the music business, Ned Tanen. His job was to make films under $1 million or, preferably, $750,000. "They said to kids who could not have gotten an appointment on the lot two weeks earlier, 'It's your movie, don't come back to us with your problems, we don't even want to know about them,'" Tanen recalled. "They were dealing with kids whom they didn't trust, didn't like their arrogant behavior, didn't like the way they dressed, didn't want to see ponytails and sandals in the commissary when they were eating. They viewed them with absolute dread." Universal simply wanted cheaply made movies that made money. "That's how, in the late '60s, early '70s," said Tanen, "it became a director's medium."[17]

Opportunities opened not only for young people in the industry—such as Peter Bogdanovich, Francis Ford Coppola, Steven Spielberg, George Lucas, and Martin Scorsese—but also for some older maverick directors, especially Sam Peckinpah and Robert Altman. Going into the late 1960s, Peckinpah was unemployable in Hollywood. Suddenly, the changing situation allowed him to jump-start his career with *The Wild Bunch,* "the *Moby Dick* of westerns." Peckinpah inverted the old western mythology, and implicitly critiqued the U.S. role in Vietnam, by producing flawed protagonists who die in a bloodbath at the film's conclusion. In the dramatic climax, four of the title characters walk down a narrow, crowded street to challenge a corrupt general who rules Mexican villages like a tyrant. "They walk as if they had found a straight line through the crooked world," the film critic Terrence Rafferty said. Unlike the final showdown in John Sturges's 1960 *The Magnificent Seven,* this one goes completely awry. The villagers do not help, and—á la Vietnam—a "limited war" turns into an indiscriminate slaughter. Just as an American officer said famously in Vietnam, "We burned the village in order to save it," *The Wild Bunch*'s protagonists become destroyers. Peckinpah's western was countermythical, showing the awful territory into which traditional western myths had led the United States. The movie was full of human weakness and failure. The considerable violence was graphic, showing blood spurting from wounds. Here, as Rafferty observed, was "a strange, dark territory that we know and we don't know, like a place in a dream: wherever we are, we've left every border behind."[18]

Midnight Cowboy also took audiences beyond familiar borders, so much so that United Artists initially applied its own X rating to the film. The plot followed the experience of an ambitious male hustler (Jon Voight in his first major screen role) who journeys from Texas to New York City to make his fortune. Instead, he falls deeper and deeper into the city's sleazy underbelly, where he ends up living in a deserted building, bonding with a homeless man (played by Dustin Hoffman). At the end, the two men break from the urban nightmare and head south to sunny Florida with dreams about starting anew. But the open road becomes a nightmare, just as it did in *Easy Rider*: Hoffman, racked with illness, dies as the bus moves along a Florida highway. The movie's treatment of urban degradation drew much criticism, but the film won three Academy Awards, including one for best picture.[19]

Over the next few years, literally dozens of bleak, despairing movies poured out of Hollywood, movies that mirrored and reinforced the anguish that shook Americans as they dealt with war, racial conflict, campus upheaval, growing cynicism, and an economic downturn. Political corruption deepened the cynicism. In 1973, Vice President Spiro Agnew resigned from office, pleading no contest to having taken bribes. In August 1974, Richard Nixon also resigned, a victim of scandals that had spread through his presidency like a "cancer," as one aide put it.

By then, the economic boom that the United States had enjoyed for most of the time since World War II had jolted to an end. America's uncontested leadership of the world economy by 1945 now faced major challenges from reconstructed nations such as Germany and Japan. As American manufacturers began to shift operations abroad in search of cheap labor, and as U.S. consumers bought cheaper imported goods rather than domestic products, the nation's industrial sector started a steep decline. In October 1973, an oil embargo by oil-producing nations, primarily in the Middle East, hammered an already reeling economy. Angry at Western nations, including the United States, for supporting Israel during the Yom Kippur War, Arab nations took the lead in enforcing the Organization of Petroleum Exporting Companies oil embargo. In the United States, oil prices quickly soared a staggering 350 percent. Transportation and energy costs spiraled.

As the economy lurched through the oil crises of 1973–74 and yet another in 1979, and as prices soared, a new term began to take hold: *stagflation*. It summed up, in the words of one historian, "a virtually inconceivable combination of galloping inflation with anemic growth and tenacious unemployment." Between 1967 and 1979, the cost of living jumped by almost 250 percent; real income, meanwhile, slumped between 1973 and 1980 by 15 percent. The growing mood of despair that crept across the nation found powerful expression in the movies.[20]

Breaking from its traditional themes of good news and hope, Hollywood entered a brief period in which doubt and disillusionment conquered the screen. *M*A*S*H* (1970) and *McCabe and Mrs. Miller* (1971), both from the director Robert Altman, were two of many examples. Altman had angered studio bosses earlier when he worked with television. But, like Peckinpah, he benefited from Hollywood's shifting currents. *M*A*S*H* was a war movie that portrayed the real enemy as the U.S. military itself. *McCabe and Mrs. Miller* turned western clichés inside out: the storied gunfighter's legends were probably untrue; the celebrated small-town democracy of the frontier was no match for the big, outside banking interests; and the hero killed the bad guys only to die in the snow, mortally wounded, while the woman he loved was stretched out dreamily in an opium den. *The Last Picture Show* (1971), one of the films that BBS contracted to do with Columbia, was as desolate a treatment of small-town America as Hollywood had ever produced. The director, Peter Bogdanovich, chose not to notify the others at BBS that he was shooting the film in black and white until he was about halfway through shooting. The movie conveyed an oppressive sense of small-town entrapment and failed dreams. In *The Candidate* (Michael Ritchie, 1972), Robert Redford played an idealistic young politician who defeated a scurrilous incumbent. But, having won political office, the Redford character asked his campaign manager: "What do we do now?" *The Parallax View* (Alan J. Pakula, 1974) was about a young journalist who unearthed a deadly conspiracy to assassinate various political leaders. Whereas, in the past, Hollywood would typically have shown the young reporter warning the public in time, in this instance the conspirators killed the reporter and framed him for another assassination. The America of these movies reeked of corruption, dashed hopes, and violence.[21]

Probably no director conveyed those themes better than Francis Ford Coppola, an outsider who believed that the way to power in Hollywood was to "double-cross the establishment." In the early 1970s, he became a real force in Hollywood via three of the darkest movies in American history: *The Godfather* (1972), *The Godfather: Part II* (1974), and *The Conversation* (1974). His breakthrough came in part because Paramount Studios was floundering. In its glory days under Adolph Zukor, Paramount had been a Hollywood gem, but, in 1970, it ranked ninth in a movie industry that was staggering through a box-office crisis despite the success of *Easy Rider* and the release of some superior movies. In 1966, Charles Bluhdorn, the multimillionaire owner of Gulf and Western, had purchased Paramount. An Austrian immigrant, he had made a fortune mainly off auto replacement parts during and right after World War II. His economic holdings by the mid-1960s were vast, but he reportedly liked the idea of owning a movie studio, although it constituted no more than 5 percent of his company's revenues. As one studio executive said: "Bluhdorn bought Paramount 'cause he figured it was an easy way to get laid." In any case, Paramount initially considered turning Mario Puzo's best-selling 1969 novel *The Godfather* into a cheap mob movie. After eight directors refused to take the assignment, Paramount turned to Coppola, then in his early thirties. The result was a brilliant film that set box-office records, jumped Paramount's profits by 55 percent over the previous year, sent Gulf and Western's stock to an all-time high, and momentarily gave Coppola tremendous creative leverage in Hollywood.[22]

Coppola had been reluctant to make a mainstream, commercial film. His real interest lay in independent movies that expressed the director's artistic vision. But he owed Warner Brothers $300,000 from earlier film efforts and could hardly turn down Paramount's invitation. Through numerous battles with Paramount, he shaped a movie that was less about organized crime than it was, in the words of the studio's vice president of creative affairs, "a metaphor for capitalism in America." The increasingly dark *The Godfather: Part II* made that point even more explicitly. "I always wanted to use the Mafia as a metaphor for America," Coppola said. "I feel that the Mafia is an incredible metaphor for this country. Both are totally capitalistic phenomena and basically have a profit motive." Here was capitalism without any romantic luster, with its exploitative edges in full view. The profit motive connects the mob to politics and huge corporations. "We're all part of the same hypocrisy, Senator," the Mafia godfather Michael Corleone tells one corrupt official. That corruption, both ruthless and violent, ultimately destroys Michael's initial innocence as well as the family that he wants to protect. The American way of life, with business at its center, resembles the criminal world of the Corleones.[23]

Coppola extended his critique of America in *The Conversation*, a devastatingly pessimistic film that explored technology's threats to privacy, the alleged neutrality of professionalism, and the difficulty of knowing anything. Things are, indeed, not what they seem.[24]

While major movies relentlessly explored the nation's unlovely side, television similarly responded to the era's social, political, and economic dislocations. Some of the most striking changes occurred in an unlikely genre: situation comedy. Through the 1960s, sitcoms had served overwhelmingly as anchors for rural, Main Street values, offering a "cultural anaesthetic" against the evening news accounts of riots, war, and demonstrations. But, in the early 1970s, three CBS programs—*The Mary Tyler Moore Show, All in the Family,* and *M*A*S*H*—broke from the conventional formulas and helped introduce what critics viewed as the "golden years" of television comedy.[25]

CBS's risky decisions to air the three programs rested on shrewd business calculations, not ideology. Robert D. Wood, the president of CBS, described himself as a political conservative but guessed that his front-running network was on the verge of slipping. Its rural-oriented programs like *The Beverly Hillbillies, Hee Haw,* and *Petticoat Junction* were popular enough to keep CBS in first place but depended on older people in less populated areas. "The wrinkles were beginning to show on the face of the CBS network," Wood recalled. Moreover, CBS had been adding affiliates in big cities, where the network's ratings were not as solid as in smaller venues. "I recognized that *Gunsmoke* and all those rural shows were doing terrifically nationally," Wood said. "It just wasn't doing much for the company-owned stations division." NBC was running second to CBS, but its viewers tended to come from higher-income groups, which spent more money—always crucial to advertisers. Wood and his allies thus made a calculated choice to shift to more realistic programming that the younger, urban audiences would like. Polls in the late 1960s suggested that a majority of such audiences did not identify with the era's social movements but nevertheless shared those movements' antiauthoritarian sensibilities and sided generally with change.[26]

Especially influential in designing the new programming were MTM Enterprises and Norman Lear. In 1970, Mary Tyler Moore; her husband, Grant Tinker; and her manager, Arthur Price, founded MTM. Tinker came to television with an English literature degree from Dartmouth and was determined to find good writers whom he would then leave to their own creative instincts. MTM thus became a "Camelot for writers," who knew that Tinker would fight to protect their scripts.[27]

The Mary Tyler Moore Show (1970–77) was MTM's first inventive creation—a sitcom that focused on neither a nuclear family nor children. Mary Tyler Moore played Mary Richards, a single woman in her thirties who worked in the newsroom of a television station. Moore refused to play either a married woman or a widow, and, as a CBS official said, she could not be a divorcée. Viewers who still associated her with her role on *The Dick Van Dyke Show* might conclude that she had divorced Dick Van Dyke, "and nobody divorces Dick Van Dyke." Moore's relationships in the show revolved around her workplace friends, a kind of surrogate family. Episodes centered on those relationships—ones in which the characters exhibited an emotional dependence on each other—rather than bizarre situations. The characters all displayed very human qualities. The middle-aged Sue Ann Nivens, for example, hosted *The Happy Homemaker* show but offscreen was sexually active. The program intimated that Mary herself had a sex life. "Don't forget to take your pill," her mother tells her father when they are in town to visit. "I won't," Mary says too quickly. The scriptwriter James L. Brooks noted the confluence of the show and the evolving women's movement: "We did not espouse women's rights, we sought to show a woman from Mary Richards' background being in a world where women's rights were being talked about." The fact that millions of single baby-boom women could identify with Richards was obviously important to the show's success. After a slow start, it became a big hit in its second year.[28]

While MTM programming soon included such sitcoms as *The Bob Newhart Show* (1972–78) and *Rhoda* (1974–79), Norman Lear broke some molds of his own with *All in the Family* (1971–78). Lear took the idea, which he had gotten from a British comedy, to ABC, in last place among the networks. Indeed, after rivaling NBC and CBS a few years earlier, ABC was slumping so badly that, according to one joke, "If you want to stop the Vietnam War, put it on ABC—it'll be over in 13 weeks." Although the network seemingly had little to lose by picking up *All in the Family*, it concluded that the show was too controversial. *Turn-On,* ABC's February 1969 effort to produce a wilder version of *Laugh-In,* had flopped after one episode. "That experience," as ABC's vice president of programming remembered, "left management shaken by anything that would bring down the wrath of the community on its head."[29]

When CBS first aired *All in the Family* in January 1971, it moved hesitantly, carefully alerting its affiliates. Yet there were signs CBS believed that a younger audience might like the show's shock effect. Hence, the network described its new program in *TV Guide* as taking "a giant step with . . . adult social satire. This series will explore American prejudices, by looking at those of one middle-class family—if viewers can take the heat." At first glance the show was traditional, focusing—as the 1950s sitcoms had done—on the domestic life of a family, in this case Archie and Edith Bunker, their daughter, and her husband. The living room provided a familiar setting. But, beyond that, the show plunged into areas that prime-time comedy had previously avoided. Topics included homosexuality, bigotry, protest, menopause, vasectomy, and miscarriage. Moreover, while most sitcoms had centered around middle-class professionals, Archie Bunker was a blue-collar worker who occasionally had to drive a cab to make ends meet and was sometimes unemployed. What especially set him apart, however, was that he was the first central TV character to exhibit some of America's uglier traits. Archie was a bigot, objecting to the "coloreds," "jungle bunnies," "Hebes," "spics," "fags,"and his "dumb Polack" son-in-law. Yet, as the actor Carroll O'Connor played him, viewers could sense his vulnerability and his frustrations with modern trends that marginalized him. His politically naive and often befuddled wife, Edith (played by Jean Stapleton)—a "dingbat," in Archie's words—was, in fact, a gentle soul who counterbalanced Archie's bigotry by exuding a tolerant innocence and bridging family differences. Her forgiving nature provided soothing reminders of the nation's better side.[30]

All in the Family jolted TV as few programs had done. A midseason replacement, it was the nation's number one show at the end of its first full season. For five years, it was the highest-rated show. It brought current public issues into prime-time television entertainment. It popularized a host of products such as T-shirts, mugs, collections of Archie's and Edith's comments, and "Archie Bunker for President" stickers. It inspired several other fine Norman Lear productions, including *Maude* (1972–78), *Sanford and Son* (1972–77), *The Jeffersons* (1975–86), *Good Times* (1974–79), and *One Day at a Time* (1975–84). (Both *The Jeffersons* and *Good Times* helped bring the black family into prime time. *One Day at a Time* introduced a divorced mother to TV.) And it stirred up considerable controversy over what kind of impact it was having, especially as issues such as race and busing racked Boston and other cities. The civil rights leader Whitney Young suspected that, "while the show tries to satirize bigotry, it only succeeds in spreading the poison and making it—by repetition—more respectable." Norman Lear thought otherwise. He believed that, by airing prejudice, he was educating Americans, pushing them to deal with it. And there was no doubt what side Lear was on. "I've always had a social conscience," he said. Archie typically got his comeuppance from other characters on the show. *All in the Family*, "along with *Mary Tyler Moore*," according to the writer Gerard Jones, "taught TV entertainment how to grapple humorously—and profitably—with the anxieties of the time."[31]

M*A*S*H (1972–83) did the same thing. Seizing on the popularity of Robert Altman's antiwar movie, it also used the Korean War to comment on issues relevant to the Vietnam era. The creator, Larry Gelbart, had cringed during the 1950s at blacklisting and Joe McCarthy–type political investigations. "I had seen people around me hurt—and that hurt," he said. Hence, he used his main character, Hawkeye Pierce (played by Alan Alda), to jab at the McCarthy-era mentality. Moreover, Gelbart felt somewhat guilty that he had moved to England in 1963 and not participated in the antiwar demonstrations in the United States. "So I think perhaps I was drawn toward something that would let me get this sort of tardy negative vote in," he guessed. "We wanted to say that war was futile. . . . We tended to make war the enemy without really saying who was fighting." The show's character Maxwell Klinger summed up Gelbart's position: "Damn Truman, damn Stalin, damn everybody."[32]

Significantly, CBS's seminal sitcoms dealt with serious social problems and, at the same time, used humor and lovable casts to capture audiences across ideological lines. Like popular culture's most successful ventures, they were both probing and soothing, and they were open to contrasting interpretations. *M*A*S*H*'s antiwar messages thus also contained appealing images of military camaraderie. Gelbart left the show after four years partly because he believed it made war more acceptable: "Given the right buddies, and the right CO, and the right kind of sense of humor, you could muddle through." Indeed, one letter to the cast said: "Boy, you guys make war look like fun." *All in the Family* also struck different chords. Some viewers could identify with Archie; others could laugh at his hapless plight. One poll showed that perhaps a third of the viewers had no quarrel with Archie's views; indeed, when a CBS study claimed that *All in the Family* mainly reinforced prejudices, the response of William Paley, the network president, was: "Destroy [the study]. Throw it out." Mary Richards on *The Mary Tyler Moore Show* was no feminist, yet she had a career, and audiences could admire her pluck in dealing with oafish, sexist males such as the newscaster Ted Baxter. Television's success—indeed, that of entertainment generally—"often comes from finding the main fault lines of value conflict in the society, and bridging them," as the media expert Todd Gitlin observed. "The successful shows find ways to enshrine, confirm, finally to soothe even acute psychological conflicts: the ones that inhabit the same human breast."[33]

Perhaps no one soothed over conflicts more effectively than Johnny Carson, who hosted NBC's *The Tonight Show* for thirty years, making it television's most profitable show. Carson brought a comforting presence to the late-night talk-variety program, which he started hosting in 1962. With his relaxed demeanor and broad smile, he never seemed far removed from the small Iowa and Nebraska towns of his childhood. Although he carefully protected his privacy and remained an elusive person, he put viewers at ease in part because he seemed so genuine. By the 1970s, he was on his way to becoming an institution. When he started joking about the Watergate scandal, Richard Nixon's resignation from office became even more likely. The humorist Art Buchwald later commented that Carson marked the line regarding what comedians could fairly say about politicians. Yet, although Carson's monologues and skits contained political bite, they were nonthreatening and unoffensive, and it was difficult to assess Carson's own politics. One of his most important contributions was in introducing a huge number of aspiring performers to a national audience. When Carson laughed at a guest's joke, he verified that individual's significance. Appearances on *The Tonight Show* jump-started numerous performers' careers. Significantly, many of the comedians—George Carlin, Richard Pryor, Woody Allen, Robin Williams, and Joan Rivers, for instance—brought countercultural identities to the show. With a judicious balancing act, the genial Carson thus accommodated new and traditional sensibilities.[34]

That same bridging of ideological lines accelerated the 1970s breakout of black comedians into the mainstream. Flip Wilson, Redd Foxx, and Richard Pryor emerged as some of the decade's most popular entertainers. In 1971, *The Flip Wilson Show* (1970–74) won TV's Emmy Award as the best variety series. *Sanford and Son* (1972–77) was another of Norman Lear's exceptionally successful "socially relevant" CBS programs. And, although the far edgier *Richard Pryor Show* (1977) lasted only a few months, it was part of Pryor's growing entertainment arsenal, including comedy albums and videos and movies.

Clerow "Flip" Wilson had grown up in a family of twenty-four children so poor that, as he put it, "even the poor looked down on me." He bounced around among thirteen foster families before joining the air force at age sixteen. There his jokes and funny stories earned him the nickname Flip. He worked in small, tough black clubs for several years before receiving bookings in the mid-1960s at the hungry i and as a guest on numerous TV shows. In 1968, his comedy album received a Grammy Award. A year later, a Flip Wilson special on NBC attracted a 42 percent share of the audience. In 1970, NBC gave him his own variety show, filmed before a live audience and featuring the many characters that Wilson had developed, including the Reverend LeRoy of the Church of What's Happening Now and the irrepressible, fun-loving Geraldine, whom Wilson played in wigs and short dresses. Whereas white comedians had typically used such black caricatures to ridicule African Americans, Wilson treated his characters with affection. Exuding a boyish charm, he brought "a distinct black voice to mainstream comedy," as one writer observed, using black street language (minus the profanity) and celebrating black life. His characters also expressed pride and independence. "When you're hot, you're hot!" Geraldine liked to brag. "When you're not, you're not!" But, importantly, the characters were safe in that they were neither angry nor rebellious. Wilson resisted political humor and the idea that he needed to be a social symbol. "I'm selling professional entertainment," he explained. "Politics is for politicians. . . . I don't have to think Black—or not think Black. I just have to entertain. I'm just a comic."[35]

Redd Foxx had a harder time containing his personal views. Before signing a big-time Las Vegas contract in 1969, he had labored for more than three decades on the fringes of the entertainment world, making risqué comedy recordings laced with social commentary and performing in the chitlin circuit's segregated theaters. "What took so long?" he asked, after he got his own show, *Sanford and Son*. The problem was that TV had stayed clear of him because his humor seemed too confrontational for whites. "White people," he quipped, "quit moving around the country like a bunch of damned gypsies. Wherever you are, we'll be there." But, by the 1970s, the country's mood had changed enough to let Lear use him as a testy but lovable old junk dealer, Fred Sanford. Foxx preferred using the explicit material of nightclubs. "It's adult," he said. "If you don't have an adult mind, get the hell out." He was, nevertheless, able to tame down his language and soften his belligerence enough to make *Sanford and Son* the most successful black-oriented show ever on TV. Although some African American critics complained that the series was "white to the core," others argued that it drew on the rich tradition of black street humor and assertive satire. Some of Foxx's references to race had considerable bite. In one episode, he answered a white police officer, who wondered whether some burglars were "colored," by saying, "Yeah . . . *white.*"[36]

Sanford and Son demonstrated the commercial viability of black sitcoms on mainstream television, paving the way for several other series in the 1970s, such as *Good Times* and *The Jeffersons.* These programs, along with Flip Wilson's, were popular among whites as well as blacks, perhaps because their characters were not angry or threatening. Fred Sanford huffed and puffed a lot, but he was harmless, likable, and content to stay within the black community. "Watching *Sanford and Son,* all that political dissent and turmoil of the 1960s seemed like no more than a bad dream," according to one interpretation.[37]

Richard Pryor's more aggressive comedy presented a greater test. Pryor grew up in a Peoria, Illinois, brothel, which his father ran, and where his mother was one of the prostitutes. His grandmother and mother both insisted that he attend church and learn the lessons of decency and dignity. Looking back, Pryor said that his childhood was "an adventure, it was two worlds," both of which found their way into his comedy routines. A ninthgrade dropout, he ended up on the black club circuit, initially trying to imitate Bill Cosby's style. The "white-bread humor," as he described it, opened up opportunities to appear as a guest on several top TV programs, including Ed Sullivan's and NBC's *Tonight Show.* "I made a lot of money being Bill Cosby, but I was hiding my personality," he recalled. "I was being a robot comic." By the mid-1960s, he was increasingly uncomfortable with his act and began incorporating sharper, rawer ethnic material about, for example, "Super Nigger." After suffering a "nervous breakdown," in his words, he returned to the stage with acts that were full of black street humor and more militancy. In a reference to Martin Luther King Jr., he joked: "I been to the mountain top, too, and what did I see? Mo' white folks with guns." But, by 1976, his jabbing humor was catching on with a wider audience. According to one critique: "He had shown that nearly undiluted African-American street humor—much of it expressed in vernacular language and little of it cloaked by middle-class propriety—could appeal to all audiences, regardless of race." He became a racial crossover star, with best-selling albums and roles in popular movies such as *Silver Streak* (Arthur Hiller, 1976). Although NBC canceled *The Richard Pryor Show* after only two months, Pryor attested to dramatic changes within American entertainment.[38]

The pace of many of those changes took a toll on popular music, which by the 1970s was increasingly fragmented. In August 1969, when over 300,000 youths gathered on a dairy farm in upstate New York for the Woodstock concert, rock and roll seemed indestructible. It pulsated with countercultural and political energy. "Woodstock signified the coming together of all tribes," asserted the guitarist Carlos Santana, one of the performers. "It became apparent that there were a lot of people who didn't want to go to Vietnam, who didn't see eye to eye with Nixon and none of that system, you know?" "There's lots and lots of us, more than anybody thought before," said Janis Joplin. "We used to think of ourselves as little clumps of weirdoes. But now we're a whole new minority group." The guitarist Jimi Hendrix was convinced that "this was only the beginning." In fact, however, Woodstock marked the end of an era—as the disaster only three months later at the Altamont Speedway suggested. At the Rolling Stones' free concert outside San Francisco, hundreds of fans suffered drug overdoses, and the Hells Angels motorcycle gang stabbed an eighteen-year-old youth to death. "Altamont was the end of the sixties," said the Jefferson Airplane's manager, Bill Thompson, referring not to the calendar but to movement sensibilities—"the whole feeling."[39]

A rapid-fire sequence of events seemed to confirm Thompson's assessment. In national politics, President Nixon's decision to send troops into Cambodia in late April 1970 set off a bloody chain of events. On May 4, national guard troops killed four demonstrators at Kent State University in Ohio. More than five hundred student protests erupted on campuses across the nation. Cheryl McCall of the underground newspaper *South End* summed up the sense of frustration and powerlessness: "I thought the war was just escalating, was never going to stop, that Nixon was absolutely crazed, that these people had taken over everything, that the Movement didn't have a chance."[40]

Developments in the music world reinforced fears that a kind of unraveling was occurring in the United States. In 1970, the Beatles released their last album, *Let It Be,* and disbanded. A sense of résignation and weariness pervaded the album, and the title song sounded like a hymn: "Mother Mary comes to me / speaking words of wisdom / Let it be, let it be." The rock critic Robert Christgau wrote: "We'd better figure out what there is for us now that we can't be Beatle fans any longer." Over the next few months, fans of Janis Joplin, Jimi Hendrix, and the Doors' Jim Morrison would also be in shock when the three performers died of drug overdoses. In early 1972, Don McLean's number one pop song "American Pie" offered up a kind of epitaph for the rock and roll era. Lasting over eight minutes, the song referred obliquely to Elvis Presley, Bob Dylan, Mick Jagger, and others, leading to "the day the music died." By most accounts, the day to which McLean referred was February 3, 1959, when a plane crash killed Buddy Holly, Ritchie Valens, and the Big Bopper. But, against the disillusioning backdrop of the early 1970s, the song seemed even more poignant. It "evoked intense feelings of collective loss, of ruined innocence and diminished potency, that gripped the nation in the Nixon years," one person remembered.[41]

One thing was sure: rock music was losing its center, splintering, moving in different directions. Awash in disillusionment, a number of musicians pulled away from politics and moved toward songs that were mellow and introspective—indeed, almost "clinically depressed." "These days nobody wants to hear songs that have a message," observed Robert Lamm of the group Chicago. Folk-rock singers like James Taylor, Carly Simon, Joni Mitchell, and Carole King focused on themes of loneliness and failed relationships. Such turning inward reminded the former student radical Todd Gitlin of the Ghost Dance phenomenon almost a century earlier among the Plains Indians as their culture disintegrated.[42]

Among the other splintering varieties of rock music were heavy-metal extravaganzas that replaced political and social messages with spectacle—flashy costumes, staged effects, and contrived shocks. An act now had to be extreme, explained one singer. If it was not: "Nobody will pay attention to you. Not for long. You have to hit them on the head." Among the most successful of these bands was Kiss, whose members wore makeup to disguise who they really were, performed in platform shoes and spandex pants, and relied on a host of special effects, from moving stage parts to smoke bombs and fake blood. By 1975, two of their albums had sold over a million copies each. Alice Cooper was another band that relished the opportunity to shock. Onstage, it chopped up baby dolls, guillotined life-size mannequins that spurted fake blood, and "hanged" the lead singer, Vince Furnier. "We were the *National Enquirer* of rock 'n' roll," bragged Furnier, who adopted the group's name and sometimes performed with his pet boa constrictor around his neck. "America is sex, death and money," he said. "We laugh at all three." *Time* magazine concluded: "With the revolt long since gone out of the music, what is left is really a new kind of vaudeville or sometimes a freak show."[43]

Such acts may have been shocking, but, as the *Rolling Stone* reporter Steve Pond observed: "Rock and roll simply wasn't dangerous anymore." He conceded that perhaps it had never really threatened the established order but that, at least in the 1960s, it had reflected a "fervent idealism" and tried to change the world. Still, by the early 1970s: "Rock music wasn't scaring anybody."[44]

Despite his outrageous stage persona, Alice Cooper was assuredly no threat to established political and economic systems. In 1968, he voted for Nixon. He despised rock groups with political associations. "Politics is boring," he said. "I hate it." In his estimation: "Madison Avenue men are the smartest in the world." Onstage, he sometimes waved over the audience a sword on which dollar bills were attached. "Do you like money?" he shouted. "How much do you like money?" Linda Ronstadt, a folk rocker who had earlier campaigned for liberal political candidates, also reflected a growing conservatism. Like Alice Cooper, she defended big business. In her opinion, Standard Oil knew more than anyone about what the country needed. "You can say what you want about big multi-nationals, running the country and stuff," she said, "but the fact remains that we need that, we need their services, we need jobs from them and they are in a better position to decide what's going to be good for the economic climate and for the rest of the world."[45]

Such comments set the tone for the loudest sound in music: "corporate rock." By the end of the 1970s, according to two musicologists, "six huge corporations—Columbia/CBS, Warner Communications, RCA Victor, Capitol-EMI, MCA, and United Artists-MGM—were responsible for over 80 percent of record sales in the United States." These companies were giant conglomerates, far from limited to the music business. RCA owned not only NBC television and radio but a range of other firms as well, including Hertz Rent-a-Car and publishers such as Random House. MCA was involved in such areas as television, movies, banking, and cemeteries. For these sprawling corporations, the music industry was a prime investment. Between 1973 and 1978, profits from recorded music doubled from $2 billion to $4 billion. During that time, prerecorded tapes were challenging the old technologies of records and were responsible for around one-third of all music sales. In 1975, small, independent labels—once the creative heart of rock and roll—produced only one of ten records. The trend toward many listening genres reflected the recording industry's effort to provide more choices to a variety of customers. Now record stores divided popular music into a host of different categories, from folk rock to heavy metal and easily listening.[46]

FM radio also became more of a corporate voice. In the late 1960s, established AM stations and networks had shrugged off FM as a venue for eggheads and hippies. Briefly, FM had enjoyed formats and broadcasting styles that were free-form. But that situation began to change in the 1970s, once industry analysts discovered how much the FM market was growing. Between 1962 and 1976, the number of FM stations nearly quadrupled, from 983 to 3,700. More significant, FM revenues between 1964 and 1974 had increased by sixteen times to almost $250 million. With more people now listening to FM than to AM, corporations began to take over FM stations. And with growing corporate ownership came a push to control FM's format. One result was the harnessing of deejays. "The day of the disc jockey who controls his individual program is quickly becoming a dinosaur," *Advertising Age* reported. Increasingly, FM stations turned to computerized, automated formats and played primarily from big-selling—multiplatinum—pop albums. Corporate owners were also much more politically cautious. When, for example, the Nixon administration warned that playing songs with drug references could jeopardize licenses, FM stations more carefully scrutinized song contents. Angrily, one renegade station sponsored an "all drug weekend," playing songs with drug references and reading from the Bill of Rights. But there was no doubt that FM's anticommercial hippie days had ended.[47]

On the musical fringes, of course, a range of subcultures continued to produce intriguing sounds, but a hint of success quickly attracted mainstream companies and corporate control. Such was the fate of disco, which sprang up on the margins but quickly became a huge corporate prize. As a *Rolling Stone* reporter observed: "Disco emerged from urban dance clubs, from an underground network of DJs, producers, independent labels and performers that made their own brand of dance music."[48]

Initially, disco allowed disenfranchised ethnic and gay groups to express themselves on the dance floor. The source of the music was not bands but deejays who played records in New York City's African American, Latin, and gay after-hours clubs. "Disco was definitely R & B dance music," recalled Nile Rodgers, who worked with several singing groups. "That was where it originated. Then it took on more blatant sexual overtones because of the gay movement." Following the June 28, 1969, riot outside New York City's Stonewall Inn, the gay liberation movement had gained momentum. On that evening, a typical police raid to reinforce laws banning intimate touching and dancing between members of the same sex, and to harass homosexuals, had sparked an angry reaction, and the customers had fought back. Disco on this level encouraged a sense of community solidarity across racial and cultural lines. It also had a democratic ambience, insofar as the focus was on the dancers, rather than a band. "Everybody secretly likes to be on stage and here we give them a huge space to do it all on," said the co-owner of a big club. Discos needed to let each dancer "feel like a star," according to another manager.[49]

The ambience fit well with the inward turn that marked much of American culture at the time. Weary of the Vietnam War (which finally ended for U.S. troops in 1973), uneasy about the economy (especially with the onset of the 1973 oil crisis and rising inflation), and cynical about politics (particularly in the wake of the Watergate scandal and Nixon's resignation), many Americans focused on their individual material needs. Disco music, as Nile Rodgers described it, "was the exact antithesis of the hippie music that preceded it. It wasn't about save the world! . . . Disco really *was* about individuality."[50]

But it was John Badham's 1977 *Saturday Night Fever* that launched disco as a mainstream popular phenomenon. Starring John Travolta, the movie focused on working-class youths who found on the disco dance floor an escape from their otherwise humdrum lives. From one perspective, the movie was a dark portrait of American life. "Life goin' nowhere / Somebody help me," sang the Bee Gees on the sound track (which sold an astounding 25 million copies). But, from another perspective, the compelling image was of the sexy, energetic Travolta finding release through his dancing. The movie was a sensation, and, in its wake, discos sprouted all over the country, even in tiny Fennimore, Wisconsin, with a population of under two thousand. According to some estimates, by 1978 there were twenty thousand discos that served over 36 million dancers. The next year, *Billboard* reported that disco constituted over one-fifth of the top singles. Nationwide, disco generated a $5 billion industry that included recordings, radio stations, magazines, clothing, and the dance halls. "The profits are astronomical," said the co-owner of perhaps most luxurious of the discos, Studio 54 in New York City. "Only the Mafia does better." By 1979, however, disco's successes had inspired a huge backlash. For one thing, it was a fad that turned boring and burned out. As the singer George Clinton said: "Nothing gets on your nerves more than some rhythm that's the same thing over and over again. It's like making love with one stroke. You can fax that in." But the opposition also had an uglier side, homophobic, racist, and sexist. "Most of the disco stars were black, female, and/or gay," as a cultural historian pointed out. "On July 12, 1979, straight America took its revenge." At a Chicago White Sox doubleheader, a local deejay burned disco records while the crowd shouted: "Disco sucks!"[51]

Country music likewise endured contradictions and controversies even as—or because—its popularity found a national audience. "Country has blanketed America," *Look* magazine reported in 1971. Second in sales only to rock, country constituted almost one-sixth of all records, rendering "the Nashville Sound . . . a misnomer. Country music is really the American Sound."[52]

A source of its popularity was the spread of white Southern culture—"redneck chic"—which moved along several paths. One was political. Amid the growing protests and upheavals in the United States, much of country music articulated the frustrations and bitterness of a so-called silent majority that sought refuge in an older, tranquil, patriotic America. Richard Nixon courted this silent majority, partly with a "Southern strategy" aimed at aligning the Republican party with conservative white Southern voters in return for judicial appointments and other favors. Nixon adopted an "us" against "them" tactic, portraying an America divided between God-fearing patriots and long-haired kooks and bums. Hoping to take advantage of the popularity of Merle Haggard's "Okie from Muskogee," which also depicted a polarized nation, he invited Haggard to a White House party. Seeking reelection in 1972, he advertised on Southern country stations and secured endorsements from the legendary Roy Acuff and Tex Ritter. Later, when trying to rescue himself from the Watergate scandal, Nixon even appeared on *The Grand Ole Opry,* extolling the strengths of country music, which he called "the heart of America": "It talks about family. It talks about religion. . . . Country music makes America a better country."[53]

It was, nevertheless, incorrect to see a neat fit between right-wing politics and country music. One of Harlan Howard's songs called for "three cheers for the good guys" who "get a tear upon their cheek / When they see Old Glory waving in the breeze." Yet Howard believed that Nixon's so-called silent majority "might agree with a lot of things the not-so-silent majority says." Johnny Cash sang that protesters' long hair "didn't really matter if the truth was there, / . . . And the lonely voice of youth cries, what is truth?" Long hair did not bother Merle Haggard, either. "I didn't give a shit how long their hair was," he said. "The thing that bothered me was that some of the people known as long-hairs were burning the flag. I didn't like that." But, when the popularity of "Okie from Muskogee" elicited an invitation to perform at the White House, he quickly recognized that the elite audience cared little for the poor, white Southerners that he (a Depression-era migrant from Oklahoma) had celebrated in songs such as "Working Man's Blues," "Hungry Eyes," and "Mama Tried." Haggard examined the faces in the White House crowd, "hoping to find just one that seemed at least interested in what I was doing. No luck." He looked at Nixon and saw "a mask I couldn't read": "It was a blank. . . . By the time I finished the third song, I didn't much give a damn." Haggard concluded that Nixon "hadn't hung out at the same place I did."[54]

Although many of country's new fans had not "hung out at the same place" as Haggard, their own experiences attracted them to the music. Economically, the downturn of the 1970s drove many job hunters from the North's sagging Frost Belt to such Sun Belt communities as Atlanta and Houston. Culturally, the disturbances of recent years made country living more appealing, with its relaxed pace and mythical independence. "Thank God I'm a Country Boy," sang John Denver in his 1975 crossover hit. As

Confederate flags sprang up across the Great Plains and the West, the country singer Tanya Tucker promised that "The South Is Gonna Rise Again."[55]

Stock-car racing, once a low-culture Southern phenomenon, attracted more and more fans across the nation. In its early days, right after World War II, informal stock-car competition had provided escape for Southern blue-collar workers who chafed under the discipline of hourly jobs. Racing around cow pastures outside cities such as Atlanta, the drivers picked up a few dollars while ignoring the rules of conduct that their employers demanded on the job. Drinking, fighting, and often crashing into each other, the contestants built local reputations as devil-may-care rebels. In those years, there were even a few female and black drivers. In 1947, William G. France, formerly a Florida gas station operator, joined several others in Daytona to form the National Association for Stock Car Auto Racing (NASCAR). Over the years, NASCAR grew into a substantial corporate enterprise. After first promoting the drivers for their wildness on and off the tracks, it moved toward cleaning up their image and imposing rules on them. South Carolina's Darlington track exemplified NASCAR's move from the outlaw regions of the culture into posher settings. In 1950, Darlington "was a chicken-shit facility run by a bunch of farmers," recalled one driver. It had one toilet, a wooden grandstand, and one telephone. Within several decades, its landscaped environs included the Azalea Terrace, whose tickets cost $500. Drivers now faced fines for cursing publicly or fighting. Stock-car racing had "lost its soul," according to the legendary driver Junior Johnson, "but it's making a lot of money."[56]

While stock-car racing's popularity enhanced Dixie's appeal among substantial chunks of the nation, a number of movies accelerated the process. *Moonrunners* (Gy Waldron, 1974) and *Thunder and Lightning* (Corey Allen, 1977), for example, celebrated good old Southern boys who were engaged in car chases, mischievous high jinks, and run-ins with corrupt, inept officials. Burt Reynolds starred in several films with similar plotlines, including *White Lightning* (Joseph Sargent, 1973) and *Gator* (Burt Reynolds and James Best, 1976). In the highly popular *Smokey and the Bandit* (Hal Needham, 1977), Reynolds and his sidekick, the country singer Jerry Reed, raced from Texas to Atlanta in an eighteen-wheeler full of bootleg beer. At the decade's end, *The Dukes of Hazzard* (1979–85) brought good old boys, stupid officials, chases, and crashing cars to the television screen in what became a top show.[57]

Although rock singers and audiences had, for the most part, come to view country music disdainfully as a bastion of white Southern bigotry and mindless patriotism, by the late 1960s a number of influential rock performers, including Bob Dylan and Gram Parsons, began to draw on it as a rich source of American music. The result was "country rock," a hybrid that merged genres into a fast-growing musical force. In 1968, the Byrds set the compass with their *Sweetheart of the Rodeo* album, catching fans by surprise. The Byrds had been a celebrated rock group, recording Dylan's "Mr. Tambourine Man" in 1965 and testing a variety of rock styles. The group's founder, Roger McGuinn, recalled that the Byrds had "always dabbled in country music," but Parsons, who was a member for only several months, "led us into this direction headlong, which we would never have done." Although the Florida-born Parsons had liked country music since his childhood, he had looked mainly to Elvis Presley and the Beatles when he organized bands in high school and college. According to McGuinn, Parsons now hoped "to be the world champion country singer" and was certain that the Byrds "could win over the country audience." *Sweetheart of the Rodeo* was a pioneering effort, from its album cover celebrating cowboy and rodeo culture to its pure country songs such as "I Am a Pilgrim" and Parsons's own "Haunting Wind." The album put country-rock music on the map. Columbia Records used its clout in Nashville to finagle an invitation for the Byrds to perform in 1968 on *The Grand Ole Opry*. "We were the first rock group ever to perform there," remembered McGuinn. The fit between rock and country was still far from comfortable, however, as the audience's shouts of "tweet tweet" and "cut your hair" demonstrated. But soon, other leading rock singers were working with country, as Dylan's 1969 *Nashville Skyline* made clear. "Are you ready for the country?" sang the innovative Neil Young. The answer was apparent in the work of a growing number of performers, including John Fogerty, Linda Ronstadt, Emmylou Harris, the Flying Burrito Brothers (which the Byrds alumni Parsons and Chris Hillman formed), Lynyrd Skynryd, and the Eagles.[58]

In notable ways, country rock constituted both a rapprochement with and a rejection of the 1960s movement cultures. Just as the hippies' counterculture often expressed a back-to-the-land idealism and identified with America's outlaw tradition, country rock evoked a cowboy mystique. The Eagles' 1973 album *Desperado* was a prominent example, but the description of "hippie cowboys" fit such Southern rockers as Charlie Daniels and Lynyrd Skynyrd. Politically, however, country rock—like rock music generally—moved in conservative directions, easing away from radical commitments and causes. As Neil Young sang in the early 1970s: "Lefting and then righting is not a crime, you know." Country rock resisted the movement side of the 1960s in another way as well. "It's sort of a backlash from the psychedelic scene, which I'm personally saturated with," explained McGuinn. McGuinn also dubbed it as "a white soul backlash": "Now the white kids are saying, 'Wait! There's soul in white music too!' and country music was it." By the 1970s, the merger of rock and country was yielding big financial dividends, but it was also replicating the familiar "kisses and collisions" that invariably marked country's quest for the popular market.[59]

In 1974, *The Grand Ole Opry* attested symbolically to country music's continuing push into the mainstream by relocating from Ryman Auditorium, where the program had aired since 1941, to a 110-acre theme park, Opryland. The Nashville sound had set the direction years earlier, of course. But, even then, the country industry had moved in crab-like fashion. It had, for instance, hardly welcomed Bob Dylan in the late 1960s. Atlantic Records in New York City, which had helped spur the rock and roll revolution, decided to challenge the Nashville producers on their own turf. In 1971, Atlantic's Jerry Wexler approached the little-known Willie Nelson in Nashville. "Nobody would record him because they thought he sung funny," recalled one producer. Wexler told Nelson that Atlantic was opening a country division and offered him a contract. "I have been looking for you a long time," Nelson replied. By then, Nelson was already jettisoning his staid suit-and-tie image and was testing traditional country dress codes, wearing a beard, letting his hair grow long, and donning a headband, for instance. "The old image of the haystacks and the hound dog chewing on the bone is gone," said one of his guitarists. "We dress and wear our hair like we want to. There's more people nowadays with long hair than without, and if they don't have long hair it's because they don't have enough."[60]

During the 1970s, Nelson and several other country musicians built reputations as outlaws—singers who defied Nashville's corporate music establishment. "Who listens to the Opry nowadays?" Waylon Jennings asked scornfully, after producing a hit album, *Ladies Love Outlaws* (1972). "Ain't nobody out there listening anymore." Jennings despised the Nashville establishment, which had ignored him for years. "They wouldn't let you do anything. You had to dress a certain way: you had to do everything a certain way," he remembered. "They kept trying to destroy me. . . . I just went about my business and did things my way." His album titles conveyed his attitude: *Lonesome, On'ry and Mean* (1973); *I've Always Been Crazy* (1978); and *Nashville Rebel* (1966). "You start messing with my music, I get mean," he warned. He considered himself far more of a rebel than Nelson was. "Willie thinks fighting the establishment is double-parking on Music Row," he laughed. But Jennings did not laugh at the label *outlaw*. "I resent it. Hey, my name is Waylon and it's Waylon's music. It's Willie's music *he* plays. It's not 'Outlaw' or 'contemporary' or 'folk-country' or 'country'—hey, man, that's *merchandising*."[61]

It was, indeed, merchandising. Jennings, Nelson, and several other outlaw singers had become popular enough by 1976 that RCA Victor combined several of their earlier recordings into an album, *Wanted: The Outlaws*, that cracked the *Billboard* Top 10 and became country's first to sell a million copies. Ultimately, it sold over 2 million. Although the anti-Nashville stance was part of an effort to return to the "hard-country" traditions of Hank Williams—complex, full of pain, anger, regret, and a fierce pride—Jennings, Nelson, and others helped take country even more into the mainstream. Jennings contended that he "couldn't go pop with a fire-cracker in [his] mouth," but, in 1977, his and Nelson's hit single "Lucken-bach, Texas" attracted tourists to the small town. Jennings conceded: "The guys that wrote the thing have never been to Luckenbach. Neither have I." The situation resembled that of Tin Pan Alley's early lyricists waxing nostal-gic about the Swanee River even though they had never seen it. Chet Atkins, very much a part of the Nashville establishment, saw little that was truly rebellious in the outlaw singers. "The only thing that's different about those guys is that they had beards."[62]

But, to people such as Roy Acuff, that difference was significant. Acuff, a *Grand Ole Opry* mainstay for over three decades, conceded that people in "hippie dress"—"long hair, beards, dirty clothes"—could be guests at the *Opry*. He was, nevertheless, certain that audiences would not accept them as they did him because he was more representative of "our good American way of life." Real country music, he emphasized, "is full of Christianity and sympathy and understanding. It helps make people better."[63]

Such a perspective helped feed the controversies around hit songs such as Tanya Tucker's "Would You Lay with Me (in a Field of Stone)" and Loretta Lynn's "The Pill." In 1974, a number of radio stations refused to play Tucker's song because of its suggestive lyrics. Although the writer, David Allen Coe, insisted that the song was really about whether a mar-riage could last until the couple rested together in a field of *tomb*stones, critics believed that the sexy, sixteen-year-old Tucker was asking for a sex-ual encounter. A year later, "The Pill" elicited a similar moral backlash. MCA had recorded it in December 1972 but withheld it for two years in order to avoid trouble. On its release, country stations such as Atlanta's WPLO suddenly received angry phone calls and a visit from a group of concerned ministers. Critics did not question Lynn's impeccable country credentials but objected, instead, to a song that openly endorsed birth con-trol. "You've set this chicken one last time / Now I've got the pill," she sang, adding: "The feelin' good comes easy now." Some critics undoubt-edly did not appreciate the song's expression of female independence, which echoed sentiments of the growing women's movement. The controversy catapulted Lynn from country star to media crossover celebrity.[64]

Invariably, of course, the issue came down to the perennial argument over how far uptown country music should go. "If you're country, you're country," insisted the singer George Jones. "If you're pop, go to New York." The longtime Nashville producer Owen Bradley worried: "We're getting the music too pop. . . . You don't go over to the caviar shelf to find the potatoes." By the 1970s, crossover hits were, nevertheless, enlarging country's audience and producing new stars, such as Dolly Parton. A prod-uct of the Tennessee hill country, Parton had started recording at age eleven and had become a familiar performer at *The Grand Ole Opry*. She described her crossover success in the mid-1970s as no threat to country music: "I'm not leaving the country, I'm taking the country with me." When her hit song "Here You Come Again" broke into the pop charts in 1977, she said: "I don't think there's a definition for country anymore. You wouldn't call my music country, you wouldn't call it pop. Why should it carry any label apart from the name of the artist?"[65]

Traditionalists might have granted Parton some maneuvering room, but they balked in 1974 when Olivia Newton-John won the Country Music Association's female singer of the year award. Newton-John had been born in England and grew up in Australia. Her recording company marketed her as a country singer. In reality, she knew so little about the Nashville world that, when she came to town to receive the award, she hoped she could meet Hank Williams—dead for over two decades. Introducing her at the award ceremony, Roy Acuff could not even correctly pronounce her name. About fifty country artists, including George Jones and Tammy Wynette, were so angry with the choice that they formed the Association of Country Entertainers to protect country from pop singers like Newton-John. The next year, when the pop singer John Denver won the Country Music Association's male singer of the year award, the more traditional Charlie Rich set fire to the slip of paper announcing Denver's name.[66]

Some critics may have questioned how country John Denver was, but one thing was certain: his sunny evocations of the wonders of rural life in such songs as "Take Me Home, Country Roads" very much reflected mainstream entertainment's renewed embrace of old certainties and myths. On April 21, 1977, for example, the Broadway musical *Annie* commenced its run of 2,377 performances. "It was a cynical, depressing time," recalled the show's creator and lyricist, Martin Charnin. "The optimist in me was looking for a project to get rid of this virus. . . . I had no interest in perpetuating cynicism." Based on the long-standing comic strip *Little Orphan Annie,* which the conservative cartoonist Harold Gray had started in the 1920s, the musical ignored contemporary problems and conveyed an optimistic message. When Annie sang that, no matter how bad things seemed to be, there was always "tomorrow," she represented, in Charnin's words, "spunk, spirit, and optimism"—antidotes "to a very terrible time."[67]

By the mid-1970s, Hollywood was also swinging back to its more customary messages of reassurance and affirmation. Even in the early 1970s, when doubts and disappointments had characterized so many films, several "law-and-order" movies had defended the status quo. John Wayne's *Chisum* (Andrew V. McLaglen, 1970) was about a patriarchal landowner who takes action in defense of the established system. President Nixon praised Wayne's character as an admirable role model and liked how "the good guys come out ahead in the Westerns, the bad guys lose." Several other very popular films applied that theme to what were, in effect, urban westerns, especially *Dirty Harry* (Don Siegel, 1971), starring Clint Eastwood as a San Francisco cop; *The French Connection* (William Friedkin, 1971), with Gene Hackman as a New York City cop; and *Death Wish* (Michael Winner, 1974), with Charles Bronson as a citizen vigilante who acts on his own to deal with criminals—all three of which inspired sequels.[68]

But Hollywood's major move back to escapist entertainment and away from skeptical treatments of American institutions and history came primarily from the efforts of Steven Spielberg, George Lucas, and Sylvester Stallone. In the early 1970s, Spielberg and Lucas had both been among the maverick directors who challenged Hollywood's traditional optimism. Spielberg at age twenty-six made *The Sugarland Express* (1974), a sad commentary on the vagaries of American justice. Based on a real-life situation, the movie sympathetically traced the tragic efforts of a young Texas couple fleeing prison terms for petty thefts and trying to get their daughter from a foster family. Audiences could feel anger when, at the movie's end, police kill the young father. When George Lucas made *American Graffiti* (1973) in twenty-eight days for $750,000, he believed that "the studio system is dead": "It died . . . when the corporations took over and the studio heads suddenly became lawyers and accountants. The power is with the people now. The workers have the means of production." With Francis Ford Coppola running interference for him, Lucas was able to get Universal Studios to provide the small budget and market his movie, which made more than $21 million. On one level, the film was a humorous treatment of a group of high school students the night after their graduation in 1962. But, on another level, it was about the end of innocence. Just around the corner rested John Kennedy's assassination, the full impact of the Vietnam War, and a time of troubles.[69]

Both directors soon moved in new directions, however—Spielberg with *Jaws* (1975) and Lucas with *Star Wars* (1977), films that a quarter of a century later, with adjustments for inflation, remained among the top seven moneymakers in movie history. Granted, *Jaws* implicitly indicted the free enterprise system by depicting how capitalist greed influenced a town's leaders to keep the beaches open despite a prowling shark. None other than the Cuban premier, Fidel Castro, recommended what he interpreted as a Marxist movie. The film might have questioned capitalism, but its spectacular box-office success sent a quite different message to the corporations: they could reap huge profits from what the studios began to identify as "blockbuster" films.[70]

Jaws helped reorient the industry's thinking about distribution, advertising, and quick, massive profits. Previously, Hollywood had relied on "platform" distribution, by which a movie opened in several big-city theaters and then gradually moved into the country's smaller venues. But, as thousands of small-town and neighborhood theaters closed, and as fewer films circulated, the studios had slowly moved toward "saturation" distribution, especially for weaker films. That system allowed for "dumping" cheap movies with short life spans on a large number of theaters at one time. But such an all-or-nothing strategy seemed too risky for big-budget films, which could not afford to flop within days of release. *Jaws* proved that saturation was well worth the gamble, particularly with an advertising blitz. Three days before the movie opened in over four hundred theaters, Universal flooded television with thirty-second ads. Not only did the movie set a box-office record, grossing over $100 million, but it also generated a souvenir side business that included *Jaws* T-shirts and shark dolls.[71]

Star Wars earned 50 percent more than *Jaws*. Moreover, along with *Jaws* and Stallone's *Rocky* (1976), it revealed some economic realities: young audiences were willing to see the same movie time and again, and they did not care that little-known actors were playing the lead roles. After United Artists and Universal had turned down his film, Lucas had struck a deal with Twentieth Century–Fox that seemed crazy at the time. He exchanged his director's fee for control of the merchandising and sequels. Sales of such items as *Star Wars* toys, lunch boxes, and T-shirts were astounding. The demand for action figures was so great that Kenner Products, a toy company, could not keep up with Christmas orders. And anticipation grew immediately for the sequel, *The Empire Strikes Back* (1980). Just as important, *Star Wars* was a very different movie from the kind that Lucas's friends, such as Francis Ford Coppola, had been making. It was quite consciously a throwback to the B-movie culture of the 1930s and 1940s, full of exciting action in which clearly defined good guys triumph over evil. Worried that "there's a whole generation growing up without any kind of fairy tales," Lucas told his wife that *Star Wars* was a movie that "ten-year-old boys would love."[72]

Those youngsters—ranging into their early teens—were, in effect, staging what one of them later described as a "coup d'etat of our local movie theaters." For them, *Star Wars* was a cultural moment similar to the one that Beatles' fans had experienced a decade earlier. The novelist Jonathan Lethem remembered watching *Star Wars* twenty-one times during the summer of its release. As the film critic Tom Shone recalled, "it was me and Lethem, and the millions of other kids just like us, who gathered together in the summer of 1977, seized our chance," and signaled change for Hollywood. "It was going to happen. We were too many." Statistics bore out Shone's assessment. Whereas the bulk of filmgoers in 1950 ranged between the ages of thirty and fifty, by the late 1980s, adolescents—a quarter of the population—constituted almost 80 percent of the movie audience.[73]

Adolescents were also crucial to the audiences that flocked to Stallone's

Rocky, another artistic throwback. Stallone, a little-known actor, wrote the screenplay about a working-class boxer who disproves his underdog status by battling the heavyweight champion to a virtual draw. Like *Star Wars, Rocky* provided "a narrative of triumph." A genuine box-office surprise, it earned $74 million on a $1 million investment and won the Academy Award for best picture.[74]

A gold-rush mentality gripped Hollywood, now in hot pursuit of film bonanzas. But, while movie blockbusters could yield fortunes, the industry's obsession with them was perilous. Saturation booking could work wonders by producing an instant hint, yet it held a movie's success hostage to its first weekend showing. "The picture, it's a flop," moaned one executive at 6:00 P.M. on a Friday night in California, the day one movie opened. He knew this already, he said, because "we got the numbers back from New York. It's over." Even well-established directors such as William Friedkin felt the pressure. There was so little room for error that "if you made a film that was not a hit," he said sardonically, "they put you under indictment."[75]

This trend spelled bad news for small studios and directors such as Robert Altman and Francis Ford Coppola. A number of independent companies that had helped energize the films of the early 1970s went bankrupt. And, at the big studios, moviemaking power shifted back to the executives and away from "troublesome" directors. Disdainful executives believed, in the words of Ned Tanen (who became Universal's head of motion pictures): "If you put four directors in charge of choosing what films are to be made in the course of a year, they'll end up shooting each other." Although Altman continued to make thoughtful critiques of American myths and values in exceptional movies such as *Nashville* (1975) and *Buffalo Bill and the Indians* (1976), the limited box-office success of his movies provided a chance to push him back to the industry's margins. "We hated Altman," said the Paramount executive Donald Simpson; he was "a pompous, pretentious asshole." Coppola, meanwhile, had embarked in 1976 on what he hoped would be a major artistic creation: *Apocalypse Now,* in which he would adapt Joseph Conrad's classic novella about imperialism, *Heart of Darkness* (1899), to gain insights into the horrors of the Vietnam War. When he finally completed the movie three years later, it was more than three times over budget. At the box office it sputtered, leading one observer to dub it *Apocalypse Now and Then.* Ultimately, it may have earned back what it cost, but, by then, the Hollywood establishment viewed Coppola as "damaged goods."[76]

While nervously waiting for Coppola to finish *Apocalypse Now,* United Artists had searched for another movie that might fill the "blockbuster gap." It turned to Michael Cimino, the young director whose searing Vietnam War movie *The Deer Hunter* (1978) had captured five Academy

Awards, including those for best film and best director. But Cimino's *Heaven's Gate* (1980) exceeded its $10 million budget within the first six weeks of filming and only a little way through the script. The final version, recut and rereleased in 1981, was a colossal failure at the box office, virtually destroying United Artists.[77]

By the end of the 1970s, the moviegoing public preferred "comedies, space fantasies, and comforting uplift," one historian concluded. The big hits included Spielberg's *Close Encounters of the Third Kind* (1977), about friendly visitors from space; nostalgic rock and roll movies such as Randal Kleiser's *Grease* (1978); and ribald comedies such as John Landis's *Animal House* (1978). Richard Donner's *Superman* (1978) suddenly made comic-book heroes mainstream movie fare, and other well-known superheroes would soon find huge audiences.[78]

What these movies documented was a growing public desire for simplicity and feeling good. The turmoil of recent years had taken a heavy emotional toll, and many people hungered for reassurance. In entertainment, many searched for escape, not relevance, as disco suggested in music venues.

Steve Martin's stand-up comedy reflected the shifting public mood as well as anything. By the age of twenty-one, Martin had been a writer for *The Smothers Brothers Comedy Hour* and other shows. "In the 1960s, the war tainted everything," he said later. "It was such a serious time." With a beard, long hair, and "old band uniform frock coats right out of *Sgt. Pepper's Lonely Hearts Club*," he provided an opening act for various rock bands. But, by 1973, he had cut his hair, shaved his beard, started wearing a white-linen three-piece suit, and moved his own act to small clubs and campuses. He also deliberately moved away from political humor and developed "a wild and craaaaazy guy" persona. He wore nose glasses, bunny ears, and a fake arrow through his head; played banjo riffs; bent balloons into various shapes; and juggled stuffed cats. During a two-month tour in late 1977, he performed in fifty cities in large venues that were almost always sold out. That year, his best-selling comedy album *Let's Get Small* won a Grammy Award and sold 1.5 million copies. In 1978, *Newsweek* called him "the hottest stand-up comic in America" and reported that he—along with Chevy Chase and Martin Mull—was "part of a counter-revolution in American comedy: white and middle-class in appearance . . . and unthreatening in its message." According to the comedian David Steinberg, Martin was "exactly right" for the times: "We are burned out on relevance and anger. He offers a special form of escape and there is no hostility in his act."[79]

With the debut of *Saturday Night Live* (*SNL*) on NBC in 1975, such humor was also evident on television. Although most of the original contributors and cast—including such talents as Chevy Chase, John Belushi,

Dan Ackroyd, and Gilda Radner—had labored in the late 1960s and early 1970s in what the writer Frank Rich described as "fringe political comedy troupes and revues," *SNL* quickly lost its bite. "The history of *SNL*," complained Rich, "is an object lesson in how the rebellious spirits of the 1960s were bought, packaged, tamed, and sold during the 1970s—thus making the country safe for the return of the complacent, business-as-usual ethic of the 1980s." NBC wanted to attract mainly the eighteen to thirty-four age group, the networks' desideratum. And the show's stars were less interested in being "video guerrillas" than in making it to prime time.[80]

Television's mid-1970s retreat from relevance was also apparent in a number of feel-good situation comedies and dramas in which the emphasis was on nostalgia, minus the political undertones of *All in the Family* or *M*A*S*H*. *The Waltons* (1972–81) made even the Great Depression look good by extolling the virtues of family togetherness. *Little House on the Prairie* (1974–83), a *Waltons*-like saga set on the Western frontier in the 1870s, showed how the Ingalls family prevailed through pluck and love. *Happy Days* (1974–84) and *Laverne and Shirley* (1976–83) brought back an idealized, innocent 1950s. Although *Chico and the Man* (1974–78) was groundbreaking in the sense that its main character was a Mexican American mechanic (played by Freddie Prinze, who was, in fact, half Hungarian, half Puerto Rican), it softened ethnic conflict with heavy doses of sentimentality. The cantankerous and seemingly bigoted garage owner emerged as caring and lovable. *Welcome Back, Kotter* (1975–79) bounced lightly through ethnic minefields in its comedic portrayal of a caring high school teacher who worked with "the Sweathogs," a superficially tough group of inner-city outcasts. "In the ragged aftermath of national division," according to one critic, the public was eager to embrace "a new, synthetic domesticity" with "themes of harmony and family, by whatever contrivances it could muster."[81]

Themes of family love and resilience were abundantly evident in TV's landmark miniseries *Roots*. The story, based on Alex Haley's best-selling book *Roots: The Saga of an American Family* (1976), traced the history of a slave family and its descendants to the late nineteenth century. In February 1977, in an unprecedented move, ABC aired the eight episodes over consecutive nights. The miniseries set audience records, with almost half the American public watching the final episode. "'Roots' Remakes TV World in Eight Nights!" declared *Variety*. Ironically, ABC had been nervous about the program. "What have you got to lose?" the producer, Stan Margulies, argued. "You're Number 3. If *Roots* fails, you'll still be Number 3." Even then, ABC discounted the advertising prices.[82]

The popular miniseries tapped the sense of ethnic awareness that was evident by the early 1970s in the black power movement and the related militance of the "unmeltable ethnics"—the sociologist Michael Novak's term for descendants of the wave of immigrants from Southern and Eastern Europe in the late nineteenth century and the early twentieth. Novak was among a growing number of individuals who believed that Americans should embrace—not deny—their ethnic identities. Francis Ford Coppola's *Godfather* films were, thus, also part of "a very conscious decision" to portray Italian American ethnicity onscreen. "I've almost never seen a movie that gave any real sense of what it was like to be an Italian-American," Coppola said. Haley's book, and the television miniseries drawn from it, echoed this growing search for cultural roots. In tandem with the *Roots* TV show, mayors in thirty cities established "Roots Week." Hundreds of colleges, universities, and high schools used Haley's book and the miniseries as the bases of courses. Guides to tracing genealogies poured from presses, stirring *Newsweek* to feature the cover story "Everybody's Search for Roots." The Continental Trailways bus company seized the moment by urging people to "Take Our Routes to Your Roots." In notable ways, the *Roots* phenomenon influenced even public policy, encouraging efforts to open sealed adoption records. Some skeptics nevertheless worried that the emphasis on ethnic identity would only exacerbate divisions within the United States, "balkanizing"—or fragmenting—the nation.[83]

Polarizing influences were certainly evident in sports. There was no better example than Muhammad Ali's comeback. Because of Ali's resistance to the draft, a substantial number of Americans viewed him with hatred, while others applauded his courage. When he came to Atlanta to resurrect his career in October 1970, he received a package that contained a black Chihuahua with its head severed and a note attached that declared: "We know how to handle black draft-dodging dogs in Georgia. Stay out of Atlanta." After someone shot a gun at Ali, a phone caller warned him he would die if he stayed in the state. "You draft-dodging bastard! We won't miss you the next time." In California, Governor Ronald Reagan pledged: "That draft dodger will never fight in my state, period."[84]

When Ali fought Joe Frazier on March 8, 1971, in New York City for the heavyweight championship, the bout itself was almost incidental to the symbolism surrounding it. Ali was a stand-in for the antiwar movement, the counterculture, and social unrest. "You won't submit to White America's old image of black fighters, you won't even submit to White America's Army," a journalist for the *Philadelphia Inquirer* reportedly told him. "They want your ass whipped in public, knocked down, ripped, stomped, clubbed, pulverized and not just by anybody, but by a real Great White Hope, and none's around." Frazier was allegedly "a surrogate 'white hope,'" a pro-establishment representative of "Patriotic America." Although Frazier cared little for politics, his supporters saw him as the "anti-Ali," a "true-blue American" who would pay back the draft dodger. Moreover, Frazier continued to call Ali by the name of Clay. Ali in turn dubbed Frazier an "Uncle Tom" who was ugly and stupid. After Frazier won a close decision, Bryant Gumbel, the young editor of *Black Sports,* walked home in tears. "Is Joe Frazier a White Champion in Black Skin?" he asked in a subsequent essay. Ali and Frazier fought two more brutal bouts, with Ali winning both of them, the last in 1975 in the Philippines.[85]

Before the third fight with Frazier, however, the thirty-two-year-old Ali defeated George Foreman in Africa, regaining his heavyweight crown. Foreman had established his patriotic credentials during the 1968 Olympic Games in Mexico City. Unlike the track stars Tommie Smith and John Carlos, who had stood on the medals stand with raised, gloved fists to protest American racism, Foreman had celebrated winning his Olympic gold medal by waving a small American flag as he walked around the ring. "Don't knock the American system to me," he wrote later. Ali was willing to criticize that system and to express black pride. "I've learned that many Africans are wiser than we are," he said in Zaire while awaiting the Foreman fight. "We in America are the savages." To his followers, Ali was a champion of the poor masses and a foe of tyrannical governments. His stunning knockout of Foreman—much bigger, six years younger, and heavily favored—added to his legendary status.[86]

On another level, however, Ali was part of a larger set of challenges to the deeply rooted Frank Merriwell view of sport. According to the "Merriwell code," athletes were supposed to subsume personal glory under an "aw-shucks" modesty, the notion of team spirit, and a love of the game. In contrast, Ali was a master of self-assertion. "I am the greatest!" he shouted when he was still Cassius Clay. Such words assuredly represented a radical break from what a black man at the time, especially in the South, was supposed to think and say. That he uttered them as an athlete was especially striking. He also described himself as "the prettiest," an uncommonly feminine description of a heavyweight boxing champion, long an icon of masculine toughness. His spouting of poetry, his "dancing" ring style, his playful disposition, and his stand as a conscientious objector also collided with images of male ruggedness. Subverting some of sport's central myths, Ali was among the first athletes to pour a "lemonade world down the drain," as *Sports Illustrated* reporter Mark Kram observed.[87]

By the 1970s, that lemonade world was, indeed, in jeopardy. Several "tell-all" books challenged the platitudes about hard work, fair play, and the joy of competition that had typically characterized athletes' memoirs. Dave Meggyesy's *Out of Their League* (1970), Johnny Sample's *Confessions of a Dirty Ballplayer* (1970), and Bernie Parrish's *They Call It a Game* (1971) presented professional football players' jaundiced views of their sport's violence, racism, political conservatism, and authoritarian structure in which owners "blacklisted" players. "Even now, after playing for fourteen years," wrote Meggyesy, an all-pro linebacker, "I can't really say that there is any worth in the game." A few years later, another all-pro defensive player, Alan Page, admitted that he did not even like football: "It really stifles you as a person." In *Ball Four* (1970), the baseball pitcher Jim Bouton described the unlovely side of his years as a New York Yankee, when he and his teammates engaged in heavy drinking and womanizing. The retired big-league baseball star Robin Roberts lashed out at Little League baseball as a "monster" that bred mainly disappointment in youngsters.[88]

An emerging group of investigative journalists similarly attacked the mythical aspects of sports. Previously, as the Los Angeles Dodgers pitcher Tommy John observed about sportswriters: "They probably knew so and so was hung over when he pitched, but they didn't expose it to the whole world. . . . Now reporters aren't holding back to protect the image of ball-players." The journalist Bill Gilbert's three-part essay in mid-1969 in *Sports Illustrated* focused on the expanding use of drugs in athletics. A rumored joke among professional athletes was that pharmacists—not players or coaches—won championships.[89]

A small cluster of movies and novels appearing by the early 1970s also emphasized the negative aspects of sport. In *Number One* (Tom Gries, 1969), Charlton Heston starred as an aging quarterback at the end of a once-glorious career who learns the problems of growing old in a society that worships youth. In Paul Wendkos's 1972 television movie *Footsteps*, Richard Crenna played a college coach who is willing to sacrifice anyone to build a winning team. Another TV movie, *Blood Sport* (Jerrold Freedman, 1974), was about a father who places great hopes on his son to become a big-time college football player. But, when the boy suffers a career-ending injury in his last high school game, the father is left to watch by himself in a darkened basement old home movies of his son's past athletic accomplishments. As Don DeLillo wrote in the novel *End Zone* (1972): "This is the custom among men who have failed to be heroes; their sons must prove that the seed was not impoverished." The sportswriter Dan Jenkins's novel *Semi-Tough* (1972) was a Book-of-the-Month Club best seller that humorously portrayed professional football players as anything but Frank Merriwells as they carouse around. "Maybe you could find some Communist chinks someplace who don't know about me," says the running back Billie Clyde Puckett, but not in America, where he thinks everyone knows about pro football: "That, and jack around with somebody else's wife or husband." Peter Gent, a former professional player for the Dallas Cowboys, also turned to fiction to dissect a sport he knew well. His *North Dallas Forty* (1973), a Literary Guild selection, was a savage tale of broken dreams and the dehumanizing side of a game in which players endure pain as well as owners and coaches who treat them as no better than jockstraps. "On Sunday forty million will be glued to their television to escape themselves and their wretched lives," says the protagonist, Phil Elliott. "But where do I go to escape? They can believe the fantasy that fills their screen. I can't." In 1977, Michael Ritchie directed the movie version of *Semi-Tough*, and, in 1979, Ted Kotcheff's *North Dallas Forty* was released.[90]

Many fans, on the other hand, had difficulty sympathizing with athletes—especially professionals—who seemed a privileged group. The unfolding player revolution thus generated little support off the field. At a time when the labor movement was flagging among many workers, it gained momentum in professional team sports. In 1966, the Major League Baseball Players Association hired a former negotiator for the United Steel Workers of America, Marvin Miller. Miller immediately championed higher salaries and retirement pensions. But many observers preferred to see professional athletics as mythical worlds of opportunity, not workplaces involving bread-and-butter issues. Fans often had trouble understanding Justice William O. Douglas's point in the 1972 Curt Flood case that baseball was "big business that is packaged with beer, with broadcasting, and with other industries." That year, the strengthened players' union greeted the new season with a thirteen-day strike, "the darkest day in sports history," according to the *Sporting News*.[91]

In the showdowns between players and management in professional sports, the owners had the advantage in an entertainment nexus that included the press, television, and advertising. By 1970, CBS alone was paying $25 million a year for the rights to televise pro football games. In turn, advertisers such as Chrysler, which spent over $13 million annually to court the sports audience, had substantial reasons to oppose strikes and other disruptions. Sports, as the journalist Leonard Shecter noted in 1969, had spawned "a sprawling five-billion-dollar-a-year industry which pretends to cater to our love of games but has evolved into that one great American institution: big business. Winning, losing, playing the game, all count far less than counting the money."[92]

Financial considerations also increasingly influenced college sports, particularly football. Athletic programs were more and more expensive, but their success greatly influenced alumni support, student enrollments, and even national prominence. In television the National Collegiate Athletic Association (NCAA) found a huge revenue source. As the NCAA president later admitted: "We were after exposure and Nielsen ratings for college football." Concerned about the sport's image, the NCAA convinced the networks to divert their cameras from political demonstrations and disturbances. In 1970, for example, the University of Buffalo band planned a halftime show, "Give Peace a Chance," that would echo student demonstrations elsewhere, not only against the war, but against racism and pollution as well. In line with the NCAA's wishes, ABC ignored the halftime activities. Shortly thereafter, the NCAA counsel drafted a provision in TV contracts whereby the network would "not telecast such disturbance . . . caused by a protest group, civil rights group, or similar organization of social dissent." The networks were no more interested in angering advertisers than was the NCAA. In that context, TV sports broadcasters resembled circus barkers touting the NCAA version of college athletics. As a result, according to one sports historian: "Colleges, through the NCAA, used the networks and the announcers' ability to promote the positive aspects of the game and cash in on the popularity of football."[93]

Tradition and finances put the sporting world on a collision course with the women's movement. Sport had long been a masculine stronghold. Over the years, a formidable rationale had developed for keeping females out of athletics. Supposedly, women were not made for sport, and, indeed, efforts to change that biological imperative would render them unattractive or perhaps even encourage lesbian desires. In 1968, *Sports Illustrated* referred to the women's Olympic track team as "dolls" and the gymnastic team as "the girlie show of sport." But, in 1972, Congress inadvertently challenged the structure and ideology of sport by passing the Educational Act. A product of the rights revolution of the 1960s, the legislation included Title IX, opposing gender discrimination: "No person in the United States shall, on the basis of sex, be excluded from participation in, be denied the benefits of, or be subjected to discrimination under any educational programs or activities receiving federal assistance." That rule, which was supposed to go into effect in 1975, would dramatically open doors for women, particularly in graduate schools. Although Title IX made no specific mention of athletics, its implications for sports were quickly apparent. In 1971, the top five university conferences awarded fewer than fifty athletic scholarships for women while allotting over five thousand to male football players. One Texas high school district gave $250,000 to the boys' sports program and only $970 to the girls'. Suggestions that Title IX applied also to sports immediately prompted cries that attempts to rectify such imbalances would gut men's programs. The NCAA president, John Fuzak, warned that universities' "public entertainment product" would suffer irrevocably. At stake, according to the Nebraska senator Roman Hruska, were "traditions and values far beyond the basic concerns of the athletic budget."[94]

The gradual breaking down of what had been a form of sexual apartheid nevertheless occurred without destroying the dominant men's programs. A virtual revolution began to occur in women's athletics. Sports participation increased among young girls; women's teams—especially in basketball—became sources of pride on a number of campuses; and professional women's leagues formed in sports such as basketball. "By 1980, women made up 30 percent of college athletes, participating in an average of five sports per school," according to one historian. Striking inequities still remained, certainly. In 1975 at the University of Texas, for example, the men's athletic department's annual telephone bill exceeded the entire operating budget of the women's athletic department. Still, overall, the percentage that women's teams received from collegiate sports budgets increased from 2 percent in 1972 to 16 percent in 1980. Meanwhile, men's "revenue sports"—football and basketball—continued to grow dramatically.[95]

A symbolic moment in the emergence of women's sports came on September 20, 1973, with the much-publicized "Battle of the Sexes" tennis match between Billie Jean King and Bobby Riggs, the self-proclaimed "number one male chauvinist in the world." King had pushed for years to open up tennis as a professional sport for women, organizing the Women's Tennis Association, helping convince the Phillip Morris Company to sponsor the Virginia Slims Circuit for women, and, in 1970, leading a boycott regarding pay inequities on professional tours. "Sometimes," she said, "I felt like a 1930s labor organizer." Riggs, an opportunistic hustler, sought to capitalize on the heated debates over feminism. Although he was fifty-five, he claimed that he could beat King, who was twenty-nine. His objective, he said, went beyond tennis, however. It was "to keep our women at home taking care of the babies—where they belong." ABC televised the match, turning it into a media circus. Riggs contended that King would not show up, given the pressure of performing in front of an audience of perhaps 50 million people. "That's the way women are," he laughed. With thirty thousand people on hand in the Houston Astrodome, and with a massive TV audience watching, the event soared to hyperbolic heights. Five bikini-dressed women—"Bobby's bosom buddies"—pulled him into the arena on a rickshaw. King entered on a litter that four well-muscled men carried. Music from the Broadway hit *Jesus Christ, Superstar* echoed across the stadium. King then proceeded to defeat Riggs. Despite the showbiz hoopla, the match helped mark the quite serious changes that were under way in women's sport.[96]

Although many traditionalists chafed at the upheavals across the sporting world, most sports fans found much to enjoy. Spectacular individual and team accomplishments continued to fascinate and amaze. In major-league baseball, for example, Hank Aaron broke Babe Ruth's seemingly inviolate record of career home runs in 1974. A year earlier, several teams had rolled to undefeated records—the Miami Dolphins in professional football, the University of Southern California in college football, and the University of California, Los Angeles, in college basketball (pushing the Bruins' consecutive winning streak to seventy-five games).

By the beginning of the 1980s, despite troubles on and off the field, sport continued to demonstrate the power of its mythology, its hold on the imagination, its capacity to reassure. Two events—one a manufactured product of the commercial culture, the other a genuine athletic triumph—

offered compelling evidence. An advertisement during the 1980 Super Bowl showed a small white boy asking "Mean Joe" Greene, the huge, fierce-looking black defensive star of the Pittsburgh Steelers, for an autograph. Greene, tired and in a sour mood, seems to shrug off the kid, who gives him a bottle of Coca-Cola. Then, suddenly, as the dejected boy walks away, he hears Greene say: "Hey, kid." As the boy turns, Greene, with the trace of a smile on his face, tosses his sweaty jersey to him. "Gee, thanks Mean Joe," replies the elated kid. Although the makers of the commercial wanted simply to sell soda, the extremely popular one-minute advertisement was packed with cultural significance. As the journalist Leon Wynter observed, it broke new ground by showing a white youth idolizing a black athlete. It facilitated the "mainstreaming of athletes and entertainers of color into commercial pop culture"—a trend that was "validated and amplified by the power of a multinational marketer on national television." On one level, the advertisement suggested an easing of racial tensions. And, at the same time, according to Wynter, it asserted consumerism's ability to give "permission to idolize [nonwhite athletes] in that most American way: to buy products associated with their names."[97]

On February 22, 1980, a few days after the airing of the "Hey, kid" ad, the lemonade characteristics of sport—its Frank Merriwell themes—were strongly evident when the underdog U.S. hockey team beat the heavily favored Soviets in the semifinals match of the winter Olympics. "Do you believe in miracles?" shouted the TV announcer Al Michaels as the electrifying match ended. The U.S. team, which went on to win the gold medal, provided a much-needed tonic at a time when the economy was reeling and Islamic revolutionaries in Iran had held fifty-two Americans hostage for more than a year.[98]

As the 1970s wound down, entertainment's mainstream generally reflected a renewed emphasis on positive themes, or at least substituting personal needs for larger causes. The quest for relevance—which had so recently influenced much of popular culture—faded. Amid a shaky economy, a growing disinterest in public affairs, an apparent decline in political idealism and activism, and balkanized audiences, the major amusement entrepreneurs struggled to find the right combinations of innovation, predictability, and reliable patrons.

The comic-book industry, for instance, tried a number of formulas. At the beginning of the decade, the Marvel and DC companies embraced the theme of relevance in which superheroes questioned existing institutions and authorities. Publishers modified the Comics Code so that portraits of political corruption were permissible. At DC, the writer Dennis O'Neil and the artist Neal Adams used the *Green Lantern/Green Arrow* series to explore a range of social issues, including racism and pollution. O'Neil, as he recalled, hoped to "awaken youngsters to the world's dilemmas, giving them an early start so they might find solutions in their maturity." His strategy was to use "fantasy rooted in the issues of the day." The Green Arrow character represented a voice from the streets, lecturing the more cautious Green Lantern in a 1970 issue to stand forcefully against the "hideous moral cancer . . . rotting our very souls." America was a beautiful country, said the Green Arrow, but it was also "terribly sick!" When an elderly black man asked Green Lantern to explain why he had not done more to help black people in America, the superhero dropped his head in shame and answered: "I can't." Meanwhile, Batman's sidekick, Robin, wrestled with the dilemma of a superhero at a time when the antihero won respect.[99]

Marvel, which now had the largest circulation in the comics business, also dealt with controversial social issues. In 1971, Marvel published a three-issue *Spider-Man* story attacking the use of drugs. A year earlier, Captain America had expressed sympathy for protesters: "In a world rife with injustice, greed, and endless war—who's to say the rebels are wrong?" And, in the wake of Watergate, he even momentarily renounced his Captain America identity, for a while becoming "Nomad," the man without a country. Marvel Comics also introduced superheroes who were not always white men—the Falcon, Luke Cage, the Black Panther, Master of Kung Fu, and the Cat. In 1978, Marvel created the Spider-Woman and, two years later, the savage She-Hulk.[100]

But, for the most part, socially conscious themes attracted a disappointingly small readership. At the end of 1976, when Captain America quit again, he did so because he was tired of fighting for causes and wanted time to discover himself. "Duty. It's always been duty," he says. "I've sacrificed everything in the name of duty. But I'll do it no longer." One startled citizen concedes: "Even Captain America deserves a private life. I say good luck to him." This turn to self-discovery fit neatly with what the writer Tom Wolfe described as the "Me Decade," characterized by an obsession with personal needs: "Remaking, remodeling, elevating, and polishing one's very self . . . and observing, studying and doting on it. (Me!)"[101]

The fact that the 1970s were profitable years for Marvel and DC reflected an important shift in the comic-book industry's business structure, demographics, and marketing strategies. In the late 1960s, large corporations had purchased DC and Marvel. Warner Communications took over DC, while Perfect Film and Chemical Corporation (later Cadence Industries) bought Marvel. The absorption of the comic-book giants into bigger businesses accompanied a change in readership. The monthly sales of DC and Marvel comics depended increasingly on an older clientele. Other comic publishers, such as Archie Comics, slumped sharply when they continued to court younger readers. This narrowing of the comic-book audience from its previously more comprehensive base was due in part to rising prices, from a dime to twenty cents or more, and occasionally even fifty cents for some issues. In 1976, DC and Marvel collaborated on a two-dollar, tabloid-size comic in which Superman battled Spider-Man. Perhaps even more important than spiraling prices, however, was the decline in retail outlets. Traditional comic retailers—particularly newsstands and small stores—were disappearing. Rarely did the expanding shopping malls stock comic books. A former high school teacher, Phil Seuling, came up with a scheme that perhaps saved the comic business: distributing directly to specialty shops. Under Seuling's system, which soon became a multimillion-dollar operation, such shops would not have to deal with wholesalers, who required them to stock all kinds of other magazines. The rise of the comic shops not only boosted the major publishers, such as Marvel and DC, but also provided outlets for raunchier, more satirical, smaller publications that spun out of the 1960s "underground comics."[102]

Relatively isolated cultural venues also proved important for musical challenges to the mainstream. "Today," wrote the music critic Jim Miller in 1982 regarding the "fragmented media marketplace," the restlessness that had earlier made rock and roll a major force was "confined to the margins of America's youth culture—and is shut off the airwaves by the timid technocrats manning our brave new world of computer print-outs." But new stirrings were in those margins, according to Miller, in "a hit-and-run guerrilla alliance of small labels, local clubs, tiny fan magazines and college radio stations . . . around the country, creating an alternative media network for the rock avant-garde."[103]

One of those alternatives was punk rock. By the mid-1970s, punk rock was showing up in New York bars via the Patty Smith Group, the Talking Heads, the Ramones, and others. Spurning such accoutrements of stardom as flashy costumes, such groups tried to reclaim the rebelliousness of early rock music from its corporate staginess. "The punks aimed to show that anybody, anywhere, could play rock & roll, that the music belonged not to the multinational corporations and big-money producers but to any kid with the guts to steal a guitar and stand on a stage," wrote Rolling Stone's Steve Pond. In their 1978 "I'm against It," the Ramones echoed the growing disillusionment with causes ("I don't care about poverty / All I care about is me") and rejected consumerism ("I don't like Burger King / I don't like anything"). But, once major companies sensed that punk rebellion was a marketable commodity, the old issue of authenticity reared its head. For example, by the late 1970s, Warner Brothers was using pretorn promotional T-shirts to advertise an album from the British punk group the Sex Pistols.[104]

Unnoticed, meanwhile, was an emerging music and style from the mean streets of New York City's South Bronx: hip-hop. By the early 1970s, like many cities such as Detroit and Cleveland, New York was awash with problems. The city was on the verge of bankruptcy, and its public image was not that of the Big Apple but of crime, ruin, and pornography. Martin Scorsese's powerful movie *Taxi Driver* (1976) conveyed a sense of the city's ruin and hopelessness. "This city here is like an open sewer," complains the protagonist, Travis Bickle, as he negotiates his taxi through a nightmare world. The collapse of old neighborhoods and rising violence devastated that once-grand symbol of American entertainment: Coney Island. According to one reporter: "Coney Island is like an old courtesan, her hair frazzled, teeth cracked, and too much rouge on her cheeks." By the early 1980s, the *Godfather* author Mario Puzo observed sadly: "It breaks your heart to see what a slothful, bedraggled harridan it has become."[105]

One of the worst "economic dead zones" among some of America's biggest cities was the South Bronx section of New York City. Hulks of burned-out buildings filled block upon block—a ravaged environment full of unemployment, violence, and drug addiction. Residents referred to the area as "Vietnam." The *New York Times* called it "a symbol of America's woes."[106]

Yet, in that improbable context, a vibrant hip-hop street culture flourished among the area's African American and Caribbean American youths. After the African American migration from the South to Northern cities had accelerated in the early twentieth century, the streets had become as influential in black communities as churches, schools, and families had traditionally been. In the tough inner cities, residents developed various survival skills and styles, including a vernacular known as "jive" talk, an often competitive form of sarcastic jabs, but also an innovative use of words to impose personal meanings on the urban experience.[107]

On the South Bronx's dangerous, gang-ridden streets in the early 1970s, some individuals sought outlets for their creative talents and energy through graffiti. There was nothing new about graffiti, certainly, but its virtual explosion in the South Bronx constituted what youths viewed as "guerrilla art." Using spray paint and felt-tipped pens, they liked particularly to slip from the Bronx's DeWitt Clinton High School into the Transit Authority Yard, where out-of-service subway cars were parked. The mostly Puerto Rican graffiti artists drew flamboyant and often intricate murals on the sides of subway cars, which subsequently transported the artwork around the city. Transit authorities cracked down on such "tagging" by increasing security and repainting the cars, but the redoubtable artists simply tagged the cars again. "It was like a virus," recalled one of the first tag artists. "They had no way of controlling it. . . . We had our way with it. We just saw it as art and a way to get recognition." Here was noncommercial, public art, existing solely as a vehicle for personal statements—a way both to interpret collapsing economic and social conditions and to impose individual meanings on alienating surroundings.[108]

A comparable kind of self-expression took the form of break dancing.

The dancers, often members of street gangs, performed in the open to the beat of music on portable boom boxes. Pickup crowds cheered them on as the dancing exhibitions became increasingly competitive.[109]

Meanwhile, at block parties and in city parks, young people danced to music that itinerant disc jockeys played from their own album collections. The mobile deejays typically showed up on street corners or in public parks with a box of records, turntables, and homemade sound systems. The procedures resembled those that had developed in Jamaica when deejays put together their own sound systems to play reggae music, which government-sponsored radio stations rejected. Many of the Bronx disc jockeys had West Indian roots. Kool Herc (Clive Campbell), for example, had moved from Kingston to the Bronx when he was twelve. Some deejays built legendary reputations through their ability to use turntables as if the tables were musical instruments. By switching back and forth between them, disc jockeys could mix the music. They could also repeat sounds by manipulating the phonograph needles along record grooves and by backspinning the records. Young Theodore Livingston (later the Grand Wizard Theodore) pioneered a technique by which he held the stylus in place while the record kept spinning. He created a rhythmic scratching noise with a musical effect—the "*wicka wicka wick*" sound that soon became "the hip-hop DJ's sonic signifier." Some deejays talked over the music, developing their own style. Rap music thus developed as "a musical form that makes use of rhyme, rhythmic speech, and street vernacular which is recited or loosely chanted over a musical soundtrack," according to one musicologist and songwriter.[110]

Influences on rap and the larger hip-hop sensibility came from many sources. Some rappers traced their techniques back to the West African bardic practice by which, as the rap veteran Afrika Bambaataa described it, a tribe's grandfather would "rap" with the children as someone played a drum. That oral expressive tradition moved historically through slave narratives, preachers' sermons, the blues of singers like Robert Johnson, the patter of African American radio disc jockeys, the verbal sparring of ghetto youths, the street jive of black comedians such as Jackie "Moms" Mabley and Redd Foxx, and the boasting rhymes of Muhammad Ali. Other influences included the improvisational schoolyard style of black basketball players such as Julius "Dr. J" Erving; kung fu movies, such as Bruce Lee's *Enter the Dragon* (Robert Clouse, 1973), in which nonwhite, non-Western martial arts specialists overcame superior forces; and films with black action heroes such as *Shaft* (Gordon Parks, 1971), *Superfly* (Gordon Parks, 1972), and *Foxy Brown* (Jack Hill, 1974). "The character John Shaft was the first movie hero I saw who looked, sounded and dressed like I wanted to look, sound and dress," recalled the actor Samuel L. Jackson. "I'd been seeing Errol Flynn, John Wayne and everybody else be heroes my whole life and, all of a sudden, here was a guy I could relate to who was heroic." The theme of rebellious outsiders who proudly asserted themselves—the cool, leather-coated detective John Shaft, for instance—won the admiration of inner-city street kids.[111]

Rap music appealed to those same youths because it articulated their own experiences on the streets. "If you don't know what's going on out there," asserted one rap artist, "you can't do rap. You can live in Beverly Hills, but your heart has to be in the streets."[112]

Initially, the hip-hop arts movement was local, noncommercial, and a means of self-expression that could make its practitioners neighborhood "stars." It shaped and gave voice to local identities via shared reference points. Its tagging, break dancing, and mixing were free of charge. "Hip Hop was not a mass market concept," the cultural commentator Nelson George insisted. "It was not a career move." It originally functioned as "a true meritocracy. You battled in the park. You rocked the house on stage." In the words of the graffiti artist and rapper Fab Five Freddie: "You make a new style. That's what life on the street is all about. What's at stake is honor and position on the street." As Kool Herc recalled: "My thing was just playing records and giving parties. I wasn't interested in making no records." And, in the 1970s, record companies had no interest in the hip-hop culture anyhow. Despite the mainstream culture's ignorance of hip-hop, homemade audiotapes were available in a kind of "underground musical economy."[113]

Not until 1979 would a rap recording indicate that the music had a commercial future. That year, Sugar Hill Studios released the single "Rapper's Delight." The company belonged to the former blues singer Sylvia Vanderpool Robinson and her husband, Joe. Although their independent rhythm and blues label had gone bankrupt, they refused to give up on the music business, naming their new recording business after a section of Harlem. Sylvia discovered rap by accident at a Harlem club. When she "heard these fellahs rappin' and saw how much people were enjoying it," she told herself: "'What a hell of a concept. I think it would be great on record!'" The Sugarhill Gang, which recorded "Rapper's Delight," was not really a rap group. It simply brought together Mike Wright (a friend of the Robinson's eldest son), Henry Jackson (a club bouncer who moonlighted in a pizza shop), and the street artist Guy O'Brien. The trio used rhyming voice-overs with a recent disco hit, "Good Times," to make "Rapper's Delight." Undoubtedly to everyone's surprise, the record jumped to the number four spot on the rhythm and blues chart and was on the pop chart for twelve weeks, rising to number thirty-six. At first, rappers such as Grandmaster Flash were irritated, wondering why Sugar Hill was able to get its material on the radio when they could not. But, ultimately, Grandmaster Flash conceded that Sugar Hill Studios "deserves undisputed credit for having turned the world on to hip hop." Although mainstream wisdom still saw little future in hip-hop, several major labels began to notice it. In the meantime, rap was able to remain close to the street consciousness from which it emerged.[114]

For the entertainment mainstream, the effort to divine public preferences was clearly largely a guessing game. "The much-wooed audience does not make 'demands,'" as a leading student of the media has written. "Public opinion, such as it is, speaks with a vast silence, or with a background yammer that is incessant, indecipherable, contradictory." Media leaders never know for sure what kinds of amusements are "winners"; otherwise, they would produce nothing but hits. Searching for the cultural zeitgeist, they instinctively fall back on a "better safe than sorry" strategy. There are dangers in being too cautious, however. Potential audiences may seek more exciting or fresh alternatives.[115]

Even undeniably popular entertainment forms would prove difficult to explain. The appeal by the late 1970s of "jiggle TV" programs—particularly, the wildly successful *Charlie's Angels* (1976–81)—was an example. The series regularly attracted over half the television audience and helped ABC challenge CBS as the top network. It was about three curvaceous female undercover detectives who worked for a boss who always commanded them over the telephone. The show unquestionably offered pure titillation for young male viewers. "Once upon a time there were three little girls," went the opening line, setting up a situation in which a male then gave instructions. One network executive actually touted the series as providing "a valuable public service. Not only does it show women how to look beautiful and lead exciting lives, but they still take their orders from a man." At CBS, the network owner, William Paley, reportedly watched the show's rising popularity and asked: "Where are *our* beautiful girls?"[116]

Charlie's Angels may have fulfilled male fantasies, but females constituted the majority of its audience. The media analyst Susan Douglas remembered both hating and loving the show. She conceded that the program made sex objects of women and, via Charlie, endorsed a patriarchal system. But she also found themes of female empowerment in the plots. Once the "angels" received their orders, they were on their own, tracking down the villains and relying on each other to get out of scrapes. Mary Murphy, a senior writer for *TV Guide*, insisted that *Charlie's Angels* marked "the beginning of girl power on television." The three women were smart, savvy, and able to take care of themselves. According to Douglas, the program was a hit because "it exploited, perfectly, the tensions between antifeminism and feminism."[117]

Various meanings may have suffused even such a seemingly frivolous TV show as *The Dukes of Hazzard* (1979–85). Pure silliness unquestionably marked the endless car chases and crashes, the predictable plots in which the good old boys foil the local bad guy (Boss Hogg) and the inept sheriff he controls, and the antics of sexy cousin Daisy. Yet the program's first producer argued that the series basically had a populist message reminiscent of "Robin Hood and Little John in Sherwood Forest": "I felt that all of us have a sense we're in Sherwood Forest today, in which the law no longer seems to work. I took that to its most extreme position, to find the comedy of it, a core of very honest people trying to do good in the middle of Sherwood Forest." Whether or not the show's dedicated fans—typically constituting 40 percent of the TV audience—shared the producer's vision was problematic. Yet who knew what subliminal meanings audiences might take from any television program, movie, comic, or other amusement form?[118]

Certainly, it was easy to misinterpret apparent trends. The perceived need by the end of the 1970s for a return to happy endings in movies, for example, might have suggested that many Americans wanted to rekindle the nation's fabled optimism, where hope trumped cynicism and doubt. But perhaps a less seismic mood shift was involved. Perhaps, as the film critic John Simon guessed at the time, audiences that by the late 1960s had wearied of "fake happy endings" had now grown tired of "fake unhappy endings." As early as 1971, the cultural commentator Lewis Lapham asserted that the emerging "fashionable despair" on movie screens was "nothing more than the necessary antithesis to an earlier illusion"—the "romantic nonsense" in which love and goodness invariably triumphed. Such despair would also engender a reaction. Gauging the timing and extent of the reaction was, nevertheless, difficult.[119]

Even the observed shift to positive messages was debatable. A strong revival of horror suggested that all was not well across the land. "The strange turn toward horror," as a writer interpreted it in 1979, indicated a declining confidence in reason and rational solutions. After considering a number of recent movies and books, he sensed that many Americans were terrified at "what the night will bring." Horror was, indeed, on the upswing. It was assuredly evident in the sensational hit movie *The Exorcist* (William Friedkin, 1973), based on William Peter Blatty's best-selling 1971 novel about a demonically possessed twelve-year-old girl. Evil also pervaded a number of subsequent movies, such as *The Omen* (Richard Donner, 1976) and *Alien* (Ridley Scott, 1979). In *Halloween* (John Carpenter, 1978), a little boy warned prophetically: "You can't kill the boogeyman." Horror was also apparent in the debut novels of Stephen King (*Carrie* in 1974) and Anne Rice (*Interview with a Vampire* in 1976). *Carrie*, which was about an outcast high school student who ultimately wreaked bloody revenge against her tormentors, represented "a ferocious howl of the outsider," in the words of the horror scholar David Skal, "a cry of class resentment and social disfranchisement that found its public at the precise moment a certain segment of the population began to suspect perhaps sub-consciously, that its safety net was about to snap."[120]

In horror entertainment, the American dream resembled a nightmare. "Disenfranchisement, exclusion, downward mobility, a struggle-to-the-death world of winners and losers [prevailed]," as Skal observed. "Familiar, civic-minded signposts are all reversed: the family is a sick joke, its house more likely to offer siege instead of shelter."[121]

By 1984, it may have been "morning in America," as President Ronald Reagan's reelection campaign asserted. Popular culture would reaffirm that image on many levels. But, per usual, it would also offer a host of more troublesome counternarratives.

12

A POP CULTURE SOCIETY

Wɪᴛʜ Rᴏɴᴀʟᴅ Rᴇᴀɢᴀɴ's ᴘʀᴇsɪᴅᴇɴᴄʏ ɪɴ ᴛʜᴇ 1980s, POL-
itics and entertainment were increasingly intertwined, yet popular culture
served as a political punching bag. Such paradoxes were legion. Business
consolidation accelerated as audiences fragmented. New technologies such
as cable expanded television's offerings while placing the networks' future
in doubt. Reagan-era upbeat triumphalism vied with reminders of serious
problems and considerable unease. Even the end of the Cold War in 1989
and an improved economy by the mid-1990s could not conceal signs of disquietude in places such as horror fiction, movies, and prime-time television
drama. Athletes such as Michael Jordan climbed new heights of celebrity,
but a range of troubles beset sports.

Amid such contradictions was a dominant fact: the role of entertainment had never been greater or more important. The flood of popular culture's images and sounds reached unprecedented levels, as advertisements,
talk shows, hundreds of cable television channels, music, magazines, and
games suffused American life. As the media scholar Todd Gitlin observed,
amusements that had been "an accompaniment *to* life" had become a
"central experience *of* life." Predictably, such a huge source of influences
on American society attracted substantial concern and opposition, again
making such things as TV programs, movies, music, and video games
heated censorship issues. No matter how much some Americans complained about popular culture, it was, nevertheless, becoming the driving
engine behind the nation's economy. During World War II and the Cold
War, national defense spending had lubricated that economy; in the 1990s,
however, employment in defense-related industries plummeted, while jobs
in entertainment shot upward. "Sitcoms," as one writer wryly observed, were
supplanting "iron and steel as principal products." Even shopping malls
depended increasingly on amusement venues to attract customers, conve-

niently merging two American pastimes: consumerism and entertainment. When the sprawling Mall of America near Minneapolis opened with a seven-acre amusement park, it drew 40 million shoppers annually—"more visitors," according to the media consultant Michael Wolf, "than Walt Disney World, Disneyland, and the Grand Canyon combined." Analogies *within* popular culture of a mainstream "big tent" and a competing variety of "side-shows" still made sense, but, in the United States as a whole, popular culture itself increasingly constituted the biggest of tents: an "entertainment economy" or, in the words of *The Nation,* "the national entertainment state."[1]

In notable ways, Ronald Reagan symbolized the movement of entertainment to the center of American life. Elected in 1980, he was the first president whose career had been in show business. Although his rhetoric invariably summoned up images of a traditional America, his career mirrored the rise of modern leisure and entertainment.[2]

Starting in the 1930s, Reagan had moved from radio broadcasting (especially as a sports announcer) to movies, a Las Vegas act, television, and advertising. In 1952, as president of the Screen Actors Guild (SAG), he had rejuvenated his career by facilitating the move into television production of the Music Corporation of America (MCA). The MCA's Lew Wasserman wanted the guild to grant his talent agency a production waiver in the fledgling television business. Blocking him, however, were long-standing SAG regulations that barred talent agencies from producing motion pictures because of inherent conflicts of interest between agents and employers. MCA was willing to pay reuse fees to performers when their TV programs were reshown, a concession that other producers refused to consider. Reagan, who for years was an MCA client and Wasserman's close friend, presided at the July 1952 meeting when SAG's governing board agreed to what were, in effect, secret terms that allowed MCA's Revue Productions to produce television programs in exchange for reuse fees. A decade later, when MCA was under investigation for possible antitrust violations, Reagan told a grand jury that he could not recall any quid pro quo between MCA and the guild. An MCA executive nevertheless remembered: "Lew always told me the waiver was Ronnie Reagan." In 1954, television's *General Electric Theater* hired Reagan as its host, resuscitating his career. The MCA waiver deal was, apparently, instrumental in Reagan's much-needed new start. "I think Ronnie did more or less what he thought he should—and then he was rewarded for it, with the GE job," said the SAG executive director Jack Dales. In 1960, Reagan again helped MCA, which had purchased Paramount Studio's pre-1948 library. Reagan returned as SAG president to help negotiate a settlement by which actors forfeited claims to TV showings of films they had made prior to 1960; in turn, the studios would establish pension and welfare plans. Reagan then stepped down as SAG president, joining MCA and Revue Productions in a joint production partnership.[3]

After Reagan entered politics, serving as California's governor for eight years and then, from 1981 to 1989, as president, he and his staff used media images to superb advantage. "I can't think of a single meeting I was at for more than an hour when someone didn't say, 'How will this play in the media?'" recalled the political strategist Lee Atwater. To make a point, Reagan liked to mention scenes or lines from movies. "Go ahead. Make my day," he said when warning Congress that he would veto a proposed law. The words were those of Dirty Harry in Clint Eastwood's *Sudden Impact* (1982). Time and again, Reagan repeated phrases or drew analogies from films. One of his most popular lines, "Win one for the Gipper," came from *Knute Rockne All American* (Lloyd Bacon, 1940), in which he himself played the Notre Dame football player George Gipp.[4]

Importantly, for much of the 1980s, Reagan related instinctively to the make-believe world that constituted the heart of popular culture. As he told one individual: "You believed it because you wanted to believe it. There's nothing wrong with that. I do it all the time." John Sears, a Reagan campaign manager, noted: "There's a generation gap between what Reagan thinks he knows about the world and the reality. His is a kind of 1952 world. He sees the world in black and white terms. . . . There were a lot of ideal worlds in Reagan's mind, and sometimes he lived in them."[5]

By the 1980s, many Americans also hungered for those ideal worlds—nostalgic places that offered escape from the troubles that had battered the nation for almost two decades. At the end of Jimmy Carter's presidency, the U.S. economy was reeling from double-digit inflation, in part because of yet another embargo on the part of the Middle Eastern oil producers. In 1979, Islamic revolutionaries toppled the shah of Iran, whom the United States had helped install in 1953. For a year, they held fifty-two Americans hostage in Tehran. The crisis added to the sense of American impotence following the disastrous intervention in Vietnam, the energy crises (which the oil embargoes exacerbated), the weakened U.S. economy (especially evident in the auto industry, where imported cars now ruled the market), and the intensification of the Cold War after the 1979 Soviet invasion of Afghanistan.

While Carter spoke to the public about a "malaise" settling over the nation, Reagan offered an upbeat message. Against Carter's pessimistic talk of America's limits, Reagan offered hope and a return to national greatness. Campaigning for president, he said that he wanted to make America strong and proud again. He indicated that he would take a firm stand against the Soviet Union, which he soon dubbed the "evil empire." He appealed nostalgically to old-fashioned patriotic values, in contrast to the beliefs of 1960s and 1970s dissenters. Several years earlier, he had delighted in using a movie comparison to describe a hippie as someone who "dresses like Tarzan, has hair like Jane, and smells like Cheetah." Not only did he win the 1980 election, but he also became the first president since Dwight Eisenhower to complete two terms. Although the economy slumped badly during Reagan's first term, it recovered enough that, by 1984, Reagan's reelection theme could be bright: "Morning in America." The stock market plunged disastrously in 1987, and a large number of scandals plagued his administration, but, nevertheless, Reagan himself remained popular. "Politics is just like show business," he explained. "You have a hell of an opening, coast for a while, and then have a hell of a close."[6]

Much of 1980s popular culture reflected Reagan's optimism, his Cold War ideology, and his emphasis on traditional ideals regarding such institutions as the family and business. It also echoed his celebration of individual heroism, masculinity, and authority. The times seemed ready once again for such ruggedly defiant characters as Mike Hammer, the tough-guy private detective who had been so popular in the early Cold War days. Since the mid-1970s, the producer Jay Bernstein had tried, without success, to interest the TV networks in resurrecting Hammer. Finally, he convinced CBS to launch a series in 1984, *Mickey Spillane's Mike Hammer.* "'Look, this isn't political,'" Bernstein told CBS, "'but . . . this show oughta get on, because the same people who vote for Reagan, whether they be Democrats or Republicans, are the kind of people who are ready for Wyatt Earp to come in and clean up the town.' And we're calling Wyatt Earp Mike Hammer." The actor Stacy Keach played the Hammer role. When the TV critic Tom Shales asked Keach "if the program constitutes reactionary entertainment, a return to simplistic bang-bang solutions to complex problems," Keach responded: "Well, yes, that's the beauty of it." Keach's six-month imprisonment in England for cocaine possession interrupted the series, but it returned in 1986 for a year as *The New Mike Hammer.*[7]

Entertainment anticipated the Reagan era. One bellwether was the revived B-movie culture of Steven Spielberg, George Lucas, and Sylvester Stallone—harking back to Saturday matinee adventure serials and pulp magazines. Another was television's smash-hit series *Dallas,* which, in the words of one TV critic, "served as an embodiment of the Reagan era before we even knew there would be a Reagan era." Starting on CBS in 1978, it enjoyed a phenomenal run of 356 episodes, until 1991. A pioneering program in some respects, it brought the daytime soap opera format into prime time with a continuing narrative from episode to episode. Miniseries such as *Roots* had used an ongoing story line, but *Dallas* popularized that format for regular evening TV dramas. Another innovation was the use of a villain as the central character: the oil man J. R. Ewing, "that human oil slick," as *Time* described him. "Once you give up on integrity," said J. R., "the rest is a piece of cake." The extremely popular series echoed the Reagan era by extolling money, big business, the Sun Belt, and conspicuous consumption. In 1984, the Republicans held their national convention in Dallas, where delegates toured J. R.'s television ranch.[8]

That year, *The Cosby Show,* which best reflected the Reagan years' rhetoric about traditional family values, launched an eight-year run as the decade's top-rated series, attracting viewers from every demographic. By featuring a stable, middle-class African American family in which the father was an obstetrician and the mother an attorney, the show challenged stereotypes of blacks as either dangerous or silly. Cosby's character, Dr. Heathcliff Huxtable, exerted parental authority with love and gentle humor. The series used small, everyday incidents in family life—such as the death of a goldfish—to make moral points about the importance of education, respect, and hard work. The plots were simple, amusing, and without real conflict. Aging baby boomers who were now raising their own families could relate to Cosby's humorous efforts to deal with his TV children. When one of the kids talked about being rich, Cosby wryly corrected him: "No, your mother and I are rich. You have nothing." Parents watching the show could also identify with Cliff Huxtable's exasperation with child rearing. "I just hope they get out of the house before we die," Cliff told his wife, Clair.[9]

However inadvertently, the series reiterated many of the themes of the Reagan administration. "Like Ronald Reagan," a student of entertainment observed, "Cliff Huxtable projected an appealing image of things as they should be, without much concern for how they were." By giving the impression that the nation had solved its race problems, the show meshed with the administration's downplaying of civil rights issues and reportedly helped confirm the beliefs of many white viewers that policies such as affirmative action were unnecessary. "If black people fail," concluded one researcher, "then white people can look at the successful people on *The Cosby Show* and say they only have themselves to blame." One journal dismissed *The Cosby Show* as "*Leave It to Beaver* in blackface." Such criticism unfortunately diminished Cosby's achievements in appealing to a huge, diverse audience and integrating elements of black history and culture into the stories. According to one media scholar: "*The Cosby Show* was able to incorporate African Americans into the type of fundamental experiences thought to be exclusively those of white America"—a significant feat.[10]

NBC's entertainment president, Brandon Tartikoff, believed, moreover, that "Bill Cosby brought masculinity back to sitcoms." In Tartikoff's opinion, audiences had wearied of male "wimps" such as Alan Alda played on programs like *M*A*S*H:* "Alan Aldaesque heroes who wore their sensitivity on their shirtsleeves." Tartikoff's statements may have been misplaced regarding the Huxtable family, in which Clair exhibited intelligence and Cliff genuinely listened to her, but Tartikoff certainly attested to the growing backlash against the women's movement.[11]

That backlash was widespread. Numerous newspaper and magazine stories described the unhappiness and sad fate that awaited feminists. Advertisements, especially for cosmetics and fashion, extolled a "feminine" look. Whereas in the early 1970s Revlon's pitch for Charlie perfume had featured independent women, by 1982 it favored women who sought marriage and a family. "We had gone a little too far with the whole women's liberation thing," said the company's executive vice president. Breck Shampoo touted the new Breck Girl as someone who "loves to cook country style," "play with her baby daughter," and do "her own housework." The fashion industry, afraid that "the women's lib movement" had made women "less fashion conscious," as one leading designer claimed, launched a series of campaigns to boost feminine apparel. "Gals like to show their legs," claimed the designer Bill Blass. In 1982, the Limited company bought Victoria's Secret, a California boutique shop, quickly turning it into a national chain with over three hundred outlets that sold intimate apparel for women. "Women want to wear very feminine lingerie now," asserted the Hollywood costume designer Bob Mackie. Like fashion designers who lamented the baneful effects of "women's lib," a number of best sellers also took aim at feminists, who were supposedly making men "soft." Identifying a masculinity crisis, books such as Robert Bly's collection of earlier essays *Iron John: A Book about Men* (1990) helped fuel a much-publicized men's movement, complete with seminars, tapes, radio shows, and retreats. A "virtual Great American Wimp Hunt" was under way.[12]

A revived masculinity found strident expression via talk radio. The number of radio stations that used a talk format (sometimes combined with news) leaped from around 200 in the early 1980s to 875 by 1992. Only country music stations were more popular. In fact, talk shows—benefiting from technology, government policy, and the shifting public mood—rescued AM radio, whose fortunes had plummeted with the rise of FM. Technology, in the form of satellites and cell phones, played a crucial role. Satellite innovations freed radio stations from having to relay shows via telephone lines and allowed managers to downlink shows more cheaply and from a wider list of selections. In 1981, the so-called shock jock Howard Stern had demonstrated satellite technology's potential by finding a national audience for his talk show from an AM station in Washington, DC. The increasingly popular cell phones allowed anonymous commuters who were driving to work to vent their opinions. Overwhelmingly, the callers were frustrated and angry men anxious to hit back at mainstream media and institutional elites who seemingly marginalized them. For the mainly white male hosts and listeners, talk shows offered a podium from which they could lambaste a range of targets, ranging from homosexuals to people on welfare, feminists, political correctness, and the well-spoken, "goody-two-shoes men" who delivered TV's evening news (e.g., "Dan Blather," as the talk show host Rush Limbaugh called CBS's Dan Rather). Talk shows thrived on controversy, combativeness, and rudeness.[13]

The strong Right political bent of the shows also owed much to the Reagan administration's deregulation policies, which, for example, allowed movie companies to own theaters again and boosted the limitations on ownership of TV stations from seven to twelve. In 1987, Reagan appointees to the Federal Communications Commission (FCC) decided that the agency would no longer enforce the Fairness Doctrine, which had been in effect since the 1934 Communications Act. In an effort to prevent one politician or political party from controlling the airwaves, the act had mandated that stations could not air one political candidate's views without giving "equal opportunities" to the opposition. The FCC's move toward deregulation meant that companies could own and consolidate many stations and that those stations could air programs without concern for political or ideological balance. "Deregulation has brought a new breed of broadcaster to whom public service matters less," complained the Media Access Project director Andrew Schwartzman. There was no doubt whose side talk radio was on: *real* men, who rejected the sensibilities of the 1960s rights revolution and resented America's perceived weakness abroad. One host "hated the Japs," and another described African Americans as "subhumanoids, savages." Hosts also prized old-fashioned masculinity. "We gotta change, we've got to go back to tough guys," said Rush Limbaugh, whose show had gone national in 1988 and, within four years, was on 529 stations, drawing listeners daily from as much as 9 percent of the population. "We're not gonna take any shit."[14]

Unlike talk radio, TV had to finesse women's issues with special care because females constituted such a large part of the audience. The assignment was challenging, particularly because over 90 percent of television writers were white males and at least some—such as the ABC producer Marshall Herskovitz—were struggling with changing female roles. "I think this is a terrible time to be a man, maybe the worst time in history," Herskovitz asserted. "Manhood has simply been devalued in recent years and doesn't carry much weight anymore." At NBC, the executive producer Jay Tares apparently agreed. "I never did get what the women's movement was all about," he said. "I still don't understand what the big problem is. No doors ever seemed closed to me."[15]

In the 1980s, feminist issues that had surfaced earlier on programs such as *The Mary Tyler Moore Show, All in the Family,* and *Maude* virtually vanished from television. Indeed, according to a Pulitzer Prize–winning media observer: "In the 1987–1988 season, the backlash's high watermark on TV, only three of twenty-two new prime-time dramas featured female leads—and only two of them were adults." The series *Cagney & Lacey* (about two female police officers who confronted such issues as breast cancer and date rape) owed its survival over seven seasons to tens of thousands of fans' letters. The CBS executive Arnold Becker explained at one point why Cagney had to appear vulnerable: "I wonder how many men there are in the U.S. today who'd be anxious to marry a hard-boiled female cop." The two detectives "were too harshly women's lib," complained another CBS executive. "We perceived them as dykes"—even though Lacey was married.[16]

"Like the country as a whole," observed one media scholar, "[the networks'] motto might have been: When in doubt, shift right." Network executives anticipated a conservative lurch in the public mood and attempted to capitalize on it, as *Mickey Spillane's Mike Hammer* demonstrated. In September 1980, when NBC's Brandon Tartikoff sensed that Reagan would become president, he immediately bought a series, *Walking Tall*, based on two popular 1970s movies about a law-and-order sheriff. The country "is looking for heroes," guessed Tony Thomopoulos, ABC Entertainment president. At CBS, an executive commissioned a script for a series called *The CIA* because he believed that America was "moving to the right." Esther Shapiro, a creator of the *Dallas*-like evening soap opera *Dynasty*, claimed: "We sort of anticipated the Reagan era, viscerally." *Dynasty* started a week before Reagan took office and soon claimed 80 million viewers. Shapiro surmised that the show satisfied Americans'—and her own—"renewed need for romance" as well as "glitz and glamour." In the 1960s, Shapiro had worn granny dresses and participated in peace marches. But, regarding her changed perspective by the time Reagan became president, she said, "I felt like dressing up again." Shortly after *Dynasty*'s debut, an ABC executive discussed his network's position: "What we're trying to get across is the message that there is a spirit in this country that is looking for a return to some basic values." By 1984, the networks were leaping with Reaganesque imagery and patriotic symbolism.[17]

Political partisanship accounted far less for such all-American messages, however, than did the drive to find audiences. Even on radio talk shows, ideology was less important than the number of listeners. "The truth is," a host conceded, "we do everything for the ratings. Yes, that's our job. I can show you the contract." Talk show celebrities developed exaggerated personas as "junkyard dogs" who used rage, disgust, and paranoia in order to attract audiences. As one host said: "I am almost completely real."[18]

On television, ABC's Roone Arledge was reportedly apolitical, but his network's star-spangled coverage of the 1984 Olympic Games in Los Angeles was loaded with messages that echoed Reagan's: America was once again standing tall and winning. Meanwhile, CBS adopted a promotional slogan: "We keep America on top of the world."[19]

Movies in the 1980s also captured that mood. Spielberg and Lucas continued to direct or produce cartoon-like adventure stories, seven of which were among the decade's top ten box-office draws. Spielberg's *E.T.: The Extra-Terrestrial* (1982), a fairy tale about an endearing little space alien who befriends a young boy, set the standard. So did Lucas's additional *Star Wars* episodes, *The Empire Strikes Back* (1980) and *Return of the Jedi* (1983). Starting with *Raiders of the Lost Ark* (1981), Spielberg and Lucas collaborated on the Indiana Jones cliff-hanger trilogy, about a 1930s-era hero who battles nasty villains. Meanwhile, between 1979 and 1990, Stallone brought back his *Rocky* boxing character four times. Seizing on the popularity of these movie heroes, toy companies such as Kenner Products created dozens of action figures, especially from the *Star Wars* movies; by 1985, Kenner had sold 250 million such toys. Games, kids' lunch boxes, and watches were additional spin-offs.[20]

The "Reaganizing" of Hollywood was evident in the themes of many other movies. Some, such as *The Big Chill* (Lawrence Kasdan, 1983), portrayed the 1960s as either fraudulent or—as in *Silkwood* (Mike Nichols, 1983)—naively idealistic. Others, such as *First Blood* (Ted Kotcheff, 1982), *The Right Stuff* (Philip Kaufman, 1983), and *Sudden Impact* (1983), warned against bungling government bureaucracies and favored authentic heroes who worked outside official regulations to achieve true justice. Others—*Risky Business* (Paul Brickman, 1983) especially—endorsed the desire for money. In a number of films—for instance, *Red Dawn* (John Milius, 1984) and *Invasion U.S.A.* (Joseph Zito, 1985)—the United States was under attack. In some—*Rambo: First Blood II* (George P. Cosmatos, 1985), *Uncommon Valor* (Ted Kotcheff, 1983), *Missing in Action* (Joseph Zito, 1984), *The Delta Force* (Menahem Golam, 1986)—Americans rescued prisoners of war still in Vietnam or in countries like Iran, weaving resentment and retaliation into narratives that exorcised recent U.S. military failures. *An Officer and a Gentleman* (Taylor Hackford, 1982) and Tony Scott's *Top Gun,* the top-grossing movie of 1986, romanticized military service. Many films—including Stallone's Rocky and Rambo movies, along with *Die Hard* (John McTiernan, 1988), *Lethal Weapon* (Richard Donner, 1987), and the Indiana Jones series—lauded traditional masculinity. A number of sports movies mixed nostalgia for idyllic settings with stories of underdog triumph—*The Natural* (Barry Levinson, 1984), *Hoosiers* (David Anspaugh, 1986), and *Field of Dreams* (Phil Alden Robinson, 1989).[21]

Meanwhile, independent women struggled with unhappiness in such movies as *Surrender* (Jerry Belson, 1987), *Broadcast News* (James L. Brooks, 1987), and *Working Girl* (Mike Nichols, 1988). "I'd like to have a child, but I don't even have a boyfriend, so how can I have a child?" moaned Cher in *Suspect* (Peter Yates, 1987). "I don't think I can do it anymore. You know, I'm tired. I'm really tired." In 1980s movies, good women sometimes took the form of rural mothers, such as those in Robert Benton's *Places in the Heart,* Mark Rydell's *The River,* and Richard Pearce's *Country*—all released in 1984. Bad women, in contrast, were typically unhinged aggressors, particularly the Glenn Close character in *Fatal Attraction* (1987), a prime example of the antifeminist backlash. Adrian Lyne, the director of *Fatal Attraction,* asserted that, when feminists talked, "it's kind of unattractive." Michael Douglas, the movie's star, approached the project feeling that he was "really tired of feminists, sick of them": "Guys are going through a terrible crisis right now because of women's unreasonable demands."[22]

There were, nevertheless, endless challenges in assessing, let alone anticipating, public sentiment. "It's kind of difficult to build a show around the mood of the country," conceded the moviemaker Brandon Stoddard, "whatever that mood may be. The other thing is, you're constantly surprised by the mood of the country." Many of the law-and-order programs that the TV networks tried in the early 1980s failed, including *Today's FBI, Strike Force,* and *McClain's Law.* "What the country seems to be attracted to for the moment," observed one industry executive, "is fantasy, escapism, *Love Boat.* . . . We misassessed the country's mood."[23]

While the public showed many signs of growing more conservative, attitudes were too fluid and ambivalent to sustain simplistic conclusions. In reality, as CBS's Herman Keld recognized, it was hard to identify trends: "I've never met anyone who knew what was going to happen two seconds from now." When, for instance, Bill Cosby first tried to interest the networks in a sitcom about a professional black family, he had no luck. Indeed, ABC quickly rejected the idea. For one thing, although Cosby's thirty-second advertisements for Jell-O and other products were highly successful, his television and movie efforts in the 1970s had been disappointments. For another, sitcoms had fallen out of fashion. In 1983, one year before *The Cosby Show* first aired, only three of the twenty-two top shows were sitcoms, and the highest ranked of those came in at only number thirteen. As Cosby recalled: "Anyone hearing that the sitcom was supposed to be dead, and suddenly, man, here's Bill Cosby wanting to do one with an *all-black* cast, had to say: 'Wrong time, wrong color.' It was all against us on paper." By chance, NBC's Brandon Tartikoff embraced the Cosby sitcom after watching the comedian on a late-night talk show discuss middle-class family life. But Tartikoff could hardly have guessed that Cosby would so rejuvenate sitcoms that, by 1987, seven were among the top ten shows and five more were in the top twenty-two. *The Cosby Show,* moreover, was instrumental in making NBC the top network.[24]

While it was difficult enough to identify trends, the trends themselves usually held multiple meanings. Although there was much talk about the "Age of Reagan," that age was more complicated than superficial "Morning in America" images suggested. "Reagan's rhetoric . . . tingles in people's ears," wrote the cultural observer Garry Wills in 1984, "but the ground is moving beneath them to other forces." Even as the president's rhetoric celebrated Americans' successes, a number of movies looked elsewhere for insight—to the Other, including primitives, marginalized individuals, and aliens. These Others emerged onscreen as happier and more admirable than much of modern society. "We," according to the message, could learn from "them." "It's curious," wrote one movie critic, "that American audiences should be so eager to identify with outsiders at a time when—or so the politicians and media pundits tell us—national pride is stronger than it has been for decades."[25]

Granted, television sitcoms had since the 1960s featured a variety of Others—a Martian on *My Favorite Martian,* the alien Mork from Ork on *Mork and Mindy,* a genie on *I Dream of Jeannie,* and even a talking horse on *Mister Ed.* But what differentiated the 1980s movie Others and their subsequent counterparts was that the world around them was more sinister and threatening. Even Spielberg's *E.T.* contained a sense of institutional and scientific menace. Sympathy for the "primitive" was evident in a host of films. *The Gods Must Be Crazy* (Jamie Uys, 1980) and *Crocodile Dundee* (Peter Faiman, 1986), contrasting the sweet innocence of Australian bushmen and backwoodsmen with the artificiality of civilization, were foreign-made movies that became surprise box-office hits. *Greystoke* (Hugh Hudson, 1984), a pessimistic recycling of the Tarzan of the Apes story, showed Tarzan escaping back to the jungle to avoid the repressed terrors of Victorian England, which displayed stuffed animals—including apes. Amazonian tribesmen in *The Emerald Forest* (John Boorman, 1985) and *The Mission* (Roland Joffé, 1986) occupied a contented world until the arrival of technology and Christian missionaries. "They still know what we have forgotten," says *The Emerald Forest*'s protagonist, an engineer whose company is damming the river. *Iceman* (Fred Schepisi, 1984) portrayed a recently discovered prehistoric man as more decent than the untrustworthy, manipulative scientists who use him to pursue fame and fortune. In *Witness* (Peter Weir, 1985), Pennsylvania's devoted Amish people contrast sharply with the residents of Philadelphia's murderous, drug-filled, big-city world. The alien from outer space in *Starman* (John Carpenter, 1984) is good and admirable, unlike the tobacco-chewing, bully-boy hunter who laughs at his concerns over a dead deer: "Bet you cried when Bambi died." The alien brings the deer back to life and offers a model for earth-lings to follow.[26]

Such movies may have allowed audiences to have it both ways. Audiences could, in effect, believe that their culture was, indeed, the best. At the same time, they could momentarily examine that culture from a more critical per-spective. In that regard, one reporter speculated that "these outsiders are ourselves looking in—they give us the opportunity both to be a part of our culture and to feel superior to it."[27]

But that process could also encourage conclusions that were critical of U.S. society and policies. In the film world of "primitive grace," the insidi-ous forces were imperialism and civilization. Several movies made clear that U.S. values were not appropriate for other peoples. "The West doesn't have answers any more," a character tells Mel Gibson's American journal-ist in Indonesia in *The Year of Living Dangerously* (Peter Weir, 1983). In *Under Fire* (Roger Spottiswoode, 1983), an American journalist, covering the Sandinista revolution in Nicaragua in 1978–79, insists: "I don't take sides. I take pictures." Yet, as he grows increasingly alienated and drops his neutral stance, audiences could not help but conclude that the United States brought nothing but trouble when it meddled in Nicaragua's affairs, a posi-tion at odds with Reagan's policies. While such movies tended to recycle familiar stereotypes of non-Americans, they also served "as paranoid fa-bles for a new world order," as the film observer John Powers noted. In them, the Third World was both threatening and a reminder of situations "that can make us feel guilty and ashamed for living so very well. We don't own history any more." Deep down, according to Powers, movies about benign primitives and the follies of Third World meddling suggested "an obvious and profound uneasiness with contemporary history. . . . There will be more isolation, more technology, more social control by govern-ment, less stability in business, more fragmentation, fewer inner certainties and more external 'danger.'"[28]

Unsettling messages dominated other highly acclaimed films of the de-cade. Martin Scorsese's *Raging Bull* (1980), a study of the real-life boxer Jake LaMotta, portrayed the ugly, frightening, abusive side of an assertive masculinity. In *Blue Velvet* (1986), David Lynch probed the terrors beneath the placid world of Reagan's America—white, middle-class, and in the na-tion's rural heartland. "I like the idea that everything has a surface which hides much more underneath," explained Lynch. "I go down in that dark-ness and see what's there." Spike Lee's *Do the Right Thing* (1989) exam-ined racial conflict. Clearly, there were movies that tested, as well as ones that affirmed, the flag-waving images of the Reagan era.[29]

Comic books reflected the same tensions. The comic industry was at a crossroads, moving increasingly from the traditional retail outlets such as newsstands and small stores to the direct-sales comic shops, which were usually limited to urban areas. Moreover, rising fuel and paper costs substantially boosted comic-book prices. By the early 1980s, the average thirty-two-page comic cost sixty cents; a few years earlier, it had sold for forty cents. The industry's changing economics forced smaller companies to the wall, especially those that continued to publish for young readers. On the other hand, the powerhouses—DC and Marvel, both of which were corporate property—prospered. They did so by appealing to older fans, a number of whom viewed comics as collectibles or valuable investments, and by licensing superhero toys, TV cartoons and series, and movies. (Between 1991 and 1996, comics shrank from 75 to 20 percent of Marvel's business.) An infusion of new talent also had an impact. The young writer-artists introduced new characters, revitalized existing ones, and also revealed the era's competing ideological currents.[30]

At Marvel Comics, John Byrne fit neatly in the Reagan camp. He associated himself with "a Middle America Bible Belt mentality" and sought to rid the comic books of the 1970s "doom, gloom, and that sort of thing." In his opinion, the Comics Guild "stank of unions," which he, a self-proclaimed "company man," found offensive. In 1975, when Byrne launched the X-Men series, he compared the Wolverine character to Clint Eastwood's Dirty Harry.[31]

Also at Marvel was Frank Miller, arguably the most influential person in the comic industry since Stan Lee. As the product of a "miserable" Vermont childhood, Miller liked to portray superheroes as somewhat disturbed emotionally, perhaps even psychotic. How else could one account for their continuing efforts to save a deeply corrupt society that hated them? Superheroes had previously been "confident symbols of hope," according to the historian Bradford Wright, but they "now spoke to the paranoia and psychosis lurking behind the rosy veneer of Reagan's America." Miller portrayed Marvel's Daredevil in endless conflict with a hopelessly debased urban environment. In 1986, Miller moved to DC Comics, where he produced a short series, *Batman: The Dark Knight Returns*, a landmark effort that quickly sold out. Batman, in this revived version, was—in Wright's words—"an older and slightly mad right-wing moralist in a dystopian Gotham City gutted by corruption and vice." The best-selling horror novelist Stephen King judged Miller's series as "probably the finest piece of comic art ever to be published in a popular edition."[32]

That same year, DC published a twelve-issue series, *The Watchmen*, that turned an even more skeptical eye on the superhero genre. Indeed, the series' inspiration was the ancient, chilling question: "Who watches the watchmen?" "I don't believe in heroes," said Alan Moore, the series' creator. "The belief in heroes . . . leads to people like Colonel Oliver North," the real-life individual who helped run—in defiance of congressional restrictions—a Reagan administration "off-the-shelf" operation that used profits from illegal weapons sales to Iran to fund guerrilla efforts to topple Nicaragua's Marxist-led government. In the pursuit of righteous goals, Moore's characters broke the law and brutally attempted to impose their will on the world.[33]

While DC and Marvel battled for comic-book supremacy, small independent companies still found some maneuvering room. In 1984, Kevin Eastman and Peter Laird paid $1,200 out of their own pockets to publish three thousand black-and-white copies of a homemade, action-figure satire, *Teenage Mutant Ninja Turtles,* about four pet store turtles who became superheroes when radioactive waste contaminated them. In the sewers, a rat taught them the martial art of ninja. Within a year, the comic went through several printings and sold over 100,000 copies. The turtles became an astounding success, especially among small children, after a little-known Hong Kong toy company, Playmates, distributed the cartoon characters as action figures. As many as nine of ten boys between the ages of three and eight reportedly owned one of them. Within several years, a hit television show, two feature movies, costumes, and video games were also on the market, turning Eastman and Laird into multimillionaires and inspiring a wave of successors, such as the Mighty Morphin Power Rangers.[34]

Although few independent comic-book publishers approached the mutant turtles' level of financial success, they nevertheless provided outlets for personal expression and critiqued the mainstream industry. The cartoonist Robert Crumb, for example, satirized much of American culture in comics such as *Despair* and *Snoid.* He also spurned mainstream respectability.[35]

Among the independents were females who regretted that comic books had become "a guy's medium," as the author Carla Sinclair said. When Sinclair accidentally discovered a copy of *Love and Rockets,* a new-style romance comic book that Jaime and Gilbert Hernandez started publishing in 1982, she became "instantly hooked." Few comic-book stores, frequented mainly by males, carried romance titles. Instead, superheroes filled the shelves. In the mid-1980s, Marvel and DC had briefly reintroduced several comics aimed at female readers, but such efforts were short-lived. Several independent ventures also had little success, and even *Love and Rockets* did not last long. By the 1980s, however, the arrival of cheap photocopying allowed a number of women to publish small runs of their own comic books, such as *Real Girl* and *Action Girl.* These women drew on the precedents of the 1970s feminist underground newspapers and, according to the illustrator Trisha Robbins, expressed "a strong political and feminist awareness they're not ashamed to talk about." A turning point subsequently occurred in mid-1991, when two all-female punk bands from the state of Washington—Bikini Kill and Bratmobile—performed in Washington, DC, popularizing such terms as *Riot Grrrl.* As Robbins explained, they used *grrrl* to link "that reclaimed word *girl* with a defiant growl." Two years later, a group of women at a San Diego comic convention formed the Friends of Lulu "to promote and encourage female readership and participation in the comic book industry." The group's motto was "Here to Save Comics." But the road ahead was steep. Many of the women cartoonists had other full-time jobs and had to depend on the mails to distribute comparatively expensive comic books.[36]

Starting in the 1980s, the future of network television was also in doubt because of new technologies—VCRs, cable TV, and remote control. Those technologies suddenly placed CBS, NBC, and ABC—the three commercial networks that had ruled television since the 1950s—on the defensive. With 90 percent of the nighttime audience through the 1970s, the networks had been the center of America's entertainment world. By the end of the 1980s, the networks' share of the television audience had slumped to 67 percent. In 1997, it slipped to 49 percent. By then, 84 percent of households owned VCRs, and over 67 percent got cable television. To deal with their declining status, the networks had to take chances, which included airing riskier kinds of programming that dealt more realistically with issues and—uncharacteristically for the medium—hinted at the darker underside of American life. "Explosive. That's the only word to describe the changes that have occurred in television during this past decade," wrote *TV Guide*'s Neil Hickey at the end of 1989. "VCRs and cable television," he predicted, "have forever changed the way we use our TV sets."[37]

Cable had emerged in the 1950s, TV's early days, as an effort to serve small, isolated towns. In eastern Pennsylvania's Mahanoy City, with a population of under five thousand, John Walson was having trouble selling television sets because surrounding mountains made reception almost impossible. On his own, he built an antenna atop a nearby mountain, got permission to run lines along the power poles, and then sold access—$100 for the hookup and $2 per month.[38]

Other entrepreneurs soon established their own cable TV systems, primarily in rural areas, typically by using utility poles and providing subscribers with a dozen or so stations. By 1964, local cable systems exceeded a thousand; during the 1970s, the number quadrupled. A few subscription cable systems operated in cities such as San Francisco, featuring sporting events and movies that were not on commercial television. But it was Home Box Office (HBO), a *Time* subsidiary in Wilkes-Barre, Pennsylvania, that made the major breakthrough: satellite-distributed services to cable systems. In 1975, HBO leased a spot on a domestic satellite that RCA launched. HBO's subscriptions soared 500 percent in one year, as viewers signed up for such programming as first-run movies and the Joe Frazier–Muhammad Ali championship fight in the Philippines—the "thrilla in Manila." In 1976,

Ted Turner established his WTBS "superstation" by putting his Atlanta channel's signal on a satellite and then distributing it to cable operators around the country. His satellite program services soon included the Cable News Network (CNN), a twenty-four-hour, all-news operation that started broadcasting in June 1980. Satellite-distributed services quickly spread to sports, music, weather, public affairs, religion, and even the soft-core Playboy Channel. By 1987, no fewer than half of American households subscribed to cable television. Subscribers paid their cable bills more promptly than they did other utility charges.[39]

The Reagan administration's deregulation policies boosted cable television. Political conservatives had long complained about the networks' alleged liberal bias. With Reagan in the White House, they had an opportunity to reshape the media. Mark Fowler, Reagan's appointment to chair the FCC, championed "the policy of 'unregulation'" to open broadcasting to the whims of the marketplace. "Television," according to Fowler, "is just another appliance. It's a toaster with pictures." One result was the appearance of broadcasters who downplayed their public service role, especially in light of the FCC's abandonment of the Fairness Doctrine. At CBS in the 1980s, the politically conservative Van Gordon Sauter, who briefly headed the news division, opposed what he believed was a "too restrictive" distinction between "news" and "entertainment." He defended "tabloid television" as "the popularization of news and information by people who don't wear the old school tie of Establishment journalism." In 1986, collisions between Sauter and those old-school journalists, who were alarmed about news coverage that slipped increasingly into entertainment, ultimately forced Sauter to resign.[40]

In truth, of course, the lines between news and entertainment had been blurring for several years. In August 1977, for instance, ABC's coverage of the arrest of New York City's "Son of Sam" serial killer resembled the sensational stories that had filled the tabloid papers over the past year as the murders had occurred. Roone Arledge, who had lifted ABC's sports division to enviable heights, had recently become head of the news division. His appointment had elicited objections from ABC News people such as Peter Jennings and Ted Koppel, who feared that Arledge would substitute gimmicks for careful reporting. Arledge hardly eased their concerns when he recommended that his staff study commercials to see how a thirty-second message could pack a wallop. The Son of Sam arrest gave Arledge an early opportunity to milk entertainment value out of a major news event. He shocked Jennings and others by bringing in the controversial reporter Geraldo Rivera to help cover the story. Shortly thereafter, Rivera joined the staff of *20/20*, which debuted in June 1978 as a "newsmagazine." *Variety* compared the program to the *National Enquirer* tabloid paper, and Arledge himself claimed to hate the program. Nevertheless, under Arledge, ABC News injected heavy doses of the tabloid style into network news.[41]

While some newscasters worried about the fate of their craft, the lifting of restrictions on commercial airtime in the 1980s unleashed a surge in "infomercials"—half-hour advertisements. "Television has become a free-wheeling bazaar of goods and services, the denizen of get-rich, lose-fat infomercials," complained one TV reporter. The Cable Act of 1984 facilitated this development and boosted the cable industry by allowing it to charge customers as much as the market allowed. Cable companies used their windfall profits to create original programming that placed the networks even more on the defensive.[42]

"Free television as we know it cannot survive alongside pay television," a CBS advertisement in *TV Guide* had warned as early as 1958, when barely 1 percent of homes with television subscribed to cable. By the 1980s, the spread of cable offerings made that dire prediction all too real, particularly as the networks tried to cope with technologies such as videocassette recorders. As VCR prices fell from some $2,000 in 1976 to about $200 in 1985, they posed a growing challenge to the networks. Whereas some 2 percent of television households had VCRs in 1979, half did by 1987. Initially, owners used their VCRs to watch videotaped movies that the Hollywood studios sold to supplement sagging theater ticket profits. Some retailers started renting the tapes despite the studios' restrictions. The result was what a sociologist described as "the rental rebellion against the movie studios"—an example of how "the day-to-day decisions of customers at thousands of mom-and-pop stores" enhanced viewers' autonomy.[43]

That autonomy expanded when viewers started recording television programs on their VCRs and then used electronic remote-control devices to fast-forward through commercials. And the remote control of television sets also allowed viewers to switch channels at will, "surfing" or "grazing" for better programs, especially during commercials. For television advertisers, who were already worried about the networks' diminishing customer base, VCRs and remote controls brought only more bad news. In 1984, General Foods reportedly wasted $1 million in paid advertising time because of viewers' ability to skip commercials.[44]

An additional threat to the networks came from nonaffiliated independent stations. Taking advantage of Reagan's deregulation policies, such stations by 1986 nearly tripled in number from the 103 that existed in 1980. By 1988, the networks' share of the prime-time audience had dropped to 68 percent, while the independents' share had grown to 20 percent. These nonnetwork stations used syndication to rerun proven hit shows such as *All in the Family.* Moreover, as the demand for syndicated programming grew, production studios began to make programs for first-run syndication. Popular offerings eventually included *Wheel of Fortune, The People's Court, The Oprah Winfrey Show,* and *Jeopardy.* Game shows served sponsors especially well. The ability to use brand-name products as prizes integrated consumer messages into the programs, thereby foiling "viewers with itchy remote control fingers," as the TV analyst Ira Rosofsky pointed out. Furthermore, according to Rosofsky, game shows were a bargain, costing on average "only $35,000, a mere fraction of a half-hour soap." Between 1980 and the 1986–87 season, the number of first-run shows in syndication jumped from twenty-five to ninety-six, much of it in the form of cheap "tabloid" programming. After his ouster from CBS, Van Gordon Sauter began to produce "reality-based" shows for syndication.[45]

Faced with deteriorating ratings, the networks abandoned their traditional search for comprehensive audiences and pursued viewers who were young, financially successful, and educated—prime targets for advertisers. As the movie industry had done earlier when it lost customers, network television aimed at smaller audiences while demonstrating more willingness to experiment outside the mainstream. Just as Hollywood had replaced the Hays Code, the networks now eased away from the 1952 production standards of the National Association of Broadcasters and began to include more sex, more violence, and earthier language. Earlier definitions of what constituted a successful program also softened. In 1964, for example, an audience share of 26 had not saved *East Side/West Side;* by the mid-1980s, an annual share of 19–22 was sufficient to keep a program on the air, especially if its demographics reaped advertising dividends.[46]

In the early 1980s, NBC especially needed to try something new. By then, the once-proud network had slipped into third place—behind ABC, at one time the network runt, and CBS. Fred Silverman, who had recently moved from CBS to NBC, proposed a new cop show, but he hardly had in mind the product that MTM Enterprises delivered: *Hill Street Blues* (1981–87). At MTM, Grant Tinker still had a formidable writing staff with credentials that rivaled English departments on many college campuses. Among the staff was Steven Bochco, a theater arts major and the son of a concert violinist, who produced *Hill Street Blues.* As *TV Guide* subsequently recognized: "Bochco brought a new style of gritty, grimy urban realism to prime-time crime shows. . . . On *Hill Street,* viewers learned to expect the unexpected—hilarity could turn to horror in an instant." The program helped move the serial format from soap operas into prime time and included a large ensemble cast with thirteen regular characters.[47]

Significantly, its resemblance to a low-budget documentary and its complicated, typically dark stories contradicted the cheerful scenarios of the Reagan years. "The appeal of a Ronald Reagan . . . to a great many people has always been solid, simple answers to very complex questions," explained Bochco, "[but] those simple, easy answers don't yield results.

They never have." A media expert later wrote: "*Hill Street Blues* was willing to walk into a 1980s no-man's land: the ghetto itself, the place of the despairing and the disenfranchised." The unorthodox characters were flawed and vulnerable. Racism sometimes reared its ugly head among even the regular characters. The dialogue was earthy. "It's a western and we're gonna have all the horseshit on the street," said Bochco. The show's philosophical viewpoint suggested "resigned hopelessness" as squad cars broke down and the police precinct crumbled. "*Hill Street* was for me always fundamentally a series about despair," Bochco recalled.[48]

NBC executives feared that the show was too grim, and its first year's dismal rating—eighty-third out of ninety-seven series—seemed to confirm their judgment. Previously, the series would have ended immediately, despite its enthusiastic reviews. Yet it survived because of its popularity with a major demographic group: affluent viewers aged eighteen to forty-nine, "a dynamite audience," according to one NBC vice president. At the end of its first season, *Hill Street Blues* received twenty-one Emmy nominations and won eight. By its third season, it was a hit, proving that literate dramas could produce quality as well as successful television programs. "Thus," wrote one TV critic, "*Hill Street* became the first show of the new cable era to make it on the strength of its demographics rather than the size of its audience."[49]

It was not the last, as NBC's *St. Elsewhere* (1982–88) quickly demonstrated. By then, the network was increasingly under the influence of Tinker, who had just become NBC's president. His hands-off style exhilarated employees, who sensed that the network was entering a creative period. Indeed, the idea for *St. Elsewhere* took shape at the very time that its model, *Hill Street Blues,* was struggling to avoid the bottom of the ratings. Tinker's description of *St. Elsewhere* as "*Hill Street Blues* in a hospital" underlined the programs' similarities. Both reworked old formulas—*Hill Street* the cop show and *St. Elsewhere* the doctor show. Both used audience demographics to survive initially abysmal ratings. Both featured troubled characters trying to survive in a broken environment. Both broke a number of prime-time rules. On *St. Elsewhere,* a main character died after contacting AIDS. Patients also died. And the series ended with the revelation that the entire set of stories had been the fantasies of an autistic child.[50]

By the end of the 1980s, MTM-style quality television was evident across the medium. Ironically, by then, MTM had become a quite different company. In the summer of 1988, it was purchased by a British company, TVS Entertainment, and, in late 1992, sold to the evangelist Pat Robertson. Meanwhile, in the fall of 1986, Tinker left NBC, after elevating it to first place by using quality dramas, *The Cosby Show,* and fast-paced entertainment like *The A-Team* (1983–87). ABC, which had plunged from first place to its worst ratings in almost three decades, now took another innovative turn with the help of people such as Bochco. By airing a number of ground-breaking series such as *Roseanne* (1988–97), *thirtysomething* (1987–91), and *China Beach* (1988–91), ABC further complicated the cultural narratives that Reagan-style conservatives favored.[51]

The sitcom *Roseanne*, which ranked as the number two show in its first season and number one the next, was notable for a number of reasons. Its main character was female. Its working-class family—the Conners—hardly fit the model of Reagan-era economics. Both parents worked in blue-collar jobs as they battled problems of unemployment, low pay, and unsympathetic bosses. Roseanne's advice on paying bills was simple: "You pay the ones marked final notice and throw the rest away." "We're not yuppies," husband Dan quipped when he learned that Roseanne was pregnant. "We're supposed to have babies when we're young and stupid." The Conners' three children were far closer to real-life people than the Beaver Cleavers had been in earlier sitcoms. "They've left for school," the parents rejoiced. "Quick—change the locks!" The program's biting humor and sardonic perspective drew heavily from the real-life difficulties of its star, Roseanne Barr. She had grown up as a Jewish outsider in heavily Mormon Salt Lake City. When she was sixteen, a car struck her, leaving her in a coma. She spent eight months in a state mental hospital. "I got pregnant the first time I ever had sex," she recalled. "My parents made me give her up for adoption." After she married, she had three more children, "lived in a car, a cabin, and a cave." After sixteen years, she finally left her abusive husband. Developing her career as a feminist comedian, she made fun of housework: "My husband asked me if we have any cheese puffs. Like he can't go and lift that couch cushion himself." And she laughed at motherhood: "I figure when my husband comes home from work, if the kids are still alive, then I've done my job." To define her TV program, she constantly battled producers, trying to make it edgier, and emphasizing that working-class families had dignity, anger, and little chance of resolving problems—particularly in thirty minutes. As the cultural commentator Barbara Ehrenreich observed: "Roseanne is the neglected underside of the eighties, bringing together its themes of poverty, obesity, and defiance."[52]

Paradoxically, in light of the Reagan-era celebration of idealized family values, television featured many troubled and violent families. During the mid-1980s, several made-for-TV movies and miniseries drew on best-selling books to produce "the family antiromance." As one observer quipped: "*This* is how families behave when they aren't watching *The Brady Bunch*." In *The Burning Bed* (Robert Greenwald, 1984), an abused wife set her husband on fire, and, in *Fatal Vision* (David Greene, 1984), a doctor murdered his family. *Nutcracker: Money, Madness and Murder* (Paul Bogart, 1987) and *At Mother's Request* (Michael Tuchner, 1987) both told of the wealthy Franklin Bradshaw family, full of abuse, secrets, and destruction. In 1984, amid an acceleration of shocking news stories and official reports of child abuse, ABC aired Randa Haines's *Something about Amelia,* about incest between a middle-class father and his thirteen-year-old daughter. The made-for-TV movie drew almost half of all television viewers the evening it aired. Its powerful message—that child abuse crossed class and cultural lines—struck a chord, and, following the show, tens of thousands of people called telephone hotlines with their own reports. Such public fascination with extreme family disorder revealed fears that the idealized traditional family was in great trouble. And, if television shows were any barometer, those fears were not subsiding in the 1990s. "Whip me, beat me . . . and give me great ratings," *Newsweek* noted of "a network obsession with women in danger." Child abuse was the subject of at least nine network movies between 1992 and 1995.[53]

Two of the most popular television series that emerged in the late 1980s were about dysfunctional families: the sitcom *Married . . . with Children* (1987–97) and the cartoon *The Simpsons* (1989–), both on the new Fox network. The fact that the shows attracted considerable fire from conservatives was full of irony because the network's founder, Rupert Murdoch, was himself politically conservative and because his move into broadcasting benefited from the deregulatory environment of Reagan's FCC. But, as one reporter noted, Murdoch had not spent millions of dollars "to compete with the Family Channel."[54]

An Australian publisher, Murdoch had made considerable money off of English tabloids before the 1970s, when he entered America's tabloid business, starting with his *National Star.* He loathed "elite journalism" and sought the largest audience he could find. In 1985, after buying several U.S. newspapers, including the *New York Post,* he purchased Twentieth Century–Fox and Metromedia, a collection of seven television stations in such big-market cities as New York and Los Angeles. At Fox, he could produce movies and television programs that he could syndicate and air on his Metromedia and other independent stations as a fourth "network." Fox was, in fact, a conglomerate, not legally a network. "In order to avoid the high costs of such a venture," as the media scholar Kristal Brent Zook explained, "Murdoch manipulated Federal Communication Commission requirements by offering just under fifteen hours of prime-time programming per week." Among his first programs, after he launched his Fox network in 1986, was a tabloid newsmagazine, *A Current Affair* (1986–96), which focused on celebrity gossip, bizarre stories, and sexy women. Murdoch favored reality shows because they were cheap to make and circumvented problems with writers. *Cops* (1989–) was one of the network's success stories, with production crews following patrol officers on their gritty, often violent rounds "out where the buses don't run."[55]

Fox targeted especially young, urban viewers. Aware that many African

Americans relied on "free" programming because they could not afford cable television, the fledgling network within seven years "was airing the largest single group of black-produced shows in television history," according to Zook. Indeed, "by 1995 black Americans (some 12 percent of the total U.S. population) were a striking 25 percent of Fox's market." Programs such as *A Different World* (1987–93) and *In Living Color* (1990–94) opened doors through which a striking number of aspiring black entertainers and producers moved—among them Keenen Ivory Wayans, Quincy Jones, Robert Townsend, Martin Lawrence, Charles Dutton, Debbie Allen, Sinbad, Yvette Lee Bowser, and Queen Latifah. Wayans believed that, in those early days, Fox "wanted to be the rebel network." Calvin Brown, a writer for *A Different World,* thought that Fox "could get away with a little more" than the other networks because it depended on blacks and teenagers. But Murdoch soon courted white "legitimacy," canceling four of Fox's six black productions in 1994 and purchasing the rights to broadcast the National Football League's Sunday games. As Murdoch expanded Fox's offerings and client base, a joke took hold that he had spotted a niche audience—half the American population. Calvin Brown regretted that black programming was one of the casualties. "We won't ever have another space in network television like that again," he predicted. Still, for a moment, Fox had provided an outlet for black voices. "Do anything you want, but make sure it's different," the Fox programmer Garth Ancier had said. "Fox is here to give you the chance to do things you can't do anywhere else." That spirit underlay the creation of *Married . . . with Children* and *The Simpsons.*[56]

In *Married . . . with Children,* according to *Newsweek,* "nasty fumes" and "snarls" issued from the fictitious Bundy household. The characters were trapped unhappily together, left with no recourse but to snipe at each other. Sentiment was absent. *The Simpsons* were more lovable but offered a startling contrast to a previous TV-sitcom family icon—the Andersons in *Father Knows Best,* who had also lived in the fictional suburb of Springfield. Unlike the Andersons, the blue-collar Simpsons exuded alienation and resentment. Bart, the ten-year-old arch nonconformist and wiseguy, quickly developed a huge fan base that worried some adults. While he received votes in student elections at Stanford University and elsewhere, one Ohio principal banned elementary students from wearing T-shirts on which Bart declared that he was an "Underachiever: And Proud of It, Man." "To be proud of being incompetent is a contradiction of what we stand for," the principal asserted. Nevertheless, with its clever satire, its cartoon format, which facilitated more radical messages, and its widely diverse and enthusiastic audience, *The Simpsons* became the longest-running sitcom ever, much to the chagrin of its critics.[57]

In numerous ways, television served as a microcosm of events and trends, not just in entertainment, but across society generally. It continued, for example, to be the main source of breaking news. More than any other medium, it provided startling, memorable scenes of the rapidly ending Cold War. In 1989, when one of the Cold War's most enduring symbols—the Berlin Wall—came down, TV cameras and commentators were on hand to capture the moment. And, in 1991, when the Persian Gulf War started with the U.S.-led invasion of Iraq in response to Iraq's takeover of Kuwait, CNN covered the event from within Baghdad itself. Indeed, for TV generally, the Gulf War was "a six-week-long ratings hit," nothing less than a "blood pumping, high-tech, all-channel media-military spectacular" of the quick military victory over the forces of Saddam Hussein. With patriotism and reverence, TV reinvigorated a victory narrative with reports of America's technological wizardry via "smart bombs" and Patriot missiles as well as reassuring messages that the United States had overcome the bad memories of Vietnam and was reconnected with its glorious past. NBC, which superimposed a fighter bomber over the American flag during its coverage of "America at War," concluded one newscast with a woman looking at the monument on Mount Rushmore and saying: "It's the freedom of the American people and of the world. And that's worth fighting for. Our forefathers did it for us."[58]

Television also reflected the tremendous acceleration of business conglomeration, hostile takeovers, and "merger mania" that characterized the U.S. economy. In the 1980s, NBC became the property of General Electric, CBS of the investor Laurence Tisch, and ABC of Capital Cities. Twenty years before, International Telephone and Telegraph's attempt to buy ABC had failed, partly on the grounds that such a takeover might threaten the integrity of the network's news coverage. General Electric's takeover of NBC raised few eyebrows, however. Nor, despite the objections of the newspeople, did GE's pressuring of NBC employees to contribute to a political action committee in order to build legislative support for the company. "Employees who elect not to participate in a giving program of this type should question their own dedication to the company and their own expectations," read a directive from GE's president.[59]

Over the next few years, mergers accelerated, creating sprawling corporate behemoths whose diversified holdings reached across much of the entertainment industry. "In 1982, 50 major corporations owned almost all of the major media outlets in the United States," reported the columnist Molly Ivins. "That included 1,787 daily newspapers, 11,000 magazines, 9,000 radio stations, 1,000 television stations, 2,500 book publishers and seven major movie studios." Further consolidation reduced those fifty corporations to twenty-nine within five years and then to nine by 1999. By

2005, the entertainment industry was basically the domain of six gigantic conglomerates—Viacom, Time Warner, NBC Universal, Sony, Fox, and Disney. "Virtually every moment of the day, in every time zone in the planet, people are watching, reading and interacting with our product," boasted Fox's Rupert Murdoch. At the 1987 annual booksellers' convention, the head of Warner Books noted sardonically: "Soon the convention will be held in the office of the lone remaining publisher." Moreover, as Robert Massie of the Authors Guild pointed out, the publishing business was shifting to "the hands of people who are not publishers."[60]

A similar trend was evident in the movie industry. As conglomerates took over, the Hollywood studios served essentially as clearinghouses for dozens of enterprises ranging from theme parks to television outlets, record companies, video rental companies, and toy and clothing manufacturers. Indeed, by 2003, Viacom, whose property included the Paramount and RKO studios, derived only 7 percent of its income from the movie business; for General Electric, the owner of Universal Studios, that figure was less than 2 percent. With a weekly average of only 12 percent of the U.S. population by then buying movie tickets at theaters—in comparison with roughly two-thirds in 1948—most movies in fact lost money at the box office. Despite substantially reduced theater audiences, motion pictures were, nevertheless, crucial to the sprawling entertainment empires. As Viacom's Sumner Redstone observed: "Without content, all the cable channels, television networks, video chains, and all the other delivery systems would be totally useless. That content is movies." Profits derived, however, not from theater ticket sales, but from the licensing of filmed entertainment for home viewing (whether for video players, cable television, or pay TV) or as "intellectual properties" such as movie characters. The fabled Hollywood of the movie moguls had become an appendage of multinational corporations with vast holdings in many businesses.[61]

In the recording industry, Motown's Berry Gordy decided in 1988 that it was impossible to compete with the gargantuan multinational corporations. He sold his fabled record company to MCA. "As I gazed from my office window across the forest of corporate buildings to the Capitol Records tower," he recalled, "I realized that many of them, too, were in the process of being taken over." Ten years later, after changing owners two more times, Motown was the property of the Seagram Corporation, a Canadian beverage business that had become the world's biggest music company.[62]

The comic-book industry was another attractive investment by the early 1990s, when Marvel and DC enjoyed flush times. Indeed, in mid-1991, Marvel Entertainment, a flourishing multimedia entertainment corporation, entered the lists of the New York Stock Exchange—a breakthrough that attested to the expanding influence of comic books. That year, the billionaire financier Ron Perelman gained a controlling interest in Marvel. In 1995, Marvel bought Heroes World, a large East Coast comic-book distributor, which became the exclusive distributor for all Marvel comics, by then numbering 150 titles per month. Despite the early 1990s prosperity at Marvel and DC, the companies constantly struggled for gimmicks to entice readers. That challenge was especially pressing because of the industry's shrinking niche audience. According to surveys, the average consumer was a twenty-year-old male who spent around twenty dollars monthly on comic books. Maintaining the loyalty of such readers was imperative. In 1988, DC killed off Batman's sidekick, Robin, after conducting a readers' phone-in poll. Although some people were shocked that DC had involved youngsters in killing a fictional child, sales soared. Four years later, DC's much-publicized "Death of Superman" issue did even better, selling over 6 million copies. Other innovative plot twists placed Batman in a wheelchair with a broken back for a year, where he watched a crazed avenging angel do his work; sent Captain America with amnesia to a parallel universe where he was a family man and construction worker who slowly rediscovered his powers; and had Spider-Man discover that he had been cloned. While such "events" sold comic books, they also threatened to become essentially meaningless—especially for investors—when, for example, Superman promptly reappeared after dying.[63]

But, in the mid-1990s, as the comic-book business increasingly became a corporate subsidiary, its economic fortunes suddenly slumped, partly because of overreach, faulty investments, and the difficulties of competing with such amusements as video and computer games. Within the three-year period 1993–96, industry sales plummeted from $1 billion to $450 million. That year, junk-bond financing and defaults on loans forced Marvel, which controlled about 35 percent of the comic-book market, to file for bankruptcy. When the billionaire corporate raider Carl Icahn tried to take control, a lengthy legal battle ensued, ending only when one of Marvel's toy companies, Toy Biz, reorganized the business. Meanwhile, by 1998, comic-book sales dropped to around $325 million, wiping out many comic-book stores. "There was a time when one in three periodicals sold in the United States was a comic book," observed the comic illustrator Trina Robbins in 1999. "Ninety percent of the nation were regular comics readers. Today that number is less than 1 percent."[64]

In 2001, Marvel broke from the Comics Code Authority and started releasing a riskier set of comics with a rating system resembling that of the movies. "We got tied up in our superhero underwear for a while," explained Marvel's editor in chief, Joe Quesada. "Marvel is growing up with the rest of the country." New titles, which sold out quickly, included some profanity and more violence. As profits started inching up again, there were even hints in one issue that Captain America was engaged in a sexual encounter.[65]

Sexual themes in entertainment were anything but new, of course, but the extent to which respectable business conglomerates brought them into the mainstream was striking. Pornography, for example, had become at least a $10 billion industry by the end of the twentieth century, and profiting from it were such highly esteemed blue-chip companies as General Motors and AT&T. Only a few years earlier, in the mid-1970s, pornographic movies had played on the amusement margins, in sleazy theaters in seedy areas. Videotapes helped revolutionize the porn business by allowing people to view movies in the privacy of their homes. By the end of the 1970s, X-rated films accounted for more than half of all recorded tape sales. Within about five years, that number dropped to 25 percent, as cable and satellite television provided easier access to pornographic and near-pornographic films and spared customers the risk of embarrassment at rental stores. The cable industry's installation of fiber-optic lines in the 1990s cut even further into the video business. Fiber optics provided household subscribers with access to hundreds of digital channels, including numerous adult pay-per-view services.[66]

In 2000, the *New York Times* reported: "The General Motors Corporation, the world's largest company, now sells more graphic sex films every year than does Larry Flynt, owner of the Hustler empire." GM owned DirecTV, which by then sold around $200 million worth of pay-per-view sex films from satellite annually. AT&T had its own hard-core sex channel on cable, Hot Network, which, according to one distributor, offered films with "real, live all-American sex—not simulated by actors." "We're in the small leagues compared to some of those companies like General Motors or AT&T," laughed Flynt. EchoStar Communications, of which Rupert Murdoch was a part owner, used its satellite to sell more graphic adult movies than did the Playboy Corporation. Meanwhile, hotel chains such as the Utah-based Marriott reaped huge profits from in-room rentals of adult movies. Such corporations kept a low profile on these investments. An AT&T official described the issue as "the crazy aunt in the attic": "Everyone knows she's there, but you can't say anything about it."[67]

While some big-name corporations used that "crazy aunt" to build an adult-viewing niche, others concentrated especially on another group of consumers: young people. These companies brilliantly honed strategies to identify and disseminate a lifestyle for youths—a culture of cool. Here, in the words of one analysis, was "the ultimate marriage of a corporation and a culture." As the twentieth century wound down, a handful of colossal enterprises dominated this youth market. The Murdoch and Disney companies were conspicuous, but Viacom was the biggest. The media scholar Robert McChesney compared the companies to imperialist nations; they constituted a "massive empire" that colonized the teen world via fashion, movies, music, television, and sports. In the late 1990s, for example, makers of the soft drink Sprite staged a highly successful advertising campaign, tying the product to hip-hop.[68]

By then, a crucial part of this empire was Music Television (MTV). The history of MTV illuminated much about incorporation, advertising, the importance of cable TV in identifying specialized audiences, and trends in the music industry. The music channel's origins rested with corporate giant American Express, one of many companies that saw rich investments in the entertainment field. In 1979, hoping to expand beyond insurance, banking, and travel, American Express bought half of Warner Communications, which was looking for a cable partner. In 1981, a $20 million investment from this joint effort launched MTV. The new venture offered marketing opportunities for advertisers to communicate with young people under age twenty-five, who tended to ignore newspapers and magazines. "Where is the Woodstock generation?" asked MTV's twenty-eight-year-old president, Robert Pittman. "They're all old and bald." Within its first year, MTV grossed $20 million in advertising from over one hundred corporations with a special interest in the youth market. Coincidentally, the music industry desperately needed energizing. It had slumped precipitously in 1979, following disco's short boom period. Indeed, industry revenues declined from the previous year for the first time since the rise of rock and roll in the mid-1950s, and that downward slide continued into 1982. Radio, so important to rock and roll's emergence, no longer helped because talk—not music—now ruled the airwaves. Faced with declining revenues, recording companies suddenly saw the potential of a television channel in marketing music.[69]

MTV's early format was unique, featuring a string of songs rather than time slots for separate programs. Its attitude was also different from that of mainstream television, deliberately conveying a sense of the irreverence and rebellion that had attracted young people to rock music. An initial challenge, however, was how to get on cable systems, especially in New York City. To that end, MTV staged an ingenious campaign in which rock stars appeared in advertisements, proclaiming, "I want my MTV!" and urging young people to get that message to local cable companies. The campaign paid off. A breakthrough occurred in September 1981, when New York City's cable system signed on. As videos resuscitated the record business, more companies produced them.[70]

It was, however, Michael Jackson's album *Thriller* that boosted MTV and changed its image in the process. In 1982, Jackson was twenty-three but had already been a highly visible performer for years. Columbia Records planned to release *Thriller,* his latest solo album, that fall with music videos, but MTV was hardly a promising outlet. The channel had quickly found an audience among white suburban teenagers across the country and virtually ignored black musicians. Perhaps only 20 of over 750 videos that MTV played in its first eighteen months included black artists. To some of its critics, the channel was racist. When Columbia threatened to keep its white artists off MTV, the channel began playing the *Thriller* videos that were already available. The fact that six of the top ten singles in the nation came from the album additionally influenced MTV. Although MTV had not wanted to pay record companies for clips, it now agreed to contribute several hundred thousand dollars to film a video for the title song. Ultimately costing $1.1 million, the video was a cultural landmark, lasting almost fifteen minutes and including a story line with scintillating choreography. The album and videos were sensations. At one point, *Thriller* was selling a million copies every four days. Two decades later, it was still the top-selling album of all time.[71]

Jackson's considerable talents were critical to his success, but so was his clean-cut persona. He shunned cigarettes, alcohol, drugs, and even such words as *funky*. One magazine contrasted him with Elvis Presley and the Beatles, who had "posed a sexual or political challenge to the status quo." Jackson, on the other hand, was "an establishment figure, perfectly in tune with the conservative America of Ronald Reagan." Substantial numbers of people nevertheless found *Thriller* anything but conservative. Some objected to the video's images of the living dead as satanic and also viewed Jackson's performance as much too suggestive. Whatever the opinion, however, no one could ignore MTV's role in the Jackson phenomenon. In a December 1983 cover story, *Time* magazine declared that music videos constituted nothing less than a "musical revolution." As *Billboard* pointed out, young people who used to say, "Yeah, I heard that song," now remarked: "Yeah, I saw that song."[72]

Rolling Stone was not alone in believing that MTV had turned rock and roll music into a series of commercials, but the channel's influence was undeniable. An "MTV look"—sexy, slick, colorful, and fast moving—spilled over into advertising, fashion, movies, and television programs such as NBC's *Miami Vice*. Music videos became a common device for promoting performers such as Cyndi Lauper, a female professional wrestler whose "Girls Just Want to Have Fun" was a big hit in late 1983. If Lauper's multicolored hair and fashions embodied the MTV look, so did the sexuality of Madonna, whose career took off suddenly in 1983 after MTV aired her videos. Music videos were crucial, not only in promoting new stars, but also in both the music industry's break from its economic doldrums and television's role in that process.[73]

By the mid-1980s, corporate sharks were all over American waters, and MTV was an attractive target, with $1 million weekly in advertising revenues and 22 million viewers between the ages of twelve and twenty-four. It was expanding and now owned other channels—Video Hits 1 (VH1); Nickelodeon, for children; and Nick at Nite, which replayed old television sitcoms. Symbolic of its changing status, MTV had started holding "corporate retreats," despite the discomfort of some employees who preferred the company's earlier, less formal atmosphere. Among the corporate raiders with an eye on media investments such as MTV was Rupert Murdoch, who was gobbling up shares of Warner Communications stock. Although Warner fended off Murdoch's takeover bid by getting help from the Chris-Kraft manufacturing company, American Express wanted out of the cable business so that it could concentrate on financial services. MTV's future was, thus, in question. Ultimately, in 1985, the burgeoning Viacom International became MTV's new owner. Since 1971, Viacom had grown from a small communications firm into a mammoth company that owned cable and syndication systems—including Lifetime and the pay-movie service Showtime—as well as TV and radio stations.[74]

Corporate consolidation and new technologies steadily transformed the music business, as they did the entertainment industry as a whole. "By 1990 six corporations collectively controlled over two-thirds of global sales of recorded music," according to a team of musicologists. Of the six, only Time Warner had an American base. The other conglomerates were Poly-Gram in the Netherlands, Sony and Matsushita in Japan, Thorn in Great Britain, and Bertelsmann in Germany. The main customers for these multinational corporations were still Americans, who spent $7.5 billion annually on 31 percent of the world's recorded music. Moreover, that music increasingly reflected the impact of digital technology. In 1982, five-inch compact discs (CDs) first appeared, providing unprecedented clarity and sound definition. A CD could hold over seventy-four minutes of sound, as opposed to around forty on a long-playing vinyl album. Within five years, CDs were outselling vinyl records. For a while, small independent recording labels stuck proudly with vinyl as an expression of nonconformity. But their holdout against CDs proved insufficient to save vinyl records, particularly after mainstream companies realized that they too might profit from underground rock, which had relied on the independents. A turning point in that regard was the release in 1991 of Nirvana's influential album *Nevermind*, which captured corporate attention by showing that "grunge" music could command substantial audiences. By marketing grunge along with other kinds of music on CDs, the major labels helped ensure the revolution in sound technology and relegate vinyl recordings to history's dustbin.[75]

In 1992, thanks in many ways to the movement of giant global corporations into the music business, *Forbes* magazine announced that America's most popular music was now country. Only six years earlier, when country's album sales had shrunk to 9 percent of the market, such an achievement seemed a pipe dream. By the mid-1990s, however, country's ascendancy was indisputable, reflecting at least partly the nation's growing conservative mood as well as the emergence of a group of new entertainers with crossover appeal and familiarity with many musical styles. Country radio's 70 million weekly listeners constituted 42 percent of the radio audience. Garth Brooks, whose album sales surpassed 60 million by 1996, was on his way to becoming America's best-selling recording artist ever. Brooks's 1991 album *Ropin' the Wind* had debuted as number one on both the country and the pop charts—the first album to do so. A 1995 survey revealed that 37 percent of Americans listened to country music each week. Meanwhile, tourists flocked to Branson, Missouri, a town of six thousand on the edge of the Ozarks that rivaled Nashville's Opryland. After the entertainer Roy Clark opened his Celebrity Theater there in 1991 to considerable fanfare, an impressive assortment of established country stars, such as Mel Tillis, also moved to the town. They hoped to avoid the hardships of touring by letting audiences come to them. By the mid-1990s, Branson had thirty-five music theaters and drew 5 million visitors annually. Within a few years, the annual number of visitors had reached 7 million. By then, Branson had more theater seats (almost sixty-two thousand) than New York City's Broadway and offered as many as eighty shows daily.[76]

Despite its soaring popularity, country music did not constitute a new musical core in American life. Indeed, it was the splintering of such a core—which Tin Pan Alley had defined for the first half of the century—that increased country's leverage. The pattern resembled that in television, where, by the 1980s, fragmentation had reduced the networks' power and allowed new channels such as MTV to find audiences. And, just as network programs such as *Hill Street Blues* had prevailed despite relatively small audiences, so a variety of music forms flourished within an expanding, yet increasingly segmented, market. A respectable showing in any of those segments could reap considerable profits, especially given the growing number of media outlets. For that reason, corporations looking to capitalize on the spreading entertainment field could hardly ignore the lucrative possibilities of "alternative" music, which had included country.[77]

Country's triumph had been a long time coming but followed a familiar trajectory from entertainment's borders to the mainstream. Via radio shows like *The Grand Ole Opry,* post–World War II honky-tonks and nickelodeons, television programs such as *Hee Haw,* and crossover artists, the onetime hillbilly music had moved far from the amusement world's periphery. Part of that success mirrored the shift in the nation's politics to the right. In the late 1960s and early 1970s, the country music establishment had generally become a source of patriotic flag-waving, not so much supporting the policies behind the Vietnam War as celebrating service to country and opposing the antiwar protesters. The popular press made much of country's association with Richard Nixon's silent majority. By the 1980s, prominent country entertainers were often conspicuous in Republican gatherings, although country music's overall conservative appeal rested less on partisan politics than on the music's nostalgic images, connotations of simpler, wholesome lifestyles, and lyrics that addressed common citizens' daily lives in clear, understandable ways.[78]

Country's soaring popularity owed much to the music's ability to tap deeply rooted but contradictory cultural needs and ideals. It combined messages that were both hedonistic and pious, rebellious and God-fearing. It celebrated home and family at the same time that it offered images of escape and rambling. It preached the joys of both individualism and companionship. It welcomed the conveniences of technology but resisted its accompanying social changes. It could be romantic and fatalistic. Its roots were in rural America and the working class, but it increasingly found middle-class and upscale audiences in the suburbs. It was nostalgic yet aware of the excitements of modernity—elements that Garth Brooks combined superbly with his cowboy hat and clothes and rock-concert devices, including cordless microphones, fireworks, and even contraptions that allowed him to swing across the stage. Although country purists had long worried that the music's journey to the cultural center jeopardized its authenticity, country— like popular culture generally—had exhibited eclectic tendencies from the start. As one scholar wrote: "Country music ain't what it used to be . . . and it really never was." Corporate America's growing interest in country music only encouraged and facilitated crossover strategies.[79]

Demographics were also crucial. Just as the earlier population shift from rural to urban America had spread jazz, rock and roll, and country, the movement from city to suburb was particularly important in widening country music's base. Formerly the music of a relatively small number of white, working-class Southerners, it now attracted middle-class suburban residents. "No longer about one particular place," wrote a student of the phenomenon, "country music had become about *every* place." The collaboration of other entertainment forms in that transition was strikingly apparent in James Bridges's 1980 hit movie *Urban Cowboy*—as important for country music as John Badham's *Saturday Night Fever* had been three years earlier for disco. In both cases, John Travolta's role was pivotal. In *Urban Cowboy*, Travolta played a blue-collar worker in Houston's oil fields who sought nighttime escape at Gilley's, a club that included mechanical bulls, cowboy memorabilia, and country bands. The movie inspired the building of clubs like Gilley's all around the country, and Travolta's cowboy attire marked a fashion trend.[80]

In the country music capital of Nashville, a mixture of apple pie and designer shoes took hold—a combination similar to that which was transforming the National Association for Stock Car Auto Racing (NASCAR) from a Southern to a national phenomenon. No American sport had arguably grown faster. By the early twenty-first century, perhaps one-fourth of the U.S. population were NASCAR fans, courtesy of drivers like Dale

Earnhardt. A high school dropout from a small North Carolina mill town, Earnhardt became stock-car racing's superstar, the legendary "No. 3" whose fearless driving earned him the nickname "the Intimidator" before it took his life in the 2001 Daytona 500 race. He was a stereotypical good old boy, the tough individual who would not let anyone push him around. "The people who love him are the people who are told, every day, what to do and what not to do, and they've got all those rules and regulations to go by," said one analysis of racing. Earnhardt allowed them to play out their own fantasies of standing up to the system. A gruff, working-class hero with corporate savvy, he was instrumental in merging the sport's country heritage with modern merchandising. In 1999 alone, his several companies, including one that marketed his souvenirs, earned $26.5 million. His success story nevertheless suggested NASCAR's dilemma in trying to bridge what the sports writer Jeff McGregor called its "red-dirt past" and "gold lamé future"—a dilemma quite familiar to country music.[81]

Country music's growing appeal—like Earnhardt's—owed much to a blending of nostalgia, chic lifestyles, and the needs of aging baby boomers. The "new traditionalism," as the reporter Jon Pareles described country's nostalgic bent, reflected a desire for roots that demographic change was pulling up. The former Reagan speechwriter Peggy Noonan believed that baby boomers—getting older, feeling the burdens of greater responsibilities, and anxious about the future—turned to entertainments "because they are the only places we can imagine progress." In Noonan's opinion, she and other "white-collar boomers have recused ourselves from a world we never made." Significantly, by the mid-1990s, country fans were more educated, wealthier, and older than rock audiences. Two-thirds of them were between the ages of twenty-five and fifty-four. Garth Brooks's music thus resembled a "kind of mid-life ballad," as one writer characterized it, weaving "tales of love, heartache, family ties and middle-aged renewal." Feelings of loss and being lost had characterized country music from its origins, certainly. But, according to Pareles, the new traditionalism had a softer edge. It smacked more of Reagan-era images of an old-fashioned America with simple rules and clear choices. Because the images resulted from looking backward "through rose-colored binoculars," they soothed and reassured. The past resembled "just one more comfy stage set," wrote Pareles, convinced that the new traditionalists were less concerned with "the passing of a way of life than eager to borrow its aura."[82]

Pareles's telling insight was accurate enough but slighted many country fans' genuine desire for security, rootedness, and a sense of place. Although country music spoke vaguely of values and belonging, it also revealed an awareness of the difficulties of building strong, meaningful bonds and relationships. Like the antiromances elsewhere in entertainment, notable elements of country acknowledged family troubles and controversial social issues. Mary Chapin Carpenter's "House of Cards" thus warned of the dangers in a town where "on the surface it looked so safe / But it was perilous underneath." And Martina McBride's "Independence Day," which was the Country Music Association's song of the year in 1995, told of a battered woman who set fire to her house and husband. Just as important, some country stars exhibited lifestyles that defied traditional values. Top singers such as Tanya Tucker and Wynonna Judd bore children out of wedlock, for example. Others wrestled with divisive issues. Reba McIntyre's "She Thinks His Name Was John" addressed the subject of AIDS, while Garth Brooks's "We Shall Be Free" was about gay rights. Nor did Brooks hesitate to speak out elsewhere on sensitive political topics. "I think," he said, "the Republicans' big problem is that they believe family values are June and Walt and 2.3 children." To Brooks, however: "It means that if a set of parents are black and white, or two people of the same sex, or if one man or one woman acts as the parent, that the children grow up happy and healthy: that's what family values are."[83]

Still, much of the new country music was decidedly upscale and oblivious to social issues, as the popularity of Billy Ray Cyrus's video for "Achy Breaky Heart" in 1992 demonstrated. Wearing a body shirt instead of familiar western garb, Cyrus turned the song into a monster crossover hit. He also helped elevate old-style line dancing into a fad that drew thousands of new country fans to the burgeoning dance clubs, where tight-fitting designer jeans, short skirts, and cowboy hats and boots were on conspicuous display. The dances became so popular that The Nashville Network (TNN) regularly aired two shows, *Wildhorse Saloon* and *Club Dance,* showing customers keeping step with the newest country recordings. Young and old adults alike moved around the floor, keeping pace with songs that were typically about individual freedom and breaking loose, yet ironically following steps that were as prescribed as those of the seventeenth-century minuet. Cyrus and line dancing attested not only to country music's exploding crossover charm but also to its popularity in foreign markets such as Japan and Brazil.[84]

But, as before, when country moved into the pop market, some performers and fans fretted that the music was losing its way, falling victim to the Nashville establishment's preference for disposable songs and prettified, cloned performers. Johnny Cash reportedly asked Waylon Jennings: "Waylon, aren't you glad that you don't wake up every morning and sound like twenty-five other singers?" Travis Tritt complained that Billy Ray Cyrus was turning country into an "ass-wiggling contest." Under pressure from his own record company, Tritt apologized, but his impressions were far from unique. According to a reporter in 1996, most of country's big, new stars were "as safe and clean as the neighborhood mall." While the industry courted a teenage audience with singers such as Shania Twain, who showed off her statuesque figure with a halter top that revealed her bare midriff, Merle Haggard concluded that even Hank Williams would have trouble in the revamped country industry. Undoubtedly, such criticism partly reflected a changing of the guard as new entertainers moved into the spotlight. It also slighted the talents of some of the younger singers, such as Twain, Faith Hill, Patty Loveless, Clint Black, and Garth Brooks, whom one traditionalist dismissed as the "anti-Hank" Williams.[85]

There were, nevertheless, legitimate concerns that, by moving up the social ladder, country music threatened to leave behind its initial working-class constituency. "Are the hats, the boots, the pickup trucks, and the honky-tonking poses all that's left of a disintegrating culture?" wondered Cash. The country music scholar Bill Malone observed that the "middle-class lenses and sensibilities" of many of the young country singers had resulted in fewer "songs that reflect experiences lived close to the margins of economic insecurity or social unrespectability." Dwight Yoakam, one of the 1980s newcomers, agreed that Nashville's favored music was "much too smooth": "It's sterile. We have a chance to educate young people, put the record straight [with strong class-based messages]." Yoakam, Steve Earle, and several other of the younger country singers genuinely identified with the working class. John Anderson's 1994 song "Country 'til I Die" reminded listeners of the distance between common laborers and snobbish, privileged, professional classes who attended fancy parties. Anderson sang about an unsophisticated truck driver's inability to get a doctor to "treat a man in [his] condition." The doctor's prognosis gave the song's title its ironic twist because the driver would quite literally be "Country 'til I Die." In 1999, Larry McCordle recorded "Murder on Music Row," which country stars Alan Jackson and George Strait subsequently released as a duet cover. According to the song: "Someone killed country music, cut out its heart and soul. They got away with murder down on music row." Most Top 40 stations would not play the song. But, in 2000, the Country Music Association demonstrated the ability of the music establishment to market dissent, recognizing "Murder on Music Row" as the recorded event of the year.[86]

Country music was more than the Nashville establishment, however. For working-class communities, where honky-tonks were part of the social fabric, the music helped define a way of life. Granted, its basis was commercial, a creation of distant recording studios and singing stars. But how local people used it was another matter. For example, at Ann's Other Place, a roadside honky-tonk tavern in a small Texas town, the jukebox and live music provided backdrop for banter and socializing. The owner leaned several old guitars against the wall, and, according to ritual, any time someone started playing one of those instruments, the jukebox would be off. On occasion, a local singer there, or elsewhere, could receive the highest of praise: favorable comparison with an established country singer. "Better than

George Jones," someone might say. In various settings, local musicians could jam over beer, joking and talking. Although the jukebox music was a commodity, individuals appropriated it, relating it to their own experiences. One man, who was nursing a beer after work and listening to Patsy Cline recordings, commented: "If anybody told me that they were gonna stop country music tomorrow I'd possibly commit suicide. . . . You can relate to this shit." A woman who had just gone through a divorce listened wistfully to Alan Jackson's "Here in the Real World," which included the lines: "The boy don't always get the girl / here in the real world." She found the song deeply moving. "That's how it is," she observed sadly. In sum, the music was a source of meaning and identity to which blue-collar constituencies continued to stake their claims, making it in effect theirs: "*real* country."[87]

Hip-hop revealed many of the same dynamics and tensions as it ballooned into a huge business. Located at first on entertainment's edges, rap music prospered by the late 1980s as corporations recognized that even slums might produce gold. Starting out as a localized, noncommercial, spontaneous art, hip-hop had developed outside the attention of white society. Indeed, in the early 1980s, radio programmers displayed a striking disinterest in any kind of black music. Astoundingly, for three weeks in October 1982, as the music producer Steve Greenberg observed: "*Not one record by an African-American could be found in the Top 20 on Billboard's pop singles or albums charts—a polarization that had not occurred since the 1940s.*" Rap thus arose in a musical as well as an urban ghetto. But, in doing so, as various accounts pointed out later, it gave voice to "the underdeveloped country of the street"—"a whole nation of street-corner kids" who crafted their own culture as they wanted it, thereby exposing "the mythical America that Tin Pan Alley had done its best to cover up." It served as "young black America's television screen." Like neighborhood gossip and folktales, it provided an ongoing "offstage" commentary on inequities, injustices, and other social wrongs. In that sense, hip-hop was "a way for the people of the ghetto to make themselves heard," as the rapper Kurtis Blow said. The rappers themselves, according to another analogy, were "seeing eye dogs" trying to help a blind society find its way.[88]

Rap's commercial possibilities had been evident in 1979, of course, with the Sugarhill Gang's "Rapper's Delight." Subsequently, several other New York rappers, such as Kurtis Blow, had also begun to find substantial audiences, primarily with party-oriented recordings. In 1982, even though radio programmers and MTV continued to ignore rap, Grandmaster Flash and the Furious Five released their influential "The Message," a grimly realistic rendering of travails in the South Bronx. They articulated a sense of the anger and despair in black inner cities—"a world like a jungle," where "the bill collectors scare my wife," where a homeless woman resided "in a bag," and where kids—surrounded by poverty, drugs, and crime—"lived so fast and died so young." It "makes me wonder, / How I keep from going under," said Grandmaster Flash. At the end of the record, the police arrest the young black men, apparently for standing on the corner. "The Message" reached number four on the rhythm and blues chart and number eighty-seven on the pop chart. It also set a political tone for much of the rap that followed. Enhancing rap's aggressive social commentary were the rap videos, whose production accelerated in the mid-1980s, featuring inner-city settings that differed sharply from most rock videos—abandoned buildings, street corners, and playgrounds.[89]

By the mid-1980s, hip-hop was breaking through mainstream barriers. In 1986, Def Jam, the independent label that the hip-hop promoter Russell Simmons had cofounded two years earlier, signed a distribution arrangement with Columbia Records. Shortly thereafter, other tiny independents, resembling "ghetto trading outposts," struck similar deals with multinational conglomerates. "Time Warner [came] around to collect their money and check on their prostitutes in the darkness of the night," joked an associate of one fledgling company. In 1986, Run-D.M.C. signed a $1.5 million deal to promote the Adidas corporation's athletic clothing. That year, the rap trio released the album *Raising Hell*, which soared to fourth on the pop chart and eighth on the R & B chart. In one of the songs, "Walk This Way," Run-D.M.C. collaborated with the well-known rock group Aerosmith. For the first time, MTV recognized the significance of a rap group, playing the "Walk This Way" video time and again. But 1988 was the real breakthrough year. MTV started its first hip-hop music show. *The Source* became the first magazine to focus on hip-hop. *Billboard* established a rap singles chart. The Grammy Awards recognized a separate rap category. And the rap group Public Enemy's album *It Takes a Nation of Millions to Hold Us Back,* an outspoken treatment of such subjects as the crack cocaine epidemic, reached number one on the R & B chart and number forty-two on the pop chart.[90]

Hip-hop's soaring popularity inspired different rap styles. Some grew from the regional competition between New York City's "old school" and the West Coast's "new school." "Gangsta"—or "reality"—rap developed a particular notoriety because of its emphasis on urban gangs, violence, and drugs. In 1989, N.W.A. (Niggaz with Attitude), calling itself the "world's most dangerous group," released the album *Straight Outta Compton* with the specific goal of "making a name for Compton and L.A.," as the band member MC Ren explained. Sounds of automatic weapons fire and police sirens punctuated such tracks as "Fuck tha Police."[91]

Significantly, the bulk of consumers of the controversial gangsta rap were white youths in the suburbs who found rap's rebelliousness and general antiauthoritarianism appealing. Although such youths' alienation from the mainstream culture often lacked a well-articulated political viewpoint, it favored oppositional attitudes. Like jazz in the 1920s or rock and roll in the 1950s, hip-hop tapped many middle-class white youths' interest in outsiders' forbidden perspectives and lifestyles. But, like 1830s minstrel shows, the black mask also contained a class element, allowing disaffected young white males from low-income housing and dead-end jobs to hit back. "There's a million of us just like me," rapped Eminem (Marshall Mathers)— himself a product of shabby settings, including Detroit's "gutter slums"— "who cuss like me / . . . who dress like me / walk, talk, and act like me." Robert Van Winkle, a white, middle-class rapper, was so determined to prove his "street" credentials that he posed as the product of a broken, ghetto home who had almost died in a gang fight. Marketing himself as Vanilla Ice, he claimed credit for his big hit "Ice, Ice Baby," although a black person, Mario Johnson, wrote and produced the music. One journalist described Van Winkle as "the Pat Boone of rap."[92]

Rap's growing popularity predictably encountered resistance on several fronts. Echoing earlier objections to jazz and rock and roll, some people within the mainstream music industry doubted that rap constituted music at all. They could only wince at the rap producer Hank Shocklee's assertion: "Music is nothing but organized noise." Another producer, Eric Sadler, observed that engineers "live by certain rules": "They're like, 'You can't do that. You don't want a distorted sound, it's not right, its's not correct.' With Hank (Shocklee) and Chuck (D) it's like, 'Fuck that it's not correct, just do this shit.' . . . You hear the shit cracklin', that's the sound we're lookin' for." The music corporations initially wavered over how to deal with rap, which drew criticism from much of mainstream society. But the solution was ultimately clear: "Does it sell? Well, sell it, then." Still, the major recording companies tended to focus on retail distribution and leave most of the production to small, "street-savvy" independent labels that typically reflected the vision of one or two people. With only $4,000 in 1984, for example, Russell Simmons and Rick Rubin had launched Def Jam Records, recording L. L. Cool J's "I Need a Beat" for $700. When that record sold over 100,000 copies, Columbia eagerly signed a $600,000 distribution deal, boosting Def Jam into a rap power. In 1997—by which time rap constituted over 9 percent of a music industry worth more than $12.5 billion—the British conglomerate EMI Records paid $100 million for half of Priority Records. Twelve years earlier, Priority had made less than $1 million. "Cause it's all about money, ain't a damn thing funny," as Grandmaster Flash and the Furious Five had said in "The Message."[93]

In yet another replay of the early opposition to jazz and rock and roll, rap's opponents attacked its language and images. Blues and rock and roll singers had earlier relied on innuendo and double entendres, but rappers freely used the infamous "F" word, explicit sexual references, and graphic descriptions of mayhem. ("I grabbed my AK[-47], my 16[-millimeter], my baby Mac [10], threw a 9[-millimeter] in the small of my back," rapped Ice-T as he described looking for a life to take. "Then we spot him, Evil E shot him, dead in the face to make sure we got him.") Critics of such rap violence sometimes betrayed a double standard. Insofar as rap provided yet another version of "true-crime pulp fiction" or short "action scenarios," as one writer noted, it resembled much of American entertainment. Rapper Schoolly D raised a pertinent question: "If Rambo can tell a story . . . and Dirty Harry . . . why can't I tell [mine]?"[94]

Some African Americans nevertheless feared that gangsta rap in particular not only sent the wrong messages to black children but also encouraged old stereotypes about knife-wielding Zip Coons that dated back to the nineteenth-century stage. Public Enemy's Chuck D favored a different historical analogy, one that linked rap to earlier subversive critiques of power such as slave tales and the blues: "It's nothin' / We ain't did before." Yet he too was apparently nervous about perpetuating ugly stereotypes. "Ten years ago," he said in 1998, "I called rap music black America's CNN. My biggest concern now is keeping it from becoming the Cartoon Network."[95]

During the late 1980s, a growing public outcry against rap mobilized authorities to take action, threatening to arrest performers such as Ice-T and N.W.A. in venues ranging from Detroit and Cincinnati to Columbus, Georgia. In May 1990, a U.S. district court judge in Florida ruled that the lyrics of 2 Live Crew's 1989 *As Nasty as They Wanna Be* were obscene. Politicians also weighed in. Sixty members of Congress protested Ice-T's "Cop Killer," whose lyrics President George H. W. Bush described as "sick." In 1992, the Democratic presidential candidate Bill Clinton criticized rapper Sister Souljah.[96]

Such attacks played out against a backdrop involving the tenuous relation between politics and popular culture. Franklin Roosevelt had, of course, made excellent use of radio. Dwight Eisenhower had filmed TV spots during his 1952 presidential campaign, although he could not believe that "an old soldier should come to this." His opponent, Adlai Stevenson, asserted that politics "isn't soap opera, this isn't Ivory Soap versus Palmolive." That same year, the vice presidential candidate Richard Nixon had salvaged his political career by delivering his famous "Checkers" TV address. John F. Kennedy had made excellent use of television. It was Ronald Reagan, however, who really demonstrated the power of the media. "The Ronald Reagan Show" ran on "all major networks, 1967–1989," as the TV analyst Steven Stark wrote. The biographer Lou Cannon believed that, for Reagan, the presidency was "the role of a lifetime." Reagan did not have to appear on entertainment programs, said the Vermont governor, Howard Dean, "because he *was* the show." Partly because Reagan was a difficult act to follow, his successor, George Herbert Walker Bush, used the media reluctantly. "I am not Ronald Reagan," he told his speechwriters. "I can't give a ten speech. Give me an eight and maybe I'll make it come out a five." The Bush administration was slow even to capitalize on talk radio, even though stridently partisan hosts such as Rush Limbaugh were fueling the so-called Republican revolution. As Bush's press secretary, Marlin Fitzwater, recalled: "There was no sense of [talk radio] as a tool. We didn't recognize what was happening." Indeed, most of Bush's advisers viewed entertainment hosts as little more than carnival barkers. Bush himself at one point dismissed NBC television's *Today* program as "some weird talk show."[97]

When Bill Clinton ran successfully for the presidency in 1992, on the other hand, he made much of his popular culture credentials in order to appeal to younger voters and distinguish himself from the old-fashioned Bush. He was a guest, for example, on radio talk programs such as Don Imus's. At one point, he appeared on MTV to answer questions from a panel of young people. Donning sunglasses, he also played a saxophone on Arsenio Hall's late-night entertainment show, launching into Elvis Presley's old hit "Heartbreak Hotel." Indeed, Clinton publicly identified himself with Presley on many occasions. "You know," Clinton told a Nashville audience, "Bush is always comparing me to Elvis in sort of unflattering ways. I don't think Bush would have liked Elvis very much, and that's just another thing that's wrong with him." Besides invoking the memory of Elvis to show that he—unlike Bush—was hip, Clinton used a variety of nontraditional media outlets to reach audiences. In that regard, he was like Ross Perot, who announced his presidential candidacy on CNN's *Larry King Live*. When Clinton spoke at the annual Radio and Television Correspondents Dinner following his election victory, he indicated that the talk show host "Larry King has liberated me from you by giving me to the American people directly."[98]

But, even as conservative politicians such as the Georgia representative Newt Gingrich shrewdly used the media to forge the much-heralded Republican revolution of the 1990s, they were quick to use popular culture as a political foil, claiming that the media belonged to "elites" and "liberals." Ironically, the end of the Cold War, which many conservatives attributed solely to Reagan, owed much to the hated counterculture. Speaking of the collapse of communism in Eastern Europe, the Czech president, Václav Havel, gave credit to the Velvet Underground, an unconventional, 1960s-rooted rock group fronted by Lou Reed that inspired a host of punk and avant-garde bands. In Eastern Europe, another recognized hero of the anti-

Communist revolution was the Mothers of Invention's innovative Frank Zappa, whose appearance fit the stereotypical image of a "long-haired hippie freak" and who fiercely resisted efforts to censor music.[99]

In any case, by the 1990s, media bashing constituted a choice political strategy. President George H. W. Bush thus publicly criticized *The Simpsons* for preaching antifamily values. "We need a nation closer to the Waltons than the Simpsons," he said. Vice President Dan Quayle objected to the sitcom *Murphy Brown* (1988–98). In the series, the broadcast news reporter Murphy Brown had a baby that resulted from a brief fling with her ex-husband. Quayle, speaking a few days later about threats to the American family, rebuked the program: "It doesn't help matters when prime-time TV has Murphy Brown, a character who supposedly epitomizes today's intelligent, highly paid professional woman, mocking the importance of fathers by bearing a child alone and calling it just another lifestyle." In 1995, Senate Majority Leader Bob Dole, who a year later would be the Republican presidential candidate, warned that "our popular culture threatens to undermine our character as a nation."[100]

However stridently politicians objected to the violent, confrontational rhetoric of what *Time* called "America's foul-mouthed culture," they nevertheless helped set the ugly tone. They facilitated the spread of the very culture they attacked. Political debate became increasingly divisive and rancorous, encouraging an "in-your-face" meanness. Indeed, one database search revealed that published articles between 1985 and 1995 on the subject of meanness in America jumped from 171 to almost 2,000. Negative campaigning reached new levels of vituperation. In one congressional campaign ad for the Republican Tom LeFever, the face of the incumbent Democrat, Vic Fazio, was changed to make it look like that of a man who had brutally killed a little girl. "It was guerrilla war," said the Minnesota congressman Vin Weber about the 1994 midterm elections and Newt Gingrich's strategy of pillorying the Democrats. "I don't think we [Republicans] could have won the House in 1994 without those sorts of tactics. But the victory came at a price, and the price was a loss of civility. And we are paying for that now." The "politics of blame" provided a convenient strategy for displacing problems onto someone else, typically well-chosen culprits. "I admit it," said the former Dan Quayle aide William Kristol, "the liberal media were never that powerful, and the whole thing [blaming the liberal media] was often used as an excuse by conservatives for conservative failures."[101]

The growing politicization of radio talk shows encouraged the breakdown in civility as hosts such as Rush Limbaugh hurled invectives at "feminazis," liberals, and Democrats. Limbaugh, with an estimated 20 million radio listeners weekly and a late-night television show that was syndicated on 250 stations, so influenced the Republican congressional victories in

1994 that the representatives dubbed him "Majority Maker." Vin Weber referred to "the Limbaugh Congress."[102]

Scurrilous talk raged across the airwaves and political discussions. One senator warned that President Clinton had "better have a bodyguard" if he entered the senator's state. Another Clinton opponent described the president as "the enemy of normal Americans." The TV evangelist Jerry Falwell advertised a videotape, *The Clinton Chronicles,* charging Clinton with dealing drugs, conspiring to murder his enemies, and conducting treasonous activities with the Russians. Such visceral hatred of Clinton flowed from convictions that the United States was engaged in nothing less than a cultural war. At the 1992 Republican convention, Pat Buchanan, a former Richard Nixon speechwriter who had himself been a presidential candidate that year, contended that religious warfare would determine the nation's soul. "It is a cultural war as critical to the kind of nation we shall be as the Cold War itself. . . . We must take back our cities, and take back our culture, and take back our country." The House majority leader, Dick Armey (R-TX), referred to the Massachusetts representative Barney Frank as "Barney Fag." The talk radio host G. Gordon Liddy instructed listeners on how they should shoot federal agents.[103]

An unsettling congruity existed between political and entertainment trends. In both spheres, malice and mean-spiritedness trumped politeness, respect, and generosity. Previously, television studio interview shows—such as those of Mike Douglas, Merv Griffin, and Dick Cavett—had been, with few exceptions, civil and friendly. But, in the late 1980s, "confrontainment," or "garbage and guts TV," proliferated rapidly. *The Morton Downey Jr. Show* (1988–89) was a harbinger of what was to come. Downey urged his audience to jeer guests. "If it moves, scream at it," he urged. He baited people, saying, "Zip it, puke breath," or, "Suck my armpit." While the audience chanted gleefully, "Mort! Mort! Mort!" he hurled insults, using such labels as "pabulum puker," "fathead," and "slime."[104]

In the 1990s, Downey-style television interview shows flourished. Indeed, talk show hosts apparently wanted "to see who could stoop the lowest and make the most noise doing it," according to one media analyst. Geraldo Rivera's confrontational show included an incident in which a neo-Nazi broke Rivera's nose during a chair-throwing fight. "It's rock-and-roll television," Rivera explained. Working like a sideshow barker in the old freak shows, Rivera focused on the bizarre and shocking: "Women who became men! They went from girly to burly! Today's *Geraldo!*" The formats of such shows resembled those in tabloid newspapers and the "true confession" magazines. Another TV talk show host, Sally Jessy Raphael, laughed: "Nobody wants to watch anything that's swarmy or tabloid or silly or unseemly—except the audience." Jerry Springer, who hosted such episodes as "Teen Transsexuals," "I'm Pregnant by My Brother," "My

Daughter Is a Teen Prostitute," and "My Boyfriend Turned Out to Be a Girl!" said that his program was "*about* outrageousness, outrageous relationships." The shows were often rowdy, loud rejections of decorum.[105]

"Trash television" drew a host of critics. William Bennett, the secretary of education under Ronald Reagan, urged advertisers to boycott programs that "parade perversity into our living rooms." Senator Joseph Lieberman, a Connecticut Democrat, believed that such shows were "degrading our culture" and making deviancy respectable. Bad taste and bad behavior were symptomatic of "demean streaks," as one newspaper headline put it, using words that implicitly suggested analogies with rap music.[106]

From another angle, however, such criticism betrayed a double standard. The comedian George Carlin observed that so-called respectable people made far too much of manners and civility. Recalling American history, he noted how members of Congress had displayed an unctuous politeness with each other during times when they and the larger society condoned slavery and Indian removal.[107]

Criticism of trash TV, as well as of rap music and other raucous forms of entertainment, often betrayed a class bias. TV talk show audiences, for example, reportedly had less money and education than did the larger population as a whole. On the more upscale *20/20*, the cohost Barbara Walters could discuss the bulimia of England's Princess Diana, but the problems and opinions of poorer people were not worthy of attention. "As long as they speak the King's English, we say it's OK," complained Jerry Springer. "But then you get someone who isn't wealthy, who doesn't have title or position, and they come on and talk about something that's important to them—all of a sudden we call that trash." Or, as the English horror writer Clive Barker aptly put it: "There's a tired old distinction that bright people will not be corrupted, but that the working classes will." Charges that trash TV constituted what William Bennett described as "cultural rot" amused Sally Jessy Raphael. She argued that moral distinctions were very clear on her show, a fact that was apparent when the audience responded to "bad" people with jeers and sympathized with victims. In that regard, the shows were, perhaps, comparable to neighborhood gossip or newspaper scandals in terms of reinforcing a community's moral values. "Like the witch doctor," argued the anthropologist Sally Engle Merry, "the media thus transform private suspicions into a public consensus."[108]

The effects of such shows were, nevertheless, debatable. Like the old freak shows, they could inflict cruelties on unsuspecting people. Humiliating such people in front of millions of viewers hardly constituted a public service. Yet it was possible to argue that the "talking tabloids" fit a longstanding popular culture tradition of challenging high culture and evoking elite opposition. "The battle over pop raunch reflects a crucial fissure in American social and political culture," observed *Time*'s Richard Corliss in

1990. Criticism of culture's rougher elements "largely ignores the ghetto, where the black underclass has built its own furious culture on the slag heap." Such criticism, according to Corliss, "discounts much of the young white working class, in tattered towns and trailer parks, who feel left out of bland, sitcom America."[109]

From this perspective, the "tabloid culture"—no less than the "street knowledge" of N.W.A.—articulated the hopes and fears of people who stood on society's margins because of their class, race, age, sexual preference, or educational limitations. The rapper Ice-T asked: "If there wasn't rap, where would the voice of the eighteen-year-old black male be? He would never be on TV, he ain't writin' no book. He is not in the movies." Like rap music, talk shows thus arguably had a democratizing influence. "On talk shows, whatever their drawbacks," contended the writer Ellen Willis, "the proles get to talk." As voices from society's underside, talk show participants represented what the media scholar Elayne Rapping described as "an emotional vanguard blowing the lid off the idea that America is anything like the place Ronald Reagan pretended to live in." In that regard, tabloid talk shows destabilized the views of powerful elites by implicitly positing multiple truths and lifestyles. And, because the shows highlighted individual differences, they were, in fact, statements of tolerance. "Norms become subject to challenge, interrogation, criticism, and therefore change," according to another cultural observer.[110]

Measuring such change—let alone the proletariat's influence—was, nevertheless, difficult. Although rap music expressed the voice of the streets, the black feminist writer bell hooks warned: "It gives people a false sense of agency. It gives them a sense that they have power over their lives when they don't." Similarly, the real winners of TV's rowdy talk shows were media tycoons such as Murdoch.[111]

Still, by the mid-1990s, the tabloid talk shows may have helped account for a curious phenomenon: despite a loud public outcry for tougher stands against crime generally, juries in notable instances were willing to find extenuating circumstances for criminal acts. In the face of reports that the Menendez brothers in California were victims of child abuse, two hung juries could not find them guilty of murdering their parents. Similarly, a jury acquitted Lorena Bobbitt of cutting off her husband's penis on the grounds that he had long abused her. "Lorena Bobbitt for Surgeon General" read some buttons outside the courtroom. The ABC analyst Jeff Greenfield wondered whether, by focusing on personal situations, the confessional formats of such shows as Sally Jessy Raphael's and Oprah Winfrey's encouraged the growth of a culture of therapy and empathy. *Oprahization* was the term that the California attorney general, Dan Lungren, applied to growing difficulties in securing convictions: "People have become so set on the *Oprah* view, they bring that into the jury box with them."[112]

Certainly, a confessional style marked much entertainment, whether it involved Sally Jessy Raphael's working-class guests or celebrities' tell-all books. Many of the talk show hosts openly discussed their own personal lives. Geraldo Rivera entitled his 1991 autobiography *Exposing Myself.* Jenny Jones acknowledged having six breast-implant operations. Ricki Lake maintained that she and her husband got "naked two hours after we met." Oprah Winfrey admitted to her audience that she had used cocaine. According to one executive producer, the willingness of the hosts "to open up," as friends would to each other, endeared them to audiences who appreciated the candor and sharing. In the case of Winfrey, such endearment contained a powerful racial subtext. As the talk show producer Belma Johnson pointed out: "We're really going to see the effect of this in the next generation, a whole generation of kids who grew up watching their mothers idolize a black woman." Still, the unsettling possibility remained that the confessional style was producing "a nation of peeping Toms," as another observer concluded. "We're voyeurs on one side of the window, and exhibitionists on the other." Here were the roots of reality TV, which, by the end of the 1990s, characterized a barrage of programs. On the Fox show *Who Wants to Marry a Millionaire,* for instance, the emergency-room nurse Darva Conger won the competition to marry the wealthy Rick Rockwell. After promptly annulling the marriage on the grounds that she valued her privacy, she posed nude for *Playboy* magazine and opened an Internet site about herself.[113]

The intensity of such fascination with personal revelations may well have been a by-product of the Cold War's end. After decades, the dreaded Communist threat was no longer something to fear. Some people guessed that this would be a mixed blessing. "One of the worst things that could happen is the fall of communism," the comedian Lenny Bruce had predicted, "because we're going to have to turn inward. We're going to hate our Congress, hate our Supreme Court, hate our president, hate our mayor. . . ."[114]

With the Cold War over, enemies that had been "out there" were now closer to home. Daytime television was obsessed with stories of betrayal and victimization. From magazines to the news, the media's tabloid fixation on the private lives of public people infused an insatiable celebrity culture with even more scandal and slander. Political nastiness and scapegoating fueled cynicism about government. "Today, we're dealing with a general coarsening of life," said one observer. "People are suspicious, hostile, paranoid." The approaching millennium added to the uneasiness. Even the 1990s general economic upturn had a paradoxical effect. According to the horror novelist Stephen King, improved economic conditions meant that Americans had more opportunity to indulge themselves by exploring the dark side.[115]

Horror moved into the 1990s entertainment mainstream with a vengeance. In January 1992, the Academy Award for best movie went to a slasher film, Jonathan Demme's 1991 *The Silence of the Lambs*. In the film, the serial killer Hannibal Lecter helped the FBI agent Clarice Starling apprehend another killer by getting her to explore her own inner demons. Hannibal then escaped prison to continue his own murderous lifestyle. The common theme in a small flood of popular thriller movies—including *Seven* (David Fincher, 1995), *Scream* (Wes Craven, 1996), *Scream 2* (Wes Craven, 1997), and *I Know What You Did Last Summer* (Jim Gillespie, 1997)—was that people should "be afraid, very afraid, and of nothing so much as yourself." Evil did not lurk in some easily identifiable monster; instead, it resided next door in very human form or in one's own scary predilections. By the end of the 1990s, several television series conveyed the same theme, particularly *The X-Files, Millennium,* and *Profiler.* "You caught the bad man?" asked the small daughter of the detective in *Millennium.* "I'm not so sure the bad man can be caught," he replied. The horror genre, according to one student of the phenomenon, pointed to "frightening realities in the real world that cannot be easily resolved. They provide lightning rods for free-floating anxieties—and we live in very anxious times."[116]

Stephen King, one of the most popular writers ever, was particularly adept at finding horror in life's mundane details. By the early 1990s, some 90 million copies of his books were in print. "There are apparently two books in every American household," quipped another horror writer, Clive Barker. "One of them is the Bible and the other one is probably by Stephen King." References to familiar brand names, song lyrics, magazines, and television programs filled his books, making them, in King's words, the "literary equivalent of Big Mac and fries." King compared himself to a brand name—the "Green Giant of horror fiction." His pop culture reference points were as much a part of his own life as they were of his novels. Born in Maine in 1947, he had as a child "often felt unhappy and different, estranged from kids my age." He sought escape through such outlets as EC Comics. In the attic, he had discovered a cache of pulp fiction that his father had collected before deserting the family when Stephen was age two. By the time Stephen was around twelve, he had started sending stories to *Famous Monsters* and pulp magazines. In King's subsequent best-selling novels, terror rested in the quotidian. "It is when the shopping cart is almost full," wrote the horror analyst David Skal, "that Stephen King inevitably brings on the newest shock or monster." He established his little shop of horrors "next door at the 7-11" convenience store, as another reader put it. Horror, in King's late-twentieth-century America, worked off an awareness that everyone might be trapped in unchangeable circumstances.[117]

King's fiction not only addressed some of the era's cultural angst but also highlighted the publishing world's eagerness to favor established best-selling authors, to the detriment of lesser-known writers. At the major publishing houses, financial and marketing people exerted greater control over which manuscripts got into print. New profit targets rose to 12–15 percent—far above the 4 percent after taxes that publishers had traditionally hoped to gain. Like the movie industry's quest for blockbusters, publishers in effect pursued franchise authors. Publishing a King novel was like winning the lottery. In hot pursuit of that lottery by the 1990s, sprawling conglomerates were taking over independent publishing houses. Gerard Howard, an editor at W. W. Norton, described the growing tensions within the publishing industry between "its two classic functions": educating and making money. "The heart of darkness at the center of today's publishing world," Howard lamented, "is a flashy, disorienting environment, a combination hall of mirrors, MTV video, commodities pit, cocktail party, soap opera, circus, fun house, and three-card monte game."[118]

Howard could just as easily have been describing the world of sports. Media influences, Reagan-era policies, and market imperatives vied with the mythical appeal of unsullied athletic heroes and competition. In the process, sport became a mammoth enterprise. Ron Wolf, the general manager of professional football's Green Bay Packers, fretted: "At some point the Super Bowl no longer became a game, but it became a show. And from that, football no longer became a game, it became a business." Professional football and many other sports had long been businesses, of course, but never such colossal corporate ventures. As commercialism swept over the sports world, virtually every aspect of athletics became a corporate commodity—from stadiums and college football bowl games bearing corporate names to NASCAR drivers and automobiles covered with corporate logos; from athletes' shoes to team uniforms; from sponsored halftime reports and televised replays to basketball's phenomenal Michael Jordan, whose product endorsements included McDonald's, Coke, Wheaties, Gatorade, and Hanes underwear; from the Dallas Cowboys' $40 million, ten-year contract in 1995 with Pepsi Cola as Texas Stadium's official soft drink to the National Collegiate Athletic Association's $1 million deal that allowed Rawlings Sporting Goods to stamp its logo on the tournament basketballs.[119]

In this intensified commercialization of sports, television once again played a pivotal role. TV brought more sports to more people than ever before, and it poured massive amounts of money into athletics. It sparked a labor upheaval in professional sports as athletes sought a fairer share of the spiraling television revenues that teams received. And it turned professional football's Super Bowl into an unofficial American holiday. No TV program attracted as many viewers. On Super Bowl weekends, Americans held more at-home parties and fewer weddings than at any other time of the year. Only on Thanksgiving did they consume more food than they did during Super Bowl gatherings.[120]

More important for sports generally, television made a wide variety of athletic events more accessible than ever before. The breakthrough came in the 1980s when several media entrepreneurs targeted niche audiences among sports fans. In 1976, Ted Turner had started using cable to transmit from his local WTBS independent station the games of his professional teams: the Atlanta Braves in baseball and the Atlanta Hawks in basketball. In 1984, seeking inexpensive programming for his "superstation," Turner sold a time slot to Vince McMahon, who wanted a larger audience for his World Wrestling Federation (WWF). McMahon admitted that professional wrestling was staged and did not represent true competition. Proudly, he said that he was in "the entertainment business." On his roster of colorful wrestlers was a former rock musician, Terry Bollea, who advertised himself as Hulk Hogan. The McMahon-Turner alliance was short-lived, however, because of personality and financial disagreements. Turner purchased the smaller National Wrestling Alliance, renaming it World Championship Wrestling (WCW), and challenged McMahon's WWF for a rapidly swelling audience. An estimated 70 percent of that audience had household incomes of under $40,000; 75 percent had no more than a high school education. One-fifth of fans were under age eighteen. Although the fan base was hardly upscale, by 1995 the WCW and WWF were grossing over $110 million from cable television pay-per-view programs. Four years later, the WWF alone was pulling in over $400 million from retail sales of merchandise. In the meantime, wrestlers like Hulk Hogan became entertainment celebrities.[121]

But the biggest moment for sports television came with the establishment in 1979 of the Entertainment and Sports Programming Network (ESPN). The brainchild of Bill Rasmussen, ESPN emerged from the small town of Bristol, Connecticut, and offered all-sports coverage around the clock. To fill the time, ESPN initially scurried to find sufficient athletic action, covering such sports as college wrestling and slow-pitch softball. Within roughly two decades, however, ESPN was responsible for almost one-fourth of all televised sports in the United States. The venture was so successful that soon a second network, ESPN2, emerged, covering such events as extreme sports and beach volleyball.[122]

In the early 1980s, ESPN virtually saved professional basketball. At the time, seventeen of twenty-three franchises were going broke, CBS was broadcasting only a few National Basketball Association (NBA) games, and advertising revenues rested "somewhere between mud wrestling and tractor pulling," as a league official admitted. One sportswriter told the NBA's commissioner, David Stern: "Nobody wants to watch ten black guys in short pants running up and down the court." ESPN nevertheless helped rebuild interest in the game and lift the NBA to new heights. The first step was to provide unprecedented coverage of college basketball, especially concerning the rise of two players—Indiana State's Larry Bird and Michigan State's Magic Johnson. The second step was to follow Bird's and Johnson's moves into the professional ranks. In 1982, ESPN started broadcasting NBA games.[123]

For universities with big-time athletic programs, television's expanded sports coverage was a cash cow. The National Collegiate Athletic Association (NCAA) negotiated lucrative TV packages but incurred the wrath of powerhouse programs that resented sharing revenues with smaller schools and conferences. In 1976, sixty-one of the major programs established the College Football Association (CFA) to gain more financial leverage. As Notre Dame's Edmund Joyce said: "We must never forget that we are in competition with the pros for the entertainment dollar."[124]

To strengthen their bargaining position and protect the established male athletic programs, the larger schools took advantage of the Reagan administration's deregulation policies. When the administration indicated in 1981 that it would review federal guidelines regarding Title IX, athletic directors were delighted. Tom Hansen, the NCAA's assistant executive director, applauded the administration's goal "to get government out of our lives, to reduce regulations." According to Hansen, the Office of Civil Rights "tries to bluff and scare you. They've been out there counting showerheads and locker stalls." Many of the traditional athletic powers hoped to end such intrusions into universities' "private" matters. Opposition to Title IX grew within the backlash against the feminist movement. At Notre Dame, Edmund Joyce resented the "militant women" who were engaged in an "irrational campaign" against football because the game allegedly proved male superiority.[125]

The quest for revenues trumped equal opportunity. As the *Houston Chronicle* summed up the issue, a "wish for fairness on the one hand" and a "devotion to capitalism on the other" produced a real dilemma. But the paper had no doubt which imperative was greater: the United States "never rewarded anyone, no matter how hard he or she worked, for producing a product void of market appeal."[126]

More than ever, the market became sports' driving force. Americans had long heralded the virtues of the free market system, but many now viewed its powers as almost magical. In late 1989, for example, when the wall dividing Berlin came down, the publisher of Harlequin Romances stationed representatives at one point to distribute 720,000 of the company's paperbacks. With the collapse of the Soviet Union, *Geraldo* promptly became the first U.S. television program that aired daily in Moscow. Educators increasingly applied market formulas to education. As universities competed for students and funds, winning athletic teams became even more useful as marketing tools. One result was that big-time college football and basketball programs were little more than entertainment businesses in a high-stakes competition for dollars. The marketing of university logo products—on everything from sweatshirts and hats to caskets—soared to over $2 million in 1993. Athletic programs drew additional income when their teams wore a particular company's shoes. In that regard, no company was more successful than Nike. Founded in the 1960s by Phil Knight, Nike become a giant transnational business. Its recognizable "Swoosh" symbol represented a "Just Do It" lifestyle. After Knight had signed up individual sports stars—especially Michael Jordan—to promote Nike's shoes, he started contracting in 1989 with universities. He would pay large amounts of money if, for example, the football teams wore his shoes and placed the familiar "Swoosh" logo on their uniforms.[127]

Although the marketplace contained riches, it could also be fickle. In colleges, the pursuit of revenues too often encouraged dishonesty. As college athletic programs battled for visibility and money, a series of scandals erupted over issues such as player recruiting, academic cheating, and drug use. In the mid-1980s, the University of Alabama football coach, Bill Curry, declared: "The system is saying, do whatever it takes to win. It is saying, 'We'll make you rich, famous and put you on TV.'" In professional sports, the quest for profits encouraged teams to shift locations—the Rams from Los Angeles to Anaheim and then to St. Louis; the Colts from Baltimore to Indianapolis; the Raiders from Oakland to Los Angeles and then back to Oakland; the Cardinals from St. Louis to Phoenix; and the Browns from Cleveland to Baltimore. The loyalty of established fans in teams' original cities meant nothing. "Sorry, Oakland," said the *Los Angeles Times,* "but we'd like to have your Raiders." When a distressed Cleveland fan learned that the Browns were relocating, he compared the news to "finding out your best friend had terminal cancer." As the fifty-year-old franchise exited Cleveland, he said: "Today, it all ended and my best friend died." Cities, competing for the prestige of having professional franchises, built expensive new sport facilities and offered other inducements. The Kansas City mayor, Emanuel Cleaver, summed up how teams boosted a city's image and pride: "Without the Chiefs and the Royals, we'd be Omaha . . . Wichita . . . Des Moines."[128]

The marketplace also stirred disputes over how to divide up sports' resources. The grasping ruthlessness of professional football's owners shocked even the NFL commissioner, Pete Rozelle. Handshakes and verbal promises no longer held much meaning. "In many ways," said Rozelle, "the NFL reminds me of the Roman Empire." As football and baseball players watched team owners strike lucrative personal deals, particularly with television, resentments grew. When the athletes organized to alter inequities and assert their rights, bitter labor disputes resulted in strikes, walkouts, and lockouts. After major-league baseball players went on strike in 1981 and NFL players in 1982, many fans expressed dissatisfaction with what they saw as overpaid athletes who substituted greed for love of the game. "What's happened to our heroes?" asked *Sports Illustrated* in 1983. The 1994 baseball strike raised the question anew, eliminating the World Series, spilling over into the next season, and lasting for 234 days.[129]

Despite fans' disgruntlement, athletics boomed in popularity. Michael Jordan dazzled fans with sheer brilliance on the basketball court. The 1998 home run race between Mark McGwire and Sammy Sosa, during which both broke the existing record of sixty-one (Sosa with sixty-six, McGwire with seventy), generated renewed enthusiasm for baseball. The soccer star Mia Hamm provided young females with a scintillating role model. In 2000, the St. Louis Rams, the worst team over the previous decade, clinched a Super Bowl victory on the game's final play. Their quarterback was Kurt Warner, a little-known backup player from a small school and the Arena Football League. In his autobiography, Warner, who had grown up in rural Iowa, tapped the continuing allure of athletics. "Sports were my refuge, my social life, and for a long time my salvation," he said. Such was the case for millions of youngsters in peewee leagues and in high schools around the nation. To ardent fans, sports dramatized the nation's cherished egalitarian values. "If you can hit .300 or score twenty points per game," as the journalist Larry Platt argued, "chances are you'll have an opportunity, no matter the color of your skin." The basketball star Charles Barkley argued that sports broke down racial lines. "In the locker room," he said, "we're all the same. It's all about merit." Sports, in many ways, had, indeed, undercut racial and gender stereotypes. According to Platt, when the NBA stars Magic Johnson and Isiah Thomas kissed playfully before the start of their teams' championship series, they showed that "the stereotype of the macho Neanderthal no longer applies to the modern athlete." Platt also noted that college football and basketball games brought a community together, uniting "town" and "gown" and providing "easily the most multicultural gathering on campus."[130]

In a sense, of course, the comedian Jerry Seinfeld joked correctly that, because players were typically not even from the cities in which their teams were located: "You're rooting for a shirt. You're cheering for laundry." Athletic teams nevertheless often provided, as the actor Dustin Hoffman observed, "a sense of community, of belonging, in a society where the glue seemed to be losing its grip."[131]

Popular culture frequently did exactly that—hold a community together—but, as always, the challenge was to understand how it did so. Television, for example, displayed a growing willingness in prime-time dramas to treat social themes in ways that appealed to older viewers and more commonly featured strong, independent female characters. But, on issues regarding criminal justice, TV conveyed a growing conservatism. As anxieties intensified about weakening social bonds, TV network dramas featuring heroic attorneys and law enforcement officials multiplied. Such shows evolved amid criticism of "liberal" judges, growing cries for the death penalty, and a strengthening victims' rights movement. Granted, moral ambiguities characterized exceptionally popular series such as the pioneering *Law & Order* and *CSI: Crime Scene Investigation* (both of which spawned several offshoots), *NYPD Blue,* and *The Practice.* Moreover, these shows' flawed protagonists typically wrestled with personal problems and weaknesses. Yet, ultimately, these series endorsed the nation's law enforcement institutions and encouraged a worldview in which alien Others jeopardized a community's fragile bonds. HBO's series *Oz,* which started in 1998, took a rare television look at what happens after courtroom sentencing. Its portrayal of prison life was stark and unsparing. But it implicitly condoned a harsh punitive ideology by showing the hopelessness of dealing with the fictional Oswald prison's incorrigibly depraved inmates, brutish men who were thoroughly unredeemable and fit only for lives behind bars.[132]

While television treatments of law and justice attested to a growing law-and-order mood that favored protecting the public through tougher sentencing, capital punishment, and more maximum-security prisons, entertainment's impact as a whole on Americans' sense of community was difficult to translate. As audiences fragmented, feelings of community became more amorphous than ever. Earlier, in the 1930s and 1940s, for instance, *Life* magazine and movies had appealed to a broad range of people. During the 1950s and 1960s, network television had done the same thing. As the twentieth century ended, however, identifying the hold of particular amusements on the public imagination was a more demanding task.

Still, in many respects, movies continued to entertain substantial audiences with creative films ranging from the animated *Toy Story* (John Lasseter, 1995) to the darkly satirical *American Beauty* (Sam Mendes, 1999). On network TV in the 1990s, millions of people got considerable pleasure from *Seinfeld,* the funny sitcom "about nothing." The genius of that inventive series was evident in the contradictory analyses of it. Some critics viewed it as "the worst, last gasp of Reaganite grasping, materialistic, narcissistic, banal self-absorption"; others saw it as subversive of Reaganesque "feel-good impulses" because its characters were basically trapped, making do with their hapless situations, and unable to reinvent themselves. Elsewhere, Coney Island, once a leading symbol of American amusements, still had its attractions. Although it had come to resemble a "poor man's" amusement place, it was showing signs of revitalization. Its legacy was mainly evident elsewhere, however, in the many other theme parks that dotted the country and especially in Las Vegas, a city whose one industry was entertainment.[133]

Indeed, while more and more of the nation became "congenial adjuncts of show business," as the media critic Neal Postman wrote in 1985, Las Vegas had arguably become its leading symbol. Like Coney Island in the early twentieth century, Las Vegas had worked to replace its unsavory "Sin City" image with a cleaned-up, "family-friendly" ambience. In 1989, the opening of the $700 million Mirage Hotel and Casino marked a turning point. "One after another," wrote the journalist Marc Cooper, "the old Rat Pack–era hotels were dynamited and in their place rose staggering Leviathans of modern, market-based entertainment." An economic boom turned Las Vegas into the fastest-growing city in the United States. Ironically, as Cooper observed, "most of those now crowding into Las Vegas are fleeing from an America where everyday life has become too much of a gamble"—the once-flourishing industrial centers of America's Rust Belt. Las Vegas's success also signified a vast change in attitudes. "What happens here, stays here," claimed a marketing campaign, thus reassuring those among the city's 36 million annual visitors who still looked to the city "as a leave-the-kids-at-home adult playground." Several decades before, in the 1950s, it had been impossible to use the word *pregnant* on *I Love Lucy;* by the century's end, America's increasingly open culture facilitated not only Las Vegas's knowing winks and glittery rise but gambling elsewhere as well. Across the country, cities and states battled budget shortfalls by legalizing lotteries, gaming tables, and slot machines. By the turn of the century, all but two states allowed some kind of gambling. In 2001 alone, according to Cooper, "51 million Americans—more than a quarter of the population over age 21—visited a casino." The revenues from more than 430 casinos reached $26.5 billion, "two and a half times what Americans spent on movie tickets, $5 billion more than they spent on DVDs and videos, and $3 billion more than on cosmetics and toiletries."[134]

By 2005, poker was one of the nation's hottest entertainments, reportedly attracting 50 million players in the United States alone. Once illegal in many places, and saddled with a reputation as shady, crooked, and dangerous, poker was finding widespread respectability. Big-time poker stars mixed with celebrities in a growing number of tournaments and television shows. The game's appeal among grassroots Americans was especially striking. "It's truly democratic," explained the poker columnist and author James McManus. "Race, fate, class, how big, or strong, or fast you are has nothing to do in determining the outcome." Luck, of course, hardly hurt, tapping the alluring outlaw tradition of get-rich schemes and risk taking that had long competed with the nation's celebration of hard work, merit, and prudence.[135]

Corporations, meanwhile, continued their own high-stakes gambling, forming mergers that threatened to turn America's entertainment into a massive mall with only several transnational owners. "The 1990s," wrote the *Baltimore Sun* reporter David Zurawik, "was a great decade for the corporate giants of the industry." Major media deals included a merger of Warner Communications and Time; the Walt Disney Company's purchase of Capital Cities/ABC; a fusion of Time Warner and the Turner Broadcasting System; and Viacom's purchase of CBS. In early 2000, America Online bought Time Warner for $183 billion, "the largest media deal in history," as the *Washington Post* observed. Among that conglomerate's massive holdings were Warner Brothers Pictures; Little, Brown publishers; Time-Life Books; magazines that included *Fortune, Life, Sports Illustrated, Vibe, People,* and *Sunset;* DC Comics; cable TV companies such as TNT, HBO, Cinemax, Black Entertainment Television, Court TV, the Home Shopping Network, and CNN; World Championship Wrestling; the Atlanta Braves and Atlanta Hawks athletic teams; recording companies ranging from Atlantic Records to Elektra and Columbia House; various theme parks, including 49 percent ownership of Six Flags; and the Book-of-the-Month Club. According to Zurawik, the coming battles would be "over who controls the wire or satellite link that brings everything from TV programs to telephone and computer data into our homes."[136]

Government's continuing deregulation policies facilitated the process of incorporation. The 1996 Telecommunications Act, for example, helped pave the way. Under federal law in 1972, no company could own more than seven FM and seven AM stations. Within twenty years, less stringent legislation allowed companies to own as many as forty stations nationwide. The 1996 law removed the total limit, although no company could own more than eight stations in any one market. "Within less than a year," reported the journalist Jeff Sharlet, "more than 1,000 mergers occurred; by 2000 four behemoths dominated the business." At the top was Clear Channel, which had started out in 1972 as one station in San Antonio but had become what one musician described as "the evil empire," owning 1,225 stations that reached 70 percent of the American public by 2003, and also owning or controlling "more live-music venues than any other company." Critics of Clear Channel described its canned music broadcasts and shrunken playlists as "robot radio." They worried, too, that the dominant company in the music business was in the hands of its founder, Lowry Mays, and his sons, who had no real interest in music. "If you don't realize that they've sent a chill throughout the creative community," said the former Reprise Records head Howie Klein, "you're living on another planet. Clear Channel pretty much can dictate what they want." Defenders argued that, prior to the 1996 legislation, over half the nation's radio stations were losing money and needed something to save them.[137]

The "entertainment economy" was full of promise and peril. It was no wonder that economic populists and moral guardians were anxious. On September 11, 2001, however, terrorist attacks on the United States suddenly posed new questions, some of which concerned the role of popular culture in a frightened nation.

EPILOGUE

Pop Culture in a Post-9/11 World

DURING THE SEVERAL MONTHS AND YEARS FOLLOWING THE terrorist attacks on September 11, 2001, Super Bowl advertisements and halftime shows provided a good guide to popular culture's varied responses to a frightening new world. In January 2002, less than five months after hijackers flew airplanes into the World Trade Center, parts of the Pentagon, and a remote Pennsylvania field, a solemn mood prevailed. "Maybe no Super Bowl will ever be as important as No. XXXVI because this one is about national confidence," proclaimed an editorial in *New Orleans* magazine. The game's initially planned Mardi Gras theme gave way to another: "Heroes, Hope, and Homeland." TV ads signaled America's resolve. The Budweiser Beer ad, for example, showed the company's famous Clydesdale horses stopping outside New York City, snorting in the cold air, and then bowing down to honor the over three thousand people who had died in the center's twin towers. Some ads simply included comments honoring the fallen. At halftime, the rock group U2 commemorated the dead by performing in front of a giant American flag and screen while the names of 9/11 victims scrolled down.[1]

Within two years, however, on February 1, 2004, the halftime show had returned to traditional showbiz glitz. The defining moment came when startled spectators suddenly had a fleeting glimpse of the singer Janet Jackson's breast. Outraged reactions on the part of viewers, politicians, and the Federal Communications Commission (FCC), which levied heavy fines on the network, indicated that another war was heating up: the familiar one over moral issues in areas such as entertainment.

By the 2004 presidential election, a widening cultural schism divided the electorate. A bloody war in Iraq, which the United States had invaded nineteen months earlier in the name of fighting terrorism, fractured the initial post-9/11 consensus. Exacerbating the fears of terrorism were anxieties about a perceived moral breakdown, which Janet Jackson's naked breast seemingly symbolized. Cultural watchdogs stepped up their offensive against "the Hollywood Left." From their perspective, much of American entertainment constituted what the conservative Dorothy Rabinowitz described as "an alternate revolting universe."[2]

In the months immediately after the 9/11 attacks, the entertainment industry rallied to the flag, as it had done during World Wars I and II. On September 21, some of the media's biggest names participated in a lengthy television appeal for funds to help victims' families, *America: A Tribute to Heroes,* carried over more than 320 national broadcast and cable networks. While dozens of stars performed, with neither introductions nor identification, celebrities in the background worked a phone bank to accept contributions. Major-league baseball games quickly added a new staple to the traditional seventh-inning stretch: the singing of "God Bless America" rather than the traditional "Take Me Out to the Ball Game." Some musicians recorded stirring appeals to national pride and strength. The country singer Toby Keith took only twenty minutes to write "Courtesy of the Red, White and Blue (the Angry American)" for an album that raced to the top of the country charts in 2002. "You'll be sorry you messed with the U. S. of A. / 'Cause we'll put a boot up your ass / It's the American way," sang Keith. "Take all the rope in Texas," he said in another song, "Find a tall oak tree / Round up all of them bad boys / Hang them high in the street for the people to see." Alan Jackson's poignant but less strident "Where Were You (When the World Stopped Turning)" received a Grammy Award as country's top song.[3]

As in World War II, the issue of patriotism and profits also surfaced. A number of companies used the emerging "war on terror" to pitch their products. This "market patriotism" raised questions about the appearance of trying to make money from a national tragedy. President George W. Bush's advice to the public hardly put such questions to rest. Bush urged citizens to continue shopping, going to Disneyland, and enjoying themselves so that terrorists would not think that they could disrupt the American lifestyle.

Against that backdrop, media people wrestled with what kinds of entertainment were now appropriate. There was considerable speculation that the horrible events of 9/11 would fundamentally alter the kinds of amusements the public required. Michael Eisner, head of Walt Disney, was convinced that "Hollywood and New York are going to change—and so will the nature of content" in films, television, and music. The comedian and talk show host Bill Maher believed that silly reality shows such as *Fear Factor*—in which competitors ate such things as pig rectums—"can't possibly work, now": "We seem to be a more sober nation." *Newsweek* agreed:

"Eating rats and bungee jumping doesn't seem so compelling anymore." A television vice president echoed that sentiment: "We are definitely moving into a kinder, gentler time," he predicted, confident that entertainment would necessarily be "more wholesome." The prevailing view appeared to be that popular culture would be less frivolous—shifting from "the great before" to "now."[4]

Some in the entertainment industry feared that many people might reject amusements as trivial and unsuited to a time of mourning and fear. But others recalled that, in previous national crises, Americans had sought respite from grim realities. If the past were any guide, according to the president of Twentieth Century–Fox Television, audiences would spurn "dark, gritty drama" in favor of "blue skies and escapist" fare.[5]

At first, caution prevailed regarding stories that featured terrorism, violence, or plots that might seem un-American. Miramax, for example, decided to delay from fall 2001 to fall 2002 the opening of Phillip Noyce's *The Quiet American,* based on Graham Greene's cynical 1955 novel about the United States in Vietnam. Harvey Weinstein at Miramax Films worried that a movie about "bad Americans" might seem "unpatriotic." Miramax finally approved a limited release of the movie, but only after the lead actor, Michael Caine, came to its defense. Because an Arnold Schwarzenegger movie, Andrew Davis's *Collateral Damage,* dealt with terrorism, Warner Brothers postponed its scheduled debut on October 7, 2001, until February 8, 2002. *The Sum of All Fears* (Phil Alden Robinson, 2002), based on a Tom Clancy best seller, was also on hold. Television was equally wary. NBC canceled a *Law & Order* miniseries about a biological attack on New York City. "I think every mainstream producer and director and studio and television executive will be very cautious about entering into a world where peoples' lives are in jeopardy," speculated the producer Brian Grazer. At the DreamWorks studio, an executive guessed that movies from the previous few years about nuclear threats and natural disasters had lost their appeal. "There are just some movies that you can't make from here on."[6]

Immediately after the 9/11 attacks, popular culture seemed particularly attentive to themes of togetherness and remembering. Many reviewers hailed Bruce Springsteen's album *The Rising* (2002) as an elegiac response to that fateful late-summer day. Television seemed ready to dish out "cultural comfort food." Whereas only three of the top thirty shows among eighteen- to forty-nine-year-olds at the beginning of the fall 2001 season were family sitcoms, that number had leaped to nine a year later. TV, overall, provided considerable family fare in series such as *Providence,* about a young female doctor who returned to her hometown to be with her widowed father, sister, and brother; *Ed,* about a New York City lawyer who took over a bowling alley in small-town Ohio so that he could court his high school girlfriend; *The Guardian,* about a corporate attorney who ended up helping children; *Judging Amy*, about a divorced female judge trying to build relationships with her daughter, brothers, and mother; and *American Dreams*, a nostalgic treatment of a family sticking together through the crises of the mid-1960s. The suspicious view of government institutions that had characterized programs such as *The X-Files* gave way to more positive treatments—for instance, *The West Wing*, about a likeable president and his staff; *First Monday*, a short-lived series concerning the Supreme Court; and three sympathetic shows about the Central Intelligence Agency, *Alias*, *The Agency*, and *24*. Patriotic themes dominated programs such as *Band of Brothers*, a miniseries celebrating America's World War II heroes that HBO aired in the fall of 2001.[7]

There was, nevertheless, a problem in attributing such programs to a new, post-9/11 mood: they had taken shape before that date. More than likely, they were simply products of yet another entertainment cycle. A fascination with World War II sacrifice had already been evident in the NBC news host Tom Brokaw's best-selling book *The Greatest Generation* (1998), the historian Stephen Ambrose's several popular volumes on the war, and the powerful Steven Spielberg movie *Saving Private Ryan* (1998). A number of movies had recently explored themes of love, sacrifice, and the importance of friendship—for example, the blockbuster hit *Titanic* (James Cameron, 1997), *Good Will Hunting* (Gus Van Sant, 1997), *As Good As It Gets* (James L. Brooks, 1997), and *Life as a House* (Irwin Winkler, 2001). And Bruce Springsteen had written "My City in Ruins"—the song on *The Rising* that appeared most directly to address the 9/11 tragedy—before the attacks. Moreover, television's fictional families might be wholesome, but they were not always conventional, and they often struggled with considerable anxieties, issues, and conflicts. TV series such as *Law & Order* frequently dealt with disturbing family problems.[8]

Within a relatively short time, it seemed that the immediate effects of 9/11 on entertainment were, in fact, negligible or, at best, ephemeral. As usual, amusements found considerable room for sex, violence, and spectacle. "People in the studios are going to continue to make the movies they think will make the most money and avoid the ones they think won't," concluded the film columnist Dave Poland one year after the attacks. "And right now, in the eyes of Hollywood, 9/11 is old news."[9]

Indeed, even worries about showing bloody, catastrophe-ridden movies quickly disappeared. Twentieth Century–Fox decided to open John Moore's *Behind Enemy Lines* in November 2001, ahead of its original screening date in 2002. The movie, about a rescue mission to save a pilot shot down behind enemy lines, reaped box-office dividends. Similarly, Ridley Scott's *Black Hawk Down* (2001), regarding the deaths of nineteen American soldiers in Somalia in 1993, enjoyed an early release in order to tap the patriotic mood. Over eight hundred political and military officials attended the Washington, DC, premiere. Secretary of Defense Donald Rumsfeld and Deputy Secretary Paul Wolfowitz described the movie as "powerful." "I think it's good for this time," Wolfowitz added. Not only did audiences attend films in record numbers right after 9/11, but they also apparently hungered for tough American heroes and military action. *Behind Enemy Lines* was so popular that, when the video version appeared less than five months after the movie's release, it included a Navy recruiting advertisement. By then, movies that studios had postponed—such as *The Sum of All Fears,* about the nuclear destruction of Baltimore, and Schwarzenegger's *Collateral Damage*—were also in circulation. "Could Terrorists Actually Detonate a Weapon of Mass Destruction on U.S. Soil?" asked a *Sum of All Fears* poster.[10]

Television too proceeded as usual. Despite predictions that mindless programs such as *Fear Factor* had no future in a more serious America, unscripted reality shows proliferated. Granted, such programs had a long history, going back to *Candid Camera* in 1948 and coming up through *Queen for a Day* in the mid-1950s and *The People's Court,* which started in 1981. In 1992, MTV's *Real World* had moved seven young adults into a house for several weeks and filmed the social dynamics. Over the next decade, and especially after 9/11, reality shows became more popular than ever. They ranged from Fox's *Who Wants to Marry a Millionaire* to CBS's trendsetting *Survivor,* in which groups of sixteen people lived in remote settings, trying to outlast each other for $1 million prizes. "On *Survivor,*" as one journalist observed, "it just happens to be a place where everyone walks around in a bathing suit, roasting rats over the campfire and openly backstabbing their co-stars." TV programmers and advertisers liked such programs because they were cheaper to produce than dramas and sitcoms. A reality show required neither scripts, nor expensive sets, nor professional casts. "It's like someone who goes to their boss and says, 'We can make something at half the cost that will make twice as much money,'" said an executive of a New York media buying firm. "The boss would say, 'Go do it, but don't embarrass us.'" Actually, the threat of embarrassment was no match for sleaziness and titillation. Fox's *Temptation Island,* which first aired in early 2001, focused on four unmarried couples who tested their feelings for each other by splitting up and then meeting a number of alluring young single males and females who tried to tempt them with sex.[11]

After 9/11, reality shows multiplied, undermining predictions about how Americans were now more generous and caring. "What a long strange trip it's been, these past 18 months," wrote the columnist Anna Quindlen in early 2003. She noted, for example, the new TV program *Are You Hot?* in which individuals posed for a panel of judges who determined who was the "hottest." Quindlen recalled that, right after the terrorist attacks, "people vowed to hug harder, call more often, keep in touch." But, within a short time, their attention seemed to be on "whether Aaron will propose to Helene or to Brooke." Quickly, audiences moved "on to the next big thing": "Your butt's too big. Your hair's too thin. You're not hot." By 2004, a number of reality shows such as *The Swan* involved "extreme makeovers," in which contestants competed for prizes by undergoing plastic surgery to make themselves more attractive. Themes of conniving, scheming, gossiping, and greed suffused many programs, including *Survivor* and *Joe Millionaire*. Although an innovative series such as *Survivor* also drew viewers because of its element of unpredictability and unscripted chance, critics could easily conclude that audiences had "a coliseum mentality," as one observer argued. "They are cheering for the lion, not the gladiator." Backstabbing was abundant on *The Apprentice*, which became a big hit in the spring of 2004. With the theme song repeating, "Money, money, money," the show focused on a dozen ambitious young people who competed for the opportunity to work for the billionaire entrepreneur Donald Trump. Each episode ended with Trump—who heavily promoted himself and his financial success—informing another of the competitors, "You're fired." According to the psychoanalyst Deborah Peel, such reality shows were "not set up to show tenderness or altruism. They're designed to promote friction, tension and bad behavior." In sum, the malice and meanness of the polarized 1990s were still powerful forces. "It's all about getting to the next step," said Chris, *Survivor*'s fall 2004 winner, on the December 12 season finale. "The hell with everybody else."[12]

One year after the 9/11 attacks, Nancy Tellum, the president of CBS Entertainment, conceded that the tragedy "really did not affect our [program] development at all." According to the media scholar Robert Thompson, the trend revealed "how quickly American popular culture can dissolve even the most horrid tragedy." As an MTV anniversary special concluded, the attack that "was supposed to have changed everything" had apparently altered little.[13]

Even the sense of national unity following the 9/11 attacks quickly began to unravel. In the few months right after 9/11, the U.S. military invasion of Afghanistan had enjoyed wide support. Afghanistan's Taliban government harbored Osama bin Laden and members of the al-Qaeda terrorist network who had planned the bloody strikes on American soil. But President Bush's decision to invade Iraq in early 2003 proved deeply divisive at home and abroad. The administration justified its historically new strategy of preemptive war against Iraq on the grounds that Saddam Hussein's regime had direct links with bin Laden and possessed weapons of mass destruction that imperiled the United States. Condoleezza Rice, the national security adviser, raised the specter of mushroom clouds rising over American cities. Secretary of State Colin Powell provided the United Nations with "proof" of the existence and location of the weapons. In March 2003, U.S. troops, with minimal international support, stormed into Iraq. Within a few weeks, Saddam Hussein's government fell. Bush, wearing a jet pilot's combat uniform, landed in a fighter plane on an American carrier to announce that the mission was accomplished. But critics of the invasion soon found ample evidence to justify their suspicions that the rationale for the Iraq War was a product of misinformation and the manipulation of evidence. Official government studies would show both that there were no weapons of mass destruction in Iraq and that Saddam Hussein was not connected to the al-Qaeda terrorists. By then, however, the administration had been able to convince a large percentage of Americans—despite evidence to the contrary—that Iraq had, indeed, possessed weapons of mass destruction and was behind the 9/11 attacks.

Public debate deteriorated. Because France refused to endorse the Bush administration's position on Iraq, three House office building cafeterias changed the name *French fries* to *freedom fries* on their menus, and cries went up to find other names for French dressing and French toast. Boycotts of French wine commenced. During a Parents' Day event at one college campus, some parents objected that a French instructor continued to teach French despite France's lack of support for the Iraq War. During the 2004 presidential election, Republicans scoffingly noted that the Democratic candidate, John Kerry, could speak French.[14]

Dubbing himself a "war president," Bush drew lines at home and abroad between the forces of good and those of "evil-doers"—between supporters and enemies of freedom. Politics quickly turned ugly. Within months of 9/11, Republicans ran TV advertisements in South Dakota in which Senate Minority Leader Tom Daschle's image morphed into bin Laden's. In Georgia's 2002 senatorial race, Republicans attacked as disloyal the Democratic incumbent Max Cleland, despite the fact that he had lost three limbs in Vietnam. The scurrilous assaults on Cleland's character worked, and his opponent won the election. Such polarizing, nasty politics helped burst the sense of togetherness that had immediately followed the 9/11 attacks and set the stage for a quick return of negative "us"-against-"them" campaigning.

Against that backdrop, some entertainment trends suggested that the Red-baiting and blacklisting techniques of the early Cold War might return. When the singer Natalie Maines of the Dixie Chicks country music group told an audience that she regretted coming from Bush's state of Texas, the reaction was vehement. A number of radio stations that belonged to the huge Clear Channel programming corporation promptly dropped the group from their playlists. *Dixie Chicked* subsequently became a term for what could happen to performers who criticized the president.[15]

In the opening months of 2003, there were other disturbing incidents.

CBS fired Ed Gernon, the producer of a four-part miniseries on Hitler's rise to power, after an interview in which he drew parallels between Hitler's Germany and recent trends in the United States. "It basically boils down to an entire nation gripped by fear, who ultimately chose to give up their civil rights and plunged the whole nation into war," Gernon had told *TV Guide* about the miniseries. According to one journalist, "politics and a strong desire not to fall foul of the Bush administration" were key factors in Gernon's firing. Elsewhere, Dale Petroskey, the president of the National Baseball Hall of Fame and a former Ronald Reagan aide, blocked the planned fifteenth anniversary showing of the baseball movie *Bull Durham* (Ron Shelton, 1988) at the museum. He did so on the grounds that the movie's stars, Susan Sarandon and Tim Robbins, were outspoken critics of the war. According to Petroskey, showing the film at this "important and sensitive" time was inappropriate because Sarandon's and Robbins's criticism hurt the United States and "could put our troops in even more danger": "As an institution, we stand behind our President and our troops in this conflict." A group calling itself Citizens against Celebrity Pundits successfully blocked Sarandon from speaking in Florida to a branch of the United Way charity organization. Elsewhere, the Visa credit card company decided not to run TV commercials featuring the actor Martin Sheen, another vocal opponent of the war. And, when the actor Danny Glover spoke against the war, the MCI telecommunications company dropped him from its ads, rather than face a threatened boycott. "The whole idea is to crush dissent," Glover insisted. "Something is happening now that is very dark and very sinister in this country, and for us to not admit it is happening is, in some ways, for us to be blind."[16]

There was, for example, a striking absence of war protest music on commercial radio stations, despite the recordings of such singers as the folk rocker John Mellencamp, the rapper Jadakiss, and country's Steve Earle. Mellencamp and Don Henley, who had performed with such country-rock groups as the Corvettes and the Eagles, placed part of the blame on "corporate-owned radio." "During Vietnam," recalled Mellencamp, "any guy with a privately owned station could play [Bob Dylan's] *Masters of War*. Now the companies who own all these stations can't afford to offend listeners and advertisers." In Henley's opinion, the fault rested with "vast media conglomerates mostly allied with this administration and its version of the FCC, which is dominated by Republicans, including Chairman Michael Powell." Two of radio's programming giants, Clear Channel and Cumulus, disagreed that politics played a role. "The free market," according to the Cumulus executive John Dickey, was the key. And that market, he insisted, had as much right to speak as did the performers. "If artists are interested in protecting their revenue streams," he predicted ominously, "they'll respond. If not, they'll suffer the consequences."[17]

That "free market" was sometimes less neutral than its proponents indicated, however. In notable instances, recording companies and radio networks tried to influence it. Hence, a U.S. version of the popular British singer George Michael's CD appeared without a song that rebuked Prime Minister Tony Blair for "dancing with Dubya." And edited copies of Jadakiss's *Why* omitted a critical reference to Bush. None other than Cumulus Media reportedly arranged a demonstration at which a tractor smashed the Dixie Chicks' CDs, tapes, and videos.[18]

Commercial considerations nevertheless predictably influenced decisions about what music to produce and circulate. John Hart, the president of a Nashville-based marketing company, maintained that country music followers had no interest in protest music. "I work with 32 stations," he said, "and I have not seen one test any of these anti-war songs." While country singers such as Emmylou Harris and Willie Nelson might question the war, their opinions counted for little against the flag-waving performances of, say, Toby Keith or Darryl Worley. In early 2003, Worley's "Have You Forgotten?" became a top radio hit. "I hear people saying we don't need this war," sang Worley. "Have you forgotten when those towers fell / We had neighbors still inside go through a living hell / And you say we shouldn't worry 'bout bin Laden / Have you forgotten?" According to Hart: "Every time we bomb somebody it's 'Hell, yeah!' . . . That's where country music is coming from."[19]

Controversy could also boost careers, however. After Linda Ronstadt infuriated fans and hotel managers in Las Vegas by praising Michael Moore's political documentary *Fahrenheit 9/11* (2004), the Artemis Records executive Danny Goldberg noted that the pop singer received more publicity than she had in a long time. "I'd love to put out a Linda Ronstadt album now," he said. "She's contemporary again."[20]

Moore's *Fahrenheit 9/11*, an unsparing critique of the Bush administration and the Iraq War, was itself a stunning example of how controversy and protest could produce box-office dividends. After Disney's Miramax division filmed the documentary, Disney refused to distribute it. According to Michael Eisner, the company did not want to damage its "nonpartisan" tradition—a curious excuse for a corporation that aired Rush Limbaugh on its ABC Radio division. Lions Gate Entertainment, a Canadian-based independent studio that was only seven years old, subsequently marketed the film with great success, setting box-office records for a documentary. Moore himself infuriated people who believed that he aided terrorism by insulting America's commander in chief during wartime. There were unsuccessful efforts, for example, to keep him from speaking and showing film clips at Utah Valley State College in Orem. A local real estate dealer interpreted Moore's coming as "a slap in the face to the citizens of this valley" and said that he would pay the students $25,000 to rescind Moore's invitation: "The issue seems to be who's in charge over here. The valley is very conservative. You know, Orem is family city USA." To counter Moore's visit, the conservative commentator Sean Hannity also spoke on campus, waiving his usual $100,000 honorarium.[21]

Fahrenheit 9/11's effectiveness in fueling opposition to Bush may have encouraged a group of well-known singers who hoped to mobilize young voters against the administration. In 2004, Bruce Springsteen and his manager, Jon Landau, were the chief organizers of a "Vote for Change" concert series. Sixteen of music's biggest acts staged over forty shows in eleven battleground states to raise money for John Kerry's campaign. The historic tour started on September 27 and lasted for fifteen days. Among the acts were R.E.M., Pearl Jam, Bonnie Raitt, the Dixie Chicks, Mellencamp, Jurassic 5, and Springsteen. "We're trying to put forward a group of progressive ideals and change the administration in the White House," Springsteen explained. Performing at one point before twenty thousand people in Washington, DC—as well as on the Sundance Channel, which broadcast the show nationally—Springsteen urged viewers: "Go to your windows, throw 'em open and tell all your neighbors—a change is comin'!"[22]

Not all musicians opposed Bush, however. Among the administration's supporters were Jessica Simpson, Ted Nugent, Alice Cooper, and Gene Simmons. Alice Cooper scoffed at the "Vote for Change" tour: "Why are we rock stars? Because we're morons. We sleep all day, we play music all night, and very rarely do we sit around reading the *Washington Journal*." Pearl Jam's Eddie Vedder—part of the "Vote for Change" effort—could not understand such thinking: "You can't spend your life, when people are getting killed, without asking serious questions about why."[23]

Republicans urged Bush backers to stay away from the "Vote for Change" concerts. The Ohio legislator Jim Trakas contended that the tour's rock stars opposed Republican values. In his opinion, Springsteen and the other performers were "serial-marrying and serial-illegitimate-child-bearing" individuals.[24]

Trakas's charges squared with the Bush campaign's targeting of Hollywood as the rival of bedrock Middle America. This strategy continued a tradition of media bashing that had been a potent Republican weapon since Richard Nixon and his administration had inveighed against snobbish liberal elites who allegedly controlled America's cultural center. The rhetoric of the political backlash, then and later, portrayed liberalism as the nation's main villain. "The whole point of being a liberal," raged the conservative author Ann Coulter in 2002, was "to feel superior to people with less money." In his 1992 autobiography, *When I Was a Kid, This Was a Free Country*, the talk show host G. Gordon Liddy contended that "left-of-center, Ivy-educated molders of public opinion" dominated such areas as "the mass news media, the entertainment business, academia." Among the creations of this liberal elite, according to Liddy, were "movies that assail and undermine the values we are attempting to inculcate in our children."[25]

By the 2004 election, pundits and commentators made much of a cultural fault line that supposedly divided the United States into "red" and "blue" states, with each color designating contrasting sets of values and lifestyles. The red states belonged to Republicans and stretched across the vast middle of the country and the South. The blue states were the strongholds of Democrats and were located mainly in the Northeast and along the West Coast. According to John Podhoretz, who had written speeches for George Bush's father: "Bush Red is a simpler place . . . where people mourn the death of NASCAR champion Dale Earnhardt, root lustily for their teams, go to church, and find comfort in old-fashioned verities." As the Bush adviser Mark McKinnon told a *New York Times* reporter about people "in the big, wide middle of America": "You know what those folks don't like? They don't like you!"[26]

This red state/blue state dichotomy was badly flawed, however. America's political map after the 2004 election revealed that the real dividing line was between cities and the countryside. In red states such as Missouri, Texas, and Alabama, for instance, St. Louis, El Paso, and Montgomery voted Democratic, and New York State's only blue shadings were in the geographically small but heavily populated urban areas. The much-ballyhooed division between "coastal liberals and heartland conservatives," as the historian Sean Wilentz observed, glossed over a perennial rural/urban split—the kind that historically had characterized cultural clashes.[27]

Still, as a metaphor of two Americas, the red/blue dichotomy was suggestive. Rupert Murdoch's Fox News Channel, for example, earned a reputation as "the Red-State Network." The channel made its debut in 1996 as an outspoken answer to the media's allegedly liberal bias. Within six years, its cable news ratings moved ahead of CNN's. Roger Ailes, Fox's CEO, had been a Republican media consultant and produced, among other things, Rush Limbaugh's television show. "There's a whole country that exists that elitists will never acknowledge," he said. "What people resent deeply out there are those in the 'blue' states thinking they're smarter." In his opinion, the intelligentsia behind most news reporting engaged in "absolute-elitist-horse-dung-Socialist thinking!" Although Ailes denied that his network was partisan, the whispered wisdom at Fox was reportedly, "We have to feed the core"—meaning conservatives. The sharply opinionated daytime anchors echoed the Bush White House, where Fox was the favorite channel. After the 9/11 attacks, Fox News pounded the war drum incessantly. Geraldo Rivera, by then working for Fox, donned a pistol and said that he personally would like to kill Osama bin Laden. One anchor dismissed the "knuckleheads" who participated in a war protest. Another anchor described France, which opposed the war, as part of an "axis of weasels." Ailes cheerfully admitted that Fox News was entertainment: "We're just getting the same girls to dance around shinier poles." Murdoch's only complaint was that the channel was not conservative enough. The writer Brian Anderson nevertheless cited Fox's rise as one reason why "we're not losing the culture wars anymore."[28]

George Bush's reelection in 2004 supplied additional fuel for arguments such as Anderson's that "a more conservative America" was emerging. In the postelection analyses, commentators made much of polls showing that 22 percent of Bush's support hinged on moral issues. Prominent among those issues were abortion and the recognition of same-sex unions, but so was the nature of American entertainment. "The folks who re-elected Bush not only voted *for* the man they felt best represents their interests, but also *against* a culture they see as alien and hostile," wrote the pro-Bush columnist Kathleen Parker. Television was "out of touch with large segments of the country," according to a Philadelphia reporter. "Red-staters, security moms, conservative Christians—whatever label you pin on the people who helped give President Bush four more years—they're not the people" who populated network television shows. Khristine Bershers of the conservative Heritage Foundation agreed. "Mostly, voters in the great expanse of America known as the 'fly-over states' . . . want to be able to watch TV with their children without having to explain what erectile dysfunction is and what Cialis might do for it," she wrote. Noting that "music and television have slowly become more risque," Bershers insisted that "the red states don't want blue-state values forced on them." Another columnist and self-described "Red Stater" took offense at "the sewage flowing from Planet Hollyweird."[29]

On February 1, 2004, Janet Jackson's "wardrobe malfunction" suddenly became "the 9/11 of the new culture war." At the end of the Super Bowl's halftime extravaganza, Justin Timberlake, who was singing with Jackson, ripped off her tear-away brassiere. Alert viewers briefly saw her right breast and—as a careful examination of video frames revealed—some nipple jewelry. Angry cries and recriminations quickly followed. An incensed Tennessee woman filed a class action suit, claiming that the incident "injured" unsuspecting viewers. Flooded with over 200,000 complaints, the Federal Communications Commission searched for who was responsible. CBS and the halftime show's producer, MTV, both denied involvement. Jackson claimed that only her bustier should have come off, not her red-lace bra as well. The day after the show, Internet searches for "Janet Jackson" set a one-day record, and over 120 stations played a hastily released single from her new album, due for release on March 30. "To me," said Sumner Redstone, who headed CBS's parent company, Viacom, "a woman's breast is not such a big deal." But the loud outcry from Congress, the public, and the FCC indicated that it was. "The chill is already here," warned *Rolling Stone* as it urged media executives to "stand up to the war on culture." The FCC looked into Oprah Winfrey's use of sexual slang during a show that she aired on teen sexuality and seemed intent as well on examining daytime soap operas.[30]

On November 15, about nine months after the Jackson incident, ABC's opening to *Monday Night Football* touched off another cultural firestorm. During the show's lead-in, a star in ABC's hit series *Desperate Housewives,* Nicolette Sheridan, wrapped in a bath towel, approached the football star Terrell Owens. She then dropped the towel, although the TV audience saw only her back from the waist up, and leaped into Owens's arms. The outrage that followed evoked apologies from ABC. The National Football League (NFL) expressed shock—to the puzzlement of some commentators, who noted that among the NFL's official sponsors was Levitra, a remedy for erectile dysfunction. Indeed, ads during the game and elsewhere on television regularly showed an alluring woman talking in a sultry fashion about how Levitra had enriched her and her mate's sexual experiences. One columnist remembered the publication over a half a century earlier of Alfred Kinsey's books on male and female sexuality in the United States. "All of a sudden," he concluded, "we're back in a pre-Kinsey world." The sportswriter Bernie Lincicome quipped: "Those of us in politically red states must, by law, be against anything that is racy, steamy and crude—not counting NASCAR, of course."[31]

Lincicome's reference to the National Association for Stock Car Auto Racing pointed to how that sport had become a symbolic marker in a culturally divided America. To its critics, NASCAR's spiraling popularity signaled much that was reprehensible—gas guzzling and pollution, racially homogenized crowds, and the world of "God and guns and guts." "What's the appeal of watching . . . traffic?" skeptics wondered. But to an estimated 75 million fans, stock-car racing resonated with the nation's attachment to speed and automobiles. Moreover, here was a sport in which feisty, daring drivers could succeed without being seven feet tall, weighing three hundred pounds, or having the natural ability to run fast. Here good old boys brought images of *Smokey and the Bandit* or *The Dukes of Hazzard* to life, risking crashes and even death in ways that hitting a ball or putting one through a hoop could not. "Cover your ears, blue America," joked one writer. "The Huns are revving their engines." During the 2004 election, Bush's supporters reportedly included many "NASCAR dads."[32]

Cultural battle lines marked even the reshowing of Steven Spielberg's powerful 1998 movie about the 1944 Normandy invasion, *Saving Private Ryan.* On Veterans Day, November 11, 2004, over sixty ABC affiliates refused to air the film because of its violence and profanity. ABC had shown it the previous two years with no problems. But this time there was a wave of objections. A radio talk show host complained: "I just don't expect the same channel that has been showing me *Jeopardy* and *Wheel of Fortune* to suddenly show me a guy getting his head blown off him." Clearly, the political winds were shifting.[33]

Additional evidence existed in the growing influence of fundamentalist Christians on entertainment. There had certainly been earlier efforts to use the media to promote religion. Silent films had included staged reenactments of the Easter passion play. In the 1920s and 1930s, some preachers had aired church services over the radio. In the record industry, gospel music had found a significant audience. For the most part, however, fundamentalist Christians had viewed popular culture with suspicion. A major exception was Marion G. "Pat" Robertson, who, in 1977, launched the cable network CBN (Christian Broadcasting Network). Initially, even Robertson had viewed TV and other entertainment forms as evil. But he had then decided that film, television, and radio were, in fact, "neutral": "It's a question of who is in control, . . . who does the programming." With that insight, in the mid-1950s he had started using a small Virginia station to promote his fundamentalist views and created *The 700 Club* program to help keep the station afloat. Eventually, Robertson syndicated *The 700 Club,* which became the pillar of CBN and one of the longest-running shows on prime-time TV. A combination talk show and newsmagazine, the program included Bible readings, prayers, and appeals for money. By 1988, Robertson's reputation had grown enough that he campaigned for the Republican presidential nomination. His surprising grassroots support supplied additional proof that fundamentalists were becoming more politically active. Other preachers such as Jerry Falwell used television to promote the ideals of the "Moral Majority." In 2004, crucial support for George Bush's reelection came from the 42 percent of Americans who claimed in a Gallup poll that they were "born again." According to one account, "more than 26 million of them turned out—23 percent of the electorate—in local church-based networks coordinated closely with the Bush campaign."[34]

By then, evangelical religion was infusing popular culture, forging what an American studies scholar described as "a parallel world of entertainment." Religion had, of course, played a prominent role throughout U.S. history—so much so that, as the writer Walter Kirn observed, "America is the revival that never ends, the camp meeting that never fully adjourns." Yet, clearly, the United States was experiencing a renewed spiritual upheaval that cut across the society, including entertainment. "Big TV, big music and big film," according to Kirn, "have left vast swaths of the country to the preacher-folk." And that part of the country helped account for an expanding evangelical Christian entertainment market. A faith-based publishing network, for example, distributed books such as the minister Rick Warren's *The Purpose Driven Life* (2002), which sold over 20 million copies in two years. "Something really big is happening, but it has been happening under the radar of the national media," contended Warren. "They've missed it entirely." Booming sales unquestionably owed much to Christian bookstores, but also to new marketing strategies that included mainstream stores like Wal-Mart and Costco.[35]

The search for wider audiences also affected fundamentalists' perspectives regarding films. "Movies are the common language of our culture," said the founder of hollywoodjesus.com, one of some three dozen such Christian Web sites that existed on the Internet by mid-2002. "We can no longer say don't see this, don't watch that. We can't do that—it's all around us." Religious groups had long monitored movies. But notable now were efforts to produce action-oriented movies with Christian messages that might attract more viewers. "You have to make films that are entertaining," insisted Peter Lalonde of the independent Cloud Ten Pictures, "otherwise nobody's going to see them. . . . We want to produce mainstream entertainment."[36]

That same goal applied to other emerging forms of Christian entertainment. There were, for example, spiritual rock concerts whose performers included the costumed "Bibleman," a character from one of several religiously oriented, computer-animated video series. By 2003, contemporary Christian music constituted the music industry's fastest-growing area. Christian nightclubs were also forming. Among them was Minneapolis's Club 3 Degrees, which banned cigarettes, liquor, and secular songs. "There's a whole world of people who live at night," explained the club's codirector. "Part of our mission is to take the Gospel into that world." In 2004, the girls' fashion magazine *Seventeen* added a faith section with personal testimonials and inspirational messages. By then, Harlequin, a top publisher of romance fiction since the mid-1960s, had added a line of Christian fiction that featured chaste heroines intent on building relationships with God as well as the males they love. Elsewhere, religion and sports mixed with added fervor. At the end of football games, members of Christian Athletes from opposing teams knelt together in prayer at midfield. Athletic merchandise now included "Jesus Sports Statues"—six-inch-high action figurines—as well as St. Christopher "sport" medals. Self-styled Christian comedians toured the country. One was Brad Stine, whose comedy hero, ironically, was George Carlin. Stine recorded at Jerry Falwell's church and performed in other religious venues, including *The 700 Club*. He was "A Conservative Unleashed," according to the title of his second DVD in 2004. Like Roger Ailes and others on the political Right, Stine believed that he was battling a "liberal-based media-entertainment structure." His targets included virtually anyone who did not take the Bible as literal truth. "This country is changing," he told one audience. "And there is, in fact, a civil war—of ideology. It's real."[37]

That theme of Americans locked in an ideological struggle over religious values and lifestyles pervaded American politics. George W. Bush's "faith-based presidency" was a powerful example. As a British observer pointed out, "the notion of America the divine" had taken on renewed energy following the 9/11 attacks and the onset of the Iraq War, with Bush very much encouraging such fervor. "I believe God wants me to be president," Bush reportedly said. According to Bruce Bartlett, who had worked in the two previous Republican administrations, Bush continually expressed a "Messianic idea of what he thinks God has told him to do." When a grassroots Christian conservative in Florida declared, "This is the very first time that I have felt that God was in the White House," the president thanked him to thunderous applause. After the president won reelection, an official of the evangelical Focus on the Family group contended that "only the Lord could have orchestrated" such a victory. Another Christian commentator, Dennis Prager, believed that nothing less than "civilization as we understand it was in the balance" and that "a beautiful man has been vindicated."[38]

Apocalyptic visions similarly permeated two of the largest manifestations of religion in popular culture—the Left Behind series of novels and Mel Gibson's 2004 movie *The Passion of the Christ*. In 1995, the Reverend Tim LaHaye had teamed up with the writer Jerry B. Jenkins to launch an end-time series of novels. LaHaye had been a cofounder of the Moral Majority as well as the founder of the American Coalition for Traditional Values, which helped reelect Ronald Reagan. He pressed a rigorously conservative political agenda. Jenkins, also an evangelical Christian, had written a comic strip and over a hundred books that, by his own admission, were not very good. But, with LaHaye providing lengthy plot outlines and Jenkins writing the action-packed narratives, their collaboration made publishing history. Working from the Bible's Book of Revelation, their twelve novels focused on the seven years following "the Rapture"—the time when Jesus was supposed to remove millions of the faithful from the earth and when those "left behind" would plunge into chaos during the rule of the Antichrist. In LaHaye and Jenkins's novels, conspiracies abound, and the villains range from proponents of gun control and abortion rights to the United Nations, the American Civil Liberties Union, the Catholic Church, some two thousand colleges, and the major media. The novels' graphic violence and horror demonstrate God's wrath. By the time the twelfth installment of the series, *Glorious Appearing*, was published in 2004, Left Behind books were outselling all other popular novels in the United States—with sales soaring to 62 million—and had inspired several films, CDs, Web sites, and even T-shirts. "In an age of terror and tumult,"

Newsweek guessed, "these books' Biblical literalism offered certitude to millions of Americans." As the protagonists of the series keep reassuring each other: "We know how it ends. We win." Statistics showed that 71 percent of the readers came from the "red state" Midwest and South.[39]

While the Left Behind novels reverberated among millions of the faithful, so did *The Passion of the Christ,* concerning Jesus's last anguished hours and crucifixion. Mel Gibson brought to the film his own personal fundamentalist passion as well as an established movie star's reputation. Although he made the film, he said, the Holy Ghost directed it. Because the actors spoke in Aramaic, Hebrew, and Latin—and the movie thus had subtitles—the film presumably held little financial promise. It was, nevertheless, a blockbuster, generating $125.2 million within five days and, after only six weeks, almost $355 million. It was "re-writing box-office history," according to the ticket tracker Paul Dergarabedian. And it did so because many churches rallied to it, even renting theaters and busing members to showings. Some people were so certain that viewing the film was a test of religious conviction that they heaped scorn on those who chose not to see it. "It's not just a movie," commented Dergarabedian. "It's a religious experience for many people." The evangelist T. D. Jakes, whose Dallas congregation numbered twenty-five thousand, believed: "Mel Gibson proves to us perhaps the next frontier of evangelism may be the movie theater."[40]

A striking irony about the Left Behind novels and Gibson's movie was the emphasis on gore and carnage despite many fundamentalists' complaints about violence in popular culture. In one of *Glorious Appearing*'s lengthy bloodbaths, "men and women soldiers and horses seemed to explode where they stood. . . . Their innards and entrails gushed to the desert floor, . . . their blood pooling and rising in the unforgiving brightness of the glory of Christ." And the relentless scourging and other brutalities that Christ endured in *The Passion of the Christ* made it "one of the cruelest movies in the history of the cinema," according to the longtime film critic David Denby. Another critic described the movie as "the Gospel according to the Marquis de Sade." The novels and the movie also shared a messianic worldview, with clear-cut divisions between good and evil. LaHaye and Gibson both conveyed the thinking of many fundamentalists that they were defending an embattled faith. "The L.A. *Times,*" Gibson told Denby, "it's an anti-Christian publication, as is the New York *Times.*" LaHaye, in turn, resented the smugness of theologians who did not take the Bible literally. "It bugs me that intellectuals look down their noses at we ordinary people."[41]

The tragic events of 9/11 and the subsequent war on terror undoubtedly facilitated apocalyptic thinking. "I think a lot of people are looking at contemporary conflict around the world and seeing it as a kind of religious war," conjectured the religion professor Elaine Pagels. It was thus hardly coincidental that, immediately after 9/11, readers flocked to the most recently published volume in the Left Behind series, *Desecration* (2001), turning it into the year's best-selling novel. Nor was it surprising that the series was popular among U.S. troops in Iraq. In that context, the cultural war accelerated abroad and at home. By the end of 2004, a *New York Times*–CBS News poll found that 70 percent of Americans believed that mass entertainment was wreaking moral havoc within the United States. The objections to Janet Jackson's breast and Nicolette Sheridan's naked back clearly expressed general anxieties about the nation's moral condition. So did the attacks in early 2005 on a video, *We Are Family*, featuring the popular cartoon character SpongeBob SquarePants. At a gathering in Washington, DC, of conservative Christians who were celebrating George Bush's second inauguration, the Focus on the Family leader James Dobson claimed that SpongeBob was part of a "pro-homosexual video." Several other religious organizations expressed similar concerns that the video undermined American values by promoting tolerance for gay and lesbian families.[42]

But blaming popular culture for America's perceived moral decline missed some larger truths while revealing selective judgments, political opportunism, and considerable hypocrisy. Mass entertainment was, ultimately, show *business*, as amusement entrepreneurs such as P. T. Barnum had long recognized. In the words of one scholar: "The religion of Hollywood is money." Historically, the ultimate arbiter of entertainment as a whole in the United States has been the revered profit motive, which most Americans celebrated as crucial to the nation's success. The famed "bottom line," sensitive to the law of supply and demand, drove the U.S. free enterprise system that politicians, entrepreneurs, and consumers extolled.[43]

And therein rested troubles for amusement watchdogs. As the columnist Robert Scheer argued, the culprit behind "immoral" entertainment was a deregulated free market, "where a right-wing mega-capitalist like Rupert Murdoch can simultaneously make millions off satires like *Married with Children* and *The Simpsons* and a right-wing news channel that wraps itself in the very 'God, country, family' tropes that those satires so crassly yet cleverly spoof." The publishing divisions of Murdoch's News Corporation similarly printed contrasting best sellers: the minister Rick Warren's *The Purpose Driven Life* and the stripper/adult film celebrity Jenna Jameson's *How to Make Love Like a Porn Star* (2004). "That's the great thing about capitalism," said Al Goldstein, the publisher of *Screw* magazine, when discussing pornography. "It's amoral, blind," and an unending source of profits.[44]

Indeed, not only had pornography become a mainstream business—with more income than professional football, basketball, and baseball combined—but its top entrepreneurs and distributors were far removed from sleazy settings and isolated backwaters. In viewpoint and organization, they fit easily with corporate America. "I've leaned toward the right in my politics," said a leading adult film director, Michael Raven. Among the sponsors of the 2001 Bush-Cheney inaugural were two leading porn providers: Marriott (via in-room X-rated movies) and General Motors (via DirecTV). Moreover, as porn became more corporate, its mainstream entrepreneurs distanced themselves from its bottom feeders. Veronica Hart, who had moved from starring in adult movies to presiding over a company that made them, argued that adult entertainment, like every business, had its "bastards." They exhibited a "carnival freak-show mentality. There has to be a geek show somewhere in our society," she said, denying that adult entertainment as a whole was part of it. Or, as Bill Asher of Vivid Pictures laughingly put it: "In truth, there's no business like porn business. Porn is the one show that no one watches but that, miraculously, never closes."[45]

ABC's surprise TV hit of late 2004, *Desperate Housewives,* was far from pornographic, but its titillating fare demonstrated once again the wide appeal of sex in entertainment and the challenges that faced moral censors. One of the top two shows of the season, it was a racy satire of suburban life, focusing humorously on marital unhappiness, infidelity, divorce, and frazzled parenthood. Yet, although the saga about "babes behaving badly" hammered "the ideal of America the Wholesome," it was extremely popular among men and women in the much-ballyhooed red states of George Bush.[46]

Once again, popular culture made generalizations difficult. Readers of the Left Behind series did not necessarily all share the authors' worldview, any more than most fans of the TV show *Buffy the Vampire Slayer* believed in the supernatural. Some Left Behind readers reportedly compared the books' mix of excitement, gore, and mystery to Stephen King novels. Among the favorite amusements of the series' younger fans were *Star Trek* and *Star Wars.* The People's Choice Awards in January 2005 also demonstrated how entertainment could cross cultural divides. In two categories of the same poll, *The Passion of the Christ* emerged as the favorite movie drama, while *Fahrenheit 9/11* was the overall favorite movie.[47]

Shifting perceptions of what constituted immorality further complicated the battles against risqué entertainment. Moralists had waged earlier wars against "Little Richard's mascara, the Beatles' hair, Lenny Bruce's language, the Smothers Brothers' politics," and Elvis Presley's gyrating hips. In retrospect, although some people continued to find a pattern of national decline in such examples, many Americans saw liberating trends and expressions of individual tastes.[48]

Indeed, the powerful American mystique regarding freedom, individualism, and opportunity owed much to popular culture's narratives, images, and personalities. Growing up in Europe after World War II, the writer Ian

Buruma was far from alone in viewing the United States as "an exotic place, where everything seemed bigger, glitzier, richer, more exciting. . . . The sexiness of pop culture was not such a trivial thing. For it had the ring of freedom, of a country with endless possibilities." Music such as rock and roll gave even provincial locales such as Memphis, Tennessee, a magical aura. Although those pop culture images rested largely on myth, "it was a potent myth," Buruma recalled. "It still held out hope to millions who were poor or persecuted, or just restless, that in America it might still be possible to find a better way of life." That myth had drawn to the United States the parents of such entertainers as John L. Sullivan, Irving Berlin, and the Marx Brothers—as well as many performers themselves, including Anna Held and Bob Hope. And, for people who were born and raised in the United States, popular culture encouraged dreams of success while effectively conveying a sense of shared values regarding family, community, and country. Movies, television, radio, novels, music, and a host of other amusements had long provided Americans with perspectives on who they were and what they wanted. There was also the inevitable allure of "the great elsewhere." One found it "somewhere over the rainbow," as Judy Garland sang in *The Wizard of Oz* (Victor Fleming, 1939). Or in a baseball diamond amid the cornfields, as in *Field of Dreams* (Phil Alden Robinson, 1989): "Build it and they will come."[49]

While military power obviously expanded America's international influence, so did its popular culture. Granted, American entertainment drew the wrath of opponents around the world as well as in the United States. But, just as rock and roll helped breach the Berlin Wall, popular culture as a whole was a potent force for change. For good reason, ABC newscaster Ted Koppel described television as "revolution in a box." The fact that America's biggest export had become pop culture assuredly owed much to technology and well-developed corporate marketers. But one could not overlook the hold of entertainment on imaginations. "American popular culture is the closest approximation today to a global lingual franca," an observer pointed out. "[Its] themes and story . . . appeal to a global sensibility: freedom, freedom of movement, freedom from family, from place, from earth, from roles."[50]

"Made-in-America pop" found consumers around the world—in Vietnam, where rock music was popular and a new chain store was named Apocalypse Now, a deliberate reference to the 1979 movie; in El Salvador, where, by 1998, 40 percent of all music sales were from the United States; and in at least sixty countries where the science fiction TV show *The X-Files* aired. *Cosmopolitan*, the beauty and fashion publication, was reportedly the world's best-selling women's magazine. *Playboy* appeared in no fewer than sixteen international editions. MTV existed in more foreign than U.S. households. In Iran, twenty years after the revolution that denounced

America as the "Great Satan," bootleg copies of the blockbuster movie *Titanic* found enthusiastic viewers, and people used the Internet to find pictures of Madonna. "You make dreams," said the editor of an Iranian film magazine of the American media, "and those dreams can be understood anywhere."[51]

Not everything about popular culture was benign, of course, as its many critics had pointed out for generations. It was too often inane, tawdry, and meretricious. Too frequently it turned American democracy into a media sideshow, sacrificing hard news for gossip, bombast, and ever-shrinking "sound bites," while substituting passive viewing for civic engagement. Too many times it equated freedom, success, and fulfillment with the acquisition of things. Too often it treated people as sex objects and reduced many groups to unflattering stereotypes. And too often its power to co-opt ideas rendered protest and dissent meaningless. Just as, in the turbulent, politically charged 1960s, Dodge had identified the purchase of a car with revolution, in 2005 a Victoria's Secret advertisement merged pictures of a tough-looking Bob Dylan with images of sexy women parading in lingerie while his new song played in the background. Similarly, a 2005 Blockbuster ad showed sign-waving protestors marching on a video rental store only to learn that their objective—the elimination of late fees—was supposedly already company policy.[52]

But—arguably more than any other aspect of American society—popular culture provided messages of diversity, tolerance, and inclusion. Time and again it celebrated victories of the "little people" over wealth, corruption, and oppression. Ironically, powerful corporations typically spun such narratives. Such fictional victories could, of course, displace attention from real political solutions and hardly disturb distributions of power and privilege. Ideals nevertheless have their own power because, sometimes, people act on them.[53]

In that regard, despite numerous paradoxes and contradictions, entertainment had the capacity to inspire and instruct. Indeed, in some ways, it engaged the real world more honestly than elected officials did. While vote-minded politicians increasingly offered simplistic reassurances and ignored difficult issues, notable elements of popular culture explored ambiguities and complexities. Clint Eastwood's powerful films *Mystic River* (2003) and *Million Dollar Baby* (2004), for example, dealt compellingly with unintended consequences and plans gone awry. And an episode of the long-running television series *ER* (one that first aired on February 11, 2005) struggled with the challenges of building a more tolerant, inclusive nation. The episode showed Kerry Weaver, one of the program's fictional doctors, at last meeting her birth mother, who had given her up for adoption as a baby. But the reunion turned sour when the born-again mother learned that Kerry was a lesbian. The mother regretted Kerry's "choice" but promised to pray for her. Deeply hurt, Kerry commented poignantly on how strange it was that, at a time when people were starving and dying in wars and terrorists flew planes into buildings, many Americans worried that homosexuals were destroying the nation. In response to her mother's belief that homosexuality is a personal failing, Kerry responded that the failing was with her mother's religion, which could not honor its own precepts. Sadness and disappointment marked the episode's conclusion, which spurned a feel-good reconciliation and simply showed mother and daughter moving in opposite directions. Meanwhile, in late 2004, DC Comics' seven-part series "Identity Crisis" became the top seller by having famed superheroes wrestle with guilt, morally questionable methods, and the issue of violence. The DC world was still "a very optimistic place," explained the editor Dan DiDio. "A tonal shift" was occurring nonetheless, and superheroes had "to work harder to get to that better future now, which is more reflective of the times we live in."[54]

Popular culture thus continued to reflect the larger society, even as it questioned and influenced it. An ongoing pattern was for pop culture to emerge from unexpected sources, bubbling up from the nether regions, from groups and individuals far removed from the corridors of power and privilege. By the early twenty-first century, for instance, hip-hop had become a dominant cultural force. No longer limited to the economically strapped urban neighborhoods whence it came, it now provided a national sound track for advertising, television, movies, and other multimedia. In 2005, Chrysler and Dodge tried to bolster their street credentials among young consumers by featuring the rappers Snoop Dogg and 50 Cent in advertising videos. Meanwhile, hip-hop fashions attracted the attention of McDonald's. The nation's largest fast-food franchise announced that among its possible choices to design new uniforms for its 300,000 employees were the rap entrepreneurs Russell Simmons and Sean "Diddy" Combs, each with his own clothing label. In retrospect, it was possible to speculate that Public Enemy's 1988 album *It Takes a Nation of Millions to Hold Us Back* constituted as much of a musical watershed as did the seminal work of, say, Louis Armstrong, Hank Williams, Elvis Presley, Bob Dylan, or the Beatles. But, even as hip-hop steadily displaced rock, whose radio ratings had dropped by almost 20 percent in six years, it was spawning other amusement forms. Reminiscent of rap's rise from New York City's South Bronx, a kind of "ghetto ballet" known as krumping gained momentum in the embattled streets of South Los Angeles, Compton, and Long Beach. Observers wondered how far this "inner-city craze" would spread.[55]

And one could only guess at what surprises technology might unleash. Video games, whose Pac Man phenomenon had drawn millions of youngsters to arcades in the late 1970s and early 1980s, ultimately opened up new worlds on personal computers. By 2005, even Disneyland, that fifty-year-old mecca of kids' fun, faced the challenge of adapting to the exploding popularity of the increasingly innovative and sophisticated video games. "Almost everything Disney does today is passive while kids today expect everything to be interactive," explained one toy consultant. Predictably, of course, despite the video-game industry's self-imposed ratings system, a game such as Grand Theft Auto (rated M ["mature"]) drew fierce criticism for its violence and sexual content. Violence in the name of patriotism was more acceptable, however. Atari's F/A 18: Operation Iraqi Freedom, for example, allowed players to bomb targets inside Iraq but enjoyed an E ("everyone") rating.[56]

Who knew what little-known amusement forms and entertainers might tap changing popular moods to achieve star status? Or which perennial entertainment favorites, such as the Miss America contest, were perhaps fading? Initiated in 1921, the contest had, in 1954, become an annual television ratings hit, drawing at one point 80 million viewers. Ultimately, however, even Miss America's swimsuit competition was no match for more titillating material increasingly available on TV and elsewhere. After half a century, the Miss America audience had declined so much that no network would air the event, which moved to an unlikely venue: CMT, cable TV's country music channel. Unquestionably, the processes by which entertainment moved in and out of society's big tent were very much continuing.[57]

Something else was certain: entertainment's appeal would not diminish. Most Americans, even in the wake of 9/11 and amid searing cultural divisions within their country, would undoubtedly have sympathized with a Chilean slum dweller's response to criticism of movies, comic books, and television sitcoms: "Don't take my dreams away from me."[58]

NOTES

PREFACE

1. Michael Mandelbaum, *The Meaning of Sports: Why Americans Watch Baseball, Football, and Basketball and What They See When They Do* (New York: Public Affairs, 2004), 1 (Cuban quote).

2. Michael Kammen, *American Culture, American Tastes: Social Change and the 20th Century* (New York: Basic, 2000), esp. 3–26, differentiates between popular culture and mass culture, which is "nonregional, highly standardized, and completely commercial," and which did not appear "until well after World War II" (18). Still, Kammen notes that the main objective of both popular and mass culture is "pleasure and commercial appeal," elements that are basic to the entertainments discussed here. Among the myriad recent interpretations of popular culture, the following are particularly helpful: George Lipsitz, *Time Passages: Collective Memory and American Popular Culture* (Minneapolis: University of Minnesota Press, 1990), esp. vi–xvi, 3–20; Lawrence W. Levine, "The Folklore of Industrial Society: Popular Culture and Its Audiences," *American Historical Review* 97 (December 1992): 1369–99; and three responses to Levine: Robin D. G. Kelley, "Notes on Deconstructing 'the Folk,'" *American Historical Review* 97 (December 1992): 1400–1408; Natalie Zemon Davis, "Toward Mixtures and Margins," *American Historical Review* 97 (December 1992): 1409–16; and T. J. Jackson Lears, "Making Fun of Popular Culture," *American Historical Review* 97 (December 1992): 1417–26.

3. On the refractive tendencies of popular culture, see Renée M. Sentilles, *Performing Menken: Adah Isaacs Menken and the Birth of American Celebrity* (Cambridge: Cambridge University Press, 2003).

4. For the sideshow–big top analogy, see James B. Twitchell, *Carnival Culture: The Trashing of Taste in America* (New York: Columbia University Press, 1992), 234, 245, 259–61. Related analogies in the study of entertainment are common. For example, Larry Starr and Christopher Waterman (*American Popular Music: From Minstrelsy to MTV* [New York: Oxford University Press, 2003], 9–10) and Paul Starr (*The Creation of the Media: Political Origins of Modern Communications* [New York: Basic, 2004], 139) discuss a "center and periphery" phenomenon.

5. Leon E. Wynter, *American Skin: Pop Culture, Big Business, and the End of White America* (New York: Crown, 2002), 1–10 (5, "preferences"; 9, "skin grafts"; 10, "*American* does not," "Oprah").

6. Lipsitz, *Time Passages*, xiv.

PROLOGUE: POPULAR CULTURE ON THE BRINK

1. Paul Johnson, *Sam Patch, the Famous Jumper* (New York: Hill & Wang, 2003), 155–60.

2. Joseph Ellis, *After the Revolution: Profiles of Early American Culture* (New York: Norton, 1979), xi–xii, 34–35, 164 (Webster quote).

3. See, e.g., James B. Twitchell, *Preposterous Violence: Fables of Aggression in Modern Culture* (New York: Oxford University Press, 1989), 48–89 (76–77, Wordsworth quote); Benjamin G. Rader, *American Sports: From the Age of Folk Games to the Age of Televised Sports,* 4th ed. (Upper Saddle River, NJ: Prentice-Hall, 1999), 2–5; Elliott J. Gorn and Warren Goldstein, *A Brief History of American Sports* (New York: Hill & Wang, 1993), 6–8.

4. Twitchell, *Preposterous Violence,* 78 (Wordsworth quote); Gorn and Goldstein, *Brief History,* 9–10 (King James quote); Leigh Eric Schmidt, *Consumer Rites: The Buying and Selling of American Holidays* (Princeton, NJ: Princeton University Press, 1995), 14 ("a dance").

5. Gorn and Goldstein, *Brief History,* 33–34 (33, "spoils"); Bruce C. Daniels, *Puritans at Play: Leisure and Recreation in Colonial New England* (New York: St. Martin's Griffin, 1995), 17–19 ("mirth," "carnal and vicious"), 66–68 (66, "sinne"), 218 ("interwoven"); Rader, *American Sports,* 7 ("glorify"); Nancy L. Struna, *People of Prowess: Sport, Leisure, and Labor in Early Anglo-America* (Urbana: University of Illinois Press, 1996), 59–63; Ellis, *After the Revolution,* 127.

6. Daniels, *Puritans at Play,* 15–24 (18, "fun"), 52–66 (54, "miscarried"), 109–17 (111, Mather), 217–20 (219, "frolics"). See also Ann Wagner, *Adversaries of Dance: From the Puritans to the Present* (Urbana: University of Illinois Press, 1997), 47–64.

7. Daniels, *Puritans at Play,* 40–42; Karen Haltunnen, *Murder Most Foul: The Killer and the American Gothic Imagination* (Cambridge, MA: Harvard University Press, 1998), 7–35; Laurence Moore, "Religion, Secularization, and the Shaping of the Culture Industry in Antebellum America," *American Quarterly* 41 (June 1989): 216–42.

8. Struna, *People of Prowess,* 5, 18, 53–57 (55, ballad).

9. Ibid., 95–99, 110 ("generation"), 126–27; T. H. Breen, "Horses and Gentlemen: The Cultural Significance of Gambling among the Gentry of Virginia," *William and Mary Quarterly* 34 (April 1977): 243–56; Rhys Isaac, *The Transformation of Virginia, 1740–1790* (Chapel Hill: University of North Carolina Press, 1982), 94–104; Rader, *American Sports,* 10–11 (10, county court). On black jockeys, see Ed Hotaling, *Wink: The Incredible Life and Epic Journey of Jimmy Winkfield* (New York: McGraw-Hill, 2005), 7–8. Later, during the Revolutionary era, according to Hotaling, the black jockey Aaron Curtis "was America's first professional athlete and star of the colonies' first premier racing region." Curtis and his wealthy master, Willie Jones, "as slave and master formed the nation's first brilliant athlete-manager combination" (8).

10. Struna, *People of Prowess,* 76, 90–94, 144–56 (144, "only game"; 156, "poorer," "debauch"), 178–79; Rader, *American Sports,* 12–14 (13, "dregs").

11. Richard Butsch, *The Making of American Audiences: From Stage to Television, 1750–1990* (Cambridge: Cambridge University Press, 2000), 21–25 (21, "favor").

12. Gordon Wood, *The Radicalism of the American Revolution* (1991; reprint, New York: Vintage, 1993), 275–76.

13. Butsch, *Making of American Audiences,* 26–31 (27, "thrown away"; 28, "Ruffians").

14. Gordon Wood, "The Shopper's Revolution," *New York Review of Books,* June 10, 2004, 26, 28; T. H. Breen, *The Marketplace of Revolution: How Consumer Politics Shaped American Independence* (New York: Oxford University Press, 2004), 31–71 (31, "empire").

15. Breen, *Marketplace of Revolution,* 156–57 (*Boston Gazette* and Tennent quotes).

16. See, e.g., Ellis, *After the Revolution,* 33–37; Rader, *American Sports,* 9 (Adams quote).

17. Robert M. Lewis, ed., *From Traveling Show to Vaudeville: Theatrical Spectacle in America, 1830–1910* (Baltimore: Johns Hopkins University Press, 2003), 5 (Connecticut, New York); Anne F. Withington, *Toward a More Perfect Union: Virtue and the Formation of American Republics* (New York: Oxford University Press, 1991), esp. 10–19, 184, 228–29, 244–49.

18. Ellis, *After the Revolution*, 113–49 (116, "exhibitions"; 128, "dictate"; 134, "homespun fare"; 145–46, "take the direction").

19. Ibid., 137 ("vilest," "incompatible"), 148–58 (150, "treasury"; 151, "trash," "fools"; 153, "shameful," "warning"; 155, "profligate," "depravity").

20. Johnson, *Sam Patch*, 3–39.

21. Ibid., 41–71 (47, "great thing"; 49, "rational amusement," "decent people," "ladies and gentlemen"; 66, "some things").

22. Ibid., 71–181 (92, Stone quote).

23. Ibid., 29, 163–69 (164, "low beginnings," "anyone"; 169, "Webster").

1. Blackface, Barnum, and Newspaper Ballyhoo

1. On Rice, see, e.g., Dale Cockrell, *Demons of Disorder: Blackface Minstrels and Their World* (Cambridge: Cambridge University Press, 1997), 69–70; and Ken Emerson, *Doo-Dah! Stephen Foster and the Rise of American Popular Culture* (New York: Simon & Schuster, 1997), 62. On Day and the penny press, see David Henkin, *City Reading: Written Words and Public Spaces in Antebellum New York* (New York: Oxford University Press, 1998), 104–8; and Isabelle Lehuu, *Carnival on the Page: Popular Print Media in Antebellum America* (Chapel Hill: University of North Carolina Press, 2000), 36–41. And, on Barnum, see Benjamin Reiss, *The Showman and the Slave: Race, Death, and Memory in Barnum's America* (Cambridge, MA: Harvard University Press, 2001), 1–2.

2. Philip B. Kunhardt Jr., Philip B. Kunhardt III, and Peter W. Kunhardt, *P. T. Barnum: America's Greatest Showman* (New York: Knopf, 1995), vi (Barnum quote).

3. Cockrell, *Demons of Disorder*, 67 ("unsophisticated"); Mel Watkins, *On the Real Side: Laughing, Lying, and Signifying—the Underground Tradition of African-American Humor That Transformed American Culture from Slavery to Richard Pryor* (New York: Simon & Schuster, 1994), 84; Emerson, *Doo-Dah!* 61–62 (61, "on everybody's tongue"); W. T. Lhamon Jr., *Raising Cain: Blackface Performance from Jim Crow to Hip Hop* (Cambridge, MA: Harvard University Press, 1998), 180–85 (181, "no single stable hand"); W. T. Lhamon Jr., *Jump Jim Crow: Lost Plays, Lyrics, and Street Prose of the First Atlantic Popular Culture* (Cambridge, MA: Harvard University Press, 2003), 3–4.

4. Jon Finson, *The Voices That Are Gone: Themes in 19th-Century American Popular Song* (New York: Oxford University Press, 1994), 161 ("anti-holiday"); Reid Mitchell, *All on a Mardi Gras Day: Episodes in the History of New Orleans Carnival* (Cambridge, MA: Harvard University Press, 1995), 3; "Police Brace for Party Time," *Spokane, WA, Spokesman-Review,* May 1, 1999, A10 (Vappu).

5. Cockrell, *Demons of Disorder*, 32–34 (32, "night hideous"), 41–42; Stephen Nissenbaum, *The Battle for Christmas* (New York: Knopf, 1996), 9.

6. Eric Lott, *Love and Theft: Blackface Minstrelsy and the American Working Class* (New York: Oxford University Press, 1995), 47.

7. Lhamon, *Jump Jim Crow*, 423 n. 17 (Rice's background); Shane White, "The Death of James Johnson," *American Quarterly* 51 (December 1999): 753–55 ("shadowland"); Lhamon, *Raising Cain*, 16, 18 (population).

8. Cockrell, *Demons of Disorder*, 86 (quotes).

9. Lott, *Love and Theft*, 41–42 (De Voe quote, Hawkins); White, "Death of James Johnson," 761–62, 766.

10. White, "Death of James Johnson," 777 ("shucked"); Nicholas E. Tawa, *High-Minded and Low-Down: Music in the Lives of Americans, 1800–1861* (Boston: Northeastern University Press, 2000), 121 (William Johnson).

11. See, e.g., Tawa, *High-Minded and Low-Down*, 108.

12. Lott, *Love and Theft*, 49–51 (49, *Tribune* quote; 50, Cotton quote; 51, "marginalized"), 248–49 n. 26; Tawa, *High-Minded and Low-Down*, 121 (Wallace quote). See also Robert C. Toll, *Blacking Up: The Minstrel Show in Nineteenth-Century America* (New York: Oxford University Press, 1974), 43–46, 51. Over a century later, the white author Norman Mailer would write a famous essay, "The White Negro" (1957), in which he praised the black male who "kept for his survival the art of the primitive" and "subsisted for his Saturday night kicks" (quoted in Lott, *Love and Theft*, 54).

13. Lott, *Love and Theft*, 24–25.

14. David Carlyon, *Dan Rice: The Most Famous Man You've Never Heard Of* (New York: Public Affairs, 2001), xiii–xiv, 4–5, 41–47 (46, "nigero singing"; 47, "negro pantomime"), 356, 362; Cockrell, *Demons of Disorder*, 96 (Dixon).

15. Lott, *Love and Theft*, 23; Catherine L. Albanese, "Savage, Sinner, and Saved: Davy Crockett, Camp Meetings, and the Wild Frontier," *American Quarterly* 33 (winter 1981): 482–501 (490, "three heads"; 494, "half horse"); Elliott J. Gorn, "'Gouge and Bite, Pull Hair and Scratch': The Social Significance of Fighting in the Southern Backcountry," *American Historical Review* 90 (February 1985): 18–43 (27, "gooseberry"); Michael Allen, *Western Rivermen, 1763–1861: Ohio and Mississippi Boatmen and the Myth of the Alligator Horse* (Baton Rouge: Louisiana State University Press, 1990), 6–8.

16. Cockrell, *Demons of Disorder*, 71; Lhamon, *Jump Jim Crow*, 96–97 (96, "now forgot," "weight in wildcats," "Alligator"), 103 ("snapping turtle").

17. Paul Johnson's *A Shopkeeper's Millennium: Society and Revivals in Rochester, New York, 1815–1837* (New York: Hill & Wang, 1978) is outstanding on how these changes played out in Rochester. For a fine summary, see also Lott, *Love and Theft*, 69–71.

18. Lott, *Love and Theft*, 72, 80, and 86 (quotes).

19. Cockrell, *Demons of Disorder*, 53–54, 57 ("antitheater"); Alexander Saxton, "Blackface Minstrelsy," in *Inside the Minstrel Mask: Readings in Nineteenth-Century Blackface Minstrelsy*, ed. Annemarie Bean, James V. Hatch, and Brooks McNamara (Hanover, NH: Wesleyan University Press, 1996), 68 ("underground theater"); Lhamon, *Raising Cain*, 136; Toll, *Blacking Up*, 69–70; Lhamon, *Jump Jim Crow*, 26–27 (26, "boots"), 102 (Rice quote).

20. Neal Gabler, *Life the Movie: How Entertainment Conquered Reality* (New York: Knopf, 1998), 28–31 (29, "democrats' revenge"); William J. Mahar, *Behind the Burnt Cork Mask: Early Blackface Minstrelsy and Antebellum American Popular Culture* (Urbana: University of Illinois Press, 1999), 268–328 (minstrelsy's misogyny).

21. Toll, *Blacking Up*, 67–71 (demeaning stereotypes); David Roediger, *The Wages of Whiteness: Race and the Making of the American Working Class*, rev. ed. (New York: Verso, 1999), 95–97, 100–107 (102–3, "vile manner"), 110–11, 115 ("new sense"), 119 ("slave ship," "both make money").

22. See Lott, *Love and Theft*; Jeff Melnick and Rachel Rubin, "Black and White Stages," *Reviews in American History* 27 (December 1999): 578 (quote).

23. Roediger, *Wages of Whiteness*, 117 (Shakespeare); Lhamon, *Jump Jim Crow*, 101 ("broder"). Roediger nevertheless cautions: "Calling oneself a white slave did not necessarily imply sympathy with the black slave" (*Wages of Whiteness*, 124).

24. Lhamon, *Raising Cain*, 139 ("lam"). Lott (*Love and Theft*) also carefully analyzes this tendency. See also Starr and Waterman, *American Popular Music*, 19.

25. See, e.g., Cockrell, *Demons of Disorder*, 94, 96; Finson, *Voices That Are Gone*, 160, 165, 169 ("science"), 170 ("skoler").

26. Cockrell, *Demons of Disorder*, 92–93. For an emphasis on the racist roots and message of the Zip Coon character, see, e.g., Barbara Lewis, "Daddy Blue: The Evolution of the Dark Dandy," in Bean, Hatch, and McNamara, eds., *Inside the Minstrel Mask*, 268.

27. Cockrell, *Demons of Disorder*, 78–79 (79, "ears of mortals"); also Finson, *Voices That Are Gone*, 167–68.

28. White, "Death of James Johnson," 757, 761; Cockrell, *Demons of Disorder*, 142 ("sound morality," "agony of tears"), 147 ("terror to all Pianos"); Philip F. Gura and James F. Bollman, *America's Instrument: The Banjo in the Nineteenth Century* (Chapel Hill: University of North Carolina Press, 1999), 2, 12–15; Lott, *Love and Theft*, 89 (Whitman quote).

29. Christine Stansell, *City of Women: Sex and Class in New York, 1789–1860* (Urbana: University of Illinois Press, 1987), 89 ("plebeian"); Lott, *Love and Theft*, 65 (minstrel tune).

30. Roediger, *Wages of Whiteness*, 120 ("carpenters"), 121 ("devil"). Note that Roediger interprets the first song a bit differently.

31. Lhamon, *Jump Jim Crow*, 106 ("Semblyman"); Roediger, *Wages of Whiteness*, 126 ("dimes"); also Finson, *Voices That Are Gone*, 166–67.

32. See Lipsitz, *Time Passages*, 63–64. Roediger (*Wages of Whiteness*, 122–27) also warns against making too much of minstrelsy's oppositional culture.

33. Bean, Hatch, and McNamara, eds., *Inside the Minstrel Mask*, xi (quote).

34. Saxton, "Blackface Minstrelsy," 70–71.

35. Starr, *Creation of the Media*, 86–90.

36. Lehuu, *Carnival on the Page*, 3–4 ("carnival"), 16–17 ("controlled world"), 156; Starr, *Creation of the Media*, 134–35.

37. Alexander Saxton, "Problems of Class and Race in the Origins of the Mass Circulation Press," *American Quarterly* 36 (summer 1984): 211–12; Reiss, *The Showman and the Slave*, 35.

38. Saxton, "Problems of Class and Race," 215 ("distress"), 217–21 (220, "hadn't any capital"), 234; Reiss, *The Showman and the Slave*, 35; Michael Schudson, *Discovering the News: A Social History of American Newspapers* (New York: Basic, 1978), 18; Lehuu, *Carnival on the Page*, 45; Starr, *Creation of the Media*, 133; Juliann Sivulka, *Soap, Sex, and Cigarettes: A Cultural History of American Advertising* (Belmont, CA: Wadsworth, 1998), 27.

39. Reiss, *The Showman and the Slave*, 36, 113; Saxton, "Problems of Class and Race," 215–16; Charles Sellers, *The Market Revolution: Jacksonian America, 1815–1846* (New York: Oxford University Press, 1991), 385–86. On Bennett and the *Herald*'s early years, see James L. Crouthamel, *Bennett's New York Herald and the Rise of the Popular Press* (Syracuse, NY: Syracuse University Press, 1989), ix–x, 1–55.

40. Lehuu, *Carnival on the Page*, 41; Henkin, *City Reading*, 118 (appearance).

41. Saxton, "Problems of Class and Race," 221 (artisan roots), 225–26 ("broom," "dull," "neglected"); Andie Tucher, *Froth and Scum: Truth, Beauty, Goodness, and the Ax Murder in America's First Mass Medium* (Chapel Hill: University of North Carolina Press, 1994), 11–12, 15 ("public"); Sellers, *Market Revolution*, 386 ("understand"); Reiss, *The Showman and the Slave*, 145 (Bennett quote).

42. Saxton, "Problems of Class and Race," 223–24; Sellers, *Market Revolution*, 386.

43. Schudson, *Discovering the News*, 60; Henkin, *City Reading*, 133 ("true," Poe quote).

44. Schudson, *Discovering the News*, 19, 25–28, 60 (news, ads; 19–20, *Daily Times* quote; 27, *Herald* quote); Saxton, "Problems of Class and Race," 211 (ads); Patricia Cline Cohen, *The Murder of Helen Jewett* (New York: Vintage, 1998), 25 (size); Henkin, *City Reading*, 108–10 (*Ledger* quote, 110). See also Lehuu, *Carnival on the Page*, 46–47; and Charles L. Ponce de Leon, *Self-Exposure: Human-Interest Journalism and the Emergence of Celebrity in America, 1890–1940* (Chapel Hill: University of North Carolina Press, 2002), 48.

45. Tucher, *Froth and Scum*, 10–11, 22, 24; Lehuu, *Carnival on the Page*, 42 (the *Herald*); Crouthamel, *Rise of the Popular Press*, 28–31 (the *Herald*); Haltunnen, *Murder Most Foul*, 199–203; Cohen, *Murder of Helen Jewett*, 25–27. Cohen provides an excellent treatment of the case.

46. Tucher, *Froth and Scum*, 60–61.

47. Reiss, *The Showman and the Slave*, 151, 160.

48. Tucher, *Froth and Scum*, 70–73, 95–96; Cohen, *Murder of Helen Jewett*, 27–37.

49. Henkin, *City Reading*, 104 ("emerging modes"), 122–24; Lehuu, *Carnival on the Page*, 49–53.

50. Reiss, *The Showman and the Slave*, 36–39 (quotes); Lott, *Love and Theft*, 76–77 (profits).

51. Reiss, *The Showman and the Slave*, 13–18 (quotes); A. H. Saxon, *P. T. Barnum: The Legend and the Man* (New York: Columbia University Press, 1989), 25–28, 33–35, 39; Kunhardt, Kunhardt, and Kunhardt, *Barnum*, 4–7, 12–13.

52. Saxon, *Barnum*, 41–44; Reiss, *The Showman and the Slave*, 14–15 (quotes); Neil Harris, *Humbug: The Art of P. T. Barnum* (Chicago: University of Chicago Press, 1973), 14–17.

53. Reiss, *The Showman and the Slave,* 17; Bluford Adams, *E Pluribus Barnum: The Great Showman and U.S. Popular Culture* (Minneapolis: University of Minnesota Press, 1997), 9–10 ("many fine ladies"), 16 ("codfish aristocracy").

54. Reiss, *The Showman and the Slave,* 1–2, 18–28; P. T. Barnum, *The Life of P. T. Barnum, Written by Himself* (1855; reprint, Urbana: University of Illinois Press, 2000), 148–49, 153 (quotes).

55. Reiss, *The Showman and the Slave,* 1, 29–33 (30, "toffish Broadway set"), 45 ("focus"), 57–59 ("righteousness"), 61, 65–66, 70.

56. Ibid., 71–75, 78–79, 88–89 ("vessel," "grotesque"), 95, 107–11, 113–17; Saxon, *Barnum,* 70, 74–77; Barnum, *Life,* 156–62 ("second look").

57. Reiss, *The Showman and the Slave,* 2, 10, 78, 89, 101, 104 (attendant), 218–19 ("puttin' on"), 222 (believing).

58. Ibid., 38, 44 (smoking), 87 ("*muskrat*," "*Lady Washington*"), 101–2 ("*no one else*"), 106.

59. Ibid., 2–3, 134–39, 148–50; Saxon, *Barnum,* 70–71.

60. Adams, *E Pluribus Barnum,* 9 (circuses); Reiss, *The Showman and the Slave,* 159 (Vivalla), 168–69 (blackface and quotes).

61. Robert Bogdan, *Freak Show: Presenting Human Oddities for Amusement and Profit* (Chicago: University of Chicago Press, 1988), 29; Andrea S. Dennett, *Weird and Wonderful: The Dime Museum in America* (New York: New York University Press, 1997), 8, 12–14, 20–21, 24; Luc Sante, *Low Life: Lures and Snares of Old New York* (New York: Random House, 1991), 12 ("capital").

62. Lott, *Love and Theft,* 76 (Barnum and the Bowery); Kunhardt, Kunhardt, and Kunhardt, *Barnum,* 32 (Broadway); Sante, *Low Life,* 10 (Broadway).

63. Barnum, *Life,* 216; Kunhardt, Kunhardt, and Kunhardt, *Barnum,* 32–34; Lewis, ed., *From Traveling Show to Vaudeville,* 49.

64. P. T. Barnum, *Barnum's Own Story: The Autobiography of P. T. Barnum, Combined and Condensed from the Various Editions Published during His Lifetime by Waldo R. Browne* (New York: Viking, 1927), 122–24.

65. Dennett, *Weird and Wonderful,* 26; Adams, *E Pluribus Barnum,* 78–79; Lewis, ed., *From Traveling Show to Vaudeville,* 29–33 (29, satirist quote).

66. Bogdan, *Freak Show,* 30–31, 33; Kunhardt, Kunhardt, and Kunhardt, *Barnum,* 113 (the Lucasies); Lewis, ed., *From Traveling Show to Vaudeville,* 48–56.

67. Dennett, *Weird and Wonderful,* 83; also Rachel Shteir, "Freak Show," *The Nation,* December 29, 1997, 41.

68. Dennett, *Weird and Wonderful,* 28–29 (Clofullia), 81–82 ("boundaries"); Bogdan, *Freak Show,* 201.

69. Bogdan, *Freak Show,* 134–37 (136, "examined," "ORANG OUTANG"; 137, "cross"); Dennett, *Weird and Wonderful,* 30–31; Adams, *E Pluribus Barnum,* 158 ("MAN AND MONKEY").

70. Adams, *E Pluribus Barnum,* 158 ("sly"); Reiss, *The Showman and the Slave,* 75 ("rhino").

71. Jon Sterngass, *First Resorts: Pursuing Pleasure at Saratoga Springs, Newport, and Coney Island* (Baltimore: Johns Hopkins University Press, 2001), 128–29 (128, "jamboree"); Tucher, *Froth and Scum,* 50–51; Luc Sante, "On the 'Big Con,'" *New York Review of Books,* June 24, 1999, 38 (Poe quote).

72. James W. Cook, *The Arts of Deception: Playing with Fraud in the Age of Barnum* (Cambridge, MA: Harvard University Press, 2001), 5 ("marketplace"); Shteir, "Freak Show" (n. 67 above), 41 ("Horatio Algers," Barnum quote); Sterngass, *First Resorts,* 129 (Lost Dauphin). On Heth, see Barnum, *Life,* 155–56, 173; Saxon, *Barnum,* 72–73; and Harris, *Humbug,* 21–22. "In a more modern sense," writes Terrence Whalen, "Barnum acted as a prototypical spin doctor" (introduction to Barnum, *Life,* xiii).

73. Barnum, *Life,* 344, 352–55.

74. Sterngass, *First Resorts,* 103–4.

75. Cook, *Arts of Deception,* 8, 16, 34–39, 49–53, 66–67, 71–72; Reiss, *The Showman and the Slave,* 105 (Poe quote); Harris, *Humbug,* 23.

76. Tucher, *Froth and Scum*, 56–57; Barnum, *Barnum's Own Story*, 26 ("fabrics," "nearly everything"), 102 ("prince"), 105–7 (Niagara), 119 ("cheated"), 125 ("advertise"); *P. T. Barnum: America's Greatest Showman* (Discovery Channel documentary, 1995) (chicken).

77. Harris, *Humbug*, 3–4, 62–65; also Kunhardt, Kunhardt, and Kunhardt, *Barnum*, 43 (proposed mermaid ad); Edward Pessen, *Jacksonian America: Society, Personality, and Politics* (Homewood, IL: Dorsey, 1969), 170 (1828 poetic observation). On Barnum and Jackson, see Saxon, *Barnum*, 42.

78. Barnum, *Barnum's Own Story*, 122 ("million"); Reiss, *The Showman and the Slave*, 96 ("crowds").

79. Stansell, *City of Women*, 90–91; Butsch, *Making of American Audiences*, 45–49 (quotes); Roediger, *Wages of Whiteness*, 99–100.

80. Lott, *Love and Theft*, 82 (drawing of Lize), 83 ("stood there," "little rough"); Stansell, *City of Women*, 91–96 (Lize; 93, Foster quote); Toll, *Blacking Up*, 15–16.

81. Roediger, *Wages of Whiteness*, 100 (Nashville); Robert C. Allen, *Horrible Prettiness: Burlesque and American Culture* (Chapel Hill: University of North Carolina Press, 1991), 66 ("no longer shone"); Stansell, *City of Women*, 91–93 ("civic scum").

82. Kunhardt, Kunhardt, and Kunhardt, *Barnum*, 39 (the Irish); Harris, *Humbug*, 33 (Tappan quote); Saxon, *Barnum*, 3 ("kicked"); Adams, *E Pluribus Barnum*, 90–91.

2. TAMING ROUGH AMUSEMENTS, 1840s–1860s

1. Karen Haltunnen, *Confidence Men and Painted Women: A Study of Middle-Class Culture in America* (New Haven, CT: Yale University Press, 1982), 186–87 (Hobsbawm quote); Sellers, *Market Revolution*, 364–95 (on what he terms "the bourgeois republic"); Stuart M. Blumin, *The Emergence of the Middle Class: Social Experience in the American City, 1760–1900* (Cambridge: Cambridge University Press, 1980), esp. 65–74 (65, "redefine"; 69, "buying"), 132 ("head-work").

2. Blumin, *Emergence of the Middle Class*, 68–257 (131, "drudgeries"). On the moral fervor of the evangelical movement, see Sellers, *Market Revolution*, 202–36; and Benjamin G. Rader, *American Ways: A Brief History of American Cultures* (New York: Harcourt, 2001), 118–21. For a succinct discussion of "middle-class ways," see Rader, *American Ways*, 135–55.

3. See, e.g., Elliott J. Gorn, *The Manly Art: Bare-Knuckle Prize Fighting in America* (Ithaca, NY: Cornell University Press, 1986), 131; and Haltunnen, *Murder Most Foul*, 140.

4. Michael Kimmel, *Manhood in America: A Cultural History* (New York: Free Press, 1996), 59 ("virtual"). On style, see, e.g., Allen, *Horrible Prettiness*, 84–87; and Haltunnen, *Confidence Men*, 65–67, 75–79.

5. Haltunnen, *Confidence Men*, 92 (number of manuals), 103–4 (*Handbook* and *Treatise* quotes); John F. Kasson, *Rudeness and Civility: Manners in Nineteenth-Century Urban America* (New York: Hill & Wang, 1990), 34–69, 112–214 (but see esp. the illustrations, 46, 61, 125); C. Dallett Hemphill, *Bowing to Necessities: A History of Manners in America, 1620–1860* (New York: Oxford University Press, 1999), 129–223. Antebellum manners functioned, according to Hemphill, as "gate-keeping devices to serve the cause of social exclusivity," erecting "class barriers more than they codified democratic opportunity" (130–31). They were, thus, an "exercise in class consolidation" (219).

6. Kimmel, *Manhood in America*, 47.

7. Gorn and Goldstein, *Brief History*, 60.

8. Saxon, *Barnum*, 39.

9. Barnum, *Life*, 207, 214.

10. Barnum, *Barnum's Own Story*, 101 ("'clap-trap'"), 118 ("quarters"), 122 ("opera").

11. Adams, *E Pluribus Barnum*, 91 ("annex"), 99 ("special place"); James W. Cook, "Mass Marketing and Cultural History: The Case of P. T. Barnum," *American Quarterly* 51 (March 1999): 182.

12. Kunhardt, Kunhardt, and Kunhardt, *Barnum*, 30–31; Barnum, *Life*, 214 (quote).

13. Kunhardt, Kunhardt, and Kunhardt, *Barnum*, 25, 79, 82–83.

14. Saxon, *Barnum*, 107 ("'drink,'" "half a score"); Laurence Senelick, *The Age and Stage of George L. Fox, 1825–1877* (Iowa City: University of Iowa Press, 1999), 120 ("hor-

ror"); Kunhardt, Kunhardt, and Kunhardt, *Barnum,* 107 ("taste"); Bruce A. McConachie, *Melodramatic Formations: American Theater and Society, 1820–1870* (Iowa City: University of Iowa Press, 1992), 161 (*"ever"*).

15. Kunhardt, Kunhardt, and Kunhardt, *Barnum,* 105.

16. Lawrence W. Levine, *Highbrow/Lowbrow: The Emergence of Cultural Hierarchy in America* (Cambridge, MA: Harvard University Press, 1988), 25–26 (Irving quotes); David Grimsted, *Melodrama Unveiled: American Theater and Culture, 1800–1850* (Berkeley and Los Angeles: University of California Press, 1968), 52–53 (Bostonian quote); Butsch, *Making of American Audiences,* 46–47 (Foster quotes); Gabler, *Life the Movie,* 11 (Trollope quote).

17. Toll, *Blacking Up,* 13 ("sovereigns"); Carlyon, *Dan Rice,* 82.

18. Allen, *Horrible Prettiness,* 55 (Trollope quote); Butsch, *Making of American Audiences,* 49 ("Boweryisms").

19. Lhamon, *Raising Cain,* 29–31, 38–46; Grimsted, *Melodrama Unveiled,* 59 (Trollope quote).

20. Butsch, *Making of American Audiences,* 73.

21. Allen, *Horrible Prettiness,* 61; Levine, *Highbrow/Lowbrow,* 89–93; Butsch, *Making of American Audiences,* 64 ("ranks").

22. Tawa, *High-Minded and Low-Down,* 18.

23. Linda Williams, *Playing the Race Card: Melodramas of Black and White from Uncle Sam to O. J. Simpson* (Princeton, NJ: Princeton University Press, 2001), esp. 15, 26, 29, 40, 43; Grimsted, *Melodrama Unveiled,* 204–48 (on what he terms the "melodramatic vision").

24. Allen, *Horrible Prettiness,* 82–84; Russel B. Nye, *The Unembarrassed Muse: The Popular Arts in America* (New York: Dial, 1970), 156; McConachie, *Melodramatic Formations,* xii (quote).

25. Allen, *Horrible Prettiness,* 73–76; Gorn and Goldstein, *Brief History,* 57; Michael Isenberg, *John L. Sullivan and His America* (Urbana: University of Illinois Press, 1994), 84–85.

26. Robert C. Toll, *On with the Show! The First Century of Show Business in America* (New York: Oxford University Press, 1976), 18–21 (21, "workingmen," "English Aristocratic Opera House," "lawful rights"); Butsch, *Making of American Audiences,* 46, 54–55, 62 (*Knickerbocker* quote), 64; McConachie, *Melodramatic Formations,* 145–53. McConachie (70–118) is also good on Forrest.

27. Butsch, *Making of American Audiences,* 71–72; Lewis, ed., *From Traveling Show to Vaudeville,* 57 (*Gleason's* quote); McConachie, *Melodramatic Formations,* 167–76 (Kimball).

28. Butsch, *Making of American Audiences,* 74–80 (78, "respectability"); Faye E. Dudden, *Women in the American Theatre: Actresses and Audiences, 1790–1870* (New Haven, CT: Yale University Press, 1994), 80 ("Manager").

29. Toll, *On with the Show!* 149–51 (*Ten Nights* quotes); Saxon, *Barnum,* 105 (play at Barnum's); Dennett, *Weird and Wonderful,* 34 (Barnum quote).

30. Kunhardt, Kunhardt, and Kunhardt, *Barnum,* 48; Barnum, *Life,* 243.

31. Kunhardt, Kunhardt, and Kunhardt, *Barnum,* 48–53, 126, 163–71; Saxon, *Barnum,* 123–30 (129, "miniature"), 207 ("attractive little man"); Harris, *Humbug,* 49–50.

32. Adams, *E Pluribus Barnum,* 98–102 (98, "taint"; 99, "one third").

33. Ibid., 42 ("womanhood"), 48 ("virginity"), 54 ("flag"); Emerson, *Doo-Dah!* 171 (Whitman quote).

34. Harris, *Humbug,* 120–21, 138 (broadside quote); David Grimsted, ed., *Notions of the Americans, 1820–1860* (New York: Braziller, 1970), 9–10 (feeling).

35. Emerson, *Doo-Dah!* 171 ("'Lindomania,'" hairbrush, Canal Street); Allen, *Horrible Prettiness,* 69 (tobacco); Harris, *Humbug,* 131 (gloves); Tawa, *High-Minded and Low-Down,* 131 (youth); Adams, *E Pluribus Barnum,* 64–65.

36. Cook, "Mass Marketing," 184; Adams, *E Pluribus Barnum,* 65–66, 68.

37. Watkins, *On the Real Side,* 85; Cockrell, *Demons of Disorder,* 146–47, 157, 169; Lewis, ed., *From Traveling Show to Vaudeville,* 68–69.

38. Mahar, *Burnt Cork Mask,* 5; Butsch, *Making of American Audiences,* 81 (quote).

39. Watkins, *On the Real Side,* 87; Cockrell, *Demons of Disorder,* 151–52 (ads and editorial); Mahar, *Burnt Cork Mask,* 372 n. 27 (Whitlock).

40. Finson, *Voices That Are Gone*, 182; Cockrell, *Demons of Disorder*, 154; Mahar, *Burnt Cork Mask*, 18 (six months), 26 (playbill); Emerson, *Doo-Dah!* 93–96 (96, "hearty laugh").

41. Mahar, *Burnt Cork Mask*, 4.

42. Cockrell, *Demons of Disorder*, 153–56; Lhamon, *Jump Jim Crow*, 31; Watkins, *On the Real Side*, 94–95 (quote).

43. Watkins, *On the Real Side*, 90–94 (including quotes); Butsch, *Making of American Audiences*, 84–85; Allen, *Horrible Prettiness*, 164–65, 170; Emerson, *Doo-Dah!* 91.

44. Butsch, *Making of American Audiences*, 86–91 (including quotes).

45. See Emerson, *Doo-Dah!* 17–56.

46. Ibid., 43.

47. Ibid., 44–47, 57–58 (57, songbooks), 99–101; also Bill C. Malone, *Don't Get above Your Raisin': Country Music and the Southern Working Class* (Urbana: University of Illinois Press, 2002), 56–59; and Mahar, *Burnt Cork Mask*, 319.

48. Emerson, *Doo-Dah!* 102 ("zigzagged"), 147, 164–68, 174.

49. Finson, *Voices That Are Gone*, 182–83; Emerson, *Doo-Dah!* 128–37, 156–60.

50. Emerson, *Doo-Dah!* 175, 182–83 (Foster quote), 205–6 ("devote").

51. Ibid., 16 ("interchange"), 183 (Foster quote), 185, 195, 205–6 ("Ethiopian melodies"), 255, 258, 279–96.

52. Butsch, *Making of American Audiences*, 93 (quote).

53. Nissenbaum, *Battle for Christmas*, 4–43 (10, "claim our right"; 13, "sensual delights"); Penne L. Restad, *Christmas in America: A History* (New York: Oxford University Press, 1995), 3–8; T. J. Jackson Lears, "Piety and Plenty," *New Republic*, January 8, 1996, 45–46.

54. Susan Davis, "'Making Night Hideous': Christmas Revelry and Public Order in Nineteenth Century Philadelphia," *American Quarterly* 34 (summer 1982): 185–99.

55. Nissenbaum, *Battle for Christmas*, 38, 48; Davis, "'Making Night Hideous,'" 195–96.

56. Nissenbaum, *Battle for Christmas*, 53–65 (53, 56, Pintard quotes); Restad, *Christmas in America*, 26–28, 46–47; Lott, *Love and Theft*, 81 (Irving quotes).

57. Nissenbaum, *Battle for Christmas*, 66–68, 71–84, 99, 108 (quote); Lears, "Piety and Plenty" (n. 53 above), 47.

58. Nissenbaum, *Battle for Christmas*, 109, 122 (quote), 132; Restad, *Christmas in America*, 64 (*Godey's* quote).

59. Restad, *Christmas in America*, 137–39; Nissenbaum, *Battle for Christmas*, 222–27.

60. Nissenbaum, *Battle for Christmas*, 136–40 (139, "intensify"), 169, 173–75, 222–29; Restad, *Christmas in America*, 56, 63, 67.

61. Both Nissenbaum (*Battle for Christmas*, x, 58, 315–19) and Restad (*Christmas in America*, viii–ix) use this concept.

62. Restad, *Christmas in America*, 67, 72–73; Lears, "Piety and Plenty" (n. 53 above), 47.

63. Schmidt, *Consumer Rites*, 39–73 (64, "Come ye Lovers"; 67, "COQUETRY cured"), 92 ("ambassadors"), 94.

64. Ibid., 14; also Lears, "Piety and Plenty" (n. 53 above), 46–47.

65. Jim Cullen, *The Art of Democracy: A Concise History of Popular Culture in the United States* (New York: Monthly Review Press, 1996), 16 (Hawthorne quote).

66. Jane Tompkins, *Sensational Designs: The Cultural Work of American Fiction, 1790–1860* (New York: Oxford University Press, 1985), 124–35, 148–53; Jane Tompkins, *West of Everything: The Inner Life of Westerns* (New York: Oxford University Press, 1992), 38, 125–28; Cullen, *Art of Democracy*, 86; David S. Reynolds, *Beneath the American Renaissance: The Subversive Imagination in the Age of Emerson and Melville* (New York: Knopf, 1988), 58, 182; Williams, *Playing the Race Card*, esp. 46–48 (47, "conventional").

67. Lehuu, *Carnival on the Page*, 102–24.

68. Saxton, "Problems of Class and Race," 219–22, 227, 234; Sellers, *Market Revolution*, 386; Schudson, *Discovering the News*, 56 (depression statistics).

69. Schudson, *Discovering the News*, 49–50 (the middle class and the penny press), 52 ("Wall Street press"), 53 ("establishment"), 55–57 (55, "dirty sheet"), 200 n. 87 ("leisure," "differs"); Henkin, *City Reading*, 106–7; Gorn, *Manly Art*, 62 (boxing); Tucher, *Froth and*

Scum, 72–73; Saxton, "Problems of Class and Race," 233 ("nigger paper"). Saxton (229–34) shows that the penny press generally reflected themes of white superiority.

70. Amy Gilman Srebnick, *The Mysterious Death of Mary Rogers: Sex and Culture in Nineteenth-Century New York* (New York: Oxford University Press, 1995), esp. 28–29 ("gang"), 73–74 ("Moral Wars"), 81–82 (versions of Rogers).

71. Schmidt, *Consumer Rites,* 77–85.

72. Gorn, *Manly Art,* 132–33, 136–39. Rader (*American Sports,* 25–30) discusses this "Victorian counterculture."

73. Gorn, "'Gouge and Bite,'" 18–43 (25, quote).

74. Gorn, *Manly Art,* 73–79, 82.

75. Ibid., 81–102, 107.

76. Haltunnen, *Murder Most Foul,* 135–71 (144, "amok"; 161, "country"; 162, "coming"; 164, "chops").

77. Ibid., 182–84 (182, "woman in the case"), 207; Dawn Keetley, "Victim and Victimizer: Female Fiends and Unease over Marriage in Antebellum Sensational Fiction," *American Quarterly* 51 (June 1999): 350–75.

78. Mahar, *Burnt Cork Mask,* 268–83 (274, "Buffalo gals"), 308–26 (308, "turkey buzzard," "scolding wife"; 324, "single feller," "de breff go").

79. Elizabeth R. Mullenix, *Wearing the Breeches: Gender on the Antebellum Stage* (New York: St. Martin's, 2000), 2, 4, 16–17, 51, 56–58 (*Herald* quote), 66, 90, 102–3, 129–233.

80. Gorn, *Manly Art,* 107, 144–47.

81. Butsch (*Making of American Audiences,* 59–61) is excellent on this trend. But see also Bruce A. McConachie, "Pacifying American Theatrical Audiences, 1820–1900," in *For Fun and Profit: The Transformation of Leisure into Consumption,* ed. Richard Butsch (Philadelphia: Temple University Press, 1990), 53–59.

82. Cook, *Arts of Deception,* 27–29.

83. Ibid., 23, 78–80, 115, 118 ("not humbug?"), 260–64 (260, "diet").

84. Kunhardt, Kunhardt, and Kunhardt, *Barnum,* 190–96. On the fate of many dime museums, see Allen, *Horrible Prettiness,* 181; Dennett, *Weird and Wonderful,* 61–65; and Sante, *Low Life,* 97–100. "Bowery museums were the true underworld of entertainment," writes Sante, "desperately cheap and small-time" (99).

85. Butsch, *Making of American Audiences,* 66–68.

86. Tompkins, *Sensational Designs,* 122–46 (145, quote).

87. Reynolds, *Beneath the American Renaissance,* 54–79 (67, Gough quote; 78, *Uncle Tom's Cabin* quote); 79, "scenes").

88. Ibid., 83 (Lippard quote), 207 (statistics and *Godey's* quote).

89. Lehuu, *Carnival on the Page,* 117–19.

90. Sterngass, *First Resorts,* 38.

91. Saxon, *Barnum,* 107–8. According to Saxon: "The first American Museum, during its years under Barnum's management, actually sold more tickets in proportion to the population than did Disneyland."

92. Kunhardt, Kunhardt, and Kunhardt, *Barnum,* 117.

3. Building an Entertainment Industry

1. John Culhane, *The American Circus: An Illustrated History* (New York: Henry Holt, 1990), 141 (schedule); Janet M. Davis, *The Circus Age: Culture and Society under the American Big Top* (Chapel Hill: University of North Carolina Press, 2002), 14 (Garland quote). Davis (*Circus Age,* 1–7), Toll (*On with the Show!* 49–51), Lewis Atherton (*Main Street on the Middle Border* [1954; reprint, New York: Quadrangle, 1966], 130–35), and Jerry Apps (*Ringlingville USA: The Stupendous Story of Seven Siblings and Their Stunning Circus Success* [Madison: Wisconsin Historical Society Press, 2005], xviii–xxii) are good on circus day and small-town excitement about circuses.

2. On these trends, see, e.g., Davis, *Circus Age,* 39–42, 52–62, 227; Harris, *Humbug,* 253 (advertisement).

3. Isenberg, *John L. Sullivan*, 205–21, 235–36; Sterngass, *First Resorts*, 3, 103–4, 109; Davis, *Circus Age*, 227–28.

4. Culhane, *American Circus*, 95–103; Nye, *Unembarrassed Muse*, 190; Saxon, *Barnum*, 231–35.

5. Finson, *Voices That Are Gone*, 124–33 (130–31, "Grandfather's Clock"); Isenberg, *John L. Sullivan*, 46 (clocks); Davis, *Circus Age*, 46–50 (building "the canvas city"), 78 (War Department); Harris, *Humbug*, 240 ("routing," "Napoleon"). Barnum was not the first circus entrepreneur to use the railroad. As early as 1850, the Spalding and Rogers Circus had employed nine railroad cars. Still, it was Barnum who definitively put the shows on rails. Nye, *Unembarrassed Muse*, 189.

6. Davis, *Circus Age*, 75 (town); Culhane, *American Circus*, 127–34 (Jumbo; 129, "lie there"); Harris, *Humbug*, 258 (the era's fascination with animals). On "Jumbomania," see also Saxon, *Barnum*, 291–300.

7. Carlyon, *Dan Rice*, xiii–xiv, 4–5, 49, 159, 206–8 (206, "unnumerable thumpings"), 249–50 (editor quote); Richard W. Flint, "The Evolution of the Circus in Nineteenth-Century America," in *American Popular Entertainment*, ed. Myron Matlaw (Westport, CT: Greenwood, 1979), 187 (Sunday-School Union).

8. Flint, "Evolution of the Circus," 188 (local attorney quotes), 190–91 (Cooperstown and street parades); Carlyon, *Dan Rice*, 6, 194, 226 ("buffoon"), 235–39, 270.

9. Harris, *Humbug*, 242 ("unobjectionable," "Moral Show"); Adams, *E Pluribus Barnum*, 165–67, 173 ("NOTHING," *Times* quote, "decency"); Flint, "Evolution of the Circus," 189 (Twain quote); Davis, *Circus Age*, 35 ("Friend," orphans, crackers). Carlyon (*Dan Rice*, esp. 84–86, 235–43, 267–73) shows how Rice also strove to clean up the circus.

10. Davis, *Circus Age*, 41 and 60–61 (Ringling Brothers), 54–56 (Bailey); Culhane, *American Circus*, 138–42 (*Times* quote, Barnum quote), 145 (statistics); Harris, *Humbug*, 271 (hoops), 280 ("vulgarity").

11. Carlyon, *Dan Rice*, 198 ("G-strings"); Adams, *E Pluribus Barnum*, 173 (scantily clad women); Bogdan, *Freak Show*, 41–46.

12. Davis, *Circus Age*, 26–29 (26, "nomadic"), 169–79.

13. Ibid., 82–85, 104–13, 115, 123–26 (124, 126, snake charmer quotes), 178; M. Alison Kibler, *Rank Ladies: Gender and Cultural Hierarchy in American Vaudeville* (Chapel Hill: University of North Carolina Press, 1999), 144, 147–48, 168–69; also Adams, *E Pluribus Barnum*, 173.

14. Kibler, *Rank Ladies*, 152 ("low"); Davis, *Circus Age*, 93–98 (93, "Lady Dainty"; 94, "good breeding"; 98, "domestic instinct"), 116 ("paradoxical"), 138–41 (avoiding censorship and "prudes"), 164 n. 67 ("Cigarette").

15. Harris, *Humbug*, 287, 291–92.

16. Paul Reddin, *Wild West Shows* (Urbana: University of Illinois Press, 1999), 60 ("Barnum"), 80 (hisses); Davis, *Circus Age*, 204 ("Friends"); William W. Savage Jr., *The Cowboy Hero: His Image in American History and Culture* (Norman: University of Oklahoma Press, 1979), 109–11. On a sanitized past, see esp. Joy S. Kasson, *Buffalo Bill's Wild West: Celebrity, Memory, and Popular History* (New York: Hill & Wang, 2000), 265–66; Daniel J. Herman, "God Bless Buffalo Bill," *Reviews in American History* 29 (June 2001): 230; and Reddin, *Wild West Shows*, 61, 75–76.

17. Reddin, *Wild West Shows*, 53–55 (54, "huge pistols"); Kasson, *Buffalo Bill's Wild West*, 11–21.

18. Reddin, *Wild West Shows*, 56–59 (57, "Hello Mamma!"; 58, "*first scalp*"); Kasson, *Buffalo Bill's Wild West*, 22–38 (24–25, "fully seven hundred"; 25, "I am sorry"; 36, "single-handed fight"). Michael Denning's *Mechanic Accents: Dime Novels and Working-Class Culture in America* (New York: Verso, 1987) is an influential study of dime novels as "the contested terrain at the intersection of the culture industry and the cultures of the working classes" (5). Yellow Hair (also, "Yellow Hand") was, in fact, a warrior, not a chief, as Cody described him. Artistic renditions of Cody's "First Scalp for Custer" appeared prominently in Cody's early Wild West programs but, later on, following such things as the Wounded Knee Massacre of 1890, became something of an embarrassment. See Paul L. Hedren, "The Contradictory Legacies of Buffalo Bill Cody's First Scalp for Custer," *Montana: The Maga-

zine of Western History 55 (spring 2005): 16–35. According to Hedren: "Cody's 'first scalp for Custer' became a legacy he created but then could never shake, though one senses that as the years passed by he wanted to very badly" (16).

19. Reddin, *Wild West Shows,* 63–65 (advertising, parades, prices, "genuinely American"); Kasson, *Buffalo Bill's Wild West,* 51 ("high toned"), 55–62; Louis S. Warren, "Cody's Last Stand: Masculine Anxiety, the Custer Myth, and the Frontier of Domesticity in Buffalo Bill's Wild West," *Western Historical Quarterly* 34 (spring 2003): 49–69 (63, "lassoing wild horses"; 65, poem). Warren argues that, in Cody's show, "this act of home defense was as present as Custer's Last Fight was absent" (54). Richard White astutely categorizes Cody's dramatic narrative as "an odd story of conquest: everything is inverted. His spectacles presented an account of Indian aggression and white defense; of Indian killers and white victims; of, in effect, badly abused conquerors" ("Frederick Jackson Turner and Buffalo Bill," in *The Frontier in American Culture,* ed. Richard White and Patricia Nelson Limerick [Berkeley and Los Angeles: University of California Press, 1994], 27).

20. Reddin, *Wild West Shows,* 60–61 (frontier anxiety), 122 (Cody at a historical juncture); also Kasson, *Buffalo Bill's Wild West,* 62, 114–20.

21. Reddin, *Wild West Shows,* 70 ("bullet"); Davis, *Circus Age,* 193 ("Strange People"), 209 (San Juan Hill [including program quotes]), 213 (Boxers [including program quotes]).

22. Davis, *Circus Age,* 131, 183 ("Bushmen"), 184 ("doomed"), 185 ("South Pacific," "cave"), 194 ("cheerleaders"), 207 (Beloit), 208 ("Philippines"), 216 ("India").

23. See Robert W. Rydell, *All the World's a Fair: Visions of Empire at America's International Expositions, 1876–1916* (Chicago: University of Chicago Press, 1984), 237 ("sliding scale"); Robert W. Rydell, *World of Fairs: The Century-of-Progress Expositions* (Chicago: University of Chicago Press, 1993), 15–24 (other examples); Davis, *Circus Age,* 192 (Sells quote).

24. L. G. Moses, *Wild West Shows and the Images of American Indians, 1883–1933* (Albuquerque: University of New Mexico Press, 1996), esp. 5–6, 25–27, 38, 44–46 (44, Black Elk quote), 103, 140–41, 173–76, 194, 272–73, 279 (Rockboy quote); Davis, *Circus Age,* 184 ("Red Man"), 186 ("worms"). Bobby Bridger (*Buffalo Bill and Sitting Bull: Inventing the West* [Austin: University of Texas Press, 2002], esp. 6–16, 316–20, 327–29) makes an arresting case for Cody as a protector of Native American culture from government agents and missionaries. Indeed, from this angle, the show became a kind of "blessed sanctuary" (328) for the native participants. Bridger acknowledges, however, that, in order to provide the requisite dramatic tension, "Cody's western melodramas" cast the Indians as "symbolic 'bad guys'" against Cody's "heroic Euroamerican's 'good guy' forces" (304–5).

25. Kasson, *Buffalo Bill's Wild West,* 213–17.

26. Finson, *Voices That Are Gone,* 200 (numbers); Toll, *Blacking Up,* 134–37, 147, 149, 154–55 (Thatcher and Dockstader quotes).

27. Toll, *Blacking Up,* 25 ("find out"), 145–48 (Haverly [including remaining quotes]), 149 (statistics).

28. Ibid., 138–39.

29. Ibid., 160–62, 166–67, 171–72, 181, 185.

30. Ibid., 195–206 (195, "'culled pussons'"; 199, "Simon Pure"; 202, "greater fidelity"; 205, "genuine sons"); Watkins, *On the Real Side,* 107–11.

31. Finson, *Voices That Are Gone,* 203–7.

32. Toll, *Blacking Up,* 209.

33. Finson, *Voices That Are Gone,* 226–30.

34. Toll, *Blacking Up,* 195 (Handy quote); Watkins, *On the Real Side,* 112.

35. Watkins, *On the Real Side,* 114.

36. W. T. Lhamon Jr., "Core Is Less," *Reviews in American History* 27 (December 1999): 567–68.

37. Nadine George-Graves, *The Royalty of Negro Vaudeville: The Whitman Sisters and the Negotiation of Race, Gender, and Class in African American Theater, 1900–1940* (New York: St. Martin's, 2000), 59–60.

38. Watkins, *On the Real Side,* 100–101 (Fletcher quote); Toll, *Blacking Up,* 221–22 (Handy and Wright).

39. Toll, *Blacking Up,* 219 (census), 222–23 (Handy quote and Kersands's salary). On Kersands's act, see ibid., 215; and Watkins, *On the Real Side,* 113.

40. Toll, *Blacking Up,* 225–28 (Handy quotes); Watkins, *On the Real Side,* 124–32; Finson, *Voices That Are Gone,* 238 (Johnson quote).

41. M. M. Manring, *Slave in a Box: The Strange Career of Aunt Jemima* (Charlottesville: University of Virginia Press, 1998), 12, 60–75 (74, "mass market"), 150–51, 182–83; Marilyn Kern-Foxworth, *Aunt Jemima, Uncle Ben, and Rastus: Blacks in Advertising, Yesterday, Today, and Tomorrow* (Westport, CT: Praeger, 1994), 63–67. Bernard Wolfe ("Uncle Remus and the Malevolent Rabbit," *Commentary,* July 1949, 31–41) examines the "grinner-giver" phenomenon of an Aunt Jemima as a white creation.

42. Karen Linn, *That Half-Barbaric Twang: The Banjo in American Popular Culture* (New York: Oxford University Press, 1991), 20–21 (concert ad and banjo teacher quote); Gura and Bollman, *America's Instrument,* frontispiece ("National Musical Instrument"), 138–39 ("iconic").

43. Gura and Bollman, *America's Instrument,* 135. For information on key banjo entrepreneurs, see ibid., 66–71 (James Ashborn), 84–85 (Frank Converse), and 108–26 (the Dobson brothers).

44. Gura and Bollman, *America's Instrument,* 139–44, 160–66.

45. Linn, *That Half-Barbaric Twang,* 3, 20–36 (29, "common sense"; 34, "lusty note"); Gura and Bollman, *America's Instrument,* frontispiece (Twain quotes).

46. Isenberg, *John L. Sullivan,* 80–81; Gorn and Goldstein, *Brief History,* 119.

47. Gorn and Goldstein, *Brief History,* 115–19; Isenberg, *John L. Sullivan,* 92–96 (94, Fox's orders); Howard Chudacoff, *The Age of the Bachelor: Creating an American Subculture* (Princeton, NJ: Princeton University Press, 1999), 187–208 (192, "vulgarity"; 191–92, "ankles and legs"); Allen, *Horrible Prettiness,* 201–3 ("gold diggers").

48. Isenberg, *John L. Sullivan,* 17–38 (background), 96–113 (101, "triple"); Jeffrey T. Sammons, *Beyond the Ring: The Role of Boxing in American Society* (Urbana: University of Illinois Press, 1990), 7.

49. Isenberg, *John L. Sullivan,* 68–69 (on the rules), 113 (Godkin quote), 117–204 (147, "challenging"), 290–93 (race).

50. Ibid., 128–32, 168–74, 183–87.

51. Ibid., 213–384 (216, "magnificent machine," "wonderful engine"; 235, "wild throwback").

52. Jules Tygiel, *Past Time: Baseball as History* (New York: Oxford University Press, 2000), 5, 10–11 (11, "more ordered"); John P. Rossi, *The National Game: Baseball and American Culture* (Chicago: Ivan Dee, 2000), 6–8.

53. Mandelbaum, *Meaning of Sports,* 40–52 (baseball's backward-looking characteristics); Gunther Barth, *City People: The Rise of Modern City Culture in Nineteenth-Century America* (New York: Oxford University Press, 1980), 148–49, 178–83, 190; Steven Gelber, "Working at Playing: The Culture of the Workplace and the Rise of Baseball," *Journal of Sport History* 10 (summer 1983): 3–22; Steven Gelber, "'Their Hands Are All Out Playing': Business and Amateur Baseball, 1845–1917," *Journal of Sport History* 11 (summer 1984): 5–27. There are several excellent histories of baseball. See, e.g., Benjamin G. Rader, *Baseball: A History of America's Game* (Urbana: University of Illinois Press, 1992); and Rossi, *National Game.*

54. Rossi, *National Game,* 9–10 (9, "mathematical wonder"); Tygiel, *Past Time,* 16–32 (21, "religious improvement"; 25, "mini-morality plays").

55. Warren Goldstein, "The Base Ball Fraternity," in *Baseball History from Outside the Lines: A Reader,* ed. John E. Dreifort (Lincoln: University of Nebraska Press, 2001), 3–17 (17, "appealed"); Rossi, *National Game,* 14.

56. Rossi, *National Game,* 12–13 (Civil War; 13, "National Wounds"); Steven A. Riess, "Professional Baseball and Social Mobility," in Dreifort, ed., *Baseball History,* 34–46; Michael S. Kimmel, "Baseball and the Reconstitution of American Masculinity, 1880–1920," in ibid., 59 (remaining quotes).

57. Ronald Story, "The Country of the Young: The Meaning of Baseball in Early American Culture," in Dreifort, ed., *Baseball History,* 19–33 (21, "counterpart," "precursor"; 25, "band of brothers"; 26, "instantaneous community").

58. Rossi, *National Game*, 15–17; Rader, *Baseball*, 25–26 (quote); Gorn and Goldstein, *Brief History*, 126–27.

59. Rossi, *National Game*, 17–33, 41–48; Riess, "Social Mobility," 35–36; Tygiel, *Past Time*, 31 (Chadwick quote).

60. Walter LaFeber, *Michael Jordan and the New Global Capitalism* (New York: Norton, 2002), 36 (Spalding).

61. Mandelbaum, *Meaning of Sports*, 4–8, 16, 52–63 (baseball's appeal and the detective novel analogy); Atherton, *Main Street*, 200–202 (small-town examples).

62. David Q. Voigt, "America's Manufactured Villain—the Baseball Umpire," in *Things in the Driver's Seat: Readings in Popular Culture*, ed. Harry R. Huebel (Chicago: Rand McNally, 1972), 46–59.

63. Kimmel, *Manhood in America*, 78–122 (84, "banker's world"; 88, "namby-pamby life"; 122, "flabby"); Judy Hilkey, *Character Is Capital: Success Manuals and Manhood in Gilded Age America* (Chapel Hill: University of North Carolina Press, 1997), 116–19; Clifford Putney, *Muscular Christianity: Manhood and Sports in Protestant America, 1880–1920* (Cambridge, MA: Harvard University Press, 2001), 118–19 ("hero").

64. Steven A. Riess, "Sport and the Redefinition of American Middle-Class Masculinity," *International Journal of the History of Sport* 8 (1991): 5–27; Kimmel, "Baseball," 59 (quote). On the ideology of sport, see Melvin L. Adelman, *A Sporting Time: New York City and the Rise of Modern Athletics, 1820–1870* (Urbana: University of Illinois Press, 1986), 269–86; and Steven A. Riess, *City Games: The Evolution of American Urban Society and the Rise of Sports* (Urbana: University of Illinois Press, 1989), 26–32, 46–47, 253–54.

65. Riess, "Redefinition," 18–19 (Whitney quote); Gorn and Goldstein, *Brief History*, 130 ("consuming").

66. Gorn and Goldstein, *Brief History*, 130–31, 154–57; Ronald A. Smith, *Sports and Freedom: The Rise of Big-Time College Athletics* (New York: Oxford University Press, 1988), 70–81.

67. Smith, *Sports and Freedom*, 92 (Remington), 96–97 (quotes).

68. See, e.g., David Wallace Adams, "More Than a Game: The Carlisle Indians Take to the Gridiron, 1892–1917," *Western Historical Quarterly* 32 (spring 2001): 30 (quote); Michael Oriard, *Reading Football: Sport, Popular Journalism, and American Culture, 1876–1913* (Chapel Hill: University of North Carolina Press, 1993), 27, 40–46; Smith, *Sports and Freedom*, 84–86; Gorn and Goldstein, *Brief History*, 160–61, 168; Mandelbaum, *Meaning of Sports*, 119–25, 164; Rader, *American Sports*, 85–88.

69. Oriard, *Reading Football*, 57–60. Hilkey (*Character Is Capital*, 15–54) discusses the subscription book industry and the proliferating success manuals.

70. Oriard, *Reading Football*, 60–70, 89–101.

71. Ibid., 89 ("formulaic"), 120–21 and 128 (wire services and syndicates), 185 ("gladiators"), 228 ("muscle").

72. Ibid., 109 ("arms"), 110 ("'best girl'"), 250–51 (New Woman, "Ivanhoe"), 252 (advantages).

73. Adams, "More Than a Game," 25–28 (26–27, "travels"), 31 ("brawn," "victorious paleface"); Oriard, *Reading Football*, 233–38 (234, "make a record"; 237, "highest type"; 238, "modernized phase").

74. Adams, "More Than a Game," 34–46 (35, cartoon; 36, "invaded the East"; 41, "no Frontier Myth"; 42, "beauty of it all"; 43, "the biggest crowd"; 45–46, "do most anything").

75. Ibid., 42 (quote).

4. "THE BILLION-DOLLAR SMILE": FROM BURLESQUE TO VAUDEVILLE AND AMUSEMENT PARKS

1. Woody Register, *The Kid of Coney Island: Fred Thompson and the Rise of American Amusements* (New York: Oxford University Press, 2001), 11 ("smile").

2. Levine, *Highbrow/Lowbrow*, 83–168 (cultural sacralization; 123, "yacht"; 134, Thomas quote; 157, Henry quote; 158, "pretty books"; 185 (Twain quote). On "the disciplining of spectatorship," see also Kasson, *Rudeness and Civility*, esp. 215–16, 233–48.

3. Toll, *On with the Show!* 208–9 ("depraved"); Allen, *Horrible Prettiness*, 92–94; Dudden, *Women in the American Theatre*, 116–18 (116–17, cheering); Butsch, *Making of American Audiences*, 95–102 (98, "Bacchus").

4. Dudden, *Women in the American Theatre*, 123–41 (130, "mentally unstable").

5. Ibid., 143–44 (143, "short-petticoated ladies," "miscellaneous legs"), 148; Allen, *Horrible Prettiness*, 105–6 (*Clipper* quotes, "bevy").

6. For a meticulous treatment of Menken, see Sentilles, *Performing Menken*, esp. 91–93 (the Mazeppa performance), 202 and 231–39 (song and photographs). See also Mullenix, *Wearing the Breeches*, 248, 343 n. 32; Dudden, *Women in the American Theatre*, 157–61; Allen, *Horrible Prettiness*, 96–100; and Toll, *On with the Show!* 213.

7. Sentilles, *Performing Menken*, 3–12 (11, "fathers"), 21–24, 220 ("wives"); Toll, *On with the Show!* 211–13 ("taming," "darling"); Rachel Shteir, *Striptease: The Untold History of the Girlie Show* (New York: Oxford University Press, 2004), 24–26.

8. Sentilles, *Performing Menken*, 16–17, 91, 94–107 (105, "bewitching").

9. Haltunnen, *Confidence Men*, 93 ("bourgeois etiquette"), 161–67 (167, "new view"), 188 ("homage"); Sentilles, *Performing Menken*, 13, 16, 61–67, 75–76, 226–27.

10. Sentilles, *Performing Menken*, esp. 1–2, 5–6, 8, 50, 115, 117, 122, 127; Dudden, *Women in the American Theatre*, 157–59.

11. Mullenix, *Wearing the Breeches*, 249–51; Sentilles, *Performing Menken*, 202.

12. Toll, *On with the Show!* 172–75; Dudden, *Women in the American Theatre*, 149–54 (150, Bennett quote); Allen, *Horrible Prettiness*, 108–17 (111–12, *Times* quote, *Clipper* quote, "take a peek"); Peter G. Buckley, "The Culture of 'Leg-Work': The Transformation of Burlesque after the Civil War," in *The Mythmaking Frame of Mind: Social Imagination and American Culture*, ed. James Gilbert et al. (Belmont, CA: Wadsworth, 1993), 115 (Twain quote), 118 (profits), 126 (Union League); Shteir, *Striptease*, 27–28; Denny M. Flinn, *Musical! A Grand Tour* (New York: Schirmer, 1997), 81–82. According to Flinn: "[*The Black Crook*] was revived in New York at least fifteen times and toured throughout the United States for the next *forty years*" (82).

13. For the various cultural and historical uses of burlesque, see Allen, *Horrible Prettiness*, 25–42, 101–4; Alan Trachtenberg, foreword to Allen, *Horrible Prettiness*, xii ("wicked fun"); and Buckley, "Culture of 'Leg-Work,'" 119 ("licentious legs").

14. Allen, *Horrible Prettiness*, 3–7 (Thompson's background and Wood's theater), 61–117 (the theatrical accommodations to the middle class and the challenges of feminized spectacle), 117 (quote). See also Butsch, *Making of American Audiences*, 74–80; and Toll, *On with the Show!* 149–59 (melodramas such as *East Lynne* and *Rip Van Winkle*; 157, "live long and prosper").

15. Allen, *Horrible Prettiness*, 137–56 (137, Allen quotes; 140, "these rebellious days"); Dudden, *Women in the American Theatre*, 164–67; Buckley, "Culture of 'Leg-Work,'" 131.

16. Buckley, "Culture of 'Leg-Work,'" 123 (*Tribune* quote); Dudden, *Women in the American Theatre*, 165 (*Times* quote); Allen, *Horrible Prettiness*, 204–14 (posters).

17. Dudden, *Women in the American Theatre*, 169; Allen, *Horrible Prettiness*, 132 ("legs and busts"), 160 ("retired"), 206–19, 225–32, 240, 259; Shteir, *Striptease*, 54.

18. Linda Mizejewski, *Ziegfeld Girl: Image and Icon in Culture and Cinema* (Durham, NC: Duke University Press, 1999), 8, 12–14 (12, quotes); David L. Chapman, *Sandow the Magnificent: Eugen Sandow and the Beginnings of Bodybuilding* (Urbana: University of Illinois Press, 1994), 57–58; Toll, *On with the Show!* 296–97. Simon Louvish (*Man on the Flying Trapeze: The Life and Times of W. C. Fields* [New York: Norton, 1997], 174) is suspicious that the Wild West show claim may have been another example of "Ziegfeldism flim-flam."

19. John F. Kasson, *Houdini, Tarzan, and the Perfect Man: The White Male Body and the Challenge of Modernity in America* (New York: Hill & Wang, 2001), 52–53; Mizejewski, *Ziegfeld Girl*, 14; Chapman, *Sandow the Magnificent*, 60–61, 75 (*Gazette* quote); Toll, *On with the Show!* 297–98.

20. Chapman, *Sandow the Magnificent*, 70–95 (the tours; 62, 84, 89, Sandow's changing costume; 93, Sandow's nutritional advice); Kasson, *Perfect Man*, 28–38, 54, 68–76 (Sandow's redefinition of masculinity; 32, 76, quotes). Kasson emphasizes that Sandow offered

"a *white* European ideal," confirming "the place of white European men on the top of the racial hierarchy" (54).

21. Mizejewski, *Ziegfeld Girl,* esp. 13, 33, 41, 45–46 ("fake story"); Louvish, *Man on the Flying Trapeze,* 175; Toll, *On with the Show!* 299–300.

22. Mizejewski, *Ziegfeld Girl,* 44 ("filthy"), 49–53 ("bodice"); Shteir, *Striptease,* 49–50; Susan Faludi, *Backlash: The Undeclared War against American Women* (New York: Crown, 1992), 173 ("lace her tight"); Susan Glenn, *Female Spectacle: The Theatrical Roots of Modern Feminism* (Cambridge, MA: Harvard University Press, 2000), 170 ("genius"). On "the complex Victorian fascination" with corsets and sexuality, see T. J. Jackson Lears, *Fables of Abundance: A Cultural History of Advertising in America* (New York: Basic, 1994), 151–53.

23. Allen, *Horrible Prettiness,* 245; William R. Leach, *Land of Desire: Merchants, Power, and the Rise of a New American Culture* (New York: Pantheon, 1993), 3 ("amuse"), 5–7 ("democratize desire"), 28–29, 34–35 ("MONEY"), 40, 63–66; Mizejewski, *Ziegfeld Girl,* 11, 91 ("Ziegfeld stage"); Glenn, *Female Spectacle,* 164–66.

24. See, e.g., David Nasaw, *Going Out: The Rise and Fall of Public Amusements* (New York: Basic, 1993), 19; Toll, *On with the Show!* 265–67; Allen, *Horrible Prettiness,* 178–79; Lawrence J. Epstein, *The Haunted Smile: The Story of Jewish Comedians in America* (New York: Public Affairs, 2001), 28 (the word *vaudeville*'s origins); also Albert F. McLean Jr., *American Vaudeville as Ritual* (Lexington: University of Kentucky Press, 1965), 19.

25. Kibler, *Rank Ladies,* 5 (vaudeville's nationally "consolidated network of commercial leisure"); John E. DiMeglio, *Vaudeville, U.S.A.* (Bowling Green, OH: Bowling Green University Popular Press, 1973), 4 ("tracks"); Toll, *On with the Show!* 267–69; Robert W. Snyder, *The Voice of the City: Vaudeville and Popular Culture in New York* (New York: Oxford University Press, 1989), 12–25.

26. Louvish, *Man on the Flying Trapeze,* 25; Toll, *On with the Show!* 269–71; Snyder, *Voice of the City,* 26–30; DiMeglio, *Vaudeville, U.S.A.,* 48, 50 (Albee quotes).

27. Snyder, *Voice of the City,* 34–41; Kibler, *Rank Ladies,* 10, 15–20; Louvish, *Man on the Flying Trapeze,* 26 (statistics).

28. Snyder, *Voice of the City,* 84–100 (95, "minor leagues").

29. Geoffrey O'Brien, "The Triumph of Marxism," *New York Review of Books,* July 20, 2000, 8; Groucho Marx, *Groucho and Me: The Autobiography* (1959; reprint, London: Virgin, 2002), 95 ("buried"), 105–6; Charles W. Stein, ed., *American Vaudeville as Seen by Its Contemporaries* (New York: Knopf, 1984), 286 ("survived," "pelted"); DiMeglio, *Vaudeville, U.S.A.,* 94 (Chaplin quote), 100 (Allen quote), 172 (Tucker quote), 187 ("sanctuaries"); Snyder, *Voice of the City,* 57 ("suspicion"). See also Benjamin McArthur, *Actors and American Culture, 1880–1920* (Philadelphia: Temple University Press, 1984), 62–65 (performers' life on the road).

30. Snyder, *Voice of the City,* 43–46 (Minnie Marx quote), 49–56 (Cantor, Burns quote, Cline, Tucker); DiMeglio, *Vaudeville, U.S.A.,* 60 (Tucker quote); Louvish, *Man on the Flying Trapeze,* 171–72 (Cantor), 181–82 (Brice).

31. O'Brien, "The Triumph of Marxism" (n. 29 above), 8; Marx, *Groucho and Me,* 77 (Groucho quote); Stein, ed., *American Vaudeville,* 286 (Harpo quote).

32. DiMeglio, *Vaudeville, U.S.A.,* 197; Glenn, *Female Spectacle,* 41–42; Isenberg, *John L. Sullivan,* 46. On the poolroom sketch, see Toll, *On with the Show!* 290–91; and McLean, *American Vaudeville as Ritual,* 127–31. On the new humor, see Alan Havig, *Fred Allen's Radio Comedy* (Philadelphia: Temple University Press, 1990), 1, 35–36; and McLean, *American Vaudeville as Ritual,* 98, 106–37.

33. Havig, *Fred Allen's Radio Comedy,* 36 (Allen quotes); Snyder, *Voice of the City,* 139 (Fields and Weber); Louvish, *Man on the Flying Trapeze,* 13 ("nut act"); Glenn, *Female Spectacle,* 41–42 (Cohan quote).

34. Louvish, *Man on the Flying Trapeze,* 206 (Burns quote); Epstein, *Haunted Smile,* xix (Berle quote).

35. Snyder, *Voice of the City,* 110–11 ("synthetic," R. E. Irwin quote); Kibler, *Rank Ladies,* 57–58, 128–29 (Tucker and May Irwin); Nasaw, *Going Out,* 53–61; DiMeglio, *Vaudeville, U.S.A.,* 111 (Waters quote). On the TOBA, see Watkins, *On the Real Side,* 365–67.

36. DiMeglio, *Vaudeville, U.S.A.,* 109, 114 (Fanton quote); Snyder, *Voice of the City,* 120 ("free thing"); Kibler, *Rank Ladies,* 126–29 (129, "big and ugly"), 133 ("sister team"), 138–40 (Wayburn); Glenn, *Female Spectacle,* 109–10 (Tanguay).

37. *New York Times,* February 10, 1999, B1 (Stephens quote); Snyder, *Voice of the City,* 113–14 (Rooney quote and brick joke); Nasaw, *Going Out,* 53 (Wynn quote); Toll, *On with the Show!* 289 (Mike joke).

38. Epstein, *Haunted Smile,* xi, xvii, 11 (statistics), 31–32 ("wrong reasons"), 62 (Benny quote); Snyder, *Voice of the City,* 123 ("Bushwick").

39. Watkins, *On the Real Side,* 174–78 (178, "artless darky"); Snyder, *Voice of the City,* 121 ("free"); Louvish, *Man on the Flying Trapeze,* 181 ("'Jonah Man'").

40. Watkins, *On the Real Side,* 174–75 (mob, Fields quote); DiMeglio, *Vaudeville, U.S.A.,* 114 (Cantor/Williams quote, Washington quote).

41. See, e.g., Epstein, *Haunted Smile,* esp. x–xxi, 20 (humor's several sides); Snyder, *Voice of the City* (Russell Brothers); Kibler, *Rank Ladies,* 56 (quote).

42. Snyder, *Voice of the City,* 34, 132; Kibler, *Rank Ladies,* 11 (quotes).

43. McLean, *American Vaudeville as Ritual,* 97 ("soubrette"); Kibler, *Rank Ladies,* 12, 42, 50–51 (50, "Miss Ronca"; 51, "a hit"), 76, 106, 208; DiMeglio, *Vaudeville U.S.A.,* 125 ("shoot another man").

44. See, e.g., Lynn Spigel, *Make Room for TV: Television and the Family Ideal in Postwar America* (Chicago: University of Chicago Press, 1992), 152.

45. Glenn, *Female Spectacle,* 48 (Shaw [including quotes]), 56–63 (Dressler and Friganza [including quotes]).

46. Toll, *On with the Show!* 278–81 (quotes). See also the excellent treatments of Tanguay in Marybeth Hamilton, *"When I'm Bad, I'm Better": Mae West, Sex, and American Entertainment* (Berkeley and Los Angeles: University of California Press, 1996), 38–44; Glenn, *Female Spectacle,* esp. 63–66, 108–10; and Snyder, *Voice of the City,* 54, 149–51.

47. Kibler, *Rank Ladies,* 14 (Pavlova), 219 n. 59 ("Vaudeville something"); Snyder, *Voice of the City,* 149–50; Louvish, *Man on the Flying Trapeze,* 75; Toll, *On with the Show!* 281 ("some people," "naughty," "never drink," "never smoke"); Glenn, *Female Spectacle,* 65–66 (song quotes); Hamilton, *"When I'm Bad, I'm Better,"* 40 ("consequences").

48. Glenn, *Female Spectacle,* 7 (Caffin quote); Kibler, *Rank Ladies,* 55, 62–66 (64, "little weasel"), 77 ("brief moments").

49. George-Graves, *Royalty of Negro Vaudeville,* xii, 13–47, 98.

50. Ibid., esp. 10–11, 84–85 (children), 101.

51. Nasaw, *Going Out,* 32–33 (quote); Snyder, *Voice of the City,* 132 ("minister"), 138–45, 153 ("institution"); Kibler, *Rank Ladies,* 8, 97 ("genius of Sophocles"), 107 ("vaudevillized").

52. On electricity (including the work of the celebrated scientist Nicola Tesla on alternating currents and the subsequent "battle of the currents" between the Edison/General Electric direct current and the Tesla/Westinghouse alternating alternative), see Pierre Berton, *Niagara: A History of the Falls* (New York: Penguin, 1992), 154–63. On electricity and the world's fair, Erik Larson, *The Devil in the White City: Murder, Magic, and Madness at the Fair That Changed America* (New York: Crown, 2003), 131.

53. Roy Rosenzweig, *Eight Hours for What We Will: Workers and Leisure in an Industrial City, 1870–1920* (Cambridge: Cambridge University Press, 1983), 171–80 (Bigelow [including quotes]); Michael Immerso, *Coney Island: The People's Playground* (New Brunswick, NJ: Rutgers University Press, 2002).

54. Sterngass, *First Resorts,* 75–99 (79, "hordes"; 98, "moved down to the sea"; 99, "toiling dwellers"); Immerso, *Coney Island,* 12–45.

55. Rosenzweig, *Eight Hours,* 1 (Worcester march, Senate testimony), 35–36, 179–80 (statistics); Sterngass, *First Resorts,* 99–100 (statistics, "unproductive time"); Immerso, *Coney Island,* 16 ("Old Ocean"), 41 (*Harper's* quote).

56. Immerso, *Coney Island,* 16 ("unwashed"); Sterngass, *First Resorts,* 99 (Strong quote).

57. Register, *Kid of Coney Island,* 14–16, 24–39, 57, 61, 68, 85 (*Sun* quote).

58. Ibid., 64 ("inventor"), 67–68, 80–81 (midway quotes).

59. Ibid., 85–91; Immerso, *Coney Island,* 6–7, 48–61; John F. Kasson, *Amusing the Mil-*

lion: *Coney Island at the Turn of the Century* (New York: Hill & Wang, 1978), 33–35; Edo McCullough, *Good Old Coney Island* (New York: Fordham University Press, 2000), 296–99 (Boynton). On Gates as Thompson's silent partner, see Register, *Kid of Coney Island*, 93–94; and McCullough, *Good Old Coney Island*, 304.

60. Immerso, *Coney Island*, 60–67 ("carnival"); Kasson, *Amusing the Million*, 63 ("world removed"), 66 ("Newport," "ordinary experience"); Register, *Kid of Coney Island*, 104 ("fairies").

61. Register, *Kid of Coney Island*, 83 ("sideshow"), 88 ("spectacle"), 91 ("deplorable"), 95–97.

62. Ibid., 81 ("masses"), 93 (concessions), 97 ("pure"); Immerso, *Coney Island*, 68 (investment).

63. Immerso, *Coney Island*, 68–82.

64. Register, *Kid of Coney Island*, 98 ("pace," general statistics); Immerso, *Coney Island*, 103 (numbers by 1910); Nasaw, *Going Out*, 86–87, 95 (examples).

65. Immerso, *Coney Island*, 81 ("slimy marsh," "dismal ugliness," "black flies"); Kasson, *Amusing the Million*, 108–9 ("new opiate").

66. Kasson, *Amusing the Million*, 50; see also Sterngass, *First Resorts*, 109.

67. Nasaw, *Going Out*, 91 ("hugged"). Kasson (*Amusing the Million*, 40–86) nicely conveys a sense of the kinds of fun that accompanied a visit to Coney Island.

68. Immerso, *Coney Island*, 107–8 ("bedlam"), 116–17 ("river").

69. Nasaw, *Going Out*, 92–93; Sterngass, *First Resorts*, 105; Immerso, *Coney Island*, 134–35, 139 (Johnson).

70. Sterngass, *First Resorts*, esp. 4, 104, 110–12; Kasson, *Amusing the Million*, 44 ("fashion"); Kathy Peiss, *Cheap Amusements: Working Women and Leisure in Turn-of-the-Century New York* (Philadelphia: Temple University Press, 1986), 136–38.

71. Sterngass, *First Resorts*, 256 (Thompson quote), 257–58 (O. Henry quote); Immerso, *Coney Island*, 133 (Tilyou quote). Sterngass (*First Resorts*, 124–25) notes that early tourist resorts helped shape these patterns in which communities of pleasure served as buffers against modern alienation.

72. Sterngass, *First Resorts*, esp. 181, 259–77 (259, "frisky"); Kasson, *Amusing the Million*, 66 ("everything"), 73–74 (machines), 82 ("danger").

73. William Howland Kenney, *Recorded Music in American Life: The Phonograph and Popular Memory, 1890–1945* (New York: Oxford University Press, 1999), 31–32.

5. THE "LEISURE PROBLEM" AT THE TURN OF THE CENTURY

1. Kasson, *Amusing the Million*, 98–105 (100, Addams quote).

2. LeRoy Ashby, *William Jennings Bryan: Champion of Democracy* (Boston: Twayne, 1987), 98–99 (White quotes, Howe quote).

3. Hiram Johnson to "My dear Boys," July 2, 1921, Hiram Johnson Papers, pt. IV, box 2, University of California, Berkeley.

4. Stefan Lorant, *The Life and Times of Theodore Roosevelt* (New York: Doubleday, 1959), 496 (Roosevelt quote); Robert Crunden, *Ministers of Reform: The Progressives' Achievement in American Civilization, 1889–1920* (New York: Basic, 1982); Ashby, *William Jennings Bryan*, 191 (Bryan quote); Hamilton, *"When I'm Bad, I'm Better,"* 10 (Addams quote).

5. See, e.g., Paul Boyer, *"In His Steps:* A Reappraisal," *American Quarterly* 23 (spring 1971): 60–78.

6. Paul O'Neill, "Frank Merriwell Is Back!" *Life*, February 11, 1972, 51–54. Nye, *Unembarrassed Muse*, 73 (I don't know).

7. Brad Leithauser, "The Awkward Age," *New York Review of Books*, December 19, 2002, 36–39.

8. Nye, *Unembarrassed Muse*, 37–40.

9. Ibid., 117–25, 132–33.

10. Roderick Nash, *The Nervous Generation: American Thought, 1917–1930* (Chicago: Rand McNally, 1970), 140 (quote).

11. See, e.g., Ponce de Leon, *Self-Exposure*, esp. 3–8, 35–36, 48–52, 59–60, 91–92, 142–54, 172–90.

12. Leithauser, "The Awkward Age" (n. 7 above), 36 (Penrod); Kasson, *Amusing the Million,* 98–102, 105 (Patten quotes).

13. Lewis A. Erenberg, *Steppin' Out: New York Nightlife and the Transformation of American Culture, 1890–1930* (Chicago: University of Chicago Press, 1981), 64–65 (64, Moskowitz quote; 65, Lippmann quote); Martin Paulsson, *The Social Anxieties of Progressive Reform: Atlantic City, 1854–1920* (New York: New York University Press, 1994), 197–98 (Addams quote); Leonard Benedict, *Waifs of the Slums and Their Way Out* (New York: Revell, 1907), 122 ("bid"). See also Derek Vaillant, *Sounds of Reform: Progressivism and Music in Chicago, 1873–1935* (Chapel Hill: University of North Carolina Press, 2003), esp. 1–125.

14. Rosenzweig, *Eight Hours,* 147–48 (Booth quotes); Dominic Cavallo, *Muscles and Morals: Organized Playgrounds and Urban Reform, 1880–1920* (Philadelphia: University of Pennsylvania Press, 1981), 41 ("grand march"), 44–45.

15. Mandelbaum, *Meaning of Sports,* 201–2, 216–17, 222–23 ("capital"), 237–41 (Auerbach quote); Gorn and Goldstein, *Brief History,* 172–76; Riess, *City Games,* 107.

16. Rosenzweig, *Eight Hours,* 151 (quotes); Riess, *City Games,* 167–68.

17. Putney, *Muscular Christianity,* esp. 1, 4–6, 98–116; Gorn and Goldstein, *Brief History,* 147 (Roosevelt quote).

18. Gorn and Goldstein, *Brief History,* 157–58 (157, "honestly"; 158, "foul play"); John S. Watterson, *College Football: History, Spectacle, Controversy* (Baltimore: Johns Hopkins University Press, 2000), 64–92 (92, "death," "lake").

19. Rossi, *National Game,* 47–72; Rader, *Baseball,* 73 ("reeked").

20. Tygiel, *Past Time,* 35–54; Steven A. Riess, *Touching Base: Professional Baseball and American Culture in the Progressive Era,* rev. ed. (Urbana: University of Illinois Press, 1999), 26–27 ("cherry tree"), 168 (Mack quote), 176 and 179 (college). McGraw ultimately joined the National League, managing the New York Giants.

21. Riess, *Touching Base,* esp. 5–53 (5, attendance figures; 16, "some kind of an article"; 28, Addams quote), 213–22. Riess effectively places Progressive Era baseball in its ideological and social contexts.

22. Gorn and Goldstein, *Brief History,* 119–20 (Roosevelt quotes), 220; Sammons, *Beyond the Ring,* 30–47 (38–40, other quotes); Riess, *City Games,* 115–16.

23. Vaillant (*Sounds of Reform,* 10–148 [111, quote]) discusses "musical progressivism's" free concerts and lessons.

24. Charles Musser, *The Emergence of Cinema: The American Screen to 1907* (Berkeley and Los Angeles: University of California Press, 1994), 57–59; Kenney, *Recorded Music in American Life,* 23–26; David Morton, *Off the Record: The Technology and Culture of Sound Recording in America* (New Brunswick, NJ: Rutgers University Press, 2000), 1–3, 77–78 (2, Edison quote); Nasaw, *Going Out,* 120–29.

25. Kenney, *Recorded Music in American Life,* 8–10, 28–30, 46–59 (50, "classes"; 51, "best"; 54, "summer home").

26. Martin W. Laforse and James A. Drake, *Popular Culture and American Life: Selected Topics in the Study of American Popular Culture* (Chicago: Nelson-Hall, 1981), 36–38 (38, "$7.00"); Morton, *Off the Record,* 45; Kenney, *Recorded Music in American Life,* 29 ("heroic").

27. Vaillant, *Sounds of Reform,* esp. 1–9, 86, 91–125 (100, "'popular'"; 103, "ennobling"; 114, "forget"; 115, "better type"; 120, "vulgar"), 286–91.

28. Kenney, *Recorded Music in American Life,* 92–93.

29. David Robinson, *From Peep Show to Palace: The Birth of American Film* (New York: Columbia University Press, 1996), 3–8; Musser, *Emergence of Cinema,* 29–40.

30. Robert Sklar, *Movie-Made America: A Cultural History of American Movies,* rev. and updated ed. (New York: Vintage, 1994), 9–13; Nasaw, *Going Out,* 130–34; Musser, *Emergence of Cinema,* 72–78; Robinson, *From Peep Show to Palace,* 38–45, 56–57.

31. Nasaw, *Going Out,* 135–38; Musser, *Emergence of Cinema,* 91–92, 100–105, 109–11, 118, 133–57; Robinson, *From Peepshow to Palace,* 53 (Edison quote), 59; Butsch, *Making of American Audiences,* 140 ("moved").

32. Nasaw, *Going Out,* 142–43 (142, quote); Kathryn Fuller, *At the Picture Show: Small-Town Audiences and the Creation of Movie Fan Culture* (Washington, DC: Smithsonian Institution Press, 1996), 8–17.

33. Musser, *Emergence of Cinema*, 178–221.

34. Steven Ross, *Working-Class Hollywood: Silent Film and the Shaping of Class in America* (Princeton, NJ: Princeton University Press, 1998), 16; Musser, *Emergence of Cinema*, 418–25; Fuller, *At the Picture Show*, 51; Butsch, *Making of American Audiences*, 141 (quotes); Nasaw, *Going Out*, 152–53, 159; Eileen Bowser, *The Transformation of Cinema, 1907–1915* (Berkeley and Los Angeles: University of California Press, 1990), 12.

35. Butsch, *Making of American Audiences*, 142–45; Daniel J. Cztirom, *Media and the American Mind: From Morse to McLuhan* (Chapel Hill: University of North Carolina Press, 1982), 48 (Sage Foundation study); Nasaw, *Going Out*, 168 (*Harper's* and Berle quotes), 170 ("called silent"); Rosenzweig, *Eight Hours*, 196 ("Kamchatka," "voicelessness"); Garth Jowett, *Film: The Democratic Art* (Boston: Little, Brown, 1976), 38–42.

36. Bowser, *Transformation of Cinema*, 1 (refinement), 3–4 ("smells"), 37–38 ("vice"); Nasaw, *Going Out*, 164 ("canned beans"), 168 (*Harper's* quote).

37. Butsch, *Making of American Audiences*, 156–57 ("promoters," "undeveloped," "patrons"); Cztirom, *Media and the American Mind*, 31–34; Nasaw, *Going Out*, 169 (Chicago study, St. Louis interviews), 175 ("unfit"); Lee Grieveson, *Policing Cinema: Movies and Censorship in Early Twentieth-Century America* (Berkeley and Los Angeles: University of California Press, 2004), 12–17 (12, "kill"), 59, 62–66. See also David Nasaw, *Children of the City: At Work and at Play* (New York: Anchor, 1985), 125–26; and Jowett, *Film*, 74–84, 88.

38. Bowser, *Transformation of Cinema*, 1 (*Harper's* quote); Kathleen McCarthy, "Nickel Vice and Virtue: Movie Censorship in Chicago, 1907–1915," *Journal of Popular Film* 5 (1976): 37–55; Grieveson, *Policing Cinema*, 67–70 (68, "uplift theater"; 70, "like to see fights").

39. Bowser, *Transformation of Cinema*, 39; Nasaw, *Going Out*, 175–80 (177, "horde"); Butsch, *Making of American Audiences*, 153–54; Grieveson, *Policing Cinema*, 22–26.

40. Ben Singer, *Melodrama and Modernity: Early Sensational Cinema and Its Contexts* (New York: Columbia University Press, 2001), esp. 19, 34–35, 59–95 (93, quote), 104.

41. Ibid., 93–95 (quote); Havig, *Fred Allen's Radio Comedy*, 3–4.

42. Sharon R. Ullman, *Sex Seen: The Emergence of Modern Sexuality in America* (Berkeley and Los Angeles: University of California Press, 1997), esp. 4–8, 14–31 (14, "array"), 72–84, 100–102, 105–16, 136. See also Erenberg, *Steppin' Out*, 61.

43. Hamilton, "*When I'm Bad, I'm Better*," 9–11.

44. Erin A. Smith, *Hard-Boiled: Working-Class Readers and Pulp Magazines* (Philadelphia: Temple University Press, 2000), 20 ("magazine revolution"); Frank M. Robinson and Lawrence Davidson, *Pulp Culture: The Art of Fiction Magazines* (Portland, OR: Collectors, 1998), 2–30; Nye, *Unembarrassed Muse*, 210–11; Kasson, *Perfect Man*, 167 ("fiction factories").

45. Tony Palmer, *All You Need Is Love: The Story of Popular Music* (New York: Penguin, 1977), 99 ("WRITTEN TO ORDER"); Finson, *Voices That Are Gone*, 154; Starr and Waterman, *American Popular Music*, 25, 31–33.

46. Palmer, *All You Need Is Love*, 100–103 ("dollar," "ear"); Edward A. Berlin, *King of Ragtime: Scott Joplin and His Era* (New York: Oxford University Press, 1994), 168; Starr and Waterman, *American Popular Music*, 29; Finson, *Voices That Are Gone*, 67–69.

47. Palmer, *All You Need Is Love*, 102–3.

48. Jody Rosen, "Two American Anthems, in Two American Voices," *New York Times*, July 29, 2000, sec. 2, p. 28; Brad Leithauser, "Let's Face the Music," *New York Review of Books*, February 22, 1999, 16, 18 ("mirror," "public," "humming"); Gary Giddins, *Visions of Jazz: The First Century* (New York: Oxford University Press, 1998), 39 ("easy"); Ann Douglas, *Terrible Honesty: Mongrel Manhattan in the 1920s* (New York: Farrar Straus Giroux, 1995), 355–56 (quote).

49. Douglas, *Terrible Honesty*, 354–57; Giddins, *Visions of Jazz*, 34–35; Rosen, "Two American Anthems" (n. 48 above), 28; Leithauser, "Let's Face the Music" (n. 48 above), 16; Starr and Waterman, *American Popular Music*, 64.

50. Rosen, "Two American Anthems" (n. 48 above), 28; Finson, *Voices That Are Gone*, 80–82 (song quotes); Starr and Waterman, *American Popular Music*, 30, 36; Palmer, *All You Need Is Love*, 107 (Caesar quote).

51. Giddins, *Visions of Jazz*, 35–37; Rosen, "Two American Anthems" (n. 48 above), 28.

52. Berlin, *King of Ragtime*, 89 ("epidemic"); Katrina Hazzard-Gordon, *Jookin': The Rise of Social Dance Formations in African-American Culture* (Philadelphia: Temple University Press, 1990), 74–86 (79, "pleasure house"; 83, "most important place"), 117–18, 162–65; Erenberg, *Steppin' Out*, 73.

53. Francis Davis, *The History of the Blues: The Roots, the Music, the People from Charley Patton to Robert Cray* (New York: Hyperion, 1995), 24–26 (Handy on "small town rounders"); Robert Palmer, *Deep Blues* (New York: Penguin, 1981), 25–43; Tim Parrish, *Walking Blues: Making Americans from Emerson to Elvis* (Amherst: University of Massachusetts Press, 2001), 77–100; Craig Werner, *A Change Is Gonna Come: Music, Race, and the Soul of America* (New York: Penguin, 1998), 65–71 (68–69, Hughes, King, and Ellison quotes), 249 (Johnson and Pendergrass quotes); Jeffrey T. Titon, *Early Downhome Blues: A Musical and Cultural Analysis*, 2nd ed. (Chapel Hill: University of North Carolina Press, 1994), xvi (Caston quote), 24, 27, 31. Titon warns: "Those who seek the origins of blues are sticking their heads in the sand" (22).

54. Davis, *History of the Blues*, 26–27 (Handy quotes, class issue), 59–60 (Walker quote); Titon, *Early Downhome Blues*, 25; Palmer, *All You Need Is Love*, 58–59, 199; Parrish, *Walking Blues*, 89 (Broonzy quote), 185–86 (Handy on the "Mississippi string band").

55. Douglas, *Terrible Honesty*, 367–68; Starr and Waterman, *American Popular Music*, 33–34. On Handy and ragtime, see Davis, *History of the Blues*, 59; and Palmer, *Deep Blues*, 105. "Because it has such a ragged movement" is the way Joplin himself explained the derivation of the music's name (Berlin, *King of Ragtime*, 45).

56. Palmer, *All You Need Is Love*, 19–31; Berlin, *King of Ragtime*, 240 (Stark quote).

57. Douglas, *Terrible Honesty*, 365–67, 376–77 (quotes); Finson, *Voices That Are Gone*, 238.

58. Palmer, *All You Need Is Love*, 107 (Berlin quote); Jeffrey Melnick, *A Right to Sing the Blues: African Americans, Jews, and American Popular Song* (Cambridge, MA: Harvard University Press, 1999), 52–55 (Sulzer quotes, Gershwin), 169–71 (Cantor); Michael Rogin, *Blackface, White Noise: Jewish Immigrants in the Hollywood Melting Pot* (Berkeley and Los Angeles: University of California Press, 1996), 155 ("feared the day"); Douglas, *Terrible Honesty*, 77 (Cantor with Williams), 361 ("be much funnier").

59. Rogin, *Blackface, White Noise*, 5 (blackface as a "rite of passage from immigrant to American"); Melnick, *Right to Sing the Blues*, 61 (inclusive).

60. David Brion Davis, "Jews and Blacks in America," *New York Review of Books*, December 2, 1999, 57 ("bonding"); Douglas, *Terrible Honesty*, 76; Melnick, *Right to Sing the Blues*, 43–44, 78 (Berlin quotes), 142, 147 ("plurality"), 150 ("first of the so-called"). According to Melnick: "'Black-Jewish relations' must be understood as a functional rhetoric which has helped situate American Jews in their current position as white ethnics" (196).

61. Berlin, *King of Ragtime*, 88 ("type"); Rosen, "Two American Anthems" (n. 48 above), 28; also Giddins, *Visions of Jazz*, 36–37; Erenberg, *Steppin' Out*, 6, 8 (Canby quote).

62. Laforse and Drake, *Popular Culture and American Life*, 35 (Edison Co. quote); Kenney, *Recorded Music in American Life*, 31–37 (36–37, lyrics; 37, Jones quote), 50–51.

63. Starr and Waterman, *American Popular Music*, 37 ("Victrola").

64. Bowser, *Transformation of Cinema*, 37 ("nothing"); Musser, *Emergence of Cinema*, 183–84 ("bald-head"), 234, 340; Sklar, *Movie-Made America*, 23.

65. Musser, *Emergence of Cinema*, 228, 347–49, 355.

66. Ross, *Working-Class Hollywood*, 36–39.

67. Ibid., xii, 63–68, 82–84; Fuller, *At the Picture Show*, 78–87. See also Kay Sloan, *The Loud Silents: Origins of the Social Problem Film* (Urbana: University of Illinois Press, 1988); Richard Koszarski, *An Evening's Entertainment: The Age of the Silent Feature Picture, 1915–1928* (Berkeley and Los Angeles: University of California Press, 1990), 223–25 (224, Weber quote).

68. Sklar, *Movie-Made America*, 33–41; Bowser, *Transformation of Cinema*, 28–35. On *The Fights of Nations*, see *Hollywoodism: Jews, Movies, and the American Dream* (Simcha Jacobovici, 1998, TV documentary).

69. Sklar, *Movie-Made America*, 40–42; Neal Gabler, *An Empire of Their Own: How the*

Jews Invented Hollywood (New York: Doubleday, 1988), 11–33 (15, "newborn person"; 18, "a lot of money"; 30, "show business"; 32, *Journal* quote); Bowser, *Transformation of Cinema*, 85; Thomas Cripps, *Hollywood's High Noon: Moviemaking and Society before Television* (Baltimore: Johns Hopkins University Press, 1997), 12, 24, 37–41.

70. Alan Dale, *Comedy Is a Man in Trouble: Slapstick in American Movies* (Minneapolis: University of Minnesota Press, 2000), 1–30 (slapstick; 16, "whaled," "effect"; 27, "condemned"); Ross, *Working-Class Hollywood*, 80 ("swat").

71. Sklar, *Movie-Made America*, 110–16; Ross, *Working-Class Hollywood*, 80–81; J. Hoberman, "The First 'Jewish' Superstar: Charlie Chaplin," in *Entertaining America: Jews, Movies, and Broadcasting*, ed. J. Hoberman and Jeffrey Shandler (New York: Jewish Museum; Princeton, NJ: Princeton University Press, 2003), 34–35 ("have me Jewish").

72. See, e.g., Sklar, *Movie-Made America*, esp. 3, 16–17.

73. Nan Enstad, *Ladies of Labor, Girls of Adventure* (New York: Columbia University Press, 1999), 162, 172–74, 191; Shelley Stamp, *Movie-Struck Girls: Women and Motion Picture Culture after the Nickelodeon* (Princeton, NJ: Princeton University Press, 2000), 102–4, 111, 121–22. In 1922, 35 percent of theaters showed serials, although, by then, more focused on male heroics (Koszarski, *Evening's Entertainment*, 164–66).

74. Singer, *Melodrama and Modernity*, 241 (statistics); Enstad, *Ladies of Labor*, 162 (audience); Lauren Rabinovitz, *For the Love of Pleasure: Women, Movies, and Culture in Turn-of-the-Century Chicago* (New Brunswick, NJ: Rutgers University Press, 1998), 102, 117–18.

75. Singer, *Melodrama and Modernity*, 231–32, 241; Enstad, *Ladies of Labor*, 161–62 (161, "strange yearnings"), 166, 193–98, 206–7; Stamp, *Movie-Struck Girls*, 125–40 (126, "desire"; 132, "finished"). See also Peiss, *Cheap Amusements*, esp. chaps. 1, 6.

76. Enstad, *Ladies of Labor*, 198; Kasson, *Perfect Man*, esp. 123.

77. Kasson, *Perfect Man*, 80–92, 98–141, 153–54.

78. Ibid., 104 ("David"), 119–24, 140, 154 ("odds").

6. POPULAR CULTURE AND MIDDLE-CLASS RESPECTABILITY IN THE EARLY TWENTIETH CENTURY

1. Kasson, *Perfect Man*, 160–66 (160, "blah"; 166, "very minor cog"), 171–72; David Traxel, "Hollywood and Vine," *New York Times Book Review*, April 4, 1999, 28 ("rotten").

2. Kasson, *Perfect Man*, 159 (quote).

3. Ibid., esp. 159, 178, 211–12, 217–18 ("hard").

4. Ronald Edsforth, "Made in the U.S.A.," in *Calvin Coolidge and the Coolidge Era: Essays on the History of the 1920s*, ed. John Earl Haynes (Washington, DC: Library of Congress, 1998), 261 ("seductive power"). Edsforth discusses the breakdown in the 1920s of a "dominant political-cultural center" (264) and argues against "any assumption that mass-consumer society and its pleasure-oriented popular culture *inevitably* generated political apathy" (250; see generally 256–66).

5. See esp. Benjamin Rader, "Compensatory Sport Heroes: Ruth, Grange, and Dempsey," *Journal of Popular Culture* 16 (spring 1983): 11–22; but also John M. Carroll, *Red Grange and the Rise of Modern Football* (Urbana: University of Illinois Press, 1999), 24; and Bruce J. Evensen, *When Dempsey Fought Tunney: Heroes, Hokum, and Storytelling in the Jazz Age* (Knoxville: University of Tennessee Press, 1996), xii–xiii.

6. Putney, *Muscular Christianity*, 161–62, 171–82 (180–81, Hall quote); Carroll, *Red Grange*, 33–34, 43–44 ("never before").

7. Putney, *Muscular Christianity*, 187–89; Watterson, *College Football*, 139–40; Rader, *Baseball*, 102–3.

8. Carroll, *Red Grange*, 52; Watterson, *College Football*, 143–46; Michael Oriard, *King Football: Sport and Spectacle in the Golden Age of Radio and Newsreels, Movies and Magazines, the Weekly and the Daily Press* (Chapel Hill: University of North Carolina Press, 2001), 262 (quotes).

9. Carroll, *Red Grange*, 59–70 (64, quote).

10. Ibid., 1–24, 66, 68–69.

11. Ibid., 82 ("privacy"), 91 (Runyon quote), 82–154 (102, "dirty little business"; 108, Halas quote); Watterson, *College Football*, 154.

12. See, e.g., Carroll, *Red Grange*, 212–13.

13. Sammons, *Beyond the Ring*, 48–50 (including quote).

14. Ibid., 51, 55 (quote), 62–64, 66–67.

15. Ibid., 51–52, 67–69; Rader, *American Sports*, 146–51; Geoffrey Perrett, *America in the Twenties: A History* (New York: Simon & Schuster, 1982), 213–16 (213, Dempsey quote). See also the fine biography by Randy Roberts, *Jack Dempsey, the Manassa Mauler* (Baton Rouge: Louisiana State University Press, 1979), 122 (Rickard quote).

16. Sammons, *Beyond the Ring*, 79; Elliott J. Gorn, "'The Manassa Mauler and the Fighting Marine': An Interpretation of the Dempsey-Tunney Fights," *Journal of American Studies* 19 (April 1985): 27–47; Evensen, *When Dempsey Fought Tunney*, xvi, 36 ("everyman"); Rader, "Compensatory Sport Heroes," 20–21; Roberts, *Jack Dempsey*, 266–70 (other quotes).

17. Evensen, *When Dempsey Fought Tunney*, xiv–xv, 45, 49–53.

18. Sammons, *Beyond the Ring*, 71–72, 78–79; Gorn, "'Manassa Mauler,'" 27–47; Evensen, *When Dempsey Fought Tunney*, xv ("clerk," "collar"); Perrett, *America in the Twenties*, 293–95 (294, "kill"); Rader, *American Sports*, 192–93.

19. Rossi, *National Game*, 100–109; Rader, *Baseball*, 99–111; David Q. Voigt, "The Chicago Black Sox and the Myth of Baseball's Single Sin," in Dreifort, ed., *Baseball History*, 96–103; Nash, *Nervous Generation*, 132 ("Boone"); Norman I. Rosenberg, "Here Comes the Judge! The Origins of Baseball's Commissioner System and American Legal Culture," in Dreifort, ed., *Baseball History*, 106–21 (117, "supreme court").

20. Rader, *Baseball*, 112–19; Rosenberg, "Here Comes the Judge!" 117 ("character bath"); Rossi, *National Game*, 103–5; Leverett T. Smith, "The Changing Style of Play: Cobb vs. Ruth," in Dreifort, ed., *Baseball History*, 124–41 (125, "superman"; 127, Cobb quote).

21. Rader, *Baseball*, 118–23; Smith, "Changing Style of Play," 134 (Lane quote), 138 (Ruth quote); Tygiel, *Past Time*, 73–85 (the media's role and other quotes).

22. Samantha Barbas, *Movie Crazy: Fans, Stars, and the Cult of Celebrity* (New York: Palgrave, 2001), 35 (statistics); Robert Knopf, *The Theater and Cinema of Buster Keaton* (Princeton, NJ: Princeton University Press, 1999), 10–15 (the vaudeville aesthetic). Paula M. Cohen (*Silent Film and the Triumph of the American Myth* [New York: Oxford University Press, 2001], 60–63) describes film comedy's evolving tendency to "subordinate the stunts to the plots" and more fully realized characters.

23. Musser, *Emergence of Cinema*, 432–33; J. Hoberman and Jeffrey Shandler, introduction to Hoberman and Shandler, eds., *Entertaining America*, 19 (Fox quotes).

24. Cohen, *Silent Film*, esp. 4–19 (7, Lindsay quote; 18, Griffith quote; 19, "voice") and 178. In this sense, the concept of "Americanization," which often implies coercion, takes on a more complex and dynamic meaning. See, e.g., Edsforth, "Made in the U.S.A.," esp. 256–62.

25. Gabler, *Empire of Their Own*, 1–3, 48–52 (Laemmle quotes), 72 ("magnate"); John Gregory Dunne, "Goldwynism," *New York Review of Books*, May 18, 1989, 28 (Warner brothers quote).

26. Gabler, *Empire of Their Own*, 41–43. On the studio system, see esp. Thomas Schatz, *The Genius of the System: Hollywood Filmmaking in the Studio Era* (New York: Henry Holt, 1988).

27. J. Hoberman and Jeffrey Shandler, "Hollywood's Jewish Question," in Hoberman and Shandler, eds., *Entertaining America*, 49 ("mongrel"), 52 ("alien"); Gabler, *Empire of Their Own*, 35 ("trespass").

28. Leslie Epstein, "Duel in the Sun," *American Prospect*, July 17, 2000, 28 (Warner quote); Gabler, *Empire of Their Own*, 79–80, 119, 154–55, 168 (Cohn quotes).

29. Gabler, *Empire of Their Own*, 27, 29 ("higher class"), 42 ("Paramount plan"), 94–102; Hoberman and Shandler, introduction, 19–22 ("peep show," "elbows"); Sklar, *Movie-Made America*, 45 ("something better"); Jowett, *Film*, 59–60 (Watson quote); Robinson, *From Peep Show to Palace*, 149 ("king"); Butsch, *Making of American Audiences*, 161 ("God"); Koszarski, *Evening's Entertainment*, 20–25 ("romance").

30. Butsch, *Making of American Audiences*, 163; Gregory A. Waller, *Main Street Amusements: Movies and Commercial Entertainment in a Southern City, 1896–1930* (Washington, DC: Smithsonian Institution Press, 1995), 68–69 (68, "nice place"; 69, "matinee"), 256–59.

31. Sklar, *Movie-Made America*, 42–44; Gabler, *Empire of Their Own*, 28–30 ("ripe"), 40, 99 ("education").

32. Sklar, *Movie-Made America*, 57–61; Gabler, *Empire of Their Own*, 90–91 (Mayer); Robert Brent Toplin, *Reel History: In Defense of Hollywood* (Lawrence: University Press of Kansas, 2002), 184–88 (186, "lightning").

33. See, e.g., Robinson, *From Peep Show to Palace*, 146–47.

34. Gabler, *Empire of Their Own*, 5–7 ("audience," "'shadow'"), 79; also 119.

35. Ibid., 40 (Zukor quote); Nasaw, *Going Out*, 214–18 (215, "promised Dad," "red blooded"; 218, "keep your hands," "fighting forces"). For a helpful listing of films that includes brief plot summaries, see Craig W. Campbell, *Reel America and World War I* (Jefferson, NC: McFarland, 1985), 149–91. See also Leslie Midkiff DeBauche, *Reel Patriotism: The Movies and World War I* (Madison: University of Wisconsin Press, 1997).

36. Ross, *Working-Class Hollywood*, 127–36 (129, "nation-wide campaign"); Nasaw, *Going Out*, 219–20.

37. Czitrom, *Media and the American Mind*, 49–50; Ross, *Working-Class Hollywood*, 40 (Goldwyn quote).

38. Gabler, *Empire of Their Own*, 43–44 (quote); Lary May, *The Big Tomorrow: Hollywood and the Politics of the American Way* (Chicago: University of Chicago Press, 2000), 57 (*Post Dispatch* quote). Erenberg (*Steppin' Out*, esp. 5–25, 60–87) offers a good overview of the building cultural wars.

39. Hoberman and Shandler, "Hollywood's Jewish Question," 51 ("motion picture influence"), 52 (state legislatures); Francis G. Couvares, *The Remaking of Pittsburgh: Class and Culture in an Industrializing City, 1877–1919* (Albany: State University of New York Press, 1984), 122 ("national hero").

40. Charles J. Maland, *Chaplin and American Culture: The Evolution of a Star Image* (Princeton, NJ: Princeton University Press, 1989), 14–24 (17, quote).

41. Hoberman and Shandler, "Hollywood's Jewish Question," 52–53 (Shuler quote); Sklar, *Movie-Made America*, 82–85; Leonard J. Leff and Jerold L. Simmons, *The Dame in the Kimono: Hollywood, Censorship, and the Production Code*, 2nd ed. (Lexington: University Press of Kentucky, 2001), 5 (Chaplin quote); Gabler, *Empire of Their Own*, 1 ("quintessence"); Lary May, *Screening Out the Past: The Birth of Mass Culture and the Motion Picture Industry* (Chicago: University of Chicago Press, 1983), 205 ("passionate").

42. Jowett, *Film*, 188 (William DeMille quote); Sklar, *Movie-Made America*, 44, 91–95 (94, "public needs"; 94, "free the subject"); Gabler, *Empire of Their Own*, 12, 35–36.

43. Ross, *Working-Class Hollywood*, 176, 200–207.

44. Jowett, *Film*, 188–89; Cohen, *Silent Film*, 160. May (*Screening Out the Past*, 209–12 [209, DeMille quote; 209–11, dialogue quotes]) is excellent on DeMille.

45. Caption taken from still of *Prodigal Daughters* in author's collection. May (*Screening Out the Past*, 122–23) discusses how these collisions were common in Mary Pickford's films.

46. See, e.g., Robert Sklar, ed., *The Plastic Age: 1917–1930* (New York: George Braziller, 1970), 17–19.

47. Barbas, *Movie Crazy*, 36–37, 41–44.

48. Ibid., 10–21 (10, "almost know"; 19, "cowardly"); Fuller, *At the Picture Show*, 114, 131.

49. Fuller, *At the Picture Show*, 133–46 (146, quote); Barbas, *Movie Crazy*, 24–25.

50. Stamp, *Movie-Struck Girls*, 7–9, 37–40 (quotes), 197–99; Fuller, *At the Picture Show*, 116; Koszarski, *Evening's Entertainment*, 30 (percentages).

51. Fuller, *At the Picture Show*, 150–65 (quotes); Barbas, *Movie Crazy*, 38–39. Quirk had edited *Popular Mechanics* before moving to *Photoplay*.

52. Barbas, *Movie Crazy*, 47–51; May, *Screening Out the Past*, 119–20; Kelly Schrum, *Some Wore Bobby Sox: The Emergence of Teenage Girls' Culture, 1920–1945* (New York: Palgrave Macmillan, 2004), 154–60. On Pickford, see also Molly Haskel, "America's Sweetheart," *New York Review of Books*, June 6, 1999, 9. Similarly, a "Charlie Chaplin Outfit"

and a host of novelty items and toys reflected the growth of what one writer described as "Chaplinitis" (see Maland, *Chaplin,* 9–14).

53. Roland Marchand, *Advertising the American Dream: Making Way for Modernity, 1920–1940* (Berkeley and Los Angeles: University of California Press, 1985), esp. 2–24 (advertising shifts), but also 117–63 (discussion of "the consumption ethic"); Barbas, *Movie Crazy,* 46 (*Movie Weekly* poem), 52–54 (53, "revolutionary change"); May, *Screening Out the Past,* 201–2 (statistics).

54. Toll, *On with the Show!* 301–26; Mizejewski, *Ziegfeld Girl,* 90 (headline); Glenn, *Female Spectacle,* 170 ("pickles").

55. Glenn, *Female Spectacle,* 170–71.

56. Ibid., 173 (quote); Toll, *On with the Show!* 317.

57. Glenn, *Female Spectacle,* 21 and 25 (photographs), 170 ("'vampire'"), 171 ("brains"), 174–75 (174, "efficiency expert"), 179–81 ("too intelligent"), 194 ("broiler"); Mizejewski, *Ziegfeld Girl,* 79 ("ragging"); Toll, *On with the Show!* 317–19 ("attract").

58. Mizejewski, *Ziegfeld Girl,* 21, 34–37, 60; Allen, *Horrible Prettiness,* 245–46 (246, "sensuality and niceness").

59. Shteir, *Striptease,* 59–60, 69–72, 84–88.

60. Ibid., 42–45 (44, Comstock quote), 59–60, 69–74 (Herk quote), 92; Glenn, *Female Spectacle,* 100; Allen, *Horrible Prettiness,* 243–44, 248–49. The raid became the subject of Roland Barber's novel *The Night They Raided Minsky's* (1967).

61. Shteir, *Striptease,* 61–65, 79; Allen, *Horrible Prettiness,* 231–32 (quotes), 248.

62. Shteir, *Striptease,* 79–82, 97; Allen, *Horrible Prettiness,* 232 (Minsky quote).

63. Francine du Plessix Gray, "Dirty Dancing," *New Yorker,* February 28, 2005, 86 (quote), 89 (dialectic), 92 (Burana quote); Allen, *Horrible Prettiness,* 285–86 (Weene quote).

64. Jill Watts, *Mae West: An Icon in Black and White* (New York: Oxford University Press, 2001), 3–62 (15, "exploiting," "darker"; 17, "hard-boiled"); Hamilton, *"When I'm Bad, I'm Better,"* 1–45 (2, "raunchy"); Claudia Roth Pierpont, "The Strong Woman," *New Yorker,* November 11, 1996, 106–7; Emily W. Leider, *Becoming Mae West* (New York: Farrar Straus Giroux, 1997), 3–6, 19–42.

65. Watts, *Mae West,* 75 ("lust," "street sweepings"); Hamilton, *"When I'm Bad, I'm Better,"* 46–55 (49, "MONSTROSITY").

66. Shteir, *Striptease,* 75–77 (Carroll quote, Shuberts, "carrot"), 98, 105; Hamilton, *"When I'm Bad, I'm Better,"* 50–51, 68–69, 71, 77–79, 93–96.

67. Watts, *Mae West,* 70–89 (75, "tour"; 86, "decency," "radical"); Hamilton, *"When I'm Bad, I'm Better,"* 55–69.

68. Watts, *Mae West,* 89–94 (92, "expect"); Leider, *Becoming Mae West,* 6 ("censorship").

69. Emily W. Leider, *Dark Lover: The Life and Death of Rudolph Valentino* (New York: Farrar Straus Giroux, 2003), 9–124 (87, villain; 88, Griffith quote; 123, *Photoplay* quote); Erenberg, *Steppin' Out,* esp. 79–86, 114–32, 146–71 (cabarets).

70. Leider, *Dark Lover,* 8 ("nice boy"), 117–24, 148–72 (159, "husband"; 168, Marion quote), 252–53 (252, "not be without").

71. Ibid., 8 ("powder puff"), 187, 219, 249–55 (254, "Vaselino"), 304 ("knickers"), 372–73 ("effeminacy"), 389–90 (*Motion Picture Magazine* quote).

72. Ibid., 4, 8, 161 ("dark people"), 386–401 (389–90, "celluloid"), 418–22.

73. Ted Gioia, *The History of Jazz* (New York: Oxford University Press, 1997), 94–95.

74. Giddins, *Visions of Jazz,* 89–90; Douglas, *Terrible Honesty,* 352 (quote); Gioia, *History of Jazz,* 5–7 (5, "blending"), 30–31, 45–46; Charles J. Gans, "Louis the Great," *Spokane, WA, Spokesman-Review,* June 29, 2000, D1; Jervis Anderson, review of *Louis Armstrong: An American Genius* by James Lincoln Collier, *New Republic,* January 30, 1984, 37 (Armstrong quote).

75. Gioia, *History of Jazz,* 78 (quotes), 84; Kenney, *Recorded Music in American Life,* 14–15.

76. Lawrence W. Levine, *The Unpredictable Past: Explorations in American Cultural History* (New York: Oxford University Press, 1993), 173–83 (culture vs. jazz; 178–79, "retrogression," *Times* quote; 181, Condon quote); Emerson, *Doo-Dah!* 253 (Carmichael quote); Douglas, *Terrible Honesty,* 377 ("the sin in syncopation"), 418 (Mezzrow quote);

Lewis A. Erenberg, *Swingin' the Dream: Big Band Jazz and the Rebirth of American Culture* (Chicago: University of Chicago Press, 1998), 10 (Sousa quote).

77. Geoffrey O'Brien, "Recapturing the American Sound," *New York Review of Books,* April 9, 1998, 49; William Youngren, "Black and White Intertwined," *Atlantic Monthly,* February 1999, 86 (Sudhalter quote), 88 ("blow"); Gioia, *History of Jazz,* 73 ("pretty notes").

78. Levine, *Unpredictable Past,* 182.

79. Kenney, *Recorded Music in American Life,* 113; Geoffrey Ward and Ken Burns, *Jazz: A History of America's Music* (New York: Knopf, 2000), 70 (*Daily News* quote), 77 (LaRocca quote).

80. Gerald Early, *The Culture of Bruising: Essays on Prizefighting, Literature, and Modern American Culture* (Hopewell, NJ: Ecco, 1994), 166–83 (168, "too tight"; 172, "strings"); Douglas, *Terrible Honesty,* 349–50 ("burlesque"), 415, 429–31 (Armstrong quotes); Starr and Waterman, *American Popular Music,* 56–59 (*Jazz*); Erenberg, *Swingin' the Dream,* 11 ("lady"); Levine, *Unpredictable Past,* 184 ("if you"); Kenney, *Recorded Music in American Life,* 63–64 (Victor); Ward and Burns, *Jazz,* 99 ("every minute"); Rogin, *Blackface, White Noise,* 113 (Baraka quote).

81. Starr and Waterman, *American Popular Music,* 60 (quote); Hamilton, *"When I'm Bad, I'm Better,"* 155 (West quote); Gilbert Osofsky, *Harlem: The Making of a Ghetto* (1964; reprint, New York: Harper & Row, 1965), 184–86 (advertisement); Douglas, *Terrible Honesty,* 337 ("Zulus"); Nathan I. Huggins, *Harlem Renaissance* (New York: Oxford University Press, 1971), 89–90 (quote).

82. Starr and Waterman, *American Popular Music,* 44–45 ("naughty diversions"), 47, 56 (Whiteman quote); Peiss, *Cheap Amusements,* 88–104 (88, "dance mad"); Erenberg, *Steppin' Out,* 160–61 (Marbury quote).

83. Starr and Waterman, *American Popular Music,* 45–47 (46, "laughing"); Erenberg, *Steppin' Out,* 158–65 ("Barbary Coast," "romping spirit"); Nasaw, *Going Out,* 106 ("fleshly," "wiggle").

84. Erenberg, *Steppin' Out,* 166–71 (quotes). On the influence of Whiteman and "sweet jazz," see Starr and Waterman, *American Popular Music,* 46, 57–59; and Burton W. Peretti, *The Creation of Jazz: Music, Race, and Culture in Urban America* (Urbana: University of Illinois Press, 1992), 94–95.

85. Erenberg, *Steppin' Out,* 153 (Castle quote), 157–58 (*McClure's* quotes).

86. Susan J. Douglas, *Listening In: Radio and the American Imagination* (New York: Times Books, 1999), 55 ("turn"); Starr and Waterman, *American Popular Music,* 40–41.

87. Kenney, *Recorded Music in American Life,* 15, 62–63 (62, "harvest").

88. Ibid., 114–18; Starr and Waterman, *American Popular Music,* 87–89; Richard A. Peterson, *Creating Country Music: Fabricating Authenticity* (Chicago: University of Chicago Press, 1997), 17, 25–32 (Brockman; 28, quotes).

89. Starr and Waterman, *American Popular Music,* 109–10 ("genius"); Kenney, *Recorded Music in American Life,* 145–48 ("pluperfect," "liquor"); Peterson, *Creating Country Music,* 5, 19.

90. Starr and Waterman, *American Popular Music,* 112–13. On the "big bang," see "Celebration," an episode of *Century of Country* (Nashville Network documentary, 1999).

91. "Celebration" (n. 90 above); Kenney, *Recorded Music in American Life,* 155; Starr and Waterman, *American Popular Music,* 114–18; Peterson, *Creating Country Music,* 43–50 (44, "go to the woods").

92. Peterson, *Creating Country Music,* 7–8 (*Variety* quote), 47, 55–56, 68–69.

93. Kenney, *Recorded Music in American Life,* 155–56.

94. Peterson, *Creating Country Music,* 16; Starr and Waterman, *American Popular Music,* 41 (100 million disks); Titon, *Early Downhome Blues,* 200 (financial statistics).

95. J. Fred MacDonald, *Don't Touch That Dial! Radio Programming in American Life from 1920 to 1960* (Chicago: Nelson-Hall, 1979), 1–14 (numbers); Michele Hilmes, *Radio Voices: American Broadcasting, 1922–1952* (Minneapolis: University of Minnesota Press, 1997), 14–15 ("shack"), 38–44. David Marc and Robert J. Thompson (*Television in the Antenna Age: A Concise History* [Malden, MA: Blackwell, 2005], 3–34) provide a brief, readable overview of radio's early technology and commercial development.

96. Hilmes, *Radio Voices*, 18, 49–56 (54, quote), 63–65; Nye, *Unembarrassed Muse*, 391 (WEAF); Mary Murphy, *Mining Cultures: Men, Women, and Leisure in Butte, 1914–41* (Urbana: University of Illinois Press, 1997), 173 ("potted palm"); Ronald A. Smith, *Play-by-Play: Radio, Television, and Big-Time College Sport* (Baltimore: Johns Hopkins University Press, 2001), 23–24.

97. MacDonald, *Don't Touch That Dial!* 24–25; Douglas, *Listening In*, 45–46; Marc and Thompson, *Television in the Antenna Age*, 31–34.

98. Douglas, *Listening In*, 6; Hilmes, *Radio Voices*, 6–7, 11; Marc and Thompson, *Television in the Antenna Age*, 44, 48.

99. Derek Vaillant, "'Your Voice Came in Last Night . . . but I Thought It Sounded a Little Scared': Rural Radio Listening and 'Talking Back' during the Progressive Era in Wisconsin, 1920–1932," in *Radio Reader: Essays in the Cultural History of Radio*, ed. Michele Hilmes and Jason Loviglio (New York: Routledge, 2002), 63–88 (63, "something with melody"; 64, "beneath the dignity"; 71, "same folks").

100. Murphy, *Mining Cultures*, 178.

101. Hilmes, *Radio Voices*, 13–16 (15, "allowed"); Douglas, *Listening In*, 17–18, 23–24, 62–99 (97–98, "hooky," "turnstile"); Peterson, *Creating Country Music*, 97–98 ("under the stars").

102. Scott Eyman, *The Speed of Sound: Hollywood and the Talkie Revolution, 1926–1930* (Baltimore: Johns Hopkins University Press, 1997), 17–35, 160 (Thalberg quote).

103. Gabler, *Empire of Their Own*, 120–35 (131–32, Warner quote); Eyman, *Speed of Sound*, 12, 56–173; Koszarski, *Evening's Entertainment*, 89–90; Schatz, *Genius of the System*, 58–61.

104. Eyman, *Speed of Sound*, 61–65; Koszarski, *Evening's Entertainment*, 83–84.

105. Eyman, *Speed of Sound*, 15, 140 ("battling mob"), 177, 243 ("upstarts"), 360 (finances). For a helpful sketch of the sound transition, see Donald Crafton, *The Talkies: American Cinema's Transition to Sound, 1926–1931* (Berkeley and Los Angeles: University of California Press, 1997), 8–13.

106. Gabler, *Empire of Their Own*, 145–46 (145, "sink or swim"); Thomas Doherty, *Pre-Code Hollywood: Sex, Immorality, and Insurrection in American Cinema, 1930–1934* (New York: Columbia University Press, 1999), 5 (end of silent-film production).

7. BATTLING THE GREAT DEPRESSION

1. Jonathan Yardley, "The Decade That Defined America," *Washington Post National Weekly Edition*, October 13–19, 2003, 33 (quote); David Kyvig, *Daily Life in the United States, 1920–1940* (2002; reprint, Chicago: Ivan Dee, 2004), 91, 105.

2. Susan Currell, *The March of Spare Time: The Problem and Promise of Leisure in the Great Depression* (Philadelphia: University of Pennsylvania Press, 2005), esp. 1–30 (19, "paramount importance"; 24, "jazz"); Steven Watts, *The Magic Kingdom: Walt Disney and the American Way of Life* (Columbia: University of Missouri Press, 1997), 66–67, 145; James Borchert, *Alley Life in Washington: Family, Community, Religion, and Folklife in the City, 1850–1970* (Urbana: University of Illinois Press, 1980), 151–52 (151, "extraordinary").

3. Russell Sanjek and David Sanjek, *American Popular Music Business in the Twentieth Century* (New York: Oxford University Press, 1991), 20–22, 47 (the phonograph industry).

4. David M. Kennedy, *Freedom from Fear: The American People in Depression and War, 1929–1945* (New York: Oxford University Press, 1999), 85–88 (quotes); Tino Balio, *Grand Design: Hollywood as a Modern Business Enterprise, 1930–1939* (Berkeley and Los Angeles: University of California Press, 1993), 13; Charles C. Alexander, *Breaking the Slump: Baseball in the Depression Era* (New York: Columbia University Press, 2002), 15.

5. Lewis A. Erenberg, "From New York to Middletown: Repeal and the Legitimization of Nightlife in the Great Depression," *American Quarterly* 38 (winter 1986): 763 (*Variety* quote); Alexander, *Breaking the Slump*, 65 ("hiding"); John B. Jones, *Our Musicals, Ourselves: A Social History of the American Musical Theater* (Lebanon, NH: Brandeis University Press, 2003), 82–83. The Ziegfeld Follies reopened in the mid-1930s, under the owner-

ship of the Shubert brothers, who added "spice" in the form of Gypsy Rose Lee, America's "number one stripper" (Shteir, *Striptease*, 177, 183).

6. Immerso, *Coney Island*, 129 ("paradise"), 142–48 (144, "half kill 'em"; 145, "more business"; 148, "last resort").

7. Culhane, *American Circus*, 203–7, 227 ("creature"); Nye, *Unembarrassed Muse*, 190–91.

8. Culhane, *American Circus*, 207–13 (210, "American boy"), 221–38.

9. Doherty, *Pre-Code Hollywood*, 17, 28, 31–32 (31, Marx quote), 45–46 ("darkened theater").

10. Balio, *Grand Design*, 4–5; Doherty, *Pre-Code Hollywood*, 6–7, 31, 45 (Hays quote). For the Code itself, see Mark A. Vieira, *Sin in Soft Focus: Pre-Code Hollywood* (New York: Abrams, 1999), 214–18; and Doherty, *Pre-Code Hollywood*, 347–59.

11. Calvin Wilson, "When Cinema Became Sin-ema," *Spokane, WA, Spokesman-Review*, January 13, 2000, D3, D8; Doherty, *Pre-Code Hollywood*, 122–23 ("Rome", "spell sex"); Vieira, *Sin in Soft Focus*, 132, 141–42.

12. Doherty, *Pre-Code Hollywood*, 176; Vieira, *Sin in Soft Focus*, 117 ("Any Time Annie").

13. Hamilton, *"When I'm Bad, I'm Better,"* 172–94 (173, Warner quotes; 176, Parsons quote); Susan McCorkle, "The Immortality of Mae West," *American Heritage* 52 (September 2001): 50, 53–54 (54, "stole everything"); Martha McPhee, "Censorship Made Me," *New York Times Book Review*, July 27, 1997, 11; Vieira, *Sin in Soft Focus*, 112–16 (116, "morsel of sin"); Balio, *Grand Design*, 15 ($21 million).

14. Hamilton, *"When I'm Bad, I'm Better,"* 178; Vieira, *Sin in Soft Focus*, 39; Wilson, "When Cinema Became Sin-ema" (n. 11 above), D8; Caryn James, "'Forbidden Hollywood,'" *Spokane, WA, Spokesman-Review*, June 1, 1993, F5.

15. David J. Skal, *The Monster Show: A Cultural History of Horror*, rev. ed. (New York: Faber & Faber, 2001), 115 ("best"), 159 ("loose"), 169 ("lives"); Balio, *Grand Design*, 298–302.

16. Skal, *Monster Show*, 159 ("sanguinary capitalist," "abandoned laborers"); David J. Skal, *Screams of Reason: Mad Scientists and Modern Culture* (New York: Norton, 1998), 129 (Karloff quote), 134–48 (era's "mad science mania"); Richard Pells, *Radical Visions and American Dreams: Culture and Social Thought in the Depression Years* (New York: Harper & Row, 1973), 269–70.

17. Vieira, *Sin in Soft Focus*, 43 ("clean up"), 50 (Joy quotes).

18. Ibid., 30–33 (Zanuck quote, "thumbs down"), 217–18 (Code quotes); Leff and Simmons, *Dame in the Kimono*, 16.

19. Robinson and Davidson, *Pulp Culture*, 52–58, 66–67; L. Glen Seretan, "The 'New' Working Class and Social Banditry in Depression America," *Mid-America* 63 (1980–81): 109–16 (111, Karpis quote; 114–15, "just as criminally"); Richard E. Meyer, "The Outlaw: A Distinctive American Folktype," *Journal of Folklore Research* 17 (June–December 1980): 102 ("roof"); Claire B. Potter, *War on Crime: Bandits, G-Men, and the Politics of Mass Culture* (New Brunswick, NJ: Rutgers University Press, 1998), 6 (Parker quote [emphasis added]), 75–105 (a discussion of "celebrity bandits," but esp. 77–79, 84–85); David E. Ruth, *Inventing the Public Enemy: The Gangster in American Culture, 1918–1934* (Chicago: University of Chicago Press, 1996), 87–105.

20. Andrew Bergman, *We're in the Money: Depression America and Its Films* (New York: New York University Press, 1971), 12–13; comments made by Ann Douglas and Warren Susman on *The Public Enemy* at the workshop "Teaching a Decade" presented at the annual meeting of the American Studies Association, Boston, October 28, 1977.

21. Michael Denning, *The Cultural Front: The Laboring of American Culture in the Twentieth Century* (New York: Verso, 1996), 256 (Bright and Faragoh); May, *Big Tomorrow*, 64, 68 (Burnett quotes), 69 (Robinson quote); Leff and Simmons, *Dame in the Kimono*, 16 (Zanuck quote).

22. Vieira, *Sin in Soft Focus*, 30, 38 (Wingate quotes). See also Currell, *March of Spare Time*, 134–38.

23. Doherty, *Pre-Code Hollywood*, 193 ("guerrilla comedians"); Stephen Merchant,

"Sibling Ribaldry," *Guardian*, July 4, 2004, 10–11 (10, "throw things"); Epstein, *Haunted Smile*, 81–93 (83–84, club, hotel).

24. Doherty, *Pre-Code Hollywood*, 196 ("sanity"); see, e.g., Raymond Durgnat, *The Crazy Mirror: Hollywood Comedy and the American Image* (New York: Delta, 1969), 150–58; Levine, *Unpredictable Past*, 229 ("nickel"); Gary Giddens, "There Ain't No Sanity Clause," *New York Times Book Review*, June 18, 2000, 6.

25. On *Freaks*, see Skal, *Monster Show*, 145–58; and Rachel Adams, *Sideshow U.S.A.: Freaks and the American Cultural Imagination* (Chicago: University of Chicago Press, 2001), 60–85.

26. Bergman, *We're in the Money*, 93–96; Doherty, *Pre-Code Hollywood*, 56–57, 161–66 (161, Warner quote).

27. Balio, *Grand Design*, 281 ("headlines" pictures, profits); Robert S. McElvaine, *The Great Depression: America, 1929–1941* (New York: Times Books, 1984), 209–10 (Little Caesar as greedy capitalist); Arthur Schlesinger Jr., *The Politics of Upheaval* (Boston: Houghton-Mifflin, 1960), 118–19 (Sinclair).

28. Doherty, *Pre-Code Hollywood*, xi, 260–61 (*Tarzan* and "naked"), 320–27 (1934); Hamilton, *"When I'm Bad, I'm Better,"* esp. 194–95, 219 (West); Leff and Simmons, *Dame in the Kimono*, 47–48 (West quote).

29. May, *Big Tomorrow*, 60–61; Edward J. Epstein, *The Big Picture: The New Logic of Money and Power in Hollywood* (New York: Random House, 2005), 29–32 (Disney; 31, "those Jews").

30. May, *Big Tomorrow*, 60–65 (60, Fox quote; 64, Burnett quote, "bloody revolting English," "Woolworth touch"); 65, "morally evil"), 146.

31. Kennedy, *Freedom from Fear*, 113–18 (113, "warehouse"), 131–54, 166 ("twins").

32. Ibid., 160–76 (Hickok). Giuliana Muscio (*Hollywood's New Deal* [Philadelphia: Temple University Press, 1997], 79) refers to the "Roosevelt effect."

33. John Lahr, "Woody Guthrie: A Life by Joe Klein," *New Republic*, October 18, 1980, 36 (quotes). On the proletarian writers, see Daniel Aaron, *Writers on the Left* (New York: Harcourt, Brace & World, 1961); and Denning, *Cultural Front*, esp. 200–282.

34. May, *Big Tomorrow*, 11–53 (13, "Mayflower"; 25, "what I read," "my parents are Cherokee"; 27, "Wall Street boys"; 28, "my kind of people"; 40, "other Americans"; 44, "bankers here"; 45, "Number One"); Jon Meacham, "What Will Rogers Could Teach the Age of Limbaugh," *Washington Monthly*, January–February 1994, 16–19.

35. Burton W. Peretti, *Jazz in American Culture* (Chicago: Ivan Dee, 1997), 61–84 (overview of swing in the 1930s); Gioia, *History of Jazz*, 129; Kenney, *Recorded Music in American Life*, 163; Gary Giddins, *Bing Crosby: A Pocketful of Dreams: The Early Years, 1903–1940* (Boston: Little, Brown, 2001), 368–69 (ARC and Victor); also Sanjek and Sanjek, *American Popular Music Business*, 47.

36. Giddins, *Bing Crosby*, 367–73 ("melody"); Kenney, *Recorded Music in American Life*, 159–61; Sanjek and Sanjek, *American Popular Music Business*, 50 ("no taste").

37. Giddins, *Bing Crosby*, 365 ("pulse"), 371 (*Variety* quote), 374–75 ("newest smash hits," "people's," "three"); Kenney, *Recorded Music in American Life*, 164–67 (statistics); John Lahr, "Sinatra's Song," *New Yorker*, November 3, 1997, 80 (statistics). According to Giddins (*Bing Crosby*, 375): "In 1939 the industry sold 50 million records; 18 million of them—36 percent of the entire market—were blue-label Deccas."

38. Kenney, *Recorded Music in American Life*, 169–73 (171, "Kapp sound"); Kathleen E. R. Smith, *God Bless America: Tin Pan Alley Goes to War* (Lexington: University Press of Kentucky, 2003), 91–92 (Tin Pan Alley); Victor Greene, "Friendly Entertainers: Dance Bandleaders and Singers in the Depression, 1929–1935," in *Prospects*, ed. Jack Salzman (Cambridge: Cambridge University Press, 1995), 197.

39. Kenney, *Recorded Music in American Life*, 171–72; Giddins, *Bing Crosby*, 374–75 (374, "Whoa"); David W. Stowe, *Swing Changes: Big-Band Jazz in New Deal America* (Cambridge, MA: Harvard University Press, 1994), 7 ("echo").

40. Ward and Burns, *Jazz*, 233–35 (233, "poorly"; 235, *Time* quote); Gioia, *History of Jazz*, 145; Erenberg, *Swingin' the Dream*, 3–4. On the "hard, hard times" for jazz, see, e.g., Ward and Burns, *Jazz*, 173–96.

41. Erenberg, *Swingin' the Dream,* 3–4 (4, *Billboard* quote); Ward and Burns, *Jazz,* 221–23 (221, *"contrast"*; 223, "trying to do," "cut this shit").

42. Erenberg, *Swingin' the Dream,* 75 (Goodman quote); Ward and Burns, *Jazz,* 234–36 (234, "defining"). Brenda D. Gottschild (*Waltzing in the Dark: African American Vaudeville and Race Politics in the Swing Era* [New York: St. Martin's, 2000], 17–20) argues that the Swing Era was under way by the late 1920s.

43. Erenberg, *Swingin' the Dream,* esp. 16, 29–30, 39 (statistic), 46 ("Carnival"), 53 (song), 70. Schrum (*Some Wore Bobby Sox,* esp. 98, 110–13, 125–27, 130, 146–68, 174) is especially useful in showing how teenagers, particularly females, adapted popular culture to their own lives.

44. Stowe, *Swing Changes,* 13–14 (quote); Erenberg, *Swingin' the Dream,* xvi, 71–83 (82, "difference"), 128–30 ("bopped," "selling"); Gioia, *History of Jazz,* 137–44. On swing culture's "aesthetic of liberation," see Gottschild, *Waltzing in the Dark,* 219–26.

45. Erenberg, *Swingin' the Dream,* 65–69 (66, "nervous," "whore in church"); Stowe, *Swing Changes,* 17–23; Ward and Burns, *Jazz,* 257–58; Gioia, *History of Jazz,* 151–52 ("Toscanini").

46. Erenberg, *Swingin' the Dream,* 35–36 ("jitterbug ecstasy," "largest crowd"), 83–88, 115–16; Stowe, *Swing Changes,* 122–28; Gottschild, *Waltzing in the Dark,* 99–101, 138–47.

47. Watterson, *College Football,* 179–86.

48. Oriard, *King Football,* 32–36, 225, 255–72 (271, "names"; 272, "rich").

49. Alexander, *Breaking the Slump,* 7–8 ("fifty per cent cut"), 16–17, 35–115, 130, 204 ("greatest force of democracy"); William M. Simons, "The Athlete as Jewish Standard Bearer: Media Images of Hank Greenberg," in Dreifort, ed., *Baseball History,* 164.

50. Alexander, *Breaking the Slump,* 5, 12–13, 204–38 (213, "race baseball"; 223, "sun"; 227–28, "segregation"; 232, Durocher quote, Traynor quote; 234, "waltz"). For a discussion of Greenlee as "Black Pittsburgh's 'Mr. Big,'" see Rob Ruck, *Sandlot Seasons: Sport in Black Pittsburgh* (1987; reprint, Urbana: University of Illinois Press, 1993), 137–69.

51. Daniel Coyle, "Invisible Men," *Sports Illustrated,* December 15, 2003, 124–36 (128, Marshall quote); Robert W. Peterson, *Pigskin: The Early Years of Pro Football* (New York: Oxford University Press, 1997), 169–80.

52. Jason Pendleton, "Jim Crow Strikes Out: Interracial Baseball in Wichita, Kansas, 1920–1935," in Dreifort, ed., *Baseball History,* 142–59 (143, Paige quote; 144, "four different races").

53. Alexander, *Breaking the Slump,* 32–33, 81 ("coolies"), 91–97 (92, "terrific importance"; 92–93, Greenberg quotes; 95, Dean quote); Simons, "Jewish Standard Bearer," 161–77.

54. Susan E. Cayleff, *Babe: The Life and Legend of Babe Didrikson Zaharias* (Urbana: University of Illinois Press, 1995), 27–82, 86, 99–111.

55. Ibid., 81–97 (86, Gallico quote; 97, "diamond," "girl"), 108 ("whiskers"), 113–34.

56. Sammons, *Beyond the Ring,* 96–113 (102, Southern press quotes; 112, Braddock quote); Chris Mead, *Champion: Joe Louis, Black Hero in White America* (New York: Penguin, 1985), xi, 1–129 (71, Baer quote).

57. Mead, *Champion,* 130–59 (134, FDR quote, Schmeling; 158, "our Negroes"; 159, Broun quote); Sammons, *Beyond the Ring,* 114–17 (Buchwald quote, Louis quote); Lawrence W. Levine, *Black Culture, Black Consciousness: Afro-American Folk Thought from Slavery to Freedom* (New York: Oxford University Press, 1977), 433–38 (Angelou quote, Malcolm X quote).

58. Douglas, *Listening In,* 208 (fight statistics).

59. Butsch, *Making of American Audiences,* 216–18; Murphy, *Mining Cultures,* 172–73 ("boundaries"); Tom Lewis, *Empire of the Air: The Men Who Made Radio* (New York: HarperCollins, 1991), 229 (RCA quote); Gerald Nachman, *Raised on Radio* (New York: Pantheon, 1998), 10 (Seldes quote); Kathy M. Newman, *Radio Active: Advertising and Consumer Activism, 1935–1947* (Berkeley and Los Angeles: University of California Press, 2004), 136 ("pleasure").

60. Statistics in Butsch, *Making of American Audiences,* 176; and Lewis, *Empire of the Air,* 230–31.

61. Lewis, *Empire of the Air,* 231 (White quote); Butsch, *Making of American Audiences,* 198 ("thanks"), 208–18 (211, "shut in still").

62. On radio and music, see Czitrom, *Media and the American Mind,* 84–85; and Lahr, "Sinatra's Song" (n. 37 above), 80. On Rice and the Hill Billies, see Peterson, *Creating Country Music,* 77–79 (78, "mules"); and Anthony Harkins, *Hillbilly: A Cultural History of an American Icon* (New York: Oxford University Press, 2004), 87–89.

63. Charles K. Wolfe, *A Good-Natured Riot: The Birth of the Grand Ole Opry* (Nashville: Country Music Foundation Press/Vanderbilt University Press, 1999), 4–23 (13, "down to earth"; 15, "Tennessee mountaineers"; 21–22, "taken largely"); Peterson, *Creating Country Music,* 69–77 (73, "difference"); Harkins, *Hillbilly,* 78–95 (discussing "constructing the hillbilly persona").

64. Peterson, *Creating Country Music,* xii, 5, 56–69; Harkins, *Hillbilly,* 74 (Peer quote).

65. Bruce Feiler, *Dreaming Out Loud: Garth Brooks, Wynonna Judd, Wade Hayes, and the Changing Face of Nashville* (New York: Avon, 1998), 85–98 (Pearl and Nashville; 87, Mencken quote; 91–92, "check," "not welcome"); Peterson, *Creating Country Music,* 81–94 (the cowboy image); Jeffrey J. Lange, *Smile When You Call Me a Hillbilly: Country Music's Struggle for Respectability, 1939–1954* (Athens: University of Georgia Press, 2004), 61, 84 (Green quote). See also Douglas B. Green, *Singing in the Saddle: The History of the Singing Cowboy* (Nashville: Country Music Foundation Press/Vanderbilt University Press, 2002), esp. 113–49 (discussion of Autry). Peter Stanfield (*Horse Opera: The Strange History of the 1930s Singing Cowboy* [Urbana: University of Illinois Press, 2002]) places the 1930s singing cowboy in an even broader historical context. Savage (*Cowboy Hero,* 79–94) traces cowboy songs from the B movies of the 1930s through the 1970s.

66. Starr and Waterman, *American Popular Music,* 123–24 (*Hit Parade* quotes); Nachman, *Raised on Radio,* 170–71.

67. Dennis McDougal, *The Last Mogul: Lew Wasserman, MCA, and the Hidden History of Hollywood* (New York: Da Capo, 2001), 9–44, 69 (Stein); Connie Bruck, "The Monopolist," *New Yorker,* April 21–28, 2003, 138; Starr and Waterman, *American Popular Music,* 123 ("Octopus"); Garry Wills, *Reagan's America: Innocents at Home* (New York: Doubleday, 1987), 261 (Teagarden quote); Smith, *God Bless America,* 79 (Tin Pan Alley revolution).

68. Smith, *God Bless America,* 40, 43, 88–89; Kenney, *Recorded Music in American Life,* 185–92; Arthur Kempton, *Boogaloo: The Quintessence of American Popular Music* (New York: Pantheon, 2003), 16–17; Starr and Waterman, *American Popular Music,* 144–45, 168. For a more detailed account, see Sanjek and Sanjek, *American Popular Music Business,* esp. 17–20, 58–78, 91–107.

69. Robert McChesney, "The Battle for the Airwaves," in *Major Problems in American History, 1920–1945,* ed. Colin Gordon (New York: Houghton Mifflin, 1999), 135–41 (141, "American system," "democracy itself"); also Robert McChesney, *Rich Media, Poor Democracy: Communications Politics in Dubious Times* (New York: New Press, 2000), 189–225.

70. Gary Cross, *An All-Consuming Century: Why Commercialism Won in Modern America* (New York: Columbia University Press, 2000), 77 (*Fortune* quote and statistics).

71. Erik Barnouw, *Tube of Plenty: The Evolution of American Television,* 2nd rev. ed. (New York: Oxford University Press, 1990), 51–56 (NBC); Lewis, *Empire of the Air,* 176–79 (NBC); MacDonald, *Don't Touch That Dial!* 46 (Mutual); Butsch, *Making of American Audiences,* 196–97 (researchers); Sivulka, *Soap, Sex, and Cigarettes,* 223; and Cross, *All-Consuming Century,* 77 (revenue).

72. Czitrom, *Media and the American Mind,* 85; MacDonald, *Don't Touch That Dial!* 231–33; Newman, *Radio Active,* 110–14; Hilmes, *Radio Voices,* 82–83, 108–10 ("ghettoization"), 151–70 (154, "drool"; 157, "neurotic"); Butsch, *Making of American Audiences,* 200–201; Murphy, *Mining Cultures,* 183; Nachman, *Raised on Radio,* 366–68, 376. According to Nachman: "The Hummerts were the General Motors of daytime radio" (380).

73. Hilmes, *Radio Voices,* 113–28 (116, Thompson quote; 123, "B damned," "average American home"), 144; Neal Gabler, *Winchell: Gossip, Power, and the Culture of Celebrity* (New York: Vintage, 1995), 110–11 ("most notorious gossip").

74. Lewis, *Empire of the Air,* 235 ("new and noisy method"), 242 (De Forest quote); Murphy, *Mining Cultures,* 190–91, 193; Newman, *Radio Active,* 3, 132–36.

75. Newman, *Radio Active,* 3–7, 110, 112, 132–33 ("worthless Joe," "we use Ivory"), 137–38.

76. Matthew Murray, "'The Tendency to Deprave and Corrupt Morals': Regulation and Irregular Sexuality in Golden Age Radio Comedy," in Hilmes and Loviglio, eds., *Radio Reader,* 140–43 (MacRorie quote), 146–47 ("*not* interested in . . . sex"); Douglas, *Listening In,* esp. 5–8 (the culture of listening).

77. Murray, "Deprave and Corrupt,'" 136–40 (137, "ain't love"; 140, "lewd"), 144. On the program, see also Lori Landay, *Madcaps, Screwballs, and Con Women: The Female Trickster in American Culture* (Philadelphia: University of Pennsylvania Press, 1998), 94–98 (95, "dismal dump").

78. See, e.g., Murray, "'Deprave and Corrupt,'" 136; and Douglas, *Listening In,* 15–17.

79. Nachman, *Raised on Radio,* 371 (Hummert quote, "every girl"); MacDonald, *Don't Touch That Dial!* 234–48 (235, "sure of"; 238, "ring"); Hilmes, *Radio Voices,* 159–64 (Frances quotes); Murphy, *Mining Cultures,* 183 ("boyfriend"); Newman, *Radio Active,* 125–27.

80. Martin P. Ely, *The Adventures of Amos 'n' Andy: A Social History of an American Phenomenon* (New York: Free Press, 1991), esp. 1–193 (54, "chose black characters"; 158–59, nonstereotypical depictions); Watkins, *On the Real Side,* 272–80 (276, "black-voice soap opera"; 277, "boycott the program"); Douglas, *Listening In,* 103–10.

81. Douglas, *Listening In,* 100–123 (101, "slapstick," "decorum"; 104, "dramas," "field day"); "peephole" joke recycled on Garrison Keillor's *Prairie Home Companion* (American Public Media), February 2, 2003.

82. Albin Krebs, "Closer to Grace: Burns Dies," *Spokane, WA, Spokesman Review,* March 10, 1996, A1, A14 ("totally sane," "feel at home"); Douglas, *Listening In,* 114–16 ("because it's empty"); Epstein, *Haunted Smile,* 23–27 (25, "couldn't afford a nurse"); Lawrence J. Epstein, *Mixed Nuts: America's Love Affair with Comedy Teams* (New York: Public Affairs, 2004), 2–15.

83. Epstein, *Haunted Smile,* 55–60 (55, "big future," "backward and forward"; 59, "faults and frailties"); Nachman, *Raised on Radio,* 52–66 (65, Benny's salary); Douglas, *Listening In,* 116–18 ("henpecked"); Margaret T. McFadden, "'America's Boy Friend Who Can't Get a Date': Gender, Race, and the Cultural Work of the Jack Benny Program, 1932–1946," *Journal of American History* 80 (June 1993): 113–34; Murray, "'Deprave and Corrupt,'" 135–36, 145–52 (146, "lavendar"; 148, "basis for identity"; 150, "weird fella").

84. Lewis, *Empire of the Air,* 231 ("laugh and dance"), 235–40 (239, Rogers quote); Nachman, *Raised on Radio,* 8 (poll). On O'Daniel, see Robert A. Caro, *The Path to Power: The Years of Lyndon Johnson* (New York: Knopf, 1982), 695–703.

85. Robert C. Toll, *The Entertainment Machine: American Show Business in the Twentieth Century* (New York: Oxford University Press, 1982), 162–64; Fran Mason, *American Gangster Cinema from* Little Caesar *to* Pulp Fiction (New York: Palgrave, 2002), 32–39; Robinson and Davidson, *Pulp Culture,* 56–57, 60, 62–65; Nachman, *Raised on Radio,* 302; MacDonald, *Don't Touch That Dial!* 167–68. See also Richard Gid Powers, *G-Men: Hoover's FBI in Popular Culture* (Carbondale: Southern Illinois University Press, 1983).

86. Doherty, *Pre-Code Hollywood,* 334 (Warner quote, Zukor quote); Epstein, *Big Picture,* 12–13, 339–40; Watts, *Magic Kingdom,* 63–100; Levine, *Unpredictable Past,* 218, 250–53; Muscio, *Hollywood's New Deal,* esp. 65–67, 75–77, 96–100.

87. Harry M. Benshoff and Sean Griffin, *America on Film: Representing Race, Class, Gender, and Sexuality at the Movies* (Malden, MA: Blackwell, 2004), 220–21, 258–59 (258, permission).

88. Ibid., 80–81, 256–57; Robert Sklar, *City Boys: Cagney, Bogart, Garfield* (Princeton, NJ: Princeton University Press, 1992), 8–9; Nachman, *Raised on Radio,* 199–201 (Lone Ranger).

89. On Carnegie, see Richard M. Huber, *The American Idea of Success* (New York: McGraw-Hill, 1971), 226–51; and Warren Susman, *Culture as History: The Transformation of American Society in the Twentieth Century* (New York: Pantheon, 1984), 165. Susman (esp. 156–64) is also helpful on the larger setting.

90. Erika Doss, introduction to *Looking at* Life *Magazine,* ed. Erika Doss (Washington, DC: Smithsonian Institution Press, 2001), 1–2 (circulation figures), 11 (Luce quotes), 13–14; Terry Smith, "*Life*-Style Modernity: Making Modern America," in ibid., 25–37; James L.

Baughman, "Who Read *Life?* The Circulation of America's Favorite Magazine," in ibid., 42 (readership figures); William Stott, *Documentary America: Expression and Thirties America* (New York: Oxford University Press, 1973), 130 ("average 1937 American").

91. Gerard Jones, *Men of Tomorrow: Geeks, Gangsters, and the Birth of the Comic Book* (New York: Basic, 2004), 1–112 (Donenfeld and the comic business's evolution; 141, reports from local dealers; 170, "junk," survey); Bradford W. Wright, *Comic Book Nation: The Transformation of Youth Culture in America* (Baltimore: Johns Hopkins University Press, 2001), 4–9 (7, "ghetto"), 13–14 ("created"); Ron Goulart, *Great American Comic Books* (Lincolnwood, IL: Publications International, 2001), 54–55, 83.

92. Wright, *Comic Book Nation*, 1, 10–26 (11, "alienated"; 13, "paradox"; 22, "super-heroes"); Goulart, *Great American Comic Books*, 73–90, 99–102, 112–14. Jones (*Men of Tomorrow*, esp. 115–16, 142–45) is excellent on Siegel and Shuster and their creation.

8. BUILDING A WARTIME CONSENSUS IN THE 1940s AND 1950s

1. Culhane, *American Circus*, 241–42.

2. Ibid., 242; Immerso, *Coney Island*, 161; Wright, *Comic Book Nation*, 31 (paper rationing).

3. Culhane, *American Circus*, 242 (*Time* quotes). On *Dumbo*, see Watts, *Magic Kingdom*, 89–91.

4. Culhane, *American Circus*, 241 ("morale"); Wright, *Comic Book Nation*, 34 ("help win"); Thomas Schatz, *Boom and Bust: American Cinema in the 1940s* (Berkeley and Los Angeles: University of California Press, 1997), 131, 139 ("effective mediums," "no censorship"); Smith, *God Bless America*, 68 ("inspiration").

5. Richard R. Lingeman, *Don't You Know There's a War On? The American Home Front, 1941–1945* (1970; reprint, New York: Paperback Library, 1971), 371–75; Wright, *Comic Book Nation*, 33–34; Goulart, *Great American Comic Books*, 128–31.

6. Wright, *Comic Book Nation*, 30–36 (30, "super-soldier," "peace-loving," "ruthless"; 35, "very much wanted"; 36, "strictly American"); also Jones, *Men of Tomorrow*, 195–202; Les Daniels, *Marvel: Five Fabulous Decades of the World's Greatest Comics* (1991; reprint, New York: Abrams, 1993), 36–43.

7. Lingeman, *Don't You Know There's a War On?* 205 (*Photoplay* quotes).

8. Schatz, *Boom and Bust*, 240 (statistics); John Bodnar, *Blue-Collar Hollywood: Liberalism, Democracy, and Working People in American Film* (Baltimore: Johns Hopkins University Press, 2003), 79 (quote).

9. Lingeman, *Don't You Know There's a War On?* 211–12 (statistics); Schatz, *Boom and Bust*, 132, 147–51.

10. Lingeman, *Don't You Know There's a War On?* 254–56; Smith, *God Bless America*, 6, 114; John Costello, *Virtue under Fire: How World War Changed Our Social and Sexual Attitudes* (Boston: Little, Brown, 1985), 120 ("razzing"). On the victory narrative, see Tom Engelhardt, *The End of Victory Culture: Cold War America and the Disillusioning of a Generation* (New York: Basic, 1995), 3–6, 16–53.

11. Smith, *God Bless America*, 87 (*Billboard* quote); Lingeman, *Don't You Know There's a War On?* 262–63 ("loneliness songs"); Jody Rosen, "Not Like the Ones We Used to Know," *Spokane, WA, Spokesman-Review,* December 18, 2003, D1; Barry Gewen, "Snow Was General All over Manhattan," *New York Times Book Review,* December 8, 2002, 14.

12. Smith, *God Bless America*, 146 (*Variety* quote); Schatz, *Boom and Bust*, 242 (Wanger quote); Costello, *Virtue under Fire*, 121 (Loesser quote).

13. Doss, introduction, 11–13 (11, "especially American"); Baughman, "Who Read *Life?*" 41–44 (41, "great backbreaker," "turned out").

14. Peterson, *Pigskin*, 138–45 (quotes); Paul D. Casdorph, *Let the Good Times Roll: Life at Home in America during World War II* (New York: Paragon, 1989), 132–34.

15. Baughman, "Who Read *Life?*" 44; Simons, "Jewish Standard Bearer," 161 (*Sporting News* quote); Rader, *Baseball*, 157 (battle cry).

16. Rossi, *National Game*, 141–44 (142, Roosevelt quote); Lingeman, *Don't You Know There's a War On?* 380–88 (380, statistics; 386, "remnants"); Rader, *Baseball*, 156–57.

17. Rader, *Baseball,* 157–58; Kathryn Jay, *More Than Just a Game: Sports in American Life since 1945* (New York: Columbia University Press, 2004), 15–16 ("play like men").

18. Gerd Horton, *Radio Goes to War: The Cultural Politics of Propaganda during World War II* (Berkeley and Los Angeles: University of California Press, 2002), 1–6, 26, 89.

19. Ibid., 83–85 ("come and buy!"), 96, 123–24 (Meservey quotes), 130–31.

20. Jones, *Our Musicals, Ourselves,* 123 (statistics); John C. Chalberg, *Rickey and Robinson: The Preacher and Player and America's Game* (Wheeling, IL: Harlan Davidson, 2000), 85 (Paige quote).

21. Smith, *God Bless America,* 149 (*Variety* quote); Horton, *Radio Goes to War,* 95; Rossi, *National Game,* 143; Wright, *Comic Book Nation,* 31; Immerso, *Coney Island,* 161–63; Culhane, *American Circus,* 242–48; Lingeman, *Don't You Know There's a War On?* 349, 353–54 (Broadway).

22. Smith, *God Bless America,* 144–52 (*Variety* quote), 158; Lahr, "Sinatra's Song" (n. 37, chap. 7 above), 80.

23. Schatz, *Boom and Bust,* 131, 153, 171–72.

24. Bill C. Malone, *Country Music, U.S.A.,* 2nd rev. ed. (Austin: University of Texas Press, 2002), 177–78, 181–83; Feiler, *Dreaming Out Loud,* 92 (*Billboard* statistics).

25. On nightclubs, see, e.g., Erenberg, "From New York to Middletown," esp. 762–63, 773–75.

26. Sally Denton and Roger Morris, *The Money and the Power: The Making of Las Vegas and Its Hold on America, 1947–2000* (New York: Knopf, 2001), 8 (quote), 95–97.

27. Ibid., 21–29 (22, "suckers"; 28, "horrible," "tourists," "every joint"), 51–52, 54.

28. Ibid., 9 ("pathology"), 54 (Siegel quote).

29. Simons, "Jewish Standard Bearer," 178.

30. Jon Wiener, "When Old Blue Eyes Was 'Red,'" *New Republic,* March 31, 1986, 21–23 (23, "wasn't born here"); Jim Cullen, "Fool's Paradise: Frank Sinatra and the American Dream," in *Popular Culture in American History,* ed. Jim Cullen (Malden, MA: Blackwell, 2001), 210–20 (217, "who the hell," "wasn't motherly"); Lahr, "Sinatra's Song" (n. 37, chap. 7 above), 77–82; Joseph Dorinson, "Frank Sinatra's House: Pride, Passion, and Politics," in *Frank Sinatra: History, Identity, and Italian American Culture,* ed. Stanislao G. Pugliese (New York: Palgrave Macmillan, 2004), 25–26; Leonard Mustazza, "Frank Sinatra and Civil Rights," in ibid., 36–37.

31. Wright, *Comic Book Nation,* 53–54.

32. Lauren R. Sklaroff, "Constructing G.I. Joe Louis: Cultural Solutions to the 'Negro Problem' during World War II," *Journal of American History* 89 (December 2002): 958–71.

33. Bodnar, *Blue-Collar Hollywood,* 55–57 (Corwin quote), 81–82, 86; J. Fred MacDonald, *Television and the Red Menace: The Video Road to Vietnam* (New York: Praeger, 1985), 7–8 ("kings and queens"); Thomas Doherty, *Projections of War: Hollywood, American Culture, and World War II,* rev. ed. (New York: Columbia University Press, 1999), 139–41.

34. George Lipsitz, *Rainbow at Midnight: Labor and Culture in the 1940s* (Urbana: University of Illinois Press, 1994), 33–40 (35, "hurt me"; 38, "same jive").

35. Ibid., 20–29 (25, Williams quote; 26, King quote).

36. John M. Blum, *V Was for Victory: Politics and American Culture during World War II* (New York: Harcourt Brace Jovanovich, 1976), 53–70 (55, "selective"; 59–61, other quotes); Judith E. Smith, *Visions of Belonging: Family Stories, Popular Culture, and Postwar Democracy, 1940–1960* (New York: Columbia University Press, 2004), 2, 21–28.

37. Peter Schrag, *The Decline of the WASP* (New York: Simon & Schuster, 1970), 13–14, 49; also May, *Big Tomorrow,* 144–45; Gary Gerstle, *American Crucible: Race and Nation in the Twentieth Century* (Princeton, NJ: Princeton University Press, 2001), 42 ("controlled assimilation"), 204–5, 255.

38. Erenberg, *Swingin' the Dream,* 185–88 (186, "pretty tunes"; 187, "just right"); Gary Giddins, "Stride and Swing," *New Yorker,* May 31, 2004, 85–87 (money, "vanilla"); Stowe, *Swing Changes,* 28 ("troublemakers"); Peretti, *Jazz in American Culture,* 90–91.

39. Erenberg, *Swingin' the Dream,* 188, 202; Stowe, *Swing Changes,* 154–55 ("the average G.I."); Peretti, *Jazz in American Culture,* 93, 97 (quote).

40. Robert Westbrook, "'I Want a Girl, Just Like the Girl That Married Harry James':

American Women and the Problem of Political Obligation in World War II," *American Quarterly* 42 (December 1990): 589–96.

41. May, *Big Tomorrow,* 163–65, 167, 172 (Hayworth and Allyson).

42. Westbrook, "'I Want a Girl,'" 596–605 (599, "pearl blond," "average legs," "one of them"; 600, "exhausted, frightened"; 605, "follow their lead"); Landay, *Madcaps, Screwballs, and Con Women,* 149–54 (149, "icon"); McDougal, *Last Mogul,* 98–99.

43. Rader, *Baseball,* 158; Rader, *American Sports,* 220 (*"more dramatic"*); Jay, *More Than Just a Game,* 16; "Baseball: Babette Ruths," *Newsweek,* July 29, 1946, 68–69.

44. Bodnar, *Blue-Collar Hollywood,* 56, 60–61, 64, 85–86; Lary May, "Making the American Consensus: The Narrative of Conversion and Subversion in World War II Films," in *The War in American Culture: Society and Consciousness during World War II,* ed. Lewis A. Erenberg and Susan E. Hirsch (Chicago: University of Chicago Press, 1996), 72–73, 81 ("realigned"); May, *Big Tomorrow,* 139–40, 148 ("top"), 151–52, 156 ("loyalty").

45. Horton, *Radio Goes to War,* 3–4, 90–93 (91, "to sell free enterprise," "doghouse"; 92, "leadership"), 98 (GM and Pennsylvania Oil ads), 115; Lingeman, *Don't You Know There's a War On?* 356–61 (357, Kleenex ad).

46. Horton, *Radio Goes to War,* 98 ("lost"), 102–8, 111 (poll), 130–32, 178.

47. Roland Marchand, "Visions of Classlessness, Quests for Dominion: American Popular Culture, 1945–1960," in *Reshaping America: Society and Institutions, 1945–1960,* ed. Robert H. Bremner and Gary Reichard (Columbus: Ohio State University Press, 1982), 163–65; Eric Avila, *Popular Culture in the Age of White Flight: Fear and Fantasy in Suburban Los Angeles* (Berkeley and Los Angeles: University of California Press, 2004), 15 (master narrative).

48. Avila (*Age of White Flight,* esp. 4–5, 32–64, 150) is excellent on these trends. Steve Gillon, *Boomer Nation: The Largest and Richest Generation and How It Changed America* (New York: Free Press, 2004), 24. See also Lizabeth Cohen, *A Consumers' Republic: The Politics of Mass Consumption in Postwar America* (New York: Knopf, 2003), esp. 194–256.

49. James T. Patterson, *Grand Expectations: The United States, 1945–1974* (New York: Oxford University Press, 1996), 77–80; J. Ronald Oakley, *God's Country: America in the Fifties* (New York: Dembner, 1986), 119–21; Gillon, *Boomer Nation,* 1–5; Landon Jones, *Great Expectations: America and the Baby Boom Generation* (1980; reprint, New York: Ballantine, 1981), 10, 20–21.

50. Avila, *Age of White Flight,* 5–11 (5, Clinton quotes), 65–105; Werner, *Change Is Gonna Come,* 183–84. For more on Clinton, see Joe McEwen, "Funk," in *The Rolling Stone Illustrated History of Rock and Roll,* ed. Anthony DeCurtis and James Henke with Holly George-Warren; orig. ed. Jim Miller (New York: Random House, 1992), 521–24; and David Szatmary, *A Time to Rock: A Social History of Rock 'n' Roll* (New York: Schirmer, 1996), 241–44.

51. Avila, *Age of White Flight,* 2, 145–84 (151, "neighborhood"; 154, "rough"; 160, "overnight," "cash"; 163, "railroads"); Rossi, *National Game,* 159–66.

52. Avila, *Age of White Flight,* 156 (Poulson quotes).

53. Engelhardt, *End of Victory Culture,* 9 ("triumphalist despair"); Henry Allen, "The Good, the Bad, and the Ugly," *Washington Post National Weekly Edition,* January 14–20, 2001, 11–12 (Updike quote); Jones, *Great Expectations,* 22 (statistics); Douglas T. Miller, *Visions of America: Second World War to the Present* (St. Paul, MN: West, 1988), 1 (*Fortune* quote).

54. Kimmel, *Manhood in America,* 223 (quote).

55. Richard M. Fried, *The Russians Are Coming! The Russians Are Coming! Pageantry and Patriotism in Cold-War America* (New York: Oxford University Press, 1998); Daniel Boorstin, *The Genius of American Politics* (Chicago: University of Chicago Press, 1953), 179 (quote); Walter A. McDougall, *The Heavens and the Earth: A Political History of the Space Age* (New York: Basic, 1985), 137 (Baruch quote); John Patrick Diggins, *The Proud Decades: America in War and Peace* (New York: Norton, 1988), 75 (catalogs, stockings).

56. Engelhardt, *End of Victory Culture,* 99–100.

57. Loren Baritz, *The Good Life: The Meaning of Success for the American Middle Class* (New York: Knopf, 1988), 224 (Piercy quote).

58. David W. Zang, *Sports Wars: Athletes in the Age of Aquarius* (Fayetteville: University of Arkansas Press, 2001), xii (Lipsyte quote); Richard O. Davies, *America's Obsession:*

Sports and Society since 1945 (New York: Harcourt Brace, 1994), vii (Warren quote); Richard M. Fried, *Nightmare in Red: The McCarthy Era in Perspective* (New York: Oxford University Press, 1990), 79 (Welker quote); Rader, *American Sports,* 280 (Crosby quote); Jay, *More Than Just a Game,* esp. 1–12, 23–27 (sport and the American way).

59. Jim Dent, *The Undefeated: The Oklahoma Sooners and the Greatest Winning Streak in College Football* (New York: Thomas Dunne, 2001), 21–22 (including quotes).

60. Michael Oriard, "Domesticated Football" (paper presented at the meeting of the Organization of American Historians, Los Angeles, April 27, 2001); Oriard, *King Football,* 162–63 (*Life* quote), 176 ("beautiful girls"), 192–98, 351 ("cheerleaders").

61. Kimmel, *Manhood in America,* 237 (*Daily News* quotes); K. A. Cuordileone, "'Politics in an Age of Anxiety': Cold War Political Culture and the Crisis in American Masculinity, 1949–1960," *Journal of American History* 87 (September 2000): 515–45; Oriard, *King Football,* 155–61 (coaches; 161, *Post* and *Collier's* quotes), 163–69 and 188–95 (middle-class ambience), 201–20 (pros).

62. Oriard, *King Football,* 201–20 (215, statistics, *Life* quote; 217, *Time* quote); Marchand, "Visions of Classlessness," 172; George Will, "Modern Life in NFL Nation," *Newsweek,* October 11, 2004, 64 (Thanksgiving Day game). On the smokestack base, see Susan Faludi, *Stiffed: The Betrayal of the American Man* (New York: Morrow, 1999), 157 ("version"), 160–64, 172–75, 185, 188 ("Commies"). On pro football's popular growth after World War II, see also Michael MacCambridge, *America's Game: The Epic Story of How Pro Football Captured a Nation* (New York: Random House, 2004), 3–115.

63. Oriard, *King Football,* 277–82; Rader, *American Sports,* 272; *City Dump: The Story of the 1951 CCNY Basketball Scandal* (George Roy and Steven Hilliard Stern, 1998, TV documentary) (Cohen quote, Kalb quote).

64. Peterson, *Pigskin,* 169–89 (185, Motley quote); Oriard, *King Football,* 308–13 (308, Griffin quote; 312, "no place"); Charles H. Martin, "Integrating New Year's Day: The Racial Politics of College Bowl Games in the American South," in *The Sporting World of the Modern South,* ed. Patrick B. Miller (Urbana: University of Illinois Press, 2002), 175–99. On Motley, see also Davies, *America's Obsession,* 34–40.

65. Before the mid-1940s, the rodeo—which grew up with the Wild West shows but far outlasted them—was arguably America's only desegregated sport. Black, Native American, and Hispanic cowboys indeed encountered prejudice, but, as Michael Allen (*Rodeo Cowboys in the North American Imagination* [Reno: University of Nevada Press, 1998], 159) has written: "There has never been a time when North American rodeo was *consistently segregated across the board.* . . . There was *never* an all-white-male rodeo era." Notably, too, from the days of Annie Oakley, rodeos allowed women participants, although the events they participated in shrank over the years.

66. Arthur R. Ashe Jr., *A Hard Road to Glory: A History of the African-American Athlete since 1946* (New York: Warner, 1988), 160–69 (164, Marble quote). A number of women in the American Tennis Association, founded in 1916 for African American players, unquestionably blazed the trail for Gibson. From the late 1930s into the 1950s, e.g., the sisters Margaret "Pete" Peters and Matilda Roumania "Repeat" Peters excelled. See John Krawczynski, "Blazing the Trail," *Spokane, WA, Spokesman Review,* July 20, 2003, C6.

67. Avila, *Age of White Flight,* 150–51 ("bagged fried chicken"); Rader, *American Sports,* 298 (admired); John Gregory Dunne, "Birth of a Salesman," *New York Review of Books,* July 15, 1999, 11.

68. Bruce Lentrall, "Black and White and Green All Over: Race Relations and the Integration of the Boston Celtics in the 1950s" (paper presented at the meeting of the Organization of American Historians, Los Angeles, April 27, 2001). Chuck Cooper was the black player drafted by the Celtics in 1950.

69. Bodnar, *Blue-Collar Hollywood,* 128 (Capra quote). On *Twelve Angry Men,* see Peter Biskind, *Seeing Is Believing: How Hollywood Taught Us to Stop Worrying and Love the Bomb* (New York: Pantheon, 1983), 10–20.

70. See May, *Big Tomorrow,* 175–213 (on "Cold War Americanism"); Garry Wills, *John Wayne's America* (New York: Simon & Schuster, 1997), 24 ("regimentation"), 149–91 (Wayne's Cold War films). See also Richard Slotkin, *Gunfighter Nation: The Myth of the*

Frontier in Twentieth-Century America (1992; reprint, New York: HarperCollins, 1993), esp. 351–65; and Randy Roberts and James S. Olson, *John Wayne, American* (New York: Free Press, 1995), 291–325.

71. Oakley, *God's Country,* 319–23; MacDonald, *Television and the Red Menace,* 126–29; Richard A. Schwartz, *Cold War Culture: Media and the Arts, 1945–1990* (1998; reprint, New York: Checkmark, 2000), 289 (Sheen); Watts, *Magic Kingdom,* 343 (Mickey Mouse Club). See also Stephen Whitfield, *The Culture of the Cold War* (Baltimore: Johns Hopkins University Press, 1991), 77–100; Patterson, *Grand Expectations,* 328–33; Thomas Doherty, *Cold War, Cool Medium: Television, McCarthyism, and American Culture* (New York: Columbia University Press, 2003), 153–60 (Sheen); and Huber, *American Idea of Success,* 314–40 (Peale).

72. Oakley, *God's Country,* 324–27 (324, Niebuhr quote; 325, Kempton quote; 326, Russell quote); William L. O'Neill, *American High: The Years of Confidence, 1945–1960* (New York: Free Press, 1986), 213 (Eisenhower quote); Biskind, *Seeing Is Believing,* 336 ("Moses, Moses"); May, *Big Tomorrow,* 206; Bodnar, *Blue-Collar Hollywood,* 134.

73. Jones, *Our Musicals, Ourselves,* 140–60 (142, "totally integrated"; 143, "eradicating"). *Carousel* played 890 times, *Flower Drum Song* 600, *The Sound of Music* 1,433.

74. Henry Koster's movie version of *Flower Drum Song* appeared in 1961; Robert Wise's *The Sound of Music* was released in 1965. Other popular 1950s musicals that appeared as films included *The Music Man* (Morton DaCosta, 1962) and *My Fair Lady* (George Cukor, 1964).

75. Watts, *Magic Kingdom,* 288–89 (quote), 358.

76. Ibid., 289–91 (291, "bursting with pride"), 313–22 (314, *Time* quote; 318, "go ahead"); MacDonald, *Television and the Red Menace,* 137 ("freedom").

77. Watts, *Magic Kingdom,* 303–8 (308, quote).

78. Ibid., 294–95 ("assimilationist"), 326–45 (327, "sanctity"); Avila, *Age of White Flight,* 132–36 (Frontierland).

79. Watts, *Magic Kingdom,* 392–96 (393, "keep it great"); Avila, *Age of White Flight,* 8–9, 12–13, 105–44 (118, "tawdry rides"; 124–25, "without extremes"; 131, "marketed," "premise"; 135, "hometown"), 175; Richard Schickel, *The Disney Version: The Life, Times, Art, and Commerce of Walt Disney* (1968; reprint, New York: Avon, 1968), 269–77.

80. Patterson, *Grand Expectations,* 189 ("Yiddish"); Whitfield, *Culture of the Cold War,* 77 (Graham quote), 129 ("hotbed").

81. Patterson, *Grand Expectations,* 189–90 (189, Sinatra quote).

82. May, *Big Tomorrow,* 203 (*Screen Guide* quotes); Roberts and Olson, *John Wayne,* 330–32 (331, Wood's will); Wills, *John Wayne's America,* 195–96. Roberts and Olson (*John Wayne,* 334, 338) say that Wayne, who was the alliance's president from March 1949 to June 1953, "played no active role" during World War II.

83. Schatz, *Boom and Bust,* 1–4, 11–21, 163–68, 289–91. On the hearings in 1947 and later, see also Larry Ceplair and Steven Englund, *The Inquisition in Hollywood: Politics in the Film Community, 1930–1960* (1980; reprint, Urbana: University of Illinois Press, 2003), 254–397.

84. See, e.g., Schatz, *Boom and Bust,* 293–95; Bruck, "The Monopolist" (n. 67, chap. 7 above), 137 (Warner); Davies, *America's Obsession,* 17–18 (bowling; 17, "country clubs"); and Kammen, *American Culture,* 92 (*Life* quote).

85. Schwartz, *Cold War Culture,* 202 ("crackpots"); May, "Making the American Consensus," 71–72 ("no more"); Doherty, *Cold War, Cool Medium,* 22 ("disloyal"). Roberts and Olson (*John Wayne,* 343–45) emphasize that the Hollywood blacklist was far from unique: across American institutions, "purging Communists was as American as motherhood, baseball, and apple pie" (343).

86. Wiener, "When Old Blue Eyes Was 'Red'" (n. 30 above), 21–23; Lahr, "Sinatra's Song" (n. 37, chap. 7 above), 84–86.

87. Whitfield, *Culture of the Cold War,* 116 (Mostel quote); Ceplair and Englund, *Inquisition in Hollywood,* 404–5, 419 (Trumbo).

88. May, *Big Tomorrow,* 208–9.

89. See, e.g., Whitfield, *Culture of the Cold War,* 132–42; Victor Navasky, *Naming Names*

(New York: Viking, 1980); and Biskind, *Seeing Is Believing*, 162–67. Biskind includes astute analyses of films such as *Blackboard Jungle* (Richard Brooks, 1955).

90. Doherty, *Cold War, Cool Medium*, 1, 4; MacDonald, *Television and the Red Menace*, 1–2; William Manchester, *The Glory and the Dream: A Narrative History of America, 1932–1972* (Boston: Little, Brown, 1974), 584–85; Douglas T. Miller and Marion Nowak, *The Fifties: The Way We Really Were* (Garden City, NY: Doubleday, 1977), 344; Thomas Doherty, *Teenagers and Teenpics: The Juvenilization of American Movies in the 1950s*, rev. ed. (Philadelphia: Temple University Press, 2002), 19 (revenues). On TV's early years, see Barnouw, *Tube of Plenty*, 70–100.

91. Doherty, *Cold War, Cool Medium*, 1–7 (1, "pact"), 23 (*Variety* quote).

92. Barnouw, *Tube of Plenty*, 109–10, 117–25 (121, "American job"; 122, "'belts'").

93. Ibid., 125–28 (128, "little creatures"); Doherty, *Cold War, Cool Medium*, 24–28 (27, "purchase price"), 35–46; MacDonald, *Television and the Red Menace*, 23–24.

94. Robert Metz, *CBS: Reflections in a Bloodshot Eye* (1975; reprint, New York: Signet, 1976), 282 ("book we live by"); Doherty, *Cold War, Cool Medium*, 28 ("these little lists").

95. Robert J. Thompson, *Television's Second Golden Age: From* Hill Street Blues *to* ER (Syracuse, NY: Syracuse University Press, 1996), 38–39.

96. See, e.g., Sivulka, *Soap, Sex, and Cigarettes*, 253–54, 264–81 (265, "Mrs. Middle Majority"; 275, Reeves quote; 279, Ogilvy); Thomas Frank, *The Conquest of Cool: Business Culture, Counter Culture, and the Rise of Hip Consumerism* (Chicago: University of Chicago Press, 1997), 24, 38–48; David Halberstam, *The Fifties* (New York: Villard, 1993), 225–27.

97. Halberstam, *The Fifties*, 501 (Reeves quote, statistics); James B. Twitchell, *Adcult USA: The Triumph of Advertising in American Culture* (New York: Columbia University Press, 1996), 93 ("selling audiences").

98. Doherty, *Cold War, Cool Medium*, 34, 68; MacDonald, *Television and the Red Menace*, 22–23.

99. Mark Goodson, "'If I'd Stood Up Earlier . . . ,'" *New York Times Magazine*, January 13, 1991, 22 ("conspiracy of silence"), 39–40, 43 (other quotes).

100. See esp. J. Fred MacDonald, "The Cold War as Entertainment in Fifties Television," *Journal of Popular Film and Television* 1 (1978): 3–31.

101. Susan J. Douglas, *Where the Girls Are: Growing Up Female in the Mass Media* (New York: Times Books, 1994), 32–33; MacDonald, *Television and the Red Menace*, 97, 101–45; Marchand, "Visions of Classlessness," 169 ("show the country").

102. Mary Ann Watson, *Defining Visions: Television and the American Experience since 1945* (New York: Harcourt Brace, 1998), 54–61 (the *Father Knows Best* and *Donna Reed Show* episodes); also David Marc, *Comic Visions: Television Comedy and American Culture* (Boston: Unwin Hyman, 1989), 52–65; Douglas, *Where the Girls Are*, 36–38; Smith, *Visions of Belonging*, 106.

103. Fried, *The Russians Are Coming!* 151–59 (156, quote).

9. COUNTERPOINTS TO CONSENSUS

1. James Naremore, *More Than Night: Film Noir in Its Contexts* (Berkeley and Los Angeles: University of California Press, 1998), epigraph (from Raymond Chandler's 1944 essay "The Simple Art of Murder").

2. Patterson, *Grand Expectations*, 61.

3. Marchand, "Visions of Classlessness," 170 (quote); *Time*, October 22, 1951; *Saturday Evening Post*, July 5, 1952.

4. See, e.g., May, "Making the American Consensus," 92–96.

5. Naremore, *More Than Night*, 254–77 (the mediascape); David Cochran, *America Noir: Underground Writers and Filmmakers of the Postwar Era* (Washington, DC: Smithsonian Institution Press, 2000), xi–xiii (xii, Farber quote), 2–3 (*Detour*). For a wide-ranging discussion of the "noir sensibility," see Paula Rabinowitz, *Black and White and Noir: America's Pulp Modernism* (New York: Columbia University Press, 2002).

6. See, e.g., Smith, *Hard-Boiled*, 18–42; Arthur Lyons, *Death on the Cheap: The Lost B Films of Film Noir* (New York: Da Capo, 2000), 13–17; Geoffrey O'Brien, *Hardboiled America: Lurid Paperbacks and the Masters of Noir*, expanded ed. (New York: Da Capo, 1997), 61–78; Allison McCracken, "Scary Women and Scarred Men: *Suspense*, Gender Trouble, and Postwar Change, 1942–1950," in Hilmes and Loviglio, eds., *Radio Reader*, 185 (horror).

7. McCracken, "Scary Women and Scarred Men," 183–205. *Suspense* lasted twenty-five years, airing 945 episodes.

8. Ibid., 198–99. See also Naremore, *More Than Night*, 259.

9. Lyons, *Death on the Cheap*, 10 (*Detour* quote). For useful overviews of film noir, see John Belton, *American Cinema/American Culture* (New York: McGraw Hill, 1994), 184–204; and the two-hour *Film in the Television Age*, part of the PBS series *American Cinema* (Alain Klarer, 1995), which Belton's volume accompanied.

10. Foster Hirsch, *Detours and Lost Highways: A Map of Neo-Noir* (New York: Proscenium, 1999), 7 (Schrader quote). On the roots of film noir, see Nicholas Christopher, *Somewhere in the Night: Film Noir and the American City* (New York: Owl, 1997), 12–17, 38–39, 54–58 (57, *Life* and *Collier's* stories), 188–89 (188, Greenberg quote); and Lyons, *Death on the Cheap*, 2, 13–19.

11. Christopher, *Somewhere in the Night*, 236–37; Lyons, *Death on the Cheap*, 2–4 (2, Mitchum quote), 29–53; Doherty, *Teenagers and Teenpics*, 18 (the indie revolution). The indie revolution was, as Doherty warns, somewhat exaggerated because the small studios depended heavily on the bigger ones for facilities and distribution. On *Detour* and Producers Releasing Corp., see also Naremore, *More Than Night*, 144–49.

12. Lyons, *Death on the Cheap*, 42 (Scorsese quote); May, *Big Tomorrow*, 227–47 (Wilder and Huston; 228, "keep track," "wonderful piece"; 235–36, "dirtied"); Robert S. Birchard, *Cecil B. DeMille's Hollywood* (Lexington: University Press of Kentucky, 2004), 342–43 ("damn"); Eddie Muller, *Dark City: The Lost World of Film Noir* (New York: St. Martin's Griffin, 1998), 10 ("distress flares").

13. Lyons, *Death on the Cheap*, 3 ("corner"), 19 ("no good"), 168–80 (list of "B noirs"). For a marvelous collection of film stills illustrating film noir's mood, themes, and images, see Alain Silver and James Ursini, *The Noir Style* (Woodstock, NY: Overlook, 1999).

14. O'Brien, *Hardboiled America*, 2–3, 16–17 (quote).

15. Ibid., 17 ("retailing"), 19–25 (19, "OUT TODAY"); Kenneth C. Davis, *Two-Bit Culture: The Paperbacking of America* (Boston: Houghton Mifflin, 1984), 12–15, 63.

16. O'Brien, *Hardboiled America*, 25; Smith, *Hard-Boiled*, 25–26.

17. O'Brien, *Hardboiled America*, 3 ("sex education"), 26 ("word went out"), 30 ("3 S's"), 41; Davis, *Two-Bit Culture*, 135–38, 154–55.

18. O'Brien, *Hardboiled America*, 102–5 (104, "shoot killers"; 105, "That Hammer!"); Halberstam, *The Fifties*, 59–60 (59, "best of taste"); Davis, *Two-Bit Culture*, 180–81; Jones, *Men of Tomorrow*, 261–62; Whitfield, *Culture of the Cold War*, 34–37; John G. Cawelti, *Adventure, Mystery, and Romance: Formula Stories as Art and Popular Culture* (Chicago: University of Chicago Press, 1976), 183–91; Max Allan Collins and James L. Traylor, *One Lonely Knight: Mickey Spillane's Mike Hammer* (Bowling Green, OH: Bowling Green University Popular Press, 1984), esp. 4–7, 33–78.

19. Walter Kirn, "Pulp Fiction," *New York Times Book Review*, November 30, 1997, 24 ("plank," "call it life"); O'Brien, *Hardboiled America*, 145–51 (149, "no familiar thing"); Sean McCann, *Gumshoe America: Hard-Boiled Crime Fiction and the Rise and Fall of New Deal Liberalism* (Durham, NC: Duke University Press, 2000), 9–10 ("only one plot"); Margot A. Henriksen, *Dr. Strangelove's America: Society and Culture in the Atomic Age* (Berkeley and Los Angeles: University of California Press, 1997), 63–64 ("funny world"). On Thompson, see also Cochran, *America Noir*, 19–38.

20. O'Brien, *Hardboiled America*, 172, 175.

21. Davis, *Two-Bit Culture*, 219–37 (219, "offensive matter"; 220, "filth, perversion," "voluptuous young women"; 228, "flood the nation"; 235, "so-called," "aberrations").

22. O'Brien, *Hardboiled America*, 27, 30 ("Gideon Bibles"), 33 ("made safe").

23. Davis, *Two-Bit Culture*, 248–53 (248, "pioneering days"; 249, "like Coca-Cola," "seat-of-the-pants"; 252, Dystel quote).

24. Jones, *Men of Tomorrow*, 234 (statistics), 236–37, 256.

25. Wright, *Comic Book Nation*, 57 (statistics), 128 (romance); Douglas, *Where the Girls Are*, 48 ("headlight comics"); Goulart, *Great American Comic Books*, 161–72.

26. Wright, *Comic Book Nation*, 56–58 (56, *Captain Marvel Adventures* quote), 72–75, 109–27; William W. Savage Jr., *Commies, Cowboys, and Jungle Queens: Comic Books and America, 1945–1954* (1990; reprint, Hanover, NH: Wesleyan University Press, 1998), 44–94.

27. Wright, *Comic Book Nation*, 75–92 (84, "remarkably perverse"); Goulart, *Great American Comic Books*, 190–200.

28. Wright, *Comic Book Nation*, 135–36, 142, 146–51; Jones, *Men of Tomorrow*, 253–57; Goulart, *Great American Comic Books*, 173–82.

29. Wright, *Comic Book Nation*, 136–42, 145, 151; Goulart, *Great American Comic Books*, 175.

30. Wright, *Comic Book Nation*, 149, 155–56.

31. James Gilbert, *A Cycle of Outrage: America's Reaction to Juvenile Delinquency in the 1950s* (New York: Oxford University Press, 1986), 91–108 (103, "perversion"; 106, "Kremlin"); Wright, *Comic Book Nation*, 92–98, 157–64, 166 ("no secure homes"); Oakley, *God's Country*, 259 ("racketeers"); Jones, *Men of Tomorrow*, 238–39 ("correspondence course"), 270–74; Goulart, *Great American Comic Books*, 206.

32. Jones, *Men of Tomorrow*, 240–41; Goulart, *Great American Comic Books*, 207.

33. Wright, *Comic Book Nation*, 165–72 (169, "there to hang"; 172, Hendrickson quote); Jones, *Men of Tomorrow*, 275–77 (276, "bastards"); Goulart, *Great American Comic Books*, 215–16 (215, "ruined").

34. Wright, *Comic Book Nation*, 172–79; Jones, *Men of Tomorrow*, 257 ("tend to discredit"), 275. On "alternative imaginative spaces," see, e.g., Kevin Glynn, *Tabloid Culture: Trash Taste, Popular Power, and the Transformation of American Television* (Durham, NC: Duke University Press, 2000), 144–45; Goulart, *Great American Comic Books*, 185, 188–89, 216–17.

35. Gerald Nachman, *Seriously Funny: The Rebel Comedians of the 1950s and 1960s* (New York: Pantheon, 2003), 50; Victor Greene, "Ethnic Comedy in American Culture," *American Quarterly* 51 (March 1999): 146–48; Epstein, *Haunted Smile*, 104–25; Marc, *Comic Visions*, 38–42.

36. Epstein, *Haunted Smile*, 167 ("offended"). On Hope, see Todd S. Purdum, "Bob Hope, Before He Became the Comedy Establishment," *New York Times*, April 20, 2003, A7; Roger Moore, "When Hope Talked, Everybody Listened," *Spokane, WA, Spokesman-Review*, July 29, 2003, A6; Vincent Canby, "A Life of Laughter," *Spokane, WA, Spokesman-Review*, July 29, 2003, A1, A7; Connie Cass, "Hope's Jokes Cure Modern Worries with Old-Fashioned Laughter," *Spokane, WA, Spokesman-Review*, July 29, 2003, A7; Marc, *Comic Visions*, 45–46 ("toastmaster"); and ABC's *Good Morning, America*, July 28, 2003 ("rubbed").

37. Tony Hendra, *Going Too Far* (New York: Doubleday, 1987), 30–32; Nachman, *Seriously Funny*, 50–51 ("audacious"), 54–58 (58, "can't hurt").

38. Hendra, *Going Too Far*, 32–39; Nachman, *Seriously Funny*, 51, 52 (Gleason quote), 59–68, 72; Epstein, *Haunted Smile*, 166–69 (*Time* quote); Phil Berger, *The Last Laugh: The World of Stand-Up Comics*, updated ed. (New York: Limelight, 1985), 64–65.

39. Nachman, *Seriously Funny*, 6, 8–17, 42 ("subdivision"), 60, 68 (Allen quote); Hendra, *Going Too Far*, 31, 35–36, 39.

40. Thomas Weyr, *Reaching for Paradise: The Playboy Vision of America* (New York: Times Books, 1978), 3–7, 15–16; James R. Petersen, *The Century of Sex: Playboy's History of the Sexual Revolution, 1900–1999* (New York: Grove, 1999), 211, 228; Max Allan Collins, George Hagenauer, and Steven Heller, *Men's Adventure Magazines in Postwar America* (London: Taschen, 2004), 6–17 (6, "spread the gospel"). For a list of the men's magazines, see Bill Devine, "Devine's Guide to Men's Adventure Magazines," in *It's a Man's World: Men's Adventure Magazines, the Postwar Pulps*, ed. Adam Parfrey (Los Angeles: Feral, 2003), 281–87.

41. Weyr, *Reaching for Paradise*, xvi, 9–11 (11, "pleasure primer," "romantic," "thorny thickets," "plan spending"), 14, 37; Richard A. Kallan and Robert D. Brooks, "The Playmate of the Month: Naked but Nice," *Journal of Popular Culture* 8 (fall 1974): 328–36 (330, "innocent"); Petersen, *Century of Sex*, 228–29, 231. As Barbara Ehrenreich points out, Hefner wanted "to reclaim *the indoors for men*" (*Hearts of Men: American Dreams and the Flight from Commitment* [New York: Anchor, 1983], 44).

42. Hendra, *Going Too Far,* 34; Nachman, *Seriously Funny,* 8, 403; Petersen, *Century of Sex,* 233.

43. Ehrenreich, *Hearts of Men,* 47 ("perfectly willing"); Schrag, *Decline of the WASP,* 198–99 (Schrag quotes).

44. Nachman, *Seriously Funny,* 72–75.

45. Lyons, *Death on the Cheap,* 19 ("nylons"), 168–80 (list of titles); Christopher, *Somewhere in the Night,* 191–95 ("action"); Muller, *Dark City,* 84–107 (94, "briefcase"); Hirsch, *Detours and Lost Highways,* 7 ("misogyny"). See also Silver and Ursini, *Noir Style,* 83–125.

46. J. Hoberman, *The Dream Life: Movies, Media, and the Mythology of the Sixties* (New York: New Press, 2003), 75 ("Sickniks," "last days of Rome"). On this "alternative culture of dissent," see Henriksen, *Dr. Strangelove's America,* 133 ("run out of places"). See also Cochran, *America Noir.*

47. On Bruce, see Andrew Kopkind, "Resurrection of a Junkie Prophet," *Ramparts,* March 1975, 45–49; Albert Goldman with Lawrence Schiller, *Ladies and Gentlemen—Lenny Bruce!* (1971; reprint, New York: Ballantine, 1974), 288–90; Nachman, *Seriously Funny,* 389–435; Hendra, *Going Too Far,* 114–45.

48. Petersen, *Century of Sex,* 232–33 (*McCall's* quote); Ehrenreich, *Hearts of Men,* 42 ("*Playboy* loved women"); Henriksen, *Dr. Strangelove's America,* 126–27 (Addams cartoons); Christopher, *Somewhere in the Night,* 188–91 (191, "subversive"), 196–201 (198, "girl").

49. Lange, *Smile When You Call Me a Hillbilly,* 61–63 (62, Cooper quotes; 63, Acuff quote), 185 (Tubb quote).

50. Malone, *Country Music, U.S.A.,* 177–84, 193–94; Lange, *Smile When You Call Me a Hillbilly,* 67–88, 223; Bill C. Malone and David Stricklin, *Southern Music/American Music,* rev. ed. (Lexington: University Press of Kentucky, 2003), 90–94.

51. Peterson, *Creating Country Music,* 162–64; Lange, *Smile When You Call Me a Hillbilly,* 76, 129, 158, 160 (statistics), 166–67; Lipsitz, *Rainbow at Midnight,* 45–55, 65.

52. Lange, *Smile When You Call Me a Hillbilly,* 76 (Dexter quote); Malone, *Country Music, U.S.A.,* 196.

53. Lange, *Smile When You Call Me a Hillbilly,* 164–65; Peterson, *Creating Country Music,* 168–71.

54. Lange, *Smile When You Call Me a Hillbilly,* 175–78 (176, Atkins quote); Mary Bufwack and Bob Oermann, "Women in Country Music," in *Popular Culture in America,* ed. Paul Buhle (Minneapolis: University of Minnesota Press, 1987), 91–97 (96, "first massively popular"); Mary A. Bufwack, "Girls with Guitars—and Fringe and Sequins and Rhinestones, Silk, Lace, and Leather," in *Reading Country Music: Steel Guitars, Opry Stars, and Honky-Tonk Bars,* ed. Cecelia Tichi (Durham, NC: Duke University Press, 1998), 167; Malone, *Country Music, U.S.A.,* 223–24.

55. Curtis W. Ellison, *Country Music Culture: From Hard Times to Heaven* (Jackson: University Press of Mississippi, 1995), 68, 76–77, 92; Peterson, *Creating Country Music,* 167–68; Malone, *Don't Get above Your Raisin',* 74–75.

56. Peterson, *Creating Country Music,* 177–78; Ellison, *Country Music Culture,* 68–77; Greil Marcus, *Mystery Train: Images of America in Rock 'n' Roll Music* (New York: Dutton, 1975), 150–51; Malone, *Don't Get above Your Raisin',* 132–34 ("no light"); Lipsitz, *Rainbow at Midnight,* 28 ("baloney"). See also Paul Hemphill, *Lovesick Blues: The Life of Hank Williams* (New York: Viking, 2005).

57. Lange, *Smile When You Call Me a Hillbilly,* 195–96 (195, Daffan quotes).

58. Ibid., 190–220 (203, Rose quote; 207, Arnold quote; 210, *Time* quote; 219, Wakely quote); Malone, *Country Music, U.S.A.,* 211, 236–37, 245.

59. Michael T. Bertrand, *Race, Rock, and Elvis* (Urbana: University of Illinois Press, 2000), 62 (Parker quote); Malone, *Country Music, U.S.A.,* 212 ("sins and worries").

60. Penny M. Von Eschen, *Satchmo Blows Up the World: Jazz Ambassadors Play the Cold War* (Cambridge, MA: Harvard University Press, 2004), 1–91 (35, Gillespie and "Students Drop Rocks"; 61, "ancestors"; 63, "go to hell"; 83, "goodwill tour of Mississippi"), 250–60 (259, "margins of diplomacy").

61. Whitfield, *Culture of the Cold War,* 96 (Spellman, *One Lonely Night* quote).

62. Ron Briley, "Hollywood and the Rebel Image in the 1950s," *Social Education* 61 (October 1997): 355–56.

63. Ibid., 353, 356–58; Biskind, *Seeing Is Believing,* 21 ("Stop! I'm a doctor"), 200–202, 207–12; Marchand, "Visions of Classlessness," 174–76 (psychology; 176, "more popular").

64. Douglas Brode, *From Walt to Woodstock: How Disney Created the Counterculture* (Austin: University of Texas Press, 2004), 53–68.

65. John H. Lenihan, *Showdown: Confronting Modern America in the Western Film* (Urbana: University of Illinois Press, 1980), 90–147 (a useful overview of the western's treatment of postwar alienation and social problems); Michael Coyne, *The Crowded Prairie: American National Identity in the Hollywood Western* (London: I. B. Tauris, 1997), 33 ("safe vessel"), 72–73; Slotkin, *Gunfighter Nation,* 385–90 ("parody"). See also Stanley Corkin, *Cowboys as Cold Warriors: The Western and U.S. History* (Philadelphia: Temple University Press, 2004), esp. 19–163 (94–106, 110–16, 120–25, *The Gunfighter*). For a discussion of the ambiguous messages in *The Searchers,* the 1956 John Ford film starring John Wayne, see also Roberts and Olson, *John Wayne,* 418–25.

66. Lenihan, *Showdown,* 117–21; Slotkin, *Gunfighter Nation,* 391–96. On Wayne, see Roberts and Olson, *John Wayne,* 348–49; and T. J. Jackson Lears, "Screw Ambiguity," *New Republic,* April 22, 1996, 40.

67. Eric Greene, *Planet of the Apes as American Myth: Race, Politics, and Popular Culture* (Hanover, NH: Wesleyan University Press, 1996), 25–26 ("ritual"), 151 ("Martian"); Engelhardt, *End of Victory Culture,* 152–53.

68. Skal, *Monster Show,* 260–61 ("keep an eye on those cars"); Skal, *Screams of Reason,* 177–91 (184, Sherdeman quotes); Henriksen, *Dr. Strangelove's America,* 50–58; Engelhardt, *End of Victory Culture,* 105–6. See also Biskind, *Seeing Is Believing,* 102–59.

69. Henriksen, *Dr. Strangelove's America,* 55 ("made the world happy").

70. Ibid., 137–38. See also the essays in Jonathan Freedman and Richard Millington, eds., *Hitchcock's America* (New York: Oxford University Press, 1999).

71. Brad Leithauser, "Lyrics in the Swamp," *New York Review of Books,* April 25, 2002, 15–17.

72. Henry Allen, "A Good Man: Charles Schulz," *Washington Post National Weekly Edition,* February 21, 2000, 30; Garry Trudeau, "You're a Good Man, Charles Schulz," *Spokane, WA, Spokesman-Review,* December 18, 1999, B6; Martin Miller, "You've Had a Good Run, Charlie Brown," *Spokane, WA, Spokesman-Review,* December 15, 1999, A1; Lawrence Chenoweth, *The American Dream of Success: The Search for the Self in the Twentieth Century* (Belmont, CA: Wadsworth, 1974), 133–35.

73. Spigel, *Make Room for TV,* 145–46, 149 (*Variety* quote).

74. Lee Winfrey, "Comedian Milton Berle Dies at 93," *Spokane, WA, Spokesman-Review,* March 28, 2002, A1, A6 (*Time* quote, "turn for the nurse"); Spigel, *Make Room for TV,* 145, 148; Steven D. Stark, *Glued to the Set: The 60 Television Shows and Events That Made Us Who We Are Today* (New York: Free Press, 1997), 8–12 (10, "anything for a laugh"; 11, *Variety* ad; 12, "never knew").

75. Stark, *Glued to the Set,* 10–14 (13, "front porches"); Marc, *Comic Visions,* 88; Spigel, *Make Room for TV,* 149 ("watch their step"); R. D. Heldenfels, "Funny-Man Berle Not So All the Time," *Spokane, WA, Spokesman-Review,* March 30, 2002, E6; Gerard Jones, *Honey, I'm Home! Sitcoms: Selling the American Dream* (New York: Grove Weidenfeld, 1992), 32–33, 63; Epstein, *Haunted Smile,* 134–35; Darden Asbury Pyron, *Liberace: An American Boy* (Chicago: University of Chicago Press, 2000), 133–35 (nationalizing shifts in television); Doherty, *Cold War, Cool Medium,* 68 ("wholesome entertainment").

76. Stark, *Glued to the Set,* 26–27; Jones, *Honey, I'm Home!* 63–64, 73–74; Doherty, *Cold War, Cool Medium,* 49–59 (51, McComas quote; 52, "lot sooner"); Schwartz, *Cold War Culture,* 25 (Arnaz quote).

77. Jones, *Honey, I'm Home!* 68–70 (68, "tantalized"); Landay, *Madcaps, Screwballs, and Con Women,* 160–95 (166, "typical"; 181, *Cosmopolitan* quote).

78. Doherty, *Cold War, Cool Medium,* 83–96, 162–89, 210–14; MacDonald, *Television and the Red Menace,* 56–57.

79. Brian Ward, *Just My Soul Responding: Rhythm and Blues, Black Consciousness, and Race Relations* (Berkeley and Los Angeles: University of California Press, 1998), 95–96 (95, "get that coon"), 102, 130–34 (130, "can't understand it"); Watson, *Defining Visions,* 31–33 (32, "turning point"; 33, "afraid of the dark"). As Ward (*Just My Soul Responding,* 133–34) shows, Cole subsequently became more publicly involved in the civil rights movement. On Cole, see also Suzanne E. Smith, *Dancing in the Street: Motown and the Cultural Politics of Detroit* (Cambridge, MA: Harvard University Press, 1999), 147–52.

80. Doherty, *Cold War, Cool Medium,* 24, 162–63.

81. Pyron, *Liberace,* 62–148 (118, "successful unknown"; 143, "lightning in a bottle"; 143–44, "backbone people"), 172 ("matinee idol"); Doherty, *Cold War, Cool Medium,* 219–20.

82. Pyron, *Liberace,* 24 ("sissy"), 35, 49–150, 213–16 (article quotes; 215, "less lavender-water"); John D'Emilio and Estelle B. Freedman, *Intimate Matters: A History of Sexuality in America* (New York: Harper & Row, 1988), 292–95 (the Cold War and the homosexuality issue).

83. Pyron, *Liberace,* 1 ("eccentricities"), 7 ("borders"), 59, 150 (idol), 151–83 (155–56, "next door neighbors"; 172, "dandelion"), 227–34, 250–55, 294; Doherty, *Cold War, Cool Medium,* 220 ("harlequin").

84. Frank Rich, "Pretty Boys," *New York Times Magazine,* December 30, 2001, 22 (Martin quote); O'Brien, "Recapturing the American Sound" (n. 77, chap. 6 above), 48 ("mellowness").

85. Nick Tosches, "Hipsters and Hoodlums," *Vanity Fair,* December 2000, 198, 200, 207; James Miller, *Flowers in the Dustbin: The Rise of Rock and Roll, 1947–1977* (New York: Simon & Schuster, 1999), 31–33; Glenn C. Altschuler, *All Shook Up: How Rock 'n' Roll Changed America* (New York: Oxford University Press, 2003), 15; Ward, *Just My Soul Responding,* 21–26 (22, Rupe quote); Lipsitz, *Rainbow at Midnight,* 336 (Lubinsky quote); Bertrand, *Race, Rock, and Elvis,* 64–65. On King Records, see Rick Kennedy and Randy McNutt, *Little Labels—Big Sound: Small Record Companies and the Rise of American Music* (Bloomington: Indiana University Press, 1999), 56–72 (61, Nathan quote).

86. Douglas, *Listening In,* 220–23 (222, "breakout listening"), 227–34; Szatmary, *Time to Rock,* 15–16 (Ertegun quote), 22–23; Miller, *Flowers in the Dustbin,* 57–61; Grace Palladino, *Teenagers: An American History* (New York: Basic, 1996), 118–22. On some of the changes in postwar radio, see Eric Rothenbuhler and Tom McCourt, "Radio Redefines Itself, 1947–1962," in Hilmes and Loviglio, eds., *Radio Reader,* 367–87.

87. Doherty, *Teenagers and Teenpics,* 14–15; Smith, *God Bless America,* 159–78 (177, "Soozie Cue"); Palladino, *Teenagers,* 63–93.

88. Palladino, *Teenagers,* 102–7 (105, quote).

89. Szatmary, *Time to Rock,* 23 (statistics); Palladino, *Teenagers,* 97–110 (110, "salient discovery"); Doherty, *Teenagers and Teenpics,* 47, 54–57 (Katzman quote).

90. Palladino, *Teenagers,* 111–15 (114, "growing underworld"), 118 ("It Jumps"); Geoffrey O'Brien, "Rock of Ages," *New York Review of Books,* December 16, 1999, 44 ("empire of the night").

91. Palladino, *Teenagers,* 124; Doherty, *Teenagers and Teenpics,* 56 ("same old glands"); Miller, *Flowers in the Dustbin,* 31; Altschuler, *All Shook Up,* 72, 74 (Ballard).

92. Altschuler, *All Shook Up,* 75 ("leerics"); Werner, *Change Is Gonna Come,* 59 (Perkins quote), 60 (Phillips quote); Miller, *Flowers in the Dustbin,* 39, 61–67 (64, Leiber quote), 105–7 (Berry quote), 125–26 (125, *Billboard* quote); David L. Chappell, "Hip Like Me: Racial Cross-Dressing in Pop Music before Elvis," in *Media, Culture, and the Modern African American Freedom Struggle,* ed. Brian Ward (Gainesville: University Press of Florida, 2001), 110–12 (Gaye quote, Berry on "Maybelline," Charles quote).

93. Bertrand, *Race, Rock, and Elvis,* 55–56 ("revised racial order"); Ward, *Just My Soul Responding,* 100–109 (attacks on rock).

94. As the songwriter-musician Steve Ashby explained to me (in conversation in Pullman, WA, August 6, 2005), musical styles like rock, country, the blues, and jazz are cross-pollinated branches from the tree of Western classical music, whose basic harmonic structure is built around chord progressions. "The 'chords' are groups of notes which 'progress' through some order until they eventually cycle back around (typically producing one or more repeated progressions). Musicians often refer to these chords with Roman numerals. Because Western music is based largely upon seven-note scales, built from a twelve-tone system, 'I' through 'VII' are typically the chords that correspond with these scale steps. 'I' could be considered home base with the chord progression wandering away and eventually returning home. Risking oversimplification, one could say that II-V-I chord progressions (or a chord cycle that was based on the second scale step, then the fifth scale step, then 'home' to the first scale step) are often considered the basic building blocks of jazz compositions. By comparison, I-IV-V chord progressions are a common characteristic of rock, country, blues, and folk music. They each have a variety of instrumentation, subject matter, and forms of delivery—but identical roots. 'Johnny B. Goode,' 'This Land Is Your Land,' 'Back in the Saddle Again,' and 'Sweet Home Chicago' have nearly identical chord progressions but represent very different musical styles."

While numerous factors contribute to the appeal of rock, jazz, country, folk, and blues styles, their accessibility comes down in part to what supposedly constitutes necessary credentials. For classical musicians, formal training/schooling has been both expected and required. But it has been less of a prerequisite for—and often even the antithesis of—early rock, jazz, country, folk, and blues. Yet, as jazz quickly evolved and branched out into increasingly complicated musical forms, it too created a higher demand on technical skills, not unlike those of more classically trained performers. And, certainly over time, in folk, the blues, country, and rock alike, a number of legendary musicians would demonstrate incredible musical virtuosity. Still, in the mid-1950s, any kid with a guitar could feel the allure of rock and roll. Armed with little more than a guitar (acoustic or electric), a handful of finger positions, and a story to tell, aspiring musicians could sense new opportunities. As outsiders for whom the school of hard knocks was typically both a reference point and a spur, they might achieve success despite their lack of musical degrees, formal training, or the stamp of approval from credentialed elites.

95. Miller, *Flowers in the Dustbin*, 73–78 (doo-wop), 114–18 (Lymon), 270 (Stones); Pete Daniel, *Lost Revolutions: The South in the 1950s* (Chapel Hill: University of North Carolina Press, 2000), 140 (Riley quote); Szatmary, *Time to Rock*, 35 (Perkins quotes); Palladino, *Teenagers*, 114 (quote).

96. Ellison, *Country Music Culture*, 247 (Twitty quote); Starr and Waterman, *American Popular Music*, 220; Palladino, *Teenagers*, 129 (sales percentage); Douglas, *Where the Girls Are*, 84 (five in the top nine); John A. Jackson, American Bandstand: *Dick Clark and the Making of a Rock 'n' Roll Empire* (New York: Oxford University Press, 1997), 39 (RCA sales). Bobbie Ann Mason (*Elvis Presley* [New York: Penguin, 2003], 76) describes 1956 as "the Year of Elvis." On some of the early trailblazers, see Nick Tosches, *Unsung Heroes of Rock 'n' Roll* (1984; reprint, New York: Da Capo, 1999). For statements of Presley's importance, see, e.g., Marcus, *Mystery Train*, 137–205; and Mikal Gilmore, *Night Beat: A Shadow History of Rock and Roll* (New York: Anchor, 1998), 18–20. *Entertainment Weekly* picked Presley as the second-greatest entertainer between 1950 and 2000, behind only the Beatles (*The 100 Greatest Entertainers, 1950–2000* [Des Moines, Iowa: Entertainment Weekly Books, 2000], 14–17). On Twitty, see also Malone, *Country Music, U.S.A.*, 381–82.

97. Peter Guralnick, *Last Train to Memphis: The Rise of Elvis Presley* (Boston: Little, Brown, 1994), 11–29 (28, "broke, man, broke"; 29, "trash we weren't"); Mason, *Elvis Presley*, 20–40 (40, "limitations"), 51; Szatmary, *Time to Rock*, 54 (MacDonald quote); Malone and Stricklin, *Southern Music/American Music*, 102–3.

98. Peter Doggett, *Are You Ready for the Country: Elvis, Dylan, Parsons, and the Roots of Country Rock* (New York: Penguin, 2000), 252 (Burgess quote); Daniel, *Lost Revolutions*, 132 ("no formal training"), 144 (Perkins quote); Bertrand, *Race, Rock, and Elvis*, 64 ("my damn babies").

99. Guralnick, *Last Train to Memphis*, 97–101 (101, Phillips quote); Mason, *Elvis Presley*, 48–49. On Phillips, see also Miller, *Flowers in the Dustbin*, 34–37.

100. Miller, *Flowers in the Dustbin*, 72 ("billion dollars" [although many sources say the figure was $1 million]); Bertrand, *Race, Rock, and Elvis*, 187 ("dug"); Marcus, *Mystery Train*, 177 ("'am I?'"); Guralnick, *Last Train to Memphis*, 134 (remaining Phillips quotes); Mason, *Elvis Presley*, 36–37, 45, 60–61 (60, "goosed it up").

101. Guralnick, *Last Train to Memphis*, 351–52.

102. Ibid., 36–51 (44, "wild-looking guys"); Marcus, *Mystery Train*, 155 ("'squirrel'"); Mason, *Elvis Presley*, 36, 40–43.

103. Marcus, *Mystery Train*, 182 ("hellbent"); Guralnick, *Last Train to Memphis*, 119 (Moore quote); comments of Charles McGovern at the session "Elvis" presented at the annual meeting of the Organization of American Historians, Los Angeles, April 28, 2001.

104. Daniel, *Lost Revolutions*, 150–52 (151, "crew cuts and muscles"; 152, "kissin' in Key West"); Erika Doss, *Elvis Culture: Fans, Faith, and Image* (Lawrence: University Press of Kansas, 1999), 123–30; Joel Williamson, "The Feminine Elvis" (paper presented at the meeting of the Organization of American Historians, Los Angeles, April 28, 2001) ("too pretty"); Guralnick, *Last Train to Memphis*, 138–39; Karal Ann Marling, *As Seen on TV: The Visual Culture of Everyday Life in the 1950s* (Cambridge, MA: Harvard University Press, 1994), 167–73, 176; Mason, *Elvis Presley*, 42–43, 56–58.

105. Williamson, "The Feminine Elvis"; Daniel, *Lost Revolutions*, 151–54, 169–71 (Scarbrough quotes); Doss, *Elvis Culture*, 130–31 (130, "face it"); Palladino, *Teenagers*, 129 ("scream"); Mason, *Elvis Presley*, 57–59.

106. Guralnick, *Last Train to Memphis*, 110 (quote); Mason, *Elvis Presley*, 54–55.

107. Nick Tosches, *Country: The Twisted Roots of Rock 'n' Roll* (1977; reprint, New York: Da Capo, 1996), 59 ("vehement," "pink teenage boys"); Guralnick, *Last Train to Memphis*, 171–73 ("no reference point"), 319 (Presley quote).

108. Williamson, "The Feminine Elvis"; McGovern's comments (n. 103 above); Altschuler, *All Shook Up*, 92 ("looking for trouble"); Miller, *Flowers in the Dustbin*, 154 ("something of a menace"); Doss, *Elvis Culture*, 49.

109. Miller, *Flowers in the Dustbin*, 133 ("mating dance," "suggestive," "animalism," "distasteful"); Miller and Nowak, *The Fifties*, 302–4 (302, "mostly nightmare"; 304, "ritualistic orgies"), 313 ("outlandish things"); Altschuler, *All Shook Up*, 38 ("carnage pots"); Ward, *Just My Soul Responding*, 109–10.

110. Altschuler, *All Shook Up*, 34, 132 (statistics); Ward, *Just My Soul Responding*, 20 (statistics); Steve Waksman, *Instruments of Desire: The Electric Guitar and the Shaping of Musical Experience* (Cambridge, MA: Harvard University Press, 1999), 2 ("boy with his guitar"), 148–66 (Berry); Miller, *Flowers in the Dustbin*, 43 (quote), 104.

111. Philip Furia, *Irving Berlin: A Life in Song* (New York: Schirmer, 1998), 254–55 (254, Leslie quote); Rosen, "Two American Anthems" (n. 48, chap. 5 above), 28; Altschuler, *All Shook Up*, 6; Szatmary, *Time to Rock*, 26 (Sinatra quotes, Martin quote, Davis quote); Ward, *Just My Soul Responding*, 90–92.

112. Furia, *Irving Berlin*, 254 ("don't like"); Altschuler, *All Shook Up*, 131 (statistics).

113. On the transistor, see Douglas, *Listening In*, 221, 225–26; and Rothenbuhler and McCourt, "Radio Redefines Itself," 378. On the 45 revolution, see Mark Coleman, *Playback: From the Victrola to MP3, 100 Years of Music, Machines, and Money* (New York: Da Capo, 2003), 64–70, 76–78.

114. O'Brien, "Rock of Ages" (n. 90 above), 44–45 ("homogenizing"); also Tosches, "Hipsters and Hoodlums" (n. 85 above), 207.

115. Guralnick, *Last Train to Memphis*, 244–63 passim, 280–96 (287, "under any circumstances"), 337–38, 351–53, 378–79 (379, "fine boy"); Altschuler, *All Shook Up*, 88–91 (90–91, "cup of tea"); Szatmary, *Time to Rock*, 50–53 (51, "unfit"); Smith, *Dancing in the Street*, 133 (Leonard quote); Mason, *Elvis Presley*, 78–82, 107–8, 111–12.

116. Williamson, "The Feminine Elvis" (the strategy of separation). On Parker, see Mason, *Elvis Presley*, 68–75 (71, "dudes"); and David Hajdu, "Hustling Elvis," *New York Review of Books*, October 9, 2003, 26–28 (26–27, Parker quotes); also David Segal, "Kingmaker," *Washington Post Weekly Edition*, September 8–14, 2003, 32–33. Guralnick's *Last Train to Memphis* has much on Parker, but the fullest source is Alanna Nash's *The Colonel:*

The Extraordinary Story of Colonel Tom Parker and Elvis Presley (New York: Simon & Schuster, 2003).

117. Williamson, "The Feminine Elvis"; Szatmary, *Time to Rock,* 56–57 (Mississippi resolution); Marling, *As Seen on TV,* 195–98.

118. O'Brien, "Rock of Ages" (n. 90 above), 44–45; Jackson, American Bandstand, ix–xi (ix, "sell it"), 40–41 (40, huckleberry quip), 49–75 (69, "ironing board"), 86–88; Altschuler, *All Shook Up,* 75–85 (79, "cleanliness"), 118–21 (120, "singing in the bathroom"); Miller, *Flowers in the Dustbin,* 55–57, 139–51; Szatmary, *Time to Rock,* 61–66 (61, statistics); Doss, *Elvis Culture,* 42–44 ("industry"). In the mid-1960s, Nelson, bored with playing sentimental ballads in nightclubs, helped popularize country rock with his Stone Canyon Band, to the displeasure of many of his previous fans. See Doggett, *Are You Ready for the Country,* 144.

119. Szatmary, *Time to Rock,* 61 (industry statistics), 148; Palladino, *Teenagers,* 129 (Presley statistics).

120. Miller, *Flowers in the Dustbin,* 148–53 (Stevenson quote), 158–63 (163, "'pop' means popular"); Nick Salvatore, "Dancing in the Streets," *New York Times Book Review,* January 12, 2003, 21 ("poker hand"); Smith, *Dancing in the Street,* esp. 6, 97, 116, 136; Ward, *Just My Soul Responding,* 258–68 (262, "general-market company"; 266, Atkins quote), 280, 394–95; Kempton, *Boogaloo,* 262 ("dialing the fire department," statistics), 268. According to Kempton, for Gordy "no place was warmer than the shadow of Ed Sullivan's smile" (*Boogaloo,* 260).

121. Miller and Nowak, *The Fifties,* 395 (Kerr quote).

122. Ibid., 265 (high school readership); Maria Reidelbach, *Completely Mad: A History of the Comic Book and Magazine* (Boston: Little, Brown, 1991), 188 (circulation and college readership).

10. POPULAR CULTURE AND 1960s FERMENT

1. Archie Loss, *Pop Dreams: Music, Movies, and the Media in the 1960s* (New York: Harcourt Brace, 1999), 2 ("core," "asylum"); Hoberman, *Dream Life,* 153 ("forever").

2. Frank, *Conquest of Cool,* 1–4 (3, "red-baiting"), 19–20 ("consumer capitalism"). For a historical analysis of advertising's power both to sanction and to subvert, see Lears, *Fables of Abundance.* Lears argues that "advertisements did more than stir up desire; they also sought to manage it—to stabilize the sorcery of the marketplace by containing dreams of personal transformation within a broader rhetoric of control" (10).

3. Frank, *Conquest of Cool,* 55–57 (Bernbach quote); Twitchell, *Adcult USA,* 28 (Reeves quote).

4. Frank, *Conquest of Cool,* 58–71; Sivulka, *Soap, Sex, and Cigarettes,* 304–7 (statistics); Lawrence A. Samuel, *Brought to You By: Postwar Television Advertising and the American Dream* (Austin: University of Texas Press, 2001), 163.

5. Frank, *Conquest of Cool,* 75–86 (80, "mush"; 83, "horseshit"), 114–15 (Reeves), 126–27; Samuel, *Brought to You By,* 59–60 (Mannes quote, "doggone"); Sivulka, *Soap, Sex, and Cigarettes,* 309–13.

6. Frank, *Conquest of Cool,* 133, 172 (Coca-Cola quote); Samuel, *Brought to You By,* 162–66 (162, *Television Magazine* quote).

7. Frank, *Conquest of Cool,* 89–91, 207 ("arise"), 230–32, 240–43, and passim (reproductions of ads); Sivulka, *Soap, Sex, and Cigarettes,* 316–17.

8. Frank, *Conquest of Cool,* 163–73 (165–66, Furr quotes).

9. Ibid., 156 ("lady"), 182–83 ("grandiose").

10. Nachman, *Seriously Funny,* 364–80 (370, "dismal failure"; 375, Conkling quote); Stan Cornyn with Paul Scanlon, *Exploding: The Highs, Hits, Hype, Heroes, and Hustlers of the Warner Music Group* (New York: HarperCollins, 2002), 31–37 (36, Starr quote), 44–45.

11. Hendra, *Going Too Far,* 154–55 ("hot under the collar," "only weapon I had"); Nachman, *Seriously Funny,* 364 ("only sane person"), 367 ("impersonal corporate bigness," "flatten personalities"), 377–78.

12. Will Haygood, "Why Negro Humor Is So Black," *American Prospect,* December 18, 2000, 31; Watkins, *On the Real Side,* 368–69.

13. Watkins, *On the Real Side,* 495–502 (495, "make jokes"; 497, *Newsweek* quote); Hendra, *Going Too Far,* 155–60.

14. O'Brien, "Recapturing the American Sound" (n. 77, chap. 6 above), 49 (*Mademoiselle* quote).

15. David Hajdu, *Positively 4th Street: The Lives and Times of Joan Baez, Bob Dylan, Mimi Baez Fariña, and Richard Fariña* (New York: Farrar Straus Giroux, 2001), 10–12 (10, Sebastian quote), 15 (Brand quote); Starr and Waterman, *American Popular Music,* 227 ("neatened"); Gilmore, *Night Beat,* 49; Jane Stern and Michael Stern, *Sixties People* (New York: Knopf, 1990), 109–11; Robert Cantwell, *When We Were Good: The Folk Revival* (Cambridge, MA: Harvard University Press, 1996), 2–6, 316–18.

16. Starr and Waterman, *American Popular Music,* 227 ("well-scrubbed"); Hajdu, *Positively 4th Street,* 192; Palmer, *All You Need Is Love,* 207 (Seeger quote). *Hootenanny* ended in September 1964.

17. O'Brien, "Recapturing the American Sound" (n. 77, chap. 6 above), 49–50; Stern and Stern, *Sixties People,* 103–4.

18. Starr and Waterman, *American Popular Music,* 277–82; Gilmore, *Night Beat,* 49; Palmer, *All You Need Is Love,* 208 (Dylan quotes); Loss, *Pop Dreams,* 57–62.

19. Douglas, *Where the Girls Are,* 84–88, 95–98.

20. Goulart, *Great American Comic Books,* 246–48 (Lee quote); Wright, *Comic Book Nation,* 180–85, 213–14.

21. Goulart, *Great American Comic Books,* 249–50; Wright, *Comic Book Nation,* 201–10 (207, "bomb is a bomb"), 217 ("green skin").

22. Goulart, *Great American Comic Books,* 250–52; Wright, *Comic Book Nation,* 210–12; Stephen Lynch, "Flawed but Believable," *Spokane, WA, Spokesman-Review,* May 1, 2002, D9 (Quesada quote); Michael Mallory, *Marvel: The Characters and Their Universe* (New York: Barnes & Noble Books, 2004), 81 (Lee quote).

23. Goulart, *Great American Comic Books,* 252–53; Wright, *Comic Book Nation,* 218–19, 223–26 (223, poll); Leslie A. Fiedler, "Up, Up, and Away—the Rise and Fall of Comic Books," *New York Times Book Review,* September 5, 1976, 11 ("scriptures").

24. Barnouw, *Tube of Plenty,* 243–48, 299–301 (300, "vast wasteland"); J. Fred MacDonald, *One Nation under Television: The Rise and Decline of Network TV* (New York: Pantheon, 1990), 136–43 (142, "magazine concept"), 153–55; Thompson, *Television's Second Golden Age,* 25–27; Samuel, *Brought to You By,* xxvii–xviii, 119–21.

25. Thompson, *Television's Second Golden Age,* 26–27; MacDonald, *One Nation under Television,* 171–72; Donald Bogle, *Primetime Blues: African Americans on Network Television* (New York: Farrar Straus Giroux, 2001), 93–113; Tom Stempel, *Storytellers to the Nation: A History of American Television Writing* (Syracuse, NY: Syracuse University Press, 1996), 86–93 (91, Salkowitz quote).

26. Marc, *Comic Visions,* 94–118; Jones, *Honey, I'm Home!* 140–47 (142, "first situation comedy"; 143, "matzoh to mayonnaise"); Stark, *Glued to the Set,* 100–103.

27. Marc, *Comic Visions,* 103; Bogle, *Primetime Blues,* 118 (Leonard quote).

28. Bogle, *Primetime Blues,* 96, 103, 106; Stark, *Glued to the Set,* 67 (Roberts quote).

29. Watson, *Defining Visions,* 142–46 (143, "best public relations"); Stempel, *Storytellers to the Nation,* 92 ("fill the house").

30. Bogle, *Primetime Blues,* 106–7 ("worthy"); Doherty, *Cold War, Cool Medium,* 72–73 ("brainwashing").

31. Lynn Spigel and Michael Curtin, introduction to *The Revolution Wasn't Televised: Sixties Television and Social Conflict,* ed. Lynn Spigel and Michael Curtin (New York: Routledge, 1997), 1–9.

32. Nachman, *Seriously Funny,* 577 (quote).

33. Bogle, *Primetime Blues,* 117–25 (123, "same aspirations"; 125, "thin lines"); Nachman, *Seriously Funny,* 564–67 (564, "showbiz backrub"; 567, "will be, on stage"), 577–79 (577, "Jackie Robinson"; 579, "not a Rochester"); Watkins, *On the Real Side,* 505–8.

34. Spigel and Curtin, introduction, 4–5.

35. Stark, *Glued to the Set,* 110 (Jethro quote); Douglas, *Where the Girls Are,* 126–38 (136, quote).

36. Julie D'Acci, "Nobody's Woman? *Honey West* and the New Sexuality," in Spigel and Curtin, eds., *The Revolution Wasn't Televised,* 72–93.

37. Molly Haskell, "Making Hay of the Blues," *New York Review of Books,* January 15, 1987, 37–39; Marc, *Comic Visions,* 220–22.

38. Marc, *Comic Visions,* 143–45 (144, "prided ourselves"); Aniko Bodroghkozy, *Groove Tube: Sixties Television and the Youth Rebellion* (Durham, NC: Duke University Press, 2001), 125 ("hippies with haircuts"), 129–34.

39. Bodroghkozy, *Groove Tube,* 123–24, 128–56 (128, "seemed complimentary"; 131–32, Tankersley quote; 146, "sick"; 155, *TV Guide* quote); Marc, *Comic Visions,* 145–49.

40. Marc, *Comic Visions,* 150–52; Stark, *Glued to the Set,* 142–47; Marc and Thompson, *Television in the Antenna Age,* 97.

41. Stempel, *Storytellers to the Nation,* 112–15 (115, Manings quotes); Marc, *Comic Visions,* 150 (ratings).

42. Rader, *American Sports,* 232–37 (Scully quote); Smith, *Play-by-Play,* 104–6 ("struggle," Arledge quotes); Jay, *More Than Just a Game,* 103–4.

43. Rader, *American Sports,* 233, 238–39. By 1972, 36 percent of Americans named pro football as their favorite sport; 21 percent favored baseball (see MacCambridge, *America's Game,* xv).

44. Rader, *American Sports,* 251–53 (Modell quote); Jay, *More Than Just a Game,* 107–9.

45. Rader, *American Sports,* 253; Jay, *More Than Just a Game,* 108–9.

46. Jay, *More Than Just a Game,* 105, 117–18 (117, "symbols of social change"); author's notes from *NFL's Greatest Moments* (ESPN), n.d. (Chiefs, Faison quote).

47. MacCambridge, *America's Game,* xvi–xvii; author's notes from *NFL's Greatest Moments* (n. 46 above) (Edwards quote).

48. Nelson George, *Hip Hop America* (New York: Viking, 1998), 146–48 (146, "buttoned-down game"); Jay, *More Than Just a Game,* 144–45 ("inventing something new").

49. Jay, *More Than Just a Game,* 58, 114 ("free"); Ashe, *Hard Road to Glory,* 95–97; Othello Harris, "Muhammad Ali and the Revolt of the Black Athlete," in *Muhammad Ali: The People's Champ,* ed. Elliott J. Gorn (Urbana: University of Illinois Press, 1995), 57–58 (57, "best country," "qualified people," "credit to my race," "fists do the talking"); Thomas R. Hietala, "Muhammad Ali and the Age of Bare-Knuckle Politics," in ibid., 120–22; Sammons, *Beyond the Ring,* 193–97.

50. Jay, *More Than Just a Game,* 114, 117–23 (117, Belafonte quote; 121, "so-called Negroes"; 123, fighting); Ashe, *Hard Road to Glory,* 97–98 (97, Malcolm X quote, "no quarrel"); Rader, *American Sports,* 301 (boycott); Zang, *Sports Wars,* 98–103; Harris, "Muhammad Ali," 58 (Patterson quote).

51. Jay, *More Than Just a Game,* 127–32; Rader, *American Sports,* 301–2.

52. Zang, *Sports Wars,* 119–39 (119, Agnew quote).

53. Ibid., 13 (Dietzel quote), 15, 30 (Parseghian quote); Jay, *More Than Just a Game,* 142 (*Sports Illustrated* quote).

54. Rader, *Baseball,* 186–92; Rossi, *National Game,* 187 ("twelve years"); Jay, *More Than Just a Game,* 153–54 ("piece of property").

55. Jay, *More Than Just a Game,* 72 (number, "minority"), 126 (Gibson quote); Samuel O. Regalado, *Viva Baseball! Latin Major Leaguers and Their Special Hunger* (Urbana: University of Illinois Press, 1998), 76 ("be that bad"), 80 (Tiant quote), 84–87 (85, "feel foolish," Dark quote), 118–24 (123, "not a dumb-head"; 124, "recognition he deserves").

56. Paul Hoch, *Rip Off the Big Game: The Exploitation of Sports by the Power Elite* (New York: Doubleday Anchor, 1972), 2–3 (Agnew quote, Babbidge quotes); *Washington Post,* November 25, 1970 (Rafferty quotes).

57. Jay, *More Than Just a Game,* 137–39 (Simpson, Lombardi quote).

58. David Maraniss, *When Pride Still Mattered: A Life of Vince Lombardi* (New York: Simon & Schuster, 1999), 240–42, 344, 471.

59. *A City on Fire: The Story of the '68 Detroit Tigers* (HBO documentary, 2002). Nevertheless, at the beginning of game five in Detroit, the angry reaction to singer Jose Feliciano's

unorthodox rendering of "The Star-Spangled Banner" was a reminder of the cultural rips in the country (see Zang, *Sports Wars*, 3–8).

60. Hoch, *Rip Off the Big Game*, 1. Zang is particularly useful on the era's politicizing of sports—a "star-spangled collision" (*Sports Wars*, 3).

61. Gilmore, *Night Beat*, 23–24.

62. Geoffrey O'Brien, "Seven Years in the Life," *New York Review of Books*, January 11, 2001, 11; Devin McKinney, *Magic Circles: The Beatles in Dream and History* (Cambridge, MA: Harvard University Press, 2003), 12 ("pain"); Miller, *Flowers in the Dustbin*, 205 ("something different"), 213–14; Douglas, *Where the Girls Are*, 113–14; David Fricke, "Beatlemania!" *Rolling Stone*, February 19, 2004, 39–44. See also *The Beatles Fortieth Anniversary Collectors Edition* (Boca Raton, FL: AMI, 2004), 4–42.

63. Terry Anderson, *The Movement and the Sixties: Protest in America from Greensboro to Wounded Knee* (New York: Oxford University Press, 1995), 93 ("hates them," "dreary old adults"); Szatmary, *Time to Rock*, 125–26 (125, *Life* quote, "spot commercials"), 128.

64. Miller, *Flowers in the Dustbin*, 192, 205–6, 210, 217; Douglas, *Where the Girls Are*, 116–19 (116, *Newsweek* quote); Ellen Willis, "'60s Rock—That Explosion of Creativity Still Lives," *TV Guide*, July 4, 1987, 10–11 ("reinventing"); Altschuler, *All Shook Up*, 183–84 (questions); McKinney, *Magic Circles*, 51 ("sexy"); Szatmary, *Time to Rock*, 127 ("talk to them").

65. Miller, *Flowers in the Dustbin*, 192, 195, 197 ("new"); O'Brien, "Seven Years in the Life" (n. 62 above), 12 ("factory").

66. Miller, *Flowers in the Dustbin*, 192; Szatmary, *Time to Rock*, 122–25 (Epstein quote, Lennon quote); McKinney, *Magic Circles*, 62–64, 115 (Harrison quote).

67. McKinney, *Magic Circles*, 131; Miller, *Flowers in the Dustbin*, 215 (quotes).

68. Miller, *Flowers in the Dustbin*, 229 ("four freaks"); *Beatles Fortieth Anniversary Collectors Edition*, 77 ("run, cry").

69. McKinney, *Magic Circles*, 58–83.

70. *Beatles Fortieth Anniversary Collectors Edition*, 77 (Harrison quote); Miller, *Flowers in the Dustbin*, 231 (McCartney quote).

71. Miller, *Flowers in the Dustbin*, 226–27; McKinney, *Magic Circles*, 103–11; Gilmore, *Night Beat*, 52–54.

72. Gilmore, *Night Beat*, 28; Starr and Waterman, *American Popular Music*, 282–87; Miller, *Flowers in the Dustbin*, 223–25; Greil Marcus, *Invisible Republic: Bob Dylan's Basement Tapes* (1997; reprint, New York: Owl, 1998), 10–31; Greil Marcus, *Like a Rolling Stone: Bob Dylan at the Crossroads* (New York: Public Affairs, 2005), 1–10 (on "Like a Rolling Stone"; 6, "pointing the direction"), 118–30 (Bloomfield quotes); Fred Goodman, *The Mansion on the Hill: Dylan, Young, Geffen, Springsteen, and the Head-On Collision of Rock and Commerce* (New York: Vintage, 1997), 7–9 (Goldberg quote, Seeger quote, Yarrow quote); Stern and Stern, *Sixties People*, 118 ("the Sullivan show"). Compare "Dylan's Electric Kiss-Off," in "50 Moments That Changed the History of Rock and Roll," special issue of *Rolling Stone*, June 24, 2004, 104.

73. Gilmore, *Night Beat*, 28–29 ("longing"); David Reyes and Tom Waldman, *Land of a Thousand Dances: Chicano Rock 'n' Roll from Southern California* (Albuquerque: University of New Mexico Press, 1998), 71–75; George Lipsitz, "Land of a Thousand Dances: Youth, Minorities, and the Rise of Rock and Roll," in *Recasting America: Culture and Politics in the Age of Cold War*, ed. Lary May (Chicago: University of Chicago Press, 1989), 276–77, 282.

74. "Sgt. Pepper's Lonely Hearts Club Band," *Rolling Stone*, December 11, 2003, 85 (Starr quote); *Beatles Fortieth Anniversary Collectors Edition*, 99 (West quote); Miller, *Flowers in the Dustbin*, 253–60 (253, McCartney quote); Starr and Waterman, *American Popular Music*, 292–95.

75. John Lahr, "Exiles on Easy Street," *New Republic*, December 14, 1984, 26–29 (26, Wolfe quote); Zang, *Sports Wars*, 20 ("switchblades"); Miller, *Flowers in the Dustbin*, 202–4 (202, "bunch of bloody amateurs"; 204, headline); Szatmary, *Time to Rock*, 134–40 (137, Oldham quote); Gilmore, *Night Beat*, 84 ("cultural changes").

76. Szatmary, *Time to Rock*, 140–42 (Townshend quote).

77. Ibid., 173 ("anything about revolt"). On Joplin, see Lucy O'Brien, *She Bop: The Definitive History of Women in Rock, Pop, and Soul* (New York: Penguin, 1996), 99–105 (103, "wrote the part"); and Gillian G. Garr, *She's a Rebel: The History of Women in Rock and Roll* (Seattle: Seal, 1992), 103–8 (104, "weirdo").

78. Szatmary, *Time to Rock*, 173–75 (173–74, Garcia quote); O'Brien, *She Bop*, 102.

79. Douglas, *Listening In*, 260–67.

80. Ibid., 269–70.

81. Ibid., 256, 269–72; Coleman, *Playback*, 84–86; Jim Ladd, *Radio Waves: Life and Revolution on the FM Dial* (New York: St. Martin's, 1991), 27–29, 35 ("shoes"), 58–60.

82. Gilmore, *Night Beat*, 29.

83. Stark, *Glued to the Set*, 56–58 (57, *Life* quote; 58, "they could understand"); Victoria E. Johnson, "Citizen Welk: Bubbles, Blue Hair, and Middle America," in Spigel and Curtin, eds., *The Revolution Wasn't Televised*, 273 (*Post* quote), 281 ("mom and dad").

84. Stark, *Glued to the Set*, 56–58 ("schism," "midwesterners," "the Geritol set's Elvis"); Johnson, "Citizen Welk," 269–71, 280 ("democracy").

85. Stark, *Glued to the Set*, 57 (Lennon sister quote); Johnson, "Citizen Welk," 273–83 (273, "clodhopper charm"; 275, "free and easy"; 278, "'square' was a compliment").

86. Stark, *Glued to the Set*, 107–11; Jones, *Honey, I'm Home!* 137–40; Marc and Thompson, *Television in the Antenna Age*, 84–85 ("anaesthetic"). In 1968, after Griffith left the show, CBS kept most of the cast together for three more years in *Mayberry RFD*.

87. Adam Parfrey, "From Pulp to Posterity: The Origins of Men's Adventure Magazines," in Parfrey, ed., *It's a Man's World*, 5–11 (7, "the way things were"); Bruce Jay Freidman, "Even the Rhinos Were Nymphos," in ibid., 13–19 (16, "'our guys'"); Josh A. Friedman, "Throw 'em a Few Hot Words," in ibid., 21, 28 (Puzo quote), 34, 40; Collins, Hagenauer, and Heller, *Men's Adventure Magazines*, 19 ("lower-tier," sales figures).

88. Adam Parfrey, "The Illustrators," in Parfrey, ed., *It's a Man's World*, 39–40 ("fear"); David Saunders, "Norman Saunders and the Evolution of Men's Magazine Illustration," in ibid., 43–47 (44, "strict censorship"); Parfrey, "The Sadistic Burlesque," in ibid., 177–213 (178, "suppressed side"), 218; Collins, Hagenauer, and Heller, *Men's Adventure Magazines*, 19, 284–407.

89. Kimmel, *Manhood in America*, 275.

90. Nicholas Dawidoff, *In the Country of Country: A Journey to the Roots of American Music* (New York: Vintage, 1998), 48–50 (Atkins quotes); Feiler, *Dreaming Out Loud*, 94. See also Paul Hemphill, *The Nashville Sound: Bright Lights and Country Music* (New York: Simon & Schuster, 1970). On country's invented traditions, see esp. Peterson, *Creating Country Music*.

91. Dawidoff, *In the Country of Country*, 70–79 (73, "ol' hillbilly"); Doggett, *Are You Ready for the Country*, xiii, 309 (Webb quote); Feiler, *Dreaming Out Loud*, 154; Starr and Waterman, *American Popular Music*, 266; Ellison, *Country Music Culture*, 92–97 (94, "feel like a whore").

92. Feiler, *Dreaming Out Loud*, 94–95 (statistics), 272 ("that is the Nashville sound"); Doggett, *Are You Ready for the Country*, 285 ("sorry"); Dawidoff, *In the Country of Country*, 49–50.

93. Hemphill, *Nashville Sound*, 149 (Ritter quotes); Doggett, *Are You Ready for the Country*, 426–27 ("don't smoke marijuana"); Rita Lang Kleinfelder, *When We Were Young: A Baby-Boomer Yearbook* (New York: Prentice-Hall, 1993), 459 (Ritter in Hall of Fame).

94. Doggett, *Are You Ready for the Country*, 5–8 (6, "shaggy-hairs"), 21–29 (23, "rednecks"), 295–300, 308–15 (311, "pet hippie"); Dawidoff, *In the Country of Country*, 192.

95. See, e.g., the annual listings in Kleinfelder, *When We Were Young*.

96. "Loose Talk," *Spokane, WA, Spokesman-Review*, February 20, 2001, D2 (Douglas quote).

97. For a discussion of such films, see Hoberman, *Dream Life*, 1–55, 69–79, 89–93. On le Carré, see Rand R. Cooper, "Company Man," *New York Times Book Review*, January 7, 2001, 10 (le Carré quote).

98. See, e.g., Lenihan, *Showdown*, 148–60.

99. See, e.g., ibid., 168–71.

100. Slotkin, *Gunfighter Nation,* 474–86; Fred Inglis, *Cruel Peace: Everyday Life and the Cold War* (New York: Basic, 1991), 98–99; Hoberman, *Dream Life,* 31–34.

101. See, e.g., Allison Graham, *Framing the South: Hollywood, Television, and Race during the Civil Rights Struggle* (Baltimore: Johns Hopkins University Press, 2001), 160–62.

102. Kevern Verney, *African Americans and US Popular Culture* (London: Routledge, 2003), 54–56; Ronald L. Davis, *Celluloid Mirrors: Hollywood and American Society since 1945* (New York: Harcourt Brace, 1997), 54 (Poitier quote).

103. Scot French, "Mau-Mauing the Filmmakers: Should Black Power Take the Rap for Killing *Nat Turner,* the Movie?" in Ward, ed., *Modern African American Freedom Struggle,* 238 (Steiger quote); Brent Staples, "Sidney Poitier's Demons," *New York Times Magazine,* April 16, 2000, 84; Ed Guerrero, *Framing Blackness: The African American Image in Film* (Philadelphia: Temple University Press, 1993), 71–77. For an interesting comparison of the screen personas of Poitier and Harry Belafonte, see Thomas Cripps, *Making Movies Black: The Hollywood Message Movie from World War II to the Civil Rights Era* (New York: Oxford University Press, 1993), 251–69, 284–94.

104. Graham, *Framing the South,* 181–82 ("protector and defender," "hillbilly from hell," "redemption"); Verney, *US Popular Culture,* 69; Davis, *Celluloid Mirrors,* 111 (Mirisch quote); Staples, "Sidney Poitier's Demons" (n. 103 above), 64 ("gray flannel suit," Mason quote); Richard S. Schickel, "The Tightrope Walker," *New York Times Book Review,* April 25, 2004, 12 ("shoeshine boy"); Guerrero, *Framing Blackness,* 74 (Baldwin quote).

105. Jones, *Our Musicals, Ourselves,* 191–96 (on the play; 193, quotes).

106. Leff and Simmons, *Dame in the Kimono,* 220 (*Playboy*); Gary Cross, *The Cute and the Cool: Wondrous Innocence and Modern American Children's Culture* (New York: Oxford University Press, 2004), 154–56.

107. Douglas, *Where the Girls Are,* 68–69 (69, "no sex life"); Petersen, *Century of Sex,* 273 ("jammed clothes drier").

108. Leff and Simmons, *Dame in the Kimono,* 200, 220, 224–29 (224, "cash infusions"; 225, "careful limits"; 227, "baggy pants"; 229, "*made* only fourteen").

109. Davis, *Two-Bit Culture,* 257–60 (258, "lifts the lid"); Halberstam, *The Fifties,* 577–86 (on the novel *Peyton Place*); Leff and Simmons, *Dame in the Kimono,* 230 (Wald quote). From 1964 to 1969, television aired a series based on *Peyton Place.*

110. See, e.g., D'Acci, "Nobody's Woman?" 77–78; and Schwartz, *Cold War Culture,* 40–41.

111. Seth Cagin and Philip Dray, *Hollywood Films of the Seventies: Sex, Drugs, Violence, Rock 'n' Roll, and Politics* (New York: Harper & Row, 1984), 32 (*The Graduate*).

112. Jon Lewis, *Hollywood v. Hard Core: How the Struggle over Censorship Saved the Modern Film Industry* (New York: New York University Press, 2000), 67–69; Davis, *Celluloid Mirrors,* 67–84 (the conglomerates).

113. Jones, *Our Musicals, Ourselves,* 237, 369. *Hello Dolly* opened in 1964 and ran on Broadway for 2,844 performances, *Funny Girl* in 1964 for 1,348 performances, *Mame* in 1966 for 1,508 performances, and *Charlie Brown* in 1967 for 1,597 performances.

114. Ibid., 241–57. *Cabaret* ran through 1,165 Broadway performances, *1776* through 1,217, and *Hair* through 1,844.

115. Denton and Morris, *The Money and the Power,* 105–46 (127, "river of wealth"; 131, Giancana quote; 146, *Life* quote, "hanging on a hook"); Tom Wolfe, "Las Vegas (What?) Las Vegas (Can't Hear You! Too Noisy) *Las Vegas!!!!*" in *Smiling through the Apocalypse: Esquire's History of the Sixties,* ed. Harold Hayes (New York: Dell, 1971), 205 ("our city").

116. Wolfe, "Las Vegas (What?)" 201–18 (209, "Monte Carlo"; 211, "resort"; 212, "wearing Capri pants"); Denton and Morris, *The Money and the Power,* 127, 181; Bernard Weinraub, "Requiem for Rats: Ring-a-Ding-Ding Baby," *New York Times,* April 13, 1998, B1, B3 ("men behaving badly").

11. Up for Grabs: Leaving the 1960s

1. Bruce Schulman, *The Seventies: The Great Shift in American Culture, Society, and Politics* (New York: Free Press, 2001), 78–79 (*Jonathan Livingston Seagull;* 79, *Time* quote, *Publishers Weekly* quote); Kleinfelder, *When We Were Young,* 602 (Bach quote).

2. Beth Bailey and David Farber (Beth Bailey and David Farber, eds., *America in the Seventies* [Lawrence: University Press of Kansas, 2004], 1–8) neatly sketch out these developments.

3. David Caute, *The Year of the Barricades: A Journey through 1968* (New York: Harper & Row, 1988), 448 (*Barb* quotes).

4. Mick LaSalle, "Ah, the '70s, When Movies Were Smart," *San Francisco Chronicle,* May 30, 2003, D5.

5. Sklar, *Movie-Made America,* 321 (statistics); Hoberman, *Dream Life,* 253.

6. Doherty, *Teenagers and Teenpics,* 1–2, 7–8, 125–27; Cagin and Dray, *Hollywood Films of the Seventies,* 50–53 (52, "there is more there," "termite art"); Davis, *Celluloid Mirrors,* 49 ("camera fell over").

7. Davis, *Celluloid Mirrors,* 99 (Newman quote), 109 (statistics).

8. Peter Biskind, *Easy Riders, Raging Bulls: How the Sex–Drugs–and–Rock 'n' Roll Generation Saved Hollywood* (New York: Simon & Schuster, 1998), 30 ("couple of rats"), 34–36 (35, "in-your-face," "go pee"), 48 ("tumbling down"). See also Hoberman, *Dream Life,* 163, 168–85.

9. Leff and Simmons, *Dame in the Kimono,* 247–71; Lewis, *Hollywood v. Hard Core,* 105–27, 133–39.

10. Leff and Simmons, *Dame in the Kimono,* 271–91; Peter Braunstein, "'Adults Only': The Construction of an Erotic City in New York during the 1970s," in Bailey and Farber, eds., *America in the Seventies,* 132 (statistics on R-rated films); "Shocker: 'Inside Deep Throat,'" *Rolling Stone,* February 10, 2005, 89 (*Deep Throat*'s profits). See also Lewis, *Hollywood v. Hard Core,* 192, 208–12; and David A. Cook, *Lost Illusions: American Cinema in the Shadow of Watergate and Vietnam, 1970–1979* (Berkeley and Los Angeles: University of California Press, 2000), 275–76.

11. Braunstein, "'Adults Only,'" 130–33 (commission quotes, "nickelodeon for the horny"), 139–40 (courts); Marc Eliot, *Down 42nd Street: Sex, Money, Culture, and Politics at the Crossroads of the World* (New York: Warner, 2001), 139–40 (Beame quote, "supermarket of porn").

12. Weyr, *Reaching for Paradise,* 248–58 (statistics), 273 (pretax earnings).

13. Ibid., 272 ("titillation"), 290–93 (290, Guccione quote); Petersen, *Century of Sex,* 353–54 (353, *Esquire* quote).

14. See, e.g., Biskind, *Easy Riders, Raging Bulls,* 43 ("dinosaurs"), 61–69, 74–75 ("Vietcong of Beverly Hills," "children of Dylan"); also Hoberman, *Dream Life,* 190–97.

15. BBS was named after Bert Schneider, Bob Rafelson, and Steve Blauner, but Nicholson was a de facto partner.

16. Biskind, *Easy Riders, Raging Bulls,* 75–77 (quote).

17. Ibid., 124–26 (quote).

18. Slotkin, *Gunfighter Nation,* 593–613 (594, "*Moby Dick*"); Terrence Rafferty, "Artist of Death," *New Yorker,* March 6, 1995, 127–29 (quotes). See also Richard Robertson, "New Directions in Westerns of the 1960s and 70s," *Journal of the West* 22 (October 1983): 43–52; Hoberman, *Dream Life,* 190, 233–35, 245–46; and Coyne, *Crowded Prairie,* 149–60. "If Westerns had acted as a safety valve," writes Coyne, "*The Wild Bunch* blasted that valve away forever" (160).

19. Leff and Simmons, *Dame in the Kimono,* 276 (the rating).

20. Schulman, *The Seventies,* 129 ("inconceivable combination"); Bailey and Farber, introduction, 2–4; Jay, *More Than Just a Game,* 157.

21. Biskind, *Easy Riders, Raging Bulls,* 76 (on Bogdanovich). For other excellent discussions of Hollywood in the 1970s, see esp. Cagin and Dray, *Hollywood Films of the Seventies;* Robert Phillip Kolker, *A Cinema of Loneliness: Penn, Kubrick, Scorsese, Spielberg, Altman,* 2nd ed. (New York: Oxford University Press, 1988); and Cook, *Lost Illusions.*

22. Jon Lewis, "If History Has Taught Us Anything . . .: Francis Coppola, Paramount Studios, and *The Godfather, Parts I, II, and III,*" in *Francis Ford Coppola's Godfather Trilogy,* ed. Nick Browne (Cambridge: Cambridge University Press, 2000), 23–24, 34; Bernard F. Dick, *Engulfed: The Death of Paramount Pictures and the Birth of Corporate Hollywood* (Lexington: University Press of Kentucky, 2001), 99–103; Biskind, *Easy Riders, Raging*

Bulls, 150 ("double-cross"), 144–47 ("easy way to get laid"). In 1998, the American Film Institute picked *The Godfather* as the third-best movie ever; *The Godfather: Part II* ranked thirty-second (*AFI's 100 Years . . . 100 Movies* [Gary Smith, 1998]). A year later, *Entertainment Weekly* ranked *The Godfather* first and *The Godfather: Part II* seventh (*The 100 Greatest Movies of All Time* [New York: Entertainment Weekly Books, 1999]).

23. Nick Browne, "Fearful A-Symmetries: Violence as History in the *Godfather* Films," in Browne, ed., *Coppola's* Godfather *Trilogy,* 11; Glenn Man, "Ideology and Genre in the *Godfather* Films," in ibid., 113, 118–22 (118, Coppola quote); Naomi Greene, "Family Ceremonies; or, Opera in *The Godfather* Trilogy," in ibid., 152–53; Lewis, "If History Has Taught Us Anything," 27–28 ("metaphor for capitalism").

24. Stephen Farber, "A Nightmare World with No Secrets," *New York Times,* May 12, 1974, sec. 2, p. 13.

25. Marc and Thompson, *Television in the Antenna Age,* 84–85 ("anaesthetic"), 94–102 (programming's shift to "relevance"); Thompson, *Television's Second Golden Age,* 28–29; Marc, *Comic Visions,* 165–66.

26. Todd Gitlin, *Inside Prime Time* (1983; reprint, New York: Pantheon, 1985), 205–11 (206, "wrinkles"; 207, "*Gunsmoke*").

27. Thompson, *Television's Second Golden Age,* 47–48. On MTM's importance, see also Marc and Thompson, *Television in the Antenna Age,* 102.

28. Thompson, *Television's Second Golden Age,* 49–54; Marc, *Comic Visions,* 167–72; Jones, *Honey, I'm Home!* 193–202 (194, "nobody divorces," Brooks quote); Stark, *Glued to the Set,* 167–70; Gitlin, *Inside Prime Time,* 214–15; Watson, *Defining Visions,* 112 ("pill").

29. Jones, *Honey, I'm Home!* 203–5; Gitlin, *Inside Prime Time,* 212 ("wrath"); Smith, *Play-by-Play,* 132 ("13 weeks").

30. Janet Staiger, *Blockbuster TV: Must-See Sitcoms in the Network Era* (New York: New York University Press, 2000), 81–83 ("giant step"); Marc, *Comic Visions,* 174–84; Jones, *Honey, I'm Home!* 205–11.

31. Staiger, *Blockbuster TV,* 89–110 (90, Young quote); Marc, *Comic Visions,* 184–87; Jones, *Honey, I'm Home!* 206–9, 212–13 (212, quote); Gitlin, *Inside Prime Time,* 212 (Lear quote).

32. Marc, *Comic Visions,* 189–99 (190, "hurt"); Gitlin, *Inside Prime Time,* 216–17 ("tardy," "damn everybody").

33. Gitlin, *Inside Prime Time,* 217–19 (217, Gelbart quote, fan mail quote); Bogle, *Primetime Blues,* 185–87 (poll, Paley quote).

34. Stark, *Glued to the Set,* 183–86; Gary Levin, "Good Night, Johnny," *Spokane, WA, Spokesman-Review,* January 24, 2005, A1; *World News Tonight* (ABC), January 24, 2005. Carson left *The Tonight Show* in 1992. He died on January 23, 2005. On the February 1, 2005, broadcast of ABC's *Good Morning, America,* one of the cohosts, Charles Gibson, recalled Buchwald's observation in an earlier interview.

35. Watkins, *On the Real Side,* 518–25 (521–22, "distinct black voice"); Bogle, *Primetime Blues,* 175–83 (181, "just a comic").

36. Watkins, *On the Real Side,* 462, 514–17 (516, "adult mind," "damned gypsies"); Bogle, *Primetime Blues,* 37–38, 187–96.

37. Bogle, *Primetime Blues,* 190.

38. Watkins, *On the Real Side,* 529–63 (531, "two worlds"; 535, "white-bread humor"; 537, "being Bill Cosby," "nervous breakdown"; 557–58, "nearly undiluted"); Nelson George, "The Rumors of His Death Have Been Greatly Exaggerated," *New York Times Magazine,* January 17, 1999, 28; Sklar, *Movie-Made America,* 332.

39. Szatmary, *Time to Rock,* 212 (Santana quote, Thompson quote); Altschuler, *All Shook Up,* 187 (Joplin quote, Hendrix quote); Caute, *Year of the Barricades,* 447–48.

40. Szatmary, *Time to Rock,* 213.

41. McKinney, *Magic Circles,* 339 (Christgau quote); Schulman, *The Seventies,* 49 ("collective loss").

42. Szatmary, *Time to Rock,* 215–16 (215, Lamm quote), 226–29; Todd Gitlin, *The Sixties: Years of Hope, Days of Rage* (New York: Bantam, 1987), 425–26; Jon Pareles, "The 70's Revisited: The Nostalgia Trail Hits Rock's Bottom," *New York Times,* April 15, 1990, H28 ("depressed").

43. Szatmary, *Time to Rock,* 235–41 (237, "hit them on the head"; 240, "*National En-quirer*"; 241, *Time* quote); Maureen Orth, "Mr. America," *Newsweek,* May 28, 1973, 65 ("sex, death and money"); Bob Greene, "Alice's New Restaurant," *Harper's,* June 1972, 16–21.

44. Steve Pond, "70s," *Rolling Stone,* September 20, 1990, 51, 53.

45. Orth, "Mr. America" (n. 43 above), 65 (voting for Nixon, "Madison Avenue men"); Greene, "Alice's New Restaurant" (n. 43 above), 18 ("like money"), 21 ("politics is bor-ing"); Szatmary, *Time to Rock,* 224 (Ronstadt quote).

46. Szatmary, *Time to Rock,* 246–49 ("corporate rock"); Starr and Waterman, *American Popular Music,* 306–7 (306, "six huge corporations"); Mark Crispin Miller, "Who Controls the Music," *The Nation,* August 25–September 1, 1997, 11.

47. Douglas, *Listening In,* 259 (statistics), 276–82 (280, *Advertising Age* quote); Starr and Waterman, *American Popular Music,* 307; Pond, "70s" (n. 44 above), 54 (multiplati-num album format).

48. Pond, "70s" (n. 44 above), 54, 110 (quote). See also Jim Miller, "Moods for Mod-erns," *New Republic,* June 30, 1979, 26.

49. Werner, *Change Is Gonna Come,* 205–8 (Rodgers quote); Schulman, *The Seventies,* 73; Szatmary, *Time to Rock,* 244 ("huge space," "star"); Braunstein, "'Adults Only,'" 142–44.

50. Werner, *Change Is Gonna Come,* 208 (Rodgers quote).

51. Schulman, *The Seventies,* 73–74, 144; Szatmary, *Time to Rock,* 245–46 (statistics, "Mafia"); Starr and Waterman, *American Popular Music,* 362–64; Werner, *Change Is Gon-na Come,* 209–11 (Clinton quote, "revenge"); Braunstein, "'Adults Only,'" 147–48.

52. Christopher S. Wren, "Country Music," *Look,* July 13, 1971, 11–12.

53. Schulman, *The Seventies,* 114 ("redneck chic"); Malone, *Country Music, U.S.A.,* 316–19, 373; Werner, *Change Is Gonna Come,* 160–62; Barbara Ching, *"Wrong's What I Do Best": Hard Country Music and Contemporary Culture* (New York: Oxford University Press, 2001), 5 ("heart of America").

54. Wren, "Country Music" (n. 52 above), 11–13 (Howard and Cash songs); Doggett, *Are You Ready for the Country,* 427 ("didn't give a shit"); Werner, *Change Is Gonna Come,* 162–63 ("at least interested"); Starr and Waterman, *American Popular Music,* 310–11, 373. For a discussion of the right-wing strains by 1974, see Florence King, "Red Necks, White Socks, and Blue Ribbon Beer," *Harper's,* July 1974, 30–34.

55. Schulman, *The Seventies,* 114–17; Starr and Waterman, *American Popular Music,* 309.

56. Daniel, *Lost Revolutions,* 89–120 (99, "bunch of farmers"; 109, Johnson quote); Josh-ua Zeitz, "Dixie's Victory," *American Heritage* 53 (August/September 2002): 46, 48–50; Karyn Charles Rybacki and Donald Jay Rybacki, "The King, the Young Prince, and the Last Confed-erate Soldier: NASCAR on the Cusp," in Miller, ed., *Sporting World,* 294–304, 318–19.

57. J. W. Williamson, *Hillbillyland: What the Movies Did to the Mountains and What the Mountains Did to the Movies* (Chapel Hill: University of North Carolina Press, 1995), 123, 133–35.

58. Doggett, *Are You Ready for the Country,* xi–xiv, 53–59 (McGuinn quotes), 427; Malone, *Country Music, U.S.A.,* 386–88; Allen, *Rodeo Cowboys,* 115, 136–37.

59. Doggett, *Are You Ready for the Country,* 59 ("psychedelic scene"), 69 ("white soul backlash"), 162–65, 401 ("kisses"), 404 ("hippie cowboys"), 420 ("righting"), 487. See also Michael Allen, "'I Just Want to Be a Cosmic Cowboy': Hippies, Cowboy Code, and the Culture of a Counterculture," *Western Historical Quarterly* 36 (autumn 2005): 275–99.

60. Malone, *Country Music, U.S.A.,* 369–70; Doggett, *Are You Ready for the Country,* 348, 351–53 (352, "sung funny," "looking for you"; 353, "old image"), 363.

61. Ching, *"Wrong's What I Do Best,"* 119 ("Opry nowadays"), 156 ("my name is Way-lon"); Doggett, *Are You Ready for the Country,* 347–51 (349, "double-parking"; 350–51, "dress a certain way"); Starr and Waterman, *American Popular Music,* 334–37; Malone, *Country Music, U.S.A.,* 398–405; Jim Paterson, "Waylon Jennings, Country Music's Ulti-mate Outlaw, Dies at 64," *Spokane, WA, Spokesman-Review,* February 14, 2002, A5 ("I get mean").

62. Ching, *"Wrong's What I Do Best,"* 6, 16, 122–23 ("couldn't go pop"); Starr and

Waterman, *American Popular Music*, 337–38; Doggett, *Are You Ready for the Country*, 347–50 (349, Atkins quote), 366–68 (368, "never been to Luckenback").

63. William Hedgepath, "Superstars, Poets, Pickers, Prophets," *Look*, July 13, 1971, 29.

64. Ching, *"Wrong's What I Do Best,"* 14–15, 32; *Controversy* (Country Music Television documentary): "Would You Lay with Me in a Field of Stone" (2003, on Tanya Tucker) and "The Pill" (2003, on Loretta Lynn); Malone, *Country Music, U.S.A.*, 306–9.

65. "The 1970's," an episode of *Century of Country* (n. 90, chap. 6 above) (Jones quote); Starr and Waterman, *American Popular Music*, 312; Wren, "Country Music" (n. 52 above), 13 (Bradley quote); Doggett, *Are You Ready for the Country*, 335, 388 (Parton quotes).

66. Starr and Waterman, *American Popular Music*, 311–12; "The 1970's," an episode of *Century of Country* (n. 90, chap. 6 above); Malone, *Country Music, U.S.A.*, 374–75, 379.

67. Jones, *Our Musicals, Ourselves*, 267–68.

68. Stephen E. Ambrose, *Nixon: The Triumph of a Politician, 1962–1972* (New York: Simon & Schuster, 1989), 369 (Nixon quote). Hoberman (*Dream Life*, 315–28, 365–77) discusses the "legal vigilantes" and "the Nixon western."

69. Biskind, *Easy Riders, Raging Bulls*, 75 (Lucas quote), 99, 317–18; Davis, *Celluloid Mirrors*, 122; Aljean Harmetz, "Our Own Past, Lost and Gone, Is in 'Graffiti,'" *New York Times*, December 2, 1973, D13.

70. Tom Shone, *Blockbuster: How Hollywood Learned to Stop Worrying and Love the Summer* (New York: Free Press, 2004), 18 (profits); Cagin and Dray, *Hollywood Films of the Seventies*, 237 (*Jaws* and Castro).

71. Sklar, *Movie-Made America*, 323–24; Davis, *Celluloid Mirrors*, 124.

72. Louis Menand, "Billion-Dollar Baby," *New York Review of Books*, July 24, 1999, 8, 11; Davis, *Celluloid Mirrors*, 122–23; Sklar, *Movie-Made America*, 328–29, 342, 357; Engelhardt, *End of Victory Culture*, 264–65 (Lucas quotes), 268–69.

73. Shone, *Blockbuster*, 10–12 (quotes); Twitchell, *Preposterous Violence*, 182 (statistics).

74. Davis, *Celluloid Mirrors*, 130; Engelhardt, *End of Victory Culture*, 264 ("triumph").

75. Biskind, *Easy Riders, Raging Bulls*, 403–4 (quotes); "The Monster That Ate Hollywood," an episode of *Frontline* (PBS, 2001); Sklar, *Movie-Made America*, 324.

76. Biskind, *Easy Riders, Raging Bulls*, 369 (Simpson quote), 372–75, 401 (Tanen quote).

77. Jon Lewis, *Whom God Wishes to Destroy . . .: Francis Coppola and the New Hollywood* (Durham, NC: Duke University Press, 1995), 46–47; Biskind, *Easy Riders, Raging Bulls*, 390–91; Cook, *Lost Illusions*, 319.

78. Sklar, *Movie-Made America*, 329, 338 (quote).

79. Tony Schwarz, "Comedy's New Face," *Newsweek*, April 3, 1978, 60–71 (61, Steinberg quote; 62, "hottest stand-up comic"; 71, "tainted everything"); Berger, *Last Laugh*, 396–402 (399, "frock coats").

80. Frank Rich, "Samurai Snobs," *New Republic*, July 28, 1986, 33–36; also Stark, *Glued to the Set*, 194–99.

81. Jones, *Honey, I'm Home!* 221–26 (226, "ragged aftermath"); also Anne Roiphe, "The Waltons," *New York Times Magazine*, November 18, 1973, 40ff.

82. Tim Brooks and Earle Marsh, *The Complete Directory to Prime Time Network and Cable TV Shows, 1946–Present*, 7th ed. (New York: Ballantine, 1999), 870–71; Stark, *Glued to the Set*, 199–201 (quotes).

83. Gerstle, *American Crucible*, 328–39 (336, Coppola quote); Michael Novak, *The Rise of the Unmeltable Ethnics* (New York: Macmillan, 1971); E. Wayne Carp, *Family Matters: Secrecy and Disclosure in the History of Adoption* (Cambridge, MA: Harvard University Press, 1998), 164–65 (*Newsweek* quote, Trailways quote), 175.

84. Hietala, "Muhammad Ali," 141 (Reagan quote), 146 ("draft-dodging dogs," "draft-dodging bastard").

85. Sammons, *Beyond the Ring*, 208–14 (209, "old image"; 212, "surrogate 'white hope'"; 213, "Patriotic America"), 218 ("knocked down"); Mark Kram, *Ghosts of Manila: The Fateful Blood Feud between Muhammad Ali and Joe Frazier* (New York: HarperCollins, 2001), 3, 150 (Gumbel quote); *Ali Frazier I: One Nation . . . Divisible* (HBO documentary, 2000) ("anti-Ali," "true-blue American," "Uncle Tom").

86. Sammons, *Beyond the Ring,* 217–18 ("don't knock"); Hietala, "Muhammad Ali," 133 ("wiser than we"). See also the movie documentary *When We Were Kings* (Leon Gast, 1996).

87. Michael Oriard, "Muhammad Ali: The Hero in the Age of Mass Media," in Gorn, ed., *Muhammad Ali,* 8–11, 13 (Kram quote); Zang, *Sports Wars,* 101–4, 111–12.

88. See, e.g., Murray Kempton, "Jock-Sniffing," *New York Review of Books,* February 11, 1971, 34–38 (38, Meggyesy quote); David Remnick, "Raging Bull," *New Yorker,* June 10, 1996, 84–86; Robin Roberts, "Strike Out Little League," *Newsweek,* July 21, 1975, 11; Charley McKenna, "Page Wants to Sack Myths about Football as a Career," *Minneapolis Tribune,* September 6, 1979, D1–D2 (Page quote); Hoch, *Rip Off the Big Game,* 65, 68–69, 107–8, 150–51, 180–84; Zang, *Sports Wars,* 65–66, 81–83.

89. Jay, *More Than Just a Game,* 148 (John quote); Hoch, *Rip Off the Big Game,* 123–25.

90. Don DeLillo, *End Zone* (1972; reprint, New York: Pocket, 1973), 14; Dan Jenkins, *Semi-Tough* (1972; reprint, New York: Signet, 1973), 3; Peter Gent, *North Dallas Forty* (1973; reprint, Toronto: Sport Media, 2003), 212–13.

91. Jay, *More Than Just a Game,* 152–56 (154, Douglas quote); Rader, *Baseball,* 186–92 (191, *Sporting News* quote).

92. Hoch, *Rip Off the Big Game,* 40 (Shecter quote), 138–39, 144.

93. Smith, *Play-by-Play,* 128–33 (133, quote).

94. Susan K. Cahn, *Coming on Strong: Gender and Sexuality in Twentieth-Century Women's Sport* (Cambridge, MA: Harvard University Press, 1995), 249–51; Jay, *More Than Just a Game,* 158–67 ("dolls," Fuzak quote, Hruska quote, statistics); Hoch, *Rip Off the Big Game,* 147 ("girlie show"); Davies, *America's Obsession,* 166–74.

95. Jay, *More Than Just a Game,* 168–71 (168, "five sports per school"); Cahn, *Coming on Strong,* 246–48. In 2005, the race car driver Danica Patrick finished fourth in the Indianapolis 500, a breakthrough moment for women in sport. *Sports Illustrated* featured her on its cover, and some people hailed her as "the woman poised to save Indy Car racing." But, even then, considerable attention focused on her "sexy" looks as an explanation for her success (Jason Whitlock, "Patrick Should Have Been Told to Go for It, Not Back Off," *The Oregonian,* June 6, 2005, E2).

96. Jay, *More Than Just a Game,* 162–64 (Riggs quotes), 171–73 (172, King quote); Cahn, *Coming on Strong,* 251–52; Joe Garner, *Stay Tuned: Television's Unforgettable Moments* (Kansas City, MO: Andrews McMeel, 2002), 152–55; Davies, *America's Obsession,* 157–66.

97. Wynter, *American Skin,* 9, 106–10.

98. See, e.g., Jay, *More Than Just a Game,* 146–47, 155, 180–81.

99. Wright, *Comic Book Nation,* 226–28 ("terribly sick!" "awaken"), 236, 240; Goulart, *Great American Comic Books,* 278 ("fantasy," "I can't"); *Comic Book Superheroes Unmasked* (Steve Kroopnick, 2003, TV documentary).

100. Daniels, *Marvel,* 152–54, 158–59, 183; Wright, *Comic Book Nation,* 230–31, 234–40, 244–46 (246, "rebels are wrong"); Goulart, *Great American Comic Books,* 280–81.

101. Wright, *Comic Book Nation,* 240 (sales); *Marvel Double Feature Starring Captain America and Iron Man* 1, no. 19 (December 1976): 7 ("duty"), 11 ("deserves a private life"); Tom Wolfe, *Mauve Gloves and Madmen, Clutter and Vine* (New York: Farrar Straus Giroux, 1976), 143.

102. Wright, *Comic Book Nation,* 230 (incorporation), 251–55; Daniels, *Marvel,* 167–69; Goulart, *Great American Comic Books,* 267–68, 286–89.

103. Jim Miller, "Is Rock on the Rocks?" *Newsweek,* April 19, 1982, 107.

104. Pond, "70s" (n. 44 above), 110; Szatmary, *Time to Rock,* 251–57; Starr and Waterman, *American Popular Music,* 345–56 (346, Ramones lyrics).

105. James Traub, "Back to the Future," *New York Times Magazine,* October 5, 2003, 17; Braunstein, "'Adults Only,'" 129–30, 146–47; Immerso, *Coney Island,* 167–76 (174–75, quotes).

106. George, *Hip Hop America,* 10 ("economic dead zones"); Werner, *Change Is Gonna Come,* 237 ("Vietnam"); Starr and Waterman, *American Popular Music,* 409 (*Times* quote).

107. Cheryl L. Keyes, *Rap Music and Street Consciousness* (Urbana: University of Illinois Press, 2002), xi–xiii, 28–29.

108. George, *Hip Hop America,* 10–12; Alexandra Marshall, "Word of Mouth," *American Prospect,* May 8, 2000, 40; Jim Fricke and Charlie Ahearn, eds., *Yes Yes Y'all: The Experience Music Project Oral History of Hip-Hop's First Decade* (Cambridge, MA: Da Capo, 2002), 13 ("virus"); Starr and Waterman, *American Popular Music,* 409.

109. George, *Hip Hop America,* 14–16; Marshall, "Word of Mouth" (n. 108 above), 40.

110. George, *Hip Hop America,* 6–7, 17–22; Keyes, *Rap Music,* 1 ("loosely chanted"), 50–59; Werner, *Change Is Gonna Come,* 237–38; Coleman, *Playback,* 142 ("sonic signifier").

111. Keyes, *Rap Music,* x, 17–32, 194, 216; George, *Hip Hop America,* 15–16, 103–6, 144–53; Barry Koltnow, "Shaft Sightings," *Spokane, WA, Spokesman-Review,* June 20, 2000, D7 (Jackson quote). For an overview of rap's roots, see also Anthony Bozza, *Whatever You Say I Am: The Life and Times of Eminem* (New York: Crown, 2003), 124–33.

112. Keyes, *Rap Music,* 5.

113. Marshall, "Word of Mouth" (n. 108 above), 40; George, *Hip Hop America,* 20–22 (21, "not a mass market concept"), 24 ("underground musical economy"), 113 ("meritocracy"); Starr and Waterman, *American Popular Music,* 409 (Freddie quote); Coleman, *Playback,* 144 (Herc quote).

114. Steve Greenberg, "Sugar Hill Records," in *The Vibe History of Hip Hop,* ed. Alan Light (New York: Three Rivers, 1999), 23–27 (24, Flash quote); Keyes, *Rap Music,* 1, 68–69 ("'hell of a concept'"); Coleman, *Playback,* 145; George, *Hip Hop America,* 29–31, 60.

115. Gitlin, *Inside Prime Time,* 226 ("much-wooed audience"); Sklar, *Movie-Made America,* 338.

116. Gitlin, *Inside Prime Time,* 71 (Paley quote), 73 ("public service").

117. Ibid., 72–73; Douglas, *Where the Girls Are,* 212–16 (213, "tensions"); Chuck Barney, "Girl Power," *Spokane, WA, Spokesman-Review,* November 19, 2000, F10 (Murphy quote).

118. Gitlin, *Inside Prime Time,* 75.

119. John Simon, "From Fake Happyendings to Fake Unhappyendings," *New York Times Magazine,* June 8, 1975, 18ff.; Lewis Lapham, "What Movies Try to Sell Us," *Harper's,* November 1971, 106–15.

120. Ron Rosenbaum, "Gooseflesh," *Harper's,* September 1979, 86–92 (86, "strange turn"); Skal, *Monster Show,* 287–361 (357, "ferocious howl"); *Sneak Previews* (Gene Siskel and Roger Ebert, PBS), episode airing April 9, 1980.

121. Skal, *Monster Show,* 354.

12. A POP CULTURE SOCIETY

1. Todd Gitlin, *Media Unlimited: How the Torrent of Images and Sounds Overwhelms Our Lives* (New York: Metropolitan, 2001), 6–24 (17, quote); Michael J. Wolf, *The Entertainment Economy: How Mega-Media Forces Are Transforming Our Lives* (New York: Times Books, 1999), xxi, 4–10 (10, quote); Geoffrey O'Brien, "Sein of the Times," *New York Review of Books,* August 14, 1997, 14 ("sitcoms"); "The Public Interest," *The Nation,* June 8, 1998, 3.

2. See esp. Wills, *Reagan's America.*

3. Ibid., 261–78; Connie Bruck, *When Hollywood Had a King: The Reign of Lew Wasserman, Who Leveraged Talent into Power and Influence* (New York: Random House, 2003), 65, 96–97, 117–23 (quotes), 185–87 (MCA and Reagan).

4. Lou Cannon, *President Reagan: The Role of a Lifetime* (New York: Simon & Schuster, 1991), 57–61, 97; Hedrick Smith, *The Power Game: How Washington Works* (New York: Random House, 1988), 402 (Atwater quote).

5. Cannon, *President Reagan,* 39 ("wanted to believe"); Frances Fitzgerald, *Way Out There in the Blue: Reagan, Star Wars, and the End of the Cold War* (New York: Simon & Schuster, 2000), 74 ("gap"), 102 ("mind").

6. Gitlin, *The Sixties,* 217 ("dresses like Tarzan"); Paul Slansky, *The Clothes Have No Emperor: A Chronicle of the American 80s* (New York: Fireside, 1989), 9 ("just like show

business"). For analyses of the political culture of the 1980s and Reagan's role in it, see Gil Troy, *Morning in America: How Ronald Reagan Invented the 1980s* (Princeton, NJ: Princeton University Press, 2005); and Daniel Marcus, *Happy Days and Wonder Years: The Fifties and the Sixties in Contemporary Cultural Politics* (New Brunswick, NJ: Rutgers University Press, 2004), esp. 5–6, 58–91.

7. Tom Shales, "Mike Hammer's No Wimp, but He Is Wising Up," *Lewiston, Idaho, Tribune,* February 5, 1984; Brooks and Marsh, *Complete Directory,* 661.

8. Sklar, *Movie-Made America,* 342 (B-movie culture); Stark, *Glued to the Set,* 218–22 (*Dallas;* 220, *Time* quote; 221, "embodiment").

9. Jones, *Honey, I'm Home!* 260–61; Stark, *Glued to the Set,* 254–58; Bogle, *Primetime Blues,* 290–92 ("before we die"); *Color Adjustment* (Marlon Riggs, 1991) ("you have nothing").

10. Jones, *Honey, I'm Home!* 261 ("projected"); Watson, *Defining Visions,* 46–47 ("themselves to blame"); Bogle, *Primetime Blues,* 292–301 (294, "blackface"; 298, "incorporate African Americans"); Stark, *Glued to the Set,* 257; Troy, *Morning in America,* 175–76, 188–89.

11. Faludi, *Backlash,* 144 ("wimps"), 154 ("masculinity"). On the Huxtables' relationships, see Bogle, *Primetime Blues,* 301–2.

12. Faludi, *Backlash,* esp. 3–45, 77–111, 169–226 (172, "less fashion conscious"; 183, Blass quote; 188, Mackie quote; 205, "gone a little too far"; 213, Breck ad quotes), 280–332; Kimmel, *Manhood in America,* 291–319 (292, "Wimp Hunt").

13. Susan J. Douglas, "Letting the Boys Be Boys: Talk Radio, Male Hysteria, and Political Discourse in the 1980s," in Hilmes and Loviglio, eds., *Radio Reader,* 485–92, 498 ("Dan Blather").

14. Ibid., 491–501 (493, "Japs," "savages"; 499, "gotta change"). But, for a slightly more detailed treatment, see Douglas, *Listening In,* 284–327. On the Fairness Doctrine, see ibid., 298–99; Starr, *Creation of the Media,* 371; and David Foster Wallace, "Host," *Atlantic Monthly,* April 2005, 67. Also Watson, *Defining Visions,* 198 (Schwartzman quote); MacDonald, *One Nation under Television,* 232 (TV ownership); Troy, *Morning in America,* 280.

15. Faludi, *Backlash,* 140–48 (147, percentage), 160 (Tares quote), 167 (Herskovitz quote).

16. Ibid., 142 ("only two of them were adults"), 151 (Becker quote), 152 ("dykes"); Thompson, *Television's Second Golden Age,* 104–9. For an informative treatment of *Cagney & Lacey,* see Julie D'Acci, *Defining Women: Television and the Case of* Cagney & Lacey (Chapel Hill: University of North Carolina Press, 1994).

17. Gitlin, *Inside Prime Time,* 219–22 (219, "shift right"; 221, "moving to the right"; 222, "looking for heroes," "some basic values"); Troy, *Morning in America,* 51, 56 (*Dynasty,* Shapiro quotes).

18. Wallace, "Host" (n. 14 above), 53 ("everything for the ratings"), 55, 64–65 (64, "almost completely real").

19. Gitlin, *Inside Prime Time,* 224; William Greider, "Terms of Endearment," *Rolling Stone,* December 20, 1984–January 3, 1985, 83, 122–26.

20. Engelhardt, *End of Victory Culture,* 268–69 (toys).

21. See, e.g., Nicholas Mills, "Reaganizing Hollywood," *Dissent,* spring 1984, 230–32; J. Hoberman, "The Fascist Guns in the West," *Radical America* 19 (1985): 53–62; and Peter Rainer, "Politicization of Films: A Mirror of Our Times," *Los Angeles Herald Examiner,* December 16, 1984, A14–A15. For additional treatments of 1980s movies, see William J. Palmer, *The Films of the Eighties: A Social History* (Carbondale: Southern Illinois University Press, 1993); Alan Nadel, *Flatlining on the Field of Dreams: Cultural Narratives in the Films of President Reagan's America* (New Brunswick, NJ: Rutgers University Press, 1997); and Stephen Prince, *A New Pot of Gold: Hollywood under the Electronic Rainbow, 1980–1989* (Berkeley and Los Angeles: University of California Press, 2000).

22. Susan Jeffords, *Hard Bodies: Hollywood Masculinity in the Reagan Era* (New Brunswick, NJ: Rutgers University Press, 1994); Faludi, *Backlash,* 112–23 (121, Lyne quote, Douglas quote), 126–39.

23. Gitlin, *Inside Prime Time,* 223–24 (223, Stoddard), 245–46 ("*Love Boat*").

24. Ibid., 23 (Keld quote); Bogle, *Primetime Blues,* 286–90 (290, Cosby quote), 294; Stark, *Glued to the Set,* 257 (statistics); Jones, *Honey, I'm Home!* 259–61 (Tartikoff, statistics).

25. Garry Wills, "The '80s Are . . . ," *GQ,* September 1984, 444 (quote); Dave Kehr, "Aliens among Us," *Chicago Tribune,* October 12, 1986, sec. 13, p. 6 ("so eager"). Marcus (*Happy Days and Wonder Years,* 7, 91–118) discusses pop culture narratives that contested the conservative nostalgia of the 1980s.

26. Kehr, "Aliens among Us" (n. 25 above), 6–8; John Powers, "Past Perfect, Future Tense: The Cult of the Primitive in '80s Films," *L.A. Weekly,* December 13–19, 1986, 51; John Powers, "Saints and Savages," *American Film* 9 (January–February 1984): 38; Harlan Kennedy, "Amazon Grace," *Film Comment* 22 (October 1986): 9–15.

27. Kehr, "Aliens among Us" (n. 25 above), 8.

28. Powers, "Saints and Savages," 40–43 ("paranoid fables"); Powers, "Past Perfect, Future Tense" (n. 26 above), 51–52 ("profound uneasiness").

29. See, e.g., Sklar, *Movie-Made America,* 351–56 (353, 355, Lynch quotes).

30. Goulart, *Great American Comic Books,* 291–93; Wright, *Comic Book Nation,* 255, 258–62; Stephen Lynch, "Heroic Measures," *Spokane, WA, Spokesman-Review,* October 6, 1996, E3 (20 percent).

31. Wright, *Comic Book Nation,* 263–66.

32. Ibid., 266–67; Goulart, *Great American Comic Books,* 293, 301–2 (King quote).

33. Gerard Jones and Will Jacobs, *The Comic Book Heroes* (Rocklin, CA: Prima, 1997), 307–8 (307, "watchmen"); Wright, *Comic Book Nation,* 271–73 (272, Moore quote).

34. Wright, *Comic Book Nation,* 283; Jones and Jacobs, *Comic Book Heroes,* 278–79, 303, 321; Goulart, *Great American Comic Books,* 303; Gary Cross, *Kids' Stuff: Toys and the Changing World of Childhood* (Cambridge, MA: Harvard University Press, 1997), 1, 215–16.

35. Goulart, *Great American Comic Books,* 284–88.

36. Trina Robbins, *From Girls to Grrrlz: A History of Female Comics from Teens to Zines* (San Francisco: Chronicle, 1999), 4 (Sinclair quotes), 81–141 (116, "not ashamed"; 135, "growl"; 140–41, "promote and encourage"). "Riot Grrrl ultimately was a fanzine-led flashpoint, a media rocket supporting the key issue—a woman's place in art and rock culture," writes Lucy O'Brien (*She Bop,* 164; also 158–64).

37. Butsch, *Making of American Audiences,* 267–69; Neil Hickey, "Decade of Change, Decade of Choice," *TV Guide,* December 9, 1989, 29.

38. Tom McGrath, *MTV: The Making of a Revolution* (Philadelphia: Running, 1996), 13.

39. Ibid., 13–17, 26; Barnouw, *Tube of Plenty,* 350–53, 493–94, 509; MacDonald, *One Nation under Television,* 223–26; Butsch, *Making of American Audiences,* 268–69 (statistics); Twitchell, *Carnival Culture,* 214 (paying bills).

40. MacDonald, *One Nation under Television,* 231–34 (231–32, Fowler quotes); Glynn, *Tabloid Culture,* 26–27 (Sauter quote).

41. Jeannette Walls, *Dish: The Inside Story on the World of Gossip* (New York: Spike, 2000), 150–65 (159, Arledge hating *20/20*); Brooks and Marsh, *Complete Directory,* 1059.

42. Watson, *Defining Visions,* 176 ("free-wheeling bazaar"), 198; Hickey, "Decade of Change" (n. 37 above), 34.

43. MacDonald, *One Nation under Television,* 132 (CBS ad); Butsch, *Making of American Audiences,* 269–71 (269, statistics; 271, "rental rebellion," "day-to-day decisions").

44. MacDonald, *One Nation under Television,* 222–23; Butsch, *Making of American Audiences,* 271–75.

45. Glynn, *Tabloid Culture,* 28–29 (numbers, Sauter); Ira Rosofsky, "As the Wheel Turns," *Village Voice,* January 27, 1987, 45; MacDonald, *One Nation under Television,* 230.

46. Thompson, *Television's Second Golden Age,* 37–42.

47. Ibid., 57–62; Gitlin, *Inside Prime Time,* 274–81; "The Twenty Top Shows of the Decade," *TV Guide,* December 9, 1989, 20. On Bochco, see also David Marc and Robert J. Thompson, *Prime Time, Prime Movers* (Syracuse, NY: Syracuse University Press, 1995), 218–30.

48. Thompson, *Television's Second Golden Age,* 35, 60–64, 71–74 (71–72, "resigned

hopelessness," "it's a western"); Stark, *Glued to the Set,* 237–39; Gitlin, *Inside Prime Time,* 273–319 (306, "simple answers"); Marc and Thompson, *Prime Time, Prime Movers,* 226 ("a series about despair"); Bogle, *Primetime Blues,* 271–78 (276, "no-man's land"); Troy, *Morning in America,* 85, 113.

49. Stark, *Glued to the Set,* 237–39 ("dynamite," "first show"); Thompson, *Television's Second Golden Age,* 66–67, 73–74; Marc and Thompson, *Prime Time, Prime Movers,* 223–24.

50. Thompson, *Television's Second Golden Age,* 58, 67, 75–96 (75, Tinker quote).

51. Ibid., 109–11; Marcus, *Happy Days and Wonder Years,* 101, 105–6.

52. Stark, *Glued to the Set,* 262–65; Watson, *Defining Visions,* 72; Barbara Ehrenreich, "The Wretched of the Hearth," *New Republic,* April 2, 1990, 28–31 (28, quote); John J. O'Connor, "Roseanne by Any Other Name Is Still Roseanne," *Lewiston, Idaho, Tribune,* August 16, 1991, D1, D4 ("pregnant," "cave"); Epstein, *Haunted Smile,* 265–67 (265–66, "cheese puffs," "done my job"); John Lahr, "Dealing with Roseanne," *New Yorker,* July 17, 1995, 42–60; Susan Douglas, "Sitcom Women: We've Come a Long Way, Maybe," *Ms.,* November/December 1995, 77.

53. Josephine Hendin, "Sexual Warfare as a Family Style," *Dissent,* spring 1986, 230–33 ("antiromance"); John Leonard, *Smoke and Mirrors: Violence, Television, and Other American Cultures* (New York: New Press, 1997), 72–95 (72, "how families behave"); John Crewdson, *By Silence Betrayed: Sexual Abuse of Children in America* (Boston: Little, Brown, 1988), ix (*Amelia*); Harry F. Waters, "Whip Me, Beat Me . . . ," *Newsweek,* November 11, 1991, 74–75; author's count of child-abuse movies.

54. Glynn, *Tabloid Culture,* 27.

55. Ibid., 27–28; Walls, *Dish,* 130–31, 231–32; Kristal Brent Zook, *Color by Fox: The Fox Network and the Revolution in Black Television* (New York: Oxford University Press, 1999), 108; MacDonald, *One Nation under Television,* 230–31. On Murdoch as a media "revolutionary," see Epstein, *Big Picture,* 58–66. On *Cops,* see Elayne Rapping, *Law and Justice as Seen on TV* (New York: New York University Press, 2003), 55–69 (56, "buses").

56. Zook, *Color by Fox,* 4–5, 11 (quotes); *Fresh Air* (Terry Gross, NPR), episode airing November 11, 2004 (niche joke).

57. Harry F. Waters, "Family Feuds," *Newsweek,* April 23, 1990, 58–61 ("fumes"); Jones, *Honey, I'm Home!* 265–66; Scott Williams, "Bart Simpson: Rebel without a Clue?" *Lewiston, Idaho, Tribune,* May 23, 1990 (T-shirt and "what we stand for"); Michael Kinsley, "Bart for President," *New Republic,* July 23, 1990, 4; Michel Marriott, "I'm Bart, I'm Black, and What about It?" *New York Times,* September 19, 1990, B1, B5.

58. Daniel C. Hallin, "Images of the Vietnam and the Persian Gulf Wars in U.S. Television," in *Seeing through the Media: The Persian Gulf War,* ed. Susan Jeffords and Lauren Rabinovitz (New Brunswick, NJ: Rutgers University Press, 1994), 53 (NBC newscast conclusion); Tom Engelhardt, "The Gulf War as Total Television," in ibid., 87 ("ratings hit"), 92 ("spectacular"). Also Michelle Kendrick, "Kicking the Vietnam Syndrome: CNN's and CBS's Video Narratives of the Persian Gulf War," in ibid., 59–76. Only later did the public learn that the actual effectiveness of smart bombs and Patriot missiles did not match the wartime hype.

59. Hickey, "Decade of Change" (n. 37 above), 31; Barnouw, *Tube of Plenty,* 509–11 ("giving program").

60. Molly Ivins, "All the News That Fits Corporate Strategy," *Spokane, WA, Spokesman-Review,* November 4, 1999, B6; David Zurawik, "Profound Changes," *Spokane, WA, Spokesman-Review,* December 29, 1999, D9; Raymond F. Betts, *A History of Popular Culture: More of Everything, Faster and Brighter* (New York: Routledge, 2004), 141 (Murdoch quote); Twitchell, *Carnival Culture,* 6–7, 84–86 (86, "lone remaining publisher"), 129 (Massie quote), 162–63, 183. On the six entertainment giants, see Epstein, *Big Picture,* 82–84, 93–105. See also Twitchell, *Preposterous Violence,* 184.

61. Epstein, *Big Picture,* 3, 14–84, and 105–25 (conglomerate wheeling and dealing and clearinghouse operations), 129 (Redstone quote); also Neil Genzlinger, "I Am Large, I Contain Multiplexes," *New York Times Book Review,* March 20, 2005, 14–15.

62. Smith, *Dancing in the Street,* 254–55 (254, Gordy quote); Epstein, *Big Picture,* 79–80 (Seagram).

63. Wright, *Comic Book Nation,* 254 (stock exchange breakthrough), 280–82 (280, sur-

veys); Jones and Jacobs, *Comic Book Heroes*, 323, 358; Goulart, *Great American Comic Books*, 313, 317, 326; Mark Kennedy, "Marvel Gives Greater Depth to Superheroes," *Spokane, WA, Spokesman-Review*, September 16, 1996; Lynch, "Heroic Measures" (n. 30 above), E3, E6.

64. Wright, *Comic Book Nation*, 283–84; Goulart, *Great American Comic Books*, 326–28, 331; Lynch, "Heroic Measures" (n. 30 above), E6 (35 percent); Robbins, *From Girls to Grrrlz*, 140.

65. Mark Niesse, "Comics Say Farewell to Code," *Spokane, WA, Spokesman-Review*, November 4, 2001, F3–F4 (F3, Quesada quote).

66. Frederick E. Allen, "When Sex Drives Technological Innovation," *American Heritage* 51 (September 2000): 19–20; Timothy Egan, "Technology Sent Wall Street into Market for Pornography," *New York Times*, October 23, 2000, sec. 8, p. 1; Christopher Stern, "Memo to Top Management: Sex Sells," *Washington Post Weekly Edition*, July 10, 2000, 17; Frank Rich, "Naked Capitalists," *New York Times Magazine*, May 20, 2001, 51–52.

67. Egan, "Technology" (n. 66 above), 1 (quotes); Stern, "Memo to Top Management" (n. 66 above).

68. "The Merchants of Cool," an episode of *Frontline* (PBS, 2001).

69. McGrath, *MTV*, 39–45; Starr and Waterman, *American Popular Music*, 369; Szatmary, *Time to Rock*, 274 (Pittman quote), 280 (advertisers).

70. McGrath, *MTV*, 47–90, 108.

71. Ibid., 99–101, 108–11; Starr and Waterman, *American Popular Music*, 370–71, 384–87; Szatmary, *Time to Rock*, 283.

72. Szatmary, *Time to Rock*, 284 ("establishment figure"), 295 (*Billboard* quote); McGrath, *MTV*, 111 (*Time* quote).

73. McGrath, *MTV*, 103–5, 108, 114–19, 122–23, 127–29.

74. Ibid., 120, 126, 134–42; Troy, *Morning in America*, 129 (statistics).

75. Starr and Waterman, *American Popular Music*, 370–71; Coleman, *Playback*, 164–71.

76. Ellison, *Country Music Culture*, xxii (*Forbes*), 235–39 (Branson); Bruce Feiler, "Gone Country," *New Republic*, February 5, 1996, 19–20; Malone, *Country Music, U.S.A.*, 417–21, 426–27; Andrea Sachs, "Twentysomethings Take to Branson," *Spokane, WA, Spokesman-Review*, February 16, 2003, H1, H5.

77. On the increasing difficulties of separating "a stylistic core" from the "periphery," see Starr and Waterman, *American Popular Music*, 406.

78. Malone, *Don't Get above Your Raisin'*, 239–46; Malone, *Country Music, U.S.A.*, 418, 431–32.

79. Starr and Waterman, *American Popular Music*, 371–72; James C. Webb, "Rednecks, White Socks, and Pina Coladas? Country Music Ain't What It Used to Be . . . and It Really Never Was," *Southern Cultures* 5 (winter 1999): 41–51. On country's dialectical themes, see, e.g., Ellison, *Country Music Culture*, xix–xx; Malone, *Don't Get above Your Raisin'*, esp. ix, 13–14, 23–24, 61, 80, 119–48; and Cecelia Tichi, *High Lonesome: The American Culture of Country Music* (Chapel Hill: University of North Carolina Press, 1994), esp. 42–49, 64–75, 87–102, 136, 144.

80. Malone, *Don't Get above Your Raisin'*, 86–87, 168; Feiler, *Dreaming Out Loud*, 38 ("one particular place").

81. Feiler, *Dreaming Out Loud*, 36–37; Jonathan Miles, "Nascar Nation," *New York Times Book Review*, May 22, 2005, 1, 10–11 (McGregor quotes). On Earnhardt, see Rybacki and Rybacki, "NASCAR on the Cusp," 295, 314–18 (316, "what to do"), 320–22; Rick Bragg, "Racer's Death Leaves Hole in Heart of His Hometown," *New York Times*, February 21, 2001, A1, A12; George Diaz, "Intimidator Gave Everything He Had to the End," *Spokane, WA, Spokesman-Review*, February 19, 2001, C1; Eddie Pells, "Earnhardt Leaves Big Void," *Spokane, WA, Spokesman-Review*, February 20, 2001, C6–C7; and Peter St. Onge, "He Lived to Win Everything," *Spokane, WA, Spokesman-Review*, February 20, 2001, C6–C7.

82. Jon Pareles, "When Country Music Moves to the Suburbs," *New York Times*, November 25, 1990, 1, 23; Ellison, *Country Music Culture*, 231 (Noonan quotes); Feiler, "Gone Country" (n. 76 above), 19–22 (statistics, "mid-life ballad").

83. Feiler, *Dreaming Out Loud*, 362 (desire for security); Feiler, "Gone Country" (n. 76 above), 23–24; Ellison, *Country Music Culture*, 259 (Brooks quote); Malone, *Country Music, U.S.A.*, 431–34.

84. Malone, *Don't Get above Your Raisin'*, 168–70; "World's Gone Country," an episode of *Century of Country* (n. 90, chap. 6 above).

85. Doggett, *Are You Ready for the Country*, 480–81, 485–89 (Cash quote, Haggard); Malone, *Country Music, U.S.A.*, 420, 426–28 (427, "anti-Hank"), 432–36; Malone, *Don't Get above Your Raisin'*, 169 (Tritt quote), 256–58; Ching, *"Wrong's What I Do Best,"* 13 ("neighborhood mall"); Feiler, *Dreaming Out Loud*, 214.

86. Malone, *Country Music, U.S.A.*, 417, 436; Malone, *Don't Get above Your Raisin'*, 254 (Cash quote), 256–57 (Malone quotes); Doggett, *Are You Ready for the Country*, 481 (Yoakam quote); Ching, *"Wrong's What I Do Best,"* 16–17 (Anderson).

87. Aaron A. Fox, *Real Country: Music and Language in Working-Class Culture* (Durham, NC: Duke University Press, 2004), ix–x, 1–2, 20–50, 145–46 (quotes), 317–21.

88. Greenberg, "Sugar Hill Records," 27; Kempton, *Boogaloo*, 358 ("underdeveloped country"), 360 ("television screen"); Luc Sante, "One Nation under a Groove," *New York Review of Books*, July 17, 2003, 23 ("whole nation"); Leonard, *Smoke and Mirrors*, 44 ("mythical America"); Tricia Rose, *Black Noise: Rap Music and Black Culture in Contemporary America* (Hanover, NH: Wesleyan University Press, 1994), 100–101, 183 ("seeing eye dogs"); Szatmary, *Time to Rock*, 336–37 (336, Blow quote).

89. Starr and Waterman, *American Popular Music*, 411–13; Greenberg, "Sugar Hill Records," 27, 29; Rose, *Black Noise*, 10 (videos).

90. Starr and Waterman, *American Popular Music*, 413–19; Kempton, *Boogaloo*, 370–71 (370, "collect their money"), 374 ("outposts"), 381. On *The Source*, see also George, *Hip Hop America*, 71.

91. Starr and Waterman, *American Popular Music*, 420–22; George, *Hip Hop America*, 42, 135–38 (135, "making a name"), 141–43. See also Cheo Hodari Coker, "N.W.A.," in Light, ed., *History of Hip Hop*, 251–53, 257–63; and Robert Marriott, "Gangsta, Gangsta: The Sad, Violent Parable of Death Row Records," in ibid., 319–25.

92. George, *Hip Hop America*, 42, 66–67; Starr and Waterman, *American Popular Music*, 414, 420; Rose, *Black Noise*, 5, 11–12; Matt Diehl, "Pop Rap," in Light, ed., *History of Hip Hop*, 124 ("Pat Boone of rap"); R. J. Smith, "Among the Mooks," *New York Times Magazine*, August 6, 2000, 39–41 (the class element; 39, Eminem lyrics). On Eminem, see also Bozza, *Whatever You Say I Am*, esp. 11–13, 19–22, 50–51, 119–21, 124, 127.

93. Rose, *Black Noise*, 6–7, 74–75 (Sadler quote), 82 (Shocklee quote), 101 ("sell it"); J. D. Considine, "The Big Willies," in Light, ed., *History of Hip Hop*, 153–55; Bill Stephney, "Money, Power, Respect: Hip Hop Economics," in ibid., 156–58; Coker, "N.W.A.," 253, 257; Nicholas Mills, *The Triumph of Meanness* (New York: Houghton Mifflin, 1997), 54 (percentage).

94. Kempton, *Boogaloo*, 365.

95. Rose, *Black Noise*, 99–100; Starr and Waterman, *American Popular Music*, 427 ("black America's CNN"); "Prophets of Rage," on Public Enemy's *It Takes a Nation of Millions to Hold Us Back* (Def Jam Records, 1988) ("ain't did before"). On criticism, see, e.g., Nathan McCall, "The Rap against Rap," *Washington Post National Weekly Edition*, November 22–28, 1993, 22–23.

96. David Mills, "The Judge vs. 2 Live Crew," *Washington Post National Weekly Edition*, June 25–July 1, 1990, 9–10; Rose, *Black Noise*, 183.

97. Edwin Diamond and Stephen Bates, *The Spot: The Rise of Political Advertising on Television* (Cambridge, MA: Harvard University Press, 1984), 35–92 (57, Eisenhower quote; 60, Stevenson quote); Stark, *Glued to the Set*, 222–31 (222, quote); Cannon, *President Reagan; Inside TV Land: Primetime Politics* (TV Land documentary, 2004) (Dean quote); Ryan J. Barilleaux and Mark J. Rozell, *Power and Prudence: The Presidency of George H. W. Bush* (College Station: Texas A&M University Press, 2004), 67 ("a ten speech"); Edwin Diamond and Robert A. Silverman, *White House to Your House: Media and Politics in Virtual America* (Cambridge, MA: MIT Press, 1995), 2–3 ("weird"); Dan Balz and Ronald Brownstein, *Storming the Gates: Protest Politics and the Republican Revival* (Boston: Little, Brown, 1996), 172 (Fitzwater quote).

98. Diamond and Silverman, *White House to Your House*, 2–12 (5, "liberated me"). On Clinton's use of popular culture and Elvis, see Marcus, *Happy Days and Wonder Years*, 155–68 (167, "always comparing me"), 173.

99. Diamond and Silverman, *White House to Your House*, 153–57 (Gingrich); David Bowman, "Forever Decadent Lou Reed," *New York Times Magazine*, April 26, 1998, 40 (Havel quote); Sean Wilentz, "Seeing Red," *New York Times Book Review*, 21 January 1996, sec. 7, p. 15.

100. Mark I. Pinsky, "Touched by the Simpsons," *Spokane, WA, Spokesman-Review*, August 21, 1999, E3 (Bush quote); Brooks and Marsh, *Complete Directory*, 694 (Quayle quote); Mills, *Triumph of Meanness*, 49 (Dole quote). Also *Inside TV Land: Primetime Politics* (n. 97 above).

101. "Dirty Words: America's Foul-Mouthed Culture" (cover story), *Time*, May 7, 1990, 92–100; Mills, *Triumph of Meanness*, 18 (database search), 26–29 (LeFever ad); Joe Klein, "The Town That Ate Itself," *New Yorker*, November 23, 1998, 79 (Weber quote); Trudy Rubin, "We Need to Blame Someone," *Spokane, WA, Spokesman-Review*, December 31, 1994, B4; *New Yorker*, May 22, 1995, 27 (Kristol quote).

102. Mills, *Triumph of Meanness*, 135; Diamond and Silverman, *White House to Your House*, 117–21, 157–58 (quotes).

103. Mills, *Triumph of Meanness*, 16–17 (17, "better have a bodyguard"), 20–21 (Buchanan quote); Philip Weiss, "Clinton Crazy," *New York Times Magazine*, February 23, 1997, 35ff.

104. Twitchell, *Carnival Culture*, 239–42 (241, Downey quotes); Troy, *Morning in America*, 278–80.

105. Watson, *Defining Visions*, 198 ("stoop the lowest"); Joshua Gamson, *Freaks Talk Back: Tabloid Talk Shows and Sexual Nonconformity* (Chicago: University of Chicago Press, 1998), 2 (Raphael quote), 37, 40, 54–55 (Rivera quote), 60, 98, 106 (Springer quote); "Springer's Harvest," *New York Times*, April 27, 1998, C8.

106. Gamson, *Freaks Talk Back*, 9 (Bennett quote, Lieberman quote); Ed Bark, "Demean Streaks," *Spokane, WA, Spokesman-Review*, August 19, 1996, B5.

107. *In Your Face, America* (CBS special, April 2, 1998).

108. Ibid. (Raphael); Gamson, *Freaks Talk Back*, 13–16 (13, Springer quote), 37; Richard Corliss, "X-Rated," *Time*, May 7, 1990, 98 (Barker quote); John Tierney, "The Upside of Gossip," *New York Times Magazine*, January 25, 1998, 15 (Merry quote); "Springer's Harvest" (n. 105 above).

109. Gamson, *Freaks Talk Back*, 15; Corliss, "X-Rated" (n. 108 above), 94.

110. Szatmary, *Time to Rock*, 337 (Ice-T quote); Gamson, *Freaks Talk Back*, 14–15 (Willis quote); Glynn, *Tabloid Culture*, 1, 8–10, 45, 64–65, 122, 144, 155–59, 184–85 (184, Rapping quote), 201 ("challenge, interrogation"); Corliss, "X-Rated" (n. 108 above), 94 (N.W.A.).

111. Mills, *Triumph of Meanness*, 54 (hooks quote).

112. Jeff Greenfield on *World News Tonight* (ABC), January 28, 1994; also Scott Simon's comments on PBS, February 12, 1994, and Miles Corwin's in the *Spokane, WA, Spokesman-Review*, February 20, 1994; Mills, *Triumph of Meanness*, 51 (Bobbitt buttons); Glynn, *Tabloid Culture*, 228 (Lungren quote). Elayne Rapping, however, argues that the Menendez trial ultimately reinforced a larger conservative trend more concerned with the fate of the victims than with why crimes have occurred. Television assisted this ideological turn and, in the process, accelerated a related tendency to see the legal system as the "solution" to a host of social and political issues (Rapping, *Law and Justice*, esp. 8–11, 34–35).

113. Kathy O'Malley, "Confessions Gain Ratings for TV Hosts," *Spokane, WA, Spokesman-Review*, February 7, 1995, D1 ("open up"), D8 ("naked two hours"); Wynter, *American Skin*, 181 (Johnson quote); Diane Holloway, "Voyeur TV," *Spokane, WA, Spokesman-Review*, July 16, 2000, F10 ("peeping Toms"); Haynes Johnson, *The Best of Times: America in the Clinton Years* (New York: Harcourt, 2001), 204–5; "Odd Move for Someone Who Wants More Privacy," *Spokane, WA, Spokesman-Review*, January 30, 2001, D2.

114. Mills, *Triumph of Meanness*, 6, 19–20; Bark, "Demean Streaks" (n. 106 above) (Bruce quote).

115. Rene Rodriquez, "Scream of the Crop," *Spokane, WA, Spokesman-Review,* November 12, 1997, D7 ("general coarsening"); "Culture of the Gothic," *Nightline* (ABC), December 10, 1997 (King); Mark Edmundson, *Nightmare on Main Street: Angels, Sadomasochism, and the Culture of Gothic* (Cambridge, MA: Harvard University Press, 1997), xi–xiv, 20–21, 65–67.

116. Edmundson, *Nightmare on Main Street,* 3–4, 59 ("be afraid"); Rodriquez, "Scream of the Crop" (n. 115 above), D3 ("frightening realities" [quoting David Skal]); Janet Maslin, "Horror Puts on Its Worst Face: The Human One," *New York Times,* December 2, 1990, 19; Haltunnen, *Murder Most Foul,* 246–47 (*Seven*); Peter Plagens, "Violence in Our Culture," *Newsweek,* April 1, 1991, 46–52; Terrence Rafferty, "See No Evil," *GQ,* October 1999, 125–30.

117. Skal, *Monster Show,* 271, 354–71 (354, Barker quote; 357, "unhappy and different"), 375 ("shopping cart"), 379 (trapped); Twitchell, *Preposterous Violence,* 104–5 (105, "Big Mac and fries," "7-11"); Twitchell, *Carnival Culture,* 105–6 ("Green Giant").

118. Twitchell, *Carnival Culture,* 73–105, 116–17 (Howard quote), 124; Andre Schiffrin, "The Corporatization of Publishing," *The Nation,* June 3, 1996, 29–32.

119. MacCambridge, *America's Game,* 394 (Pepsi), 430 (Wolf quote); Jay, *More Than Just a Game,* 192–94 (Rawlings), 200–204; Dunne, "Birth of a Salesman" (n. 67, chap. 8 above), 12 (Jordan).

120. MacCambridge, *America's Game,* 428–29 (Super Bowl).

121. Jay, *More Than Just a Game,* 182, 205; Louis M. Kyriakoudes and Peter A. Coclanis, "'The Tennessee Test of Manhood': Professional Wrestling and Southern Cultural Stereotypes," in Miller, ed., *Sporting World,* 281–82 (statistics); *The Unreal Story of Professional Wrestling* (Chris Mortensen, 1999) (McMahon quote).

122. Jay, *More Than Just a Game,* 182, 205–6; Wolf, *Entertainment Economy,* 221–23.

123. Jay, *More Than Just a Game,* 201–2; Dunne, "Birth of a Salesman" (n. 67, chap. 8 above), 12 ("mud wrestling"); Wynter, *American Skin,* 98–99 ("short pants").

124. Jay, *More Than Just a Game,* 189, 191 (Joyce quote); Watterson, *College Football,* 332–52 (on "the CFA revolt").

125. Jay, *More Than Just a Game,* 184–87.

126. Ibid., 188.

127. Ibid., 189–94; Twitchell, *Carnival Culture,* 7 (Harlequin, *Geraldo*); LaFeber, *New Global Capitalism,* 54–67 (Nike).

128. Jay, *More Than Just a Game,* 189–90, 194–200 (198, Curry quote), 208–13 (209, *Times* quote); Watterson, *College Football,* 353–78; MacCambridge, *America's Game,* 343–55, 390 (Cleaver quote); Faludi, *Stiffed,* 155 ("best friend"). See also Davies, *America's Obsession,* 137–55 (sports as a business).

129. MacCambridge, *America's Game,* 355 (Rozelle quote); Jay, *More Than Just a Game,* 148 (*Sports Illustrated* quote), 152, 156–57, 218; Rossi, *National Game,* 203–7.

130. MacCambridge, *America's Game,* 409–11 (Warner quote); Larry Platt, *New Jack Jocks: Rebels, Race, and the American Athlete* (Philadelphia: Temple University Press, 2002), 2–9 (8, "multicultural gathering"; 9, Barkley quote), 35 ("macho Neanderthal"), 175 ("chances are").

131. Platt, *New Jack Jocks,* 11 (Seinfeld joke); Dustin Hoffman on *Good Morning, America* (ABC), October 20, 2004.

132. Ted Johnson, "All Grown Up with Somewhere to Go," *TV Guide,* October 23, 1999, 23–27; Susan Douglas, "Signs of Intelligent Life on TV," *Ms.,* May/June 1995, 78–81; Rapping, *Law and Justice,* 13–18, 23–47, 80–99. As Rapping notes, movie treatments of prison life, particularly *Murder in the First* (Mark Rocco, 1995) and *The Shawshank Redemption* (Frank Darabont, 1994), featured heroic convicts, unlike those in *Oz.*

133. O'Brien, "Sein of the Times" (n. 1 above), 12–14; Immerso, *Coney Island,* 177–87; Wolf, *Entertainment Economy,* 3 (Las Vegas).

134. Neil Postman, *Amusing Ourselves to Death: Public Discourse in the Age of Show Business* (New York: Penguin, 1985), 3–4; Marc Cooper, "America's Last Honest Place," *The Nation,* May 24, 2004, 28–30; Adam Goldman, "Vegas Clearly the Place to Be," *Spo-*

kane, WA, Spokesman-Review, December 26, 2004, H6; Christina Almeida, "Las Vegas: More Than Gambling," *Spokane, WA, Spokesman-Review,* December 28, 2004, A7; Michael Connolly, *The Narrows* (London: Orion, 2004), 108–9 ("adult playground").

135. *CBS Sunday Morning,* July 17, 2005. On the culture's enduring fascination with luck, see T. J. Jackson Lears, *Something for Nothing: Luck in America* (New York: Penguin, 2003).

136. On Viacom's, Time Warner's, and other conglomerate holdings, see "The Media Nation" foldout in *The Nation,* June 8, 1998, 20–28; Leonard, *Smoke and Mirrors,* 287–89; Sharon Walsh, "The Future Is Here," *Washington Post National Weekly Edition,* March 20, 2000, 19 ("largest media deal"); Paul Farhi, "In Television, Big Is Now Clearly Better," *Washington Post National Weekly Edition,* September 20, 1999, 21; Zurawik, "Profound Changes" (n. 60 above), D9; Susan Faludi, "The Malling of the Media," *The Nation,* May 27, 1996, 10; "The National Entertainment State," *The Nation,* June 3, 1996, 23–26; Gene Lyons, "The Media Is the Message," *Harper's,* October 2003, 79 (AOL/Warner holdings); and Miller, "Who Controls the Music" (n. 46, chap. 11 above), 11–12, and the accompanying "The Media Nation: Music" foldout, 27–30.

137. Jeff Sharlet, "Big World: How Clear Channel Programs America," *Harper's,* December 2003, 37–45 (38–39, "1,000 mergers," "evil empire," "more live-music venues"); Damien Cave, "Clear Channel: Inside Music's Superpower," *Rolling Stone,* September 2, 2004, 53–54 (53, Klein quote).

EPILOGUE: POP CULTURE IN A POST-9/11 WORLD

1. Thomas Frank, "Down and Out in the Red Zone," *The Baffler,* no. 15 (2002): 3 (quote), 11.

2. Eric Alterman, "Money for Nothing," *The Nation,* December 13, 2004, 13 (quotes).

3. Lynn Spigel, "Entertainment Wars: Television Culture after 9/11," *American Quarterly* 56 (June 2004): 250–51 (*Tribute*); Mark Binelli, "The Battle Hymn of Toby Keith," *Rolling Stone,* January 22, 2004, 43; Jon Pareles, "Amid Grammy Award Glee, September 11 Somberness Remains," *New York Times,* February 24, 2003, B1.

4. Ellen Goodman, "Game Shows Torture to Play, Watch," *Spokane, WA, Spokesman-Review,* January 27, 2002, B6 (Eisner quote, Maher quote, "kinder, gentler"); "Finding Our New Voice," *Newsweek,* October 1, 2001, 6 ("bungee jumping"); James Poniewozik, "The Culture Comes Home," *Time,* November 19, 2001, 126 ("great before"); *After 9/11: Pop Goes On* (MTV anniversary special, September 11, 2002); Spigel, "Entertainment Wars," 235, 241.

5. Sharon Waxman, "The Great Escape," *Washington Post Weekly Edition,* January 14–20, 2002, 21; Bernard Weinraub, "After the Attacks: Hollywood Film Industry for Now Scratches Violence for Family Fare and Patriotism," *New York Times,* September 16, 2001, sec. 1, p. 7 ("dark, gritty drama," "blue skies").

6. Noy Thrupkaew, "Paved with Good Intentions," *American Prospect,* April 2003, 45 (Weinstein quote); Weinraub, "After the Attacks" (n. 5 above), 7 ("just some movies," Grazer quote); Jonathan Markovitz, "Reel Terror Post 9/11," in *Film and Television after 9/11,* ed. Wheeler W. Dixon (Carbondale: Southern Illinois University Press, 2004), 202; Spigel, "Entertainment Wars," 235–36, 242–45.

7. Poniewozik, "The Culture Comes Home" (n. 4 above), 126; Joshua Gamson, "Double Agents," *American Prospect,* December 3, 2001, 38–39; Tom Nawrocki and Matt Weatherford, "Fall Preview Television," *Rolling Stone,* October 11, 2001, 101; Rapping, *Law and Justice,* 174 ("cultural comfort food," statistics).

8. Poniewozik, "The Culture Comes Home" (n. 4 above); "Great Unknown," *Spokane, WA, Spokesman Review,* September 8, 2002, F3, F6; Rapping, *Law and Justice,* 174–75.

9. "Great Unknown" (n. 8 above), F6 (Poland quote); Wheeler W. Dixon, "Introduction: Something Lost—Film after 9/11," in Dixon, ed., *Film and Television after 9/11,* 3, 16; *After 9/11* (n. 4 above).

10. Peter Travers, "Black Hawk Down," *Rolling Stone,* January 31, 2002, 57; Rebecca

Bell-Metereau, "The How-To Manual, the Prequel, and the Sequel in Post-9/11 Cinema," in Dixon, ed., *Film and Television after 9/11,* 145 (*Sum of All Fears* poster); Markovitz, "Reel Terror Post 9/11," 211 (Rumsfeld quote, Wolfowitz quote); Rick Lyman, "Moviegoers Are Flocking to Forget Their Troubles," *New York Times,* June 21, 2002, business section, 1, 6; Waxman, "The Great Escape" (n. 5 above).

11. Leslie Kelly, "Survivor Mania," *Spokane, WA, Spokesman-Review,* July 18, 2000, D1, D7 ("back-stabbing"); David Bauder, "Fox Promise to Drop Reality Shows Sounds Familiar," *Spokane, WA, Spokesman-Review,* February 26, 2000, A5 ("'don't embarrass us'"); Marc and Thompson, *Television in the Antenna Age,* 121, 126–28. On the first TV reality shows, such as *Candid Camera,* see Anna McCarthy, "'Stanley Milgram, Allen Funt, and Me': Postwar Social Science and the 'First Wave' of Reality TV," in *Reality TV: Remaking Television Culture,* ed. Susan Murray and Laurie Ouellette (New York: New York University Press, 2004), 19–39. Chad Raphael ("The Political Economic Origins of Reali-TV," in ibid., 119–36) discusses the industry uses of reality TV during the 1980s and 1990s.

12. Anna Quindlen, "Are You Hot? Is It Nuclear?" *Newsweek,* February 24, 2003, 76; John Curran, "Homeless," *Spokane, WA, Spokesman-Review,* April 27, 2005, D9 ("cheering for the lion"); Holloway, "Voyeur TV" (n. 113, chap. 12 above), F10 (Peel quote). On reality TV, see the essays in Murray and Ouellette, eds., *Reality TV.* See also the useful analysis of *Survivor* in Mary Beth Haralovich and Michael W. Trosset, "'Expect the Unexpected': Narrative Pleasure and Uncertainty due to Chance in *Survivor,*" in ibid., 75–96.

13. "Great Unknown" (n. 8 above), F6 (Tellum quote, Thompson quote; Dixon, "Introduction," 3, 16, 24; *After 9/11* (n. 4 above).

14. Richard C. Crepeau, "Sport and Society," message posted to H-Arete, April 10, 2003, archived at http://www.h-net.org/~arete (printout in author's possession); Sean Loughlin, "House Cafeterias Change Names for 'French' Fries and 'French' Toast," *CNN.com/Inside Politics,* March 12, 2003. http://www.cnn.com/2003/ALLPOLITICS/03/11/sprj.irq.fries.

15. Alisa Solomon, "Art Makes a Difference," *The Nation,* November 8, 2004, 28 ("Dixie Chicked").

16. Andrew Gumbel, "Hollywood Revives McCarthyist Climate by Silencing and Sacking War Critics," *Independent/UK,* April 21, 2003 (Gernon quote, "fall foul"); Stephen A. Smith, "Speaking Out Not Popular Thing to Do," *Spokane, WA, Spokesman-Review,* April 15, 2003, C1; Crepeau, "Sport and Society" (n. 14 above) (Petroskey quotes); "Actor Glover Rips Boycott," *Spokane, WA, Spokesman-Review,* May 19, 2003, A2 (Glover quote).

17. Elysa Gardner, "Artists Risk Rocking the Boat When Rocking the Vote," *USA Today,* August 5, 2004, D2.

18. Ibid., D2; Gumbel, "Hollywood Revives McCarthyist Climate" (n. 16 above).

19. John Gerome, "Patriotic Tunes," *Spokane, WA, Spokesman-Review,* July 4, 2004, F4 (Hart quotes); "New Country Song Makes Statement on War," *Spokane, WA, Spokesman-Review,* March 2, 2003, F4 (Worley lyrics).

20. Gardner, "Artists Risk Rocking the Boat" (n. 17 above), D2 (Goldberg quote).

21. David Gates, "Agent Provocateur," *Newsweek,* June 28, 2004, 28–29 (28, "nonpartisan"); Johnnie L. Roberts, "The Lions' Reign," *Newsweek,* July 12, 2004, 42–43; Paul Foy, "Michael Moore Stirs Opponents in Utah," *Spokane, WA, Spokesman-Review,* October 19, 2004, C3 ("who's in charge").

22. Larry McShane, "Against Bush," *Spokane, WA, Spokesman-Review,* August 5, 2004, D7 ("progressive ideals"); Colleen McCain Nelson, "Rockers Attempt to Rock the Vote," *Spokane, WA, Spokesman-Review,* October 3, 2004, A7; David Fricke, "Taking It to the Streets," *Rolling Stone,* September 2, 2004, 37–48; David Fricke, "Showdown in D.C.," *Rolling Stone,* November 11, 2004, 19–22 (19, "throw 'em open").

23. "Rock for Bush," *Rolling Stone,* September 2, 2004, 48; Nelson, "Rockers Attempt to Rock the Vote" (n. 22 above), A7 (Cooper quote); McShane, "Against Bush" (n. 22 above), D7 (Vedder quote).

24. Nelson, "Rockers Attempt to Rock the Vote" (n. 22 above), A7.

25. Thomas Frank, *What's the Matter with Kansas? How Conservatives Won the Heart of America* (New York: Metropolitan, 2004), 115–17 (Liddy quotes, Coulter quote).

26. Frank (ibid., 13–27 [20–21, Podhoretz quote]) critiques the red/blue state concept, as does Mark Danner ("How Bush Really Won," *New York Review of Books,* January 13, 2005, 48–53). Ron Suskind, "Faith, Certainty, and the Presidency of George W. Bush," *New York Times Magazine,* October 17, 2004, 64 (McKinnon quote).

27. Sean Wilentz, "It Wasn't Morality That Divided Bush and Kerry Voters—It Was . . . ," http://hnn.us/articles/8548.html. According to John Nichols, "Urban Archipelago: Progressive Cities in a Conservative Sea," *The Nation,* June 20, 2005, 13–14: "Every American city with a population of more than 500,000 voted for John Kerry in 2004, as did about half the cities with populations between 50,000 and 500,000." For a critique of the red state/blue state map as a way of understanding the election, see Adolph A. Reed Jr., "The 2004 Election in Perspective: The Myth of 'Cultural Divide' and the Triumph of Neoliberal Ideology," *American Quarterly* 57 (March 2005): 1–15.

28. See esp. Ken Auletta, "Vox Fox," *New Yorker,* May 26, 2003, 58–73 (63, "core"; 64, "knuckleheads," "weasels"); Marshall Sella, "The Red-State Network," *New York Times Magazine,* June 24, 2001, 26ff. (29, "Socialist thinking"; 30, "thinking they're smarter," "shinier poles"). Brian Anderson, "We're Not Losing the Culture Wars Anymore," *City Journal,* autumn 2003, http://www.city-journal.org/html/13_4_were_not_losing.html.

29. Kathleen Parker, "Color the Democrats Totally Clueless," *Spokane, WA, Spokesman-Review,* November 6, 2004, B4; Ellen Gray, "Election Results Could Affect Small-Screen Landscape," *Spokane, WA, Spokesman-Review,* November 6, 2004, E7 ("out of touch"); Khristine Bershers, "Moral of Election? The Left Doesn't Get It," *Spokane, WA, Spokesman-Review,* November 11, 2004, B7; Dave Oliveria, "We Red Staters Can Get Offended, Too," *Spokane, WA, Spokesman-Review,* December 12, 2004, B6 ("Planet Hollyweird"). Danner ("How Bush Really Won" [n. 26 above], 49) cautions against reading too much into the "moral values" poll and argues that "the 2004 election turned on a fulcrum of fear" of terrorism and threats to national security. Still, as Thomas Frank ("What's the Matter with Liberals?" *New York Review of Books,* May 12, 2005, 46–51, 47) points out, fear and the national security issue meshed easily with the moral values issue: "shooting war and cultural war" merged.

30. Damien Cave, "Janet's Fallout," *Rolling Stone,* March 4, 2004, 13–14 ("the new culture war"); Damien Cave, "The Jackson Blame Game," *Rolling Stone,* March 4, 2004, 14; "Time to Fight," *Rolling Stone,* April 29, 2004, 22 (Redstone quote, "chill is already here").

31. Jon Carroll, *San Francisco Chronicle,* November 19, 2004 ("pre-Kinsey world"); "Stupid Is as Stupid Does," *Spokane, WA, Spokesman-Review,* November 23, 2004, C2 (Lincicome quote).

32. Miles, "Nascar Nation" (n. 81, chap. 12 above), 1, 10–11.

33. *World News Tonight* (ABC), November 11, 2004 (quote); Jonathan Alter, "A Shabby Fiesta of Hypocrisy," *Newsweek,* November 29, 2004, 56.

34. Marc and Thompson, *Television in the Antenna Age,* 111 ("in control"). On CBN, see, e.g., Brooks and Marsh, *Complete Directory,* 906; Dana Milbank, "Religion Infuses Politics, Starting from the Grass Roots," *Spokane, WA, Spokesman-Review,* November 7, 2004, A1, A11 ("more than 26 million"); and Suskind, "Presidency of George W. Bush" (n. 26 above), 51 (poll). On radio, see Douglas C. Abrams, *Selling the Old-Time Religion: American Fundamentalists and Mass Culture, 1920–1940* (Athens: University of Georgia Press, 2001); and Tona J. Hangen, *Redeeming the Dial: Radio, Religion, and Popular Culture in America* (Chapel Hill: University of North Carolina Press, 2002).

35. Melani McAlister, "An Empire of Their Own," *The Nation,* September 22, 2003, 31 ("parallel"); Walter Kirn, "God's Country," *New York Times Magazine,* May 2, 2004, 17–18; Rachel Donadio, "Faith-Based Publishing," *New York Times Book Review,* November 28, 2004, 35 ("under the radar").

36. Mark I. Pinsky, "Thumbs Up from God," *Spokane, WA, Spokesman-Review,* May 18, 2002, E3 ("common language"); Steven Rea, "Spiritual Screenings," *Spokane, WA, Spokesman-Review,* January 11, 2003, E3 (Lalonde quote); also Danny M. Boyd, "Faith Flicks," *Spokane, WA, Spokesman-Review,* February 3, 2001, E3.

37. Advertisement for "Festival 2002," *Spokane, WA, Spokesman-Review,* August 18,

2002, A8 (Bibleman); McAlister, "Empire of Their Own" (n. 35 above), 31; Rea, "Spiritual Screenings" (n. 36 above) (computer animations); Adrian Campo-Flores, "'Get Your Praise On,'" *Newsweek,* April 19, 2004, 56–57 ("live at night"); David Briggs, "Pulpit Fiction Unveiled," *Spokane, WA, Spokesman-Review,* October 12, 1997, A1 (Harlequin); Rachel Zoll, "Fashion Magazine Adds Touch of Faith," *Spokane, WA, Spokesman-Review,* September 14, 2004, 14; Richard C. Crepeau, "Sport and Society," message posted to H-Arete, August 1, 2001, archived at http://www.h-net.org/~arete (printout in author's possession); Jeff Baenen, "Comic Book Faith," *Spokane, WA, Spokesman-Review,* June 4, 2005, E3; Adam Green, "Standup for the Lord," *New Yorker,* August 9, 16, 2004, 46–52 (Stine; 47, "a civil war"). See also Eileen Luhr, "Metal Missionaries to the Nation: Christian Heavy Metal Music, 'Family Values,' and Youth Culture, 1984–1994," *American Quarterly* 57 (March 2005): 103–28.

38. George Monbiot, "America Is a Religion," *Guardian Weekly,* August 7–13, 2003, 13 ("America the divine"); Joan Didion, "Mr. Bush and the Divine," *New York Review of Books,* November 6, 2003, 82–86 (83, "God wants me"); Suskind, "Presidency of George W. Bush" (n. 26 above), 46 (Bartlett quote), 51 ("very first time"), 64 (McKinnon); Milbank, "Religion Infuses Politics" (n. 34 above), A11 ("orchestrated," Prager quote); Alan Cooperman, "A Faith-Based President," *Washington Post National Weekly Edition,* September 20–26, 2004, 6–7.

39. David Gates, "The Pop Prophets," *Newsweek,* May 24, 2004, 45–47 (47, "terror and tumult"); McAlister, "Empire of Their Own" (n. 35 above), 31–34 (33, "how it ends"). See also Linton Weeks, "By the Book," *Spokane, WA, Spokesman-Review,* July 27, 2002, E3; Gershom Gorenberg, "Intolerance: The Bestseller," *American Prospect,* September 23, 2002, 44–47; Gene Lyons, "The Apocalypse Will Be Televised," *Harper's,* November 2004, 85–90; Robert Dreyfuss, "Reverend Doomsday," *Rolling Stone,* February 19, 2004, 46–50; and Didion, "Mr. Bush and the Divine" (n. 38 above), 81–82.

40. David Germain, "'Passion' Easily Takes Weekend Spot," *Spokane, WA, Spokesman-Review,* March 2, 2004, D7; David Germain, "'Passion' Again the No. 1 Movie," *Spokane, WA, Spokesman-Review,* April 13, 2004, D7 (Dergarabedian quotes); Geneive Abdo and Lou Carlozo, "No to 'Passion,'" *Spokane, WA, Spokesman-Review,* May 1, 2004, E3; David Briggs, "New Jesus Film Portrays Hope amid Despair," *Spokane, WA, Spokesman-Review,* August 7, 2004, E3 (Jakes quote); David Denby, "The Jesus War," *New Yorker,* September 15, 2003, 69 (Holy Ghost as director).

41. Lyons, "The Apocalypse Will Be Televised" (n. 39 above), 90 ("seemed to explode"); David Denby, "Nailed," *New Yorker,* March 1, 2004, 86 ("one of the cruelest"); David Ansen, "So What's the Good News?" *Newsweek,* March 1, 2004, 60 ("de Sade"); Denby, "The Jesus War" (n. 40 above), 58–71 (69, "anti-Christian publication"); Gates, "Pop Prophets" (n. 39 above), 48 ("intellectuals").

42. David Kirkpatrick, "Why Jesus Is Becoming More Macho," *New York Times,* April 4, 2004 (Pagels quote); Gates, "Pop Prophets" (n. 39 above), 46 (*Desecration*); Robert Scheer, "The Invisible Hand Holds the Remote," *Los Angeles Times,* November 30, 2004, B13; Celeste Kennel-Shank, "Kid's Video on Tolerance Attacked," *Spokane, WA, Spokesman-Review,* January 21, 2005, A3; Sean Kirst, "It's a Talking Sponge, for Crying Out Loud," *Spokane, WA, Spokesman-Review,* January 24, 2005, A11 ("pro-homosexual video"); Richard Goldstein, "Cartoon Wars," *The Nation,* February 21, 2005, 6–8.

43. See, e.g., Alter, "Shabby Fiesta" (n. 33 above), 56. Gary Strauss, "Talk of Religion No Longer Taboo in Hollywood," *Spokane, WA, Spokesman-Review,* July 9, 2005, E3 ("religion of Hollywood").

44. Scheer, "Invisible Hand" (n. 42 above), B13; Frank, *What's the Matter with Kansas?* 133–34; Donadio, "Faith-Based Publishing" (n. 35 above), 35 (best sellers); "The Business of Kink," an episode of *Pornucopia: Going Down in the Valley* (HBO documentary, 2004) (Goldstein quote).

45. Rich, "Naked Capitalists" (n. 66, chap. 12 above), 51–56 (52, Asher quote; 56, Hart quote), 80–82 (80, Raven quote), 92.

46. Marc Peyser and David J. Jefferson, "Sex and the Suburbs," *Newsweek,* November 29, 2004, 49–54; Richard Goldstein, "Red Sluts, Blue Sluts," *The Nation,* January 3, 2005,

20 ("babes," "America the Wholesome"); Nancy Franklin, "Women Gone Wild," *New Yorker,* January 17, 2005, 92–93.

47. McAlister, "Empire of Their Own" (n. 35 above), 35–36; *People's Choice Awards Show* (CBS), January 9, 2005.

48. Leonard Pitts Jr., "We Are Abscessed with Pop Culture," *Spokane, WA, Spokesman-Review,* August 12, 2000, B6.

49. Ian Buruma, "The Election and America's Future," *New York Review of Books,* November 4, 2004, 8; Gitlin, *Media Unlimited,* 23 ("the great elsewhere").

50. Gitlin, *Media Unlimited,* 172 (Koppel quote), 178 ("franca"); Paul Farhi and Megan Rosenfeld, "Exporting America," *Washington Post National Weekly Edition,* November 30, 1998, 6–7 ("global sensibility").

51. Farhi and Rosenfeld, "Exporting America" (n. 50 above); John Lancaster, "Embracing the Great Satan's Culture," *Washington Post National Weekly Edition,* December 14, 1998, 8–9 ("make dreams").

52. See, e.g., the hard-hitting critique in Postman's classic *Amusing Ourselves to Death;* also Gitlin, *Media Unlimited,* 164–74.

53. For a defense of, e.g., TV's capacity to surprise and exhibit a social conscience as well as a discussion of its ambiguous relation with business, see Leonard, *Smoke and Mirrors,* 6–14, 102, 105–9, 289–90.

54. Pico Iyer, "The End of Happy Endings?" *New York Times Magazine,* February 8, 2004, 20–22; Anthony Breznican, "Heroes of New Comic Book Series Not So Super," *Spokane, WA, Spokesman-Review,* September 12, 2004, F3, F7 (DiDio quote). Steven Johnson (*Everything Bad Is Good for You: How Today's Popular Culture Is Actually Making Us Smarter* [New York: Riverhead, 2005]) argues that "popular culture has, on average, grown more complex and intellectually challenging over the past thirty years" (xiii). "The cultural race to the bottom is a myth. . . . All around us the world of mass entertainment grows more demanding and sophisticated, and our brains happily gravitate to that newfound complexity" (198–99).

55. Bill Werde, "Rock Radio No Longer Rolling," *Rolling Stone,* March 24, 2005, 11–12; Rafer Guzman, "Hip-Hop Carries Standard More Than Rock," *Spokane, WA, Spokesman-Review,* July 3, 2005, D4; "Iacocca's Top Car Guy, but Lacks Street Cred," *Spokane, WA, Spokesman-Review,* July 8, 2005, A15; Daisy Nguyen, "Film 'Rize' Documents Power of Krumping," *Spokane, WA, Spokesman-Review,* July 5, 2005, B7; Guy Trebay, "The Clowning, Rump-Shaking, Wilding-Out Battle Dancers of South Central L.A.," *New York Times Magazine,* June 19, 2005, 28–33; "McDonald's Wants Fashionable New Uniforms," *Spokane, WA, Spokesman-Review,* July 6, 2005, A9.

56. Gary Gentile, "Where's the Magic?" *Spokane, WA, Spokesman-Review,* July 15, 2005, A12, A15; Ron Harris, "Sex in Video Game Has Panel on Hot Seat," *Spokane, WA, Spokesman-Review,* July 19, 2005, A1, A4. For a discussion of the active participation that video games require, see Johnson, *Everything Bad,* 41–60, 152–54. And, for a brief sketch of video games' move from arcades to the parlor, see Cross, *The Cute and the Cool,* 159–61.

57. Curran, "Homeless" (n. 12 above), D9 (Miss America).

58. Gitlin, *Media Unlimited,* 198 ("dreams"). Crucial here is "the fun of it, the entry into a fantastic world elsewhere" (Lears, "Making Fun of Popular Culture," 1426).

BIBLIOGRAPHY

SCHOLARLY ARTICLES

Adams, David Wallace. "More Than a Game: The Carlisle Indians Take to the Gridiron, 1892–1917." *Western Historical Quarterly* 32 (spring 2001): 25–53.

Albanese, Catherine L. "Savage, Sinner, and Saved: Davy Crockett, Camp Meetings, and the Wild Frontier." *American Quarterly* 33 (winter 1981): 482–501.

Allen, Frederick E. "When Sex Drives Technological Innovation." *American Heritage* 51 (September 2000): 19–20.

Allen, Michael. "'I Just Want to Be a Cosmic Cowboy': Hippies, Cowboy Code, and the Culture of a Counterculture." *Western Historical Quarterly* 36 (autumn 2005): 275–99.

Bailey, Beth, and David Farber. Introduction to *America in the Seventies*, ed. Beth Bailey and David Farber, 1–8. Lawrence: University Press of Kansas, 2004.

Baughman, James L. "Who Read *Life*? The Circulation of America's Favorite Magazine." In *Looking at* Life *Magazine*, ed. Erika Doss, 41–51. Washington, DC: Smithsonian Institution Press, 2001.

Bell-Metereau, Rebecca. "The How-To Manual, the Prequel, and the Sequel in Post-9/11 Cinema." In *Film and Television after 9/11*, ed. Wheeler W. Dixon, 142–62. Carbondale: Southern Illinois University Press, 2004.

Boyer, Paul. "*In His Steps*: A Reappraisal." *American Quarterly* 23 (spring 1971): 60–78.

Braunstein, Peter. "'Adults Only': The Construction of an Erotic City in New York during the 1970s." In *America in the Seventies*, ed. Beth Bailey and David Farber, 129–56. Lawrence: University Press of Kansas, 2004.

Breen, T. H. "Horses and Gentlemen: The Cultural Significance of Gambling among the Gentry of Virginia." *William and Mary Quarterly* 34 (April 1977): 243–56.

Briley, Ron. "Hollywood and the Rebel Image in the 1950s." *Social Education* 61 (October 1997): 353–58.

Browne, Nick. "Fearful A-Symmetries: Violence as History in the *Godfather* Films." In *Francis Ford Coppola's* Godfather *Trilogy*, ed. Nick Browne, 1–22. Cambridge: Cambridge University Press, 2000.

Buckley, Peter G. "The Culture of 'Leg-Work': The Transformation of Burlesque after the Civil War." In *The Mythmaking Frame of Mind: Social Imagination and American Culture*, ed. James Gilbert et al., 113–34. Belmont, CA: Wadsworth, 1993.

Bufwack, Mary A. "Girls with Guitars—and Fringe and Sequins and Rhinestones, Silk, Lace, and Leather." In *Reading Country Music: Steel Guitars, Opry Stars, and Honky-Tonk Bars*, ed. Cecelia Tichi, 153–87. Durham, NC: Duke University Press, 1998.

Bufwack, Mary, and Bob Oermann. "Women in Country Music." In *Popular Culture in America*, ed. Paul Buhle, 91–97. Minneapolis: University of Minnesota Press, 1987.

Butsch, Richard. "Bowery B'hoys and Matinee Ladies: The Re-Gendering of Nineteenth-Century Theater Audiences." *American Quarterly* 46 (September 1994): 374–405.

Chappell, David L. "Hip Like Me: Racial Cross-Dressing in Pop Music before Elvis." In *Media, Culture, and the Modern African American Freedom Struggle,* ed. Brian Ward, 104–21. Gainesville: University Press of Florida, 2001.

Coker, Cheo Hodari. "N.W.A." In *The Vibe History of Hip Hop,* ed. Alan Light, 251–53, 257–63. New York: Three Rivers, 1999.

Considine, J. D. "The Big Willies." In *The Vibe History of Hip Hop,* ed. Alan Light, 153–55, 158–63. New York: Three Rivers, 1999.

Cook, James W. "Mass Marketing and Cultural History: The Case of P. T. Barnum." *American Quarterly* 51 (March 1999): 175–86.

Cullen, Jim. "Fool's Paradise: Frank Sinatra and the American Dream." In *Popular Culture in American History,* ed. Jim Cullen, 205–28. Malden, MA: Blackwell, 2001.

Cuordileone, K. A. "'Politics in an Age of Anxiety': Cold War Political Culture and the Crisis in American Masculinity, 1949–1960." *Journal of American History* 87 (September 2000): 515–45.

D'Acci, Julie. "Nobody's Woman? *Honey West* and the New Sexuality." In *The Revolution Wasn't Televised: Sixties Television and Social Conflict,* ed. Lynn Spigel and Michael Curtin, 72–93. New York: Routledge, 1997.

Davis, Natalie Zemon. "Toward Mixtures and Margins." *American Historical Review* 97 (December 1992): 1409–16.

Davis, Susan. "'Making Night Hideous': Christmas Revelry and Public Order in Nineteenth-Century Philadelphia." *American Quarterly* 34 (summer 1982): 185–99.

Devine, Bill. "Devine's Guide to Men's Adventure Magazines." In *It's a Man's World: Men's Adventure Magazines, the Postwar Pulps,* ed. Adam Parfrey, 280–87. Los Angeles: Feral, 2003.

Diehl, Matt. "Pop Rap." In *The Vibe History of Hip Hop,* ed. Alan Light, 121–25, 128–33. New York: Three Rivers, 1999.

Dixon, Wheeler W. "Introduction: Something Lost—Film after 9/11." In *Film and Television after 9/11,* ed. Wheeler W. Dixon, 1–28. Carbondale: Southern Illinois University Press, 2004.

Dorinson, Joseph. "Frank Sinatra's House: Pride, Passion, and Politics." In *Frank Sinatra: History, Identity, and Italian American Culture,* ed. Stanislao G. Pugliese, 23–31. New York: Palgrave Macmillan, 2004.

Doss, Erika. Introduction to *Looking at* Life *Magazine,* ed. Erika Doss, 1–21. Washington, DC: Smithsonian Institution Press, 2001.

Douglas, Susan J. "Letting the Boys Be Boys: Talk Radio, Male Hysteria, and Political Discourse in the 1980s." In *Radio Reader: Essays in the Cultural History of Radio,* ed. Michele Hilmes and Jason Loviglio, 485–503. New York: Routledge, 2002.

Edsforth, Ronald. "Made in the U.S.A." In *Calvin Coolidge and the Coolidge Era: Essays on the History of the 1920s,* ed. John Earl Haynes, 244–70. Washington, DC: Library of Congress, 1998.

Engelhardt, Tom. "The Gulf War as Total Television." In *Seeing through the Media: The Persian Gulf War,* ed. Susan Jeffords and Lauren Rabinovitz, 81–95. New Brunswick, NJ: Rutgers University Press, 1994.

Erenberg, Lewis A. "From New York to Middletown: Repeal and the Legitimization of Nightlife in the Great Depression." *American Quarterly* 38 (winter 1986): 761–78.

Flint, Richard W. "The Evolution of the Circus in Nineteenth-Century America." In *American Popular Entertainment,* ed. Myron Matlaw, 187–95. Westport, CT: Greenwood, 1979.

Freidman, Bruce Jay. "Even the Rhinos Were Nymphos." In *It's a Man's World: Men's Adventure Magazines, the Postwar Pulps,* ed. Adam Parfrey, 12–19. Los Angeles: Feral, 2003.

French, Scot. "Mau-Mauing the Filmmakers: Should Black Power Take the Rap for Killing *Nat Turner,* the Movie?" In *Media, Culture, and the Modern African American Freedom Struggle,* ed. Brian Ward, 233–54. Gainesville: University Press of Florida, 2001.

Friedman, Josh A. "Throw 'Em a Few Hot Words." In *It's a Man's World: Men's Adventure Magazines, the Postwar Pulps,* ed. Adam Parfrey, 21–36. Los Angeles: Feral, 2003.

Gelber, Steven. "'Their Hands Are All Out Playing': Business and Amateur Baseball, 1845–1917." *Journal of Sport History* 11 (summer 1984): 5–27.

———. "Working at Playing: The Culture of the Workplace and the Rise of Baseball." *Journal of Sport History* 10 (summer 1983): 3–22.

Gilbert, James. "Popular Culture." *American Quarterly* 35 (spring/summer 1983): 141–54.

Goldstein, Warren. "The Base Ball Fraternity." In *Baseball History from Outside the Lines: A Reader,* ed. John E. Dreifort, 3–17. Lincoln: University of Nebraska Press, 2001.

Gorn, Elliott J. "'Gouge and Bite, Pull Hair and Scratch': The Social Significance of Fighting in the Southern Backcountry." *American Historical Review* 90 (February 1985): 18–43.

———. "'The Manassa Mauler and the Fighting Marine': An Interpretation of the Dempsey-Tunney Fights." *Journal of American Studies* 19 (April 1985): 27–47.

Greenberg, Steve. "Sugar Hill Records." In *The Vibe History of Hip Hop,* ed. Alan Light, 23–33. New York: Three Rivers, 1999.

Greene, Naomi. "Family Ceremonies; or, Opera in *The Godfather* Trilogy." In *Francis Ford Coppola's Godfather Trilogy,* ed. Nick Browne, 133–55. Cambridge: Cambridge University Press, 2000.

Greene, Victor. "Ethnic Comedy in American Culture." *American Quarterly* 51 (March 1999): 144–59.

———. "Friendly Entertainers: Dance Bandleaders and Singers in the Depression, 1929–1935." In *Prospects,* ed. Jack Salzman, 181–207. Cambridge: Cambridge University Press, 1995.

Hallin, Daniel C. "Images of the Vietnam and the Persian Gulf Wars in U.S. Television." In *Seeing through the Media: The Persian Gulf War,* ed. Susan Jeffords and Lauren Rabinovitz, 45–57. New Brunswick, NJ: Rutgers University Press, 1994.

Haralovich, Mary Beth, and Michael W. Trosset. "'Expect the Unexpected': Narrative Pleasure and Uncertainty due to Chance in *Survivor.*" In *Reality TV: Remaking Television Culture,* ed. Susan Murray and Laurie Ouellette, 75–96. New York: New York University Press, 2004.

Harris, Othello. "Muhammad Ali and the Revolt of the Black Athlete." In *Muhammad Ali: The People's Champ,* ed. Elliott J. Gorn, 54–69. Urbana: University of Illinois Press, 1995.

Hedren, Paul L. "The Contradictory Legacies of Buffalo Bill Cody's First Scalp for Custer." *Montana: The Magazine of Western History* 55 (spring 2005): 16–35.

Herman, Daniel J. "God Bless Buffalo Bill." *Reviews in American History* 29 (June 2001): 228–37.

Hietala, Thomas R. "Muhammad Ali and the Age of Bare-Knuckle Politics." In *Muhammad Ali: The People's Champ,* ed. Elliott J. Gorn, 117–53. Urbana: University of Illinois Press, 1995.

Hoberman, J. "The Fascist Guns in the West." *Radical America* 19 (1985): 53–62.

———. "The First 'Jewish' Superstar: Charlie Chaplin." In *Entertaining America: Jews, Movies, and Broadcasting,* ed. J. Hoberman and Jeffrey Shandler, 34–39. New York: Jewish Museum; Princeton, NJ: Princeton University Press, 2003.

Hoberman, J., and Jeffrey Shandler. "Hollywood's Jewish Question." In *Entertaining America: Jews, Movies, and Broadcasting,* ed. J. Hoberman and Jeffrey Shandler, 47–75. New York: Jewish Museum; Princeton, NJ: Princeton University Press, 2003.

———. Introduction to *Entertaining America: Jews, Movies, and Broadcasting,* ed. J. Hoberman and Jeffrey Shandler, 15–22. New York: Jewish Museum; Princeton, NJ: Princeton University Press, 2003.

Johnson, Victoria E. "Citizen Welk: Bubbles, Blue Hair, and Middle America." In *The Revolution Wasn't Televised: Sixties Television and Social Conflict,* ed. Lynn Spigel and Michael Curtin, 265–85. New York: Routledge, 1997.

Kallan, Richard A., and Robert D. Brooks. "The Playmate of the Month: Naked but Nice." *Journal of Popular Culture* 8 (fall 1974): 328–36.

Keetley, Dawn. "Victim and Victimizer: Female Fiends and Unease over Marriage in Antebellum Sensational Fiction." *American Quarterly* 51 (June 1999): 350–75.

Kelley, Robin D. G. "Notes on Deconstructing 'the Folk.'" *American Historical Review* 97 (December 1992): 1400–1408.

Kendrick, Michelle. "Kicking the Vietnam Syndrome: CNN's and CBS's Video Narratives of the Persian Gulf War." In *Seeing through the Media: The Persian Gulf War,* ed. Susan Jeffords and Lauren Rabinovitz, 59–76. New Brunswick, NJ: Rutgers University Press, 1994.

Kennedy, Harlan. "Amazon Grace." *Film Comment* 22 (October 1986): 9–15.

Kimmel, Michael S. "Baseball and the Reconstitution of American Masculinity, 1880–1920." In *Baseball History from Outside the Lines: A Reader,* ed. John E. Dreifort, 47–61. Lincoln: University of Nebraska Press, 2001.

Kyriakoudes, Louis M., and Peter A. Coclanis. "'The Tennessee Test of Manhood': Professional Wrestling and Southern Cultural Stereotypes." In *The Sporting World of the Modern South,* ed. Patrick B. Miller, 276–93. Urbana: University of Illinois Press, 2002.

Lears, T. J. Jackson. "Making Fun of Popular Culture." *American Historical Review* 97 (December 1992): 1417–26.

Lentrall, Bruce. "Black and White and Green All Over: Race Relations and the Integration of the Boston Celtics in the 1950s." Paper presented at the meeting of the Organization of American Historians, Los Angeles, April 27, 2001.

Levine, Lawrence W. "The Folklore of Industrial Society: Popular Culture and Its Audiences." *American Historical Review* 97 (December 1992): 1369–99.

Lewis, Barbara. "Daddy Blue: The Evolution of the Dark Dandy." In *Inside the Minstrel Mask: Readings in Nineteenth-Century Blackface Minstrelsy,* ed. Annemarie Bean, James V. Hatch, and Brooks McNamara, 257–72. Hanover, NH: Wesleyan University Press, 1996.

Lewis, Jon. "If History Has Taught Us Anything . . .: Francis Coppola, Paramount Studios, and *The Godfather, Parts I, II, and III.*" In *Francis Ford Coppola's* Godfather *Trilogy,* ed. Nick Browne, 23–56. Cambridge: Cambridge University Press, 2000.

Lhamon, W. T., Jr. "Core Is Less." *Reviews in American History* 27 (December 1999): 566–71.

Lipsitz, George. "Land of a Thousand Dances: Youth, Minorities, and the Rise of Rock and Roll." In *Recasting America: Culture and Politics in the Age of Cold War,* ed. Lary May, 267–84. Chicago: University of Chicago Press, 1989.

Luhr, Eileen. "Metal Missionaries to the Nation: Christian Heavy Metal Music, 'Family Values,' and Youth Culture, 1984–1994." *American Quarterly* 57 (March 2005): 103–28.

MacDonald, J. Fred. "The Cold War as Entertainment in Fifties Television." *Journal of Popular Film and Television* 1 (1978): 3–31.

Man, Glenn. "Ideology and Genre in the *Godfather* Films." In *Francis Ford Coppola's* Godfather *Trilogy,* ed. Nick Browne, 109–32. Cambridge: Cambridge University Press, 2000.

Marchand, Roland. "Visions of Classlessness, Quests for Dominion: American Popular Culture, 1945–1960." In *Reshaping America: Society and Institutions, 1945–1960,* ed. Robert H. Bremner and Gary Reichard, 163–90. Columbus: Ohio State University Press, 1982.

Markovitz, Jonathan. "Reel Terror Post 9/11." In *Film and Television after 9/11,* ed. Wheeler W. Dixon, 201–25. Carbondale: Southern Illinois University Press, 2004.

Marriott, Robert. "Gangsta, Gangsta: The Sad, Violent Parable of Death Row Records." In *The Vibe History of Hip Hop,* ed. Alan Light, 319–25. New York: Three Rivers, 1999.

Martin, Charles H. "Integrating New Year's Day: The Racial Politics of College Bowl Games in the American South." In *The Sporting World of the Modern South,* ed. Patrick B. Miller, 175–99. Urbana: University of Illinois Press, 2002.

May, Lary. "Making the American Consensus: The Narrative of Conversion and Subversion in World War II Films." In *The War in American Culture: Society and Consciousness during World War II,* ed. Lewis A. Erenberg and Susan E. Hirsch, 71–102. Chicago: University of Chicago Press, 1996.

McCarthy, Anna. "'Stanley Milgram, Allen Funt, and Me': Postwar Social Science and the 'First Wave' of Reality TV." In *Reality TV: Remaking Television Culture,* ed. Susan Murray and Laurie Ouellette, 19–39. New York: New York University Press, 2004.

McCarthy, Kathleen. "Nickel Vice and Virtue: Movie Censorship in Chicago, 1907–1915." *Journal of Popular Film* 5 (1976): 37–55.

McChesney, Robert. "The Battle for the Airwaves." In *Major Problems in American History, 1920–1945,* ed. Colin Gordon, 135–41. New York: Houghton Mifflin, 1999.

McConachie, Bruce A. "Pacifying American Theatrical Audiences, 1820–1900." In *For Fun and Profit: The Transformation of Leisure into Consumption,* ed. Richard Butsch, 47–70. Philadelphia: Temple University Press, 1990.

McCorkle, Susan. "The Immortality of Mae West." *American Heritage* 52 (September 2001): 48–57.

McCracken, Allison. "Scary Women and Scarred Men: *Suspense,* Gender Trouble, and Postwar Change, 1942–1950." In *Radio Reader: Essays in the Cultural History of Radio,* ed. Michele Hilmes and Jason Loviglio, 183–207. New York: Routledge, 2002.

McEwen, Joe. "Funk." In *The Rolling Stone Illustrated History of Rock and Roll: The Definitive History of the Most Important Artists and Their Music,* 3rd ed., ed. Anthony DeCurtis and James Henke with Holly George-Warren; orig. ed. Jim Miller, 521–25. New York: Random House, 1992.

McFadden, Margaret T. "'America's Boy Friend Who Can't Get a Date': Gender, Race, and the Cultural Work of the Jack Benny Program, 1932–1946." *Journal of American History* 80 (June 1993): 113–34.

Melnick, Jeff, and Rachel Rubin. "Black and White Stages." *Reviews in American History* 27 (December 1999): 572–79.

Meyer, Richard E. "The Outlaw: A Distinctive American Folktype." *Journal of Folklore Research* 17 (June–December 1980): 94–124.

Moore, Laurence. "Religion, Secularization, and the Shaping of the Culture Industry in Antebellum America." *American Quarterly* 41 (June 1989): 216–42.

Murray, Matthew. "'The Tendency to Deprave and Corrupt Morals': Regulation and Irregular Sexuality in Golden Age Radio Comedy." In *Radio Reader: Essays in the Cultural History of Radio,* ed. Michele Hilmes and Jason Loviglio, 135–56. New York: Routledge, 2002.

Mustazza, Leonard. "Frank Sinatra and Civil Rights." In *Frank Sinatra: History, Identity, and Italian American Culture,* ed. Stanislao G. Pugliese, 33–45. New York: Palgrave Macmillan, 2004.

Oriard, Michael. "Muhammad Ali: The Hero in the Age of Mass Media." In *Muhammad Ali: The People's Champ,* ed. Elliott J. Gorn, 5–23. Urbana: University of Illinois Press, 1995.

———. "Domesticated Football." Paper presented at the meeting of the Organization of American Historians, Los Angeles, April 27, 2001.

Parfrey, Adam. "From Pulp to Posterity: The Origins of Men's Adventure Magazines." In *It's a Man's World: Men's Adventure Magazines, the Postwar Pulps,* ed. Adam Parfrey, 5–10. Los Angeles: Feral, 2003.

———. "The Illustrators." In *It's a Man's World: Men's Adventure Magazines, the Postwar Pulps,* ed. Adam Parfrey, 39–40. Los Angeles: Feral, 2003.

———. "The Sadistic Burlesque." In *It's a Man's World: Men's Adventure Magazines, the Postwar Pulps,* ed. Adam Parfrey, 177–213. Los Angeles: Feral, 2003.

Pendleton, Jason. "Jim Crow Strikes Out: Interracial Baseball in Wichita, Kansas, 1920–1935." In *Baseball History from Outside the Lines: A Reader,* ed. John E. Dreifort, 142–59. Lincoln: University of Nebraska Press, 2001.

Powers, John. "Saints and Savages." *American Film* 9 (January–February 1984): 38–43.

Rader, Benjamin. "Compensatory Sport Heroes: Ruth, Grange, and Dempsey." *Journal of Popular Culture* 16 (spring 1983): 11–22.

Raphael, Chad. "The Political Economic Origins of Reali-TV." In *Reality TV: Remaking Television Culture,* ed. Susan Murray and Laurie Ouellette, 119–36. New York: New York University Press, 2004.

Reed, Adolph A., Jr. "The 2004 Election in Perspective: The Myth of 'Cultural Divide' and the Triumph of Neoliberal Ideology." *American Quarterly* 57 (March 2005): 1–15.

Riess, Steven A. "Sport and the Redefinition of American Middle-Class Masculinity." *International Journal of the History of Sport* 8 (1991): 5–27.

————. "Professional Baseball and Social Mobility." In *Baseball History from Outside the Lines: A Reader*, ed. John E. Dreifort, 34–46. Lincoln: University of Nebraska Press, 2001.

Robertson, Richard. "New Directions in Westerns of the 1960s and 70s." *Journal of the West* 22 (October 1983): 43–52.

Rosenberg, Norman I. "Here Comes the Judge! The Origins of Baseball's Commissioner System and American Legal Culture." In *Baseball History from Outside the Lines: A Reader*, ed. John E. Dreifort, 105–21. Lincoln: University of Nebraska Press, 2001.

Rothenbuhler, Eric, and Tom McCourt. "Radio Redefines Itself, 1947–1962." In *Radio Reader: Essays in the Cultural History of Radio*, ed. Michele Hilmes and Jason Loviglio, 367–87. New York: Routledge, 2002.

Rybacki, Karyn Charles, and Donald Jay Rybacki. "The King, the Young Prince, and the Last Confederate Soldier: NASCAR on the Cusp." In *The Sporting World of the Modern South*, ed. Patrick B. Miller, 294–325. Urbana: University of Illinois Press, 2002.

Saunders, David. "Norman Saunders and the Evolution of Men's Magazine Illustration." In *It's a Man's World: Men's Adventure Magazines, the Postwar Pulps*, ed. Adam Parfrey, 43–47. Los Angeles: Feral, 2003.

Saxton, Alexander. "Blackface Minstrelsy." In *Inside the Minstrel Mask: Readings in Nineteenth-Century Blackface Minstrelsy*, ed. Annemarie Bean, James V. Hatch, and Brooks McNamara, 67–85. Hanover, NH: Wesleyan University Press, 1996.

————. "Problems of Class and Race in the Origins of the Mass Circulation Press." *American Quarterly* 36 (summer 1984): 211–34.

Seretan, L. Glen. "The 'New' Working Class and Social Banditry in Depression America." *Mid-America* 63 (1980–81): 107–17.

Simons, William M. "The Athlete as Jewish Standard Bearer: Media Images of Hank Greenberg." In *Baseball History from Outside the Lines: A Reader*, ed. John E. Dreifort, 160–79. Lincoln: University of Nebraska Press, 2001.

Sklaroff, Lauren R. "Constructing G.I. Joe Louis: Cultural Solutions to the 'Negro Problem' during World War II." *Journal of American History* 89 (December 2002): 958–71.

Smith, Leverett T. "The Changing Style of Play: Cobb vs. Ruth." In *Baseball History from Outside the Lines: A Reader*, ed. John E. Dreifort, 123–41. Lincoln: University of Nebraska Press, 2001.

Smith, Terry. "*Life*-Style Modernity: Making Modern America." In *Looking at Life Magazine*, ed. Erika Doss, 25–39. Washington, DC: Smithsonian Institution Press, 2001.

Spigel, Lynn. "Entertainment Wars: Television Culture after 9/11." *American Quarterly* 56 (June 2004): 235–70.

Spigel, Lynn, and Michael Curtin. Introduction to *The Revolution Wasn't Televised: Sixties Television and Social Conflict*, ed. Lynn Spigel and Michael Curtin, 1–18. New York: Routledge, 1997.

Stephney, Bill. "Money, Power, Respect: Hip Hop Economics." In *The Vibe History of Hip Hop*, ed. Alan Light, 156–58. New York: Three Rivers, 1999.

Story, Ronald. "The Country of the Young: The Meaning of Baseball in Early American Culture." In *Baseball History from Outside the Lines: A Reader*, ed. John E. Dreifort, 19–33. Lincoln: University of Nebraska Press, 2001.

Trachtenberg, Alan. Foreword to *Horrible Prettiness: Burlesque and American Culture*, by Robert C. Allen, xi–xiv. Chapel Hill: University of North Carolina Press, 1991.

Vaillant, Derek. "'Your Voice Came in Last Night . . . but I Thought It Sounded a Little Scared': Rural Radio Listening and 'Talking Back' during the Progressive Era in Wisconsin, 1920–1932." In *Radio Reader: Essays in the Cultural History of Radio*, ed. Michele Hilmes and Jason Loviglio, 63–88. New York: Routledge, 2002.

Voigt, David Q. "America's Manufactured Villain—the Baseball Umpire." In *Things in the Driver's Seat: Readings in Popular Culture*, ed. Harry R. Huebel, 46–59. Chicago: Rand McNally, 1972.

————. "The Chicago Black Sox and the Myth of Baseball's Single Sin." In *Baseball History from Outside the Lines: A Reader*, ed. John E. Dreifort, 95–103. Lincoln: University of Nebraska Press, 2001.

Warren, Louis S. "Cody's Last Stand: Masculine Anxiety, the Custer Myth, and the Frontier of Domesticity in Buffalo Bill's Wild West." *Western Historical Quarterly* 34 (spring 2003): 49–69.

Webb, James C. "Rednecks, White Socks, and Pina Coladas? Country Music Ain't What It Used to Be . . . and It Really Never Was." *Southern Cultures* 5 (winter 1999): 41–51.

Westbrook, Robert. "'I Want a Girl, Just Like the Girl That Married Harry James': American Women and the Problem of Political Obligation in World War II." *American Quarterly* 42 (December 1990): 587–614.

Whalen, Terrence. Introduction to *The Life of P. T. Barnum, Written by Himself* (1855), vii–xxxvii. Urbana: University of Illinois Press, 2000.

White, Richard. "Frederick Jackson Turner and Buffalo Bill." In *The Frontier in American Culture,* ed. Richard White and Patricia Nelson Limerick, 6–65. Berkeley and Los Angeles: University of California Press, 1994.

White, Shane. "The Death of James Johnson." *American Quarterly* 51 (December 1999): 753–95.

Williamson, Joel. "The Feminine Elvis." Paper presented at the meeting of the Organization of American Historians, Los Angeles, April 28, 2002.

Wolfe, Tom. "Las Vegas (What?) Las Vegas (Can't Hear You! Too Noisy) *Las Vegas!!!!*" In *Smiling through the Apocalypse: Esquire's History of the Sixties,* ed. Harold Hayes, 201–18. New York: Dell, 1971.

Zeitz, Joshua. "Dixie's Victory." *American Heritage* 53 (August/September 2002): 46–55.

BOOKS

Aaron, Daniel. *Writers on the Left.* New York: Harcourt, Brace & World, 1961.

Abrams, Douglas C. *Selling the Old-Time Religion: American Fundamentalists and Mass Culture, 1920–1940.* Athens: University of Georgia Press, 2001.

Adams, Bluford. *E Pluribus Barnum: The Great Showman and U.S. Popular Culture.* Minneapolis: University of Minnesota Press, 1997.

Adams, Rachel. *Sideshow U.S.A.: Freaks and the American Cultural Imagination.* Chicago: University of Chicago Press, 2001.

Adelman, Melvin L. *A Sporting Time: New York City and the Rise of Modern Athletics, 1820–1870.* Urbana: University of Illinois Press, 1986.

Alexander, Charles C. *Breaking the Slump: Baseball in the Depression Era.* New York: Columbia University Press, 2002.

Allen, Michael. *Rodeo Cowboys in the North American Imagination.* Reno: University of Nevada Press, 1998.

———. *Western Rivermen, 1763–1861: Ohio and Mississippi Boatmen and the Myth of the Alligator Horse.* Baton Rouge: Louisiana State University Press, 1990.

Allen, Robert C. *Horrible Prettiness: Burlesque and American Culture.* Chapel Hill: University of North Carolina Press, 1991.

Altschuler, Glenn C. *All Shook Up: How Rock 'n' Roll Changed America.* New York: Oxford University Press, 2003.

Ambrose, Stephen E. *Nixon: The Triumph of a Politician, 1962–1972.* New York: Simon & Schuster, 1989.

Anderson, Terry. *The Movement and the Sixties: Protest in America from Greensboro to Wounded Knee.* New York: Oxford University Press, 1995.

Apps, Jerry. *Ringlingville USA: The Stupendous Story of Seven Siblings and Their Stunning Circus Success.* Madison: Wisconsin Historical Society Press, 2005.

Ashby, LeRoy. *William Jennings Bryan: Champion of Democracy.* Boston: Twayne, 1987.

Ashe, Arthur R., Jr. *A Hard Road to Glory: A History of the African-American Athlete since 1946.* New York: Warner, 1988.

Atherton, Lewis. *Main Street on the Middle Border.* 1954. Reprint, New York: Quadrangle, 1966.

Avila, Eric. *Popular Culture in the Age of White Flight: Fear and Fantasy in Suburban Los Angeles.* Berkeley and Los Angeles: University of California Press, 2004.

Bailey, Beth, and David Farber, eds. *America in the Seventies*. Lawrence: University Press of Kansas, 2004.

Balio, Tino. *Grand Design: Hollywood as a Modern Business Enterprise, 1930–1939*. Berkeley and Los Angeles: University of California Press, 1993.

Balz, Dan, and Ronald Brownstein. *Storming the Gates: Protest Politics and the Republican Revival*. Boston: Little, Brown, 1996.

Barbas, Samantha. *Movie Crazy: Fans, Stars, and the Cult of Celebrity*. New York: Palgrave, 2001.

Barilleaux, Ryan J., and Mark J. Rozell. *Power and Prudence: The Presidency of George H. W. Bush*. College Station: Texas A&M University Press, 2004.

Baritz, Loren. *The Good Life: The Meaning of Success for the American Middle Class*. New York: Knopf, 1988.

Barnouw, Erik. *Tube of Plenty: The Evolution of American Television*. 2nd rev. ed. New York: Oxford University Press, 1990.

Barnum, P. T. *Barnum's Own Story: The Autobiography of P. T. Barnum, Combined and Condensed from the Various Editions Published during His Lifetime by Waldo R. Browne*. New York: Viking, 1927.

———. *The Life of P. T. Barnum, Written by Himself*. 1855. Reprint, Urbana: University of Illinois Press, 2000.

Barth, Gunther. *City People: The Rise of Modern City Culture in Nineteenth-Century America*. New York: Oxford University Press, 1980.

The Beatles Fortieth Anniversary Collectors Edition. Boca Raton, FL: AMI, 2004.

Bean, Annemarie, James V. Hatch, and Brooks McNamara, eds. *Inside the Minstrel Mask: Readings in Nineteenth-Century Blackface Minstrelsy*. Hanover, NH: Wesleyan University Press, 1996.

Belton, John. *American Cinema/American Culture*. New York: McGraw Hill, 1994.

Benedict, Leonard. *Waifs of the Slums and Their Way Out*. New York: Revell, 1907.

Benshoff, Harry M., and Sean Griffin. *America on Film: Representing Race, Class, Gender, and Sexuality at the Movies*. Malden, MA: Blackwell, 2004.

Berger, Phil. *The Last Laugh: The World of Stand-Up Comics*. Updated ed. New York: Limelight, 1985.

Bergman, Andrew. *We're in the Money: Depression America and Its Films*. New York: New York University Press, 1971.

Berlin, Edward A. *King of Ragtime: Scott Joplin and His Era*. New York: Oxford University Press, 1994.

Berton, Pierre. *Niagara: A History of the Falls*. New York: Penguin, 1992.

Bertrand, Michael T. *Race, Rock, and Elvis*. Urbana: University of Illinois Press, 2000.

Betts, Raymond F. *A History of Popular Culture: More of Everything, Faster and Brighter*. New York: Routledge, 2004.

Birchard, Robert S. *Cecil B. DeMille's Hollywood*. Lexington: University Press of Kentucky, 2004.

Biskind, Peter. *Easy Riders, Raging Bulls: How the Sex–Drugs–and–Rock 'n' Roll Generation Saved Hollywood*. New York: Simon & Schuster, 1998.

———. *Seeing Is Believing: How Hollywood Taught Us to Stop Worrying and Love the Bomb*. New York: Pantheon, 1983.

Blum, John M. *V Was for Victory: Politics and American Culture during World War II*. New York: Harcourt Brace Jovanovich, 1976.

Blumin, Stuart M. *The Emergence of the Middle Class: Social Experience in the American City, 1760–1900*. Cambridge: Cambridge University Press, 1980.

Bodnar, John. *Blue-Collar Hollywood: Liberalism, Democracy, and Working People in American Film*. Baltimore: Johns Hopkins University Press, 2003.

Bodroghkozy, Aniko. *Groove Tube: Sixties Television and the Youth Rebellion*. Durham, NC: Duke University Press, 2001.

Bogdan, Robert. *Freak Show: Presenting Human Oddities for Amusement and Profit*. Chicago: University of Chicago Press, 1988.

Bogle, Donald. *Primetime Blues: African Americans on Network Television.* New York: Farrar Straus Giroux, 2001.

Boorstin, Daniel. *The Genius of American Politics.* Chicago: University of Chicago Press, 1953.

Borchert, James. *Alley Life in Washington: Family, Community, Religion, and Folklife in the City, 1850–1970.* Urbana: University of Illinois Press, 1980.

Bowser, Eileen. *The Transformation of Cinema, 1907–1915.* Berkeley and Los Angeles: University of California Press, 1990.

Bozza, Anthony. *Whatever You Say I Am: The Life and Times of Eminem.* New York: Crown, 2003.

Breen, T. H. *The Marketplace of Revolution: How Consumer Politics Shaped American Independence.* New York: Oxford University Press, 2004.

Bridger, Bobby. *Buffalo Bill and Sitting Bull: Inventing the West.* Austin: University of Texas Press, 2002.

Brode, Douglas. *From Walt to Woodstock: How Disney Created the Counterculture.* Austin: University of Texas Press, 2004.

Brooks, Tim, and Earle Marsh. *The Complete Directory to Prime Time Network and Cable TV Shows, 1946–Present.* 7th ed. New York: Ballantine, 1999.

Browne, Nick, ed. *Francis Ford Coppola's Godfather Trilogy.* Cambridge: Cambridge University Press, 2000.

Bruck, Connie. *When Hollywood Had a King: The Reign of Lew Wasserman, Who Leveraged Talent into Power and Influence.* New York: Random House, 2003.

Butsch, Richard. *The Making of American Audiences: From Stage to Television, 1750–1990.* Cambridge: Cambridge University Press, 2000.

Cagin, Seth, and Philip Dray. *Hollywood Films of the Seventies: Sex, Drugs, Violence, Rock 'n' Roll, and Politics.* New York: Harper & Row, 1984.

Cahn, Susan K. *Coming on Strong: Gender and Sexuality in Twentieth-Century Women's Sport.* Cambridge, MA: Harvard University Press, 1995.

Campbell, Craig W. *Reel America and World War I.* Jefferson, NC: McFarland, 1985.

Cannon, Lou. *President Reagan: The Role of a Lifetime.* New York: Simon & Schuster, 1991.

Cantwell, Robert. *When We Were Good: The Folk Revival.* Cambridge, MA: Harvard University Press, 1996.

Carlyon, David. *Dan Rice: The Most Famous Man You've Never Heard Of.* New York: Public Affairs, 2001.

Caro, Robert A. *The Path to Power: The Years of Lyndon Johnson.* New York: Knopf, 1982.

Carp, E. Wayne. *Family Matters: Secrecy and Disclosure in the History of Adoption.* Cambridge, MA: Harvard University Press, 1998.

Carroll, John M. *Red Grange and the Rise of Modern Football.* Urbana: University of Illinois Press, 1999.

Casdorph, Paul D. *Let the Good Times Roll: Life at Home in America during World War II.* New York: Paragon, 1989.

Caute, David. *The Year of the Barricades: A Journey through 1968.* New York: Harper & Row, 1988.

Cavallo, Dominic. *Muscles and Morals: Organized Playgrounds and Urban Reform, 1880–1920.* Philadelphia: University of Pennsylvania Press, 1981.

Cawelti, John G. *Adventure, Mystery, and Romance: Formula Stories as Art and Popular Culture.* Chicago: University of Chicago Press, 1976.

Cayleff, Susan E. *Babe: The Life and Legend of Babe Didrikson Zaharias.* Urbana: University of Illinois Press, 1995.

Ceplair, Larry, and Steven Englund. *The Inquisition in Hollywood: Politics in the Film Community, 1930–1960.* 1980. Reprint, Urbana: University of Illinois Press, 2003.

Chalberg, John C. *Rickey and Robinson: The Preacher and Player and America's Game.* Wheeling, IL: Harlan Davidson, 2000.

Chapman, David L. *Sandow the Magnificent: Eugen Sandow and the Beginnings of Bodybuilding.* Urbana: University of Illinois Press, 1994.

Chenoweth, Lawrence. *The American Dream of Success: The Search for the Self in the Twentieth Century.* Belmont, CA: Wadsworth, 1974.

Ching, Barbara. *"Wrong's What I Do Best": Hard Country Music and Contemporary Culture.* New York: Oxford University Press, 2001.

Christopher, Nicholas. *Somewhere in the Night: Film Noir and the American City.* New York: Owl, 1997.

Chudacoff, Howard. *The Age of the Bachelor: Creating an American Subculture.* Princeton, NJ: Princeton University Press, 1999.

Cochran, David. *American Noir: Underground Writers and Filmmakers of the Postwar Era.* Washington, DC: Smithsonian Institution Press, 2000.

Cockrell, Dale. *Demons of Disorder: Blackface Minstrels and Their World.* Cambridge: Cambridge University Press, 1997.

Cohen, Lizabeth. *A Consumers' Republic: The Politics of Mass Consumption in Postwar America.* New York: Knopf, 2003.

Cohen, Patricia Cline. *The Murder of Helen Jewett.* New York: Vintage, 1998.

Cohen, Paula M. *Silent Film and the Triumph of the American Myth.* New York: Oxford University Press, 2001.

Coleman, Mark. *Playback: From the Victrola to MP3, 100 Years of Music, Machines, and Money.* New York: Da Capo, 2003.

Collins, Max Allan, George Hagenauer, and Steven Heller. *Men's Adventure Magazines in Postwar America.* London: Taschen, 2004.

Collins, Max Allan, and James L. Traylor. *One Lonely Knight: Mickey Spillane's Mike Hammer.* Bowling Green, OH: Bowling Green State University Popular Press, 1984.

Connolly, Michael. *The Narrows.* London: Orion, 2004.

Cook, David A. *Lost Illusions: American Cinema in the Shadow of Watergate and Vietnam, 1970–1979.* Berkeley and Los Angeles: University of California Press, 2000.

Cook, James W. *The Arts of Deception: Playing with Fraud in the Age of Barnum.* Cambridge, MA: Harvard University Press, 2001.

Corkin, Stanley. *Cowboys as Cold Warriors: The Western and U.S. History.* Philadelphia: Temple University Press, 2004.

Cornyn, Stan, with Paul Scanlon. *Exploding: The Highs, Hits, Hype, Heroes, and Hustlers of the Warner Music Group.* New York: HarperCollins, 2002.

Costello, John. *Virtue under Fire: How World War Changed Our Social and Sexual Attitudes.* Boston: Little, Brown, 1985.

Couvares, Francis G. *The Remaking of Pittsburgh: Class and Culture in an Industrializing City, 1877–1919.* Albany: State University of New York Press, 1984.

Coyne, Michael. *The Crowded Prairie: American National Identity in the Hollywood Western.* London: I. B. Tauris, 1997.

Crafton, Donald. *The Talkies: American Cinema's Transition to Sound, 1926–1931.* Berkeley and Los Angeles: University of California Press, 1997.

Crewdson, John. *By Silence Betrayed: Sexual Abuse of Children in America.* Boston: Little, Brown, 1988.

Cripps, Thomas. *Hollywood's High Noon: Moviemaking and Society before Television.* Baltimore: Johns Hopkins University Press, 1997.

———. *Making Movies Black: The Hollywood Message Movie from World War II to the Civil Rights Era.* New York: Oxford University Press, 1993.

Cross, Gary. *The Cute and the Cool: Wondrous Innocence and Modern American Children's Culture.* New York: Oxford University Press, 2004.

———. *An All-Consuming Century: Why Commercialism Won in Modern America.* New York: Columbia University Press, 2000.

———. *Kids' Stuff: Toys and the Changing World of Childhood.* Cambridge, MA: Harvard University Press, 1997.

Crouthamel, James L. *Bennett's* New York Herald *and the Rise of the Popular Press.* Syracuse, NY: Syracuse University Press, 1989.

Crunden, Robert. *Ministers of Reform: The Progressives' Achievement in American Civilization, 1889–1920.* New York: Basic, 1982.

Culhane, John. *The American Circus: An Illustrated History.* New York: Henry Holt, 1990.

Cullen, Jim, ed. *Popular Culture in American History.* Malden, MA: Blackwell, 2001.

——. *The Art of Democracy: A Concise History of Popular Culture in the United States.* New York: Monthly Review Press, 1996.

Currell, Susan. *The March of Spare Time: The Problem and Promise of Leisure in the Great Depression.* Philadelphia: University of Pennsylvania Press, 2005.

Czitrom, Daniel J. *Media and the American Mind: From Morse to McLuhan.* Chapel Hill: University of North Carolina Press, 1982.

D'Acci, Julie. *Defining Women: Television and the Case of* Cagney & Lacey. Chapel Hill: University of North Carolina Press, 1994.

Dale, Alan. *Comedy Is a Man in Trouble: Slapstick in American Movies.* Minneapolis: University of Minnesota Press, 2000.

Daniel, Pete. *Lost Revolutions: The South in the 1950s.* Chapel Hill: University of North Carolina Press, 2000.

Daniels, Bruce C. *Puritans at Play: Leisure and Recreation in Colonial New England.* New York: St. Martin's Griffin, 1995.

Daniels, Les. *Marvel: Five Fabulous Decades of the World's Greatest Comics.* 1991. Reprint, New York: Abrams, 1993.

Davies, Richard O. *America's Obsession: Sports and Society since 1945.* New York: Harcourt Brace, 1994.

Davis, Francis. *The History of the Blues: The Roots, the Music, the People from Charley Patton to Robert Cray.* New York: Hyperion, 1995.

Davis, Janet M. *The Circus Age: Culture and Society under the American Big Top.* Chapel Hill: University of North Carolina Press, 2002.

Davis, Kenneth C. *Two-Bit Culture: The Paperbacking of America.* Boston: Houghton Mifflin, 1984.

Davis, Ronald L. *Celluloid Mirrors: Hollywood and American Society since 1945.* New York: Harcourt Brace, 1997.

Dawidoff, Nicholas. *In the Country of Country: A Journey to the Roots of American Music.* New York: Vintage, 1998.

DeBauche, Leslie Midkiff. *Reel Patriotism: The Movies and World War I.* Madison: University of Wisconsin Press, 1997.

DeCurtis, Anthony, and James Henke, eds., with Holly George-Warren; Jim Miller, orig. ed. *The Rolling Stone Illustrated History of Rock and Roll: The Definitive History of the Most Important Artists and Their Music,* 3rd ed. New York: Random House, 1992.

DeLillo, Don. *End Zone.* 1972. Reprint, New York: Pocket, 1973.

D'Emilio, John, and Estelle B. Freedman. *Intimate Matters: A History of Sexuality in America.* New York: Harper & Row, 1988.

Dennett, Andrea Stulman. *Weird and Wonderful: The Dime Museum in America.* New York: New York University Press, 1997.

Denning, Michael. *The Cultural Front: The Laboring of American Culture in the Twentieth Century.* New York: Verso, 1996.

——. *Mechanic Accents: Dime Novels and Working-Class Culture in America.* New York: Verso, 1987.

Dent, Jim. *The Undefeated: The Oklahoma Sooners and the Greatest Winning Streak in College Football.* New York: Thomas Dunne, 2001.

Denton, Sally, and Roger Morris. *The Money and the Power: The Making of Las Vegas and Its Hold on America, 1947–2000.* New York: Knopf, 2001.

Diamond, Edwin, and Stephen Bates. *The Spot: The Rise of Political Advertising on Television.* Cambridge, MA: Harvard University Press, 1984.

Diamond, Edwin, and Robert A. Silverman. *White House to Your House: Media and Politics in Virtual America.* Cambridge, MA: MIT Press, 1995.

Dick, Bernard F. *Engulfed: The Death of Paramount Pictures and the Birth of Corporate Hollywood.* Lexington: University Press of Kentucky, 2001.

Diggins, John Patrick. *The Proud Decades: America in War and Peace.* New York: Norton, 1988.

DiMeglio, John E. *Vaudeville, U.S.A.* Bowling Green, OH: Bowling Green University Popular Press, 1973.

Dixon, Wheeler W., ed. *Film and Television after 9/11.* Carbondale: Southern Illinois University Press, 2004.

Doggett, Peter. *Are You Ready for the Country: Elvis, Dylan, Parsons, and the Roots of Country Rock.* New York: Penguin, 2000.

Doherty, Thomas. *Cold War, Cool Medium: Television, McCarthyism, and American Culture.* New York: Columbia University Press, 2003.

———. *Teenagers and Teenpics: The Juvenilization of American Movies in the 1950s.* Rev. ed. Philadelphia: Temple University Press, 2002.

———. *Pre-Code Hollywood: Sex, Immorality, and Insurrection in American Cinema, 1930–1934.* New York: Columbia University Press, 1999.

———. *Projections of War: Hollywood, American Culture, and World War II.* Rev. ed. New York: Columbia University Press, 1999.

Doss, Erika, ed. *Looking at* Life *Magazine.* Washington, DC: Smithsonian Institution Press, 2001.

———. *Elvis Culture: Fans, Faith, and Image.* Lawrence: University Press of Kansas, 1999.

Douglas, Ann. *Terrible Honesty: Mongrel Manhattan in the 1920s.* New York: Farrar Straus Giroux, 1995.

Douglas, Susan J. *Listening In: Radio and the American Imagination.* New York: Times Books, 1999.

———. *Where the Girls Are: Growing Up Female in the Mass Media.* New York: Times Books, 1994.

Dreifort, John E., ed. *Baseball History from Outside the Lines: A Reader.* Lincoln: University of Nebraska Press, 2001.

Dudden, Faye E. *Women in the American Theatre: Actresses and Audiences, 1790–1870.* New Haven, CT: Yale University Press, 1994.

Durgnat, Raymond. *The Crazy Mirror: Hollywood Comedy and the American Image.* New York: Delta, 1969.

Early, Gerald. *The Culture of Bruising: Essays on Prizefighting, Literature, and Modern American Culture.* Hopewell, NJ: Ecco, 1994.

Edmundson, Mark. *Nightmare on Main Street: Angels, Sadomasochism, and the Culture of Gothic.* Cambridge, MA: Harvard University Press, 1997.

Ehrenreich, Barbara. *Hearts of Men: American Dreams and the Flight from Commitment.* New York: Anchor, 1983.

Eliot, Marc. *Down 42nd Street: Sex, Money, Culture, and Politics at the Crossroads of the World.* New York: Warner, 2001.

Ellis, Joseph. *After the Revolution: Profiles of Early American Culture.* New York: Norton, 1979.

Ellison, Curtis W. *Country Music Culture: From Hard Times to Heaven.* Jackson: University Press of Mississippi, 1995.

Ely, Martin P. *The Adventures of Amos 'n' Andy: A Social History of an American Phenomenon.* New York: Free Press, 1991.

Emerson, Ken. *Doo-Dah! Stephen Foster and the Rise of American Popular Culture.* New York: Simon & Schuster, 1997.

Engelhardt, Tom. *The End of Victory Culture: Cold War America and the Disillusioning of a Generation.* New York: Basic, 1995.

Enstad, Nan. *Ladies of Labor, Girls of Adventure.* New York: Columbia University Press, 1999.

Epstein, Edward J. *The Big Picture: The New Logic of Money and Power in Hollywood.* New York: Random House, 2005.

Epstein, Lawrence J. *Mixed Nuts: America's Love Affair with Comedy Teams.* New York: Public Affairs, 2004.

———. *The Haunted Smile: The Story of Jewish Comedians in America.* New York: Public Affairs, 2001.

Erenberg, Lewis A. *Swingin' the Dream: Big Band Jazz and the Rebirth of American Culture.* Chicago: University of Chicago Press, 1998.

———. *Steppin' Out: New York Nightlife and the Transformation of American Culture, 1890–1930.* Chicago: University of Chicago Press, 1981.

Evensen, Bruce J. *When Dempsey Fought Tunney: Heroes, Hokum, and Storytelling in the Jazz Age.* Knoxville: University of Tennessee Press, 1996.

Eyman, Scott. *The Speed of Sound: Hollywood and the Talkie Revolution, 1926–1930.* Baltimore: Johns Hopkins University Press, 1997.

Faludi, Susan. *Stiffed: The Betrayal of the American Man.* New York: Morrow, 1999.

———. *Backlash: The Undeclared War against American Women.* New York: Crown, 1992.

Feiler, Bruce. *Dreaming Out Loud: Garth Brooks, Wynonna Judd, Wade Hayes, and the Changing Face of Nashville.* New York: Avon, 1998.

Finson, Jon. *The Voices That Are Gone: Themes in 19th-Century American Popular Song.* New York: Oxford University Press, 1994.

Fitzgerald, Frances. *Way Out There in the Blue: Reagan, Star Wars, and the End of the Cold War.* New York: Simon & Schuster, 2000.

Flinn, Denny M. *Musical! A Grand Tour.* New York: Schirmer, 1997.

Fox, Aaron A. *Real Country: Music and Language in Working-Class Culture.* Durham, NC: Duke University Press, 2004.

Frank, Thomas. *What's the Matter with Kansas? How Conservatives Won the Heart of America.* New York: Metropolitan, 2004.

———. *The Conquest of Cool: Business Culture, Counter Culture, and the Rise of Hip Consumerism.* Chicago: University of Chicago Press, 1997.

Freedman, Jonathan, and Richard Millington, eds. *Hitchcock's America.* New York: Oxford University Press, 1999.

Fricke, Jim, and Charlie Ahearn, eds. *Yes Yes Y'all: The Experience Music Project Oral History of Hip-Hop's First Decade.* Cambridge, MA: Da Capo, 2002.

Fried, Richard M. *The Russians Are Coming! The Russians Are Coming! Pageantry and Patriotism in Cold-War America.* New York: Oxford University Press, 1998.

———. *Nightmare in Red: The McCarthy Era in Perspective.* New York: Oxford University Press, 1990.

Fuller, Kathryn. *At the Picture Show: Small-Town Audiences and the Creation of Movie Fan Culture.* Washington, DC: Smithsonian Institution Press, 1996.

Furia, Philip. *Irving Berlin: A Life in Song.* New York: Schirmer, 1998.

Gabler, Neal. *Life the Movie: How Entertainment Conquered Reality.* New York: Knopf, 1998.

———. *Winchell: Gossip, Power, and the Culture of Celebrity.* New York: Vintage, 1995.

———. *An Empire of Their Own: How the Jews Invented Hollywood.* New York: Doubleday, 1988.

Gamson, Joshua. *Freaks Talk Back: Tabloid Talk Shows and Sexual Nonconformity.* Chicago: University of Chicago Press, 1998.

Garner, Joe. *Stay Tuned: Television's Unforgettable Moments.* Kansas City, MO: Andrews McMeel, 2002.

Garr, Gillian G. *She's a Rebel: The History of Women in Rock and Roll.* Seattle: Seal, 1992.

Gent, Peter. *North Dallas Forty.* 1973. Reprint, Toronto: Sport Media, 2003.

George, Nelson. *Hip Hop America.* New York: Viking, 1998.

George-Graves, Nadine. *The Royalty of Negro Vaudeville: The Whitman Sisters and the Negotiation of Race, Gender, and Class in African American Theater, 1900–1940.* New York: St. Martin's, 2000.

Gerstle, Gary. *American Crucible: Race and Nation in the Twentieth Century.* Princeton, NJ: Princeton University Press, 2001.

Giddins, Gary. *Bing Crosby: A Pocketful of Dreams: The Early Years, 1903–1940.* Boston: Little, Brown, 2001.

———. *Visions of Jazz: The First Century.* New York: Oxford University Press, 1998.

Gilbert, James. *A Cycle of Outrage: America's Reaction to Juvenile Delinquency in the 1950s*. New York: Oxford University Press, 1986.

Gillon, Steve. *Boomer Nation: The Largest and Richest Generation and How It Changed America*. New York: Free Press, 2004.

Gilmore, Mikal. *Night Beat: A Shadow History of Rock and Roll*. New York: Anchor, 1998.

Gioia, Ted. *The History of Jazz*. New York: Oxford University Press, 1997.

Gitlin, Todd. *Media Unlimited: How the Torrent of Images and Sounds Overwhelms Our Lives*. New York: Metropolitan, 2001.

———. *The Sixties: Years of Hope, Days of Rage*. New York: Bantam, 1987.

———. *Inside Prime Time*. 1983. Reprint, New York: Pantheon, 1985.

Glenn, Susan. *Female Spectacle: The Theatrical Roots of Modern Feminism*. Cambridge, MA: Harvard University Press, 2000.

Glynn, Kevin. *Tabloid Culture: Trash Taste, Popular Power, and the Transformation of American Television*. Durham, NC: Duke University Press, 2000.

Goldman, Albert, with Lawrence Schiller. *Ladies and Gentlemen—Lenny Bruce!* 1971. Reprint, New York: Ballantine, 1974.

Goodman, Fred. *The Mansion on the Hill: Dylan, Young, Geffen, Springsteen, and the Head-On Collision of Rock and Commerce*. New York: Vintage, 1997.

Gorn, Elliott J., ed. *Muhammad Ali: The People's Champ*. Urbana: University of Illinois Press, 1995.

———. *The Manly Art: Bare-Knuckle Prize Fighting in America*. Ithaca, NY: Cornell University Press, 1986.

Gorn, Elliott J., and Warren Goldstein. *A Brief History of American Sports*. New York: Hill & Wang, 1993.

Gottschild, Brenda D. *Waltzing in the Dark: African American Vaudeville and Race Politics in the Swing Era*. New York: St. Martin's, 2000.

Goulart, Ron. *Great American Comic Books*. Lincolnwood, IL: Publications International, 2001.

Graham, Allison. *Framing the South: Hollywood, Television, and Race during the Civil Rights Struggle*. Baltimore: Johns Hopkins University Press, 2001.

Green, Douglas B. *Singing in the Saddle: The History of the Singing Cowboy*. Nashville: Country Music Foundation Press/Vanderbilt University Press, 2002.

Greene, Eric. *Planet of the Apes as American Myth: Race, Politics, and Popular Culture*. Hanover, NH: Wesleyan University Press, 1996.

Grieveson, Lee. *Policing Cinema: Movies and Censorship in Early Twentieth-Century America*. Berkeley and Los Angeles: University of California Press, 2004.

Grimsted, David. *Melodrama Unveiled: American Theater and Culture, 1800–1850*. Berkeley and Los Angeles: University of California Press, 1968.

———, ed. *Notions of the Americans, 1820–1860*. New York: Braziller, 1970.

Guerrero, Ed. *Framing Blackness: The African American Image in Film*. Philadelphia: Temple University Press, 1993.

Gura, Philip F., and James F. Bollman. *America's Instrument: The Banjo in the Nineteenth Century*. Chapel Hill: University of North Carolina Press, 1999.

Guralnick, Peter. *Last Train to Memphis: The Rise of Elvis Presley*. Boston: Little, Brown, 1994.

Hajdu, David. *Positively 4th Street: The Lives and Times of Joan Baez, Bob Dylan, Mimi Baez Fariña, and Richard Fariña*. New York: Farrar Straus Giroux, 2001.

Halberstam, David. *The Fifties*. New York: Villard, 1993.

Haltunnen, Karen. *Murder Most Foul: The Killer and the American Gothic Imagination*. Cambridge, MA: Harvard University Press, 1998.

———. *Confidence Men and Painted Women: A Study of Middle-Class Culture in America*. New Haven, CT: Yale University Press, 1982.

Hamilton, Marybeth. *"When I'm Bad, I'm Better": Mae West, Sex, and American Entertainment*. Berkeley and Los Angeles: University of California Press, 1996.

Hangen, Tona J. *Redeeming the Dial: Radio, Religion, and Popular Culture in America.* Chapel Hill: University of North Carolina Press, 2002.

Harkins, Anthony. *Hillbilly: A Cultural History of an American Icon.* New York: Oxford University Press, 2004.

Harris, Neil. *Humbug: The Art of P. T. Barnum.* Chicago: University of Chicago Press, 1973.

Havig, Alan. *Fred Allen's Radio Comedy.* Philadelphia: Temple University Press, 1990.

Hayes, Harold, ed. *Smiling through the Apocalypse: Esquire's History of the Sixties.* New York: Dell, 1971.

Hazzard-Gordon, Katrina. *Jookin': The Rise of Social Dance Formations in African-American Culture.* Philadelphia: Temple University Press, 1990.

Hemphill, C. Dallett. *Bowing to Necessities: A History of Manners in America, 1620–1860.* New York: Oxford University Press, 1999.

Hemphill, Paul. *The Nashville Sound: Bright Lights and Country Music.* New York: Simon & Schuster, 1970.

———. *Lovesick Blues: The Life of Hank Williams.* New York: Viking, 2005.

Hendra, Tony. *Going Too Far.* New York: Doubleday, 1987.

Henkin, David. *City Reading: Written Words and Public Spaces in Antebellum New York.* New York: Oxford University Press, 1998.

Henriksen, Margot A. *Dr. Strangelove's America: Society and Culture in the Atomic Age.* Berkeley and Los Angeles: University of California Press, 1997.

Hilkey, Judy. *Character Is Capital: Success Manuals and Manhood in Gilded Age America.* Chapel Hill: University of North Carolina Press, 1997.

Hilmes, Michele. *Radio Voices: American Broadcasting, 1922–1952.* Minneapolis: University of Minnesota Press, 1997.

Hilmes, Michele, and Jason Loviglio, eds. *Radio Reader: Essays in the Cultural History of Radio.* New York: Routledge, 2002.

Hirsch, Foster. *Detours and Lost Highways: A Map of Neo-Noir.* New York: Proscenium, 1999.

Hoberman, J. *The Dream Life: Movies, Media, and the Mythology of the Sixties.* New York: New Press, 2003.

Hoberman, J., and Jeffrey Shandler. *Entertaining America: Jews, Movies, and Broadcasting.* New York: Jewish Museum; Princeton, NJ: Princeton University Press, 2003.

Hoch, Paul. *Rip Off the Big Game: The Exploitation of Sports by the Power Elite.* New York: Doubleday Anchor, 1972.

Horton, Gerd. *Radio Goes to War: The Cultural Politics of Propaganda during World War II.* Berkeley and Los Angeles: University of California Press, 2002.

Hotaling, Ed. *Wink: The Incredible Life and Epic Journey of Jimmy Winkfield.* New York: McGraw-Hill, 2005.

Huber, Richard M. *The American Idea of Success.* New York: McGraw-Hill, 1971.

Huggins, Nathan I. *Harlem Renaissance.* New York: Oxford University Press, 1971.

Immerso, Michael. *Coney Island: The People's Playground.* New Brunswick, NJ: Rutgers University Press, 2002.

Inglis, Fred. *Cruel Peace: Everyday Life and the Cold War.* New York: Basic, 1991.

Isaac, Rhys. *The Transformation of Virginia, 1740–1790.* Chapel Hill: University of North Carolina Press, 1982.

Isenberg, Michael. *John L. Sullivan and His America.* Urbana: University of Illinois Press, 1994.

Jackson, John A. American Bandstand: *Dick Clark and the Making of a Rock 'n' Roll Empire.* New York: Oxford University Press, 1997.

Jay, Kathryn. *More Than Just a Game: Sports in American Life since 1945.* New York: Columbia University Press, 2004.

Jeffords, Susan. *Hard Bodies: Hollywood Masculinity in the Reagan Era.* New Brunswick, NJ: Rutgers University Press, 1994.

Jenkins, Dan. *Semi-Tough.* 1972. Reprint, New York: Signet, 1973.

Johnson, Haynes. *The Best of Times: America in the Clinton Years.* New York: Harcourt, 2001.

Johnson, Paul. *Sam Patch, the Famous Jumper.* New York: Hill & Wang, 2003.

———. *A Shopkeeper's Millennium: Society and Revivals in Rochester, New York, 1815–1837.* New York: Hill & Wang, 1978.

Johnson, Steven. *Everything Bad Is Good for You: How Today's Popular Culture Is Actually Making Us Smarter.* New York: Riverhead, 2005.

Jones, Gerard. *Men of Tomorrow: Geeks, Gangsters, and the Birth of the Comic Book.* New York: Basic, 2004.

———. *Honey, I'm Home! Sitcoms: Selling the American Dream.* New York: Grove Weidenfeld, 1992.

Jones, Gerard, and Will Jacobs. *The Comic Book Heroes.* Rocklin, CA: Prima, 1997.

Jones, John B. *Our Musicals, Ourselves: A Social History of the American Musical Theater.* Lebanon, NH: Brandeis University Press, 2003.

Jones, Landon. *Great Expectations: America and the Baby Boom Generation.* 1980. Reprint, New York: Ballantine, 1981.

Jowett, Garth. *Film: The Democratic Art.* Boston: Little, Brown, 1976.

Kammen, Michael. *American Culture, American Tastes: Social Change and the 20th Century.* New York: Basic, 2000.

Kasson, John F. *Houdini, Tarzan, and the Perfect Man: The White Male Body and the Challenge of Modernity in America.* New York: Hill & Wang, 2001.

———. *Rudeness and Civility: Manners in Nineteenth-Century Urban America.* New York: Hill & Wang, 1990.

———. *Amusing the Million: Coney Island at the Turn of the Century.* New York: Hill & Wang, 1978.

Kasson, Joy S. *Buffalo Bill's Wild West: Celebrity, Memory, and Popular History.* New York: Hill & Wang, 2000.

Kempton, Arthur. *Boogaloo: The Quintessence of American Popular Music.* New York: Pantheon, 2003.

Kennedy, David M. *Freedom from Fear: The American People in Depression and War, 1929–1945.* New York: Oxford University Press, 1999.

Kennedy, Rick, and Randy McNutt. *Little Labels—Big Sound: Small Record Companies and the Rise of American Music.* Bloomington: Indiana University Press, 1999.

Kenney, William Howland. *Recorded Music in American Life: The Phonograph and Popular Memory, 1890–1945.* New York: Oxford University Press, 1999.

Kern-Foxworth, Marilyn. *Aunt Jemima, Uncle Ben, and Rastus: Blacks in Advertising, Yesterday, Today, and Tomorrow.* Westport, CT: Praeger, 1994.

Keyes, Cheryl L. *Rap Music and Street Consciousness.* Urbana: University of Illinois Press, 2002.

Kibler, M. Alison. *Rank Ladies: Gender and Cultural Hierarchy in American Vaudeville.* Chapel Hill: University of North Carolina Press, 1999.

Kimmel, Michael. *Manhood in America: A Cultural History.* New York: Free Press, 1996.

Kleinfelder, Rita Lang. *When We Were Young: A Baby-Boomer Yearbook.* New York: Prentice-Hall, 1993.

Knopf, Robert. *The Theater and Cinema of Buster Keaton.* Princeton, NJ: Princeton University Press, 1999.

Kolker, Robert Phillip. *A Cinema of Loneliness: Penn, Kubrick, Scorsese, Spielberg, Altman.* 2nd ed. New York: Oxford University Press, 1988.

Koszarski, Richard. *An Evening's Entertainment: The Age of the Silent Feature Picture, 1915–1928.* Berkeley and Los Angeles: University of California Press, 1990.

Kram, Mark. *Ghosts of Manila: The Fateful Blood Feud between Muhammad Ali and Joe Frazier.* New York: HarperCollins, 2001.

Kunhardt, Philip B., Jr., Philip B. Kunhardt III, and Peter W. Kunhardt. *P. T. Barnum: America's Greatest Showman.* New York: Knopf, 1995.

Kyvig, David. *Daily Life in the United States, 1920–1940.* 2002. Reprint, Chicago: Ivan Dee, 2004.

Ladd, Jim. *Radio Waves: Life and Revolution on the FM Dial.* New York: St. Martin's, 1991.

LaFeber, Walter. *Michael Jordan and the New Global Capitalism*. New York: Norton, 2002.

Laforse, Martin W., and James A. Drake. *Popular Culture and American Life: Selected Topics in the Study of American Popular Culture*. Chicago: Nelson-Hall, 1981.

Landay, Lori. *Madcaps, Screwballs, and Con Women: The Female Trickster in American Culture*. Philadelphia: University of Pennsylvania Press, 1998.

Lange, Jeffrey J. *Smile When You Call Me a Hillbilly: Country Music's Struggle for Respectability, 1939–1954*. Athens: University of Georgia Press, 2004.

Larson, Erik. *The Devil in the White City: Murder, Magic, and Madness at the Fair That Changed America*. New York: Crown, 2003.

Leach, William R. *Land of Desire: Merchants, Power, and the Rise of a New American Culture*. New York: Pantheon, 1993.

Lears, T. J. Jackson. *Something for Nothing: Luck in America*. New York: Penguin, 2003.

———. *Fables of Abundance: A Cultural History of Advertising in America*. New York: Basic, 1994.

Leff, Leonard J., and Jerold L. Simmons. *The Dame in the Kimono: Hollywood, Censorship, and the Production Code*. 2nd ed. Lexington: University Press of Kentucky, 2001.

Lehuu, Isabelle. *Carnival on the Page: Popular Print Media in Antebellum America*. Chapel Hill: University of North Carolina Press, 2000.

Leider, Emily W. *Dark Lover: The Life and Death of Rudolph Valentino*. New York: Farrar Straus Giroux, 2003.

———. *Becoming Mae West*. New York: Farrar Straus Giroux, 1997.

Lenihan, John H. *Showdown: Confronting Modern America in the Western Film*. Urbana: University of Illinois Press, 1980.

Leonard, John. *Smoke and Mirrors: Violence, Television, and Other American Cultures*. New York: New Press, 1997.

Levine, Lawrence W. *The Unpredictable Past: Explorations in American Cultural History*. New York: Oxford University Press, 1993.

———. *Highbrow/Lowbrow: The Emergence of Cultural Hierarchy in America*. Cambridge, MA: Harvard University Press, 1988.

———. *Black Culture, Black Consciousness: Afro-American Folk Thought from Slavery to Freedom*. New York: Oxford University Press, 1977.

Lewis, Jon. *Hollywood v. Hard Core: How the Struggle over Censorship Saved the Modern Film Industry*. New York: New York University Press, 2000.

———. *Whom God Wishes to Destroy . . .: Francis Coppola and the New Hollywood*. Durham, NC: Duke University Press, 1995.

Lewis, Robert M., ed. *From Traveling Show to Vaudeville: Theatrical Spectacle in America, 1830–1910*. Baltimore: Johns Hopkins University Press, 2003.

Lewis, Tom. *Empire of the Air: The Men Who Made Radio*. New York: HarperCollins, 1991.

Lhamon, W. T., Jr. *Jump Jim Crow: Lost Plays, Lyrics, and Street Prose of the First Atlantic Popular Culture*. Cambridge, MA: Harvard University Press, 2003.

———. *Raising Cain: Blackface Performance from Jim Crow to Hip Hop*. Cambridge, MA: Harvard University Press, 1998.

Light, Alan, ed. *The Vibe History of Hip Hop*. New York: Three Rivers, 1999.

Lingeman, Richard R. *Don't You Know There's a War On? The American Home Front, 1941–1945*. 1970. Reprint, New York: Paperback Library, 1971.

Linn, Karen. *That Half-Barbaric Twang: The Banjo in American Popular Culture*. New York: Oxford University Press, 1991.

Lipsitz, George. *Rainbow at Midnight: Labor and Culture in the 1940s*. Urbana: University of Illinois Press, 1994.

———. *Time Passages: Collective Memory and American Popular Culture*. Minneapolis: University of Minnesota Press, 1990.

Lorant, Stefan. *The Life and Times of Theodore Roosevelt*. New York: Doubleday, 1959.

Loss, Archie. *Pop Dreams: Music, Movies, and the Media in the 1960s*. New York: Harcourt Brace, 1999.

Lott, Eric. *Love and Theft: Blackface Minstrelsy and the American Working Class.* New York: Oxford University Press, 1995.

Louvish, Simon. *Man on the Flying Trapeze: The Life and Times of W. C. Fields.* New York: Norton, 1997.

Lyons, Arthur. *Death on the Cheap: The Lost B Films of Film Noir.* New York: Da Capo, 2000.

MacCambridge, Michael. *America's Game: The Epic Story of How Pro Football Captured a Nation.* New York: Random House, 2004.

MacDonald, J. Fred. *One Nation under Television: The Rise and Decline of Network TV.* New York: Pantheon, 1990.

———. *Television and the Red Menace: The Video Road to Vietnam.* New York: Praeger, 1985.

———. *Don't Touch That Dial! Radio Programming in American Life from 1920 to 1960.* Chicago: Nelson-Hall, 1979.

Mahar, William J. *Behind the Burnt Cork Mask: Early Blackface Minstrelsy and Antebellum American Popular Culture.* Urbana: University of Illinois Press, 1999.

Maland, Charles J. *Chaplin and American Culture: The Evolution of a Star Image.* Princeton, NJ: Princeton University Press, 1989.

Mallory, Michael. *Marvel: The Characters and Their Universe.* New York: Barnes & Noble Books, 2004.

Malone, Bill C. *Country Music, U.S.A.* 2nd rev. ed. Austin: University of Texas Press, 2002.

———. *Don't Get above Your Raisin': Country Music and the Southern Working Class.* Urbana: University of Illinois Press, 2002.

Malone, Bill C., and David Stricklin. *Southern Music/American Music.* Rev. ed. Lexington: University Press of Kentucky, 2003.

Manchester, William. *The Glory and the Dream: A Narrative History of America, 1932–1972.* Boston: Little, Brown, 1974.

Mandelbaum, Michael. *The Meaning of Sports: Why Americans Watch Baseball, Football, and Basketball and What They See When They Do.* New York: Public Affairs, 2004.

Manring, M. M. *Slave in a Box: The Strange Career of Aunt Jemima.* Charlottesville: University of Virginia Press, 1998.

Maraniss, David. *When Pride Still Mattered: A Life of Vince Lombardi.* New York: Simon & Schuster, 1999.

Marc, David. *Comic Visions: Television Comedy and American Culture.* Boston: Unwin Hyman, 1989.

Marc, David, and Robert J. Thompson. *Prime Time, Prime Movers.* Syracuse, NY: Syracuse University Press, 1995.

———. *Television in the Antenna Age: A Concise History.* Malden, MA: Blackwell, 2005.

Marchand, Roland. *Advertising the American Dream: Making Way for Modernity, 1920–1940.* Berkeley and Los Angeles: University of California Press, 1985.

Marcus, Daniel. *Happy Days and Wonder Years: The Fifties and the Sixties in Contemporary Cultural Politics.* New Brunswick, NJ: Rutgers University Press, 2004.

Marcus, Greil. *Like a Rolling Stone: Bob Dylan at the Crossroads.* New York: Public Affairs, 2005.

———. *Invisible Republic: Bob Dylan's Basement Tapes.* 1997. Reprint, New York: Owl, 1998.

———. *Mystery Train: Images of America in Rock 'n' Roll Music.* New York: Dutton, 1975.

Marling, Karal Ann. *As Seen on TV: The Visual Culture of Everyday Life in the 1950s.* Cambridge, MA: Harvard University Press, 1994.

Marx, Groucho. *Groucho and Me: The Autobiography.* 1959. Reprint, London: Virgin, 2002.

Mason, Bobbie Ann. *Elvis Presley.* New York: Penguin, 2003.

Mason, Fran. *American Gangster Cinema from* Little Caesar *to* Pulp Fiction. New York: Palgrave, 2002.

May, Lary. *The Big Tomorrow: Hollywood and the Politics of the American Way.* Chicago: University of Chicago Press, 2000.

———, ed. *Recasting America: Culture and Politics in the Age of Cold War.* Chicago: University of Chicago Press, 1989.

———. *Screening Out the Past: The Birth of Mass Culture and the Motion Picture Industry.* Chicago: University of Chicago Press, 1983.

McArthur, Benjamin. *Actors and American Culture, 1880–1920.* Philadelphia: Temple University Press, 1984.

McCann, Sean. *Gumshoe America: Hard-Boiled Crime Fiction and the Rise and Fall of New Deal Liberalism.* Durham, NC: Duke University Press, 2000.

McChesney, Robert. *Rich Media, Poor Democracy: Communications Politics in Dubious Times.* New York: New Press, 2000.

McConachie, Bruce A. *Melodramatic Formations: American Theater and Society, 1820–1870.* Iowa City: University of Iowa Press, 1992.

McCullough, Edo. *Good Old Coney Island.* New York: Fordham University Press, 2000.

McDougal, Dennis. *The Last Mogul: Lew Wasserman, MCA, and the Hidden History of Hollywood.* New York: Da Capo, 2001.

McDougall, Walter A. *The Heavens and the Earth: A Political History of the Space Age.* New York: Basic, 1985.

McElvaine, Robert S. *The Great Depression: America, 1929–1941.* New York: Times Books, 1984.

McGrath, Tom. *MTV: The Making of a Revolution.* Philadelphia: Running, 1996.

McKinney, Devin. *Magic Circles: The Beatles in Dream and History.* Cambridge, MA: Harvard University Press, 2003.

McLean, Albert F., Jr. *American Vaudeville as Ritual.* Lexington: University of Kentucky Press, 1965.

Mead, Chris. *Champion: Joe Louis, Black Hero in White America.* New York: Penguin, 1985.

Melnick, Jeffrey. *A Right to Sing the Blues: African Americans, Jews, and American Popular Song.* Cambridge, MA: Harvard University Press, 1999.

Metz, Robert. *CBS: Reflections in a Bloodshot Eye.* 1975. Reprint, New York: Signet, 1976.

Miller, Douglas T. *Visions of America: Second World War to the Present.* St. Paul, MN: West, 1988.

Miller, Douglas T., and Marion Nowak. *The Fifties: The Way We Really Were.* Garden City, NY: Doubleday, 1977.

Miller, James. *Flowers in the Dustbin: The Rise of Rock and Roll, 1947–1977.* New York: Simon & Schuster, 1999.

Miller, Patrick B., ed. *The Sporting World of the Modern South.* Urbana: University of Illinois Press, 2002.

Mills, Nicholas. *The Triumph of Meanness.* New York: Houghton Mifflin, 1997.

Mitchell, Reid. *All on a Mardi Gras Day: Episodes in the History of New Orleans Carnival.* Cambridge, MA: Harvard University Press, 1995.

Mizejewski, Linda. *Ziegfeld Girl: Image and Icon in Culture and Cinema.* Durham, NC: Duke University Press, 1999.

Morton, David. *Off the Record: The Technology and Culture of Sound Recording in America.* New Brunswick, NJ: Rutgers University Press, 2000.

Moses, L. G. *Wild West Shows and the Images of American Indians, 1883–1933.* Albuquerque: University of New Mexico Press, 1996.

Mullenix, Elizabeth R. *Wearing the Breeches: Gender on the Antebellum Stage.* New York: St. Martin's, 2000.

Muller, Eddie. *Dark City Dames: The Wicked Women of Film Noir.* New York: Regan, 2001.

———. *Dark City: The Lost World of Film Noir.* New York: St. Martin's Griffin, 1998.

Murphy, Mary. *Mining Cultures: Men, Women, and Leisure in Butte, 1914–41.* Urbana: University of Illinois Press, 1997.

Murray, Susan, and Laurie Ouellette, eds. *Reality TV: Remaking Television Culture.* New York: New York University Press, 2004.

Muscio, Giuliana. *Hollywood's New Deal.* Philadelphia: Temple University Press, 1997.

Musser, Charles. *The Emergence of Cinema: The American Screen to 1907.* Berkeley and Los Angeles: University of California Press, 1994.

Nachman, Gerald. *Seriously Funny: The Rebel Comedians of the 1950s and 1960s.* New York: Pantheon, 2003.

———. *Raised on Radio.* New York: Pantheon, 1998.

Nadel, Alan. *Flatlining on the Field of Dreams: Cultural Narratives in the Films of President Reagan's America.* New Brunswick, NJ: Rutgers University Press, 1997.

Naremore, James. *More Than Night: Film Noir in Its Contexts.* Berkeley and Los Angeles: University of California Press, 1998.

Nasaw, David. *Going Out: The Rise and Fall of Public Amusements.* New York: Basic, 1993.

———. *Children of the City: At Work and at Play.* New York: Anchor, 1985.

Nash, Alanna. *The Colonel: The Extraordinary Story of Colonel Tom Parker and Elvis Presley.* New York: Simon & Schuster, 2003.

Nash, Roderick. *The Nervous Generation: American Thought, 1917–1930.* Chicago: Rand McNally, 1970.

Navasky, Victor. *Naming Names.* New York: Viking, 1980.

Newman, Kathy M. *Radio Active: Advertising and Consumer Activism, 1935–1947.* Berkeley and Los Angeles: University of California Press, 2004.

Nissenbaum, Stephen. *The Battle for Christmas.* New York: Knopf, 1996.

Novak, Michael. *The Rise of the Unmeltable Ethnics.* New York: Macmillan, 1971.

Nye, Russel B. *The Unembarrassed Muse: The Popular Arts in America.* New York: Dial, 1970.

Oakley, J. Ronald. *God's Country: America in the Fifties.* New York: Dembner, 1986.

O'Brien, Geoffrey. *Hardboiled America: Lurid Paperbacks and the Masters of Noir.* Expanded ed. New York: Da Capo, 1997.

O'Brien, Lucy. *She Bop: The Definitive History of Women in Rock, Pop, and Soul.* New York: Penguin, 1995.

The 100 Greatest Entertainers, 1950–2000. Des Moines, Iowa: Entertainment Weekly Books, 2000.

The 100 Greatest Movies of All Time. New York: Entertainment Weekly Books, 1999.

O'Neill, William L. *American High: The Years of Confidence, 1945–1960.* New York: Free Press, 1986.

Oriard, Michael. *King Football: Sport and Spectacle in the Golden Age of Radio and Newsreels, Movies and Magazines, the Weekly and the Daily Press.* Chapel Hill: University of North Carolina Press, 2001.

———. *Reading Football: Sport, Popular Journalism, and American Culture, 1876–1913.* Chapel Hill: University of North Carolina Press, 1993.

Osofsky, Gilbert. *Harlem: The Making of a Ghetto.* 1964. Reprint, New York: Harper & Row, 1965.

Palladino, Grace. *Teenagers: An American History.* New York: Basic, 1996.

Palmer, Robert. *Deep Blues.* New York: Penguin, 1981.

Palmer, Tony. *All You Need Is Love: The Story of Popular Music.* New York: Penguin, 1977.

Palmer, William J. *The Films of the Eighties: A Social History.* Carbondale: Southern Illinois University Press, 1993.

Parfrey, Adam, ed. *It's a Man's World: Men's Adventure Magazines, the Postwar Pulps.* Los Angeles: Feral, 2003.

Parrish, Tim. *Walking Blues: Making Americans from Emerson to Elvis.* Amherst: University of Massachusetts Press, 2001.

Patterson, James T. *Grand Expectations: The United States, 1945–1974.* New York: Oxford University Press, 1996.

Paulsson, Martin. *The Social Anxieties of Progressive Reform: Atlantic City, 1854–1920.* New York: New York University Press, 1994.

Peiss, Kathy. *Cheap Amusements: Working Women and Leisure in Turn-of-the-Century New York.* Philadelphia: Temple University Press, 1986.

Pells, Richard. *Radical Visions and American Dreams: Culture and Social Thought in the Depression Years.* New York: Harper & Row, 1973.

Peretti, Burton W. *Jazz in American Culture.* Chicago: Ivan Dee, 1997.

———. *The Creation of Jazz: Music, Race, and Culture in Urban America.* Urbana: University of Illinois Press, 1992.

Perrett, Geoffrey. *America in the Twenties: A History.* New York: Simon & Schuster, 1982.

Pessen, Edward. *Jacksonian America: Society, Personality, and Politics.* Homewood, IL: Dorsey, 1969.

Petersen, James R. *The Century of Sex: Playboy's History of the Sexual Revolution, 1900–1999.* New York: Grove, 1999.

Peterson, Richard A. *Creating Country Music: Fabricating Authenticity.* Chicago: University of Chicago Press, 1997.

Peterson, Robert W. *Pigskin: The Early Years of Pro Football.* New York: Oxford University Press, 1997.

Platt, Larry. *New Jack Jocks: Rebels, Race, and the American Athlete.* Philadelphia: Temple University Press, 2002.

Ponce de Leon, Charles L. *Self-Exposure: Human-Interest Journalism and the Emergence of Celebrity in America, 1890–1940.* Chapel Hill: University of North Carolina Press, 2002.

Postman, Neil. *Amusing Ourselves to Death: Public Discourse in the Age of Show Business.* New York: Penguin, 1985.

Potter, Claire B. *War on Crime: Bandits, G-Men, and the Politics of Mass Culture.* New Brunswick, NJ: Rutgers University Press, 1998.

Powers, Richard Gid. *G-Men: Hoover's FBI in Popular Culture.* Carbondale: Southern Illinois University Press, 1983.

Prince, Stephen. *A New Pot of Gold: Hollywood under the Electronic Rainbow, 1980–1989.* Berkeley and Los Angeles: University of California Press, 2000.

Putney, Clifford. *Muscular Christianity: Manhood and Sports in Protestant America, 1880–1920.* Cambridge, MA: Harvard University Press, 2001.

Pyron, Darden Asbury. *Liberace: An American Boy.* Chicago: University of Chicago Press, 2000.

Rabinovitz, Lauren. *For the Love of Pleasure: Women, Movies, and Culture in Turn-of-the-Century Chicago.* New Brunswick, NJ: Rutgers University Press, 1998.

Rabinowitz, Paula. *Black and White and Noir: America's Pulp Modernism.* New York: Columbia University Press, 2002.

Rader, Benjamin G. *American Ways: A Brief History of American Cultures.* New York: Harcourt, 2001.

———. *American Sports: From the Age of Folk Games to the Age of Televised Sports.* 4th ed. Upper Saddle River, NJ: Prentice-Hall, 1999.

———. *Baseball: A History of America's Game.* Urbana: University of Illinois Press, 1992.

Rapping, Elayne. *Law and Justice as Seen on TV.* New York: New York University Press, 2003.

Reddin, Paul. *Wild West Shows.* Urbana: University of Illinois Press, 1999.

Regalado, Samuel O. *Viva Baseball! Latin Major Leaguers and Their Special Hunger.* Urbana: University of Illinois Press, 1998.

Register, Woody. *The Kid of Coney Island: Fred Thompson and the Rise of American Amusements.* New York: Oxford University Press, 2001.

Reidelbach, Maria. *Completely Mad: A History of the Comic Book and Magazine.* Boston: Little, Brown, 1991.

Reiss, Benjamin. *The Showman and the Slave: Race, Death, and Memory in Barnum's America.* Cambridge, MA: Harvard University Press, 2001.

Restad, Penne L. *Christmas in America: A History.* New York: Oxford University Press, 1995.

Reyes, David, and Tom Waldman. *Land of a Thousand Dances: Chicano Rock 'n' Roll from Southern California*. Albuquerque: University of New Mexico Press, 1998.

Reynolds, David S. *Beneath the American Renaissance: The Subversive Imagination in the Age of Emerson and Melville*. New York: Knopf, 1988.

Riess, Steven A. *Touching Base: Professional Baseball and American Culture in the Progressive Era*. Rev. ed. Urbana: University of Illinois Press, 1999.

———. *City Games: The Evolution of American Urban Society and the Rise of Sports*. Urbana: University of Illinois Press, 1989.

Robbins, Trina. *From Girls to Grrrlz: A History of Female Comics from Teens to Zines*. San Francisco: Chronicle, 1999.

Roberts, Randy. *Jack Dempsey, the Manassa Mauler*. Baton Rouge: Louisiana State University Press, 1979.

Roberts, Randy, and James S. Olson. *John Wayne, American*. New York: Free Press, 1995.

Robinson, David. *From Peep Show to Palace: The Birth of American Film*. New York: Columbia University Press, 1996.

Robinson, Frank M., and Lawrence Davidson. *Pulp Culture: The Art of Fiction Magazines*. Portland, OR: Collectors, 1998.

Roediger, David. *The Wages of Whiteness: Race and the Making of the American Working Class*. Rev. ed. New York: Verso, 1999.

Rogin, Michael. *Blackface, White Noise: Jewish Immigrants in the Hollywood Melting Pot*. Berkeley and Los Angeles: University of California Press, 1996.

Rose, Tricia. *Black Noise: Rap Music and Black Culture in Contemporary America*. Hanover, NH: Wesleyan University Press, 1994.

Rosenzweig, Roy. *Eight Hours for What We Will: Workers and Leisure in an Industrial City, 1870–1920*. Cambridge: Cambridge University Press, 1983.

Ross, Steven. *Working-Class Hollywood: Silent Film and the Shaping of Class in America*. Princeton, NJ: Princeton University Press, 1998.

Rossi, John P. *The National Game: Baseball and American Culture*. Chicago: Ivan Dee, 2000.

Ruck, Rob. *Sandlot Seasons: Sport in Black Pittsburgh*. 1987. Reprint, Urbana: University of Illinois Press, 1993.

Ruth, David E. *Inventing the Public Enemy: The Gangster in American Culture, 1918–1934*. Chicago: University of Chicago Press, 1996.

Rydell, Robert W. *World of Fairs: The Century-of-Progress Expositions*. Chicago: University of Chicago Press, 1993.

———. *All the World's a Fair: Visions of Empire at America's International Expositions, 1876–1916*. Chicago: University of Chicago Press, 1984.

Sammons, Jeffrey T. *Beyond the Ring: The Role of Boxing in American Society*. Urbana: University of Illinois Press, 1990.

Samuel, Lawrence A. *Brought to You By: Postwar Television Advertising and the American Dream*. Austin: University of Texas Press, 2001.

Sanjek, Russell, and David Sanjek. *American Popular Music Business in the Twentieth Century*. New York: Oxford University Press, 1991.

Sante, Luc. *Low Life: Lures and Snares of Old New York*. New York: Random House, 1991.

Savage, William W., Jr. *Commies, Cowboys, and Jungle Queens: Comic Books and America, 1945–1954*. 1990. Reprint, Hanover, NH: Wesleyan University Press, 1998.

———. *The Cowboy Hero: His Image in American History and Culture*. Norman: University of Oklahoma Press, 1979.

Saxon, A. H. *P. T. Barnum: The Legend and the Man*. New York: Columbia University Press, 1989.

Schatz, Thomas. *Boom and Bust: American Cinema in the 1940s*. Berkeley and Los Angeles: University of California Press, 1997.

———. *The Genius of the System: Hollywood Filmmaking in the Studio Era*. New York: Henry Holt, 1988.

Schickel, Richard. *The Disney Version: The Life, Times, Art, and Commerce of Walt Disney.* 1968. Reprint, New York: Avon, 1968.

Schlesinger, Arthur, Jr. *The Politics of Upheaval.* Boston: Houghton-Mifflin, 1960.

Schmidt, Leigh Eric. *Consumer Rites: The Buying and Selling of American Holidays.* Princeton, NJ: Princeton University Press, 1995.

Schrag, Peter. *The Decline of the WASP.* New York: Simon & Schuster, 1970.

Schrum, Kelly. *Some Wore Bobby Sox: The Emergence of Teenage Girls' Culture, 1920–1945.* New York: Palgrave Macmillan, 2004.

Schudson, Michael. *Discovering the News: A Social History of American Newspapers.* New York: Basic, 1978.

Schulman, Bruce. *The Seventies: The Great Shift in American Culture, Society, and Politics.* New York: Free Press, 2001.

Schwartz, Richard A. *Cold War Culture: Media and the Arts, 1945–1990.* 1998. Reprint, New York: Checkmark, 2000.

Sellers, Charles. *The Market Revolution: Jacksonian America, 1815–1846.* New York: Oxford University Press, 1991.

Senelick, Laurence. *The Age and Stage of George L. Fox, 1825–1877.* Iowa City: University of Iowa Press, 1999.

Sentilles, Renée M. *Performing Menken: Adah Isaacs Menken and the Birth of American Celebrity.* Cambridge: Cambridge University Press, 2003.

Shone, Tom. *Blockbuster: How Hollywood Learned to Stop Worrying and Love the Summer.* New York: Free Press, 2004.

Shteir, Rachel. *Striptease: The Untold History of the Girlie Show.* New York: Oxford University Press, 2004.

Silver, Alain, and James Ursini. *The Noir Style.* Woodstock, NY: Overlook, 1999.

Singer, Ben. *Melodrama and Modernity: Early Sensational Cinema and Its Contexts.* New York: Columbia University Press, 2001.

Sivulka, Juliann. *Soap, Sex, and Cigarettes: A Cultural History of American Advertising.* Belmont, CA: Wadsworth, 1998.

Skal, David J. *Screams of Reason: Mad Scientists and Modern Culture.* New York: Norton, 1998.

———. *The Monster Show: A Cultural History of Horror.* Rev. ed. New York: Faber & Faber, 2001.

Sklar, Robert. *Movie-Made America: A Cultural History of American Movies.* Rev. and updated ed. New York: Vintage, 1994.

———. *City Boys: Cagney, Bogart, Garfield.* Princeton, NJ: Princeton University Press, 1992.

———, ed. *The Plastic Age: 1917–1930.* New York: George Braziller, 1970.

Slansky, Paul. *The Clothes Have No Emperor: A Chronicle of the American 80s.* New York: Fireside, 1989.

Sloan, Kay. *The Loud Silents: Origins of the Social Problem Film.* Urbana: University of Illinois Press, 1988.

Slotkin, Richard. *Gunfighter Nation: The Myth of the Frontier in Twentieth-Century America.* 1992. Reprint, New York: HarperCollins, 1993.

Smith, Erin A. *Hard-Boiled: Working-Class Readers and Pulp Magazines.* Philadelphia: Temple University Press, 2000.

Smith, Hedrick. *The Power Game: How Washington Works.* New York: Random House, 1988.

Smith, Judith E. *Visions of Belonging: Family Stories, Popular Culture, and Postwar Democracy, 1940–1960.* New York: Columbia University Press, 2004.

Smith, Kathleen E. R. *God Bless America: Tin Pan Alley Goes to War.* Lexington: University Press of Kentucky, 2003.

Smith, Ronald A. *Play-by-Play: Radio, Television, and Big-Time College Sport.* Baltimore: Johns Hopkins University Press, 2001.

———. *Sports and Freedom: The Rise of Big-Time College Athletics.* New York: Oxford University Press, 1988.

Smith, Suzanne E. *Dancing in the Street: Motown and the Cultural Politics of Detroit.* Cambridge, MA: Harvard University Press, 1999.

Snyder, Robert W. *The Voice of the City: Vaudeville and Popular Culture in New York.* New York: Oxford University Press, 1989.

Spigel, Lynn. *Make Room for TV: Television and the Family Ideal in Postwar America.* Chicago: University of Chicago Press, 1992.

Spigel, Lynn, and Michael Curtin, eds. *The Revolution Wasn't Televised: Sixties Television and Social Conflict.* New York: Routledge, 1997.

Srebnick, Amy Gilman. *The Mysterious Death of Mary Rogers: Sex and Culture in Nineteenth-Century New York.* New York: Oxford University Press, 1995.

Staiger, Janet. *Blockbuster TV: Must-See Sitcoms in the Network Era.* New York: New York University Press, 2000.

Stamp, Shelley. *Movie-Struck Girls: Women and Motion Picture Culture after the Nickelodeon.* Princeton, NJ: Princeton University Press, 2000.

Stanfield, Peter. *Horse Opera: The Strange History of the 1930s Singing Cowboy.* Urbana: University of Illinois Press, 2002.

Stansell, Christine. *City of Women: Sex and Class in New York, 1789–1860.* Urbana: University of Illinois Press, 1987.

Stark, Steven D. *Glued to the Set: The 60 Television Shows and Events That Made Us Who We Are Today.* New York: Free Press, 1997.

Starr, Larry, and Christopher Waterman. *American Popular Music: From Minstrelsy to MTV.* New York: Oxford University Press, 2003.

Starr, Paul. *The Creation of the Media: Political Origins of Modern Communications.* New York: Basic, 2004.

Stein, Charles W., ed. *American Vaudeville as Seen by Its Contemporaries.* New York: Knopf, 1984.

Stempel, Tom. *Storytellers to the Nation: A History of American Television Writing.* Syracuse, NY: Syracuse University Press, 1996.

Stern, Jane, and Michael Stern. *Sixties People.* New York: Knopf, 1990.

Sterngass, Jon. *First Resorts: Pursuing Pleasure at Saratoga Springs, Newport, and Coney Island.* Baltimore: Johns Hopkins University Press, 2001.

Stott, William. *Documentary America: Expression and Thirties America.* New York: Oxford University Press, 1973.

Stowe, David W. *Swing Changes: Big-Band Jazz in New Deal America.* Cambridge, MA: Harvard University Press, 1994.

Struna, Nancy L. *People of Prowess: Sport, Leisure, and Labor in Early Anglo-America.* Urbana: University of Illinois Press, 1996.

Susman, Warren. *Culture as History: The Transformation of American Society in the Twentieth Century.* New York: Pantheon, 1984.

Szatmary, David. *A Time to Rock: A Social History of Rock 'n' Roll.* New York: Schirmer, 1996.

Tawa, Nicholas E. *High-Minded and Low-Down: Music in the Lives of Americans, 1800–1861.* Boston: Northeastern University Press, 2000.

Thompson, Robert J. *Television's Second Golden Age: From* Hill Street Blues *to* ER. Syracuse, NY: Syracuse University Press, 1996.

Tichi, Cecelia. *High Lonesome: The American Culture of Country Music.* Chapel Hill: University of North Carolina Press, 1994.

Titon, Jeffrey T. *Early Downhome Blues: A Musical and Cultural Analysis.* 2nd ed. Chapel Hill: University of North Carolina Press, 1994.

Toll, Robert C. *The Entertainment Machine: American Show Business in the Twentieth Century.* New York: Oxford University Press, 1982.

———. *On with the Show! The First Century of Show Business in America.* New York: Oxford University Press, 1976.

———. *Blacking Up: The Minstrel Show in Nineteenth-Century America.* New York: Oxford University Press, 1974.

Tompkins, Jane. *West of Everything: The Inner Life of Westerns.* New York: Oxford University Press, 1992.

———. *Sensational Designs: The Cultural Work of American Fiction, 1790–1860.* New York: Oxford University Press, 1985.

Toplin, Robert Brent. *Reel History: In Defense of Hollywood.* Lawrence: University Press of Kansas, 2002.

Tosches, Nick. *Unsung Heroes of Rock 'n' Roll.* 1984. Reprint, New York: Da Capo, 1999.

———. *Country: The Twisted Roots of Rock 'n' Roll.* 1977. Reprint, New York: Da Capo, 1996.

Troy, Gil. *Morning in America: How Ronald Reagan Invented the 1980s.* Princeton, NJ: Princeton University Press, 2005.

Tucher, Andie. *Froth and Scum: Truth, Beauty, Goodness, and the Ax Murder in America's First Mass Medium.* Chapel Hill: University of North Carolina Press, 1994.

Twitchell, James B. *Adcult USA: The Triumph of Advertising in American Culture.* New York: Columbia University Press, 1996.

———. *Carnival Culture: The Trashing of Taste in America.* New York: Columbia University Press, 1992.

———. *Preposterous Violence: Fables of Aggression in Modern Culture.* New York: Oxford University Press, 1989.

Tygiel, Jules. *Past Time: Baseball as History.* New York: Oxford University Press, 2000.

Ullman, Sharon R. *Sex Seen: The Emergence of Modern Sexuality in America.* Berkeley and Los Angeles: University of California Press, 1997.

Vaillant, Derek. *Sounds of Reform: Progressivism and Music in Chicago, 1873–1935.* Chapel Hill: University of North Carolina Press, 2003.

Verney, Kevern. *African Americans and US Popular Culture.* London: Routledge, 2003.

Vieira, Mark A. *Sin in Soft Focus: Pre-Code Hollywood.* New York: Abrams, 1999.

Von Eschen, Penny M. *Satchmo Blows Up the World: Jazz Ambassadors Play the Cold War.* Cambridge, MA: Harvard University Press, 2004.

Wagner, Ann. *Adversaries of Dance: From the Puritans to the Present.* Urbana: University of Illinois Press, 1997.

Waksman, Steve. *Instruments of Desire: The Electric Guitar and the Shaping of Musical Experience.* Cambridge, MA: Harvard University Press, 1999.

Waller, Gregory A. *Main Street Amusements: Movies and Commercial Entertainment in a Southern City, 1896–1930.* Washington, DC: Smithsonian Institution Press, 1995.

Walls, Jeannette. *Dish: The Inside Story on the World of Gossip.* New York: Spike, 2000.

Ward, Brian, ed. *Media, Culture, and the Modern African American Freedom Struggle.* Gainesville: University Press of Florida, 2001.

———. *Just My Soul Responding: Rhythm and Blues, Black Consciousness, and Race Relations.* Berkeley and Los Angeles: University of California Press, 1998.

Ward, Geoffrey, and Ken Burns. *Jazz: A History of America's Music.* New York: Knopf, 2000.

Watkins, Mel. *On the Real Side: Laughing, Lying, and Signifying—the Underground Tradition of African-American Humor That Transformed American Culture from Slavery to Richard Pryor.* New York: Simon & Schuster, 1994.

Watson, Mary Ann. *Defining Visions: Television and the American Experience since 1945.* New York: Harcourt Brace, 1998.

Watterson, John S. *College Football: History, Spectacle, Controversy.* Baltimore: Johns Hopkins University Press, 2000.

Watts, Jill. *Mae West: An Icon in Black and White.* New York: Oxford University Press, 2001.

Watts, Steven. *The Magic Kingdom: Walt Disney and the American Way of Life.* Columbia: University of Missouri Press, 1997.

Werner, Craig. *A Change Is Gonna Come: Music, Race, and the Soul of America.* New York: Penguin, 1998.

Weyr, Thomas. *Reaching for Paradise: The* Playboy *Vision of America.* New York: Times Books, 1978.

Whitfield, Stephen. *The Culture of the Cold War.* Baltimore: Johns Hopkins University Press, 1991.

Williams, Linda. *Playing the Race Card: Melodramas of Black and White from Uncle Sam to O. J. Simpson.* Princeton, NJ: Princeton University Press, 2001.

Williamson, J. W. *Hillbillyland: What the Movies Did to the Mountains and What the Mountains Did to the Movies.* Chapel Hill: University of North Carolina Press, 1995.

Wills, Garry. *John Wayne's America.* New York: Simon & Schuster, 1997.

———. *Reagan's America: Innocents at Home.* New York: Doubleday, 1987.

Withington, Anne F. *Toward a More Perfect Union: Virtue and the Formation of American Republics.* New York: Oxford University Press, 1991.

Wolf, Michael J. *The Entertainment Economy: How Mega-Media Forces Are Transforming Our Lives.* New York: Times Books, 1999.

Wolfe, Charles K. *A Good-Natured Riot: The Birth of the Grand Ole Opry.* Nashville: Country Music Foundation Press/Vanderbilt University Press, 1999.

Wolfe, Tom. *Mauve Gloves and Madmen, Clutter and Vine.* New York: Farrar Straus Giroux, 1976.

———. *The Purple Decades.* New York: Berkley, 1983.

Wood, Gordon. *The Radicalism of the American Revolution.* 1991. Reprint, New York: Vintage, 1993.

Wright, Bradford W. *Comic Book Nation: The Transformation of Youth Culture in America.* Baltimore: Johns Hopkins University Press, 2001.

Wynter, Leon E. *American Skin: Pop Culture, Big Business, and the End of White America.* New York: Crown, 2002.

Zang, David W. *Sports Wars: Athletes in the Age of Aquarius.* Fayetteville: University of Arkansas Press, 2001.

Zook, Kristal Brent. *Color by Fox: The Fox Network and the Revolution in Black Television.* New York: Oxford University Press, 1999.

INDEX